P9-CQG-878

FIFTH
CANADIAN
EDITION

SOCIAL PSYCHOLOGY

FIFTH CANADIAN EDITION

SOCIAL PSYCHOLOGY

ELLIOT ARONSON
University of California, Santa Cruz

TIMOTHY D. WILSON
University of Virginia

BEVERLEY FEHR
University of Winnipeg

ROBIN M. AKERT
Wellesley College

Toronto

Vice-President, Editorial Director: Gary Bennett
Editor-in-Chief: Michelle Sartor
Acquisitions Editor: Matthew Christian
Sponsoring Editor: Carolin Sweig
Marketing Manager: Lisa Gillis
Supervising Developmental Editor: Suzanne Schaan
Developmental Editor: Megan Burns
Lead Project Manager: Ioana Gagea
Manufacturing Manager: Susan Johnson
Production Editor: Vasundhara Sawhney, Cenveo Publisher Services
Copy Editor: Deborah Cooper-Bullock
Proofreader: Susan Adlam
Index: Belle Wong
Compositor: Cenveo Publisher Services
Photo Researcher: Indu Arora
Permissions Researcher: Amanda Campbell
Art Director: Julia Hall
Cover and Interior Designer: Miriam Blier
Cover Image: Ryan McVay/Getty Images

Credits and acknowledgments for material borrowed from other sources and reproduced, with permission, in this textbook appear on the appropriate page within the text and on page 577.

---

10 9 8 7 6 5 4 3 2 1 [CKV]

Library and Archives Canada Cataloguing in Publication

Social psychology / Elliot Aronson ... [et al.]—5th Canadian ed.

Includes bibliographical references and index.
ISBN 978-0-13-216539-6

1. Social psychology—Textbooks. I. Aronson, Elliot

HM1033.S62 2012 302 C2011-906927-X

ISBN 978-0-13-216539-6

To my grandchildren: Jacob, Jason, Ruth, Eliana, Natalie, Rachel, and Leo Aronson. My hope is that your wonderful capacity for empathy and compassion will help make the world a better place.

—E.A.

To my family, Deirdre Smith, Christopher, and Leigh Wilson

—T.D.W.

To my children, Genevieve and Everett

—B.F.

To my mentor, colleague, and friend, Dane Archer

—R.M.A.

Brief Contents

Contents

CHAPTER 12 Prejudice Causes and Cures 372

Preface

When we began writing this book, our overriding goal was to capture the excitement of social psychology. We have been pleased to hear, in many kind letters and email messages from professors and students, that we succeeded. One of our favourites was from a student who said that the book was so interesting that she always saved it for last, to reward herself for finishing her other work. With that one student, at least, we succeeded in making our book an enjoyable, fascinating story, not a dry report of facts and figures.

Our goal in *Social Psychology*, Fifth Canadian edition, is to capture the excitement of social psychology for students in Canada by presenting the field in a Canadian context. In the novel *Tamarind Mem* (1996), Indo-Canadian writer Anita Rau Badami tells the story of two young girls growing up in India whose parents sought to enhance their status by emulating British ways. To keep abreast of British fashion and hairstyles, the girls' mother faithfully subscribed to an expensive British magazine. One of the daughters, Kamini, recalls that the magazine also contained a children's story that usually focused on the sandwich and ginger-beer picnics of two young British girls, Nora and Tilly. Kamini comments, "I liked Nora and Tilly but wished that they had different names—Gauri and Geetha, perhaps, or Mini and Bani" (Badami, 1996, p. 24).

This quotation captures the sentiment of your Canadian author, Beverley Fehr, who taught social psychology for years using the U.S. edition of this text. Although her students always enjoyed the book, she felt that they would have been happier if the news stories, historical examples, and statistics reflected their Canadian experience. In short, she was convinced that social psychology would come alive for students in Canada when they discovered the relevance of social psychological theories and concepts to the society in which they live.

What's New in This Edition?

We are pleased to add a new **How Would You Use This?** feature found at the end of most chapters that we believe will appeal greatly to students. In Chapter 8, for example, we point out to students that sooner or later they will be part of a group that needs to make an important decision, and invite them to think about how they might use concepts from the chapter to ensure that the group makes the best decision it can. The purpose of this feature is to encourage students to think critically about the material and apply it to their own lives.

Throughout the printed text, you will find the following icons that link you to related content on MyPsychLab. In the Pearson eText, these icons are hyperlinked directly to the online resources:

Watch Observe fascinating video clips related to key topics and concepts covered in each chapter. If you are a visual learner, this feature is for you!

Simulate Engage in practical experiments and observe the outcomes of other simulations that put concepts into action and bring the text to life.

Explore Dive into a deeper understanding of critical concepts by exploring a variety of interesting and challenging activities.

Listen Listen to informative audio files that complement a specific topic you are learning about.

Connect to MyPsychLab These boxes connect you to MyPsychLab where you will become more engaged with the material as you stretch your critical-thinking skills through writing assignments and improve your understanding of concepts by taking part in stimulating experiments.

In addition, the Fifth Canadian edition has been substantially updated with nearly 350 new Canadian articles and more than 200 non-Canadian sources. Here is a sampling of the new research that is covered:

- **Chapter 2, "Methodology: How Social Psychologists Do Research"** includes a new section titled "New Frontiers in Social Psychology." This section discusses new methods and approaches that social psychologists have adopted in recent years, including cross-cultural research, evolutionary psychology, and social neuroscience. We also present recent work by York University researcher Pepler and colleagues (2011) on the effectiveness of bullying interventions and research conducted at the University of Manitoba (Nowatzki & Morry, 2009) and the University of Windsor (Ip & Jarry, 2008) on the consequences of internalizing body images promoted in the media.
- **Chapter 3, "Social Cognition: How We Think about the Social World,"** has been updated in many ways. For example, in the section on automatic thought, we describe a recent study conducted by researchers at the University of Calgary and the University of Western Ontario and at Essex University showing when people are subliminally exposed to legal concepts (e.g., lawyer) they become more competitive, more self-interested, and more likely to see other people as untrustworthy (Callan, Kay, Olson, Brar, & Whitefield, 2010). We also present research out of the University of Waterloo on the "smart unconscious," which focuses on automatic attitudes in marriages (Murray, Holmes, & Pinkus, 2010). Finally, we have added a major new section titled "Cultural Differences in Thinking" that discusses recent research by Taka Masuda and colleagues at the

University of Alberta on holistic versus analytic thinking in different cultures.

- **In Chapter 4, "Social Perception: How We Come to Understand Other People,"** we have updated the section on nonverbal communication, discussing several recent studies that address the evolutionary significance of facial expressions of emotion (e.g., the work on pride and shame by Tracy & Matsumoto, 2008), recent research conducted at the University of Toronto by Aviezer and colleagues (2011) on the malleability of emotion perception, and recent cross-cultural studies by Masuda, Ito, and colleagues looking at the extent to which Canadians and Japanese people pay attention to the context when interpreting emotion expressions. In the section on attribution, we discuss recent work by researchers at universities in Ontario showing that when we are faced with an innocent person's misfortune (either ours or someone else's), we preserve our belief in a just world by convincing ourselves that, down the road, good things will happen to even out the score (Anderson, Kay, & Fitzsimons, 2010; Gaucher, Hafer, Kay, & Davidenko, 2010). For example, Danielle Gaucher and colleagues (2010) found that athletes (basketball players and hockey players) who had high "just world" beliefs expressed confidence that officials' calls would balance out to be fair in the long run.
- **Chapter 5, "Self-Knowledge and the Need to Maintain Self-Esteem,"** contains a new section on self-control that discusses recent research on self-regulation. There is also increased coverage of cultural differences in the self, including a new study by University of British Columbia researcher Steve Heine and colleagues (2008) examining cultural differences in self-awareness. Many new Canadian studies on social comparison are discussed, including recent studies conducted at the University of Toronto (Trottier, Polivy, & Herman, 2007; Tiggerman & Polivy, 2010) and at Ryerson University (Want, Vickers, & Amos, 2009) which show that when women are exposed to thin models the resultant social comparison produces body dissatisfaction.
- **In Chapter 6, "Attitudes and Attitude Change: Influencing Thoughts, Feelings, and Behaviour,"** we have added several new Canadian studies on the theory of planned behaviour, including application of theory to pro-environment behaviours, such as reducing car use (Abrahmse, Steg, Gifford, & Vlek, 2009), as well as behavioural intentions toward people with mental illness (Norman, Sorrentino, Windell, Ye, Szeto, & Manchanda, 2010). We also present recent Canadian studies on the elaboration likelihood model, including research showing that when people are under cognitive load, they are more likely to take the peripheral route (Sinclair, Moore, Mark, Soldat, & Lavis, 2010; White & Willness, 2009). In our discussion of cognitive dissonance, we present a recent study by University of Waterloo researchers showing how parents use dissonance reduction to justify the costs of having a child (Eibach & Mock, 2011). We also include recent research on the biological basis of dissonance, including research on brain activity during the experience of dissonance and dissonance reduction. Finally, we discuss new Canadian studies that have used hypocrisy induction to persuade youth to quit smoking and young children to play safely on playground equipment.
- **In Chapter 7, "Conformity: Influencing Others,"** we discuss new Canadian research on social norms relevant to the lives of our students, including a recent study on how students' perceptions of social norms influence whether they attend classes or take them online (Bassili, 2008), how much alcohol they consume (Arbour-Nicitopoulos, Kwan, Lowe, Taman, & Faulkner, 2010), and how much they eat (Feeney, Polivy, Pliner, & Sullivan, 2001; Leone, Pliner, & Herman, 2007). In the "Social Influence and Women's Body Image" section, we feature several new Canadian studies, including a successful intervention developed at Wilfrid Laurier University and the University of Waterloo that focuses on challenging social norms concerning body ideals (Strahan, Lafrance, Wilson, Ethier, Spencer, & Zanna, 2008). We also include fascinating new research out of McMaster University on conformity in rats (Galef & Whiskin, 2008). In addition, we present University of Toronto research on "loyal deviance," which offers a new perspective on motivations for dissenting from the group (Packer & Chasteen, 2010). In the section on obedience, we present research out of Simon Fraser University examining whether watching Milgram's classic film has a positive effect on moral development (Sheppard & Young, 2007).
- **Chapter 8, "Group Processes: Influence in Social Groups,"** includes new research out of the University of Waterloo on why groups sometimes perform better than individuals (Malcolmson, Reynolds, & Smilek, 2007). Groundbreaking new studies on social dilemmas, including research out of the University of Toronto and Northeastern University, show that consistent cooperation is the most beneficial strategy for everyone (Weber & Murnighan, 2008), and research out of McMaster University demonstrates the complex strategies that groups develop for dealing with free loaders (Kiyonari & Barclay, 2008). We also have updated the section on leadership, including a new section on transformational leadership that cites many recent Canadian studies. Our section on gender and leadership is updated and includes a 2010 review by Budworth (York University) and Mann (Guelph University) that documents the challenges that women in leadership positions continue to face.
- **Chapter 9, "Interpersonal Attraction: From First Impressions to Close Relationships,"** has been substantially

revised, starting with a new section featuring a dozen recent Canadian studies on the formation of relationships online. The chapter also includes recent Canadian research on the similarity-attraction hypothesis, with a focus on research showing that perceptions of similarity predict attraction more strongly than actual similarity. The section on physical attractiveness moves beyond the traditional focus on facial beauty to include new Canadian research on attractiveness and height, foot size, leg length, and finger length. We also present recent research conducted at the University of Western Ontario showing that the emphasis that people place on looks occurs at an automatic level (Sritharan, Heilpern, Wilbur, & Gawronski, 2010). The section on evolution and love has been expanded and includes a new section that focuses on how the menstrual/ovulatory cycle affects women's perceptions of male attractiveness. Included here is research out of Saint Mary's University showing that women's perceptions of a man's attractiveness are also influenced by his sexual history and whether he is seeking a long- or short-term relationship (Williams, Fisher, & Cox, 2008). We also have added new material that describes recent neuroscience research identifying the areas of the brain that are activated when people are passionately in love. A second major addition is to the attachment styles section, which focuses on recent research on the genetic contribution to attachment styles. "The Role of Commitment in Maintaining Relationships" section has been heavily revised to include recent work by Lydon and colleagues at McGill University on the devaluation of attractive alternatives as a commitment-maintaining strategy (e.g., Linardatos & Lydon, 2011). We also include new research on forgiveness as a relationship maintenance strategy (Lydon, Menzies-Tolman, Burton, & Bell, 2008). Finally, when discussing the deterioration of relationships, we present new research by Cheryl Harasymchuk at Carleton University and Beverley Fehr at the University of Winnipeg on relational boredom as a threat to relationship satisfaction.

- **Chapter 10, "Prosocial Behaviour: Why Do People Help?"**, includes fascinating new research out of the University of Western Ontario showing selective reciprocity in infants (Dunfield & Kuhlmeier, 2010). In the section on the evolutionary explanation of prosocial behaviour, we present a recent analysis of the beneficiaries of wills in British Columbia that supports inclusive fitness theory (Webster, Bryan, Crawford, McCarthy, & Cohen, 2008). In discussing the debate over whether true altruism exists, we present recent Canadian research documenting costly altruism among HIV patients (Balfour, Corace, Tasca, Tremblay, Routy, & Angel, 2010). We also include a new "Socioeconomic Differences in Prosocial Behaviour" section that focuses on recent research conducted in Canada and the United States showing that poor people are more generous and helpful because they tend to be more compassionate than wealthy people (Piff, Kraus, Côté, Cheng, & Keltner, 2010). We also discuss a recent analysis of the personalities of Canadians who have won the Governor General's caring and bravery awards (Walker & Frimer, 2007).
- **Chapter 11, "Aggression: Why We Hurt Other People,"** includes several new Canadian studies on the relation between alcohol and aggression (e.g., Wells, Graham, & Tremblay, 2009; Wells, Mihic, Tremblay, Graham, & Demers, 2008) and a recent Canadian study on the link between testosterone and aggression (Carrè, Gilchrist, Morrisey & McCormick, 2010). We have also expanded coverage of violence in intimate relationships, citing many new Canadian studies, as well as new Canadian research on bullying and cyberbullying. New research on the effects of violent media is presented, including the results of a recent meta analysis on the link between violent video games and aggression (Anderson et al., 2010). The section on the role of social exclusion in aggressive behaviour has also been updated and expanded.
- **Chapter 12, "Prejudice: Causes and Cures,"** is substantially updated and revised, featuring 55 new Canadian sources. We have included a new "Measurement of Prejudice" section that highlights Canadian innovations in assessing prejudice at an implicit level (e.g., Clow & Olson, 2010; Gawronski, Peters, Brochu, & Strack, 2008) and the development of subtle paper-and-pencil scales, including the Modern Homonegativity Scale developed by University of Saskatchewan researchers (Morrison, Morrison, & Franklin, 2009). We also present new research by University of Manitoba researcher Jacquie Vorauer and colleagues on the relation between prejudice and acceptance of multiculturalism (Vorauer & Sasaki, 2010; Vorauer, Gagnon, & Sasaki, 2009). We include new Canadian research on gender discrimination (Alksnis, Desmarais, & Curtis, 2008; Gaucher, Friesen, & Kay, 2011), including research conducted in Canada and Belgium showing that children apply gender stereotypes automatically (Banse, Gawronski, Rebetz, Gutt, & Morton, 2010). Another new section features work conducted at the University of Waterloo by Danielle Gaucher and colleagues on injunctification which shows that prejudice is perpetuated because people are motivated to justify the status quo (e.g., Kay et al., 2009). In the individual differences section, we present recent research out of Brock University by Gordon Hodson and colleagues on social dominance orientation and prejudice (Costello & Hodson, 2010; Hodson, Hogg, & MacInnis, 2009; Hodson, Rush & MacInnis, 2010; Hodson, MacInnis, & Rush, 2010). The chapter also features many new Canadian studies on stereotype threat and how its effects can be overcome.

- **Social Psychology in Action 1, "Social Psychology and the Environment,"** begins with University of Victoria researcher Robert Gifford's (2008) analysis of the barriers to engaging in pro-environmental behaviours. We updated the section on using social norms to change environmental attitudes and behaviours, including recent research by Graham, Koo, and Wilson (2011) on how to get students to conserve energy by driving less. We also added a new "Intrinsic Motivation and Implementation Plans" section that features the work of University of Ottawa researchers showing that when people are intrinsically motivated, they engage in many more pro-environmental behaviours than when they are extrinsically motivated (Pelletier & Sharp, 2007). We present their suggestions for increasing intrinsic motivation (Pelletier & Sharp, 2008), which includes formulating specific implementation plans (drawing on work by McGill University researcher Richard Koestner and colleagues).
- **Social Psychology in Action 2, "Social Psychology and Health,"** has been updated with new Canadian studies showing a link between interpersonal stress and health problems. In addition, several new Canadian studies are presented on the relation between perceived control and physical and emotional health among university students and the elderly. Also included is new research from the University of Saskatchewan showing that people who are high in self-efficacy are more likely to engage in optimal levels of physical activity (Nickel & Spink, 2010a). We also discuss recent research on the positive effects of an attributional retraining intervention with first-year students at the University of Manitoba (Haynes, Clifton, Daniels, Perry, Chipperfield, & Ruthig, 2011; Haynes, Daniels, Stupinsky, Perry, & Hladkyj, 2008) and a similar intervention used by a St. Thomas University, Fredericton, researcher with people learning a new sport (Le Foll, Rascle, & Higgins, 2008). In the section on social support, we feature new research by Nancy Collins and colleagues that uses virtual reality technology to experimentally show the positive benefits of a responsive, supportive partner (Kane, McCall, & Collins, 2011; Collins & Feeney, 2000, 2004).
- **Social Psychology in Action 3, "Social Psychology and the Law,"** has been updated considerably. For example, we present many new Canadian studies on the accuracy of eyewitness testimony, including a recent meta analysis on lay people's knowledge of the pitfalls of eyewitness testimony (Desmarais & Read, 2011). We also discuss new Canadian research on police lineups, including a new computer program (developed in collaboration with researchers at the University of Ontario Institute of Technology), in which photographs are displayed by a "virtual" officer (Cutler, Daugherty, Babu, Hodges, & Van Wallendael, 2009). In the section on expert testimony, we present articles on the admissibility of expert evidence in Canada (Glancy & Bradord, 2007), as well as an article by University of British Columbia researchers cautioning experts to be mindful that the results of staged crimes may not generalize to the real world (Yuille, Ternes, & Cooper, 2010). We also present new Canadian research on techniques for eliciting confessions (and false confessions), including work by Memorial University researchers (King & Snook, 2009), researchers at St. Mary's University (Smith, Stinson, & Patry, 2009), and interviews with inmates at a Quebec penitentiary (Deslauriers-Varin, Beauregard, & Wong, 2011). Several recent studies on false memories are discussed as well as an article on a Supreme Court of Canada decision on the inadmissibility of witness testimony obtained via hypnosis (Patry, Stinson, & Smith, 2009).

Social psychology comes alive for students when they understand the whole context of the field: how theories inspire research, why research is performed as it is, and how further research triggers yet new avenues of study. We have tried to convey our own fascination with the research process in a down-to-earth, meaningful way and have presented the results of the scientific process in terms of the everyday experience of the reader; however, we did not want to "water down" our presentation of the field. In a world where human behaviour can be endlessly surprising and where research results can be quite counterintuitive, students need a firm foundation on which to build their understanding of this challenging discipline.

The main way we try to engage students is with a storytelling approach. Social psychology is full of good stories, such as how the Holocaust inspired investigations into obedience to authority and how reactions to the marriage of the crown prince of Japan to Masako Owada, a career diplomat, illustrates cultural differences in the self-concept. By placing research in a real-world context, we make the material more familiar, understandable, and memorable. Each chapter begins with a real-life vignette that illustrates the concepts to come. We refer to this event at several points in the chapter, clarifying to students the relevance of the material they are learning. Examples of the opening vignettes include the tragic death of Reena Virk, a Victoria teenager who was brutally murdered in 1997 while onlookers participated in tormenting her; we describe the legal battle to convict her killers that continued to 2009 (Chapter 7, "Conformity: Influencing Others"). In addition, we describe some amazing acts of altruism by Canadians including Allen and Violet Large, a retired couple near Halifax, who won an $11.25 million dollar lottery in 2010 and donated nearly all of it to charity (Chapter 10, "Prosocial Behaviour: Why Do People Help?").

We also weave "mini-stories" into each chapter that both illustrate specific concepts and bring the material to life. For each one, we first describe an example of a real-life phenomenon that is designed to pique students' interest. These stories are taken from current events, literature, and our own lives. Next, we describe an experiment that attempts to explain the phenomenon. This experiment is typically described in some detail because we believe that students should not only learn the major theories in social psychology, but also understand and appreciate the methods used to test those theories. For example, in Chapter 10, we point out how a January 17, 2011, headline that said "Woman freezes to death as neighbours ignore screams" bears an eerie resemblance to the Kitty Genovese headlines back in 1964. In the recent case, the screams came from a 66-year-old Toronto woman with dementia who had wandered out of her house on a night when the temperature was -28°C. According to the police, there were signs that the disoriented woman tried to get into a car for shelter; scratch marks were also found on the screen door of a nearby home. Neighbours heard the woman screaming but did nothing, and no one called 911. One neighbour reported that she had looked out of her window when she heard the screams and saw someone stumbling in the cold, but ignored it. By the time the woman's husband noticed that she was missing, she had frozen to death a few blocks from her home. We use this tragedy to pique students' interest in the classic Latané and Darley studies on bystander intervention. We invite you to thumb through the book to find more examples of these mini-stories.

Last but not least, we discuss the methods used by social psychologists in some detail. How can "boring" details about methodology be part of a storytelling approach, you might ask? We believe that part of what makes the story of social psychology so interesting is explaining to students how to test hypotheses scientifically. In recent years, the trend has been for textbooks to include only short sections on research methodology and to provide only brief descriptions of the findings of individual studies. In this book, we integrate the science and methodology of the field into our story in several ways.

First, we devote an entire chapter to methodology (Chapter 2). We use our storytelling approach by presenting two compelling real-world problems related to violence and aggression: Does pornography promote violence against women? Why don't bystanders intervene more to help victims of violence? We then use actual research studies on these questions to illustrate the three major scientific methods (observational research, correlational research, and experimental research). Rather than a dry recitation of methodological principles, the scientific method unfolds like a story with a "hook" (what are the causes of real-world aggression and apathy toward violence?) and a moral (such interesting, real-world questions can be addressed scientifically). We have been pleased by the positive reactions to this chapter in the previous editions.

Second, we describe prototypical studies in more detail than most texts. We discuss how a study was set up, what the research participants perceived and did, how the research design derives from theoretical issues, and the ways in which the findings support the initial hypotheses. We often ask readers to pretend that they were participants so they can better understand the study from the participants' point of view. Whenever pertinent, we've also included anecdotal information about how a study was done or came to be; these brief stories allow readers insights into the heretofore hidden world of creating research. See, for example, the description of how Nisbett and Wilson (1977) designed one of their experiments on the accuracy of people's causal inferences in Chapter 5 and the description of the origins of Aronson's jigsaw puzzle technique in Chapter 12.

And finally, we include a balanced coverage of classic and modern research. The field of social psychology is expanding rapidly, and exciting new work is being done in all areas of the discipline. With the extensive new material included in this Fifth Canadian edition, the book provides thorough coverage of up-to-date, cutting-edge research. But by emphasizing what is new, some texts have a tendency to ignore what is old. We have tried to strike a balance between the latest research findings and classic research in social psychology. Some older studies (e.g., early work in dissonance, conformity, and attribution) deserve their status as classics and are important cornerstones of the discipline. For example, unlike several other current texts, we present detailed descriptions of the Festinger and Carlsmith (1959) dissonance study (Chapter 6), and the Asch (1956) and Sherif (1936) conformity studies (Chapter 7). We then bring the older theories up to date, following our discussions of the classics with modern approaches to the same topics. This allows students to experience the continuity and depth of the field, rather than regarding it as a collection of studies published in the past few years.

Supplements to the Text

A really good textbook should become part of the classroom experience, supporting and augmenting the professor's vision for his or her class. *Social Psychology*, Fifth Canadian edition, offers a number of supplements that will enrich both the professor's presentation of social psychology and the student's understanding of it.

Student Supplements

- MyPsychLab *(www.MyPsychLab.com)* **The moment you know.** Educators know it. Students know it. It's that inspired moment when something that was difficult to understand suddenly makes perfect sense. Our MyLab products have been designed and refined with a single purpose in mind—to help educators create that moment of understanding with their students.

  MyPsychLab delivers **proven results** in helping individual students succeed. It provides **engaging experiences** that personalize, stimulate, and measure learning for each student. And, it comes from a **trusted partner** with educational expertise and an eye on the future.

MyPsychLab can be used by itself or linked to any learning management system. To learn more about how MyPsychLab combines proven learning applications with powerful assessment, visit www.MyPsychLab.com.

MyPsychLab—the moment you know.

- **CourseSmart for Students** CourseSmart goes beyond traditional expectations–providing instant, online access to the textbooks and course materials you need at an average savings of 60%. With instant access from any computer and the ability to search your text, you'll find the content you need quickly, no matter where you are. And with online tools like highlighting and note-taking, you can save time and study efficiently. See all the benefits at www.coursesmart.com/students.

Instructor Supplements

- **Instructor's Resource Manual** Includes lecture ideas, teaching tips, suggested readings, chapter outlines, student projects and research assignments, Try It! exercises, critical-thinking topics and discussion questions, and a media resource guide.
- **Pearson MyTest** MyTest from Pearson Education Canada is a powerful assessment generation program that helps instructors easily create and print quizzes, tests, and exams, as well as homework or practice handouts. Questions and tests can all be authored online, allowing instructors ultimate flexibility and the ability to efficiently manage assessments at any time, from anywhere. MyTest for *Social Psychology*, Fifth Canadian edition, includes approximately 2000 questions. These questions are also available in Microsoft Word format (see Test Item File, below).
- **Test Item File** Each question in this 2000-question test bank is referenced to the corresponding text page number, topic, and skill level. The test bank is available both as a Test Item File in Microsoft Word format and in MyTest format (see above).
- **PowerPoint Presentations** These presentations cover the key concepts in each chapter.
- **Image Library** Figures and tables from the text are provided in electronic format.
- peerScholar Firmly grounded in published research, peerScholar is a powerful online pedagogical tool that helps develop your students' critical- and creative-thinking skills. peerScholar facilitates this through the process of creation, evaluation, and reflection. Working in stages, students begin by submitting a written assignment. peerScholar then circulates their work for others to review, a process that can be anonymous or not depending on your preference. Students receive peer feedback and evaluations immediately, reinforcing their learning and driving the development of higher-order thinking skills. Students can then re-submit revised work, again depending on your preference. Contact your Pearson Representative to learn more about peerScholar and the research behind it.
- **Pearson Custom Library** For enrollments of at least 25 students, you can create your own textbook by choosing the chapters that best suit your own course needs. *To begin building your custom text, visit www.pearsoncustomlibrary.com.* You may also work with a dedicated Pearson Custom editor to create your ideal text—publishing your own original content or mixing and matching Pearson content. *Contact your local Pearson Representative to get started.*
- **Technology Specialists** Pearson's Technology Specialists work with faculty and campus course designers to ensure that Pearson technology products, assessment tools, and online course materials are tailored to meet your specific needs. This highly qualified team is dedicated to helping schools take full advantage of a wide range of educational resources, by assisting in the integration of a variety of instructional materials and media formats. Your local Pearson Education sales representative can provide you with more details on this service program.
- **CourseSmart for Instructors** CourseSmart goes beyond traditional expectations–providing instant, online access to the textbooks and course materials you need at a lower cost for students. And even as students save money, you can save time and hassle with a digital eTextbook that allows you to search for the most relevant content at the very moment you need it. Whether it's evaluating textbooks or creating lecture notes to help students with difficult concepts, CourseSmart can make life a little easier. See how when you visit www.coursesmart.com/instructors.

Acknowledgments

Elliot Aronson is delighted to acknowledge the collaboration of his son, Hal Aronson, an environmental sociologist. Hal's insights and creativity were of enormous value in bringing the current edition up to date. He would also like to acknowledge the general contributions of his best friend (who also happens to be his wife of 55 years), Vera Aronson. Vera, as usual, provided a great deal of inspiration for his ideas and acted as the sounding board for and supportive critic of many of his semi-formed notions, helping to mould them into more sensible analyses.

Tim Wilson would like to thank his graduate mentor, Richard E. Nisbett, who nurtured his interest in the field and showed him the continuity between social psychological research and everyday life. He thanks his parents, Elizabeth and Geoffrey Wilson, for their overall support. Most of all, he thanks his wife, Deirdre Smith, and his children, Christopher and Leigh, for their love, patience, and understanding, even when the hour was late and the computer was still on.

Beverley Fehr would like to thank her colleagues at the University of Winnipeg and her social psychology colleagues at the University of Manitoba for their enthusiasm and support throughout this project. Beverley would also like to express immense gratitude to her highly skilled, super-efficient research assistant, Erin Larson. On a more personal note, Beverley's children, Genevieve and Everett, were an invaluable source of joy and energy. Finally, Beverley would like to thank the staff at Frenchway Café, where much of her writing was done, for their warmth, friendliness, and the countless refills of coffee.

No book can be written and published without the help of a great many people working with the authors behind the scenes, and this book is no exception. Beverley would like to thank the people at Pearson Education Canada who worked with her on this text. She would like to express appreciation to Megan Burns, developmental editor, for her competence, patience, support, and understanding throughout this project. Beverley would also like to thank sponsoring editor Carolin Sweig for her encouragement, warmth, and enthusiasm, and project manager Sarah Lukaweski, copy editor, Deborah Bullock-Cooper, and proofreader, Susan Adlam for their expertise, conscientiousness, and patience in dealing with an author who struggled to meet deadlines because of her passion for including "just one more" Canadian study.

Robin Akert is beholden to Prof. Jonathan Cheek, Prof. Julie Donnelly, Nan Vaida, Melody Tortosa, and Lila Mc-Cain for their interest in her work, their feedback and advice, their unconditional support, and their wonderful senses of humour. She also wishes to thank her students in social psychology. Their intelligence, perspicacity, dedication, and joie de vivre are her continuing sources of energy and motivation for this book. She is deeply grateful to her family, Michaela and Wayne Akert, and Linda and Jerry Wuichet; their enthusiasm and boundless support have sustained her on this project as on all the ones before it. Finally, no words can express her gratitude and indebtedness to Dane Archer, mentor, colleague, and friend, who opened the world of social psychology to her and who has been her guide ever since.

Finally, we would like to thank the many colleagues who read one or more chapters of previous editions of the book. Reviewers of this Fifth Canadian edition included the following:

Theresa Bianco, Concordia University
Michael Boisvert, Fanshawe College
Sue Ludwig, Grant MacEwan University
Tom Murphy, University of Western Ontario
Kim O'Neil, Carleton University
Simon Sherry, Dalhousie University
Gillian Watson, University of British Columbia.

About the Authors

Elliot Aronson

When I was a kid, we were the only Jewish family in a virulently anti-Semitic neighborhood. I had to go to Hebrew school every day, late in the afternoon. Being the only youngster in my neighborhood going to Hebrew school made me an easy target for some of the older neighborhood toughs. On my way home from Hebrew school, after dark, I was frequently waylaid and roughed up by roving gangs shouting anti-Semitic epithets.

I have a vivid memory of sitting on a curb after one of these beatings, nursing a bloody nose or a split lip, feeling very sorry for myself and wondering how these kids could hate me so much when they didn't even know me. I thought about whether those kids were taught to hate Jews or whether, somehow, they were born that way. I wondered if their hatred could be changed—if they got to know me better, would they hate me less? I speculated about my own character. What would I have done if the shoe were on the other foot—that is, if I were bigger and stronger than they—would I be capable of beating them up for no good reason?

I didn't realize it at the time, of course, but eventually I discovered that these were profound questions. And some thirty years later, as an experimental social psychologist, I had the great good fortune to be in a position to answer some of those questions and to invent techniques to reduce the kind of prejudice that had claimed me as a victim.

Elliot Aronson is one of the most renowned social psychologists in the world. In 2002 he was chosen as one of the 100 most eminent psychologists of the twentieth century. He is currently Professor Emeritus at the University of California at Santa Cruz and Distinguished Visiting Professor at Stanford University.

Dr. Aronson is the only person in the 110-year history of the American Psychological Association to have received all three of its major awards: for distinguished writing, distinguished teaching, and distinguished research. Many other professional societies have honored his research and teaching as well. These include the American Association for the Advancement of Science, which gave him its highest honor, the Distinguished Scientific Research award; the American Council for the Advancement and Support of Education, which named him Professor of the Year of 1989; and the Society for the Psychological Study of Social Issues, which awarded him the Gordon Allport prize for his contributions to the reduction of prejudice among racial and ethnic groups. In 1992, he was named a Fellow of the American Academy of Arts and Sciences. He has served as president of the Western Psychological Association as well as president of the Society of Personality and Social Psychology.

Tim Wilson

One day, when I was 8, a couple of older kids rode up on their bikes to share some big news: They had discovered an abandoned house down a country road. "It's really neat," they said. "We broke a window and nobody cared!" My friend and I hopped onto our bikes to investigate. We had no trouble finding the house—there it was, sitting off by itself, with a big, jagged hole in a first-floor window. We got off of our bikes and looked around. My friend found a baseball-sized rock lying on the ground and threw a perfect strike through another first-floor window. There was something exhilarating about the smash-and-tingle of shattering glass, especially when we knew there was nothing wrong with what we were doing. After all, the house was abandoned, wasn't it? We broke nearly every window in the house and then climbed through one of the first-floor windows to look around.

It was then that we realized something was terribly wrong. The house certainly did not look abandoned. There were pictures on the wall, nice furniture, books in shelves. We went home feeling frightened and confused. We soon learned that the house was the residence of an elderly couple who were away on vacation. Eventually my parents discovered what we had done and paid a substantial sum to repair the windows. For years, I pondered this incident: Why did I do such a terrible thing? Was I a bad kid? I didn't think so, and neither did my parents. How, then, could a good kid do such a bad thing? Even though the neighborhood kids said the house was abandoned, why couldn't my friend and I see the clear signs that someone lived there? How crucial was it that my friend was there and threw the first rock? Although I didn't know it at the time, these reflections touched on several classic social psychological issues, such as whether only bad people do bad things, whether the social situation can be powerful enough to make good people do bad things, and the way in which our expectations about an event can make it difficult to see it as it really is. Fortunately, my career as a vandal ended with this one incident. It did, however, mark the beginning of my fascination with basic questions about how people understand themselves and the social world—questions I continue to investigate to this day.

Tim Wilson did his undergraduate work at Williams College and Hampshire College and received his Ph.D. from the University of Michigan. Currently Sherrell J. Aston Professor of Psychology at the University of Virginia, he has published numerous articles in the areas of introspection, attitude change, self-knowledge, and affective forecasting, as well as the recent book, Strangers to Ourselves: Discovering the Adaptive Unconscious. *His research has received the support of the National Science Foundation and the National Institute for Mental Health. He has been associate editor of the* Journal of Personality and Social Psychology *and a member of the Social and Groups Processes Review Committee at the National Institute of Mental*

Health. He has been elected twice to the Executive Board of the Society for Experimental Social Psychology and is a Fellow in the American Psychological Society and the Society for Personality and Social Psychology. In 2009, he was named a Fellow of the American Academy of Arts and Sciences. Wilson has taught the Introduction to Social Psychology course at the University of Virginia for more than twenty years. In 2001 he was awarded an All University Outstanding Teaching Award.

Beverley Fehr

I suspect that many social psychologists, like me, didn't start out with the intention of becoming social psychologists. I was attending university as a music major, taking psychology courses for interest. I enjoyed them, but kept experiencing a vague sense of disappointment—each course wasn't quite what I had thought psychology would be about. When I enrolled in a social psychology course that was offered one summer, I was delighted to have finally found what I was looking for. One day, as part of a class exercise, our professor handed out copies of Rubin's (1970) love and liking scale for us to complete with reference to a romantic partner and a friend. (This scale is still widely used in close relationships research today.) I was dating someone at the time about whom I cared deeply, although I had a feeling that he was not a particularly good choice as a long-term partner. I was astonished, when we scored the scale, that the love score for this person was extremely high, but the liking score was distressingly low! Quite aside from the personal implications of this result, I was utterly fascinated that social psychologists could use the scientific method to gain insight into issues that are highly relevant to people's everyday lives. This, and other experiences in that class, prompted me to reconsider my career choice and I ended up changing my major to psychology. I suspect that this experience may also have played a role in my eventual decision to become a social psychologist who studies close relationships.

Beverley Fehr graduated with a B.A. (Hons.) from the University of Winnipeg where she was awarded the Gold Medal for the highest standing in psychology. She received her M.A. (under the guidance of Jim Russell) and her Ph.D. (under the guidance of Dan Perlman) from the University of British Columbia. Her doctoral thesis on lay people's conceptions of love and commitment won the Iowa/International Network for the Study of Personal Relationships Dissertation Prize. She has published numerous articles and book chapters on the topics of emotion and close relationships. Her book Friendship Processes *(1996) was awarded the 1997 Outstanding Academic Book Award by Choice: Current Reviews for Academic Libraries. Beverley's research is supported by grants from the Social Sciences and Humanities Research Council of Canada and the Fetzer Institute. She is past president of the International Association for Relationships Research, has served as associate editor of the* Journal of Personality and Social Psychology, *and is a fellow of the Canadian Psychological Association.*

Robin Akert

One fall day, when I was about 16, I was walking with a friend along the shore of the San Francisco Bay. Deep in conversation, I glanced over my shoulder and saw a sailboat capsize. I pointed it out to my friend, who took only a perfunctory interest and went on talking. However, I kept watching as we walked, and I realized that the two sailors were in the water, clinging to the capsized boat. Again I said something to my friend, who replied, "Oh, they'll get it upright, don't worry."

But I was worried. Was this an emergency? My friend didn't think so. And I was no sailor; I knew nothing about boats. But I kept thinking, "That water is really cold. They can't stay in that water too long." I remember feeling very confused and unsure. What should I do? Should I do anything? Did they really need help?

We were near a restaurant with a big window overlooking the bay, and I decided to go in and see if anyone had done anything about the boat. Lots of people were watching but not doing anything. This confused me too. Very meekly, I asked the bartender to call for some kind of help. He just shrugged. I went back to the window and watched the two small figures in the water. Why was everyone so unconcerned? Was I crazy?

Years later, I reflected on how hard it was for me to do what I did next: I demanded that the bartender let me use his phone. In those days before "911," it was lucky that I knew there was a Coast Guard station on the bay, and I asked the operator for the number. I was relieved to hear the Guardsman take my message very seriously.

It had been an emergency. I watched as the Coast Guard cutter sped across the bay and pulled the two sailors out of the water. Maybe I saved their lives that day. What really stuck with me over the years was how other people behaved and how it made me feel. The other bystanders seemed unconcerned and did nothing to help. Their reactions made me doubt myself and made it harder for me to decide to take action. When I later studied social psychology in college, I realized that on the shore of the San Francisco Bay that day, I had experienced the "bystander effect" fully: The presence of other, apparently unconcerned bystanders had made it difficult for me to decide if the situation was an emergency and whether it was my responsibility to help.

Robin Akert graduated summa cum laude from the University of California at Santa Cruz, where she majored in psychology and sociology. She received her Ph.D. in experimental social psychology from Princeton University. She is currently a Professor of psychology at Wellesley College, where she was awarded the Pinanski Prize for Excellence in Teaching early in her career. She publishes primarily in the area of nonverbal communication and recently received the AAUW American Fellowship in support of her research. She has taught the Social Psychology course at Wellesley College for nearly thirty years.

Special Tips for Students

The two quotes in the margin below, taken together, sum up everything you need to know to be a proficient student: Be an active, creative consumer of information, and make sure it sticks! How do you accomplish these two feats? Actually, it's not difficult at all. Like everything else in life, it just takes some work—some clever, well-planned, purposeful work. Here are some suggestions about how to do it.

Get to Know the Textbook

Believe it or not, in writing this book, we thought very carefully about the organization and structure of each chapter. Things are the way they appear for a reason, and that reason is to help you learn the material in the best way possible. Here are some tips on what to look for in each chapter.

There is then creative reading as well as creative writing.

–Ralph Waldo Emerson, *1837*

Key terms are in boldface type in the text so that you'll notice them. We define the terms in the text, and that definition appears again in the margin. These marginal definitions are there to help you out if later in the chapter you forget what something means. The marginal definitions are short and easy to find. You can also look up key terms in the alphabetical Glossary at the end of this textbook.

Make sure you notice the headings and subheadings. The headings are the skeleton that holds a chapter together. They link together like vertebrae. If you ever feel lost, look back to the last heading and the headings before that one—this will give you the "big picture" of where the chapter is going. It should also help you see the connections between sections.

The summary at the end of each chapter is a succinct shorthand presentation of the chapter information. You should read it and make sure there are no surprises when you do so. If anything in the summary doesn't ring a bell, go back to the chapter and reread that section. Most important, remember that the summary is intentionally brief, whereas your understanding of the material should be full and complete. Use the summary as a study aid before your exams. When you read it over, everything should be familiar and you should have that wonderful feeling of knowing more than is in the summary (in which case you are ready to take the exam).

I am a kind of burr, I shall stick.

—William Shakespeare, *1604*

Be sure to do the Try It! exercises. They will make concepts from social psychology concrete and help you see how they can be applied to your own life. Some of the Try It! exercises replicate social psychology experiments. Other Try It! exercises reproduce self-report scales so you can see where you stand in relation to other people. Still other Try It! exercises are short quizzes that illustrate social psychological concepts.

Just Say No to the Couch Potato Within

Because social psychology is about everyday life, you might lull yourself into believing that the material is all common sense. Don't be fooled. The material is more complicated than it might seem. Therefore, we want to emphasize that the best way to learn it is to work with it in an active, not passive, fashion. You can't just read a chapter once and expect it to stick with you. You have to go over the material, wrestle with it, make your own connections to it, question it, think about it, interact with it. Actively working with material makes it memorable and makes it your own. Because it's a safe bet that someone is going to ask you about this material later and you're going to have to pull it out of memory, do what you can to get it into memory now. Here are some techniques to use:

- Go ahead and be bold—use a highlighter! Go crazy—write in the margins! If you underline, highlight, circle, or draw little hieroglyphics next to important points, you will remember them better. We recall taking exams in university where we not only remembered the material but could actually see in our minds the textbook page it was written on and the little squiggles and stars we'd drawn in the margin.
- Read the textbook chapter before the applicable class lecture, not afterward. This way, you'll get more out of the lecture, which will introduce new material. The chapter will give you the big picture, as well as a lot of detail. The lecture will enhance that information and help you put it all together. If you don't read the chapter first, you may not understand some of the points made in the lecture or realize that they are important.
- Here's a good way to study material: Write out a difficult concept or a study (or say it out loud to yourself) in your own words, without looking at the book or your notes. Can you do it? How good was your version? Did you omit anything important? Did you get stuck at some point, unable to remember what comes next? If so, you now know that you need to go over that information in more detail. You can also study with someone else, describing theories and studies to each other and seeing if you're making sense.
- If you have trouble remembering the results of an important study, try drawing your own version of a graph of the findings (you can use our data graphs for an idea of how to proceed). If all the various points in a theory are confusing you, try drawing your own flowchart of how it works. You will probably find that you remember the research results much better in pictorial form than in words and that the theory isn't so confusing (or missing a critical part) if you've outlined it. Draw information a few times and it will stay with you.
- Remember, the more you work with the material, the better you will learn and remember it. Write it in your own words, talk about it, explain it to others, or draw visual representations of it.
- Last but not least, remember that this material is a lot of fun. You haven't even started reading the book yet, but we think you're going to like it. In particular, you'll see how much social psychology has to tell you about your real, everyday life. As this course progresses, you might want to remind yourself to observe the events of your daily life with new eyes, the eyes of a social psychologist, and to try to apply what you are learning to the behaviour of your friends, acquaintances, strangers, and, yes, even yourself. Make sure you use the Try It! exercises and visit the website. You will find out how much social psychology can help us understand our lives. When you read newspapers or magazines or watch the nightly news, think about what social psychology has to say about such events and behaviours—we believe you will find that your understanding of daily life is richer.

We suspect that 10 years from now you may not remember all the facts, theories, and names you learn now. Although we hope you will remember some of them, our main goal is for you to take with you into your future a great many of the broad social psychological concepts presented herein. If you open yourself to social psychology's magic, we believe it will enrich the way you look at the world and the way you live in it.

FIFTH CANADIAN EDITION

SOCIAL PSYCHOLOGY

1 Introduction to Social Psychology

THE TASK OF THE PSYCHOLOGIST IS TO TRY TO UNDERSTAND and predict human behaviour. Different kinds of psychologists go about this in different ways, and in this book we will attempt to show you how social psychologists do it. Let's begin with a few examples of human behaviour. Some of these might seem important; others might seem trivial; one or two might seem frightening. To a social psychologist, all of them are interesting. Our hope is that by the time you finish reading this book you will find all of these examples as fascinating as we do. As you read, try to think about how you would explain why each event unfolded as it did.

- "Canadians amaze with their giving"; "Canadians rush to help Haiti, overloading web servers." Headlines such as these were a daily occurrence in Canadian newspapers, as story after story documented the extent to which Canadians were moved to assist the victims of the January 2010 earthquake in Haiti. Assistance included benefit concerts, school bake sales, fundraising drives at sports events, and extended hours at the offices of relief organizations so that all of the donations could be accommodated. One person who helped is Neil Bauman, a 41-year-old architect from Saint John, New Brunswick. He volunteered to travel to Haiti with other Red Cross delegates to help build short-term and long-term shelter for people who had lost their homes in the quake. He acknowledged that it was stressful to be away for a month, leaving behind his wife and his two- and four-year-old sons. But he and his family were willing to pay the price to respond to those who were so severely in need (Robinson, 2010).

  What would make a person such as Neil Bauman leave his young family for a month in order to reach out to complete strangers in a faraway country? Why did so many Canadians open their hearts and their wallets to help the earthquake victims?

- You are taking a break in a student lounge with your friends. The television in the room is set on the CBC News Network. The top story of the day is Prime Minister Stephen Harper's visit to the United States to meet with President Barack Obama concerning cross-border security. The cameras zoom in as the leaders sign a 10-page declaration that allows, among other things, border agents in both countries to exchange information more freely, including information about airline travellers. Commentators and members of the opposition parties who are interviewed criticize the deal, arguing that these measures erode the privacy of Canadian citizens and undermine the sovereignty of Canada as a country. You agree with these views. Just as you are opening your mouth to speak, your friend Maria says, "All of this reaction to the new border security deal is ridiculous. Why shouldn't Canada and the U.S. exchange information if it will keep the border safer?" Steve chimes

OUTLINE

Jean-François Caudron was subjected to severe initiations as a rookie, but remembers his teammates with fondness.

in, "Not only that, but the U.S. is Canada's major trade partner. If we can work together on security issues, it will only help our economy." He further points out that the cost of post-9/11 border delays is approximately $14 billion per year. "I agree that Canadians are overreacting," says Emily. "It's not as though we're giving our country to the Americans just because Harper signed this declaration." All eyes turn to you.

What would you say? Would you state your own opinion or conform to your friends' unanimous attitude? Would it surprise you to learn that when placed in a similar situation most university students would go along with the majority opinion rather than appear odd or out of step?

- On the cover of the March 6, 2000, issue of *Maclean's*, a headline reads, "A barbaric rite of passage: hazing in university athletics." The article begins with the story of Jean-François Caudron from St-Hubert, Quebec, the recipient of a hockey scholarship from the University of Vermont. As a rookie, he was subjected to a hazing that involved shaving his pubic hair, painting his toenails, and drinking warm beer until he vomited. Based on his experiences on Canadian hockey teams, Jean-François knew there was no escaping rookie night: "You knew about this night and you were nervous. You feel pressure that you have to do it." One might expect that Jean-François would have nothing but bad memories about his hazing experiences. However, he describes it this way: "[O]nce it was over, I was so happy. I really felt part of the team" (O'Hara, 2000).

Why would Jean-François feel so happy to be part of a team that inflicted pain, embarrassment, and humiliation on him?

- In the mid-1980s, residents of Quebec were introduced to the Order of the Solar Temple—a cult founded by Luc Jouret and his partner Joseph Di Mambro. Prominent citizens, including the highly respected mayor of Richelieu and his wife, joined the cult. They were taught that the only redemption from their sins was to experience death by fire, which would transport them to the star Sirius, where they would be reborn. Suicides were to take place during the spring or autumn equinox. The cult attracted worldwide attention in October 1994 when 53 cult members, including the mayor of Richelieu and his wife, died in a combined mass murder-suicide. An elaborate system of explosives was used to set fire to the buildings they inhabited in Quebec and Switzerland. Nearly a year later, another 16 cult members, including several children, died in a remote village in France. So far, at least 74 members of this cult have died.

How can people agree to kill themselves and their own children? Were they crazy? Were they under some kind of hypnotic spell? How would you explain it?

We now have presented several questions about human social behaviour—questions we find fascinating. Why do people sometimes go to great lengths to help complete strangers, as Neil Bauman did when he left his young family for a month in order to build shelters for earthquake victims? When people disagree on issues such as the need for heightened security measures, why are they likely to go along with the majority rather than voice their true opinion? Why did Jean-François Caudron like being part of hockey teams that forced him to endure barbaric hazing rituals? And how could large numbers of people be induced to kill their own children and themselves in Quebec, Switzerland, and France? In this chapter, we will consider what these examples have in common and why they are of interest to us. We will also put forth some reasonable explanations based upon social psychological research.

What Is Social Psychology?

At the heart of social psychology is the phenomenon of social influence: We are all influenced by other people. When we think of social influence, the kinds of examples that readily come to mind are direct attempts at persuasion, whereby one person deliberately tries to change another person's behaviour. This is what happens in an advertising campaign when creative individuals employ sophisticated techniques to persuade us to buy a particular brand of toothpaste, or during an election campaign when similar techniques are used to get us to vote for a particular political candidate. Direct attempts at persuasion also occur when our friends try to get us to do something we don't really want to do ("Come on, have another beer—everyone else is in") or when the schoolyard bully uses force or threats to make smaller kids to part with their lunch money or completed homework.

These attempts at direct social influence form a major part of social psychology, and will be discussed in our chapters on conformity, attitudes, and group processes. To the social psychologist, however, social influence is broader than attempts by one person to change another person's behaviour. Social influence extends beyond behaviour—it includes our thoughts and feelings, as well as our overt acts. In addition, social influence takes on many forms other than deliberate attempts at persuasion. We are often influenced merely by the presence of other people. Moreover, even when we are not in the physical presence of other people, we are still influenced by them. Thus, in a sense, we carry our mothers, fathers, friends, and teachers around with us, as we attempt to make decisions that would make them proud of us.

On a more subtle level, each of us is immersed in a social and cultural context. Social psychologists are interested in studying how and why our thoughts, feelings, and behaviours are shaped by the entire social environment. Taking all these factors into account, we can define **social psychology** as the scientific study of the way in which people's thoughts, feelings, and behaviours are influenced by the real or imagined presence of other people (Allport, 1985).

Social Psychology
The scientific study of the way in which people's thoughts, feelings, and behaviours are influenced by the real or imagined presence of other people

The Power of Social Interpretation

Other disciplines, such as anthropology and sociology, are also interested in how people are influenced by their social environment. Social psychology is distinct, however, primarily because it is concerned not so much with social situations in any objective sense, but rather with how people are influenced by their interpretation, or **construal**, of their social environment. To understand how people are influenced by their social world, social psychologists believe, it is more important to understand how they perceive, comprehend, and interpret the social world than it is to understand the objective properties of the social world itself (Lewin, 1943).

Construal
The way in which people perceive, comprehend, and interpret the social world

As you can see from Ross's research as discussed in Connections (below), construal is important and has wide ramifications. Consider a murder trial. The prosecution may be able to present compelling evidence, such as DNA tests, that it believes will have a decisive impact on the verdict. But no matter how powerful the evidence might be, the final verdict will always hinge on precisely how each member of the jury construes that evidence—and these construals may rest on a variety of events and perceptions that may or may not bear objective relevance to the case. Such construal processes can produce very different outcomes. In the O. J. Simpson trial in the United States, even though objective evidence concerning DNA and hair and fibre samples was presented, the jury decided that Simpson was not guilty of murdering his ex-wife and her friend. Now consider the recent (March 2011) second-degree murder conviction of Mark Edward Grant for killing Candace Derksen in Winnipeg in November 1984. The then 13-year-old Candace was walking home from school when she disappeared. Her frozen body was found six weeks later in a nearby storage shed. Her hands and feet had been bound with twine. The murder remained unsolved for 26 years when the police came forward with DNA evidence linking Mark Edward Grant to the crime. Grant's lawyer argued that the DNA evidence proved only that Grant had been at that location, not that he was Candace's killer. His lawyer also maintained that the DNA evidence was contaminated. (Given that DNA testing was not available in 1984, most of the case's investigators did not wear gloves, gowns, or masks when gathering the evidence.) However, in this case, the Queen's Bench jury was persuaded by the DNA evidence and handed down a guilty verdict. Grant's lawyer plans to appeal.

CONNECTIONS 

The Role of Construal in Conflict Negotiations

A special kind of construal is what Lee Ross calls "naïve realism." Ross is a social psychologist who has been working closely with Israeli and Palestinian negotiators. These negotiations frequently run aground because of naïve realism—the conviction all of us have that we perceive things "as they really are" (Pronin, Gilovich, & Ross, 2004; Ehrlinger, Gilovich, & Ross, 2005). We assume that other reasonable people see things the same way that we do.

> [E]ven when each side recognizes that the other side perceives the issues differently, each thinks that the other side is biased while they themselves are objective and that their own perceptions of reality should provide the basis for settlement. (Pronin, Gilovich, & Ross, 2004)

Although both the Israelis and the Palestinians understand intellectually that the other side perceives the issues differently, both sides resist compromise, fearing that their "biased" opponent will benefit more than they. In a simple experiment, Ross took peace proposals created by Israeli negotiators, labelled them as Palestinian proposals, and asked Israeli citizens to judge them. The Israelis liked the Palestinian proposals attributed to Israel more than they liked the Israeli proposals attributed to the Palestinians. Ross concludes, "If your own proposal isn't going to be attractive to you when it comes from the other side, what chance is there that the *other* side's proposal is going to be attractive when it comes from the other side?" (Pronin, Gilovich, & Ross, 2004). The hope is that once negotiators on both sides become fully aware of this phenomenon, and how it impedes conflict resolution, a reasonable compromise will be more likely.

Another distinctive feature of social psychology is that it is an experimentally-based science. As scientists, we test our assumptions, guesses, and ideas about human social behaviour empirically and systematically, rather than relying on folk wisdom, common sense, or the opinions and insights of philosophers, novelists, political pundits, our grandmothers, and others wise in the ways of human beings. As you will see, conducting systematic experiments in social psychology presents many challenges—primarily because we are attempting to predict the behaviour of highly sophisticated organisms in a variety of complex situations.

As scientists, our goal is to find objective answers to a wide array of important questions: What are the factors that cause aggression? How might people reduce prejudice? What causes two people to like or love each other? Why do certain kinds of advertisements work better than others? The specific ways in which social psychologists conduct experiments to meet these challenges will be illustrated throughout this book.

We will spend most of this introductory chapter expanding on the issues raised in the preceding paragraphs: what social psychology is and how it is distinct from other, related disciplines. A good place to begin is with what social psychology is not.

Some Alternative Ways of Understanding Social Influence

Let's take another look at the examples at the beginning of this chapter. Why did people behave the way they did? One way to answer this question might simply be to ask them. For example, we could ask Jean-François Caudron why he was so happy to be part of a hockey team that inflicted pain on him or ask followers of Luc Jouret why they joined the cult. The problem with this approach is that people are not always aware of the origins of their own responses (Gilbert, 2008; Nisbett & Wilson, 1977; Wilson, 2002). It is unlikely that Caudron knows why the hazing he experienced made him feel like part of the team or that the members of the Solar Temple know why they got pulled into a cult.

Folk Wisdom Journalists, social critics, and novelists have many interesting things to say about these situations. Such commentary is generally referred to as *folk wisdom* or *common sense*. There is no shortage of folk theories for events such as the Solar Temple tragedy. When cult members kill themselves and their children at the request of their leader, explanations range from the view that the leader must have employed hypnotism and drugs to weaken the resistance of his followers, to suspicion that the people who were attracted to his cult must have been disturbed, self-destructive individuals in the first place. Such speculations, because they underestimate the power of the situation, are almost certainly incorrect—or at the very least oversimplified. Indeed, what is most striking about members of the Solar Temple cult is that they tended to be highly respected, well-functioning members of society—including a mayor, a journalist, a civil servant, and a sales manager.

Don't get us wrong. A great deal can be learned about social behaviour from journalists, social critics, and novelists—and in this book we quote from all of these. There is, however, at least one problem with relying entirely on such sources: More often than not, they disagree with one another, and there is no easy way of determining which of them is correct.

Consider what folk wisdom has to say about the factors that influence how much we like other people. On the one hand, we know that "birds of a feather flock together," and with a little effort, each of us could come up with many examples in which we liked and spent time with people who shared our backgrounds and interests. But, on the other hand, folk wisdom *also* tells us that "opposites attract," and if we tried, we could come up with examples in which people with backgrounds and interests different from our own did attract us. Which is correct? Similarly, are we to believe that "out of sight is out of mind" or that "absence makes the heart grow fonder"; that "haste makes waste" or that "he who hesitates is lost"?

Unfortunately, because so-called common sense frequently turns out to be wrong or oversimplified, people tend not to learn from previous incidents. The Solar Temple tragedy was probably the first mass suicide involving Canadians, but certainly not the first or the last event of this kind. In 1978, nearly 800 members of a California-based religious cult died in Jonestown, Guyana, when they drank a deadly mixture of Kool-Aid and cyanide in response to a command from their leader, the Reverend Jim Jones. Subsequent doomsday cults capitalized on fears that the millennium would bring about the end of the world, and managed to persuade their followers to take their lives and those of their children. For example, the leaders of the Ugandan Movement for the Restoration of the Ten Commandments of God persuaded parents that handing over their children to die was the only way to prevent them from falling into the hands of Satan. On March 17, 2000, hundreds of people, many of whom were children, were led into a sealed chapel that was set on fire (Associated Press, 2000). Hundreds of other cult members and their children died in other ways. While it is difficult to determine the exact number of casualties, most reports suggest that between 800 and 1000 people

Charismatic leaders are able to persuade people to willingly hand over their children to be mistreated, sexually abused, and, in some cases, even killed. Warren Jeffs, leader of the Yearning for Zion Mormon sect, continues to receive support from his followers.

perished, placing this cult on the same horrific scale as the California-based Jonestown cult (Wasswa, 2002).

Still more recently, in April 2008, more than 400 children—one of them Canadian—were seized by Child Protective Services authorities in Texas. There were allegations that young girls, and perhaps some boys, were beaten, starved, and forced to have sex with much older men. Their parents were followers of Warren Jeffs, the leader of the Yearning for Zion Mormon sect. At the beginning of 2011, the RCMP began investigating allegations that two 12-year-old girls and one 13-year-old girl from Bountiful, British Columbia, were taken to the United States by their parents to marry Warren Jeffs. This event was part of a larger investigation that included marriage documents for nine teenage girls (eight from Bountiful) that were seized during the Texas raid. Jeffs claimed that he had orders from God to marry at least three young virgins, and preferably many more. He also held the belief that "spiritual marriages" of girls as young as age 13 to men in their forties and fifties should be arranged. Moreover, there were reports of Jeffs reassigning wives and children to other men in the sect. In August 2011, this charismatic leader was charged with sexual assault of children and was sentenced to life plus 20 years to be served in a Texas prison.

It is difficult for most people to grasp just how powerful a cult can be in affecting the hearts and minds of relatively normal people. Accordingly, the general population is eager to find someone to blame. Often people blame the victims themselves, accusing them of stupidity or of suffering from mental illness. Fixing blame may make us feel better by resolving our confusion, but it is no substitute for understanding the complexities of the situations that produced those events.

Philosophy Throughout history, philosophy has been a major source of insight about human nature. Indeed, the work of philosophers is part of the foundation of contemporary psychology. This has more than mere historical significance. In recent decades, psychologists have looked to philosophers for insights into the nature of consciousness (e.g., Dennett, 1991) and how people form beliefs about the social world (e.g., Gilbert, 1991). Sometimes, however, even great thinkers find themselves in disagreement with one another. When this occurs, how is one to know who is right? Are there some situations where philosopher A might be right, and other conditions under which philosopher B might be right? How would you determine this?

We social psychologists address many of the same questions that philosophers address, but we attempt to look at these questions scientifically—even concerning that great human mystery, love. In 1663, the great Dutch philosopher Benedict Spinoza offered a highly original insight. He proposed that if we love someone whom we formerly hated, that love will be greater than if hate had not preceded it. Spinoza's proposition is beautifully worked out. His logic is impeccable. But how can we be sure that it holds up? What are the conditions under which it does or doesn't hold? These are empirical questions for the social psychologist.

One of the tasks of the social psychologist is to make educated guesses (called *hypotheses*) about the specific situations under which one outcome or the other would occur. Just as a physicist performs experiments to test hypotheses about the nature of the physical world, the social psychologist performs experiments to test hypotheses about the nature of the social world. The task of the social psychologist is to design well-controlled experiments sophisticated enough to tease out the situations that would result in one or another outcome. This enriches our understanding of human nature and allows us to make accurate predictions once we know the key aspects of the prevailing situation. We will discuss the scientific methods that social psychologists use in Chapter 2.

The major reason we have conflicting philosophical positions (just as we have conflicting folk aphorisms) is that the world is a complicated place. Small differences in the situation might not be easily discernible, yet these small differences might produce very different effects.

To elaborate on this point, let's return to our earlier discussion about the kinds of people we like and the relationship between absence and liking. We would suggest that there are some conditions under which birds of a feather flock together and other conditions under which opposites do attract. Similarly, there are some conditions under which absence makes the heart grow fonder, and others under which out of sight does mean out of mind. Social psychologists have conducted careful research that specifies the conditions under which each of these statements is true, as you will see in Chapter 9.

Social Psychology Compared with Sociology

Social psychology's focus on social behaviour is shared by several other disciplines in the social sciences, most notably sociology. Both disciplines are concerned with the influence of social and societal factors on human behaviour. There are important differences, however. One such difference is the level of analysis. Social psychology is a branch of psychology, rooted in the study of *individuals*, with an emphasis on the psychological processes going on in their hearts and minds. *For the social psychologist, the level of analysis is the individual in the context of a social situation.* For example, to understand why people intentionally hurt one another, the social psychologist focuses on the specific psychological processes that trigger aggression in specific situations. To what extent is aggression preceded by a state of frustration? If people are feeling frustrated, under what conditions will they vent their frustration with an overt, aggressive act? What factors might preclude an aggressive response by a frustrated individual? Besides frustration, what other factors might cause aggression? We will address these questions in Chapter 11.

Sociology is more concerned with broad societal factors that influence events in a society. Thus, the focus is on such topics as social class, social structure, and social institutions. Of course, because society is made up of collections of people, some overlap is bound to exist between the domains of sociology and social psychology. The major difference is that sociology, rather than focusing on the psychology of the individual, looks toward society at large. Sociologists, like social psychologists, are interested in aggressive behaviour, but sociologists are more likely to be concerned with why a particular society (or group within a society) produces different levels and types of aggression in its members. Sociologists might ask, for example, why the murder rate in the United States is so much higher than in Canada. Within Canada, why is the murder rate higher in some social classes than in others? How do changes in society relate to changes in aggressive behaviour?

The difference between social psychology and sociology in level of analysis reflects another difference between the disciplines—namely, what they are trying to explain. *The goal of social psychology is to identify universal properties of human nature that make everyone susceptible to social influence, regardless of social class or culture.* The laws governing the relationship between frustration and aggression, for example, are hypothesized to be true of most people in most places—not just members of one social class, age group, or race.

Social psychology is a young science that developed mostly in North America. Many of its findings have not yet been tested in other cultures to see if they are indeed universal. Nevertheless, our goal as social psychologists is to discover such laws. Fortunately, cross-cultural research is increasing, and as it continues to grow, we are learning more about the extent to which these laws are universal. This type of cultural expansion is extremely valuable because it sharpens theories, either by demonstrating their universality or by leading us to discover additional variables, the incorporation of which will ultimately help us make more accurate predictions of human social behaviour. We will encounter many examples of cross-cultural research in subsequent chapters.

Social Psychology Compared with Personality Psychology

If you are like most people, when you read the examples that opened this chapter and started thinking about how those events might have come about, you probably wondered about the strengths, weaknesses, flaws, and quirks of the personality of the individuals involved. Why did parents in Bountiful, British Columbia, hand over their daughters—as young as 12 and 13 years old—to be married to Warren Jeffs? Most of us explain these kinds of behaviours in terms of the personalities of the people involved.

What might these character traits be? Some people are leaders and others are followers; some people are bold and others are timid; some people are public-spirited and others are selfish.

Individual Differences The aspects of people's personalities that make them different from other people

Asking—and trying to answer—questions such as these is the work of personality psychologists. When trying to explain social behaviour, personality psychologists generally focus their attention on **individual differences**—the aspects of people's personalities that make them different from other people. For example, to explain why the people in the Solar Temple cult ended their own lives and those of their children it seems natural to point to their personalities. Perhaps they were all "conformist types" or weak-willed; maybe they were even psychotic. The insights of personality psychologists increase our understanding of human behaviour, but social psychologists are convinced that explaining behaviour primarily in terms of personality factors ignores a critical part of the story: the powerful role played by social influence. Remember that it was not just a handful of people who died in a ski resort in Quebec and in two villages in Switzerland. It is thought that, in all, 74 people lost their lives to the Solar Temple cult. In the Jonestown tragedy in northern Guyana, nearly 800 Americans took their own lives, and in the Ugandan cult, at least that many—many of whom were children—perished. More than 400 children from the Texas polygamy sect were removed by authorities because of allegations of rape and sexual exploitation, while their mothers continued to deny that there was wrongdoing. Although it is conceivable that all of these people were psychotic, that explanation is highly improbable. If we want a deeper, richer, more thorough explanation of these tragic events, we need to understand what kind of power and influence the charismatic leaders of these cults possess, the nature of the impact of living in a closed society cut off from other points of view, and myriad other factors that might have contributed to these tragic outcomes.

These two different approaches can be illustrated with an everyday example. Suppose you stop at a roadside restaurant for a cup of coffee and a piece of pie. The waitress comes to take your order, but you are having a hard time deciding which kind of pie you want. While you are hesitating, she impatiently taps her pen against her order book, rolls her eyes toward the ceiling, scowls at you, and finally snaps, "Hey, I haven't got all day, you know!"

The people in this photo can be studied from a variety of perspectives: as individuals and as members of a family, a social class, an occupation, a culture, a region, and on and on.

What do you conclude about this event? When faced with such a situation, most people would conclude that the waitress is a nasty or unpleasant person; consequently, they would be reluctant to enter that particular restaurant again—especially when that nasty person was on duty. That would certainly be understandable. However, suppose we were to tell you that the waitress is a single parent and was kept awake all night by the moaning of her youngest child, who has a painful terminal illness; that her car broke down on her way to work and she has no idea where she will find the money to have it repaired; that when she finally arrived at the restaurant, she learned that her co-worker was too drunk to work, requiring her to cover twice the usual number of tables; and that the short-

TABLE 1.1 Social Psychology Compared with Related Disciplines

Sociology	Social Psychology	Personality Psychology
Provides general laws and theories about societies, not individuals.	Studies the psychological processes people have in common with one another that make them susceptible to social influence.	Studies the characteristics that make individuals unique and different from one another.

order cook kept screaming at her because she was not picking up the orders fast enough to please him? Given all this information, you might revise your judgment and conclude that she is not necessarily a nasty person—just an ordinary person under enormous stress.

The key fact remains that when trying to account for a person's behaviour in a complex situation, the overwhelming majority of people will jump to the conclusion that the behaviour was caused by the personality of the individual involved rather than consider the influence of the situation. And this fact—that we often fail to take the situation into account—is important to a social psychologist, for it has a profound impact on how human beings relate to one another.

In sum, social psychology is located somewhere between its closest intellectual cousins, sociology and personality psychology (see Table 1.1). Social psychology shares with sociology an interest in situational and societal influences on behaviour but focuses more on the psychological makeup of individuals that renders them susceptible to social influence. Social psychology shares with personality psychology an emphasis on the psychology of the individual, but rather than focusing on what makes people different from one another, it emphasizes the psychological processes shared by most people that make them susceptible to social influence.

The Power of Social Influence

When trying to convince people that their behaviour is greatly influenced by the social environment, the social psychologist is up against a formidable barrier: All of us tend to explain people's behaviour in terms of their personalities (e.g., the case of the waitress discussed earlier). This barrier is known as the **fundamental attribution error**—the tendency to explain people's behaviour in terms of personality traits, thereby underestimating the power of social influence. While reading this book, try to suspend judgment for a short time and consider the possibility that to understand why people do what they do, it is important to look closely at the nature of the social situation. The accompanying Try It! exercise may help you do just that.

Explore on **mypsychlab**
Fundamental Attribution Error

Fundamental Attribution Error
The tendency to overestimate the extent to which people's behaviour stems from internal, dispositional factors and to underestimate the role of situational factors

TRY IT! Social Situations and Behaviour

1. Think about one of your friends or acquaintances whom you regard as a shy person. For a moment, try not to think about that person as "shy" but rather as someone who has difficulty relating to people in some situations but not in others.
2. Make a list of the social situations that you think are most likely to bring out your friend's "shy" behaviour.
3. Make a list of the social situations that might bring forth more outgoing behaviour on his or her part. (For example, if someone showed a real interest in one of your friend's favourite hobbies or topics of conversation, it might bring out behaviour that could be classified as charming or vivacious.)
4. Try to create a social environment in which this would be accomplished. Pay close attention to the effect it has on your friend's behaviour.

Watch on mypsychlab
Social Influence

Underestimating the Power of Social Influence

When we underestimate the power of social influence, we experience a feeling of false security. For example, when trying to explain why people do repugnant or bizarre things—such as the members of the Solar Temple cult taking their own lives or killing their own children—it is tempting, and in a strange way comforting, to write off the victims as flawed human beings. Doing so helps the rest of us believe that the repugnant or bizarre thing could never happen to us. However, by failing to appreciate fully the power of the situation, we tend to oversimplify complex situations, and oversimplification decreases our understanding of the causes of a great deal of human behaviour. Among other things, this oversimplification can lead us to blame the victim in situations in which the individual was overpowered by social forces too difficult for most of us to resist—as in the Solar Temple tragedy.

The head monkey at Paris puts on a traveller's cap, and all the monkeys in America do the same.

—Henry David Thoreau, *philosopher (1817–1862)*

To take a more mundane example, imagine a situation in which people are playing a two-person game wherein each player must choose one of two strategies. They can play competitively, where they try to win as much money as possible and ensure that their partner loses as much as possible, or they can play cooperatively, where they try to ensure that both they and their partner win some money. We will discuss the details of this game ("The Prisoner's Dilemma") in Chapter 8. For now, it is important to note that people can use only two basic strategies when playing the game—competitive or cooperative. How do you think your friends would play this game? Few people find this question difficult to answer; most people have a sense of the relative competitiveness of their friends. "Well," you might say, "I am certain that my friend Sam, who is a cutthroat business major, would play this game more competitively than my friend Richard, who is a really caring, loving person." That is, we think about our friends' personalities and answer accordingly. We usually do not think much about the nature of the social situation when making our predictions.

CONNECTIONS

The Fundamental Attribution Error: When We Blame the Victims of Violence

The tendency to explain others' behaviour as stemming from internal rather than situational factors can lead to tragic consequences, including a tendency to blame victims for their plight. Even if people are made aware of the situational factors responsible for the plight of disadvantaged members of society (e.g., inadequate nutrition, disrupted family life), they may still see such individuals as responsible for their misfortune. This tendency extends even to victims of violence. For example, women who are sexually assaulted are often seen as having somehow "caused" the attack (Morry & Winkler, 2001; Harrison & Abrishami, 2004), and battered wives are often seen as responsible for their abusive husbands' behaviour (Summers & Feldman, 1984).

Research conducted at Carleton University (Kristiansen & Giulietti, 1990) and at Mount Saint Vincent University (Perrott, Miller, & Delaney, 1997) has shown that people justify blaming victims of violence by assuming that the person must have done something to provoke the attack. Kristiansen and Giulietti (1990) asked participants to read the following scenario:

> Mrs. X explained that as she was late coming home from work, she was preparing leftovers. Upon hearing this, Mr. X got upset and angry. He argued that as she has a family to attend to, Mrs. X should ensure that she gets home on time.

Some participants received the provocation version of this scenario. For these participants, the scenario went on to read:

Mrs. X then became upset. She began to yell at Mr. X, and as her anger heightened, she began to shout various obscenities at him, calling him a "nagging bastard."

All participants then read the same ending:

Mrs. X then went into the kitchen to prepare dinner. Mr. X followed her. He grabbed her by the arm and slapped her, knocking her to the floor, and kicked her several times. He subsequently left the house.

In this study, participants who received the provocation information assigned more blame to the victim than those who did not receive this information. This tendency to see other people as responsible for their plight can result in tragic consequences, such as seeing the victims of abuse and violence as responsible for their suffering.

But how accurate are such predictions? Should the social situation be considered? To find out, Liberman, Samuels, and Ross (2004) conducted the following experiment. First, they chose a group of students at Stanford University who were considered by the resident assistants in their dorm to be either especially cooperative or especially competitive. The researchers did this by describing the game to the resident assistants and asking them to think of students in their dormitories who would be most likely to adopt the competitive or cooperative strategy. As expected, the resident assistants had no trouble thinking of students who fit each category.

Next, Liberman, Samuels and Ross invited these students to play the game in a psychology experiment. There was one added twist: The researchers varied a seemingly minor aspect of the social situation—namely, what the game was called. They told half the participants that it was the "Wall Street Game" and half that it was the "Community Game." Everything else about the game was identical. Thus, because people who were judged as either competitive or cooperative played the game under one of two names, the experiment resulted in four conditions.

Again, most of us go through life assuming that what really counts is an individual's personality—not something as trivial as what a game is called. Some people seem competitive by nature and would relish the opportunity to go head to head with a fellow student. Others seem much more cooperative and would achieve the most satisfaction by ensuring that no one lost too much money and no one's feelings were hurt. Right? Not so fast! As seen in Figure 1.1, even as trivial an aspect of the situation as the name of the game made a tremendous difference in how people behaved. When it was called

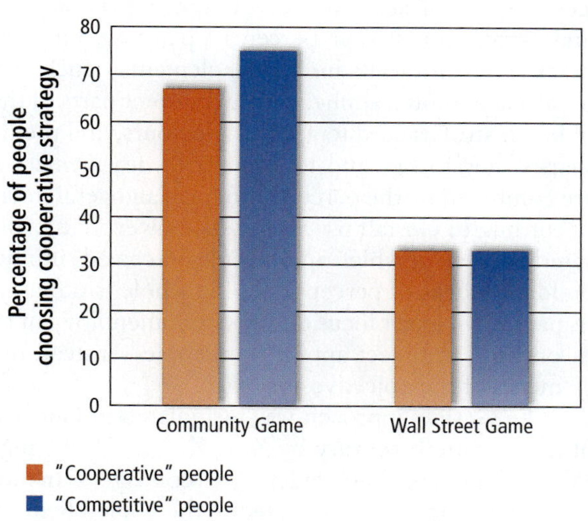

FIGURE 1.1

What influences how cooperative people will be—their personalities or the nature of the social situation?

In this situation, the student's personality made no measurable difference in the student's behaviour. The students who were labelled "competitive" (by the resident assistants in their dormitories) were no more likely to adopt the competitive strategy than those labelled "cooperative." However, the name of the game—whether it was called the Wall Street Game or the Community Game—did make a tremendous difference. Such seemingly minor aspects of the social situation can have powerful effects on people's behaviour, overwhelming the differences in their personalities.

(Adapted from Liberman, Samuels, & Ross, 2004)

the Wall Street Game, only one-third of the people responded cooperatively, whereas when it was called the Community Game, approximately two-thirds of the people responded cooperatively. The name of the game conveyed strong social norms about what kind of behaviour was appropriate in this situation. In Chapter 7, we will see that social norms shape people's behaviour in powerful ways.

This is not to say that personality differences do not exist or are unimportant; they do exist and frequently are of great importance. But we have learned that social and environmental situations are so powerful that they have dramatic effects on almost everyone. That is the domain of the social psychologist.

The Subjectivity of the Social Situation

We have argued that the social situation often has profound effects on human behaviour. But what exactly do we mean by the social situation? One strategy for defining it would be to specify the objective properties of the situation, such as how rewarding it is to people, and then to document the behaviours that follow from these objective properties. For example, dogs come when they are called because they have learned that compliance is followed by positive reinforcement (e.g., food or fondling). Although the rewards and punishments in an organism's environment undoubtedly influences its behaviour, human social behaviour cannot be fully understood by confining our observations to the physical properties of a situation. Instead, it is important to look at the situation from the viewpoint of the people in it, to see how they construe the world around them (Griffin & Ross, 1991; Ross & Nisbett, 1991). For example, if a person approaches you, slaps you on the back, and asks you how you are feeling, is that rewarding or not? On the surface, it might seem like a reward. After all, isn't that person's interest in you a good thing? In actuality, it is a complex situation that depends on your thoughts and feelings. You might construe the meaning differently, depending on whether the question is asked by a close friend of yours who is deeply concerned that you might be working too hard, a casual acquaintance simply passing the time of day, or an automobile salesperson intending to sell you a used car. This would be the case even if the question were worded the same and asked in the same tone of voice. In responding to the salesperson's question, it is unlikely that you will begin a detailed description of the pains you've been having in your kidney—something you might do in response to your closest friend's inquiry.

Gestalt Psychology

A school of psychology stressing the importance of studying the subjective way in which an object appears in people's minds, rather than the objective physical attributes of the object

This emphasis on construal, the way people interpret the social situation, has its roots in an approach called Gestalt psychology. Initially proposed as a theory of how people perceive the physical word, **Gestalt psychology** holds that we should study the subjective way in which an object appears in people's minds (the gestalt, or whole), rather than the way in which the objective physical attributes of the object combine. One way to try to understand how people perceive a painting, for example, would be to break it down into its individual elements—such as the exact amounts of primary colours applied to the different parts of the canvas, the types of brush strokes used to apply the colours, and the different geometric shapes they form—and to attempt to determine how these elements are combined by the perceiver to form an overall image of the painting. According to Gestalt psychologists, however, it is impossible to understand the way in which an object is perceived simply by studying these building blocks of perception. The whole is different from the sum of its parts. One must focus on the phenomenology of the perceiver—that is, on how an object appears to people—instead of on the individual elements of the objective stimulus.

In the 1930s, a woman reads a government-sponsored storefront sign urging the German people to boycott Jewish businesses. This was an early step that eventually led to the Holocaust.

The Gestalt approach was formulated in Germany in the first part of the twentieth century by Kurt Koffka, Wolfgang Kohler, and Max Wertheimer, and their students and colleagues. In the late 1930s, several of these psychologists emigrated to the United States to escape the Nazi regime and subsequently had such a major influence on psychology that one observer remarked, "If I were required to name the one person who had had the biggest impact on the field, it would have to be Adolf Hitler" (Cartright, 1979, p. 84). Among these immigrants was Kurt Lewin, who is generally considered to be the founding father of modern experimental social psychology. As a young German-Jewish professor, Lewin directly experienced the anti-Semitism rampant in Nazi Germany. This experience profoundly affected his thinking, and once in the United States, he helped shape social psychology and directed it toward a deep interest in the exploration of causes and cures of prejudice and ethnic stereotyping.

As a theorist, Lewin took the bold step of applying Gestalt principles beyond the perception of objects to social perception—how people perceive other people and their motives, intentions, and behaviours. Lewin was the first scientist to fully realize the importance of taking the perspective of the people in any social situation to see how they construe (e.g., perceive, interpret, distort) this social environment. Social psychologists soon began to focus on the importance of considering subjective situations (how they are construed by people). These early social psychologists and their key statements are presented on the following pages.

Such construals can be rather simple, as in the example of the question "How are you feeling?" discussed earlier. Other construals might appear simple but are, in reality, remarkably complex. Suppose, for example, that Maria gives Shawn a kiss on the cheek at the end of their first date. How will Shawn respond to the kiss? We would say that it depends on how he construes the situation. Does he interpret it as a first step—a sign of awakening romantic interest on Maria's part? Or does he see it as an aloof, sisterly expression—a signal that Maria wants to be friends but nothing more? Or does he see it as a sign that Maria is interested in him but wants things to go slow in their developing relationship?

Were Shawn to misconstrue the situation, he might commit a serious blunder; he might turn his back on what could have been the love of his life, or he might express passion inappropriately. In either case, we believe that the best strategy for understanding Shawn's reaction would be to find a way to determine his construal of Maria's behaviour, rather than to dissect the objective nature of the kiss itself (e.g., its length, degree of pressure). But how are these construals formed? Stay tuned.

Kurt Lewin—"If an individual sits in a room trusting that the ceiling will not come down, should only his 'subjective probability' be taken into account for predicting behaviour or should we also consider the 'objective probability' of the ceiling's coming down as determined by engineers? To my mind, only the first has to be taken into account" (1943).

(Archives of the History of American Psychology, The University of Akron)

Where Construals Come From: Basic Human Motives

How will Shawn determine why Maria kissed him? If it is true that subjective and not objective situations influence people, then we need to understand how people arrive at their subjective impressions of the world. What are people trying to accomplish when they interpret the social world? Again, we could address this question from the perspective of people's personalities. What is it about Shawn, including his upbringing, family background, and unique experiences, that makes him view the world the way he does? As we have discussed, such a focus on individual differences in people's personality, while valuable, misses what is usually of far greater importance: the effects of the social situation on people. To understand these effects, we need to understand the fundamental laws of human nature, common to all, that explain why people construe the social world the way they do.

We human beings are complex organisms; at a given moment, myriad intersecting motives underlie our thoughts and behaviours. Over the years, social psychologists have found that two of these motives are of primary importance: *the need to be accurate* and *the need to feel good about ourselves*. As we go through life, there are times when each of these motives pulls us in the same direction. Often, however, we find ourselves in situations in which these two motives tug us in opposite directions—situations in which we must face up to the fact that we have behaved foolishly or immorally in order to perceive the world accurately.

Connect to MyPsychLab
To take a survey on what motivates you, go to MyPsychLab

Fritz Heider—"Generally, a person reacts to what he thinks the other person is perceiving, feeling, and thinking, in addition to what the other person may be doing" (1958).

(Archives of the History of American Psychology, The University of Akron)

Leon Festinger—"The way I have always thought about it is that if the empirical world looks complicated, if people seem to react in bewilderingly different ways to similar forces, and if I cannot see the operation of universal underlying dynamics, then that is my fault. I have asked the wrong questions; I have, at a theoretical level, sliced up the world incorrectly. The underlying dynamics are there, and I have to find the theoretical apparatus that will enable me to reveal these uniformities."

Leon Festinger, one of social psychology's most innovative theorists, was quick to realize that it is precisely when these two motives tug an individual in opposite directions that we can gain our most valuable insights into the workings of the human heart and mind. An example will clarify. On May 19, 2005, the Liberal Party needed the support of Chuck Cadman, a Member of Parliament sitting as an Independent, on a budget amendment vote in order to stay in power. The Conservative Party, led by Stephen Harper, needed Cadman's vote to force an election. At the time, Cadman was critically ill with cancer. His wife, Dona, later claimed that the Conservatives had offered her dying husband a $1 million life insurance policy two days before the crucial vote. The so-called Cadman affair came to light in 2008. One of the revelations was a recording of an interview with Stephen Harper in July 2005, conducted by Vancouver journalist Tom Zytaruk shortly after Cadman's death. In the interview, Harper said that he was aware that representatives of the Conservative Party had engaged in discussions with Cadman but maintained that the financial offer "was only to replace financial considerations he might lose due to an election" (Harper, as quoted in "Opposition MPs Grill PM," 2008). Members of the opposition challenged this statement, pointing out that the dying Cadman would not have been able to run in an election. Tom Flanagan, former chief adviser to Stephen Harper, admitted that he and others tried to persuade Cadman to rejoin the Conservative caucus, despite the fact that Cadman was seriously ill. (Cadman sat as a Conservative before becoming an Independent member of parliament). The last of these discussions took place mere hours before the critical vote. In reflecting on these events, Flanagan comments, "This last desperate try with Cadman shows how we were all caught up in the attempt to force an election . . .. It's an excellent example of how the passions of politics lead to decisions that later make you scratch your head" (Flanagan, as quoted in Geddes, 2008).

Did Stephen Harper also admit that the behaviour of the Conservatives was out of line in this case? Not a chance. When the Cadman affair was brought to light, Harper, who by then was Canada's prime minister, defended the actions of the Conservatives and categorically denied that any deal had been offered to Cadman in the form of life insurance for his widow. Moreover, he launched a lawsuit against the Liberal Party for claiming that he knew of an offer to bribe Cadman to change his vote. On September 17, 2008, Harper's lawsuit was postponed until after the October 14, 2008, election. Lawyers for the Liberal Party accused Harper's legal team of deliberately delaying the proceedings lest some unpleasant facts come to light that could jeopardize the election. In June 2009, Harper dropped the lawsuit altogether.

It is doubtful that truth of the Cadman affair will ever be fully known given that the key witness is no longer living. What is clear is that Harper's response to this situation has been self-justification. Sometimes the need for self-justification can fly in the face of the need to be accurate. This is how many Canadians construe the Chuck Cadman affair. According to an Ipsos-Reid poll conducted in March 2008, 44 percent of respondents believe that the Conservatives did make an offer to Chuck Cadman, and nearly one-third believe that Steven Harper is not telling the truth (Russell, 2008).

The Self-Esteem Approach: The Need to Feel Good about Ourselves

Self-Esteem

People's evaluations of their own self-worth—that is, the extent to which they view themselves as good, competent, and decent

Most people have a strong need to maintain reasonably high **self-esteem**—to see themselves as good, competent, and decent (Aronson, 1992; Aronson, 1998; Baumeister, 1993; Kunda, 1990; Tavris & Aronson, 2007). The reason people view the world the way they do can often be traced to this underlying need to maintain a favourable image of themselves. Given the choice between distorting the world in order to feel good about themselves and representing the world accurately, people often take the first option.

Justifying Past Behaviour Suppose a couple gets divorced after 10 years of a marriage made difficult by the husband's irrational jealousy. Suppose the husband blames the breakup of his marriage on the fact that his ex-wife was not sufficiently responsive or attentive to his needs, rather than admitting the truth, namely that his jealousy and possessiveness drove her away. His interpretation serves an important purpose—it makes him feel better about himself. It is very difficult to own up to major deficiencies in ourselves, even when the cost is seeing the world inaccurately. The consequence of this distortion, of course, is that it decreases the probability that the individual will learn from experience. In his next relationship, the husband in our example is likely to run into the same problems.

We do not mean to imply that people totally distort reality, denying the existence of all information that reflects badly on them; such extreme behaviour is rare outside of mental institutions. Yet it is often possible for normal people to put a slightly different spin on the existing facts, one that puts them in the best possible light. Consider Roger—everybody knows someone like Roger. He's the guy whose shoes are almost always untied and who frequently has coffee stains on the front of his shirt or mustard stains around his lips. Most observers might consider Roger to be a slob, but Roger might see himself as casual and non-compulsive. The fact that people distort their interpretation of reality so that they feel better about themselves is not surprising, even to the most casual observer of human behaviour. But the ways in which this motive operates are often startling. An understanding of this phenomenon can shed light on behaviour that would otherwise be mystifying.

Suffering and Self-Justification Let's go back to one of our early scenarios: the case of Jean-François Caudron. Why did Jean-François feel happy to be a part of hockey teams that made him endure rookie-night hazings? Perhaps his teammates were usually such a great bunch of guys that he was able to overlook their behaviour on rookie night. That is quite possible. But a far more compelling possibility involves the hazing itself. Specifically, we would contend, a major factor that increased Jean-François' liking for his teammates was, in fact, the unpleasant hazing ritual he experienced. That sounds a little strange. Why would something so unpleasant cause Jean-François to like his team? Doesn't it seem obvious that people like things that are associated with rewards rather than punishments? Not necessarily.

Connect to MyPsychLab
To access the Critical Thinking question on hazing, go to MyPsychLab

Here's how it works. If Jean-François goes through a hazing in order to be accepted by a team of mean-spirited players who do nasty things to one another, he will feel like a fool: "Why did I go through all that pain and embarrassment in order to be accepted by a bunch of jerks? Only a moron would do a thing like that." To avoid feeling like a fool, he will try to justify his decision to undergo the hazing by seeing his team in the best possible light.

Our desire to maintain self-esteem can have surprising consequences. Social psychological research demonstrates that when people submit to a painful or embarrassing initiation in order to join a group, they need to justify the experience to avoid feeling foolish. One way they do that is to decide that the initiation was worth it because the group is so wonderful. While a sports or military hazing may be silly or dangerous, at the same time, it does build cohesiveness.

But what about situations in which people experience severe hazings—more severe than having their toenails painted and being forced to drink warm beer until they vomit? Surely, under these conditions people wouldn't decide that they really want to belong to the group, would they? As it turns out, they often do. Consider the case of Dee Brasseur, one of Canada's first female military pilots. Her applications to fly with the elite all-male Snowbirds jet team were repeatedly turned down because of her gender. She also endured harassment, assault, and even rape during her 21-year career in the military. "Battle fatigue" caused by years of gender discrimination eventually forced her to retire. How does Dee Brasseur sum up her feelings toward the military? "I still love it . . .. I would recommend it to anybody, despite what occurred" (Branswell, 1998).

While an unmotivated observer might consider these costs of belonging to a group to be high, people such as Jean-François Caudron and Dee Brasseur who have experienced them are motivated to see the experiences differently. Jean-François, like many athletes, considers hazing a small price to pay for the sense of team solidarity that it creates. And Dee remains fiercely loyal to the military.

Does this sound unbelievable? Are people actually more attracted to groups that subject them to pain and abuse? As far-fetched as it may sound, a series of well-controlled laboratory experiments conducted in the 1950s and 1960s demonstrated conclusively that the more unpleasant the procedure the participants underwent to get into a group, the more they liked the group (Aronson & Mills, 1959; Gerard & Mathewson, 1966). This phenomenon will be discussed more thoroughly in Chapter 6. The important points to remember here are that

- human beings are motivated to maintain a positive picture of themselves, in part by justifying their past behaviour, and that
- under certain specific conditions, this leads them to do things that at first glance might seem surprising or paradoxical—for example, they may prefer people and things for whom they have suffered over people and things they associate with pleasure.

The Social Cognition Approach: The Need to Be Accurate

Even when people are bending the facts to cast themselves in as favourable a light as they can, they do not completely distort reality. It would not be very adaptive to live in a fantasy world, believing, for example, that the car speeding toward you as you step off the curb is really a mirage or that your future spouse will be Katy Perry or Christiano Ronaldo. In fact, human beings are quite skilled at thinking, contemplating, and deducing. One of the hallmarks of being human is the ability to reason. As a species, human beings have developed truly amazing logical and computational abilities. In our lifetimes, we have witnessed such extraordinary cognitive achievements as the invention and development of computers, the exploration of outer space, and the conquering of many human diseases.

Moreover, on a more common—but perhaps more important—level, it is impossible to observe the cognitive development of a child without being awestruck. Just think of the vast gains in knowledge and reasoning that occur in the first few years of life. In a relatively short time, we see a child transform from a squirming, helpless newborn, who seems to do little but eat, cry, and sleep, into a sophisticated, garrulous four-year-old, who can utter complex sentences, hatch diabolic plots to frustrate a younger sibling, and evoke consternation and pride in parents.

Social Cognition

How people think about themselves and the social world; more specifically, how people select, interpret, remember, and use social information

Social Cognition Given the amazing cognitive abilities of our species, it makes sense that social psychologists, when formulating theories of social behaviour, would take into consideration the way in which human beings think about the world. We call this the cognitive approach to social psychology, or **social cognition** (Fiske & Taylor, 1991; Kunda, 1999; Nisbett & Ross, 1980). Researchers who attempt to understand social behaviour from the perspective of social cognition begin with the assumption that people try to view the world as accurately as possible. Accordingly, human beings are viewed by researchers as amateur sleuths who are doing their best to understand and predict their social world.

But this is by no means easy, because we almost never know all the facts we need to make the most accurate judgment of a given situation. Whether it is a relatively simple decision, such as which breakfast cereal is the best combination of nutrition and tastiness, or a slightly more complex decision, such as our desire to buy the best car we can for under $1800, or a much more complex decision, such as choosing a marriage partner who will make us deliriously happy for the rest of our lives, it is almost never easy to gather all the relevant facts in advance. Moreover, we make countless decisions every day; even if there were a way to gather all the facts for each decision, we simply lack the time and the stamina to do so.

Does this sound a bit overstated? Aren't most decisions fairly easy? Let's take a closer look. We will begin by asking you a simple question: Which breakfast cereal is better for you, Lucky Charms or 100% Natural from Quaker? If you are like most of our students, you answered, "100% Natural from Quaker." After all, Lucky Charms is a kid's cereal, full of sugar and cute little marshmallows. There is even a picture of a leprechaun on the box, for goodness' sake. And 100% Natural has a picture of raw wheat on the box, the box is the colour of natural wheat, and doesn't *natural* mean "good for you"? If that is the way you reasoned, you have, understandably, fallen into a common cognitive trap—you have generalized from the package to the product. A careful reading of the ingredients (in small print on the package) will inform you that although Lucky Charms has a bit more sugar in it than 100% Natural, the latter contains far more fat—so much so that the respected journal *Consumer Reports* has judged it to be less healthful than Lucky Charms. Even in the simple world of cereals, things are not always what they seem.

Expectations about the Social World To add to the difficulty, sometimes our expectations about the social world get in the way of our accurate perception of it. Our expectations can even change the *nature* of the social world. Imagine, for example, that you are an elementary school teacher dedicated to improving the lives of your students as best you can. You are aware at the beginning of the academic year of how each student performed on standardized intelligence tests. Early in your career, you were pretty sure, but not *entirely* sure, that these tests could gauge each child's true potential. But after several years of teaching, you have gradually become certain that these tests are accurate. Why the change? Almost without fail, you have come to see that the kids who got high scores on these tests are the ones who did the best in your classroom, and the kids who got low scores performed poorly in class.

This scenario doesn't sound all that surprising, except for one key fact: You might be very wrong about the validity of the intelligence tests. It might be that the tests weren't very accurate but that you unintentionally treated the kids with high scores and the kids with low scores differently, making it look as if the tests were accurate. This result is exactly what Robert Rosenthal and Lenore Jacobson (1968) found in their investigation of a phenomenon called the *self-fulfilling prophecy*. They entered elementary school classrooms and administered a test. They then informed each teacher that according to the test, a few specific students were "bloomers" who were about to take off and perform extremely well. In actuality, the test showed no such thing; the children labelled as bloomers were chosen by drawing names out of a hat and thus were no different, on average, from any of the other kids. Lo and behold, on returning to the classroom at the end of the school year, Rosenthal and Jacobson found that the bloomers were performing extremely well. The mere fact that the teachers were led to expect these students to do well caused an improvement in their performance. This striking phenomenon is no fluke; it has been replicated a number of times in a wide variety of schools (Rosenthal, 1995).

How did this result come about? Although this outcome seems almost magical, it is embedded in an important aspect of human nature. If you were one of those teachers and were led to expect two or three specific students to perform well, you would be more likely to treat those students in special ways—paying more attention to them, listening to them with respect, calling on them more frequently, encouraging them, and trying to teach them more challenging material. This in turn would almost certainly make these students feel happier, more respected, more motivated, and smarter; and *voilà* —the prophecy is fulfilled. Thus, even when we are trying to perceive the social world as accurately as possible, we can err in many ways, ending up with the wrong impressions. We will explain why—and the conditions under which social perception is accurate—in Chapters 3 and 4.

Other Motives: Ensuring Our Survival

We want to reiterate what we stated earlier: The two major sources of construals we have emphasized here—the need to maintain a positive view of ourselves (the self-esteem approach) and the need to view the world accurately (the social cognition approach)—are the most important of our social motives. But they are certainly not the only motives influencing people's thoughts and behaviours. As noted earlier, we human beings are complex organisms, and under various conditions, a variety of motives influence what we think, feel, and do. Biological drives such as hunger and thirst, of course, can be powerful motivators, especially under circumstances of extreme deprivation. At a more psychological level, we can be motivated by fear or by the promise of love, favours, and other rewards involving social exchange. These motives will be discussed at length in Chapters 9 and 10. Still another significant motive is the need for control. Research has shown that people feel they need to exert some control over their environment (Langer, 1975; Taylor, 1989). When people experience a loss of control, such that they believe they have little or no influence over whether good or bad things happen to them, there are a number of important consequences, as we discuss in the Social Psychology and Health module. At a very fundamental level, human behaviour is motivated by the need to survive. We discuss this motive next.

Natural Selection

The process by which heritable traits that promote survival in a particular environment are passed along to future generations, because organisms with that trait are more likely to reproduce

The Evolutionary Approach Evolutionary theory was developed by Charles Darwin (1859) to explain the ways in which animals adapt to their environments. Central to the theory is **natural selection**, which is the process by which heritable traits that promote survival in a particular environment are passed along to future generations, because organisms with that trait are more likely to produce offspring. A common example is how giraffes came to have long necks. In an environment where food is scarce, giraffes who happened to have long necks could feed on foliage that other animals couldn't reach. These giraffes were more likely to survive and produce offspring than other giraffes, the story goes, and the "long-neck" gene thus became common in subsequent generations.

Evolutionary Psychology

The attempt to explain social behaviour in terms of genetic factors that evolved over time according to the principles of natural selection

In biology, evolutionary theory is used to explain how different species acquired physical traits such as long necks. But what about social behaviours, such as the tendency to be aggressive toward a member of one's own species or the tendency to be helpful toward others? Is it possible that social behaviours have genetic determinants that evolve through the process of natural selection, and if so, is this true in human beings as well as animals? These are the questions posed by **evolutionary psychology**, which attempts to explain social behaviour in terms of genetic factors that evolved over time according to the principles of natural selection. The core idea is that evolution occurs very slowly, such that social behaviours that are prevalent today are due at least in part to adaptations to environments in our distant past (Buss, 2005; Schaller, Simpson, & Kenrick, 2006). We will discuss how evolutionary theory explains social behaviour in upcoming chapters (e.g., Chapter 9 on interpersonal attraction, Chapter 10 on prosocial behaviour, and Chapter 11 on aggression). Here we mention that a lively debate has arisen over the testability of evolutionary hypotheses. Because current behaviours are thought to be adaptations to environmental conditions that existed thousands of years ago, psychologists make their best guesses about what those conditions were and how specific kinds of behaviours gave people a reproductive advantage. But these hypotheses are obviously impossible to test with the experimental method. And just because hypotheses sound plausible does not mean they are true. For example, some scientists now believe that giraffes did not acquire a long neck in order to eat leaves in tall trees. Instead, they suggest, long necks first evolved in male giraffes to gain an advantage in fights with other males over access to females (Simmons & Scheepers, 1996). Which of these explanations is true? It's difficult to tell. On the other hand, evolutionary approaches can generate novel hypotheses about social behaviour that can be tested with the other methods described in this chapter.

Social Psychology and Social Problems

To recapitulate, social psychology can be defined as the scientific study of social influence. Social influence can best be understood by focusing on the major roots of human behaviour. It might have occurred to you to ask why we want to understand social influence in the first place. Who cares? And what difference does it make whether a behaviour has its roots in the desire to be accurate, the desire to bolster our self-esteem, or the desire to survive and pass on our genes?

There are several answers to these questions. The most basic answer is simple: We are curious. Social psychologists are fascinated by human social behaviour and want to understand it on the deepest possible level. In a sense, all of us are social psychologists. We all live in a social environment, and we are all more than mildly curious about such issues as how we become influenced, how we influence others, and why we fall in love with some people, dislike others, and are indifferent to still others.

Many social psychologists have another reason for studying the causes of social behaviour: to contribute to the solution of social problems. From the very beginning of our young science, social psychologists have been keenly interested in such social problems as the reduction of hostility and prejudice, and the increase of altruism and generosity. Contemporary social psychologists have continued this tradition and have broadened the issues of concern to include endeavours such as inducing people to conserve natural resources such as water and energy (Dickerson, Thibodeau, Aronson, & Miller, 1992), educating people to practise safer sex to reduce the spread of AIDS (Aronson, 1997a, 1998; Stone, Aronson, Crain, Winslow, & Fried, 1994), understanding the relationship between viewing violence on television and violent behaviour (Eron, Huesmann, Lefkowitz, & Walder, 1996; Josephson, 1987), and developing effective negotiation strategies for the reduction of international conflict (Kelman, 1997). The ability to understand and explain complex and dysfunctional social behaviour brings with it the challenge to change it. For example, given the associated health risks, there has been increased pressure on governments to persuade people to stop smoking. In 2000, Canadian cigarette packages began to display the largest, most graphic warning images and messages anywhere in the world. The federal government's intent was to frighten people into stopping (or not starting) smoking. As you have probably seen, the images include pictures of a cancerous mouth, of premature infants with warnings to pregnant women not to smoke (because of the link between smoking and sudden infant death syndrome), and of brain fragments with a warning that smoking leads to increased risk of strokes. This seems consistent with common sense. If you want people to do something they aren't inclined to do, why not scare the daylights out of them?

This is certainly not a stupid idea. When researchers at the University of Waterloo compared the effects of warning messages on cigarette packages in Canada, the United Kingdom, Australia, and the United States, they concluded that Canada's large, graphic warnings were the most effective (Hammond, Fong, Borland, Cummings, McNeill, & Driezen, 2007). However, according to Health Canada, they are not effective enough. This conclusion was based on a poll conducted in 2007, which showed that the percentage of smokers who reported that the images were ineffective was on the rise. Health Canada's research also suggested that bigger, even more graphic images would be more persuasive. In February 2011, Health Canada unveiled even more graphic images on cigarette packages that cover 75 percent of the outside panel. Moreover, fear-producing images and messages are displayed on the inside of cigarette packages, making Canada the first country in the world to do so. Clearly, the Canadian government is convinced that the best way to get people to stop smoking is to make them terrified of the consequences. As we shall see in subsequent chapters, there are many dysfunctional acts (e.g., cigarette smoking, drunk driving) for which the induction of fear can and does motivate people to take rational, appropriate action to preserve their health (Petty, 1995).

However, based on years of systematic research on persuasion, social psychologists have realized that this approach is not effective in all situations. For example, the fear-inducing approach has been applied to obesity, for which it has had little effect. (We discuss this further in Chapter 7.) Similarly, in the case of AIDS, we now know that appeals to fear do not produce the desired effect of persuading people to practise safer sex. Rather, the research evidence suggests that most people do not want to be thinking about dying or contracting a painful illness while they are getting ready to have sex. Such thoughts can interfere, to say the least, with the romance of the occasion. Moreover, most people do not enjoy using condoms because they feel that interrupting the sexual act destroys the mood. As demonstrated in a study with French-Canadian university students, people who feel that condoms are inconvenient are less likely to use them (Hébert, Bernard, deMan, & Farrar, 1989). Given these considerations, when people have been exposed to frightening messages, instead of engaging in rational problem-solving behaviour, most tend to reduce that fear by engaging in denial; for example, in research conducted at various universities in Ontario, students expressed beliefs such as "It can't happen to me," "Surely none of my friends have AIDS," and "This person I've just met doesn't seem like the type who would sleep around" (MacDonald, Zanna, & Fong, 1996; Maticka-Tyndale, Herold, & Mewhinney, 1998).

The astute reader will see that the process of denial stems not from the desire to be accurate but from the desire to maintain self-esteem. That is, if people can succeed in convincing themselves that their sexual partners could not possibly have AIDS, then they can continue to engage in unprotected sex while maintaining a reasonably positive picture of themselves as rational individuals. By understanding the conditions under which self-esteem maintenance prevails, social psychologists have been able to contribute important insights into AIDS education and prevention, as we will discuss (Aronson, 1997a; Aronson, Fried, & Stone, 1991; Stone et al., 1994).

Does fear motivate people to stop smoking? Social psychologists investigate this kind of relevant social issue.

Throughout this book, we will examine many similar examples of the applications of social psychology. Likewise, we will discuss some of the underlying human motives and characteristics of the social situations that produce significant social behaviours, with the assumption that if we are interested in changing our own or other people's behaviour, we must first know something about these fundamental causes. Although most of the studies discussed are concerned with such fundamental causes, in the process, they also address critical social problems, including the effects of mass media on attitudes and behaviour (Chapter 6), violence and aggression (Chapter 11), and prejudice (Chapter 12). For the benefit of the interested reader, we have also included three separate modules that apply social psychology to contemporary issues involving the environment, health, and law. Your instructor may assign them at any time during the semester or may decide not to assign them at all, leaving that decision to your own curiosity.

HOW WOULD YOU USE THIS?

Thinking Like a Social Psychologist

You're consulting for the Department of National Defense. During a brainstorming session General Smith presents an idea for attracting new recruits to the Canadian Armed Forces. His notion is to make boot camp more appealing: While keeping the training rigorous, the idea is to make the living conditions more comfortable (e.g., air conditioning, gourmet food, comfortable beds). You realize that although on the surface this sounds like a good idea, there may be some unintended consequences regarding the cohesiveness and camaraderie within each platoon. What might these unintended consequences be?

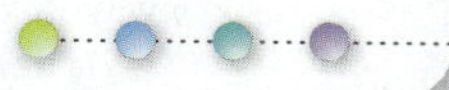

Summary

- **What Is Social Psychology?** The scientific study of the way in which people's thoughts, feelings, and behaviours are influenced by the real or imagined presence of other people. Social psychologists are interested in understanding how and why the social environment shapes the thoughts, feelings, and behaviours of the individual.
  - **The Power of Social Interpretation** To understand social influence it is more important to understand how people *perceive and interpret* the social world than it is to understand that world objectively. The term *construal* refers to the world as it is interpreted by the individual.
  - **Some Alternative Ways of Understanding Social Influence** Social psychologists approach the understanding of social influence differently than philosophers, journalists, or the layperson. Social psychologists develop explanations of social influence through experiments in which the variables being studied are carefully controlled.
  - **Social Psychology Compared with Sociology** A fundamental way in which the two disciplines vary is in their *level of analysis*. Social psychology is rooted in the study of the individual's internal psychological processes; *the level of analysis for social psychology is the individual in the context of a social situation*. In contrast, sociologists focus their analysis on groupings of people organized in social categories such as family, race, religion, and economic class. While sociologists aim to study larger social processes such as historical and political changes or how larger social structures (e.g., race, class, gender, sexual orientation) shape an individual's life chances, the orientation of the social psychologist is on the internal processes that take place within individuals. Social psychologists seek to identify universal *properties of human nature* that make everyone susceptible to social influence regardless of social class or culture. Sociologists seek to explain *properties of societies*.
  - **Social Psychology Compared with Personality Psychology** When trying to explain social behaviour—how an individual acts within a social context (in relation to others)—personality psychologists explain the behaviour in terms of the person's individual character traits. Although social psychologists would agree that personalities do vary, they explain social behaviour in terms of the *power of the social situation* (as it is construed by the individual) to shape how one acts.
- **The Power of Social Influence** Social psychologists have discovered, through rigorous empirical research, that individual behaviour is powerfully influenced by the social environment.
  - **Underestimating the Power of Social Influence** People tend to explain behaviour in terms of individual personality traits and underestimate the power of social influence in shaping individual of social influence in shaping individual behaviour. Social psychological researchers have shown time and again that social and environmental situations are usually more powerful than personality differences in determining an individual's behaviour.
  - **The Subjectivity of the Social Situation** Human beings are sense-making creatures; they are constantly interpreting things. How humans will behave in a given situation is not determined by the objective conditions of a situation but rather by how they perceive it (construal).
- **Where Construals Come From: Basic Human Motives** The way in which an individual construes (perceives,

comprehends, and interprets) a situation is largely shaped by the two basic *human motives: the need to be accurate* and *the need to feel good about ourselves*. At times these two motives tug in opposite directions; for example, when an accurate view of how we acted in a situation would reveal that we behaved selfishly.

- **The Self-Esteem Approach: The Need to Feel Good about Ourselves** Most people have a strong need to see themselves as good, competent, and decent. People often distort their perception of the world to preserve their self-esteem.
- **The Social Cognition Approach: The Need to Be Accurate** The social cognition perspective is an approach to social psychology that takes into account the way in which human beings think about the world: Individuals are viewed as trying to gain accurate understandings so that they can make effective judgments and decisions that range from which cereal to eat to whom they will marry. In actuality, individuals typically act on the basis of incomplete and inaccurately interpreted information.
- **Other Motives: Ensuring Our Survival** Human behaviour also is motivated by a very basic need: the need for survival—of oneself and one's offspring. This evolutionary perspective has been used to explain various social psychological phenomena, including mate selection, prosocial behaviour, and aggression.

Social Psychology and Social Problems Social psychological theories about human behaviour have been applied effectively to deal with a range of contemporary problems that include prejudice, energy shortages, the spread of AIDS, unhealthy habits, and violence in the schools. When recommending interventions to deal with serious social problems, it is imperative to act on the basis of scientifically grounded theories about human construal and behaviour.

Methodology

How Social Psychologists Do Research

IN 1993, THE PARLIAMENTARY STANDING COMMITTEE ON Communications and Culture published a report on the effects of television violence titled "Television Violence: Fraying Our Social Fabric." This report was triggered, at least in part, by a petition initiated by 13-year-old Virginie Larivière, whose 11-year-old sister had been robbed, sexually assaulted, and murdered. Larivière was convinced that television violence was responsible for her sister's death. She and her family gathered more than 1.3 million signatures from Canadians across the country. The petition called for a boycott of violent television programming and for federal government legislation to reduce the violent content of television programming. The 11 members of Parliament who served on the Standing Committee interviewed the chair of the Canadian Radio-television and Telecommunications Commission, professors, executives from the Canadian Association of Broadcasters, and the president of the Canadian Film and Television Production Association (now the Canadian Media Production Association). Based on these interviews and various reports, the committee decided there was not enough evidence to support the conclusion that violence on television contributes to violent behaviour: "Many factors contribute to violence in society and the part played by television violence can only be estimated and amounts to an unknown fraction." As a result, the committee recommended against legislating a reduction in violent content in television programming, preferring industry self-regulation and public education instead.

The question of whether television violence produces violent behaviour is an extremely important one, particularly in light of allegations—such as those made by Virginie Larivière—that violence on television plays a role in brutal, deadly assaults on innocent people. However, as the Standing Committee on Communications and Culture discovered, different experts have different opinions, making it difficult to draw firm conclusions. How can one decide who is right? Is this a case where majority opinion rules, or is there a more scientific way to determine the answers?

Consider, now, a 1995 report commissioned by the federal Department of Canadian Heritage to address the same question. This report, entitled "Television Violence: A Review of the Effects on Children of Different Ages," was prepared by social psychologist Wendy Josephson, who analyzed the results of hundreds of scientific studies. Her conclusion was that television violence does increase aggressive behaviour—at least among children predisposed toward aggression. She pointed out that "although the group especially at risk might be a minority of viewers, they are likely to be the majority of aggressors." Josephson's conclusion, based on a careful analysis of scientific evidence, was quite different from the conclusion reached by the Standing Committee on Communications and Culture, which relied on reports and interviews with individuals—many of whom were from the television industry. In this chapter, we will examine the kinds of research methods that allow us to scientifically answer important questions about the causes of violence.

Social Psychology: An Empirical Science

A fundamental principle of social psychology is that many social problems, such as the causes of and reactions to violence, can be studied scientifically (Wilson, Aronson, & Carlsmith, in press; Reis & Judd, 2000). Before we discuss how social psychological research is done, we begin with a warning: The results of some of the experiments you encounter will seem obvious, because the topic of social psychology is something with which we are all intimately familiar: social behaviour and social influence. Note that this separates social psychology from other sciences. When you read about an experiment in particle physics, it is unlikely that the results will connect with your personal experiences and have a ring of familiarity. We don't know about you, but none of your authors has ever thought, "Wow! That experiment on quarks was just like what happened to me while I was waiting for the bus yesterday" or "My grandmother always told me to watch out for quarks, positrons, and antimatter." When reading about the results of a study on helping behaviour or aggression, however, it is quite common to think, "Aw, come on, I could have predicted that. That's the same thing that happened to me last Friday."

I love games. I think I could be very happy being a chess player or dealing with some other kinds of games. But I grew up in the Depression. It didn't seem one could survive on chess, and science is also a game. You have very strict ground rules in science, and your ideas have to check out with the empirical world. That's very tough and also very fascinating.

—Leon Festinger, 1977

The thing to remember is that when we study human behaviour, the results may appear to have been predictable—in retrospect. Indeed, there is a well-known human tendency called the **hindsight bias**, whereby people exaggerate how much they could have predicted an outcome *after* knowing that it occurred (Bradfield & Wells, 2005; Fischhoff, Gonzalez, Lerner, & Small, 2005; Fessel, Epstude, & Roese, 2009; Metcalfe & Finn, 2011). A recent study found that the tendency to think that we "knew it all along" is already apparent among three-year-olds and was alive and well among the elderly Vancouver residents sampled (Bernstein, Erdfelder, Meltzoff, Peria, & Loftus, 2001). Hindsight is 20/20, as the saying goes. This phenomenon was illustrated in a study by Roese and Olson (1996). They asked students at the University of Western Ontario to read a story, based on World War I events, about a young British soldier who devised a plan to save a small village that was about to be invaded. In one condition, participants were told that the soldier managed to convince others in the military to accept his plan and the village was saved. When asked how predictable this outcome was, they felt it was obvious all along that the village would be saved. In another condition, participants were told that the soldier's plan was rejected and the village was destroyed. When asked how predictable this outcome was, these participants thought it was obvious that the village would be destroyed! As this study shows, the opposite finding of an experiment might seem just as obvious as the results that actually were obtained. The trick is to predict what will happen in an experiment *before* you know how it turns out.

Hindsight Bias

The tendency for people to exaggerate how much they could have predicted the outcome after knowing that it occurred

To find out for yourself what we mean when we say not all findings that may seem obvious can actually be predicted in advance, take the accompanying Try It! quiz.

TRY IT! Social Psychology Quiz

Take a moment to answer the questions below, each of which is based on social psychological research. While the correct answers may seem obvious in retrospect, many are difficult to guess in advance.

1. Suppose an authority figure asks university students to administer near-lethal electric shocks to another student who has not harmed them in any way. What percentage of these students will agree to do it?
2. If you give children a reward for doing something they already enjoy doing, they will subsequently like that activity (a) more, (b) the same, or (c) less.
3. Who do you think would be happiest with their choice of a consumer product, such as an art poster? (a) People who spend several minutes thinking about why they like or dislike each poster. (b) People who choose a poster without analyzing the reasons for their feelings.
4. Repeated exposure to a stimulus, such as a person, a song, or a painting, will make you like it (a) more, (b) the same, or (c) less.
5. You ask an acquaintance to do you a favour—for example, to lend you $10—and he or she agrees. As a result of doing you this favour, the person will probably like you (a) more, (b) the same, or (c) less.
6. When making a complex decision, is it best to (a) decide right away without further thought, (b) think carefully about the different options, or (c) find something to distract you for a while, and then make up your mind?
7. In Canada and the United States, female university students tend not to do as well as male students on math tests. Under which of the following circumstances will women do as well as men? (a) They are told that there are no gender differences on a test. (b) They are told that women tend to do better on a difficult math test, because under these circumstances, they rise to the challenge. (c) They are told that men outperform women under almost all circumstances.
8. Which statement about the effects of advertising is most true? (a) Subliminal messages implanted in advertisements are more effective than normal, everyday advertising. (b) Normal, everyday advertising, such as television ads for painkillers or laundry detergents, are more effective than subliminal messages implanted in ads. (c) Both kinds of advertising are equally effective. (d) Neither type of advertising is effective.
9. In public settings, (a) women touch men more, (b) men touch women more, or (c) there is no difference—men and women touch each other equally.
10. Which things in their past do people regret the most? (a) Actions they performed that they wish they had not. (b) Actions they did not perform that they wish they had. (c) It depends on how long ago the events occurred.

Go to www.MyPsychLab.com for the answers.

Each answer is based on well-established social psychological research. In our experience as teachers, we have found that few of our students get all the answers correct. Findings that seem obvious in retrospect may not be easy to predict in advance.

Social psychology is an empirical science with a well-developed set of methods to answer questions about social behaviour, such as the ones about violence with which we began this chapter. These methods are of three types: the *observational method*, the *correlational method*, and the *experimental method*. Any of these methods can be used to explore a specific research question; each is a powerful tool in some ways and a weak tool in others. Part of the creativity in conducting social psychological research involves choosing the right method, maximizing its strengths, and minimizing its weaknesses.

In this chapter, we will discuss these methods in detail. We, the authors of this book, are not primarily textbook writers—we are social scientists who have done a great deal of research in social psychology. As such, we will try to provide you with an understanding of both the joy and the difficulty of doing research. The joy comes in unravelling the clues about the causes of interesting and important social behaviours, just as a sleuth gradually unmasks the culprit in a mystery. Each of us finds it exhilarating that we have the tools to provide definitive answers to questions that philosophers have debated for centuries. At the same time, as seasoned researchers we have learned to temper this exhilaration with a heavy dose of humility, for the practical and ethical constraints involved in creating and conducting social psychological research are formidable.

Formulating Hypotheses and Theories

There is lore in science that brilliant insights come all of a sudden, as when Archimedes shouted, "Eureka! I have found it!" when the solution to a problem flashed into his mind. While such insights do sometimes occur suddenly, science is a cumulative process, and researchers typically generate hypotheses from previous theories and research. We define a **theory** as an organized set of principles that can be used to explain observed phenomena. We define a **hypothesis** as a testable statement or idea about the relationship between two or more variables. We will be discussing many theories and hypotheses as we proceed through this book.

Theory

An organized set of principles that can be used to explain observed phenomena

Hypothesis

A testable statement or idea about the relationship between two or more variables

Inspiration from Earlier Theories and Research

Many studies stem from a researcher's dissatisfaction with existing theories and explanations. After reading other people's work, a researcher might believe that he or she has a better way of explaining people's behaviour (e.g., why they fail to help in an emergency). Social psychologists, like scientists in other disciplines, engage in a continual process of theory refinement: They develop a theory, test specific hypotheses derived from that theory, and, based on the results, revise the theory and formulate new hypotheses.

Hypotheses Based on Personal Observations

Researchers often observe a phenomenon in everyday life that they find curious and interesting. They then construct a theory about why this phenomenon occurred and design a study to see if they are right.

Consider the murder of Kitty Genovese. Genovese was attacked while walking to her car and brutally murdered in the alley of an apartment complex. The attack lasted 45 minutes. No fewer than 38 of the apartment residents admitted later that they had rushed to their windows after hearing Genovese's screams for help. However, not one of these bystanders attempted in any way to help her—none of them even telephoned the police.

As you might imagine, the Kitty Genovese murder received a great deal of publicity. Reporters, commentators, and pundits of all kinds came forward with their personal theories about why the bystanders had done nothing. Most people blamed Genovese's neighbours' failure to intervene on the apathy, indifference, and callousness that big-city life breeds. Two social psychologists who taught at universities in New York, however, had a different idea. Bibb Latané and John Darley got to talking one day about the Genovese murder. Here is how Latané describes it: "One evening after [a] downtown cocktail party, John Darley . . . came back with me to my 12th Street apartment for a drink. Our common complaint was the distressing tendency of acquaintances, on finding that we called ourselves social psychologists, to ask why New Yorkers were so apathetic" (Latané, 1987, p. 78). Instead of focusing on "what was wrong with New Yorkers," Latané and Darley (1968) thought it would be more interesting and more important to examine the

Kitty Genovese was attacked in this area in full view of her neighbours. Why didn't anyone call the police?

TABLE 2.1 A Summary of Research Methods

Method	Focus	Question Answered
Observational	Description	What is the nature of the phenomenon?
Correlational	Description	What is the relation between variable X and variable Y?
Experimental	Causality	Is variable X a cause of variable Y?

social situation in which Genovese's neighbours found themselves: "We came up with the insight that perhaps what made the Genovese case so fascinating was itself what made it happen—namely, that not just one or two, but 38 people had watched and done nothing" (Latané, 1987, p. 78).

The researchers had the hunch that, paradoxically, the more people who witness an emergency, the less likely it is that any given individual will intervene. Genovese's neighbours might have assumed that someone else had called the police, a phenomenon Latané and Darley (1968) referred to as the *diffusion of responsibility*. Perhaps the bystanders would have been more likely to help had each thought he or she alone was witnessing the murder.

After a researcher has a hypothesis, whether it comes from a theory, previous research, or an observation of everyday life, how can he or she tell if it is true? In science, idle speculation will not do; the researcher must collect data to test his or her hypothesis. This requires the precise specification of how the variables that will be examined will be measured or manipulated, known as an **operational definition.** We will give some examples of operational definitions when we discuss the various methods that can be used to testhypotheses such as Latané and Darley's. These include the observational method, the correlational method, and the experimental method (see Table 2.1).

Operational Definition
The precise specification of how variables are measured or manipulated

The Observational Method

Watch on **mypsychlab**
Naturalistic Observation

A lot can be learned by an astute observer of human behaviour. If the goal is to describe what a particular group of people or type of behaviour is like, the **observational method** is very useful. This is the technique whereby a researcher observes people and systematically records measurements of their behaviour. This method varies according to the degree to which the observer actively participates in the scene. At one extreme, the observer neither participates nor intervenes in any way; instead, the observer is unobtrusive and tries to blend in with the scenery as much as possible. The method by which researchers attempt to understand a group or culture by observing it from the inside without imposing any preconceived notions they might have is known as **ethnography**. The goal is to understand the richness and complexity of the group by observing it in action. Ethnography is the chief method of cultural anthropology, the study of human cultures and societies. As social psychology broadens its focus by studying social behaviour in different cultures, ethnography is increasingly being used to describe different cultures and generate hypotheses about psychological principles (Fine & Elsbach, 2000; Hodson, 2004; Uzzel, 2000).

Observational Method
The technique whereby a researcher observes people and systematically records measurements of their behaviour

Ethnography
The method by which researchers attempt to understand a group or culture by observing it from the inside without imposing any preconceived notions they might have

Consider this example from the early years of social psychological research. In the 1950s, a group of people in the U.S. Midwest predicted that the world would come to an end in a violent cataclysm on a specific date. They also announced that they would be rescued in time by a spaceship that would land in their leader's backyard. Assuming that the end of the world was not imminent, Leon Festinger and his colleagues thought it would be interesting to observe this group closely and chronicle how they reacted when their beliefs and prophecy were disconfirmed (Festinger, Riecken, & Schachter, 1956). To monitor the hour-to-hour conversations of this group, the social psychologists found it necessary to join the group and pretend that they too believed the world was about to end. In case you are wondering what happened when the world didn't actually end, the cult members still clung to their beliefs and assumed that a spaceship would eventually come to rescue them. Many became even more committed to the belief system and renewed their efforts to convert others. The cult members needed to assure themselves that the spaceship rescue would still take place, so visitors to the group were often perceived as coming to them from outer space to deliver messages.

Watch on **mypsychlab** Bullying

To give a more recent example, Debra Pepler at York University and Wendy Craig at Queen's University have developed a particularly unobtrusive method for observing bullying behaviour in school settings (Atlas & Pepler, 1998; Craig & Pepler, 1997; Pepler & Craig, 1995; Pepler, Craig, O'Connell, Atlas, & Charach, 2004). The children wear waist pouches containing small microphones, while a hidden video camera films their interactions. Thus, children can freely roam over relatively large areas (e.g., school playgrounds) while having their behaviour recorded. This combination of audio and visual technology allows the researchers to observe overt physical acts of aggression, as well as more subtle forms of bullying, such as indirect aggression and verbal threats or insults. (Subtle forms of bullying are especially difficult to detect when researchers rely on more traditional methods, such as standing outside a playground fence and making check marks whenever they notice particular behaviours.)

The waist-pouch microphone technology also addresses an age-old problem in observational research—namely, that people change their behaviour when they are being observed. Bullies, for example, tend not to engage in bullying when adults are around (Craig & Pepler, 1997; Pepler et al., 2004). Therefore, an advantage of using unobtrusive measures, such as Pepler and Craig's, is that researchers can observe spontaneous, naturally occurring behaviour.

In all observational research—regardless of whether observers are on the spot or later analyze videotapes or audiotapes—it is important for the researchers to clearly define the behaviours of interest. For example, in Pepler and Craig's research an episode is classified as bullying only if there is a power imbalance between the individuals involved, if there is intent to harm on the part of the person doing the bullying, and if the victim shows distress (Atlas & Pepler, 1998; Craig & Pepler, 1997; Pepler et al., 2004). (Note that the importance of clearly defining the behaviours of interest applies to all psychological research not just to observational studies.) Let's take a closer look at one of the criteria that Pepler and colleagues use to define bullying, namely a power imbalance. Are you able to come up with an operational definition of this variable that would be useful in the context of observing playground interactions? Pepler and Craig operationally defined a power imbalance as a discrepancy in terms of height and weight between the children involved. In other words, in situations involving aggression on the playground, the researchers assume that a bigger child is likely to be in a position of power relative to a smaller child.

If the researchers were interested in observing bullying in, for example, a corporate boardroom, they presumably would specify a different operational definition of power imbalance—perhaps the discrepancy between the individuals' status in the corporation (e.g., vice-president versus manager).

CONNECTIONS

Using Observational Research to Develop Anti-Bullying Programs

Observational research can be used to address important social problems. For example, Debra Pepler and colleagues' research on bullying has led to the development of an anti-bullying intervention program that has been used in schools across Canada (Pepler et al., 1994; Pepler et al., 2004; Pepler, Jiang, & Craig, 2006). This program, modelled after a successful intervention program developed in Norway and Sweden (Olweus, 1996, 1997, 2004), educates children, teachers, administrators, and parents about the problem of bullying. Children are taught how to respond when they are the victims of bullying and how to intervene when they observe incidents of bullying. Teachers are trained to be vigilant for instances of bullying and to make swift interventions. This program (and others like it all around the world; see Smith, Pepler, & Rigby, 2004) has met with mixed success. In a recent comprehensive assessment of the effectiveness of this intervention in three Toronto schools, Pepler and colleagues found that a decrease in bullying (based on children's self-reports and playground observations) is most likely to be seen among children who bully moderately often (Pepler et al., 2006; 2011). Children who bully at a high rate do not seem to benefit. (These children tend to have more serious problems that are beyond the scope of a school-based bullying intervention.) Moreover, the improvement in the behaviour of the moderate bullies takes time; at a six-month follow-up, the intervention did not appear to be having a significant effect. However, decreases in bullying and victimization were evident in the longer-term (18 months later).

One of the many challenges facing those who administer anti-bullying programs is that schools and teachers vary tremendously in terms of the support for, and resources dedicated to, such programs. Moreover, anti-bullying programs have not been particularly successful at getting peers to intervene, despite the fact that peer intervention generally stops bullying. This latter point is critical because, according to Pepler, "Research indicates that when students intervene, in 57 per cent of the cases the bullying stops within 10 seconds . . . so we really need to empower our children to know what to do in bullying situations" (Pepler, as quoted in "Don't Stand By . . . Stand Up," 2006). This has been the focus of more recent interventions, which are aimed at encouraging bystanders to speak up—to tell a teacher, parent, guidance counsellor, or others until the situation is addressed. For example, children might watch films of bullying incidents and participate in role-modelling exercises in which they rehearse how and when to intervene (Rigby & Johnson, 2006–2007). It is encouraging that research on the dynamics of bullying is leading to the development of anti-bullying programs all over the world.

But, you might be wondering, how can we be sure that the observers are presenting an accurate portrayal of social behaviour? In observational research—whether observing children's behaviour on a playground or the behaviour of members of doomsday cults—it is important to establish **interjudge reliability**, which is the level of agreement between two or more people who independently observe and code a set of data. By showing that two or more judges independently come up with the same observations, researchers ensure that the observations are not the subjective impressions of one individual.

Interjudge Reliability
The level of agreement between two or more people who independently observe and code a set of data; by showing that two or more judges independently come up with the same observations, researchers ensure that the observations are not the subjective impressions of one individual

Archival Analysis

Another form of the observational method is **archival analysis**, whereby the researcher examines the accumulated documents, or archives, of a culture (Mullen, Rozell, & Johnson, 2001; Simonton, 1999). Diaries, novels, suicide notes, popular music lyrics, television shows, movies, magazine and newspaper articles, and advertising, for example, all tell us a great deal about how a society views itself. Much like our earlier example, specific, well-defined categories are created and then applied to the archival source. Archival analysis is a powerful form of observational research because it allows a unique look at the values and interests of a culture. (If you want to try your hand at archival analysis, see the accompanying Try It! exercise.)

Archival Analysis
A form of the observational method whereby the researcher examines the accumulated documents, or archives, of a culture (e.g., diaries, novels, magazines, and newspapers)

To give an example, Eric Patton at Saint Joseph's University, Philadelphia, and Gary Johns at Concordia University in Montreal analyzed portrayals of women's absenteeism in the workplace by examining the content of articles published in the *New York Times* over the last 100 years (Patton & Johns, 2007). Although there was some variation across time, women generally were portrayed as missing work because of familial and domestic obligations. Moreover, their absenteeism was viewed negatively.

Archival studies have found that women and men are portrayed differently in advertisements. What are the differences in the way the men and woman are portrayed in these photos? To learn more about these differences, complete the Try It! exercise on the next page.

The researchers suggest that this portrait of women's absenteeism serves to perpetuate gender stereotypes and may lead to discrimination in the workplace.

To give another example, researchers at York University used archival analysis to examine the relation between body ideals (as portrayed in magazines such as *Playboy* and *Playgirl*) and the body sizes of average young women and men (Spitzer, Henderson, & Zivian, 1999). It turns out that the body sizes of *Playboy* models and beauty pageant winners have decreased over time to the point where, currently, nearly 100 percent of these women are underweight according to Health Canada's guidelines. The researchers comment that "clearly the North American ideal for female beauty as portrayed in the media is at a weight deemed to be dangerous by Canadian and World Health officials" (p. 559). Interestingly, the body mass index of North American women actually has increased in the past four decades (somewhat more so for American than Canadian women). Thus, the average woman's body is now further from the cultural ideal than it was 40 years ago.

As for men's bodies, Spitzer and colleagues found that the body sizes of *Playgirl* centrefolds and average young men have both increased over time. However, as a look around your classroom probably will verify, the average guy doesn't look like a *Playgirl* centrefold. The bodies of *Playgirl* centrefolds have increased dramatically in muscle, not fat, whereas for average men, increases have tended to occur in the other direction.

Findings such as these lead us inexorably to some disturbing questions: Does the ideal of thinness for women contribute to body dissatisfaction and destructive behaviours such as bulimia or excessive exercise that could ultimately end in death? The deaths of high-profile anorexic models, such as Brazilian model Ana Carolina Reston, who weighed only 40 kilograms (88 pounds), shocked some governments into taking action aimed at changing the cultural ideal of thinness. In April 2008, the French government introduced a law that would make it a crime to promote excessive thinness in the fashion industry, not only in shows but also on websites, in magazines, and in advertisements. In Spain, fashion-show organizers banned models with a body mass index under 18 (starvation level) from fashion runways. Canada decided not to follow suit (Agrell, 2008).

The fashion industry has come under criticism for using models that are dangerously thin.

In addition to using starvation-weight models, the fashion industry recently has come under criticism for touching up photos of already-thin models to make their waists and legs look even thinner (and their breasts larger). In October 2010, the Canadian clothing retailer Jacob aligned itself with the "no retouching" camp, arguing that by not retouching photos of models, it is promoting more realistic body images. The model used in one of its advertisements is tall, thin and wears size 4 clothing—which the company argues is more realistic than the size 0 that is typically worn by models. Some would argue that even at size 4, the tall, slender Jacob's model does not represent the average woman's body size.

We could also ask whether the muscular ideal for men contributes to dangerous behaviours such as anabolic steroid use. To answer such questions, researchers must use research methods such as the correlational method and the experimental method. These methods will be discussed next.

Archival Analysis: Body Image and the Media

Try doing your own archival analysis to see how the ideal body types for women and men are portrayed in the media. Choose three or four magazines that differ in their topic and audience: for example, a news magazine such as *Maclean's*, a "women's" beauty magazine such as *Glamour*, a "men's" magazine such as *GQ*, and a fitness magazine such as *Shape* or *Muscle & Fitness*. For each magazine, open the pages randomly until you find a photograph of a woman's or a man's body. Repeat this so you look at two or three such photographs in each magazine.

- What is the ideal body type for women portrayed in these magazines? What is the ideal body type for men portrayed in these magazines? In answering these questions, note the following:
  - (a) the ideal weight portrayed
  - (b) the ideal muscle-to-fat ratio
  - (c) other characteristics (e.g., width of shoulders relative to waist, size of bust/chest).
- Does the ideal body type portrayed in the magazines seem attainable for each gender? Are the ideals that are portrayed healthy?

According to research conducted at the University of Manitoba and the University of Winnipeg (Morry & Staska, 2001; Nowatzki & Morry, 2009), internalizing the body ideals portrayed in the media can be harmful to your health. The researchers found that women who frequently read beauty magazines were more likely to accept the societal ideal of thinness for females. Internalization of this ideal was associated with greater body dissatisfaction and with higher incidence of eating disorders. In other recent research along these lines, it was found that media portrayals of the ideal women's body have a particularly negative impact on those women for whom body image is an important part of their self-definition (Ip & Jarry, 2008). In this experiment, female students at the University of Windsor participated in an experiment, supposedly on consumer responses, in which they were required to evaluate advertisements. Participants in the body ideals condition rated magazine advertisements featuring thin models; participants in the control condition rated advertisements for products. It was found that women exposed to thin models subsequently reported lower appearance self-esteem than women in the control condition. Those for whom body image was important were especially affected by exposure to thin models—they subsequently placed even greater emphasis on body image and reported greater dissatisfaction with their own bodies.

And what about men? Morry and Staska (2001) found that men who frequently read fitness magazines were more likely to internalize the muscular ideal, which in turn was associated with body dissatisfaction, disordered eating behaviours, and steroid use. The bottom line, regardless of your sex, is to beware of too readily accepting the ideals portrayed in the media—it could be dangerous to your physical and emotional health.

The Correlational Method

Research Methods

Social scientists usually want to do more than document social behaviour—they want to understand relations between variables and to be able to predict when different kinds of social behaviour will occur. The correlational method is ideal for answering questions about whether two variables are related—and, if so, determining the strength of that relation. We define the **correlational method** as a technique in which researchers systematically measure two or more variables and assess the relation between them (i.e., how much one can be predicted from the other). Many important questions about human social behaviour can be answered using the correlational method, such as whether people's level of compassion is related to how much money they donate toward famine relief, whether the amount of time spent reading beauty magazines is associated with the acceptance of the body ideal of thinness, and whether attitudes toward condom use are related to the frequency with which condoms are actually used.

Correlational Method

The technique whereby researchers systematically measure two or more variables and assess the relation between them (i.e., how much one can be predicted from the other)

Correlation Coefficient

A statistic that assesses how well you can predict one variable based on another (e.g., how well you can predict people's weight from their height)

Researchers look at such relations by calculating the **correlation coefficient**, which is a statistic that assesses how well you can predict one variable based on another—for example, how well you can predict people's weight from their height. A positive correlation means that increases in the value of one variable are associated with increases in the value of the other variable. Height and weight are positively correlated; the taller people are, the more they tend to weigh. A negative correlation means that *increases* in the value of one variable are associated with *decreases* in the value of the other. We might expect, for example, that as the number of classes a student skips goes up, the student's mark in the course will go down—the more classes cut, the lower the grade. It is also possible, of course, for two variables to be completely uncorrelated, so that a researcher cannot predict one variable from the other. Knowing someone's shoe size will not allow you to predict how many books that person owns.

Correlation coefficients are expressed as numbers that can range from −1.00 to +1.00. A correlation of +1.00 means that two variables are perfectly correlated in a positive direction; thus, by knowing people's standing on one variable, the researcher can predict exactly where they stand on the other variable. In everyday life, of course, perfect correlations are rare; for example, one study found that the correlation between height and weight was +0.47 in a sample of men aged 18 to 24 (Freedman, Pisani, Purves, & Adhikari, 1991). This means that, on average, the taller people were heavier than the shorter people, but there were exceptions. A correlation of −1.00 means that two variables are perfectly correlated in a negative direction. Thus, a correlation of −0.47 would tell you that, on average, the more classes students skip, the lower their grades, but, once again, there are exceptions. Finally, a correlation of zero means that two variables are not correlated. It may surprise you that the correlation between having positive attitudes toward condom use and actually using them is disturbingly close to zero: +0.23 in a sample of French-Canadian university students (Hébert et al., 1989). Thus, if you know that someone has positive attitudes toward using condoms, this information will not allow you to make a very accurate prediction about whether the person actually will use one the next time he or she has sex.

Connect to MyPsychLab

To take a survey on participating in a research study, go to MyPsychLab

Surveys

The correlational method is often used in **surveys**, research in which a representative sample of people are asked questions about their attitudes or behaviour. Surveys are a convenient way to measure people's attitudes; for example, people can be telephoned and asked which candidate they will support in an upcoming election or how they feel about a variety of social issues. Researchers often apply the correlational method to survey results, to predict how people's responses to one question predict their other responses. Political scientists, for example, might be interested in whether people's attitudes toward a specific issue, such as gun control, predict how they will vote. Psychologists often use surveys (questionnaires) to help understand social behaviour and attitudes—for example, by seeing whether the amount of pornography that men see is correlated with their attitudes toward women.

Surveys

Research in which a representative sample of people are asked questions about their attitudes or behaviour

Surveys have a number of advantages, one of which is that they allow researchers to judge the relationship between variables that are often difficult to observe, such as how often people engage in safer sex. For example, Herold and Mewhinney (1993) wanted to know whether people who had positive attitudes toward the use of condoms would be more likely to engage in safer sex. To answer this question, they asked women and men in various singles bars in southern Ontario to complete a survey that assessed their agreement with attitude statements such as "If I were to have sex with someone I just met, I would be uncomfortable suggesting to my partner that we use a condom." Respondents also were asked about the frequency with which they actually used condoms. (As mentioned earlier, the correlation between positive attitudes toward condoms and the frequency of using them is surprisingly low.)

Another advantage of surveys is the ability to sample representative segments of the population. Answers to a survey are useful only if they reflect the responses of people in general—not just the people actually tested (called the *sample*). Survey researchers go to great lengths to ensure that the people they sample are typical. They select samples that are representative of the population on a number of characteristics important to a given research question (e.g., age, educational background, religion, gender, income level). They also make sure to use a **random selection** of people from

Random Selection

A way of ensuring that a sample of people is representative of a population, by giving everyone in the population an equal chance of being selected for the sample the population at large, which is a way of ensuring that a sample of people is representative. As long as the sample is selected randomly, it can be assumed that the responses are a reasonable match to those of the population as a whole. (Random selection also is important when researchers conduct experiments—which we discuss later.)

CONNECTIONS

Random Selection in Political Polls

There are some famous cases whereby people tried to generalize from samples that were not randomly selected—to their peril. In the fall of 1936, a weekly magazine in the United States called *The Literary Digest* conducted a large survey asking readers for whom they planned to vote in the upcoming presidential election. The magazine obtained the names and addresses of its sample from telephone directories and automobile registration lists. The results of its survey of 2 million people indicated that the Republican candidate, Alf Landon, would win by a landslide. There never was a President Landon; instead, Franklin D. Roosevelt won every state but two. What went wrong with *The Literary Digest* 's poll? In the depths of the Great Depression, many people could not afford telephones or cars. Those who could afford these items were, by definition, doing well financially, were frequently Republican, and overwhelmingly favoured Alf Landon. However, the majority of the voters were poor—and overwhelmingly supported the Democratic candidate, Roosevelt. By using a list of names that excluded the less affluent members of the population, *The Literary Digest* created a nonrepresentative sample. *The Literary Digest* never recovered from this methodological disaster and went out of business shortly after publishing its poll.

The Literary Digest

NEW YORK OCTOBER 31, 1936

Topics of the day

LANDON, 1,293,669; ROOSEVELT, 972,897

Final Returns in The Digest's Poll of Ten Million Voters

Well, the great battle of the ballots in the Poll of ten million voters, scattered throughout the forty-eight States of the Union, is now finished, and in the table below we record the figures received up to the hour of going to press.

These figures are exactly as received from more than one in every five voters polled in our country—they are neither weighted, adjusted nor interpreted.

Never before in an experience covering more than a quarter of a century in taking polls have we received so many different varieties of criticism—praise from many; condemnation from many others—and yet it has been just of the same type that has come to us every time a Poll has been taken in all these years.

A telegram from a newspaper in California asks: "Is it true that Mr. Hearst has purchased THE LITERARY DIGEST?" A telephone message only the day before these lines were written: "Has the Republican National Committee purchased THE LITERARY DIGEST?" And all types and varieties, including: "Have the Jews purchased THE LITERARY DIGEST?" "Is the Pope of Rome a stockholder of THE LITERARY DIGEST?" And so it goes—all equally absurd and amusing. We could add more to this list, and yet all of these questions in recent days are but repetitions of what we have been experiencing all down the years from the very first Poll.

Problem—Now, are the figures in this Poll correct? In answer to this question we will simply refer to a telegram we sent to a young man in Massachusetts the other day in answer to his challenge to us to wager $100,000 on the accuracy of our Poll. We wired him as follows:

"For nearly a quarter century, we have been taking Polls of the voters in the forty-eight States, and especially in Presidential years, and we have always merely mailed the ballots, counted and recorded those returned and let the people of the Nation draw their conclusions as to our accuracy. So far, we have been right in every Poll. Will we be right in the current Poll? That, as Mrs. Roosevelt said concerning the President's reelection, is in the 'lap of the gods.'

"We never make any claims before election but we respectfully refer you to the opinion of one of the most quoted citizens to-day, the Hon. James A. Farley, Chairman of the Democratic National Committee. This is what Mr. Farley said October 14, 1932:

"'Any sane person can not escape the implication of such a gigantic sampling of popular opinion as is embraced in THE LITERARY DIGEST straw vote. I consider this conclusive evidence as to the desire of the people of this country for a change in the National Government. THE LITERARY DIGEST poll is an achievement of no little magnitude. It is a Poll fairly and correctly conducted.'"

In studying the table of the voters from

The statistics and the material in this article are the property of Funk & Wagnalls Company and have been copyrighted by it; neither the whole nor any part thereof may be reprinted or published without the special permission of the copyright owner.

Final Report "Literary Digest" 1936 Presidential Poll

Sound like ancient history? Think again. In a recent interview, Canada's first celebrity pollster Allan Gregg (chair of Harris/Decima) reported that response rates to telephone surveys have dropped by 15 percent because more people are using cellphones, have call display, or simply hang up. The result is that telephone polls are now most likely to be answered by the elderly, rural dwellers, and the less educated. In contrast, polls that are conducted online are more likely to be answered by those who are younger, more affluent, and better educated. In both cases, the resultant samples are unrepresentative of the population at large, which, according to *Ottawa Citizen* journalist Susan Riley, may be one reason why polls are showing such contradictory results (Riley, 2011). For example, "one week the Conservative gender gap is gone, the next week 'oops it's back'" (Gregg, as cited in Riley, 2011).

A potential problem with survey data is the accuracy of the responses. Straightforward questions—regarding what people think about an issue or what they typically do—are relatively easy to answer. For example, in plebiscites held in 2002 and 2008, residents of Brandon, Manitoba, were asked a question about a hotly contested issue: "Do you favour the establishment of a casino in the city of Brandon?" This kind of straightforward question tends to produce straightforward answers. More than half of voters (56 percent in 2002; 57 percent in 2008) responded "No." As a result, no casino was built. Although casino developers have made subsequent overtures, city council has remained steadfast in its resolve not to have a casino within city limits, based on these results (Goerzen, 2011). In social psychological research, however, participants are generally not asked a single question with a yes or no answer.

And as the question becomes more complex, it is even more challenging to elicit accurate answers. Asking respondents to predict how they might behave in some hypothetical situation or to explain why they behaved as they did in the past is an invitation to inaccuracy (Schuman & Kalton, 1985; Schwarz, 1999; Schwarz, Groves, & Schuman, 1998). Often people simply don't know the answer—but they think they do. Richard Nisbett and Tim Wilson (1977) demonstrated this phenomenon of "telling more than you can know" in a number of studies in which people often made inaccurate reports about why they responded the way they did. Their reports about the causes of their responses pertained more to their theories and beliefs about what should have influenced them than to what actually influenced them. (We discuss these studies at greater length in Chapter 5.)

Explore on **mypsychlab**
Correlations Do Not Show Causation

Limits of the Correlational Method: Correlation Does Not Equal Causation

The major shortcoming of the correlational method is that it tells us only that two variables are related, whereas the goal of the social psychologist is to identify the *causes* of social behaviour. We want to be able to say that A causes B, not just that A is related to, or correlated with, B.

If a researcher finds a correlation between two variables, there are three possible causal relations between these variables. For example, researchers have found a correlation between the amount of violent television children watch and how aggressive they are (Eron, 1982). One explanation of this correlation is that watching TV violence causes kids to become more violent. It is equally probable, however, that the reverse is true: that kids who are aggressive to begin with are more likely to watch violent television. Or there might be no causal relation between these two variables; instead, both television watching and violent behaviour could be caused by a third variable, such as having neglectful parents who do not pay much attention to their kids. (Experimental evidence does support one of these causal relationships; we will discuss which one in Chapter 11.) When we use the correlational method, it is wrong to jump to the conclusion that one variable is causing the other to occur. *Correlation does not prove causation.*

Unfortunately, one of the most common methodological errors in the social sciences is for a researcher to forget this adage. Drawing causal conclusions from correlational data also frequently occurs in everyday life. Consider, for example, a column in the *Winnipeg Free Press* featuring Tillie the Rainmaker. It all began in 1986 when Tillie took a trip to Sacramento, California. As soon as she stepped off the plane, the skies poured with rain, ending a six-week drought. Until then, Tillie had seen herself as an average Jewish grandmother. But at that moment, she realized that she had special powers. Tillie claims to have ended many droughts and extinguished major forest fires since then. Winnipeg rabbi Alan Green is a strong supporter of Tillie and her work. "I can't prove scientifically that there is cause-and-effect," says Green. But he does believe that such things are possible. Besides, he says, "It's a freely offered gift . . .. There can be no harm" (Reynolds, 2000, p. D3).

Tillie Goren believes that she has the ability to end droughts because on several occasions when she has visited a drought-stricken area, it has started to rain. Is this a case of correlation or causation?

In a letter to the editor the following week, a psychology professor suggested that a more likely explanation for Tillie's special powers is that

TRY IT! Correlation Does Not Equal Causation

It can be difficult to remember that when two variables are correlated, it doesn't necessarily mean that one caused the other; correlation does *not* allow us to make causal inferences. For each of the following examples, think about why the correlation was found. Even if it seems obvious which variable was causing the other, are there alternative explanations?

Correlation Does Not Equal Causation Quiz

1. Recently, a politician extolled the virtues of the Boy and Girl Scouts organizations. In his salute to the Scouts, the politician mentioned that few teenagers convicted of street crimes had been members of the Scouts. In other words, he was positing a negative correlation between activity in Scouting and frequency of criminal behaviour. Why might this be?
2. A recent study reported that the more milk children drank, the more weight they gained. One researcher concluded that children who need to control their weight should not drink much milk. Is this a valid conclusion?
3. A recent study of soldiers stationed on army bases found that the number of tattoos a soldier had was correlated positively with his becoming involved in a motorcycle accident. Why?
4. Recently, it was reported that a correlation exists between people's tendency to eat breakfast in the morning and how long they live, such that people who skip breakfast die at a younger age. Does eating Cheerios lead to a long life?
5. A recent study found that adolescents who are religious are less likely to commit crimes and more likely to wear seat belts than adolescents who are not religious. Does religion make people more likely to obey the law?
6. A research study found that having a pet in childhood is correlated with a reduced likelihood of becoming a juvenile delinquent in adolescence. Why is this?
7. "Hyper-texting teens more likely to have sex, do drugs" reads a headline in the November 10, 2010, issue of the *Winnipeg Free Press* (Stobbe, 2010). The article describes a study in which it was found that teenagers who text at least 120 times per day are three and one-half times more likely to have sex than teens who are not hyper-texters. Hyper-texters were also more likely to binge drink, get in a fight, and use drugs. How would you explain this correlation?

Go to www.MyPsychLab.com for answers.

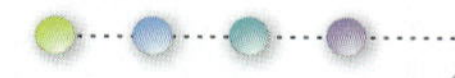

she and her rabbi inferred causality from correlational events (Double deception, 2000). In some cases, this inference might be quite harmless, as Rabbi Green points out. However, it is not sound scientific practice, and the consequences can be quite serious, as demonstrated by a study of birth control methods and sexually transmitted diseases (STDs) in women (Rosenberg, Davidson, Chen, Judson, & Douglas, 1992). These researchers examined the records of women who had visited a clinic for STDs, noting which method of birth control they used and whether they had STDs. Surprisingly, the researchers found that women who relied on condoms had significantly more STDs than women who used diaphragms or contraceptive sponges. This result was widely reported in the popular press, along with the conclusion that the use of diaphragms and sponges caused a lower incidence of disease. Some reporters urged women whose partners used condoms to switch to other methods.

Can you see the problem with this conclusion? The fact that the incidence of disease was correlated with the type of contraception women used is open to a number of causal interpretations. Perhaps the women who used sponges and diaphragms had sex with fewer partners. (In fact, condom users were more likely to have had sex with multiple partners in the previous month.) Perhaps the partners of women who relied on condoms were more likely to have STDs than the partners of women who used sponges and diaphragms. There is simply no way of knowing. Thus, the conclusion that the use of diaphragms and sponges offers protection against STDs cannot be drawn from this correlational study.

Other examples of the difficulty of inferring causality from correlational studies are shown in the accompanying Try It! quiz.

Simulate on **mypsychlab**
Aggression and Prosocial Behaviour

The Experimental Method: Answering Causal Questions

Experimental Method
The method in which the researcher randomly assigns participants to different conditions and ensures that these conditions are identical except for the independent variable (the one thought to have a causal effect on people's responses)

The only way to determine causal relations is with the **experimental method**. Here, the researcher systematically orchestrates the event so that people experience it in one way (e.g., they witness an emergency along with other bystanders) or another way (e.g., they witness the same emergency but as the sole bystander). The experimental method is the method of choice in most social psychological research, because it allows the experimenter to make causal inferences. For this reason, the experimental method is the crown jewel of social psychological research design.

The experimental method always involves direct intervention on the part of the researcher. Let's return for a moment to Latané and Darley's hypothesis, discussed earlier, that the more people who witness an emergency the less likely it is that any given individual will intervene. By carefully changing only one aspect of the situation (e.g., group size), they could test whether this aspect is the cause of the behaviour in question (e.g., whether people help in an emergency). Sound simple? Actually, it isn't. Staging an experiment to test Latané and Darley's hypothesis involves severe practical and ethical difficulties. What kind of emergency should be used? Ideally (from a scientific perspective), it should be as true to the Genovese case as possible. Accordingly, you would want to stage a murder that passersby could witness. In one condition, you could stage the murder so that only a few onlookers were present; in another condition, you could stage it so that a great many onlookers were present.

Obviously, no scientist in his or her right mind would stage a murder for unsuspecting bystanders. But how can we arrange a realistic situation that is upsetting enough to be similar to the Genovese case without it being too upsetting? In addition, how can we ensure that each bystander experiences the same emergency except for the variable whose effect we want to test—in this case, the number of bystanders?

Theory is a good thing, but a good experiment lasts forever.

—Pyotr Leonidovich Kapitsa, *Nobel physicist (1894–1984)*

Let's see how Latané and Darley (1968) dealt with these problems. Imagine you were a participant in their experiment. You arrive at the scheduled time and find yourself in a long corridor with doors to several small cubicles. An experimenter greets you and takes you into one of the cubicles, mentioning that five other students, seated in the other cubicles, will be participating with you. The experimenter leaves after giving you a pair of headphones with an attached microphone. You put on the headphones, and soon you hear the experimenter explaining to everyone that he is interested in learning about the kinds of personal problems that college students experience. To ensure that people will discuss their problems openly, he explains, each participant will remain anonymous; each will stay in his or her separate room and communicate with the others only via the intercom system. Further, the experimenter says, he will not be listening to the discussion, so that people will feel freer to be open and honest. Finally, the experimenter asks that participants take turns presenting their problems, each speaking for two minutes, after which each person will comment on what the others said. To make sure this procedure is followed, he says, only one person's microphone will be turned on at a time.

The group discussion then begins. You listen as the first participant admits that he has found it difficult to adjust to college. With some embarrassment, he mentions that he sometimes has seizures, especially when under stress. When his two minutes are up, you hear the other four participants discuss their problems, after which it is your turn. When you have finished, it is the first person's turn to speak again. To your astonishment, after he makes a few further comments, he seems to begin to experience a seizure:

> I—er—um—I think I—I need—er—if—if could—er—er—somebody er—er—er—er—er—er—give me a little—er—give me a little help here because—er—I—er—I'm—er—er—h—h—having a—a—a real problem—er—right now and I—er—if somebody could help me out it would—it would—er—er s—s—sure be—sure be good... because—er—there—er—er—a cause I—er—I—uh—I've got a—a one of the—er—sei—er—er—things coming on and—and—and I could really—er—use some help so if somebody would—er—give me a little h—help—uh—er—er—er—er—c—could somebody—er—er—help—er—uh—uh—uh (choking sounds)... I'm gonna die—er—er—I'm... gonna die—er—help—er—er—seizure—er (chokes, then quiet). (Darley & Latané, 1968, p. 379)

What would you have done in this situation? If you were like most of the participants in the actual study, you would have remained in your cubicle, listening to your fellow student having a seizure, and done nothing about it. Does this surprise you? Latané and Darley kept track of the number of people who left their cubicle to find the victim or the experimenter before the end of the victim's seizure. (This was their operational definition of helping.) Only 31 percent of the participants helped in this way. Fully 69 percent of the students remained in their cubicles and did nothing—just as Kitty Genovese's neighbours failed to offer her assistance in any way.

Does this finding prove that the failure to help was because of the number of people who witnessed the seizure? How do we know that it wasn't because of some other factor? We know because Latané and Darley included two other conditions in their experiment. In these conditions, the procedure was identical to that described above, with one crucial difference: The size of the discussion group was smaller, meaning that fewer people were witnesses to the seizure. In one condition, the participants were told that there were three other people in the discussion group aside from themselves (the victim plus two others). In another condition, participants were told that there was only one other person in their discussion group (namely, the victim). In this latter condition, each participant believed that he or she was the only one who could hear the seizure. Did the size of the discussion group make a difference? As you'll see in a moment, it did.

Connect to MyPsychLab
To access the Critical Thinking question on Bullying, go to MyPsychLab

Independent and Dependent Variables

The number of people witnessing the emergency in the Latané and Darley study was the **independent variable**, which is the variable a researcher changes or varies to see if it has an effect on some other variable. The **dependent variable** is the variable a researcher measures to see if it is influenced by the independent variable; the researcher hypothesizes that the dependent variable will be influenced by the level of the independent variable. That is, the dependent variable is hypothesized to depend on the independent variable (see Figure 2.1). Latané and Darley found that their independent variable—the number of bystanders—did have an effect on the dependent variable—whether they tried to help. When the participants believed that four other people were witnesses to the seizure, only 31 percent offered assistance. When the participants believed that only two other people were aware of the seizure, the amount of helping behaviour increased to 62 percent of the participants. When the participants believed that they were the only person listening to the seizure, nearly everyone helped (85 percent). Thus, Latané and Darley were successful in identifying one important determinant of whether people help—the number of bystanders who are present.

Simulate on **mypsychlab**
Distinguishing Independent and Dependent Variables

Independent Variable
The variable a researcher changes or varies to see if it has an effect on some other variable

Dependent Variable
The variable a researcher measures to see if it is influenced by the independent variable; the researcher hypothesizes that the dependent variable will be influenced by the level of the independent variable

FIGURE 2.1
Independent and dependent variables in experimental research.

These results indicate that the number of bystanders strongly influences the rate of helping, but it does not mean that the size of the group is the only cause of people's decision to help. After all, when there were four bystanders, one-third of the participants still helped; conversely, when participants thought they were the only witness, some of them failed to help. Obviously, other factors influence helping behaviour—the bystanders' personalities, their prior experience with emergencies, and so on. Nonetheless, Latané and Darley succeeded in identifying one important determinant of whether people help, namely the number of bystanders present.

Independent Variable	Dependent Variable
The variable that is hypothesized to influence the dependent variable. Participants are treated identically except for this variable.	The response that is hypothesized to depend on the independent variable. All participants are measured on this variable.
Example: Latané and Darley (1968)	
The number of bystanders	**How many participants helped?**
Participant + Victim	85%
Participant + Victim + Two others	62%
Participant + Victim + Four others	31%

Internal Validity in Experiments

How can we be sure that the differences in help across conditions in the Latané and Darley (1968) seizure study were a result of the different numbers of bystanders who witnessed the emergency? Could this effect have been caused by some other aspect of the situation? Again, this is the beauty of the experimental method. We can be sure of the causal connection between the number of bystanders and helping because Latané and Darley made sure that everything about the situation was the same in the different conditions except the independent variable, the number of bystanders. Keeping everything the same but the independent variable is referred to as *internal validity*. Latané and Darley were careful to maintain high internal validity by ensuring that everyone witnessed the same emergency. They prerecorded the supposed other participants and the victim, and played their voices over the intercom system.

You may have noticed, however, that there was a key difference between the conditions of the Latané and Darley experiment other than the number of bystanders: Different people participated in the different conditions. Maybe the observed differences in helping were a result of characteristics of the participants instead of the independent variable. The people in the sole witness condition might have differed in any number of ways from their counterparts in the other conditions, making them more likely to help. Maybe they were more likely to have had loving parents, to know something about epilepsy, or to have experience helping in emergencies. If either of these possibilities is true, it would be difficult to conclude that it was the number of bystanders, rather than something about the participants' backgrounds, that led to differences in helping.

Fortunately, there is a technique that allows experimenters to minimize differences among participants as the cause of the results: **random assignment to condition.** This is the process whereby all participants have an equal chance of taking part in any condition of an experiment; through random assignment, researchers can be relatively certain that differences in the participants' personalities or backgrounds are distributed evenly across conditions. Because Latané and Darley's participants were randomly assigned to the conditions of their experiment, it is very unlikely that the ones who knew the most about epilepsy all ended up in one condition. Knowledge about epilepsy should be randomly (i.e., roughly evenly) dispersed across the three experimental conditions. This powerful technique is the most important part of the experimental method.

Random Assignment to Condition

The process whereby all participants have an equal chance of taking part in any condition of an experiment; through random assignment, researchers can be relatively certain that differences in the participants' personalities or backgrounds are distributed evenly across conditions

Even with random assignment, however, there is always the (very small) possibility that different characteristics of people did not distribute themselves evenly across conditions. For example, if we randomly divide a group of 40 people into two groups, it is possible that more of those who know the most about epilepsy will by chance end up in one group than in the other—just as it is possible to get more heads than tails when you flip a coin 40 times. This is a possibility we take seriously in experimental science. The analyses of our data come with a **probability level (p-value)**, which is a number, calculated with statistical techniques, that tells researchers how likely it is that the results of their experiment occurred by chance and not because of the independent variable. The convention in science, including social psychology, is to consider results *significant* (trustworthy) if the probability level is less than 5 in 100 that the results might be attributable to chance factors, and not the independent variables studied. For example, if we flipped a coin 40 times and got heads 40 times, we would probably assume that this was very unlikely to have occurred by chance and that there was something wrong with the coin. (We might check the other side to ensure that it wasn't one of those trick coins with heads on both sides!) Similarly, if the results in two conditions of an experiment differ significantly from what we would expect by chance, we assume that the difference was caused by the independent variable (e.g., the number of bystanders present during the emergency). The *p*-value tells us how confident we can be that the difference was attributable to chance rather than to the independent variable.

Probability Level (*p*-Value)
A number, calculated with statistical techniques, that tells researchers how likely it is that the results of their experiment occurred by chance and not because of the independent variable(s); the convention in science, including social psychology, is to consider results significant if the probability level is less than 5 in 100 that the results might be attributable to chance factors and not the independent variables studied

To summarize, the key to a good experiment is to maintain high **internal validity**, which we can now define as making sure that the independent variable, and *only* the independent variable, influences the dependent variable. This is accomplished by controlling all extraneous variables (other variables that could conceivably affect the independent variable) and by randomly assigning people to different experimental conditions (Campbell & Stanley, 1967). When internal validity is high, the researcher is in a position to judge whether the independent variable causes the dependent variable. This hallmark of the experimental method sets the technique apart from the observational and correlational methods: Only the experimental method can answer causal questions.

Internal Validity
Ensuring that nothing other than the independent variable can affect the dependent variable; this is accomplished by controlling all extraneous variables and by randomly assigning people to different experimental conditions

External Validity in Experiments

For all of the advantages of the experimental method, there are some drawbacks. By virtue of gaining enough control over the situation so as to randomly assign people to conditions and rule out the effects of extraneous variables, the situation can become somewhat artificial and distant from real life. For example, one could argue that Latané and Darley strayed far from the original inspiration for their study, the Kitty Genovese murder. What does witnessing a seizure while participating in a laboratory experiment in a college building have to do with a brutal murder in New York? How often in everyday life does anyone have discussions with other people through an intercom system? Did the fact that the participants knew they were in a psychology experiment influence their behaviour?

These are important questions that concern **external validity**, which is the extent to which the results of a study can be generalized to other situations and other people. Note that two kinds of generalizability are at issue: the extent to which we can generalize from the situation constructed by an experimenter to real-life situations (generalizability across *situations*), and the extent to which we can generalize from the people who participated in the experiment to people in general (generalizability across *people*).

External Validity
The extent to which the results of a study can be generalized to other situations and to other people

Generalizability across Situations Research in social psychology is sometimes criticized for being conducted in artificial situations, such as psychology experiments at a university, that cannot be generalized to real life. To address this problem, social psychologists attempt to increase the generalizability of their results by making their studies as realistic as possible. We can refer to the extent to which an experiment is

Mundane Realism

The extent to which an experiment is similar to real-life situations

Psychological Realism

The extent to which the psychological processes triggered in an experiment are similar to psychological processes that occur in everyday life; psychological realism can be high in an experiment, even when mundane realism is low

Cover Story

A description of the purpose of a study given to participants that is different from its true purpose; cover stories are used to maintain psychological realism

similar to real-life situations as the experiment's **mundane realism** (Aronson & Carlsmith, 1968). It can be difficult to achieve realism in a laboratory setting—especially when people are placed in situations they would rarely, if ever, encounter in everyday life, such as what occurred in Latané and Darley's group discussion of personal problems over an intercom system.

It is more important to ensure that a study is high in **psychological realism**—how similar the psychological processes triggered in an experiment are to psychological processes that occur in everyday life (Aronson, Wilson, & Brewer, 1998). Even though Latané and Darley staged an emergency that in significant ways was unlike ones encountered in everyday life, was it psychologically similar to real-life emergencies? Were the same psychological processes triggered? Did the participants have the same types of perceptions and thoughts, make the same types of decisions, and choose the same types of behaviours that they would have in a real-life situation? If so, then the study is high in psychological realism and we can generalize the results to everyday life.

Psychological realism is heightened if people feel involved in a real event. To accomplish this, experimenters often tell participants a **cover story**—a disguised version of the study's true purpose. You might have wondered why Latané and Darley told people that the purpose of the experiment was to study the personal problems of college students. It certainly would have been easier to say, "We are interested in how people react to emergencies, so at some point during the study we are going to stage an accident, and then we'll see how you respond." We think you will agree, however, that such a procedure would be very low in psychological realism. In real life, no one knows when emergencies are going to occur and we are not given time to plan responses to them. If participants knew that an emergency was about to happen, the kinds of psychological processes triggered would have been quite different from those of a real emergency, reducing the psychological realism of the study.

Further, as discussed earlier, people don't always know why they do what they do, or even what they will do until it happens. Therefore, describing an experimental situation to participants and then asking them to respond normally will produce responses that are, at best, suspect. For example, after describing the Latané and Darley seizure experiment to our students, we usually ask them to predict how they would respond, just as we asked you earlier. Invariably, most of our students think they would have helped the victim, even when they know that in the condition in which the group size was six, most people did not help. Unfortunately, we cannot depend on people's predictions about what they would do in a hypothetical situation; we can find out what people will really do only when we construct a situation that triggers the same psychological processes as occur in the real world.

A good deal of social psychological research takes place in laboratory settings. How do social psychologists generalize from the findings of these studies to life outside the laboratory?

Generalizability across People Recall that social psychologists study the way in which people in general are susceptible to social influence. Latané and Darley's experiment documented an interesting, unexpected example of social influence, whereby the mere knowledge that others were present reduced the likelihood that people helped. But what have we learned about people in general? The participants in their study were 52 male and female students at New York University who received course credit for participating. Would the study have turned out the same if a different population had been used? Would the number of bystanders have influenced helping behaviour had the participants been middle-aged blue-collar workers instead of university students? Canadian instead of American? Nova Scotians instead of New Yorkers?

The only way to be certain that the results of an experiment represent the behaviour of a particular population is to ensure that participants are randomly selected from that population. Ideally, samples in experiments should be randomly selected, just as they are in surveys. Unfortunately, it is impractical and expensive to select random samples for social psychology experiments. It is difficult enough to convince a random sample of people to agree to answer a few questions over the telephone as part of a political poll, and such polls can cost thousands of dollars to conduct. Imagine the difficulty Latané and Darley would have had convincing a random sample of Americans to board a plane to New York to take part in their study, not to mention the cost of such an endeavour. Even trying to gather a random sample of students at New York University would not have been easy; each person contacted would have had to agree to spend an hour in Latané and Darley's laboratory.

Of course, concerns about practicality and expense are not good excuses for poor science. Many researchers address this problem by studying basic psychological processes that make people susceptible to social influence, assuming that these processes are so fundamental that they are universally shared. In that case, participants for social psychology experiments don't really have to come from every corner of Earth. Of course, as we shall discuss in this textbook, some social psychological processes do vary in different subgroups and different cultures and in those cases, diverse samples of people have to be studied. The question then is "How can researchers tell whether the processes they are studying are universal?"

Replications Suppose a researcher claims that her study is high in psychological realism—that it has thus captured psychological functioning as it occurs in everyday life—and that it doesn't matter that only Introductory Psychology students at one university participated because these psychological processes are universal. Should we take her word for it?

Not necessarily. The ultimate test of an experiment's external validity is **replication**—conducting the study over again, generally with different subject populations or in different settings. Sometimes researchers will also use different methods, to see if they still get the same results. Do we think that Latané and Darley found the results they did only because their participants knew they were in a psychology experiment? If so, then we should try to replicate their study in an experiment conducted outside the laboratory. Do we think that their results are limited to only certain kinds of emergencies? Then we should try to replicate the results with a different emergency. Do we think that only New Yorkers would be so unhelpful? Then we should try to replicate the study with participants from different parts of the United States and in different countries. Only with such replications can we be certain about how generalizable the results are.

Replication

Repeating a study, generally with different subject populations, in different settings, or by using different methods

When many studies of one problem are conducted, the results can vary. Several studies might find an effect of the number of bystanders on helping behaviour, for example, whereas a few do not. How can one make sense out of this? Does the number of bystanders make a difference or not? Fortunately, a statistical technique called **meta analysis** averages the results of two or more studies to see if the effect of an independent variable is reliable. Earlier, we discussed *p*-levels, which tell us the probability that the findings of one study are attributable to chance or to the independent variable. A meta analysis essentially does the same thing, except that it finds an average from the results of many different studies. If, say, an independent variable is found to have an effect in only one of 20 studies, the meta analysis will tell us that that one study was probably an exception and that, on average, the independent variable is not influencing the dependent variable. If an independent variable is having an effect in most of the studies, the meta analysis is likely to tell us that, on average, it does influence the dependent variable.

Meta Analysis

A statistical technique that averages the results of two or more studies to see if the effect of an independent variable is reliable

Most of the findings you will read about in this book have been replicated in different settings and with different populations, thereby demonstrating that they are reliable phenomena that are not limited to the laboratory or to Introductory Psychology students. For example, Latané and Darley's original findings have been replicated numerous times. Increasing the number of bystanders has been found to inhibit helping behaviour with many kinds of people, including children, university students, and future ministers (Darley & Batson, 1973; Latané & Nida, 1981); in Israel (Schwartz & Gottlieb, 1976); in small towns and large cities in the United States (Latané & Dabbs, 1975); in a variety of settings, such as psychology laboratories, city streets, and subway trains (Harrison & Wells, 1991; Latané & Darley, 1970; Piliavin & Piliavin, 1972; Piliavin, Dovidio, Gaertner, & Clark, 1981); and with a variety of types of emergencies, such as seizures, potential fires, fights, and accidents (Latané & Darley, 1968; Shotland & Straw, 1976; Staub, 1974), as well as with less serious events, such as having a flat tire (Hurley & Allen, 1974). Given that many of these replications have been conducted in real-life settings (e.g., on a subway train), people could not possibly have known that an experiment was being conducted. We will frequently point out similar replications of the major findings we discuss in this book.

Simulate on **mypsychlab**
Observational Studies

The Basic Dilemma of the Social Psychologist

When we conduct experiments in psychology, there is almost always a trade-off between internal and external validity—that is, between

(a) having enough control over the situation to ensure that no extraneous variables are influencing the results and to randomly assign people to conditions, and

(b) ensuring that the results can be generalized to everyday life.

Field Experiments
Experiments conducted in natural settings, rather than in the laboratory

One of the best ways to increase external validity is by conducting **field experiments.** In a field experiment, people's behaviour is studied outside the laboratory, in its natural setting. A field experiment is identical in design to a laboratory experiment (e.g., the researcher controls the occurrence of an independent variable to see what effect it has on the dependent variable), except that it is conducted in a real-life setting. The participants in a field experiment are unaware that the events they experience are in fact an experiment. The external validity of such an experiment is high because it is taking place in the real world, with real people who are more diverse than a typical university student sample.

Many such field studies have been conducted in social psychology. For example, Latané and Darley (1970) tested their hypothesis about group size and bystander intervention in a convenience store outside New York City. Two "robbers"—with the full knowledge and permission of the cashier and manager of the store—waited until there were either one or two other customers at the checkout counter. Then they asked the cashier to name the most expensive beer the store carried. The cashier answered the question and then said he would have to check in the back to see how much of that brand was in stock. While the cashier was gone, the robbers picked up a case of beer in the front of the store, declared, "They'll never miss this," put the beer in their car, and drove off.

Because the robbers were rather burly fellows, no one attempted to intervene directly to stop the theft. But when the cashier returned, how many people would help by telling him that a theft had just occurred? The number of bystanders had the same inhibiting effect on helping behaviour as in the laboratory seizure study. Significantly fewer people reported the theft when there was another witness/customer in the store than when they were alone.

Real life can best be captured by doing a field experiment such as Latané and Darley's (1970) beer theft study, but it is difficult to control all extraneous variables in such studies. For example, the astute reader will have noticed that Latané and Darley's study was unlike laboratory experiments in an important respect: People could not be randomly assigned to the alone or in-pairs conditions. If this were the only study Latané and Darley had performed, we could not be certain whether the kinds of people who prefer to shop alone, compared with the kinds of people who prefer to shop with a friend, differ in ways that might influence helping behaviour. By randomly assigning people to conditions in their laboratory studies, Latané and Darley were able to rule out such alternative explanations.

The trade-off between internal and external validity has been referred to as the *basic dilemma of the social psychologist* (Aronson & Carlsmith, 1968). The challenge is to devise a study that maximizes both. Wendy Josephson's (1987) study on the relation between television violence and aggressive behaviour is an example of one that rose to this challenge and elegantly captured both internal validity and external validity. In this study, boys in grades 2 and 3 from 13 schools in Winnipeg watched either a violent or a nonviolent television show. Internal validity was achieved by controlling the television show the participants watched. For example, Josephson ensured that the violent and nonviolent shows were equivalent in terms of excitement, liking, and physiological arousal. This level of control ensured that any differences in subsequent behaviour between the two groups were because of differences in violent content, rather than other variables that might be associated with violent programming, such as excitement. Internal validity was further enhanced by random assignment of participants to either the violent or the nonviolent condition. External validity was maximized by having the participants play floor hockey in their school gymnasium (an activity typical for boys this age) after they had finished viewing the television segment. (As you will see in Chapter 11, in social psychological research, aggression is often assessed in terms of the severity of electric shocks administered to another research participant—a procedure that may be high in internal validity, but that certainly lacks external validity.)

In Josephson's (1987) study, observers recorded instances of aggression during the hockey game. The observers were unaware whether the boys had seen the violent or the nonviolent show. This procedure is known as keeping observers "blind" to the experimenter's hypothesis. To make the observation as natural as possible, participants were told that the observers would be doing "play by plays" just the way they do in "real" hockey games. The observers spoke into microphones, noted the number on a child's jersey, and recorded the kind of aggression that occurred. (One of the observers was Wendy Josephson's mother, who apparently had to swallow hard before repeating some of the instances of verbal aggression!) The results of this study indicated that exposure to violent programming did, in fact, increase aggression—but only among boys who were predisposed toward aggression.

Generally, both internal and external validity are not captured in a single experiment. Most social psychologists opt first for internal validity, conducting laboratory experiments in which people are randomly assigned to different conditions and all extraneous variables are controlled; here, there is little ambiguity about which variable is causing which result. Other social psychologists prefer external validity to control, conducting most of their research in field studies. And many social psychologists do both. Taken together, both types of studies meet the requirements of the perfect experiment.

New Frontiers in Social Psychology

Social psychologists are always looking for new approaches to investigating human social behaviour. In recent years, there has been a proliferation of cross-cultural research. An even more recent development is the area of social neuroscience, which involves the use of brain imaging techniques to try to discover which social psychological processes are biologically based. Both cross-cultural research and social neuroscience research are important in helping us understand which human social behaviours are universal and "hard wired" into the brain and which are more likely to be culturally-specific products of socialization.

Cross-Cultural Research

Social psychology largely began as a Western science, conducted by Western social psychologists with Western participants. This raises the question of how universal the findings are. To find out whether psychological processes differ in different cultures, social psychologists conduct **cross-cultural research** (Heine, 2008; Heine & Buchtel, 2009; Kitayama & Cohen, 2007; Moghaddam, Taylor, & Wright, 1993; Nisbett, 2003; Norenzayan & Heine, 2005). Some findings in social psychology are culture-dependent, as we shall see throughout this book. In Chapter 3, for example, we will see that Westerners and East Asians rely on fundamentally different kinds of thought

Cross-Cultural Research
Research conducted with members of different cultures to see whether the psychological processes of interest are present across cultures or whether they are specific to a single culture

to perceive and understand the social world. In Chapter 5, we'll discuss cultural differences in the very way people define themselves. Many Western (i.e., European and North American) cultures tend to emphasize individualism and independence, whereas many Eastern (i.e., Asian) cultures emphasize collectivism and interdependence (Heine, 2003; Heine & Buchtel, 2009; Heine & Hamamura, 2007).

Conducting cross-cultural research is not simply a matter of travelling to another culture, translating materials into the local language, and replicating a study there (Heine, Buchtel, & Norenzayan, 2008; Heine, Lehman, Peng, & Greenholtz, 2002; van de Vijver & Leung, 1997). Researchers have to guard against imposing their own viewpoints and definitions, learned from their own culture, onto another culture with which they are unfamiliar. They must also be sure that their independent and dependent variables are understood in the same way in different cultures (Bond, 1988; Lonner & Berry, 1986). Even items on questionnaires might be answered differently. Researchers at the University of British Columbia recently discovered that when giving people rating scales (e.g., rating how well a personality trait such as "extrovert" describes a person, using a scale from 1 = not at all to 7 = extremely), people of East Asian heritage tend to endorse the midpoints of scales whereas people of European-Canadian heritage are more likely to endorse the end points (i.e., make more extreme ratings; Hamamura, Heine, & Paulhus, 2007). Thus, a researcher might conclude that two cultures are very different because members of those cultures responded so differently to a questionnaire, when, in reality, the two cultures might actually be quite similar in terms of the construct in question. One of the ways of getting around this issue is to observe people's behaviour, rather than rely exclusively on questionnaires. As we discuss in Chapter 3, psychologists have developed computer-administered tasks (e.g., assessing how long it takes someone to respond to images presented on a computer screen) that may be less subject to the kinds of biases that might creep in when participants use self-report scales. Most cross-cultural researchers are sensitive to these issues, and as more and more cross-cultural research is conducted carefully, we will be able to determine which social psychological processes are universal and which are culture-bound.

Social Neuroscience

As we have seen, social psychology is concerned with how people's thoughts, feelings, and behaviours are influenced by the real or imagined presence of other people. Most research studies in social psychology, then, study just that—thoughts, feelings,

Some basic psychological processes are universal, whereas others are shaped by the culture in which one lives. Are people's self-concepts shaped by cultural rules of how people must present themselves, such as the requirement by the Taliban regime in Afghanistan that women cover themselves from head to toe (left)? Are people's ideas about their relationships to their family and social groups influenced by cultural practices, such as cradling one's child while at work, as this woman from Indonesia (right) is doing? Cross-cultural research is challenging but necessary to explore how culture influences the basic ways in which people think about and interact with others.

and behaviours. Human beings are biological organisms, however, and social psychologists have become increasingly interested in the connection between biological processes and social behaviour. These include the study of hormones and behaviour, the human immune system, and neurological processes in the human brain. To study the brain and its relation to behaviour, psychologists use sophisticated technologies, including electroencephalography (EEG), in which electrodes are placed on the scalp to measure electrical activity in the brain, and functional magnetic resonance imaging (fMRI), in which people are placed in scanners that measure changes in blood flow in their brains. Social psychologists take these measurements while participants think about and process social information, allowing researchers to map the correlates of different kinds of brain activity to social information processing. This kind of research is in its infancy but promises to open up a whole new area of inquiry into the relationship of the brain to behaviour (Harmon-Jones & Winkielman, 2007; Lieberman, 2007; Ochsner, 2007). For example, as we discuss in Chapter 9, social psychologists have made considerable progress in identifying the areas of the brain that are activated when people fall madly, passionately in love.

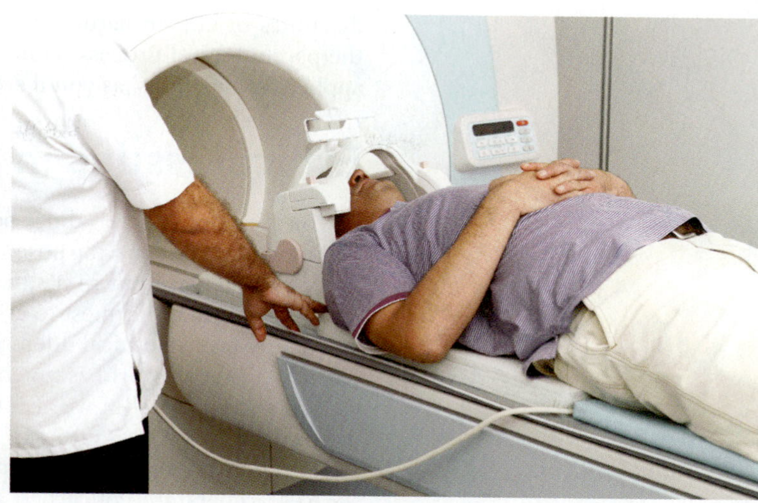

Social psychologists are studying the brain and its relation to behaviour. They use technologies such as electroencephalography (EEG), in which electrodes are placed on the scalp to measure electrical activity in the brain, and functional magnetic resonance imaging (fMRI), in which people are placed in scanners that measure changes in blood flow in their brains. Social psychologists take these measurements while participants think about and process social information, allowing researchers to map the correlates of different kinds of brain activity to social information processing.

Basic versus Applied Research

You may have wondered how people decide which specific topic to study. Why would a social psychologist decide to study helping behaviour or the effects of violent television on aggression? Is he or she simply curious? Or does the social psychologist have a specific purpose in mind, such as trying to reduce violence?

The goal in **basic research** is to find the best answer as to why people behave the way they do, purely for reasons of intellectual curiosity. The researchers aren't directly trying to solve a specific social or psychological problem. In contrast, the goal in **applied research** is to solve a particular social problem; building a theory of behaviour is usually secondary to solving the specific problem, such as alleviating racism, reducing violence, or stemming the spread of AIDS.

Basic Research

Studies that are designed to find the best answer as to why people behave the way they do and that are conducted purely for reasons of intellectual curiosity

Applied Research

Studies designed specifically to solve a particular social problem; building a theory of behaviour is usually secondary to solving the specific problem

In social psychology, the distinction between basic and applied research is fuzzy. Even though researchers may label themselves as either basic or applied scientists, the endeavours of one group are not independent of those of the other group. There are countless examples of advances in basic science that at the time had no known applied value but later proved to be the key to solving a significant social or medical problem. As we discuss later in this book, for instance, basic research with dogs, rats, and fish on the effects of feeling in control of one's environment has led to the development of techniques to improve the health of elderly nursing home residents (Langer & Rodin, 1976; Schulz, 1976; Seligman, 1975). Similarly, research on attribution has been used to help new students cope with the transition to university or college (Wilson & Linville, 1982, 1985).

There is nothing so practical as a good theory.

—Kurt Lewin, *1951*

Most social psychologists would agree that to solve a specific social problem, it is vital to have a good understanding of the psychological processes responsible for it. Kurt Lewin (1951), one of the founders of social psychology, coined a phrase that has become a motto for the field: "There is nothing so practical as a good theory." He meant that to solve such difficult social problems as violence or racial prejudice, one must first understand the underlying psychological dynamics of human nature and social interaction. Even when the goal is to discover the psychological processes underlying social behaviour, the findings often have clear applied implications, as you'll see throughout this book.

Ethical Issues in Social Psychology

As you read this chapter, did it bother you to learn that researchers sometimes mislead people about the true purpose of their study or that in Latané and Darley's seizure study people were put in a situation that might have been upsetting? This study illustrates that in their quest to create realistic, engaging situations, social psychologists frequently face an ethical dilemma. For scientific reasons, we want our experiments to resemble the real world as much as possible and to be as sound and well controlled as we can make them. But we also want to avoid causing our research participants stress, discomfort, or unpleasantness. These two goals often conflict as the researcher goes about the business of creating and conducting experiments.

Researchers are concerned about the health and welfare of the individuals participating in their experiments. Researchers are also in the process of discovering important information about human social behaviour—such as bystander intervention, prejudice, conformity, aggression, and obedience to authority. Many of these discoveries are bound to benefit society. Indeed, given the fact that social psychologists have developed powerful tools to investigate such issues scientifically, many scholars feel it would be immoral not to conduct these experiments. To gain insight into such critical issues, however, researchers must create vivid events that are absorbing for the participants. Some of these might make the participants uncomfortable, such as witnessing someone having a seizure. We can't resolve this dilemma by making pious claims that participants never experience discomfort in an experiment or by insisting that all is fair in science and forging blindly ahead. Clearly, the problem calls for a middle ground.

Watch on **mypsychlab**
Becoming a Grandparent

Informed Consent
Agreement to participate in an experiment, granted in full awareness of the nature of the experiment which has been explained in advance

Deception
The procedure whereby participants are misled about the true purpose of a study or the events that will actually transpire

The dilemma would be less problematic if researchers could obtain **informed consent** from their participants before their participation. To obtain informed consent, the researcher explains the nature of the experiment to participants before it begins and asks for their agreement to participate. If participants are made fully aware of the kinds of experiences they are about to undergo and state that they are willing to participate, the ethical dilemma is resolved. In many social psychology experiments, this sort of description is feasible—and where it is feasible, it is done. But sometimes it is impossible. Suppose Latané and Darley (1970) had told their participants that a seizure was about to be staged, that it wouldn't be a real emergency, and that the hypothesis stated they should offer help. As we explained earlier, such a procedure would be bad science. In this kind of experiment, it's essential that the participant experience contrived events as if they were real; this is called a deception experiment. **Deception** in social psychological research involves misleading participants about the true purpose of a study or the events that transpire. (Note that not all research in social psychology involves deception.)

Simulate on **mypsychlab**
Ethics of Psychological Research

Guidelines for Ethical Research

To ensure that the dignity and safety of research participants are protected, the Canadian Psychological Association has published a set of ethical principles that apply to psychology research and clinical practice conducted in Canada; the guidelines that pertain to psychological research are summarized in Figure 2.2. In addition, a set of ethics guidelines called the Tri-Council Policy Statement governs research conducted at Canadian universities. All psychology research is reviewed by a Research Ethics Board to ensure that the strict guidelines of the Tri-Council Policy Statement are met. Any aspect of the experimental procedure that this committee judges to be stressful or upsetting must be changed or eliminated before the study can be conducted. (Note that many of the experiments you will read about in this book

Ethical Principles of Psychologists in the Conduct of Research

1. Respect for dignity of persons. The central ethical principle underlying psychological research is respect for human dignity. This principle forms the foundation for the other principles that follow.
2. Informed consent. As much as possible, the researcher should describe the procedures to participants before they take part in a study, and document their agreement to take part in the study as it was described to them.
3. Minimizing harm. Psychologists must take steps to avoid harming their research participants.
4. Freedom to withdraw. Participants must be informed that they are free to withdraw from a study at any point, and that there will be no negative consequences for doing so.
5. Privacy and confidentiality. All information obtained from individual participants must be held in strict confidence.
6. Use of deception. Deception may be used only if there are no other viable means of testing a hypothesis, and only if a Research Ethics Board rules that it does not put participants at undue risk. After the study, participants must be provided with a full description and explanation of all procedures, in a post-experimental interview called the debriefing.

FIGURE 2.2

Procedures for the protection of participants in psychological research.

(Adapted from the Canadian code of ethics for psychologists [Canadian Psychological Association, 2000] and Ethical principles of psychologists in the conduct of research [American Psychological Association, 2003])

were conducted before ethics committees were established, which occurred in the early 1970s at most universities. Some of these experiments would not receive ethics approval today.)

In all research studies, participants must be told that they can withdraw at any time, for any reason, without fear of consequences for doing so. They must also be assured of the anonymity and confidentiality of their responses. When deception is used, a post-experimental interview, called the debriefing session, is crucial and must occur. **Debriefing** is the process of explaining to the participants, at the end of the experiment, the true purpose of the study and what exactly transpired. If any participants experienced discomfort, the researchers attempt to alleviate it. Debriefing is particularly important when participants have been given false feedback in an experiment (e.g., being told that they failed on a test when, in fact, the feedback was "rigged" by the experimenter). There is evidence that people continue to believe the false feedback that they've been given (regardless of whether it was positive or negative), even after being told that it was fake (Ross, Lepper, & Hubbard, 1975). In recent research conducted at Simon Fraser University, McFarland and colleagues (2007) showed that to counteract this tendency, researchers should explain not only that the score was fake, but also that the test itself was a bogus, invalid test. Otherwise, people have a tendency to cling to their test score and still think that it tells them something about their abilities (McFarland, Cheam, & Buehler, 2007).

Debriefing

Explaining to the participants, at the end of the experiment, the true purpose of the study and exactly what transpired

The debriefing session also provides an opportunity to inform the participants about the goals and purpose of the research, thereby serving an important educational function. The best researchers question their participants carefully after the experiment and listen to what they say, regardless of whether deception was used in the experiment. (For a detailed description of how debriefing interviews should be conducted, see Aronson, Ellsworth, Carlsmith, & Gonzalez, 1990.)

In our experience, nearly all participants understand and appreciate the need for deception, as long as the time is taken in the post-experimental debriefing session to fully discuss the purpose of the research and to explain why alternative procedures could not be used. Researchers who have investigated the impact of participating in deception studies have consistently found that people do not object to the kinds of mild discomfort and deceptions typically used in social psychological research (e.g., Christensen, 1988; Finney, 1987; Gerdes, 1979). For example, in a study at the University of Manitoba, attitudes toward deception research were assessed in 1970 and again, 20 years later, in 1990 (Sharpe, Adair, & Roese, 1992). At each time, there was no evidence that students who had participated in deception studies felt negatively about their experience. In fact, participants who had been deceived were more likely to agree with arguments in favour of deception research than were those who had not experienced deception. And, importantly, those who had experienced deception did not show greater distrust of psychologists. Some studies have even found that people who participated in deception experiments said they had learned more and enjoyed the experiments more than did those who participated in nondeception experiments, even if they had experienced some stress and conflict during the study (Latané & Darley, 1970; Smith & Richardson, 1983). We do not mean to imply that all deception is beneficial. Nonetheless, if mild deception is used and time is spent after the study discussing the deception with participants and explaining why it was necessary, the evidence shows that people will not be harmed.

HOW WOULD YOU USE THIS?

As we have seen in this chapter, social psychologists use empirical methods to test hypotheses about social behaviour. Now that you know something about these methods, you are in a good position to judge the quality of research findings you read about in newspapers and magazines. For example, as we saw, one of the most common mistakes is for people to assume that because two variables are correlated with each other, one caused the other. We hope that when you hear about correlational findings in the media, a little light will go off in your head that causes you to challenge any causal conclusions that are drawn. Suppose, for example, that you are browsing through a promotional brochure for the *Consumers Reports on Health* newsletter, as one of us recently was, and you came across this tidbit: "Need more motivation to exercise? Exercise leads to better sex. In one study, men who exercised were five times as likely to achieve normal sexual function as a less-active group." Did the little light go off? This is a correlational finding—men who exercised more functioned better sexually—and we cannot draw the conclusion that it is the exercise that "leads to" (e.g., causes) better sex. Can you think of alternative explanations of this finding? Better yet, can you design an experiment that would test the hypothesis that exercise helps people's sex lives?

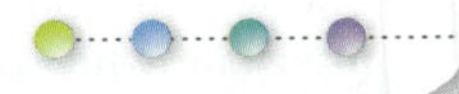

Summary

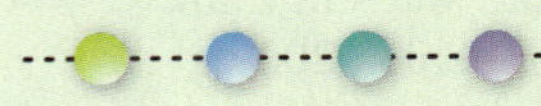

- **Social Psychology: An Empirical Science** A fundamental principle of social psychology is that human social behaviour can be studied scientifically.
- **Formulating Hypotheses and Theories** Social psychological research often begins with a theory about why people behave the way they do. Researchers come up with hypotheses that can be scientifically tested, based on their theories or their observations of human social behaviour.
  - **Inspiration from Earlier Theories and Research** Hypotheses often come from earlier theories or research findings. For example, researchers may conduct studies to test an alternative explanation of previous experiments.
  - **Hypotheses Based on Personal Observations** Many hypotheses come from observations of everyday life, such as Latané and Darley's hunches about why people failed to help Kitty Genovese.
- **The Observational Method** The observational method, whereby researchers observe people and systematically record their behaviour, is useful for describing the nature of a phenomenon and generating hypotheses. One form of the observational method is ethnography, the method by which researchers attempt to understand a group or culture by observing it from the inside, without imposing any preconceived notions they might have.
  - **Archival Analysis** Another form of the observational method is archival analysis, whereby researchers examine documents or archives, such as looking at photographs in magazines to see how men and women are portrayed.
- **The Correlational Method** The correlational method, whereby two or more variables are systematically measured and the relationship between them assessed, is very useful when the goal is to predict one variable from another. For example, researchers might be interested in whether there is a correlation between the amount of violent television programs children watch and how aggressive they are.

- **Surveys** The correlational method is often applied to the results of surveys, in which a representative group of people are asked questions about their attitudes and behaviours. To make sure that the results are generalizable, researchers randomly select survey respondents from the population at large.
- **Limits of the Correlational Method: Correlation Does Not Equal Causation** Social psychologists are usually interested in determining causality, such as whether watching violent television programs *causes* children to be more aggressive. The major limitation of the correlational method is that it cannot determine causality. If two variables, A and B, are correlated (such as television watching and aggression), it could be that A is causing B (e.g., television watching makes kids aggressive), B is causing A (e.g., aggressive kids like to watch violent television), or that some third variable, C, is causing both A and B (e.g., something about the way kids are raised makes them want to watch more violent television programs and makes them more aggressive).

The Experimental Method: Answering Causal Questions The only way to determine causality is to use the experimental method, in which the researcher randomly assigns participants to different conditions and ensures that these conditions are identical except for the independent variable.

- **Independent and Dependent Variables** The independent variable is the one that the researchers vary to see if it has a causal effect (e.g., how much television children watch); the dependent variable is what researchers measure to see if it is affected (e.g., how aggressive children are).
- **Internal Validity in Experiments** Experiments should be high in internal validity, which means that people in all conditions are treated identically, except for the independent variable (e.g., how much television children watch).
- **External Validity in Experiments** External validity—the extent to which researchers can generalize their results to other situations and people—is accomplished by increasing the realism of the experiment, particularly its psychological realism (the extent to which the psychological processes triggered in the experiment are similar to the psychological processes triggered in everyday life). It is also accomplished by replicating the study with different populations of participants.
- **The Basic Dilemma of the Social Psychologist** When researchers conduct experiments, there is always a trade-off between internal validity (having control over the experiment and randomly assigning participants to conditions) and external validity (ensuring that the results can be generalized to the "real world"). This trade-off is known as the basic dilemma of the social psychologist.

New Frontiers in Social Psychology In recent years social psychologists have developed new ways of investigating social behaviour.

- **Cross-Cultural Research** To study the ways in which culture shapes people's thoughts, feelings, and behaviour, social psychologists conduct cross-cultural research. Doing so is not simply a matter of replicating the same study in different cultures. Researchers have to guard against imposing their own viewpoints and definitions, learned from their culture, onto another culture with which they are unfamiliar.
- **Social Neuroscience** Social psychologists have become increasingly interested in the connection between biological processes and social behaviour. These include the study of hormones and behaviour, the human immune system, and neurological processes in the human brain.

Basic Versus Applied Research As in any other science, some social psychology studies are basic research experiments (designed to answer basic questions about why people do what they do), whereas others are applied studies (designed to find ways to solve specific social problems).

Ethical Issues in Social Psychology Social psychologists are concerned with the welfare of their research participants.

- **Guidelines for Ethical Research** Canadian psychologists carefully follow the Canadian Psychological Association's guidelines, which specify procedures such as obtaining informed consent, the participant's right to leave the study at any time, ensured anonymity and confidentiality, and debriefing following an experiment, particularly if deception (a cover story about the supposed purpose of the study) has been used.

Social Cognition

How We Think about the Social World

OUTLINE

KEVIN CHAPPELL WAS ON HIS WAY TO THE TOP. IT WAS 1988 and the 29-year-old man with an IQ of 147 had just been accepted to medical school, had graduated at the top of his class from Trent University, and was working on a master's degree. He was also an avid soccer player and had played lead guitar in a rock and roll band. On January 30, 1988, he decided to go for a run after a hard day of studying. It was a dark, rainy evening, and as he crossed a street, he was hit by a car. From that moment, Chappell's life was changed immeasurably. He sustained severe brain damage, leaving him unable to recognize things. He could see objects but didn't know what they were—a condition known as visual agnosia. There are very few people in the world with visual agnosia—so, not surprisingly, Chappell's condition attracted the attention of neuropsychologists.

Psychologist Gordon Winocur, a specialist in memory at Trent University, met Chappell just after he had been diagnosed with visual agnosia. Chappell didn't touch the cup of coffee that Dr. Winocur had served him, which wasn't unusual for someone with this diagnosis. Why would you pick up a cup of coffee if you don't recognize what it is? One day, however, Chappell happened to run into Winocur and greeted him by name. Winocur was stunned. How could someone who didn't recognize objects know who he was?

It became apparent that Chappell does recognize one thing: faces. He doesn't recognize arms, legs, or feet. He doesn't recognize faces that are upside down or sideways, but he does recognize faces that are upright. This ability probably makes him unique in the world. Winocur teamed up with two neuropsychologists, Morris Moscovitch from the University of Toronto and Marlene Behrmann from Carnegie Mellon University in Pittsburgh, to formally study Kevin Chappell. Their findings were published in the science journal *Nature*, in 1992 (Behrmann, Winocur, & Moscovitch, 1992). In follow-up research, it was shown that Kevin Chappell's ability to recognize faces extends to photographs of faces, caricatures, and cartoon faces. He can even recognize faces made up of objects—although he isn't able to recognize the objects themselves (Gauthier, Behrmann, & Tarr, 1999; Moscovitch, Winocur, & Behrmann, 1997).

To recognize an object, we have to be able to perceive its parts, synthesize them, and match them to the representation of that object stored in our brain. Dr. Moscovitch comments that "Kevin seems to be fine at identifying the bits and pieces . . .. It's his ability to integrate the information rapidly and then match it to the internal representation that seems to be impaired" (Scott, 2002).

Because of a brain injury, Kevin Chappell, shown here standing between his two sons, lives in a world of unidentifiable objects.

A writer interviewing Chappell, then age 44, shows him a pair of sunglasses. "It's brown with bits of silver and two horns," Chappell says. But what is it? Chappell has no idea. "I don't know what I see," he replies, "I have to guess" (Scott, 2002). It is difficult to imagine what Kevin Chappell's world must be like. When we enter a classroom, for example, we do not see a bunch of objects that have platforms parallel to the floor connected to four legs with another flat surface at a right angle that we then mentally assemble to figure out what they are. Instead of having to pause and think, "Let's see. Oh, yes, those are chairs," we quickly, unconsciously, and effortlessly categorize the objects as chairs. The fact that we do this automatically allows us to use our conscious mind for other, more important purposes ("What's going to be on the quiz today?" or "Should I strike up a conversation with that cute guy in the third row?") Similarly, when we encounter people we know, the process of recognizing them requires little effort on our part, thereby allowing us to focus on our interaction with them.

Watch on **mypsychlab**
Social Cognition

In this chapter we will explore social cognition, which is the way people think about themselves and the social world—how they select, interpret, remember, and use social information to make judgments and decisions. Not only are we able to recognize chairs and other physical objects without any apparent effort, but we are also able to make complex judgments about people at lightning speed. Of course, we also occasionally make mistakes, and sometimes these mistakes are costly. In this chapter you will see how sophisticated we are as social thinkers, as well as the kinds of mistakes we are prone to make.

It is the mind which creates the world about us, and even though we stand side by side in the same meadow, my eyes will never see what is beheld by yours.

—George Gissing, *The Private Papers of Henry Ryecroft, 1903*

To understand how people think about the social world and how accurate their impressions are likely to be, one needs to distinguish between two different kinds of social cognition. One kind of thought is quick and automatic—as when we effortlessly classify an object as a chair. Other times, we pause and think about ourselves and our environment, and carefully contemplate what is going on around us. You may have spent hours deliberating over important decisions in your life, such as where to go to university or college, what to choose as your major, and whether to break up with your boyfriend or girlfriend. This is the second kind of social cognition—controlled thinking, which is more effortful and deliberate. Often, the automatic and controlled modes of social cognition work very well together. Think of a plane that can fly on automatic pilot, monitoring hundreds of complex systems and adjusting instantly to changes in atmospheric conditions. The autopilot does just fine most of the time, though occasionally it is important for the human pilot to take over and fly the plane manually. Humans, too, have an "automatic pilot" that monitors their environment, draws conclusions, and directs their behaviour. But people can also "override" this automatic type of thinking and analyze a situation slowly and deliberately. We will begin by examining the nature of automatic thinking.

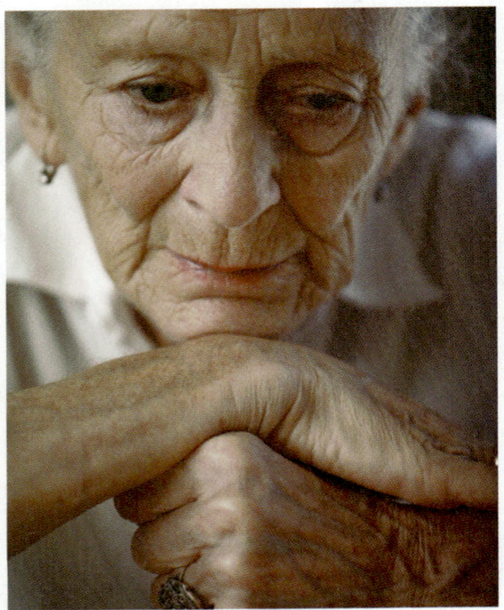
When people engage in controlled thinking, they consider something slowly and deliberately.

On Automatic Pilot: Low-Effort Thinking

People typically size up a new situation very quickly: They figure out who is there, what is happening, and what might happen next. Often these quick conclusions are correct. When you attended your first university class, for example, you probably made quick assumptions about who people were (the person standing at the lectern was the professor) and how to behave. We doubt that you confused the class with a birthday party. And you probably reached these conclusions without even being aware that you were doing so.

Imagine a different approach. Every time you encounter a new situation, you stop and think about it slowly and deliberately, like Rodin's statue *The Thinker*. When you are introduced to someone new, you have to excuse yourself for 15 minutes while you analyze what you have learned and how much you like the person. When you drive down an unfamiliar road, you have to pull over and analyze its twists and turns before knowing how to proceed. Sounds exhausting, doesn't it? Instead, we form impressions of people quickly and effortlessly, and navigate new roads without much conscious analysis of what we are doing. We see an object with two dark lenses attached to curved arms and immediately know that those are sunglasses. We do these things by engaging in an automatic analysis of our environments, based on our past experiences and knowledge of the world. **Automatic thinking** is thought that is generally nonconscious, unintentional, involuntary, and effortless (Bargh, 2007; Bargh & Ferguson, 2000; Wegner & Bargh, 1998).

Connect to MyPsychLab
To access the Critical Thinking question on gender stereotypes, go to MyPsychLab

Automatic Thinking
Thinking that is nonconscious, unintentional, involuntary, and effortless

People as Everyday Theorists: Automatic Thinking with Schemas

Automatic thinking helps us understand new situations by relating them to our prior experiences. When we meet someone new, we don't start from scratch to figure out what he or she is like; we categorize the person as "an engineering student" or "like my cousin Helen." The same goes for places, objects, and situations. When we walk into a fast-food restaurant we've never visited, we know, without thinking, not to wait at a table for a waiter and a menu. We know that we have to go to the counter to order because our mental "script" automatically tells us that this is what we do in fast-food restaurants, and we assume that this one is no different.

More formally, people use **schemas**, which are mental structures that organize our knowledge about the social world. These mental structures influence the information we notice, think about, and remember (Bartlett, 1932; Heine, Proulx, & Vohs, 2006; Janicik & Larrick, 2005; Markus, 1977). The term *schema* is very general; it encompasses our knowledge about many things—other people, ourselves, social roles (e.g., what a librarian or an engineer is like), and specific events (e.g., what usually happens when people eat a meal in a restaurant). In each case, our schemas contain our basic knowledge and impressions that we use to organize what we know about the social world and interpret new situations.

Simulate on **mypsychlab**
Schemas

Schemas
Mental structures people use to organize their knowledge about the social world around themes or subjects and that influence the information people notice, think about, and remember

Schemas also influence the way in which we process information. For example, there is evidence that information relevant to a particular schema is processed more quickly than information unrelated to it. To illustrate this phenomenon, Gardner, MacIntyre, and Lalonde (1995) asked English-speaking students living in Quebec to rate the characteristics of various groups (e.g., English Canadians, French Canadians, males, females). Participants were faster when rating the stereotypical characteristics of each group than when rating its nonstereotypical characteristics; for example, when the target group was males, characteristics such as *rugged*, *impatient*, and *talkative* were rated more quickly than characteristics such as *irreligious*, *artistic*, and *impolite*.

Theory helps us to bear our ignorance of facts.

—George Santayana, *The Sense of Beauty, 1896*

We also tend to "fill in the blanks" with schema-consistent information (Lenton & Bryan, 2005). In a study by Kunda, Sinclair, and Griffin (1997), students at the University of Waterloo were told that Michael was either a salesperson or an actor, and that his friends described him as very extroverted. They were then asked, "What kinds of behaviours do you suppose they have in mind when they describe him

Explore on mypsychlab
Confirmation Bias

this way?" The researchers found that when told that Michael was a salesperson, participants generated pushy descriptions (e.g., "speaks loudly," "monopolizes conversations"), whereas when Michael was described as an actor, they generated descriptions such as "life of the party" and "not afraid of the spotlight." In another study by these researchers, participants read about John the lawyer versus John the construction worker, and were asked to generate examples of aggressive behaviour that John might perform. John the lawyer was seen as more likely to argue, whereas John the construction worker was seen as more likely to punch and fight (Kunda, Sinclair, & Griffin, 1997). In other words, given a label, we fill in the blanks with all kinds of schema-consistent information. As we discuss next, this tendency to "fill in the blanks" allows for more efficient information processing, but it also can have tragic consequences.

Stereotypes about Race and Violence When applied to members of a social group such as one of gender or race, schemas are commonly referred to as *stereotypes*, which we will discuss in detail in Chapter 12. For now, we point out that stereotypes can be applied rapidly and automatically when we encounter other people. For example, experiments have been conducted on the effects of people's stereotypes about African-Americans and crime (Payne, Shimizu, & Jacoby, 2005; Payne, 2006). In one study, participants saw photographs of black and white faces. Next, they were asked to identify as quickly as possible objects that were shown on a computer screen. Participants who had seen pictures of black faces were more likely to misidentify a tool as a gun than were participants who had seen white faces (Payne, 2001). Other researchers have shown that the converse is also true—when a crime object, such as a gun, was displayed on a computer screen, white university students and police officers were quicker to identify black faces than white faces (Eberhardt, Goff, Purdie, & Davies, 2004).

In related research, people performed a task that mirrors the kind of dilemma that police officers encounter in real life (Correll, Park, Judd, & Wittenbrink, 2002). Specifically, non-black participants played a video game in which they saw photographs of young men in realistic settings, such as in a park, at a train station, and on a sidewalk. Half of the men were African-American, and half were white. And half of the men in each group were holding a handgun and half were holding a nonthreatening object such as a cellphone, wallet, or camera. Participants were instructed to press a button labelled "shoot" if the man in the picture had a gun and a button labelled "don't shoot" if he did not. Like a real police officer, they had very little time to make up their minds (just over half a second). Participants won or lost points on each round of the game, modelled after the risks and benefits faced by officers in real life. Participants earned 5 points for not shooting someone who did not have a gun and 10 points for shooting someone who did have a gun. They lost 20 points if they shot someone who was not holding a gun and lost 40 points if they failed to shoot someone who was holding a gun (which, in real life, would be the most life-threatening situation for a police officer).

In a study by Correll and colleagues (2002), people played a video game in which they saw photographs of men who were holding a handgun or a non-threatening object, such as a cellphone, as in the picture shown here. Half of the men were black and half were white. Participants were instructed to press a button labelled "shoot" if the man had a gun and a button labelled "don't shoot" if he did not. Similar to a situation that would be encountered by a real police officer, they had very little time to make up their minds (just over half a second). The most common mistake people made was to "shoot" a black man who was not holding a gun, like the man in this picture.

The results? Participants were especially likely to pull the trigger when the people in the pictures were black, whether or not they were holding a gun. This "shooter bias" meant that people made relatively few errors when a black person was in fact holding a gun but also that they made the most errors, shooting an unarmed

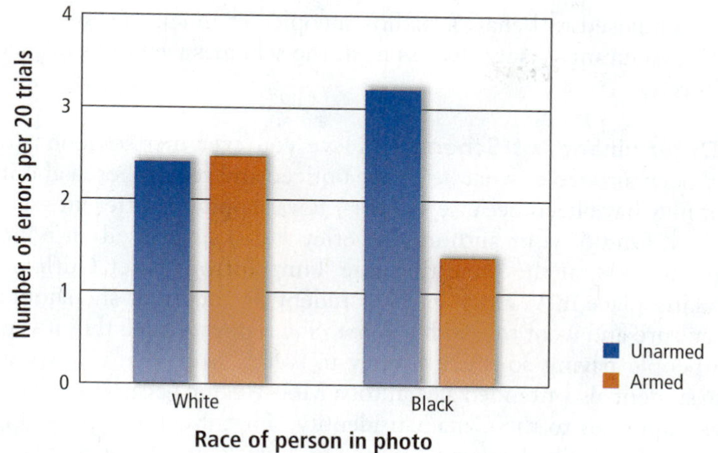

FIGURE 3.1

Errors made in "shooting" people in video game.

Participants played a video game in which they were supposed to "shoot" a man if he was holding a gun and withhold fire if he was not. People were influenced by the race of the men in the pictures. As seen in the figure, people were prone to make mistakes by "shooting" black men who were unarmed.

(Adapted from Correll et al., 2002)

person, when a black person was not holding a gun (see Figure 3.1). When the men in the picture were white, participants made about the same number of errors whether the men were armed or unarmed.

Sadly, these effects are not limited to the laboratory. In 1999, police officers in the Bronx mistakenly thought that Amadou Diallo, a black man, was reaching for a gun when he was simply reaching for his wallet. Police fired a total of 41 shots at Diallo, killing him instantly.

Recent studies have shown that even the physical environment can trigger automatic thinking about race and crime. For example, researchers at the University of British Columbia found that the negative stereotype of black people—especially traits relevant to danger (e.g., crime)—came to mind more quickly for participants who were seated in a dark room, compared with participants who were seated in a brightly lit room (Schaller, Park, & Mueller, 2003). This tendency was particularly pronounced among those who regard the world as a dangerous place. In another series of studies conducted by American and Canadian researchers, faces of black or white men were presented on a computer. Some participants were seated in a closed booth during the experiment; others were placed in a grassy, open field. Participants who associated black men with danger were faster to respond to fight-related words when in the closed-in booth; those who held the same stereotype but were in an open field were faster to respond to escape or flight words. Reactions to white men did not differ as a function of the physical environment in which the experiment took place (Cesario, Plaks, Hagiwara, Navarrete, & Higgins, 2010). In all these studies, people had to respond so quickly that they had little time to control their reactions or think about what they were doing. Their responses were the result of automatic thinking that is rooted in the pervasive stereotypes in North American culture about black people and violence.

Needless to say, the effects we have been discussing are not limited to stereotypes about black people. On January 31, 2005, Winnipeg police officers were searching for suspects in a home invasion. Eighteen-year-old Matthew Dumas was in the vicinity, although he was not a suspect. However, police officers noticed that he had a metal object up his sleeve. The object turned out to be a screwdriver. He was ordered to drop it, and when he refused, one of the officers fired two shots at him. Dumas died shortly afterward. At an inquest held in June 2008, Morris Swan-Shannacappo, grand chief of the Southern Chiefs Organization, pointed to similar shootings of Aboriginal men. "We know Matthew was racially profiled . . .. If he had not been aboriginal he would not have been stopped" (Swan-Shannacappo, as quoted in Rollason, 2008, p. A5).

We should keep in mind that stereotypes based on people's race are a special case of a more general phenomenon: people's organization of the world into schemas (Kunda, 1999). In addition to schemas about classes of people, for example, we have schemas about specific individuals (e.g., what Aunt Jane is like), social roles (e.g., how mothers are supposed to behave), or how people act in specific situations (e.g., at a party or in a restaurant). As we discuss next, the schemas we hold can vary depending on our culture.

Cultural Determinants of Schemas Have you ever met someone from another culture and been amazed at what he or she noticed and remembered about your country? If so, it may have been because the person was applying different schemas to what he or she saw. One of your authors (Beverley Fehr) supervised an honours student from China in 2008, at the same time the Tim Hortons Brier Curling Championship was taking place in Winnipeg. The student decided that she should experience Canadian culture and went to watch a game. She reported back that it was very amusing to see people paying so much money to watch "a couple of guys mopping the floor." The student also attended a Manitoba Moose game because she had learned that hockey was important to the Canadian identity. That event also proved mystifying—and amusing—to her. She later commented on how "cute" it was that large men, who looked even bigger with all of their padded clothing, would be put in tiny, little "punishment boxes."

As this example illustrates, although everyone uses schemas to understand the world, the *content* of our schemas is influenced by our culture. One researcher, for example, interviewed a Scottish settler and a local Bantu herdsman in Swaziland, a small country in southeast Africa (Bartlett, 1932). Both men had been present at a complicated cattle transaction that had transpired a year earlier. The Scottish man had little memory about the details of the transaction; he had to consult his records to remember how many cattle were bought and sold and for how much. The Bantu man, when asked, promptly recited from memory every detail of the transaction, including from whom each ox and cow had been bought, the colour of each ox and cow, and the price of each transaction. The Bantu people's memory for cattle is so good that they do not bother to brand them; if a cow happens to wander away and get mixed up with a neighbour's herd, the owner simply goes over and takes it back, having no trouble distinguishing his cow from dozens of others.

Cattle are a central part of the Bantu economy and culture, and as a result, the Bantu have well-developed schemas about cattle. To a person who grew up in a different culture, one cow might look like any other; this person undoubtedly has well-developed schemas about things that are quite foreign to the Bantu, such as transactions on the Toronto Stock Exchange, foreign movies, or, for that matter, why people would pay big bucks to watch someone "mop the floor."

By now you might be wondering why we have schemas in the first place. We turn to this issue next.

The Function of Schemas: Why Do We Have Them? Earlier we discussed some of the negative consequences of schemas, cases in which people "fill in the blanks" in erroneous ways (e.g., assuming a black person's cellphone is a gun). However, we should point out that the consequences of "filling in the blanks" are not always harmful. One of your authors (Beverley Fehr) once attended a fundraising breakfast for a counselling centre. Guest speaker Pamela Wallin (now a senator in the Canadian government) described an early incident that nearly cost her her broadcasting career—or so she thought. The setting was the G7 economic summit in Quebec, and CTV had managed to arrange interviews with the British prime minister and the chancellor of West Germany. Wallin excitedly announced to viewers that they should stay tuned, because after the commercial break they would be interviewing then prime minister Margaret Thatcher and chancellor Helmut "Shit." Convinced that she had just committed career suicide, Wallin fled the studio. The first few people she ran into commented that for a moment they thought she had mispronounced chancellor Schmidt's name but then realized that the vacuum cleaner had been on, or that they hadn't had their morning coffee yet, or . . .. In short, the fact that Wallin said *shit* on television was so inconsistent with people's schemas of her that they convinced themselves they must have heard wrong—that she really must have said *Schmidt*.

If schemas can sometimes make us misperceive the world, why do we have them? Schemas are typically very useful for helping us organize and make sense of the world and to fill in the gaps of our knowledge. Think back, for a moment, to our opening story about Kevin Chappell, a man who lives in a world of unidentifiable objects. What would it be like to have no schemas about the social world? What if everything you encountered was inexplicable, confusing, and unlike anything else you'd ever known? Tragically, this is what happens to people who suffer from a neurological disorder called Korsakov's syndrome. People who suffer from Korsakov's syndrome also have difficulty forming schemas, just as Kevin Chappell does because of his visual agnosia. This can be so unsettling—even terrifying—that some people with Korsakov's syndrome go to great lengths to try to impose meaning on their experiences. The neurologist Oliver Sacks gives the following description of a patient with Korsakov's syndrome named Mr. Thompson:

> He remembered nothing for more than a few seconds. He was continually disoriented. Abysses of amnesia continually opened beneath him, but he would bridge them, nimbly, by fluent confabulations and fictions of all kinds. For him they were not fictions, but how he suddenly saw, or interpreted, the world. Its radical flux and incoherence could not be tolerated, acknowledged, for an instant—there was, instead, this strange, delirious, quasi-coherence, as Mr. Thompson, with his ceaseless, unconscious, quick-fire inventions, continually improvised a world around him . . . *for such a patient must literally make himself (and his world) up every moment.* (Sacks, 1987; emphasis in original)

In short, it is so important to us to have continuity, to relate new experiences to our past schemas, that people who lose this ability invent schemas where none exist.

Schemas are particularly useful when we encounter information that is confusing or ambiguous because they help us figure out what is going on. Consider a classic study by Harold Kelley (1950), in which students in different sections of an economics class were told that a guest lecturer would be filling in that day. To create a schema about what the guest lecturer would be like, Kelley told the students that the economics department was interested in how different classes reacted to different instructors and that the students would receive a brief biographical note about the instructor before he arrived. The note contained information about the instructor's age, background, and teaching experience. It also gave one of two descriptions of his personality. One version said, "People who know him consider him to be a rather cold person, industrious, critical, practical, and determined." The other version was identical, except that the phrase "a rather cold person" was replaced with "a very warm person." The students were randomly given one of these personality descriptions.

I know that often I would not see a thing unless I thought of it first.

—Norman Maclean, *A River Runs through It*, 1976

The guest lecturer then conducted a class discussion for 20 minutes, after which the students rated their impressions of him. How humorous was he?

People who know him consider him to be a rather cold person, industrious, critical, practical, and determined.

People who know him consider him to be a very warm person, industrious, critical, practical, and determined.

How sociable? How considerate? Given that there was some ambiguity in this situation—after all, the students had seen the instructor for only a brief time—Kelley hypothesized that they would use the schema provided by the biographical note to fill in the blanks. This is exactly what happened. The students who expected the instructor to be warm gave him significantly higher ratings than did the students who expected him to be cold, even though all of the students had observed the same teacher behaving in the same way. Students who expected the instructor to be warm were also more likely to ask him questions and to participate in the class discussion.

> *It is a capital mistake to theorize before you have all the evidence. It biases the judgment.*
>
> —Sherlock Holmes (Sir Arthur Conan Doyle), *1898*

It is important to note that there is nothing wrong with what Kelley's students did. As long as people have reason to believe their schemas are accurate, it is perfectly reasonable to use them to resolve ambiguity. If a suspicious-looking character approaches you in a dark alley and says, "Take out your wallet," your schema about such encounters tells you the person wants to steal your money, not admire pictures of your family. This schema helps you avert a serious, and perhaps deadly, misunderstanding. The danger comes when we automatically apply schemas that are not accurate, such as assuming that a black person reaching into his pocket is about to produce a gun.

CONNECTIONS 

Reconstructing the Movies: Schemas Affect What You Remember

We don't remember exactly what occurred in a given setting as if our minds were a film camera recording precise images and sounds. Instead, we remember some information that was there—particularly information our schemas lead us to notice and pay attention to—and we remember other information that was never there but that we have unknowingly added later (Darley & Akert, 1993; Markus & Zajonc, 1985). If you ask people what is the most famous line of dialogue in the classic Humphrey Bogart and Ingrid Bergman movie *Casablanca*, they will probably say, "Play it again, Sam." Similarly, if you ask them what is one of the most famous lines from the 1966–69 *Star Trek* television series, they will probably say, "Beam me up, Scotty." Here is a piece of trivia that might surprise you: Both of these lines of dialogue are reconstructions—the characters in the movie and the television series never said them.

Which Schemas Are Applied? Accessibility and Priming The social world is full of ambiguous information that is open to interpretation. Imagine for example that while you are riding on a city bus, a man gets on and sits beside you. He mutters incoherently to himself, stares at everyone on the bus, and repeatedly rubs his face with one hand. How would you make sense of his behaviour? You have several schemas you could use. What dictates your choice? Your impression of the man on the bus can be affected by **accessibility**, the extent to which schemas and concepts are at the forefront of our minds and therefore are likely to be used when we are making judgments about the social world (Higgins, 1996a; Sanna & Schwarz, 2004; Wyer & Srull, 1989).

Accessibility

The extent to which schemas and concepts are at the forefront of people's minds and are therefore likely to be used when making judgments about the social world

Schemas can be accessible for three reasons: First, some schemas are chronically accessible because of past experience (Chen & Andersen, 1999; Dijksterhuis & van Knippengerg, 1996; Higgins & Brendl, 1995; Rudman & Borgida, 1995). This means that these schemas are constantly active and ready to use to interpret ambiguous situations. For example, if there is a history of alcoholism in your family, traits describing an alcoholic are likely to be chronically accessible to you, increasing the likelihood that these traits will come to mind when you are thinking about the behaviour of the man on the bus. If someone you know suffers from mental illness, however, then thoughts about how mentally ill people behave are more likely to be accessible than are thoughts about alcoholics, leading you to interpret the man's behaviour very differently.

There is evidence that people who are targets of prejudice or discrimination are more likely to interpret ambiguous situations as discriminatory, presumably because discrimination schemas become chronically accessible for them. In a recent study, black Canadian and white Canadian participants read scenarios describing ambiguous interpersonal situations (e.g., being served last in a restaurant; a new work colleague seems to be getting preferential treatment from the boss). The person in the scenario (i.e., the server in the restaurant scenario; the boss in the workplace scenario) was described as either the same race as the participant or a different race (i.e., white for black participants; black for white participants). Black Canadians were much more likely to attribute the ambiguous behaviours to racial discrimination when the server or boss was described as white than were white Canadians who read that the server or boss was black (Outten, Giguère, Schmitt, & Lalonde, 2010). Presumably, black Canadians' greater experience with racial discrimination made it more likely that a discrimination schema was accessible and therefore became the lens through which they interpreted the ambiguous behaviours.

Second, schemas can become accessible because they are related to a current goal. The concept of mental illness might not be chronically accessible to you, but if you are studying for a test in your abnormal psychology class and need to learn about different kinds of mental disorders, this concept might be temporarily accessible. As a consequence, you might be likely to notice the man on the bus and interpret his behaviour as a sign of a mental disorder—at least until your test is over and you no longer have the goal to learn about mental illness (Forster, Liberman, & Higgins, 2005; Kuhl, 1983; Martin & Tesser, 1996).

Finally, schemas can become temporarily accessible because of our recent experiences (Bargh, 1996; Higgins & Bargh, 1987; Oishi, Schimmack, & Colcombe, 2003; Stapel & Koomen, 2000). This means that a particular schema or trait is not always accessible but happens to be primed by something people have been thinking about or doing before encountering an event. Suppose, for example, that right before the man on the bus sat down, you were reading Ken Kesey's *One Flew Over the Cuckoo's Nest*, a novel about patients in a mental hospital. Given that thoughts about mental patients are at the forefront of your mind, you would probably assume that the man's strange behaviour was attributable to mental illness. If, on the other hand, thoughts about alcoholism were fresh in your mind—for example, you had just looked out the window and seen a person leaning against a building drinking a bottle of wine—you would probably assume that the man on the bus was drunk (see Figure 3.2). These are examples of **priming**, the process by which

Priming
The process by which recent experiences increase the accessibility of a schema, trait, or concept

Is this man an alcoholic or just down on his luck? Our judgments about other people can be influenced by schemas that are accessible in our memories. If you had just been talking to a friend about a relative who had an alcohol problem, you might be more likely to think that this man has an alcohol problem as well, because alcoholism is accessible in your memory.

FIGURE 3.2

How we interpret an ambiguous situation: The role of accessibility and priming.

recent experiences increase the accessibility of a schema, trait, or concept, making it more likely that you will use this information to interpret a new event—such as the behaviour of the man on the bus. Reading Kesey's novel primes traits pertaining to mental illness, making it more likely that these traits will be used to interpret a new event, such as the behaviour of the man on the bus, even though this new event is completely unrelated to the original event that primed those traits.

In what has become the classic demonstration of priming effects, Tory Higgins, Stephen Rholes, and Carl Jones (1977) told participants that they would be taking part in two unrelated studies. In the first, a perception study, they would have to identify different colours while memorizing a list of words. In the second, a reading comprehension study, they would be asked to read a paragraph about someone named Donald and then give their impressions of him. This paragraph is shown in Figure 3.3. Take a moment to read it. What do you think of Donald?

You might have noticed that many of Donald's actions are ambiguous, interpretable in either a positive or a negative manner. Take the fact that he piloted a boat without knowing much about it and wants to sail across the Atlantic Ocean. You could put a positive spin on these acts, deciding that Donald has an admirable sense of adventure. Or you might give the same behaviour a negative spin, assuming that Donald is quite a reckless and foolhardy individual.

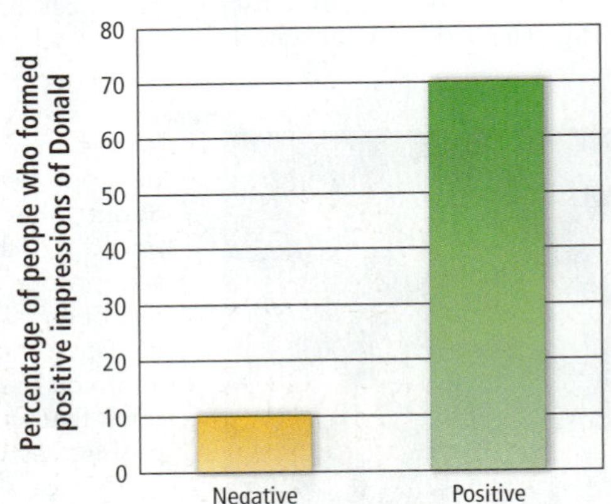

Description of Donald

Donald spent a great deal of time in his search of what he liked to call excitement. He had already climbed Mt. McKinley, shot the Colorado rapids in a kayak, driven in a demolition derby, and piloted a jet-powered boat—without knowing very much about boats. He had risked injury, and even death, a number of times. Now he was in search of new excitement. He was thinking, perhaps, he would do some skydiving or maybe cross the Atlantic in a sailboat. By the way he acted, one could readily guess that Donald was well aware of his ability to do many things well. Other than business engagements, Donald's contacts with people were limited. He felt he didn't really need to rely on anyone. Once Donald made up his mind to do something it was as good as done no matter how long it might take or how difficult the going might be. Only rarely did he change his mind—even when it might well have been better if he had.

FIGURE 3.3

Priming and accessibility.

People read the paragraph about Donald and formed an impression of him. In a prior study, some people had memorized words that could be used to interpret Donald in a positive way (e.g., adventurous, self-confident), while others had memorized words that could be used to interpret Donald in a negative way (e.g., reckless, conceited). As seen in the graph, those who had memorized the positive words formed a much more positive impression of Donald than did those who had memorized the negative words.

(Adapted from Higgins, Rholes, & Jones, 1977)

How did the participants interpret Donald's behaviour? As expected, it depended on whether positive or negative traits were primed. In the first study, the researchers divided people into two groups and gave them different words to memorize. People who had first memorized the words *adventurous*, *self-confident*, *independent*, and *persistent* later formed positive impressions of Donald, viewing him as a likeable man who enjoyed new challenges. People who had first memorized *reckless*, *conceited*, *aloof*, and *stubborn* later formed negative impressions of Donald, viewing him as a stuck-up person who took needlessly dangerous chances.

But it was not memorizing just any positive or negative words that influenced people's impressions of Donald. In other conditions, research participants memorized words that were also positive or negative, such as *neat* or *disrespectful*. However, these traits did not influence their impressions of Donald because the words did not apply to Donald's behaviour. Thoughts, then, have to be both accessible and *applicable* before they will act as primes, exerting an influence on our impressions of the social world.

Priming is a good example of automatic thinking because it occurs quickly, unintentionally, and unconsciously. When judging others, people are usually not aware that they are applying concepts or schemas that they just happened to be thinking about earlier. As we discuss next, people also apply concepts or schemas that happen to be on their minds when interpreting their own behaviour.

In a recent study, University of Toronto researchers primed a meal schema by having some participants consume an appetizer, a main course, and then dessert at a nicely-set table. Participants in the non-meal condition received exactly the same food items, but ate them in random order while standing at a counter. (These participants were required to make ratings of the foods in terms of sweetness, saltiness, and so on.) The researchers hypothesized that those who had a meal schema primed would eat less when they were subsequently offered more food (pasta), because it would be on their minds that they had just eaten a meal. Participants in the non-meal condition were expected to eat more because they did not have a meal schema primed, even though they ate exactly the same amount as those in the meal condition. Indeed, in what was supposedly a second, unrelated study on the effects of carbohydrates on reading performance, the researchers found that participants in the meal condition ate significantly less pasta than those in the non-meal condition (Pliner & Zec, 2007). Thus, the schemas that are primed can actually affect how much you eat!

It is also the case that primes can affect your perceptions of other people and your own behaviour even when you are not consciously aware of the prime. In a recent fascinating program of research, Mitchell Callan and colleagues (2010) hypothesized that subliminally priming participants with legal concepts would lead to more competitiveness, perceptions of others as untrustworthy, and greater self-interest compared to a control condition. This hypothesis was tested in a series of studies with students from the University of Calgary, the University of Western Ontario, and the University of Essex in the United Kingdom. The basic paradigm was to present either legal terms (e.g., *lawyer*, *judge*) or neutral words (*prior*, *activity*) on a computer screen too quickly to be consciously perceived. In one of the studies, participants then read an ambiguous description of a meeting between two people who exchanged opinions. Those who had been primed with legal concepts perceived the people in the scenario as more competitive and less trustworthy than those who received the neutral prime. In a subsequent study, participants who were subliminally primed with legal concepts actually behaved more competitively while playing a game than participants primed with neutral words. In yet another study, those who were primed with legal concepts expressed more opposition to a government policy that was not in their self-interest (Callan, Kay, Olson, Brar, & Whitefield, 2010). These findings illustrate that priming effects can operate outside of conscious awareness, and can influence not only how we perceive others but also how we behave ourselves.

Self-Fulfilling Prophecy

The case whereby people have an expectation about what another person is like, which influences how they act toward that person, which, in turn, causes that person to behave consistently with their original expectations

Making Our Schemas Come True: The Self-Fulfilling Prophecy People are not always passive recipients of information—they often act on their schemas, and in doing so, can change the extent to which these schemas are supported or contradicted. In fact, people can inadvertently make their schemas come true by the way they treat others. This is called a **self-fulfilling prophecy**, and it operates as follows: we have an expectation about what another person is like that influences how we act toward that person, which in turn, causes that person to behave consistently with our expectations. In other words, our expectations come true. Figure 3.4 illustrates this self-perpetuating cycle of self-fulfilling prophecy.

In what has become one of the most famous studies in social psychology, Robert Rosenthal and Lenore Jacobson (1968) examined whether teachers' expectations for students can have self-fulfilling effects. They administered an IQ test to all students in an elementary school and told the teachers that some of the students had scored so well that they were sure to "bloom" academically in the upcoming year. In fact, the students identified as "bloomers" were chosen randomly by the researchers. As we discussed in Chapter 2, the use of random assignment means that, on average, the students designated as bloomers were no smarter or more likely to bloom than any of the other kids. The only way in which these students differed from their peers was in the minds of the teachers. (Neither the students nor their parents were told anything about the results of the test.)

FIGURE 3.4

The self-fulfilling prophecy: A sad cycle in four acts.

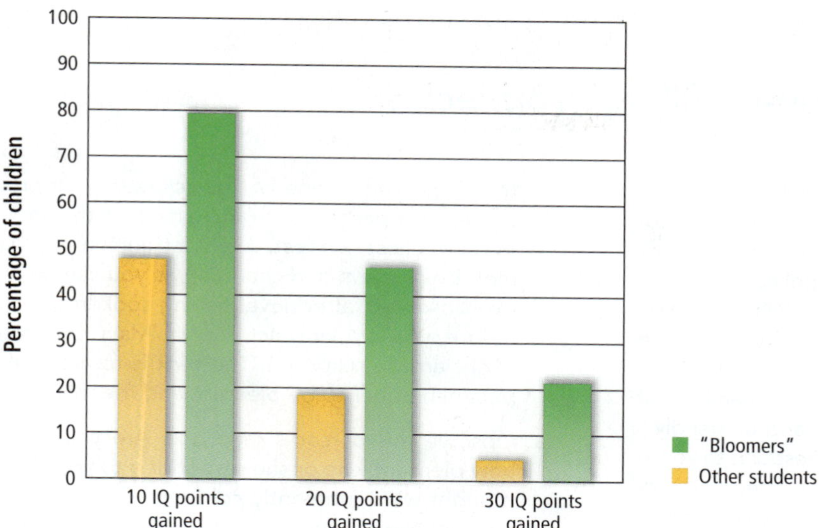

FIGURE 3.5

The self-fulfilling prophecy. Percentage of first and second graders who improved on an IQ test over the course of the school year.

Those whom the teachers expected to do well actually improved more than did the other students.

(Adapted from Rosenthal & Jacobson, 1968)

After creating the expectation in the teachers' minds that some of the kids would do especially well, Rosenthal and Jacobson waited to see what would happen. They observed the classroom dynamics periodically over the school year, and at the end of the year they tested all the children again with an actual IQ test. Did the prophecy come true? Indeed it did—the students in each class who had been labelled as bloomers showed significantly higher gains in their IQ scores than did the other students (see Figure 3.5). The teachers' expectations had become reality. Rosenthal and Jacobson's findings have since been replicated in a number of experimental and correlational studies (Babad, 1993; Blank, 1993; Madon, Guyll, Spoth, & Willard, 2004; Madon, Guyll, Buller, Scherr, Willard, & Spoth, 2008; Jussim & Harber, 2005).

Prophecy is the most gratuitous form of error.

—George Eliot *(Mary Ann Evans Cross), 1871*

Teachers can unintentionally make their expectations about their students come true by treating some students differently from others.

TRY IT! Avoiding Self-Fulfilling Prophecies

1. Examine some of your own schemas and expectations about social groups, especially groups you don't particularly like. These might be members of a particular race or ethnic group, of a rival university, of a political party, or people with a particular sexual orientation. Why don't you like members of this group? "Well," you might think, "one reason is that whenever I interact with francophones (substitute anglophones, Jews, Muslims, gays, or members of any other social group), they seem cold and unfriendly." And you might be right. Perhaps they do respond to you in a cold and unfriendly fashion. Not, however, because they are this way by nature but because they are responding to the way you have treated them.
2. Try this exercise to counteract the self-fulfilling prophecy. Find someone who is a member of a group you dislike and strike up a conversation. For example, sit next to this person in one of your classes or approach him or her at a party. Try to imagine that this individual is the friendliest, kindest, sweetest person you have ever met. Be as warm and charming as you can be. Don't go overboard—if, after never having spoken to this person before, you suddenly act like Mr./Ms. Congeniality, you might arouse suspicion. The trick is to act as if you expect him or her to be pleasant and friendly.
3. Observe this person's reactions. Are you surprised by how pleasantly he or she responded to you? People you thought were inherently cold and unfriendly will probably behave in a warm and friendly manner themselves, in response to the way you have treated them. If this doesn't work on your first encounter with the person, try it again on one or two occasions. In all likelihood, you will find that friendliness really does breed friendliness.

Did the teachers in the Rosenthal and Jacobson (1968) study callously decide to give more encouragement and attention to the bloomers? Not at all. Most teachers are dedicated and try not to treat some students in a more advantageous manner than others. Far from being a conscious, deliberate act, the self-fulfilling prophecy is instead an example of automatic thinking (Chen & Bargh, 1997). Interestingly, the teachers in the Rosenthal and Jacobson (1968) study reported that they spent slightly less time with the students who were labelled as bloomers. In subsequent studies, however, teachers have been found to treat bloomers (i.e., the students they expect to do better) differently in four general ways: (1) They create a warmer emotional climate for bloomers, giving them more personal attention, encouragement, and support; (2) they give bloomers more material to learn and material that is more difficult; (3) they give bloomers more and better feedback on their work; and (4) they give bloomers more opportunities to respond in class and give them longer to respond (Brophy, 1983; Jussim, 1986; Rosenthal, 1994; Snyder, 1984).

A distressing implication of the fact that self-fulfilling prophecy occurs automatically is that our schemas may be quite resistant to change. Suppose a teacher has the schema that boys possess innate ability that makes them superior in math to girls. "But Mr. Jones," we might say, "how can you hold such a belief? There are plenty of girls who do very well in math." Mr. Jones would probably be unconvinced because he would have data to support his schema. "In my classes over the years," he might reply, "nearly three times as many boys as girls have excelled at math." His error lies not in his characterization of the evidence but in his failure to realize his role in producing it. Robert Merton referred to this process as a "reign of error," whereby people can "cite the actual course of events as proof that [they were] right from the very beginning" (1948). See the accompanying Try It! exercise for a way to overcome your own self-fulfilling prophecies.

To summarize, we have seen that the amount of information we face every day is so vast that we have to reduce it to a manageable size. In addition, much of this information is ambiguous or difficult to decipher. One way we deal with this "blooming, buzzing, confusion," in William James' words (1890), is to rely on schemas, which help us reduce the amount of information we need to take in and help us interpret ambiguous information. These schemas are applied quickly, effortlessly, and unintentionally; in short, they are one form of automatic thinking. Another form of automatic thinking is to apply specific rules and shortcuts when thinking about the social world. These shortcuts are, for the most part, extremely useful, but as we will see, they too can sometimes lead to erroneous inferences about the world.

Mental Strategies and Shortcuts: Heuristics

Think back to your decision about where to apply to university. How did you narrow down your list from the schools you considered to the ones to which you actually applied? One strategy would be to investigate thoroughly each of the more than 70 universities in Canada as well as all of the community colleges. You could read every catalogue from cover to cover, visit every campus, and interview as many faculty members, deans, and students as you could find. Getting tired yet? Such a strategy would, of course, be prohibitively time-consuming and costly. Instead of considering every university and college, most high school students narrow down their choice to a small number of options and find out what they can about these schools.

This example is like many decisions and judgments we make in everyday life. When deciding which job to accept, what car to purchase, or whom to marry, we usually do not conduct a thorough search of every option ("Okay, it's time for me to get married; I think I'll consult the census lists of unmarried adults in my city and begin my interviews tomorrow"). Instead, we use mental strategies and shortcuts that make the decision easier, allowing us to get on with our lives without turning every decision into a major research project. These shortcuts do not always lead to the best decision. For example, if you had exhaustively studied every college and university in Canada, maybe you would have found one that you liked better than the one you attend now. Mental shortcuts are efficient, however, and usually lead to good decisions in a reasonable amount of time (Gigerenzer, 2008; Gilovich & Griffin, 2002; Griffin & Kahneman, 2003; Nisbett & Ross, 1980).

What shortcuts do people use? One, as already discussed, is to use schemas to understand new situations. Rather than starting from scratch when examining our options, we often apply previous knowledge and schemas. We have many schemas, about everything from colleges and universities (e.g., what community colleges are like versus what universities are like) to other people. When making specific kinds of judgments and decisions, however, we do not always have a ready-made schema to apply. At other times, there are too many schemas that could apply, and it is not clear which one to use. What do we do?

At times like these, people often use mental shortcuts called **judgmental heuristics.** The word *heuristics* comes from the Greek word meaning "to discover"; in the field of social cognition, heuristic refers to the mental shortcuts people use to make judgments quickly and efficiently. Before discussing these heuristics, we should note that they do not guarantee people will make accurate inferences about the world. In fact, we will document many mental errors in this chapter. However, keep in mind that people use heuristics for a reason: Most of the time, they are highly functional and serve us well.

Simulate on **mypsychlab**
Heuristics

Judgmental Heuristics
Mental shortcuts people use to make judgments quickly and efficiently

How Easily Does It Come to Mind? The Availability Heuristic Suppose you are sitting in a restaurant with several friends one night, when it becomes clear that the waiter made a mistake with one of the orders. Your friend Michael ordered the veggie burger with onion rings but instead got the veggie burger with fries. "Oh, well," he says, "I'll just eat the fries." This starts a discussion of whether he should have sent back his order, and some of your friends accuse Michael of being unassertive. He turns to you and asks, "Do you think I'm an unassertive person?" How would you answer this question?

One way, as we have seen, would be to call on a ready-made schema that provides the answer. If you know Michael well and have already formed a picture of how assertive he is, you can recite your answer easily and quickly: "Don't worry, Michael, if I ever need a used-car salesman, you'd be the first person I'd call." Suppose, though, that you've never really thought about how assertive Michael is and have to think about your answer. In such a situation, you might rely on how easily different examples come to mind. If it is easy to think of times when Michael acted assertively (e.g., that time he stopped someone from butting in line in front of him at the movies), you will conclude that Michael is a pretty assertive guy. If it is easier to think of times when Michael acted unassertively (e.g., that time he let a phone solicitor talk him into buying an expensive long-distance calling plan), you will conclude that he is pretty unassertive.

Availability Heuristic

A mental shortcut whereby people base a judgment on the ease with which they can bring something to mind

This mental shortcut is called the **availability heuristic**, which is basing a judgment on the ease with which you can bring something to mind (Oppenheimer, 2004; Rothman & Hardin, 1997; Schwarz & Vaughn, 2002). The first studies demonstrating the availability heuristic were conducted by Tversky and Kahneman (1973) at the Hebrew University of Jerusalem. (Daniel Kahneman, who took a position at the University of British Columbia from 1978 to 1986, won the Nobel Prize in Economics in 2002 for his research on the psychology of decision making. In 2007, he received the highest honour bestowed by the American Psychological Association, the Award for Outstanding Lifetime Contributions to Psychology.) In one of their studies, participants were presented with the names of famous and nonfamous people. When asked to recall the names, participants were more likely to remember the famous ones, even though there were fewer famous than non-famous names on the list. Presumably, the famous names were more available in memory. When other participants were asked to estimate the number of male and female names, they gave higher estimates for the gender that was famous. For example, if a list contained the names of 19 famous women and 20 non-famous men, participants believed there had been a greater number of women's names than men's on the list. Tversky and Kahneman's findings have been replicated in research conducted in other countries, including Canada (McKelvie, 1995, 1997).

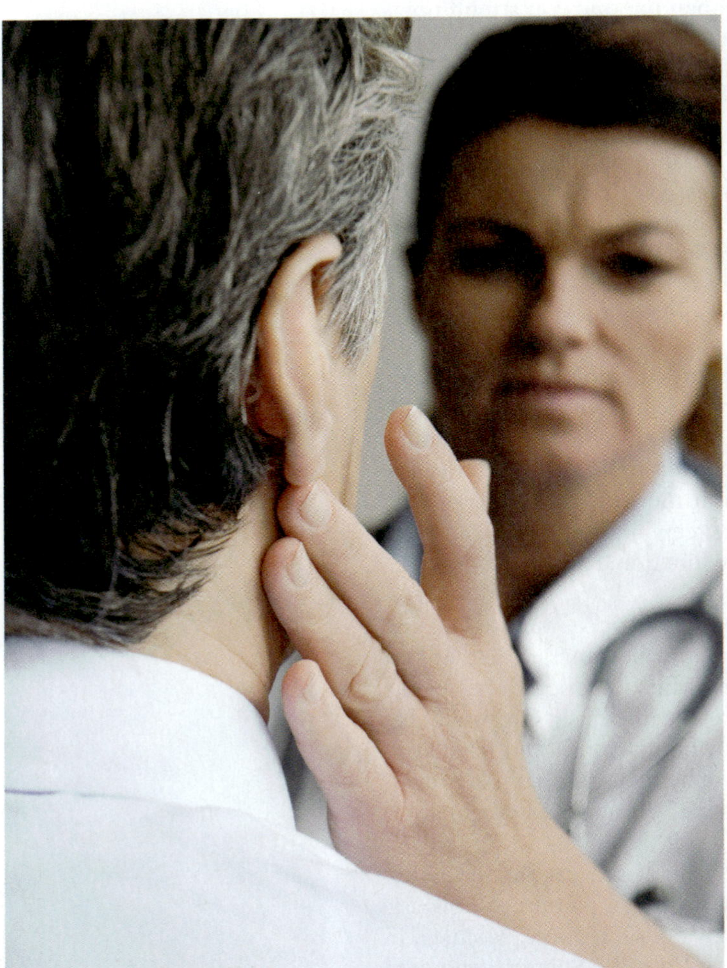

Physicians have been found to use the availability heuristic when making diagnoses. Their diagnoses are influenced by how easily they can bring to mind different diseases.

There are many situations in which the availability heuristic is a good strategy. To return to our earlier example, if you can easily bring to mind several times when Michael stood up for his rights, he probably is an assertive person; if you can easily bring to mind several times when he was timid or meek, he probably is not an assertive person. The trouble with the availability heuristic is that sometimes what is easiest to bring to mind is not typical of the overall picture, leading to faulty conclusions. When physicians are diagnosing diseases, for example, it might seem a relatively straightforward matter for them to observe people's symptoms and figure out what disease, if any, they have. Sometimes, though, medical symptoms are ambiguous and might be a sign of several different disorders. Do doctors use the availability heuristic, whereby they are more likely to consider diagnoses that come to mind easily? Several studies of medical diagnoses suggest that the answer is yes (Eraker & Politser, 1988; Fox, 1980; Travis, Phillippi, & Tonn, 1989; Weber, Bockenholt, Hilton, & Wallace, 1993).

Consider Dr. Robert Marion's diagnosis of Nicole, a bright, sweet, nine-year-old patient. Nicole was normal in every way, except that once or twice a year she had strange, neurological attacks, characterized by disorientation, insomnia, slurred words, and strange mewing sounds. Nicole had been hospitalized three times, had seen more than a dozen specialists, and had undergone many diagnostic tests, including CT scans, brain-wave tests, and virtually every blood test there is. The doctors were stumped; they could not figure out what was wrong with her. Within minutes of seeing her, however, Dr. Marion correctly diagnosed her problem as a rare, inherited blood disorder called acute intermittent porphyria (AIP). The blood chemistry of people with this disorder often gets out of sync, causing a variety of neurological symptoms. It can be controlled with a careful diet and by avoiding certain medications.

How did Dr. Marion diagnose Nicole's disorder so quickly, when so many other doctors failed to do so? He had just finished writing a book on the genetic diseases of historical figures, including a chapter on George III of England, who—you guessed it—suffered from AIP. "I didn't make the diagnosis because I'm a brilliant diagnostician or because I'm a sensitive listener," reports Dr. Marion. "I succeeded where others failed because [Nicole] and I happened to run into each other in exactly the right place, at exactly the right time" (Marion, 1995). In other words, Dr. Marion used the availability heuristic. AIP happened to be available in his memory, making the diagnosis easy. Though this was a happy outcome of the use of the availability heuristic, it is easy to see how it can go wrong.

Take the case of Dr. Harrison Alter, an emergency-room physician working on a Navajo reservation in Tuba City, Arizona (Groopman, 2007). Over a three-week period, Dr. Alter had seen dozens of people with viral pneumonia. One day, Blanche Begaye (not her real name), a woman in her sixties, appeared in the emergency room. She was breathing very rapidly and had a fever. She had taken Aspirin, but her condition had only gotten worse. Her lungs sounded fine, and a chest X-ray did not show signs of pneumonia. Her white-cell blood count was not elevated (which would be expected if she had pneumonia), although an analysis of her blood electrolytes showed that her blood was slightly acidic. Dr. Alter's diagnosis was that Begaye was in the early stages of pneumonia. He admitted Begaye, ordered an IV, and placed her in the care of an internist. Shortly thereafter, the internist took Dr. Alters aside and said, "That's not a case of viral pneumonia. She has aspirin toxicity" (Groopman, 2007). Dr. Alter immediately knew that the internist was right: "She was an absolutely classic case—the rapid breathing, the shift in blood electrolytes—and I missed it" (Groopman, 2007). Dr. Alter's misdiagnosis illustrates the downside of using the availability heuristic. The fact that he had recently seen so many patients with viral pneumonia meant that this was the first diagnosis that came to mind when he saw Blanche Begaye.

Do people use the availability heuristic to make judgments about themselves? It might seem that we have well-developed ideas about our own personalities, such as how assertive we are. However, it turns out that often we do not have firm schemas about our own traits (Kunda et al., 1993; Markus, 1977). In those cases, might we make judgments about ourselves based on how easily we can recall examples of our own behaviour? To find out, Norbert Schwarz and his colleagues (1991) performed a clever experiment in which they altered how easy it was for people to bring to mind examples of their own past behaviours. In one condition, they asked people to think of six times they had acted assertively. Most people found this to be pretty easy; examples came to mind quickly. In another condition, the researchers asked people to think of 12 times they had acted assertively. This was much more difficult; people had to try hard to think of this many examples. All participants were then asked to rate how assertive they thought they really were.

The question was, did people use the availability heuristic (the ease with which they could bring examples to mind) to infer how assertive they were? As seen on the left side of Figure 3.6, they did. People who were asked to think of six examples rated themselves as relatively assertive, because it was easy to think of six examples ("Hey, this is easy—I guess I'm a pretty assertive person"). It might surprise you to learn that people asked to think of 12 examples rated themselves as relatively unassertive, because it was difficult to think of 12 examples ("Hmm, this is hard—I must not be a very assertive person"). Other people were asked to think of either 6 or 12 times they had acted *un*assertively, and similar results were found—those asked to think of six examples rated themselves as more unassertive than those who were asked to think of 12 examples (see the right side of Figure 3.6; Schwarz, Bless, Strack, Klumpp,

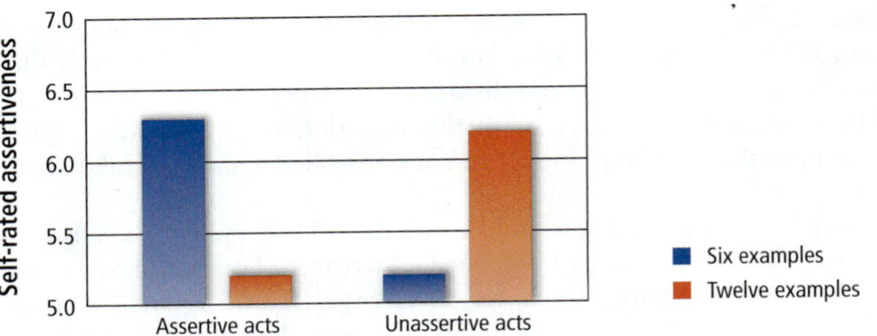

FIGURE 3.6

Availability and assertiveness.

People who were asked to think of six times they behaved assertively found it easy to do so and therefore concluded that they were pretty assertive people. People who were asked to think of 12 times they behaved assertively found it difficult to think of so many examples and therefore concluded that they were not very assertive people (see the left side of the graph). Similar results were found among people asked to think of either 6 or 12 times they behaved unassertively (see the right side of the graph). These results show that people often base their judgments on availability, or how easily they can bring information to mind.

(Adapted from Schwarz et al., 1991)

Rittenhauer-Schtaka, & Simmons, 1991). In short, people use the availability heuristic—the ease with which they can bring examples to mind—when making judgments about themselves and other people. It might interest you to learn that a devious professor actually used this technique to improve his course evaluations. He asked his students to list either 2 ways or 10 ways that the course could be improved and then to rate their overall impression of the course. Who gave the course the highest ratings? Those asked to list 10 ways in which it could be improved, because they found it difficult to come up with that many ways that the course was lacking and thought, "If I can't come up with that many criticisms, it must be a great course!" (Fox, 2006).

How Similar Is A to B? The Representativeness Heuristic Suppose, for example, that you attend a university in Alberta. One day you meet a student named Lyne standing in line for one of the food outlets on campus. Lyne is fashionably dressed, orders a café au lait and a croissant, and from the way she pronounces *croissant*, it's apparent she speaks French. Which province do you think Lyne is from? Because Lyne seems similar to many people's stereotype of a Quebecer, you might guess Quebec, or at least seriously entertain this possibility. If so, you would be using the **representativeness heuristic**, which is a mental shortcut whereby people classify something according to how similar it is to a typical case—such as how similar Lyne is to your conception of a typical Quebecer (Gilovich & Savitsky, 2002; Kahneman & Frederick, 2002; Kahneman & Tversky, 1973; Tversky & Kahneman, 1974).

Representativeness Heuristic

A mental shortcut whereby people classify something according to how similar it is to a typical case

Categorizing things according to representativeness is often a perfectly reasonable thing to do. If you did not use the representativeness heuristic, how else would you decide where Lyne comes from? Should you just randomly choose a province? Actually, there is another source of information you might use. If you knew nothing about Lyne, it would be wise to guess that she was from Alberta, because at Alberta universities there are more in-province than out-of-province students. If you guessed Alberta, you would be using what is called **base rate information**, or information about the relative frequency of members of different categories in the population (e.g., the percentage of students at Alberta universities who are from Alberta).

Base Rate Information

Information about the frequency of members of different categories in the population

What do people do when they have both base rate information (e.g., knowing that there are more students from Alberta than from Quebec at a university) and contradictory information about the person in question (e.g., encountering Lyne, who dresses fashionably and speaks French)? Kahneman and Tversky (1973) found that people do not use base rate information sufficiently, paying most attention to how representative the information about the specific person is of the general category (e.g., Quebecers). (This tendency also has been confirmed in recent research conducted in Canada and Belgium [De Neys & Glumicic, 2008].) While this is not a bad strategy if the information about the person is reliable, it can get you into trouble when the information is flimsy. Returning to our example of Lyne, given that the base rate of students from Quebec attending universities in Alberta is low, you would need to have very good evidence that Lyne was from Quebec before ignoring the base rate and guessing that she is one of the few exceptions. And given that it is not unusual to find people from Alberta who dress well, speak French, and enjoy café au lait and croissants, you would, in this instance, be wise to use the base rate.

CONNECTIONS

Personality Tests and the Representativeness Heuristic

Suppose you took a personality test, such as one of the many that are available online, and received the following feedback:

> You have a need for other people to like and admire you, and yet you tend to be critical of yourself. While you have some personality weaknesses you are generally able to compensate for them. You have considerable unused capacity that you have not turned to your advantage. Disciplined and self-controlled on the outside, you tend to be worrisome and insecure on the inside. At times you have serious doubts as to whether you have made the right decision or done the right thing. You prefer a certain amount of change and variety and become dissatisfied when hemmed in by restrictions and limitations. You also pride yourself as an independent thinker and do not accept others' statements without satisfactory proof. But you have found it unwise to be too frank in revealing yourself to others. At times you are extroverted, affable, and sociable, while at other times you are introverted, wary, and reserved. Some of your aspirations tend to be rather unrealistic.

"Wow," you might think. "This test is amazing; it is uncanny how well it captured who I am." If so, you are not alone. Bertram Forer (1949) gave this feedback to a group of students and asked them to rate how well it described them, on a scale from 0 = very poor to 5 = excellent. The average rating was 4.26—a phenomenon that has come to be known as the Barnum effect, after the circus owner and showman P. T. Barnum.

Why do most people believe that this personality description describes them so well? One culprit is the representativeness heuristic: The statements are vague enough that virtually everyone can find a past behaviour that is similar (representative of) to the feedback. Consider the statement, "At times you have serious doubts as to whether you have made the right decision or done the right thing." All of us can think of times this was true of us, that is, of examples that are representative of this statement. Who hasn't second-guessed themselves about an important decision, such as where to go to school or what major to choose? Similarly, all of us can think of times when we were independent thinkers and times when we revealed too much about ourselves. The reason the feedback seems to describe us so well is that we do not go beyond the representative examples that come to mind and think, "Actually, there are just as many times when I didn't feel or act this way."

How do heuristics influence your thinking? Take the accompanying Try It! quiz to find out.

TRY IT! Reasoning Quiz

Answer each of the following questions:

1. Consider the letter *r* in the English language. Do you think that this letter occurs more often as the first letter of words (e.g., rope) or more often as the third letter of words (e.g., park)?
   a. more often as the first letter
   b. more often as the third letter
   c. about equally often as the first and third letter
2. Which of these do you think causes more fatalities in Canada?
   a. accidental death
   b. death from strokes
   c. each causes about the same number of deaths
3. Suppose you flipped a fair coin six times. Which sequence is more likely to occur? (H = heads, T = tails)
   a. H T T H T H
   b. H H H T T T
   c. both sequences are equally likely
4. After observing the sequence T T T T T, what is the probability that the next coin flip will be heads?
   a. less than 0.5
   b. 0.5
   c. greater than 0.5

Go to www.MyPsychLab.com for the answers.

The Pervasiveness of Automatic Thinking

Part of the definition of automatic thinking is that it occurs unconsciously. Although it might seem magical that we can think without being aware that we are thinking, social psychologists are increasingly reaching the conclusion that we can do just that (Bargh, 2007; Bargh & Morsella, 2008; Dijksterhuis & Nordgren, 2006; Hassin, Uleman, & Bargh, 2005; Stapel & Koomen, 2006; Wilson, 2002). If we had to rely on slow, conscious thinking alone we would be in a pickle because we often need to make very fast decisions about what is happening around us, what to pay attention to, and which of our goals to pursue. We would be left scratching our heads while the world whizzed by. As we have seen, these fast, unconscious processes can sometimes lead to tragic errors. Most of the time, however, unconscious thinking is critical to navigating our way through the world.

Have you ever been chatting with someone at a party and suddenly realized that someone across the room mentioned your name? The only way this could happen is if, while you were engaged in conversation, you were unconsciously monitoring the other conversations to see if something important came up (such as your name). This *cocktail party phenomenon* has been demonstrated in several experiments (Harris & Pashler, 2004; Moray, 1959).

Unconscious thinking may also be involved when we have competing goals and are not sure which one to act on. Suppose, for example, that you are taking a difficult course in which the professor grades on a curve, guaranteeing that only a few people will get As. A classmate you don't know very well tells you he is having difficulty with some of the material and asks whether you will join him to have coffee and go over your notes for the class. On the one hand, you want to be helpful, satisfying your goal of being a caring, compassionate person. On the other hand, you want to satisfy your goal of doing well in the class and are hesitant to hurt your chances by raising someone else's grade. Which goal do you act on? You could mull this over for a while, consciously weighing your options. However, often it is our nonconscious mind that chooses the goal for us in such situations, basing the decision in part on which goal has been recently activated or primed. For example, John Bargh and colleagues (2001) asked students to play a game in which they had to choose to cooperate or be competitive with another student. Just prior to playing the game, they completed a task (supposedly for another professor) in which they had to make sentences out of a list of words. In one condition, many of the words had to do with cooperation, such as *helpful*, *fair*, and *share*. In the control condition, the words were unrelated to cooperation or competition, such as *salad* and *umbrella*. (It is important in this kind of study that participants do not realize that there is a connection between the sentence-making task and the cooperation game.) It turns out that the people who made sentences out of words having to do with cooperation were significantly more likely to cooperate in the game with the other student than were students in the control condition. The words were sufficient to prime the goal of being cooperative unconsciously, without people knowing that they had made such a choice at all (Bargh, Gollwitzer, Lee-Chai, Barndollar, & Trötschel, 2001).

Outside consciousness there rolls a vast tide of life which is perhaps more important to us than the little isle of our thoughts which lies within our ken.

—E. S. Dallas

There is even evidence that our unconscious minds can do better at some tasks than our conscious minds. Suppose you were shopping for an apartment, and after looking at several places you narrowed your choice to four possibilities. You have a great deal of information about each apartment, including its location, cost, size, whether it has free Internet access, and so on. Each apartment has pros and cons, making it difficult to decide which one to rent. How should you go about making up your mind? Given the importance of this decision, most of us would spend a lot of time thinking about it, consciously analyzing the alternatives to determine what our best option is. Surely, you might think, this would be better than *avoiding* conscious thought about the apartments, by, say, spending several minutes memorizing words for a vocabulary test in your Spanish class and then choosing one of the apartments.

As absurd as this last approach might sound, research by Dijksterhuis (2004) suggests that it might actually produce the best choice (see also Dijksterhuis & Nordgren, 2005). He gave people a lot of information about four apartments in a short amount of time, which made it difficult for them to determine right away that one of the apartments was, in fact, superior to the others (that is, which one had the highest ratio of good to bad attributes). He then randomly assigned people to one of three conditions. In the *immediate choice* condition, he asked people to choose the apartment they thought was the best right away. In the *conscious thought* condition, he asked people to think carefully about the apartments for three minutes and then choose the best one. In the *unconscious thought* condition, he gave people a distracting task for three minutes so that they could not think about the apartments consciously, with the assumption that they would continue to think about the apartments unconsciously.

Who was most likely to choose the best apartment? As seen in Figure 3.7, it was people in the unconscious thought condition. Because people in this condition could not consciously think about the apartments, something else must have happened that produced the best choice. In subsequent research, it was found that when people were distracted they were still working on the task unconsciously, organizing the information in a way that made the best choice more apparent to them.

Research on unconscious thought is in its infancy, and we would not yet recommend that you find something to distract you whenever you are faced with an important choice. It is becoming clearer, however, that automatic, nonconscious thinking is far more pervasive than previously thought, and that this kind of thinking can lead to good decisions.

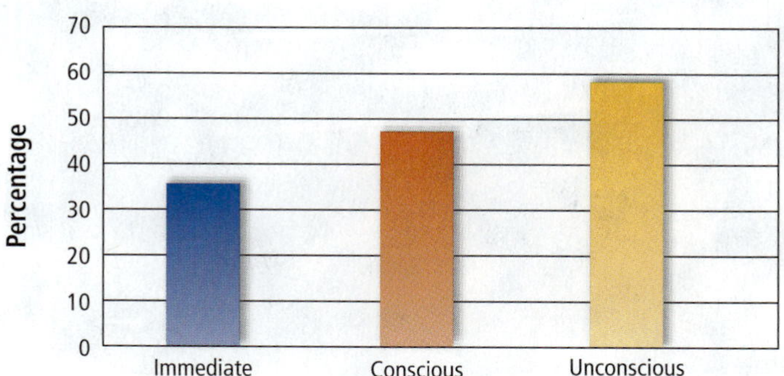

FIGURE 3.7

The power of unconscious thinking.

After receiving a great deal of information about four apartments, participants chose one immediately (immediate condition), or thought about the apartments consciously for three minutes (conscious condition), or were distracted for three minutes, allowing their unconscious to work unimpeded (unconscious condition). People in the latter condition were most likely to pick the apartment that had the most positive qualities and the fewest negative qualities.

(Adapted from Dijksterhuis, 2004)

In fact, recent research suggests that unconscious thinking may play a role in relationship happiness. Researchers at the University of Buffalo and at the University of Waterloo had couples in the first few months of marriage complete a variety of questionnaires with respect to how they felt about their partner and their relationship (Murray, Holmes, & Pinkus, 2010). They also completed daily diaries for two weeks in which they reported on events in their day, how their partner reacted, marital satisfaction on that day, and the like. Four years later, the researchers assessed the participants' automatic attitudes toward their spouse assessed by examining if on a computer task the spouse's name was more likely to be associated with pleasant or unpleasant words. It was found that the dynamics of the relationship were better reflected in people's automatic attitudes than in conscious reports of what their relationship was like. For example, those people who felt rejected by their partner on a given day and responded by becoming cold and distant later showed less positive automatic attitudes toward their partner, which was not detected in their conscious evaluations of their partner or their relationship. The researchers refer to this as the "smart unconscious" that picks up on relationship dynamics that conscious reflection may not (Murray et al., 2010).

At this point, you might be wondering why we have spent so much time on the automatic, nonconscious type of social cognition. Didn't we say earlier that there are two modes of thinking: automatic and controlled? Isn't it possible to think about the social world slowly, carefully, and deliberately, such as when someone takes time to sit down and really think a problem through? Indeed it is. We've spent so much time on automatic thinking, however, because it is so pervasive and dominates much of people's mental lives. Just as modern jetliners fly mostly on automatic pilot, so do people rely a great deal on automatic thinking to get through their days. However, just as an airline pilot can take control of the plane when trouble occurs, controlled thinking takes over and influences our behaviour when unusual events occur—sometimes for better, and sometimes for worse.

Controlled Social Cognition: High-Effort Thinking

Racial profiling—official action toward people based on their race, ethnicity, or national origin instead of their behaviour—has received a great deal of attention since the events of September 11, 2001. Because the terrorists who flew the planes into

Do you think racial profiling is playing a role in this situation?

the World Trade Center towers, a field in Pennsylvania, and the Pentagon were of Middle Eastern descent, some people feel that anyone who looks as if he or she might be of a similar background should receive special scrutiny when flying on commercial airlines. On the New Year's Eve after the attacks, Michael Dasrath and Edgardo Cureg boarded a Continental Airlines flight from New Jersey to Tampa. Dasrath was a U.S. citizen who was born in South America, and Cureg was a U.S. resident from the Philippines. Both had successfully passed through extensive security checks. Dasrath, seated in first class, was removed from the plane when a woman complained that he made her uncomfortable. Cureg was also removed from the flight, allegedly because he made other passengers nervous. Neither man posed a threat but, because they had brown skin, they were singled out and refused service.

These examples of racial profiling bear some similarities to the tragedy involving Jean Charles de Menezes, a 27-year old Brazilian man gunned down by London police in 2005, shortly after the subway bombings in that city. Members of Britain's Muslim community expressed alarm and concern that police were targeting men whose race or physical characteristics resembled those of the men accused on the subway bombings. In both cases, innocent people were suspected of a crime because of the colour of their skin. In other respects, however, the examples are quite different. In de Menezes' case, the police had very little time to react—seconds or less—as he approached a subway station. More than likely, the police officers' automatic thinking took over. In the case of the men removed from the airplane, however, the airline officials presumably had ample time to think about and consider their actions. Racial prejudice can thus be the result of automatic thinking or of conscious, deliberative thinking—an issue we will take up in detail in Chapter 12. For now, we use this example to illustrate the more conscious, controlled type of social cognition.

Controlled thinking is defined as thinking that is conscious, intentional, voluntary, and effortful. People can usually turn on or turn off this type of thinking at will and are fully aware of what they are thinking. Further, this kind of thinking is effortful in the sense that it requires mental energy. People have the capacity to think in a conscious, controlled way about only one thing at a time; they cannot be thinking about what they will eat for lunch today at the same time they are thinking through a complex math problem. Automatic thinking, in contrast, can occur in the background with no conscious effort at all.

Connect to MyPsychLab
Practice your controlled thinking! To participate in an experiment on depth of processing, go to MyPsychLab

Controlled Thinking
Thinking that is conscious, intentional, voluntary, and effortful

Thinking about What Might Have Been: Counterfactual Reasoning

When do people go off automatic pilot and think about things more slowly and consciously? One circumstance is when they experience a negative event that was a "close call," such as failing a test by just a point or two. Under these conditions, people engage in **counterfactual thinking**—mentally changing some aspect of the past as a way of imagining what might have been (Kahneman & Miller, 1986; Kahneman & Tversky, 1982; Markman, Gavanski, Sherman, & McMullen, 1995; Roese, 1997; Roese & Olson, 1997; Sanna, Carter, & Small, 2006). "If only I hadn't fallen asleep while studying the night before the test," you might think, "I would have gotten a better grade," or "If only I had worked up the courage to ask Michelle, she might be going out with me instead of my best friend." If you had mustered up the courage to ask out Michelle and the two of you were now head over heels in love, chances are you probably wouldn't be spending much time agonizing over how the outcome could have been different.

Counterfactual Thinking
Mentally changing some aspect of the past as a way of imagining what might have been

There is considerable evidence that we are most likely to engage in counterfactual thinking when we "just missed" avoiding a negative event. For example, missing a plane by five minutes causes more counterfactual thinking ("If only I had driven a little faster," "If only I hadn't stopped to pick up a coffee") and more regret than missing a plane by half an hour (Kahneman & Miller, 1986; Miller, Turnbull, & McFarland, 1990). Similarly, if you sold a winning lottery ticket to your sister one hour before the draw, you would experience more regret than if you had sold the ticket two weeks earlier

(Miller & Taylor, 2002). As you might expect, people also feel greater sympathy for others in near-miss situations. To demonstrate this, Miller and McFarland (1986) had students at Simon Fraser University read a scenario in which a man attempted to walk to safety after his plane crashed in an isolated northern area. Those who were told that the man perished 0.4 kilometres from the nearest town awarded greater compensation to his family than did those who were told that he died 120 kilometres from the nearest town.

The use of hypothetical scenarios such as these is common in counterfactual research. In addition to the scenarios we have discussed, students at the University of British Columbia have been asked to imagine a man taking an unusual route home and having an accident (Kahneman & Tversky, 1982; Mandel & Lehman, 1996). Students at the University of Western Ontario have been asked to imagine a man catching or missing a flight out of Pearson Airport in Toronto (Roese & Olson, 1996), getting a good or poor grade on a project with a classmate (Roese & Olson, 1993), or going on a blind date that ends in disaster (Roese & Olson, 1995). The researchers then assess whether the participants engage in counterfactual thinking, the emotions they would experience in that situation, and so on. However, it is important to note that the effects that we have been discussing are not limited to people's reactions to hypothetical scenarios (Branscombe, Owen, Garstka, & Coleman, 1996; Davis & Lehman, 1995). Indeed, as Davis, Lehman, Wortman, Silver, and Thompson (1995)

Who do you think would be happier: the silver or bronze medallist in an athletic competition? Research by Medvec, Madey, and Gilovich (1995) suggests that bronze medallists are happier because it is more difficult for them to engage in counterfactual reasoning—imagining ways in which they could have won the event. This certainly seems to have been true for Canada's Clara Hughes (left), a speed skater, shown here after winning the bronze medal in the Women's 5000 metres event at the 2010 Vancouver Olympics. By contrast, Cheryl Bernard (right), the Canadian women's curling skip whose team placed second in the same Olympics, hangs her head after losing the gold to the Swedish team. "Eventually, this silver's going to feel really great," a teary-eyed Bernard said in a post-game interview, "Just right now, the gold was very close" (Hicks, 2010).

have demonstrated, counterfactual thoughts have a huge impact on people's emotional reactions to actual events. These researchers interviewed people who had experienced the trauma of losing a spouse or child in a car accident or the death of an infant from sudden infant death syndrome. They discovered that thoughts such as, "If only I had done something differently, my spouse [child] would still be alive" were common. In fact, for half of the participants, these kinds of thoughts persisted four to seven years later. Sadly, the more they engaged in such counterfactual thinking, the greater their distress. Similar findings were obtained when Davis and colleagues (1996) interviewed spinal cord injury victims. As expected, the more these people imagined ways in which the tragedy could have been averted, by mentally "undoing" the circumstances preceding it, the more distress they reported (Davis, Lehman, Silver, & Wortman, 1996).

Counterfactual reasoning can also lead to some paradoxical effects on emotions. For example, who do you think would be happier: an Olympic athlete who won a silver medal (came in second) or an Olympic athlete who won a bronze medal (came in third)? Though you might think that the athlete who performed better (the silver medal winner) would be happier, that is not what Victoria Medvec, Scott Madey, and Tom Gilovich (1995) predicted. They reasoned that the silver medal winner should feel worse, because he or she could more easily imagine having won the event and would therefore engage in more counterfactual reasoning. To see if they were right, they analyzed videos of the 1992 Olympics. Both immediately after their event and while athletes received their medals, silver medal winners appeared less happy than bronze medal winners. Analyses of media interviews with the athletes confirmed that the thoughts of silver medallists were focused on "I almost won . . . ," whereas bronze medallists focused on "At least I did this well . . .." Subsequent research has confirmed these findings (e.g., Medvec, Madey, & Gilovich, 2002) and shown that silver medallists are particularly unhappy if they expected to get gold, whereas bronze medallists are particularly happy if they did not expect to win a medal at all (McGraw, Mellers, & Tetlock, 2005).

Earlier we described controlled thinking as conscious, intentional, voluntary, and effortful, but different kinds of controlled thought meet these requirements to different degrees. Counterfactual reasoning is clearly conscious and effortful; we know we are obsessing about the past, and this kind of thinking can take up so much mental energy that we cannot think about anything else. It is not, however, always intentional or voluntary. Even when we want to stop dwelling on the past and move on to something else, it can be difficult to turn off the "if only" thinking that characterizes counterfactual reasoning. This is not so good if counterfactual thinking results in rumination, whereby people repetitively focus on negative things in their lives. Rumination has been found to be a contributor to depression (Lyubomirsky, Caldwell, & Nolen-Hoeksema, 1993). Thus, it is not advisable to ruminate constantly about a bad test grade to the point where you can't think about anything else.

Counterfactual thinking actually can be useful, however, if it focuses people's attention on ways that they can cope better in the future. Research conducted at the University of Western Ontario (Haynes, Sorrentino, Olson, Szeto, Wirkki, & O'Connor, 2007; Roese, 1994; Roese & Olson, 1997) and at the University of British Columbia (Mandel & Lehman, 1996) shows that counterfactual thinking involves thinking not only about why an event occurred, but also about how various outcomes could have been avoided. This latter aspect can have beneficial effects. For example, in one study, Roese (1994) asked students at the University of Western Ontario to think of an exam they had written in the past year on which they had performed very poorly. Some participants were then asked to "list some specific actions that, in retrospect, could have been taken to have improved your exam score." These students subsequently expressed greater intentions to perform success-enhancing behaviours in the future (e.g., studying), and in fact, actually worked harder to improve their performance compared with students who were asked to focus on actions that could have made the outcome even worse. Research conducted at the University of British Columbia produced similar findings (Nasco & Marsh, 1999).

Moving beyond academic settings, researchers at Defence Research and Development Canada and at City University in the United Kingdom asked prisoners to generate counterfactuals (e.g., "I probably wouldn't have been convicted, if only I had . . .") or, in the control condition, to report on the facts of their case (Mandel & Dhami, 2005). The results suggested that generating counterfactuals might be beneficial in helping offenders not to re-offend.

Researchers at the University of British Columbia have shown that people generate more counterfactuals when asked to focus on *self-improvement* (writing down ways they could learn or be improved by negative situations such as being in a car accident or experiencing a relationship breakup) than when asked to focus on *self-enhancement* (what they could do to make themselves "feel better" in such situations; White & Lehman, 2005b). Thus, counterfactual thinking can be useful when it motivates us to take steps to prevent similar outcomes from occurring in the future.

Finally, we note that there is an exception. A team of researchers from three Canadian universities recently found that not everyone is motivated to do better after generating counterfactuals for a poor performance on a test or an assignment. Specifically, for students who are high in perfectionism (e.g., who believe that their best is never good enough), generating counterfactuals may not have a positive, motivating effect (Sirois, Monforton, & Simpson, 2010).

Thought Suppression and Ironic Processing

Thought Suppression
The attempt to avoid thinking about something a person would prefer to forget

Instead of ruminating about something, we might simply do our best not to think about it. How successful are we at **thought suppression**—the attempt to avoid thinking about something we would prefer to forget, such as a lost love, an unpleasant encounter with one's boss, or a delectable piece of cheesecake in the refrigerator? That depends on the interaction of two processes, one relatively automatic and the other relatively controlled (Wegner, 1992, 1994; Wegner, Wenzlaff, & Kozak, 2004). The automatic part of the system, called the *monitoring process*, searches for evidence that the unwanted thought is about to intrude on consciousness. Once the unwanted thought is detected, the more controlled part of the system, called the *operating process*, comes into play. This is the effortful, conscious attempt to distract oneself by finding something else to think about. These two processes operate in tandem, like two parents conspiring to keep their kids away from junk-food outlets at a mall. One parent's job, akin to the monitoring process, is to keep a watch out for the food joints and to let the other parent know when they are in the vicinity ("McDonald's alert!"). The other parent's job, akin to the operating process, is to divert the kids' attention away from the fast-food places ("Hey, kids, look at the giant picture of SpongeBob in that store window!"). This system works pretty well as long as each process (parent) does its job—one ever alert for the topic we want to avoid and the other diverting our attention from this topic.

What happens, though, when the controlled operating process is unable to do its job because the person is tired or preoccupied? The monitoring process continues to find instances of the unwanted thought, which then intrude on consciousness unchecked by the controlled process. A state of hyperaccessibility results, in which the unwanted thought occurs with high frequency. If the parent who is supposed to distract the children falls down on the job, for example, the kids will become even more aware that fast-food joints are in the vicinity because they will keep hearing the monitoring parent point them out (Renaud & McConnell, 2002; Wenzlaff & Bates, 2000).

The irony is that when we are trying our best not to think about something (e.g., you are on guard not to think about jokes about short people because your height-challenged boss is standing next to you), those thoughts are especially likely to pop into our minds. When we are tired or preoccupied—that is, under *cognitive load*—it is even more likely that these thoughts will spill out unchecked.

The standard procedure in thought suppression experiments is to ask participants not to think of a white bear. And, as you may have guessed, thoughts of white bears are especially likely pop into your mind when you are asked not to think of them. Would it make a difference if the thoughts that you were told to suppress had great personal significance to you? To find out, researchers at the University of Toronto and the University of British Columbia recruited samples of religious and nonreligious university students for their experiment. The religious students were practising Christians whose faith was highly personally significant to them. All participants read a vignette that ended with a blasphemous thought: "While looking at the crucifix, you suddenly have a thought, 'Jesus Christ was not the Messiah; Jesus Christ was just a raving lunatic!' The thought is accompanied by an image of Jesus Christ as a psychotic homeless man roaming the streets talking to himself" (Corcoran & Woody, 2009, p. 1027).

Participants in the thought suppression condition were instructed to "try as hard as you can to suppress all thoughts related to the story you read"; participants in the "do not suppress" condition were told that they could think about whatever they liked, including the story. Religious participants experienced more anxiety when having thoughts about the story than did nonreligious participants and rated their thoughts as more unacceptable. The key finding was that intrusive thoughts about the story persisted longer for religious participants who were told to suppress their thoughts compared to participants in the other conditions (Corcoran & Woody, 2009).

Before leaving this topic, we should note that there can be an emotional and physical cost to thought suppression. In research conducted at the University of New Brunswick and the University of Waterloo, students were asked about the types of thoughts that they had tried to suppress in the last month. The vast majority of students (76 percent) reported trying to suppress worries, followed by obsessive thoughts, depressing thoughts, anger, and jealous thoughts. Unfortunately, the strategies that the students reported for trying to control unwanted thoughts (e.g., distraction) tended not to be effective. Moreover, failure to control unwanted thoughts took its toll; anxiety and frustration were the most common emotional responses associated with failure to control unwanted thoughts (Clark & Purdon, 2009). In another study, women who had had an abortion were asked how much they had tried to suppress thoughts about the abortion (Major & Gramzow, 1999). The more the women reported that they tried not to think about the abortion, the greater their reported psychological distress.

Thought suppression can also have an adverse affect on your health. Researchers asked medical school students to write about a personal topic once a day for three days (Petrie, Booth, & Pennebaker, 1998). After each writing episode, some participants were asked to suppress all thoughts about what they had just written for five minutes. These participants showed a significant decrease in immune system functioning compared with those who did not suppress their thoughts. As you will see in the Social Psychology and Health module, it is generally better to open up about your problems by writing about or discussing them than to try to suppress your thoughts about the problems.

A Portrayal of Social Thinking

By now we have seen two rather different modes of social cognition: one that is effortless, involuntary, unintentional, and unconscious (automatic thinking) and another that is more effortful, voluntary, intentional, and conscious (controlled thinking). We have also discussed that both kinds of thinking can lead to consequential errors. Matthew Dumas' death may have been the result of an automatic assumption made by the Winnipeg police officer who shot him, based on his race. Other kinds of racial prejudice, such as racial profiling, can be the result of more controlled thinking. So how good a thinker is the typical human being anyway? How can we reconcile the fact that human beings have amazing cognitive abilities that have resulted in dazzling cultural and intellectual achievements with the fact that, at the same time, humans are prone to making consequential mental errors such as the ones documented in this chapter?

One way of addressing this question is to ask which kind of thinking—automatic or controlled—is more important in human functioning. The answer to this question has engendered a lively debate among social psychologists. It is fair to say that there has been an increasing appreciation of the role of automatic thinking in human thought; more and more research has shown that people operate on automatic pilot when thinking about the social world. Some researchers have gone so far as to argue that the role of conscious, controlled thinking actually may be quite limited in human functioning (Bargh, 2007; Bargh & Chartrand, 1999; Wegner, 2002, 2004; Wilson, 2002). Others have argued that although it can be difficult, it is possible to gain conscious control over unwanted automatic responses, such as prejudiced ones (Devine, 1989b; Devine & Monteith, 1999; Fiske, 1989a). Debate over these fundamental issues, such as the role of consciousness in human functioning, is likely to generate a good deal of research in the next several years.

What is clear is that despite the troubles they can cause, both kinds of thinking are extremely useful. It would be difficult to live without the ability to process information about the social world automatically and make quick assumptions about our environment; we would be like a primitive, extremely slow computer, chugging away constantly as we tried to understand what was happening around us. And it is clearly to our advantage to be able to switch to controlled mode, where we can think about ourselves and our social world more slowly and carefully.

The following portrait of the social thinker is emerging: People are very sophisticated social thinkers who have amazing cognitive abilities. No one has yet been able to construct a computer that comes close to matching the power of the human brain. But there is plenty of room for improvement. The shortcomings of social thinking we have documented can be tragic, as demonstrated by the examples of racial prejudice in this chapter (Gilovich, 1991; Nisbett & Ross, 1980; Quattrone, 1982; Slusher & Anderson, 1989). Perhaps the best metaphor of human thinking is that people are "flawed scientists"—brilliant thinkers who are attempting to discover the nature of the social world in a logical manner but do not do so perfectly. People are often blind to truths that don't fit their schemas and sometimes treat others in ways that make their schemas come true—something that good scientists would never do.

Improving Human Thinking

One purpose of controlled thinking is to provide checks and balances for automatic thinking. Thus, when trouble occurs, controlled thinking may "kick in." How successful are people at correcting their mistakes? Can they be taught to do better?

Overconfidence Barrier

The barrier that results when people have too much confidence in the accuracy of their judgments; people's judgments are usually not as correct as they think they are

One approach is to make people a little more humble about their reasoning abilities. Often we have greater confidence in our judgments than we should (Blanton, Pelham, De Hart, & Carvallo, 2001; Buehler, Griffin, & Ross, 2002; Vallone, Griffin, Lin, & Ross, 1990). For example, research conducted in Canada and Britain has shown that if people are able to answer a few difficult questions correctly, they tend to overestimate just how much general knowledge they have (Griffin & Buehler, 1999). Anyone trying to improve human inference is thus up against an **overconfidence barrier** (Metcalfe, 1998). Many people seem to think that their reasoning processes are just fine the way they are; hence, there is no need for remedial action. One approach, then, might be to address this overconfidence directly, getting people to consider the possibility that they might be wrong. This tack was taken by Lord, Lepper, and Preston (1984), who found that when people were asked to consider the opposite point of view to their own, they realized there were other ways to construe the world than their own way; consequently, they made fewer errors in their judgments (Anderson, Lepper, & Ross, 1980; Hirt, Kardes, & Markman, 2004; Mussweiler, Strack, & Pfeiffer, 2000).

The greatest of all faults, I should say, is to become conscious of none.

—Thomas Carlyle, *essayist (1795–1881)*

Another approach is to directly teach people some basic statistical and methodological principles about how to reason correctly, with the hope that they will apply these principles in their everyday lives. Many of these principles are already taught in courses in statistics and research design, such as the idea that if you want to generalize from a sample of information (e.g., a group of welfare mothers) to a population (e.g., all welfare mothers), you must have a large, unbiased sample. Do people who take such courses apply these principles in their everyday lives? Are they less likely to make the kinds of mistakes we have discussed in this chapter? A number of studies have provided encouraging answers to these questions, showing that people's reasoning processes can be improved by university statistics courses, graduate training in research design, and even brief one-time lessons (Fong, Krantz, & Nisbett, 1986; Malloy, 2001; Nisbett, Krantz, Jepson, & Kunda, 1983; Nisbett, Fong, Lehman, & Cheng, 1987; Schaller, Asp, Rosell, & Heim, 1996). Thus, there is reason to be cautiously optimistic—we say cautiously because a study conducted at Concordia University found that training in statistics and research methods does not guarantee the transfer of these concepts to everyday life. Specifically, Mill, Gray, and Mandel (1994) found that in order to improve reasoning abilities, it was necessary to introduce tutorial sessions that focused explicitly on the application of course material to reasoning in everyday contexts (e.g., evaluating claims made by politicians, choosing between competing products).

The sign of a first-rate intelligence is the ability to hold two opposed ideas at the same time.

—F. Scott Fitzgerald *(1896–1940)*

In summary, there is reason to be hopeful about people's ability to overcome the kinds of mistakes we have documented in this chapter. And you don't have to go to graduate school to do it. Sometimes it helps simply to consider the opposite, as participants in the Lord and colleagues (1984) study did. Beyond this, formal training in statistics helps, at both the graduate and undergraduate levels—especially if your instructor illustrates how these principles apply in real-life situations. So, if you were dreading taking a university statistics course, take heart: It might not only satisfy a requirement for your major but improve your reasoning as well!

Modest doubt is called the beacon of the wise.

—William Shakespeare, *Troilus and Cressida, 1601*

Cultural Differences in Thinking

So far we have been focusing on the distinction between automatic versus controlled thinking. But there are also other ways of thinking—some of which depend on culture. To illustrate how culture creates differences in how people think, take a quick look at the first picture on this page. Okay, now take a quick look at the picture right beneath it: Did you notice any differences between the two pictures? Your answer might depend on the culture in which you grew up. Richard Nisbett at the University of Michigan, Takahiko Masuda, at the University of Alberta, and their colleagues have found that people who grow up in Western cultures tend to have an **analytic thinking style**, a type of thinking in which people focus on the properties of objects without considering their surrounding context. For example, Westerners are most likely to focus on the planes because they are the main objects in the pictures. They thus are more likely to notice changes in these objects, such as the fact that the passenger plane has more windows in the second picture than in the first (Masuda & Nisbett, 2006).

Take a quick look at these two photos and see whether you notice any differences between them. As discussed in the text, the differences you notice may have to do with the culture in which you grew up.

People who grow up in East Asian cultures (e.g., China, Japan, Korea) tend to have a **holistic thinking style**, a type of thinking in which people focus on the "whole picture"—that is, on the object (or person) and the context that surrounds that object, as well as on the relationships that exist between the objects (Masuda & Nisbett, 2001; Nisbett, 2003; Nisbett, 2001; Norenzayan & Nisbett, 2000). For example, East Asians are more likely to notice changes in the background of the pictures, such as the fact that the shape of the control tower changes from one to the other. (Note that in the actual study people saw 20-second videos of these scenes and tried to find all the differences between them. The pictures on this page are the last scenes from these two videos.) In more recent research, Masuda and colleagues hypothesized that a holistic thinking style would be associated with information-rich cultural products. To test this idea, they analyzed the content of portal pages of East Asian and North American government and university websites (Wang, Masuda, Ito, & Rashid, under review). As predicted, East Asian websites contained

Analytic Thinking Style

A type of thinking in which people focus on the properties of objects without considering their surrounding context; this type of thinking is common in Western cultures

Holistic Thinking Style

A type of thinking in which people focus on the overall context, particularly the ways in which objects relate to one another; this type of thinking is common in East Asian cultures (e.g., China, Japan, Korea)

much more information than Canadian and American websites. In another study in this series, the researchers reasoned that in cultures in which a lot of information tends to be presented, people have to develop efficient information search strategies. To test this, they asked East Asian and Canadian students attending the University of Alberta to find target objects on information-rich webpages. As predicted, East Asians were faster at this task than Canadians (Wang et al., *under review*). In Chapter 4 we will see that holistic versus analytic thinking also influences the perception of emotions in other people.

Recent research suggests that something very interesting is going on, at a physiological level, in people who engage in analytic versus holistic thinking. Trey Hedden and colleagues (2008) used functional magnetic resonance imaging (fMRI) to examine where in the brain cultural experience affects perceptual processing. Their participants, East Asians and European-Americans, underwent fMRI while making judgments about the length of lines inside boxes. Some of the participants were told to ignore the box around each line ("ignore context") and some were told to pay attention to the box around each line ("attend to context"). While participants were equally accurate at judging the lengths of the lines, they showed significantly more brain activity when they had to follow the instructions that were the opposite of their cultural thinking style. That is, American participants showed greater activation in higher-order cortical regions (frontal and parietal areas) when told to pay attention to the context, while East Asian participants showed greater activity in the same brain regions when told to ignore the context. Greater cortical activation means that the participant had to exert more attention (in a sense, had to work harder cognitively) when asked to perceive objects in a way that was not typical for him or her (Hedden, Katay, Aron, Markus, & Gabrieli, 2008).

A second group of researchers used event-related potentials (ERPs) to measure brain activity (Lewis, Goto, & Kong, 2008). While fMRI indicates which brain regions are active, ERPs provide a more fine-grained analysis of the onset and offset of neural firing. These researchers also presented participants with a series of simple perceptual tasks that involved visual information about "targets" and context. In an interesting twist, their participants were all Americans who had grown up in American culture but were of two different ethnic backgrounds: European-American or East Asian-American. The pattern of ERPs indicated that the European-American participants paid more attention to the targets while the East Asian-American participants paid more attention to the context surrounding the targets.

Where do these differences in holistic versus analytic thinking come from? According to recent research, one answer may be found by looking at actual differences in the environments in these cultures. Miyamoto, Nisbett, and Masuda (2006) took photographs in randomly chosen city scenes in Japan and the United States. They matched the scenes as best they could; for example, the sizes of the cities were equivalent, as were the buildings that were photographed in each city (e.g., hotels and public elementary schools). The researchers hypothesized that the scenes in the Japanese cities would be "busier"; that is, they would contain more objects that competed for people's attention than the scenes in the American cities. They were right. The Japanese scenes contained significantly more information and objects than the American scenes.

Could this be one reason why Americans focus more on a foreground object whereas East Asians focus more on the overall context? To find out, Miyamoto and colleagues did a second study in which they showed the pictures of American or Japanese cities to a sample of American and Japanese university students (Miyamoto, Nisbett, & Masuda, 2006). The students were asked to imagine that they were in the scene depicted in the each picture, with the idea that the Japanese pictures would prime holistic thinking whereas the American pictures would prime analytic thinking. Then the students completed the same airplane picture task described on the preceding page, in which they tried to detect the differences between two similar pictures. As predicted, the people who saw the photos of Japanese cities were more likely to detect changes in the *background* of the test pictures, whereas people who saw the pictures of the American cities were more likely to detect changes in the *main object* of the pictures. This finding suggests that people in all cultures are capable of thinking holistically or analytically. Other research conducted with students at Queen's University and students at Beijing University in China also has shown that analytic and holistic reasoning can be primed. Specifically, Canadian participants who received a holistic prime gave similar responses to Chinese participants (Spina, Ji, Guo, Zhang, Li, & Fabrigar, 2010).

An analogy that is often used is that the human mind is like a toolbox, filled with specific tools to help people think about and act in the social world. All humans have access to the same tools, but the culture in which they grew up can influence the ones they use the most (Norenzayan & Heine, 2005). If you live in a house that has screws instead of nails, you will use your screwdriver more than a hammer, but if your house contains nails and not screws, the screwdriver won't get much use. Thus, people have the same tools in their mental toolbox, but the environment in which they live, or even the environment which has been recently primed, triggers a reliance on one of the styles (Norenzayan, Choi, & Peng, 2007). Or, as John Gabrieli puts it, "Culture is not changing how you see the world, but rather how you think and interpret" (Gabrieli, as quoted in Goldberg, 2008, p. C3).

HOW WOULD YOU USE THIS?

By definition it is difficult to recognize our own automatic thinking, because it is nonconscious, unintentional, involuntary, and effortless. We don't have a special window through which we can watch our automatic minds at work, which makes it difficult to know the extent to which we are making quick assumptions about other people and the extent to which these assumptions are correct. Can you think of any indirect clues that suggest to people that they have made incorrect automatic assumptions about other people? For example, think back to the section of the chapter on self-fulfilling prophecies. Is there some way a middle-school teacher could tell whether he or she is making false assumptions about the math abilities of the boys and girls in his or her class? What about you in your everyday life: When you meet someone for the first time and get to know him or her, how can you tell whether your initial assumptions are correct? Would it help to compare notes with other people who know this person?

Summary

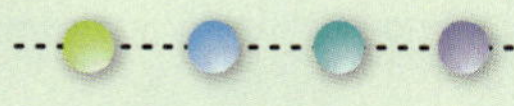

- **On Automatic Pilot: Low-Effort Thinking** A great deal of social cognition—how people think about themselves and the social world—involves automatic thinking, which is nonconscious, unintentional, involuntary, and effortless.
  - **People as Everyday Theorists: Automatic Thinking with Schemas** An important part of automatic thinking is using our past knowledge to organize and interpret new information. More specifically, people use schemas, which are mental structures that people use to organize their knowledge about the social world around themes or subjects and that influence what people notice, think about, and remember. Relying on schemas is adaptive and functional because schemas help reduce ambiguity, but people can be overzealous. For example, schemas tend to persist, even when we are confronted with contradictory information. Schemas also can cause problems such as self-fulfilling prophecies, whereby a schema or expectation about another person influences how we act toward that person, which causes that person to behave consistently with our expectation.

- **Mental Strategies and Shortcuts: Heuristics** Another form of automatic thinking is the use of judgmental heuristics, which are mental shortcuts people use to make judgments quickly and efficiently. Examples are the availability heuristic, whereby people base a judgment on the ease with which they can bring something to mind, and the representativeness heuristic, whereby people classify something according to how similar it is to a typical case. People also have a tendency to ignore base rate information—the prior probability that something or someone belongs in that classification. Heuristics are extremely useful and often produce accurate judgments but can be misused, producing faulty judgments.
- **The Pervasiveness of Automatic Thinking** Recent research suggests that a great deal of human thought occurs outside of conscious awareness. People unconsciously monitor what is going on around them, in case something important occurs that requires their conscious attention. Even people's goals can be unconsciously activated.

Controlled Social Cognition: High-Effort Thinking Not all social cognition is automatic; we also engage in controlled thinking, which is conscious, intentional, voluntary, and effortful.

- **Thinking about What Might Have Been: Counterfactual Reasoning** One form of controlled thinking is counterfactual reasoning, whereby people mentally change some aspect of the past as a way of imagining what might have been.
- **Thought Suppression and Ironic Processing** Another kind of controlled thinking is thought suppression, which is the attempt to avoid thinking about something. Research shows that thought suppression often backfires, causing people to think more about the topic they are trying to forget—especially when people are tired or distracted.

A Portrayal of Social Thinking In this chapter we documented several ways in which social cognition can go wrong, producing faulty judgments. We should keep in mind, however, that humans are very sophisticated social thinkers who have amazing cognitive abilities. People are like "flawed scientists"—brilliant thinkers who are attempting to discover the nature of the social world in a logical manner but do not do so perfectly.

- **Improving Human Thinking** People are affected by an overconfidence barrier, whereby they are too confident in the accuracy of their judgments. Research shows that some kinds of thinking, such as statistical reasoning, can be improved dramatically with training—such as taking a course in statistics.
- **Cultural Differences in Thinking** The human mind is like a toolbox, filled with specific tools to help people think about and act in the social world. All humans have access to the same tools, but the culture in which they grew up can influence the tools they use the most. Western cultures tend to emphasize an analytic thinking style, a type of thinking in which people focus on the properties of objects without considering their surrounding context. People who grow up in East Asian cultures tend to have a holistic thinking style, a type of thinking in which people focus on the overall context, particularly the ways in which objects relate to one another.

Social Perception

How We Come to Understand Other People

OUTLINE

AS YOU HAVE NO DOUBT NOTICED, OTHER PEOPLE ARE NOT easy to figure out. Why are they the way they are? Why do they do what they do? How frequently and urgently we pose these questions is demonstrated in this touching story, sent in by a reader to the *New York Times:*

> After ending an office romance, a female friend of mine threw a bag full of her former paramour's love letters, cards, and poems into an outside dumpster. The following day he called and wanted to know why she would throw out his letters. She was stunned. He explained that a homeless person going through the garbage read the correspondence and called the number found on a piece of stationery. The homeless man was curious as to why two people who seemed so in love could now be apart. "I would have called you sooner," the man told the former boyfriend, "but this was the first quarter I was given today." (De Marco, 1994)

The homeless man was down on his luck—no home, no money, reduced to rifling through garbage cans—and yet that endless fascination with the human condition still asserted itself. He needed to know why the couple broke up. He even spent his only quarter to find out.

We all have a fundamental fascination with explaining other people's behaviour. But the reasons why others behave as they do are usually hidden from us. All we have to go on is observable behaviour: what people do, what they say, their facial expressions, gestures, and tone of voice. Unfortunately, we can't read other people's minds; we can't know, truly and completely, who they are and what they mean. Instead, we rely on our impressions and theories, putting them together as well as we can, hoping they will lead to reasonably accurate and useful conclusions.

Our desire to understand people is so fundamental that it carries over into our hobbies and recreational lives. We go to movies, read novels, watch soap operas, and "people-watch" at airports because thinking about the behaviour of even strangers and fictional characters fascinates us. This basic aspect of human cognition has been exploited brilliantly by "reality TV" programmers, who cast television shows with real people instead of actors, and place them in unusual or difficult situations. This relatively new genre of television has proved to be a powerhouse. Since the original version of *Survivor*, shot in 2000, reality shows have crowded the top 10 list of most-watched shows every year. Why are these shows so popular? Because we enjoy figuring people out. We do it all day long, as a necessary part of social survival, and then we go home, turn on the television, and do it for fun and entertainment. Take, for example, two popular reality shows that are particularly interesting from a social psychological perspective: *Survivor* and *American Idol* (and its now defunct Canadian counterpart, *Canadian Idol*). In *Survivor*, the contestants scheme, lie, and form secret alliances as, one by one, they vote their fellow contestants off the show in hope of being the last survivor and collecting the reward of $1 million. In a typical segment, we see one contestant form an alliance with another and then turn around and betray that person without blinking an eye. When are the contestants lying and when are they telling the truth? And what are they really like as people—are they deceitful, manipulative opportunists or are they just playing the game? In the latest incarnation of *Survivor*, eliminated contestants are sent to Redemption Island where they duel with other eliminated contestants to gain the chance to return to *Survivor* and compete for the $1 million. This latest twist sparks even more devious plotting, backstabbing, and scheming.

In *American Idol*, we watch an array of contestants compete to be named the favourite singer and winner of a lucrative recording contract. The compelling aspects of the show are threefold: The contestants are very much "real people," with a variety of backgrounds; their talent varies, so much so that the early episodes of the show present people who truly can't sing (but naively think they can); and the judges can be very critical and even cruel in their feedback. In short, an emotional train wreck is put into motion, wherein some contestants will be embarrassed and maligned, and will dissolve into tears on camera. Clearly, viewers enjoy watching this real-life emotional spectacle and competition; *American Idol* has become the most popular show on U.S. television since it first debuted in 2002. And viewers play a critical role in the process—they vote someone off the show each week. Although interest in the show is waning somewhat, in the 2009 *American Idol* finale, a record number of votes—approximately 88 million—were cast once the show got down to two finalists (Melisurgo, 2010). More Americans voted in that *Idol* finale than had voted in any election for a U.S. president. Viewers so enjoy making these decisions that many websites (including online betting sites) have spontaneously arisen to allow them to communicate with one another about the show (Arthur, 2006).

Social Perception

The study of how we form impressions of other people and make inferences about them.

Why do we spend so much time and energy observing and trying to explain the behaviour of others? Because doing so helps us understand and predict our social world (Heider, 1958; Kelley, 1967). In this chapter, we discuss **social perception**—the study of how we form impressions of other people and make inferences about them. One important source of information that we use is nonverbal behaviour, such as facial expressions, body movements, and tone of voice.

Connect to MyPsychLab

To access the Critical Thinking question on speed dating, go to MyPsychLab

Nonverbal Behaviour

What do we know about people when we first meet them? We know what we can see and hear, and even though we know we should not judge a book by its cover, this kind of easily observable information is critical to our first impressions. For example, physical characteristics such as attractiveness influence the way we judge others (Hatfield & Sprecher, 1986a). We also pay a great deal of attention to what people say. After all, our most noteworthy accomplishment as a species is the development of verbal language. But people's words are only part of the story. We communicate volumes without words (Ambady & Rosenthal, 1992, 1993; De Paulo & Friedman, 1998; Gifford, 1991, 1994). **Nonverbal communication** refers to how people communicate, intentionally or unintentionally, without words. Facial expressions, tone of voice, gestures, body position and movement, the use of touch, and eye gaze are the most frequently used and most revealing channels of nonverbal communication (Henley, 1977; Knapp & Hall, 2006).

Nonverbal Communication

The way in which people communicate, intentionally or unintentionally, without words; nonverbal cues include facial expressions, tone of voice, gestures, body position and movement, the use of touch, and eye gaze

Interestingly, our ability to read nonverbal cues is not limited to members of our species. Researchers at the Université du Québec à Montréal photographed cats expressing different emotions (e.g., fear was produced by running a vacuum cleaner; Thibault, Bourgeois, & Hess, 2006). It turned out that people were remarkably accurate at identifying the cats' emotions. We also are not the only species that can read nonverbal communication. For example, dogs are adept at reading not only "dog nonverbals" but human nonverbals as well, and dogs even outperform chimpanzees when it comes to understanding human nonverbal cues (Hare & Tomasello, 2005). Nonetheless, human nonverbal communication is particularly eloquent and sophisticated.

In other research conducted at the Université du Québec à Montréal using facial electromyography (recording the movements of facial muscles), it has been shown that we automatically mimic other people's facial expressions, such as happiness, sadness, and disgust (Hess & Blairy, 2001). The extent of mimicry differs, depending on our gender and the gender of the person with whom we are interacting. For example, women are especially likely to mimic other people's smiles (Hess & Bourgeois, 2010). It is also the case that we are more likely to mimic when we like our interaction partner or consider him or her to be a member of our group (Bourgeois & Hess, 2008). Hess and colleagues (2010) suggest that our tendency to mimic other people's facial expressions may reflect empathy—the capacity to feel what someone else is feeling.

This capacity may even be hard-wired into our brains. Recent research in neuroscience has found that humans (and our close relatives, primates) have a special kind of brain cell called *mirror neurons*. These neurons respond when we perform an action *and* when we see someone else perform the same action (Gallese, Fadiga, Fogassi, & Rizzolatti, 1996). For example, when we see someone crying, these mirror neurons fire automatically and involuntarily, just as if we were crying ourselves. Bruno Wicker and colleagues (2003) investigated the role of mirror neurons in the emotion of disgust. They used functional magnetic resonance imaging (fMRI) to look at the pattern of brain cells firing in research participants as they performed two different tasks: smelling obnoxious, gross odours and watching a film of an actor wrinkling his face with a disgusted look. The researchers found that feeling disgusted oneself (from smelling something gross) and observing someone else's facial expression of disgust activated the same region of a participant's brain (Wicker, Keysers, Plailly, Royet, Gallese, & Rizzolatti, 2003). Thus, one way that we are able to connect with each other emotionally is through the activation of these mirror neurons. At least some of the time, as researcher Vittorio Gallese put it, "We don't have to *think* about what other people are . . . feeling, we simply *know*"—in short, we feel it too (Gallese, as quoted in Winerman, 2005, p. 50).

Nonverbal cues serve many functions in communication. They help people express their emotions, their attitudes, and their personality. For example, you express "I'm angry" by narrowing your eyes, lowering your eyebrows, staring intently, and setting your mouth in a thin, straight line. You convey the attitude "I like you" with smiles and extended eye contact. And you convey the personality trait of being an extravert with broad gestures and frequent changes in voice pitch and inflection (Knapp & Hall, 2006).

Nonverbal cues can also substitute for a verbal message. Hand gestures, such as flashing the "okay" sign (forming a circle with the thumb and forefinger and the rest of the fingers curved above the circle) or drawing a finger across your throat, convey clear messages without any words at all (Ekman, 1965).

Nonverbal forms of communication have typically been studied individually, in their separate "channels" (e.g., eye gaze or gestures), even though in everyday life nonverbal cues of many kinds occur all at the same time in a dazzling orchestration of information (Archer & Akert, 1980, 1984). Let's focus on a few of these channels.

An eye can threaten like a loaded and leveled gun, or can insult like hissing or kicking; or, in its altered mood, by beams of kindness, it can make the heart dance with joy.

—Ralph Waldo Emerson, *The Conduct of Life, 1860*

Facial Expressions of Emotion

The crown jewel of nonverbal communication is the facial expressions channel. This aspect of communication has the longest history of research, beginning with Charles Darwin's (1872) book *The Expression of the Emotions in Man and Animals*. Its primacy is attributable to the exquisite communicativeness of the human face (Kappas, 1997; McHugo & Smith, 1996; Wehrle, Kaiser, Schmidt, & Scherer, 2000). Look at the accompanying photographs; you can probably figure out the meaning of these expressions with very little effort.

Simulate on **mypsychlab**
Facial Expressions of Emotion

Encode

To express or emit nonverbal behaviour, such as smiling or patting someone on the back

Decode

To interpret the meaning of the nonverbal behaviour other people express, such as deciding that a pat on the back was an expression of condescension and not kindness

Darwin's research on facial expressions has had a major impact on the field in many areas. We will focus on his belief that the primary emotions conveyed by the face are universal—the idea that all human beings everywhere **encode** or express these emotions in the same way, and all human beings can **decode** or interpret them with equal accuracy. Darwin's (1872) interest in evolution led him to believe that nonverbal forms of communication were species-specific and not culture-specific. He maintained that facial expressions were vestiges of once-useful physiological reactions—for example, if early hominids ate something that tasted terrible, they would have wrinkled their noses in displeasure (from the bad smell) and expelled the food from their mouths. Note that the photograph showing the disgusted expression demonstrates this sort of reaction. Such facial expressions then acquired evolutionary significance; being able to communicate such emotional states (e.g., the feeling of disgust, not for food but for another person or a situation) had survival value for the developing species (Hansen & Hansen, 1988; Izard, 1994; McArthur & Baron, 1983; Susskind, Cusi, Feiman, Grabski, & Anderson, 2008). For example, being able to perceive that another person is angry (and therefore potentially dangerous) would have greater evolutionary significance for early humans—it might have meant the difference between life and death. D. Vaughn Becker and colleagues (2007) have intriguing results in this area. They found that research participants were faster and more accurate at decoding angry expressions on male faces and at detecting happy expressions on female faces. Furthermore, when researchers subtly manipulated (via computer-generated faces) how male or female the face looked, and the strength of the emotion shown, researchers again found a strong connection between anger and men's faces, and happiness and women's faces. The researchers suggest that from an evolutionary perspective, the costs and benefits of perceiving anger and happiness would vary depending on whether the encoder was male or female (Becker, Kenrick, Neuberg, Blackwell, & Smith, 2007).

When the eyes say one thing, and the tongue another, a practiced man relies on the language of the first.

—Ralph Waldo Emerson, *The Conduct of Life*, 1860

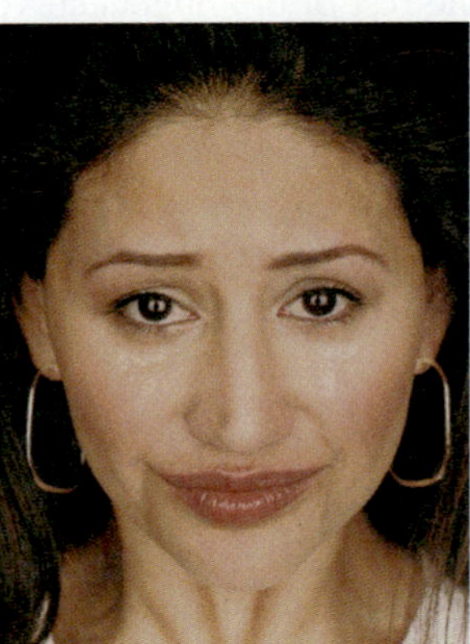

These photographs depict facial expressions of the six major emotions. Can you guess the emotion expressed on each face?

ANSWERS: (clockwise, beginning with upper-left photo): anger, fear, disgust, sadness, surprise, and happiness.

Was Darwin right? Are facial expressions of emotion universal? According to Paul Ekman and Walter Friesen, the answer is yes, at least for six major emotions: anger, happiness, surprise, fear, disgust, and sadness (Ekman & Friesen, 1986). To demonstrate that the facial expressions of these emotions are universal, Ekman and Friesen (1971) travelled to New Guinea, where they studied the decoding ability of the South Fore, a preliterate society that had had little contact with Western civilization. They told the Fore people brief stories with emotional content and then showed them photographs of American men and women expressing the six emotions. The Fore participants' job was to match the facial expressions of emotion to the stories. The researchers concluded that the Fore people were almost as accurate as American research participants had been. They then asked the Fore people to demonstrate, while being photographed, facial expressions that would match the stories they were told. When these photographs were shown to American research participants, they were also decoded quite accurately. Based on these and other data, it is generally accepted that the ability to interpret these six emotions is universal—part of being human, and not a product of people's cultural experience (Biehl et al., 1997; Ekman, 1993, 1994; Ekman et al., 1987; Elfenbein & Ambady, 2002; Izard, 1994).

Simulate on mypsychlab
Recognizing Facial Expressions of Emotions

Watch on mypsychlab
Basic Emotions

Subsequently, other emotions have been added to this list of basic emotions. These additions tend to be emotions that are involved in social interaction (and, therefore, probably occurred later in evolution)—namely, contempt (Haidt & Keltner, 1999; Matsumoto & Ekman, 2004; see the photo on this page), pride, embarrassment, anxiety, shame, and guilt (Ekman, O'Sullivan, & Matsumoto, 1991; Harrigan & O'Connell, 1996; Keltner & Shiota, 2003; Tracy & Robins, 2006, 2007). A team of researchers from several universities in Canada and Europe have recently found that pain has an identifiable facial expression (Simon, Craig, Gosselin, Belin, & Rainville, 2008). We note that much research on emotion continues to focus on the original six basic emotions identified by Ekman and colleagues.

Are Facial Expressions of Emotion Universal? Not all emotion theorists have agreed with Ekman's conclusion that there are six (or more) universal facial expressions. As we shall see, there are some thorny issues involved in drawing conclusions about universality. One issue concerns the level of accuracy that participants must achieve in order to conclude that a given facial expression is being perceived in the same way across cultures. For example, when Ekman and Friesen (1975) showed photographs of their six basic emotions to participants in the United States, Brazil, Chile, Argentina, Japan, and New Guinea, at least 82 percent of participants in each culture labelled their happiness facial expression as such. However, these percentages were substantially lower for some of the other emotions. For example, the fear expression was identified by only 54 percent of participants in both Argentina and New Guinea, and less than half (44 percent) of the New Guinea participants recognized the disgust expression.

According to Russell, Suzuki, and Ishida (1993), there is even less agreement when participants are asked to name the emotion shown in a face, rather than to select emotion terms from a list in which the number of emotion terms matches the number of faces (a common procedure in Ekman and Friesen's studies). Russell and colleagues approached adults in various public places in Canada, Greece, and Japan, and showed them photographs of the six basic facial expressions of emotions, plus contempt. Once again, the facial expression of happiness was identified by the majority of respondents in each country, whereas recognition rates for the other emotions were much lower. For example, only 14 percent of Japanese participants generated fear-related words for the fear expression. The contempt photograph was not labelled as such by participants in any of the cultures. Similar findings have been obtained in studies conducted with Canadian, Chinese, Japanese, Indian, and European participants (Elfenbein, Beaupré, Lèvesque, & Hess, 2007; Hess & Blairy, 2001; Hess, Philippot, & Blairy, 1998; Mandal, Bryden, & Bulman-Fleming, 1996; Yik, Meng, & Russell, 1998; Yik & Russell, 1999). Elfenbein and colleagues (2007) recently compared the facial expressions of Canadians and Africans and found evidence of variability. Interestingly, the cultural differences

Recent research suggests that "contempt" may be a universally recognized expression.

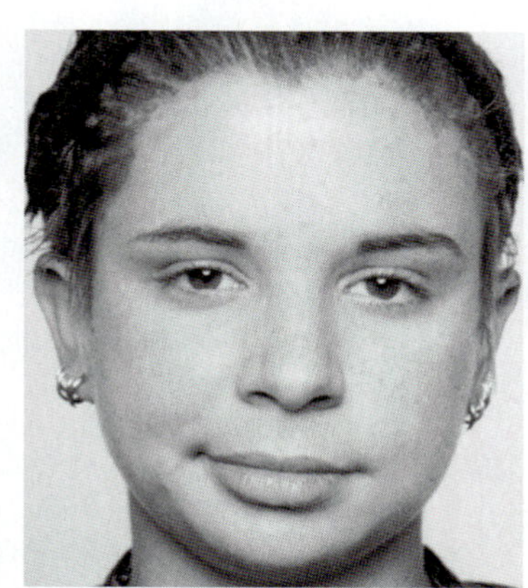

were most pronounced for social emotions such as contempt and anger and least pronounced for reflex-based emotions such as disgust and surprise. If the perception of certain basic emotions is universal, people in all cultures should be able to identify all of these emotions with relative ease. This does not appear to be the case. The Try It! exercise on the next page encourages you to come up with your own answer to the question of how many basic facial expressions of emotion exist.

The claim of universality also suggests that basic facial expressions of emotion should be easily identified regardless of the context in which they are perceived. This also does not appear to be the case. In a series of studies conducted at the University of British Columbia, James Russell and Beverley Fehr (1987) found that the judgment of a given facial expression depended on what other faces were presented. If, for example, participants were exposed to a happy face and then a neutral face, the neutral face was perceived as sad. If a sad face was encountered first, the neutral face appeared happy. Most important, these effects were not limited to neutral faces. An angry face was perceived as sad, for example, when participants were first exposed to an expression such as disgust. Similar results were found in a more recent series of experiments conducted at McMaster University (Rutherford, Chattha, & Krysko, 2008). Researchers at the University of Toronto and at the Hebrew University of Jerusalem recently have shown that the context (e.g., a disgust face in a fear context) influences which parts of the face people fixate on (e.g., eyes versus mouth) in trying to decode the emotion being expressed (Aviezer, Hassin, Ryan, Grady, Susskind, Anderson, Moscovitch, & Bentin, 2008). The situation a person is in also can influence the emotion read from a face. Consider, for example, the facial expression of the woman in the middle of the top row on page 92. Most people perceive this face as showing fear. Do you agree? At the University of British Columbia, Carroll and Russell (1996) found that an intense fear expression was perceived as anger if participants were told that the person had just experienced an extremely frustrating situation.

One final note on this topic: As you may recall from Chapter 3, people in East Asian cultures are more likely to be *holistic* thinkers, focusing on the focal object and the context in which it is situated. People in Western cultures tend to be *analytic* thinkers, focusing on the central object and paying little, if any, attention to the context. This difference in thinking style influences the perception of facial expressions of emotion (Masuda, Ellsworth, Mesquita, Leu, Tanida, & Van de Veerdonk, 2008). For example, University of Alberta researcher Takahiko Masuda and colleagues (2008) presented research participants in the United States and Japan with cartoon drawings of people in groups. One person in each cartoon was the central figure, shown in the foreground. This person had a facial expression that was happy, sad, angry, or neutral. The other people in the group had facial expressions that either matched the central figure or were different. The participants' task was to judge the central person's emotion. The researchers found that the facial expressions on the group members' faces had little effect on Americans' ratings of the central figure. If that figure was smiling broadly, he received a high rating for "happy." It didn't matter what the rest of the group was expressing. In comparison, the facial expressions of the group members had a significant effect on the Japanese participants' ratings of the central figure. A broad smile was interpreted as very happy if the group members were also smiling; the same broad smile was interpreted as significantly less happy if the other group members were looking sad or angry. In short, the meaning of the cartoon character's facial expression changed given his "context"—what the other characters standing next to him were feeling (Masuda et al., 2008).

Interestingly, Masuda and colleagues (2008) measured the eye-tracking movements of the participants as they looked at the cartoons. The Japanese spent more time looking at the cartoon characters in the background than did the Americans. Both groups began by looking at the central character, but after one second, the Japanese started to scan their eyes over the other characters significantly more than did the Americans. As Dr. Denise Park puts it, using a camera analogy, "The Americans are more zoom and the East Asians are more panoramic" (Parks, as quoted in Goldberg, 2008, p. C1).

How Many Universal Facial Expressions of Emotion Are There?

How many universal facial expressions of emotion are there? Come up with your own answer the next time you are with a group of friends. You can take turns posing facial expressions of emotion while the others in the group try to guess the emotion that is being conveyed. Here are some emotions you may wish to focus on:

1. **Happiness, sadness, anger, fear, disgust, surprise** These are the six facial expressions originally identified as universal by Ekman and Friesen (1975). If these are basic, universal facial expressions, it should be relatively easy for the people doing the posing to show those emotions on their faces. It should also be easy for the rest of the group to identify the emotion being displayed.
2. **Contempt** This is an emotion that Paul Ekman has more recently added to the list of universal facial expressions. Is contempt easily conveyed via facial expression? Was it easily recognized?
3. **Embarrassment** Research by Dacher Keltner (1995; Keltner & Shiota, 2003) suggests that embarrassment has a distinctive facial expression—the person turns his or her head away, looks down and to the side, and smiles with pressed lips. Is this how embarrassment looked when it was posed in your group? Should it be considered a universal facial expression?
4. **Heroism, humour/amusement, love, peace, wonder** Are these emotions easily conveyed via facial expression? According to an analysis of ancient Hindu writings, these emotions—along with anger, disgust, fear, sadness, and shame/embarrassment—may be universal (Hejmadi, Davidson, & Rozin, 2000). When participants in India and the United States were presented with videotaped expressions of these emotions (conveyed via facial expression and body movement), they were quite accurate at identifying them.
5. **Pride and shame** Recently, psychologists have suggested that pride, and its opposite, shame, should be added to the list of universal emotions (Tracy & Robins, 2007; Tracy & Robins, 2008; Tracy & Matsumoto, 2008).
6. **Pain** A group of researchers from a number of Canadian universities recently found that people can recognize the facial expression of pain (Simon, Craig, Gosselin, Belin, & Rainville, 2008).

So, exactly how many universal facial expressions of emotion are there? Which emotions should be included in that set? If you and your friends disagree, take heart—emotion researchers aren't quite sure either.

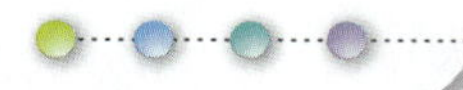

This is not to say that North Americans are completely oblivious to the context in which faces are perceived. Indeed, in a recent series of studies, Canadian and Japanese participants were presented with happy and sad faces and were asked to identify, as quickly as possible, whether each face was showing positive or negative emotions. The faces were presented on a background of different landscapes that were either positive or negative in appearance. Both Canadians and Japanese were faster at identifying facial expressions when the expression and background matched (e.g., happy face in a pleasant landscape) than when the expression and background conflicted (Ito, Masudo, & Hoiki, 2011). However, in general, it is the case that East Asians pay more attention to the context than do Westerners.

Why Is Decoding Sometimes Inaccurate? Emotion theorists do agree, however, on some other factors that limit the accuracy with which facial expressions are decoded. First, people frequently display **affect blends** (Ekman & Friesen, 1975), wherein one part of their face registers one emotion while another part registers a different emotion. Take a look at the photographs on the next page and see if you can tell which two emotions are being expressed in each face. In the photograph on the left, we see a blend of anger (the eye and eyebrow region) and disgust (the nose and mouth region). (It may help to cover half the photograph with your hand to see each emotion clearly.) This is the sort of expression you might display if a person told you something that was both horrible and inappropriate—you'd be disgusted with the content and angry that the person had told you. Second, at times, people try to appear less emotional than they are so that no one will know how they really feel. For example, if someone says something mean to you,

Affect Blend

A facial expression in which one part of the face registers one emotion while another part of the face registers a different emotion

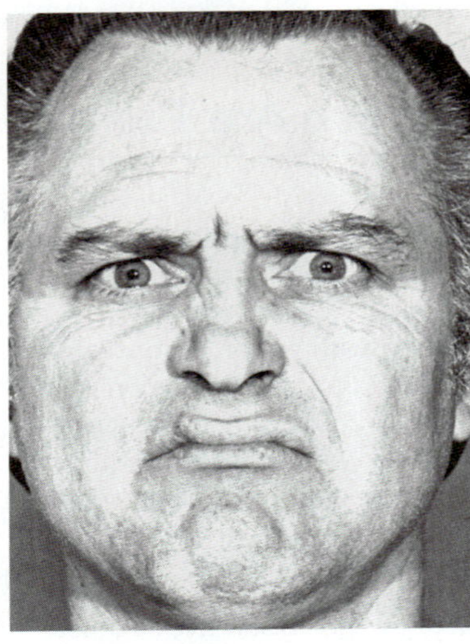
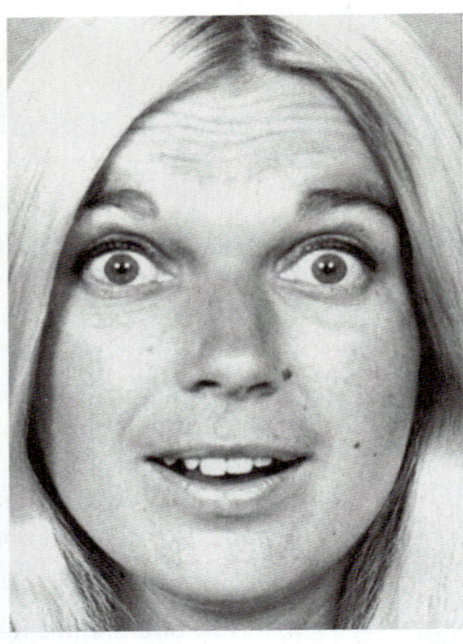

Often people express more than one emotion at the same time. Can you tell which emotions these people are expressing? The answers are printed below.

(Adapted from Ekman & Friesen, 1975)

ANSWERS: The man is expressing a blend of anger and disgust. The woman is expressing a blend of surprise and happiness.

you may hide your hurt feelings, allowing nothing to show on your face. A third reason that decoding facial expressions can be difficult has to do with culture. We turn to this topic next.

Culture and Nonverbal Communication

For decades, Paul Ekman and his colleagues have studied the influence of culture on the display of emotions (Ekman & Davidson, 1994; Ekman & Friesen, 1969). They have concluded that **display rules** are particular to each culture and dictate what kind of emotional expression people are supposed to show. For example, in many cultures, it is considered appropriate for men to display "powerful" emotions such as anger, contempt, and disgust, and for women to display "powerless" emotions such as fear and sadness. This gender difference has been found in research conducted with Canadian, American, and Japanese participants (Fehr & Baldwin, 1996; Hareli, Shomrat, & Hess, 2009; Sadfar, Friedlmeier, Matsumoto, Kwantes, Kakai, & Shigemasu, 2009). Thus, when Canadian novelist Robertson Davies portrays a funeral scene in *Murther and Walking Spirits* (1991) with the phrase, "they sat in rows of weeping men and grim-faced women," he realizes that this description runs contrary to cultural norms, and adds an explanation: "For in our day there has been a reversal which makes it perfectly all right for a man to give way to feeling, whereas women must show no such weakness." So far, the reversal about which Davies speaks appears to exist only in fiction.

Display Rules

Culturally determined rules about which emotional expressions are appropriate to show

In Japan, traditional cultural rules dictate that women should not exhibit a wide, uninhibited smile (Ramsey, 1981). Japanese women will generally hide their wide smiles behind their hands, while Western women are allowed—indeed, encouraged—to smile broadly and frequently (Henley, 1977; Hess & Bourgeois, 2010; La France, Hecht, & Paluck, 2003).

In collectivist cultures, the expression of strong negative emotions is discouraged because doing so can disrupt group harmony. Thus, in Japan, people tend to cover up negative facial expressions with smiles and laughter and to display fewer facial expressions in general compared to Canadians and Americans (Aune & Aune, 1996; Gudykunst, Ting-Toomey, & Nishida, 1996; Leathers, 1997; Yuki, Maddux, & Masuda, 2007; Sadfar et al., 2009).

In India, also a collectivist country, expressions of fear and anger are not very distinct, making it difficult for both Canadians and Indians to identify them (Mandal, Bryden, & Bulman-Fleming, 1996). Indians also judge fear and anger as more unpleasant than do Canadians. The researchers suggest that because of collectivist cultural norms, Indians probably have less experience displaying these emotions and perceive them as more aversive when expressed. A recent study that included over 5000 participants from 32 different countries (including Canada) confirms that the more individualistic a culture, the more likely it is that the expression of emotion is encouraged (Matsumoto, Yoo, Fontaine, Anguas-Wong, Arriola, Ataca, & Grossi, 2008). In contrast, in collectivist cultures such as Japan, Korea, and China, moderation is prescribed (Leu, Mesquita, Ellsworth, ZhiYong, Huijuan, Buchtel, Karasawa, & Masuda, 2010).

There are, of course, other channels of nonverbal communication. These nonverbal cues are shaped by culture as well. Eye contact and eye gaze are particularly powerful nonverbal cues. In North America, most people become suspicious when a person doesn't "look them in the eye" while speaking, and they find talking to someone who is wearing dark sunglasses disconcerting. However, as you can see in Figure 4.1, in other parts of the world, direct eye gaze is considered invasive or disrespectful.

Cultural Differences in Nonverbal Communication

Many forms of nonverbal behaviour are specific to a given culture. Not only do some of the nonverbal behaviours of one culture mean nothing in another, but the same nonverbal behaviour can exist in two cultures but have very different meanings in each. Such nonverbal differences can lead to misunderstanding when people from different societies interact. Some of these cultural differences are noted here.

Eye contact and gaze

In North American culture, direct eye contact is valued; a person who won't "look you in the eye" is perceived as being evasive or even untruthful. However, in many parts of the world, direct eye contact is considered disrespectful, especially with superiors. For example, in Nigeria, Puerto Rico, and Thailand, children are taught not to make direct eye contact with their teachers and other adults. Many Aboriginal people in North America use minimal eye contact as well. Japanese use far less direct eye contact than North Americans. In contrast, Arabs use a great deal of eye contact, with a gaze that would be considered piercing by people from some other cultures.

Personal space and touching

Societies vary in whether they are high-contact cultures, in which people stand close to each other and touch frequently, or low-contact cultures, in which people maintain more interpersonal space and touch less often. High-contact cultures include Middle Eastern, South American, and southern European countries. Low-contact cultures include North American countries, northern European countries, Asian countries, and most North American Aboriginal cultures. Cultures also differ in how appropriate they consider same-sex touching among friends. For example, in Korea and Egypt, men and women hold hands, link arms, or walk hip to hip with their same-sex friends, and these nonverbal behaviours carry no sexual connotation. In North America, such behaviour is much less common, particularly between male friends.

Hand and head gestures

The "OK" sign: In North America, this sign means "OK." In Japan, this hand gesture means "money; in France, it means "zero"; in Mexico, it means "sex"; and in Ethiopia, it means "homosexuality." Finally, in some South American countries, like Brazil, it is an obscene gesture, carrying the same meaning as the American "flipping the bird" sign.

The "thumb up" gesture: In North America, this sign means "OK." Several European countries have a similar meaning for this gesture; for example, in France it means "excellent!" In Japan, the same gesture means "boyfriend," while in Iran and Sardinia, it is an obscene gesture.

The "hand-purse" gesture: This gesture, which is formed by straightening the fingers and thumb of one hand and bringing them together so the tips touch, pointing upwards, has no clear meaning in North American culture. However, in Italy, it means "What are you trying to say?"; in Spain, it means "good"; in Tunisia, it means "slow down"; and in Malta, it means "you may seem good, but you are really bad."

Nodding the head: In North America, nodding one's head up and down means "Yes" and shaking it from side to side means "No." However, in some parts of Africa and India, the opposite is true: nodding up and down means "No," and shaking from side to side means "Yes." In Korea, shaking one's head from side to side means "I don't know" (which in North America is communicated by a shrug of the shoulders). Finally, Bulgarians indicate disagreement by throwing their heads back and then returning them to an upright position—which is frequently mistaken by North Americans as meaning agreement.

FIGURE 4.1
Cultural differences in nonverbal communication.

Cultures also vary greatly in what is considered normative use of personal space (Hall, 1969). For example, in countries such as Canada and the United States, most people like to have a bubble of open space, at least 0.5 metres in radius, surrounding them; in comparison, in some other cultures, strangers will think nothing of standing right next to each other, to the point of touching (see Figure 4.1). Differences in personal space can lead to misunderstandings when people of different cultures interact. For example, when Neil Malamuth was at the University of Manitoba, he helped organize a student exchange program in which North American students travelled to Israel. On one occasion, he organized a dance so the students from the two countries could get to know one another. Because of cultural differences in personal space, there were some unintended consequences:

> The scripted behaviour for an Israeli female in slow dances is generally not to have direct bodily contact with her dancing partner unless she is intimately involved with him. North American scripts, as you know, frequently prescribe body contact in such dances even when no intimacy is involved or desired. The consequence of the different cultural scripts was that the Israeli males thought that the North American women with whom they danced desired immediate sexual intimacy. The North American males dancing with Israeli partners, on the other hand, seemed very uncomfortable in being kept at a physical distance and later reported that they had been thinking that the Israelis must have found something about them highly offensive. (Malamuth, 1983)

Gestures of the hands and arms are also a fascinating means of communication. We are adept at understanding certain gestures, such as the "okay" sign (see Figure 4.1) and "giving someone the finger" (also known as the "up yours" gesture; Wolfgang & Wolofsky, 1991), in which one bends all the fingers down at the first knuckle except the longest, middle finger. Gestures such as these, for which there are clear, well-understood definitions, are called **emblems** (Archer, 1997a; Ekman & Friesen, 1975). The important point about emblems is that they, too, are not universal; each culture has devised its own emblems. For example, Wolfgang and Wolofsky (1991) photographed actors displaying 23 different Canadian emblems. They asked Canadians and students from Asian, Latin, and Mediterranean countries to identify them. Overall, identification rates were high because even the participants from other countries already had some exposure to Canadian emblems. However, Canadians showed the highest rate of correct identification (97 percent). Thus, when the late prime minister Pierre Trudeau gave protesters "the finger," it was a clear communicative sign that protesters and the media at the time had no difficulty interpreting. In some parts of Europe, however, one would have to make a quick gesture with a cupped hand under one's chin to convey the same message.

Emblems

Nonverbal gestures that have well-understood definitions within a given culture; they usually have direct verbal translations, such as the "okay" sign

In more recent research, English Canadians, French Canadians, and people in Germany were asked to indicate the gestures they would use to communicate numbers (e.g., "How would you order three beers in a bar?"). It was found that the gestures used to signal numerals differed by culture. For example, Germans were more likely to use their thumb to indicate the first numeral; English and French Canadians were more likely to start with their index finger (Pika, Nicoladis, & Marentette, 2009).

In conclusion, many forms of nonverbal behaviour are specific to a given culture. A gesture that has meaning in one culture may not mean anything in another. Moreover, the same nonverbal behaviour can exist in two cultures, but have very different meanings in each. Such nonverbal differences can lead to misunderstanding when people from different societies interact.

CONNECTIONS

The Email Dilemma: Communicating without Nonverbal Cues

There you are, working at 4:00 in the morning on your psychology paper, which is due the next afternoon. You have a question and decide to email your professor, figuring there may be a chance he'll respond the next morning. You add a little joke about "waiting until the last minute" to do your paper, when in fact the complexity of your question should indicate that you've been working on it for days. Next morning, a blistering email arrives from your professor, criticizing you for not taking the assignment seriously. Oh dear. Your professor didn't get that you were joking.

This scenario demonstrate the dilemma of email communication: Words go out, but there are no nonverbal cues to give them additional meaning. Humour, sarcasm, sadness, and other emotions are stripped away and your words stand alone, potentially open to misinterpretation. Sometimes we try to clarify our words by inserting *emoticons*, like this one: ☺. Although many emoticons exist, they can be inappropriate if your message is a formal one, and they are often difficult to interpret. For example, what does "%-(" or ";~/" mean? ("I'm confused" and "I'm unsure," respectively; Kruger, Epley, Parker, & Ng, 2005).

Do email writers realize to a sufficient extent that the loss of nonverbal cues can be a problem? Research by Justin Kruger and colleagues (2005) suggests no. They conducted a study where college students were given a number of topics about which to communicate (e.g., dorm life, dating), which were matched to one of four emotions: sarcasm, sadness, anger, or seriousness. Their job was to construct a statement on the topic that successfully conveyed the associated emotion. They communicated their statements in one of three ways: face-to-face to another person; to another person but using their voice only; or via an email. Finally, participants communicated their messages to either a stranger or a close friend.

Before they delivered their statements, participants were asked to what extent they thought they had successfully communicated the emotion in their message. As you can see in Figure 4.2, this anticipated accuracy is very high. Participants were very confident of their communicative abilities. Regardless of the mode of interaction, they felt they'd communicated accurately almost 90 percent of the time. Next, the message recipients were asked to indicate what emotion was in the message—the actual accuracy. As Figure 4.2 shows, recipients were significantly less likely to get the emotional meaning if the message was communicated via email. To make these results even more worrisome, participants' friends did no better at decoding the correct emotion than did complete strangers! Thus, email writers were overconfident about their ability to communicate emotion with words alone—they thought they had communicated clearly, but in fact, they had not (Kruger et al., 2005).

The moral of the story: Relying on words alone, as occurs in email, means using an impoverished medium of communication. Be careful. Be very, very careful when you email. You can easily be misunderstood, and those misunderstandings (as we'll see throughout this chapter) can have serious effects on your interactions with others. And remember too that you are very likely to think your meaning is clear to the recipient of an email, when in fact, it may be clear only to *you*.

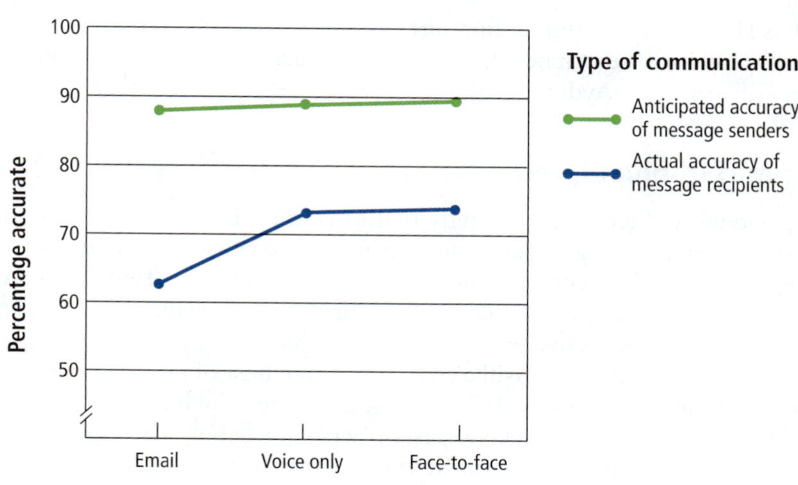

FIGURE 4.2

Accuracy at communicating emotions in three types of messages.

Although message senders were highly confident they could communicate sarcasm, sadness, anger, and seriousness in all of the three types of messages, they were in fact most likely to fail to communicate the emotions accurately over email. This occurred whether the email recipients were their friends or strangers.

(Adapted from Kruger et al., 2005)

To summarize, you can learn a great deal about people from their nonverbal behaviour, including their attitudes, emotions, and personality traits. Nonverbal behaviour offers many bits of information—"data" that we then use to construct our overall impressions or theories about others. But nonverbal cues are just the beginning of social perception. We turn now to the cognitive processes people use when forming impressions of others.

Connect to MyPsychLab
What do you think has influenced your personality? To take a survey on what has shaped your personality, go to MyPsychLab

Implicit Personality Theories: Filling in the Blanks

As we saw in Chapter 3, when people are unsure about the nature of the social world, they use their schemas to fill in the gaps (Fiske & Taylor, 1991; Kunda, 1999). Thus, when we are trying to understand other people, we can use just a few observations of a person as a starting point, and then, using our schemas, create a much fuller understanding of what that person is like (Kim & Rosenberg, 1980). Schemas allow us to form impressions quickly, without having to spend weeks with people to figure out what they are like.

Implicit Personality Theory
A type of schema people use to group various kinds of personality traits together; for example, many people believe that if someone is kind, he or she is generous as well

This kind of schema is called an **implicit personality theory**, a term which refers to people's ideas about what kinds of personality traits go together (Asch, 1946; Schneider, 1973; Sedikides & Anderson, 1994; Sherman & Klein, 1994; Werth & Foerster, 2002). We use a few known traits to determine what other qualities the person has. If someone is kind, our implicit personality theory tells us that he or she is probably also generous; similarly, we assume that a stingy person is also irritable.

But relying on implicit personality theories, like any schemas, can also lead us astray. For example, University of British Columbia researchers found that if someone was shy, people tended to assume that the person was also unintelligent—an assumption that simply was not true (Paulhus & Morgan, 1997). Believe it or not, our implicit personality theories can even cost us our lives! How? A team of researchers in the United States and Canada found that university students relied on implicit personality theories to determine whether they should use condoms in sexual situations (Williams, Kimble, Covell, Weiss, Newton, Fisher, & Fisher, 1992). If people knew their partner and liked him or her, they assumed that he or she couldn't possibly be HIV positive. If they didn't know their partner, they relied on superficial characteristics, such as the person's age, how he or she dressed, or even whether the person was from a large city versus a small town. For example, if a potential sexual partner didn't dress provocatively or wasn't from a large city, participants assumed that a condom wasn't necessary. The researchers concluded that people place themselves at considerable risk by relying on such implicit personality theories because these variables are not accurate indicators of whether a sexual partner actually has HIV or AIDS. Similar findings have been obtained in more recent studies conducted by a team of researchers from universities across Canada (Knäuper, Kornik, Atkinson, Guberman, & Aydin, 2005).

Others are to us like the "characters" in fiction, external and incorrigible; the surprises they give us turn out in the end to have been predictable—unexpected variations on the theme of being themselves.

—Mary McCarthy, *novelist and essayist, 1912–1989*

Culture and Implicit Personality Theories

Implicit personality theories are strongly tied to culture. Like other beliefs, they are passed from generation to generation in a society. One culture's implicit personality theory might be very different from another culture's (Anderson, 1995; Chiu, Morris, Hong, & Menon, 2000). For example, a strong implicit personality theory in our culture involves physical attractiveness. We presume that "what is beautiful is good"—that people with physical beauty will also have a whole host of other wonderful qualities (Dion, Berscheid, & Walster, 1972; Eagly, Ashmore, Makhijani, & Longo, 1991; Jackson, Hunter, & Hodge, 1995). Consistent with this belief, when Dion and Dion (1987) showed visitors to the Ontario Science Centre photographs of attractive and

Implicit personality theories differ from culture to culture. Westerners assume that there is an artistic type of person: someone who is creative, intense, temperamental, and unconventional—for example, poet/songwriter Leonard Cohen (left). The Chinese have no such implicit personality theory. They have a category of *shi gú* person—someone who is worldly, devoted to family, socially skillful, and somewhat reserved (right). Westerners do not have this implicit personality theory.

unattractive individuals, more positive qualities (e.g., kind, considerate, sincere) were attributed to the attractive individuals. Participants also predicted that attractive individuals would experience more successes in life.

Dion, Pak, and Dion (1990) wondered whether physical attractiveness stereotyping might be less likely to occur in collectivist cultures (e.g., China) where social judgments are more likely to be based on group-related attributes (e.g., family, position in a social group) than on characteristics of the individual. Indeed, they found that Chinese students at the University of Toronto who were highly involved in Toronto's Chinese community—who, therefore, were probably more collectivist—were less likely to assume that an attractive person possessed desirable personality traits compared with students who were not as involved in the Chinese community.

Cultural variation in implicit personality theories was also demonstrated in an intriguing study by Hoffman, Lau, and Johnson (1986). They noted that different cultures have different ideas about personality types. In Western cultures, there is a kind of person who has an artistic personality: a person who is creative, intense, and temperamental, and who has an unconventional lifestyle. The Chinese, however, do not have a schema or implicit personality theory for an artistic type. Conversely, in China there are categories of personality that do not exist in Western cultures; for example, a *shi gú* person is someone who is worldly, devoted to family, socially skillful, and somewhat reserved. Hoffman and colleagues hypothesized that these culturally specific implicit personality theories would influence the way people form impressions of others. To test this hypothesis, they wrote stories, in English and Chinese, describing a person behaving like an artistic type or a *shi gú* type, without using those labels. They gave the stories written in English to a group of unilingual English speakers and to a group of Chinese–English bilingual participants. They gave the stories written in Chinese to another group of Chinese–English bilingual participants. The task for participants was to write down their impressions of the characters in the stories. The researchers then examined whether the participants listed traits that were not used in the stories but fit the artistic or *shi gú* personality type. In other words, they looked at whether participants used their implicit personality theories to "fill in the blanks." For example, the term *unreliable* was not mentioned in the "artistic personality type" story but is consistent with that implicit personality theory.

As seen in Figure 4.3, when the unilingual English speakers read about the characters, they formed an impression that was more consistent with the artistic type than with the *shi gú* type. This was also the case for the Chinese–English bilingual participants who read the descriptions in English. However, Chinese–English bilingual participants

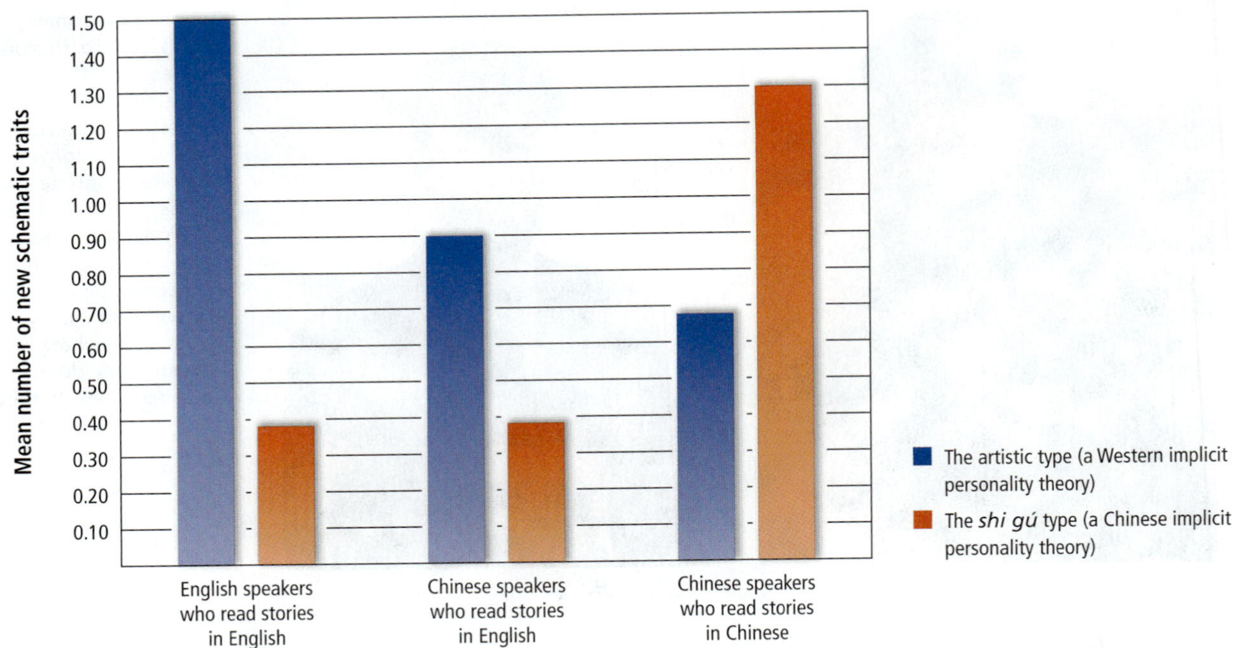

FIGURE 4.3

Implicit personality theories: How our culture and language shape our impressions of other people.

People formed impressions of characters in stories that were consistent with the implicit personality theory contained in their language. For example, when Chinese–English bilinguals read stories about people in English, they were likely to form impressions consistent with a Western implicit theory, the artistic personality. When Chinese–English bilingual participants read the same stories in Chinese, they were likely to form impressions consistent with a Chinese implicit theory, the *shi gú* personality.

(Adapted from Hoffman, Lau, & Johnson, 1986)

who read the descriptions in Chinese showed the opposite pattern of results. Their impression of the character was more consistent with the *shi gú* type than with the artistic type because the Chinese language provides a convenient label or implicit personality theory for this kind of person.

These results are consistent with a well-known argument by Benjamin Whorf (1956) that the language people speak influences the way they think about the world. Characters described identically were perceived differently by the bilingual research participants, depending on the language—and therefore the implicit personality theory—used. Consequently, one's culture and one's language produce widely shared implicit personality theories, and these theories can influence the kinds of inferences people make about each other.

In the beginning was not the word, not the deed, not the silly serpent. In the beginning was why? Why did she pluck the apple? Was she bored? Was she inquisitive? Was she paid? Did Adam put her up to it? If not, who did?

—John le Carré, *The Russia House*, 1989

Causal Attribution: Answering the "Why" Question

We have seen that when we observe other people, we make guesses about their personalities, such as how friendly or outgoing they are, often based on their nonverbal behaviour. And once we get this far, we use our implicit personality theories to fill in the blanks. If a person is friendly, she must be sincere as well. Or, more disturbingly, if a person is likeable, he or she must not have AIDS.

However, nonverbal behaviour and implicit personality theories are not fail-safe indicators of what a person is really thinking or feeling. If you meet an acquaintance and she says, "It's great to see you!" does she really mean it?

Perhaps she is acting more thrilled than she really feels, out of politeness. Perhaps she is outright lying. The point is that even though nonverbal communication is sometimes easy to decode and implicit personality theories can streamline the way we form impressions, there is still substantial ambiguity as to what a person's behaviour really means. Why did that acquaintance behave as she did? To answer this "why" question, we use our immediate observations to form more elegant and complex inferences about what people really are like and what motivates them to act as they do. How we go about answering these questions is the focus of **attribution theory**, the study of how we infer the causes of our own and other people's behaviour.

Attribution Theory
A description of the way in which people explain the causes of their own and other people's behaviour

The Nature of the Attributional Process

Fritz Heider is frequently referred to as the father of attribution theory. His influential book defined the field of social perception, and his legacy is still very much evident in current research (Singer & Frith, 2006; Surian, Caldi, & Sperber, 2007; Trope & Gaunt, 2003). Heider (1958) discussed what he called "naive" or "common sense" psychology. In his view, people are like amateur scientists trying to understand other people's behaviour by piecing together information until they arrive at a reasonable explanation or cause. Heider was intrigued by what seemed reasonable to people and how they arrived at their conclusions.

One of Heider's (1958) most valuable contributions is a simple dichotomy: When trying to decide why people behave as they do—for example, why a father just yelled at his young daughter—we can make one of two attributions. One option is to make an **internal attribution**, deciding that the cause of the father's behaviour was something about him—his disposition, personality, attitudes, or character—an explanation that assigns the causes of his behaviour internally. For example, we might decide that the father has poor parenting skills and disciplines his child in inappropriate ways. Alternatively, we might make an **external attribution**, deciding that something about the situation, not the person's personality or attitudes, caused the behaviour. If we conclude that the man yelled because his daughter had just stepped into the street without looking, we would be making an external attribution for his behaviour. (See the accompanying Try It! exercise.)

Internal Attribution
The inference that a person is behaving in a certain way because of something about him or her, such as his or her attitude, character, or personality

External Attribution
The inference that a person is behaving a certain way because of something about the situation he or she is in; the assumption is that most people would respond the same way in that situation

Notice that our impression of the father will be very different, depending on the type of attribution we make. If we make an internal attribution, we'll have a negative impression of him. If we make an external attribution, we won't learn much about him—after all, most parents would have done the same thing if they were in that situation and their child had just disobeyed them by stepping into the street. Quite a difference!

This internal/external attribution dichotomy plays an extraordinarily important role in even the most intimate parts of our lives. Indeed, spouses in happy, satisfied marriages

According to Fritz Heider (1958), we tend to see the causes of a person's behaviour as internal. So when we see a homeless person, we will most likely at first assume that he is at fault for being poor—perhaps lazy or drug-addicted. If you knew the person's situation—that perhaps he has lost his job because of a plant closing or has a spouse whose medical bills have bankrupted them—you might come up with a different, external attribution.

Watch on **mypsychlab**
Attribution

make very different attributions about their partners than spouses in troubled, distressed marriages. Satisfied spouses tend to make internal attributions for their partners' positive behaviours (e.g., "She helped me because she's such a generous person") and external attributions for their partners' negative behaviours (e.g., "He said something mean because he's so stressed at work this week"). In contrast, spouses in distressed marriages tend to display the opposite pattern: Their partners' positive behaviours are chalked up to external causes (e.g., "She helped me because she wanted to impress our friends"), while negative behaviours are attributed to internal causes (e.g., "He said something mean because he's a self-centred jerk"). When an intimate relationship becomes troubled, this second pattern of attributions about one's partner only makes the situation worse and can have dire consequences for the health and future of the relationship (Bradbury & Fincham, 1991; Fincham, Bradbury, Arias, Byrne, & Karney, 1997; Karney & Bradbury, 2000).

Another of Heider's (1958) important contributions was his observation that people generally prefer internal attributions over external ones. Although either type of attribution is always possible, Heider noted that we tend to see the causes of a person's behaviour as residing in that person. We are perceptually focused on *people*—they are who we notice—while the *situation*, which is often difficult to see and hard to describe, can be overlooked (Bargh, 1994; Carlston & Skowronski, 1994; Gilbert, 1998b; Jones, 1979, 1990; Jones & Davis, 1965).

Simulate on **mypsychlab**
Impression Formation and Attribution

The Covariation Model: Internal versus External Attributions

Covariation Model
A theory stating that to form an attribution about what caused a person's behaviour, we systematically note the pattern between the presence (or absence) of possible causal factors and whether or not the behaviour occurs

The first, essential step in the process of social perception is determining how people decide whether to make an internal or an external attribution. Harold Kelley's (1967, 1973) major contribution to attribution theory was the idea that we notice and think about more than one piece of information when we form an impression of another person. For example, let's say that you ask your friend to lend you her car, and she says no. Naturally, you wonder why. In formulating an answer, Kelley's theory, called the **covariation model,** states that you will systematically examine multiple instances of behaviour, occurring at different times and in different situations. Has your friend

TRY IT! Listen as People Make Attributions

Probably most of us have been in a situation in which we've told another person about something that happened to us (e.g., getting the job that 100 people applied for) and had the person respond with, "It was meant to be." Or, you might have found that special someone who assures you that fate has brought you together. How common are fate attributions? Who is most likely to make them? The next time you are with a diverse group of people, describe a few improbable events, such as two brothers meeting after decades of separation, or finding the love of your life and discovering that the two of you had been in the same kindergarten class. Try to come up with both positive and negative unlikely events. Listen to the kinds of attributions people make. How many of them attribute these outcomes to fate or say things like "it was meant to be"? It turns out that some people are more likely to engage in fate attributions than others, according to a recent study. The participants in this research were students at the University of British Columbia. Some students were EuroCanadian; others were of East Asian heritage. Within each group, some students identified themselves as Christian, while others said they were nonreligious. All participants were presented with a series of improbable events (e.g., the brothers reuniting example given above). Both culture and religion were associated with making fate attributions. Specifically, participants of East Asian heritage and Christians attributed more events to fate than did EuroCanadians and nonreligious participants (Norenzayan & Lee, 2010).

refused to lend you her car in the past? Does she lend it to other people? Does she normally lend you other possessions of hers?

Kelley, like Heider before him, assumed that when we are in the process of forming an attribution, we gather information, or data, that will help us reach a judgment. The data we use, according to Kelley, are how a person's behaviour "covaries" or changes across time, place, different actors, and different targets of the behaviour. By discovering covariation in people's behaviour (e.g., your friend refuses to lend you her car; she agrees to lend it to others), you are able to reach a judgment about what caused their behaviour.

When we are forming an attribution, what kinds of information do we examine for covariation? Kelley (1967, 1972, 1973) identified three key types of information: *consensus*, *distinctiveness*, and *consistency*. Let's describe these types of information through an example. You are working at your part-time job in a clothing store and you observe your boss yelling at another employee, Hannah, telling her in no uncertain terms that she's an idiot. Without any conscious effort on your part, you pose the attributional question: "Why is the boss yelling at Hannah and being so critical—is it something about the boss or something about the situation that surrounds and affects him?"

Now let's look at how Kelley's model of covariation assessment answers this question. **Consensus information** refers to how other people behave toward the same stimulus—in this case, Hannah. Do other people at work also yell at Hannah and criticize her? **Distinctiveness information** refers to how the actor (the person whose behaviour we are trying to explain) responds to other stimuli. Does the boss yell at and demean other employees in the store? **Consistency information** refers to the frequency with which the observed behaviour between the same actor and the same stimulus occurs across time and circumstances. Does the boss yell at and criticize Hannah regularly and frequently, whether the store is busy with customers or empty?

According to Kelley's theory, when these three sources of information combine into one of two distinct patterns, a clear attribution can be made. People are most likely to make an *internal attribution*—deciding the behaviour was a result of something about the boss—when the consensus and distinctiveness of the act are low, but consistency is high (see Figure 4.4). We would be pretty confident that the boss yelled

Consensus Information

Information about the extent to which other people behave the same way as the actor does toward the same stimulus

Distinctiveness Information

Information about the extent to which one particular actor behaves in the same way to different stimuli

Consistency Information

Information about the extent to which the behaviour between one actor and one stimulus is the same across time and circumstances

Why did the boss yell at his employee Hannah?			
People are likely to make an ***internal attribution***—it was something about the boss—if they see this behaviour as	***low*** in consensus: The boss is the only person working in the store who yells at Hannah	***low*** in distinctiveness: The boss yells at all the employees	***high*** in consistency: The boss yells at Hannah almost every time he sees her
People are likely to make an ***external attribution***—it was something about Hannah—if they see this behaviour as	***high*** in consensus: All of the employees yell at Hannah too	***high*** in distinctiveness: The boss doesn't yell at any of the other employees	***high*** in consistency: The boss yells at Hannah almost every time he sees her
People are likely to think it was something peculiar about the particular circumstances in which the boss yelled at Hannah if they see this behaviour as	***low or high*** in consensus	***low or high*** in distinctiveness	***low*** in consistency: This is the first time that the boss has yelled at Hannah

FIGURE 4.4

The covariation model.

Why did the boss yell at his employee Hannah? To decide whether a behaviour was caused by internal (or dispositional) factors, or external (or situational) factors, people use consensus, distinctiveness, and consistency information.

at Hannah because he is a mean and vindictive person if we knew that no one else yells at Hannah, that the boss yells at other employees, and that the boss yells at Hannah every chance he gets. People are likely to make an *external attribution* (in this case, about Hannah) if consensus, distinctiveness, and consistency are all high. Finally, when consistency is low, we cannot make a clear internal or external attribution and so resort to a special kind of external or *situational attribution*, one that assumes something unusual or peculiar is going on in these circumstances—for example, the boss just received very upsetting news and lost his temper with the first person he saw.

The covariation model assumes that people make causal attributions in a rational, logical way. People observe the clues, such as the distinctiveness of the act, and then draw a logical inference about why the person did what he or she did. Several studies have confirmed that people often do make attributions the way that Kelley's model says they should (Gilbert, 1998b; Hewstone & Jaspars, 1987; White, 2002)—with two exceptions. First, studies have shown that people don't use consensus information as much as Kelley's theory predicted; they rely more on consistency and distinctiveness information when forming attributions (McArthur, 1972; Wright, Luus, & Christie, 1990). Second, people don't always have the relevant information they need on all three of Kelley's dimensions. For example, you may not have consistency information because this is the first time you have ever asked your friend to borrow her car. In these situations, research has shown that people proceed with the attributional process by using the information they do have, and if necessary, making inferences about the "missing data" (Fiedler, Walther, & Nickel, 1999; Kelley, 1973).

To summarize, the covariation model portrays people as master detectives, deducing the causes of behaviour as systematically and logically as Sherlock Holmes would. However, as we saw in Chapter 3, sometimes people aren't that accurate or rational when forming judgments about others. Attributions can be biased or distorted when people use mental shortcuts (see Chapter 3). In the next section, we discuss some specific errors or biases that plague the attributional process. One shortcut is very common, at least in Western cultures, namely assuming that people do what they do because of the kind of people they are, not because of the situation they are in.

The Correspondence Bias: People as Personality Psychologists

On September 22, 1999, Nadia Hama made newspaper headlines when her 18-month-old daughter Kaya fell 47 metres from the Capilano Suspension Bridge in North Vancouver, British Columbia. People in the media and on the street were quick to blame Hama, accusing her of deliberately throwing Kaya off the bridge. The accusations mounted as it came to light that her daughter had Down syndrome and that Hama had looked into placing her for adoption. In short, Hama was portrayed as a bad mother who intentionally tried to kill her child. Other people agreed that Hama may have tried to kill her child, but pointed to situational factors in explaining her behaviour. They focused on the extremely high levels of stress in her life—raising a handicapped child, being embroiled in an ugly divorce, and not receiving child-care payments from her estranged husband. Not surprisingly, Hama explained her behaviour as situationally caused—maintaining that baby Kaya's fall was accidental.

Whether we make internal or external attributions for someone's behaviour can have serious consequences. In Hama's case, those who made internal attributions concluded that she was a cold-hearted murderer; in contrast, those who made external attributions felt compassion, sympathy, and pity. Quite a difference! Perhaps even more important, the fate of Hama rested on the attributions made for baby Kaya's fall. Ultimately, police and Crown prosecutors did not find sufficient evidence to charge her with either attempted murder or criminal negligence causing bodily harm (D'Angelo, 2000).

Other research has shown that when people are convicted of committing crimes, attributions play a role in the severity of sentencing. Linda Coates (1997) recorded the kinds of attributions made by judges in transcripts of 70 cases of sexual assault in British Columbia. The kind of attributions made had important implications for sentencing:

If the assault was seen as the result of a decision to be violent or of the offender's violent nature, the sentence was harsher than if situational or external attributions were made (e.g., the assault was attributed to stress or negative mood).

The pervasive, fundamental theory or schema most of us have about human behaviour is that people do what they do because of the kind of people they are, not because of the situation they are in. Thus, in Hama's case, people's first impulse was to attribute her behaviour to being a bad mother and cold-hearted murderer. When thinking this way, we are more like personality psychologists, who see behaviour as stemming from internal dispositions and traits, than social psychologists, who focus on the impact of social situations on behaviour. This tendency to infer that people's behaviour corresponds to or matches their dispositions and personality has been called the **correspondence bias** (Fiske & Taylor, 1991; Gilbert & Malone, 1995; Jones, 1979, 1990). The correspondence bias is so pervasive that many social psychologists call it the *fundamental attribution error* (Heider, 1958; Jones, 1990; Ross, 1977; Ross & Nisbett, 1991).

Correspondence Bias
The tendency to infer that people's behaviour corresponds to or matches their disposition (personality)

There have been many empirical demonstrations of the tendency to see people's behaviour as a reflection of their dispositions and beliefs, rather than as influenced by the situation (Gawronski, 2003a, 2003b; Jones, 1979, 1990; Miller, Ashton, & Mishal, 1990; Riggs & Gumbrecht, 2005). In a classic study, Edward Jones and Victor Harris (1967) asked university students to read a fellow student's essay that either supported or opposed Fidel Castro's rule in Cuba, and then to guess how the author of the essay really felt about Castro. In one condition, the researchers told the students that the author freely chose which position to take in the essay, thereby making it easy to guess how he or she really felt. If the author chose to write in favour of Castro, then clearly he or she must indeed be sympathetic to Castro. In another condition, however, the students learned that the author did not have any choice about which position to take—he or she had been assigned the position as a participant in a debate. Logically, if we know someone could not choose the topic, we should not assume the writer believes what he or she wrote. Yet the participants in this study, and in dozens of others like it, assumed that the author really believed what he or she wrote, even when they knew he or she could not choose which position to take. As seen in Figure 4.5, people moderated their guesses a little bit—there was not as much difference in people's estimates of the author's attitude in the pro-Castro and anti-Castro conditions—but they still assumed that the content of the essay reflected the author's true feelings.

Now imagine the following situation. You are in a psychology experiment on the "accuracy of first impressions." When you arrive at the lab, you discover that you are in the experiment with a very attractive, opposite-sex person who happens to be single. The experimenter tells this person that his or her task is to write down his or her impression of you. Your job is to assess the accuracy of his or her impression. The two of you are ushered into separate rooms. A little while later, the experimenter returns with the other person's write-up on his or her impressions of you. You notice that the instructions to your partner state that she or he should feel free to express either

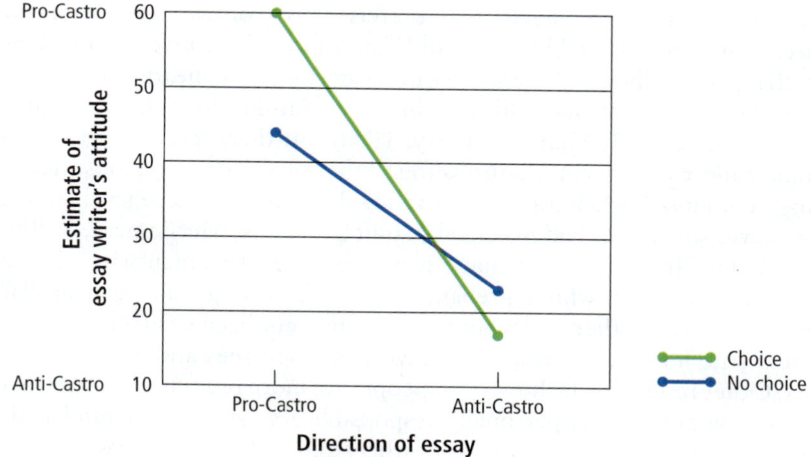

FIGURE 4.5
The correspondence bias.
Even when people knew that the author's choice of an essay topic was externally caused (i.e., in the no-choice condition), they assumed that what he or she wrote reflected how he or she really felt about Castro. That is, they made an internal attribution for the author's behaviour.
(Adapted from Jones & Harris, 1967)

a positive or negative impression of you. With your heart pounding, you read what she or he wrote. It turns out that this very attractive, available person had nothing but good things to say about you! You are then asked a number of questions such as how attracted you are to him or her, whether you would like to go on a date with him or her, and whether you think that your partner really believed what she or he had written about you.

What we have been describing so far is the *no constraint* condition of an experiment conducted by McGill University researchers (Gagné, Khan, Lydon, & To, 2008). There was another condition in this experiment, the *constraint* condition, in which the participants received the same positive assessment from the attractive partner (who, as you've probably figured out, was a confederate). But in this case, the participants saw that his or her instructions were to provide a positive impression of them.

Based on what you know about the correspondence bias, you can probably anticipate the results. Even when people knew that the attractive confederate had been instructed to write something positive about them, they tended to make a dispositional attribution—they believed that the positive feedback reflected the confederate's true opinion of them. However, there were a few interesting qualifiers having to do with the participants' relationship status and self-esteem. It turned out that people who were currently in a dating relationship and who had low self-esteem were less likely to make a dispositional attribution for the positive feedback in the constraint condition than in the no constraint condition. Thus, the correspondence bias has some limits; but, in general, if someone tells us we are wonderful, our tendency is to believe that they really mean it—even if we know they were told to say so.

Why is the correspondence bias, the tendency to explain behaviour in terms of people's dispositions, referred to as the fundamental attribution error? It is not always wrong to make an internal attribution; clearly, people frequently do what they do because of the kind of people they are. However, there is ample evidence that social situations can have a strong impact on behaviour—indeed, the major lesson of social psychology is that these influences can be extremely powerful. Research on the correspondence bias tells us that people tend to underestimate these influences when explaining other people's behaviour. Even when a situational constraint on behaviour is obvious, as in the Jones and Harris (1967) experiment, people persist in making internal attributions (Lord, Scott, Pugh, & Desforges, 1997; Newman, 1996; Ross, 1977; Ross, Amabile, & Steinmetz, 1977; Ross & Nisbett, 1991).

Blaming the Victim: A Consequence of the Correspondence Bias Even if people are made aware of the situational factors responsible for the plight of disadvantaged members of our society (e.g., inadequate nutrition, disrupted family life), they may still see these individuals as responsible for their misfortune. Guimond and Dubé (1989), for example, found that Anglophone students viewed Francophones themselves, rather than situational factors, as responsible for their lower economic status in Quebec.

Another way in which the correspondence bias leads to victim blaming is when people decide that victims could have exercised control over a situation but didn't. Research conducted at the University of Windsor and the University of Manitoba has shown that people who attribute serious illnesses (e.g., HIV, heart disease, lung cancer) to controllable factors are more likely to blame victims for their illness (Mantler, Schellenberg, & Page, 2003; Menec & Perry, 1998). Further, recent research conducted with lung cancer patients in Manitoba found that caregivers were most likely to make blaming attributions when a patient continued to smoke—more so than when he or she had never smoked or had managed to quit (Lobchuk, McClement, McPherson, & Cheang, 2008). In yet another study, it was found that women who gave birth to a disabled child and for whom prenatal diagnostic testing had been available were blamed more than mothers for whom this test had not been available (Lawson, 2003). This held true for a large sample of university employees and a group of Canadian doctors. Other research has shown that people are more prejudiced toward overweight people if they are seen as personally responsible for being fat (Crandall, D'Anello, Sakalli, Lazarus, Wieczorkowska, & Feather, 2001). Finally, in research conducted at Lakehead University, Rotenberg (1998) found that students were less accepting of a lonely student if they attributed his or her loneliness to controllable factors. Thus, the consequences of our tendency to explain other people's behaviour in dispositional terms can lead to tragic consequences, including a tendency to blame those who are victimized or stigmatized for their plight.

The Role of Perceptual Salience in the Correspondence Bias Why do we fall prey to the correspondence bias? One reason is that when we try to explain someone's behaviour, our focus of attention is usually on the person, not on the surrounding situation (Heider, 1958; Jones & Nisbett, 1972). In fact, the situational causes of another person's behaviour are practically invisible to us (Gilbert, 1998b; Gilbert & Malone, 1995). If we don't know what happened to a person earlier in the day (e.g., she received an F on her midterm), we can't use that situational information to help us understand her current behaviour. Even when we know her situation, we still don't know how she interprets it—for example, the F may not have upset her because she's planning to drop the course anyway. If we don't know the meaning of the situation for her, we can't accurately judge its effects on her behaviour.

What information does that leave us? Although the situation may be close to invisible, the individual is extremely "perceptually prominent"—people are what our eyes and ears notice. And what we notice seems to be the reasonable and logical cause of the observed behaviour (Heider, 1958). We can't see the situation, so we ignore its importance. People, not the situation, have **perceptual salience** for us; we pay attention to them and, as a result, we tend to think that they alone cause their behaviour.

Perceptual Salience
Information that is the focus of people's attention; people tend to overestimate the causal role of perceptually salient information

Several studies have confirmed the importance of perceptual salience, including a particularly elegant one by Shelley Taylor and Susan Fiske (1975). In this study, two male students engaged in a "get acquainted" conversation. (They were actually both accomplices of the experimenters and were following a script during their conversation.) At each session, six actual research participants also took part. They sat in assigned seats, surrounding the two conversationalists (see Figure 4.6). Two of them sat on each side of the actors; they had a clear, profile view of both individuals. Two observers sat behind each actor; they could see the back of one actor's head but the face of the other. Thus, who was visually salient—that is, who the participants could see the best—was cleverly manipulated in this study.

Be not swept off your feet by the vividness of the impression, but say, 'Impression, wait for me a little. Let me see what you are and what you represent.'

—Epictetus, Discourses, *AD 101*

After the conversation, the research participants were asked questions about the two men—for example, who had taken the lead in the conversation, and who had chosen the topics to be discussed? As you can see in

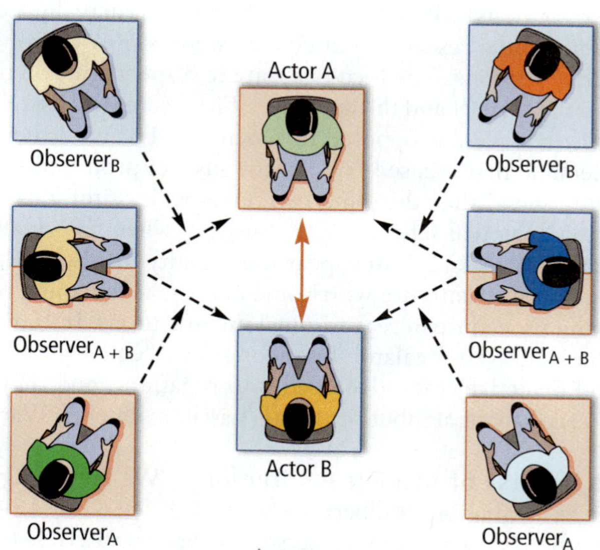

FIGURE 4.6
Manipulating perceptual salience.

This is the seating arrangement for two actors and the six research participants in the Taylor and Fiske study. Participants rated each actor's impact on the conversation. The researchers found that people rated the actor they could see more clearly as having the largest role in the conversation.

(Adapted from Taylor & Fiske, 1975)

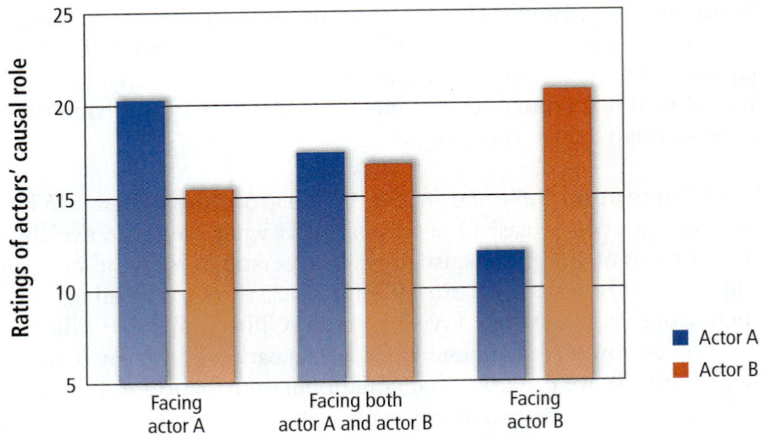

FIGURE 4.7

The effects of perceptual salience.

These are the ratings of each actor's causal role in the conversation. People thought that the actor they could see better had the most impact on the conversation.

(Adapted from Taylor & Fiske, 1975)

Figure 4.7, the person the participants thought had the greater impact on the conversation was the one they could see best. Even though all the observers heard the same conversation, those who were facing actor A thought *he* had taken the lead and chosen the topics, whereas those who were facing actor B thought *he* had taken the lead and chosen the topics. In comparison, those who could see both students equally well thought both were equally influential.

Perceptual salience, or our visual point of view, helps explain why the correspondence bias is so widespread. We focus our attention more on people than on the surrounding situation because the situation is so difficult to see or know; we underestimate or even forget about the influence of the situation when we are explaining human behaviour. This tendency can have some very disturbing implications. Let's say you have been picked up by the police as a potential suspect in a crime (though, of course, you are innocent). Back at the police station, you reach the point in the process where a detective says you will now be "interviewed." You've watched enough episodes of *Law and Order* to know that this is the "interrogation" part. The detective tells you that you will be videotaped while answering questions, for possible later use in a court of law. As a student of social psychology, you should immediately ask, "Will the camera be focused only on me, or will it show me and the detective who's asking questions?" Why, you ask? Because recent research on videotaped police interrogations has shown that perceptual salience can trigger the correspondence bias, affecting how guilty the suspect is judged to be (Lassiter, 2002). In one study, Lassiter and colleagues (2007) presented 21 courtroom judges (who also had previous experience as both prosecutors and criminal defense attorneys) and 24 police officers (who had extensive experience conducting interrogations) with a videotape of a suspect (actually a confederate) confessing to a crime. These research participants were shown one of three videotaped camera-perspective versions: The focus was on the suspect only; on the detective only; or equal focus on the suspect and the detective. They were then asked to rate how "voluntary" the confession was, as opposed to "coerced." For both the judges and police officers, the videotape that focused only on the suspect produced significantly higher ratings of "voluntariness" than the other two versions (Lassiter, Diamond, Schmidt, & Elek, 2007). The perceptual salience of the suspect, when shown all alone, triggered a correspondence bias, making him appear more guilty than when he was not as perceptually salient. These results are worrisome because videotaping only the suspect is standard operating procedure in real criminal investigations. In fact, only one country in the world thus far, New Zealand, has adopted an "equal-focus" camera perspective (suspect and detective) for videotaped interrogations, and they have done so in response to concerns about attributional bias (Lassiter, Ratcliff, Ware, & Irvin, 2006).

Two-Step Process of Attribution

Analyzing another person's behaviour first by making an automatic internal attribution and only then thinking about possible situational reasons for the behaviour, after which one may adjust the original internal attribution

The Two-Step Process of Making Attributions We go through a **two-step process** when we make attributions (Gilbert, 1989, 1991, 1993; Krull, 1993). First, we make an internal attribution; we assume that a person's behaviour was due to something about

FIGURE 4.8
The two-step process of attribution.

that person. In the second step, we attempt to adjust this attribution by considering the situation the person was in. But we often don't make enough of an adjustment in this second step. Indeed, when we are distracted or preoccupied, we often skip the second step, making an extreme internal attribution (Gilbert & Hixon, 1991; Gilbert & Osborne, 1989; Gilbert, Pelham, & Krull, 1988). Why? Because the first step (making the internal attribution) occurs quickly and spontaneously, whereas the second step (adjusting for the situation) requires more effort and conscious attention (see Figure 4.8).

We will engage in this second step of attributional processing if we consciously slow down and think carefully before reaching a judgment, if we are motivated to reach as accurate a judgment as possible, or if we are suspicious about the behaviour of the target person, for example, believing that he or she is lying or has ulterior motives (Hilton, Fein, & Miller, 1993; Risen & Gilovich, 2007; Webster, 1993).

Culture and the Correspondence Bias The two-step attributional process may vary by culture. Although the jury is still out, it appears that the first step—making the initial, dispositional attribution, may be universal, whereas, the second step—adjusting the initial attribution to take the situation into account—may be more culturally specific. We have already discussed North American research showing that even when people are informed that the person whose essay they are reading was told to express particular views, people still tend to believe that those views reflect the person's true attitudes. The same thing happens in Korea, Japan, and China: Participants believe the content of the person's essay indicates what he or she is really like (Choi & Nisbett, 1998; Krull et al., 1999; Kashima, Siegel, Tanaka, & Kashima, 1992; Kitayama & Masuda, 1997; Masuda & Kitayama, 1996, 2003).

Watch on mypsychlab Cultural Psychology: Kaiping Peng

But what if we made the situation more salient in an essay-writing type of study? Would participants from collectivistic cultures show less of a correspondence bias than participants from individualistic cultures? Collectivist (often Asian) cultures emphasize group membership, interdependence, and conformity to group norms (Fletcher & Ward, 1988; Markus & Kitayama, 1991; Newman, 1991; Triandis, 1990; Zebrowitz-McArthur, 1988). These cultural values suggest that people would be socialized to take situational factors into account. In several studies, the researchers made the situational information more salient by having the participants go through the same procedure as the target person they are judging. Like the target, the observers are also assigned to write an essay on a position they did not choose. Sometimes they are also given prepared statements to include in their essays. When later asked to judge the target's attitude, the observers should realize that the target was just as constrained by the situation as they were, so the content of the target's essay shouldn't reveal much about the target. What happens? American participants still show the correspondence bias when judging the target person; they still think the essay tells them something about what the target is really like. But in collectivist cultures, participants take this situational information into account and make far fewer dispositional attributions about the target (Choi & Nisbett, 1998; Kitayama & Masuda, 1997; Masuda & Kitayama, 1996).

These cultural differences are not limited to experiments in which people read essays. Joan Miller (1984) asked people of two cultures—Hindus living in India and Americans living in the United States—to think of various examples of behaviours performed by their friends, and to explain why those behaviours occurred. American participants preferred dispositional explanations for the behaviours; they were more likely to say that the causes of their friends' behaviours were the kinds of people they are, rather than the situation or context in which the behaviours occurred. In contrast, Hindu participants preferred situational explanations for their friends' behaviours (Miller, 1984).

Another study compared attributions made for crimes in Chinese- and English-language newspapers. Specifically, Michael Morris and Kaiping Peng (1994) targeted two similar crimes, both mass murders, one committed by a Chinese graduate student in Iowa, the other committed by a white postal worker in Michigan. The researchers coded all of the news articles about the two crimes that appeared in the *New York Times* and the *World Journal*, a Chinese-language U.S. newspaper. As you can see in Figure 4.9, journalists writing in English made significantly more dispositional attributions about both mass murderers than did journalists writing in Chinese. For example, English-language reporters described one murderer as a "darkly disturbed man" with a "sinister edge" to his personality. Chinese-language reporters, when describing the same murderer, emphasized more situational causes, such as "not getting along with his adviser" and his "isolation from the Chinese community."

Finally, in a more recent study, Chiu, Morris, Hong, and Menon (2000) asked members of the public in the United States and Hong Kong to read a scenario about patients who got sick because a pharmacy worker made an error while mixing medicines. As expected, Americans made more dispositional attributions (assigning responsibility to the worker), whereas the Chinese were more likely to assign responsibility to the clinic (e.g., poor management, incompetent training of workers). This cultural difference was even more pronounced in a follow-up laboratory study when some participants answered the questions while performing another task. Presumably under these conditions, participants engaged in automatic processing (see Chapter 3), with the result

FIGURE 4.9

The role of culture in the correspondence bias.

Newspaper articles about two murderers, appearing in English- and Chinese-language newspapers, were coded for the types of attributions made. Journalists writing in English made significantly more dispositional attributions about both the Chinese and the Anglo-American murderer than did journalists writing in Chinese.

(Adapted from Morris & Peng, 1994)

that American participants were especially likely to blame the worker and Chinese participants were especially likely to blame the clinic. A more recent study conducted with business students at the University of Regina and at the University of Hokkaido, Japan similarly found that Japanese participants were more likely to make situational attributions during business transactions, whereas Canadian participants were more likely to make dispositional attributions (Branzei, Vertinsky, & Camp, 2007).

In conclusion, the research conducted so far suggests that people everywhere probably start off at the same point, showing the correspondence bias: They automatically make dispositional attributions about other people. In collectivist cultures, what happens next is that people look to the situation: They revise and correct their first impressions, taking the situation into account, especially if the situational information is particularly salient and noticeable (Choi, Dalal, Kim-Prieto, & Park, 2003; Lieberman, Jarcho, & Obayashi, 2005; Trope & Gaunt, 2000). Westerners tend to avoid this second step. Their first impression, the dispositional attribution, sticks (Choi et al., 2003; Hedden, Ketay, Aron, Markus, & Gabrieli, 2008; Knowles, Morris, Chiu, & Hong, 2001; Lewis, Goto, & Kong, 2008).

Research has shown that when forming attributions, people in collectivistic cultures such as Japan's are more likely to take situational information into account than are people in individualistic cultures.

Before leaving this topic we should point out that Westerners are capable of coming up with situational explanations, but only if they are motivated to think more deeply (Lee, Hallahan, & Herzog, 1996; Webster, 1993) or if they are given attributional training. In recent research conducted by American and Canadian researchers, white university students were first taught the difference between situational and dispositional attributions. Participants in the situational attribution training condition were then shown photographs of black men on a computer screen, along with sentences describing negative stereotypic behaviours (e.g., "arrived at work an hour late"). A situational explanation (e.g., "the power went off and reset his alarm") and a dispositional explanation (e.g., "he is an irresponsible person") then appeared on the screen. The task for participants was to select the situational explanation. In a subsequent, supposedly unrelated study, these participants were less likely to automatically associate black faces with negative stereotype words compared to participants who had not been trained to make situational attributions (Stewart, Latu, Kawakami, & Myers, 2010).

The Actor/Observer Difference

An interesting twist on the correspondence bias is that it does not apply across the board. Whereas we tend to attribute other people's behaviour to internal causes, we look beyond ourselves, to the situation, to explain our own behaviour. Thus, if we see a woman yelling at her child in a grocery store, we are quick to make the attribution that she's a mean, bad parent. The woman, however, would probably explain her behaviour in more situational terms, such as sleep deprivation or the stress she's under since she lost her job. This difference in attributions is called the **actor/observer difference** (Hansen, Kimble, & Biers, 2001; Jones & Nisbett, 1972; Robins, Spranca, & Mendelsohn, 1996). The letter to Rhona Raskin (see Figure 4.10) is an interesting demonstration of the actor/observer difference. The writer focuses on the external forces affecting her life and shaping her behaviour. Raskin, however, will have none of it. She makes a strong, internal attribution, declaring that the woman herself, not the situation, is the cause of her problems.

Actor/Observer Difference

The tendency to see other people's behaviour as dispositionally caused, while focusing more on the role of situational factors when explaining one's own behaviour

There have been countless demonstrations of the actor/observer difference. For example, University of British Columbia social psychologist Peter Suedfeld (2003) examined the attributions made by survivors of the Holocaust (i.e., their explanations for why they survived). Participants in the control group—Jews who had been safe from Nazi persecution—were asked to explain why some Jews survived the Holocaust. Survivors were most likely to make situational attributions, reporting that they had survived because of the help and support of other people or because of luck, fate, or help from God. In contrast, those in the control group (who were explaining the behaviour of the survivors) were more likely to mention internal factors, such as the

FIGURE 4.10

Actor/observer differences in attribution.

The advice column letter and its response depict actor/observer differences in attribution. Schoeneman and Rubanowitz (1985) examined letters to the "Ann Landers" and "Dear Abby" advice columns and found strong evidence for actor/observer differences. Letter writers tended to attribute their problems to external factors, whereas the advice columnists tended to make dispositional attributions to the letter writers. Similarly, in this column, the writer attributes her problems to the behaviour of the girlfriend of the man with whom she has become sexually involved rather than to her own behaviour. Rhona Raskin, on the contrary, puts the blame squarely on the letter writer's shoulders and tells her to shape up.

Dear Rhona:

I get harassing phone calls throughout the day from a woman whose boyfriend I know. Honestly, I was just friends with this guy, but since all this pestering started we've become sexually involved. I am not looking to steal him away from her—it's just great sex! It seems to work for him too. I suspect that he's never been the faithful type to begin with. I've asked her to stop bothering me but to no avail. Is this all destined to blow up into ugliness for me?

HARASSED

Dear H:

Your pleasure centre is wired to danger. It's my only explanation for a woman who'd even CONSIDER continuing to boink a guy who is so thoughtless that he not only cheats on his girlfriend, but also leaves a trail of crumbs to his co-conspirator. You act as though the girlfriend's behaviour is beyond belief. Really, it's yours that needs investigation. Yes, she is stalking you and there are restraining orders that can be put in place, but imagine all the effort that will take. And how predictably catty—two women fighting over a man. Oh right, you only care for the sensational part while the girlfriend wants the whole package. Go meditate on the concept of karma. Yours needs an overhaul.

survivors' determination and persistence. Also in line with the actor/observer difference, there is evidence that people perceive more consistency in the attitudes of other people than in their own attitudes, as demonstrated in a series of studies conducted at Memorial University (Grant, Button, Hannah, & Ross, 2003).

> *Resemblances are the shadows of differences. Different people see different similarities and similar differences.*
>
> —Vladimir Nabokov, *Pale Fire, 1962*

Perceptual Salience Revisited Why, at times, do the attributions made by actors and observers diverge so sharply? One reason is our old friend perceptual salience (Jones & Nisbett, 1972). As mentioned earlier, we notice other people's behaviour more than their situation. When it comes to ourselves, we notice our own situation more than our own behaviour. None of us is so egotistical or self-centred that we walk through life constantly holding up a full-length mirror in order to observe ourselves. We are looking outward; perceptually salient to us are other people, objects, and the events that unfold. As a result, when the actor and the observer think about what caused a given behaviour, they are swayed by the information that is most salient and noticeable to them: the actor for the observer and the situation for the actor (Malle & Knobe, 1997; Nisbett & Ross, 1980; Ross & Nisbett, 1991; Storms, 1973).

The Role of Information Availability in the Actor/Observer Difference The actor/observer difference occurs for another reason as well. Actors have more information about themselves than observers do. Actors know how they've behaved over the years; they know what happened to them that morning. Thus, they are far more aware than observers are of both the similarities and the differences in their behaviour across time and across situations (Balcetis & Dunning, 2008; Jones & Nisbett, 1972; Krueger, Ham, & Linford, 1996; Malle & Knobe, 1997). In Kelley's (1967) terms, actors have far more consistency and distinctiveness information about themselves than observers do. For example, if you are quiet and sit alone at a party, an observer is likely to make a dispositional attribution about you ("Gee, that person is quite an introvert"). In fact, you may know that this is not how you usually behave at a party. Maybe you are just feeling tired or depressed by some recent bad news. It is not surprising, then, that actors' self-attributions usually reflect situational factors, because they know more about how their behaviour varies from one situation to the next than do most observers, who see them in limited contexts.

Finally, we should note that social psychologists have also examined the link between culture and the actor/observer difference (Van Boven, White, Kamanda, & Gilovich, 2003). For example, Incheol Choi and Richard Nisbett (1998) examined the actor/observer difference among American and Korean research participants. These groups did not differ in the attributions they made to themselves—the "actors." They both made situational attributions for their behaviour. They differed only in the attributions they formed about another person, and in a way we've seen already in our discussion of the correspondence bias: Americans were more likely to think that the other person's behaviour derived from his or her disposition, whereas Koreans were more likely to think that the other person's behaviour was caused by the situation.

So far, our discussion of the mental shortcuts people use when making attributions has covered the role of perceptual salience and information availability. But what about a person's needs, desires, hopes, and fears—do these more emotional factors also create biases in our attributions? Are you motivated to see the world in certain ways because these views make you feel better, both about yourself and life in general? The answer is yes. The shortcuts discussed next have a motivational basis; they are attributions that protect our self-esteem and our belief that the world is a safe and just place.

Self-Serving Attributions

Imagine that Alison goes to her chemistry class one day with some apprehension because she will find out how she did on the midterm. When the professor returns her exam, Alison sees that she has received an A. What will Alison think is the reason for her great grade? It probably will come as no surprise that people tend to take personal credit for their successes but blame their failures on external events that were beyond their control. Therefore, Alison is likely to think that her success was due to the fact that she's good at chemistry and just plain smart.

How can we explain this departure from the typical actor/observer pattern of attributions? The answer is that when people's self-esteem is threatened, they often make **self-serving attributions**. Simply put, these attributions refer to our tendency to take credit for our successes (by making internal attributions) but to blame others or the situation (by making external attributions) for our failures. Many studies have shown that people make internal attributions when they do well on a task but make external attributions when they do poorly (McAllister, 1996; Miller & Ross, 1975; Pronin, Lin & Ross, 2002; Robins & Beer, 2001).

Self-Serving Attributions

Explanations for one's successes that credit internal, dispositional factors and explanations for one's failures that blame external, situational factors

A particularly interesting arena for studying self-serving attributions is professional sports. When explaining their victories, athletes and coaches point overwhelmingly to aspects of their own teams or players (Sherman & Kim, 2005). In fact, in an analysis of professional athletes' and coaches' explanations for their teams' wins and losses, it was found that 80 percent of the attributions for wins were to internal factors. Losses were more likely to be attributed to external factors (Lau & Russell, 1980). Consider, for example, a headline that appeared in the sports section of the August 15, 2008, *National Post:* "Humidity wears down Dancevic." Frank Dancevic, from Niagara Falls, Ontario, competed in his first Olympics in men's tennis in Beijing. He won the first set in a match against ninth-seeded Stanislas Wawrinka, but lost the next two. This is how he explained his loss: "The humidity started getting to me as the match went on in the second set and it started sapping away at my body." He also pointed to the smog and pollution in Beijing: "I feel like my lungs are burning from the pollution and smog . . .. It's a huge factor" (Dancevic, as quoted in Arthur, 2008). In other words, Dancevic made self-serving attributions—blaming the loss on external factors rather than himself.

According to research on self-serving bias, we tend to blame our failures on external factors. Canadian tennis player, Frank Dancevic, blamed his disappointing performance at the Olympics on external factors such as heat and humidity.

We should note that there are some exceptions. For example, experienced athletes are less likely to make self-serving attributions than are less experienced ones. Experienced athletes realize that losses sometimes are their fault and that wins are not

TRY IT! Self-Serving Attributions in the Sports Pages

Do athletes and coaches tend to take credit for their wins but make excuses for their losses? Find out for yourself the next time you read the sports section of the newspaper or watch television interviews after a game. Analyze the sports figures' comments to see what kinds of attributions they make about the cause of their performance. Is the pattern a self-serving one? For example, after a win, does the athlete make such internal attributions as "We won because of excellent teamwork; our defensive line really held today" or "My serve was totally on"? After a loss, does the athlete make such external attributions as, "All the injuries we've had this season have really hurt us" or "That line judge made every call against me"?

According to the research, these self-serving attributions should occur more often than the opposite pattern in which, for example, a winner says, "We won because the other team played so badly it was like they were dead" (external), or a loser says, "I played terribly today. I stank" (internal).

Finally, think about why people make self-serving attributions. If, for example, a famous athlete such as Sidney Crosby attributes his team's loss to factors outside himself, do you think he is protecting his self-esteem (i.e., trying to look good in front of others) or making the most logical attribution he can, given his experience (i.e., he's so talented, most team losses really aren't his fault)?

always because of them (Roesch & Amirkhan, 1997). Consider the attributions made by Susan Nattrass, an Olympic athlete from Edmonton. Beijing was the sixth Olympics for this very experienced trap shooter. How did she explain her disappointing 11th place finish? She placed the blame squarely on her own shoulders: "I moved my eyes instead of letting the bird go and then moving my eyes. It's trying too hard. I was excited, so I moved before I really saw it" (Nattrass, as quoted in Hall, 2008). You can explore self-serving attributions by sports figures in the accompanying Try It! exercise.

The self-serving bias has a number of important implications that extend well beyond the world of sports. For example, it leads people to believe that their actions are rational and defensible, but that the actions of others are unreasonable and unjustified. This phenomenon was demonstrated by Sande, Goethals, Ferrari, and Worth (1989), who found that American students attributed positive motives to the United States for both positive actions (e.g., saving whales trapped in ice) and negative actions (e.g., building more nuclear-powered submarines). However, these same actions were attributed to negative, self-serving motives if participants were told the actions had been performed by the former Soviet Union. Apparently one participant remarked that the only reason Soviets would save trapped whales was to slaughter and eat them later; another participant assumed that the whales must have been blocking Soviet shipping lanes! Canadian students tended to attribute similar motives to U.S. and Soviet actions.

Self-serving biases also tend to creep in whenever we work on tasks with others (Sande, Ellard, & Ross, 1986; Shestowsky, Wegener, & Fabrigar, 1998; Zanna & Sande, 1987). For example, in a classic study conducted at the University of Waterloo, Ross and Sicoly (1979) found that students working on a group project had very good memories when asked to recall their contributions to the project. However, their memories were considerably poorer when asked to recall the contributions of the other group members. As you may have observed, this tendency extends even to our closest relationships. In another study, Ross and Sicoly (1979) asked married couples living in student housing at the University of Waterloo to indicate the extent to which each spouse assumed responsibility for 20 different activities (e.g., cooking, deciding how money should be spent, resolving conflicts). Each person tended to overestimate his or her contribution, such that when the husband's and wife's estimates of responsibility were added, the total was greater than 100 percent!

Finally, a recent study of people in campgrounds in the Canadian Rockies National Park found evidence of self-serving biases when campers were asked "Compared to the average camper, please indicate how likely you think your visiting the campground will affect the conditions listed below." Participants were given a list of possible impacts (e.g., disturbing wildlife and vegetation, leaving garbage behind, contributing to the local economy). Perhaps not surprisingly, these campers believed that their behaviours were less likely to have a negative impact relative to "the average camper" and more likely to have a positive impact (Van Winkle & MacKay, 2008).

Culture and the Self-Serving Bias Research suggests that, like the other attributional biases we have discussed, the self-serving bias has a strong cultural component as well. In a meta analysis of 266 studies conducted all over the world, Amy Mezulis and her colleagues (2004) found that, on the one hand, the self-serving bias is strongest in the United States and some other Western countries—Canada, Australia, and New Zealand. It is also prevalent in Africa, Eastern Europe, and Russia. On the other hand, some Asian cultures displayed a markedly low or even absent level of self-serving bias: Japan, the Pacific Islands, and India (Mezulis, Abramson, Hyde, & Hankin, 2004). In many traditional Asian cultures, the values of modesty and harmony with others are highly valued. For example, Chinese students are expected to attribute their success to other people, such as their teachers or parents, or to other aspects of the situation, such as the high quality of their school (Bond, 1996; Leung, 1996). Their cultural tradition does not encourage them to attribute their success to themselves (such as to their talent or intelligence), as students in Western countries are encouraged to do. Several studies have found that Chinese students take less credit for their successes than do American students (Anderson, 1999; Lee & Seligman, 1997).

What about failure? Recall that in individualistic cultures such as that of the United States, people tend toward the self-serving bias, looking outside of themselves—to the situation—to explain failure. In collectivist cultures such as China's, the reverse is true: People attribute failure to internal causes, not to external ones (Anderson, 1999; Oishi, Wyer, & Colcombe, 2000). (In Chapter 5, we will discuss research showing that Asian students tend not to believe success feedback but readily accept failure feedback, whereas Canadian students show just the opposite tendency.) In fact, in some Asian cultures, such as Japan and Korea, self-critical attributions are extremely common and an important "glue" that holds groups together. When one criticizes one's self (the opposite of a self-serving attribution), others offer sympathy and compassion, which strengthens the interdependence of the group members (Kitayama & Uchida, 2003; Kitayama, Markus, Matsumoto, & Norasakkunkit, 1997).

Defensive Attributions People also alter their attributions to deal with other kinds of threats to their self-esteem. One of the most difficult things to understand in life is the occurrence of tragic events, such as sexual assaults, terminal diseases, and fatal accidents. Even when they happen to strangers we have never met, they can be upsetting. They remind us that if such tragedies can happen to someone else, they can happen to us. One way we deal with this is by making **defensive attributions**, which are explanations for behaviour that defend us from feelings of vulnerability and mortality.

Defensive Attributions

Explanations for behaviour that avoid feelings of vulnerability and mortality

Belief in a Just World One kind of defensive attribution is to believe that bad things happen only to bad people—or at least, only to people who make stupid mistakes or poor choices. Therefore, bad things won't happen to us because we won't be that stupid or careless. Melvin Lerner (1980; Lerner & Simmons, 1966), formerly at the University of Waterloo, has called this the **belief in a just world**—the assumption that people get what they deserve and deserve what they get. By using this attributional bias, the perceiver does not have to acknowledge that there is randomness in life—that an accident or a criminal or unemployment may be just around the corner for an innocent person.

Belief in a Just World

A form of defensive attribution wherein people assume that bad things happen to bad people and that good things happen to good people

A review of 66 experiments that have been conducted since the 1980 review published by Lerner confirms that there is solid research evidence that people engage in this kind of defensive attribution (Hafer & Bègue, 2005). What if a random, awful event happens to another person? How do we deal with that kind of threat to our belief in a just world? For example, in an ingenious set of experiments, Carolyn Hafer (2000a) at Brock University demonstrated that the more people's belief in a just world was threatened by hearing about an attack on an innocent person, the more likely they were to derogate the victim's character and to distance themselves from the victim. Presumably, by doing so they were able to convince themselves that bad things happen only to bad people—and since they themselves are good, surely no misfortune will befall them. More recently, researchers at universities in Ontario have shown that another way of preserving just-world beliefs when faced with an innocent person's misfortune (either ours or someone else's) is to convince ourselves that, down the road, good things will happen to even out the score (Anderson, Kay, & Fitzsimons, 2010; Gaucher, Hafer, Kay, & Davidenko, 2010). For example, Danielle Gaucher and colleagues found that athletes (basketball players and hockey players) who had high just-world beliefs expressed confidence that officials' calls would balance out to be fair in the long run (Gaucher et al., 2010).

Another way that we can alleviate our distress at the prospect of something awful happening is to convince ourselves that there is a higher power in control. A recent study conducted at the University of Waterloo found that when participants were primed with words such as *random* and *chance* they reported significantly higher beliefs in God and other supernatural sources of control than when primed with negative words that did not connote randomness (e.g., *slimy*, *poorly;* Kay, Moscovitch, & Laurin, 2010).

What are the functions of just-world beliefs? According to Hafer (2000b, 2002), such beliefs motivate us to invest in our future. The idea is that we will not be very motivated to plan ahead and make long-term investments if we believe that the world is an unfair, unjust place. To test this idea, Hafer (2000b) asked Brock University students to write an essay about their plans after graduation; other students were asked to write about their current university courses and activities. Later, all students saw a video of a young woman named Sarah who was seeing a counsellor because she had recently contracted a sexually transmitted disease. In the "innocent victim" version of the videotape, Sarah said that she and her partner had used a condom but it had broken during sex. In the "not innocent" version, Sarah admitted that no condom had been used. Who was most likely to blame Sarah for contracting the disease, even when she was portrayed as an innocent victim? You guessed it—the students who earlier had been asked to focus on their long-term goals and plans. Presumably, these participants most needed to be reassured that their long-term investments would be rewarded according to principles of fairness and justice. By blaming Sarah for her fate, they were able to maintain this belief.

Finally, research conducted by Mitch Callan and colleagues with students at the University of Calgary and at the University of Western Ontario shows that people are so motivated to maintain the belief that the world is a just place that they will engage in irrational thinking to preserve this belief (Callan, Ellard, & Nicol, 2006; Callan, Sutton, & Dovale, 2010). In this research, participants were told that a man named David was seriously injured when he was hit by a car. Participants in the immoral condition were also told that David was having an affair with his travel agent, named Susanne. Participants in the moral condition were told that David had asked Susanne to book a vacation for his family. Those who were told that David was having an affair were more likely to think that the accident occurred because he was having an affair and that he deserved to be in the accident. When participants were placed under cognitive load (having to memorize numbers while answering questions about David), these findings were even more pronounced, suggesting that this kind of thinking tends to be automatic (Callan et al., 2010). Thus, even though the two events (the affair and the accident) were completely unrelated, participants linked them to preserve their belief that the world is a just place. Does this sound far-fetched? Consider the horrific stabbing and beheading of Tim McLean—a passenger riding a Greyhound bus that was travelling from Winnipeg to Edmonton on August 2, 2008. The murder was clearly unprovoked. In fact, McLean was sleeping when he was first attacked. How does one preserve a belief in a just world in the face of such a shocking, tragic event? According to one religious group in Kansas, God sent a man to behead McLean as punishment for Canada's liberal stance on homosexuality, abortion, and adultery. Members of this group planned to attend McLean's funeral in order to convey this message (Gackle, 2008). This example shows that there seems to be no limit to the lengths that people will go to assure themselves that the world is a just place where people get what they deserve.

Consequences of Just-World Beliefs: Blaming Victims of Violence Suppose a female student on your campus was the victim of a date rape by a male student. How do you think you and your friends would react? Would you wonder if she'd done something to trigger the sexual assault? Was she acting suggestively earlier in the evening? Had she invited the man into her room? Research by Elaine Walster (Hatfield; 1966) and others has focused on such attributions (e.g., Burger, 1981; Lerner & Miller, 1978; Stormo, Lang, & Stritzke, 1997). In several experiments, it has been found that the victims of crimes or accidents are often seen as causing their fate. Perrott and Webber (1996) presented students at Mount Saint Vincent University with scenarios in which a man or a woman was attacked. Overall, there was greater blaming of female victims than of male victims. Similarly, people tend to believe that rape victims are to blame for the sexual assault (Bell, Kuriloff, & Lottes, 1994; Burt, 1980; Lambert & Raichle, 2000). Those who believe in rape myths (e.g., women falsely report rape to get attention) are especially likely to engage in victim blaming, as shown by research conducted at the University of Manitoba (Morry & Winkler, 2001) and the University of Saskatchewan (Clarke & Lawson, 2009). It is also the case that battered wives are frequently seen as responsible for their abusive husbands' behaviour (Summers & Feldman, 1984). According to research conducted at Carleton University (Kristiansen & Giulietti, 1990) and at Mount Saint Vincent University (Perrott, Miller, & Delaney, 1997), women are especially likely to be blamed for domestic assaults if they are seen as having done something to provoke their partner (see the second Connections box in Chapter 1).

CONNECTIONS

Attributional Biases: Present in the Courtroom?

Sadly, the tendency to blame victims extends to the courtroom. Consider, for example, the 1998 case of *R.v. Ewanchuk*. The complainant in this case was a 17-year-old woman who was raped by a man while he was interviewing her for a job. The man was 45-year-old Steve Ewanchuk, a contractor with a history of convictions for rape and aggravated sexual assault. At the time of this incident, he was under a court order not to hire any females under the age of 18. The young woman testified in the Alberta Court of Queen's Bench that she did not consent to Ewanchuk's advances and in fact felt very afraid during their encounter. The trial judge, however, held her responsible for not having communicated her fear and ruled that consent had been implied. As a result, Ewanchuk was acquitted. The case then went to the Alberta Court of Appeal. One of the appeal judges commented that Ewanchuk's actions were "far less criminal than hormonal" and suggested that the 17-year-old should have taken actions to stop him by using "a well-chosen expletive, a slap in the face, or, if necessary, a well-directed knee" (*R.v. Ewanchuk*, 1998). Once again, Ewanchuk was acquitted. This decision was finally overturned by the Supreme Court of Canada in 1999, which ruled that there is no such thing as implied consent. One of the Supreme Court judges, Madam Justice L'Heureux-Dubé, wrote, "This case is not about consent, since none was given. It is about myths and stereotyping." These myths include the belief that a woman could resist a sexual attack if she really wanted to, that women deserve to be raped because of the way they dress, and so on.

Despite the Supreme Court's ruling, there has been lingering concern that women who are the victims of sexual assault will be further victimized by rape myths and by victim blaming when they appear in the courtroom (L'Heureux-Dubé, 2001; Tang, 2000). It turns out that these concerns are valid. On February 24, 2011, Kenneth Rhodes was convicted of raping a 26-year-old woman on a dark highway outside of Thompson, Manitoba. He was given a two-year conditional sentence, which means that he remains free in the community. Bench Justice Robert Dewar believed that jail time was not necessary because the victim's appearance (wearing a tube top, high heels, and make up) sent signals that "sex was in the air." Justice Dewar characterized Mr. Rhodes as a "clumsy Don Juan" who misunderstood the victim's intentions. Justice Dewar's verdict sparked outrage across the country and was seen as violating the Supreme Court's (1999) ruling on implied consent. At the time of writing, an investigation has been launched into the judge's decision. In the meantime, he has been banned from cases involving sexual assault.

As for Steve Ewanchuk, on November 8, 2005, he was convicted of repeatedly sexually assaulting an eight-year-old girl. The Crown attempted to have him labelled as a dangerous offender, which would have kept him behind bars indefinitely. However, on January 26, 2007, an Edmonton judge rejected the dangerous offender label, choosing instead to declare Steve Ewanchuk a long-term offender—meaning that he will be supervised in the community for 10 years after serving the term for his most recent conviction.

To end on a more positive note, you may be less vulnerable to making these kinds of attributions simply because you are taking this course! Guimond and Palmer (1996) studied the attributions of social science and commerce students at an Ontario university over a three-year period. The two groups of students made similar attributions for poverty and unemployment in their first year of university. However, by their third year, commerce students were more likely to make dispositional attributions—blaming the poor for their poverty and the unemployed for their unemployment—whereas social science students were more likely to make situational attributions. Similar results were obtained in a subsequent study comparing the attributions of social science and engineering students in a Canadian Armed Forces college (Guimond, 1999).

HOW WOULD YOU USE THIS?

You're going to spend your whole life making attributions about other people. You simply can't survive if you don't. You'll need to make decisions about what kind of people they "really" are. Someone you can love? Someone you can't trust? How can you do that accurately? That is the question. So much rides on "accuracy" in this area of life, and yet we often have, at best, imperfect knowledge upon which to base our judgments. Here's what you can do: First, remember that attributions come in two "flavors," internal and external. Remind yourself, often, to think about both as potential causes for another's behaviour. If you find yourself relying too much on one type (perhaps falling prey to an attributional bias), force yourself to consider the other possibility. Play fair, in other words, when you make attributions. Human behaviour is remarkably complex and is often a product of both the individual and the situation. Second, be humble. When you're forming an attribution about another, think of it as a "hypothesis," one that you're working on but are willing to change when new information becomes available. Third, acknowledge when you've been right but also acknowledge when you've been wrong. Incorrect attributions can be an immense learning experience. In fact, we call that "gaining wisdom." So go out there, and be wise!

Summary

- **Nonverbal Behaviour.** Nonverbal communication is used to express emotion, convey attitudes, and communicate personality traits.
  - **Facial Expressions of Emotion** Six major emotions are considered universal, encoded and decoded similarly by people around the world; they have evolutionary significance. There is debate, however, over whether these six are basic and whether they are perceived differently in different cultures. Affect blends occur when one part of the face registers one emotion and another part, a different emotion.
  - **Culture and Nonverbal Communication** Other channels of nonverbal communication include eye gaze, touch, personal space, gesture, and tone of voice. Display rules are particular to each culture and dictate what kinds of emotional expressions people are supposed to show. Emblems are gestures with well-defined meanings and are culturally determined.
- **Implicit Personality Theories: Filling in the Blanks** To understand other people, we observe their behaviour, but we also infer their feelings, traits, and motives. To do so, we use general notions or schemas about which personality traits go together in one person.
  - **Culture and Implicit Personality Theories** Implicit personality theories, or schemas, are shared by people in a culture but not necessarily by people in other cultures.
  - **Causal Attribution: Answering the "Why" Question** According to attribution theory, we try to determine why people do what they do in order to uncover the feelings and traits that are behind their actions. This helps us understand and predict our social world.
  - **The Nature of the Attributional Process** When trying to decide what causes people's behaviour, we can make one of two attributions: an internal (dispositional) attribution or an external (situational) attribution.
  - **The Covariation Model: Internal versus External Attributions** The covariation model focuses on observations of behaviour across time, place, actors, and targets of the behaviour. It examines how the perceiver chooses either an internal or an external attribution. We make such choices by using consensus, distinctiveness, and consistency information.
  - **The Correspondence Bias: People as Personality Psychologists** People also use various mental shortcuts when making attributions, including the use of schemas and theories. One common shortcut is the correspondence bias, the tendency to believe that people's behaviour corresponds to (matches) their dispositions. A reason for this bias is that a person's behaviour has greater perceptual salience than does the surrounding situation. The two-step process of attribution states that the initial and automatic attribution tends to be dispositional, but it can be altered by situational information at the second step.
  - Although people from individualistic and collectivistic cultures both demonstrate the correspondence bias, members of collectivist cultures are more sensitive to situational causes of behaviour and more likely to rely on situational explanations, as long as situational variables are salient.
  - **The Actor/Observer Difference** The actor/observer difference is an amplification of the correspondence bias: We tend to see other people's behaviour as dispositionally caused, although we are more likely to see our own behaviour as situationally caused. The actor/observer effect occurs because perceptual salience and information availability differ for the actor and the observer.
  - **Self-Serving Attributions** People's attributions are also influenced by their personal needs. Self-serving attributions occur when people make internal attributions for their successes and external attributions for their failures. Defensive attributions help people avoid feelings of vulnerability. One type of defensive attribution is the belief in a just world, in which we believe that bad things happen to bad people and good things happen to good people.

5 Self-Knowledge and the Need to Maintain Self-Esteem

"WHO I AM BECAUSE OF WHO SHE WAS" IS THE title of a memoir by Canadian writer Eva Tihanyi. In the story, Tihanyi reflects on the role her Hungarian-born grandmother played in shaping her sense of self. Eva Tihanyi was raised by her grandmother for much of her life and dedicated one of her books to her with these words: "My grandmother, Elizabeth Kalán Tihanyi, without whom I would not have become who I am." Exactly who is Eva Tihanyi? She answers that question this way: "Who I am is a dogma-hating feminist who insists on thinking for herself; a wife who has maintained her own idea of what it is to be a wife; a mother who loves her son unconditionally but has not sacrificed her own self to do so; a teacher who believes that a classroom is an exciting forum rather than a jail; a writer for whom writing is not just an act of putting words on paper but also a way of viewing the world" (Tihanyi, 1999, p. 102).

If you were asked to answer the question "Who am I?" what responses would you give? Would they be similar to or different from those of Eva Tihanyi? How did you become who you are? Were particular people influential in developing your sense of self?

More generally, what is the nature of the self, and how do people discover it? As we will discuss, the process by which people come to know themselves, and how they evaluate this knowledge, is a fascinating one. We now turn to these questions.

Eva Tihanyi (age six) and her grandmother, Elizabeth Kalán Tihanyi, at the Budapest airport in 1962. Eva was about to board the plane that brought her to Canada to be reunited with her parents.

OUTLINE

The Nature of the Self

Watch on mypsychlab
Self-Awareness Task

Who are you? How did you come to be this person you call "myself"? One of the founders of psychology, William James (1842–1910), described the basic duality of our perception of self. First, the self is composed of one's thoughts and beliefs about oneself, or what James (1890) called the "known" or more simply the "me." Second, the self is also the active processor of information, the "knower" or the "I." In modern terms, we refer to the "known" aspect of the self as the **self-concept**, which is the contents of the self (our knowledge about who we are), and to the "knower" aspect as **self-awareness**, which is the act of thinking about ourselves. These two aspects of the self combine to create a coherent sense of identity. Your self is both a book—full of fascinating contents collected over time—and the reader of that book—who at any moment can access a specific chapter or add a new one. In this chapter, we will focus on these aspects of the self: the nature of the self-concept and how people come to know themselves through self-awareness. In the last part of the chapter, we will focus on self-esteem: whether we evaluate our self positively or negatively.

Self-Concept
The contents of the self; that is, our knowledge about who we are

Self-Awareness
The act of thinking about ourselves

A good place to begin is with the question of whether humans are the only species with a sense of self. Some fascinating studies suggest that we are not alone in this regard. Gallup (1977; Gallup & Suarez, 1986) placed a mirror in an animal's cage until the animal became familiar with it. The animal was then briefly anaesthetized and an odourless red dye was painted on its brow or ear (called the "rouge test"). What happens when the animal wakes up and looks in the mirror? Chimpanzees and orangutans immediately touch the area of their heads that contains the red spot. Dolphins also

Researchers have examined whether species other than humans have a self-concept by seeing whether they recognize that an image in a mirror is themselves and not another member of their species. The same procedure has been used with humans, revealing that people develop a self-concept at about the age of two.

show signs of recognizing themselves in mirrors (Emery & Clayton, 2005; Reiss & Marino, 2001). These studies indicate that chimps and orangutans, and possibly dolphins, have a rudimentary self-concept. They realize that the image in the mirror is them and not another animal, and recognize that they look different from the way they looked before (Gallup, Anderson, & Shillito, 2002; Heschl & Buckart, 2006; Posada & Colell, 2007).

What about humans? Researchers have used a variation of the rouge test with humans and found that self-recognition develops at around two years of age (Courage, Edison, & Howe, 2004; Lewis & Ramsay, 2004). This finding was recently confirmed by researchers at Dalhousie University using a variety of tests, including the rouge test (Moore, Mealiea, Garon, & Povinelli, 2007). As we grow older, this self-concept, of course, becomes more complex. Psychologists have studied how people's self-concept changes from childhood to adulthood by asking people of different ages to answer a simple question: "Who am I?" Typically, a child's self-concept is concrete, with references to clear-cut, easily observable characteristics such as age, sex, neighbourhood, and hobbies. For example, a nine-year-old answered the question "Who am I?" this way: "I have brown eyes. I have brown hair. I have brown eyebrows . . .. I'm a boy. I have an uncle that is almost seven feet tall" (Montemayor & Eisen, 1977). As we mature, we place less emphasis on physical characteristics and more emphasis on our psychological states (e.g., our thoughts and feelings), our traits or characteristics, and considerations of how other people judge us (Hart & Damon, 1986; Montemayor & Eisen, 1977; Sande, Goethals, & Radloff, 1988). Thus, we might define ourselves as an extrovert, a cautious person, a spiritual person, an only child, a worrier, someone who is not very interested in politics, and so on.

Functions of the Self: Self-Regulation

We have seen that people develop a self-concept at an early age. But why do humans have self-concepts in the first place? One answer is that the self serves an executive function, regulating people's behaviour, choices, and plans for the future, much like the chief executive officer of a corporation (Baumeister & Vohs, 2003; Carver & Scheier, 1998; Higgins, 1989, 2005; Leary, 2004). We appear to be the only species that can imagine events that have not yet occurred and engage in long-term planning, and it is the self that does this planning and exerts control over our actions (Gilbert, 2006). Regulating our behaviour and choices in optimal ways, of course, can be easier said than done, as anyone who has been on a diet or tried to quit smoking knows.

In Chapter 3, we discussed a form of self-control that does not work very well and often backfires, namely *thought suppression*, whereby we try to push thoughts out of our minds. Often, the more we try not to think about something, such as an ex-boyfriend or the chips on the counter, the more those thoughts come to mind. An interesting question, then, is how the self engages in self-regulation. When we face a difficult choice ("Should I go to the party or study for my midterm?"), what determines how successful we will be at exerting self-control? According to an intriguing theory of self-control called the self-regulatory resource model, self-control is a limited resource, like a muscle that gets tired with frequent use but then rebounds in strength (Baumeister & Hetherington, 1996; Baumeister, Vohs, & Tice, 2007; Vohs, Baumeister, & Ciarocco, 2005). The idea is that people have a limited amount of energy to devote to self-control and that spending it on one task limits the amount that can be spent on another task, just as going for a 10 kilometre run makes it difficult to then immediately play a game of basketball.

This idea has been tested by having participants exert self-control on one task and then assessing whether this reduces their ability to exert control on a subsequent, completely unrelated task (Muraven, Rosman, & Gagné, 2007). In one study, for example, people who were instructed to suppress a thought (don't think about a white bear) were worse at trying to regulate their emotions on a second task (try not to laugh while watching a comedy film), compared with people who did not first have to suppress their thoughts (Muraven, Tice, & Baumeister, 1998). Although the tasks were quite different, the researchers suggested that the first task depleted the resource people use to control their behaviours and feelings, making it difficult to engage in a subsequent act of self-control. More recent research has shown that if people are asked to make a very positive impression on another person (a task that presumably requires some effort), they subsequently show more depletion (e.g., lowered persistence on tasks, more likely to "blurt" things out) compared with when they are told to act neutral (Vohs et al., 2005).

These findings help explain why we often fail at self-control when we are under stress. Former smokers, for example, are more likely to take up smoking again when experiencing life's slings and arrows. Dealing with stress depletes the "self resource," so there is less to spend in other areas. Similarly, efforts at self-control are more likely to fail at night, when the self resource has been depleted by a day of making choices and resisting temptations; dieters are more likely to break their diets at night, and bulimics are more likely to engage in binge eating at night (Baumeister, Muraven, & Tice, 2000). People are best at self-control when they are well rested and not too stressed out.

Before leaving this topic, we want to point out that a recent study conducted with University of Toronto students found neural evidence that is consistent with the self-regulation model. In this experiment, the brain activity of participants was recorded while they performed a task that required self-control, namely suppressing their emotions while watching movies depicting animals suffering and dying. (In the control condition, participants saw the same movies but were not instructed to suppress their feelings.) Those who engaged in self-control later made more errors on a task that required intense concentration than did participants in the control group, just as would be expected, based on the self-regulation model. Interestingly, these participants showed weakened neural response (relative to the control group) in the area of the brain that monitors and detects errors (Inzlicht & Gutsell, 2007).

The Content of the Self: Self-Schemas

Suppose that over the course of a day, Sarah and Caitlin play volleyball together and watch an old movie on TV. How will they organize, remember, and think about these experiences? It depends on their self-schemas. As we saw in Chapter 3, a schema is a body of knowledge that helps us organize what we know about the social world; schemas influence the information we notice, think about, and remember. Similarly, we have **self-schemas**—an organized body of knowledge about ourselves—our attitudes, our likes and dislikes, our personality traits, and so on (Markus, 1977; Oyserman, Kemmelmeir, Fryberg, Brosh, & Hart-Johnson, 2003; Shadel, Cervone, Niaura, & Abrams, 2004; von Hippel, Hawkins, & Schooler, 2001). Say that Sarah, on the one hand, plays a lot of sports and that athleticism is an important part of her self-schema. She is likely to think about and remember the volleyball game more than the movie. Caitlin, on the other hand, has performed in several plays and loves to act. Because acting is more likely to be part of her self-schema, she will think about and remember the movie more than the volleyball game.

Self-Schemas

An organized body of knowledge about the self (e.g., attitudes, preferences, traits) that influences what people notice, think about, and remember about themselves

Self-schemas have a number of advantages. Try this experiment out on your friends. Divide your friends into two groups, and read them a list of 20 adjectives, such as *warm*, *colourful*, *quiet*, and *soft*. Ask one group of your friends to think about how much each adjective describes themselves, and ask the other group to think about how much each adjective describes someone else. Then ask both groups to write down as many of the words as they can remember. More than likely you will find a **self-reference effect**, which is the tendency for people to remember information better if they relate it to themselves (Markus, 1977; Kihlstrom, Beer, & Klein, 2003; Symons & Johnson, 1997). Integrating information with our self-schemas helps us organize the information better and connect it to other information about ourselves, which makes it more likely that we will remember it later.

Self-Reference Effect

The tendency for people to remember information better if they relate it to themselves

Of course, as we learned in Chapter 3, our schemas can also bias memory processes. At the University of Waterloo, Ziva Kunda and colleagues (Kunda, Fong, Sanitioso, & Reber, 1993; Sanitioso, Kunda, & Fong, 1990) found that our desire to see ourselves in a positive light can influence which of our past actions we are most likely to remember. For example, in one of their studies, participants were told that research shows that the trait of introversion is associated with professional success; others were told that extroversion is associated with success. All participants were then asked to list behaviours they had performed that were relevant to the dimension of introversion/extroversion. Those who were led to believe that introversion was associated with success were more likely to remember introverted, rather than extroverted, behaviours they had performed. The opposite was true for those who were led to believe that extroversion was associated with success (Sanitioso, Kunda, & Fong, 1990). According to the researchers, when people are motivated to see themselves as possessing a desired quality or trait, they conduct a selective memory search for examples of past behaviours consistent with that trait. This body of evidence then allows them to draw the "rational" conclusion that the desirable trait is part of their self-schemas.

Self-Concept Clarity Research conducted by Jennifer Campbell at the University of British Columbia suggests that some of us have a clearer sense of who we are than others. Self-concept clarity is defined as the extent to which knowledge about the self is stable, and clearly and consistently defined (Campbell, 1990; Campbell, Trapnell, Heine, Katz, Lavallee, & Lehman, 1996). Self-concept clarity has important cognitive and emotional implications (Campbell & Fehr, 1990; Campbell, Assanand, & Di Paula, 2000). For example, Campbell and colleagues have found that people who are low in self-concept clarity tend to have low self-esteem, are depression-prone, and are more neurotic and less aware of their internal states than those who are high in self-concept clarity. Further, they tend to engage in chronic self-analysis and rumination—an involuntary, negative form of self-focus associated with threat or uncertainty (e.g., "Sometimes it's hard for me to shut off thoughts about myself"). Conversely, people low in self-concept clarity are less likely to engage in positive forms of self-focus such as reflection (e.g., "I love exploring my 'inner self'"; Campbell et al., 1996).

Other Canadian researchers have replicated these findings. For example, the link between low self-concept clarity and low self-esteem has been found with diverse samples ranging from university students of different nationalities and ethnicities to members of a First Nations community (Stinson, Holmes, Wood, Forest, Gaucher, & Kath, 2010; Usborne & Taylor, 2010). Regarding depression, a recent longitudinal study of mothers (most of whom were Canadian) confirmed that people with low self-concept clarity are more likely to experience depression; in this research, the association between low self-concept clarity and depression was strongest for women with low self-esteem (Lee-Flynn, Pomaki, DeLongis, Biesanz, & Puterman, 2011). Finally, research conducted at Brandon University in Manitoba has shown that university students who are low in self-concept clarity also are more likely to engage in self-handicapping (creating excuses in advance so that if one does poorly on a task, one can avoid self-blame; Thomas & Gadbois, 2007). Thus, not having a clear, confident sense of who you are can have negative effects on your thoughts and emotions. To find out where you stand in terms of self-concept clarity, see the accompanying Try It! exercise.

People had very different reactions to Masako Owada's decision to give up her promising career to marry Crown Prince Naruhito of Japan—in part because of cultural differences in the importance of independence versus interdependence.

Cultural Differences in Defining the Self

In June 1993, Masako Owada, a 29-year-old Japanese woman, married Crown Prince Naruhito of Japan. Masako was a very bright career diplomat in the foreign ministry, educated at Harvard and Oxford. She spoke five languages and was on the fast track to a prestigious diplomatic career. Her decision to marry the prince surprised some observers because it meant she would have to give up her career. Indeed, she gave up any semblance of an independent life, becoming subservient to the prince and the rest of

TRY IT! A Measure of Self-Concept Clarity†

Instructions: Indicate the extent to which you agree or disagree with each of these statements.

	Strongly Disagree				Strongly Agree
1. My beliefs about myself often conflict with one another.*	1	2	3	4	5
2. One day I might have one opinion of myself and on another day I might have a different opinion.*	1	2	3	4	5
3. I spend a lot of time wondering about what kind of person I really am.*	1	2	3	4	5
4. Sometimes I feel that I am not really the person that I appear to be.*	1	2	3	4	5
5. When I think about the kind of person I have been in the past, I'm not sure what I was really like.*	1	2	3	4	5
6. I seldom experience conflict between the different aspects of my personality.	1	2	3	4	5
7. Sometimes I think I know other people better than I know myself.*	1	2	3	4	5
8. My beliefs about myself seem to change very frequently.*	1	2	3	4	5
9. If I were asked to describe my personality, my description might end up being different from one day to another day.*	1	2	3	4	5
10. Even if I wanted to, I don't think I could tell someone what I'm really like.*	1	2	3	4	5
11. In general, I have a clear sense of who I am and what I am.	1	2	3	4	5
12. It is often hard for me to make up my mind about things because I don't really know what I want.*	1	2	3	4	5

†This Self-Concept Clarity Scale was developed by Campbell, Trapnell, Heine, Katz, Lavallee, & Lehman (1996) to measure the extent to which people have a stable, clear, and consistently defined sense of self. The items with asterisks (*) are reverse-scored. To find out how you score on this scale, first reverse your answers to the items with asterisks. If you answered 5, change it to a 1; if you answered 4, change it to a 2, and so on. Then sum your ratings on all 12 questions. The higher your score, the more clearly defined your sense of self is. Among Canadian students, average scores on this scale range from 38 to 43. The researchers expected that in less individualist cultures, such as Japan, scores would be lower on this scale. Indeed, when University of British Columbia students completed the Self-Concept Clarity Scale, the average score was 40; when students in Japan completed the scale, the average score was 35.

the royal family and spending much of her time participating in rigid royal ceremonies. Although some people had hoped that she would modernize the monarchy, apparently this has not happened: "so far the princess has not changed the imperial family as much as it has changed her" ("Girl born to Japan's princess," 2001).

Independent View of the Self
Defining oneself in terms of one's own internal thoughts, feelings, and actions, and not in terms of the thoughts, feelings, and actions of other people

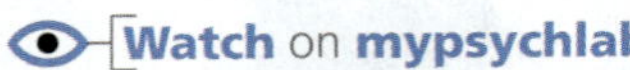
Watch on **mypsychlab**
Cognition, Emotion, and Motivation Across Cultures: Shinobu Kitayama

How do you feel about Masako's decision to marry the prince? Your answer may say something about the nature of your self-concept and the culture in which you grew up. In many Western cultures, people have an **independent view of the self**, which is defining oneself in terms of one's own internal thoughts, feelings, and actions, and not in terms of the thoughts, feelings, and actions of other people (Heine, Lehman, Markus, & Kitayama, 1999; Kitayama & Markus, 1994; Kitayama & Uchida, 2005; Markus & Kitayama, 1991, 2001; Oyserman & Lee, 2008; Triandis, 1995). Westerners learn to define themselves as quite separate from other people and to value independence and uniqueness. Thus, many Western observers were mystified by Masako's decision to marry the prince. Some assumed she was coerced into the marriage by a backward, sexist society that did not properly value her worth as an individual with an independent life of her own.

In contrast, many Asian and other collectivist cultures have an **interdependent view of the self**, which is defining oneself in terms of one's relationships to other people and recognizing that one's behaviour is often determined by the thoughts, feelings, and actions of others. Connectedness and interdependence between people is valued, whereas independence and uniqueness are frowned on. For example, people from Asian cultures are more likely to see themselves in terms of communal qualities such as being kind, accepting, and loyal, whereas Canadians are more likely to see themselves in terms of individual characteristics such as having an exciting personality and being physically attractive, interesting, and so on (Anthony, Holmes, & Wood, 2007; Hong & Woody, 2007). Similarly, when asked to complete sentences beginning with "I am...," people from Asian cultures are more likely to refer to social groups, such as one's family or religious group, than are people from Western cultures (Bochner, 1994; Triandis, 1989). Thus, to many Japanese and other Asians, Masako Owada's decision to give up her career was not at all surprising: It was a positive, natural consequence of her view of herself as connected and obligated to others, such as her family and the royal family. What is viewed as positive and normal behaviour by one culture might be viewed very differently by another.

Interdependent View of the Self

Defining oneself in terms of one's relationships to other people; recognizing that one's behaviour is often determined by the thoughts, feelings, and actions of others

The squeaky wheel gets the grease.

—North American proverb

We do not mean to imply that every member of a Western culture has an independent view of the self and that every member of an Asian culture has an interdependent view of the self. Within cultures there are differences in the self-concept, and these differences are likely to increase as contact between cultures increases. It is interesting to note, for example, that Masako's decision to marry the prince was unpopular among at least some young Japanese women, who felt that her choice was not a positive sign of interdependence but a betrayal of the feminist cause in Japan (Sanger, 1993). Women in Japan are joining the workforce in record numbers, and more women are postponing or forgoing marriage in favour of careers (Faiola, 2004). And the restricted life in the Imperial Household seems to have taken its toll on Princess Masako. In 2004, she stopped making public appearances, and the press office for the royal family announced that she was receiving therapy for depression (Carpenter, 2008).

The nail that stands out gets pounded down.

—Japanese proverb

Consider again Jennifer Campbell's notion of self-concept clarity. It might already have occurred to you that self-concept clarity is probably a Western phenomenon, given that it is based on a premise that the self is a stable configuration of internal traits that govern behaviour across situations. The sense of self might be less clear in cultures in which the self is perceived as interdependent (i.e., based on relationships with others). To find out, Campbell and her colleagues (1996) administered the Self-Concept Clarity Scale to Canadian and Japanese students. (See the Try It! exercise on page 128.) Japanese participants did, in fact, have lower self-concept clarity than Canadian participants. Moreover, self-concept clarity was not as strongly linked to self-esteem for the Japanese participants as it was for the Canadian participants (Campbell et al., 1996). Similarly, a recent study found that Koreans living in Vancouver reported lower self-concept clarity than European-Canadians in that city (Hong & Woody, 2007).

In summary, the difference between an independent and an interdependent sense of self is real and has interesting consequences for communication between different cultures. Indeed, differences in the sense of self are so fundamental that it is difficult for people with independent selves to appreciate what it is like to have an interdependent self, and vice versa. Western readers might find it difficult to appreciate the Asian sense of interdependence; similarly, many Japanese find it difficult to comprehend that North Americans could possibly know who they are, separate from the social groups to which they belong.

Gender Differences in Defining the Self

There is a stereotype that when women get together, they talk about interpersonal problems and relationships, whereas when men get together, they talk about sports or politics—anything but their feelings. Research suggests that there is some truth to the stereotype (Fehr, 1996) and that it reflects a difference in women's and men's self-concepts (Baumeister & Sommer, 1997; Cross, Bacon, & Morris, 2000; Cross & Madson, 1997; Gabriel & Gardner, 1999, 2004). Specifically, women's self-concepts reflect more *relational* interdependence, meaning that they focus more on their close relationships, such as how they feel about their romantic partner, a friend, or their child (Brewer & Gardner, 1996). Indeed, in recent research conducted at the University of Waterloo, women rated relational traits (e.g., warm, affectionate, loving) as more self-descriptive than did men (Anthony et al., 2007; see also Guimond, Chatard, Martinot, Crisp, & Redersdorff, 2006). This gender difference also has been found in a series of studies conducted by an international team of researchers that included John Adair from the University of Manitoba. The researchers administered the sentence completion test ("I am...") to thousands of participants in as many as 15 different cultures. Women were found to hold a more relational view of the self—but only in individualist cultures (e.g., Canada, white South Africa, New Zealand). In collectivist cultures that emphasize interdependence (e.g., China, Ethiopia, black South Africa), women and men were equally likely to hold a relational view of the self (Watkins, Adair et al., 1998; Watkins, Akande et al., 1998).

This is not to say that men in individualist cultures are completely lacking in interdependence. Quite the contrary. According to research by Cross and Madson (1997), interdependence is part of men's conception of self, but it is not the kind of relational interdependence shown by women. Rather, men tend to define themselves in terms of social groups, such as the sports teams to which they belong (Cross, Bacon, & Morris, 2000; Cross & Madson, 1997; Gabriel & Gardner, 1999). This is known as *collective* interdependence (Gabriel & Gardner, 1999). To see how much your self-concept is based on a sense of relational interdependence, answer the questions in the accompanying Try It! exercise.

When interpreting gender differences such as these, it is important to keep in mind the bigger picture. Even though women and men differ in their self-conceptions, overall, the psychological differences between women and men are far fewer than the similarities (Deaux & La France, 1998; Fehr & Broughton, 2001).

Connect to MyPsychLab
Do you think you're normal? To take a survey to asses your emotions and attitudes towards experiences, go to MyPsychLab

Knowing Ourselves through Introspection

Introspection
The process whereby people look inward and examine their own thoughts, feelings, and motives

We've seen that the culture in which people grow up and their gender help shape their self concept. But how do people learn who they are in the first place? How did you discover those things that make you uniquely *you*? We will now discuss how people gain self-knowledge. "Well", you might say, "It's not exactly a surprise; I just think about myself. No big deal." In other words, you rely on **introspection**—you look inward and examine the "inside information" that you, and you alone, have about your thoughts, feelings, and motives, just as the quotation by C. S. Lewis suggests. And indeed, you do find some answers when you introspect. But there are two interesting things about introspection. First, people do not rely on this source of information as often as you might think—surprisingly, people spend very little time thinking about themselves. According to one study, only 8 percent of thoughts are about the self; most of the time, people are thinking about work, chores, and time (Csikszentmihalyi & Figurski, 1982). Second, even when people do introspect, the reasons for their feelings and behaviour can be hidden from conscious awareness (Wilson, 2002; Wilson & Dunn, 2004). As Nietzsche observed, much of the self may be unknown. In short, self-scrutiny isn't all it's cracked up to be. If this was your only source of knowledge about yourself, you would be in trouble.

There is one thing, and only one in the whole universe which we know more about than we could learn from external observation. That one thing is [ourselves]. We have, so to speak, inside information; we are in the know.

—C. S. Lewis, *1960*

A Measure of Relational Interdependence†

Instructions: Indicate the extent to which you agree or disagree with each of these statements.

	Strongly Disagree						Strongly Agree
1. My close relationships are an important reflection of who I am.	1	2	3	4	5	6	7
2. When I feel close to someone, it often feels to me like that person is an important part of who I am.	1	2	3	4	5	6	7
3. I usually feel a strong sense of pride when someone close to me has an important accomplishment.	1	2	3	4	5	6	7
4. I think one of the most important parts of who I am can be captured by looking at my close friends and understanding who they are.	1	2	3	4	5	6	7
5. When I think of myself, I often think of my close friends or family also.	1	2	3	4	5	6	7
6. If a person hurts someone close to me, I feel personally hurt as well.	1	2	3	4	5	6	7
7. In general, my close relationships are an important part of my self-image.	1	2	3	4	5	6	7
8. Overall, my close relationships have very little to do with how I feel about myself.	1	2	3	4	5	6	7
9. My close relationships are unimportant to my sense of what kind of person I am.	1	2	3	4	5	6	7
10. My sense of pride comes from knowing who I have as close friends.	1	2	3	4	5	6	7
11. When I establish a close friendship with someone, I usually develop a strong sense of identification with that person.	1	2	3	4	5	6	7

†To compute your score, first reverse the rating you gave to questions 8 and 9. That is, if you circled a 1, change it to a 7; if you circled a 2, change it to a 6; if you circled a 7, change it to a 1; and so on. Then total your answers to the 11 questions. High scores reflect more of a tendency to define yourself in terms of relational interdependence. Cross, Bacon, and Morris (2000) found that women tend to score higher than men; in eight samples of university students, women averaged 57.2 and men averaged 53.4. Recent research suggests that how you score on this scale can have implications for your love life! In a study conducted at McGill University, participants first visualized their romantic partner and then were presented with a list of negative partner behaviours (e.g., "Your partner criticizes something you say"). Those who scored high on this scale made more benign (positive, forgiving) attributions for negative partner behaviours than those who scored low on this scale (Linardatos & Lydon, 2011a). The researchers suggest that people who are high in relational interdependence are more likely to respond to situations in ways that help maintain their relationships.

(Adapted from Cross, Bacon, & Morris, 2000)

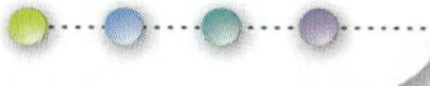

Focusing on the Self: Self-Awareness Theory

As just discussed, we do not focus on ourselves very often. However, sometimes we turn the spotlight of consciousness on ourselves, particularly when we encounter something in the environment that triggers self-awareness, such as watching ourselves on a videotape or seeing our reflection in the mirror. According to **self-awareness theory**, when we focus our attention on ourselves, we evaluate and compare our current behaviour

Self-Awareness Theory
The idea that when people focus their attention on themselves, they evaluate and compare their behaviour with their internal standards and values

> *We are unknown, we knowers, ourselves to ourselves; this has its own good reason. We have never searched for ourselves—how should it then come to pass, that we should ever find ourselves?*
>
> —Friedrich Nietzsche, *1918*

against our internal standards and values (Carver, 2003; Duval & Silvia, 2002; Duval & Wicklund, 1972; Phillips & Silvia, 2005; Wiekens & Stapel, 2008). In short, we become self-conscious, in the sense that we become objective, judgmental observers of ourselves. Let's say that you feel that you should quit smoking, and one day you catch an image of yourself in a store window smoking a cigarette. How do you think you would feel?

Seeing your reflection will make you aware of the disparity between your behaviour and your internal standards. If you can change your behaviour to match your internal guidelines (e.g., quit smoking), you will do so. If you feel you can't change your behaviour, then being in a state of self-awareness will be very uncomfortable because you will be confronted with disagreeable feedback about yourself. This dissatisfaction with ourselves can be painful. As a result, we take steps to alleviate the discomfort of unpleasant realizations about the self. Figure 5.1 illustrates this process—how self-awareness makes us conscious of our internal standards and directs our subsequent behaviour.

> *I swear to you . . . that to be overly conscious is a sickness, a real, thorough sickness.*
>
> —Fyodor Dostoevsky, *Notes from Underground, 1864*

Consider, for example, a study by Sophia Moskalenko and Steven Heine (2003). These researchers told some participants that they had done very poorly on a task that reflected their level of intelligence. Others were told that they had done well. Moskalenko and Heine reasoned that the participants who were given the failure feedback would be highly motivated to escape self-awareness and therefore would be most likely to pay attention to a video that was on in the room. And that is exactly what happened.

Sometimes people go even further in their attempt to escape the self. Roy Baumeister (1991) has pointed out that such diverse activities as alcohol abuse, binge eating, sexual masochism, and suicide have one thing in common: All are effective ways of turning the internal spotlight away from oneself. Getting drunk, for example, is one way of avoiding negative thoughts about oneself (at least temporarily). Suicide, of course, is the ultimate way of ending self-scrutiny. The fact that people regularly engage in harmful behaviours is an indication of how aversive self-focus can be (Hull, 1981; Hull & Young, 1983; Hull, Young, & Jouriles, 1986).

> *I have often wished I had time to cultivate modesty . . .. But I am too busy thinking about myself.*
>
> —Dame Edith Sitwell *(1887–1964)*

We hasten to add that self-awareness does not inevitably have negative effects. According to Baumeister (1991), people sometimes escape self-awareness through more positive means, such as religious expression and spirituality. It is also important to point out that self-focus is not always unpleasant. If you have just experienced a major success, focusing on yourself can be pleasant indeed because it highlights your positive accomplishments (Greenberg & Musham, 1981; Silvia & Abele, 2002). Similarly, a recent study found that people feel good about themselves when self-awareness is created by having their Facebook profile displayed on a computer screen, rather than having them see their reflection in a mirror. The researchers suggest that people present their ideal self on Facebook and other social networking sites, rather than their actual self (which, presumably, is the self that is activated when they see themselves in a mirror; Gonzales & Hancock, 2011). Finally, self-focus can also be a way of keeping you out of trouble, by reminding you of your sense of right and wrong. For example, several studies have found that when people are self-aware (e.g., in front of a mirror), they are more likely to follow their moral standards, such as avoiding the temptation to cheat on a test (Beaman, Klentz, Diener, & Svanum, 1979; Diener & Wallbom, 1976; Gibbons, 1978).

Thus, self-awareness can have negative or positive effects. And in those cases in which self-awareness feels aversive, those bad feelings can be alleviated in either a constructive or a destructive manner.

Cultural Differences in Self-Awareness

Virtually all the work we have described so far has been conducted with samples of people from Western countries (primarily North Americans). Given that people who grow up in East Asian cultures tend to have a more interdependent view of the

FIGURE 5.1

Self-awareness theory: The consequences of self-focused attention.

When people focus on themselves, they compare their behaviour with their internal standards.

(Adapted from Carver & Scheier, 1981)

self, defining themselves in terms of their relationships to other people, is it possible that they differ in how self-aware they tend to be? Recent research indicates that the answer is yes. Dov Cohen and colleagues have found that East Asians are more likely to have an *outside perspective on the self*, viewing themselves through the eyes of other people. People who grow up in Western cultures are more likely to have an *insider perspective on the self*, focusing on their own private experiences without considering how other people see them (Cohen, Hoshino-Browne, & Leung, 2007).

Another way of saying this is that East Asians may be in a chronic state of self-awareness, because they are more likely to be seeing themselves through the eyes of other people. Because East Asians are already self-aware, they should be less influenced by cues such as mirrors. This is exactly what Steve Heine and colleagues found in a recent program of research (Heine, Takemoto, Moskalenko, Lasaleta, & Henrich, 2008). In Heine and colleagues' first study, Americans who rated themselves with a mirror present were more dissatisfied with themselves (reported a larger "gap" or discrepancy between their actual and ideal selves) than when there was no mirror present. For Japanese participants, dissatisfaction with self did not differ depending on whether a mirror was present. These results are shown in Figure 5.2. In their second study, Heine and colleagues found that Canadian university students placed in front of a mirror were less likely to cheat on a test than those who were not in front of a mirror (as has been found in past research with North American participants). The mirror had no impact on the rate of cheating among Japanese participants. As the authors note, the Japanese participants in these studies acted as if they had "mirrors in their heads" and therefore did not need an actual mirror to see themselves from an outside perspective (Heine et al., 2008).

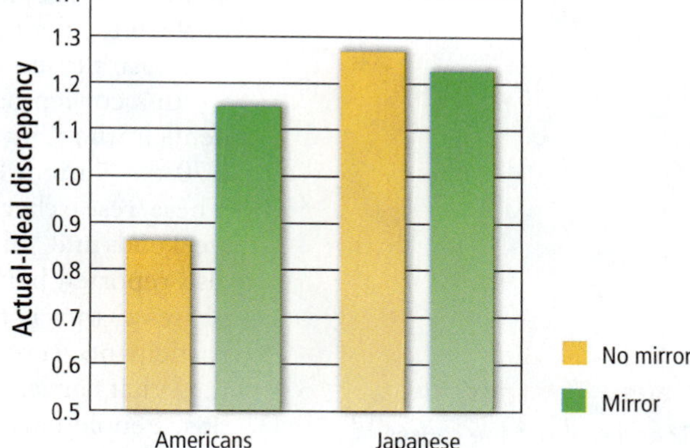

FIGURE 5.2

Effects of mirror on Japanese and American college students.

American college students who filled out a questionnaire in front of a mirror noticed more discrepancies between their ideal and actual selves than did American college students who filled out the questionnaire without a mirror present. The presence of a mirror had no effect on the answers of Japanese college students.

Interestingly, in a series of studies conducted at the University of Manitoba and the University of Waterloo, Jacquie Vorauer and colleagues (Vorauer & Ross, 1999; Vorauer, 2001) found that when people were made to feel self-aware, they tended to assume that another person also would have this heightened access to their traits. This tendency was particularly pronounced among those high in interdependence (Vorauer & Cameron, 2002).

Thus, it would appear that Westerners can adopt an outside perspective on the self, but the "default" tends to be an insider perspective, whereas for East Asians, the default tends to be an outsider's perspective.

Judging Why We Feel the Way We Do: Telling More than We Can Know

Even when we are self-aware and introspect to our heart's content, it can be difficult to know *why* we feel the way we do. This is not to say that we are thinkers without a clue—we are aware of the final result of our thought processes (e.g., deciding that we are in love); however, we are often unaware of the cognitive processing that led to the result. It's as if the magician pulled a rabbit out of a hat: You see the rabbit, but you don't know how it got there. How do we deal with this rabbit problem?

Even though we often don't know why we feel a certain way, it seems we are always able to come up with an explanation. Richard Nisbett and Tim Wilson referred to this phenomenon as "telling more than we know" because people's explanations of their feelings and behaviour often go beyond what they can reasonably know (Nisbett & Ross, 1980; Nisbett & Wilson, 1977a). For example, in one study, university students were asked to keep journals of their moods every day for five weeks (Wilson, Laser, & Stone, 1982). The students also kept track of things that might affect their daily moods, such as the weather and how much they had slept the night before. At the end of the five weeks, the students estimated how much their mood was related to these other variables. Wilson and colleagues found that in many cases, people were wrong about what predicted their mood; for example, most people believed that the amount of sleep they got predicted how good a mood they were in the next day, when in fact this wasn't true—amount of sleep was unrelated to people's moods.

In a conceptually similar study, McFarlane, Martin, and Williams (1988) had students at the University of British Columbia keep track of their moods every day for a 70-day period. Later, the students were asked to recall what their moods had been. These researchers found that participants "remembered" more positive moods on weekends and "bluer Mondays" than they actually experienced. Interestingly, women also reported having been in worse moods during their premenstrual and menstrual phases than was the case. (In fact, during the menstrual phase of their cycle, female participants were actually in an especially pleasant mood!)

Causal Theories

Theories about the causes of one's own feelings and behaviours; typically, we learn such theories from our culture (e.g., "absence makes the heart grow fonder")

What participants in these studies relied on, at least in part, were their **causal theories**. People have many theories about what influences their feelings and behaviour and often use these theories to help them explain why they feel the way they do (e.g., "I am in a bad mood—I bet it's because I got only four hours of sleep last night, or because it's Monday, or because it's 'that time of the month'"). We learn many of these theories from the culture in which we grow up. The only problem, as discussed in Chapter 3, is that our schemas and theories are not always correct and thus can lead to incorrect judgments about the causes of our actions.

Consider this example of causal theories in action from some researchers who have studied them. One night, Dick Nisbett and Tim Wilson were meeting in an office at the University of Michigan. They were trying to think of ways to test the hypothesis that people rely on causal theories when trying to uncover the reasons for their feelings, judgments, and actions. Brilliant insights were not forthcoming, and the researchers were frustrated by their lack of progress. Then they realized that a source of their frustration (or so they thought) was the annoying whine of a vacuum cleaner that a custodial worker was operating right outside their office. This realization led them to wonder whether distracting background noises are more bothersome than people think. Maybe this was an example of the very kind of situation they were looking for—one that would influence people's judgments but would be overlooked when people explained their behaviour.

After shutting the door, Nisbett and Wilson (1977) designed a study to test this possibility. They showed participants a documentary in the presence of an annoying noise. About a minute into the film, a "construction worker" (actually Nisbett) turned on a power saw right outside the door to the room and ran the saw intermittently until Wilson, the experimenter, went to the door and asked him to please stop sawing until the film was over. At the end of the film, the participants rated how much they enjoyed it. The experimenter then asked them whether the hallway noise had influenced their evaluations. To see if the noise really did have an effect, there was a control condition in which other participants viewed the film without any distracting noise. The hypothesis was that the noise would lower people's evaluation of the film but that people would not realize the noise was responsible for the negative evaluation.

Does this seem like a reasonable hypothesis? It did to the researchers; but, as it turns out, they were completely wrong. The participants who watched the film with the annoying background noise did not like it any less than did those who saw the film without the distracting noise (in fact, they liked it slightly more). However, when the participants were asked how much the noise had influenced their ratings, most people reported that it had lowered their ratings of the film. Thus, even though the noise had no detectable effect on people's feelings about the film, it influenced their explanations for their feelings.

Thus, introspecting about our past actions and our current thoughts does not always yield the right answer about why we feel the way we do. How else might we find out what kind of person we are? We now turn to another source of self-knowledge: observation of our own behaviour.

Knowing Ourselves by Observing Our Own Behaviour

Suppose that a friend asks you how much you like classical music. You hesitate because you never listened to classical music when you were growing up, but lately you have found yourself listening to symphonies on the radio every now and then. "Well, I don't know," you reply. "I guess I like some kinds of classical music. Just yesterday, I listened to a Beethoven symphony on the radio while I was driving to work." In giving this response, you used an important source of self-knowledge: observations of your own behaviour.

Self-perception theory argues that when our attitudes and feelings are uncertain or ambiguous, we infer these states by observing our behaviour and the situation in which it occurs (Bem, 1972). Let's consider each part of this theory. First, we infer our inner feelings from our behaviour only when we are not sure how we feel. If you've always known that you are a classical music lover, then you do not need to observe your behaviour to figure this out (Andersen, 1984; Andersen & Ross, 1984). However, if you aren't sure how much you like classical music, you are especially likely to use your behaviour as a guide to how you feel. This effect was demonstrated by Chaiken and Baldwin (1981) with University of Toronto students. First, the researchers assessed whether the participants had well-defined attitudes toward protecting the environment. Then they asked participants to check off which behaviours from a list of pro- or anti-environmental actions they had performed (e.g., "I frequently leave on lights in rooms I'm not using") as a way of reminding them of their past behaviour. The researchers hypothesized that being reminded of their past behaviour would influence only the participants whose attitudes were more uncertain. Indeed, participants with less clearly defined environmental attitudes were

Self-Perception Theory

The theory that when our attitudes and feelings are uncertain or ambiguous, we infer these states by observing our behaviour and the situation in which it occurs

I've always written poems . . . . I never know what I think until I read it in one of my poems.

—Virginia Hamilton Adair, *1913–1996*

strongly affected by these behavioural cues—those who were reminded of their pro-environmental behaviour subsequently reported that they held pro-environmental attitudes, whereas those who were reminded of their anti-environmental behaviour later reported more negative environmental attitudes. In contrast, being reminded of their past behaviour had little effect on the participants who already had clear attitudes on this issue.

Self-perception theory also claims that people evaluate whether their behaviour really reflects how they feel or whether the situation they are in made them act that way. If you freely choose to listen to the classical music station—that is, no one makes you do it—you are especially likely to conclude that you listen to that station because you love classical music. If it is your roommate and not you who always tunes in to the classical station, you are unlikely to conclude that you listen to classical music because you love it.

Intrinsic versus Extrinsic Motivation

An interesting implication of self-perception theory is that if people are given rewards for engaging in certain activities, they may conclude that they actually don't enjoy that activity. Instead, they may think that they are just participating in the activity for the reward. Let's say you love to play the piano. You spend many hours happily practising, simply enjoying the act of making music and the feeling that you are getting better. We would say that your interest in playing the piano stems from **intrinsic motivation**, which is the desire to engage in an activity because you enjoy it or find it interesting, not because of **extrinsic motivation**—external rewards or pressures (Durik & Harackiewicz, 2007; Harackiewicz, Durik, & Barron, 2005; Lepper, Corpus, & Iyengar, 2005; Ryan & Deci, 2000).

Intrinsic Motivation
The desire to engage in an activity because we enjoy it or find it interesting, not because of external rewards or pressures

Extrinsic Motivation
The desire to engage in an activity because of external rewards or pressures, not because we enjoy the task or find it interesting

Whether our behaviour is motivated by intrinsic versus extrinsic factors has a number of far-reaching effects (Koestner & Losier, 2002; Losier & Koestner, 1999; Vallerand, 1997; Vallerand & Ratelle, 2002). For example, a Canadian research team found that intrinsic motivation was positively correlated with persistence (over a two-year period) among competitive swimmers (Pelletier, Fortier, Vallerand, & Brière, 1996) and with maintaining interest in repetitive figure skating tasks, as demonstrated with competitive figure skaters from clubs in the Ottawa–Carleton area (Green-Demers, Pelletier, Stewart, & Gushue, 1998). Similarly, Bailis and Segall (2004) found that intrinsic motivation was correlated with continuing one's membership (over a two-year period) in a Winnipeg wellness centre. In the domain of academics, intrinsic motivation has been correlated with positive language learning outcomes (e.g., feeling competent speaking French in a sample of French immersion students; Noels, Clément, & Pelletier, 1999), and with remaining in school rather than dropping out, as has been shown in several studies with French-Canadian high school students (Koestner & Losier, 2002; Vallerand, Fortier, & Guay, 1997; see also Guay, Mageau, & Vallerand, 2003). Intrinsic motivation is also associated with actively seeking information about environmental issues (e.g., nuclear waste, pesticides in food) and engaging in pro-environmental behaviours (e.g., recycling, conserving resources, purchasing environmentally friendly products), as demonstrated in several studies of Ontario residents (Pelletier, 2002; Séguin, Pelletier, & Hunsley, 1999).

Finally, intrinsic motivation also has relationship benefits. For example, partners who are motivated to be in a relationship for its own sake, rather than to receive external benefits or rewards, are more likely to view relationship problems as "challenges" rather than "hassles" (Blais, Sabourin, Boucher, & Vallerand, 1990), to engage in more constructive conflict resolution (Knee, Lonsbary, Canevello, & Patrick, 2005), and to report greater relationship satisfaction (Blais et al., 1990). Interestingly, according to a recent program of research conducted in Quebec, intrinsic motivation in non-relational domains also has positive a "spill over" effect on relationships. More specifically, in a series of studies with student and non-student samples, it was found that the more passionate participants were about their work, a sport, or other activity, the higher the quality of their interpersonal relationships (Philippe, Vallerand, Houlfort, Lavigne, & Donahue, 2010).

The Overjustification Effect Return, for a moment, to our earlier example of the joy you experienced while playing the piano. Now let's say your parents get the brilliant idea of rewarding you with money for playing the piano. They figure that this will make you practise even harder. After all, rewards work, don't they? However, your parents have now added an extrinsic reason for you to play the piano. Unfortunately, extrinsic rewards can undermine intrinsic motivation. Whereas before you played the piano because you loved it, now you're playing it so that you'll get the reward. What was once play is now work. The sad outcome is that replacing intrinsic motivation with extrinsic motivation makes people lose interest in the activity they initially enjoyed. This result is called the **overjustification effect**, whereby people view their behaviour as caused by compelling extrinsic reasons (e.g., a reward), making them underestimate the extent to which their behaviour was caused by intrinsic reasons (e.g., their enjoyment of the activity; Deci, Koestner, & Ryan, 1999a, 1999b; Harackiewicz, 1979; Lepper, 1995; Lepper, Henderlong, & Gingras, 1999).

Overjustification Effect
The case whereby people view their behaviour as caused by compelling extrinsic reasons, making them underestimate the extent to which their behaviour was caused by intrinsic reasons

Preserving Intrinsic Interest Does society's reward system wreak havoc with intrinsic motivation? Fortunately, there are conditions under which overjustification effects don't come into play. Rewards will undermine interest only if interest was high initially (Calder & Staw, 1975; Tang & Hall, 1995). If a child has no interest in reading, then getting him or her to read by offering free pizzas is not a bad idea, because there is no initial interest to undermine.

Also, the type of reward makes a difference. So far, we have discussed **task-contingent rewards**, meaning that people get them only for performing a task, regardless of how well they do it. Sometimes **performance-contingent rewards** are used, whereby the reward depends on how well people perform the task. For example, grades are performance-contingent because you get a high reward (an A) only if you do well. This type of reward is less likely to decrease interest in a task—and may even increase interest—because it conveys the message that you are good at the task (Deci & Ryan, 1985). Thus, rather than giving kids a reward for playing math games regardless of how well they do (i.e., a task-contingent reward), it is better to reward them for doing well in math. However, even performance-contingent rewards must be used with care because they, too, can backfire. Although people like the positive feedback these rewards convey, they do not like the apprehension caused by being evaluated (Harackiewicz, 1989; Harackiewicz, Manderlink, & Sansone, 1984). The trick is to convey positive feedback without making people feel nervous and apprehensive about being evaluated. A recent study conducted by American and Canadian researchers also shows that performance contingent rewards lead to worse performance than task contingent rewards if rewards are taken away for poor performance (e.g., losing money every time you make a mistake; Muraven, Rosman, & Gagné, 2007). Thus, rewards must be doled out in a way that they can be earned if one performs well, but not set up so that they are taken away if one performs poorly.

Task-Contingent Rewards
Rewards that are given for performing a task, regardless of how well the task is done

Performance-Contingent Rewards
Rewards that are based on how well we perform a task

Making children read for external reasons can lead to an overjustification effect, whereby they infer that they have no intrinsic interest in reading.

Knowing Ourselves through Social Interaction

People are not solitary seekers of self-knowledge, but social beings who often see themselves through the eyes of other people. James (1890) stressed the importance of social relationships in people's definition of self, noting that they can have different "selves" that develop in response to different social situations. For example, the self that you present to your friends is probably different than the self you present when interacting with your social psychology professor. Not only is it true that we present ourselves differently to different people, but it is also the case that other people shape how we view ourselves. It's as if other people reflect their image of us back for us to see.

Seeing Ourselves through the Eyes of Others: The Looking-Glass Self

Looking-Glass Self

The idea that we see ourselves through the eyes of other people and incorporate their views into our self-concept

The idea that we see ourselves through the eyes of other people—either present or imagined—and incorporate their views into our self-concept is called the **looking-glass self** (Cooley, 1902; Mead, 1934). Mark Baldwin and colleagues have explored this idea in an ingenious set of experiments (Baldwin, 1992; Baldwin & Meunier, 1999; Baldwin & Sinclair, 1996; Baldwin, Granzberg, Pippus, & Pritchard, 2003). Imagine you were a participant in one of their studies. Think of an older member of your family. Try to form a vivid picture of this person in your mind. Imagine that this person is sitting beside you. Focus on the colour of the person's eyes or hair, and then focus on the sound of the person's voice. Imagine talking to this person.

Simulate on **mypsychlab**
Multiple Selves

Now imagine reading a story about a woman who engages in sexually permissive behaviour. How much do you think you would enjoy the story? Not very much, according to Baldwin and Holmes (1987). They found that female students at the University of Waterloo who had previously imagined older family members rated a *Cosmopolitan* magazine story about a woman's permissive sexual behaviour as less enjoyable than women who had imagined their (presumably more permissive) university friends. In a follow-up study, Baldwin and colleagues primed a sense of self as a Catholic among Catholic women at the University of Waterloo through subliminal exposure to a picture of then Pope John Paul II looking disapproving (Baldwin, Carrell, & Lopez,

The looking-glass self. In one study (Baldwin, Carrell, & Lopez, 1990), students were subliminally exposed either to a photo of the chair of their department, scowling, or to a photo of a post-doctoral student, smiling. Those exposed to their scowling department head subsequently rated their own research more negatively than did those exposed to the friendly post-doctoral student. In another study (Baldwin et al., 1990), participants were subliminally exposed either to a picture of a scowling man unknown to them or to a picture of Pope John Paul II, altered to look particularly disapproving. Practising Catholic women rated themselves more negatively after reading a sexually permissive passage when they had been exposed to the picture of the disapproving pope.

1990). Other participants were exposed to the scowling face of a man who was unfamiliar to them—and therefore should not have had implications for their sense of self. All participants then read the same sexually permissive passage. As expected, practising Catholic women who were exposed to the disapproving countenance of the pope rated themselves more negatively than did those who were exposed to the disapproving face of an unfamiliar man. Presumably for the practising Catholics, the pope was an especially relevant internal audience (Baldwin et al., 1990).

In yet another study in this series (Baldwin et al., 1990), graduate students at the University of Michigan were asked to evaluate their recent research ideas. For some of the students, an evaluative authority figure was primed by subliminal exposure (flashing a slide so quickly that the participants weren't consciously aware of what had been shown) to the scowling face of their program director. Other students were exposed to an approving figure—the warm, friendly face of a post-doctoral student (John Ellard, now a social psychology professor at the University of Calgary). Students who were exposed to the scowling face of their program director subsequently evaluated their research ideas more negatively than did those exposed to the friendly face of the post-doctoral student.

Who we are, then, is determined, at least in part, by the internal audience we have in mind. If, on the one hand, we are reminded of a significant person in our lives who seems critical or disapproving, we will tend to see ourselves as possessing negative traits (e.g., immoral or incompetent). On the other hand, if we happen to have a supportive, approving internal audience in mind, we are more likely to view ourselves as having positive characteristics.

Knowing Ourselves by Comparing Ourselves with Others

Connect to MyPsychLab
To access the Critical Thinking question on eating disorders and the media, go to MyPsychLab

We also come to know ourselves through comparison with other people. Imagine that you are at a buffet with all kinds of delectable offerings. As you load your plate, you may be wondering whether it looks as though you are eating too much. How might you find out? Probably by looking at how much the people around you are eating. If they are eating more than you are, you will likely feel just fine about your heaped plate. If they are eating less than you, you may feel a little sheepish or embarrassed. In fact, recent research conducted with female students at the University of Toronto found exactly that—when a confederate ate more than they did, the participants concluded that they had eaten an appropriate amount. If the confederate ate less than they did, the research participants saw their food intake as less appropriate. The confederate also was better liked when she ate more, rather than less, than the participants—presumably because she made the participants feel as though their behaviour was appropriate (Leone, Herman, & Pliner, 2008).

This example illustrates Leon Festinger's (1954) **social comparison theory**, which holds that people learn about their own abilities and attitudes by comparing themselves with other people. The theory revolves around two important questions: When do you engage in social comparison? With whom do you compare yourself?

Social Comparison Theory
The idea that we learn about our own abilities and attitudes by comparing ourselves with other people

The answer to the first question is that you socially compare when there is no objective standard for you to measure yourself against and when you experience some uncertainty about yourself in a particular area, such as wondering whether you are eating an appropriate amount in public settings (Suls & Fletcher, 1983; Suls & Miller, 1977).

As to the second question—with whom do people compare themselves?—not surprisingly, people find it most informative to compare themselves with others who are similar to them on the attribute or dimension in question (Goethals & Darley, 1977; Goffin, Jelley, Powell, & Johnson, 2009; Miller, 1982; Wheeler, Koestner, & Driver, 1982; Zanna, Goethals, & Hill, 1975). For example, if you are wondering about your artistic ability, it will not be very informative to compare yourself with Picasso—one of the great artists of the twentieth century. It also will not be that informative to compare your artistic endeavours with the finger painting and scribbles of your four-year-old sister. It is better to compare yourself with the other people in your drawing class, if your goal is to assess your own abilities.

The Need to Feel Good about Ourselves

As we have discussed, people are motivated to understand themselves. It is also the case that people need to feel good about themselves. We now turn to the topic of self-evaluation.

Social Comparison Revisited

Downward Social Comparison

The process whereby we compare ourselves with people who are worse than we arein a particular trait or ability

Constructing an accurate image of ourselves is only one reason that we engage in social comparison. We also use social comparison to boost our egos. Is it important to you to believe that you are a fabulous artist-in-the-making? Then compare yourself with your little sister—you have her beat! This use of **downward social comparison**—comparing yourself with people who are worse than you in a particular trait or ability—is a self-protective, self-enhancing strategy (Aspinwall & Taylor, 1993; Buunk, Oldersma, & de Dreu, 2001; Davison, Pennebaker, & Dickerson, 2000). Indeed, there is considerable evidence that if you compare yourself with people who are less smart, less talented, or in poorer health than you are, you'll feel very good about yourself. For example, Joanne Wood, Shelley Taylor, and Rosemary Lichtman (1985) found evidence of downward comparison in interviews with cancer patients. The vast majority of patients spontaneously compared themselves with other cancer patients who were more ill than they were, presumably as a way of making themselves feel more optimistic about the course of their own condition. Wood and colleagues also examined spontaneous social comparisons in everyday life by having students at the University of Waterloo keep track of times when they compared themselves with another person over a three-week period (Wood, Michela, & Giordano, 2000). An analysis of these diaries confirmed that people were most likely to spontaneously engage in downward social comparisons when they wanted to feel better about themselves.

Evidence of downward social comparisons making people feel better has been found in many other domains as well. For example, researchers at universities in Ontario and Israel found that the more frequently employees engaged in downward social comparison—comparing themselves to co-workers who were worse off in terms of performance, salary, and the like—the greater the job satisfaction and commitment (Brown, Ferris, Heller, & Keeping, 2007). University of Manitoba researchers asked elderly people (with an average age of 85 years) about the strategies they engaged in when facing restrictions on a particular activity or task. Making downward social comparison (reminding oneself that others are worse off) was correlated with life satisfaction (Bailis, Chipperfield, Perry, Newall, & Haynes, 2008). Finally, in a recent program on life regrets conducted with older adults living in Montreal, it was found that when people felt that there wasn't anything they could do about their regret, engaging in downward social comparison (i.e., believing that other people their age had even more severe regrets) was associated with positive emotional well-being and better health (Bauer & Wrosch, 2011).

In an interesting twist on this issue, Anne Wilson at Wilfrid Laurier University and Michael Ross at the University of Waterloo suggested that we might even be able to get a self-esteem boost by comparing our current performance with our own past performance (Ross & Wilson, 2002; Wilson & Ross, 2000, 2001; see also Redersdorff & Guimond, 2006). We are still using downward social comparison, but in this case, the target of comparison is a "past" self instead of another person. For example, in one of Wilson and Ross's studies (2000), a participant mentioned that her "university student" self was more outgoing and sociable than her former shy, reserved "high school student" self. In related research, Cameron, Ross, and Holmes (2002) showed that if we are forced to think about a time when we behaved badly in a relationship, we will bend over backward to show how much we and our relationships have improved since then. In other words, when we are reminded of a negative "past" self, we restore our self-esteem by focusing on how much better our current self is.

It is important to point out that downward comparison does not inevitably result in increased self-esteem and well-being. According to Penelope Lockwood (2002), comparing ourselves with someone who is worse off will make us feel good only if we don't feel vulnerable to that person's negative outcomes. In one of her studies, first-year students at the University of Toronto who were doing well academically read about the experiences of another first-year student who was struggling. In this situation, students showed the usual self-enhancement effect of downward social comparison. They could feel good about the fact that they, themselves, were not experiencing academic difficulties. Quite the opposite occurred, however, when participants were presented with a situation that could, in fact, happen to them. This time, first-year students read about a recent graduate who did well in university at the outset but then declined in academic performance over his four years at the University of Toronto. After he graduated, he could find work only in fast-food restaurants. In this case, downward social comparison had a negative effect. Those who were asked to imagine experiencing a similar fate felt worse about themselves than students in a control group (who wrote about a typical day in their lives). Thus, comparing ourselves with someone who is worse off can make us feel better about ourselves—but only if we are confident that the other person's fate cannot befall us.

There is little satisfaction in the contemplation of heaven for oneself if one cannot simultaneously contemplate the horrors of hell for others.

—P. D. James, *The Children of Men, 1992*

How do we feel if we instead compare ourselves with someone who is better than we are in a particular trait or ability—thereby engaging in **upward social comparison**? According to Lockwood and Kunda (1997, 1999, 2000), the answer is "It depends." In general, comparing ourselves to someone who is outperforming us is threatening to our self-esteem. For example, in their research on social comparison in the workplace, Brown and colleagues (2007) found that the more frequently employees engaged in upward social comparison—comparing themselves to co-workers with better performance and higher salary—the lower their job satisfaction and commitment. In another recent study, a team of Canadian and American researchers found that when participants were outperformed by a confederate on a competitive task, they tried to restore their self-esteem by outperforming the confederate on a subsequent task (Pliner, Rizvi, & Remick, 2009). However, upward social comparison can sometimes have positive consequences, as was shown in a program of research by Lockwood and Kunda (1999).

Upward Social Comparison
The process whereby we compare ourselves with people who are better than we are in a particular trait or ability

Imagine that you were a participant in one of their studies. Think of a peak academic experience that made you especially proud. If you are like the math, biology, and computer science students at the University of Waterloo who participated in this study, you would have no trouble coming up with an answer. Now imagine reading an article in your campus newspaper that describes a student of the same gender as you who has had a stellar academic career. This person has won all kinds of awards, and university officials are raving about how truly outstanding this student is. How do you feel now? If you suddenly don't feel so good, you are not alone. Lockwood and Kunda (1999) found that when participants' "best" self had been activated, it was depressing for them to be exposed to a "superstar." They tended not to feel very good about themselves, and their motivation to study hard took a dive.

What if, instead of describing your "best" self, you focused on your "usual" self? Other participants in this study did just that—they were simply asked to describe what they had done the day before. For these participants, reading about the superstar student was inspiring. They imagined that they, too, could achieve greatness, and as a result they felt very good about themselves—even better than participants who focused on their usual self but did not read about the superstar. (These results are shown in Figure 5.3.)

Thus, when we focus on our actual or usual self, exposure to outstanding others inspires us to generate higher hopes and aspirations for ourselves than we would have

FIGURE 5.3

Effects of upward social comparison on self-enhancement.

People who focused on their usual self evaluated themselves more positively following exposure to a "superstar" than did people who were not exposed to a superstar. However, people who focused on their "best" self evaluated themselves more negatively following exposure to a superstar than did those who were not exposed to a superstar (Lockwood & Kunda, 1999).

Prime type	No superstar	Superstar
Usual self	7.16	8.04
"Best" self	8.18	7.49

Self-rating (0–10)

if we hadn't been exposed to the superstar. However, if we happen to be focusing on our best or ideal self, it can be discouraging to realize that someone else has already surpassed our highest hopes and dreams.

In sum, the kinds of social comparisons we engage in depend on the nature of our goals (Lockwood, Sadler, Fyman, & Tuck, 2004). If we want to feel good, we can engage in downward comparison and compare ourselves with our past selves or to those who are less fortunate. Doing so will make us look better by comparison—as long as we're convinced that we are not vulnerable to the same misfortunes. Upward social comparisons generally make us feel bad—it is threatening to our self-esteem to be outperformed by others, unless we feel that it is possible for us to achieve the superstars' level of performance. In that case, upward social comparison can have positive effects and motivate us to pursue our dreams.

Watch on **mypsychlab** Body Image part 1: Kianna, 12 Years Old

Before leaving this topic, we should make one final point. The research we have been discussing focuses on comparisons with others whom we may not even know (e.g., reading about another student who has done well). Recent research shows that social comparison has very different effects when the person we are comparing ourselves with is our romantic partner (Pinkus, Lockwood, Schimmack, & Fournier, 2008). When our romantic partner is the comparison target, we actually feel better after engaging in upward social comparisons (focusing on domains in which your partner outperforms you) than in downward social comparisons (focusing on areas in which you perform better than your partner). Why might this be the case? Pinkus and colleagues suggest that in romantic relationships, we experience high levels of empathy (e.g., sharing in the joy of our partner's success rather than being threatened by it) and shared fate—meaning that our partner's outcomes affect us. Thus, if your partner gets a hefty raise and you don't, you can still feel happy, because you are likely to benefit from his or her good fortune.

"Of course you're going to be depressed if you keep comparing yourself with successful people."

CONNECTIONS

Do Models Make Us Feel Bad about Ourselves?

It is no secret that in our culture the ideal body type for women is thin—super thin. As we mentioned in Chapter 2, the ideal portrayed in the media is getting thinner, at a time when the average weight for women is actually increasing. What effect does it have on women to constantly encounter images of super-thin models? Based on social comparison theory, we would expect that seeing super-thin models would make women feel bad. Research suggests that this is the case. In a recent study conducted at the University of Toronto, female participants read about a woman who was described as either thin, average weight, or overweight. It was found that participants, especially those who were chronic dieters, used the weight of the thin woman as a standard of comparison. Specifically, these women perceived themselves as more overweight and reported more body dissatisfaction and lower appearance self-esteem than chronic dieters who read a description of an average-weight woman. (Comparing themselves to an overweight person did not make the participants feel better about their own weight; Trottier, Polivy, & Herman, 2007.)

In a subsequent study, Tiggerman and Polivy (2010) asked female participants to rate advertisements from women's magazines that featured thin models. Participants in the appearance condition were asked to rate how thin they were compared to the models in the ads. Participants in the intelligence condition were asked to rate how intelligent they were compared to the models. Those in the appearance condition engaged in upward social comparison—they perceived themselves as less thin and less attractive than the models. Women in the intelligence condition engaged in downward social comparison—they rated themselves as somewhat more intelligent and educated than the models. It probably comes as no surprise that the women who compared their appearance to that of the models reported more negative moods and body dissatisfaction than those in the intelligence condition.

But, you may be thinking, the women who participated in these studies were explicitly instructed to focus on the weight or appearance of another woman. This doesn't necessarily mean that every time a gorgeous model shows up in a commercial that women will feel bad about themselves. Or does it? Researchers from Ryerson University in Toronto recently required female participants to watch a 10 minute clip from an episode of the TV show *Friends*. The plot line in this segment revolved around a thin, attractive woman. However, she did not wear revealing clothing and there were no close-up shots or references to her appearance. The participants in this study were told that they would be required to report on how much they enjoyed the segment. Before actually seeing it, participants in a weight and shape intervention condition were given material that was intended to mitigate the effects of exposure to the thin, attractive woman. Specifically, they read an article saying that the body shapes of TV actors are unrealistic, body weight is partly genetically determined, there are health risks of being underweight, and so on. The idea was to communicate that televised images of women's bodies are unrealistic and unattainable, with the hope that this might reduce the tendency to engage in social comparison. Participants in the control condition simply viewed the 10 minute segment. The results? Women who simply watched the show reported greater body dissatisfaction than participants who received the weight and shape intervention (Want, Vickers, & Amos, 2009).

Social Comparison and Culture

It probably won't surprise you to learn that the kinds of social comparisons that people make and the reasons for engaging in social comparison differ by culture. For example, in a series of studies, Lockwood, Marshall, and Sadler (2005) found that European-Canadians were more motivated by positive role models (e.g., a student who had experienced academic success) compared with Asian-Canadians, who were more likely to be motivated by negative role models (e.g., a student who had experienced academic failures). The researchers suggest that people from collectivist cultures are more concerned with avoiding failure than with achieving success, whereas just the opposite is true in individualistic cultures.

Recent research also shows that people from collectivist cultures seek self-improvement to a greater extent than do those from individualist cultures, and this, too, affects the kind of social comparison information that is sought. For example, White and Lehman (2005b) found that Asian-Canadians were more likely than European-Canadians to choose to compare their performance with that of someone who did better than they did on a task (upward social comparison), rather than comparing themselves with a person who did worse than they did (downward social comparison). In other words, unlike European-Canadians, Asian-Canadians did not capitalize on an opportunity to get a self-esteem boost but, rather, used social comparison information to identify areas for self-improvement. Earlier we also discussed research showing that people enhance their self-esteem by viewing their current self more positively than their past self. As you might expect, Japanese people are less likely to engage in this kind of self-enhancement than are Canadians (Ross, Heine, Wilson, & Sugimori, 2005).

Self-Discrepancy Theory

Listen on **mypsychlab**
Roger's View of Adjustment

The work of E. Tory Higgins and his colleagues (Higgins, 1987, 1989, 1996, 1999; Higgins, Klein, & Strauman, 1987) is concerned with understanding how violations of personal standards influence how people feel about themselves. In particular, these researchers have taken a close look at the nature of the emotional distress that occurs when we perceive ourselves as not measuring up to our ideals and standards. **Self-discrepancy theory** posits that we become distressed when our sense of who we truly are—our actual self—is discrepant from our personal standards or desired self-conceptions. For Higgins and colleagues, these standards are reflected most clearly in the beliefs we hold about the type of person we aspire to be—our "ideal" self—and the type of person we believe we should be—our "ought" self. Comparing our actual self with our ideal and ought-to-be selves provides us with an important means of self-evaluation.

Self-Discrepancy Theory
The theory that we become distressed when our sense of who we truly are—our actual self—is discrepant from our personal standards or desired self-conceptions

What happens when we become aware that we have failed to measure up to our own standards? Consider the predicament of Sarah, a first-year university student who has always had very high academic standards. In terms of self-discrepancy theory, academic competence is a central component of her ideal self. In her first semester at a competitive, prestigious university, however, Sarah has discovered that As are now much more difficult to come by. As a matter of fact, in her Introductory Chemistry course—a prerequisite for her major—she barely managed to earn a C. Given this scenario, how is Sarah likely to experience this discrepancy between her ideal and actual selves?

To begin with, we might imagine that the threat to her self-concept as a high achiever would almost certainly generate fairly strong levels of emotional discomfort—for example, disappointment in herself and perhaps an unaccustomed sense of uncertainty regarding her abilities. Self-discrepancy research supports this view. In a series of studies, Higgins and colleagues (Higgins, 1989; Higgins, Bond, Klein, & Strauman, 1986) have found that when people are made mindful of a discrepancy between their actual and ideal selves, they tend to experience a pattern of feelings involving dejection, sadness, dissatisfaction, and other depression-related emotions.

On the contrary, what if Sarah had encountered a self-discrepancy involving her "ought" self—that is, not the ideal self she aspired to but the "should-be" self she felt obligated to uphold? Imagine that being a top-notch student was not enormously significant to Sarah. Instead, suppose that her parents had always held this standard as highly important, and that Sarah, out of respect for them, tried to achieve academic excellence. How then would Sarah experience this discrepancy between her actual and "ought" selves in the face of a mediocre performance in her first semester at university? Research by Higgins and colleagues indicates that, in this case, Sarah would be likely to experience fear, worry, tension, and other anxiety-related emotions.

More recent research shows that discrepancies between our ideal and "ought" selves are especially likely to produce negative emotion when we are feeling self-aware (e.g., sitting in front of a mirror while contemplating who we are, who we should be, and who we would ideally like to be; Phillips & Silvia, 2005).

How do people cope with the negative feelings generated by either of these forms of self-discrepancy? According to the theory, self-discrepancies not only produce emotional discomfort but also provoke strivings to minimize the gap between the actual and the ideal, or the actual and "ought" selves. Thus, Sarah, who is coping with her lacklustre performance in chemistry, might convince herself that the grading was unfair or that her chemistry instructor was totally inept, or might in some other way interpret her mediocre performance in the most positive light possible. Of course, justifying her actions in order to maintain self-esteem—while a self-protective strategy in the short run—might not be the most adaptive approach Sarah could adopt. Rather, she would undoubtedly benefit far more from reassessing her situation—concluding perhaps that maintaining her high academic standards might require greater effort than she had been accustomed to exerting in the past when her courses were less challenging.

Self-discrepancy theory posits that we are distressed when our sense of who we truly are does not match our desired self-conception. For this high-achieving student, finding out she's done poorly on a test would generate strong levels of emotional discomfort.

Self-Discrepancies and Culture In cultures that emphasize interdependence, self-criticism is valued because group members are expected to continually strive to improve themselves in order to function harmoniously with others (Heine et al., 1999). Heine and Lehman (1999) reasoned that this emphasis on self-criticism might lead people in Asian cultures to experience larger discrepancies between their ideal and actual self than people in Western cultures. Indeed, in research conducted at the University of British Columbia and at Ritsumeikan University in Kyoto, Japan, they found that Japanese students viewed their actual self as falling short of their ideal self—particularly in traits they regarded as important—to a greater extent than did the Canadian students. Interestingly, discrepancies between the actual and ideal selves were not as depressing for Japanese students as they were for Canadian students. Heine and Lehman suggest that the Japanese participants may have been accustomed to thinking of their inadequacies as areas for improvement and therefore found it less upsetting that they weren't measuring up to their ideals.

Self-Evaluation: Biased or Accurate?

So far we have been operating on the assumption that people—at least in individualistic cultures—have a need to feel good about themselves. One way of feeling good about ourselves is to distort or exaggerate our positive qualities. We might even convince ourselves that we are better than most other people. Such positive illusions certainly can bolster self-esteem. That said, probably most of us don't want to live in a fantasy world in which we are fooling ourselves about the kind of person we are. In fact, we might even want other people to "tell it like it is" so that we develop an accurate picture of who we are. Consequently, it seems we are caught between wanting to view ourselves in the most positive possible light and wanting an accurate assessment of what we are really like. Given these conflicting motives, do our self-evaluations tend to show a positivity bias or do they tend to be accurate? Let's examine the evidence for each side of this issue.

Self-Enhancement: Wanting to Feel Good about Ourselves, Regardless of the Facts

Take a moment to answer the following questions: How attractive are you compared with the average student (of your gender) at your university? How adaptive are you compared with the average student? How well are you able to get along with others compared with the average student?

Chances are you see yourself as better than the average student with regard to at least some of these qualities, or perhaps even all of them. One way of boosting our self-esteem is to hold unrealistically positive views of ourselves, a tendency known as **self-enhancement**. "Well," you might be thinking, "in my case, it really isn't unrealistic to have a positive view of myself—I really am a great person." We don't doubt that you *are* a great person. The problem, however, is that most people have a tendency to think this way, and it really isn't possible for everyone to be better than most people, is it? This is why self-enhancement is defined as an unrealistically positive view of oneself.

Self-Enhancement
An unrealistically positive view of oneself

Research confirms that we really do paint quite a flattering picture of ourselves. For example, when Heine and Lehman (1999) asked students at the University of British Columbia the kinds of questions with which we began this section, they found that participants tended to view themselves as better than the average student. In research along the same lines, Jennifer Campbell (1986) found that students at the University of British Columbia showed a false uniqueness effect—they believed that many other students shared their weaknesses but that they were unique in their strengths. Similarly, researchers at Simon Fraser University have found that people tend to rate themselves as happier, more intelligent, more ethical, and even as having stronger emotional reactions than those around them (McFarland & Miller, 1990; Miller & McFarland, 1987).

Does engaging in this kind of unrealistic thinking actually make us feel better about ourselves? Apparently so. According to a program of research conducted at the University of British Columbia by Del Paulhus and colleagues, the more we distort reality to paint a flattering picture of ourselves, the higher our self-esteem (Paulhus, 1998; Yik, Bond, & Paulhus, 1998). Similarly, in recent research conducted at the University of Manitoba, it was found that elderly people who self-enhanced in the domain of physical activity (e.g., saw themselves as more active and energetic than their peers) reported higher life satisfaction than those who did not (Bailis et al., 2008).

Self-Enhancement and Culture As we have seen, self-enhancement is largely a phenomenon of individualistic cultures. Unrealistically positive self-views are not common in collectivist, interdependent cultures. In fact, in Asian cultures, the tendency is to hold a negative view of oneself—a phenomenon known as *self-effacement* (Chen, Bond, Chan, Tang, & Buchtel, 2009; Heine et al., 1999; Heine, 2001, 2003). This tendency is established at a relatively young age. For example, Kwok (1995) found that grade 4 students in Hong Kong rated themselves lower in scholastic competence, athletic competence, physical appearance, and overall self-worth than did grade 4 students in Canada. Interestingly, this was the case even though the Chinese students performed better than the Canadian children on standardized math tests. At the university level, Heine and colleagues have found that Japanese students see themselves as worse than their peers, whereas Canadian students view themselves as superior to their peers. Self-effacement is particularly pronounced among Japanese students after they are given failure feedback. In contrast, failure feedback does nothing to tarnish the positive self-view of Canadians (Heine, Kitayama, & Lehman, 2001; for related findings, see Endo, Heine, & Lehman, 2000; Heine & Renshaw, 2002).

In conceptually-related research, students working on group projects at the University of British Columbia and at the Chinese University of Hong Kong were asked to rate one another's personality traits (Yik et al., 1998). Canadian students showed classic self-enhancement—they rated themselves more positively than the other group members rated them. Just the opposite was found for Chinese students—they rated themselves more negatively than their peers rated them. Given findings such as these, it is perhaps not surprising that Asian university students score lower on measures of self-esteem than do Canadian students (Campbell et al., 1996; Endo et al., 2000; Heine & Lehman, 1997b; Sato & Cameron, 1999).

As you might expect, these findings are not unique to students. A recent study found that adults from Korea living in Vancouver scored higher on measures of self-criticism than European-Canadians in that city (Hong & Woody, 2007).

Might people evaluate themselves differently depending on the cultural identity that is activated? To find out, Ross, Xun, and Wilson (2002) asked Chinese-born students who had lived in Canada for an average of seven years to complete a questionnaire on various aspects of the self. The questionnaire was written in either Chinese or English. Participants who answered in Chinese described themselves in more collectivist terms, were more self-effacing, and scored lower on a self-esteem measure than the participants who completed the questionnaire in English. In fact, the responses of Chinese participants who answered in English were more similar to those of a comparison group of Canadian-born students than they were to Chinese participants responding in Chinese. In short, the language used primed different senses of self—the Chinese language brought to mind the participants' collectivist, self-effacing self, whereas the English language activated their individualistic, self-enhancing self.

Before leaving this topic, we consider one final question: Might people in Asian countries in fact secretly engage in self-enhancement but not feel comfortable openly bragging about themselves on questionnaires? To find out, Heine, Takata, and Lehman (2000) designed a study in which they measured self-enhancement in a subtle way—namely, by examining whether students believed or accepted certain kinds of feedback. In this research, students at the University of British Columbia and at Nara University in Japan took a computerized mathematical judgment test. Later, participants were asked who had performed better on the test—they or the average student at their university? To answer this question, they were given (false) information on how they had performed on each trial and how the average student had performed. Participants were told that they could keep viewing trials until they had enough information to answer the question. Participants in the success condition were given higher scores than the average student on most trials; for participants in the failure condition, the average student's scores generally were higher. The critical question was how many of these trials participants would want to view before making a decision about whether they had performed better than the average student. As shown on the left side of Figure 5.4, in Canada, participants in the failure condition tended to view more trials than participants in the success condition. In other words, Canadians found it hard to believe that they had done worse than the average student and therefore needed ample "proof" that that was the case. However, if the feedback indicated that they had outperformed the average student, they did not need to see many trials to be convinced. In other words, Canadians showed self-enhancement. In Japan, participants showed exactly the opposite pattern. They did not have to see many trials in which they had been outperformed before concluding that the average student had performed better than they had (see the right side of Figure 5.4). However, when it came to concluding that they had performed better than the average student, they needed plenty of proof—Japanese participants in the success condition viewed the greatest number of trials. These results are consistent with self-effacement.

More recently, these researchers reasoned that if cultural differences in self-enhancement are merely due to self-presentation biases (i.e., East Asian people believing that they should present themselves in a negative light, while secretly believing that they are great), then cultural differences should disappear when people are under cognitive load. As you may recall from other cognitive load studies, the idea is that people's "true" attitudes emerge when their cognitive resources are taxed in some way—it's more difficult to control your responses when your brain is occupied with doing a complex task. To test this idea, students at the University of British Columbia and students at Hokkaido University in Japan performed self-ratings while under high or low cognitive load (keeping an eight-digit number in mind versus keeping a one-digit number in

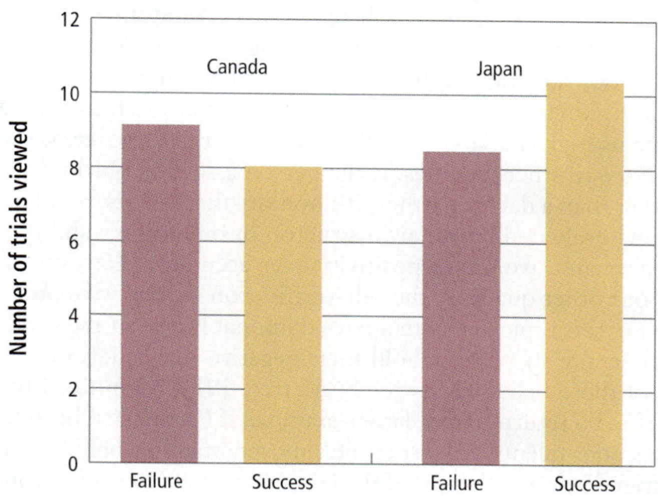

FIGURE 5.4

Cultural differences in self-enhancement.

When Canadian participants received feedback that they had performed worse than the average student, they needed greater "proof" that this had been the case than when they received feedback that they had performed better than the average student. Japanese students found it easy to believe that they had performed poorly but hard to believe that they had performed well.

(Based on Heine, Takata, & Lehman, 2000)

mind). It turned out that Japanese participants self-enhanced less than Canadian participants regardless of cognitive load. Thus, it was not the case that Japanese people reported more positive self-views when their self-evaluations were assessed in a way that tapped into their "true" feelings (Falk, Heine, Yuki, & Takemura, 2009).

Based on these and other findings, Heine and colleagues have concluded that when it comes to self-enhancement, people from Eastern cultures simply don't do it! A meta-analysis of 81 studies examining self-enhancement among North Americans and East Asians supports this conclusion (Heine, 2003; Heine & Hamamura, 2007).

Self-Verification: Wanting to Know the Truth about Ourselves

So far we have focused on research showing that, at least in North America, people tend to be highly motivated to feel good about themselves, to the point that they will happily distort reality in order to maintain a positive self-concept. But according to William Swann and colleagues, people are also motivated to know the truth about themselves—even if the truth hurts (Giesler, Josephs, & Swann, 1996; Swann, 1990, 1996; Swann & Hill, 1982; Swann & Pelham, 1988; Swann & Schroeder, 1995). According to Swann's **self-verification theory,** people have a need to seek confirmation of their self-concept, whether that self-concept is positive or negative. In some circumstances, this tendency can conflict with the desire to uphold a favourable view of oneself.

Self-Verification Theory

A theory suggesting that people have a need to seek confirmation of their self-concept, whether the self-concept is positive or negative; in some circumstances, this tendency can conflict with the desire to uphold a favourable view of oneself

Consider, for example, Patrick, who has always thought of himself as a lousy writer with poor verbal skills. One day he is working on a term paper with a friend, who remarks that she thinks his paper is skillfully crafted, beautifully written, and superbly articulate. How will Patrick feel? He should feel pleased and gratified, we might predict on the one hand, because the friend's praise gives Patrick's self-esteem a boost. On the other hand, Patrick's friend has given him feedback that challenges his longstanding view of himself as a poor writer, and he might be motivated to maintain this negative view. Why? For two reasons. First, it can be unsettling and confusing to have our views of ourselves "disconfirmed"; if we changed our self-concept every time we encountered someone with a different opinion of us, it would be impossible to maintain a coherent sense of self. Second, self-verification theory holds that it can be uncomfortable to interact with people who view us differently from the way we view ourselves. People who don't know us might have unrealistic expectations, and it would be embarrassing to have them discover that we are not as smart or as artistic or as creative as they think we are. Better to let them know our faults at the outset.

In short, when people with negative self-views receive positive feedback, opposing needs go head to head—the desire to feel good about themselves by believing the positive feedback (i.e., self-enhancement needs) versus the desire to maintain a consistent, coherent picture of themselves and avoid the embarrassment of being found out (i.e., self-verification needs). Which needs win out? According to Swann and colleagues, whether we want to have accurate, rather than positive, feedback depends on two things: the dimension on which we are being evaluated and the nature of the relationship we have with the person doing the evaluating (Swann, Bosson, & Pelham, 2002; for related findings, see Katz & Joiner, 2002, and Sciangula & Morry, 2009). For example, when it comes to a quality such as physical attractiveness, we want dating partners to give us high marks—regardless of the facts. However, we want the truth when it comes to our other qualities. If the person assessing our looks is a friend or a roommate, rather than a dating partner, it's honesty that counts. Similarly, if our artistic ability is being evaluated by our art instructor, or our athletic ability is being evaluated by our teammates, we prefer positivity over accuracy. However, if these people are evaluating our other qualities, the self-verification motive wins out.

Before leaving this topic, we note a few additional limits on the need to self-verify. First, people generally strive to uphold their negative self-beliefs only when they are highly certain of those beliefs (Maracek & Mettee, 1972; Swann & Ely, 1984; Swann & Pelham, 1988). To return to our earlier example, if Patrick had been less thoroughly convinced of his poor talents as a writer, he almost certainly would have been more receptive to his friend's praise. Second, if the consequences of being improperly evaluated are not too great—for example, if our contact with these individuals is sufficiently rare that it is unlikely they will discover we are not who we appear to be—then even people with negative views prefer positive feedback (Aronson, 1992). Finally, if people feel there is nothing they can do to improve their abilities, they generally prefer positive feedback to accurate feedback. Why remind ourselves that we are terrible if there is nothing we can do about it? If, however, people feel that a negative self-attribute can be changed with a little work, they prefer accurate feedback because this information can help them figure out what they need to do to get better (Steele, Spencer, & Josephs, 1992).

HOW WOULD YOU USE THIS?

This chapter was concerned with the nature of the self and the way in which people come to know their own attitudes, traits, and abilities. What is this topic doing in a book on social psychology, which is concerned with the way in which people's thoughts and behaviours are influenced by other people? Nothing is as personal as our self-knowledge, but as we have seen even our private thoughts and beliefs are formed in a social context. Can you think of examples from your own life in which your views of yourself were shaped by your parents, friends, or teachers? Or, more broadly, by the community and culture in which you live? (See pages 127–129 on cultural influences on the self.) Now let's turn the question around: Can you think of examples in which you have influenced someone else's self-views, such as a sibling, a close friend, or a romantic partner? Suppose, for example, that you have a friend who could use a bit of a confidence boost; he or she has an unrealistically negative view of his or her abilities (e.g., in academics, music, athletics, driving ability). Based on what you have learned in this chapter, can you think of a couple of ways in which you might help this person gain confidence? (See, for example, pages 136–137 on intrinsic versus extrinsic motivation and pages 140–142 on downward social comparison.)

Summary

- **The Nature of the Self** In this chapter, we have explored how people come to know and evaluate themselves. The self-concept refers to the contents of the self—namely one's knowledge of one's own thoughts, beliefs, and personality traits.
    - **Functions of the Self: Self-Regulation** The self serves to regulate people's behaviour, choices, and plans for the future. Research on the self-regulatory resource model suggests that we have a limited amount of energy to devote to exercising self-control. Self-control is more difficult when we are depleted (e.g., feeling stressed or sleep-deprived).
    - **The Content of the Self: Self-Schemas** People organize information about themselves into self-schemas, which are knowledge structures about the self that help people understand, explain, and predict their own behaviour. One advantage of self-schemas is that people can remember information better if they relate it to themselves. This is known as the self-reference effect. People differ in the extent to which their sense of self is clearly defined. Having low self-concept clarity is associated with negative thoughts and feelings.
    - **Cultural Differences in Defining the Self** People who grow up in Western cultures tend to have an independent view of the self, whereas people who grow up in Asian cultures tend to have an interdependent view of the self.
    - **Gender Differences in Defining the Self** Women tend to have relational interdependence, focusing more on close relationships, whereas men tend to have collective interdependence, focusing on their membership in larger groups.
- **Knowing Ourselves through Introspection** Introspection is the process whereby people look inward and examine their own thoughts, feelings, and motives.
    - **Focusing on the Self: Self-Awareness Theory** According to self-awareness theory, when people focus

on themselves, they evaluate and compare their current behaviour to their internal standards and values.

- **Cultural Differences in Self-Awareness** Research indicates that people from Eastern cultures are more likely to see themselves through the eyes of other people, whereas people from Western cultures are more likely to focus on their own private experiences, without considering how other people see them.
- **Judging Why We Feel the Way We Do: Telling More than We Can Know** According to research on "telling more than we can know," when people introspect about why they feel the way they do, they often use causal theories, many of which are learned from their culture. When people think about the reasons for their attitudes, they assume that their attitudes match the reasons that are plausible and easy to verbalize, leading to reasons-generated attitude change.

- **Knowing Ourselves by Observing Our Own Behaviour** Another way that people gain self-knowledge is by observing their own behaviour. Self-perception theory argues that when our attitudes and feelings are uncertain or ambiguous, we infer these states by observing our own behaviour and the situation in which it occurs.
  - **Intrinsic versus Extrinsic Motivation** An overjustification effect occurs when people focus on the extrinsic reasons for their behaviour and underestimate their intrinsic reasons. The kinds of rewards that are given also make a difference. Task-contingent rewards are given for doing a task, regardless of how well it is done. Performance-contingent rewards are based on how well people perform the task. Generally, performance-contingent rewards are less likely to undermine intrinsic motivation because they convey the message that you are good at the task.
- **Knowing Ourselves through Social Interaction** Social relationships are important in people's definition of self.
  - **Seeing Ourselves through the Eyes of Others: The Looking-Glass Self** According to the looking-glass self, our sense of who we are is based on others' perceptions of us. These perceptions become internalized and can influence our sense of self at any given time.
- **Knowing Ourselves by Comparing Ourselves to Others** We also know ourselves through comparison with others. Social comparison theory states that we will compare ourselves with others when we are unsure of our standing on some attribute and there is no objective criterion we can use. Typically, we choose to compare ourselves with similar others, for this is most diagnostic.
- **The Need to Feel Good about Ourselves** We also engage in social comparison to satisfy another basic human need: the need to maintain self-esteem.
  - **Social Comparison Revisited** Downward social comparison, comparing ourselves with those who are inferior on the relevant attribute, can make us feel better about ourselves—so long as we are confident that we are not vulnerable to their plight. Upward social comparison, comparing ourselves with those who are superior on the relevant attribute, can make us feel better about ourselves if we are focusing on our actual (usual) self, but it can make us feel worse about ourselves if we are focusing on our best or ideal self.
  - **Social Comparison and Culture** In collectivist cultures, people are more likely to compare themselves to people who outperform them (upward social comparison), whereas in individualist cultures, people are more likely to compare themselves to people who perform worse than them (downward social comparison).
  - **Self-Discrepancy Theory** According to self-discrepancy theory, we will feel bad about ourselves when our actual self falls short of the self we feel we should be (our "ought" self) or the self we would like to be (our "ideal" self). Discrepancies between our actual and ideal selves produce feelings of dejection and depression, whereas discrepancies between our actual self and our "ought" self produce feelings of anxiety.
- **Self-Evaluation: Biased or Accurate?** One way of feeling good about ourselves is to distort or exaggerate our positive qualities. On the contrary, sometimes we want other people to "tell it like it is" so that we develop an accurate picture of who we are. Consequently, it seems we are caught between wanting to view ourselves in the most positive possible light and wanting an accurate assessment of what we are really like.
  - **Self-Enhancement: Wanting to Feel Good about Ourselves, Regardless of the Facts** Research on self-enhancement suggests that the need to feel good about ourselves is so strong that we tend to hold unrealistically positive views of ourselves.
  - **Self-Verification: Wanting to Know the Truth about Ourselves** In contrast, self-verification theory holds that we want accurate information about what we are like—even if it is not flattering. Generally, people opt for self-enhancement rather than self-verification. Finally, it is important to realize that self-enhancement is limited to individualistic (Western) cultures. In collectivist (Eastern) cultures, people are more likely to be self-critical, a phenomenon known as self-effacement.

6 Attitudes and Attitude Change

Influencing Thoughts, Feelings, and Behaviour

MARCH 1997. QUEBEC POLICE WERE STUNNED WHEN they learned that five people had committed suicide in Saint-Casimir, a village west of Quebec City. The people who died were members of the Solar Temple cult (discussed in Chapter 1). The cult was led by Luc Jouret and his right-hand man, Joseph Di Mambro. Those who joined the Solar Temple cult were mainly wealthy professionals, including the mayor of Richelieu, Quebec, his wife, people in upper management positions at Hydro-Québec, a journalist, and a civil servant. Jouret was a charismatic spiritual leader with formidable powers of persuasion. A cult member interviewed by *Maclean's* reported, "He asked all of us to empty our bank accounts" (Laver, 1994). She and her husband sold their property in Switzerland and handed over the proceeds—$300 000—to Jouret. Others followed suit. Most disturbing of all, Jouret convinced cult members that the world was about to be destroyed by fire and that the only salvation was to take a "death voyage" by ritualized suicide to the star Sirius, where they would be reborn.

The cult attracted worldwide attention in October 1994, when buildings used by Jouret and his followers in a small village in Switzerland, and a chalet owned by Di Mambro in Morin Heights, Quebec, erupted in flames. Swiss firefighters discovered a chapel in which 22 cult members, cloaked in ceremonial robes, lay in a circle, with their faces looking up at a Christ-like figure resembling Jouret. In Morin Heights, police found the bodies of cult members clad in ceremonial robes and wearing red and gold medallions inscribed with the initials *T. S.* (Temple Solaire). At the end of the day, the death toll was 53 people, including several children. It is believed that both Jouret and Di Mambro died in the Swiss fires. So did the mayor of Richelieu, Quebec, and his wife (Laver, 1994).

Sadly, the 1994 deaths did not put an end to the cult. Some of the remaining followers continued to take death voyages. Although Quebec police believed that the Solar Temple had run its course by 1997, the five suicides in Saint-Casimir brought the total to 74 deaths in Canada and Europe over a five-year period.

How could intelligent, rational people be persuaded to hand over their money and even their lives to a charismatic leader? As we shall discuss in this chapter, people can be swayed by appeals to their fears, hopes, and desires. We will also show that once people change their attitudes, a powerful process of self-justification

OUTLINE

Luc Jouret, leader of the Order of the Solar Temple cult, died in the 1994 mass murder–suicide along with 52 other cult members.

sets in. People feel a strong need to justify their decisions, and in the process of doing so, become even more committed to their decision. But first, what exactly is an attitude, and how is it changed? These questions, which are some of the oldest in social psychology, are the subject of this chapter.

The Nature and Origin of Attitudes

Attitude

An evaluation of a person, object, or idea

Each of us *evaluates* our worlds. We form likes and dislikes of virtually everything we encounter; indeed, it would be odd to hear someone say, "My feelings toward anchovies, snakes, chocolate cake, and Stephen Harper are completely neutral." Simply put, **attitudes** are evaluations of people, objects, or ideas (Ajzen & Fishbein, 2005; Crano & Prislin, 2006; Eagly & Chaiken, 2007; Fazio, 2007; Olson & Zanna, 1993; Petty, Cacioppo, Strathman, & Priester, 2005). Attitudes are evaluative in that they consist of a positive or negative reaction toward someone or something. Sometimes people actually experience ambivalence, or "mixed feelings." For example, research conducted at the University of Waterloo has shown that some people have ambivalent attitudes toward feminists—they see feminists in both positive and negative terms (MacDonald & Zanna, 1998)—and toward issues such as capital punishment and abortion (Newby-Clark, McGregor, & Zanna, 2002). According to research conducted at the University of Western Ontario, some of us have ambivalent attitudes toward Canada's Native peoples (Bell & Esses, 1997, 2002) and toward Asian immigrants to Canada (Maio, Bell, & Esses, 1996). Our point is that people are not neutral observers of the world but constant evaluators of what they see. We can elaborate further on our definition of an attitude by stating more precisely what we mean by an "evaluation." An attitude is made up of three components:

- an *affective* component, consisting of emotional reactions toward the attitude object (e.g., another person or a social issue),
- a *cognitive* component, consisting of thoughts and beliefs about the attitude object, and
- a *behavioural* component, consisting of actions or observable behaviour toward the attitude object.

Consider your attitude toward a particular model of car, such as a Toyota Prius. What is your affective reaction when you see the car? Perhaps it triggers feelings of pleasure or excitement. If you are a Canadian autoworker examining a new foreign-made model, you may feel anger or resentment. What is your cognitive reaction? What beliefs do you hold about the car's attributes? Perhaps you admire the hybrid engine in the Prius that makes it one of the most fuel-efficient cars you can buy. And what about your behavioural reaction? Do you go to the dealership to test drive the car and actually buy one? These components combine to form your overall attitude toward the Prius.

Where Do Attitudes Come From?

Social psychologists have focused primarily on the way that attitudes are created by people's affective, cognitive, and behavioural experiences. One important finding is that not all attitudes are created equally. Although attitudes have affective, cognitive, and behavioural components, any given attitude can be based more on one type of experience than another (Zanna & Rempel, 1988).

Affectively Based Attitude

An attitude based primarily on people's emotions and feelings about the attitude object

Affectively Based Attitudes An attitude based more on emotions and feelings than on an objective appraisal of pluses and minuses is called an **affectively based attitude** (Breckler & Wiggins, 1989; Zanna & Rempel, 1988). Sometimes we simply like a certain brand of car, regardless of whether it gets good gas consumption or whether it has enough cupholders. Occasionally we even feel very positive about something—such as another person—in spite of having negative beliefs. An example is falling in love with someone despite knowing that the person has a history of being untrustworthy.

As a guide to which attitudes are likely to be affectively based, consider the topics that etiquette manuals suggest should not be discussed at a dinner party: politics, sex, and religion. People seem to vote more with their hearts than their minds—for example, basing their decision to vote for a political candidate on how they feel about the person or the party, rather than on a well-reasoned evaluation of the policies (Abelson, Kinder, Peters, & Fiske, 1982; Granberg & Brown, 1989). The nephew of one of the authors (Beverley Fehr) learned this first hand when he was campaigning for a political candidate in Calgary. One of the questions he asked when he knocked on people's doors was whether they were happy with the Conservative candidate currently serving in that riding. A frequent response in this Conservative stronghold was, "Yes. I think he's doing a great job." The member of Parliament in that riding was actually a woman!

We never desire passionately what we desire through reason alone.

—François de la Rochefoucauld, *Maxims, 1665*

That is the way we are made; we don't reason; where we feel, we just feel.

—Mark Twain, *A Connecticut Yankee in King Arthur's Court, 1889*

Where do affectively based attitudes come from? One source is people's values, such as their religious and moral beliefs. Attitudes about such issues as abortion, the death penalty, and premarital sex are often based on one's value system (Hodson & Olson, 2005; Murray, Haddock, & Zanna, 1996; Schwartz, 1992; Smith, Bruner, & White, 1956). For example, in a study conducted at the University of Western Ontario, Maio and Olson (1995) varied the message on posters soliciting donations for cancer research. In the value-expressive condition, the poster read, "Save people's lives, help researchers find a cure for cancer and *help others live*"; in the non-value condition, the message ended with "and *protect your future*." For participants in the value-expressive condition (help others live), there was a positive correlation between altruistic values and having favourable attitudes toward donating to cancer research. In contrast, in the non-values condition (protect your future), there was no relation between altruistic values and attitudes toward donating money.

Affectively based attitudes have three things in common:

1. they do not result from a rational examination of the issues;
2. they are not governed by logic (e.g., persuasive arguments about the issues seldom change an affectively based attitude);
3. they are often linked to people's values, so that trying to change them challenges those values (Katz, 1960; Smith, Bruner, & White, 1956).

Attitudes toward abortion, the death penalty, and premarital sex are examples of affectively based attitudes that are likely to be based on people's value systems.

Cognitively Based Attitudes Sometimes our attitudes are based primarily on the relevant facts, such as the objective merits of an automobile. How many kilometres per litre of gas does the car get? Does it have air conditioning? To the extent that a person's evaluation is based primarily on beliefs about the properties of an attitude object, it is a **cognitively based attitude**. The purpose of this kind of attitude is to classify the pluses and minuses of an object so we can quickly tell whether it is worth our while to have anything to do with it (Katz, 1960; Murray, Haddock, & Zanna, 1996; Smith, Bruner, & White, 1956). Consider your attitude toward a utilitarian object such as a vacuum cleaner. Your attitude is likely to be based on your beliefs about the objective merits of particular brands, such as how well they vacuum up dirt and how much they cost—not on how sexy they make you feel! How can we tell whether an attitude is more affectively or cognitively based? See the accompanying Try It! exercise for one way of measuring the bases of people's attitudes.

Cognitively Based Attitude

An attitude based primarily on a person's beliefs about the properties of an attitude object

Behaviourally Based Attitudes A **behaviourally based attitude** stems from people's observations of how they behave toward an attitude object. This may seem a little odd—how do we know how to behave if we don't already know how we feel? According to Daryl Bem's (1972) *self-perception theory* (discussed in Chapter 5), under certain circumstances people don't know how they feel until they see how they behave. Suppose, for example, that you asked a friend how much she enjoys exercising. If she replies, "Well, I guess I like it, because I always seem to be going for a run or heading over to the gym," we would say she has a behaviourally based attitude. Her attitude is based more on an observation of her own behaviour than on her cognition or affect.

Behaviourally Based Attitude

An attitude based primarily on observations of how one behaves toward an attitude object

How can I know what I think till I see what I say?

—Graham Wallas, *The Art of Thought*, 1926

Comparing Affective, Cognitive, and Behavioural Bases of Attitudes As we have been discussing, not all attitudes are created in the same way. Geoffrey Haddock, Mark Zanna, and Victoria Esses have conducted a series of studies, mostly with University of Waterloo students, to determine which attitudes are most likely to be based on affective, cognitive, or behavioural experiences (Esses, Haddock, & Zanna, 1993; Haddock & Zanna, 1994, 1998; Haddock, Zanna, & Esses, 1993, 1994). It turns out that when attitudes are negative toward particular groups, they are often cognitively based. More specifically, these researchers found that people's attitudes toward homosexuals and Pakistanis were based on a kind of cognition that they called symbolic beliefs—namely, beliefs that these groups threaten their value system (Esses, Haddock, & Zanna, 1993; Haddock, Zanna, & Esses, 1993). Attitudes toward other social groups that were studied (English Canadians, French Canadians, and Native Canadians) were more positive; these attitudes were more likely to be based on affect—how the participants felt about these groups (Haddock, Zanna, & Esses, 1993). Haddock and Zanna (1998) also found that attitudes toward social issues such as capital punishment were more likely to be based on how people felt about the issue (affect), rather than on their thoughts about it (cognition). Thus, when it comes to our attitudes concerning different social groups, it appears that if we dislike the group, our attitudes are likely to have a cognitive basis—specifically, the belief that the group threatens our value system. Attitudes toward groups that we like are apt to be based on our feelings toward that group (i.e., affect). In short, different attitudes have different bases.

Connect to MyPsychLab

Do you prefer cats or dogs? To participate in an experiment on implicit and explicit attitudes about your preference, go to MyPsychLab

Explicit versus Implicit Attitudes

Explicit Attitudes

Attitudes that we consciously endorse and can easily report

Watch on **mypsychlab**
Implicit Attitudes

Implicit Attitudes

Attitudes that are involuntary, uncontrollable, and at times unconscious

Once an attitude develops, it can exist at two levels. **Explicit attitudes** are ones we consciously endorse and can easily report; they are what we think of as our evaluations when someone asks us a question such as "What is your opinion on imposing carbon taxes?" or "What is your opinion on imposing carbon taxes, compared with that of other students at your university or college?" (Olson, Goffin, & Haynes, 2007). People can also have **implicit attitudes**, which are involuntary, uncontrollable, and at times unconscious evaluations (Bassili & Brown, 2005; Fazio & Olson, 2003; Gawronski &

TRY IT! Affective and Cognitive Bases of Attitudes

Complete this questionnaire to see how psychologists measure the affective and cognitive components of attitudes.

1. Record the number on each scale that best describes your feelings toward snakes:

hateful	−3	−2	−1	0	1	2	3	loving
sad	−3	−2	−1	0	1	2	3	delighted
annoyed	−3	−2	−1	0	1	2	3	happy
tense	−3	−2	−1	0	1	2	3	calm
bored	−3	−2	−1	0	1	2	3	excited
angry	−3	−2	−1	0	1	2	3	relaxed
disgusted	−3	−2	−1	0	1	2	3	accepting
sorrowful	−3	−2	−1	0	1	2	3	joyful

2. Record the number on each scale that best describes the traits or characteristics of snakes:

useless	−3	−2	−1	0	1	2	3	useful
foolish	−3	−2	−1	0	1	2	3	wise
unsafe	−3	−2	−1	0	1	2	3	safe
harmful	−3	−2	−1	0	1	2	3	beneficial
worthless	−3	−2	−1	0	1	2	3	valuable
imperfect	−3	−2	−1	0	1	2	3	perfect
unhealthy	−3	−2	−1	0	1	2	3	wholesome

Once you have answered these questions, sum all your responses to Question 1, and all your responses to Question 2. These scales were developed by Crites, Fabrigar, and Petty (1994) to measure the affective and cognitive components of attitudes. Question 1 measures the affective component of your attitude toward snakes; you were asked to rate your feelings about them. Question 2 measures the cognitive component of attitudes; you were asked to rate your beliefs about the characteristics of snakes. Most people's attitudes toward snakes are more affectively than cognitively based. If this was true of you, your total score for Question 1 should depart more from zero (in a negative direction, for most people) than your total score for Question 2.

Now, substitute "vacuum cleaners" for "snakes" for Questions 1 and 2, and mark the scales again. Most people's attitudes toward a utilitarian object such as a vacuum cleaner are more cognitively than affectively based. If this was true of you, your total score for Question 2 should depart more from zero than your total score for Question 1.

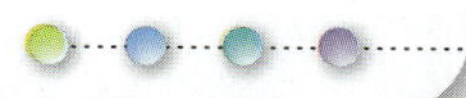

Bodenhausen, 2006; Greenwald & Banaji, 1995; Rydell & Gawronski, 2009; Stanley, Phelps, & Banaji, 2008; Wilson, Lindsey, & Schooler, 2000).

Consider Sam, a white, middle-class university student who genuinely believes that all races are equal and who abhors any kind of racial bias. This is Sam's explicit attitude, in the sense that it is his conscious evaluation of members of other races that governs how he chooses to act. For instance, consistent with his explicit attitude, Sam recently signed a petition in favour of affirmative action policies at his university. However, Sam has grown up in a culture in which there are many negative stereotypes about minority groups, and it is possible that some of these negative ideas have seeped into him in ways of which he is not fully aware (Devine, 1989a). When he is around people from Pakistan, for example, perhaps some negative feelings are triggered automatically and unintentionally. If so, he has a negative implicit attitude toward Pakistanis, which is likely to influence behaviours he is not monitoring or controlling, such as how nervous he acts around them (Dovidio, Kawakami, & Gaertner, 2002). (We will discuss such automatic prejudice in Chapter 12; see also our discussion of automatic thinking in Chapter 3).

People can have explicit and implicit attitudes toward the same subject. Explicit attitudes are those we consciously endorse and can easily report; implicit attitudes are involuntary, uncontrollable, and, at times, unconscious.

A variety of techniques have been developed to measure people's implicit attitudes, some of which we discussed in Chapter 3. One of the most popular is the Implicit Association Test (IAT; Gawronski & Bodenhausen, 2005; Greenwald, McGhee, & Schwartz, 1998; Greenwald & Nosek, 2001), in which people categorize words or pictures on a computer. (Rather than going into detail about how this test works, we encourage you to visit a website where you can take the test yourself and read more about how it is constructed: https://implicit.harvard.edu/implicit.)

Research on implicit attitudes is in its infancy, and psychologists are actively investigating their origins, how to measure them, and their relation to explicit attitudes. For example, University of Western Ontario researchers Bertram Gawronski and Etienne LeBel (2008) found that implicit and explicit attitudes tend to be positively correlated when people are asked to reflect on their feelings about an attitude object (e.g., how they feel about Coke versus Pepsi), but are not necessarily related when they are asked to focus on cognitions about the attitude object (e.g., listing reasons why they prefer Coke or Pepsi; Gawronski & LeBel, 2008). As to the question of where implicit attitudes come from, Rudman, Phelan, and Heppen (2007) found evidence that implicit attitudes are rooted more in people's childhood experiences, whereas explicit attitudes are rooted more in their recent experiences. We will return to a discussion of implicit attitudes in Chapter 12 as they apply to stereotyping and prejudice.

When Attitudes Predict Behaviour

It might seem that once we know someone's attitudes, it would be easy to predict their behaviour. Knowing, for example, that someone holds positive attitudes toward a politician should enable you to predict whether that person will vote for that politician in the next election. Right? Actually, the relation between attitudes and behaviour is not nearly so straightforward as one might expect.

In the early 1930s, Richard LaPiere (1934) embarked on a sightseeing trip across the United States with a young Chinese couple. Because prejudice against Asians was commonplace among Americans at that time, he was apprehensive about how his Chinese friends would be treated. At each hotel, campground, and restaurant they entered, LaPiere worried that his friends would confront anti-Asian prejudice and that they would be refused service. Much to his surprise, of the 251 establishments he and his friends visited, only one refused to serve them.

If actions are to yield all the results they are capable of, there must be a certain consistency between them and one's intentions.

—François de la Rochefoucauld, *Maxims, 1665*

After his trip, LaPiere wrote a letter to each establishment that he and his friends had visited, asking if it would serve a Chinese visitor. Of the many establishments who replied, only one said it would. More than 90 percent said they definitely would not (the rest said they were undecided). People's attitudes—as expressed in their response to LaPiere's written inquiry—were in stark contrast to their actual behaviour toward LaPiere's Chinese friends.

LaPiere's study was not, of course, a controlled experiment. As he acknowledged, there are several possible reasons why his results did not show consistency between people's attitudes and behaviour. For example, he had no way of knowing whether the proprietors who answered his letter were the same people who had served him and his friends. Further, people's attitudes could have changed in the months that passed between the time they served the Chinese couple and the time they received the letter. Nonetheless, the lack of correspondence between people's attitudes and what they actually did was so striking that we might question the assumption that behaviour routinely follows from attitudes. Indeed, when Allan Wicker (1969) reviewed dozens of more methodologically sound studies, he reached the same conclusion: People's attitudes are poor predictors of their behaviour.

How can this be? Does a person's attitude toward Asians or political candidates really tell us nothing about how he or she will behave? How can we reconcile LaPiere's findings—and other studies like it—with the fact that many times behaviour and attitudes *are* consistent? Stay tuned for the answer.

The Theory of Planned Behaviour

In subsequent research, social psychologists have discovered that attitudes can actually predict behaviours quite well—but only under certain conditions (DeBono & Snyder, 1995; Fazio, 1990; Zanna & Fazio, 1982). What are these conditions? According to the **theory of planned behaviour** (Ajzen & Fishbein, 1980, 2005; Ajzen & Sexton, 1999; Fishbein & Ajzen, 1975), the best predictor of people's planned, deliberate behaviour is their intention (i.e., whether they intend to perform the behaviour in question), which, in turn, is determined by three things: their attitudes toward the specific behaviour, their subjective norms, and their perceived behavioural control (see Figure 6.1). Let's consider each of these in turn.

Connect to MyPsychLab
To access the Critical Thinking question on smoking, go to MyPsychLab

Theory of Planned Behaviour
A theory that the best predictors of a person's planned, deliberate behaviours are the person's attitudes toward specific behaviours, subjective norms, and perceived behavioural control

Specific Attitudes The theory of planned behaviour holds that only *specific attitudes* toward the behaviour in question can be expected to predict that behaviour. In one study, researchers asked a sample of married women about their attitudes toward birth control pills, ranging from the general (the women's attitude toward birth control) to the specific (their attitude toward using birth control pills during the next two years; see Table 6.1). Two years later, the women were asked whether they had used birth control pills at any time since the last interview. As Table 6.1 shows, the women's general attitude toward birth control did not predict their use of birth control at all. This general attitude did not take into account other factors that could have influenced their decision, such as concern about the long-term effects of the pill and their attitudes toward other forms of birth control. The more specific the question was about the act of using birth control pills, the better this attitude predicted their actual behaviour (Davidson & Jaccard, 1979).

This study helps explain why LaPiere (1934) found such inconsistency between people's attitudes and behaviours. His question to the proprietors—whether they would serve "members of the Chinese race"—was very general. Had he asked a much more specific question—such as whether they would serve an educated, well-dressed, well-to-do Chinese couple accompanied by a white American professor—the proprietors might have given an answer that was more in line with their behaviour.

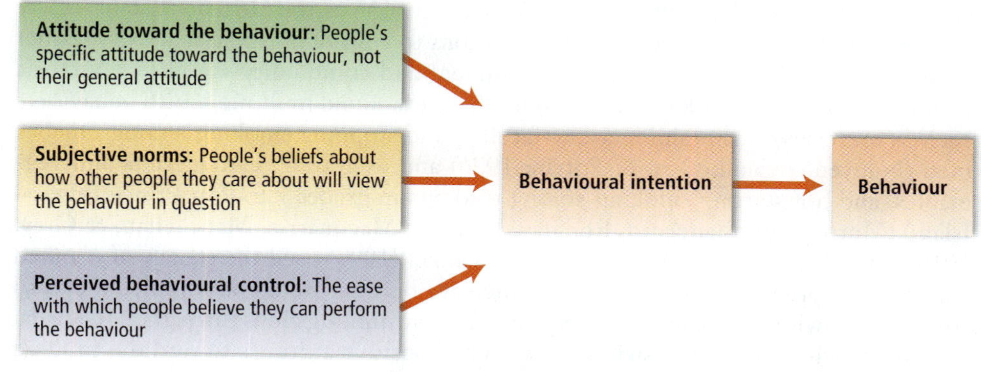

FIGURE 6.1
The theory of planned behaviour.

According to this theory, the best predictors of people's behaviours are their behavioural intentions. The best predictors of their intentions are their attitudes toward the specific behaviour, their subjective norms, and their perceived control of the behaviour.

(Adapted from Ajzen & Fishbein, 1980)

TABLE 6.1 Specific Attitudes Are Better Predictors of Behaviour*

Different groups of women were asked about their attitudes toward birth control. The more specific the question, the better it predicted their actual use of birth control.

Attitude Measure	Attitude Behaviour Correlation
Attitude toward birth control	0.08
Attitude toward birth control pills	0.32
Attitude toward using birth control pills	0.53
Attitude toward using birth control pills during the next two years	0.57

* If a correlation is close to 0, there is no relationship between the two variables. The closer the correlation is to 1, the stronger the relationship between attitudes and behaviour.

Source: Adapted from Davidson & Jaccard, 1979.

Subjective Norms In addition to measuring attitudes toward the behaviour, we also need to measure people's subjective norms—their beliefs about how the people they care about will view the behaviour in question (see Figure 6.1). To predict someone's intentions, it can be as important to know these beliefs as to know his or her attitudes. For example, suppose we want to predict whether Kristen intends to go to a heavy metal concert. We happen to know that she can't stand heavy metal music. Based on her negative attitude, we would probably say she won't go. Suppose, however, that we also know that Kristen's best friend, Malcolm, really wants her to go. Knowing this subjective norm—her belief about how a close friend views her behaviour—we might make a different prediction.

Perceived Behavioural Control Finally, as seen in Figure 6.1, people's intentions are influenced by perceived behavioural control, which is the ease with which people believe they can perform the behaviour. If people think it is difficult to perform the behaviour, such as sticking to a gruelling exercise regimen, they will not form a strong intention to do so. If people think it is easy to perform the behaviour, such as remembering to buy milk on the way home from work, they are more likely to form a strong intention to do so.

There is considerable research support for the idea that asking people about these determinants of their intentions—attitudes toward specific behaviours, subjective norms, and perceived behavioural control—increases the ability to predict their behaviour. Most of this research has focused on behaviours related to health and fitness, such as remaining smoke-free among Quebec high school students (Hill, Boudreau, Amyot, Dery, & Godin, 1997) and among University of Prince Edward Island students (Murnaghan, Blanchard, Rodgers, La Rosa, Macquarrie, MacClellan, & Gray, 2009); exercise among women and men living in Alberta (Courneya & Friedenreich, 1997, 1999; McCormack, Spence, Berry, & Doyle-Baker, 2009) and women and men living in Victoria, British Columbia (Kliman & Rhodes, 2008); participation in exercise classes for the elderly offered at the University of Western Ontario (Estabrooks & Carron, 1999); and, in a recent study, intentions to engage in physical activity, rather than watch television, among university student and community samples in Victoria (Rhodes & Blanchard, 2008). Some studies have examined multiple health behaviours such as exercising, maintaining a low-fat diet, and stopping smoking among Quebec men (Nguyen, Beland, Otis, & Potvin, 1996) and exercising, eating fruits and vegetables, and not starting smoking among students in grades 7 to 9 in Prince Edward Island (Murnaghan, Blanchard, Rodgers, La Rosa, Macquarrie, MacClellan, & Gray, 2010). In a final example, Mummery and Wankel (1999) used the theory of planned behaviour to predict whether a cycle of intensive training would be completed by 116 competitive swimmers (aged 11 to 18 years) from swimming clubs throughout Canada. Consistent with the theory, swimmers who had positive attitudes toward the training cycle, who believed that important people in their life wanted them to complete it, and who believed that they were capable of doing so were most likely to report that they intended to complete the upcoming cycle of training. Importantly, swimmers with these intentions also were the most likely to actually complete their training.

More recently, the theory of planned behaviour has been applied in other areas, such as predicting whether people will engage in pro-environmental behaviours such as reducing car use, as tested in a sample of office workers in Victoria (Abrahmse, Steg, Gifford, & Vlek, 2009). At the University of Western Ontario, Norman and colleagues (2010) recently used the theory to predict behavioural intentions toward people with mental illness (e.g., schizophrenia, depression). To assess behavioural intentions, they asked questions such as "Would you recommend this person for a job?"; "Would you support this person marrying someone in your family?" and so on. Consistent with the theory, specific attitudes and subjective norms (perceived behavioural control was not assessed in these studies) were found to predict behavioural intentions among university students and community service club members (Norman, Sorrentino, Windell, Ye, Szeto, & Manchanda, 2010).

Finally, we note that culture may play a role in the importance placed on these determinants of behavioural intentions. In a recent study, Hosking and colleagues (2009) predicted that personal attitudes would be a stronger predictor of behavioural intentions in individualistic cultures, whereas social norms would be a stronger predictor of intentions in collectivist cultures. These predictions were tested in large samples of smokers in two Southeast Asian countries and four Western countries (including Canada). It turned out that, as predicted, personal attitudes toward smoking predicted intentions to quit more strongly in Western countries than in Southeast Asian countries. Contrary to predictions, however, the influence of social norms did not vary significantly by culture. The researchers conclude that even in individualistic countries, such as Canada, we are still influenced by how we think the important people in our lives view our behaviour (Hosking, Borland, Yong, Fong, Zanna, Laux, & Omar, 2009).

Below, we will focus on how the theory of planned behaviour applies to an important social issue: persuading people to engage in safer sex.

The Theory of Planned Behaviour: Implications for Safer Sex

There is one area in which people's attitudes are often inconsistent with their behaviour, even though the consequences can be fatal. The inconsistency takes the form of having positive attitudes toward using condoms, expressing intentions to use condoms, but then failing to actually use them in sexual encounters (Hynie & Lydon, 1996). For example, in a study conducted with patrons of various dating bars in southern Ontario, nearly 100 percent of the participants agreed with statements such as "If I were to have sex with someone I just met, I would have no objections if my partner suggested that we use a condom" (Herold & Mewhinney, 1993). However, these favourable attitudes toward condom use did not translate into safer sex practices. Only 56 percent of the people at the bar who engaged in casual sex had used a condom in their most recent sexual encounter. Even more frightening, a mere 29 percent of the women and men who had engaged in casual sex in the past year reported that they always used a condom.

Why would people with positive attitudes toward condom use risk their lives by not using condoms? Perhaps the theory of planned behaviour can provide some clues. As you'll recall, according to this theory, attitudes are not the only predictor of behaviour. Subjective norms, perceived behavioural control, and behavioural intentions also play a role. Can these variables help us understand why people so often fail to use condoms, despite having positive attitudes toward condom use? Let's take a look at some studies.

Subjective Norms People's beliefs about how others view the behaviour in question are an important determinant of their behaviour. One study found that 65 percent of

If people fear a negative reaction, they are less likely to raise the issue of condom use with a potential sexual partner.

the students at a high school in Nova Scotia believed that their sexually active friends use condoms (Richardson, Beazley, Delaney, & Langille, 1997). Such beliefs should promote condom use. Indeed, there is evidence that whether university students use condoms depends on the norms for sexual behaviour that operate among their friends (Winslow, Franzini, & Hwang, 1992). For example, researchers at York University and Queen's University found that social norms (the belief that others in one's social group think that using condoms is important) predicted intentions to use condoms. Importantly, subjective norms also predicted actual condom use, as reported in a follow-up study six weeks later (Hynie, MacDonald, & Marques, 2006). Of course, social norms may vary depending on the situation. For example, students from various universities in eastern Ontario on "break loose" vacations in Daytona Beach, Florida, report that it is more acceptable to have casual sex while on such vacations than while at home (Maticka-Tyndale, Herold, & Mewhinney, 1998, 2001; Mewhinney, Herold, & Maticka-Tyndale, 1995). Unfortunately, the norm of permissive sexuality that evolves in such settings is accompanied by a low rate of condom use (Eiser & Ford, 1995).

Our beliefs about how our sexual partner feels about condom use is another example of a subjective norm. If we anticipate a negative reaction from our partner, we are less likely to use condoms. Several studies conducted in Montreal have shown that women, in particular, anticipate a negative reaction from their partner if they provide condoms (Hynie & Lydon, 1995; Maticka-Tyndale, 1992).

Perceived Behavioural Control If people think it is difficult to perform a behaviour, they will not form strong intentions to do so. At first glance, using condoms might seem like an easy thing to do. However, that is actually not the case. A study conducted with sexually active students at the University of British Columbia found that those who were embarrassed about buying condoms bought them less often than did those who were not embarrassed (Dahl, Gorn, & Weinberg, 1998). Further, in a series of studies conducted at McGill University, it was found that people can feel awkward about bringing up the topic of condoms during a sexual encounter (Hynie, Lydon, Cote, & Wiener, 1998; Hynie & Lydon, 1996). In short, the more difficult you find it to perform behaviours such as buying condoms or bringing up the topic with your partner, the less likely you are to actually use them.

Behavioural Intentions The importance of intentions in predicting condom use has been demonstrated in studies of the Latin American community in Montreal, the English-speaking Caribbean community in Toronto, and the South Asian community in Vancouver (Godin, Maticka-Tyndale, Adrien, Manson-Singer, Willams, & Cappon, 1996), as well as in a survey of first-year university students across Canada (Hawa, Munro, & Doherty-Poirier, 1998). What factors might affect people's intentions to use condoms? Researchers at the University of Waterloo and at Queen's University (MacDonald & Martineau, 2002; MacDonald, Fong, Zanna, & Martineau, 2000; MacDonald, Zanna, & Fong, 1996) have found a number of answers to this question. One factor is mood. In a study conducted with female university students, MacDonald and Martineau (2002) found that participants who were in a bad mood were more likely to report intentions to engage in sexual intercourse without a condom than those who were in a good mood. Women who were low in self-esteem were especially likely to intend to engage in unprotected sex when they were in a bad mood. The researchers suggest that people with low self-esteem who are experiencing negative mood may be especially worried about the threat of rejection and therefore may be less likely to insist on condom use.

Tara MacDonald and colleagues also have found that for both women and men, alcohol intoxication is associated with lower intentions to use condoms—even among those who have positive attitudes toward condom use (MacDonald, Zanna, & Fong, 1996; MacDonald et al., 2000). The researchers explain that when people are intoxicated, their ability to process information is impaired, such that they are able to focus only on the most immediate aspects of the situation (e.g., short-term pleasure) rather than on the long-term consequences of their actions. These findings are alarming, given that alcohol is present in many of the settings in which people are likely to encounter cues that promote casual sex (e.g., bars, parties, vacations; Maticka-Tyndale, Herold, & Mewhinney, 1998, 2001).

In summary, even the most positive of attitudes toward condom use do not guarantee that people will practise safer sex. The theory of planned behaviour suggests that other variables must be taken into account as well, including subjective norms, perceived behavioural control, and behavioural intentions.

Attitude Change

As we have seen, attitudes do not necessarily translate into behaviour. However, this fact does not stop people from trying to change our attitudes, hoping our behaviour will follow. Advertisers, for example, assume that changing people's attitudes toward products will result in increased sales, and politicians assume that positive feelings toward a candidate will result in a vote for that candidate on election day. But what is the best way to change people's attitudes? As you'll see next, this question has fascinated social psychologists for decades. Here are some of their answers.

Of the modes of persuasion furnished by the spoken word, there are three kinds. The first kind depends on the personal character of the speaker; the second on putting the audience into a certain frame of mind; the third on the proof, or apparent proof, provided by the words of the speech itself.

—Aristotle, Rhetoric, *350 BCE*

Persuasive Communications and Attitude Change

Suppose the Canadian Cancer Society has given you a five-figure budget to come up with an anti-smoking campaign that could be used nationwide. You have many decisions ahead of you. Should you pack your public service announcement with facts and figures? Or should you take a more emotional approach in your message, including frightening visual images of diseased lungs? Should you hire a famous movie star to deliver your message, or a Nobel Prize–winning medical researcher? Should you take a friendly tone and acknowledge that it is difficult to quit smoking, or should you take a hard line and tell smokers to (as the Nike ads put it) "just do it"? You can see the point—it's not easy to figure out how to construct a truly **persuasive communication**, one that advocates a particular side of an issue.

Persuasive Communication

Communication (e.g., a speech or television advertisement) advocating a particular side of an issue

Fortunately, social psychologists have conducted many studies on what makes a persuasive communication effective, beginning with Carl Hovland and colleagues (Hovland, Janis, & Kelley, 1953). These researchers conducted experiments on the conditions under which people are most likely to be influenced by persuasive communications. In essence, they studied "who says what to whom," looking at the *source of the communication* (e.g., how expert or attractive the speaker is); the *communication itself* (e.g., the quality of the arguments; whether the speaker presents both sides of the issue); and the *nature of the audience* (e.g., which kinds of appeals work with hostile versus friendly audiences). Because these researchers were at Yale University, this approach to the study of persuasive communications is known as the **Yale Attitude Change Approach**.

Yale Attitude Change Approach

The study of the conditions under which people are most likely to change their attitudes in response to persuasive messages; researchers in this tradition focus on "who said what to whom"—that is, on the source of the communication, the nature of the communication, and the nature of the audience

This approach has yielded a great deal of useful information on how people change their attitudes in response to persuasive communications. Some of this information is summarized in Figure 6.2. Regarding the source of the communication, for example, research has shown that speakers who are credible, trustworthy, attractive, or likeable are more persuasive than those who are not. In a study on the effects of speaker credibility, students at the University of Waterloo listened to a tape-recorded speech in which it was argued that vigorous exercise is actually harmful (Ross, McFarland, Conway & Zanna, 1983). Participants in the credible condition were told that the speaker was Dr. James Rundle, a world authority on the effects of exercise; those in the non-credible condition were told that the speech was delivered by a local representative of the Fat Is Beautiful organization. As you might expect, participants were more influenced by the message when it was attributed to a credible source. More recent research conducted at the University of Alberta shows that people are more likely not

FIGURE 6.2
The Yale Attitude Change Approach.

The Yale Attitude Change Approach

The effectiveness of persuasive communications depends on who says what to whom.

Who: The Source of the Communication

- Credible speakers (e.g., those with obvious expertise) persuade people more than speakers lacking in credibility (Hovland & Weiss, 1951; Jain & Posavac, 2000).
- Attractive speakers (whether because of physical or personality attributes) persuade people more than unattractive speakers do (Eagly & Chaiken, 1975; Petty, Wegener, & Fabrigar, 1997).

What: The Nature of the Communication

- People are more persuaded by messages that do not seem to be designed to influence them (Petty & Cacioppo, 1986; Walster & Festinger, 1962).
- Is it best to present a one-sided communication (one that presents only arguments favouring your position) or a two-sided communication (one that presents arguments for and against your position)? In general, two-sided messages work better, if you are sure to refute the arguments on the other side (Crowley & Hoyer, 1994; Igou & Bless, 2003; Lumsdaine & Janis, 1953).
- Is it best to give your speech before or after someone arguing for the other side? If the speeches are to be given back to back and there will be a delay before people have to make up their minds, it is best to go first. Under these conditions, there is likely to be a *primacy effect,* wherein people are more influenced by what they hear first. If there is a delay between the speeches and people will make up their minds right after hearing the second one, it is best to go last. Under these conditions, there is likely to be a *recency effect,* wherein people remember the second speech better than the first one (Haugtvedt & Wegener, 1994; Miller & Campbell, 1959).

To Whom: The Nature of the Audience

- An audience that is distracted during the persuasive communication will often be persuaded more than one that is not (Festinger & Maccoby, 1964; Albarracin & Wyer, 2001).
- People low in intelligence tend to be more influenceable than people high in intelligence, and people with moderate self-esteem tend to be more influenceable than people with low or high self-esteem (Rhodes & Wood, 1992).
- People are particularly susceptible to attitude change during the impressionable ages of 18 to 25. Beyond those ages, people's attitudes are more stable and resistant to change (Krosnick & Alwin, 1989; Sears, 1981).

only to remember arguments from a credible source, but also to change their behaviour accordingly (Jones, Sinclair, & Courneya, 2003).

Research inspired by the Yale Attitude Change approach has been important in identifying the determinants of effective persuasion. However, it has not been clear which aspects of persuasive communications are most important—that is, when one factor should be emphasized over another. For example, let's return to that job you have with the Canadian Cancer Society—it wants to see your ad next month! If you were to read the many Yale Attitude Change studies, you would find much useful information about who should say what to whom in order to construct a persuasive communication. However, you might also find yourself saying, "Gee, there's an awful lot of information here, and I'm not sure where I should place the most emphasis. Should I worry most about who delivers the ads? Or should I worry more about the content of the message itself?"

The Central and Peripheral Routes to Persuasion Some well-known attitude researchers have asked the same questions: When is it best to stress factors central to the communication—such as the strength of the arguments—and when is it best to stress factors peripheral to the logic of the arguments—such as the credibility or attractiveness of the person delivering the speech? An answer is provided by two influential theories of persuasive communication: Shelly Chaiken's **heuristic-systematic persuasion model** (Chaiken, 1987; Chaiken, Liberman, & Eagly, 1989; Chaiken, Wood, & Eagly, 1996; Chen & Chaiken, 1999), and Richard Petty and John Cacioppo's

Heuristic-Systematic Model of Persuasion
The theory that there are two ways in which persuasive communications can cause attitude change: people either process the merits of the arguments (known as *systematic processing*) or are swayed by factors that are peripheral to the message itself, such as "Experts are always right" (known as *heuristic processing*)

Elaboration Likelihood Model
The theory that there are two ways in which persuasive communications can cause attitude change: the *central route* occurs when people are motivated and have the ability to pay attention to the arguments in the communication, and the *peripheral route* occurs when people do not pay attention to the arguments but are instead swayed by surface characteristics (e.g., who gave the speech)

elaboration likelihood model (Petty & Cacioppo, 1986; Petty & Wegener, 1999; Petty, Cacioppo, Strathman, & Priester, 2005). These theories specify when people will be influenced by what the speech says (i.e., the logic of the arguments) and when they will be influenced by more superficial characteristics (e.g., who gives the speech or how long it is).

To sell a product, it is effective to have a credible, trustworthy celebrity, such as Wayne Gretzky, provide an endorsement.

Both theories state that under certain conditions, people are motivated to pay attention to the facts in a communication and so will be most persuaded when these facts are logically compelling. That is, sometimes people elaborate on what they hear, carefully thinking about and processing the content of the communication. Chaiken (1980) calls this *systematic processing*; Petty and Cacioppo (1986) call this the *central route to persuasion*. Under other conditions, people are not motivated to pay attention to the facts; instead they notice only the surface characteristics of the message, such as how long it is and who is delivering it. The logic of the arguments does not have much persuasive power in this case because people are not paying close attention to what the communicator is saying. Instead, they are persuaded if the message is long, or if the communicator is attractive or an expert. Chaiken (1980) calls this *heuristic processing*, and Petty and Cacioppo (1986) call this the *peripheral route to persuasion*, because people are swayed by things peripheral to the message itself.

What determines whether people take the central versus the peripheral route to persuasion? The key is whether people have the motivation and ability to pay attention to the facts. If people are truly interested in the topic and motivated to pay close attention to the arguments, they are more likely to take the central route. Similarly, if people have the ability to pay attention—for example, if nothing is distracting them—they will also take the central route (see Figure 6.3). If people are bored, tired, or otherwise not able to concentrate, they will tend to take the peripheral route. For example, researchers at Brock University found that people were more likely to take the central route when the message was presented in clear, comprehensible language; they relied on the peripheral route when arguments were presented using complicated, jargon-laden language (Hafer, Reynolds, & Obertynski, 1996). In more recent research conducted with students at the University of Alberta, it was found that when under cognitive load (performing a demanding counting task), participants were persuaded by peripheral factors such as the likeability of the source rather than the strength of the arguments (Sinclair, Moore, Mark, Soldat, & Lavis, 2010). Similarly, researchers at the University of Calgary and at Brock University recently found that when participants were under cognitive load, they evaluated "hypocritical" companies (e.g., a cigarette manufacturing company campaigning to decrease rates of smoking among youth) less negatively than participants who were not under cognitive load and therefore were able to process the information and recognize the incongruity (White & Willness, 2009). Finally, according to research conducted with Canadian and American university students, when people have positive perceptions of a brand (i.e., positive perceptions of the country from which the brand originates and the country in which it is manufactured, such as a plasma television from Japan versus Peru), they take the heuristic route and are not influenced by central route information such as the pluses and minuses of the product (Carvalho, Samu, & Sivaramakrishnan, 2011).

The ability to kill or capture a man is a relatively simple task compared with changing his mind.

—Richard Cohen, 1991

Now that you know a persuasive communication can change people's attitudes in either of two ways—via the central or the peripheral route—you may be wondering what difference it makes. As long as people change their attitudes, should any of us care how they got to that point? If we are interested in creating long-lasting attitude change, we should care a lot. People who base their attitudes on a careful analysis of the arguments are more likely to maintain this attitude over time, are more likely to behave consistently with this attitude, and are more resistant to counter-persuasion than people who base their attitudes on peripheral cues (Chaiken, 1980; Mackie, 1987; Martin, Hewstone, & Martin, 2003; Petty, Haugvedt, & Smith, 1995; Petty & Wegener, 1999). For example, Perlini and Ward (2000) attempted to increase knowledge of AIDS

FIGURE 6.3

The elaboration likelihood model.

The elaboration likelihood model describes how people change their attitudes when they hear persuasive communications.

among high school students in Sault Ste. Marie by providing them with scripts describing characters who either had AIDS or were medical experts on AIDS. The purpose of these scripts was to create awareness of how AIDS can be prevented, how it is contracted, and so on. The participants then acted out these various scripts in a role play. Other participants received the same information, but it was delivered via a lecture or videotape. The researchers reasoned that the active participation required by the role-play exercise would invoke the central route to persuasion. And indeed four weeks later, the role-play participants showed more positive attitudes toward AIDS prevention than did participants in the other groups. Those in the role-play condition also showed the greatest improvement in knowledge of AIDS prevention.

Fear and Attitude Change

Now you know exactly how to construct your ad for the Canadian Cancer Society, right? Well, not quite. Before people will consider your carefully constructed arguments, you have to get their attention. If you are going to show your anti-smoking ad on television, for example, how can you be sure that people will watch your ad rather than head for the refrigerator? One way to get people's attention is to scare them. This type of persuasive message is called a **fear-arousing communication**. Public service ads often take this approach by trying to scare people into practising safer sex, wearing their seat belts, and staying away from drugs. As mentioned in Chapter 1, in 2000,

Fear-Arousing Communication

A persuasive message that attempts to change people's attitudes by arousing their fears

Health Canada requires that all cigarette packs display pictures that warn about the dangers of smoking. Do you think this ad would scare people into quitting?

the Canadian government began to place frightening images on cigarette packages—larger and more graphic than those used anywhere else in the world. In February 2011, Health Canada released even more graphic images, covering 75 percent of the outside panel of a cigarette package. It was announced that fear-producing images and messages would also be displayed on the inside of cigarette packages, making Canada the first country in the world to do so. Clearly, the Canadian government is convinced that the best way to get people to stop smoking is to make them terrified of the consequences.

But does fear actually induce people to change their attitudes? It depends on whether the fear influences people's ability and motivation to pay attention to and process the arguments in a message. If a moderate amount of fear is created, and if people believe that listening to the message will teach them how to reduce this fear, they will be motivated to analyze the message carefully and will likely change their attitudes via the central route (Petty, 1995; Rogers, 1983).

Consider a study by Leventhal, Watts, and Pagano (1967), who showed a group of smokers a graphic film depicting lung cancer and gave them pamphlets with specific instructions about how to quit smoking. These people reduced their smoking significantly more than did people who were shown only the film or only the pamphlet. Why? Watching the film scared people and giving them the pamphlet reassured them that there was a way to reduce this fear—by following the instructions on how to quit. Seeing only the pamphlet didn't work very well, because there wasn't the fear to motivate people to read it carefully. Seeing only the film didn't work very well either, because people were likely to tune out a message that raised fear but did not give information about how to reduce it. This may explain why some attempts to frighten people into changing their attitudes and behaviour fail: They succeed in scaring people but do not provide specific recommendations for them to follow. When specific recommendations are offered, people will be more likely to accept them, particularly if they are feeling vulnerable and worried that they are at risk for experiencing the feared event (Das, de Wit, & Stroebe, 2003; De Hoog, Stroebe, & de Wit, 2005; Ruitter, Abraham, & Kok, 2001).

A recent study suggests that fear might also be effective in preventing people from starting to smoke (Sabbane, Bellavance, & Chebat, 2009). Participants in this study were teenagers in Montreal who were non-smokers (a small number were occasional smokers). They were asked to evaluate a website that displayed an image of diseased gums and teeth with the text "Smoking causes mouth disease," or a website with only the text, or, in the control condition, a website with only an image of a package of cigarettes (with no warning image). Participants who were exposed to the frightening image plus the text were more likely to report intentions not to smoke than participants in the other two conditions. Presumably, the text alone did not evoke a sufficient level of fear to be effective.

Fear-arousing communications also will fail if they are so strong that they are overwhelming. If people are scared to death, they will become defensive, deny the importance of the threat, and be unable to think rationally about the issue (Janis

& Feshbach, 1953; Jepson & Chaiken, 1990; Liberman & Chaiken, 1992). For example, in a recent study conducted by researchers in Australia and at the University of Calgary, male and female drivers were exposed to frightening ads depicting the consequences of driving drunk or of speeding. Young male drivers claimed that the ads would be effective in promoting safer driving for other people but did not influence them. Not surprisingly, these participants were less likely to report intentions not to drink and drive or not to speed compared to female drivers who saw the ads (Lewis, Watson, & Tay, 2007). According to researchers at Concordia University and McGill University, humour can be an effective tool for reducing distress among people who find fear-producing messages especially threatening. In a series of studies, Conway and Dubé (2002) showed that for those who were most threatened by the fear-producing messages, the use of humour resulted in greater attitude change and intention to enact the desired behaviours (e.g., using sunscreen to avoid skin cancer, using condoms to avoid AIDS) than did nonhumorous messages.

So, if you have decided to arouse people's fear in your ad for the Canadian Cancer Society, keep these points in mind: First, try to create enough fear to motivate people to pay attention to your arguments, but not so much fear that people will tune out or distort what you say. You may even want to throw in a bit of humour for the benefit of those who find fear-inducing messages especially distressing. Second, include some specific recommendations about how to stop smoking, so people will be reassured that paying close attention to your arguments will help them reduce their fear.

Advertising and Attitude Change

How many times, in a given day, does someone attempt to change your attitudes? Be sure to count every advertisement you see or hear, because advertising is nothing less than an attempt to change your attitude toward a consumer product, be it a brand of laundry detergent, a type of automobile, or a political candidate. Don't forget to include ads you get in the mail, calls from telemarketers, and signs you see on the sides of buses, as well as those ever-present television commercials and ads that pop up on websites. How many did you come up with? You might be surprised at the answer. According to some estimates, we encounter 300 to 400 advertisements per day (Pratkanis & Aronson, 1991).

You can tell the ideals of a nation by its advertisements.

—George Norman Douglas, *South Wind, 1917*

Even in our most private moments, we are not immune from advertisements, as witnessed by the proliferation of advertisements placed in public washrooms—above the hand dryers and even on the inside doors of washroom stalls. A curious thing about advertising is that most people think it works on everyone but themselves (Wilson & Brekke, 1994). However, it turns out that we are influenced by advertising more than we think. Indeed, there is substantial evidence indicating that advertising works—when a product is advertised, sales tend to increase (Lodish, Abraham, Kalmenson, Lievelsberger, Lubetkin, Richardson, & Stevens, 1995; Ryan, 1991; Wells, 1997).

Tailoring Advertisements to People's Attitudes Which types of ads work the best? It depends on the type of attitude we are trying to change. As we saw earlier, some attitudes are based more on beliefs about the attitude object (cognitively based attitudes), whereas others are based more on emotions and values (affectively based attitudes). Several studies have shown that it is best to fight fire with fire. If an attitude is cognitively based, try to change it with rational arguments; if it is affectively based, try to change it using emotion (Fabrigar & Petty, 1999; Snyder & DeBono, 1989). In one study, for example, Sharon Shavitt (1990) gave people advertisements for different kinds of consumer products. Some of the items were utilitarian products, such as air conditioners and coffee. People's attitudes toward such products tend to be based on an appraisal of the utilitarian aspects of the products (e.g., how energy-efficient an air conditioner is) and thus are cognitively based. Other items were designated as social identity products, such as perfume and greeting cards. People's attitudes toward these types of products are based more on their values and concerns about their social identity and so are more affectively based.

As seen in Figure 6.4, people reacted most favourably to the ads that matched the type of attitude they had. If people's attitudes were cognitively based (e.g., toward air conditioners or coffee), the ads that focused on the utilitarian aspects of these products were most successful. If people's attitudes were more affectively based (e.g., toward perfume or greeting cards), the ads that focused on values and social identity concerns were most successful. Thus, if you ever get a job in advertising, the moral is to know what type of attitude most people have toward your product, and then tailor your advertising accordingly.

Recent research by Haddock and colleagues (2008) also suggests that you should pay attention to individual differences in people. It turns out that those who are high in need for cognition are more likely to be persuaded by cognitively based messages, whereas people who are high in need for affect are more likely to be persuaded by affectively based messages. For example, in one study in this series, participants who were high in need for affect reported the most positive attitudes toward lemphurs (a fictional animal) when they were described in ways that induced positive emotions (e.g., lemphurs make beautiful sounds that emulate a kitten purring). Participants high in need for cognition reported the most positive attitudes when given "the facts" (e.g., lemphurs are social animals who closely care for their offspring; Haddock, Maio, Arnold, & Huskinson, 2008).

Do you think this ad will work better with people who have affectively based or cognitively based attitudes toward cars? In general, ads work best if they are tailored to the kind of attitude they are trying to change. Given that this ad seems to be targeting people's emotions (indeed, it doesn't present any information about the car, such as its safety record, gas mileage, or reliability), it will probably work best on people whose attitudes are affectively based.

Cultural Differences in Advertising As we discussed in Chapter 5, there are differences in people's self-concept across cultures; Western cultures tend to stress independence and individualism, whereas many collectivist (e.g., Asian) cultures stress interdependence. Sang-pil Han and Sharon Shavitt (1994) reasoned that these differences in self-concept might also reflect differences in the kinds of attitudes people have toward consumer products. Perhaps advertisements that stress individuality and self-improvement might work better in Western cultures, whereas advertisements that stress one's social group might work better in Asian cultures. To test this hypothesis, the researchers created ads for the same product that stressed either independence (e.g., an ad for shoes said, "It's easy when you have the right shoes") or interdependence (e.g., "The shoes for your family") and showed them to Americans and Koreans. Americans were persuaded most by the ads stressing independence; Koreans were persuaded most by the ads stressing interdependence. Han and Shavitt (1994) also analyzed actual magazine advertisements in the United States and Korea, and found that these ads were, in fact, different. American ads tended to emphasize individuality, self-improvement, and benefits of the product for the individual consumer, whereas Korean ads tended to emphasize the family, concerns about others,

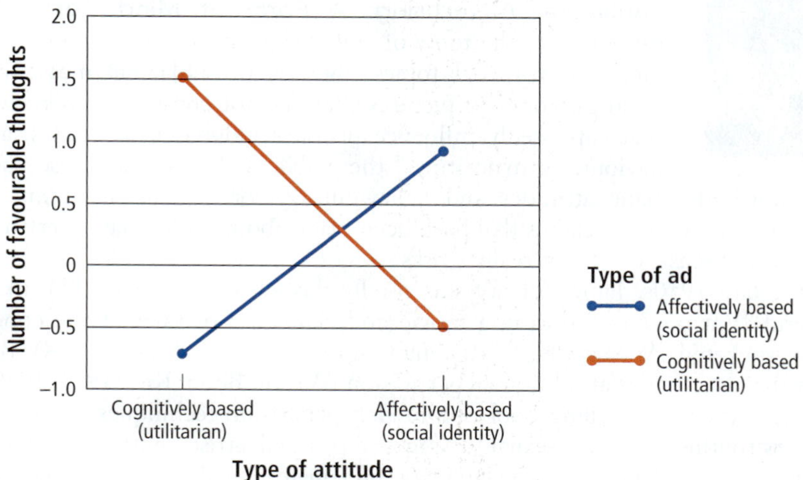

FIGURE 6.4

Effects of affective and cognitive information on affectively and cognitively based attitudes.

When people had cognitively based attitudes (e.g., toward air conditioners and coffee), cognitively based advertisements that stressed the utilitarian aspects of the products worked best. When people had more affectively based attitudes (e.g., toward perfume and greeting cards), affectively based advertisements that stressed values and social identity worked best. (The higher the number, the more favourable the thoughts people listed about the products after reading the advertisements.)

(Adapted from Shavitt, 1990)

and benefits for one's social group. More recently, researchers in Canada and China designed advertisements for digital cameras that were intended to appeal to people in individualist cultures ("Achieve Genuine Self-Expression") or collectivist cultures ("Share the Joy with Those You Love"). These ads were evaluated by North American consumers. As predicted, North Americans responded more favourably to the individualist ads than to the collectivist ads (Teng, Laroche, & Zhu, 2007). A recent meta analysis confirms that advertisements contain more individualistic content in Western cultures such as North America and more collectivistic content in countries such as Japan, Korea, China, and Mexico (Morling & Lamoreaux, 2008).

CONNECTIONS 

Do Media Campaigns to Reduce Drug Use Work?

Smoking and drinking are common in movies, and sometimes public figures admired by youth glamourize the use of drugs and alcohol. Advertising, product placement, and the behaviour of admired figures can have powerful effects on people's behaviour, including tobacco and alcohol use (Pechmann & Knight, 2002; Saffer, 2002). This raises an important question: Do public service ads designed to reduce people's use of drugs such as alcohol, tobacco, and marijuana work?

By now you know that changing people's attitudes and behaviour can be difficult, particularly if people are not very motivated to pay attention to a persuasive message or are distracted while trying to pay attention. If persuasive messages are well crafted, they can have an effect, however, and we have seen many successful attempts to change people's attitudes in this chapter. What happens when researchers take these techniques out of the laboratory and try to change real-life attitudes and behaviour, such as people's attraction to and use of illegal drugs?

A meta analysis of studies that tested the effects of a media message (conveyed via television, radio, electronic, and print media) on substance abuse (including illegal drugs, alcohol, and tobacco) in youths was encouraging (Derzon & Lipsey, 2002). After a media campaign that targeted a specific substance, such as tobacco, kids were less likely to use that substance. Television and radio messages had bigger effects than messages in the print media (Ibrahim & Glantz, 2007).

A recent meta analysis showed that public campaigns to reduce drug use can work. Do you think this ad is effective, based on what you have read in this chapter?

Subliminal Messages
Words or pictures that are not consciously perceived but that supposedly influence people's judgments, attitudes, and behaviours

Subliminal Advertising: A Form of Mind Control? We cannot leave the topic of advertising without discussing one of its most controversial topics: the use of **subliminal messages**—defined as words or pictures that are not consciously perceived but that supposedly influence people's judgments, attitudes, and behaviour. A majority of the public believes that these messages can unknowingly shape attitudes and behaviour (Zanot, Pincus, & Lamp, 1983). Given the near-hysterical claims that have been made about subliminal advertising, it is important to discuss whether it really works.

In the late 1950s, James Vicary supposedly flashed the messages "Drink Coca-Cola" and "Eat popcorn" during a movie and claimed that sales at the concession stand skyrocketed. Apparently, Vicary made up these claims (Weir, 1984). But that was not the last attempt at subliminal persuasion. Wilson Bryan Key (1973, 1989), who has written several bestselling books on hidden persuasion techniques, maintains that advertisers routinely implant sexual messages in print advertisements, such as the word *sex* in the ice cubes of an ad for gin, and male and female genitalia in everything from pats of butter to the icing in an ad for cake mix. In addition, there is a large market for audiotapes containing subliminal messages to help people lose weight, stop smoking, improve their study habits, raise their self-esteem, and even shave a few strokes off their golf scores. In 1990, sales of subliminal self-help tapes were estimated to be $50 million (Krajick, 1990). Are subliminal messages effective? Do they really make us more likely to buy consumer products, or help us to lose weight and stop smoking?

There is no scientific evidence that implanting sexual images in advertising boosts sales of the product. The public is very aware of the technique, however—so much so that some advertisers have begun to poke fun at subliminal messages in their ads.

Debunking the Claims about Subliminal Advertising Few of the proponents of subliminal advertising have conducted scientific studies to back up their claims. Fortunately, social psychologists have conducted careful, controlled experiments on subliminal perception, allowing us to evaluate the sometimes outlandish claims that are being made. Simply stated, there is no evidence that the types of subliminal messages used in everyday life have any influence on people's behaviour. Hidden commands to eat popcorn do not cause us to line up at the concession stand and buy popcorn any more than we normally would do, and the subliminal commands on self-help tapes do not (unfortunately!) help us to quit smoking or lose a few pounds (Broyles, 2006; Merikle, 1988; Moore, 1995; Pratkanis, 1992; Trappey, 1996). For example, one study randomly assigned people to listen to a subliminal self-help tape designed to improve memory or one designed to improve self-esteem. Neither of the tapes had any effect on people's memory or self-esteem (Greenwald, Spangenberg, Pratkanis, & Eskenazi, 1991). Even so, participants were convinced that the tapes had worked, which is why subliminal tapes are such a lucrative business.

Evidence for Subliminal Influence in the Lab We've seen that subliminal messages are ineffective when used in advertising. But there is some evidence for such effects in carefully controlled laboratory studies. Recall that in Chapter 5 we discussed research by Baldwin, Carrell, and Lopez (1990), who flashed slides of a scowling program director, a friendly post-doctoral student, or a disapproving-looking pope so quickly that they were not consciously perceived. Nevertheless, these images did have the predicted effects on participants' self-evaluations. Several other researchers have found similar effects of pictures or words flashed at subliminal levels (e.g., Bargh & Pietromonaco, 1982; Bornstein & Pittman, 1992; Dijksterhuis & Aarts, 2002; Dijksterhuis, Aarts, & Smith, 2005). However, all successful demonstrations of subliminal stimuli have been conducted under meticulous laboratory conditions that are difficult to reproduce in everyday life. Researchers have to ensure that the illumination of the room is just right, that people are seated just the right distance from a viewing screen, and that nothing else is occurring to distract them as the subliminal stimuli are flashed. Research conducted at the University of Waterloo shows that people also have to be motivated to accept the persuasive message (Strahan, Spencer, & Zanna, 2002). For example, in one of these studies, participants in the experimental condition were subliminally primed with words such as *dry* and *thirsty*. Participants in a control condition were subliminally exposed to neutral words. Later, those in the experimental group were more persuaded by an advertisement for "Superquencher" drinks than those in the control group. But even in the laboratory there is no evidence that subliminal messages can get people to act counter to their wishes, values, or personalities, making them march off to the supermarket to buy drinks when they're not thirsty or vote for candidates they despise.

Ironically, the hoopla surrounding subliminal messages has obscured a significant fact about advertising: Ads are more powerful when we can consciously perceive them. As we have discussed, there is ample evidence that the ads people encounter in everyday life and perceive consciously can have substantial effects on their behaviour—even though they do not contain subliminal messages. It is interesting that people fear subliminal

TRY IT! Advertising and Mind Control

Here is an exercise on people's beliefs about the power of advertising that you can try on your friends. Ask 10 or so friends the following questions—preferably friends who have not had a course in social psychology! See how accurate their beliefs are about the effects of different kinds of advertising.

1. Do you think you are influenced by subliminal messages in advertising? (Define subliminal messages for your friends as words or pictures that are not consciously perceived but that supposedly influence people's judgments, attitudes, and behaviours.)
2. Do you think you are influenced by everyday advertisements that you perceive consciously, such as television ads for laundry detergent and painkillers?
3. Suppose you had a choice to listen to one of two speeches that argued against a position you believe in, such as whether marijuana should be legalized. In Speech A, a person presents several arguments against your position. In Speech B, all of the arguments are presented subliminally—you will not perceive anything consciously. Which speech would you rather listen to, A or B?

Tally results for each person in a table like the one below:

Question 1	Question 2	Question 3
Yes	Yes	Yes
No	No	No

Go to www.MyPsychLab.com to see if your results match those of scientific studies. Show off your knowledge to your friends. Ask them why they are more wary of subliminal messages than everyday advertising, when it is everyday advertising and not subliminal messages that changes people's minds. Why do you think people are most afraid of the kinds of ads that are least effective? What does this say about people's awareness of their own thought processes?

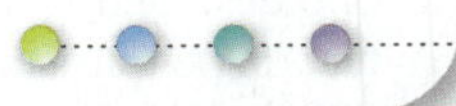

advertising more than they do regular advertising, when regular advertising is so much more powerful (Wilson, Houston, & Meyers, 1998). (Test the power of advertising with your friends or fellow students with the accompanying Try It! exercise.)

Resisting Persuasive Messages

By now, you are no doubt getting nervous (and not just because the chapter hasn't ended yet!). With all of these clever methods to change your attitudes, are you ever safe from persuasive communications? Indeed you are, or at least you can be, if you use some strategies of your own. Here's how to ensure that all of those persuasive messages that bombard you don't turn you into a quivering mass of constantly changing opinion.

Attitude Inoculation

One approach is to get people to consider the arguments for and against their attitude before someone attacks it. The more people have thought about pro and con arguments beforehand, the better they can ward off attempts to change their minds by using logical arguments. William McGuire (1964) demonstrated this by using what he called **attitude inoculation**—the process of making people immune to attempts to change their attitudes by exposing them to small doses of the arguments against their position. Having considered the arguments beforehand, people should be relatively immune to the effects of the communication—just as exposing them to a small amount of a virus can inoculate them against exposure to the full-blown viral disease. For example, in one study, McGuire (1964) "inoculated" people by giving them brief, weak arguments against beliefs that most members of a society accept uncritically, such as the idea that we should brush our teeth after every meal. Two days later, people came back and read a much stronger attack on the truism, one that contained a series of logical arguments about why brushing your teeth too frequently is a bad idea. The

Attitude Inoculation

The process of making people immune to attempts to change their attitudes by exposing them to small doses of the arguments against their position people who had been inoculated against these arguments were much less likely to change their attitudes compared to a control group who had not been. Why? Those inoculated with weak arguments had the opportunity to think about why these arguments were unfounded and were therefore in a better position to contradict the stronger attack they heard two days later. The control group, never having considered why people should or should not brush their teeth frequently, was particularly susceptible to the strong communication arguing that they should not.

The logic of McGuire's inoculation approach can be extended to real-world situations such as peer pressure. Consider Jake, a 13-year-old who is hanging out with some classmates, many of whom are smoking cigarettes. The classmates begin to make fun of Jake for not smoking and dare him to take a puff. Many 13-year-olds, faced with such pressure, would cave in. But suppose we immunized Jake to such social pressures by exposing him to mild versions of them and showing him ways to combat these pressures. We might have him role-play a situation in which a friend calls him a wimp for not smoking a cigarette and teach him to respond by saying, "I'd be more of a wimp if I smoked it just to impress you." Would this help him resist the more powerful pressures exerted by his classmates?

Several programs designed to prevent smoking in adolescents suggest that it would. For example, McAlister and colleagues (1980) used a role-playing technique with seventh graders much like the one described above. The researchers found that these students were significantly less likely to smoke three years after the study, compared with a control group that had not participated in the program. This result is encouraging and has been replicated in similar programs designed to reduce smoking (Chassin, Presson, & Sherman, 1990; Hoffman, Monge, Chou, & Valente, 2007).

Inoculation is also effective in resisting attacks on our attitudes. Bernard, Maio, and Olson (2003) had participants at the University of Western Ontario generate various kinds of arguments supporting the value of equality. A control group was not required to generate any arguments. Later, those who had formulated arguments were less likely to be persuaded by messages attacking the value of equality. Importantly, there is evidence that if people are able to resist an attack on their attitudes, they may actually come to hold those attitudes with greater certainty as a result (Tormala & Petty, 2002).

The chief effect of talk on any subject is to strengthen one's own opinions and, in fact, one never knows exactly what he does believe until he is warmed into conviction by the heat of the attack and defense.

—Charles Dudley Warner, *Backlog Studies, 1873*

Being Alert to Product Placement

In an episode of the television show *Desperate Housewives*, Gabrielle needs to find work while her husband is in prison. She lands a job at the local mall, where she promotes a new car model. Was it a coincidence that the car was a Buick LaCrosse? Apparently not; according to some reports, the show had an agreement with Buick to promote their cars by incorporating them into the script (Guthrie, 2005).

When an advertisement comes on during a television show, people often press the mute button on the remote control (or the fast-forward button if they've recorded the show). To counteract this tendency to tune out, advertisers look for ways of displaying their wares during the show itself, referred to as *product placement*. In other words, companies pay the makers of a television show or movie to incorporate their product into the script. In the movie *E.T.: The Extra-Terrestrial*, for example, Elliott left a trail of Reese's Pieces to draw out E.T., after which sales of the candy boomed. More than 40 products were shown in the hit movie *Iron Man*, including both Apple and Well computers, cars made by Audi, Ford, and Rolls-Royce, and the magazines *Vanity Fair* and *Rolling Stone*. In a recent analysis of the impact of product placement, researchers at Arizona State University and at McMaster University examined daily stock returns for firms whose products were featured in successful movies aired in 2002. The firms analyzed in this study gained an average of $296.5 million in market value following the release of a film that showcased their products (Wiles & Danielova, 2009).

Product placement, in which a commercial product is incorporated into the script of a movie or television show, has become common practice.

One reason product placement may be so successful is that people do not realize that someone is trying to influence their attitudes and behaviour. People's defenses are down; when we see E.T. eating Reese's Pieces, we don't think about the fact that someone is trying to influence our attitudes, and we don't generate counter-arguments (Burkley, 2008; Levitan & Visser, 2008). Children can be especially vulnerable. One study, for example, found that the more often children in grades 5 to 8 had seen movies in which adults smoked cigarettes, the more positive were their attitudes toward smoking (Sargent, Dalton, Beach, Mott, Tickle, Ahrens, & Heatherton, 2002; see also Wakefield, Flay, & Nichter, 2003). Not surprisingly, parents object to the placement of products in children's films, particularly the placement of unethical products such as cigarettes, alcohol, and fast food, as found in a recent study conducted in Canada and in the United Kingdom. In fact, nearly half of the respondents felt that product placement in films is more objectionable than traditional television commercials (Hudson, Hudson, & Peloza, 2008). In the same vein, researchers at universities in Ontario and Manitoba recently found that, at least under some circumstances, telling people that a radio program they were listening to had been paid for by a particular brand that was featured on the show caused them to evaluate the product and the radio show more negatively (Wei, Fischer, & Main, 2008).

This leads to the question of whether forewarning people that someone is about to try to change their attitudes is an effective tool against product placement or persuasion more generally. It turns out that it is. Several studies have found that warning people about an upcoming attempt to change their attitudes makes them less susceptible to that attempt. When people are forewarned, they analyze what they see and hear more carefully and as a result are likely to avoid attitude change. Without such warnings, people pay little attention to the persuasive attempts and tend to accept them at face value (Knowles & Linn, 2004; Wood & Quinn, 2003). So, before sending the kids off to the movies, it is good to remind them that they are likely to encounter several attempts to change their attitudes.

Simulate on **mypsychlab**
Cognitive Dissonance

Explore on **mypsychlab**
Cognitive Dissonance & Attitude Change

Changing Our Attitudes because of Our Behaviour: The Theory of Cognitive Dissonance

We have been focusing on persuasion—those times when other people attempt to change your attitudes. But there is another route to attitude change that might surprise you. Sometimes people change their attitudes not because another person is trying to get them to do so but, rather, because their own behaviour prompts them to do so. How does this happen? As we discuss next, this can happen when people behave in ways that contradict, or are inconsistent with, their attitudes. This realization produces discomfort. One way to alleviate the discomfort is for people to change their attitudes and bring them in line with their behaviour. Let's take a look at how this process works.

Leon Festinger was the first to investigate the precise workings of this powerful phenomenon, and he elaborated his findings into what is arguably social psychology's most important and most provocative theory: the theory of cognitive dissonance (Festinger, 1957). **Cognitive dissonance** is defined as the uncomfortable feeling we experience when our behaviour is at odds with our attitudes or when we hold attitudes that conflict with one another. Dissonance most often occurs whenever we do something that makes us feel stupid or immoral (Aronson, 1968, 1969, 1992, 1998; Thibodeau & Aronson, 1992). It always produces discomfort, and because discomfort is unpleasant, we are motivated to take steps to reduce it (Zanna & Cooper, 1974). How do we know this is the case? Take a moment to place yourself in the following situation.

Cognitive Dissonance

A feeling of discomfort caused by the realization that one's behaviour is inconsistent with one's attitudes or that one holds two conflicting attitudes

If you are like most university students, the idea of taking a class at 6:30 A.M. isn't particularly inviting. Imagine, however, that you are asked to write an essay in favour of 6:30 A.M. classes and that your arguments might affect whether your university actually adopts such a policy. As you start writing, you begin to experience an uneasy feeling, the kind of discomfort that social psychologists refer to as cognitive dissonance. You really do not want your classes to begin at 6:30 A.M.; yet, here you are, formulating compelling arguments for why such a policy should be implemented. This is just the situation in which some students at the University of Alberta found themselves, and most of them showed classic dissonance reduction—they changed their attitudes to become consistent with the position they were endorsing (Wright, Rule, Ferguson, McGuire, & Wells, 1992). In other words, they decided that the idea of 6:30 A.M. classes wasn't so bad after all.

That's not the whole story, however. Before writing the essay, some participants were given a drug—supposedly to improve memory—and were told either that the drug would have no side effects or that the drug would make them tense. The researchers expected that participants who were told the drug would make them tense would not experience dissonance because they would attribute their uneasy feelings to the drug ("Oh, right—I took a pill that's supposed to make me feel tense; that's why I'm feeling this way"). And if they weren't experiencing dissonance, they wouldn't need to change their attitudes, would they? Indeed, participants in this condition were most likely to retain their negative views toward 6:30 A.M. classes, despite writing an essay promoting such a policy.

Given that the experience of dissonance is unpleasant and uncomfortable, we will take steps to alleviate the discomfort. How? As we saw in the Wright and colleagues (1992) study, one option is to attempt to justify our behaviour through changing one of the dissonant cognitions. Most often, this takes the form of changing our attitudes to bring them in line with our behaviour. A recent study conducted by researchers at the University of Manitoba and at Queen's University found that we are likely to take this route when the attitude in question isn't particularly important to us. If the attitude matters and we've just focused on how important it is, we are less likely to reduce dissonance by changing that attitude (Starzyk, Fabrigar, Soryal, & Fanning, 2009). But that still leaves us with other options. We could reduce dissonance by changing our behaviour to bring it in line with the dissonant cognition. We could also attempt to justify our behaviour by adding new cognitions. These different ways of reducing dissonance are illustrated in Figure 6.5.

To illustrate, let's look at a behaviour that millions of people engage in several times a day—smoking cigarettes. If you are a smoker, you are likely to experience dissonance because you know that this behaviour can produce a painful, early death. How can you reduce this dissonance? The most direct way is to change your behaviour—to give up smoking. Your behaviour would then be consistent with your knowledge of the link between smoking and cancer. While many people have succeeded in doing just that, it's not easy—many have tried to quit and failed. What do these people do? It would be wrong to assume that they simply swallow hard and prepare to die. They don't. Instead, they try to reduce their dissonance in a different way: by convincing themselves that smoking isn't as bad as they thought.

Smokers can come up with pretty creative ways to justify their smoking. Some succeed in convincing themselves that the data linking cigarette smoking to cancer are inconclusive. Others will add new cognitions—for example, the erroneous belief that filters trap most of the harmful chemicals, thus reducing the threat of cancer. Some will add a cognition that allows them to focus on the vivid exception: "Look at old Sam Carouthers—he's 90 years old, and he's been smoking a pack a day since he was 15. That proves it's not always bad for you." Still others will add the cognition that smoking is an extremely enjoyable activity, one for which it is worth risking cancer. Others even succeed in convincing themselves that, all things considered, smoking is worthwhile because it relaxes them, reduces nervous tension, and, in this way, actually improves their health.

Watch on **mypsychlab**
Cognitive Dissonance: Need to Justify Our Actions

FIGURE 6.5
How we reduce cognitive dissonance.

These justifications may sound silly to the non-smoker. That is precisely our point. People experiencing dissonance will often go to extreme lengths to reduce it. We did not make up the examples of denial, distortion, and justification listed above; they are based on actual examples generated by people who have tried and failed to quit smoking. Similar justifications have been generated by people who try and fail to lose weight, who refuse to practise safer sex, or who receive bad news about their health (Aronson, 1997b; Croyle & Jemmott, 1990; Goleman, 1982; Kassarjian & Cohen, 1965; Leishman, 1988). To escape from dissonance, people will engage in quite extraordinary rationalizing.

This youngster may be thinking, "There's nothing wrong with putting on a little extra weight. After all, some professional football players weigh more than 140 kilograms and earn millions of dollars a year. Pass the fries."

Decisions, Decisions, Decisions

Every time we make a decision, we experience dissonance. How come? Let's pretend that you are trying to decide which of two attractive people to date: Chris, who is funny and playful, but a bit irresponsible, or Pat, who is interesting and smart, but not very spontaneous. You agonize over the decision but eventually decide to pursue a relationship with Pat. After you've made the decision, you will experience dissonance because, despite Pat's good qualities, you did choose to be with someone who is not very spontaneous and you turned down someone who is playful and funny. We call this **post-decision dissonance.**

Cognitive dissonance theory predicts that to feel better about the decision, you will do some mental work to try to reduce the dissonance. What kind of work? You would convince yourself that Pat really was the right person for you and that Chris actually would have been a lousy choice. An early experiment by Jack Brehm (1956) illustrates this phenomenon. Brehm posed as a representative of a consumer testing service and asked women to rate the attractiveness and desirability of several kinds of appliances, such as toasters and electric coffee makers. Each woman was told that as a reward for having participated in the survey she could have one of the appliances as a gift. She was given a choice between two of the products she had rated as being equally attractive. After she made her decision, her appliance was wrapped up and given to her. Twenty minutes later, each woman was asked to re-rate all of the products. Brehm found that after receiving the appliance of their choice, the women rated its attractiveness somewhat higher than they had done the first time. Not only that, but they drastically lowered their rating of the appliance they had decided to reject. In other words, following a decision, to reduce dissonance, we change the way we feel about the chosen and not chosen alternatives—cognitively spreading them apart in our own minds to make ourselves feel better about the choice we made.

Once we have committed a lot of time or energy to a cause, it is nearly impossible to convince us that the cause is unworthy.

Post-Decision Dissonance

Dissonance that is inevitably aroused after a person makes a decision; such dissonance is typically reduced by enhancing the attractiveness of the chosen alternative and devaluing the rejected alternatives

Much of the research conducted since Brehm's classic study has adopted this methodology. Participants first evaluate a set of items; they then are given a choice between two items they found attractive; once they have made their choice, they again rate the items to see if their evaluations have changed. A consistent finding is that people rate the chosen item more positively and the rejected item more negatively than they did before making their decision (Gilbert & Ebert, 2002). Research conducted at the University of Western Ontario has demonstrated that these effects occur even when people's evaluations are assessed at an implicit (unconscious) level (Gawronski, Bodenhausen, & Becker, 2007).

The Permanence of the Decision Decisions vary in terms of how permanent they are—that is, how difficult they are to revoke. It is a lot easier, for instance, to go back to a car dealership to exchange a defective new car for another one than to extricate yourself from an unhappy marriage: the more permanent and less revocable the decision, the greater the need to reduce dissonance.

An excellent place to investigate the significance of irrevocability is the racetrack. Experienced bettors typically spend a great deal of time poring over the "dope sheets," trying to decide which horse to put their money on. When they make a decision, they head for the betting windows. While they are standing in line, they have already made their decision but, we would hypothesize, because it is still revocable, they have no urge to reduce dissonance. However, once they get to the window and place their bet—even if it's for only $2—there is no turning back. Thirty seconds later, they cannot go back and tell the nice person behind the window that they have changed their mind. If irrevocability is an important factor, one would expect greater dissonance reduction among bettors a few minutes after placing the bet than a few minutes before placing the bet.

In a simple but clever experiment, Knox and Inkster (1968) intercepted people at the Exhibition Park Race Track in Vancouver who were on their way to place $2 bets and asked them how certain they were that their horses would win. The investigators also intercepted other bettors just as they were leaving the $2 window, after having placed their bets, and asked them the same question. Almost invariably, people who had already placed their bets gave their horses a much better chance of winning than did those who had yet to place their bets. Since only a few minutes separated one group from another, nothing "real" had occurred to increase the probability of winning; the only thing that had changed was the finality of the decision—and thus the dissonance it produced.

The Decision to Behave Immorally Needless to say, life is made up of more than just decisions about kitchen appliances and racehorses: often our decisions involve moral and ethical issues. When is it okay to lie to a friend, and when is it not? When is an act stealing, and when is it borrowing? Resolving moral dilemmas is a particularly interesting area in which to study dissonance. Believe it or not, dissonance reduction following a difficult moral decision can cause people to behave either more *or less* ethically in the future—it can actually change their system of values.

Take the issue of cheating on an exam. Suppose you are a third-year university student taking the final exam in a chemistry course. You have always wanted to be a surgeon and you know that your admission to medical school depends heavily on how well you do in this course. The key question on the exam involves some material you know well, but you experience acute anxiety and draw a blank. You simply cannot think. You happen to be sitting behind the smartest person in the class and notice that she has just written down her answer to this question. You could easily read it if you chose to. Time is running out. What do you do? Your conscience tells you it's wrong to cheat—and yet if you don't cheat, you are certain to get a poor grade. And if you get a poor grade, there goes medical school.

Regardless of whether you decide to cheat, you are doomed to experience dissonance. If you cheat, your cognition that "I am a decent, moral person" is dissonant with your cognition that "I have just committed an immoral act." If you decide to resist temptation, your cognition that "I want to become a surgeon" is dissonant with your cognition that "I could have acted in a way that would have ensured a good grade and admission to medical school, but I chose not to. Wow, was that stupid!"

In this situation, some students decide to cheat; others decide not to. What happens to the students' attitudes about cheating after their decision? For students who decide to cheat, an efficient path of dissonance reduction would be to adopt a more lenient attitude toward cheating, convincing themselves that it is a victimless crime that doesn't hurt anybody, and that everybody does it, so it's not really that bad. Students who manage to resist the temptation to cheat also could reduce dissonance by changing their attitude about the morality of the act—but this time in the opposite

Once an individual makes a final and irrevocable decision, he or she has a greater need to reduce dissonance. At the racetrack, for example, once bettors have placed their bet, their certainty is greater than it is immediately before they've placed it.

direction. That is, to justify giving up a good grade, they would have to convince themselves that it is dishonest and immoral to cheat and that only a despicable person would do such a thing.

The dissonance reduction that occurs for these students—regardless of whether they cheated—is not merely a rationalization of their behaviour but an actual change in their system of values; individuals faced with this kind of choice will undergo either a softening or a hardening of their attitudes toward cheating on exams, depending on whether they decided to cheat.

These speculations were put to the test by Judson Mills (1958) in an experiment performed at an elementary school. Mills first measured the attitudes of sixth graders toward cheating. He then had them participate in a competitive exam, offering prizes to the winners. The situation was arranged so it was almost impossible to win without cheating. Moreover, Mills made it easy for the children to cheat on the exam and created the illusion that they could not be detected. Under these conditions, as one might expect, some of the students cheated and others did not. The next day, the sixth graders were again asked to indicate how they felt about cheating. Children who had cheated became more lenient toward cheating, and those who had resisted the temptation to cheat adopted a harsher attitude toward cheating.

After he cheats, he will try to convince himself that everybody would cheat if they had the chance.

Classic experiments conducted in the laboratory often inspire contemporary research in the real world. A case in point: While conducting research among mid-level business executives in India, two social psychologists came up with some interesting data pertinent to Mills' results (Viswesvaran & Deshpande, 1996). They reasoned that executives who were in the process of making a decision about whether to behave ethically were in a vulnerable state. On the one hand, they wanted to behave ethically; on the other hand, they were undoubtedly concerned that they might need to behave unethically to succeed. The investigators found that executives who had substantial reason to believe that managerial success could be achieved only through unethical behaviour experienced far greater dissonance (in the form of job dissatisfaction) than those who were given no reason to believe this. Our prediction is that if the researchers had returned a year or two later, they would have found a reduction in dissonance in this group; that is, as with Mills' participants, most of those who behaved unethically would have found a way to justify that behaviour after the fact.

Dissonance, the Brain, and Evolution

Neuroscientists have recently shown that cognitive dissonance and its reduction are reflected in the way the brain processes information. In a study of people who were required to process dissonant or consonant information while in an fMRI scanner, Drew Westen and colleagues (2006) found that the reasoning areas of the brain virtually shut down when people were confronted with dissonant information. The emotion circuits of the brain lit up happily when consonance was restored. As the researchers put it, people twirl the "cognitive kaleidoscope" until the pieces fall into the pattern they want to see, and then the brain repays them by activating circuits involved in pleasure—not unlike, they note, what addicts feel when they get a fix (Westen, Blagov, Harenski, Kilts, & Hammon, 2006).

Other experiments support the notion that cognitive dissonance developed evolutionarily, suggesting that it has survival value. Recall the study by Brehm (1956) in which homemakers ranked appliances, and then, after getting to keep an appliance of their choice, lowered their ranking of the previously attractive appliance they did not choose. In a study by Egan, Santos, and Bloom (2007), monkeys were placed in a similar situation, only they were choosing between different coloured M&Ms instead of kitchen appliances. Like the homemakers, they reduced their liking for the colour

Going through a lot of effort to become a soldier will increase the recruit's feelings of cohesiveness and pride in the corps.

M&Ms not chosen. Additional support for the biological basis of cognitive dissonance comes from research showing that left frontal cortical activity is involved in the dissonance reduction process (E. Harmon-Jones, C. Harmon-Jones, Fearn, Sigelman, & Johnson, 2008).

The Justification of Effort

Suppose you expend a great deal of effort to get into a particular club, and it turns out to be a totally worthless organization, consisting of boring, pompous people engaged in trivial activities. You would feel pretty foolish, wouldn't you? This situation would produce a fair amount of dissonance; your cognition that you are a sensible, adept human being is dissonant with your cognition that you worked hard to get into a worthless club. How would you reduce this dissonance? You might start by finding a way to convince yourself that the club and the people in it are nicer, more interesting, and more worthwhile than they appeared to be at first glance. Activities and behaviours are open to a variety of interpretations; if people are motivated to see the best in people and things, they will tend to interpret these ambiguities in a positive manner. We call this the **justification of effort**—the tendency for individuals to increase their liking for something they have worked hard to attain.

Justification of Effort

The tendency for individuals to increase their liking for something they have worked hard to attain

In a classic experiment, Elliot Aronson and Judson Mills (1959) explored the link between effort and dissonance reduction. In this study, university students volunteered to join a group that would meet regularly to discuss various aspects of the psychology of sex. To be admitted to the group, they volunteered to go through a screening procedure. For one-third of the participants, the procedure was extremely demanding and unpleasant; for a second one-third of participants, it was only mildly unpleasant; and the final one-third was admitted to the group without undergoing any screening procedure. Each participant was then allowed to listen in on a discussion being conducted by the members of the group they would be joining. The discussion was arranged so it was as dull and bombastic as possible. After the discussion was over, each participant was asked to rate it in terms of how much he or she liked it, how interesting it was, how intelligent the participants were, and so forth. The major findings are shown in Figure 6.6.

Rating for the discussion group (higher rating means greater liking)

100

90

80

Control (no initiation)

Mild initiation

Severe initiation

Severity of initiation

FIGURE 6.6

The tougher the initiation, the more we like the group.

The more effort we put into gaining group membership, the more we like the group we have just joined.

(Adapted from Aronson & Mills, 1959)

The results supported the predictions. Participants who underwent little or no effort to get into the group did not enjoy the discussion very much. They were able to see it for what it was—a dull and boring waste of time. Participants who went through a severe initiation, however, succeeded in convincing themselves that the same discussion, though not as scintillating as they had hoped, was dotted with interesting and provocative tidbits, and therefore, in the main, was a worthwhile experience. In short, they justified their effortful initiation process by interpreting all the ambiguous aspects of the group discussion in the most positive manner possible.

To turn to a real-life example, think about the tremendous cost, effort, and sacrifice involved in raising a child. How do parents justify the huge expenditure of time, money, and other resources? Based on what you know so far, you are probably in a position to make a prediction, based on cognitive dissonance theory, which is exactly what University of Waterloo researchers recently did. In the study, parents in the dissonance condition were given information on how much it costs to raise a child until 18 years of age. Other parents were given the same information, but also were told that adult children often support their aging parents, such that parents in old age frequently are more financially secure than elderly people without children. It was predicted that parents in the cost condition would experience dissonance and would reduce it by idealizing parenthood. Indeed, these parents expressed greater agreement with statements such as "There is nothing more rewarding in life than raising a child" than parents in the control condition who were given information about costs and the long-term benefits of having children (Eibach & Mock, 2011). In a follow-up study, the researchers found that parents for whom dissonance was created by reminding them of the costs of raising a child also were more likely to claim that there was nothing as enjoyable in life as spending time with their children!

In summary, if a person agrees to go through an effortful, difficult, or an unpleasant experience to attain some goal or object, that goal or object becomes more attractive. As we mentioned in Chapter 1, it is not unusual for people in the military or on sports teams to be subjected to barbaric, cruel hazing rituals. On the face of it, you might expect that the victims of hazings would despise those who made them suffer. However, by now you are probably in a better position to understand the reactions of people such as Dave Tremblay. When Dave Tremblay, a former Quebec Nordiques prospect, joined the Pickering Panthers of the Ontario Hockey Association, he was blindfolded, shaved, and forced to sit in a hot liniment that badly burned his genitals. A few years later, he was hazed again when he received a hockey scholarship from a U.S. university. That time, he was sick for days, suffering from alcohol poisoning. How does he remember the teammates who inflicted this cruelty on him? Remarkably, with fondness: "They came by and checked on us when it was over . . .. They didn't just beat the crap out of us and leave us" (O'Hara, 2000). If it weren't for cognitive dissonance theory, such a reaction would be difficult to understand!

External Justification

A person's reason or explanation for dissonant behaviour that resides outside the individual (e.g., to receive a large reward or avoid a severe punishment)

Internal Justification

The reduction of dissonance by changing something about oneself (e.g., one's attitude or behaviour)

Counter-Attitudinal Advocacy

The process that occurs when a person states an opinion or attitude that runs counter to his or her private belief or attitude

The Psychology of Insufficient Justification

Imagine your best friend invites you to the first performance of a band that he has proudly put together. The vocalist is awful, the bass player shows little talent, and as it turns out, your friend should have kept up with his saxophone lessons. Afterward, your friend excitedly asks you how you enjoyed the band. How do you respond? You hesitate. Chances are you go through something like the following thought process: "Jeremy seems so happy and excited. Why should I hurt his feelings and possibly ruin our friendship?" So you tell Jeremy that the band was great. Do you experience much dissonance? We doubt it. Your belief that it is important not to cause pain to people you like provides ample **external justification** for having told a harmless lie.

Counter-Attitudinal Advocacy What happens, on the other hand, if you say something you don't really believe and there isn't a good external justification for doing so? That is, what if Jeremy sincerely needed to know your opinion of the band because he was thinking of quitting school to devote his life to music? If you still tell him the band was great, you will experience dissonance. When you can't find external justification for your behaviour, you will attempt to find **internal justification**—that is, you will try to reduce dissonance by changing something about your attitudes or behaviour. How can you do this? You might begin looking for positive aspects of the band—some evidence of creativity or potential that might be realized with a little more practice or a few new talented band members. If you look hard enough, you will probably find something. Within a short time, your attitude toward the band will have moved in the direction of the statement you made—and that is how saying becomes believing. This phenomenon is referred to as **counter-attitudinal advocacy**, a process that occurs when a person states an opinion or attitude that runs counter to his or her private belief or attitude. When we do this with little external justification, we start to believe the lie we told.

"How do I look?" your friend asks. Do you tell him the truth? Chances are you don't. Your concern about his feelings provides enough external justification for telling a white lie, so you experience little dissonance.

This proposition was first tested in a groundbreaking experiment by Leon Festinger and J. Merrill Carlsmith (1959). In this experiment, university students were induced to spend an hour performing a series of excruciatingly boring and repetitive tasks. The experimenter then told them that the purpose of the study was to determine whether people would perform better if they had been told in advance that the tasks were interesting. They were each informed that they had been randomly assigned to the control condition—that is, they had not been told anything in advance. However, he explained, the next participant, a young woman who was just arriving in the anteroom, was going to be in the experimental condition. The experimenter said that he needed to convince her that the task was going to be interesting and enjoyable. Since it was much more convincing if a fellow student rather than the experimenter delivered this message, would the participant do so? With this request, the experimenter induced the participants to lie about the task to another student.

Half of the students were offered $20 for telling the lie (a large external justification), while the others were offered only $1 for telling the lie (a very small external justification). After the experiment was over, an interviewer asked the lie-tellers how much they had enjoyed the tasks they had performed earlier in the experiment. The results validated the hypothesis. Students who had been paid $20 for lying—that is, for saying that the tasks had been enjoyable—rated the activities as the dull and boring experiences they were. But those who were paid only $1 for saying that the task was enjoyable rated the task as significantly more enjoyable. In other words, people who had received an abundance of external justification for lying told the lie but didn't believe it, whereas those who told the lie without a great deal of external justification succeeded in convincing themselves that what they said was closer to the truth.

Using Counter-Attitudinal Advocacy to Tackle Social Problems Can research on counter-attitudinal advocacy be used to solve social problems? Would it be possible, for example, to get people to endorse a policy favouring a minority community and then see whether attitudes become more positive toward that community? Absolutely. In an important set of experiments, Mike Leippe and Donna Eisenstadt (1994, 1998) demonstrated that laboratory experiments on counter-attitudinal advocacy can be applied directly to important societal problems—in this case, race relations and racial prejudice. They induced white students at an American university to write a counter-attitudinal essay publicly endorsing a controversial proposal at their university—to double the funds available for academic scholarships for African-American students. Because the total funds were limited, this meant cutting by half the scholarship funds available to white students. As you might imagine, this was a highly dissonant situation. How might they reduce dissonance? The best way would be to convince themselves that they really believed deeply in that policy. Moreover, dissonance theory would predict that their general attitude toward African-American people would become more favourable and much more supportive. And that is exactly what Leippe and Eisenstadt found.

In a more recent experiment along the same lines, Son Hing, Li, and Zanna (2002) focused on "aversive racists" (those low in explicit prejudice but high in implicit prejudice). In the study, the experimental group first wrote essays about why it was important to treat minority students fairly. They were later instructed to write about two situations in which they reacted to an Asian more negatively than they thought they should have. This created feelings of hypocrisy, and therefore dissonance, in the experimental group. Subsequently, this group of students showed evidence of a reduction in prejudicial behaviour. Specifically, participants in the hypocrisy condition recommended less of a budget cut to the Asian Student Association at the University of Waterloo than did participants in a control condition.

In the past two decades, this aspect of dissonance theory—the induction of hypocrisy—has also been applied to another important societal issue: the prevention of the spread of AIDS. As we discussed earlier in this chapter, although college and university students are aware that AIDS is a serious problem, a surprisingly small percentage use condoms every time they have sex. Is there anything that can be done about this? Elliot Aronson and colleagues (Aronson, Fried, & Stone, 1991; Stone et al., 1994) have had considerable success at convincing people to use condoms by employing a variation of the counter-attitudinal advocacy paradigm. They asked university students to compose a speech describing the dangers of AIDS and advocating the use of condoms every single time a person has sex. In one condition, the students merely composed the arguments. In another condition, the students composed the arguments and then recited them in front of a video camera, after being informed that the videotape would be played to an audience of high school students. In addition, half of the students in each condition were made mindful of their own failure to use condoms, by having them make a list of the circumstances in which they had found it particularly difficult, awkward, or impossible to use them.

Essentially, then, the participants in one condition—those who made a video for high school students after having been made mindful of their own failure to use condoms—were in a state of high dissonance. This was caused by their being made aware of their own hypocrisy; they were fully aware of the fact that they were preaching behaviour to high school students that they themselves were not practising. To remove the hypocrisy, they would need to start practising what they were preaching. And that is exactly what Aronson and colleagues found. Later, when the students were given the opportunity to purchase condoms very cheaply, those in the hypocrisy condition were the most likely to buy them. A follow-up telephone interview several months after the experiment demonstrated that the effects were long-lasting. People in the hypocrisy condition reported far greater use of condoms than did those in the control conditions.

Hypocrisy induction also has been used to address road rage. In one study in a series conducted by Takaku (2006), a driving simulation was set up so that the participants accidentally cut off another driver. Being reminded of their own driving mistakes in this way resulted in greater forgiveness of the mistakes of other drivers.

Recently, researchers have shown that hypocrisy induction is even effective when used with young children. More specifically, Morrongiello and Mark (2008) used hypocrisy induction to get children to refrain from engaging in risky, unsafe behaviours on school playground equipment. Hypocrisy was induced by having school children in Guelph, Ontario, make a list of risky playground behaviours that they had previously engaged in. They were then asked to sign a "Safe Play on Playgrounds" poster and to make a radio commercial promoting safe play. Children for whom dissonance was created by making them aware of their hypocrisy later reported that they intended to engage in far fewer risky behaviours than children in a control group. This effect held at a one-month follow up (Morrongiello & Mark, 2008).

We end by noting that recent research suggests that hypocrisy induction may be especially effective with people who have high self-esteem. In a study aimed at quitting smoking, researchers at the University of Western Ontario found that people with high self-esteem were more likely than people with low self-esteem to reduce dissonance in the most direct way, namely by quitting smoking (Peterson, Haynes, & Olson, 2008). Similarly, a study that created dissonance by confronting drivers with the environmental costs of driving rather than using public transportation found that people with high self-esteem expressed a willingness to change their behaviour and use public transportation, whereas those with low self-esteem were more likely to rationalize their driving (e.g., arguing that environmental concerns are exaggerated; Holland, Meertens, & Van Vugt, 2002).

The Power of Mild Punishment If you really want to stop someone from behaving badly (e.g., trying to stop a bully from beating up little kids) you should dish out punishment—and make sure it is severe enough to have a deterrent effect. Right? Not so, according to dissonance theory. Dissonance theory would predict just the opposite. Give the bully mild punishment. Then, when the bully stops beating up little kids, dissonance is created. "I like beating up little kids, but I'm not doing it. Why?" He doesn't have a convincing answer to this question because the threat is so mild it doesn't produce a superabundance of justification. In short, this is **insufficient punishment**. This dissonance can be reduced by deciding "I guess I stopped because it's really not that much fun after all." In contrast, if this bully had received severe punishment, he or she would have ample external justification for having stopped ("I'm not beating up kids because I'll get kicked out of school if a teacher sees me"). In this case, the behaviour may decrease, but probably only when a teacher isn't around. In other words, true attitude change hasn't taken place.

Insufficient Punishment

The dissonance aroused when individuals lack sufficient external justification for having resisted a desired activity or object, usually resulting in individuals devaluing the forbidden activity or object

Parents can intervene to stop bullying after it takes place, but what might they do to make it less likely to happen in the future?

These speculations were put to the test by Elliot Aronson and J. Merrill Carlsmith (1963) in an experiment with preschoolers. In this study, the experimenter first asked each child to rate the attractiveness of several toys. He then pointed to a toy that the child considered to be among the most attractive and told the child that he or she was not allowed to play with it. Half of the children were threatened with mild punishment (the experimenter said he would be annoyed) if they disobeyed; the other half were threatened with severe punishment (the experimenter said he would be very angry, would take their toys away, and would never come back again). The experimenter then left the room for several minutes to provide the children with the time and opportunity to play with the other toys and to resist the temptation of playing with the forbidden toy. None of the children played with the forbidden toy.

The experimenter then returned to the room and asked each child to rate how much he or she liked each of the toys. Initially, all the children had wanted to play with the forbidden toy but, during the temptation period, all of them had refrained from playing with it. Clearly, the children were experiencing dissonance. How did they respond? The children who had received a severe threat had ample justification for their restraint. They knew why they hadn't played with the toy and therefore they had no reason to change their attitude toward it. These children continued to rate the forbidden toy as highly desirable; indeed, some even found it more desirable than they had before the threat.

But what about the others? Without much external justification for avoiding the toy, the children in the mild threat condition needed an internal justification to reduce their dissonance. They succeeded in convincing themselves that the reason they hadn't played with the toy was that they didn't really like it. They rated the forbidden toy as less attractive than they had at the beginning of the experiment. Subsequent research showed that these effects are quite long-lasting (Freedman, 1965). The implications for child rearing are fascinating. Parents who use punishment to encourage their children to adopt positive values should keep the punishment mild—barely enough to produce a change in behaviour—and then the values will follow.

> *We do not love people so much for the good they have done us as for the good we have done them.*
>
> —Leo Tolstoy, *1869*

The Aftermath of Bad Deeds

Imagine that you realize that your actions have hurt another person. How would you react? Would you be especially kind to this person to make up for your transgression? Sadly, that is not what dissonance theory would predict. According to dissonance theory, when we hurt someone, we come to dislike or hate that person as a way of justifying our cruelty. This phenomenon was demonstrated in an early experiment performed by Keith Davis and Edward E. Jones (1960). Participants watched a young man (a confederate) being interviewed and then provided him with an analysis of his shortcomings as a human being. Specifically, the participants were told to tell the young man that they believed him to be a shallow, untrustworthy, boring person. The participants succeeded in convincing themselves that they didn't like the victim of their cruelty—after the fact. In short, after saying things they knew were certain to hurt him, they convinced themselves that he deserved it. They found him less attractive than they had prior to saying the hurtful things to him.

How can we induce this child to give up playing with an attractive toy?

These effects can operate on quite a subtle level, as when we tell disparaging jokes about particular groups. Even though it may seem like harmless fun, we end up evaluating the group more negatively as a means of justifying our put-downs, as demonstrated in a program of research conducted at the University of Western Ontario (Hobden & Olson, 1994; Maio, Olson, & Bush, 1997). For example, participants who were asked to recite disparaging jokes about Newfoundlanders later reported more negative stereotypes of this group than those who recited nondisparaging jokes.

When civilians such as the elderly, women, and children are targets of military violence, the soldiers committing the violence will be inclined to derogate or dehumanize their victims to reduce their own dissonance. Here, Master Corporal Clayton Matchee of the Canadian Airborne Regiment smiles and points at Somali teenager Shidane Arone, whom members of the regiment tortured and beat to death in 1993. This photo, taken by one of the soldiers, shows the dehumanization of Somali people in the eyes of the soldiers.

Do people in real-world situations also use dissonance to justify cruel actions toward another human being? Sadly, the answer appears to be yes. In March 1993, Canadian soldiers from the elite Canadian Airborne Regiment on a peacekeeping mission in Somalia captured 16-year-old Shidane Arone trying to sneak into their compound. He was tied up, savagely beaten, and tortured to death. A court martial later learned that one of the soldiers beat Arone with a wooden riot baton, a metal pipe, and his feet and fists. Other soldiers joined in. According to newspaper reports, the young Somali boy's cries of "Canada, Canada, Canada" as he drifted in and out of consciousness could be heard across the compound. Canadians were shocked and deeply disturbed by this incident. Perhaps most shocking was that the soldiers posed for "trophy" photographs—in one photograph, soldiers posed beside the unconscious Somali boy; in another photograph, a soldier held the boy's head up by jamming a wooden baton into his bloody mouth; still others showed a soldier holding a gun to Arone's head. What was so chilling about these photographs was the broad smiles on the soldiers' faces. As James Travers, the editor of the *Ottawa Citizen*, commented, "They not only tortured, beat, and killed him, but were obviously playing when they did this" (Boadle, 1994). How could anyone gleefully torture and murder a 16-year-old boy? By deciding that he deserved it. It may seem absurd to suggest that Canadian peacekeepers could convince themselves that an unarmed, civilian boy deserved to be beaten to death for trying to enter their compound. However, as various inquiries into this tragedy revealed, some of the higher-ranking officers had issued orders to "abuse" any Somali intruders. While the soldiers who committed these atrocities were aware that it was illegal to torture or kill anyone they captured, the fact that some of their superiors advocated punishing intruders appears to have been all the justification they needed. In short, the soldiers may have convinced themselves that Arone deserved what he got.

Another way in which people reduce dissonance for having committed cruel acts is to derogate or dehumanize their victim. According to the report of the Somalia Commission of Inquiry, the Canadian soldiers referred to the Somali people as "gimmes," "smufties," and "nignogs" (Canada, 1997). Unfortunately, history keeps repeating itself. In 2005, Americans in charge of the Abu Ghraib prison near Baghdad tortured and killed Iraqi prisoners. The images of torture and humiliation bore a chilling resemblance to the photos of Shidane Arone. One of the striking similarities was the dehumanization of the victims—the prisoners were shown naked, with hoods over their faces, or crawling on all fours with leashes around their necks.

Ironically, success at dehumanizing the victim virtually guarantees a continuation or even an escalation of the cruelty. It becomes easier to hurt and kill "subhumans" than to hurt and kill fellow human beings. Reducing dissonance in this way has sobering future consequences: it increases the likelihood that the atrocities people are willing to commit will become greater and greater through an endless chain of violence followed by self-justification (in the form of dehumanizing the victim), followed by greater violence and still more intense dehumanization. In this manner, unbelievable acts of human cruelty—such as the Nazi Final Solution that led to the murder of 6 million European Jews, the murders of 2 million Cambodians in Pol Pot's killing fields in the 1970s, and the massacre of 600 000 Tutsis in Rwanda in 1994—can occur. Unfortunately, such atrocities are not a thing of the past but are as recent as today's newspaper.

Avoiding the Rationalization Trap

The tendency to reduce dissonance by justifying our behaviour can lead us into an escalation of rationalizations that can be disastrous. We call this the **rationalization trap**—the potential for dissonance reduction to produce a succession of self-justifications that

Rationalization Trap
The potential for dissonance reduction to produce a succession of self-justifications that ultimately result in a chain of stupid or immoral actions

ultimately results in a chain of stupid or irrational actions. The irony, of course, is that to avoid thinking of ourselves as stupid or immoral, we set the stage to increase our acts of stupidity or immorality.

Is there a way that people can be persuaded not to rationalize their behaviour when they make mistakes? A clue as to how such behaviour might come about can be found in research on self-affirmation (Steele, 1988). **Self-affirmation theory** suggests that people can reduce the impact of a dissonance-arousing threat to their self-concept by focusing on and affirming their competence on some dimension unrelated to the threat.

Self-Affirmation Theory

A theory suggesting that people will reduce the impact of a dissonance-arousing threat to their self-concept by focusing on and affirming their competence on some dimension unrelated to the threat

Research by Claude Steele and colleagues (Steele, 1988; Steele & Liu, 1981; see also Aronson, Cohen, & Nail, 1998; White & Argo, 2009) shows how self-affirmation comes about. Suppose that immediately after Mary acted cruelly, but before she had an opportunity to derogate her victim, she was reminded of the fact that she had recently donated several units of blood to Canadian Blood Services or that she had recently received a high score on her physics exam. This self-affirmation would likely provide her with the ability to resist engaging in typical dissonance-reducing behaviour. In effect, Mary might be able to say, "It's true—I just did a cruel thing. But I am also capable of some really fine, intelligent, and generous behaviour." In a series of clever experiments, Steele and colleagues demonstrated that if—prior to the onset of dissonance—you provide people with an opportunity for self-affirmation, they will generally grab it (Steele, 1988; Steele & Liu, 1981). According to a recent series of studies conducted by researchers at universities in the United States and Canada, self-affirmation has beneficial effects (e.g., participants score higher on an integrity scale) even when it is created implicitly (i.e., outside of conscious awareness; Sherman, Cohen, Nelson, Nussbaum, Bunyan, & Garcia, 2009).

Both salvation and punishment for man lie in the fact that if he lives wrongly, he can befog himself so as not to see the misery of his position.

—Leo Tolstoy *(1828–1910)*

But can self-affirmation actually serve as a cognitive buffer, protecting a person from caving in to temptation and committing a cruel or immoral act? In an early experiment on cheating (Aronson & Mettee, 1968), university students were first given a personality test, and then given false feedback that was either positive (i.e., aimed at temporarily raising self-esteem) or negative (i.e., aimed at temporarily lowering self-esteem), or they received no information at all. Immediately afterward, they played a game of cards in which, to win a large pot, they could easily cheat without getting caught. The results were striking. Students in the high self-esteem condition were able to resist the temptation to cheat to a far greater extent than were the students in the other conditions. In short, a temporary boost in self-esteem served to inoculate these students against cheating, because the anticipation of doing something immoral was more dissonant than it would otherwise have been. Thus, when they were put in a tempting situation, they were able to say to themselves, "Terrific people like me don't cheat." And they didn't (see also Spencer, Josephs, & Steele, 1993; Steele, Spencer, & Lynch, 1993).

Recent studies conducted by University of British Columbia researchers point to another promising approach for avoiding the rationalization trap (Aquino, Reed, Thau, & Freeman, 2007). In this research, participants were primed with moral identity words (e.g., *caring*, *honest*, *helpful*) or in the control condition, with positive, but not moral, words (e.g., *happy*, *open-minded*). Participants also were asked to write stories about themselves by using these words. Later, they were exposed to pictures and newspaper articles about prisoner abuses in Abu Ghraib prison and at Guantanamo Bay. Those whose moral identity was made salient (that is, brought to the forefront of their minds) subsequently reported more negative emotions in response to these abuses than those in the control condition.

Thus, there is evidence that affirming people in some way (e.g., boosting their self-esteem) or reminding them of their morals may reverse the rationalization trap. We find these results encouraging.

Dissonance, Self-Affirmation, and Culture According to Heine and Lehman (1997a), the experience of dissonance may be unique to cultures in which the self is defined as independent. If, on the one hand, the focus in a culture is on the individual (as in North America), it becomes important for the individual to behave in ways that are consistent with his or her attitudes, because the person's behaviour is seen as diagnostic of what he or she is really like. On the other hand, if the self is defined in relation to others, as is the case in Asian cultures, behaviour is more likely to be tailored to the demands of the group. If an individual behaves in an attitude-inconsistent way, others are likely to invoke situational explanations. (You may recall from our discussion of the correspondence bias in Chapter 4 that people in Asian cultures do, in fact, make more situational attributions for others' behaviour than do those in Western cultures.) Based on this reasoning, Heine and Lehman hypothesized that people in Asian cultures should experience little dissonance when their attitudes and behaviours are inconsistent.

To test this idea, the researchers conducted a study in which students at the University of British Columbia and Japanese students visiting Vancouver signed up for a marketing research study. First, the researchers administered a bogus personality test. Then participants were asked to rate the desirability of 10 CDs. In the meantime, their personality tests supposedly had been scored. Some participants received positive personality feedback and others received negative feedback. (Participants in a control group did not receive any personality information.) Next, participants were given a choice between their fifth- and sixth-ranked CDs. After they made their selection, they were asked to again rate all 10 CDs.

Canadian participants in the control group showed classic dissonance reduction—they rated the chosen CD higher than they had previously and the rejected CD lower than they had previously. However, consistent with self-affirmation theory, those who received positive personality feedback did not engage in dissonance reduction. Because they had been reminded of what wonderful people they were, and they did not feel a need to reduce dissonance by changing their ratings of the CDs. Those who received negative feedback were especially likely to engage in dissonance reduction.

What about the Japanese participants? They did not show dissonance reduction in any of the conditions. Japanese students felt as badly as Canadian students did about the negative personality feedback and were more likely than the Canadian participants to believe that it was accurate. However, they did not reduce dissonance by changing their ratings of the CDs, even under these circumstances.

In an interesting twist, Hoshino-Browne and colleagues (2005) examined whether East Asians might experience dissonance when they have to make a decision that affects a member of their group. In this research, students at the University of Waterloo and at Kyoto University in Japan rated the 10 dishes they would prefer most at a new Chinese restaurant (the self condition) or rated the 10 dishes a close friend would prefer (the friend condition). Later, participants were shown coupons for the fifth- and sixth-ranked dishes and were told to select one. Those in the self condition were asked to once again rate their preferences for all of the dishes; those in the friend condition rated their friend's preferences. European-Canadian participants showed classic post-decision dissonance in the self condition—they now rated the dish for which they had chosen the coupon more positively and the "rejected" dish (i.e., the coupon for the dish they didn't select) more negatively than they had before. East Asian participants did not show this effect. However, in the friend condition, the results were opposite—here European-Canadians did not show evidence of dissonance reduction, but Asian participants did. In other words, European-Canadians tended to justify their decisions when they made choices for themselves, whereas East Asians tended to justify their decisions when they made choices for a close other (Hoshino-Browne, Zanna, Spencer, Zanna, Kitayama, & Lackenbauer, 2005).

In follow-up studies, the researchers examined the role of two different types of self-affirmation in reducing dissonance—either an independent self-affirmation (e.g., writing about a value that uniquely describes you) or an interdependent self-affirmation (writing about why a certain value is held by you and your family members). As you can probably guess, an independent self-affirmation diminished the need for dissonance reduction among European-Canadians; an interdependent self-affirmation diminished the need for dissonance reduction among East Asians. Interestingly, both kinds of self-affirmation were effective for bicultural participants (i.e., East Asians living in Canada who strongly identified with both cultures). Hoshino-Browne and colleagues (2005) conclude that for self-affirmation to protect people from engaging in dissonance reduction, it is important to affirm a culturally valued trait.

The Solar Temple Revisited

At the beginning of this chapter, we raised a vital question regarding the followers of Luc Jouret and Joseph Di Mambro of the Solar Temple. How could intelligent people allow themselves to be led into what, to the overwhelming majority of us, is obviously senseless and tragic behaviour—resulting in mass murder–suicides? Needless to say, the situation is a complex one; there were many factors operating, including the charismatic, persuasive power of each of these leaders, the existence of a great deal of social support for the views of the group from other members of the group, and the relative isolation of each group from dissenting views, producing a closed system—a little like living in a room full of mirrors.

In addition to these factors, we are convinced that the single most powerful force was the existence of a great deal of cognitive dissonance. You know from reading this chapter that when individuals make an important decision and invest heavily in that decision in terms of time, effort, sacrifice, and commitment, the result is a strong need to justify those actions and that investment. The more they sacrifice and the harder they work, the greater the need to convince themselves that their views are correct; indeed, they may even begin to feel sorry for those who do not share their beliefs. The members of the Solar Temple cult sacrificed a great deal for their beliefs; they abandoned their friends and families, relinquished their money and possessions, and if they were female, subjected themselves to sexual exploitation. All of these sacrifices served to increase their commitment to the cult. Those of us who have studied the theory of cognitive dissonance were not surprised to learn that intelligent, respected, professional people could be persuaded that through death by fire, they could escape the imminent apocalypse on Earth and be reborn on the star Sirius. To begin to question these beliefs would have produced too much dissonance to bear. Although tragic and bizarre, the death voyages of the Solar Temple members are not unfathomable. They are simply an extreme manifestation of a process—cognitive dissonance—that we have seen in operation over and over again.

HOW WOULD YOU USE THIS?

You have a friend who drives after drinking. You keep telling him that this activity is dangerous. He says he can handle it. How could you get him to change his behaviour?

Hint: Think about the research on getting students to practise safe sex (use condoms); think about the "hypocrisy induction."

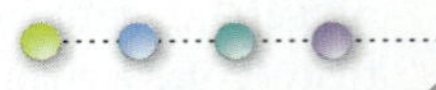

Summary

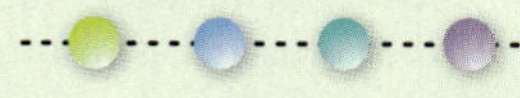

The Nature and Origin of Attitudes An attitude is a person's enduring evaluation of people, objects, and ideas.

- **Where Do Attitudes Come From?** Affectively based attitudes stem more from people's emotions and values. Cognitively based attitudes stem more from people's beliefs about the properties of the attitude object. Behaviourally based attitudes are formed according to people's actions toward the attitude object.
- **Explicit Versus Implicit Attitudes** Once an attitude develops, it can exist at two levels. Explicit attitudes are those we consciously endorse and can easily report. Implicit attitudes are involuntary, uncontrollable, and at times unconscious.

When Attitudes Predict Behaviour Under what conditions will people's attitudes dictate how they actually behave?

- **The Theory of Planned Behaviour** According to the theory of planned behaviour, the best predictors of people's behaviours are their intentions to perform the behaviour. Intentions, in turn, are a function of people's attitude toward the specific act in question, subjective norms (people's beliefs about how others view the behaviour in question), and how much people believe they can control the behaviour.
- **The Theory of Planned Behaviour: Implications for Safer Sex** The theory of planned behaviour is useful in understanding why people frequently express positive attitudes toward using condoms but often fail to use them. People are unlikely to use condoms if (1) they believe that their peers are not using condoms or that their partner would disapprove (*subjective norms*); (2) they find it embarrassing to buy condoms or bring up the topic with their partner (*perceived behavioural control*); and (3) if their intentions to use condoms are undermined (e.g., by excessive alcohol consumption).

Attitude Change Social psychologists have examined several ways in which people's attitudes can be changed. Attitudes often change in response to social influence.

- **Persuasive Communications and Attitude Change** Attitudes can change in response to a persuasive communication. According to the Yale Attitude Change Approach, the effectiveness of a persuasive communication depends on aspects of the communicator, or source of the message; aspects of the message itself (e.g., its content); and aspects of the audience. The heuristic-systematic model of persuasion and the elaboration likelihood model specify when people are persuaded more by the strength of the arguments in the communication and when they are persuaded more by surface characteristics. When people have both the motivation and ability to pay attention to a message, they take the central route to persuasion, in which they pay close attention to the strength of the arguments. When they have low motivation or ability, they take the peripheral route to persuasion, in which they are swayed by surface characteristics, such as the attractiveness of the speaker.
- **Fear and Attitude Change** Fear-arousing communications can cause lasting attitude change if a moderate amount of fear is aroused and people believe they will be reassured by the content of the message.
- **Advertising and Attitude Change** The many advertisements that we are bombarded with in the course of a day are intended to change our attitudes. Social psychologists have conducted research to evaluate which advertising techniques are most effective. Appeals to emotion work best if the attitude is based on affect; appeals to utilitarian features (pluses and minuses of the product) work best if the attitude is based on cognition. There is no evidence that subliminal messages in advertisements have any influence on people's behaviour. Subliminal influences have been found, however, under controlled laboratory conditions.

Resisting Persuasive Messages Researchers have studied a number of ways that people can avoid being influenced by persuasive messages.

- **Attitude Inoculation** One way is to expose people to small doses of arguments against their position, which makes it easier for them to defend themselves against a persuasive message they hear later.
- **Being Alert to Product Placement** Increasingly, advertisers are paying to have their products shown prominently in television shows and movies. Forewarning people about attempts to change their attitudes, such as product placement, makes them less susceptible to attitude change.

Changing Our Attitudes because of Our Behaviour: The Theory of Cognitive Dissonance According to cognitive dissonance theory, people experience discomfort (dissonance) when they behave in ways that are inconsistent with their attitudes or when they hold two conflicting attitudes. To reduce the dissonance, people either (1) change their behaviour to bring it in line with their cognitions about themselves, (2) justify their behaviour by changing one of their cognitions, or (3) attempt to justify their behaviour by inventing new cognitions.

- **Decisions, Decisions, Decisions** Decisions arouse dissonance because they require choosing one thing and not the other. The thought that we may have made the wrong choice causes discomfort. After the choice is final, the mind diminishes the discomfort through solidifying the case for the item chosen.
- **Dissonance, the Brain, and Evolution** Recent research shows that dissonance and dissonance reduction are reflected in the way that the brain processes information. The fact that monkeys show dissonance reduction suggests that it may have survival value.

- **The Justification of Effort** People tend to increase their liking for something they have worked hard to attain, even if the thing they attained is not something they would otherwise like. This explains, for example, the intense loyalty the initiated feel for a team or a group after undergoing hazing.
- **The Psychology of Insufficient Justification** When people express an opinion counter to their attitudes (counter-attitudinal advocacy) for low external justification (e.g., a small reward), they find an internal justification for their behaviour, coming to believe what they said. In other words, they change their attitudes so that they are in line with their behaviour. The internal process of self-justification has a much more powerful effect on an individual's long-term values and behaviours than a situation in which the external justifications are evident. If people avoid doing something desirable for insufficient punishment, they will come to believe that the activity wasn't that desirable after all. Thus, mild punishment is more effective at getting people to refrain from negative behaviours than severe punishment.
- **The Aftermath of Bad Deeds** If we do harm to another, to reduce the threat to our self-image that could come from doing a bad deed, we tend to justify the bad deed by derogating the victim. That is, we come to believe that the victim deserved the harm or, in more extreme cases, that he or she is less than human. Reducing dissonance in this way can result in a rationalization trap, whereby we set the stage for increasing acts of stupidity or immorality.
- **Avoiding the Rationalization Trap** According to self-affirmation theory, we can avoid the rationalization trap by reminding ourselves of our competencies in other areas. It is also useful to remind ourselves that we are good and decent people.
- In Western, individualistic cultures, people experience dissonance when they make decisions for themselves; in Eastern, collectivist cultures, people experience dissonance when they make decisions for close others. Independent self-affirmations reduce dissonance in individualistic cultures; interdependent self-affirmations reduce dissonance in collectivist cultures.

7 Conformity

Influencing Others

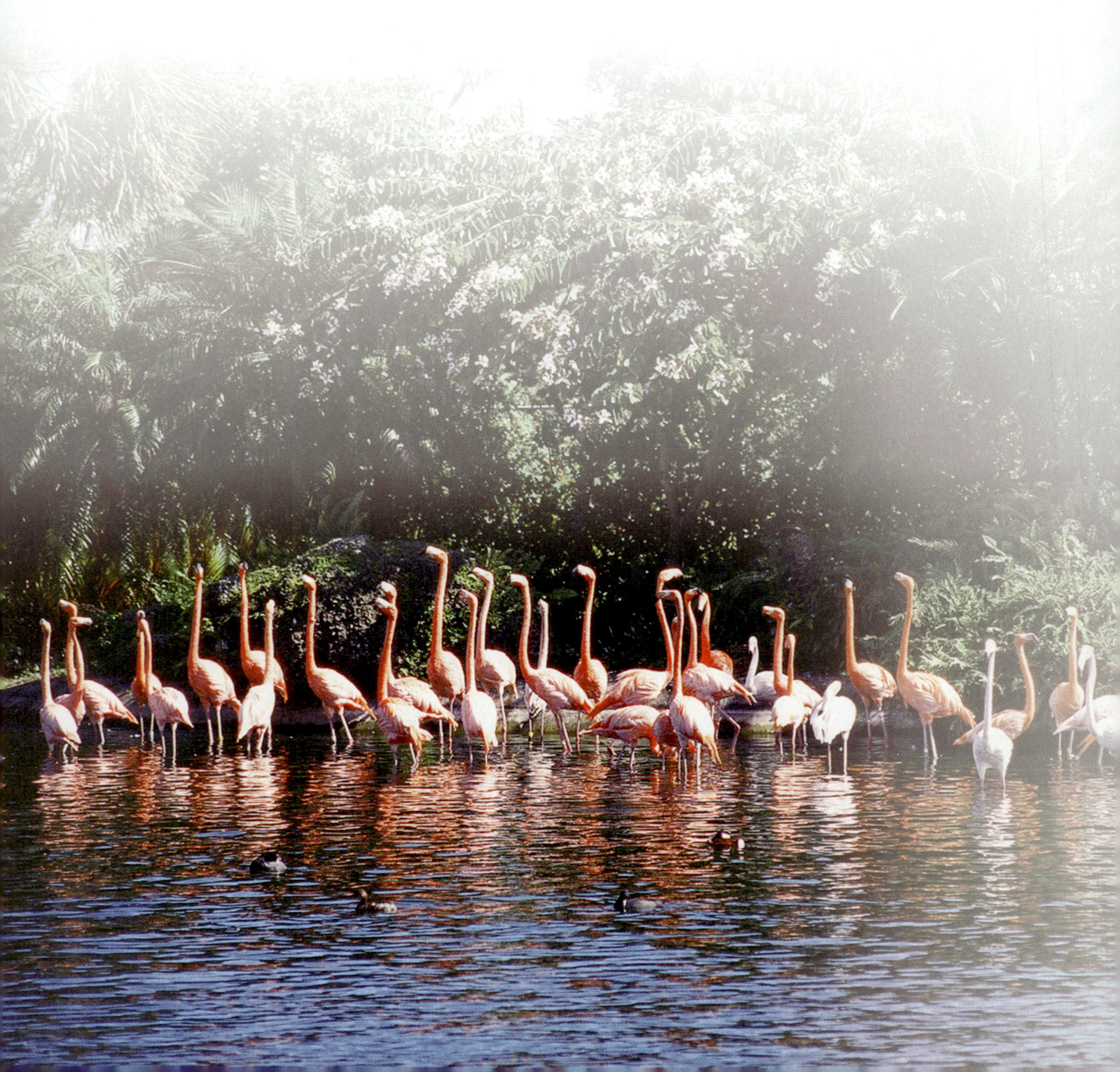

THE JUDGMENT BROUGHT DOWN BY MR. JUSTICE MACAULAY on May 10, 1999, begins with the statement "Reena Virk died on November 14, 1997, after a vicious beating" (*R.* v. *Warren Paul Glowatski*, 1999). The transcript of the trial documents the events that led to the tragic death of this 14-year-old girl. During an exchange with Reena Virk, a student at her school extinguished a lit cigarette on her forehead. Other friends of this student joined in and began beating Virk. One girl testified that she grabbed a lighter and tried to set Virk's hair on fire; others began punching and kicking Virk in the head and face. According to the pathologist's report, Virk's head injuries alone were severe enough to be life-threatening. She also suffered massive internal injuries. The pathologist considered the force of these injuries to be comparable with crush injuries that would result from being run over by a car. The unconscious Virk was dragged by Kelly Ellard and Warren Glowatski to the Gorge waterway not far from downtown Victoria, where she was drowned. Apparently, Ellard smoked a cigarette as she stood with one foot on Virk's head, holding it under water.

Glowatski and eventually Ellard were charged with second-degree murder. Six other girls involved in the beating were given sentences ranging from a 60-day conditional sentence to one year in jail. Glowatski appealed his conviction, but it was upheld by the appeal court. He served time in prison and was granted parole in 2010. Ellard was tried three times; her third trial resulted in a second-degree murder conviction in April 2005. She appealed. The appeal court overturned her conviction in September 2008, and ordered a fourth trial. The Crown appealed to the Supreme Court of Canada. In June 2009, the Supreme Court of Canada upheld the 2005 second-degree murder conviction. "Kelly Ellard goes to prison. Finally." is how one writer summed up this 10-year legal battle (www2.macleans.ca/2009/06/12/kelly-ellard-goes-to-prison-finally/).

Canadians were horrified by Reena Virk's brutal death. How could ordinary high school students in Victoria, British Columbia, engage in such savage acts against a defenceless 14 year old? Why did some students participate in the beatings rather than attempt to stop this tragedy? Sadly, as we shall see, the need to conform to a group probably played a role in Virk's murder.

Facebook has added a new dimension to such tragedies. In February 2011, a 14-year-old boy attending Shaftesbury High School in Winnipeg was bullied in

OUTLINE

Reena Virk, a B.C. teenager, was savagely beaten by her schoolmates, and then drowned by two other teenagers. She died on November 14, 1997.

ways that bore an eerie resemblance to the Reena Virk case. The boy was attacked by a 14-year-old girl, who taunted him, slammed him into the side of a car, and kicked him. As many as 40 students watched the assault. Rather than intervening, they joined in, taunting, cheering, and throwing cigarette butts at the boy. One of the students videotaped the attack, and the recording was posted on Facebook. Although the attack wasn't fatal, mental health professionals commented on the emotional damage caused by having the attack distributed on the Internet and explained that it would be retraumatizing for the boy each time he saw it or knew that others were watching it. Needless to say, watching the video was a traumatic experience for the boy's family as well. His mother commented, "In the 11th or 12th centuries, you would be crucified and the crowd would throw vegetables. Now in the 21st century you have 40-plus people throw cigarettes—and they look so happy. It just shocks me." She went on to say, "At that moment, watching the video, I died a bit and my heart broke. I don't know where the pieces are" (Rollason, 2011).

Under what conditions and for what reasons are we likely to fall under the influence of others? That is the key question to be addressed in this chapter.

Conformity: When and Why

Connect to MyPsychLab
To access the Critical Thinking question on the holocaust, go to MyPsychLab

Conformity
A change in behaviour as a result of the real or imagined influence of other people

Think for a moment about the word **conformity**, which we can define as a change in behaviour as a result of the real or imagined influence of other people (Kiesler & Kiesler, 1969). Although we will be focusing on human conformity in this chapter, we note that research suggests that that the pressure to conform may be shared with other species. Researchers at McMaster University recently demonstrated that rats will conform to the behaviour of other rats—even when it could be costly to do so. For example, rats who were given toxic food that made them sick later avoided that food; however, if they were exposed to other rats eating it, they ate it, too (Galef & Whiskin, 2008). The researchers concluded that the tendency to conform to the behaviour of others is so powerful that it can override behaviours that promote survival, such as avoiding poisonous food.

Do as most do, and [people] will speak well of thee.

—Thomas Fuller (1608–1661)

It were not best that we should all think alike; it is difference of opinion that makes horse races.

—Mark Twain (1835–1910)

Turning to human conformity, which of the two quotations on this page do you find more appealing? Which one best describes your immediate reaction to the word *conformity*?

We wouldn't be surprised if you preferred the Mark Twain quotation. North American culture stresses the importance of not conforming (Hofstede, 1986; Markus, Kitayama, & Heiman, 1996). This is part of being in an individualistic culture—one that emphasizes being independent, thinking for yourself, and standing up for yourself. We want to be perceived as people who make up our own minds—not as spineless, weak conformists; not as puppets, but players (Cialdini, 2005; Hornsey & Jetten, 2005; Pronin, Berger, & Molouki, 2007). As a result, we maintain the belief that our behaviour is not influenced by others, even when reality suggests otherwise. This phenomenon was illustrated in a program of research by Jacquie Vorauer and Dale Miller (1997). They asked students at the University of Manitoba to rate how satisfied they felt with their intellectual abilities. Before making their ratings, they were allowed to see the same ratings supposedly given by another student. Were participants influenced by the other student's responses? Yes, they were. Specifically, if the other student provided a positive self-assessment, participants also evaluated themselves positively—more so than if the other student had provided a negative self-assessment. Most importantly, participants were not aware that they had been influenced by the other student's responses. The bottom line is that we probably conform a lot more than we realize (or want to admit).

Indeed, people do conform—sometimes in extreme and surprising ways, as suggested by the deaths of 74 Solar Temple cult members (discussed in Chapter 6). But you might argue that is an unusual case—surely most people do not conform to this extent. We might convince ourselves that the followers of Luc Jouret and Joseph Di Mambro were disturbed people who were somehow predisposed to do what charismatic leaders told them to do. There is, however, another more chilling possibility. Maybe most of us would have acted the same way, had we been exposed to the same long-standing conformity pressures. Perhaps almost anyone would have conformed had he or she been put in these same extreme situations. If this statement is true, we should be able to find other situations in which people, put under strong social pressures, conform to surprising degrees. Unfortunately, we do not have to look very far to find such instances.

Watch on **mypsychlab**
Infomercial Example: Robert Cialdini

We opened this chapter with the deeply disturbing story of Reena Virk, who died at the hands of a group of high school students. Once one of the students began attacking Virk, others did, too. In Chapter 6, we described the chilling story of Shidane Arone, who was tortured to death by Canadian peacekeepers in Somalia. In that situation as well, one soldier began beating the boy and others joined in. And, of course, the Holocaust in World War II provides countless horrific examples of conformity at its worst.

The examples we have seen so far are all cases of conformity with bad consequences: Human beings lost their lives as a result of people going along with others. However, conformity is not simply "good" or "bad" in and of itself. Rather than labelling conformity as "good" or "bad," the social psychologist is interested in *why* people conform. Knowing why and when people are influenced by others will help us understand whether a given act of conformity in their own life is wise or foolish. To return to the example of the Solar Temple cult, some members probably conformed because they did not know what to do in a confusing or unusual situation; the behaviour of the people around them served as a cue about how to respond, and so they decided to act in a similar manner. Other people probably conformed because they did not wish to be ridiculed or punished for being different from everybody else; they chose to act the way the group expected them to, so they wouldn't be rejected or disapproved of by group members. Let's see how each of these reasons for conforming operates.

Informational Social Influence: The Need to Know What's "Right"

Watch on **mypsychlab**
Social Influence: Robert Cialdini

One of the important things we get from interacting with other people is information. There are many situations in which we don't know what to do, or even know what is happening. Unfortunately, life, unlike our clothing, does not come with labels attached, telling us what is going on and how we should respond. Instead, the social world is frequently ambiguous and ill-defined. For example, how should you address your psychology professor—as Dr. Berman, Professor Berman, Ms. Berman, or Patricia? How should you vote on a proposal to increase your tuition to expand student services? Is the scream you just heard coming from a person joking with friends or from the victim of a mugging?

In these and many other everyday situations, we feel uncertain about what to think or how to act. We simply don't know enough to make a good or accurate choice. Fortunately, we have a powerful and useful source of knowledge available to us—the behaviour of other people. Asking others what they think or watching what they do helps us reach a definition of the situation (Kelley, 1955; Thomas, 1928). When we subsequently act like everyone else, we are conforming—but not because we are weak, spineless individuals with no self-reliance. Instead, the influence of other people leads us to conform because we see them as a source of information to guide our behaviour.

This is called **informational social influence** (Cialdini, 1993, 2000; Cialdini & Goldstein, 2004; Deutsch & Gerard, 1955).

Informational Social Influence
Conforming because we believe that others' interpretation of an ambiguous situation is more correct than ours and will help us choose an appropriate course of action

As an illustration of how other people can be a source of information, imagine you are a participant in a classic experiment by Muzafer Sherif (1936). In the first phase of the study, you are seated alone in a dark room and asked to focus your attention on a dot of light 5 metres away. The experimenter asks you to estimate in centimetres how far the light moves. You stare earnestly at the light and, yes, it moves a little. You say, "About 5 centimetres," though it is not easy to tell exactly. The light disappears and then comes back; you are asked to judge again. The light seems to move a little more, and you say, "10 centimetres." After several of these trials, the light seems to move about the same amount each time—about 5 to 10 centimetres. Now, the interesting thing about this task is that the light was not actually moving at all. It looked as if it was moving because of a visual illusion called the *autokinetic effect*. If you stare at a bright light in a uniformly dark environment (e.g., a star on a dark night), the light will appear to waver. This occurs because you have no stable reference point to anchor the position of the light. The distance that the light appears to move varies from person to person but becomes consistent for each person over time. In Sherif's (1936) experiment, the participants all arrived at their own, stable estimates during the first phase of the study, but these estimates differed from person to person. Some people thought the light was moving only 2.5 centimetres or so, whereas others thought it was moving as much as 25 centimetres.

> *'It's always best on these occasions to do what the mob do.' 'But suppose there are two mobs?' suggested Mr. Snodgrass. 'Shout with the largest,' replied Mr. Pickwick.*
>
> —Charles Dickens, *The Pickwick Papers*, 1836–1837

Sherif chose to use the autokinetic effect because he wanted a situation that would be ambiguous—where the correct definition of the situation would be unclear to his participants. In the second phase of the experiment, a few days later, the participants were paired with two other people, each of whom had had the same prior experience alone with the light. Now the situation became a truly social one, as all three made their judgments out loud. Remember, the autokinetic effect is experienced differently by different people; some see a lot of movement, some do not see much at all. After hearing their partners give judgments that were different from their own, what did people do? Over the course of several trials, people reached a common estimate, and each member of the group conformed to that estimate. These results indicate that people were using one another as a source of information, coming to believe that the group estimate was the correct one (see Figure 7.1).

Private Acceptance
Conforming to other people's behaviour out of a genuine belief that what they are doing or saying is right

An important feature of informational social influence is that it can lead to **private acceptance**, whereby people conform to the behaviour of others because they genuinely believe that these other people are correct. It might seem equally plausible that people publicly conformed to the group but privately maintained the belief that the light was moving only a small amount. For example, maybe someone privately believed that the light was moving 25 centimetres but announced that it had moved

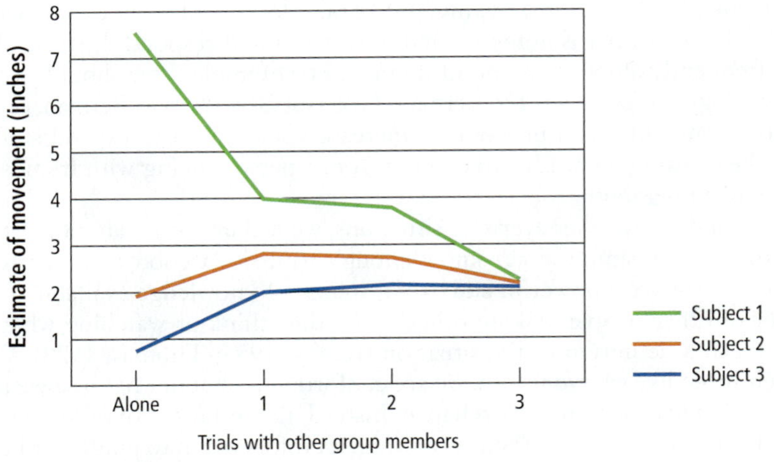

FIGURE 7.1

One group's judgments in Sherif's (1936) autokinetic studies.

People estimated how far a point of light appeared to move in a dark room. When they saw the light by themselves, their estimates varied widely. When they were brought together in groups and heard other people announce their estimates, they conformed to the group's estimate of how much the light moved.

(Adapted from Sherif, 1936)

7.5 centimetres (the group estimate) to avoid looking silly or foolish. This would be a case of **public compliance**, whereby a person conforms publicly without necessarily believing in what the group is saying or doing. Sherif casts doubt on this interpretation, however, by asking people to judge the lights once more by themselves, after participating in groups. Even though they no longer had to worry about looking silly in front of other participants, they continued to give the answer the group had given earlier. These results suggest that people were relying on one another to define reality and came to privately accept the group estimate.

Public Compliance

Conforming to other people's behaviour publicly, without necessarily believing in what they are doing or saying

In everyday life, of course, we are rarely asked to judge how much a stationary light is moving. However, there are many common situations in which we rely on other people to help us define what is going on. Think about the first time you were at the symphony or at a jazz concert. You knew that you would applaud at some time—but exactly when? After a solo? Only at the end of a piece? What about standing ovations, or shouting for an encore? No doubt, you looked to others in the audience to help you learn the appropriate way of showing approval in each setting. Later research has shown that information conformity does, indeed, occur in real-life situations (Baron, Vandello, & Brunsman, 1996; Levine, Higgins, & Choi, 2000). It has also revealed another variable that affects informational social influence: how important it is to the individual to be accurate at the task. It may surprise you to learn that when participants are convinced that the task is important, they are *more* likely to conform to the group than participants who are led to believe the task is unimportant. In other words, when we are facing an important decision, we are even more likely to rely on other people for information and guidance. In short, informational social influence is pervasive in our day-to-day lives.

When People Conform to Informational Social Influence

What kinds of situations are most likely to produce conformity because of informational social influence? We will discuss three: ambiguous situations, crises, and situations in which an expert is present.

When the Situation Is Ambiguous You may have had the experience of hearing a fire alarm in a building. What did you do? If you are like most people, you turned to the people around you to see if the situation was an emergency. If, on the one hand, other people seemed unconcerned and weren't making moves to leave the building, you probably decided that there wasn't a need to evacuate. On the other hand, if other people started rushing toward the emergency exit doors, your behaviour would probably be quite different. When you are unsure of the correct response, the appropriate behaviour, or the right idea, you will be most open to influence from others. Research shows that the more uncertain you are, the more you will rely on others (Baron, Vandello, & Brunsman, 1996; Tesser, Campbell, & Mickler, 1983; Walther, Bless, Strack, Rackstraw, Wagner, & Werth, 2002).

When Shidane Arone entered the compound of the Canadian peacekeepers in Somalia, the soldiers experienced considerable ambiguity about how to handle such a situation. One of the commanding officers had given an order that the soldiers should "abuse" intruders. During the court martial, the defence argued that the officer's instruction was that physical force could be used to capture intruders and that the term *abuse* did not imply that torture was acceptable. Regardless of what was intended, it seems that soldiers did not have a clear sense of what should be done if they caught someone entering their compound. More generally, reports of investigations of these events suggest that the peacekeepers had not been well prepared for their mission. As we discuss later, investigations into the abuses of Iraqi prisoners at the hands of American soldiers similarly revealed that the soldiers were not given clear instructions on what should be done with detainees. In such situations, when ambiguity abounds, people are especially likely to be influenced by the actions of those around them. Tragically, as the Shidane Arone case illustrates, such actions can result in the loss of lives.

Connect to MyPsychLab
Emotions can influence behaviour, especially in a crisis situation. To take a survey on how you deal with your emotions, go to MyPsychLab

When the Situation Is a Crisis When the situation is a crisis, we usually do not have time to stop and think about exactly which course of action we should take. We need to act and act now. If we feel scared and panicky, and are uncertain what to do, it is only natural for us to see how other people are responding—and to do likewise. Unfortunately, the people we imitate may also feel scared and panicky, and not behave rationally.

Consider what happened on Halloween night in 1938. Orson Welles, the gifted actor and future film director, and the Mercury Theatre broadcast a radio play based loosely on H. G. Wells' 1898 science-fiction fantasy *The War of the Worlds*. Remember that this was the era before television; radio was a source of entertainment, with music, comedy, and drama programs, and the only source for fast-breaking news. That night, Welles and his fellow actors put on a radio drama of a cataclysm—the invasion of Earth by hostile Martians—that was so realistic and effective that at least 1 million listeners in the United States became frightened, and several thousand were panic-stricken (Cantril, 1940). The result was a **contagion**—the rapid transmission of emotions or behaviour through a crowd, in this case, the listening audience. Why were so many Americans convinced that what they had heard was a real news report of an invasion by aliens? One reason is that the play parodied existing radio news shows very well, and many listeners missed the beginning of the broadcast, when it was clearly labelled as a play, because they had been listening to the nation's number-one-rated show, *Charlie McCarthy*, on another station. Another culprit, however, was informational social influence. Many people were listening with friends and family, and naturally turned to one another out of uncertainty to see whether they should believe what they had heard. Seeing looks of concern and worry on their loved ones' faces added to the panic people were beginning to feel. "We all kissed one another and felt we would all die," reported one listener (Cantril, 1940).

Contagion
The rapid transmission of emotions or behaviour through a crowd

Closer to home, Luc Jouret, a leader of the Solar Temple cult, apparently was convinced that the world was coming to an end and managed to persuade his followers that this was true (see Chapter 6). Needless to say, this constituted a crisis for those who accepted this belief, and they turned to him for guidance. Sadly, they believed him when he said that death by fire was the correct course of action so they could be reborn on the star Sirius. Such instances of mind control, or brainwashing, can actually qualify as extreme cases of informational social influence. When people believe that they are in a crisis situation, they are more likely to succumb to these forms of influence.

When Other People Are Experts Typically, the more expertise or knowledge a person has, the more valuable he or she will be as a guide in an ambiguous or crisis situation (Allison, 1992; Bickman, 1974; Cialdini & Trost, 1998). For example, a passenger who sees smoke coming out of an airplane engine will probably look around for the flight attendants to check their reaction; they have more expertise than the vacationer in the next seat. However, experts are not always reliable sources of information. Imagine the fear felt by the young man who was listening to Welles' broadcast of *The War of the Worlds* and called his local police department for an explanation—only to discover that the police also thought the events described on the radio were actually happening.

The *New York Times* headlined the 1938 *War of the Worlds* incident. Partly because of informational social influence, many listeners believed that the fictional radio broadcast by Orson Welles and the Mercury Theatre players about an invasion by Martians was true.

The role of experts in exerting informational social influence was examined by Serge Guimond (1999) in a study of students in a military college who were training to become Canadian Armed Forces officers. He found that students in the social sciences became more liberal in their views over their three years in college (e.g., became less willing to blame the victims of poverty and unemployment), whereas engineering students became more conservative. Guimond concluded that the students' attitudes had changed as a result of informational social influence—in this case, the information they learned from their professors in these courses.

When Informational Conformity Backfires

The War of the Worlds incident reminds us that using other people as a source of information can be dangerous. If other people are misinformed, we will adopt their mistakes and misinterpretations. Depending on others to help us reach a definition of the situation can sometimes lead to an inaccurate definition indeed. An example of extreme and misdirected informational social influence is **mass psychogenic illness** (Bartholomew & Wessely, 2002; Colligan, Pennebaker, & Murphy, 1982), the occurrence of similar physical symptoms in a group of people for which there is no known physical or medical cause.

Mass Psychogenic Illness

The occurrence of similar physical symptoms in a group of people for which there is no known physical or medical cause

Consider, for example, the "toxic bus" case. On May 25, 2004, as a man disembarked from a Vancouver bus, he made a comment to the driver to the effect that the driver was about to have a bad day. Shortly afterward, the driver began to feel nauseated and started vomiting. He checked if any of the other passengers were feeling ill. A passenger seated behind him reported having a headache and thought that there was a suspicious smell on the bus. Fearing that there had been a chemical attack, the driver placed a distress call. Other passengers began to feel sick, as did several of the paramedics who were called to the scene. Six passengers and three paramedics were taken to a Vancouver hospital. Some of them were vomiting. Others complained of a burning sensation in their eyes. Nineteen people, including the driver, passengers, emergency personnel, and journalists were quarantined. Vancouver Police began to search for the man who had made the mysterious comment. In early June of that year, Vancouver's chief medical health officer announced that the medical symptoms experienced by those involved were not consistent with chemical poisoning. Moreover, tests of the bus had not revealed the presence of toxic chemicals. He concluded that the symptoms were a case of mass psychogenic illness. The allegation that the medical symptoms were brought on by anxiety over a possible chemical attack outraged the paramedics who had become ill. The Vancouver Police took their side, stating that "you're talking about two very senior ambulance attendants and they're not going to have psychosomatic symptoms" (Crawford, 2004; "Chemical Probably Cause of Bus Mystery," as cited in Bartholomew & Wessely, 2007). The police arranged for additional experts to test the bus. These tests revealed the presence of methyl chloride. However, this did little to clarify matters. Given that methyl chloride is common in the environment, there was controversy over whether the levels found were sufficient to cause poisoning. Moreover, other "nontoxic" buses were not tested, so there was no way of knowing whether the toxic bus had higher levels of methyl chloride than other buses. Psychiatrists from Australia and Britain analyzed the "toxic bus" case and concluded that the medical symptoms experienced were, in fact, attributable to mass psychogenic illness (Bartholomew & Wessely, 2007). According to these psychiatrists, in the post-9/11 world, people's fears of terrorist attacks—including the use of chemical or biological attacks—are heightened. They explained the symptoms experienced by those involved in the toxic bus incident as an anxiety reaction. Needless to say, this interpretation was vehemently rejected by the ambulance attendants who became ill (Bartholomew & Wessely, 2007). The controversy has inspired a play, "The Toxic Bus Incident," that opened in Halifax, in April 2009. It would appear that the toxic bus case is a modern-day example of informational conformity gone awry.

Ninety-nine percent of the people in the world are fools, and the rest of us are in great danger of contagion.

—Thornton Wilder, *The Matchmaker*, 1938

What is particularly interesting about modern cases of mass psychogenic illness (as well as other peculiar forms of informational conformity) is the powerful role that mass media play in their dissemination. Through television, radio, newspapers, magazines, the Internet, and email, information is spread quickly and efficiently to all segments of the population. Whereas in the Middle Ages it took 200 years for the "dancing manias" (a kind of psychogenic illness) to criss-cross Europe (Sirois, 1982), it takes only minutes for most of the inhabitants of the planet to learn about an unusual event today. Luckily, the mass media also have the power to quickly squelch these uprisings of contagion by introducing more logical explanations for ambiguous events.

Resisting Informational Social Influence

Relying on others to help us define what is happening can be an excellent idea—or it can be a tragedy in the making. How can we tell when other people are a good source of information and when we should resist other people's definition of a situation? First, it is important to remember that it is possible to resist illegitimate or inaccurate informational social influence. Some Solar Temple cult members refused to take their own lives. Not every student on the scene participated in the fatal attack on Reena Virk. And not every soldier in the Canadian Airborne Regiment participated in the beating death of Shidane Arone. Similarly, during *The War of the Worlds* broadcast, not all listeners panicked (Cantril, 1940). Some engaged in rational problem solving: They checked other stations on the radio dial and discovered that no other station was broadcasting the same news. Instead of relying on others and being caught up in the contagion and mass panic, they searched for and found information on their own.

Yes, we must, indeed, all hang together or, most assuredly, we shall all hang separately.

—Benjamin Franklin, *at the signing of the Declaration of Independence, 1776*

One reason that the decision about whether to conform is so important is that it influences how people define reality. If you decide to accept other people's definition of a situation, you will come to see the world as they do. If you decide to reject other people's definition of a situation, you will come to see the world differently from the way they do. This basic fact about how we define reality has been demonstrated in an interesting program of research conducted at the University of Waterloo (Buehler & Griffin, 1994; Griffin & Buehler, 1993).

In one study, Roger Buehler and Dale Griffin (1994) asked students to read newspaper reports of a real, highly controversial incident in which an African-Canadian teenager driving a stolen car was shot and killed by white police officers. Many of the details of the situation were ambiguous, such as how much the youth had threatened the officers and how much the officers had feared for their lives. Buehler and Griffin first asked participants how they interpreted the situation. How fast was the victim's car going? Was the victim trying to ram the police car? Did he realize that his pursuers were the police? What were the police officers thinking and feeling? Each participant was then told that other participants believed that the police were 75 percent responsible and the victim was 25 percent responsible. After indicating whether they agreed with this assessment, the participants were told that their original responses had supposedly been lost in a computer crash and were again asked how they interpreted the situation. Here's the critical question: Did participants now interpret the situation differently, depending on whether they agreed with other people's assessments?

The answer is yes. As shown in Figure 7.2, people who agreed with the group that the police were mainly responsible changed their interpretations to be consistent with

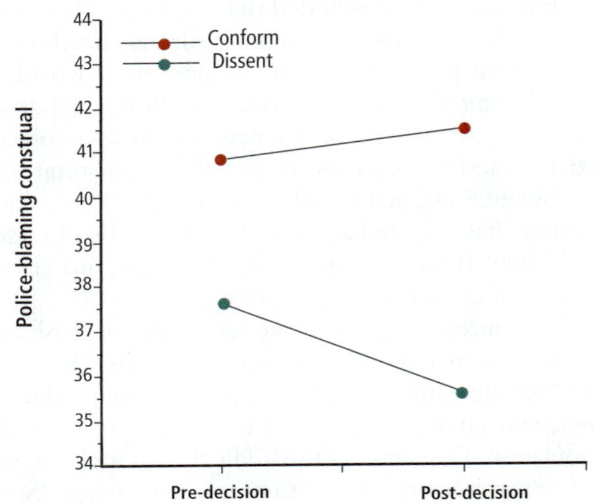

FIGURE 7.2

Pre-decision and post-decision construals by conformity decision.

People who conformed to the group's opinion that the police were to blame for the death of an African-Canadian teenager subsequently formed a more police-blaming interpretation of the event. Those who decided not to conform to the group (i.e., the dissenters) later reinterpreted the situation such that the police were seen as less blameworthy.

Source: Bueler, R. & Griffin, D. (1994). Change-of-meaning effects in conformity and dissent: Observing construal processes over time. *Journal of Personality and Social Psychology, 67*, 989. Copyright © 1994 by the American Psychological Association. Reprinted with permission.

the group opinion—they now believed that the victim had not threatened the police and that police had not feared for their lives. What about the people who did not conform? Interestingly, they also changed their interpretations, but in the opposite direction—they now believed that the victim's car was about to ram the police and that the police were in fear for their lives. It is remarkable that once we have formed an opinion of a situation, we may interpret that same situation quite differently a mere 10 minutes later to bolster our decision to go along with, or deviate from, the majority opinion.

Decisions about whether to conform to informational influence, then, will affect not only people's behaviour, but also their interpretation of reality (Bless, Strack, & Walther, 2001; Hoffman, Granhag, See, & Loftus, 2001). Thus, it is important to consider carefully whether other people's reactions to a situation are any more legitimate than your own. Ask yourself these questions:

- Do other people know more about what is going on than I do? Is there an expert handy, someone who should know more?
- Do the actions of other people or experts seem sensible? If I behave the way they do, will it go against my common sense, or against my internal moral compass—my sense of right and wrong?

By knowing how informational social influence works in daily life, you are in a better position to know when it is useful and when it is not.

Normative Social Influence: The Need to Be Accepted

Watch on **mypsychlab**
Peer Pressure part 1: Tim, 18 Years Old

In the 1990s, in Rio de Janeiro, Brazil, teenage boys and girls engaged in a reckless game: They "surfed" on the tops of trains, standing with arms outstretched as the trains sped along. An average of 150 teenagers died each year from this activity, and 400 more were injured by falling off the trains or hitting the 3000-volt electric cable; despite these facts, the surfing continued (Arnett, 1995). More recently, in the United States and Australia, teenagers surfing speeding cars has become a growing problem, resulting in severe injuries and deaths (Daniel & Nelson, 2004). In Canada, every year, drugs such as ecstasy claim the lives of young people. A Toronto Public Health report (2000) documented that in the previous two years there were 13 ecstasy-related deaths in Ontario alone. A nationwide survey published in 2005 found that 2.5 percent of university students had used ecstasy during the past year. That number doubled (5.4 percent) when non-university students of the same age were surveyed (Adlaf, Demers, & Gliksman, 2005). More recent statistics show that the use of ecstasy and other drugs has declined from 2004 to 2009 (CAMH, 2004; CADMUS, 2009). However, a brief look at the news media makes it clear that there are still far too many tragedies. For example, on March 25, 2009, police were called to a wedding celebration at the Paul First Nation, west of Edmonton. Four teenage girls had become seriously ill after taking ecstasy. The girls were rushed to the hospital; 14-year-old Leah Dominique House and 15-year-old Trinity Dawn Bird died shortly thereafter. To give another example, at the time of writing, a 17-year-old boy from Strathmore, Alberta, faces trafficking charges after a 19-year-old and a 15-year-old male were found in a skateboard park in a state of medical distress after taking ecstasy obtained from him. The two teenagers were taken to the local hospital, where the 15-year-old boy died. The 19-year-old was flown to Calgary for more intensive treatment.

Why do these young people engage in such risky behaviour? Why does anyone follow the group's lead when the resulting behaviour is less than sensible and may even be dangerous? We doubt that these young people risk their lives as a result of informational conformity—it is difficult to argue that a participant at a rave would say, "Gee, I don't know what to do. A stranger wants to sell me drugs that might kill me. I guess it must be a good idea; I see other people doing it."

The desire to be accepted and liked by others can lead to highly dangerous behaviour. Here, Brazilian teenagers "surf" on top of trains because it has become the popular thing to do in their peer group.

These examples tell us that there is another reason why we conform, aside from the need for information. We also conform so we will be liked and accepted by other people. This is known as **normative social influence.** This type of conformity results in public compliance with the group's beliefs and behaviours but not necessarily in private acceptance (Cialdini, Kallgren, & Reno, 1991; Deutsch & Gerrard, 1955; Levine, 1999; Nail, McDonald, & Levy, 2000). We human beings are by nature a social species. Few of us could live happily as hermits, never seeing or talking to another person. Through interactions with others, we receive emotional support, affection, and love, and we partake of enjoyable experiences. Given this fundamental human need for social companionship, it is not surprising that we often conform to be accepted by the group to which we belong. Groups have certain expectations about how the group members should behave, and members in good standing conform to these rules, or **social norms.** Members who do not are perceived as different, difficult, and eventually deviant. Deviant members can be ridiculed, punished, or even rejected by the other group members (Kruglanski & Webster, 1991; Levine, 1989; Miller & Anderson, 1979; Schachter, 1951). University of Western Ontario researchers Leslie Janes and James Olson (2000) conducted a series of studies on what they referred to as "jeer pressure." Participants observed someone either ridiculing another person or engaging in self-ridicule. Those who observed someone else being ridiculed later showed the greatest conformity to their peers. Why might this be? According to Janes and Olson, groups use ridicule as a means of punishing group members who fail to comply with the group's norms. Thus, when we observe someone else being ridiculed, we will be especially likely to go along with the group to avoid being the next target.

Normative Social Influence

The influence of other people that leads us to conform in order to be liked and accepted by them; this type of conformity results in public compliance with the group's beliefs and behaviours but not necessarily in private acceptance

Social Norms

The implicit or explicit rules a group has for the acceptable behaviours, values, and beliefs of its members

Normative social influence is another reason why soldiers in Canada's Airborne Regiment participated in the torture and fatal beating of Shidane Arone and why high school students in Victoria participated in the brutal beating and drowning of Reena Virk. In the case of Virk, fears of being rejected or punished by the group didn't end at the scene. Later, when giving statements to the police and testifying in court, some of the students lied because they were afraid of the consequences of "ratting" on their friends.

Conformity and Social Approval: The Asch Line Judgment Studies

Customs do not concern themselves with right or wrong or reason. But they have to be obeyed; one reasons all around them until [one] is tired, but [one] must not transgress them, it is sternly forbidden.

—Mark Twain *(1835–1910)*

You probably don't find it too surprising that people sometimes conform to be liked and accepted by others. After all, if the group is important to us and if it is a matter of wearing the right kind of clothing or using the right cool words, why not go along? But surely we won't conform when we are certain that the group's behaviour is wrong and the pressures are coming from a group that we don't care all that much about. Or will we?

To find out, Solomon Asch (1951, 1956) conducted a series of classic studies exploring the parameters of normative social influence. Asch initiated this program of research because he believed that there are limits to how much people will conform. Naturally, people conformed in the Sherif studies, he reasoned, given that the situation was highly ambiguous—trying to guess how much a light was moving. Asch believed, however, that when a situation was completely unambiguous, people would act like rational, objective problem solvers. When the group said or did something that contradicted an obvious truth, surely people would reject social pressures and decide for themselves what was going on.

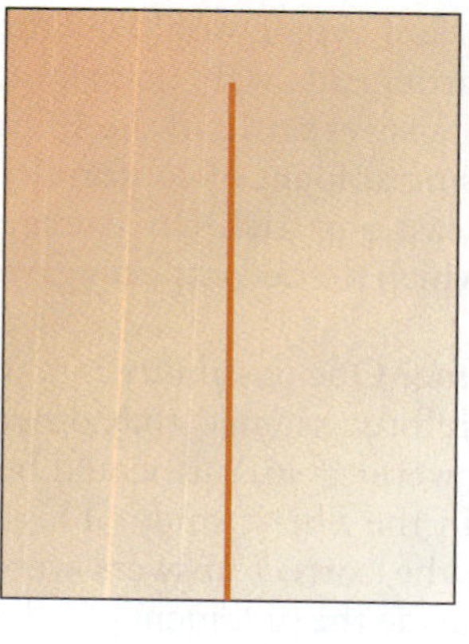

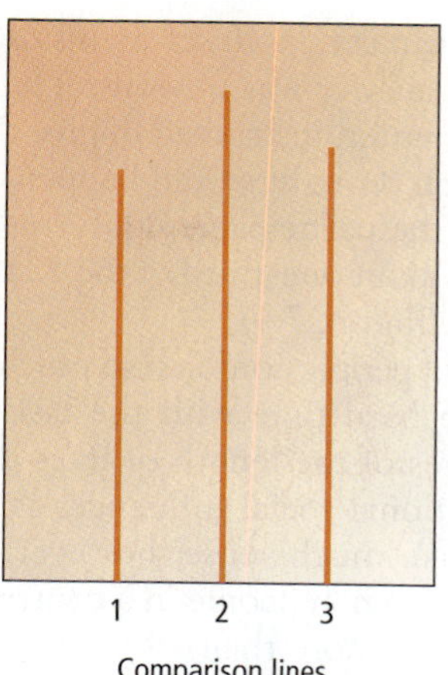

FIGURE 7.3

The judgment task in Asch's line studies.

In a study of normative social influence, participants judged which of the three comparison lines on the right was closest in length to the standard line on the left. The correct answer was obvious (as it is here). However, members of the group (actually confederates) said the wrong answer out loud. Now the participant is in a dilemma. Should he say the right answer and go against the whole group, or should he conform to their behaviour and give the obviously wrong answer?

(Adapted from Asch, 1956)

Simulate on **mypsychlab**
Conformity

To test his hypothesis, Asch conducted the following study. Had you been a participant, you would have been told that this was an experiment on perceptual judgment and that you would be taking part with seven other students. Here's the scenario: The experimenter shows everyone two cards, one with a single line, the other with three lines, labelled 1, 2, and 3. He asks each of you to announce aloud which of the three lines on the second card is closest in length to the line on the first card (see Figure 7.3). It is crystal clear that the correct answer is the second line. Not surprisingly, each participant says, "Line 2." Your turn comes next to last, and, of course, you say it's line 2 as well. The last participant concurs. The experimenter then presents a new set of cards and asks the group members to again make their judgments and announce them out loud. Again, the answer is obvious, and everyone gives the correct answer.

At this point, you are probably thinking to yourself, "What a boring experiment! How many times will we have to judge these silly lines? I wonder what's for dinner tonight." As your mind starts to wander, something surprising happens. The experimenter presents the third set of lines and again the answer is obvious—line 3 is clearly the closest in length to the target line. But the first participant announces that the correct answer is line 1! "Geez," you think, "this guy must be so bored that he fell asleep." The second person also announces that he, too, believes line 1 is the correct answer. The third, fourth, fifth, and sixth participants concur; then it is your turn to judge. By now, you are probably looking at the lines very closely to see if you missed something. But no, line 3 is clearly the correct answer. What will you do? Will you bravely blurt out, "Line 3," or will you go along with the group and give the obviously incorrect answer, "Line 1"?

Participants in an Asch conformity study. The real participant is seated in the middle. He is surrounded by the experimenter's accomplices who have just given the wrong answer on the line task.

As you can see, Asch set up a situation to see if people would conform even when the correct answer was obvious. The other participants were actually accomplices of the experimenter, instructed to give the wrong answer on 12 of the 18 trials. Contrary to what Asch thought would happen, a surprising amount of conformity occurred: 76 percent of the participants conformed on at least one trial. On average, people conformed on about one-third of the 12 trials on which the accomplices gave the incorrect answer (see Figure 7.4).

Why did people conform so much of the time? One possibility is that people genuinely had a hard time with the task and therefore assumed that other people were better judges of the length of lines than they were. If so, this would be another case of informational social influence, as we saw in the Sherif study. This interpretation doesn't make much sense, however, because the correct answers were obvious—so much so that when people in a control group made the judgments by themselves, they were accurate more than 99 percent of the time. Instead, normative pressures came into play. Even though the other participants were strangers, the fear of being the lone dissenter was very strong, causing people to conform, at least occasionally. One participant had this to say about why he conformed: "Here was a group; they had a definite idea; my idea disagreed; I didn't want particularly to make a fool of myself . . .. I felt I was definitely right . . . [but] they might think I was peculiar" (Asch, 1955). These are classic normative reasons for conforming. People know that what they are doing is wrong but go along anyway so as not to feel peculiar or look like a fool. These reasons illustrate an important fact about normative pressures: In contrast to informational social influence, normative pressures usually result in *public compliance without private acceptance*—that is, people go along with the group even if they do not believe in what they are doing or think it is wrong (Cialdini, Reno, & Kallgren, 1990; Cialdini & Trost, 1998; Deutsch & Gerard, 1955; Sorrels & Kelley, 1984).

It isn't difficult to keep alive, friends—just don't make trouble—or if you must make trouble, make the sort of trouble that's expected.

—Common Man in Robert Bolt's A Man for All Seasons, 1966

What is especially surprising about Asch's results is that people were concerned about looking foolish in front of complete strangers. It is not as if the participants were in danger of being ostracized by a group that was important to them. Nor was there any risk of open punishment or disapproval for failing to conform, or of losing the esteem of people they really cared about, such as friends and family members. Yet decades worth of research indicates that conformity for normative reasons can occur simply because we do not want to risk social disapproval, even from complete strangers we will never see again (Crutchfield, 1955; Tanford & Penrod, 1984). As Moscovici (1985) comments, the Asch studies are "one of the most dramatic illustrations of conformity, of blindly going along with the group, even when the individual realizes that by doing so he turns his back on reality and truth."

In a variation of his study, Asch (1957) demonstrated the power of social disapproval in shaping a person's behaviour. The confederates gave the wrong answer 12

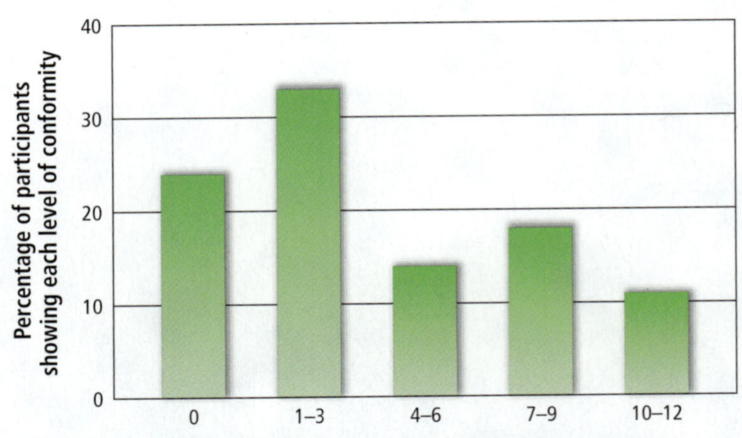

FIGURE 7.4

Results of the Asch line judgment study.

Participants in the Asch line study showed a surprisingly high level of conformity, given how obvious it was that the group was wrong in its judgments: Seventy-six percent of the participants conformed on at least one trial; only 24 percent of participants never conformed at all (see the bar labelled zero). Most participants conformed on one to three of the 12 trials when the group gave the wrong answer. However, a sizeable number of participants conformed to the group's response nearly every time it gave the wrong answer (see the two bars on the right).

(Adapted from Asch, 1957)

out of 18 times, as before, but this time the participants wrote their answers on a piece of paper, instead of saying them out loud. Thus, people did not have to worry about what the group thought of them, because the group would never find out what their answers were. Conformity dropped dramatically, occurring on an average of only 1.5 of the 12 trials.

Recent research by Gregory Berns and colleagues has provided biological evidence for just how unpleasant and uncomfortable it is to resist normative social influence (Berns, Chappelow, Zink, Pagnoni, Martin-Skurski, & Richards, 2005). The researchers used functional magnetic resonance imaging (fMRI) to examine the alterations in brain activity of research participants as they either normatively conformed to a group's judgment or maintained their independence and disagreed with the group. During the task, the participant completed one-third of the trials with no knowledge of the answers of four other people, who they believed were also doing the task. On the remaining two-thirds of the trials, the participant saw the four group members' answers on a visual display. Half the time, the group had all chosen the wrong answers, and the other half of the time, they had all chosen the right answers.

Now, what did the participants do, and most importantly, what areas of their brains were activated when they did it? First, participants did conform to the group's wrong answers some of the time, on average, for 41 percent of the trials. (This level of normative conformity is similar to that found in the Asch [1951, 1956] studies.) On the baseline trials, in which the participants answered alone, the fMRI indicated brain activity in the posterior brain areas dedicated to vision and perception. When the participants conformed to the group's wrong answers, activation occurred in the same areas; however, when participants chose to give the right answer and thus disagree with the group and their unanimous wrong answer, the visual and perceptual areas of the brain were not activated. Instead, different areas of the brain became active—the amygdala, an area devoted to negative emotions, and the right caudate nucleus, an area devoted to modulating social behaviour (Berns et al., 2005). This brain imaging research supports the idea that normative social influence occurs because people feel negative emotions, such as discomfort and tension, when they stand up for their beliefs and go against the group.

When People Conform to Normative Social Influence

Although conformity is commonplace, we are not lemmings who always do what everyone else is doing. And we certainly do not agree on all issues, such as abortion, affirmative action, or same-sex marriages. Exactly when are people most likely to conform to normative pressures? The answer to this question is provided by Bibb Latané's (1981) **social impact theory**. According to this theory, the likelihood that you will respond to social influence from other people depends on three variables:

1. *Strength*: How important is the group to you?
2. *Immediacy*: How close is the group to you in space and time during the influence attempt?
3. *Number*: How many people are in the group?

Social Impact Theory

The theory that conforming to social influence depends on the strength of the group, its immediacy, and the number of other people in the group

Social impact theory predicts that conformity will increase as strength and immediacy increase. Clearly, the more important a group is to us, and the more we are in its presence, the more likely we will be to conform to its normative pressures. Number, however, operates in a different manner. As the size of the group increases, each additional person has less of an influencing effect—going from 3 people to 4 makes more of a difference than going from 53 people to 54; in other words, when the group is small, adding another member will increase conformity pressure—but if a group is large, adding yet another voice to the chorus doesn't have much effect. Latané (1981) constructed a mathematical model that captures these hypothesized effects of strength, immediacy, and number, and has applied this formula to the results of many conformity studies. The formula has done a good job of predicting the actual amount of conformity that occurs (Bourgeois & Bowen, 2001;

Simulate on mypsychlab
Social Influence

TRY IT! Fashion: Normative Social Influence in Action

You can observe social impact theory in action by focusing on fashion—specifically, the clothes and accessories that you and your group of friends wear, as well as the "look" of other groups on campus. You can also observe what happens when you break those normative rules for fashion—for example, by dressing in a way that deviates from that of your group. When you are with a group of friends and acquaintances, examine carefully how everyone is dressed. Pretend you are from another culture and not acquainted with the norms of this group; this will help you notice details you might otherwise overlook. For example, what kinds of pants, shoes, shirts, jewellery, and so on are worn by this group? Are there similarities in their haircuts? Can you discover their fashion "rules"?

Next, spend some time "people watching" on campus; specifically, observe what other groups of people are wearing. Can you discern different subgroups on your campus, defined by their style of dress? If so, there are different types of normative conformity operating on your campus; groups of friends are dressing according to the rules of their subgroup and not according to the rules of the campus as a whole.

Finally, if you are brave, break the fashion rules of your normative group. You can do this subtly or you can be very obvious! (Do be sensible, however, and don't get yourself arrested!) For example, if you're male, you could wear a skirt around campus. That would definitely attract attention; you will be rebelling against normative influence in a very major way! If you're female, you'll have to get more creative to break the normative rules (since women's fashion includes pants, blazers, and other typically male clothing). You could wear a large, green garbage bag (with holes cut out for your head and arms) over your clothing. In either case, simply walk around campus as usual—as if you don't notice you are wearing anything strange. The interesting part will be how people react to you. What will your friends say? Will strangers stare at you?

Your group of friends, as well as the students at your school in general, may well have the qualities that social impact theory discusses—the group is important to you; the group size is more than three; and the group is unanimous—which is the case if your friends or your university or college has definite fashion norms. If you stop conforming to this normative social influence, the other group members will exert some kind of pressure on you, to try to get you to return to conformity.

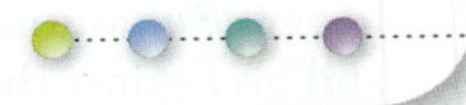

Latané, 1981; Latané & Bourgeois, 2001; Latané & L'Herrou, 1996). For example, gay men who lived in communities that were highly involved in AIDS-awareness activities (where strength, immediacy, and number would all be high) reported feeling more social pressure to avoid risky sexual behaviour and stronger intentions to do so than did men who lived in less involved communities (Fishbein et al., 1993). Similarly, as we mentioned in Chapter 6, whether people use condoms depends, at least in part, on the norms for sexual behaviour that operate in their group of friends.

Finally, in a recent study conducted by John Bassili (2008), students at the University of Toronto were asked how they thought other students felt about taking classes face to face versus online. They also reported on how many of their Introductory Psychology classes they had attended in person versus watched online. It turned out that participants were influenced by what they thought was the norm among other students. Those participants who believed that other students preferred online classes were more likely to go this route; those who believed that other students preferred face-to-face lectures were more likely to attend classes in person. (It may interest you to know that whether the students attended lectures or watched them online did not affect their performance on exams.) (The accompanying Try It! exercise gives you a chance to observe and experience normative pressures in action.)

Social impact theory covers conformity to all kinds of social influence. For our present purposes, let's examine in more detail what it says about the conditions under which people will conform to normative social pressures.

When the Group Size Is Three or More As you just saw, conformity increases as the number of people in the group increases—up to a point. Imagine you are a participant in

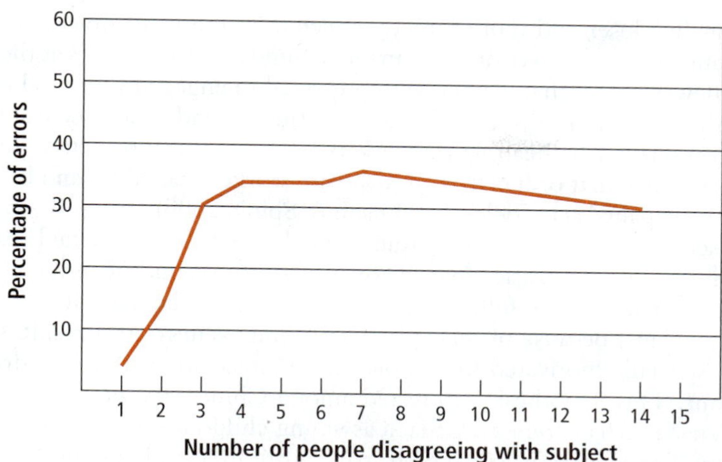

FIGURE 7.5

Effects of group size on conformity.

Asch varied the size of the unanimous majority and found that once the majority numbered four people, adding more people had little influence on conformity.

(Adapted from Asch, 1955)

Solomon Asch's study, where you judged the length of lines. If there are only you and one other participant, and the latter gives a blatantly wrong answer about the length of the lines, will you be less likely to cave in and conform to that person's response than if there are five other participants all giving the wrong answer? What if there are 15 people in the majority? Asch (1955) studied this question, and as you can see in Figure 7.5, conformity increases as the number of people in the group increases, but once the majority reaches about four or five in number (Bond, 2005; Bond & Smith, 1996; Gerard, Wilhelmy, & Conolley, 1968; McGuire, 1968), conformity pressures peak just as social impact theory suggests.

Finally, we want to acknowledge that research conducted at the University of British Columbia by Campbell and Fairey (1989) suggests the effects of group size depend on the kind of social influence that is operating. According to these researchers, in situations in which the group is clearly wrong, conformity will be motivated by normative influence; the participants will conform in order to be accepted by the group. And in these situations, the size of the group should matter. A participant might not feel much pressure to conform when the first person gives an incorrect response. However, conformity pressure will mount as each additional group member also gives the same incorrect response. In contrast, in situations in which the group is making a judgment that may be correct, participants will turn to the group as a source of information. Here, group size is less likely to matter. Once the first group member has given his or her response, it adds very little information if two, three, or four group members also provide the same response.

Thus, the size of a group is most likely to affect conformity under the conditions we have been discussing here: when normative social influence is operating. And as we have seen, it does not take an extremely large group to create normative social influence.

When the Group Is Important Another tenet of social impact theory is that the strength of the group—defined as how important the group is to us—makes a difference. Normative pressures are much stronger when they come from people whose friendship, love, and respect we cherish, because there is a large cost to losing this love and respect. Thus, groups to which we are highly attracted and with which we strongly identify will exert more normative influence on us than groups to which we have little or no attachment (Abrams et al., 1990; Guimond, 1999; Hogg, 1992; Nowak, Szamrej, & Latané, 1990; Packer & Chasteen, 2010). For example, in a recent test of this aspect of social impact theory, a team of Canadian researchers found that railroad workers were more influenced by norms about safety that they believed were held by their co-workers than the norms they believed were held by management (Turner, Chmiel, Hershcovis, & Walls, 2010). The researchers point out that workers

Hain't we got all the fools in town on our side? And ain't that a big enough majority in any town?

—Mark Twain, *The Adventures of Huckleberry Finn, 1884*

are relationally closer and more directly affected by the work practices of their co-workers compared to supervisors or managers. Similarly, researchers at the University of Saskatchewan found that women who preferred to engage in physical activity with others (rather than alone) were influenced by their friends (e.g., seeing their friends being active) but not by health-care workers telling them to be active. In fact, there was some evidence that orders from health-care workers backfired and had a negative effect on participants' activity levels (Wilson & Spink, 2009).

In a fascinating study, Tafarodi, Kang, and Milne (2002) reasoned that members of bicultural visible minorities (e.g., people who are second-generation Canadians) might feel that they are not fully accepted as members of the majority group (i.e., European-Canadians) because of their physical distinctiveness. As a result, such people might be especially motivated to conform to the majority in terms of dress, speech, or behaviour. This hypothesis was tested among Chinese women—who were either born in Canada or had come to Canada as young children—attending the University of Toronto. The women were asked to participate in a study on aesthetic judgment and were told they would be required to rate how much they liked various pieces of art presented on a computer screen. The computer "happened" to display various sets of ratings of each painting, including those supposedly given by Chinese-Canadians and by European-Canadians. Half of the participants completed their ratings in view of a mirror (intended to remind them of their visible-minority appearance); the other half completed the ratings without a mirror. Tafarodi and colleagues hypothesized that the participants who were reminded of their distinctive appearance would be most likely to conform to the ratings of the majority (i.e., European-Canadians). And that is exactly what happened. Thus, when we are attracted to a group and are reminded that we don't quite fit in, we are especially motivated to conform.

If you can get a few allies to agree with you, it's easier to buck the majority and believe some rather strange things. Ernst Zundel, a German Holocaust denier who was deported from Canada to Germany in 2005 for propagating hate, tries through his books and website to get people to believe that the Holocaust never happened, despite the massive amount of documented evidence to the contrary. When he arrived in Germany, Zundel faced charges of inciting hatred, libel, and disparaging the dead. On February 15, 2007, he was convicted and sentenced to a five-year term in a German prison. He was freed on March 1, 2010. Zundel continues to have followers all around the world.

When the Group Is Unanimous Normative social influence is most powerfully felt when everyone in the group says or believes the same thing—for example, when your group of friends all believe that *101 Dalmatians* was the greatest movie ever made. Resisting such unanimous social influence is difficult or even impossible—unless you have an ally. If another person disagrees with the group—say, by nominating the first *Star Wars* movie as the best movie ever—this nonconformist behaviour will help you to buck the tide as well.

To test the importance of having an ally, Asch (1955) conducted another version of his conformity experiment. In this variation, he had six of the seven confederates give the wrong answer, whereas one confederate gave the right answer on every trial. Now, the participant was not alone. Having even one ally dramatically helped him resist normative pressures. People conformed on an average of only 6 percent of the trials in this study, compared with 32 percent in the version where all of the confederates gave the wrong answer. Several other studies have found that observing another person resist normative social influence emboldens the individual to do the same (Allen & Levine, 1969; Morris & Miller, 1975; Nemeth & Chiles, 1988).

This effect of allies produces some interesting anomalies in everyday life—people who hold unpopular beliefs are able to maintain them in the face of group pressure if they can convince at least a few others to agree with them. For example, since the seventeenth century, there have been proponents of the hollow Earth theory—the idea that an unknown civilization resides at the centre of Earth. Now, American scientists and a Utah adventure guide, Steve Currey, claim to have pinpointed the exact location of the hole that leads to Earth's hollow core. Apparently it can be found in the Arctic Sea, just beyond Canada's Arctic Islands (Foot, 2007). In 2006, Steve Currey organized a North Pole Inner Earth Expedition. People were invited to take the journey to the centre of the Earth, at a mere cost of US$20 000. When Currey suddenly died of brain cancer, Brooks Agnew, a Kentucky-based physicist stepped in. He planned to make the journey to the centre of Earth sometime in 2009 and convinced a band of believers to join him. In anticipation of this event, Randy Freeman, a Yellowknife writer, warned that "besides heaps of throwaway cash, prospective cruisers should bring along enough gullibility to swallow an outlandish theory that, despite centuries of scorn, refuses to die" (Foot, 2007). Criticism such as this has not deterred Brooks Agnew. According to the North Pole Inner Earth Expedition website, although the 2009 journey did not take place because of a lack of funds, it will occur by 2012, so long as enough people step up and donate (www.npiee.org).

Gender Differences in Conformity Is it the case that women and men differ in how readily they conform to social pressures? For many years, the prevailing wisdom has been to answer this question in the affirmative: Women are more conforming than men (Crutchfield, 1955). For decades, this finding was presented as a fact. More recently, researchers have taken an objective look at this question by conducting meta analyses. (Recall from Chapter 2 that a meta analysis is a statistical technique that allows you to combine the results across a large number of studies and come up with a meaningful statistical summary.) Alice Eagly and Linda Carli (1981), for example, performed a meta analysis of 145 studies on influenceability that included more than 21 000 participants. Consistent with previous literature, they found that, on average, men are less easily influenced than women. But the size of the difference is very small.

Not only are sex differences in influenceability small but they depend on the type of conformity pressures impinging on people. Gender differences are especially likely to be found in group-pressure situations in which an audience can directly observe how much you conform (e.g., the Asch study in which answers were given in the presence of all participants). When faced with this kind of social pressure, women are more likely to conform than are men. For example, in recent research conducted in Canada and Japan, women conformed more than men on a group conformity task (Cadsby, Hamaguchi, Kawagoe, Maynes, & Song, 2007). In situations in which conformity is private (e.g., the Asch study in which participants answered privately), gender differences in influenceability virtually disappear. Eagly (1987) suggests that this pattern of results stems from the social roles men and women are taught in our society. Women are taught to be more agreeable and supportive, whereas men are taught to be more independent in the face of direct social pressures. Further, Eagly points out that both women and men are more likely to exhibit such gender-consistent behaviours in public situations in which everyone can see how they respond (e.g., the Asch-type conformity study). But, once again, it is important to keep in mind that the size of these differences is small.

One other finding in this area is surprising and controversial. The gender of the researchers conducting conformity studies makes a difference, too. Eagly and Carli (1981) found that male researchers were more likely than female researchers to find that men conformed less than women. They suggest that researchers may be more likely to use experimental materials and situations that are familiar to their own gender. Male researchers, for example, may be more likely than female researchers to study how people conform to persuasive messages about sports. As we noted earlier, people are more likely to conform when confronted with an unfamiliar, ambiguous situation; thus, women may be more likely to conform in the unfamiliar situations designed by male experimenters.

A study by Sistrunk and McDavid (1971) speaks to this issue. These researchers constructed a questionnaire in which some topics were more familiar to men (e.g., mechanics), some were more familiar to women (e.g., fashion), and others were gender neutral. Interestingly, women conformed more than men on the masculine items, men conformed more than women on the feminine items, and women and men conformed equally on the gender-neutral items. The same pattern of findings was obtained in a similar study conducted with University of Saskatchewan students (Maupin & Fisher, 1989).

When the Group's Culture Is Collectivist Is it the case that the society in which one is raised affects the frequency of normative social influence? Perhaps not surprisingly, the answer is yes. Rod Bond and Peter Smith (1996) conducted a meta analysis of 133 Asch line judgment studies in 17 countries. Participants in collectivist cultures showed higher rates of conformity on the line task than did participants in individualist cultures. In fact, in individualist cultures, including Canada (Lalancette & Standing, 1990), the rate of conformity in Asch-type studies has been declining. In contrast, in collectivist cultures, conformity is considered a valued trait—not a negative one, as in North America. Agreeing with others is not considered an act of submission or cowardice in collectivist cultures but rather an act of tact and sensitivity (Hodges & Geyer, 2006; Smith & Bond, 1999). Because emphasis is on the group and not the individual, people in such cultures value normative social influence because it promotes harmony and supportive relationships in the group (Guisinger & Blatt, 1994; Kim et al., 1994; Markus, Kitayama, & Heiman, 1996). We want to underscore that this emphasis on one's group is critical—some researchers have found that when Japanese students participate in Asch-type studies in which the others in the experiment are strangers, they conform even less than do North Americans (Frager, 1970; Williams & Sogon, 1984).

In a recent intriguing study, Monica Stelzl and Clive Seligman (2009) examined whether people with dual national identities associate different values with each of those identities. Students at the University of Western Ontario who were of South-East or East-Asian descent were asked to rate the importance of a number of values (e.g., power, hedonism, conformity) to themselves as Canadians and as Asians. Interestingly, when rating the values in terms of their identity as Asians, conformity was ranked first. When these same participants performed the ratings in terms of their identity as Canadians, conformity ranked near the bottom—seventh out of ten. These effects held regardless of whether the participants were first- or second-generation immigrants, and regardless of the degree of acculturation to Canada.

J.W. Berry (1967; Kim & Berry, 1993) explored the issue of conformity as a cultural value by comparing two cultures that had very different strategies for accumulating food. He hypothesized that societies that relied on hunting or fishing would value independence, assertiveness, and adventurousness in their members—traits that are needed to find and bring home food—whereas societies that were primarily agricultural would value cooperativeness, conformity, and acquiescence—traits that make close living and interdependent farming more successful. Berry compared the Inuit of Baffin Island in Canada, a hunting and fishing society, with the Temne of Sierra Leone, Africa, a farming society, on an Asch-type conformity task. The Temne showed a significant tendency to accept the suggestions of the group, while the Inuit almost completely disregarded them. One Temne put it this way: "When the Temne people choose a thing, we must all agree with the decision—this is what we call cooperation" (Berry, 1967, p. 417). In contrast, the few times the Inuit did conform to the group's wrong answer, they did so with "a quiet, knowing smile" (Berry, 1967, p. 417).

The extent to which conformity is valued varies across cultures. Hunting cultures that prize independence and assertiveness, such as that of the Inuit, show low levels of conformity.

Finally, researchers at the University of British Columbia recently have examined another possible origin of cultural differences in conformity, namely pathogen prevalence (Murray, Trudeau, & Schaller, 2011). Specifically, the researchers correlated the rates of conformity reported for 17 countries analyzed in the Bond and Smith (1996) study cited earlier with records on the prevalence of disease-causing pathogens (e.g., tuberculosis, leprosy, malaria) in each country. It turns out that the greater the prevalence of pathogens, the higher the degree of conformity in a country. Murray and colleagues suggest that the threat of infectious disease may cause a culture to promote greater conformity to social norms (e.g., bathing norms, norms about defecating near water sources, norms concerning social contact).

The Consequences of Normative Social Influence

We have seen that people are highly motivated to conform to social norms. What are the consequences of going along with the group? As you might expect, it depends on what the group is doing. Normative social influence can be used for good or ill. To begin with the positive, Richard Martin at the University of Regina and John Randal, at Victoria University of Wellington, New Zealand (2009) recently examined the role of social influence in increasing donations at a New Zealand art gallery. They "stacked" a clear plastic donation box with either small bills and change (totalling $50) or with larger bills (totalling $200). The idea was that the large bills would convey the message that the social norm was to give generously. And in fact, those who made a donation contributed more in the $200 condition than in the $50 condition. Normative social influence also has been used to promote pro-environmental behaviours. In a recent study, Jessica Nolan and colleagues (2008) gave a sample of California residents information urging them to conserve electrical energy in their homes. The household members received one of four messages: three of these presented basic reasons to conserve (to protect the environment, to benefit society, or to save money), and the fourth message contained a message designed to invoke conformity to social norms (participants were told that the majority of their neighbours conserved electrical energy). The researchers then measured actual energy usage from the homes' electrical metres. They found that the normative message, containing information about the behaviour of their neighbours, caused people to conserve significantly more energy than did the other three messages (Nolan, Schultz, Cialdini, Goldstein, & Griskevicius, 2008).

In a study along the same lines, Goldstein, Cialdini, and Griskevicius (2008) tested whether normative influence could be used to encourage hotel patrons to re-use their towels, given that the lack of success with the standard hotel management technique of posting signs to "reuse your bath towels and save energy." The researchers placed signs in hotel bathrooms that conveyed social normative information ("Almost 75% of guests who are asked to participate in our new resource savings program do help by using the towels more than once"). A significantly greater number of guests re-used their towels in this condition, compared to those who received a standard "help save the environment" appeal.

There are many occasions, however, in which conforming to a group's social norms can have deadly consequences, as illustrated by our earlier examples of train surfing and ecstasy use. How can we be sure that normative conformity is to blame? This is where carefully-controlled social psychology research comes to the rescue. Before getting into the particulars, take a moment to think about the other students at your college or university. How many of them would you say have used alcohol, cigarettes, or marijuana in the last month? When more than 1000 students at the University of Toronto were asked this question, the estimates were very high: 96 percent for alcohol, 87 percent for cigarettes, and 77 percent for marijuana. It turns out that these perceptions were not particularly accurate—the actual rates of substance use in the last month among these students were 66 percent for alcohol, 13.5 percent for cigarettes, and 13.5 percent for marijuana. Does it matter that the participants were so off-base in terms of their perceptions of the group's norms? It matters a lot! The researchers found that the students' perceptions of the social norms were the strongest predictor of whether they had used these substances in the last month. More specifically, students "were twice as likely to use cigarettes, over 3 times as likely to use marijuana and 7 times as likely to consume alcohol in the past 30 days if they perceived the typical student to have used these substances in the past 30 days" (Arbour-Nicitopoulos, Kwan, Lowe, Taman, & Faulkner, 2010, p. 193).

CONNECTIONS

Can Normative Social Influence Be Used to Reduce Students' Binge Drinking?

Research conducted in the United States shows that students typically overestimate how much their peers drink each week (Berkowitz, 2004; Lewis, Lee, Patrick, & Fossos, 2007; Perkins, 2007). This suggests a path for intervention—perhaps if students were made aware of what the social norms really are, they would modify their behaviour accordingly. Indeed, over the past few years, a new technique, the "social norms approach," has replaced prior "scare" tactics as a way to combat binge drinking on hundreds of colleges and universities in the United States. This method involves giving students accurate information about the (lower) drinking levels on their campus. By reducing ambiguity about drinking norms and giving students a new definition of the situation, it is hoped that they will conform to this information and reduce their own alcohol intake.

Whether the social norms approach works is currently being debated by researchers (Lederman, Stewart, Goodhart, & Laitman, 2003; Schemo, 2003). The major problem with this approach is that sometimes it "boomerangs." That is, some students, who already drink very little (or not at all), find out what the "average amount" is on their campus and *increase* their own alcohol intake to be like everyone else! In short, the public service message meant to decrease alcohol consumption can actually have the effect of increasing it (Perkins, Haines, & Rice, 2005; Wechsler, Nelson, Lee, Seiber, Lewis, & Keeling, 2003). For this approach to work, one needs to remember that there are two types of people receiving your message: Those performing the socially undesirable behaviour at an *above average* level (and you want to convince them to decrease it) and those who are performing the socially undesirable behaviour at a *below average* level (and you want them to continue what they're doing—you don't want them to "boomerang" and increase their activity of the undesirable behaviour).

Perhaps a lesson can be taken from those trying to get people to reduce their energy consumption—it has been found that people who use less energy than the average will maintain their low level of use if, in addition to information about social norms, a smiley face is placed on the sheet of information that records their low rate of energy consumption (Shultz, Cialdini, Goldstein, & Griskevicius, 2007). Thus, rewarding people for not complying with undesirable social norms might help mitigate this "backfiring" effect.

The Cost of Resisting Normative Social Influence

One way to observe the power of normative social pressure is to see what happens when people resist it. If a person refuses to do as the group asks and thereby violates its norms, what happens? Think for a moment about the norms that operate in your group of friends. Some friends have an egalitarian norm for making group decisions. For example, when choosing a movie, such groups will ensure that everyone gets to state a preference; the choice is then discussed until agreement is reached. Think about what would happen if, in a group with this kind of norm, you stated at the outset that you wanted to see only the latest Batman movie and weren't going to the movies with your friends otherwise. Your friends would be surprised by your behaviour; they would also be annoyed with you, or even angry. If you continued to disregard the friendship norms of the group by failing to conform to them, two things would happen. First, the group would try to bring you "back into the fold," chiefly through increased communication with you. Teasing comments and long discussions would ensue as your friends tried to figure out why you were acting so strangely and as they tried to get you to conform to their expectations (Garfinkle, 1967). If these discussions didn't work, your friends would most likely curtail communication with you (Festinger & Thibaut, 1951; Gerard, 1953). Now, in effect, you would be rejected (Abrams, Marques, Bown, & Henson, 2000; Hornsey, Jetten, McAuliffe, & Hogg, 2006; Milgram & Sabini, 1978).

> *Success or failure lies in conformity to the times.*
>
> —Niccolò Machiavelli, *The Prince, 1513*

Stanley Schachter (1951) demonstrated how the group responds to an individual who ignores the group's normative influence. He asked groups of university students to read and discuss a case history of "Johnny Rocco," a juvenile delinquent. Most of the students took a middle-of-the-road position about the case, believing that Rocco should receive a judicious mixture of love and discipline. Unbeknown to the participants, however, Schachter had planted an accomplice in the group, who was instructed to disagree with the group's recommendations. He consistently argued that Rocco should receive the harshest amount of punishment, regardless of what the other group members argued.

How was the deviant treated? He received the most comments and questions from the real participants throughout the discussion, until near the end, when communication with him dropped sharply. The other group members had tried to convince the deviant to agree with them; when it appeared that wouldn't work, they ignored him. In addition, they punished the deviant. After the discussion, they were asked to nominate one group member who should be eliminated from further discussions if the size of the group had to be reduced. They nominated the deviant. They were also asked to assign group members to various tasks in future discussions. You guessed it—they assigned the unimportant or boring jobs, such as taking notes, to the deviant.

Krista Piche paid a high price for not conforming to the military code of silence after being sexually assaulted by a petty officer. She filed a complaint, despite being advised by a medical warrant officer not to do so. Military brass responded by forcing her to work alongside the man who had assaulted her and repeatedly denied her requests for a transfer. Even though a career with the military had been her lifelong dream, these consequences of nonconformity made her life so unbearable that she eventually left the military.

Are the findings of Schachter's 1951 study relevant today? Consider the case of Master Seaman Biden, a military police officer with 20 years of service in the Canadian Forces. He was injected with the anthrax vaccine during the 1991 Persian Gulf War and subsequently experienced medical problems. When he learned that the vaccine was out of date and that the Michigan manufacturer of the drug had been charged by the U.S. government for numerous health violations, he wrote a letter to his member of Parliament. Subsequently, Biden received a scathing letter from his commanding officer because members of the military are expected not to voice complaints publicly. He was ordered to stop talking to the media and was ostracized at work. Biden told an *Ottawa Citizen* reporter that he was assigned menial jobs that were usually done by junior privates: "He cleaned rifles while junior officers sat idle, sipping coffee" (Blanchfield, 2000). The parallels between Biden's experience and the way in which participants in Schachter's 1951 study treated a deviant group member are striking.

As we have seen, social groups are well versed in how to bring a nonconformist into line. According to John Bassili (2003), we are keenly aware of the negative consequences of expressing views that contradict those of the majority, which is why we are so reluctant to express minority opinions. He conducted a series of studies in which University of Toronto students were telephoned and asked about their attitudes on various issues (e.g., exams, hospitals). A computer recorded how long it took them to respond to each question. When participants believed their attitude was in a minority position, they took longer to give their response than when they believed their attitude was held by the majority of University of Toronto students.

Under what conditions are people most likely to dissent from the group's norms? You might think that nonconformity would be more likely if we couldn't care less about the group. However, recent research conducted at the University of Toronto shows that we are most likely to defy the group when the group matters a lot to us—a phenomenon that the researchers refer to as "loyal deviance." In such cases, the motivation for nonconformity is to prevent the group from the consequences of making a bad decision (Packer & Chasteen, 2010).

Overcoming Normative Social Influence

Can we find the courage to resist normative pressure? Fortunately, there are some strategies that work. First, simply be aware that social normative influence is operating. Is the presence of others causing you to change your behaviour from what you think is right? The second step of resistance is to take action. More specifically, try to find an ally. We know that having an ally helps us resist normative pressures. Thus, if you are in a situation in which you don't want to go along with the crowd but you fear repercussions if you don't, try to find another person—or better yet, a group—who thinks the way you do.

Finally, it is important to remember that conforming to normative influence most of the time earns you the right to deviate occasionally without serious consequences. This interesting observation was made by Edwin Hollander (1958, 1960), who stated that conforming to a group over time earns you **idiosyncrasy credits,** much like putting money in the bank. Thus, your past conformity allows you, at some point in the

Idiosyncrasy Credits

The credits a person earns, over time, by conforming to a group's norms; if enough idiosyncrasy credits are earned, the person can, on occasion, behave in a deviant manner without retribution from the group future, to deviate from the group (or act idiosyncratically) without getting into too much trouble. If you refuse to drive your friends and yourself home because you've had a few drinks, for example, they may not become upset with you if you have followed their friendship norms in other areas in the past—you've earned the right to be different, to deviate from their normative rules in this area. Thus, resisting normative influence may not be as difficult or as scary as you might think, especially if you have earned idiosyncrasy credits within a group.

Social Influence in Everyday Life

Social influence operates on many levels in our daily lives. For example, although few of us are slaves to fashion, we nonetheless tend to wear what is considered appropriate and stylish at a given time. The wide ties worn in the 1970s gave way to narrow ties in the 1980s. Similarly, women's hemlines dropped from mini to maxi and rose again in the 1990s. Social influence is at work whenever you notice a "look" shared by people in a certain group. No doubt, a few years from now current fashions will look dated and silly, and none of us will conform to them.

Fads are another fairly frivolous example of social influence. Certain activities or objects can suddenly become popular and sweep the country. In the late 1950s, every girl had to have a hula hoop or risk social ostracism. University students swallowed live goldfish in the 1930s, crammed as many people as possible into phone booths in the 1950s, and "streaked" (ran naked) at official gatherings in the 1970s. These fads seem silly now, but ask yourself, could there be "fads" that people are following now?

To provide another example, popular music is a big part of students' lives. You're likely to download music, discovering bands before they make it big, and to share your musical finds with your friends. In fact, music likes and dislikes are one of the ways that young adults communicate who they are to their peers (Rentfrow & Gosling, 2006). But there's so much music and so little time. How do you learn about new bands? Do you think that other people's knowledge influences you? And once you've heard a new song, does knowing that it's popular (or unpopular) influence your liking for it? Salganik, Dobbs, and Watts (2006) conducted an ingenious study to find out. They created an online music marketplace that attracted 14 341 participants. When participants entered the site, they were asked if they wanted to take part in a study about musical tastes. After agreeing, they were (unknown to them) randomly assigned to one of two conditions: the independent condition or the social influence condition. Those in the independent condition saw a list of 48 songs. They could decide which songs to listen to. After listening, they were asked to rate the song and could download the song for free, if they wished.

In 1969, hippie fashions in clothing and hairstyles were all the rage.

The social influence condition was the same but for one difference. The same 48 songs were listed, but next to each song was the number of downloads it had received from others. Note that these were real download counts, as truly occurred when the other participants decided they wanted a song. Thus, in the social influence condition, participants could use informational social influence. They could look at the download numbers and immediately sample just those songs that had the highest numbers, shortening their task and increasing the odds they'd find some good songs. In fact, participants in this condition tended to download the popular choices and avoid the non-popular ones. Normative social influence was probably operating, too; knowing that others liked a certain song enough to download it in high numbers suggests that it's a hip song, perhaps soon to break out on the radio, and one wouldn't want to be left out of this group of people "in the know."

Social Influence and Women's Body Image A more sinister form of social influence involves people's attempts to conform to cultural definitions of an attractive body. Although many, if not most, world societies consider plumpness in

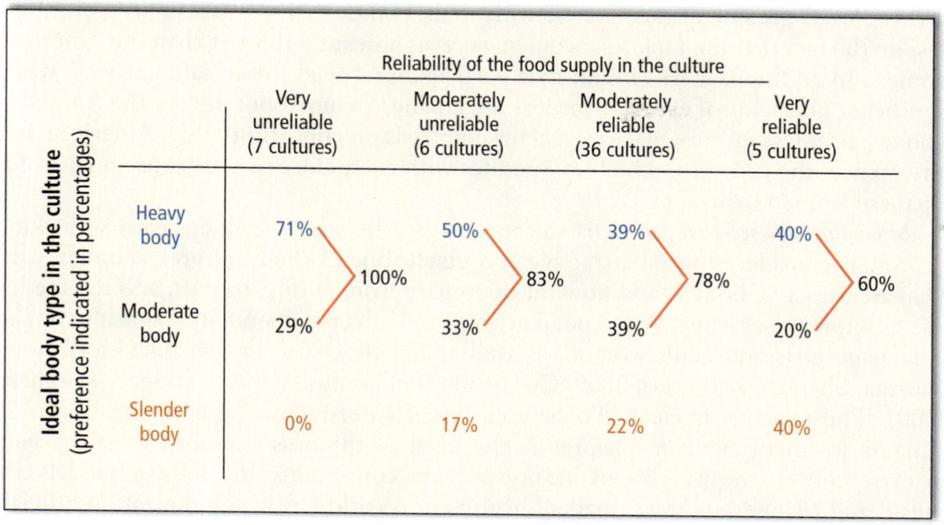

Ideal body type in the culture (preference indicated in percentages)	Very unreliable (7 cultures)	Moderately unreliable (6 cultures)	Moderately reliable (36 cultures)	Very reliable (5 cultures)
	Reliability of the food supply in the culture			
Heavy body	71%	50%	39%	40%
(Heavy + Moderate)	100%	83%	78%	60%
Moderate body	29%	33%	39%	20%
Slender body	0%	17%	22%	40%

FIGURE 7.6

What is the "ideal" female body across cultures?

Researchers divided 54 cultures into groups, depending on the reliability of their food supply. They then determined what was considered to be the "ideal" female body in each culture. Heavy female bodies were considered most beautiful in cultures with an unreliable food supply. Furthermore, the moderate to heavy body range was preferred by the majority in all cultures except those with a very reliable food supply. Only in cultures in which food was readily available was the slender body valued, and only in this type of culture did the majority prefer a body in the slender to moderate range.

(Adapted from Anderson et al., 1992)

females attractive, Western culture—particularly North American culture—currently values thinness in the female form (Fouts & Burggraf, 1999; Grossbard, Lee, Neighbors, & Larimer, 2009; Thompson & Heinberg, 1999; Weeden & Sabini, 2005).

For example, at Simon Fraser University, Judith Anderson and colleagues (1992) analyzed what people in 54 cultures considered to be the ideal female body. The researchers also assessed how reliable the food supply was in each culture. They hypothesized that in societies in which food was frequently scarce, a heavy body would be considered the most beautiful—these would be women who had enough to eat and therefore would be healthy and fertile. As you can see in Figure 7.6, their hypothesis was supported. Heavy bodies for women were preferred over slender or moderate ones in cultures with unreliable food supplies. Furthermore, heavy to moderate bodies were preferred by the vast majority in all cultures. The exception was cultures with very reliable food supplies (such as that of the United States)—only in these cultures did the majority prefer moderate to slender female bodies (Anderson, Crawford, Nadeau, & Lindberg, 1992).

Have North Americans always considered thinness to be the ideal standard for the female body? Analyses of photographs of women in magazines such as *Ladies' Home Journal* and *Vogue* show a startling series of changes in the cultural definition of female bodily attractiveness during the twentieth century (Silverstein et al., 1986). At the turn of the twentieth century, an attractive woman was voluptuous and heavy; by the flapper period of the 1920s, the preferred look for women was rail-thin and flat-chested. The ideal body type changed again in the 1940s, when World War II pin-up girls, such as Betty Grable, exemplified a heavier standard. The curvaceous, heavier female body remained popular during the 1950s; witness, for example, Marilyn Monroe. However, the "swinging 1960s" fashion look, exemplified by the reed-thin British model Twiggy, introduced a very thin silhouette again. This extremely thin standard of feminine physical attractiveness continues to this day. In fact, a recent meta analysis of this research indicates that North American women have adopted the "thin is beautiful" standard even more strongly in the 2000s than in the 1990s (Grabe, Ward, & Hyde, 2008).

Interestingly, the standards for physical attractiveness for Japanese women have also undergone changes in recent decades. Since World War II, the preferred look has taken on a "Westernized" element: long-legged, thin bodies, or what is called the *hattou shin* beauty (Mukai, Kambara, & Sasaki, 1998). This cultural shift has had an effect—Japanese women experience strong normative pressures to be thin (Mukai, 1996). In fact, Mukai and colleagues (1998) found that college-aged Japanese women were even more likely than American women to perceive themselves as being overweight. They

No woman can be too slim or too rich.

—Wallis Simpson, *Duchess of Windsor (1896–1986)*

also reported greater dissatisfaction with their bodies than American women did—despite the fact that the Japanese women were significantly thinner than the American women. In addition, it was found that participants' "need for social approval" was a significant predictor of eating disorders for Japanese women but not for the American women. Japanese culture places a greater emphasis on conformity than American culture; hence, the pressure to be thin operates with even more serious consequences for Japanese women (Mukai et al., 1998).

Informational social influence is the mechanism by which women learn what kind of body is considered to be attractive at a given time in their culture. Women learn what an attractive body is and how they compare from family, friends, and the media. For example, researchers have coded articles and advertisements in magazines aimed at teenage girls and adult women, as well as female characters on television shows (Barriga, Shapiro, & Jhaveri, 2009; Cusumano & Thompson, 1997; Fouts & Burggraf, 2000). The message is clear: To be considered an attractive female, one has to be thin. As we mentioned in Chapter 2, the ideal of thinness has been taken to such an extreme that the weights of beauty pageant contestants and *Playboy* models are considered "dangerous" by Canadian health and World Health Organization officials (Spitzer, Henderson, & Zivian, 1999). Moreover, the "ideals" are getting thinner at a time when average young women in Canada and the United States are getting heavier. Thus, women are getting a strong message that their bodies are not conforming to cultural standards of beauty. What are the consequences of this message? Research on body image indicates that women tend to perceive themselves as overweight and as heavier than they actually are (Cohn & Adler, 1992), and that this effect is heightened if they've just been exposed to media portrayals of thin women (Bessenoff, 2006; Fredrickson et al., 1998; Grube, Ward, & Hyde, 2008).

Watch on **mypsychlab**
Body Image part 2: Kianna, 12 Years Old

To give a recent example, researchers at Wilfrid Laurier University and the University of Waterloo conducted a series of studies on how sociocultural norms influence adolescent girls and women. The experiment was presented to participants as a study of long-term memory. Female university students were shown a series of commercials and were asked to remember them in as much detail as possible. Participants in the control condition watched commercials featuring various products (e.g., cellphone, gas station). Participants in the experimental condition saw the same commercials plus two commercials featuring very thin, attractive women (e.g., supermodels wearing Victoria's Secret bras). Women who were exposed to the attractive, thin models later based their self-esteem more on their appearance

Cultural standards for women's bodies change rapidly. Whereas today's female models and movie stars tend to be lean and muscle-toned, many female icons of the 1940s and 1950s, such as Marilyn Monroe, were curvaceous, heavier, and less muscular.

and reported greater body dissatisfaction than did women in the control group. The authors sum up this finding as "Victoria's dirty secret" (Strahan, Lafrance, Wilson, Ethier, Spencer, & Zanna, 2008).

Normative social influence explains women's attempts to create the ideal body through dieting and, more disturbingly, through eating disorders such as anorexia nervosa and bulimia (Bearman, Stice, & Chase, 2003; Morry & Staska, 2001; Stice & Shaw, 2002). As early as 1966, researchers found that 70 percent of high school girls surveyed were unhappy with their bodies and wanted to lose weight (Heunemann et al., 1966; Hill, Oliver, & Rogers, 1992). Currently, it is estimated that as many as 80 percent of girls want to be thinner. The sociocultural pressure for thinness operating on women is a potentially fatal form of normative social influence. Between 200 000 and 300 000 Canadian women aged 13 to 40 currently have anorexia nervosa; twice as many have bulimia. These illnesses are fatal for 10 to 15 percent of those affected (Support, Concern and Resources for Eating Disorders, 2002).

> *You cannot make a man by standing a sheep on its hind-legs. By standing a flock of sheep in that position, you can make a crowd of men.*
>
> —Sir Max Beerbohm, *Zuleika Dobson*, 1911

Social Influence and Men's Body Image What about cultural definitions of the attractive *male* body? Have those changed over time as well? Do men engage in conformity, too, trying to achieve the perfect body? Until recently, there was very little research on these questions, but studies conducted in the past decade suggest that yes, cultural norms have changed, in that men are beginning to come under the same pressure to achieve the ideal body that women have experienced for decades (Cafri, Thompson, Ricciardelli, McCabe, Smolak, & Yesalis, 2005; Cafri & Thompson, 2004; Grossbard, Lee, Neighbors, & Larimer, 2009; Olivardia, Pope, Borowiecki, & Cohane, 2004; Wojtowicz & von Ranson, 2006). Specifically, the ideal body for males is much more muscular now than it was in the past. For example, Harrison Pope and colleagues (1999) analyzed male-oriented action figure toys, such as G. I. Joe dolls, by measuring their waists, chests, and biceps. The changes in G. I. Joe from 1964 to 1998 are startling. The researchers found that the toy figures had grown much more muscular over time, far exceeding the muscularity of even the largest human bodybuilders (Pope, Olivardia, Gruber, & Borowiecki, 1999).

In another study, Pope and colleagues (2000) coded advertisements in two women's magazines, *Glamour* and *Cosmopolitan*, since 1950, for how often male and female models were pictured in some state of undress. For women, the percentage remained at about 20 percent over the decades, but for men a change was clear. In 1950, less than 5 percent of ads showed men in some state of undress; by 1995, that figure had risen to as much as 35 percent (Pope, Phillips, & Olivardia, 2000).

To describe one last study by Pope and colleagues (2000), men in the United States, France, and Austria were asked to alter a computer image of a male body in terms of fat and muscle until it reflected, first, their own bodies; second, the body they'd like to have; and finally, the body they thought women would find most attractive. The men were quite accurate in the depiction of their own bodies. Remarkably, men in all three countries chose an ideal body that had on average 12.5 kilograms more muscle than their own! This ideal standard was also the body they chose for what they thought women would find attractive. (In fact, when women participants completed the task, they chose a very normal, typical-looking male body as their ideal; Pope, Phillips, & Olivardia, 2000).

These data suggest that informational and normative social influence may be operating on men, as well as on women. Ida Jodette Hatoum and Deborah Belle (2004) investigated this issue by focusing on the relationship between media consumption and bodily concerns in a sample of college men. They found that reading male-oriented magazines such as *Maxim*, *Details*, *Esquire*, *Men's Fitness*, and *Men's Health*, all of which present the hypermuscular male body, was significantly correlated with negative feelings about one's own body. (These researchers

Has the North American cultural ideal of the male body changed over time? Harrison Pope and colleagues (1999) measured the waist, chest, and biceps of the most popular action figure toys over three decades, including G. I. Joe dolls, pictured here. The researchers suggest that such images of the male body may contribute to body image disorders in boys.

also found that the more men were exposed to these male-directed magazines (as well as to movies), the more they valued thinness in women.) It probably comes as no surprise that adolescent and young men are responding to this pressure by developing strategies to achieve the ideal "six-pack" body (Bergstrom & Neighbors, 2006; McCabe & Ricciardelli, 2003a, 2003b; Ricciardelli & McCabe, 2003). As we mentioned in Chapter 2, men—especially those who read fitness magazines (which, of course, portray very muscular bodies)—are engaging in dangerous behaviour such as crash dieting and using risky substances such as anabolic steroids or ephedrine (Cafri et al., 2005; Morry & Staska, 2001; Spitzberg & Rhea, 1999).

Can the effects of social norms regarding body ideals be overcome? To find out, Strahan and colleagues (2008) followed up their "Victoria's dirty secret" study with a field study in which they tested an intervention intended to reduce the impact of social norms. Participants in this study were male and female adolescents from different schools in Ontario. Those in the intervention condition participated in two sessions that included discussions of body image ideals, how unrealistic appearance ideals are (e.g., showing "real-life" versus touched-up photos of celebrities), risks associated with trying to conform to these unattainable ideals, and so on. Participants also created arguments against social norms about appearance and made posters challenging these norms. Participants in the control group attended sessions on the benefits of volunteerism. The results? Both male and female participants who received the body image intervention were more likely to reject appearance norms and less likely to internalize these norms. Strahan and colleagues also assessed the extent to which these students based their self-esteem on their appearance. Girls in the control group based their self-esteem more strongly on appearance than did boys, confirming a basic finding in the literature: that females' feelings of self-worth are more strongly tied to appearance than males' self-esteem is tied to appearance. In fact, boys' self-esteem was unaffected by the intervention. However, girls in the intervention group were less likely to base their self-esteem on appearance than girls in the control group. The results are encouraging and suggest that it is possible to help people withstand normative pressures to conform.

Minority Influence: When the Few Influence the Many

We shouldn't end our discussion of social influence by leaving the impression that the individual never has an effect on the group. As Serge Moscovici (1985, 1994; Moscovici, Mucchi-Faina, & Maass, 1994) says, if groups really did succeed in silencing nonconformists, rejecting deviants, and persuading everyone to go along with the majority point of view, then how could change ever be introduced into society? We would all be like robots, marching along with everyone else in monotonous synchrony, never able to adapt to changing reality.

Minority Influence

The case in which a minority of group members influences the behaviour or beliefs of the majority

Instead, Moscovici (1985, 1994) argues, the individual, or the minority of group members, can influence the behaviour or beliefs of the majority. This is called **minority influence**. How can a minority influence a majority? The key is consistency. People with minority views must express the same view over time, and different members of the minority must agree with one another. If a person in the minority wavers between two different viewpoints or if two individuals express different minority views, the majority will dismiss them as people who have peculiar and groundless opinions. If, however, the minority expresses a consistent unwavering view, the majority is likely to take notice and may even adopt the minority view (Moscovici & Nemeth, 1974).

Never let anyone keep you contained, and never let anyone keep your voice silent.

—Adam Clayton Powell *(1865–1953)*

In a meta analysis of nearly 100 studies, Wendy Wood and colleagues described how minority influence operates (Wood, Lundgren, Ouellette, Busceme, & Blackstone, 1994). People in the majority can cause other group members to conform through normative influence. People in the minority can rarely influence others through normative means—the majority has little concern for how the minority views them. In fact, majority group members may be loath to agree publicly with the minority; they don't want anyone to think they agree with the unusual or strange views of the minority. Minorities, therefore, exert their influence on the group via the other principal method: informational social influence. The minority introduces new, unexpected information to the group and causes the group to examine the issues more carefully. Such careful examination may cause the majority to realize that the minority view has merit, leading the group to adopt all or part of the minority's view. In short, majorities often cause public compliance because of normative social influence, whereas minorities can produce private acceptance because of informational social influence (De Dreu & De Vries, 2001; Levine, Moreland, & Choi, 2001; Wood, Pool, Leck, & Purvis, 1996).

Compliance: Requests to Change Your Behaviour

We have discussed two main reasons why people conform: because other people serve as a useful source of information (informational social influence) and because of pressures to follow social norms (normative social influence). We will now look at how these reasons for conformity apply to some familiar situations in which you might be asked to do something you really do not want to do. Some of these situations are quite common, such as a salesperson pressuring you into subscribing to some magazines or a charity trying to get you to donate money to its cause. Others are less common but more frightening, such as an authority figure asking you to do something that is against your morals. When and why will people conform in these situations?

We will begin with the case of **compliance**—that is, a change in behaviour in response to a direct request from another person. We can hardly make it through a day without a request from someone asking us to do something we would rather not do, be it a letter from a charity asking for money, a telephone call (invariably during dinner) from someone selling time-share vacation property, or a friend wanting to borrow $25. Social psychologists have studied when and why people are likely to comply with these kinds of requests.

Compliance
A change in behaviour in response to a direct request from another person

The Door-in-the-Face Technique

Suppose you have agreed to go door to door to ask people to donate money to the Canadian Heart Association. Here is a good way to get people to give. First, ask people to donate a large amount of money, with the full expectation that they will refuse. When someone answers the door, you might say, "Hello, I'm asking for donations to the Canadian Heart Association. Do you think you could donate $500?" Once people refuse, you immediately retreat to a more reasonable request: "Well, okay, but do you think you could donate $5?" This approach is called the **door-in-the-face technique**, because the first request is purposefully so large that people will want to slam the door shut. Several studies show that it works well in getting people to agree to the second, more reasonable request (Cialdini & Trost, 1998; Patch, Hoang, & Stahelski, 1997; Reeves et al., 1991; Wang, Brownstein, & Katzev, 1989).

Door-in-the-Face Technique
A technique to get people to comply with a request, whereby people are presented first with a large request, which they are expected to refuse, and then with a smaller, more reasonable request, to which it is hoped they will acquiesce

Robert Cialdini and colleagues (1975) decided to see if they could get students to volunteer to chaperone problem adolescents on a two-hour trip to the zoo. When they approached students on a university campus, only 17 percent agreed to this request. In another condition, before asking people to go on the zoo trip, the experimenter made a very large request. The students were asked if they would be willing to work as unpaid counsellors at a juvenile detention centre. The experimenter went on to explain that the position would require two hours of their time per week and that they would have to make a commitment for a minimum of two years. Not surprisingly, no one agreed to such a large request. When students refused, the experimenter said, "Well, we also have another program you might be interested in," and went on to ask if they would chaperone the zoo trip. These students were three times more likely to agree to go on the zoo trip than were the students asked this smaller request alone (Cialdini, Vincent, Lewis, Catalan, Wheeler, & Darby, 1975).

Reciprocity Norm

A social norm by which the receipt of something positive from another person requires you to reciprocate, or behave similarly, in response

The **reciprocity norm** says that if people do something nice for us, we should reciprocate by doing something nice for them (Cialdini & Trost, 1998; Cialdini, Green, & Rusch, 1992; Uehara, 1995; Whatley et al., 1999). Salespeople and charities capitalize on this tendency for people to follow the reciprocity norm mindlessly. They give us a small gift, such as greeting cards, personalized address labels, or free food to taste in the grocery store. Their plan is to make us feel obligated to reciprocate by buying their product or giving money to their cause (Church, 1993; James & Bolstein, 1992). To illustrate how strong the reciprocity norm is—and how mindlessly people follow it—one researcher chose some names at random out of the telephone book and sent each person a Christmas card, signed with his name (Kunz & Woolcott, 1976). Most people sent a card back to him, even though he was a complete stranger!

In the case of the door-in-the-face technique, the reciprocity norm is invoked when the person backs down from an extreme request to a smaller one. We feel as if the requester is doing us a favour by changing his or her position, trying to meet us halfway; because of the reciprocity norm, we then feel obligated to return the favour and appear reasonable too.

One disadvantage of the door-in-the-face technique is that it is likely to be short-lived. Once people have agreed to the smaller request, they have met their obligation by meeting the requester halfway; therefore, they will not be more likely to agree to subsequent requests. Suppose, for example, that your goal is to get people to donate money to the Canadian Heart Association on a regular basis. Once you have retreated from your request for $500 to the more reasonable request for $5 and your neighbour has met you halfway by agreeing, his or her obligation is over. If you ask for another $5 next month, he or she may well feel exploited, thinking, "This person sure is pushy. You'd think I'd get a break after being so reasonable last time." So what should you do if you want long-term compliance? Stay tuned.

The Foot-in-the-Door Technique

Put yourself in the following situation: You are participating in a study in order to fulfill your Introductory Psychology research requirement. At the end of the study, the experimenter asks if you would mind spending 5 or 10 minutes rating some materials for her next study. You agree to help her out. Then she makes another request. Would you volunteer to spend a few extra hours participating in research—over and above the hours required for your research requirement—so that some graduate students can complete their studies?

This is a situation in which University of Western Ontario students found themselves in research conducted by Gorassini and Olson (1995). They were participants in a study on the **foot-in-the-door technique**, a compliance technique in which people are presented first with a small request, to which they are expected to acquiesce, followed by a larger request, to which it is hoped they will also acquiesce. The expression *foot in the door* comes from salespeople who discovered that they were more likely to make a sale if they could get the customer to agree to an initial smaller request, such as letting them into the house to display their products. Thus, this technique is the opposite of the door-in-the-face method.

Foot-in-the-Door Technique

A technique to get people to comply with a request, whereby people are presented first with a small request, to which they are expected to acquiesce, followed by a larger request, to which it is hoped they will also acquiesce

Does the foot-in-the door strategy work? According to the personal experience of one of your authors (Beverley Fehr), this technique is quite effective—even when used on a social psychologist who is familiar with it! Here is her story:

> I was a new assistant professor at the University of Winnipeg, teaching psychology courses for the first time. In October of that year, my department chair approached me and made a request. Would I agree to teach the social psychology class of a colleague who had become ill? It would involve only a class or two . . .. I was extremely busy preparing lectures for my own classes, but I reluctantly agreed. After all, it was only a class or two . . .. At the end of that week, my department chair made another request. Would I be kind enough to teach my colleague's class for another week while things got sorted out? Again, I reluctantly agreed.

> Before I knew it, I had taught the rest of the course, and in December I found myself making up the final exam and grading it!
>
> I am convinced that if my department chair had come to me at the outset and presented only the large request ("Would you teach someone else's class for the rest of the semester and compose the final exam and grade it?"), I would have explained that I already had more than a full schedule teaching my own classes for the first time and therefore, unfortunately, I would have to decline.

The effectiveness of the foot-in-the-door technique is not limited to the personal experience of your authors. In a classic study, Jonathan Freedman and Scott Fraser (1966) tested whether homeowners would agree to put up a large, obtrusive sign in their front yards that said "Drive Carefully." When someone came to their door and asked the homeowners to do this, only 17 percent agreed. But what if they had agreed earlier to a smaller request? The researchers first asked a different group of homeowners to sign a petition indicating that they were in favour of safe driving. Just about everyone agreed to this innocuous request. Two weeks later, a different individual approached these homeowners and asked them to put the sign in their front yard. Though the sign was just as big and obtrusive as the sign used in the control group, these homeowners were over three times more likely to agree to put it in their front yard.

A recent meta analysis confirms the effectiveness of the foot-in-the-door technique (Burger, 1999). Interestingly, it works for a very different reason than does the door-in-the-face technique. Instead of invoking a reciprocity norm, it triggers a change in self-perception. By agreeing to the small request, people come to view themselves as the kind of person who helps others. Once this self-image is in place, it makes people more likely to agree to the second, larger request, even when it comes later. So, if you are collecting money for the Canadian Heart Association and want your neighbours to donate on a long-term basis, first ask them for a small amount, such as 50 cents or $1. If they agree, they will come to view themselves as the kind of people who give to this worthy cause, increasing the likelihood that future donations will be forthcoming (Burger, 1986; Cialdini, 1993; Cialdini, Trost, & Newsom, 1995; Dillard, 1991; Dolin & Booth-Butterfield, 1995). If you are trying to create long-term compliance, the foot-in-the door technique is a good way to go.

Watch on **mypsychlab**
Car Salesman Example: Robert Cialdini

Lowballing

Lowballing
An unscrupulous strategy whereby a salesperson induces a customer to agree to purchase a product at a very low cost, and then subsequently raises the price; frequently, the customer will still make the purchase at the inflated price

Another technique for inducing compliance is called **lowballing** (Cialdini et al., 1978; Weyant, 1996). Robert Cialdini, a distinguished social psychologist, temporarily joined the sales force of an automobile dealership to observe this technique closely. Here's how it works: You enter a car showroom, intent on buying a particular car. Having already priced it at several dealerships, you know that you can purchase it for about $22 000. You are approached by a personable, middle-aged man, who tells you that he can sell you one for $20 000. Excited by the bargain, you agree to the deal and, at the salesperson's request, write out a cheque for the down payment. Meanwhile, you rub your hands in glee, as you imagine yourself driving home in your shiny new bargain. Alas, 10 minutes later, the salesperson returns, looking forlorn. He tells you that in his zeal to give you a good deal, he made an error in calculation and the sales manager caught it. The price of the car actually comes to $22 499. You are disappointed. Moreover, you are pretty sure that you can get it a bit cheaper elsewhere.

The decision to buy is not irrevocable. Yet, research by Cialdini and colleagues (1978) suggests that far more people will go ahead with the deal than if the original asking price had been $22 499, even though the reason for purchasing the car from this particular dealer—the bargain price—no longer exists. Why?

Lowballing works for at least three reasons. First, while the customer's decision to buy is certainly reversible, a commitment of sorts does exist—through the act of signing a cheque for a down payment. This creates the illusion of irrevocability, even though—if the car buyer really thought about it—he or she would quickly realize that it is a nonbinding contract. However, in the razzle-dazzle world of high-pressure sales, even temporary illusion can have powerful consequences. Second, this commitment triggers the anticipation of an exciting event—in this case, driving out with a new car. To thwart the anticipated event by not going ahead with the deal would produce disappointment. Third, while the final price is substantially higher than the customer thought it would be, it is probably only slightly higher than the price at another dealership. Under these circumstances, the customer in effect says, "Oh, what the heck. I'm already here, I've already filled out the forms, I've already written out the cheque—why wait?" And off he or she goes, in a shiny, new car.

CONNECTIONS 

Do You Use "Reverse" Psychology?

Have you ever used "reverse" psychology to get someone to do something that they really don't want to do? One of your authors (Beverley Fehr) remembers negotiations with her mother about whether she could wait until the evening to do the lunch dishes and the dinner dishes all at once, so that afternoon playtime wasn't disrupted by dishwashing duties. "But if you let them pile up," her mother would say, "It will take you an hour to do them all." After dinner, your author would furiously attack the dishes and proudly announce that she had managed to do all of the dishes in a mere 20 minutes. "Reverse psychology works again," her mother would say, smiling.

Surprisingly, the concept of reverse psychology—eliciting compliance by strategically getting someone to contradict you—is something that appears in lay people's vocabularies but is not a term that has actually been used in the field of psychology, until recently. University of Toronto researcher Geoff MacDonald and colleagues (2011) explored whether people actually use reverse psychology (which they refer to as *strategic self-anticonformity*). In their first study, they asked participants to describe times when they had used strategic self-anticonformity. People had no difficulty coming up with examples (e.g., a male participant told his partner that she didn't really need him, so that she would tell him that she did). Moreover, there are two reasons to use strategic self-anticonformity: to elicit attitudinal or behavioural compliance from another person (e.g., getting the dishes cleaned quickly) or to elicit a reassuring or affirming message from another person (e.g., wanting to hear that you are needed). Of the two, using strategic self-anticonformity to gain reassurance was most common. As for effectiveness, participants in this study gave an average success rating of 6.60 on a scale in which 1 = not at all successful and 9 = complete success (MacDonald, Nail, & Harper, 2011). In a follow-up study, the researchers found that strategic self-anticonformity is used as least as often as the kinds of compliance strategies traditionally studied by social psychologists (e.g., foot-in-the-door, door-in-the face). They conclude that strategic self-anticonformity should be added to this list.

Obedience to Authority

Watch on mypsychlab
Adolescent Behaviour: Health and Lifestyle Choices

Obedience
Conformity in response to the commands of an authority figure

The kinds of compliance we have just discussed can be annoying; a skillful salesperson, for example, can make us buy something we don't really need. Rarely, however, do such instances of everyday compliance have life-or-death consequences. Yet, unfortunately, another kind of social influence can be extremely serious and even tragic: **obedience**—conformity in response to the commands of an authority figure—to hurt or kill a fellow human being.

Consider the My Lai massacre during the Vietnam War. On the morning of March 16, 1968, a company of U.S. soldiers boarded helicopters that would take them to the village of My Lai. One of the helicopter pilots radioed that he saw Vietcong soldiers below. The troops jumped out of the helicopters with rifles firing. They soon realized that the pilot was wrong: There were no enemy fighters. Instead, the soldiers found several villagers—women, children, and elderly men—cooking their breakfast over small fires. Inexplicably, the leader of the platoon, Lieutenant William Calley, ordered one of the soldiers to kill the villagers. Other soldiers began firing, and the carnage spread. The Americans rounded up and systematically murdered all the villagers of My Lai. They shoved women and children into a ravine and shot them; they threw hand grenades into huts of cowering villagers. Though no one knows the exact number of deaths, the estimates range from 450 to 500 people (Hersh, 1970).

Why did the soldiers obey Lieutenant Calley's order to kill the innocent villagers? We suspect that all of the reasons people conform combined to produce this atrocity. The behaviour of the other soldiers made the killing seem like the right thing to do (*informational influence*); the soldiers wanted to avoid rejection and ridicule from their peers (*normative influence*); and the soldiers followed the social norm for obedience to authority too readily, without questioning or taking personal responsibility for what they were doing (i.e., mindless conformity). It was the power of these conformity pressures—not personality defects in the soldiers—that led to the tragedy. This makes the incident all the more frightening because it implies that similar incidents can occur with any group of soldiers if similar conformity pressures are present.

The twentieth century was marked by repeated atrocities and genocides—in Armenia, Germany, Ukraine, Rwanda, Cambodia, Bosnia, and Afghanistan, to name just a few. One of the most important questions facing the world's inhabitants is "Where does obedience end and personal responsibility begin?" The philosopher Hannah Arendt (1965) argued that most participants in the Holocaust in World War II were not sadists or psychopaths who enjoyed the mass murder of innocent people but ordinary citizens subjected to complex and powerful social pressures. She covered the trial of Adolf Eichmann, the Nazi official responsible for the transportation of Jews to the death camps, and concluded that he was not the monster that many people made him out to be; rather, he was a commonplace bureaucrat like any other bureaucrat,

Under strong social pressure, individuals will conform to the group, even when this means doing something immoral. During the Vietnam War, U.S. soldiers massacred several hundred Vietnamese civilians—elderly men, women, and children—in the village of My Lai. This award-winning photograph of some of the victims chilled North Americans. Why did the soldiers commit this atrocity? The social influence pressures of conformity and obedience can cause decent people to commit indecent acts.

Victims of the Holocaust in World War II at Nordhausen, Germany, in April 1945. According to social psychologists, most of the German guards and citizens who participated in the Holocaust were not madmen but ordinary people exposed to extraordinary social influences.

who did what he was told without questioning his orders (Miller, 1995).

Our point is not that the soldiers at My Lai, or Adolf Eichmann, or, closer to home, the Canadian peacekeepers who killed Shidane Arone in Somalia be excused for the crimes they committed. The point is that it is too easy to explain their behaviour as the acts of crazy people. It is more fruitful—and indeed more frightening—to view their behaviour as the acts of ordinary people exposed to extraordinary social influence. But how do we know whether this interpretation is correct? How can we be sure that it was social influence and not the work of evil people that produced these atrocities? The way to find out is to study social pressure in the laboratory under controlled conditions. We could take a sample of ordinary citizens, subject them to various kinds of social influence, and see to what extent they will conform and obey. Can an experimenter influence ordinary people to commit immoral acts, such as inflicting severe pain on an innocent bystander? Stanley Milgram (1963, 1974, 1976) decided to find out, in what has become the most famous series of studies in social psychology.

Imagine you were a participant in one of Milgram's studies (1963, 1974). You answer an ad in the paper asking for participants in a study on memory and learning. When you arrive at the laboratory, you meet another participant, a 47-year-old, somewhat overweight, pleasant-looking fellow. The experimenter explains that one of you will play the role of a teacher and the other that of a learner. You draw a slip of paper out of a hat and discover that you will be the teacher. It turns out that your job is to teach the other participant a list of word pairs (e.g., *blue–box*, *nice–day*) and then test him on the list. The experimenter instructs you to deliver an electric shock to the learner whenever he makes a mistake, because the purpose of the study is to examine the effects of punishment on learning.

You watch as the other participant—the learner—is strapped into a chair in an adjacent room and as electrodes are attached to his arm. You are seated in front of a shock generator whose 30 switches deliver varying levels of shock in 15-volt increments, from 15 to 450 volts. Labels accompany these switches, from "Slight Shock," to "Danger: Severe Shock," to an ominous "XXX" beside the highest levels (see the accompanying photos). The experimenter tells you that the first time the learner makes a mistake, you should give him a shock of 15 volts—the smallest amount—and then increase the amount by 15 volts for each subsequent mistake he makes. So you will know what the shocks feel like, the experimenter gives you a sample shock of 45 volts, which is rather painful.

You read the list of word pairs to the learner and then begin the testing phase. After announcing the first word of a pair, you give four possible answers; the learner responds by pressing one of four switches, which illuminates a light on the answer box

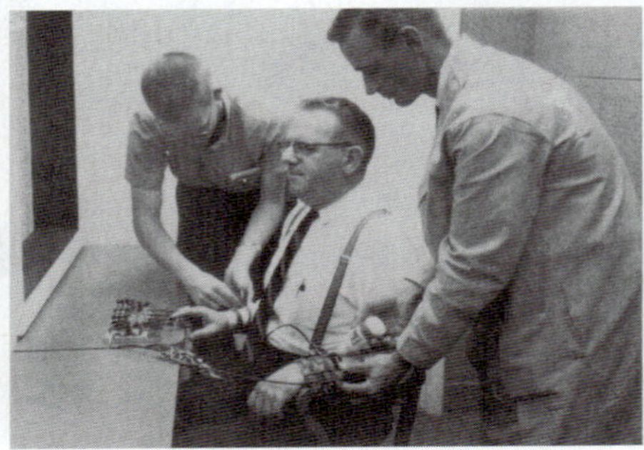

The shock generator used in the Milgram (1974) experiments (left). The learner (an accomplice of the experimenter) is strapped into the chair, and electrodes are attached to his arm (right).

in front of you. Everything begins smoothly, as the learner gets the first few answers right. Then he gets some wrong and, as instructed, you deliver a shock for each one, increasing the voltage as you have been instructed.

At this point, you are probably becoming concerned about the number and severity of the shocks you will have to give. When you get to the 75-volt level, the learner, whom you can hear over an intercom, emits a painful "Ugh!" Perhaps you pause and ask the experimenter what you should do. "Please continue," he responds. As the learner continues to make mistakes, you deliver a few more shocks. The learner protests, shouting, "Ugh! That's all! Get me out of here!" You look at the experimenter with grave concern. He tells you, "It is absolutely essential that you continue" (see Figure 7.7).

What would you do? How many people do you think would continue to obey the experimenter and increase the level of shock until they had delivered the maximum amount (450 volts)? When this question was posed to psychology majors at Yale University, they

Watch on **mypsychlab**
Classic Footage of Milgram's Obedience Study

Learner's Protests

75 volts: Ugh!

90 volts: Ugh!

105 volts: Ugh! (louder)

120 volts: Ugh! Hey this really hurts.

135 volts: Ugh!!

150 volts: Ugh!!! Experimenter! That's all. Get me out of here. I told you I had heart trouble. My heart's starting to bother me now. Get me out of here, please. My heart's starting to bother me. I refuse to go on. Let me out.

165 volts: Ugh! Let me out! (shouting)

180 volts: Ugh! I can't stand the pain. Let me out of here! (shouting)

195 volts: Ugh! Let me out of here. Let me out of here. My heart's bothering me. Let me out of here! You have no right to keep me here! Let me out! Let me out of here! Let me out! Let me out of here! My heart's bothering me. Let me out! Let me out!

210 volts: Ugh! Experimenter! Get me out of here. I've had enough. I won't be in the experiment any more.

225 volts: Ugh!

240 volts: Ugh!

255 volts: Ugh! Get me out of here.

270 volts: Ugh! (Agonized scream) Let me out of here. Let me out of here. Let me out of here. Let me out. Do you hear? Let me out of here.

285 volts: Ugh! (Agonized scream)

300 volts: Ugh! (Agonized scream) I absolutely refuse to answer any more. Get me out of here. You can't hold me here. Get me out. Get me out of here.

315 volts: Ugh! (Intensely agonized scream) I told you I refuse to answer. I'm no longer part of this experiment.

330 volts: Ugh! (Intense and prolonged agonized scream) Let me out of here. Let me out of here. My heart's bothering me. Let me out, I tell you. (Hysterically) Let me out of here. Let me out of here. You have no right to hold me here. Let me out! Let me out! Let me out of here! Let me out!

Instructions Used by the Experimenter to Achieve Obedience

Prod 1: Please continue *or* Please go on.

Prod 2: The experiment requires that you continue.

Prod 3: It is absolutely essential that you continue.

Prod 4: You have no other choice; you must go on.

The prods were always made in sequence: Only if prod 1 had been unsuccessful could prod 2 be used. If the subject refused to obey the experimenter after prod 4, the experiment was terminated. The experimenter's tone of voice was at all times firm but not impolite. The sequence was begun anew on each occasion that the subject balked or showed reluctance to follow orders.

Special prods. If the subject asked whether the learner was likely to suffer permanent physical injury, the experimenter said:

Although the shocks may be painful, there is no permanent tissue damage, so please go on. [Followed by prods 2, 3, and 4 if necessary.]

If the subject said that the learner did not want to go on, the experimenter replied: Whether the learner likes it or not, you must go on until he has learned all the word pairs correctly. So please go on. [Followed by prods 2, 3, and 4 if necessary.]

FIGURE 7.7

Transcripts of the learner's protests and the experimenter's prods to achieve obedience in Milgram's obedience study.

(Adapted from Milgram, 1963, 1974)

estimated that only about 1 percent of the population would go to this extreme. A sample of middle-class adults and a panel of psychiatrists made similar predictions. However, having read our discussion of conformity thus far, you are probably not as optimistic. Whereas no one would have believed that such travesties as the Holocaust in World War II or the My Lai massacre in Vietnam could have occurred, they did. Like the people who committed these horrific acts, most of Milgram's participants succumbed to the pressure of an authority figure. The average maximum amount of shock delivered was 360 volts, and 62.5 percent of the participants delivered the 450-volt shock, the maximum amount. A full 80 percent of the participants continued giving the shocks even after the learner, who earlier had mentioned that he had a heart condition, screamed, "Let me out of here! Let me out of here! My heart's bothering me. Let me out of here! . .. Get me out of here! I've had enough. I won't be in the experiment any more" (Milgram, 1974).

It is important to know that the learner was actually an accomplice of the experimenter and play-acted his role; he did not receive any actual shocks. (See the learner's script in Figure 7.7.) It is equally important to note that the study was very convincingly done, so that people believed they really were shocking the learner. Here is Milgram's description of one participant's response to the teacher role:

> I observed a mature and initially poised businessman enter the laboratory smiling and confident. Within 20 minutes he was reduced to a twitching, stuttering wreck, who was rapidly approaching a point of nervous collapse. He constantly pulled on his earlobe and twisted his hands. At one point he pushed his fist into his forehead and muttered, "Oh God, let's stop it." And yet he continued to respond to every word of the experimenter and obeyed to the end. (Milgram, 1963)

When you think of the long and gloomy history of man, you will find more hideous crimes have been committed in the name of obedience than in the name of rebellion.

—C. P. Snow, "Either-Or"

It seems particularly disturbing that in the Milgram studies, obedience occurred "across the board." Milgram's research participants ranged in age from their twenties to their fifties and included blue-collar, white-collar, and professional workers. Although most of his research participants were men, Milgram obtained the same rate of obedience in the one study he conducted with female participants. More recently, Burger (2009) replicated Milgram's research (with many ethical precautions such as having a clinical psychologist present to intervene if a participant appeared to be distressed). Rates of obedience did not vary as a function of gender, age, ethnicity, or education. Also, the few personality variables that were examined (e.g., empathy) did not produce clear-cut findings. Thus, it appears that no one is immune from the pressure to obey authority (Blass, 2004).

It is also important to point out that although we might dismiss Milgram's findings as a vestige of an earlier time when people were more conforming, the rate of obedience in Burger's (2009) very recent research does not differ significantly from that obtained in the original Milgram studies. A recent review confirms that rates of obedience in Milgram-type studies have remained consistent over time (Blass, 2004).

Watch on **mypsychlab**
Milgram's Obedience Study

Milgram's studies raise an important but disturbing question: Why did ordinary, decent people conform to the wishes of the experimenter, to the point to which they, at least in their own minds, were inflicting great pain on another human being? Why were the students, middle-class adults, and psychiatrists so wrong in their predictions about what people would do? The reasons we have just discussed for why people conform combined in a dangerous way. Let's take a close look at how this worked in the Milgram experiments.

The Role of Normative Social Influence

First, it is clear that normative pressures made it difficult for people to refuse to continue. As we have seen, if someone really wants us to do something, it can be difficult to say no. This is particularly true when the person is in a position of authority over us. Milgram's participants probably believed that if they refused to continue, the experimenter would be disappointed, hurt, or maybe even angry—all of which put pressure on them to continue. It is important to note that this study, unlike the Asch study, was set up so the experimenter actively attempted to get people to conform, giving such stern commands as "It is absolutely essential that you continue." When an authority figure is so insistent that we obey, it is difficult to say no (Blass, 2000, 2003; Hamilton, Sanders, & McKearney, 1995; Miller, 1986). For example, research conducted at the University of British Columbia has shown that obedience is highest in the presence of a directive authority figure. (Interestingly, if the authority figure is removed from the scene, there can be a backfiring effect such that people begin to behave contrary to what the authority figure has commanded them to do [Conway & Schaller, 2005].) Similarly, in a recent series of studies, researchers at the University of Halle-Wittenberg, Germany, and at the University of Western Ontario found that when teachers were asked to make hiring decisions, their choice of applicants was influenced by directives from the principal—in this case, the principal's preference for East German over West German applicants. The teachers who were most committed to their school were most likely to obey the principal and recommend East German applicants for the job—even when there were better qualified West German applicants in the pool. The researchers conclude that obedience to an authority figure may be at least partly responsible for employment discrimination (Petersen & Dietz, 2008).

The fact that normative pressures were present in the Milgram experiments is clear from a variation of the study that he conducted (1974). This time there were three teachers, two of whom were confederates of the experimenter. One confederate was instructed to read the list of word pairs; the other was instructed to tell the learner whether his response was correct. The real participant's job was to deliver the shocks, increasing their severity with each error, as in the original experiment. At 150 volts, when the learner gave his first vehement protest, the first confederate refused to continue despite the experimenter's command that he do so. At 210 volts, the second confederate refused to continue. The result? Seeing their peers disobey made it much easier for the actual participant to disobey as well. In this experiment, only 10 percent of the participants gave the maximum level of shock (see Figure 7.8). This result is similar to Asch's finding that people did not conform nearly as much when one accomplice bucked the majority and consistently gave the correct answer.

The Role of Informational Social Influence

Despite the power of the normative pressures in Milgram's original study, they are not the sole reason people complied. The experimenter was authoritative and insistent, but he did not point a gun at participants and tell them to "conform or else." The participants were free to get up and leave any time they wanted to. Why didn't they, especially when the experimenter was a stranger they had never met before and probably would never see again?

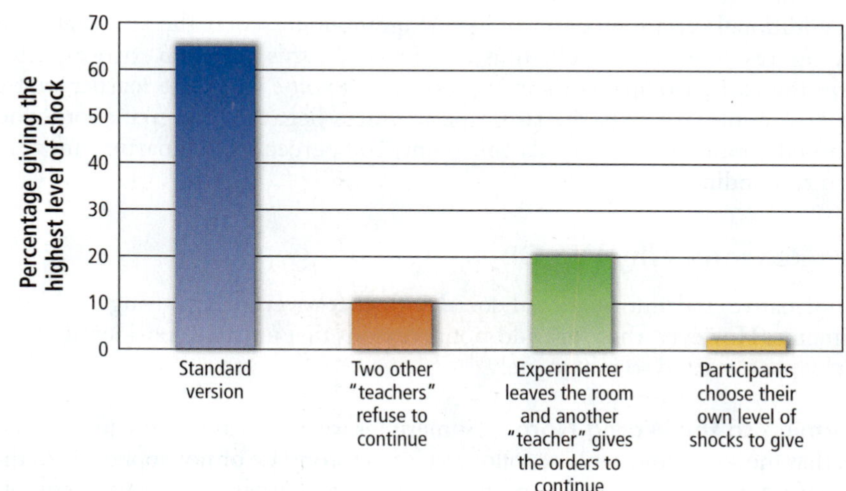

FIGURE 7.8

The results of different versions of the Milgram experiment.

Obedience is highest in the standard version in which the participant is ordered to deliver increasing levels of shock to another person (left bar). Obedience drops when other participants model disobedience or when the authority figure is not present (two middle bars). Finally, when no orders are given to increase the shocks, almost no participants do so (right bar). The contrast in behaviour between the far-left and far-right bars indicates just how powerful the social norm of obedience is.

(Adapted from Milgram, 1974)

As we saw earlier, when people are in a confusing situation and unsure of what they should do, they use other people to reach a definition of the situation. Informational social influence is especially powerful when the situation is ambiguous, when it is a crisis, and when the other people in the situation have some expertise. The situation faced by Milgram's participants was clearly confusing, unfamiliar, and upsetting. It all seemed straightforward enough when the experimenter explained it to them, but then it turned into something else altogether. The learner cried out in pain, but the experimenter told the participant that while the shocks were painful, they did not cause any permanent tissue damage. The participant didn't want to hurt anyone, but he or she had agreed to be in the study and to follow directions. When in such a state of conflict, it was only natural for the participants to use an expert—the experimenter—to help them decide what they should do (Darley, 1995; Krakow & Blass, 1995; Meeus & Raaijmakers, 1995).

Another version of the experiment that Milgram performed supports the idea that informational influence was operative. This version was identical to the original one except for two critical changes. First, the experimenter never said which shock levels were to be given, leaving this decision up to the teacher (the real participant). Second, the situation was arranged so the experimenter was "unexpectedly" called away from the experiment. The participant was instructed to continue on, and another "teacher"—actually, a confederate, who was supposedly there to record how long it took the learner to respond—said that he had just thought of a good system: How about if they increased the level of shock each time the learner made a mistake? He insisted that the real participant follow this procedure.

Note that in this situation the expertise of the person giving the commands has been removed. And in this situation, people were much less likely to use the nonexpert as a source of information about how they should respond. As seen in Figure 7.8, in this version, obedience dropped from 65 percent of participants giving the maximum amount of shock to only 20 percent. The fact that 20 percent still obeyed suggests that some people were so uncertain about what to do that they used even a nonexpert as a guide.

More recent research conducted at the University of British Columbia confirms that people are less likely to obey when they perceive that the authority figure is actually not an expert (Conway & Schaller, 2005). For example, in one study, participants were presented with a scenario in which they were employees having to choose between two computer network systems. Participants in the nonexpert condition were told that the boss did not know anything about computers; those in the expert condition were told that the boss had an advanced degree in computer networking. In both conditions, the boss issued a command to vote for one of the systems under consideration. Those who believed the boss did not have expertise were less likely to obey this order (even when told that the other employees all went along with it) than those who were told he had competence in this area.

An additional variation conducted by Milgram underscores the importance of authority figures as experts in eliciting obedience. In this variation, two experimenters gave the real participants their orders. At 150 volts, when the learner first cried out that he wanted to stop, the two experimenters began to disagree about whether they should continue the study. At this point, 100 percent of the participant teachers stopped responding.

Other Reasons Why We Obey

Both normative and informational social influences were very strong in Milgram's experiments. However, there are additional reasons that must be considered to explain fully why people acted so inhumanely.

Conforming to the Wrong Norm Sometimes we are on automatic pilot and don't realize that the social norm we are following is inappropriate or not applicable to the situation we are in. We don't mean to imply that Milgram's participants were completely mindless or unaware of what they were doing. All were terribly concerned about the plight of the victim. The problem was that they were caught in a web of conflicting norms, and it was difficult to determine which one to follow. At the beginning of the experiment, it was perfectly reasonable to obey the norm that says, "Obey expert, legitimate authority figures." The experimenter was confident and knowledgeable, and the study seemed a reasonable test of an interesting hypothesis. So, why not cooperate and do as they were told? But then gradually the rules of the game changed and this "obey authority" norm was no longer appropriate. The experimenter, who seemed so reasonable before, was asking people to inflict great pain on a fellow participant. But once people are following one norm, it can be difficult to switch midstream, realizing that this norm is no longer appropriate and that another norm—"Do not inflict needless harm on a fellow human being"—should be followed (Conway & Schaller, 2005; Modigliani & Rochat, 1995). We suspect that if, halfway through the experiment, Milgram's participants had been told to take a 15-minute break and go sit in a room by themselves, rather than continue with the fast-paced experiment, many more would have realized that they should no longer follow the norm to obey authority and would have refused to continue.

Self-Justification Second, it is important to remember that the experimenter asked people to increase the shocks in very small increments. The participants did not go from giving a small shock to giving a potentially lethal one. Instead, at any given point they were faced with the decision about whether to increase the amount of shock they had just given by 15 volts. As we saw in Chapter 6, every time a person makes an important or difficult decision, dissonance is produced, with resultant pressures to reduce it. An effective way of reducing dissonance produced by a difficult decision is to tell oneself that the decision was fully justified. However, because reducing dissonance provides a justification for the preceding action, in some situations, it makes a person vulnerable to pressures leading to an escalation of the chosen activity. Thus, in the Milgram study, once the participants agreed to administer the first shock, it created pressure on them to continue to obey. As the participants administered each successive level of shock, they had to justify it in their minds. Once a particular shock level was justified, it became very difficult for them to find a place where they could draw the line and stop. How could they say, in effect, "Okay, I gave him 200 volts, but not 215—never 215"? Each succeeding justification laid the groundwork for the next shock and would have been dissonant with quitting; 215 volts is not that different from 200, and 230 is not that different from 215. Those who did break off the series did so against enormous internal pressure to continue.

Mika Haritos-Fatouros (1988; see Staub, 1989) reports that this incremental approach was used by the Greek military dictatorship of the late 1960s to train torturers. In his interviews with former torturers, Haritos-Fatouros learned that their first contact with political prisoners was to bring them food and "occasionally" give them some blows. Next, they were put on guard while others conducted torture sessions. Then, they would take part in a few group floggings or beatings and the last step—being in charge of a torture session—"was announced suddenly to the [man] by the commander-in-chief without leaving him any time for reflection" (Haritos-Fatouros, 1988).

It's Not about Aggression Before leaving our discussion of the Milgram studies, we should mention one other possible interpretation of his results. Did the participants act so inhumanely because there is an evil side to human nature, lurking just below the surface, ready to be expressed on the flimsiest excuse? After all, it was socially acceptable to inflict harm on another person in the Milgram experiment; in fact, participants were ordered to do so. Perhaps this factor allowed the expression of a universal aggressive urge.

To test this hypothesis, Milgram conducted another version of his study. Everything was the same except that the experimenter told the participants they could choose any level of shock they wished to give the learner when he made a mistake. Milgram gave people permission to use the highest levels, telling them there was a lot to be learned from all levels of shock. This instruction should have allowed any aggressive urges to be expressed unchecked. Instead, the participants chose to give very mild shocks (see Figure 7.8). Only 2.5 percent of the participants gave the maximum amount of shock. Thus, the Milgram studies do not show that people have an evil streak that seeps through when the surface is scratched. Rather, these studies demonstrate that social pressures can combine in insidious ways to make humane people act in an inhumane manner.

Watch on **mypsychlab**
The Power of the Situation: Phil Zimbardo

According to Philip Zimbardo (2007), the findings of Milgram's obedience studies provide insight into the horrific treatment and deaths of prisoners in Iraq's Abu Ghraib prison at the hands of U.S. soldiers. Zimbardo argues that many of the conditions that promoted the inflicting of pain on the learner in the Milgram experiments applied to the situation in Iraq in 2005. The American soldiers were in an unfamiliar, ambiguous situation in which the rules kept changing. The soldiers feared repercussions if they did not comply with orders from authority figures to torture and kill (Dittman, 2004; Hersh, 2004; Zimbardo, 2007). In most cases, the abuse began gradually and then escalated to more extreme forms. The soldiers did not feel personally responsible for their behaviour. In short, the conditions that were found to produce evil in the Milgram experiments, conducted more than 30 years ago, were reproduced in the Abu Ghraib prison. And in this real-world context, the results were even more dire. Sadly, the words of Stanley Milgram still apply to the kinds of atrocities, such as the treatment of the Iraqi prisoners, we are witnessing today:

> Even Eichmann was sickened when he toured the concentration camps, but in order to participate in mass murder he had only to sit at a desk and shuffle papers. At the same time the man in the camp who actually dropped Cyclon-B into the gas chambers is able to justify his behavior on the grounds that he is only following orders from above. Thus there is fragmentation of the total human act; no one man decides to carry out the evil act and is confronted with its consequences. The person who assumes full responsibility for the act has evaporated. Perhaps this is the most common characteristic of socially organized evil in modern society. (Milgram, 1976, pp. 183–184)

Epilogue: A Look at the Minority Who Disobeyed We have been focusing on the fact that nearly two-thirds of the participants in the Milgram study obeyed the experimenter and delivered the highest level of shock. However, this means that approximately one-third of the participants disobeyed. Can anything be learned from those who refused to continue giving the learner shocks? Recently, a Canadian researcher, Dominic Packer, conducted a meta analysis of Milgram's studies to find out (Packer, 2008). Specifically, Packer examined whether the learner's expression of pain, his request to be released from the experiment, or perhaps both had contributed to disobedience. It was found that in all of Milgram's studies, disobedience was most likely to occur at 150 volts. This was not the first time the learner expressed pain, but it was the first time he asked to be let out of the experiment (see Figure 7.7). It is striking that the learner's expression of pain was not enough to invoke disobedience. According to Packer, these findings have implications for the humane treatment of prisoners:

> In response to global terrorism, the legal rights previously afforded to prisoners of war (e.g., Geneva conventions) have been reconsidered and, in part, replaced with assurances that interrogations will not cause undue pain. These assurances assume that agents of the law are as capable of appropriately responding to pain as they are of respecting well-specified legal rights. This reanalysis of Milgram's data suggests that this may not be the case. (Packer, 2008, p. 303)

To end on a more encouraging note, there is some evidence that simply watching Milgram's classic film can have beneficial effects. Jerry Sheppard and Marnie Young (2007) showed students enrolled in a Business, Ethics, and Society class at Laurentian University the Milgram obedience film. (Students in the control group were not shown the film.) Those who saw the film subsequently exhibited a higher level of moral reasoning. These effects were strongest for women. Thus, becoming aware of the powerful way in which obedience to an authority figure can cause us to behave in ways we would normally consider unthinkable makes it more likely that we will take the moral high road.

HOW WOULD YOU USE THIS?

The topics of conformity and obedience bring to mind the great opening sentence in Charles Dickens' novel *A Tale of Two Cities*: "It was the best of times, it was the worst of times." These types of social influence are incredibly useful in maintaining social order. Without them, life would be chaotic, even dangerous. However, they have their "dark side" as well, even to the point of promoting and enabling genocide. What can you do to protect yourself from the potentially negative effects of social influence? Probably the most difficult is informational conformity; by definition, you conform to others because you don't know what's going on. Therefore, it is very difficult to know if they're wrong. Typically, it's best to rely on an expert instead of a nonexpert, but even this advice can be tricky. Resisting normative conformity is more straightforward. You'll know what the right thing to do is, but will you be able to withstand the disapproval of others? Remember that having an ally will help you to stand up to group pressure. Obedience also presents a fairly straightforward scenario. You'll know when you've been given an order that goes against your ethical or moral beliefs. As with normative conformity, it will be a matter of whether you are willing and able to experience the repercussions of your disobedience. Luckily, learning about these types of social influence will make you more aware in the future of when it is appropriate to agree with the group and when it is not.

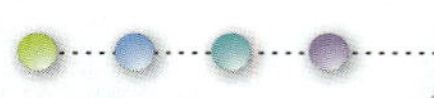

Summary

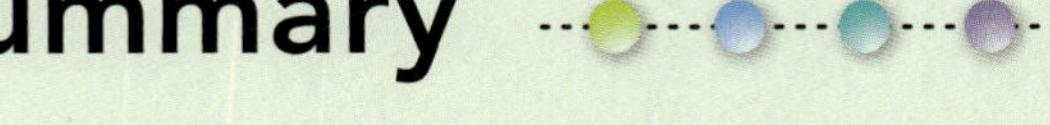

- **Conformity: When and Why** Conformity occurs when people change their behavior because of the real (or imagined) influence of others. People conform for two main reasons: because of informational and normative social influences.
- **Informational Social Influence: The Need to Know What's "Right"** Informational social influence occurs when people do not know what is the correct (or best) thing to do or say. They look to the behaviour of others as an important and needed source of information, and they use it to choose appropriate courses of action for themselves. Informational social influence usually results in private acceptance, wherein people genuinely believe in what other people are doing or saying.
  - **When People Conform to Informational Social Influence** People are more likely to conform to informational social influence when the situation is ambiguous, a crisis, or if experts are present.
  - **When Informational Conformity Backfires** Using other people as a source of information can backfire when they are wrong about what's going on. Contagion occurs when emotions and behaviours spread rapidly throughout a group; one example is mass psychogenic illness.
  - **Resisting Informational Social Influence** You can best resist the inappropriate use of others as a source of information by evaluating whether the information you are receiving is from a legitimate expert. Also, check the information you are getting against your internal moral compass.
- **Normative Social Influence: The Need to Be Accepted** Normative social influence occurs when we change our behaviour to match that of others because we want to remain a member of the group and continue to gain the advantages of group membership. We conform to the group's social norms, implicit or explicit rules for acceptable behaviours, values, and attitudes. Normative social influence usually results in public compliance but not private acceptance of other people's ideas and behaviours.

- **Conformity and Social Approval: The Asch Line Judgment Studies** In a series of classic studies, Solomon Asch found that people would conform, at least some of the time, to the obviously wrong answer of the group.
- **When People Conform to Normative Social Influence** Social impact theory specifies when normative social influence is most likely to occur by referring to the strength, immediacy, and size of the group. We are more likely to conform when the group is one we care about, when the group members are unanimous in their thoughts or behaviours, when the group has three or more members, and when we are members of collectivist cultures. Past conformity gives people idiosyncrasy credits, allowing them to deviate from the group without serious consequences.
- **The Consequences of Normative Social Influence** The consequences of normative social influence can be positive (e.g., conforming to norms concerning pro-environmental behaviours such as energy conservation) or negative (e.g., going along with dangerous or unhealthy behaviours performed by the group, such as binge drinking).
- **The Cost of Normative Social Influence** Resisting normative social influence can lead to ridicule, ostracism, and even rejection by the group.
- **Overcoming Normative Social Influence** We can resist inappropriate normative pressures by taking the time to stop and become aware of what social norms are operating, by finding an ally, and by gathering idiosyncrasy credits over time from a group whose membership we value.
- **Social Influence in Everyday Life** Normative social influence operates on many levels in social life: It influences our eating habits, hobbies, fashion, body image, and so on, and it promotes correct (polite) behaviour in society.

Minority Influence: When the Few Influence the Many Under certain conditions, an individual (or small number of people) can influence the majority. The key is consistency in the presentation of the minority viewpoint.

Compliance: Requests to Change Your Behaviour Another form of social influence is compliance—conforming in response to requests from others.

- **The Door-in-the-Face Technique** An effective compliance technique is the door-in-the-face technique, in which a person starts out with a big request in order to get people to agree to a second, smaller request. This technique works because of the reciprocity norm; when the requester retreats from the larger to the smaller request, it puts pressure on people to reciprocate by agreeing to the smaller request.
- **The Foot-in-the-Door Technique** This technique is also effective; here the requester starts out with a very small request to get people to agree to a larger request.
- **Lowballing** Another effective compliance technique is lowballing, in which a person makes a commitment to an attractive offer. The deal is then changed so that the offer is no longer as attractive. Nevertheless, the person tends to go along with this much less attractive deal.

Obedience to Authority In the most famous series of studies in social psychology, Stanley Milgram examined obedience to authority figures. He found chilling levels of obedience, to the point to which a majority of participants administered what they thought were near-lethal shocks to a fellow human being.

- **The Role of Normative Social Influence** Normative pressures make it difficult for people to stop obeying authority figures. They want to please the authority figure by doing a good job.
- **The Role of Informational Social Influence** The obedience experiment was a confusing situation for participants, with competing, ambiguous demands. Unclear about how to define what was going on, they followed the orders of the expert.
- **Other Reasons Why We Obey** Participants conformed to the wrong norm: They continued to follow the "obey authority" norm when it was no longer appropriate. It was difficult for them to abandon this norm for three reasons: the fast-paced nature of the experiment; the fact that the shock levels increased in small increments; and their loss of a feeling of personal responsibility.

8 Group Processes

Influence in Social Groups

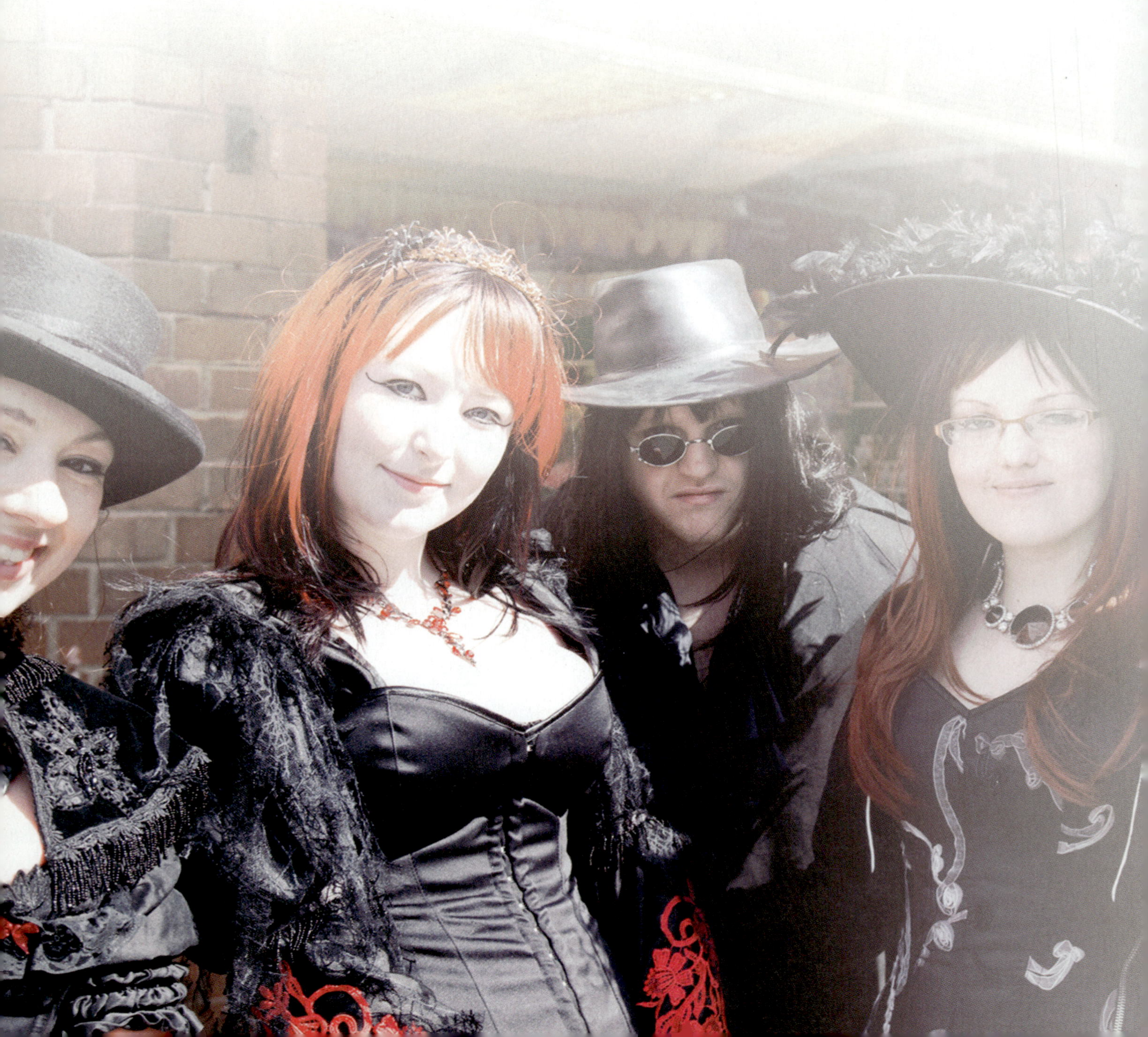

IN 1998, CANADIAN MILITARY OFFICIALS MADE A DECISION TO vaccinate Canadian soldiers against anthrax, a deadly biological weapon, before deploying them to the Persian Gulf. One soldier who had served in the military for 26 years, Sergeant Michael Kipling, refused to be vaccinated. For his disobedience, Kipling was court-martialled.

During the court martial, several facts came to light. One was that the anthrax vaccine was not licensed for use in Canada and, therefore, Health Canada had recommended that the military seek informed consent from soldiers before administering the drug. Another fact was that the military's legal advisers had made a similar recommendation. Canada's highest military commanders decided to ignore the advice of Health Canada and of their own lawyers, however, and imposed the vaccine on soldiers without their consent.

What were the consequences of making this decision? One consequence is the continuing debate over whether the medical symptoms experienced by half of the 4500 Canadians involved in the Gulf War are the result of the anthrax vaccine. Louise Richard, for example, was a healthy, athletic military nurse when she left for the Persian Gulf in 1991. Now she is too ill to work. She suffers from fatigue, depression, memory loss, gastrointestinal problems, and excessive bleeding. She has also lost all of her hair and has started to lose her teeth. Military officials blame the medical symptoms experienced by Gulf War veterans on stress and possible exposure to chemical warfare. Military personnel such as Michael Kipling and Louise Richard believe that the anthrax vaccine is to blame.

Statistics Canada, with the cooperation of Canada's defence department, conducted a four-year study and concluded that Gulf War veterans do not suffer higher mortality and cancer rates than military personnel who were not deployed to Kuwait. These results, released on November 3, 2005, further angered Gulf War veterans, who accused the government of biasing the research to avoid paying millions of dollars in disability benefits. Critics pointed out that the study focused only on cancer rates, rather than on the range of symptoms, such as those experienced by Louise Richard, that have come to be known as Gulf War syndrome (Blanchfield, 2005).

There was yet another, very serious, consequence of this decision. According to Canada's chief military judge, Colonel Guy Brais, who presided over Michael Kipling's court martial, the military's decision to impose the vaccine violated the human rights of soldiers such as Kipling. In his decision, Judge Brais agreed with the defence that the vaccine Kipling had been ordered to take could have been unsafe, and that his common law and Charter rights were therefore violated. In his words, "The government . . . could never be justified

OUTLINE

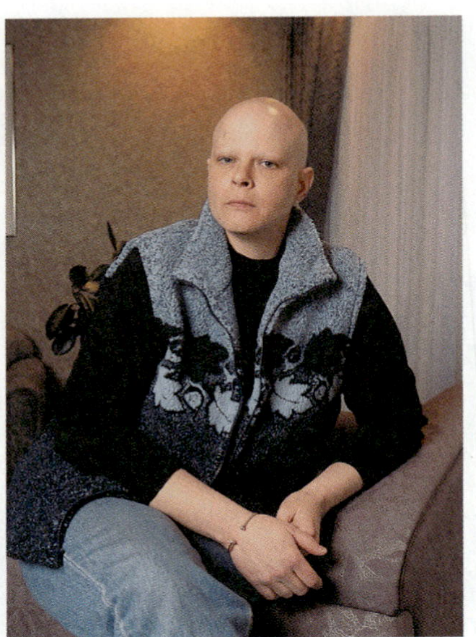

Louise Richard before and after her tour of duty in the 1991 Persian Gulf War. She believes that the anthrax vaccine is responsible for her mysterious illnesses.

to impose inoculation of soldiers with unsafe and dangerous vaccines" (Brais, as quoted in Edmonds, 2000).

Why would military officials ignore the advice of Health Canada and their own lawyers to impose a potentially unsafe vaccine on Canadian soldiers? Surely, Canada's top military commanders wouldn't be prepared to place Canadian soldiers at risk. And, surely, they wouldn't want to administer a possibly dangerous substance without obtaining informed consent from the soldiers. Or would they?

In this chapter, we will focus on how people interact in groups, and how groups can end up making decisions that have tragic consequences.

What Is a Group?

Group

A collection of three or more people who interact with one another and are interdependent, in the sense that their needs and goals cause them to rely on one another

A **group** is defined as a collection of three or more people who interact with one another and are interdependent, in the sense that their needs and goals cause them to rely on one another (Cartwright & Zander, 1968; Lewin, 1948). (Two people are generally considered to be a dyad rather than a group; Levine & Moreland, 2006). Groups, then, are more than a bunch of people who happen to be occupying the same space. Rather, groups are people who have assembled together for a common purpose, such as citizens meeting to solve a community problem, or people who have gathered to blow off steam at a party. Think for a moment about the number of groups to which you belong. Don't forget to include your family, campus groups, community groups (such as churches or synagogues), sports teams, and more temporary groups (such as your classmates in a small seminar). All of these count as groups because you interact with the other group members and you are interdependent, in the sense that you influence them and they influence you.

Why People Join Groups

Why do people join groups? Forming relationships with other people fulfills a number of basic human needs. So basic, in fact, that there may be an innate need to belong to social groups. Roy Baumeister and Mark Leary (1995) argue that in our evolutionary past, there was a substantial survival advantage to establishing bonds with other people. People who bonded together were better able to hunt and grow food, find mates, and care for children. Consequently, the need to belong has become innate and is present in all societies. Consistent with this view, people in all cultures are motivated to form relationships with other people and to resist the dissolution of these relationships (Gardner, Pickett, & Brewer, 2000; Manstead, 1997). Not surprisingly, perhaps, groups become an important part of our identity, helping us to define who we are (Dion, 2000; Tropp & Wright, 2001).

Research by James Cameron (1999) suggests that the groups to which we belong even play an important role in defining who we expect to be in the future. He asked students at Mount Allison University how much they agreed with statements such as "In a group of Mount Allison students, I really feel that I belong." Feeling a part of the university was associated with positive self-esteem and well-being. Moreover, students who had a sense of belonging also believed that being a Mount Allison student would help them become the self they aspired to be in the future.

Group membership also plays an important role in motivating people to become involved in social change. For example, Patrick O'Neill (2000) examined collective action among a variety of groups, including board members of a transition house for battered women in Nova Scotia, peace activists in Vancouver, and members of a lower-class Montreal neighbourhood protesting the establishment of a toxic waste dump in their community. Across groups, O'Neill found that those who identified most strongly with their group were most likely to engage in social action. As we discuss next, groups also help establish social norms, the explicit or implicit rules defining what is acceptable behaviour.

Groups have a number of benefits. Other people can be an important source of information. Groups are also an important part of our identity, helping us define who we are, and serve as a source of social norms, the explicit or implicit rules defining what is acceptable behaviour.

The Composition and Functions of Groups

The groups to which you belong probably vary in size from three or three members to several dozen members. Most social groups, however, range in size from three to six members (Desportes & Lemaine, 1998; Levine & Moreland, 1998). This is a result, in part, of our definition of social groups as involving interaction between members. If groups become too large, you cannot interact with all of the members. For example, the college or university you attend is not a social group, because you are unlikely to meet and interact with every student there.

Another important feature of groups is that the members tend to be alike in age, sex, beliefs, and opinions (George, 1990; Levine & Moreland, 1998; Magaro & Ashbrook, 1985). There are two reasons for the homogeneity of groups. First, many groups attract people who are already similar before they join (Feld, 1982). Second, groups operate in ways that encourage similarity in the members (Moreland, 1987). This can happen in a number of important ways, some of which we discussed in Chapter 7.

Social Norms As we saw in Chapter 7, *social norms* are a powerful determinant of our behaviour. If you belong to a political party, you can probably think of social norms present in your group, such as whether you participate in protest marches and how you are supposed to feel about rival political parties. These norms may not be shared by the members of other groups to which you belong, such as your mosque, church, or synagogue. Social norms are powerful determinants of human behaviour, as shown by what happens if people violate them too often: They are shunned by other group members and, in extreme cases, pressured to leave the group (Schachter, 1951; see Chapter 7).

Social Roles

Shared expectations by group members about how particular people in the group are supposed to behave

Social Roles Most groups also have well-defined **social roles**—which are shared expectations about how particular people are supposed to behave (Hare, 2003). Whereas norms specify how all group members should behave, roles specify how people who occupy certain positions in the group should behave. A boss and an employee in a business occupy different roles and are expected to act in different ways in that setting. Like social norms, roles can be very helpful, because people know what to expect from each other. When members of a group follow a set of clearly defined roles, they tend to be satisfied and perform well (Barley & Bechky, 1994; Bettencourt & Sheldon, 2001).

Connect to MyPsychLab

To access the Critical Thinking question on college student drinking, go to MyPsychLab

Watch on mypsychlab

Interview with Philip Zimbardo: The Stanford Prison Experiment

There are, however, potential costs to social roles. People can get so into a role that their personal identity and personality are lost. Suppose, for example, that you agreed to take part in a two-week psychology experiment in which you were randomly assigned to play the role of either a prison guard or a prisoner in a simulated prison. You might think that the role you were assigned to play would not be very important—after all, everyone knows it is only an experiment and that people are just pretending to be guards or prisoners. Philip Zimbardo and his colleagues, however, had a different hypothesis. They believed that social roles can be so powerful that they can take over our personal identities, and we become the role we are playing. To see if this is true, Zimbardo and colleagues conducted an unusual study. They converted rooms in the basement of the psychology department at Stanford University into a mock prison and paid students to play the role of either guard or prisoner (Haney, Banks, & Zimbardo, 1973). The role each student played was determined by the flip of a coin. The "guards" were outfitted with a uniform of khaki shirts and pants, a whistle, a police nightstick, and reflecting sunglasses; the "prisoners" were outfitted with a loose-fitting smock with an identification number stamped on it, rubber sandals, a cap made from a nylon stocking, and a locked chain attached to one ankle.

Watch on mypsychlab

The Stanford Prison Experiment

The researchers planned to observe the students for two weeks to see whether they began to act like real prison guards and prisoners. As it turned out, the students quickly assumed these roles—so much so that the researchers had to end the experiment after only six days. Many of the guards became quite abusive, thinking of creative ways to verbally harass and humiliate the prisoners. The prisoners became passive, helpless, and withdrawn. Some prisoners, in fact, became so anxious and depressed that they had to be released from the study earlier than others.

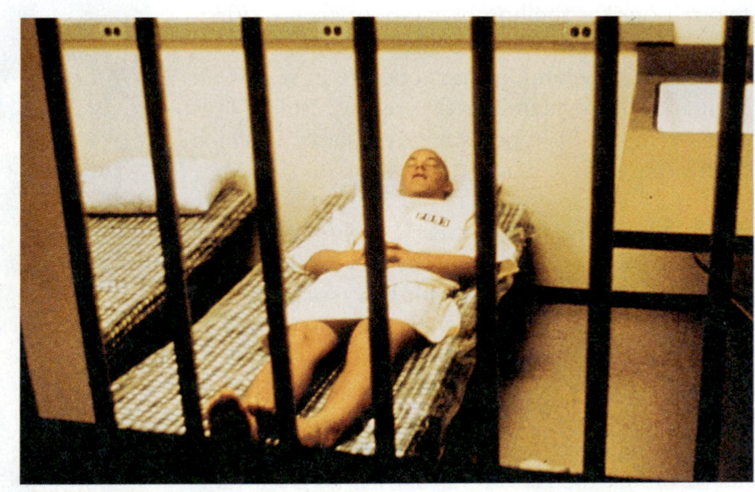

Philip Zimbardo and his colleagues randomly assigned students to play the role of prisoner or guard in a mock prison. The students assumed these roles all too well. Those playing the role of guard became quite aggressive, whereas those playing the role of prisoner became passive, helpless, and withdrawn. People got into their roles to the point to which their personal identities and sense of decency somehow were lost.

Remember, everyone knew that they were in a psychology experiment and that the "prison" was only make-believe. However, people embraced their roles to such an extent that their personal identities and sense of decency somehow were lost.

In Chapter 7, we referred to Philip Zimbardo's observation that many of the factors that contributed to the high levels of obedience in the classic Milgram study also were present in the recent abuse of Iraqi prisoners by American soldiers in Abu Ghraib prison. Zimbardo believes that the same psychological processes that operated in his mock prison, set up in a university basement more than 30 years ago, also were present in Abu Ghraib: the role of prison guard, the anonymity, and the dehumanization of the prisoners all contributed to the tragic loss of decency among the Americans in charge of the prison (Zimbardo, 2007). It was easy to dehumanize the prisoners, given that the guards didn't speak their language and that many of the prisoners were naked (because of a shortage of prison suits). "You start looking at these people as less than human," said one guard, "and you start doing thing to 'em that you would never dream of" (Zimbardo, 2007, p. 352).

Most groups have a number of well-defined social roles, which are shared expectations in a group about how particular people are supposed to behave. Roles can be very helpful, because people know what to expect from each other. However, people can get so far into a role that their personal identities and personalities get lost, sometimes with tragic consequences. Some people think that the abuse at the Abu Ghraib prison in Iraq was due to soldiers getting too far into their roles as prison guards.

This is not to say that the American soldiers should be excused for their actions. The abuse came to light when one of the guards reported what was going on, and as in Zimbardo's study, there were some guards who treated the prisoners well. Thus, not everyone was caught in the web of their social roles, unable to resist. But as much as we would like to think that we would be one of these heroes, the lesson learned from the Zimbardo study—and from Milgram's obedience studies (discussed in Chapter 7)—is that most of us would be unable to resist the social influences in these powerful situations, and perhaps would perform acts we thought we were incapable of performing.

Gender Roles Not all social roles involve such extreme behaviour, of course. Even in everyday life, however, roles can be problematic when they are arbitrary or unfair, such as societal expectations based on people's gender. All societies have expectations about how people who occupy the roles of women and men should behave. In many cultures, women are expected to assume the role of wife and mother, with only limited opportunities to pursue other careers. Even in countries such as Canada, in which women can pursue careers, the options remain limited by gender-role stereotyping. (We discuss this issue in greater detail in Chapter 12.) For example, Lupaschuk and Yewchuk (1998) asked children in grades 4 to 12 residing in a rural community in Alberta what their lives would be like if they woke up the next day and discovered they were the other sex. The results showed that the occupational aspirations of boys and girls are influenced by traditional gender-role expectations. For example, a male junior high student remarked that if he were a girl, "people would expect me to do women's work like clean house or be a secretary." The researchers concluded that women are still constrained by expectations that they will pursue traditional occupations, and that child care and housework remain their responsibility. More recent research confirms that women are still expected to pursue gender stereotypic occupations (Alksnis, Desmarais, & Curtis, 2008). To experience the pressure to conform to social roles first-hand, see the accompanying Try It! exercise.

Connect to MyPsychLab
To take a survey on how gender affects you, go to MyPsychLab

Watch on **mypsychlab**
Adults' Perceptions of Boys and Girls

This is not to say that role expectations haven't changed at all. In 1976, for example, 39 percent of women with children under the age of 16 were part of the paid workforce; by 2004, this number had risen to 73 percent (Canada, 2005f), at which it remains according to 2009 Statistics Canada data. However, even in 2004, two-thirds of employed women were working in traditional female-dominated occupations (e.g., teaching, nursing, service, and clerical)—a number that hasn't changed much over the past decade (Canada, 2005f). This difference in roles translates into a difference in earnings. Lisa Stickney at Temple University, Pennsylvania and Alison Konrad at the University of Western Ontario (2007) analyzed data gathered by the International Social Survey Program and found that in 26 of the 28 countries surveyed (including

TRY IT! What Happens When You Violate a Role?

Pick a behaviour that is part of a gender role in your culture and deliberately violate it. For example, if you are male, you might decide to put on makeup or carry a purse to your next class. If you are female, you might decide to dress like a male for a formal occasion, by wearing a jacket and tie. Keep a journal describing how others react to you. More than likely, you will encounter a good deal of social disapproval, such as people staring at you or questioning your behaviour. For this reason, you want to avoid role violations that are too extreme.

The social pressure that is brought to bear on people who do not conform explains why it can be so difficult to break out of the roles to which we are assigned, even when those roles are arbitrary. Of course, there is safety in numbers; when enough people violate role expectations, others do not act nearly so negatively, and as a result, the roles begin to change. For example, it is now much more acceptable for men to wear earrings than it was 25 years ago. To illustrate this safety in numbers, enlist the help of several same-sex friends and violate the same role expectation together. Again, note carefully how people react to you. Did you encounter more or less social disapproval in the group than you did as an individual?

Canada), women still earn significantly less than men. In Canada, women make up 70 percent of part-time workers and 60 percent of minimum-wage earners. These low-paying jobs tend not to come with benefits (e.g., a pension) or job security (Statistics Canada, 2009). Even women who are in full-time employment are disadvantaged financially. According to Statistics Canada, the average woman who works full time makes 71.4 cents for every dollar earned by a man who works similar hours (Statistics Canada, 2009). Moreover, women are still expected to maintain the traditional role of child-rearer and household manager. Conflict results, because women are expected to "do it all"—maintain a career, raise the children, clean the house, and attend to their husband's needs (Brislin, 1993; Eagly & Diekman, 2003). Not surprisingly, many women who work long days and have children at home report feeling time-stressed (Statistics Canada, 2006).

Women's growth in the workforce has necessitated a change in men's roles, as well. According to the Statistics Canada Converging Family Roles survey, in 1986, 54 percent of men reported carrying out household duties. By 2006, this number had risen to 69 percent. (In comparison, 90 percent of women reported steadily performing household duties over that period.) The number of hours per day that men spent on household tasks also increased, rising from 1.8 hours to 2.2 hours (Sanders, 2006). However, women in Canada still spend an average of two hours more per day than men do on household chores, child care, and the like (Statistics Canada, 2008). For example, a recent large-scale survey found that women in Canada spend about 4.2 hours per day doing domestic work compared to 2.5 hours for men (Abma, 2011). Research also shows that the more the husbands engage in household chores and errands, the better their wives' emotional health (Harris, 2008). Some reports even claim that when a husband does chores, the couple's sex life gets a boost! An Edmonton mother can vouch for the positive effects of a husband doing chores: "Just the fact that he would do something to ease the load is a huge turn-on," she says—far greater than the effects of receiving flowers or other gifts (Harris, 2008).

Group Cohesiveness
Qualities of a group that bind members together and promote liking among them

Group Cohesiveness Another important aspect of group composition is how tightly knit the group is. **Group cohesiveness** is defined as qualities of a group that bind members together and promote liking among them (Dion, 2000; Hogg, 1993; Holtz, 2004). If a group has formed primarily for social reasons, such as a group of friends who like to go to the movies together on weekends, then the more cohesive the group is, the better. This is pretty obvious; would you rather spend your free time with a bunch of people who don't care for one another or with a tightly knit bunch of people who feel committed to one another? As might be expected, the more cohesive a group is, the more its members are likely to stay in the group, take part in group activities, and try to recruit like-minded members (Levine & Moreland, 1998; Pickett, Silver, & Brewer, 2002; Sprink & Carron, 1994). One drawback of group cohesiveness, however, is that the group members' concern with maintaining good relations can get in the way of finding good solutions to problems. We will return to this issue later in the chapter, when we discuss group decision making.

How Groups Influence the Behaviour of Individuals

Do you act differently when other people are around? Simply being in the presence of other people can have a variety of effects on your behaviour. We will begin by looking at how a group affects your performance on something with which you are very familiar: taking a test in a class.

Social Facilitation: When the Presence of Others Energizes Us

It is time for the final exam in your psychology class. You have spent countless hours studying the material, and you feel ready. When you arrive, you see that the exam is scheduled in a tiny, packed room. You squeeze into an empty desk, elbow to elbow with your classmates. The professor arrives and says that if any students are bothered by the close quarters, they can take the test by themselves in one of several smaller rooms down the hall. What should you do?

The question is whether the mere presence of others will affect your performance (Geen, 1989; Guerin, 1993; Kent, 1994; Sanna, 1992). The presence of other people can mean one of two things: (1) performing a task with others who are doing the same thing you are, or (2) performing a task in front of an audience that is not doing anything except observing you. Note that the question is a basic one about the mere presence of other people, even if they are not part of a group that is interacting. Does their presence make a difference?

To answer this question, we need to talk about insects—cockroaches, in fact. Believe it or not, a classic study using cockroaches as research participants suggests an answer to the question of how you should take your psychology test. Robert Zajonc and colleagues built a contraption to see how cockroaches' behaviour was influenced by the presence of their peers (Zajonc, Heingartner, & Herman, 1969). The researchers placed a bright light (which cockroaches dislike) at the end of a runway and timed how long it took a roach to escape the light by running to the other end, where it could scurry into a darkened box (see the left side of Figure 8.1). The question was "Did roaches perform this simple feat faster when they were by themselves or when they were in the presence of other cockroaches?" You might be wondering how the researchers managed to persuade other cockroaches to be spectators. They did so by placing extra roaches in clear plastic boxes next to the runway. These roaches were in the bleachers, so to speak, observing the solitary cockroach do its thing (see Figure 8.1). It turned out that the individual cockroaches performed the task faster when they were in the presence of other roaches than when they were by themselves.

Now, we would not give advice on how you should take your psychology test based on one study that used cockroaches. But the story does not end here. There have been dozens of studies on the effects of the mere presence of others, involving human beings as well as other species such as ants and birds (e.g., Aiello & Douthitt, 2001;

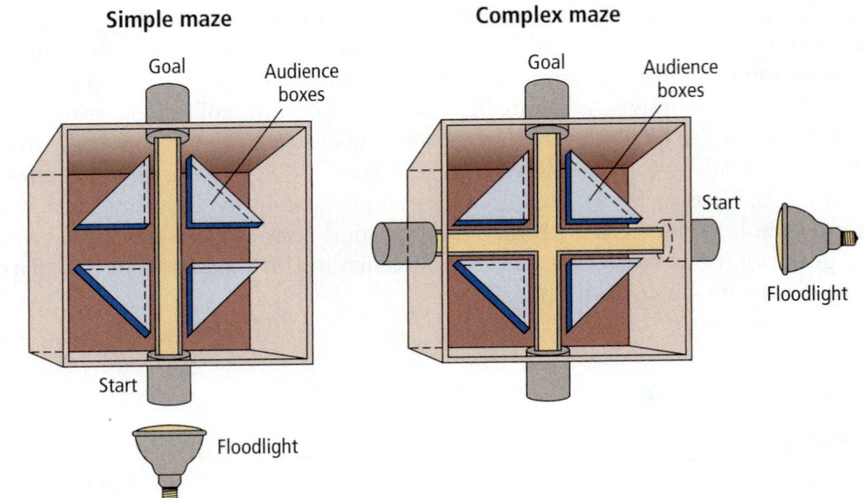

FIGURE 8.1

Cockroaches and social facilitation.

In the maze on the left, cockroaches had a simple task: to go from the starting point down the runway to the darkened box. They performed this feat faster when other roaches were watching than when they were alone. In the maze on the right, the cockroaches had a more difficult task. It took them longer to solve this maze when other roaches were watching than when they were alone.

(Adapted from Zajonc, Heingartner, & Herman, 1969)

Mere social contact begets . . . a stimulation of the animal spirit that heightens the efficiency of each individual workman.

—Karl Marx, *Das Kapital, 1867*

Rajecki, Kidd, & Ivins, 1976; Thomas, Skitka, Christen, & Jungena, 2002; Zajonc & Sales, 1966). There is a remarkable consistency to the findings of these studies. As long as the task is relatively simple and well learned—as escaping a light is for cockroaches—the mere presence of others improves performance. In one of the first social psychology experiments ever done, Norman Triplett (1898) asked children to wind up fishing line on a reel, either by themselves or in the presence of other children. They did so faster when in the presence of other children.

Simple versus Difficult Tasks Before concluding that you should stay in the crowded classroom to take your exam, we need to consider another set of findings. Remember that we said the presence of others enhances performance on simple well-learned tasks. Escaping a light is old hat for a cockroach, and winding fishing line on a reel is not difficult, even for a child. What happens when the task is more difficult and done in the presence of others? To find out, Zajonc and colleagues (1969) included another condition in the cockroach experiment. This time, the cockroaches had to solve a maze that had several runways, only one of which led to the darkened box (see the right side of Figure 8.1). When working on this more difficult task, the opposite pattern of results occurred. The roaches took longer to solve it when other roaches were present than when they were alone. Many other studies have also found that people and animals do worse in the presence of others when the task is difficult (e.g., Bond & Titus, 1983; Geen, 1989).

Arousal and the Dominant Response In an influential article published in 1965, Robert Zajonc offered an elegant theoretical explanation for why the presence of others facilitates a well-learned or dominant response but inhibits a less practised or new response. His argument has two steps: First, the presence of others increases physiological arousal (i.e., our bodies become more energized). Second, when such arousal exists, it is easier to do something that is simple (called the *dominant response*) but more difficult to do something complex or learn something new. Consider, for example, something that is second nature to you, such as riding a bicycle or writing your name. Arousal, caused by the presence of other people watching you, should make it even easier to perform these well-learned behaviours. But let's say you have to do something more complex, such as learning a new sport or working on a difficult math problem. Now arousal will lead you to feel flustered and not do as well as if you were alone (Schmitt, Gilovich, Goore, & Joseph, 1986). This phenomenon is known as **social facilitation**—the tendency for people to do better on simple tasks, but worse on complex tasks, when they are in the presence of others and their individual performance can be evaluated.

Social Facilitation

The tendency for people to do better on simple tasks, but worse on complex tasks, when they are in the presence of others and their individual performance can be evaluated

Simulate on **mypsychlab**
Social Facilitation

Research on social facilitation finds that people do better on a well-learned task when in the presence of others than when they are alone. If students have studied hard and know the material well, they might be better off taking an exam in a room with many other people.

Suppose, for example, that you decide to stop at a local pool hall and shoot a few racks. Will you perform better or worse if people are watching you wield your pool cue? As we have seen, it should depend on whether shooting pool is a simple or complex task for you. This is what James Michaels and colleagues (1982) found in a field study conducted in the pool hall of a university student union. A team of four students observed several different players from a distance, until they found ones who were experienced (defined as those who made at least two-thirds of their shots) or novices (defined as those who made no more than one-third of their shots). They then casually approached the table and watched people play.

Imagine that you are one of the players. There you are, shooting pool, when suddenly you notice four strangers standing around watching you. What will happen to your performance? The prediction made by social facilitation theory is clear. If you have played so much pool that you would feel comfortable challenging Minnesota Fats, the arousal caused by the presence of others should improve your game. If you are a novice and feel as if you are all thumbs, the arousal caused by the presence of others should make your game go to pieces. This is exactly what was found. The novices made significantly fewer of their shots when they were observed, whereas the experts made significantly more of their shots (Michaels, Blommel, Brocato, Linkous, & Rowe, 1982).

Why the Presence of Others Causes Arousal Why does the presence of others lead to arousal? Researchers have developed three theories to explain the role of arousal in social facilitation:

1. Other people cause us to become particularly alert and vigilant.
2. They make us apprehensive about how we're being evaluated.
3. And they distract us from the task at hand.

The first explanation suggests that the presence of other people makes us more alert. When we are by ourselves reading a book, we don't have to pay attention to anything but the book; we don't have to worry that the lamp will ask us a question. When someone else is in the room, however, we have to be alert to the possibility that he or she will do something that requires us to respond. Because people are less predictable than lamps, we are in a state of greater alertness in their presence. This alertness, or vigilance, causes mild arousal. The beauty of this explanation—the one preferred by Robert Zajonc (1980)—is that it explains both the animal and the human studies. A solitary cockroach need not worry about what the cockroach in the next room is doing.

However, it needs to be alert when in the presence of another member of its species—and the same goes for human beings.

The second explanation focuses on the fact that people are not cockroaches and are frequently concerned about how other people are evaluating them. When other people can see how you are doing, the stakes are raised. You feel as if the other people are evaluating you, and you will feel embarrassed if you do poorly and pleased if you do well. This concern about being judged, called *evaluation apprehension*, can cause mild arousal. According to this view, then, it is not the mere presence of others but the presence of others who are evaluating us that causes arousal and subsequent social facilitation (Blascovich, Mendes, Hunter, & Salomon, 1999; Bond, Atoum, & VanLeeuwen, 1996; Muller & Butera, 2007).

The third explanation centres on how distracting other people can be (Baron, 1986; Huguet et al., 1999; Muller, Atzeni, & Fabrizio, 2004). It is similar to Robert Zajonc's (1980) notion that we need to be alert when in the presence of others, except that it focuses on the idea that *any* source of distraction—be it the presence of other people or noise from the party going on in the apartment upstairs—will put us in a state of conflict, because it is difficult to concentrate on what we are doing. Trying to pay attention to two things at once produces arousal, as anyone knows who has ever tried to read the newspaper while a two-year-old clamours for attention. Consistent with this interpretation, there is evidence that nonsocial sources of distraction, such as a flashing light, cause the same kinds of social facilitation effects as does the presence of other people (Baron, 1986).

We have summarized research on social facilitation in the upper half of Figure 8.2. (We will discuss the lower half in a moment.) This figure illustrates that there is more than one reason that the presence of other people is arousing. The consequences of this arousal, however, are the same. When an individual is around other people, that individual does better on tasks that are simple and well learned, but worse on tasks that are complex and require them to learn something new.

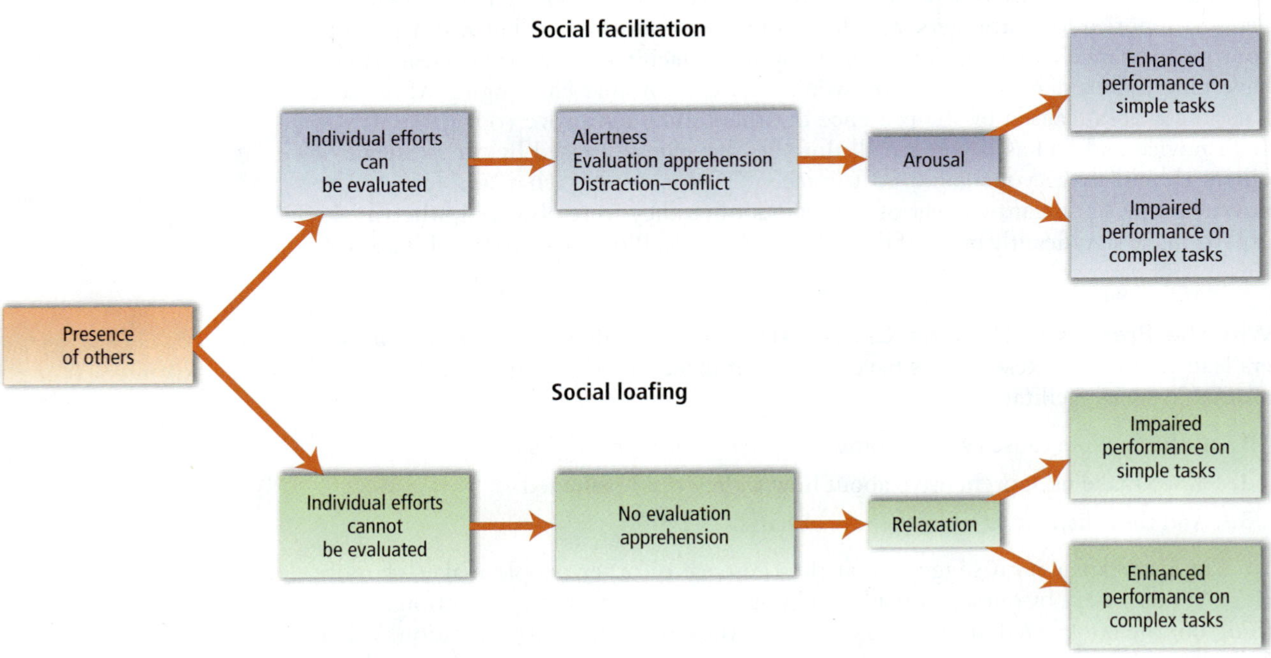

FIGURE 8.2

Social facilitation and social loafing.

The presence of others can lead to social facilitation or social loafing. The important variables that distinguish the two are evaluation, arousal, and the complexity of the task.

(Adapted from Cottrell et al., 1968)

Where, then, should you take your psychology exam? We can now recommend that you should take your exam in the presence of your classmates, assuming you know the material well, so that it is relatively simple for you to recall it. The arousal produced by being elbow to elbow with your classmates should improve your performance. We can also conclude, however, that when you study for an exam—that is, when you learn new material—you should do so by yourself and not in the presence of others. In this situation, the arousal caused by others will make it more difficult to concentrate.

Finally, we end by noting that it is not only the presence of real people who can influence our behaviour—so can the presence of our favourite TV characters as well. In a recent study, university students performed a simple or complex task while a picture of their favourite TV character or some other TV character was displayed on a computer screen. When the TV character was a favourite—such as George from *Grey's Anatomy*—it was as if a real person was in the room: People did better on the simple task but worse on the complex task. When the TV character wasn't a favourite, their performance was unaffected (Gardner & Knowles, 2008).

Social Loafing: When the Presence of Others Relaxes Us

When you take your psychology exam, your individual efforts will be evaluated; that is, you will be graded on the test. This is typical of the research on social facilitation we have reviewed. People are working on something—either alone or in the presence of others—and their individual efforts are easily observed and evaluated. Often when you are in the presence of others, however, your efforts cannot be distinguished from those of the people around you. Such is the case when you clap after a concert (i.e., no one can tell how loudly you are clapping) or when you play an instrument in a band (i.e., your instrument blends in with all the others).

These situations are just the opposite of the kinds of social facilitation settings we have just considered. In social facilitation, the presence of others puts the spotlight on you, making you aroused. However, if being with other people means we can merge into a group, becoming less noticeable than when we are alone, we should become relaxed. Will this relaxation produced by becoming lost in the crowd lead to better or worse performance? Once again, the answer depends on whether we are working on a simple or a complex task.

Let's first consider simple tasks, such as trying to pull as hard as you can on a rope. The question of how working with others would influence performance on such a task was first studied in the 1880s by the French agricultural engineer Max Ringelmann (1913). He found that when a group of men pulled on a rope, each individual exerted less effort than when he did it alone. A century later, social psychologists Bibb Latané, Kipling Williams, and Stephen Harkins (1979) called this **social loafing**, which is the tendency for people to do worse on simple tasks, but better on complex tasks, when they are in the presence of others and their individual performance cannot be evaluated. Social loafing in groups has since been found for a variety of simple tasks, such as clapping your hands, cheering loudly, and thinking of as many uses for an object as you can (Karau & Williams, 2001; Shepperd & Taylor, 1999).

Social Loafing
The tendency for people to do worse on simple tasks, but better on complex tasks, when they are in the presence of others and their individual performance cannot be evaluated

What about complex tasks? Recall that when our performance in a group cannot be identified, we become more relaxed. Recall also our earlier discussion of the effects of arousal on performance: Arousal enhances performance on simple tasks but impairs performance on complex tasks. By the same reasoning, becoming relaxed impairs performance on simple tasks—as we have just seen—but improves performance on complex tasks (Jackson & Williams, 1985). The idea is that when people are not worried about being evaluated, they should be less likely to tense up on a difficult task and therefore do it better as a result. This process is illustrated in the lower half of Figure 8.2.

Research conducted at Queen's University suggests that similar processes may affect the quality of ideas generated by a group. One problem with the use of techniques

Which of us . . . is to do the hard and dirty work for the rest—and for what pay?

—John Ruskin *(1819–1900)*

such as brainstorming is that people worry that others may evaluate their ideas negatively—even though the point of brainstorming is to express whatever ideas come to mind without fear of criticism. Cooper and colleagues proposed that computers might provide an important vehicle for improving the quality of a group's ideas—computers allow for interaction between people, yet participants can remain anonymous, thereby reducing their evaluation apprehension (Cooper, Gallupe, Pollard, & Cadsby, 1998). Indeed, the researchers found that participants in anonymous electronic groups found it easier to generate ideas and reported lower evaluation apprehension than did those in non-anonymous (i.e., electronic or in-person) discussion groups. Participants in anonymous electronic discussion groups also generated the greatest number of controversial ideas. This is supposed to be one of the benefits of brainstorming. However, there was an unexpected twist to these findings—it turned out that the kind of controversy generated under these conditions was not very desirable. In fact, some of the ideas generated by the anonymous electronic groups were highly offensive. For the discussion topic "How to reduce the spread of AIDS," for example, participants generated ideas such as "Burn AIDS carriers at the stake like witches" and "Set a trap encouraging gays to come out of the closet and then eliminate them." The researchers observed that if one group member generated an inappropriate idea, it could set off a vicious cycle of group members attempting to outdo one another. Those who were offended by these responses simply stopped contributing ideas. Cooper and colleagues concluded that the use of computers can have benefits such as allowing for interaction while preserving anonymity, thereby lowering evaluation apprehension, but that safeguards may be necessary to ensure that the generation of controversial ideas does not spiral out of control.

Gender and Cultural Differences in Social Loafing: Who Slacks Off the Most? Jane and John are working with several classmates on a class project, and no one can assess their individual contributions. Who is more likely to slack off and let the others do most of the work—John or Jane? If you said John, you are probably right. Karau and Williams (1993) reviewed more than 150 studies of social loafing and found that the tendency to loaf is stronger in men than in women. Why? As discussed in Chapter 5, women tend to be higher than men in *relational interdependence*, which is the tendency to focus on and care about personal relationships with others. Perhaps it is this focus that makes women less likely to engage in social loafing when in groups (Eagly, 1987; Wood, 1987).

Research also has found that the tendency to loaf is stronger in Western cultures than in Asian cultures, which may be due to the different self-definitions prevalent in these cultures (Karau & Williams, 1993). Asians are more likely to have an *interdependent view of the self*, which is a way of defining oneself in relation to other people (see Chapter 5). This self-definition may reduce the tendency toward social loafing when in groups. We should not, however, exaggerate these gender and cultural differences. Women and members of Asian cultures do engage in social loafing when in groups; they are just less likely to do so than men or members of Western cultures (Chang & Chen, 1995).

To summarize, you need to know two things to predict whether the presence of others will help or hinder your performance: whether your individual efforts can be evaluated and whether the task is simple or complex. If your performance can be evaluated, the presence of others will make you alert and aroused. This will lead to social facilitation effects, whereby people do better on simple tasks but worse on complex tasks (see upper half of Figure 8.2 on page 244). If your efforts cannot be evaluated (i.e., you are one cog in a machine), you are likely to become more relaxed. This leads to social loafing effects, whereby people do worse on simple tasks but better on complex tasks (see lower half of Figure 8.2).

These findings have numerous implications for the way in which groups should be organized. If you are a manager who wants your employees to work on a relatively simple problem, a little evaluation apprehension is not such a bad thing—it should improve performance. On the one hand, you shouldn't place your employees in groups in which their individual performance cannot be observed, because social loafing (lowered performance on simple tasks) is likely to result. On the other hand, if you want your employees to work on a difficult, complex task, then lowering their evaluation apprehension—by placing them in groups in which their individual performance cannot be observed—is likely to result in better performance.

Deindividuation: Getting Lost in the Crowd

So far, we have discussed the ways in which a group affects how hard people work and how successfully they learn new things. However, as was demonstrated by the Queen's University study on brainstorming in anonymous electronic discussion groups (Cooper et al., 1998), being in a group can also cause **deindividuation**, which is the loosening of normal constraints on behaviour, leading to an increase in impulsive and deviant acts (Lea, Spears, & de Groot, 2001). In other words, getting lost in a crowd—or hiding behind the anonymity of the Internet—can lead to an unleashing of behaviours that individuals would never dream of doing otherwise (Lee, 2004).

Deindividuation
The loosening of normal constraints on behaviour when people are in a group, leading to an increase in impulsive and deviant acts

Throughout history, there have been many examples of groups of people committing horrendous acts that no individual would do on his or her own. In Chapter 6, we discussed the chilling murder of a Somali teen by Canadian peacekeepers. In Chapter 7, we described the My Lai massacre during the Vietnam War, in which a group of American soldiers systematically murdered hundreds of defenceless women, children, and elderly men. We have also referred to the more recent abuse of Iraqi prisoners at the hands of American soldiers in Abu Ghraib prison. In Europe, mobs of soccer fans sometimes attack and bludgeon one another. Closer to home, male hockey fans report that the greater the number of male friends with whom they attend a game, the greater the probability that they will become involved in a fight, as shown by research conducted in Alberta (Russell & Arms, 1998). The United States also has a shameful history of white people lynching African-American people. Brian Mullen (1986) analyzed newspaper accounts of 60 lynchings committed in that country between 1899 and 1946, and discovered an interesting fact: The more people there were in the mob, the greater the savagery and viciousness with which they killed their victims. Mullen also found that people who participated in these lynchings often did so cloaked in the anonymity of white robes and hooded masks. Similarly, Robert Watson (1973) studied 24 cultures and found that warriors who hid their identity before going into battle—by using face and body paint—were significantly more likely to kill, torture, or mutilate captive prisoners than were warriors who did not hide their identities.

A chilling Canadian example of this phenomenon occurred on November 14, 1999, when 15-year-old Matti Baranovski and his friends were approached in a Toronto park by a group of youths looking for a fight. One of the youths wore ski goggles; another covered the lower half of his face with a blue bandana. Still others wore masks or balaclavas to disguise themselves. The youths approached Matti's friends, took their cigarettes, and searched their wallets for money. When Matti questioned what they were doing, they turned on him, viciously punching and kicking him in the head and body. The last kick in the face broke his neck. Matti died from these injuries. The trial for three of the accused finally ended in July 2003. Meir Mariani and William Cochrane were charged with manslaughter. Daniel Weitz, a Canadian-Israeli soldier, was acquitted. In trying to understand why such violence can occur, some analysts pointed to the fact that the attackers were in a group and that they were wearing disguises. As noted in one newspaper story, "Disguises tend to make those wearing them capable of far more terrible acts of violence than would normally occur" (Simmie, 1999, p. A3).

When people lose their identity in a group, they are more likely to commit impulsive and deviant acts. Matti Baranovski, a Toronto teen, was brutally beaten to death in November 1999 by a group of youths wearing balaclavas, masks, goggles, and other disguises. Here, his grieving mother lays a wreath on the casket at his funeral.

If you can keep your head when all about you are losing theirs . . .

—Rudyard Kipling, "If," 1909

Why Does Deindividuation Lead to Impulsive Acts? Exactly what is it about deindividuation that leads to impulsive—and often violent—acts? There are three factors. First, the presence of others, or the wearing of uniforms and disguises, makes people feel less accountable for their actions because it reduces the likelihood that any individual will be singled out and blamed (Diener, 1980; Prentice-Dunn & Rogers, 1989; Zimbardo, 1970). Second, the presence of others lowers self-awareness, thereby shifting people's attention away from their moral standards. As discussed in Chapter 5, it is difficult to focus inward on ourselves and outward on the world around us at the same time; consequently, at any given point, we vary as to how self-aware we are (Carver & Scheier, 1981; Duval & Wicklund, 1972). One consequence of focusing on ourselves is that we are reminded of our moral standards, making us less likely to behave in a deviant or antisocial manner (e.g., "I believe that hurting other people is wrong; I'm not going to throw a drink at this soccer fan—even if he is cheering for the 'wrong' team"). If we are focusing on our environment, however, self-awareness will be low and we will be more likely to forget our moral standards and act impulsively.

Finally, deindividuation also increases the extent to which people obey the group's norms, as shown in a meta analysis of more than 60 studies (Postmes & Spears 1998). When group members are together and deindividuated, they are more likely to act according to the group norms than other norms such as "It is wrong to hurt another human being." This latter explanation can account for why deindividuation does not always lead to aggressive or antisocial behaviour—it depends on what the norm of the group is. Imagine that you are at a raucous party at which everyone is dancing wildly to very loud music. To the extent that you feel deindividuated—it is dark, and you are dressed similarly to other people—you are more likely to join the group and let loose on the dance floor. If the group is angry and the norm is to act violently, then deindividuation will make people in the group act aggressively. Thus, it is the specific norm of the group that determines whether deindividuation will lead to positive or negative behaviours (Gergen, Gergen, & Barton, 1973; Johnson & Downing, 1979).

CONNECTIONS

Sports and Aggression: Does What You Wear Change Who You Are?

Most of us do not encounter lynch mobs, wars, and masked attackers on a day-to-day basis. It is not as uncommon, however, to be asked to wear uniforms that make us look like everyone else in the vicinity—a situation that might also make us feel less accountable for our actions and hence more aggressive. Does wearing a uniform, such as on a sports team, actually increase aggressiveness? A study by Rehm, Steinleitner, and Lilli (1987) indicates that it does. They randomly assigned fifth graders in German schools to various five-person teams, and then watched the teams play handball against each other. All of the members of one team wore orange shirts and all of the members of the other team wore their normal street clothes. The children who wore the orange shirts, and who were therefore harder to tell apart, played the game significantly more aggressively than did the easier-to-identify children who wore their everyday clothing.

Even the colour of a uniform can make a difference. Mark Frank and Thomas Gilovich (1988) noted that in virtually all cultures, the colour black is associated with evil and death. They examined penalty records and recorded the colour of uniforms worn by teams in the National Hockey League and the National Football League from 1970 to 1986. Interestingly, teams that wore black uniforms ranked near the top of their leagues in terms of penalties. Moreover, if a team switched to a non-black uniform, there was an immediate decrease in the number of penalties. These researchers also conducted an experiment in which participants played a game wearing either white or black uniforms. Those who wore black uniforms showed greater aggressiveness than did those who wore white uniforms.

In a hockey game in March 2004, Colorado Avalanche player Steve Moore suffered a broken neck and other injuries after being hit from behind by Todd Bertuzzi of the Vancouver Canucks. The National Hockey League fined the Canucks and suspended Bertuzzi; he was reinstated in August 2005, 17 months after the attack. He also pleaded guilty to assault in a Vancouver court and was given a sentence of one year's probation and community service. Moore has been unable to play again and has sued Bertuzzi and the Vancouver Canucks for more than $40 million in lost income and damages. The lawsuit is scheduled to go to court in the fall of 2012. The ill-fated game took place in Vancouver, which meant that Bertuzzi was wearing the dark-coloured uniform that Canucks players use during home games. Might Bertuzzi's assault have been less severe if the game had been played in Colorado, where he would have being wearing the "away" white uniform? Although we can't be sure, the research we have been discussing does raise the possibility that the colour of the uniform partly affected the attack.

Thus, something as seemingly superficial as whether we are wearing a uniform while playing our favourite sport—as well as the colour of that uniform—can affect our level of aggressiveness.

Group Decisions: Are Two (or More) Heads Better than One?

We have just discussed that the presence of other people influences individual behaviour in a number of interesting ways. We turn now to one of the major functions of groups: to make decisions. In the Canadian judicial system, many verdicts are determined by groups of individuals (juries) rather than single individuals (see the Social Psychology and the Law module for a discussion of jury decision making). The Supreme Court of Canada is made up of nine justices—not a solitary sage member of the judiciary. Similarly, governmental and corporate decisions are frequently made by groups of people who meet to discuss the issues, and all Canadian prime ministers have a cabinet and the Privy Council to advise them.

Is it true that two (or more) heads are better than one? Most of us assume that the answer to this question is yes. A lone individual may be subject to all sorts of whims and biases, whereas several people together can exchange ideas, catch each other's errors, and reach better decisions. We have all taken part in group decisions in which we listened to someone else and thought to ourselves, "Hmm, that's a really good point—I would never have thought of that." In general, groups will do better than individuals if people are motivated to search for the answer that is best for the entire group and not just for themselves (De Dreu, Nijstad, & van Knippenberg, 2008) and if they rely on the person with the most expertise (Davis & Harless, 1996). In fact, according to recent research, even the highest-performing individuals do better if they work in a group. In this study, students working in groups (ranging in size from three to five people) were given math problems to solve. Groups of three or more solved the problem in about six equations. In comparison, when the very top students in each group worked alone, on average, they solved the problem in 6.5 equations (Laughlin, Hatch, Silver, & Boh, 2006). In another recent study conducted at the University of Waterloo, participants were required to search for visual symbols on a computer screen. Participants who worked in pairs performed better than those who did the task alone. The reason was that pairs tended to divide up the screen, such that each person had to search only his or her "half" of the screen (Malcolmson, Reynolds, & Smilek,

2007). Sometimes, though, two heads are not better than one (Kerr & Tindale, 2004). Several factors, as we will see, can cause groups to actually make worse decisions than individuals.

Process Loss: When Group Interactions Inhibit Good Problem Solving

One problem is that a group will do well only if the most talented member can convince the others that he or she is right—which is not always easy, given that many of us bear a strong resemblance to mules when it comes to admitting that we are wrong (Henry, 1995; Laughlin, 1980; Maier & Solem, 1952). You undoubtedly know what it's like to try to convince a group to follow your idea, be faced with opposition and disbelief, and then have to sit there and watch the group make the wrong decision. This is called **process loss**, which is defined as any aspect of group interaction that inhibits good problem solving (Hurley & Allen, 2007; Steiner, 1972). Process loss can occur for a number of reasons. Groups might not try hard enough to find out who the most competent member is and instead rely on somebody who really doesn't know what he or she is talking about. The most competent member might find it difficult to disagree with everyone else in the group—recall our discussion of normative conformity pressures in Chapter 7. Other causes of process loss involve communication problems within the group—in some groups, people don't listen to one another; in others, one person is allowed to dominate the discussion while the others tune out (Sorkin, Hays, & West, 2001; Watson, Johnson, Kumar, & Critelli, 1998).

Process Loss

Any aspect of group interaction that inhibits good problem solving

Failure to Share Unique Information Another interesting example of process loss is the tendency for groups to focus on what its members already know in common, failing to discuss information that some members have but others do not (Geitemeier & Schulz-Hardt, 2003; Stasser & Titus, 1985). Consider a medical team trying to decide on the course of treatment of a person with abdominal pain. All members share some knowledge, such as the fact that the patient is a male in his fifties with a history of digestive problems. Some members of the team, however, know things that the other members do not. The doctor who first examined the patient in the emergency room may be the only one who knows that the patient had mussels for dinner that night, whereas one of the attending physicians may be the only one to have seen the results of a blood test showing that the patient has an abnormally high white blood cell count. Obviously, to make the most informed decision, the group needs to pool all the information and use it to decide on the best course of treatment.

Nor is the people's judgement always true: The most may err as grossly as the few.

—John Dryden, *Absalom and Achitophel*, 1682

As obvious as this is, there is a funny thing about groups: They tend to focus on the information they share and ignore unique information known only to one or a few members of the group. In one study, for example, participants met in groups of four to discuss which candidate for student body president was the most qualified (Stasser & Titus, 1985). In the shared information condition, each participant was given the same packet of information to read: data indicating that candidate A was the best choice for office. As seen in the upper row of Figure 8.3, all participants in this condition knew that candidate A had eight positive qualities and four negative qualities, making him superior to the other candidates. Not surprisingly, when this group met to discuss the candidates, almost all of the members chose candidate A.

In the unshared information condition, each participant received a different packet of information. As seen in the lower row of Figure 8.3, each person knew that candidate A had two positive qualities and four negative qualities. However, the two positive qualities cited in each person's packet were unique, different from those listed in other participants' packets. Everyone learned that candidate A had the same four negative qualities; thus, if the participants shared the information in their packets, they would learn that candidate A had a total of eight positive qualities and four negative qualities—just as people in the shared information condition knew. Most of the groups in the unshared

FIGURE 8.3

When people are in groups, do they share information that only they know?

Participants in a study met to discuss candidates for an election. In the shared information condition (upper row of figure), each person was given the same positive and negative facts about the candidates. Candidate A was clearly the superior candidate, and most groups preferred him. In the unshared information condition (lower row of figure), each person was given the same four negative facts about candidate A, as well as two unique positive facts. In discussion, these people focused on the information they all shared and failed to mention the unique information; these groups no longer saw candidate A as superior.

(Adapted from Stasser & Titus, 1985)

information condition never realized that candidate A had more good than bad qualities, because they focused on the information they shared rather than on the information they did not share. As a result, few of these groups chose candidate A.

Subsequent research has focused on ways to get groups to concentrate more on unshared information (Campbell & Stasser, 2006; Postmes, Spears, & Cihangir, 2001; Scholten, van Knippenberg, Nijstand, & De Dreu, 2007; Stasser & Birchmeier, 2003). One way of accomplishing this is to make sure that group discussions last long enough to get beyond what everybody already knows. Unshared information is more likely to be brought up later in the discussion (Fraidin, 2004; Larson Christenson, Franz, & Abbott, 1998; Larson, Foster-Fishman, & Franz, 1998). Another approach is to assign different group members to specific areas of expertise so they know that they alone are responsible for certain types of information. If only one doctor's job is to monitor the blood tests, he or she is more likely to bring up this information and other members are more likely to pay attention to it (Stasser, Stewart, & Wittenbaum, 1995; Stewart & Stasser, 1995).

This last lesson has been learned by many couples, who know to rely on each other's memories for different kinds of information. One member of a couple might be responsible for remembering social engagements, while the other might be responsible for remembering when to pay the bills (Wegner, Erber, & Raymond, 1991). The combined memory of two people that is more efficient than the memory of either individual is called **transactive memory** (Hollingshead, 2001; Wegner, 1995). By learning to specialize their memories and knowing what their partner is responsible for, couples often do quite well in remembering important information. The same can be true of groups of strangers, if they develop a system whereby different people are remembering different parts of a task (Ellis, Porter, & Wolverton, 2008; Lewis, Belliveau, Herndon, & Keller, 2007; Moreland, 1999; Moreland, Argote, & Krishnan, 1996). In sum, the tendency for groups to fail to share important information known to only some of the members can be overcome if people learn who is responsible for what kinds of information and take the time to discuss these unshared data (Stasser, 2000).

Transactive Memory

The combined memory of two people that is more efficient than the memory of either individual

Groupthink: Many Heads, One Mind A possible limitation of research on group problem solving is that most studies use people who have never met before and give them tasks that are unfamiliar and sometimes trivial. Would groups do better if their members were used to working with one another and if they were dealing with important, real-world problems? Our opening example of the Canadian military's decision to administer the anthrax vaccine suggests not. Let's see why.

Watch on mypsychlab
Bay of Pigs

Groupthink

A kind of thinking in which maintaining group cohesiveness and solidarity is more important than considering the facts in a realistic manner

Using real-world events, Irving Janis (1972, 1982) developed an influential theory of group decision making that he called **groupthink**—defined as a kind of thinking in which maintaining group cohesiveness and solidarity is more important than considering the facts in a realistic manner. According to Janis's theory, groupthink is most likely to occur when certain preconditions are met, such as when the group is highly cohesive, isolated from contrary opinions, and ruled by a directive leader who makes his or her wishes known. When these preconditions of groupthink are met, several symptoms appear (outlined in Figure 8.4). The group begins to feel it is invulnerable and can do no wrong. Group members do not voice contrary views (self-censorship) because they are afraid of ruining the high morale or *esprit de corps* of the group, or because they are afraid of being criticized by others. If anyone does voice a contrary viewpoint, the rest of the group is quick to criticize that person, pressuring him or her to conform to the majority view. The perilous state of groupthink causes people to reach an inferior decision (see right side of Figure 8.4). The group does not consider the full range of alternatives, does not develop contingency plans, and does not adequately consider the risks of its preferred choice.

The only sin which we never forgive in each other is difference of opinion.

—Ralph Waldo Emerson, *Society and Solitude, 1870*

Groupthink may well have been behind the decision of military leaders to go ahead with the anthrax vaccine despite the fact that Health Canada had not approved it and military lawyers had advised against it. Can you think of other major decisions that were plagued by groupthink? One example is of NASA launching the space shuttle *Challenger* in 1986, despite the objections of engineers who said that the freezing temperatures presented a severe danger to the rubber O-rings—the seals that eventually failed during the launch, causing the rocket to explode and kill all aboard. More recently, social

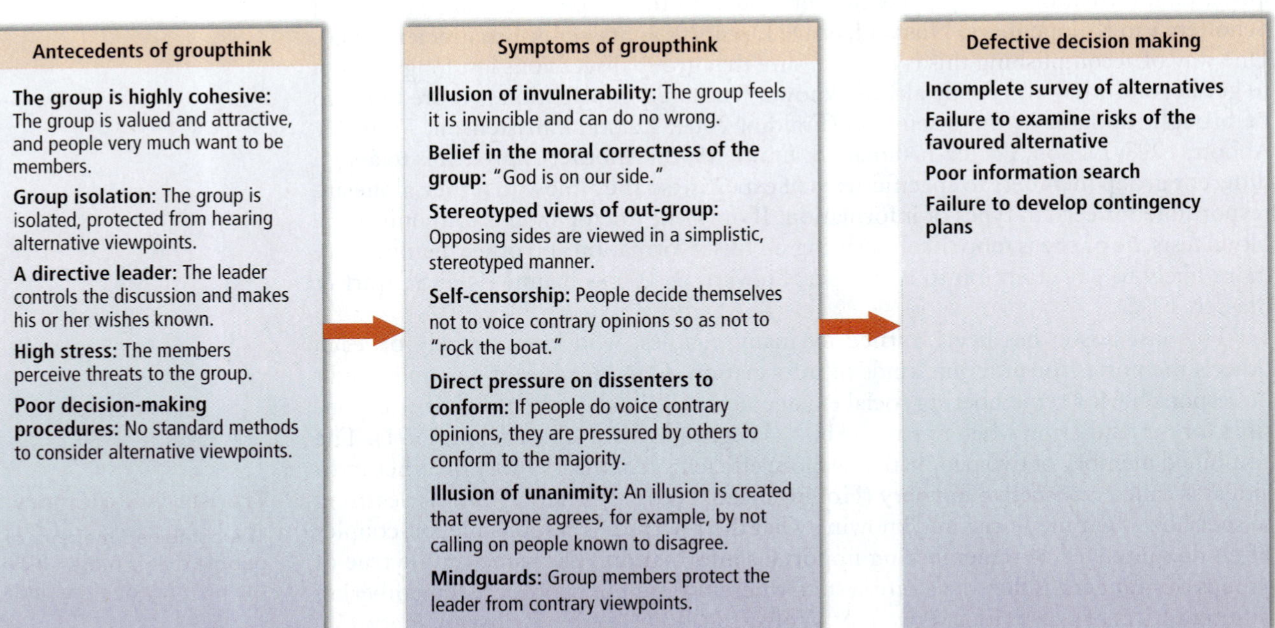

FIGURE 8.4
Groupthink: Antecedents, symptoms, and consequences.

Under some conditions, maintaining group cohesiveness and solidarity is more important to a group than considering the facts in a realistic manner (see antecedents in first panel). When this happens, certain symptoms of groupthink occur, such as the illusion of invulnerability (see symptoms in middle panel). These symptoms lead to defective decision making (see final panel).

(Adapted from Janis, 1982)

"All those in favor say 'Aye.'"
"Aye." *"Aye."* *"Aye."* *"Aye."* *"Aye."*

psychologists and political pundits have analyzed whether then U.S. president George W. Bush's decision to invade Iraq in 2003 was a product of groupthink. Although a definitive answer has not been reached, it appears that many of the symptoms of groupthink were present (Aronson, Wilson, & Akert, 2010).

Closer to home, in October 2005, Canadian newspapers trumpeted the release of Peter C. Newman's scathing portrayal of former prime minister Brian Mulroney, including how he handled the Meech Lake Accord in 1990 (Newman, 2005). In June of that year, Mulroney and the provincial premiers met behind closed doors for seven days to make a decision regarding constitutional reform. The conditions were ripe for groupthink. The politicians met in isolation—away from the media, their constituents, and their advisers. The meetings took place shortly before the Accord would have to be ratified, leaving little time to discuss alternatives. Mulroney was a persuasive, directive leader who managed to convince the premiers that the Meech Lake Accord was the answer to Canada's unity problems, and that failure to sign the accord would place the country in political and economic peril. His goal in these discussions was to ensure that dissenters conformed. This was the context of his infamous quip that one simply needed to know when to roll the dice and the Meech Lake Accord would be a done deal. The final decision was reached when the most prominent dissenter, the premier of Quebec, was absent. Under these conditions, the group reached consensus—a consensus that unravelled as soon as the prime minister and the premiers emerged from their cloistered environment and returned to Ottawa and the provinces. The Meech Lake Accord faced a sudden death when several provinces refused to endorse it.

Since Janis first proposed his theory, it has been put to the test by a number of researchers (Adlag & Fuller, 1993; Ahlfinger & Esser, 2001; Hodson & Sorrentino, 1997;

The decision to launch the space shuttle *Challenger*, which exploded because of defective O-ring seals, appears to have been the result of groupthink on the part of NASA officials, who disregarded engineers' concerns about the quality of the seals.

Hogg & Hains, 1998; Mohamed & Wiebe, 1996; Tetlock, Peterson, McGuire, Chang, & Field., 1992; Turner, Pratkanis, Probasco, & Leve, 2006; Turner, Pratkanis, & Struckman, 2007). The upshot, according to a recent review, is that defective decision making may be more common than the original theory assumed. Janis's theory held that a specific set of conditions had to be met for groupthink to occur, namely the antecedents listed on the left side of Figure 8.4 (e.g., the group has to be highly cohesive). It now appears that groupthink can occur even when some of these antecedents are missing. It may be enough for people to identify strongly with the group, have clear norms about what the group is supposed to do, and have low confidence that the group can solve the problem (Baron, 2005; Henningsen, Henningsen, Eden, & Cruz, 2006). It is thus all the more important that groups be aware of the potential for groupthink and take steps to avoid it.

Avoiding the Groupthink Trap A wise leader can take several steps to ensure that his or her group is immune to this style of decision making (Flowers, 1977; McCauley, 1989; Zimbardo & Andersen, 1993):

- **Remain impartial.** The leader should not take a directive role but should remain impartial.
- **Seek outside opinions.** The leader should invite outside opinions from people who are not members of the group and who are therefore less concerned with maintaining group cohesiveness.
- **Create subgroups.** The leader should divide the group into subgroups that first meet separately and then meet together to discuss their different recommendations.
- **Seek anonymous opinions.** The leader might also take a secret ballot or ask group members to write down their opinions anonymously; doing so would ensure that people give their true opinions, uncensored by a fear of recrimination from the group.

Group Polarization: Going to Extremes

Maybe you are willing to grant that groups sometimes make poor decisions. Surely, though, groups will usually make less-risky decisions than a lone individual will—one individual might be willing to bet the ranch on a risky proposition, but if others help make the decision, they will interject reason and moderation—or will they? The question of whether groups or individuals make more risky decisions has been examined in numerous studies. Participants are typically given the Choice Dilemmas Questionnaire, a series of stories that present a dilemma for the main character and ask the reader to choose how much probability of success there would have to be before the reader would recommend the risky alternative (Kogan & Wallach, 1964). People choose their answers alone and then meet in a group to discuss the options, arriving at a unanimous group decision for each dilemma.

Many of the initial studies found, surprisingly, that groups make riskier decisions than individuals do. An example of an item from a Choice Dilemmas Questionnaire about a chess player appears in the accompanying Try It! exercise. When deciding alone, participants said the chess player should make the risky gambit only if there were at least a 30 percent chance of success. But after discussing the problem with others in a group, people said the chess player should go for it, even if there were only a 10 percent chance of success (Wallach, Kogan, & Bem, 1962). Findings such as these became known as the *risky shift*. But further research made it clear that such shifts were not the full story. It turns out that groups tend to make decisions that are more extreme in the same direction as the individuals' initial predispositions, which, in the case of the chess problem, happened to be risky.

What would happen if people were initially inclined to be conservative? In such cases, groups tend to make even more conservative decisions than individuals do. Consider this problem: Domenic, a young married man with two children, has a secure but low-paying

Choice Dilemmas Questionnaire

You will need four or five friends to complete this exercise. First, copy the following questionnaire and give it to each of your friends to complete by themselves, without talking to one another. Do not tell anyone that he or she will be discussing the questionnaire with the others. Then bring everyone together and ask them to discuss the dilemma and arrive at a unanimous decision. They should try to reach consensus such that every member of the group agrees at least partially with the final decision. Finally, compare people's initial decisions (made alone) with the group decision. Who made the riskier decisions on average: people deciding by themselves or the group?

As discussed in the text, groups tend to make riskier decisions than individuals on problems such as these. Did you find the same thing? Why or why not? If the group did make a riskier decision, was it due more to the persuasive arguments interpretation discussed in the text, the social comparison interpretation, or both?

The Choice Dilemmas Questionnaire

A low-ranked participant in a national chess tournament, playing an early match against a highly favoured opponent, has the choice of attempting or not attempting a deceptive but risky manoeuvre that might lead to quick victory if it is successful or to almost certain defeat if it fails. Please indicate the lowest probability of success that you would accept before recommending that the chess player play the risky move.

_______ 1 chance in 10 of succeeding
_______ 3 chances in 10 of succeeding
_______ 5 chances in 10 of succeeding
_______ 7 chances in 10 of succeeding
_______ 9 chances in 10 of succeeding
_______ I would not recommend taking the chance.

(Adapted from Wallach, Kogan, & Bem, 1962)

job and no savings. Someone gives him a tip about a stock that will triple in value if the company's new product is successful but will plummet if the new product fails. Should Domenic sell his life insurance policy and invest in the company? Most people recommend a safe course of action here: Domenic should buy the stock only if the new product is certain to succeed. When they talk it over in a group, people become even more conservative, deciding that the new product would have to have a nearly 100 percent chance of success before they would recommend that Domenic buy stock in the company.

The tendency for groups to make decisions that are more extreme than the initial inclinations of the members—toward greater risk if the group members' initial tendency is to be risky and toward greater caution if the group members' initial tendency is to be cautious—is known as **group polarization** (Brown, 1965; Ohtsubo, Masuchi, & Nakanishi, 2002; Rodrigo & Ato, 2002; Teger & Pruitt, 1967). Group polarization occurs for two main reasons. According to the persuasive arguments interpretation, all individuals bring to the group a set of arguments—some of which other individuals have not considered—to support their initial recommendation. For example, one person might stress that cashing in the life insurance policy is an unfair risk to Domenic's children, should he die prematurely. Another person might not have considered this possibility; upon hearing it, she becomes more conservative as well. The result is that group members end up with a greater number of arguments in support of their position than they initially started out with. A series of studies supports this interpretation of group polarization (Burnstein & Sentis, 1981; Burnstein & Vinokur, 1977).

Group Polarization
The tendency for groups to make decisions that are more extreme than the initial inclinations of their members

According to the social comparison interpretation, when people discuss an issue in a group, they first check how everyone else feels. What does the group value—being risky or being cautious? To be liked, many people then take a position that is similar to everyone else's but a little more extreme. In this way, the individual supports the group's values and also presents himself or herself in a positive light—a person in the vanguard, an impressive thinker. This interpretation of group polarization has also received research support (Blaskovich, Ginsburg, & Veach, 1975; Brown, 1986; Isenberg, 1986; Zuber, Crott, & Werner, 1992).

Leadership in Groups

A critical question we have not considered yet is the role of the leader in group decision making. The question of what makes a great leader has long intrigued psychologists, historians, and political scientists (Bass, 1990, 1997; Chemers, 2000; Fiedler, 1967; Hogg, 2001; Hollander, 1985; Klenke, 1996; Simonton, 1987). One of the best-known answers to this question is the **great person theory**, which maintains that certain key personality traits make a person a good leader, regardless of the situation the leader faces. If the great person theory is true, we ought to be able to isolate the key aspects of personality that make someone a great leader. Is it a combination of intelligence, charisma, and courage? Is it better to be introverted or extroverted? Should we add a dollop of ruthlessness to the mix as well, as Niccolò Machiavelli suggested in 1513, in his famous treatise on leadership, *The Prince*? Or do highly moral people make the best leaders?

Great Person Theory

The theory that certain key personality traits make a person a good leader, regardless of the situation the leader faces

Leadership and Personality In the numerous studies that have been conducted, only weak relationships have been found between specific personal characteristics and leadership. Compared with nonleaders, leaders tend to be slightly more intelligent, more extroverted, more driven by the desire for power, more charismatic, more socially skilled, more adaptive and flexible, and more confident in their leadership abilities (Albright & Forziati, 1995; Chemers, Watson, & May, 2000; Judge, Bono, Ilies, & Gerhardt, 2002; Van Vugt, 2006). What is most telling, however, is the absence of strong relationships. Moreover, surprisingly few personality characteristics correlate with leadership effectiveness. Bradley and colleagues (2002) followed Canadian Forces officer candidates over a five-year period and found little relation between personality variables and leadership ability—only one trait emerged as particularly useful in predicting who would make a good leader, and that was dominance. Why might that be? The researchers suggest that "military operations are not the place for insecure people" (Bradley, Nicol, Charbonneau, & Meyer, 2002).

There is a modest but positive relationship between intelligence and leadership effectiveness (Simonton, 1985; Stogdill, 1974). Supreme Court Chief Justice Beverley McLachlin, pictured here, graduated with a gold medal from the University of Alberta and is described as having an "unquenchable intellectual curiosity."

University of British Columbia social psychologist Peter Suedfeld and his colleagues have identified another correlate of leadership effectiveness, namely *integrative complexity*—the ability to recognize more than one perspective on an issue and to be able to integrate these various perspectives (Ballard & Suedfeld, 1988; Suedfeld, Conway III, & Eichorn, 2001). These researchers have found substantial correlations between integrative complexity and greatness among Canadian prime ministers and other prominent leaders.

Simonton (1987, 2001) gathered information on 100 personal attributes of all U.S. presidents, such as their family backgrounds, educational experiences, occupations, and personalities. Only three of these variables—height, family size, and the number of books a president published before taking office—correlated with how effective the presidents were in office, as rated by historians. Presidents who were tall, came from small families, and had published many books were more likely to be great leaders. The other 97 characteristics, including personality traits, were not related to leadership effectiveness at all.

We should point out that different ways of analyzing these markers of presidential greatness can produce different results. Stewart McCann (1992) at the University College of Cape Breton analyzed the same data Simonton did, using slightly different statistical techniques. His conclusion was that personological factors do predict greatness—more so than Simonton's analysis would suggest. The variables that emerged as important in McCann's analysis were IQ, height, attractiveness, tidiness, and achievement drive. Specifically, great presidents tend to be smart, tall, not good-looking, messy, and achievement-oriented. However, even this list is rather short.

photo: Jean-Marc Carisse

The great charisma of Pierre Elliot Trudeau contributed to his rise as fifteenth prime minister of Canada in 1968. Trudeau was also the Canadian prime minister with the highest integrative complexity (Suedfeld, Conway III, & Eichorn, 2001). Overall, however, there is surprisingly little evidence that traits such as charisma, dominance, and self-confidence predict who will become an effective leader.

Leadership Styles Although great leaders may not have specific kinds of personalities, they do appear to adopt specific kinds of leadership styles. **Transactional leaders**, on the one hand, set clear, short-term goals and reward people who meet them. **Transformational leaders**, on the other hand, inspire followers to focus on common, long-term goals (Bass, 1998; Burns, 1978). Transactional leaders do a good job of making sure the needs of the organization are met and that things run smoothly. It is transformational leaders, however, who think outside the box, identify important long-term goals, and inspire their followers to toil hard to meet these goals.

Transactional Leaders
Leaders who set clear, short-term goals and reward people who meet them

Transformational Leaders
Leaders who inspire followers to focus on common, long-term goals

Most of the research has focused on transformational leaders. For example, Kara Arnold at Memorial University and colleagues have found that transformational leadership is associated with psychological well-being in samples of health-care workers, funeral directors, and dental hygienists (Arnold, Turner, Barling, Kelloway, & McKee, 2007). The results of a large-scale study conducted with Canadian military officers and their members showed that the members reported high job satisfaction and positive attitudes toward officers who were transformational leaders (Ivey & Kline, 2010). Transformational leadership also has positive effects in school settings. In a study of nearly 500 French Canadian school teachers, principals' transformational leadership and transactional leadership was positively correlated with teachers' confidence that they could do their job effectively (Dussault, Payette, & Leroux, 2008). Researchers at Université Laval found that transformational leadership on the part of principals, vice-principals, and teachers was associated with fostering community and civic engagement among students attending school in a low-income, multicultural neighbourhood in Quebec City (Bader, Horman, & Lapointe, 2010).

Interestingly, these leadership styles are not closely linked with personality traits; it is not as if people are "born" to be one or the other type of leader (Judge, Colbert, & Ilies, 2004). This suggests that it should be possible to develop interventions to foster these kinds of leadership. In a recent study, Jane Mullen at Mount Allison University and Kevin Kelloway at St. Mary's University (2009) did just that. Managers from 21 health-care organizations in Eastern Canada were randomly assigned to transformational leadership training or to a control group that did not receive an intervention. Two kinds of transformational leadership interventions were designed. One was intended to foster general transformational leadership through lectures, discussion, and developing personalized plans for goal setting and goal attainment; the other was focused specifically on transformational leadership in the area of occupational safety. Managers in the latter group received the same training, except that the lectures, goal setting, and so on were specifically focused on the topic of leadership in the area of workplace safety. Employees supervised by these managers subsequently reported on the safety climate of the workplace, rate of injury, and so on. Although both kinds of leadership training had positive effects, when employees were asked specifically about the extent to which their manager promoted safety outcomes, the managers that had undergone the safety-specific transformational leadership training received the highest marks. The results suggest that leaders can be taught to adopt a transformational leadership style and that when a specific outcome such as occupational safety is desired, transformational leadership training that targets that specific area is most effective (Mullen & Kelloway, 2009).

Finally, we point out that transformational and transactional leadership styles are not mutually exclusive; in fact, the most effective leader is one who adopts both styles, as a meta analysis by Judge and Piccolo (2004) shows (see also Dussault et al., 2008, discussed earlier). If no one was minding the day-to-day operation of an organization, and people were not being rewarded for meeting short-term objectives, the organization would suffer. At the same time it is important to have a charismatic leader who inspires people to think about long-term objectives as well.

Leadership: The Right Person in the Right Situation As you know by now, one of the most important tenets of social psychology is that to understand social behaviour, it is not enough to consider personality traits alone. We must take the social situation into account as well. The inadequacy of the great person theory does not mean that personal characteristics are irrelevant to good leadership. Instead, being good social psychologists, we should consider both the nature of the leader and the situation in which the leading takes place. This view of leadership states that it is not enough to be a great person; you have to be the right person at the right time in the right situation. For example, the relationship between prime ministerial greatness and integrative complexity varies, depending on the situation. Generally, when people are under stress, their level of integrative complexity decreases—it is more difficult to see other points of view, integrate them, and come up with complex solutions when in crisis mode. Peter Suedfeld and his colleagues made the discovery that great leaders show just the opposite pattern: They increase in integrative complexity during a crisis and then return to their usual level of complexity afterward (Ballard & Suedfeld, 1988; Suedfeld, Conway III, & Eichorn, 2001). Although Pierre Trudeau had the highest integrative complexity among Canadian prime ministers, according to the work of Suedfeld and colleagues, consider the example of Lester B. Pearson, Canada's prime minister from 1963 to 1968. During the Suez invasion in 1956, when he was a minister in the federal government, he managed to negotiate an end to the fighting—an achievement that earned him the 1957 Nobel Peace Prize. Moreover, he came up with the idea of United Nations peacekeeping and was instrumental in bringing it to fruition. Interestingly, Pearson's integrative complexity—as coded from speeches he made during that time—increased during the Suez crisis and then returned to its usual (still high) level once the crisis had ended. Situational factors—in this case, a crisis situation—influenced how the qualities of a leader were manifest.

A comprehensive theory of leadership therefore needs to focus on characteristics of the leader, his or her followers, and the situation (Hollander, 1958; House, 1971; Laschinger, Finegan, & Wilk, 2011; Sternberg & Vroom, 2002). The best-known theory of this type is the **contingency theory of leadership** (Fiedler, 1967, 1978). According to Fiedler, there are two kinds of leaders: those who are task-oriented and those who are relationship-oriented. The **task-oriented leader** is concerned more with getting the job done than with the feelings of and relationships among the workers. The **relationship-oriented leader** is concerned primarily with the feelings of and relationships among the workers. Task-oriented leaders do well in *high control* work situations—situations in which the leader has excellent interpersonal relationships with subordinates, his or her position in the company is clearly perceived as powerful, and the work to be done by the group is structured and well defined. They also do well in *low control* work situations—situations in which the leader has poor relationships with subordinates and the work to be done is not clearly defined. When situational control is very high, people are happy, everything is running smoothly, and there is no need to worry about people's feelings and relationships. The leader who pays attention only to the task will get the most accomplished. When situational control is very low, the task-oriented leader is best at taking charge and imposing some order on a confusing, ill-defined work environment. Relationship-oriented leaders, however, are most effective in situations that are *moderate control* work situations. Under these conditions, the wheels are turning fairly smoothly but some attention to the squeakiness caused by poor relationships and hurt feelings is needed. The leader who can soothe such feelings will be most successful (see Figure 8.5).

Contingency Theory of Leadership

The theory that leadership effectiveness depends both on how task-oriented or relationship-oriented the leader is, and on the amount of control and influence the leader has over the group

Task-Oriented Leader

A leader who is concerned more with getting the job done than with the feelings of and relationships among the workers

Relationship-Oriented Leader

A leader who is concerned primarily with the feelings of and relationships among the workers

The contingency theory of leadership has been supported in studies of numerous types of leaders, including business managers, college administrators, military

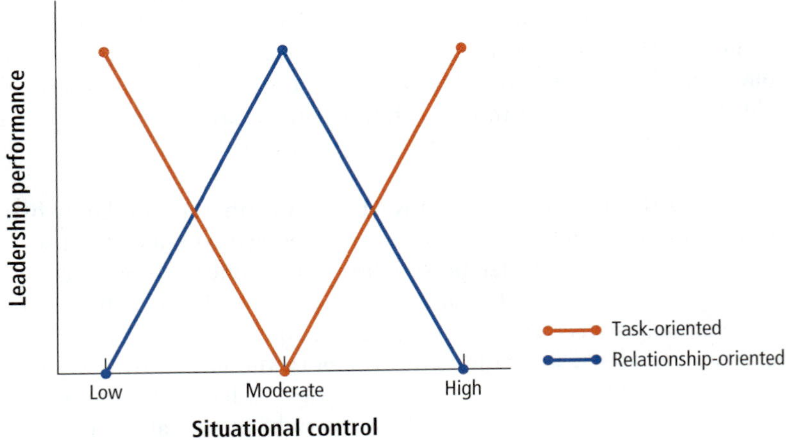

FIGURE 8.5

Fiedler's contingency theory of leadership

According to Fiedler, task-oriented leaders perform best when situational control is high or low, whereas relationship-oriented leaders perform best when situational control is moderate.

(Fiedler, 1967, 1978)

commanders, and postmasters (Chemers, 2000; Peters, Hartke, & Pohlmann, 1985; Schriesheim, Tepper, & Tetrault, 1994; Van Vugt & De Cremer, 1999).

> *Leadership cannot really be taught. It can only be learned.*
>
> —Harold Geneen, *1984*

Gender and Leadership An old adage says that because of sex discrimination, a woman has to be "twice as good as a man" to advance. No doubt barriers to advancement are breaking down, but they have by no means disappeared. In Canada, women make up 46.7 percent of the workforce (Canada, 2001) and 58 percent of all people who hold university degrees. (It may interest you to know that in psychology, 70 percent of the doctorates are awarded to women.) However, according to a survey conducted by the Canadian Association for University Teachers, women are still under-represented in academic positions, particularly at the senior level. For example, only 18 percent of full professors at Canadian universities are women (CAUT Bulletin, 2006). Similarly, only 19.5 percent of the chiefs leading the 615 First Nations of Canada are women (Voyageur, 2011). In the United States, only 12 of the CEOs of *Fortune 500* companies are women; more than 85 percent of the boards of directors of these companies are men, as are more than 84 percent of the corporate officers (Catalyst, 2008).

Watch on **mypsychlab**
Psychology of Gender: Alice Eagly

Alice Eagly and her colleagues have undertaken several reviews of the literature on gender and leadership (Carli & Eagly, 1999; Eagly & Karau, 2002; Eagly, Karau, & Makhijani, 1995; Eagly, Johannesen-Schmidt, & van Engen, 2003). The bad news is that there are two forms of prejudice against women. First, if women behave in the way they are "supposed" to behave according to societal norms—namely, in a *communal* fashion (i.e., concerned with the welfare of others, warm, helpful, kind, affectionate)—they are often perceived as having less leadership potential. This is because people typically expect successful leaders to be more *agentic* (i.e., assertive, controlling, dominant, independent, self-confident) than communal, especially in high-powered positions such as the head of a large corporation or the leader of a country. Second, once women become leaders, they are evaluated more negatively than men when they exhibit agentic leadership behaviour, again because these behaviours are contrary to how women are "supposed" to behave.

According to a recent review by Marie-Hélène Budworth at York University and Sara Mann at the University of Guelph (2010), women are expected to be modest and not draw attention to their accomplishments, which is another reason that they are less likely to be selected for leadership positions. Not only is it difficult for women to attain top leadership positions, but when they do, they are often put in precarious positions in which it is difficult to succeed. Michelle Ryan and her colleagues have identified what they call a "glass cliff" (Ryan, Haslam, Hersby, Kulich, & Atkins, 2008). Even when women have broken through the "glass ceiling" into top leadership positions, they are more likely than men to be put in charge of units that are in crisis and in which the risk of failure is high. Ryan and her colleagues found this to be true in studies of hiring in real-world companies, as well as in controlled laboratory studies in which people read descriptions of companies and recommended people for leadership positions. Participants were more likely to recommend a woman when an organizational unit was in crisis and a man when the unit was running smoothly, which makes it more likely that women will fail in their leadership positions.

One reason for the "glass cliff" is that women are perceived to be better at crisis management, particularly when there are interpersonal problems that need to be dealt with. As mentioned earlier, women are expected to be communal and men are expected to be agentic. But these expectations can have some pernicious effects in the way that women are evaluated (Biernat, Crandall, Young, Kobrynowicz, & Halpin, 1998). If a woman's style of leadership is stereotypically "masculine" (e.g., autocratic, "bossy," and task-oriented), she is evaluated more negatively than are men who have the same style (Budworth & Mann, 2010; Eagly & Carli, 2003; Eagly, Makhijani, & Klonsky, 1992). This is especially true if men are doing the evaluating (Butler & Geis, 1990).

However, even when women use a transformational leadership style—a style that is generally regarded as effective—they are evaluated negatively by their male subordinates as shown in a recent study conducted with male and female managers of industrial organizations and school vice-principals in Canada. Specifically, the researchers found

Research shows that women seeking leadership roles can find themselves in a double bind. If they conform to society's expectations about how they ought to behave by being warm and communal, they are often perceived to have low leadership potential. If they become leaders and act in ways that leaders are expected to act—namely, in agentic, forceful ways—they are often perceived negatively for not "acting as a woman should."

that the more women used this leadership style with male subordinates, the lower the performance rating they received from them (female subordinates, however, responded positively to a woman's transformational leadership). Male leaders' performance was rated as equally effective by both male and female subordinates—regardless of their levels of transformational leadership (Ayman, Korabik, & Morris, 2009).

Thus, there is a double bind for women. If they conform to societal expectations about how they ought to behave by being warm and communal, they are often perceived to have low leadership potential. If they succeed in attaining a leadership position and act in ways that leaders are expected to act—namely, in agentic, forceful ways, they are often perceived negatively for not acting as a woman "should." This double bind was vividly illustrated in the 2008 U.S. Democratic presidential race. Presidential candidate Hillary Clinton was frequently criticized for being cold and aloof. When she shed tears during a media interview in the midst of her gruelling campaign schedule, some commentators accused her of being too emotional and questioned whether she had what it took to be president of the United States. Others accused her of manufacturing the tears to combat her "ice queen" image. In commenting on this, Kim Campbell, who in 1993 served as Canada's only female prime minister, remarked that women in leadership are in a lose-lose situation. She put it this way, "Damned if you do, and damned if you don't" and went on to say that "It's a real risk for a woman to show emotion . . .. But if you don't, you'll be attacked for not caring enough" (Campbell, as quoted in Panetta, 2008).

The better news is that prejudice toward women leaders appears to be lessening. In a 1953 Gallup poll 63 percent of the people interviewed said that they preferred a man as a boss, 5 percent preferred a woman, and 25 percent had no preference. In a similar poll conducted in 2002, it was found that 32 percent preferred a man as a boss, 19 percent preferred a woman, and 49 percent stated that they had no preference (Eagly & Karau, 2002). Further, there is a growing recognition that effective leaders must be able to act in stereotypical female (communal) ways as well as stereotypical male (agentic) ways (Eagly & Karau, 2002). In the words of Kim Campbell, "Neither sex has a monopoly on these qualities. There are more differences within the sexes than between them . . .. You just have to let people do the job so that you begin to change your mind about . . . what a president of the United States looks like, and what a prime minister of Canada looks like" (Campbell, as quoted in Panetta, 2008).

I wonder men dare trust themselves with men.

—*William Shakespeare, Timon of Athens, 1600–1608*

Conflict and Cooperation

We have just examined how people work together to make decisions; in these situations, group members have a common goal. Often, however, people have incompatible goals, placing them in conflict. This can be true of two individuals such as romantic partners who disagree about who should clean the kitchen, or two groups, such as a labour union and company management, who disagree over wages and working conditions. It can also be true of two nations, as in the case of the long-standing conflict between Israel and its Arab neighbours, or between peoples, as with the Shiites, Sunnis, and Kurds in Iraq. The opportunity for interpersonal conflict exists whenever two or more people interact. Sigmund Freud (1930) went so far as to argue that conflict is an inevitable by-product of civilization because the goals and needs of individuals often clash with the goals and needs of their fellow human beings. The nature of conflict and how it can be resolved has been the topic of a great deal of social psychological research (Cohen & Insko, 2008; Deutsch, 1973; Levine & Thompson, 1996; Pruitt, 1998; Thibaut & Kelley, 1959).

Many conflicts are resolved peacefully, with little rancour. Couples can sometimes find a way to resolve their differences in a mutually acceptable manner, and labour disputes are sometimes settled with a friendly handshake. All too often, however, conflict erupts into open hostility. People may resort to violence to resolve their differences, as the murder rate in our country attests. Warfare between nations remains an all-too-common solution to international disputes. In fact, when wars over the past five centuries are examined, the twentieth century ranks first in the severity of wars—defined as the number of deaths per war—and ranks second in their frequency (Levy & Morgan, 1984). Between 1972 and 1976, fewer than 2000 people were killed by terrorists. Unfortunately, this number has been increasing rapidly; between 2002 and 2006, the number exceeded 30 000 (Cohen & Insko, 2008). Obviously, it is of great importance to find ways of resolving conflicts peacefully.

Sometimes, people are able to resolve conflicts peacefully, such as a couple that has an amicable divorce. Other times conflicts escalate into rancour and violence. Social psychologists have performed experiments to test ways in which conflict resolution is most likely to occur.

Social Dilemmas

What is best for individuals is not always best for the group as a whole. Consider a recent publishing venture by the novelist Stephen King. He wrote two installments of a novel called *The Plant* and posted them on the Internet, asking his readers to pay US$1 per installment. The deal he offered was simple: If at least 75 percent of the people who downloaded the installments paid the fee, he would keep writing and posting new installments. If fewer than 75 percent of the people paid up, he would stop writing, and no one would get the rest of the novel. King devised a classic **social dilemma**, a conflict in which the most beneficial action for an individual, if chosen by most people, will have harmful effects on everyone (Weber, Kopelman, & Messick, 2004). It was to any individual's financial advantage to download King's novel free of charge and let other people pay. If too many people took this approach, however, everyone would lose, because King said he would stop writing the novel. At first, people acted for the good of all; more than 75 percent paid for the first installment. As with many social dilemmas, however, people eventually acted in their own self-interest, to the detriment of all. The number of people who paid for their later installments dropped below 75 percent, and King stopped posting new ones, saying on his website that the book was "on hiatus."

Social Dilemma

A conflict in which the most beneficial action for an individual, if chosen by most people, will have harmful effects on everyone

One of the most common ways of studying social dilemmas in the laboratory is with a game called the Prisoner's Dilemma. In this game, two people have to choose one of two options without knowing what the other person will choose. However, the number of points they win depends on the options chosen by both people. Suppose, for example, that you were playing the game with a friend. As shown in the accompanying Try It! exercise you have to choose option X or option Y without knowing which option your friend will choose. Your payoff—the amount of money you win or lose—depends on the choices of both you and your friend. For instance, if both you and your friend choose option X, you both win $3. If, however, you choose option Y and your friend chooses option X, you win $6 and your friend loses $6. Which option would you choose?

Many people begin by choosing Y. At worst, you will lose $1; at best, you will win the highest possible amount, $6. Choosing option X raises the possibility that both sides will win some money, but this is also a risky choice. If your partner chooses Y while you choose X, you stand to lose a great deal. Because people do not know how much they can trust their opponent, option Y frequently seems like the safest choice (Rapoport & Chammah, 1965). The rub is that both players will probably think this way, ensuring that both sides lose (see the lower right corner of the table in the Try It! exercise).

People's actions in these games seem to mirror many conflicts in everyday life. To find a solution that is desirable to both parties, people must trust each other. Often, they do not, and this lack of trust leads to an escalating series of competitive moves, so that in the end no one wins (Batson & Ahmad, 2001; Insko & Schopler, 1998; Kelley & Thibaut, 1978; Pruitt, 1998). Two countries locked in an arms race may feel that they cannot afford to disarm, out of fear that the other side will take advantage of their weakened position. The result is that both sides add furiously to their stockpile of weapons, neither side gaining superiority over the other and both spending money they could better use to solve domestic problems (Deutsch, 1973). Such an escalation

TRY IT! The Prisoner's Dilemma

	Your Options	
Your Friend's Options	Option X	Option Y
Option X	You win $3 Your friend wins $3	You win $6 Your friend loses $6
Option Y	You lose $6 Your friend wins $6	You lose $1 Your friend loses $1

Instructions: Play this version of the Prisoner's Dilemma game with a friend. First, show the table above to your friend and explain how the game works. On each trial of the game, you and your friend can choose option X or option Y, without knowing what the other will choose. You should each write your choice on a folded piece of paper, both of which are then opened at the same time. The dollar amounts in the table represent imaginary money that you and your friend win or lose on each trial. For example, if you choose option X on the first trial and your friend chooses option Y, you lose an imaginary $6 and your friend wins an imaginary $6. If both of you choose option Y, you both lose an imaginary $1. Play the game for 10 trials and keep track of how much "money" each of you wins or loses. Did you and your friend choose the cooperative option (option X) or the competitive option (option Y) more often? Why? Did a pattern of trust or mistrust develop over the course of the game?

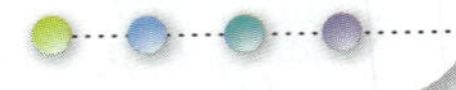

of conflict is also seen among couples who are divorcing. Sometimes, the goal seems to be to hurt the other person rather than to further one's own or the children's needs. In the end, both suffer because, metaphorically speaking, both partners choose option Y too often.

Increasing Cooperation in Social Dilemmas Such escalating conflict, though common, is not inevitable. Many studies have found that when people play a Prisoner's Dilemma game or engage in similar social dilemma tasks, they will under certain conditions adopt the more cooperative response, ensuring that both sides end up with a positive outcome. Not surprisingly, if people are playing the game with a friend or if they expect to interact with their partner in the future, they are more likely to adopt a cooperative strategy that maximizes both their own profits and those of their partner (Cohen & Insko, 2008; Pruitt & Kimmel, 1977). In addition, growing up in some societies, such as Asian cultures, seems to foster a more cooperative orientation than growing up in the West does (Bonta, 1997; Markus & Kitayama, 1991). In a recent study conducted with Chinese students in Hong Kong, it was found that showing symbols of Chinese culture before the game (e.g., a Chinese dragon) made people more cooperative, whereas showing them symbols of Western culture (e.g., an American flag) made them more competitive (Wong & Hong, 2005).

Another proven strategy is to allow individuals, rather than opposing groups, to resolve a conflict, because two individuals who play Prisoner's Dilemma are more likely to cooperate than two groups who play the same game (Schopler & Insko, 1999). The reason for this is that people are more likely to assume that another individual is cooperative at heart and can be trusted, but that most groups of individuals will, given the opportunity, stab us in the back. Greater trust of individuals than groups was confirmed in a recent study conducted with a sample of business students in Canada (Song, 2009).

Even playing social dilemma games with a small, rather than a large, group increases the chances of cooperation, as demonstrated in a study by Gerard Seijts at the University of Manitoba and Gary Latham at the University of Toronto (2000).

Participants in this study were told that they could invest money in either a personal account or a joint account. Any money placed in the joint account would be doubled and divided equally among the group members. This is a classic dilemma because you can make the most money if you put your money in a personal account and then benefit from the money others have put into the joint account. However, if everyone in the group adopts this strategy, it will not be very profitable. The greatest earnings result when the group adopts a cooperative strategy and everyone invests all of their money in the joint account. Seijts and Latham found that participants in three-person groups were more cooperative than participants in seven-person groups and, as a result, made more money. Members of seven-person groups were more likely to focus on maximizing their own gains rather than those of the group.

To increase cooperation, you can also try the **tit-for-tat strategy**—which is a way of encouraging cooperation by at first acting cooperatively but then always responding the way your opponent did (i.e., cooperatively or competitively) on the previous trial. This strategy communicates a willingness to cooperate as well as an unwillingness to sit back and be exploited if the other party does not cooperate. The tit-for-tat strategy is usually successful in getting the other person to respond with a cooperative, trusting response (Axelrod, 1984; Messick & Liebrand, 1995; Parks & Rumble, 2001; Sheldon, 1999; Van Lange, Ouwerkerk, & Tazelaar, 2002). The analogy to the arms race would be to match not only any military buildup made by an unfriendly nation but also any conciliatory gesture, such as a ban on nuclear testing.

Tit-for-Tat Strategy

A means of encouraging cooperation by at first acting cooperatively but then always responding the way your opponent did (i.e., cooperatively or competitively) on the previous trial

What about the strategy of cooperating consistently throughout? Wouldn't that work? J. Mark Weber at the University of Toronto and J. Keith Murnighan at Northwestern University (2008) recently explored whether consistent cooperators are "suckers or saviours" in social dilemma situations. In an impressive series of studies, they showed that consistent contributors (i.e., those who contribute to the group on each round) create a norm of cooperation in the group, with the result that each member of the group, including the consistent contributor, walks away with a greater payout than members of groups that do not contain a consistent contributor. The researchers also found that high-status consistent contributors (e.g., a Ph.D. student in a group with undergraduate students) encourage greater consistent contributing than low-status group members (e.g., a part-time secretary). However, even groups with a low-status consistent contributor end up with greater profits than groups without a consistent contributor. This provides definitive evidence that consistently modelling cooperative behaviour benefits everyone, including the consistent contributor who stands to lose the most by contributing every time (Weber & Murnighan, 2008).

In other research along these lines, Kiyonari and Barclay (2008) found that cooperators are evaluated more positively by the other group members than "free loaders" (i.e., those who benefit from the other group members' contributions, while failing to contribute themselves). They conducted a series of studies in which they gave group members the opportunity to punish (having money taken away) or reward (getting additional money) cooperators and freeloaders. Not surprisingly, freeloaders were more likely to be punished; cooperators were more likely to be rewarded. The researchers also examined how the group members who doled out rewards and punishments were perceived by the rest of the group. Those who handed out rewards were perceived positively by the rest of the group. Those who dished out punishment were evaluated negatively by the rest of the group. Thus, even though freeloaders could be perceived as "deserving" punishment, people seem to realize that punishment is not the best way to promote social good. Interestingly, those who failed to reward cooperative behaviours also were negatively perceived by the group, suggesting that failing to promote the collective good is frowned upon as well. Kiyonari and Barclay conclude that cooperation is more likely to be maintained by a reward system rather than a punishment system. Finally, we note that research conducted at the University of Guelph and at two universities in Japan has shown that freeloading is less likely when the rewards at stake are large rather than small; when freeloading is reduced, groups can arrive at decisions that are beneficial to everyone and they do so more easily and efficiently (Cadsby et al., 2007).

Using Threats to Resolve Conflict

My own belief is that Russian and Chinese behavior is as much influenced by suspicion of our intentions as ours is by suspicion of theirs. This would mean that we have great influence over their behavior—that by treating them as hostile, we assure their hostility.

—J. William Fulbright (1905–1995)

When caught in a conflict, many of us are tempted to use threats to get the other party to cave in to our wishes, believing that we should, in the words of Teddy Roosevelt, "speak softly and carry a big stick." Parents commonly use threats to get their children to behave, and teachers often threaten their students with demerits or a visit to the principal. Threats are often used on an international scale, as well, to further the interests of one nation over another (Turner & Horvitz, 2001).

A classic series of studies by Morton Deutsch and Robert Krauss (1960, 1962) indicates that threats are not an effective means of reducing conflict. These researchers developed a game in which two participants imagined they were in charge of trucking companies, one named Acme Trucking Company and one named Bolt Trucking Company. The goal of each company was to transport merchandise as quickly as possible to a destination. The participants were paid 60 cents for each "trip" but had 1 cent subtracted for every second it took them to make the trip. The most direct route for each company was over a one-lane road, on which only one truck could travel at a time. This placed the two companies in direct conflict, as seen in Figure 8.6. If Acme and Bolt both tried to take the one-lane road, neither truck could pass and both would lose money. Each company could take an alternative route, but this was much longer, guaranteeing that they would lose at least 10 cents on each trial.

How did the participants respond to this dilemma? After a while, most of them worked out a solution that allowed both trucks to make a modest amount of money. They took turns, one waiting until the other person crossed the one-lane road, and then they would take that route as well.

In another version of the study, the researchers gave Acme a gate that could be lowered over the one-lane road, thereby blocking Bolt from using that route with a

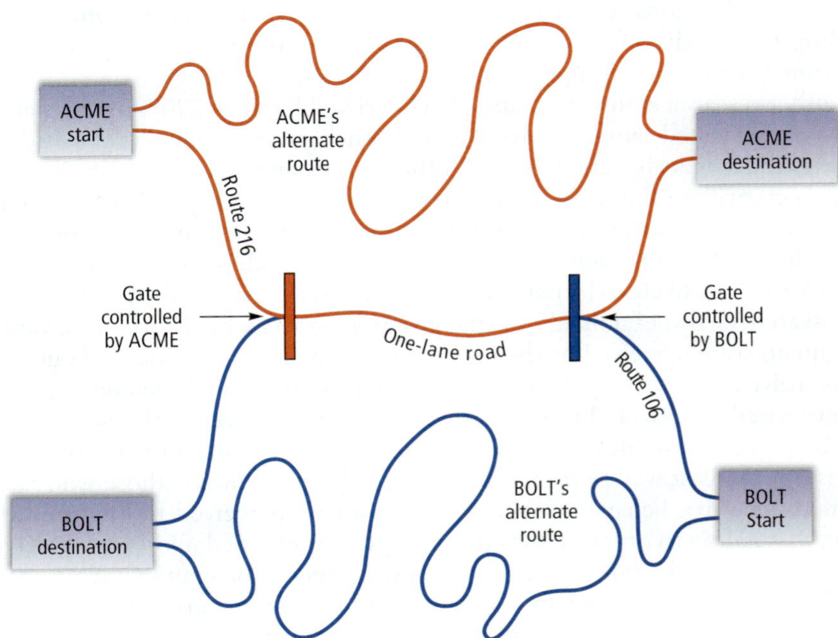

FIGURE 8.6
The trucking game.

Participants play the role of head of either Acme Trucking Company or Bolt Trucking Company. To earn money, they have to drive their trucks from the starting point to their destination as quickly as possible. The quickest route is the one-lane road, but both trucks cannot travel on this road at the same time. In some versions of the studies, participants were given gates that they used to block the other's progress on the one-lane road.

(Adapted from Deutsch & Krauss, 1960)

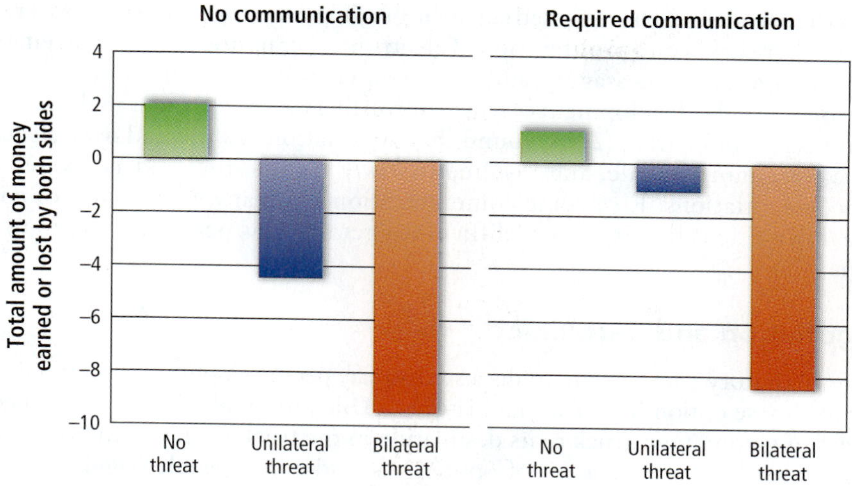

FIGURE 8.7

Results of the trucking game studies.

The left panel shows the total amount of money the participants made (summed over Acme and Bolt) when they could not communicate. When threats were introduced by giving one or both sides a gate, both sides lost more money. The right panel shows the amount of money the participants made when they were required to communicate on every trial. Once again, giving them each a gate reduced their winnings.

(Adapted from Deutsch & Krauss, 1962)

unilateral threat condition. You might think that using force—the gate—would increase Acme's profits, because all Acme had to do was threaten Bolt to "stay off the one-lane road or else." In fact, quite the opposite happened. When one side had the gate, both participants lost more than when neither side had the gate—as seen in the left panel of Figure 8.7 This figure shows the total amount earned or lost by both sides. The Acme participants won slightly more than the Bolt participants when they had the gate but won substantially more when neither side had a gate. The Bolt participants did not like to be threatened and often retaliated by parking their truck on the one-lane road, blocking the other truck's progress. Meanwhile, the seconds ticked away and both sides lost money.

What would happen if the situation were more equitable, with both sides having a gate? Surely, they would learn to cooperate very quickly, recognizing the stalemate that would ensue if both of them used their gate, right? To the contrary, both sides lost more money in the bilateral threat condition than in any of the other conditions (as you can see in the left panel of Figure 8.7). The owners of the trucking companies both threatened to use their gate and did so with great frequency. Once Acme used the gate to block Bolt, Bolt retaliated and blocked Acme the next time its truck came down the road—producing a stalemate that was not in either of their interests.

Effects of Communication There is a way in which the trucking game does not approximate real life: The two sides were not allowed to communicate with each other. Would the two adversaries work out their differences if they could talk them over? To find out, Deutsch and Krauss ran a version of their study in which the participants were required to communicate over an intercom on every trial. Surely, if people were forced to talk to each other, they would cooperate more. But, as shown in the right panel of Figure 8.7, no dramatic increase in profits occurred. Making people communicate reduced losses somewhat when Acme alone had the gate (the unilateral threat condition) but failed to increase cooperation in either of the two other conditions (no threat, bilateral threat). Overall, requiring people to communicate did not raise profits dramatically. Why not?

The problem with the communication in the trucking studies is that it did not foster trust. In fact, people used the intercom to convey threats. In a later version of their trucking study, Krauss and Deutsch specifically instructed people in how to communicate, telling them to work out a solution that was fair to both parties—one that they would be willing to accept if they were in the other person's shoes. Under these conditions, verbal communication increased the amount of money both sides made, because it fostered trust instead of adding fuel to the competitive fires (Deutsch, 1973, 1990; Kerr & Kaufman-Gilliland, 1994; Krauss & Deutsch, 1966; Pruitt, 1998).

In the decades that have passed since the original trucking game studies were conducted, there has been a proliferation of electronic communication such as email, instant messaging, text messaging, and video-conferencing. Does the mode of communication affect the development of trust? According to a recent meta analysis, it does. Stuhlmacher and Citera (2005) found that negotiations conducted over electronic media were more hostile, and resulted in lower profits, than old-fashioned face-to-face negotiations. Electronic communication has many advantages, of course, but a down side is that it is more difficult to get to know people and learn to trust them.

Negotiation and Bargaining

In the laboratory games we have discussed so far, people's options are limited. They have to choose option X or Y in the Prisoner's Dilemma, and they have only a couple of ways of getting their truck to its destination in the trucking game. In everyday life, people often have a wide array of options. Consider two people haggling over the price of a car. Either the buyer or the seller can give in to all of the other's demands, to some of them, or to none of them; either party can walk away from the deal at any time. Given that there is considerable latitude in how people can resolve the conflict, communication between the parties is all the more important. By talking, bargaining, and negotiating, people can arrive at a satisfactory settlement. **Negotiation** is defined as a form of communication between opposing sides in a conflict, in which offers and counter-offers are made and a solution occurs only when both parties agree (DeDreu, Beersma, Steinel, & Van Kleef, 2007; DeDreu, Weingart, & Kwon, 2000; Galinsky, Mussweiler, & Medvec, 2002; Thompson, 2005). How successful are people at negotiating mutually beneficial solutions?

Negotiation

A form of communication between opposing sides in a conflict, in which offers and counter-offers are made and a solution occurs only when both parties agree

Integrative Solution

A solution to a conflict whereby the parties make trade-offs on issues according to their different interests; each side concedes the most on issues that are unimportant to it but important to the other side

One limit to successful negotiation is that people often assume they are locked in a conflict in which only one party can come out ahead. They don't realize that solutions favourable to both parties are available. A couple getting a divorce, for example, might lock horns and find it impossible to reach a financial settlement, until they realize that they have different priorities. Perhaps it is most important to one person to keep the furniture and the season tickets to the opera, whereas the other might want the china and the art collection. This type of compromise, called an **integrative solution**, is an outcome in which the parties in a conflict make trade-offs on issues according to their

Former prime minister Paul Martin, Canadian Assembly of First Nations chief Phil Fontaine, and other government and Aboriginal leaders sign the Kelowna Accord in 2005. The accord designated funding to improve the employment, living conditions, and education of Aboriginal peoples. The Accord was heralded by Aboriginal leaders because it involved a process of consultation and cooperation that brought federal government leaders, provincial ministers, territorial leaders, and Aboriginal leaders to the table. (Paul Martin's Liberal Party subsequently lost the election. Prime Minister Stephen Harper's Conservative Party has not implemented the Accord, despite calls from Aboriginal leaders to do so.)

different interests; each side concedes the most on issues that are unimportant to it but important to the other side.

It might seem that such integrative solutions would be relatively easy to achieve. After all, the two parties simply have to sit down and figure out which issues are most important to each. However, people often find it difficult to identify integrative solutions (De Dreu et al., 2007; Moran & Ritov, 2007; Thompson, 1997). One barrier is a tendency for us to assume that what is important to us is obvious to everyone—including our opponent. However, this assumption is not necessarily warranted, as demonstrated in a study by Vorauer and Claude (1998). These researchers had students at the University of Manitoba participate in negotiation sessions; others observed the sessions. When later questioned, negotiators assumed that it was obvious what their goals had been during the interaction. This was especially true for negotiators who had been asked to reflect on their goals before entering the negotiation—probably a common occurrence in real-life negotiation situations. Importantly, even though negotiators believed that their goals were obvious, observers were no better than chance at identifying these goals.

If uninvolved outside observers are unable to tell what is important to us, chances are that those with whom we are engaged in conflict will be even less able to do so. Indeed, there is evidence that the more people have at stake in a negotiation, the more biased are their perceptions of their opponent. They will tend to distrust proposals made by the other side and to overlook interests they have in common (O'Connor & Carnevale, 1997; Ross & Ward, 1995, 1996). This is one reason why people often use neutral mediators to solve labour disputes, legal battles, and divorce proceedings. Mediators are often in a better position to recognize that there are mutually agreeable solutions to a conflict (Carnevale, 1986; Kressel & Pruitt, 1989; Ross & La Croix, 1996).

The bottom line? When you are negotiating with someone, it is important to keep in mind that integrative solutions are often possible. Try to gain the other side's trust and communicate your own interests in an open manner (ideally in person or with the help of a mediator). Remember that the way you construe the situation is not necessarily the same as the way the other party construes the situation. You may well discover that the other side communicates its interests more freely as a result, increasing the likelihood that you will find a solution beneficial to both parties.

> *Yet there remains another wall. This wall constitutes a psychological barrier between us, . . . [a] barrier of distorted and eroded interpretation of every event and statement . . .. I ask, why don't we stretch our hands with faith and sincerity so that together we might destroy this barrier?*
>
> —*Former Egyptian president Anwar al-Sadat, speaking before the Israeli Knesset, 1977*

HOW WOULD YOU USE THIS?

Chances are you will soon find yourself in a group that needs to make a decision. Perhaps you are involved in a student organization that is making budget decisions or part of a group of students deciding how to proceed on a class project. Based on what you have learned in this chapter, will you act any differently to make sure that your group makes the best decision? What kinds of *process loss* should you be alert to, for example, that might impede good decision making? (See page 250.) How can you make sure that people share information that others don't have? (See page 250.) Is it possible that you and your friends will be subject to *groupthink*, and if so, how can you prevent it? (See page 252.) Lastly, can you predict who is likely to become the leader in your groups and how effective he or she will be? What should you do to increase the chances that you will be chosen as the leader? (See pages 256–260.) Good luck!

Summary

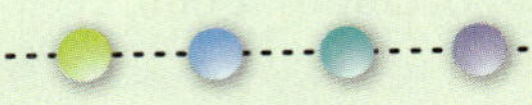

- **What Is a Group?** A group consists of three or more people who interact with one another and are interdependent.
  - **Why People Join Groups** The *need to belong* to groups may be innate. Groups also serve as a source of information about the social world and are an important part of our social identities. People are very sensitive to rejection from groups and do what they can to avoid it.
  - **The Composition and Functions of Groups** Groups tend to consist of homogeneous members, in part because groups have social norms that people are expected to obey. Groups also have well-defined social roles, shared expectations about how people are supposed to behave. People can get so far into a social role that their personal identities and personalities get lost. Group cohesiveness, qualities of a group that bind members together and promote liking between members, is another important property of groups that influences the group's performance.
- **How Groups Influence the Behaviour of Individuals** Research has compared the performance of people who are by themselves versus in groups.
  - **Social Facilitation: When the Presence of Others Energizes Us** When people's individual efforts on a task can be evaluated, the mere presence of others leads to social facilitation: Their performance is enhanced on simple tasks but impaired on complex tasks.
  - **Social Loafing: When the Presence of Others Relaxes Us** When people's individual efforts cannot be evaluated, the mere presence of others leads to social loafing: Performance is impaired on simple tasks but enhanced on complex tasks. Social loafing is more prevalent among men than women, and more prevalent in Western than Asian cultures.
  - **Deindividuation: Getting Lost in the Crowd** The mere presence of others can also lead to deindividuation, which is the loosening of normal constraints on behaviour when people are in groups and are feeling anonymous.
- **Group Decisions: Are Two (or More) Heads Better than One?** Research has compared how people make decisions when they are by themselves versus in groups.
  - **Process Loss: When Group Interactions Inhibit Good Problem Solving** Groups make better decisions than individuals if they are good at pooling ideas and listening to the expert members of the group. Often, however, process loss occurs, which is any aspect of group interaction that inhibits good decision making. For example, groups often focus on the information they have in common and fail to share unique information. Tightly knit, cohesive groups are also prone to groupthink, which occurs when maintaining group cohesiveness and solidarity becomes more important than considering the facts in a realistic manner.
  - **Group Polarization: Going to Extremes** Group polarization causes groups to make more extreme decisions in the direction toward which its members were initially leaning; these group decisions can be more risky or more cautious, depending on which attitude is valued in the group.
  - **Leadership in Groups** There is little support for the great person theory, which argues that good leadership is a matter of having the right personality traits. Leaders do adopt specific kinds of leadership styles, such as transactional (leaders who set clear short-term goals and reward people who meet them) or transformational (leaders who inspire followers to focus on common, long-term goals). Leadership effectiveness is a function of both the kind of person a leader is and the nature of the work situation. Research on Fiedler's contingency theory of leadership has found that leadership performance depends on whether a group has a task-oriented leader or a relationship-oriented leader and on whether the work environment is high or low in situational control. There is a double bind for women leaders: If they conform to societal expectations about how they ought to behave—namely, being warm and communal—they are often perceived as having low leadership potential. If they succeed in attaining a leadership position and act in ways that leaders are expected to act—namely, in agentic, forceful ways—they are often perceived negatively for not acting as a woman "should."
- **Conflict and Cooperation** Research has examined how people resolve conflicts when they have incompatible goals.
  - **Social Dilemmas** These occur when the most beneficial action for an individual will, if chosen by most people, have harmful effects on everyone. A commonly studied social dilemma is the Prisoner's Dilemma, in which two people must decide whether to look out for only their own interests or for their partner's interests as well. Creating trust is crucial in solving this kind of conflict.
  - **Using Threats to Resolve Conflict** Research has found that, on the one hand, using threats tends to escalate rather than resolve conflicts.Communication, on the other hand, resolves conflict only when it promotes trust.
  - **Negotiation and Bargaining** When two sides are negotiating and bargaining it is important to look for an integrative solution, whereby each side concedes the most on issues that are unimportant to it but are very important to its adversary.

Interpersonal Attraction

From First Impressions to Close Relationships

"THEN I MET NINA." THESE FOUR LITTLE WORDS changed a man's life. Several years ago, Bradley Bird, a Canadian newspaper writer in his early forties, was on a trip, covering a series of sad, dark events—the experiences of Chechen refugees and conflict in Kosovo and Kurdish Turkey. As he wearily boarded a bus in Georgia (in the Caucasus region near Russia), bracing himself for the 20-hour ride to northeast Turkey for one last story, a woman took the seat beside him. She was a tall, attractive, raven-haired woman in her thirties. As the bus headed into the night, the woman turned to him and asked his name. Bradley recalls, "I looked at her seriously for the first time and was pleased to see a face as lovely as I'd ever beheld, with dark mysterious eyes, a perfect nose, and full red lips" (Bird, 2001).

The woman's name was Nina. To Bradley's surprise, he found himself asking her if there was a man in her life. She answered, "No." He surprised himself still more by saying, "You need me, and I need you." Because she said she spoke only a little English, he repeated it to make sure she understood. She smiled, and they gazed into each other's eyes. It was midnight and the driver turned off the interior lights. Her arm brushed against his in the darkness. "The sensation was incredible," Bradley exclaims, "electric, and I couldn't stop myself; I gave her arm a gentle squeeze." Nina reciprocated.

At first they tried to hide their feelings from the other passengers, but 12 hours into the ride, they were unable to contain their joy. Bradley informed the driver that his plans had changed and he would now stay on the bus an additional 13 hours so he could have more time with Nina. The driver and passengers began to celebrate with them. An older, heavy man brought out a bottle of vodka to mark the occasion. Bradley reports that by then, he and Nina were inseparable and began to make plans for her to come to Canada. He begged to accompany her to Sofia, Bulgaria, where she was going to visit her sister, but she refused. So he got off the bus in Istanbul. Instead of flying home as scheduled, he waited there for three weeks, hoping to catch Nina on her way back to Georgia. During that time, he tried to reach Nina at her sister's, but the phone number she had given him didn't work. Reluctantly, he returned home and immediately sent her the documents she would need to get a visa. It was May.

Nina wrote back, assuring Bradley of her desire to be with him. She also told him that he would have to return to Turkey and plead her case to the Canadian embassy there. By this time, it was August, and Bradley had accepted a teaching position. What to do now? The answer was clear. Bradley promptly quit his job and spent the next few months trying to reach Nina to make arrangements for them to meet in Turkey. The phone lines were always busy or not working. In December,

OUTLINE

he decided he simply had to take action. He booked a flight to Turkey and two tickets to return to Canada. He managed to track down Nina's sister in Bulgaria and asked her to let Nina know that he was coming. "Oh, Bradley," she said, "Nina is back with her husband. Her daughter insisted on it." With those words, Bradley's dream of a life with Nina was shattered. But Bradley Bird isn't bitter. In his words, "I will always be grateful to Nina for giving me 33 of the happiest hours of my adult life" (Bird, 2001).

As Bradley Bird's experience illustrates, the need to love and be loved is one of the most fundamental human needs. Despite all of the warning signs—the fact that he had just met this woman and knew nothing about her and the fact that she had given him the wrong phone number for her sister in Bulgaria—Bradley just couldn't help himself. He fell in love with the mysterious Nina, and it changed his life. This man in his forties, who had experienced other relationships (he was once married), describes the bus ride with Nina as the happiest 33 hours of his adult life!

What, exactly, is love, and why are we so motivated to seek it? Or perhaps the question should be "Why are we so motivated to seek it even when it comes at a high cost?" Research conducted by Susan Boon and Karen Pasveer (1999) at the University of Calgary suggests that people are well aware of the risks associated with relationships. One of their research participants, a 26-year-old woman, wrote the following:

> Some of my friends who aren't in relationships are dying to get into one. I don't understand why because most of the time it's a more hurtful than it is an enjoyable experience. I told them, "Enjoy being single because it's more fun and I think it's a lot less hassle." Getting into a relationship . . . falling for somebody, and you're bound to set yourself up for a lot of hurt . . . and misery. (p. 317)

Despite the potential for hurt and misery, most people are highly motivated to find love. Why? This is one of the basic questions to be addressed in this chapter.

We will discuss the antecedents of attraction, from the initial liking of two people meeting for the first time to the love that develops in close relationships. We will also discuss how people maintain relationships once they have been formed, as well as the processes whereby relationships end. As we present this research, you may want to think about how you can put these social psychological findings to good use in your own life—although we can't guarantee that a thorough reading of this chapter will save you from completely rearranging your life because of a chance meeting with a gorgeous, mysterious stranger on a bus.

Major Antecedents of Attraction

Connect to MyPsychLab
To access the Critical Thinking question on attraction, go to MyPsychLab

When social psychologist Ellen Berscheid asked people of various ages what made them happy, at or near the top of their lists were making and maintaining friendships and having positive, warm relationships (Berscheid, 1985; Berscheid & Peplau, 1983; Berscheid & Reis, 1998). The absence of meaningful relationships with other people makes people feel lonely, worthless, hopeless, helpless, powerless, and alienated (Baumeister & Leary, 1995; Hartup & Stevens, 1997; Peplau & Perlman, 1982; Stroebe & Stroebe, 1996). We start this chapter with research on what attracts people to each other in the first place.

Contrary to popular belief, I do not believe that friends are necessarily the people you like best; they are merely the people who got there first.

—Sir Peter Ustinov, Dear Me, 1977

The Person Next Door: The Propinquity Effect

One of the simplest determinants of interpersonal attraction is proximity. The people who, by chance, you see and interact with most often are most

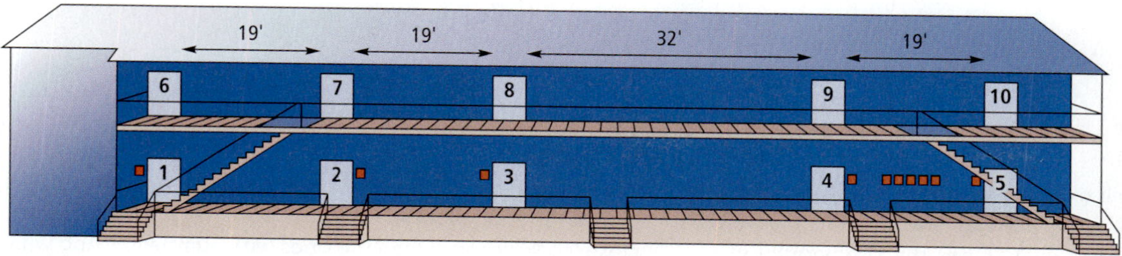

FIGURE 9.1

The floor plan of a Westgate West building.

All of the buildings in the MIT housing complex had the same floor plan.

(Adapted from Festinger, Schachter, & Back, 1950)

likely to become your friends and lovers (Aron, Fisher, Strong, Acevedo, Riela, & Tsapelas, 2008; Berscheid & Reis, 1998; Fehr, 1996; Moreland & Beach, 1992; Newcomb, 1961; Tsai, 2006). This includes people in your city, in your neighbourhood, and on your street. Now, this might seem obvious. However, the striking thing about proximity and attraction, or the **propinquity effect** as social psychologists call it, is that it works on a micro level.

Propinquity Effect

The finding that the more we see and interact with people, the more likely they are to become our friends

Consider a classic study conducted in a housing complex for married students at the Massachusetts Institute of Technology (MIT). Leon Festinger, Stanley Schachter, and Kurt Back (1950) tracked friendship formation among the couples in the various apartment buildings. For example, one section of the complex, Westgate West, consisted of 17 two-storey buildings, each having 10 apartments. The residents had been assigned to their apartments at random as vacancies opened up, and nearly all of them were strangers when they moved in. The researchers asked the residents to name their three closest friends in the housing project. Just as the propinquity effect would predict, 65 percent of the residents mentioned people who lived in the same building, even though the other buildings were not far away. Even more striking was the pattern of friendships within a building. Each Westgate West building was designed as shown in the drawing in Figure 9.1. The researchers found that 41 percent of the next-door neighbours indicated that they were close friends, 22 percent of those who lived two doors apart did so, and only 10 percent of those who lived on opposite ends of the hall did so.

Festinger and colleagues (1950) demonstrated that attraction and propinquity rely not only on actual physical distance, but also on the more psychological, functional distance. *Functional distance* is defined as certain aspects of architectural design that make it likely that some people will come into contact with each other more often than with others. For example, consider the friendship choices of residents of apartments 1 and 5 in Figure 9.1. Couples living at the foot of the stairs, and in one case near the mailboxes, saw a great deal of upstairs residents. Sure enough, residents in apartments 1 and 5 throughout the complex had more friends upstairs than did dwellers in the other first-floor apartments. (You can map out propinquity effects in your life with the accompanying Try It! exercise.)

Close friendships are often formed in university, in part because of propinquity.

TRY IT! Mapping the Effect of Propinquity in Your Life

In this exercise, you will examine the relationship between who your friends and acquaintances are and the place(s) where you spend time regularly. Does the propinquity effect explain who your friends are?

First, pick a physical space to focus on. You could choose your dormitory, apartment building, or the building in which you work. (We'll use a dormitory as an example.) Draw a rough floor plan of your dormitory. (You can decide whether you need to draw just your floor or more of the building.) Include the location of all dorm room doors, the stairs or elevator, and so on. Mark your room with a large X.

Second, think about who your close friends are on the floor; mark each of their rooms on your drawing with the number 1. Next, think about who your other friends are; mark each of their rooms with the number 2. Finally, think about your acquaintances, people you say hello to or chat with briefly now and then; mark each of their rooms with the number 3.

Now, examine the pattern of friendships on your drawing. Are your friends clustered near your room in physical space? Are the rooms with numbers 1 and 2 among the closest to your room in physical space? Are they physically closer to your room than the ones with number 3? And what about the rooms that didn't get a number (meaning that you don't really know these people or interact with them)—are these rooms the farthest from yours?

Finally, examine your "propinquity map" for the presence of functional distance. Do aspects of the architectural design of your dorm or building make you more likely to cross paths with some residents than others? For example, the location of the bathroom, kitchen, living room, stairs or elevator, and mailboxes can play an important role in propinquity and friendship formation. These are all places you go to frequently; when walking to and from them, you pass some people's dorm rooms but not others'. Are the people who live along your path the ones you know best? If so, propinquity has played a big role in determining the people with whom you have formed relationships!

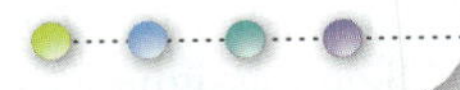

Mere Exposure Effect

The finding that the more exposure we have to a stimulus, the more apt we are to like it

Simulate on mypsychlab
Mere Exposure

The propinquity effect works because of familiarity, or the **mere exposure effect**—the more exposure we have to a stimulus, the more apt we are to like it. We see certain people a lot, and the more familiar they become, the more friendship blooms. Interestingly, in a recent set of studies, it was shown that familiarity leads to attraction regardless of whether interactions are face-to-face or online (Reis, Maniaci, Caprariello, Eastwick, & Finkel, 2011).

A good example of propinquity and mere exposure effects is your classroom. All semester long, you see the same people. Does this increase your liking for them? Richard Moreland and Scott Beach (1992) tested this hypothesis by planting female research confederates in a large university classroom. The women did not interact with the professor or the other students; they simply walked in and sat quietly in the first row, where everyone could see them. The confederates differed in how many classes they attended, from 15 meetings down to the control condition of zero. At the end of the semester, the students in the class were shown slides of the women, whom they rated on several measures of liking and attraction. As you can see in Figure 9.2, mere exposure had a definite effect on liking. Even though they had never interacted, the more often the students had seen the women in class, the more they liked them. These findings have been replicated in many other studies of university students' friendships (e.g., documenting that you are most likely to form friendships with people who sit close to you in class), children's friendships, and friendships among military and police trainees (Back, Schmukle, & Egloff, 2008; Fehr, 2008; Foster, 2005; Gifford-Smith & Brownell, 2003; Segal, 1974; Sykes, 1983).

Of course, if you feel negatively toward the person in question, then, not surprisingly, the more exposure you have to him or her, the greater your dislike (Swap, 1977). For example, during the 2005–06 federal election campaign, the Conservative Party ran a number of ads prominently featuring Stephen Harper. These ads seemed to backfire—undecided voters said that the ads persuaded them to vote for the Liberals

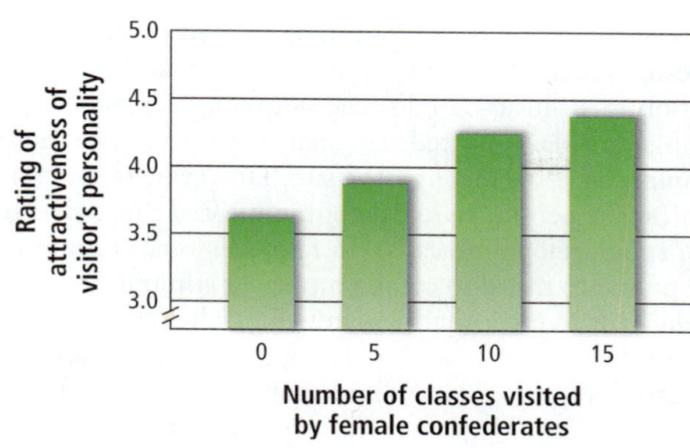

FIGURE 9.2

The effect that mere exposure in the classroom has on attraction.

The more often students saw a female confederate in their classroom, the more positively they rated her personality, even though they had never interacted with her.

(Adapted from Moreland & Beach, 1992)

or NDP instead of for the Conservative Party. One newspaper writer dubbed this "The Harper Effect: The more we see him, the less we like him" (Panetta, 2005). Nevertheless, Stephen Harper managed to win that election and become the prime minister of Canada. However, the likeability issue surfaced again in the 2008 election. In one poll, 55 percent of Canadians agreed with the statement "there is something about Stephen Harper I just don't like" (Bryden, 2008). However, once again, Stephen Harper managed to override his likeability deficit and win the election. He did so again in 2011. Thus, unless our feelings toward someone are negative, familiarity generally breeds attraction and liking (Bornstein, 1989; Bornstein & D'Agostino, 1992; Griffin & Sparks, 1990; Moreland & Zajonc, 1982; Zajonc, 1968).

Forming Relationships Online So far we have been focusing on the kind of familiarity that develops when you rub shoulders with another person in the course of your day. However, these days, strangers can get to know each other through social networking sites, email, and online chat rooms. Computer-mediated communication offers a twist on the propinquity effect; the fact that someone is thousands of kilometres away no longer means you can't encounter him or her. Are online relationships the same as those formed in everyday life? Do online relationships survive when they move from the computer screen to face-to-face interactions? Social psychologists are beginning to explore these questions. Laboratory experiments have shown that people report being more comfortable revealing their "true" self to a partner over the Internet compared with a face-to-face interaction (Bargh, McKenna, & Fitzsimons, 2002; McKenna, Green, & Gleason, 2002). Interestingly, McKenna and colleagues (2002) found that participants also tended to report more liking for an Internet partner than a partner they met in person—even when, unbeknownst to them, it was actually the same person! These studies have focused on interactions between strangers.

Do these kinds of interactions lead to lasting relationships? Let's start with friendships. Here the research has produced mixed results (see Fehr, 2008, for a review). Some studies have found that the "rich get richer," meaning that people who are extroverted and have good social skills use the Internet as another way of acquiring even more friends. Other studies have shown that online friendships are more likely to be formed by lonely, introverted people who may lack the social skills required to form relationships in person. This has become known as the social compensation hypothesis. Whether or not that is a good thing is a matter of debate. Some scholars argue that computer-mediated communication is a blessing for those who find it difficult to form friendships face to face. Others argue that those who are lacking in social skills will become even more isolated if they retreat from the "real world" and conduct their social lives online. A recent study conducted with high school students in Ontario found support for the social compensation hypothesis among boys (i.e., socially anxious boys had better friendship quality if they engaged in online chatting) and support for the "rich get richer" hypothesis among girls (Desjarlais & Willoughby, 2010). It will take some time (and a lot more research) before a definitive conclusion on this issue can be reached.

Another issue is whether relationships can be formed exclusively online or whether at some point face-to-face interaction is necessary. Baym and Ledbetter (2009) studied friendship formation in a music-based social network, *Last.fm*. Respondents from 48 countries, including Canada, reported that shared musical taste motivated friendship formation and communication through the site. However, these relationships tended not to develop unless the people involved communicated through other means as well (e.g., face to face, email, telephone calls). In fact, it is very common for relationships that have formed online to move to offline modes of communication (Fehr, 2008). At some point, people want to meet that person behind the screen.

Watch on **mypsychlab**
IT Video: Public Speaking

Finally, we note that recent research shows that people report opening up more and being more satisfied with their offline than their online friendships. This was found in a study of female bloggers in Canada, the United States, and the United Kingdom (Bane, Cornish, Erspamer, & Kampman, 2010) and with students at Wilfrid Laurier University (Buote, Wood, & Pratt, 2009). Finally, it should be acknowledged that these days, people are increasingly relying on texting, instant messaging, and the like even with their offline friends, as shown in a large-scale study of Canadian high school students (Blais, Craig, Pepler, & Connolly, 2008) and students at the University of Western Ontario (Quan-Hasse, 2007). Thus, the Internet does play an important role in maintaining friendships regardless of whether they were formed online or offline.

And what about romantic relationships? People often disclose more personal information more quickly when interacting with a potential dating partner online rather than face-to-face. As a result, online relationships may form more quickly and become intimate sooner than offline relationships. However, early research shows that these relationships can fizzle just as quickly as they started up. In online interactions, it's also easier to manipulate the self that is presented to others. Disillusionment can set in when the person you meet doesn't live up to the image presented online (McKenna, 2008; Sprecher, Wenzel, & Harvey, 2008). While there is still much to be learned about Internet relationships, the data suggest that because of computers, propinquity may soon no longer be a prerequisite for the formation of relationships.

Similarity

Similarity

Attraction to people who are like us

Complementarity

Attraction to people who are opposite to us

Although propinquity does affect relationship choices, it is also the case that we don't become good friends or lovers with everyone who is near us in physical space (or cyberspace, for that matter). The "fuel" is the match between our interests, background, attitudes, and values and those of the other person. Are we more attracted to people who are like us (the concept of **similarity**), or are we more attracted to people who are our opposites (the concept of **complementarity**)? Folk wisdom may suggest that "opposites attract," but research evidence proves that it is similarity, not complementarity, that draws people together (Berscheid & Reis, 1998).

Dozens of tightly controlled experiments have shown, for example, that if all you know about a person whom you've never met is his or her opinions on several issues, then the more similar those opinions are to yours, the more you will like him or her (Byrne, 1997; Byrne & Nelson, 1965; McPherson, Smith-Lovin, & Cook, 2001). And what happens when you do meet? In a classic study, Theodore Newcomb (1961) randomly assigned male students at the University of Michigan to be roommates in a particular dormitory at the start of the school year. The critical question was "Would similarity predict friendship formation?" The answer is yes. The men became friends with those who were demographically similar (e.g., shared a rural background) as well as with those who were similar in attitudes and values (e.g., were also engineering majors or also held liberal political views).

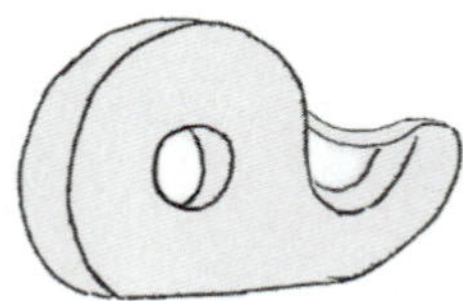

"I don't care if she is a tape dispenser. I love her."

Since Newcomb conducted this research, dozens of studies have demonstrated that similarity in many domains is an important predictor of attraction in both friendships and romantic relationships (see Fehr, 1996, 2008). Much of this research has focused on similarity of attitudes and values. Similarity effects are generally not as strong for personality. Recent research conducted with students at Brock University and at the University of Calgary found that similarity effects are most likely to be found for traits that are related to one's value system (e.g., honesty; Lee, Ashton, Pozzebon, Visser, Bourdage, & Ogunfowora, 2009). In another recent study conducted with adolescents living in Montreal, it was found that similarity in personality was strongest for reciprocated friendship pairs (i.e., the friendship is mutual; Linden-Andersen, Markiewicz, & Doyle, 2009). We are also more likely to be attracted to someone who enjoys the same kinds of leisure activities that we do (Werner & Parmelee, 1979). In fact, according to a study conducted at the University of Waterloo, for some people, similarity in terms of activity preferences is a stronger predictor of attraction than is similarity of attitudes (Jamieson, Lydon, & Zanna, 1987). We also are attracted to people who are similar to us in terms of interpersonal style and communication skills (Burleson & Samter, 1996).

Finally, we note that similarity effects seem to be strongest in individualistic cultures. For example, Heine and colleagues found that Canadians place more emphasis on similarity in terms of personality, activity preferences, and the like than do people in Japan (Heine, Foster, & Spina, 2009).

Why is similarity so important in attraction? There are several possibilities. First, we tend to think that people who are similar to us will be inclined to like us. Given this reasonable assumption, we take the first steps and initiate a relationship (Berscheid, 1985; Condon & Crano, 1988). Second, people who are similar provide us with important social validation for our characteristics and beliefs—that is, they provide us with the feeling that we are right in our views and our thinking (Byrne & Clore, 1970). Finally, the rewards-of-interaction explanation offers another reason for why similarity leads to attraction (Berscheid & Walster (Hatfield), 1978; Burleson, 1994). According to this explanation, if a person feels the same way we do on important issues, we assume it would be enjoyable to spend time with him or her. Conversely, it is not very pleasant to interact with someone who disagrees with us on everything (Rosenbaum, 1986).

A few final comments before leaving this topic. Although we have been focusing on research showing that similarity leads to attraction, there is also evidence that attraction can lead to perceptions of similarity. In other words, the more attracted we are to someone, the more similar we assume that person is to us. For example, one study found that students in dating relationships and married couples living in the Kitchener-Waterloo area overestimated the degree of similarity between themselves and their partner. The greater the similarity they perceived, the more understood they felt by their partner. Feelings of understanding, in turn, predicted relationship satisfaction (Murray, Holmes, Bellavia, Griffin, & Dolderman, 2002). According to a program of research conducted by Marian Morry at the University of Manitoba, the link between attraction and perceived similarity holds true for romantic

An administrator in a college housing office sorts through roommate applications, placing them in piles according to their similar answers to questions about living habits and interests.

Life is to be fortified by many friendships. To love, and to be loved, is the greatest happiness of existence.

—Sydney Smith, *1771–1845*

relationships, same-sex friendships, and cross-sex friendships (Morry, 2005a, 2007). Interestingly, these perceptions may not be all that accurate. For example, in a recent study conducted at the University of Toronto, Li and Chignell (2010) found that people reading blogs were more attracted to authors they perceived as similar to themselves in terms of personality (especially the traits of agreeableness and openness), even though there wasn't much evidence of actual personality similarity. Other Canadian researchers have found that people perceive greater personality similarity between themselves and their friends than actually exists (Lee et al., 2009; Linden-Andersen et al., 2009). In fact, in a recent meta analysis, Montoya and colleagues found that in long-term relationships, "perceived" similarity predicted liking and attraction better than "actual" similarity did. Thus, feeling similar to another is so important that we will create beliefs about the similarity between ourselves and intimate others, believing such similarities exist even when they don't (Montoya, Horton, & Kirchner, 2008).

Reciprocal Liking

Reciprocal Liking
When you like someone and that person also likes you

Most of us like to be liked. Not surprisingly, **reciprocal liking**—liking someone who likes us in return—is one of the prime determinants of interpersonal attraction (Berscheid & Walster (Hatfield), 1978; Condon & Crano, 1988; Kenny, 1994; Kubitscheck & Hallinan, 1998; Secord & Backman, 1964). Liking is so powerful it can even make up for the absence of similarity. In one experiment, for example, when a young woman expressed interest in male research participants simply by maintaining eye contact, leaning toward them, and listening attentively, the men expressed great liking for her despite the fact that they knew she disagreed with them on important issues (Gold, Ryckman, & Mosley, 1984). Similarly, a recent study conducted at McMaster University found that participants were most attracted to confederates (male and female actors) when they behaved in ways that communicated interest and liking (Clark, 2008).

Interestingly, reciprocal liking can come about because of a self-fulfilling prophecy (see Chapter 3), as demonstrated in an experiment by Rebecca Curtis and Kim Miller (1986). University students who did not know one another took part in the study in pairs. The researchers led some students to believe that they were liked by the student with whom they would be paired. Other students were led to believe that they were disliked by their partner for the study. The pairs of students were then given an opportunity to have a conversation. Just as predicted, those individuals who thought they were liked behaved in more likeable ways with their partner; they disclosed more about themselves, disagreed less about the topic under discussion, and generally behaved in a warmer, more pleasant manner than did those individuals who thought they were disliked. As a result, their partners ended up liking them—more so than did the partners of students who believed they were disliked.

We should note that reciprocal liking effects can occur only if you like yourself in the first place. People with negative self-concepts tend to be skeptical about others actually liking them and therefore do not necessarily reciprocate liking (Swann, Stein-Seroussi, & McNulty, 1992).

The Effects of Physical Attractiveness on Liking

Propinquity, similarity, and reciprocal liking are not the only determinants of who we will come to like. We also are affected by people's looks—their physical attractiveness. How important is physical appearance to our first impressions of people? A classic study by Walster (Hatfield) and her colleagues revealed a surprising answer (Walster (Hatfield), Aronson, Abrahams, & Rottman, 1966). These researchers matched 752 incoming students at the University of Minnesota for a blind date at a dance during orientation week. The students had previously taken a battery of personality and aptitude tests; however, the researchers paired them up at random. On the night of the dance, the couples spent a few hours together dancing and chatting. They then evaluated their date and indicated whether they would like to date that person again. Of the many possible characteristics that could have determined whether they liked each other—such as their partner's intelligence, independence, sensitivity, or sincerity—the overriding determinant was physical attractiveness. What's more, there was no great difference between men and women on this score.

In more recent research, female students at Laurentian University were presented with photographs of an attractive or unattractive man along with information that he either was or was not involved in sports and was either high or low in status. Participants were most interested in dating and forming a long-term relationship with men who were portrayed as attractive, participated in sports, and were high status. However, attractiveness was the most important variable of these three (Schulte-Hostedde, Eys, & Johnson, 2008). Interestingly, research conducted at the University of Western Ontario shows that these effects occur at both an automatic (unconscious) level and when people make more conscious, deliberate evaluations (Sritharan, Heilpern, Wilbur, & Gawronski, 2010). In this study, female students were shown the dating profile of a 22-year-old male student, supposedly from an online dating site. The researchers included either a very attractive or a very unattractive photograph along with information about the male student's qualities (e.g., ambitious or not ambitious). It turned out that that the women's automatic first impressions were influenced only by the man's looks, not his other qualities. When an attractive photograph accompanied the description, participants expressed greater liking for the man and a greater desire to go out with him than when the description was accompanied by an unattractive photo. When making more conscious, deliberate evaluations, the women were influenced by both looks and the man's qualities (Sritharan et al., 2010).

The powerful role that physical appearance plays in attraction is not limited to heterosexual relationships. When gay men participated in a "blind date" study like the original University of Minnesota study, they responded just as the heterosexual men and women had in the earlier study: The physical attractiveness of their dates was the strongest predictor of their liking for them (Sergios & Cody, 1985).

Oh, what vileness human beauty is, corroding, corrupting everything it touches.

—Orestes, *408* BCE

These findings raise a perplexing issue. When people are asked about the qualities they desire in a dating partner or a mate, physical attractiveness is not at the top of the list (Buss & Barnes, 1986). Yet when it comes to people's actual behaviour—what people do rather than what they say—appearance seems to be the only thing that matters, at least in situations in which strangers are forming their first impressions of each other. Are people unaware of the importance they place on looks, or are they simply unwilling to admit that they so highly value such a superficial characteristic?

Beauty is a greater recommendation than any letter of introduction.

—Aristotle, *fourth century* BCE

To find out, Hadjistavropoulos and Genest (1994) designed a clever study. They presented female students at the University of Saskatchewan with photographs of men varying in physical attractiveness, along with descriptions of their (supposed) personality traits. The researchers found that attractive men were rated as more desirable to date than were unattractive men. Moreover, attractiveness was the strongest predictor of desirability—more so than personality information. So far, this sounds just like the other studies we have been describing. But here's the interesting twist: Some of the participants were connected to an impressive-looking apparatus that they were told was a highly accurate lie detector. The researchers reasoned that if, on the one hand, people aren't aware of the emphasis they place on looks, lie detector participants should give the same responses as participants who are not connected to a lie detector. If, on the other hand, people are aware that they base their evaluations of people on looks but feel they shouldn't admit it, then those who are attached to a lie detector should be more likely to "confess" to this than those who are not. And that is exactly what happened. The findings suggest that we are aware of the value we place on looks—but as long as we can get away with it, we won't admit it.

Simulate on mypsychlab
Perceptions of Attractiveness

What Is Attractive? Is physical attractiveness "in the eye of the beholder," or do we share some of the same notions of what is beautiful and handsome? From early childhood on, the media tell us what is beautiful. Moreover, this specific definition of beauty is associated with goodness. For example, illustrators of most traditional children's books, as well as the people who draw the characters in Disney movies, have taught us that the heroines—as well as the princes who woo and win them—all look alike. They all have regular features—small, pert noses; big eyes; shapely lips; blemish-free complexions—and slim, athletic bodies: pretty much like Barbie and Ken dolls.

Bombarded as we are with media depictions of attractiveness, it is not surprising to learn that we share a set of criteria for defining beauty (Fink & Penton-Voak, 2002; Tseëlon, 1995). Look at the photographs below of models and actors who are considered very attractive in Western cultures. Can you describe the facial characteristics that have earned them this label? Michael Cunningham (1986) designed a creative study to determine these standards of beauty. He asked male university students to rate the attractiveness of 50 photographs of women, taken from a college yearbook and from an international beauty pageant program. Cunningham then carefully measured the relative size of the facial features in each photograph.

Research has found that we share some standards of beauty. In females, large eyes, prominent cheekbones and narrow cheeks, high eyebrows, and a small chin are associated with beauty; in males, large eyes, prominent cheekbones, and a large chin are rated as most beautiful. Today's popular actors—such as Natalie Portman, Ziyi Zhang, Patrick Dempsey, and Will Smith—fit these criteria.

He found that high attractiveness ratings were given to faces with large eyes, a small nose, a small chin, prominent cheekbones and narrow cheeks, high eyebrows, large pupils, and a big smile. Cunningham and colleagues also examined women's ratings of male attractiveness in the same manner. They found that higher attractiveness ratings of men were associated with large eyes, prominent cheekbones, a large chin, and a big smile (Cunningham, Barbee, & Pike, 1990). There is some overlap in the men's and women's ratings—both sexes admire large eyes in the opposite sex; these are considered to be a "baby face" feature, for newborn mammals have very large eyes for the size of their face. Baby face features are thought to be attractive because they elicit feelings of warmth and nurturance in perceivers—take, for example, our response to babies, kittens, and puppies (e.g., Berry, 1995; McArthur & Berry, 1987; Zebrowitz, 1997; Zebrowitz & Montepare, 1992). Both sexes also admire prominent cheekbones in the opposite sex, an adult feature that is found only in the faces of those who are sexually mature. Note that the female face that is considered beautiful has more baby face features (small nose, small chin) than the handsome male face, suggesting that beauty in the female, more so than in the male, is associated with childlike qualities.

We note that although Cunningham and colleagues found that a big smile was considered attractive in both male and female faces, when men's and women's faces are directly compared, smiling women's faces are rated as more attractive than smiling men's faces, according to a recent study conducted at McMaster University and at the University of Stirling, Scotland (Penton-Voak & Chang, 2008). Interestingly, a recent study conducted with participants at Wilfrid Laurier University found that perceptions of facial attractiveness also depend on the perceivers' height. Specifically, Geldart (2008) found that for tall people, a face with a larger forehead and smaller chin was considered most attractive, whereas short people had the opposite preference. Thus, your visual point of view may affect what you find most attractive.

More recently, researchers have extended this line of work to the body, rather than just the face, making the kinds of detailed, fine-grained measurements that have been applied to facial features. Let's start with the feet. Research conducted with men and women in Canada and Australia confirms what you might expect, namely that for women, having small feet is considered more attractive than having larger feet. When it came to men's feet, the findings were reversed, such that having big feet was considered more attractive than having small feet. One last finding: Men were more attracted by women's feet than women were by men's feet. The researchers also hypothesized that men might be more attracted to women's shoes than vice versa, but that was not the case (Voracek, Fisher, Rupp, Lucas, & Fessler, 2007).

Moving from length of feet to length of legs, a recent large-scale study examined the attractiveness of leg length (specifically, the leg-to-body ratio) in 27 different nations. Overall, average leg-to-body ratios were considered more attractive than extremes. (However, legs that were extremely long generally were preferred over legs that were extremely short.) Participants in Canada, Europe, and Africa perceived long legs in males and females as more attractive than did participants in Asia and Latin America (Sorokowski, Szmajke, Sorokowska, Cunen, Fabrykant, Zarafshani . . . & Fang, 2011).

Finally, at Brock University, Anthony Bogaert and colleagues have been assessing the relation between finger length and physical attractiveness (Bogaert, Fawcett, & Jamieson, 2009). Specifically, these researchers divide the length of the second (index) finger and by the length of the fourth (ring) finger, which is known as a 2D:4D ratio. A longer index finger results in a ratio higher than 1, whereas a longer ring finger results in a ratio of less than 1. What does all of this have to do with attractiveness? It turns out that men with a low 2D:4D ratio are rated as more physically attractive (both self-reported and as rated by women) than men with a high 2D:4D ratio. A low 2D:4D ratio is associated with masculinity (higher levels of prenatal exposure to male hormones), whereas a high 2D:4D is associated with femininity. The authors suggest that heterosexual women are attracted to masculine men because male hormones are markers of reproductive fitness (e.g., sperm quality, dominance/competitiveness; Bogaert et al., 2009). (We discuss evolutionary explanations such as this in greater detail later in this chapter.)

Cultural Standards of Beauty Are people's perceptions of what is a beautiful or handsome face similar across cultures? According to a review of this literature by University of Toronto social psychologist Karen Dion (2002), the answer is a surprising yes (see also Cunningham et al., 1995; Jones & Hill, 1993; McArthur & Berry, 1987; Rhodes et al., 2001). Even though racial and ethnic groups do vary in specific facial features, people from a wide range of cultures agree on what is attractive in the human face. When researchers have asked participants from various countries, ethnicities, and racial groups to rate the physical attractiveness of photographed faces of people who also represent various countries, ethnicities, and racial groups, the participants' ratings agree to a remarkable extent. For example, one review of this literature found that correlations between participants' ratings ranged from 0.66 to 0.93 (Langlois & Roggman, 1990), which are very strong correlations (see Chapter 2). A meta analysis of many studies also found evidence for cross-cultural agreement in what constitutes a beautiful or handsome face (Langlois, Kalakanis, Rubenstein, Larson, Hallam, & Smoot, 2000). Although there is some variability from person to person, across large groups a consensus emerges: Perceivers think that some faces are just better looking than others, regardless of cultural background (Berscheid & Reis, 1998).

Assumptions about Attractive People As you have probably observed, beauty "matters"—even when it shouldn't. We are attracted to that which is beautiful, and that can lead to unfair treatment. For example, in a study conducted with premature babies, it was found that neonatal nurses responded more positively to cuter babies and gave them better care. As a result, cuter babies gained weight more quickly and were discharged sooner than the less attractive babies (Badr & Abdallah, 2001). An analysis of national survey data gathered by the Institute for Social Research at York University revealed that attractiveness and income also are positively correlated—at least for men (Roszell, Kennedy, & Grabb, 1989). More recent studies have documented that good-looking people earn 10 to 15 percent more than their less good-looking counterparts (French, 2002; Mobius & Rosenblatt, 2006). To give a final example, a recent study conducted in Finland found that good-looking political candidates—especially female candidates—get more votes (Poutvara, Berggren, & Jordahl, 2006).

One reason that physically attractive people get preferential treatment has to do with the assumptions that we make about attractive individuals, namely that they possess a host of desirable traits. Karen Dion, Ellen Berscheid, and Elaine Walster (Hatfield) (1972) have called this the "what is beautiful is good" stereotype (Ashmore, Solomon, & Longo, 1996; Brigham, 1980; Hatfield & Sprecher, 1986a). In fact, a recent study conducted at the University of British Columbia found that people attribute more positive qualities to physically attractive people than to less attractive people after a mere three minutes of interaction (Lorenzo, Biesanz, & Human, 2010).

Most research on the "what is beautiful is good" stereotype has been conducted with young people, usually university students. An exception is a study by Perlini, Bertolissi, and Lind (1999), who showed photographs of attractive and unattractive younger and older women to first-year university students and to senior citizens living in Sault Ste. Marie, Ontario. The researchers found that participants attributed more positive qualities to attractive women—regardless of their age. There was, however, one exception. Senior men attributed more positive qualities to attractive young women than to attractive older women. Thus, it appears that the "what is beautiful is good" stereotype applies across the lifespan, with one exception—older men seem to perceive that what is beautiful *and younger* is good. (Unfortunately, older women are all too aware of the emphasis that is placed on youth in our culture. A study conducted with women ages 50 to 70 living in Vancouver found that the majority engaged in some form of beauty modification, for example wrinkle creams or surgical procedures, even if they believed that "natural" aging was more authentic and pure; Clarke & Griffin, 2007.)

Luckily for those of us who do not look like supermodels, the stereotype is relatively narrow, affecting people's judgments about an individual only in specific areas. Meta analyses have revealed that physical attractiveness has the largest effect on both men's and women's attributions when they are making judgments about social competence.

The beautiful are thought to be more sociable, extroverted, and popular than the less attractive. They are also seen as more sexual, happier, and more assertive (Eagly, Ashmore, Makhijani, & Longo, 1991; Feingold 1992a). According to a recent study conducted at Memorial University, intelligence and liberal attitudes should also be added to this list (Snook, Grant, & Button, 2009).

Interestingly, the stereotype that the beautiful are particularly gifted in the area of social competence has some research support; highly attractive people do develop good social interaction skills and report having more satisfying interactions with others than do the less attractive (Berscheid & Reis, 1998; Feingold, 1992b; Reis, Nezlek, & Wheeler, 1980; Reis et al., 1982). Thus, there appears to be a kernel of truth in the "what is beautiful is good" stereotype. The reason is that beautiful people, from a young age, receive a great deal of social attention that helps them develop good social skills, which, in turn, may lead to other positive outcomes, such as interpersonal and occupational success. You probably recognize the self-fulfilling prophecy at work here, a concept we discussed in Chapter 3. The way we treat people affects how they behave and, ultimately, how they perceive themselves.

Can a "regular" person be made to act like a "beautiful" one through the self-fulfilling prophecy? Mark Snyder, Elizabeth Decker Tanke, and Ellen Berscheid (1977) decided to find out. They gave male university students a packet of information about another research participant, which included a photograph. The photograph was of either an attractive woman or an unattractive woman. The purpose of the photograph was to invoke the men's stereotype that "what is beautiful is good"—that the woman would be more warm, likeable, poised, and fun to talk to if she was physically attractive than if she was unattractive. The men then had a telephone conversation with a woman, whom they were told was the woman in the photograph; they actually spoke with a different woman. Did the men's beliefs create reality? Yes—the men who thought they were talking to an attractive woman responded to her in a warmer, more sociable manner than did the men who thought they were talking to an unattractive woman. Not only that, but the men's behaviour influenced how the women themselves responded. When observers later listened to a tape recording of the women's half of the conversation, they rated the women whose male partners thought they were physically attractive as more attractive, confident, animated, and warmer than the women whose male partners thought they were unattractive. In short, if a man thought he was talking to an attractive woman, he spoke to her in a way that brought out her best and most sparkling qualities.

This study was later replicated with the male and female roles switched. Andersen and Bem (1981) showed female participants a photograph of either an attractive or an unattractive man; the women then had a phone conversation with him. The men on the other end of the line were unaware of the women's belief about them. Just as in the Snyder, Tanke, and Berscheid (1977) study, the women acted on their stereotype of beauty, and the unknowing men responded accordingly.

Does the "what is beautiful is good" stereotype operate across cultures? The answer appears to be yes. One study found that in South Korea and in North America, people believe that physically attractive people are more socially skilled, friendly, and well adjusted. However, in Canada and the United States, the "beautiful" stereotype includes traits that are valued in individualistic cultures (e.g., strong, dominant). In South Korea, the stereotype includes traits that are valued in collectivist cultures—traits that reflect integrity and concern for others (e.g., honest, empathic; Wheeler & Kim, 1997). Based on her review of this research on this topic, Karen Dion (2002) concluded that physical attractiveness stereotyping occurs cross-culturally, although more so in individualistic societies, which place greater weight on qualities of the individual, including his or her appearance.

Attraction and the Misattribution of Arousal

Imagine that you go to see a scary movie with an extremely attractive date. As you are sitting there, you notice that your heart is thumping and you are a little short of breath. Is this because you are wildly attracted to your date or because the movie is terrifying you? It is unlikely that you could say, "Fifty-seven percent of my arousal is due to the fact that my date is gorgeous, 32 percent is due to the scary movie, and 11 percent is due to indigestion from all the popcorn I ate." Because of this difficulty in pinpointing the precise causes of our arousal, we sometimes form mistaken emotions. You might think that most of your arousal is a sign of attraction to your date, when in fact a lot of it is due to the movie (or maybe even indigestion).

Misattribution of Arousal

The process whereby people make mistaken inferences about what is causing them to feel the way they do

Many studies have demonstrated the occurrence of such **misattribution of arousal**, whereby people make mistaken inferences about what is causing them to feel the way they do (Ross & Olson, 1981; Schachter, Silversting, & Perlick, 1977; Storms & Nisbett, 1970; Valins, 1966; Zillman, 1978). Consider, for example, an intriguing field experiment by Donald Dutton and Arthur Aron (1974). Imagine you are one of the participants (all of whom were men). You are one of many people visiting the Capilano Canyon in scenic North Vancouver. Spanning the canyon is a narrow, 137-metre suspension bridge made of wooden planks attached to wire cables. You decide to walk across it. When you get a little way across, the bridge starts to sway from side to side. You feel as though you are about to tumble over the edge and you reach for the handrails, but they are so low that it feels even more likely that you will topple over. Then, you make the mistake of looking down. You see nothing but a sheer 70-metre drop to rocks and rapids below. You become more than a little aroused: Your heart is thumping, you breathe rapidly, and you begin to perspire. At this point, an attractive young woman approaches you and asks whether you could fill out a questionnaire for her, as part of a psychology project on the effects of scenic attractions on people's creativity. You decide to help her out. After you complete the questionnaire, the woman thanks you and says she would be happy to explain her study in more detail. She tears off a corner of the questionnaire, writes down her name and phone number. How attracted do you think you would be to this woman? Would you phone her and ask her out?

When people are aroused, in this case because of crossing a scary bridge, they often misattribute this arousal to the wrong source—such as attraction to the person they are with.

Think about this for a moment, and now imagine that the same woman approaches you under different circumstances. You decide to take a leisurely stroll farther up the Capilano River. You notice a wide sturdy bridge made of heavy cedar planks. The bridge has high handrails, even though it is situated only 3 metres above a shallow rivulet that runs into the main river. You are peaceably admiring the scenery when the woman asks you to fill out her questionnaire. How attracted do you feel toward her now? Dutton and Aron's prediction is clear: If you are on the high, scary bridge, you will be considerably aroused and will mistakenly think some of this arousal is the result of attraction to the beautiful woman. This is exactly what happened in the actual experiment. Half of the men (50 percent) who were approached on the high suspension bridge telephoned the woman later, whereas relatively few of the men (12.5 percent) who were approached on the low, sturdy bridge called her. (As you probably have guessed, the woman was a confederate—someone hired by the researchers—and she approached only men who were not accompanied by a woman.) This type of misattribution of arousal has been found in subsequent studies with both women and men as participants (Meston & Frohlich, 2003; Zillman, 1978).

A television series called *Love in the Wild*, launched in the summer of 2011, seems to be capitalizing on misattribution of arousal. In the show, women and men who are looking for love are paired up and engage in extreme high-arousal activities, such as navigating crocodile-infested waters and bat-infested caves. The pair that wins the high-arousal challenge of the day is rewarded with a night together in romantic, luxurious accommodation that producers describe as overflowing with everything the pair could possibly need for an intimate night of romance. The show's producers promise that "sparks will fly" (NBC.com, 2011).

In summary, we have discussed four major determinants of attraction: propinquity, similarity, reciprocal liking, and physical attractiveness. After getting to this point in the chapter, you should be in a pretty good position to make a favourable first impression the next time you meet someone. Suppose you want Chloe to like you. You should hang around her (preferably on a high, scary bridge) so you become familiar, emphasize your similarity to her, and find ways of showing that you like her. It also wouldn't hurt to look your best. But what if you want to do more than make a good impression? What if you want to have a close friendship or a romantic relationship? Stay tuned.

Forming Close Relationships

Early research on interpersonal attraction focused almost exclusively on first impressions. Why? Primarily because long-term, close relationships are much more difficult to study scientifically than first impressions. As we explained in Chapter 2, random assignment to different conditions is the hallmark of an experiment. When studying first impressions, a researcher can randomly assign you to a get-acquainted session with someone who is similar or dissimilar to you. However, a researcher can't randomly assign you to the similar or dissimilar "lover" condition and make you have a relationship! However, as we will show, important strides have been made toward understanding how close relationships are formed.

Defining Love

In the opening of this chapter, we described Bradley Bird's falling-in-love experience. But what, exactly, is love? For centuries, philosophers, poets, and novelists have grappled with this question. More recently, social psychologists have attempted to provide a scientific answer. One of the first to attempt at a scientific analysis of love was Zick Rubin (1970, 1973). He defined love as feelings of intimacy, attachment, and passion, and argued that love is a feeling distinct from liking. Subsequently, social psychologists attempted to dive deeper into the study of love and reached a conclusion that you may already have discovered. There probably isn't a single, simple definition of love because love comes in many forms. According to Ellen Berscheid (2006, 2010), there are four basic kinds of love: passionate or romantic love, companionate (friendship-based) love, compassionate love, and attachment love. Most of the research in social psychology has focused on passionate love and companionate love, which will be the focus in this chapter.

Watch on **mypsychlab**
Love Marriage: Scherazade and Roderick, late 30's

Love is something so divine, Description would but make it less; 'Tis what I feel, but can't define, 'Tis what I know, but can't express.

—Beilby Porteus *(1731–1808)*

Try to reason about love, and you will lose your reason.

—French proverb

Companionate versus Passionate Love If you have ever been in love, think back to how you felt about your sweetheart when you first got to know him or her. You probably felt a combination of giddiness, longing, joy, and anxiety—the kinds of feelings that Bradley Bird experienced when he met Nina. The ancient Greeks considered this strange, bewildering set of feelings to be a form of madness, causing all sorts of irrational and obsessional acts. Though times have changed, most people are familiar with the torment—and exhilaration—that comes with falling in love. Now think about how you feel toward your mother or your brother or a very close friend. You might also use the word *love* to describe how you feel about these important people in your life, but in this case the feelings are probably quite different from the feelings you have for your sweetheart.

Ellen Berscheid and Elaine Walster (Hatfield) (1974, 1978) attempted to capture this distinction when they proposed that there are two major kinds of love: companionate and passionate. (As mentioned earlier Ellen Berscheid has now expanded this list to four major kinds of love.) **Companionate love** is defined as the feelings of intimacy and affection we feel toward someone with whom our lives are deeply intertwined. People can experience companionate love in nonsexual relationships, such as

Companionate Love
The feelings of intimacy and affection we feel toward someone with whom our lives are deeply intertwined

The Passionate Love Scale

Explore on mypsychlab
Passionate Love Scale

These items ask you to describe how you feel when you are passionately in love. Think of the person you love most passionately right now. (If you are not in love right now, think of the last person you loved passionately. If you have never been passionately in love, think of the person whom you came closest to caring for in that way.) Choose your answer by remembering how you felt at the time when your feelings were the most intense.

For each of the 15 items, choose the number between 1 and 9 that most accurately describes your feelings. The answer scale ranges from 1, "not at all true," to 9, "definitely true." Write the number you choose next to each item.

1	2	3	4	5	6	7	8	9
Not at all true				Moderately true				Definitely true

1. I would feel deep despair if __________ left me.
2. Sometimes, I feel I can't control my thoughts; they are obsessively on __________.
3. I feel happy when I am doing something to make __________ happy.
4. I would rather be with __________ than anyone else.
5. I'd get jealous if I thought __________ were falling in love with someone else.
6. I yearn to know all about __________.
7. I want __________—physically, emotionally, and mentally.
8. I have an endless appetite for affection from __________.
9. For me, __________ is the perfect romantic partner.
10. I sense my body responding when __________ touches me.
11. __________ always seems to be on my mind.
12. I want __________ to know me—my thoughts, my fears, and my hopes.
13. I eagerly look for signs indicating __________'s desire for me.
14. I possess a powerful attraction for __________.
15. I get extremely depressed when things don't go right in my relationship with __________.

Scoring: Add up your scores for the 15 items. The total score can range from a minimum of 15 to a maximum of 135. The higher your score, the more your feelings for the person reflect passionate love.

(Adapted from Hatfield & Sprecher, 1986b)

Passionate Love

The feelings of intense longing, accompanied by physiological arousal, we feel for another person; when our love is reciprocated, we feel great fulfillment and ecstasy; but, when it is not, we feel sadness and despair

close friendships or familial relationships, or in sexual relationships, in which they experience feelings of intimacy but not a great deal of heat and passion. **Passionate love** involves an intense longing for another person. When things are going well—that is, the other person loves us, too—we feel great fulfillment and ecstasy. When things are not going well, we feel great sadness and despair. This kind of love is characterized by obsessive thoughts about the loved one, as well as heightened physiological arousal wherein we actually feel shortness of breath and a thumping heart when we are in our loved one's presence (Regan, 1998; Regan & Berscheid, 1999).

Elaine Hatfield and Susan Sprecher (1986b) developed a questionnaire to measure passionate love. Passionate love, as measured by this scale, consists of strong uncontrollable thoughts, intense feelings, and overt acts toward the target of one's affection. Find out if you are experiencing (or have experienced) passionate love, by filling out the accompanying Try It! questionnaire.

If you just completed the Passionate Love Scale, you will be reminded that falling in love is an extraordinary feeling—you are giddy, euphoric, full of energy, and close to obsessed with your new beloved. These powerful emotions, experienced by people in many different cultures, suggest that passionate/romantic love may have evolved as a primary component of the human mating system. Is something special happening in our brains when we fall in love? To find out, a team of researchers recruited university students in New York who described themselves as currently being "intensely in love" (Aron, Fisher, Mashek, Strong, Li, & Brown, 2005). They asked these research participants to bring two photographs to the experimental session: one of their beloved and one of an acquaintance of the same age and sex as their beloved. After filling out some questionnaires (including the Passionate Love Scale on page 286), the participants were ready for the main event. They slid into a functional MRI (fMRI) scanner, which records increases and decreases in blood flow in the brain. These changes in blood flow indicate which parts of the brain have neural activity at any given time.

This scene from the movie *Twilight* exemplifies the early stages of love.

The researchers found that two specific areas deep within the brain were activated when participants looked at the photographs of their romantic partner and were not activated when they looked at the photograph of their acquaintance. Furthermore, those participants who reported higher levels of passionate love showed greater activation in these areas when looking at their beloved than those who reported lower levels (Aron et al., 2005). These two brain areas were the ventral tegmental area (VTA) and the caudate nucleus, which communicate with each other as part of a circuit. A great deal is already known about what causes these areas of the brain to fire and what kind of processing they do—and now, this knowledge can be applied to the experience of passionate love.

Specifically, prior research has found that the VTA becomes highly active when people ingest cocaine—a drug that induces feelings of pleasure, euphoria, restlessness, sleeplessness, and loss of appetite (reactions that are reminiscent of falling in love, as well). The VTA, rich in the neurotransmitter dopamine, also fires when people eat chocolate. Thus, the VTA is a major "reward" and "motivation" centre of the brain, as is the caudate nucleus. For example, fMRI studies of gamblers' brains as they gambled show greatly increased activity in these dopamine-rich areas when they win, a rewarding (and motivating) event for them (Aron et al., 2005). Thus, when people say that falling in love is "like a drug" or "like winning the lottery," they're right. All these experiences activate the same areas of the brain: dopamine-rich centres of pleasure, reward, and motivation (Bartels & Zeki, 2000, 2004; Fisher, 2004).

"Ordinary" People's Definition of Love So far we have been discussing social psychologists' answers to the question "What is love?" Beverley Fehr (1988, 1994; Fehr & Russell, 1991) has been interested in how ordinary people define love. This is an important issue because the way in which people define love can determine how they act in their close relationships (e.g., deciding whether they are truly "in love," deciding whether they are experiencing the kind of love that leads to commitment). In an initial set of studies, Fehr (1988) asked students at the University of British Columbia to define love. Specifically, participants were asked to list the features or characteristics of the concept of love. The definitions of love that were generated included both companionate features (e.g., warmth, intimacy, caring) and passionate features (e.g., heart rate increases, sexual attraction, thinking about the other person all the time). In follow-up research, other participants were shown these features and were asked to rate which were most important in defining love. As shown in Table 9.1, contrary to the stereotype that university students would view love only in passionate terms, Fehr found that companionate love was seen as capturing the meaning of love more so than passionate love. Moreover, participants reported that they relied on the level of companionate love, rather than the level of passionate love, when deciding whether a relationship was progressing or deteriorating.

These studies have been replicated by researchers on the east coast of Canada (Button & Collier, 1991) and on the west coast of the United States (Aron & Westbay,

TABLE 9.1 Ratings of Features of Love*

Highest Ratings		Lowest Ratings	
Trust	7.50	Thinking about the other all the time	4.45
Caring	7.28	Energy	4.28
Honesty	7.17	Heart rate increases	4.26
Friendship	7.08	Euphoria	4.12
Respect	7.01	Gazing at the other	4.10
Concern for the other's well-being	7.00	Seeing only the other's good qualities	3.45
Loyalty	7.00	Butterflies in stomach	3.41
Commitment	6.91	Uncertainty	2.88
Accepting the other the way she/he is	6.82	Dependency	2.81
Supportiveness	6.78	Fear? Scary	2.28

*Ratings were made on a scale in which 1 = extremely poor feature of love and 8 = extremely good feature of love. The features of love to which students at the University of British Columbia assigned the highest ratings portray companionate love; the features that received the lowest ratings portray passionate love.

Source: Fehr, 1988.

1996; Luby & Aron, 1990). Participants in these studies have shown remarkable agreement on the features of love. The companionate features of love are especially likely to be mentioned and also consistently receive the highest importance ratings. These findings suggest that, at least within North America, people tend to agree on the meaning of love (Fehr, 2001, in press). Fehr and Russell (1991) examined ordinary people's conceptions of love from a slightly different angle by asking students at the University of British Columbia and at the University of Winnipeg to list different types of love. They found that the kinds of love listed could be grouped into companionate kinds of love (e.g., friendship love, familial love, maternal love) and passionate kinds of love (e.g., romantic love, passionate love, infatuation, sexual love). Once again, the companionate kinds of love were regarded as capturing the true meaning of love. Thus, ordinary people's view of love fits nicely with Berscheid and Walster (Hatfield)'s companionate/passionate distinction (Fehr, 2001, 2006). Love is seen as including both companionate and passionate aspects, although the companionate aspect is considered to be the essence of love.

Gender and Love

Who is all mushy and romantic when it comes to love? Who is practical and solid? If you are like many people, you will answer "women" to the first question and "men" to the second. But think back to our opening story of Bradley Bird and you may come up with a different answer—one that is more consistent with the results of social psychological research. Indeed, when social psychologists began to conduct research on this question, they found that men fall in love more quickly than women and are more likely to endorse romantic beliefs such as "true love lasts forever." Men are also more likely than women to report having experienced love at first sight—as Bradley Bird can attest. In contrast, women hold a more practical, friendship-based orientation to love (essentially, a companionate view of love). One of the first studies that discovered these gender differences was conducted by Kenneth Dion and Karen Dion (1973) at the University of Toronto. These differences in how women and men view love continue to be found, even among culturally diverse participants (Dion & Dion, 1993; Galperin & Haselton, 2010; Hendrick & Hendrick, 1986, 1992; Rubin, Peplau, &

Hill, 1981; Sprecher & Metts, 1989). (We will discuss this research in greater detail in the following section.)

However, researchers are beginning to realize that there also are similarities in women's and men's definitions and experience of love (Hendrick & Hendrick, 1995). In studies conducted at the University of Winnipeg, Beverley Fehr and Ross Broughton (2001) obtained the classic finding, namely, that men gave higher ratings to romantic, passionate love than did women, and women gave higher rating to companionate love than did men. However, when they looked at how high or low these ratings were, they discovered that even though men rated romantic, passionate love higher than did women, both sexes gave this kind of love a low rating (indicating that it did not capture their idea of what love is). And even though women had rated companionate love higher than men did, both sexes gave this kind of love the highest rating (indicating that this kind of love best fit their conceptions of what love is). It was concluded that women's and men's views of love are actually more similar than has been thought.

While people all over the world experience love, how love is defined varies across cultures.

Watch on mypsychlab

Arranged Marriage: Rati and Subas, 20's

Culture and Love

Throughout this book, we have noted that Western and Eastern cultures vary in important ways, with Western cultures emphasizing that the individual is autonomous and self-sufficient, and defined in terms of his or her personal qualities. Eastern cultures, in contrast, tend to be collectivistic, emphasizing the individual's loyalty to the group and defining him or her through membership in the group (Heine et al., 1999; Hofstede, 1984; Hui & Triandis, 1986; Markus, Kitayama, & Heiman, 1996; Triandis, 1995). According to Karen Dion and Kenneth Dion (1993, 1996, 2001), romantic love has less value in collectivist societies than in individualist societies. In individualist societies, romantic love is a heady, highly personal experience; one immerses oneself in the new partner and often virtually ignores friends and family for a while. The decision as to whom to become involved with or marry is for the most part a personal one. In comparison, in collectivist cultures, the individual in love must take into account the wishes of family and other group members; in fact, marriages are often by arrangement, with the respective families matching up the bride and groom (Adams, Anderson, & Adonu, 2004; Fiske, Kitayama, Markus, & Nisbett, 1998; Levine, Sato, Hashimoto, & Verma, 1995). For example, in West Africa, relationships with one's parents, siblings, and relatives are considered more important and influential than the more recent relationship one has formed with one's spouse. In many areas of West Africa, happily married couples do not live in the same house, nor do they expect to sleep together every night. In stark contrast to the pattern of intimate relationships in individualistic cultures, their connection and obligation to extended family takes precedence over that to their spouse. In individualistic cultures, the opposite is typically true (Adams, Garcia, Purdie-Vaughns, & Steele, 2004).

Consistent with these cultural differences, research has shown that people in individualistic cultures (e.g., the United States, Canada) value passionate love more than people from collectivist cultures (e.g., Asian countries) do. For example, in one study, university students in 11 countries around the world were asked, "If a man [woman] had all the qualities you desired, would you marry this person if you were not in love with him [her]?" The researchers found that marrying for love was most important to participants in Western and Westernized countries (e.g., the United States, Brazil, England, and Australia) and of least importance to participants in less-developed Eastern countries (e.g., India, Pakistan, and Thailand; Levine et al., 1995). More recently, in a large-scale study of 48 nations, Schmitt and colleagues found that scores on a love and romance scale were highest in Canada and the United States and lowest in East Asia (Schmitt, Youn, Bond, Brooks, Frye, Johnson . . . & Stoka, 2009). This is not to say that passionate love is nonexistent in collectivist cultures. Reviewing the anthropological research on 166 societies, William Jankowiak and Edward Fischer (1992; Jankowiak, 1995) found evidence for passionate love in 147 of them, as you can see in

TABLE 9.2 Cross-Cultural Evidence for Passionate Love Based on Anthropological Research in 166 Societies

Cultural Area	Passionate Love Present	Passionate Love Absent
Mediterranean	22 (95.7%)	1 (4.3%)
Sub-Saharan Africa	20 (76.9%)	6 (23.1%)
Eurasia	32 (97.0%)	1 (3.0%)
Insular Pacific	27 (93.1%)	2 (6.9%)
North America	24 (82.8%)	5 (17.2%)
South and Central America	22 (84.6%)	4 (15.4%)

Source: Data from Jankowiak & Fischer, 1992.

Table 9.2. However, as we discuss next, people in collectivist cultures are most likely to value and identify with companionate love.

Many studies have shown that people from collectivist cultures value companionate love more than people from individualistic cultures do (Dion & Dion, 1993; Gao, 1993; Jankowiak, 1995; Ting-Toomey & Chang, 1996). As Dion and Dion (1993) point out, companionate love is a "style of love that would not disrupt a complex network of existing family relationships" (p. 465). Indeed, considerable research confirms that in collectivist cultures familial relationships play an important role in the choice of romantic partners. For example, in one study, participants were presented with a scenario in which Chinese parents who had moved to Canada were upset that their child was dating a European-Canadian. Chinese-Canadian students were more likely to support the parents, whereas European-Canadian students were more likely to support the child (Uskul, Lalonde, & Cheng, 2007). According to Richard Lalonde and colleagues (e.g., Giguère & Lalonde, 2010; Lalonde & Giguère, 2008), young people from East Asian cultures living in Canada experience conflict because their parents want them to choose mates with more traditional qualities but, at the same time, these young people are influenced by the norms that are operating in Canada. It has also been shown in this work that the greater the identification that young Asian-Canadians have with their East Asian heritage, the more traditional the qualities that they want in a mate (see Marshall, 2010, for similar findings).

The results of these studies indicate that the concept of romantic love is to some extent culturally specific (Dion & Dion, 1996; Gao & Gudykunst, 1995; Hatfield & Rapson, 1996, 2002; Hatfield & Sprecher, 1995; Sprecher, Aron, Hatfield, Cortese, Potapova, & Levitskaya, 1994; Zhang, & Kline, 2009). Love can vary in definition and behaviour in different societies. We all love, but we do not necessarily all love in the same way—or at least we don't describe it in the same way. Robert Moore noted, in summarizing his research in the People's Republic of China, "Young Chinese do fall deeply in love and experience the same joys and sorrows of romance as young Westerners do. But they do so according to standards that require . . . the individual [to] sacrifice personal interests for the sake of the family . . .. This means avoiding fleeting infatuations, casual sexual encounters, and a dating context [in which] family concerns are forgotten" (Moore, 1998, p. 280).

Why Do We Love?

We began this chapter by asking, "Why are people so highly motivated to seek loving relationships?" If you were to ask a group of social psychologists this question, you would probably get a number of answers, depending on each psychologist's theoretical persuasion. Chances are that two of the answers would be "It's all about survival" (evolutionary theories) and "It's all about your mother" (attachment theories). Probably each of these theories tells part of the story. As you read about them, you may wish to think about which theory seems to best explain your motivation for seeking love.

Evolutionary Explanations of Love

The basic tenet of evolutionary biology is that an animal's "fitness" is measured by its reproductive success—that is, its ability to pass on its genes to the next generation. Reproductive success is not just part of the game; it *is* the game. Has human behaviour evolved in specific ways to maximize reproductive success? Evolutionary psychologists say yes; they argue that males and females have very different agendas because of their differing roles in producing offspring. For women, reproduction is costly in terms of time, energy, and effort, and this means that they must consider carefully when and with whom to reproduce. In comparison, reproduction has few costs for males. The evolutionary approach argues that reproductive success for the two sexes translates into two very different behaviour patterns. Male animals would do best to pursue frequent pairings with many females, and female animals would do best to pair infrequently and only with a carefully chosen male (Berkow, 1989; Symons, 1979).

What does this have to do with falling in love? According to David Buss and colleagues (1985, 1988a, 1996a, 1996b; Buss & Schmitt, 1993), the **evolutionary approach** explains the different strategies of men and women in romantic relationships. Women, facing high reproductive costs, will look for a man who can supply the resources and support she needs to bear a child. Men will look for a woman who appears capable of reproducing successfully. More specifically, men will respond to the physical appearance of women, since age and health denote reproductive fitness; women will respond to the economic and career achievements of men, since these variables represent resources they and their offspring will need (Buss, 1988b; see also Weeden & Sabini, 2005). The Bradley Bird and Nina relationship described at the beginning of this chapter would seem to fit this profile. He was swept off his feet by her beauty; she may have been attracted to him because of the better life he could offer her.

Several studies have found support for these predictions. For example, Buss and colleagues (1989, 1990, 1996a, 1996b) asked more than 9000 adults in 37 countries, including various regions of Canada, how important and desirable various characteristics were when choosing a marriage partner. In general, the women valued ambition, industriousness, and good earning capacity in a potential mate more than the men did. The men valued physical attractiveness in a mate more than the women did (Buss & Barnes, 1986; Buss & Schmitt, 1993; Hatfield & Sprecher, 1995; Lundy, Tan, & Cunningham, 1998; Regan & Berscheid, 1997). Other survey studies have found that men prefer spouses who are younger than they are—youth indicating greater reproductive fitness, while women prefer spouses around their own age (Buss, 1989; Kenrick & Keefe, 1992). We should point out, however, that in mate selection studies, the top characteristics on both women's and men's lists are the same, and they include someone who is warm and loving, honesty, trustworthiness, and a pleasant personality (see Fehr, in press). It is also the case that both women and men focus on physical attractiveness when it comes to having a short-term fling. When it comes to having a long-term relationship, both women and men focus less on looks and more on whether this person has desired qualities of a long-term mate (Gangestad, Garver-Apgar, Simpson, & Cousins, 2007; Little, Burriss, Jones, DeBruine, & Caldwell, 2008; Regan & Berscheid, 1997).

A recent topic of interest in evolutionary psychology is whether ovulation affects women's mate preferences. The findings of a number of different studies suggest that this is the case. It has been found, for example, that when women are at the most fertile point of their cycle, they are more likely to engage in mate-attracting behaviours such as wearing more sexy, revealing clothing, than they do at other times of their cycle (Durante, Li, & Haselton, 2008; Haselton, Mortezai, Pillsworth, Belske-Rechek, & Frederick, 2007). Near ovulation, women also report feeling more attractive and express greater interest in going to places where they can meet men (Haselton & Gangestad, 2006). Interestingly, when they are most fertile, women find masculine-looking

Watch on **mypsychlab**
Relationships and Love

Men seek to propagate widely, whereas women seek to propagate wisely.

—Robert Hinde, *Animal Behaviour, 1984*

Watch on **mypsychlab**
Evolution and Sex: Michael Bailey

Evolutionary Approach
An approach derived from evolutionary biology that states that men and women are attracted to different characteristics in each other—men are attracted by women's appearance; women are attracted by men's resources—because this maximizes their reproductive success

men most attractive—more so than they do when they are in a low-fertility part of their cycle (Johnston, Hagel, Franklin, Fink, & Grammer, 2001). More masculine features are indicators of testosterone and are believed to be associated with good health. Research also has shown that women who feel that their current partners are not very good "catches" are more likely to be flirtatious and interested in having an affair during high-fertility phases (Haselton & Gangestad, 2006; Pillsworth, & Haselton, 2006).

Finally, since it is to our evolutionary advantage to avoid close genetic others as sexual partners, it may interest you to learn that during times of peak fertility, young women avoid their fathers. More specifically, a recent study tracked the frequency and duration of young women's cellphone calls during times of high and low fertility. Fathers were less likely to be called and calls were of shorter duration when the participants were at the highest risk of conception (Lieberman, Pillsworth, & Haselton, 2011). The basic point of the evolutionary approach to love is that strategies evolved in our ancestral environments which helped males and females produce healthy offspring, perpetuating the species. The research we have discussed suggests that these strategies are still with us—affecting us, unconsciously, when we decide with whom to become involved intimately.

It may have occurred to you that the data we have been discussing could be explained in other ways. Indeed, the evolutionary approach to love has attracted its share of criticism and generated considerable controversy (Bradshaw, Bubier, & Sullivan, 1994; McKelvie & McLellan, 1993, 1994; Schmitt et al., 2009). Some social psychologists argue that the theory is untestable; we can't do an experiment to prove that evolutionary forces are the primary cause of current human behaviour (Sternberg & Beall, 1991). Others suggest that it is an oversimplification of extremely complex human behaviour (Travis & Yeager, 1991). It has also been argued that findings such as men valuing physical attractiveness and youth in a partner can be explained in terms of decades of conditioning by advertising and media images (Hatfield & Rapson, 1993).

Still other researchers note that around the world women have less power, status, wealth, and other resources than men do. If women need to rely on men to achieve economic security, they must consider this characteristic when choosing a mate. In comparison, men are generally free to choose a woman by using more frivolous criteria such as good looks (Rosenblatt, 1974). Interestingly, in an analysis of several countries, Gangestad (1993) found that the more economic power women had in a given culture, the more women were interested in a physically attractive man. A more recent study found that both women and men from wealthy families wanted a partner who was also wealthy. This study also found that both women and men who were good-looking wanted to find their match: a beautiful or handsome mate (Buston & Emlen, 2003). So, as you can see, when discussing human mate preference, it is difficult to disentangle nature (inborn preferences) from nurture (cultural norms and gender roles). The evolutionary approach is an interesting, exciting, and controversial theory; further theorizing and research will reveal more about the role that biology plays in love.

CONNECTIONS

Does Your Face Reveal Your "Intentions"?

Wouldn't life be easier if all you had to do was look at someone's face to know whether that person was interested in a short-term fling or a serious, long-term relationship? Recent research suggests that this may actually be the case! Lynda Boothroyd and colleagues (2008) administered a test to a group of British university students that assessed the extent to which they were open to short-term sexual relationships. They then took photos of those participants who scored very high on this scale and photos of those who scored low (i.e., those who were not open to casual sexual relationships). The photographs were then arranged in pairs, such that the photo of a person who was interested in casual sex would be paired with a photo of a person who was not open to casual sex. A new group of participants was shown these pairs and asked to "choose the individual that you feel is more open to short-term relationships, one-night stands, and the idea of sex without love."

Were participants able to correctly identify who was open to casual sex and who wasn't? It turns out that women were good at making these kinds of judgments. In fact, they were able to do this when looking at female and male faces. Men were somewhat less accurate (Boothroyd, Jones, Burt, DeBruine, & Perrett, 2008). A follow-up study found that women rated the men who were open to casual sex as less attractive for a long-term relationship than the men who were not open to casual sex. Keep in mind that these women didn't know these men's attitudes toward casual sex—all they had to go on was a photograph. Interestingly, it didn't matter if the researchers used actual photographs or composites (such as those shown on the next page) in which they averaged faces of women and men who were open to casual sex and then averaged the faces of women and men who were not open to casual sex.

In research along the same lines conducted at Saint Mary's University, it was found that women gave higher attractiveness ratings to a man's face when he was described as desiring a long-term rather than a short-term relationship and when he was described as having little rather than a lot of sexual experience (Williams, Fisher & Cox, 2008).

How should these findings be interpreted? According to evolutionary theory, women and men have different "agendas" when they play the mating game. Men want to ensure successful reproduction (i.e., passing on their genes), whereas women want to find a partner who can be counted on to provide the resources required to raise offspring. From an evolutionary perspective, it would be advantageous for women to be able to detect which men are good long-term prospects. It would also be advantageous to be able to figure out sooner rather than later who is not a good long-term prospect, to avoid making a costly mistake. This may be why women need only to glance at a man's face to figure out his "intentions" and why they perceive men who have "slept around" a lot and who are interested in short-term flings as less attractive than men who seem to be better long-term prospects.

An interesting side note: Which person in the pairs of accompanying photographs do you find more attractive? In Boothroyd and colleagues' (2008) studies, both women and men rated the photographs of the women who were open to casual sex (the lower photo) as more attractive than the photographs of the women who were not open to casual sex (the upper photo). On the other hand, men who were open to casual sex (the photo on the right) were not rated as more attractive but were rated as more masculine looking than men who were not open to casual sex (photo on the left) by both women and men.

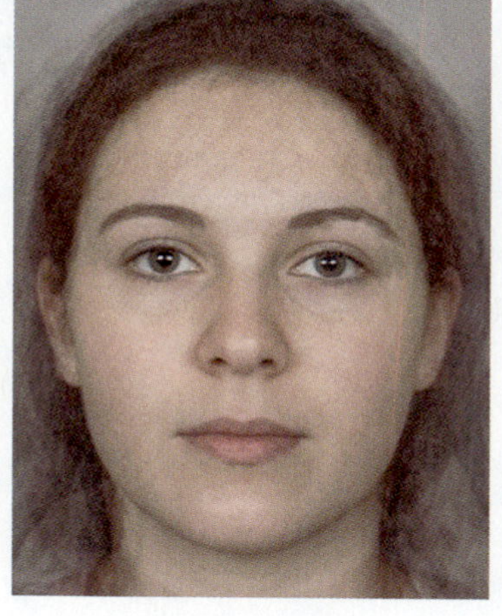

Not open to casual sex.

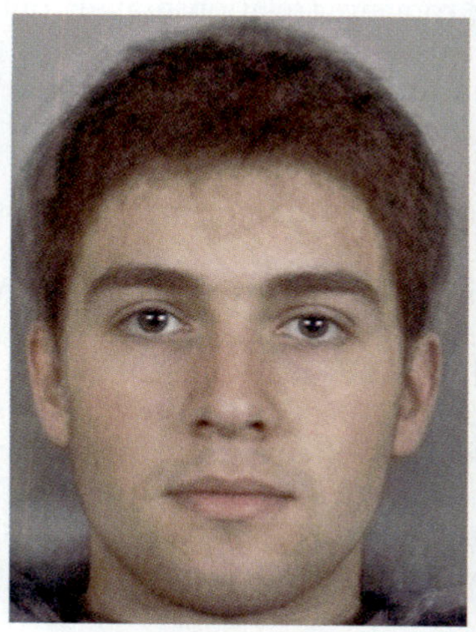

Not open to casual sex.

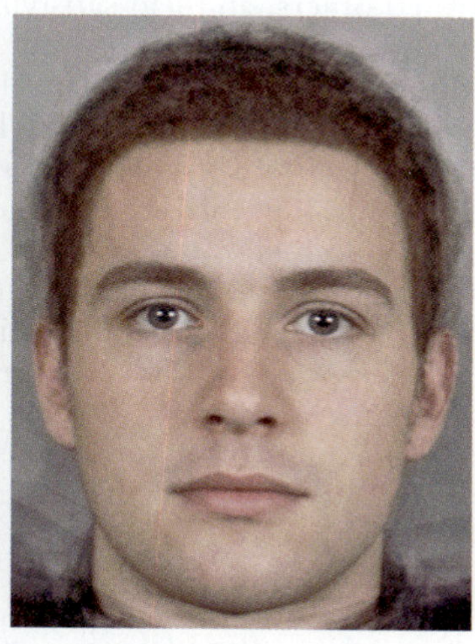

Open to casual sex.

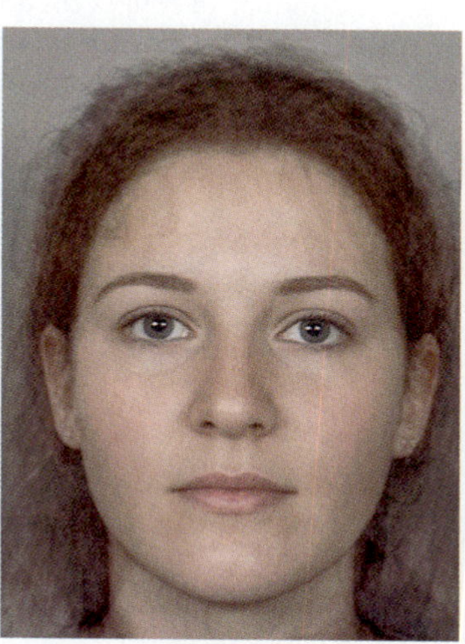

Open to casual sex.

Attachment Styles and Intimate Relationships

The evolutionary approach takes the long view—how people act today is based on behaviour patterns that evolved from our species' hominid past. Another theory of love also focuses on the past, but on the more recent past; **attachment theory** states that our behaviour in adult relationships is based on our experiences as infants with our parents or caregivers. This approach draws on the groundbreaking work of John Bowlby (1969, 1973, 1980) and Mary Ainsworth (Ainsworth, Blehar, Waters, & Wall, 1978) on how infants form bonds to their primary caregivers (usually their mother). The theory of **attachment styles** states that the kinds of bonds we form early in life influence the kinds of relationships we form as adults. Ainsworth and her colleagues (1978) identified three types of relationships between infants and their mothers.

Attachment Theory

The theory that our behaviour in adult relationships is based on our experiences as infants with our parents or caregivers

Attachment Styles

The expectations people develop about relationships with others based on the relationship they had with their primary caregiver when they were infants

Parent-Child Attachments: Ross Thompson

Secure Attachment Style

An attachment style characterized by trust, a lack of concern with being abandoned, and the view that one is worthy and well liked

Avoidant Attachment Style

An attachment style characterized by a suppression of attachment needs, because attempts to be intimate have been rebuffed; people with this style find it difficult to develop intimate relationships

Anxious/Ambivalent Attachment Style

An attachment style characterized by a concern that others will not reciprocate one's desire for intimacy, resulting in higher-than-average levels of anxiety

Connect to MyPsychLab

To take a survey to assess your experiences with the father-figure in your life, go to MyPsychLab

- Infants with a **secure attachment style** typically have caregivers who are responsive to their needs and who show positive emotions when interacting with them. These infants trust their caregivers, are not worried about being abandoned, and come to view themselves as worthy and loved.
- Infants with an **avoidant attachment style** typically have caregivers who are aloof and distant, rebuffing the infant's attempts to establish intimacy. These infants desire to be close to their caregiver but learn to suppress this need, as if they know that attempts to be intimate will be rejected. People with this style find it difficult to become close to other people.
- Infants with an **anxious/ambivalent attachment style** typically have caregivers who are inconsistent and overbearing in their affection. These infants are unusually anxious, because they can never predict when and how their caregivers will respond to their needs. People with this style desperately seek closeness to others but experience mixed, conflicted feelings even when they are in a loving relationship.

The key assumption of attachment theory is that the particular attachment style we learn as infants and young children typically stays with us throughout life and generalizes to all of our relationships with other people (Fraley & Shaver, 2000; Hartup & Laursen, 1999; Mikulincer & Shaver, 2005, 2007). In a groundbreaking study, Cindy Hazan and Phillip Shaver (1987) asked adults to choose one of three descriptions designed to capture the three kinds of attachment styles described above, according to how they typically felt in romantic relationships. The researchers also asked people questions about their current and past relationships. The results of this study were consistent with an attachment theory perspective. Securely attached adults reported that they easily became close to other people, readily trusted others, and had satisfying romantic relationships. People with an avoidant style reported that they were uncomfortable becoming close to others, found it difficult to trust others, and had less satisfying romantic relationships. People with an anxious/ambivalent style also tended to have less satisfying relationships but of a different type: They were likely to be obsessive and preoccupied with their relationships, fearing that their partners did not want to be as intimate or close as they desired.

These findings have been replicated in literally hundreds of studies (see Mikulincer & Shaver, 2007). For example, at the University of Toronto, Keelan, Dion, and Dion (1994) found that people who were securely attached maintained high levels of satisfaction, commitment, and trust in their romantic relationship over the four-month period of the study, whereas those who were insecurely attached (i.e., avoidant and anxious-ambivalent) showed decreases in satisfaction, commitment, and trust over time. Although most of the research has focused on heterosexual relationships, a recent study conducted with female same-sex couples in Canada and the United States similarly found that avoidant and anxious attachment are negatively correlated with relationship satisfaction (Horne & Biss, 2009).

Watch on mypsychlab

Attachment in Infants

Attachment theory predicts that the attachment style we learn as infants stays with us throughout life and generalizes to our relationships with other people.

Considerable research shows that people with insecure attachment (anxious or avoidant) tend to have difficulty forming relationships in the first place. Anxious people are desperate to be in a relationship, but at the same time, are terrified of rejection. In a series of studies conducted at the University of Manitoba, Vorauer and colleagues (2003) found that people with anxious attachment are so afraid of rejection in a romantic relationship that they overestimate how much romantic interest they are communicating to a potential partner. The problem is that the target of their overtures may not even realize that an overture is being made (Vorauer, Cameron, Holmes, & Pearce, 2003). More recently, researchers at McGill University observed how people high in anxiety behave in speed dating situations (avoidant people aren't very motivated to form relationships, so, not surprisingly, tend not to sign up for speed dating). In the sessions, participants had three-minute interactions with members of the opposite sex (16 to 23, depending on the session) and, for each person, indicated whether they wanted to pursue further contact. Anxiously-attached people's desperation was evident in these choices—they were unselective, meaning that they wanted to pursue a lot of the people they had met. Sadly, this interest tended not to be reciprocated—the participants who were highest in anxious attachment tended to be the least popular (i.e., not selected for further contact by their speed dating partners; McClure, Lydon, Baccus, & Baldwin, 2010).

In my very own self, I am part of my family.

—D. H. Lawrence
(1885–1930)

Even when anxious people manage to form relationships, they continue to be haunted by fears of rejection because now they worry that their partner will reject them. Sadly, these beliefs may become a reality. Murray, Griffin, Rose, and Bellavia (2003) found that married people with insecure attachment were more likely to internalize experiences of rejection from their partner, which led to decreases in self-esteem. This sensitivity to rejection predicted a decline in the partner's satisfaction over the course of a year (Murray et al., 2003).

Not surprisingly, people's attachment style also affects how they handle conflict and problems in their relationships. University of Western Ontario researcher Lorne Campbell and his colleagues had a large sample of dating couples participate in a two-week diary study in which they recorded the amount of conflict and social support as well as the overall quality they perceived in their dating relationship (Campbell, Simpson, Boldry, & Kashy, 2005). The researchers found that attachment anxiety was correlated with reports of high levels of conflict. In fact, anxiously attached participants reported more conflicts than their partners did. Moreover, in a follow-up laboratory session, when discussing an actual conflict, participants who were high in attachment

TABLE 9.3 Measuring Attachment Styles

Secure style	47%*	It is relatively easy for me to become emotionally close to others. I am comfortable depending on others and having others depend on me. I don't worry about being alone or having others not accept me.
Preoccupied (anxious) style	14%	I want to be completely emotionally intimate with others, but I often find that others are reluctant to get as close as I would like. I am uncomfortable being without close relationships, but I sometimes worry that others don't value me as much as I value them.
Dismissive avoidant style	18%	I am comfortable without close emotional relationships. It is very important for me to feel independent and self-sufficient, and I prefer not to depend on others or have them depend on me.
Fearful avoidant style	21%	I am somewhat uncomfortable getting close to others. I want emotionally close relationships, but I find it difficult to trust others completely, or to depend on them. I sometimes worry that I will be hurt if I allow myself to become too close to others.

*The percentages in each category are based on a sample of Introductory Psychology students.

Source: Adapted from Bartholomew, K. & Horowitz, L. M. (1991). Attachment styles among young adults: A test of a four-category model. *Journal of Personality and Social Psychology, 61,* 226–244. Copyright © 1991 by the American Psychological Association. Adapted with permission.

anxiety reported greater distress during the interaction than participants who were low in attachment anxiety—even if their partner had responded in a positive manner (Campbell et al., 2005). A recent study of married and co-habiting couples in Quebec found that anxious and avoidant attachment styles are also associated with sexual difficulties in a relationship. For example, avoidant people limited intimacy by avoiding sexual encounters. Anxious men had sex less often if they felt their partner was pressuring them; anxious women avoided sex, especially if they were with an avoidant man (Brassard, Shaver, & Lussier, 2007).

In another study, Lussier, Sabourin, and Turgeon (1997) examined the relation between attachment style and coping strategies among a sample of French Canadian cohabiting and married couples. They found that when difficulties arose, secure participants reported using active task-centred coping strategies that were aimed at solving problems. These strategies were associated with marital well-being. As you might expect, avoidant participants tended to use passive, avoidant strategies. Anxious/ambivalent participants used passive, emotion-focused coping strategies—strategies that were associated with marital distress.

It probably will not surprise you to learn that when a relationship ends, anxious attachment is associated with more rumination, brooding, preoccupation, regret, and less positive adjustment to the breakup, as shown by a recent study conducted in Victoria (Saffrey & Ehrenberg, 2007).

In an important conceptual development pertaining to avoidant attachment, Simon Fraser University researcher Kim Bartholomew proposed that there are actually two kinds of avoidant attachment (Bartholomew, 1990; Bartholomew & Horowitz, 1991). People with a **fearful avoidant style** consciously desire intimate relationships but avoid them because they are afraid to trust others and worry that they will be hurt if they allow themselves to become too close to another person. People with a **dismissive avoidant style** claim that they do not need close relationships, preferring to be independent and self-sufficient. Bartholomew developed a scale to assess secure attachment, preoccupied attachment (similar to the anxious/ambivalent attachment discussed earlier), and these two avoidant styles (Bartholomew & Horowitz, 1991; see Table 9.3). Research has shown that people with a fearful avoidant style have a negative view of themselves and of other people, whereas people with a dismissive avoidant style have a positive view of themselves but a negative view of others (Bartholomew & Horowitz, 1991). People with a fearful style also report greater distress when a romantic relationship ends than do those with a dismissive style (Sprecher, Felmlee, Metts, Fehr, & Vanni, 1998).

Fearful Avoidant Style

A type of avoidant attachment in which close relationships are avoided because of mistrust and fears of being hurt

Dismissive Avoidant Style

A type of avoidant attachment in which the person is self-sufficient and claims not to need close relationships

Multiple Attachment Representations Please reread the attachment descriptions in Table 9.3. For each description, try to think of a relationship—with a romantic partner, friend, or parent—in which you felt that way. When students at the University of Winnipeg were asked to do so, most of them were able to think of relationships that matched each style (Baldwin, Keelan, Fehr, Enns, & Koh-Rangarajoo, 1996). Indeed, it is now acknowledged that rather than possessing one single attachment style that applies to all of our relationships, we can have different kinds of attachment to different people in our lives (Fraley, 2002; Pitman & Scharfe, 2010; Simpson, Rholes, Campbell, & Wilson, 2003). For example, Ross and Spinner (2001) asked students at the University of New Brunswick and adults from the adjacent community to fill out the Bartholomew and Horowitz (1991) scale for four specific relationships (e.g., mother, friend). The researchers found that relationship-specific attachment ratings are not necessarily the same as people's reports of their general attachment style—"Knowing, for example, that an individual is securely attached to his or her mother tells us relatively little about whether that individual is also securely attached in other relationships" (Ross & Spinner, 2001).

A similar conclusion was reached by McGill University researchers Tamarha Pierce and John Lydon (2001). In a series of studies, they found that people's overall attachment style is correlated with, but distinct from, their attachment in specific relationships (e.g., mother, father, best friend, and romantic partner). Interestingly, over time, attachment to specific partners changed in the direction of global overall attachment, rather than vice versa. In other words, if you are generally secure, your attachment in specific relationships will tend to become secure, whereas your attachment in any particular relationship is less likely to change your overall style.

Findings such as these have led researchers such as Mark Baldwin and Beverley Fehr (1995; Baldwin et al., 1996) to suggest that attachment styles might best be conceptualized as schemas—mental structures that people use to organize information—rather than as stable personality traits. As we discussed in Chapter 3, schemas are resistant to change but not impossible to change. In the context of attachment theory, this is good news, because it implies that people can learn new and healthier ways of relating to others than they experienced in infancy (Kirkpatrick & Hazan, 1994; Kojetin, 1993). Indeed, there is mounting evidence that even if people had unhappy relationships with their parents, they are not doomed to a lifetime of unhappy relationships.

The Genetic Contribution to Attachment Styles Your attachment style is clearly shaped by your "environment"—your caregivers as a child, and the friends and romantic partners with whom you interact as an adult. Do your genes affect your attachment style, too? Two recent studies explored just this question. Omri Gillath and colleagues collected saliva samples from their research participants, from which their DNA was extracted (Gillath, Shaver, Baek, & Chun, 2008). DNA sequences were tested for the presence and number of specific alleles related to the neurotransmitters dopamine and serotonin. The researchers also had participants rate themselves on attachment anxiety and avoidance. They found that the presence of a particular dopamine allele pattern was significantly related to attachment anxiety, and a particular serotonin allele pattern was significantly related to attachment avoidance. The strength of these relationships indicated that genes accounted for about 20 percent of the variability in attachment anxiety and avoidance (Gillath et al., 2008). Thus, a person's genotype may predispose him or her to a specific attachment style, which will then be further affected, one way or the other, by influences in the environment.

Donnellan and colleagues (2008) conducted a study in which they compared the anxiety and avoidance attachment scores of monozygotic (MZ) twins (identical twins) and dizygotic (DZ) twins (fraternal twins) who were in their twenties. Each pair of twins had grown up together and had presumably experienced similar caregiving. Of course, MZ twins share the same genes, while DZ twins are no more similar genetically than any two siblings. Using behavioural genetic statistical modelling to compare MZ and DZ twins, the researchers determined that genetic effects accounted for 45 percent of the variability in attachment anxiety and 39 percent of the variability in attachment avoidance. Most of the remaining variability was due to the environment, but not the shared environment of the childhood home. Instead, the researchers found that nonshared aspects of the environment affected the participants' scores on attachment anxiety and avoidance. Nonshared experiences (meaning "not shared by one's twin") would principally involve the relationships that the participants had had as adults (Donnellan, Burt, Levendosky, & Klump, 2008). This is another indicator that attachment styles can be fluid and are capable of changing over the course of a lifetime. While we await more research on the heritability of attachment styles, it currently appears that one's genes account for 20 to 45 percent of the anxious and avoidant styles, with one's environment accounting for the rest.

In summary, we began this section with the important question "Why do we love?" According to evolutionary theories, we love to increase our chances of reproduction, thereby ensuring the survival of our species. According to attachment theory, we learned lessons about how worthy we are of love from our primary caregiver, and those lessons determine whether we seek loving relationships as well as the quality of those relationships.

Maintaining Close Relationships

So far we have been focusing on how relationships begin. However, this is only the first chapter in the story of a relationship. Granted, some relationships read a lot like short stories—they may consist of only one chapter; other relationships, however, may evolve into novels, with many chapters. Social psychologists also have something to say about the process of maintaining a relationship once it has been formed.

Social Exchange Theories

Social exchange and equity theories are based on the simple notion that relationships operate on an economic model of costs and benefits, in much the way that the marketplace operates (Blau, 1964; Homans, 1961; Kelley & Thibaut, 1978; Thibaut & Kelley, 1959). **Social exchange theory** states that how people feel about a relationship depends on their perception of the rewards they receive from the relationship and their perception of the costs they incur, as well as their perception of what kind of relationship they deserve, and the probability that they could have a better relationship with someone else. In other words, we "buy" the best relationship we can get, one that gives us the most value for our emotional dollar. The basic concepts of social exchange theory are *reward*, *cost*, *outcome*, *comparison level*, and *comparison level for alternatives* (Thibaut & Kelley, 1959).

Social Exchange Theory

The theory that how people feel about a relationship depends on their perceptions of the rewards and costs of the relationship, the kind of relationship they deserve, and the probability that they could have a better relationship with someone else

Rewards are the positive, gratifying aspects of the relationship that make it worthwhile and reinforcing. They include the positive personal characteristics and behaviour of your relationship partner (e.g., similarity, attractiveness, sense of humour) and your ability to acquire external resources by virtue of knowing this person (e.g., gaining access to money, status, activities, or other interesting people; Lott & Lott, 1974). Costs are, obviously, the other side of the coin; all friendships and romantic relationships have some costs attached to them (e.g., putting up with the annoying habits and characteristics of the other person). The outcome of the relationship is based on a calculation of the **reward/cost ratio**—you can think of it as a mathematical formula in which outcome equals rewards minus costs. (If you come up with a negative number, your relationship is not in good shape.)

Reward/Cost Ratio

The notion that there is a balance between the rewards that come from a relationship and the personal cost of maintaining the relationship; if the ratio is not favourable, the result is dissatisfaction with the relationship

How satisfied you are with your relationship depends on another variable—your **comparison level**, or your expectations about the levels of rewards and costs that you deserve in a relationship (Kelley & Thibaut, 1978; Thibaut & Kelley, 1959). Some people have a high comparison level, expecting to receive many rewards and incur few costs in their relationships. If a given relationship doesn't match this comparison level, people will be unhappy and unsatisfied. In contrast, people who have a low comparison level would be happy in the same relationship, because they expect relationships to be difficult and costly.

Comparison Level

People's expectations about the levels of rewards and costs that they deserve in a relationship

Finally, your satisfaction with a relationship also depends on your perception of the likelihood that you could replace it with a better one—or your **comparison level for alternatives.** There are a lot of people out there. Could a relationship with a different person—or even being alone—give you a better outcome, or greater rewards for fewer costs, than your current relationship does? People who have a high comparison level for alternatives—perhaps because they believe the world is full of fabulous people dying to meet them or because they are not afraid to be on their own—are more likely to get out of a relationship. People with a low comparison level for alternatives will be more likely to stay in a costly relationship because, to them, what they have is not great but they don't think they could find anything better out there.

Comparison Level for Alternatives

People's expectations about the level of rewards and punishments they would receive in an alternative relationship

Rewards, costs, and alternatives do not tell the whole story, however. As you may have observed, many people do not leave their partners, even when they are dissatisfied and their alternatives look bright. Caryl Rusbult and her colleagues would agree; they say that we need to consider at least one additional factor to understand close relationships: a person's level of investment in the relationship (Kelley, 1983; Rusbult, 1980, 1983, 1991; Rusbult, Martz, & Agnew, 1998). In her **investment model** of close relationships, Rusbult defines investments as anything that people have put into a relationship that will be lost if they leave it—tangible things, such as financial resources and possessions (e.g., a house), as well as intangible things, such as the emotional welfare of one's children, or time and emotional energy spent building the relationship. As seen in Figure 9.3, the greater the investment individuals have in a relationship, the less likely they are to leave, even if satisfaction is low and alternatives are available. In short, to predict whether people will stay in an intimate relationship, according to the investment model, we need to know (1) how satisfied they are with the relationship (i.e., the level of rewards minus costs); (2) whether they believe that attractive alternatives are available; and (3) the extent of their investment in the relationship.

What, after all, is our life but a great dance in which we are all trying to fix the best going rate of exchange?

—Malcolm Bradbury, *1992*

Investment Model

The theory that people's commitment to a relationship depends on their satisfaction with the relationship in terms of rewards, costs, and comparison level; their comparison level for alternatives; and how much they have invested in the relationship that would be lost by leaving it

To test this model, Rusbult (1983) asked students involved in heterosexual dating relationships to fill out questionnaires over a seven-month period. Every three weeks or so, people answered questions about each of the components of the model shown in Figure 9.3. Rusbult also kept track of whether the students stayed in the relationships

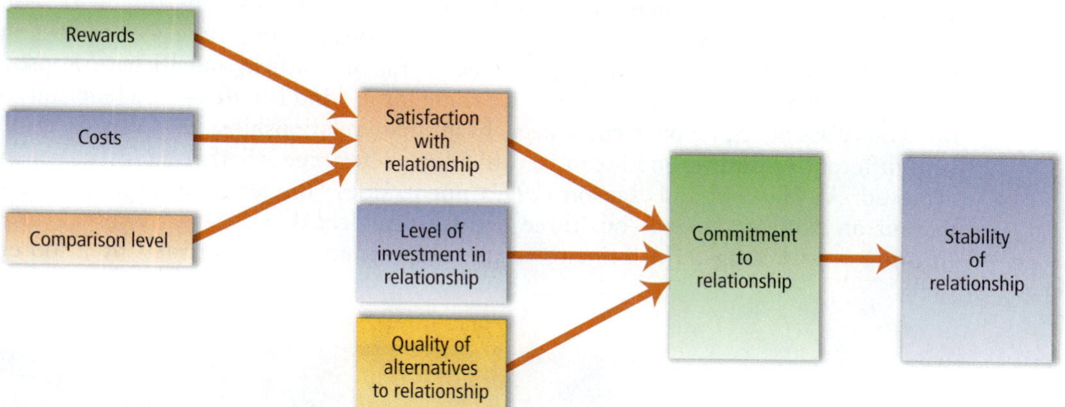

FIGURE 9.3

The investment model of commitment.

People's commitment to a relationship depends on three variables: how satisfied they are (i.e., rewards minus costs), how much they feel they have invested in the relationship, and whether they have good alternatives to this relationship. These commitment variables in turn predict how stable the relationship will be. A woman who feels, for example, that the costs exceed the rewards in her relationship would have low satisfaction; if she also felt she had little invested in the relationship and another very attractive person was expressing interest in her, she would have a low level of commitment. The end result is low stability; most likely, she would break up with her current partner.

(Adapted from Rusbult, 1983)

or broke up with their partner. Consistent with the model, people's satisfaction, alternatives, and investments all predicted how committed they were to the relationship and whether it lasted. Subsequent studies have found similar results for married couples of diverse ages, for women in abusive relationships, for lesbian and gay couples, for close friends, and for residents of the United States, the Netherlands, and Taiwan (Lin & Rusbult, 1995; Rusbult, 1991; Rusbult & Buunk, 1993; Rusbult & Martz, 1995; Rusbult, Olson, Davis, & Hannon, 2001; see review by Rusbult & Van Lange, 2003).

Equity Theory

Equity Theory
The theory that people are happiest with relationships in which the rewards and costs that a person experiences, and the contributions that he or she makes to the relationship are roughly equal to the rewards, costs, and contributions of the other person

Some researchers have criticized social exchange theory for ignoring an essential variable in relationships—the notion of fairness. Proponents of **equity theory** argue that people are not just out to get the most rewards for the least cost; they are also concerned about equity in their relationships, wherein the rewards and costs they experience and the contributions they make to the relationship are comparable with the rewards, costs, and contributions of the other person (Homans, 1961; Walster (Hatfield), Walster, & Berscheid, 1978). These theorists describe equitable relationships as the most happy and stable type. In comparison, inequitable relationships result in one person feeling overbenefited (i.e., getting a lot of rewards, incurring few costs, devoting little time or energy to the relationship) or underbenefited (i.e., getting few rewards, incurring a lot of costs, devoting a lot of time and energy to the relationship).

According to equity theory, both underbenefited and overbenefited partners should feel uneasy about this state of affairs, and both should be motivated to restore equity to the relationship. This makes sense for the underbenefited person. Who wants to continue feeling miserable? But why should the overbenefited individual want to give up what social exchange theory indicates is a cushy deal—lots of rewards for little cost and little work? Hatfield and Walster (1978) argue that equity is all about fairness; people will eventually feel uncomfortable or even guilty if they get more than they deserve in a relationship. However, let's face facts—being overbenefited just doesn't feel as bad as being underbenefited, and research has, in fact, borne out that inequity is perceived as more of a problem by the underbenefited individual (Buunk & Prins, 1998; Clark & Chrisman, 1994; Hatfield, Greenberger, Traupmann, & Lambert, 1982; Sprecher, 1998; Sprecher & Schwartz, 1994; Traupmann et al., 1981; Van Yperen & Buunk, 1994).

Does equity theory operate in long-term relationships the same way it does in new or less intimate relationships? Not exactly. Elaine Hatfield and Richard Rapson (1993) note that in casual relationships we trade for in-kind benefits—you lend someone your class notes, he buys you a beer. In intimate relationships, however, we trade very different resources, and it can be difficult to determine whether equity has been achieved. As Hatfield and Rapson (1993) put it, does "dinner at an expensive restaurant on Monday balance out three nights of neglect due to a heavy workload"? In other words, long-term intimate relationships seem to be governed by a looser

Close relationships can have either exchange or communal properties. Family relationships are typically communal; acquaintanceships are typically based on exchange, though they can become communal if they grow into friendships.

give-and-take notion of equity, rather than a rigid tit-for-tat strategy (Kollack, Blumstein, & Schwartz, 1994; Laursen & Hartup, 2002; Vaananen, Buunk, Kivimaki, Pentti, & Vahteva, 2005).

According to Margaret Clark and Judson Mills, interactions between new acquaintances or casual friends are governed by equity concerns and are called **exchange relationships.** In exchange relationships, people keep track of who is contributing what and feel taken advantage of when they feel they are putting more into the relationship than they are getting out of it. However, interactions between close friends, family members, and romantic partners are governed less by an equity norm and more by a desire to help each other in times of need (Clark, 1984, 1986; Clark & Mills, 1979, 1993; Mills & Clark, 1982, 1994, 2001). In these **communal relationships**, people give in response to the other's needs, regardless of whether they are repaid. In fact, a critical feature of communal relationships is the perception that the other person will respond to one's needs with behaviours that communicate understanding and caring (Clark & Monin, 2006; Lemay, Clark, & Feeney, 2007; Reis, Clark & Holmes, 2004). These two kinds of relationships are summarized in Figure 9.4.

Exchange Relationships
Relationships governed by the need for equity (i.e., for a comparable ratio of rewards and costs)

Communal Relationships
Relationships in which people's primary concern is being responsive to the other person's needs

In a series of experiments, Margaret Clark and her colleagues varied whether people desired an exchange or a communal relationship with another person, and then observed the extent to which they were concerned with equity in the relationship. In these experiments, participants interacted with an interesting person and were told either that this person was new to the area and wanted to meet new people—thereby increasing their interest in establishing a communal relationship with the person—or that the other person was married and visiting the area for only a brief time—thereby making them more inclined to favour an exchange relationship with the person (Clark, 1984; Clark & Mills, 1979; Clark & Waddell, 1985; Williamson & Clark, 1989, 1992). As predicted, people in the exchange condition operated according to the equity norm. People in the communal condition, thinking there was a chance for a long-term relationship, were relatively unconcerned with a tit-for-tat accounting of who was contributing what. These results are not

The friendships which last are those wherein each friend respects the other's dignity to the point of not really wanting anything from him.

—Cyril Connolly
(1903–1974)

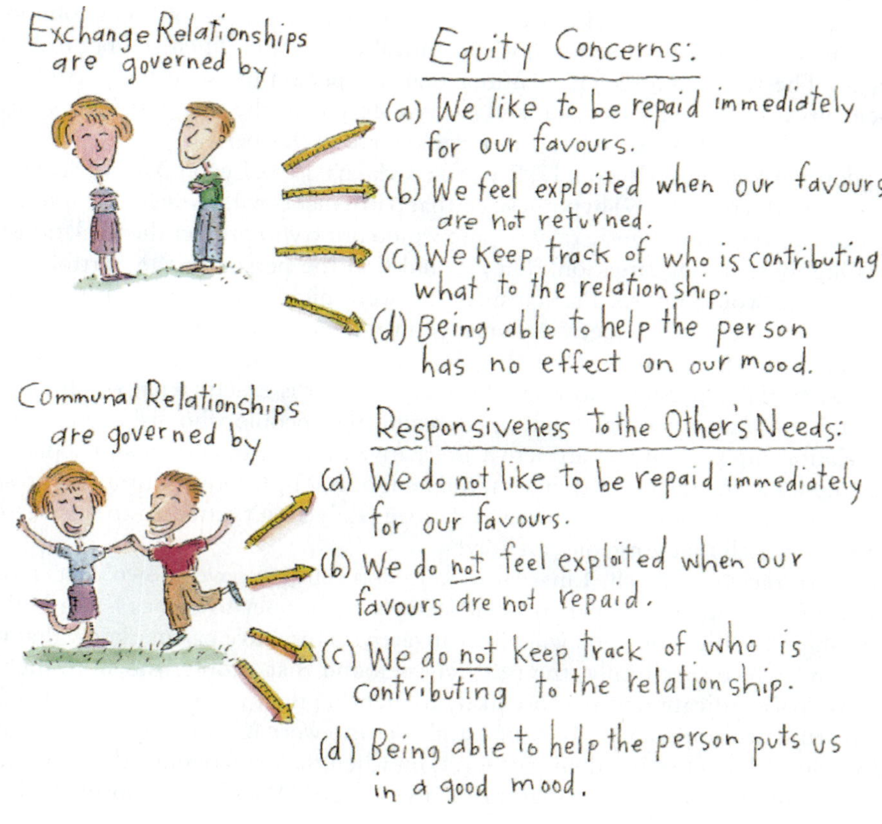

FIGURE 9.4
Exchange versus communal relationships.

limited to exchange and communal relationships created in the laboratory. Other studies show that ongoing friendships are more communal than relationships between strangers (Clark, Mills, & Corcoran, 1989).

Are people in communal relationships completely unconcerned with equity? No. As we saw earlier, people do feel distressed if they believe their intimate relationships are inequitable (Canary & Stafford, 2001; Walster et al., 1978). However, equity takes on a somewhat different form in communal relationships than it does in less intimate ones. In communal relationships, the partners are more relaxed about what constitutes equity at any given time; they believe that things will eventually balance out and a rough kind of equity will be achieved over time (Lemay & Clark, 2008; Lemay, Clark, & Feeney, 2007). If this is not the case—if they come to feel there is a chronic imbalance—the relationship may end.

The Role of Commitment in Maintaining Relationships

Every relationship faces challenges—a loss of passion over time, fights with in-laws, and temptations such as the single, attractive co-worker in the office next door. The "glue" that holds relationships together under these kinds of circumstances is commitment. As we discuss next, commitment operates in various ways—all of which serve to keep relationships together.

Commitment and Resisting Attractive Alternatives What do people do to preserve their relationship when an attractive alternative partner comes along? This important question has been addressed in a series of ingenious experiments by McGill University researcher John Lydon and colleagues. Imagine that you are a participant in their research and that you happen to be dating, cohabiting, or married. You are told that the purpose of the experiment is to find out how well computers do at matching people for romantic relationships. In the first session, you pose for a photograph and fill out a questionnaire about yourself so a portfolio can be created. When you arrive for your second session, a research assistant tells you that this time you will be evaluating another person's portfolio. You are given a photograph of an extremely attractive person of the opposite sex. The information in the person's portfolio indicates that this person is currently not romantically involved. Then the bombshell is dropped. The research assistant mentions that this person has seen the portfolios of participants in the previous session and has chosen you as the best match for himself or herself. You are then asked how attracted you are to this person.

Lydon and colleagues (Lydon, 1999; Lydon & Zanna, 1990; Lydon, Meana, Sepinwall, Richards, & Mayman, 1999) hypothesized that participants with only low or moderate commitment to their romantic relationship would not try to protect their relationship in this highly tempting situation. They would find the person in the portfolio very attractive and would say so. Participants who were highly committed to their relationships, however, were expected to engage in relationship maintenance efforts—in this case, by convincing themselves that they really were not all that attracted to this gorgeous, available person who wanted them. And that is exactly what was found. In follow-up research, Lydon and colleagues found that people who are committed to their relationship also rate an attractive alternative as less attractive than people who are less committed (Lydon, Fitzsimons, & Naidoo, 2003). In other words, we protect our relationship by convincing ourselves that we really aren't attracted to this person, who really isn't all that gorgeous, anyway!

In more recent research, Linardatos & Lydon (2011b) have shown that if your relationship is an important part of your identity (they refer to this as being high in relationship identification), you will let an attractive alternative partner know that you are "taken." More specifically, the researchers found that people who were high in relationship identification were more likely to mention their partner while conversing with an attractive confederate. In contrast, those who were low in relationship identification avoided mentioning their partner, even when the confederate asked questions that were intended to bring out that information (e.g., "What do you normally do on the weekend?"). In another study in this series, Linardatos and Lydon (2011b) found that people high in relationship identification spent less time looking at pictures of attractive people than those whose relationship identification was low. They were also more committed to their partners and, importantly, when contacted up to three years later, were more likely to report that the relationship was still intact.

In other research, Lydon and colleagues have examined gender differences in responding to attractive alternatives (Lydon, Menzies-Tolman, Burton, & Bell, 2008). It turns out that when women are tempted by an attractive, available person of the opposite sex, they react by shoring up their commitment to their current partner. Men are less likely to do so. However, this gender difference disappears when men receive coaching on how to protect their relationships. Specifically, in one of their studies, men were asked to imagine being approached by an attractive alternative. Participants in the experimental group were asked to think "When the guy/girl approaches, I will _______ to protect my relationship." Men who rehearsed relationship-protecting strategies were more likely later to avoid the attractive alternative than those in the control condition.

Finally, another successful strategy for resisting alternatives is to have people "relive" an experience of love for their partner. In a recent study, Gonzaga and colleagues (2008) asked people to think about a time when they felt either love or sexual desire for their dating partner. Next, all participants were asked to suppress thoughts about attractive alternatives. Those who thought about love were better able to push thoughts of an attractive alternative out of their minds and actually remembered fewer details about him or her than those who were asked to think about an experience of sexual desire. It was also the case that feelings of love, but not sexual desire, predicted commitment to the relationship (Gonzaga, Haselton, Smurda, Davies, & Poore, 2008).

Commitment and Forgiveness There is also evidence that when we are committed to our partners we are more forgiving of their mistakes and shortcomings. For example, Menzies-Tolman and Lydon (2005) found that the more committed people were to their relationships, the more forgiving they were of their partner's transgressions. More specifically, those who were high in commitment rated their partner's wrongdoings as less severe and were more likely to respond constructively compared with those who were less committed. Follow-up studies showed that women are more likely than men to respond to relationship transgressions with constructive, accommodating responses (Lydon et al., 2008).

Research by Caryl Rusbult and colleagues confirms that commitment leads to greater forgiveness (Rusbult & Agnew, 2010). In one of their studies, people were primed with either low or high commitment (by having them write out their thoughts about independence or dependence, respectively). Later, in a supposedly unrelated experiment, participants were asked how they would react to a series of partner betrayals. Participants who were primed with high commitment reported more forgiveness in these situations than those primed with low commitment (Finkel, Rusbult, Kumashiro, & Hannon, 2002).

In conclusion, research shows that when people are committed to their relationships, they take steps to protect their relationship when an attractive alternative comes on the scene, perceive their partner's transgressions as less severe, and react more constructively when their partner does something wrong. All of these behaviours contribute to relationship maintenance and stability.

The Role of Positive Illusions

Relationships have inevitable conflicts and disappointments. During these times, we may experience doubts about our choice of partner and question whether ours really is a good relationship. Research conducted at the University of Waterloo suggests that under these circumstances we maintain our relationships by indulging in **positive illusions**—that is, fantasies in which we convince ourselves that we have the most wonderful partner and the most wonderful relationship in the world—regardless

Positive Illusions

Idealization of our romantic relationships and partners in order to maintain the relationship of the facts. This process of idealization has been explored in several studies by Sandra Murray, John Holmes, and their colleagues. (Sandra Murray received the prestigious American Psychological Association Award for Distinguished Early Career Contributions for this work.)

In one of their first studies, Murray and Holmes (1993) investigated whether people deal with doubts and uncertainties by weaving stories in which their partner's flaws are reinterpreted as virtues. In attempting to test this hypothesis, the researchers faced a challenge: How does one get people to have doubts about their partner? Here's how Murray and Holmes did it. Students in dating relationships were asked whether their partner tended to initiate conflicts. As expected, most participants reported that they did not have the kind of partner who starts fights. Those in the experimental group then read a fake *Psychology Today* article in which it was argued that engaging in conflict can be healthy for a relationship. This information was intended to threaten participants' views of their partner. Participants in the control group read an unrelated story. Later, when asked again whether their partner initiated conflict, participants in the experimental group—but not those in the control group—changed their tune. They now reported that they, in fact, had partners who quite enjoyed a good fight! The researchers suggest that by taking this kind of poetic licence, these participants were able to maintain a positive view of their partner and their relationship.

In a subsequent study, Murray and Holmes (1999) identified another way in which we maintain our relationships: by finding redeeming features in our partner's faults. Specifically, when they asked students at the University of Waterloo to write out their dating partner's faults, approximately half of their participants engaged in "yes, but" refutations. For example, one woman reported that her partner had a tendency to overreact to situations but added that she had come to realize that he did so only to protect her.

The creative storytelling that people in these studies engaged in suggests that we are highly motivated to maintain positive perceptions of our partners and our relationships, regardless of the facts. Do we actually hold idealistic, rather than realistic, views of our partners? To find out, Murray, Holmes, and Griffin (1996a) asked dating and married couples to rate their own attributes, their partner's attributes, and attributes of an ideal partner. Take, for example, the case of Lucia and Mario. If Lucia's perception of Mario is accurate (i.e., based on reality), the way in which she rates him in terms of intelligence, humour, and consideration should be very similar to how Mario rates himself on these attributes. If, however, Lucia holds an idealistic view of Mario, she should rate him more positively than he rates himself. And that is exactly what these researchers found. In fact, participants' ratings of their partner closely resembled their ratings of an ideal partner. These findings have been confirmed in subsequent research (Murray et al., 2000; Murray et al., 2002; Murray, Holmes, & Griffin, 1996a). We should note, however, that the effects we have been discussing tend to be stronger for women than for men. In a series of studies conducted at McGill University and Université de Moncton, it was found that men tend to engage in positive illusions only if they are highly committed to a relationship, whereas women are more likely to hold unrealistically positive perceptions of their partner regardless of their level of commitment (Gagné & Lydon, 2003).

The assumption in this research has been that people view their partner in highly positive ways as a means of maintaining their relationships. Is it actually beneficial to see our partners in idealistic ways? Wouldn't relationships be better off if we perceived our partners as they really are? Apparently not. In fact, it would seem that the rosier the glasses through which we view our partners, the better. Murray and Holmes have consistently found that the more people idealize their partners and the more that their partner idealizes them, the greater their satisfaction with the relationship (Murray & Holmes, 1997, 1999; Murray et al, 2000; Murray, Holmes, & Griffin, 1996a). According to recent research conducted at the University of Manitoba, relationship satisfaction is particularly high when we idealize our partners in terms of traits that are important to relationships (e.g., caring, loving, affectionate) rather than in terms of less relationship-relevant traits (e.g., talkative, reserved; Sciangula & Morry, 2009). Moreover, idealization is more likely to occur in romantic relationships (i.e., dating and marital relationships) than in friendships (Morry, Reich, & Kito, 2010).

Idealization also has survival value: relationships in which partners idealize one another are most likely to endure. For example, Murray, Holmes, and Griffin (1996b) conducted a longitudinal study in which they measured idealization and satisfaction among dating couples several times over a one-year period. The researchers found that couples who idealized each other at the outset experienced the greatest increases in satisfaction over the course of the year and the greatest decreases in conflicts and doubts. These couples also were more likely to be together a year later than were couples who did not idealize one another. Perhaps most astonishing was the finding that over time people began to live up to the idealized image their partner had of them. Stated differently, individuals who idealized their partners ultimately created the partners they wished for. Thus, in the world of close relationships, dreams can actually come true!

But you may be thinking, surely over time, idealization could lead to disappointment as people get to know who their partner "really" is. This important question was examined in a recent study in which married couples were studied over the first 13 years of their marriage. It was found that couples who had positive illusions about their spouse at the newlywed stage reported greater feelings of marital love than couples who started their marriage with less idealistic views of each other (Miller, Niehuis, & Huston, 2006). Thus, positive illusions seem to be beneficial for relationships. However, we note that Fletcher and Kerr (2010) recently conducted a meta analysis of the research on idealization and concluded that people also temper their illusions with a dose of reality—as evidenced by the fact that many relationships do end.

Ending Close Relationships

As you may know first hand, some relationships resemble nightmares more than dreams come true. In Canada, just over one-third of marriages end in divorce (Canada, 2002). The dissolution of other kinds of relationships is not publicly recorded. However, in longitudinal studies of dating relationships, a typical finding is that half of the couples break up within a few years, with gay and lesbian relationships showing some of the highest rates of dissolution (Sprecher, 1994; Sprecher & Fehr, 1998). And even though people tend not to break up with friends formally, the loss of friendships is a common experience (Fehr, 1996). Thus, in addition to studying what love is and how it blooms, social psychologists study the end of the story—how it dies.

Why Relationships End

As you might expect, the reasons that relationships end are complex and multifaceted. Moreover, different kinds of relationships end for different reasons. For example, common reasons given for the dissolution of marriage are financial difficulties, unemployment, alcoholism, sexual infidelity, low religiosity, and premarital pregnancy (Sprecher & Fehr, 1998; White, 1990). Not all of these reasons would apply to dating relationships or friendships. There are, however, some important commonalities across relationships.

One place to look for clues is among the predictors of attraction. If the factors that initially attracted you to someone are no longer present, the relationship is likely to be in trouble. For example, at the beginning of this chapter we identified similarity as an important predictor of attraction; as you might expect, if spouses, friends, or dating partners become dissimilar, the relationship is vulnerable to dissolution (Fehr, 1996; Sprecher & Fehr, 1998). Statements such as "We grew apart" or "We seemed to be going in different directions" reflect the role of dissimilarity in the breakup of relationships.

In a fascinating study, Diane Felmlee (1995) asked 300 university students to focus on a romantic relationship that had ended and to list the qualities that had first attracted them to the person and the characteristics they ended up disliking most about the person. Felmlee found that 30 percent of these breakups could be classified as "fatal attractions." In other words, the qualities that were initially so attractive (e.g., "He's so unusual and different," "She's so exciting and unpredictable") became the very reasons

Recent research suggests that sheer boredom is one reason that couples may become dissatisfied with their relationships.

why the relationship ended (e.g., "He and I have nothing in common," "I can never count on her"). "Fatal attractions" were most likely to occur for qualities on which the partners were dissimilar.

The theories of relationships discussed earlier also shed light on the issue of why relationships end. Social exchange theorists, for example, find that relationships are likely to end when rewards are low and costs are high, when attractive alternatives are available to one or both partners, or when the partners have invested little in the relationship (Rusbult, 1983; Rusbult, Martz, & Agnew, 1998). Equity also plays a role in the ending of relationships. People are likely to end relationships that they feel are inequitable—particularly if they are feeling underbenefited.

Finally, there is another reason that relationships end—a reason few of us are willing to admit: sheer boredom. According to Aron and Aron (1986a, 1996), as another person becomes familiar to us, there is less that is new and exciting for us to discover about him or her. The day-to-day routine of living together may lead people to feel that they are in a rut and are missing out on excitement and passion (Baumeister & Bratslavsky, 1999; Fincham & Bradbury, 1993). In a recent program of research conducted at the University of Manitoba and the University of Winnipeg, Cheryl Harasymchuk has found that in both dating and marital relationships, boredom is associated with less enjoyment and excitement in relationships, and with lower relationship satisfaction (Harasymchuk, 2008; Harasymchuk & Fehr, 2008, 2011). This research also has shown that boredom is a unique challenge in relationships—reflecting the loss of something positive that was once present but now is missing—it is not the same as other negative processes such as conflict or hostility. According to University of Windsor researcher John La Gaipa (1982) boredom is also an issue in friendships. He maintains that friendships may end because of boredom, but that boredom is not considered a socially acceptable basis for terminating a friendship. Thus, when asked why a friendship ended, people are likely to mention reasons such as disloyalty or betrayals of trust. We suspect that people who terminate a marriage would be especially likely to offer such reasons, even if the culprit was sheer boredom.

The Process of Breaking Up

Ending a relationship is one of life's more painful experiences. The pain is greatest for the person who is being rejected. If you have ever broken up with someone, however, you may be all too aware that it is no fun telling someone that you no longer want to be with him or her. Consequently, it probably does not come as a surprise that people often use passive avoidance strategies when terminating a relationship. For example, Baxter (1982) asked people about the strategies they would use to end a romantic relationship or a friendship. She identified four major strategies from these accounts: withdrawal/avoidance, positive tone (e.g., trying to prevent "hard feelings"), manipulative strategies (e.g., getting a third party to communicate the bad news), and open confrontation. For both types of relationships, people reported that they would be most likely to use positive tone strategies. They also said they would use withdrawal/avoidance strategies, especially for friendship terminations. Open confrontation was a more likely strategy for ending romantic relationships.

Other research has shown that passive strategies such as withdrawal or avoidance are especially likely to be used in friendships, which people generally opt to let fade away (Fehr, 1996). In contrast, dating or marital relationships are less likely to simply wither on the vine—especially if one partner still wants the relationship to continue. Thus, more direct methods are generally necessary for these sorts of breakups (Baxter, 1985).

The Experience of Breaking Up

How do people feel when their relationship ends? One important factor is the role they played in the decision to end the relationship (Helgeson, 1994; Lloyd & Cate, 1985). For example, when Robin Akert (1998) asked a sample of university students to focus on their most important former romantic relationship, she found that the single most powerful predictor of reactions to breakups was whether you were the one who did the breaking up or the one who was "dumped." Not surprisingly, if your partner broke up with you, you were miserable—participants in this situation reported high levels of loneliness, depression, unhappiness, and anger, and virtually all reported experiencing physical disorders (e.g., upset stomach, trouble sleeping) in the weeks after the breakup. In contrast, those who did the breaking up experienced the lowest levels of upset, pain, and stress, although they were not exempt from negative effects—they tended to experience guilt and unhappiness. Those who reported that the breakup was mutual fell in the middle of these two groups—they were not as upset or hurt as those who had been dumped, but they suffered more than those who did the breaking up.

> *Love is like war; easy to begin but very hard to stop.*
>
> —H. L. Mencken

The degree of distress experienced after a breakup is influenced by other factors as well. For example, Sprecher and colleagues found that in addition to responsibility for the breakup, social exchange variables played a role (Sprecher, Felmlee, Metts, Fehr, & Vanni, 1998). As you might expect based on our earlier discussion of social exchange theory, people who reported high levels of relationship satisfaction and commitment were much more distressed when the relationship ended than those who were less satisfied and committed. Also consistent with social exchange theory, people experienced less distress if they were interested in an alternative relationship, but more distress if attractive alternatives were available to their former partner. The good news is that the participants reported that they felt significantly less distressed currently than they had immediately after the breakup. Thus, if by some unfortunate circumstance your heart has been broken, take comfort in the fact that time really does heal wounds.

HOW WOULD YOU USE THIS?

If there was ever a chapter in a textbook that had something to say about your "real" life, this chapter is probably it. Romantic relationships and friendships are an integral part of our lives, and wonderful as they are, they are also frequently confusing and even upsetting. While the information in this chapter could help you when you're "falling in love," you'll probably be too distracted by your new partner to even think about research studies on attraction. However, when things go bad, this information can really be of help. Apply the various terms and theories to your predicament—do they help shed some light on what is going on? For example, are you and your friend or romantic partner seeing the relationship differently, perhaps one of you as an "exchange" and the other as "communal?" Does one or the other of you have an attachment style that is causing problems? Are the two of you dissimilar in areas that are important to you? Are there cultural differences that might explain what's going on? If your loved one is thinking of ending the relationship, is it because he or she has encountered an attractive alternative partner? Should your relationship end, remind yourself of the research showing that as painful as breakups can be, people truly do get over them.

Summary

Major Antecedents of Attraction

- **The Person Next Door: The Propinquity Effect** In the first part of this chapter, we discussed the variables that cause initial attraction between two people. One such variable is physical proximity, or the propinquity effect: People who you come into contact with the most are the most likely to become your friends and lovers. This occurs because of mere exposure: Familiarity with any stimulus produces liking for it.
- **Similarity** Similarity between people, whether in attitudes, values, leisure preferences, or personality traits is also a powerful cause of attraction and liking. The weakest similarity effects tend to be found for personality.
- **Reciprocal Liking** In general, we like others who like us.
- **The Effects of Physical Attractiveness on Liking** Physical attractiveness also plays an important role in attraction. People from different cultures perceive facial attractiveness quite similarly. The "what is beautiful is good" stereotype indicates that people assume that physical attractiveness is associated with other desirable traits.
- **Attraction and the Misattribution of Arousal** Attraction can also occur because of misattribution of arousal—mistakenly assuming that feelings of physiological arousal from some other source are caused by the presence of an attractive person in our environment.

Forming Close Relationships

- **Defining Love** Social psychologists make a distinction between companionate love—feelings of intimacy and affection for those with whom our lives are intertwined—and passionate love—feelings of intense longing and arousal. Ordinary people's definitions of love include both companionate and passionate love, with an emphasis on the former.
- **Gender and Love** Men hold a more romantic, passionate view of love than do women, whereas women hold a more companionate view of love. However, research suggests that both men and women see companionate love as capturing the true meaning of love—more so than passionate love.
- **Culture and Love** Although love is a universal emotion, cultural variations in the definition of love do occur. Love has a somewhat different emphasis in collectivistic and individualistic cultures.

Why Do We Love?

We discussed two theories that address the question of why we form relationships: evolutionary theory and attachment theory.

- **Evolutionary Explanations of Love** Evolutionary psychology explains love in terms of genetic factors that evolved over time according to the principles of natural selection. Men and women are attracted to different characteristics in each other because this maximizes their reproductive success. Women's attraction to men depends on whether they are in a high or low fertility time in their ovulatory cycle.
- **Attachment Styles and Intimate Relationships** People's relationship with their primary caregiver in infancy is a significant determinant of the quality of their close relationships as adults; there is evidence that attachment is also partly genetically determined. There are three types of attachment relationships: secure, anxious/ambivalent, and avoidant. Avoidant attachment has been further subdivided into preoccupied and fearful avoidant styles.

Maintaining Close Relationships

- **Social Exchange Theories** Social exchange theory argues that how satisfied people feel in their relationships depends on their assessment of the reward/cost ratio in their relationship. To determine whether people will stay in a relationship, we also need to know their comparison level (the outcomes they have come to expect in relationships) and their comparison level for alternatives (their expectations about how happy they would be in other relationships or alone). According to the investment model of close relationships, to predict whether a relationship will last, we need to know each person's level of satisfaction, comparison level for alternatives, and how much has been invested in the relationship.
- **Equity Theory** Equity theory states that we are happiest when relationships are fair—when what we contribute is comparable with what our partner contributes. Further, the notion of equity is different in long-term versus short-term relationships. Short-term relationships are usually exchange relationships, in which people are concerned about a fair distribution of rewards and costs. Long-term, intimate relationships are usually communal relationships, in which people are less concerned with an immediate accounting of who is contributing what and are more concerned with helping their partner when he or she is in need.
- **The Role of Commitment in Maintaining Relationships** People who are committed to their partners are more likely to resist attractive alternative partners. They also tend to be more forgiving of a partner's transgressions.
- **The Role of Positive Illusions** The more we idealize our partner, the greater our satisfaction with a relationship and the more likely that the relationship will endure.

Ending Close Relationships

- **Why Relationships End** Relationships end for a number of reasons, including dissimilarity between the partners, fatal attractions in which the qualities in a person that once were attractive become the very qualities that repel, and sheer boredom.

- **The Process of Breaking Up** People tend to use passive strategies when ending relationships, although these strategies may not be effective for ending romantic relationships.
- **The Experience of Breaking Up** A powerful variable that predicts how a person will weather a breakup is the role he or she plays in the decision to terminate the relationship.

10 Prosocial Behaviour

Why Do People Help?

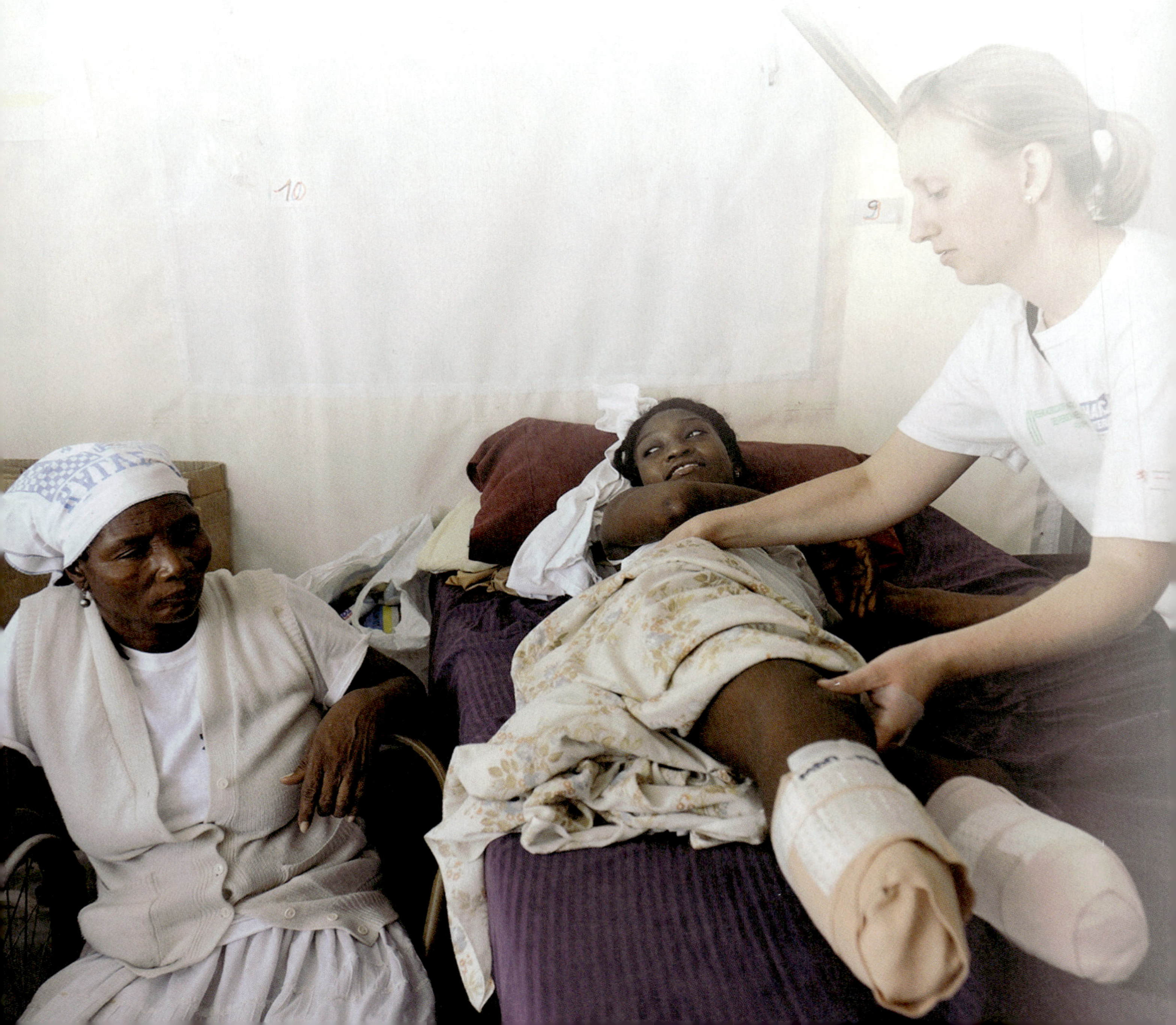

I

N CHAPTER 2, WE DESCRIBED HOW DURING THE BRUTAL STABBING death of Kitty Genovese, neighbours heard her screams for help. Many even watched the assault through their window. Yet, no one intervened. No one even called the police. This tragic event, which took place more than 40 years ago in New York City, may seem far removed from today. But is it? Read on.

January 17, 2011. Headlines such as "Woman freezes to death as neighbours ignore screams" bear an eerie resemblance to the headlines about Kitty Genovese back in 1964. In this case, the screams came from a 66-year-old Toronto woman with dementia who had wandered out of her house in the night. The temperature was –28°C. According to the police, there were signs that the disoriented woman tried to get into a car for shelter. Scratch marks also were found on the screen door of a nearby home. Neighbours heard the woman screaming but did nothing. No one called 911. One neighbour reported that she had looked out of her window when she heard the screams; although she saw someone stumbling in the cold, she ignored her. By the time the woman's husband noticed that she was missing, she had frozen to death a few blocks from her Scarborough home.

June 3, 2006. The lead article in the *Winnipeg Free Press* begins with this question: "How could nearly a dozen Winnipegers turn their backs on a Good Samaritan who lay bleeding and unconscious on a Portage Avenue sidewalk?" (McIntyre, 2006). It all began when a panhandler started harassing a woman standing at a bus stop. Murray Aklwenzie, a 60-year-old man, noticed and politely asked the panhandler to leave the woman alone. The panhandler then turned on Aklwenzie. The attack left Aklwenzie with a crushed skull and other near-fatal injuries. At least a dozen passersby witnessed the scene but did nothing as Aklwenzie lay there, unconscious and bleeding. What about the woman who Aklwenzie had stepped in to help? She hopped on her bus when it arrived and never even notified the police.

December 6, 2002. Breann Voth, a teenager from Port Coquitlam, British Columbia, was on her way to catch the morning bus when she was murdered. Investigations into her death revealed that Voth's cries for help were heard in at least 15 households—yet, no one called the police. Her naked body was found later that morning on the banks of the Coquitlam River.

Based on these events, what is your view of human nature? Are human beings inclined to respond when they see another person in need? Can people be counted on to help? Now consider the following stories:

On August 15, 2009, Tina Moores of Grand Falls-Windsor, Newfoundland, noticed that a young girl was being carried into deeper water by a strong current. She immediately jumped into the water to try to save the girl. Once she reached her, she managed to hold the girl's head above water. However, it was a struggle

OUTLINE

Justice Peck is one of many people who exhibit prosocial behaviour. What makes some people help others even at considerable cost to themselves?

and Tina began to lose strength. Tina's sister noticed and began swimming toward them. By then, some people in a boat arrived and managed to get the little girl and Tina's sister to shore. Meanwhile, Tina was drifting further away. By the time another boat with her husband in it reached her, it was too late. On September 23, 2010, Tina Maryann Moores was posthumously awarded a Carnegie medal for heroism for sacrificing her life to save that of a young child.

In April 2008, a 14-year-old boy, Justice Peck, was about to go to bed in his Prince George, British Columbia, home when he thought he smelled smoke coming from his neighbour's duplex. He rushed over and opened the outside door to the home. The stairs were engulfed in fire. Peck jumped through the flames and alerted the occupants—a single mother with two young boys. They smashed a front window and climbed through it to safety. "If it wasn't for Justice," the mother said, "we would all be dead" (Peebles, 2008, p. A2).

On November 4, 2010, Allen and Violet Large, a retired couple who live near Halifax, got some potentially life-changing news—they had won an $11.25 million dollar lottery! Four months later, nearly all the money was spent. Sports cars? Cruises? Mansions? Not at all: Allen and Violet's lifestyle remains modest (before retirement, he was a steelworker and she worked in a cosmetics factory). They still drive their 5-year-old truck and their 13-year-old car. They don't have a microwave or voicemail. Even so, they decided that other people needed the money more than they did. So they donated their winnings to close family members and a very long list of charities, ranging from animal-protection agencies to churches to health-care services. They kept a mere 2 percent for themselves in case of emergency. When the lottery winners were announced, the media in Nova Scotia commented that unlike many lottery winners, this big win would not change the lives of Allen and Violet Large. That has been the case. But it certainly has changed the lives of many others (Moore, 2010).

Based on reading these stories, what is your view of human nature now? Are human beings inclined to respond when they see another person in need? Can people be counted on to help?

Why Do People Help?

Connect to MyPsychLab

To access the Critical Thinking question on the domesticated gene, go to MyPsychLab

Prosocial Behaviour

Any act performed with the goal of benefiting another person

Altruism

The desire to help others, even if it involves a cost to the helper

Why is it that sometimes people perform acts of great self-sacrifice and heroism, whereas at other times they behave in uncaring, heartless ways, ignoring the desperate pleas of those in need? In this chapter, we will consider the major determinants of **prosocial behaviour**—which we define as any act performed with the goal of benefiting another person (Penner, Dovidio, Piliavin, Schroeder, 2005; Mikulincer & Shaver, 2010). Sometimes people act in a prosocial manner out of self-interest—hoping to get something in return. But in this chapter, we will be particularly concerned with prosocial behaviour motivated by **altruism**—which is the desire to help another person or group of people, even if it involves a cost to the helper (Post, Underwood, Schloss, & Harlbut, 2002). For example, Murray Aklwenzie risked his life by intervening when a woman was being harassed at a bus stop. Tina Moores sacrificed her life to save a child from drowning.

In another example, a recent study examined the motivations HIV-infected men and women in Ottawa and Montreal had for participating in HIV vaccine trials. There were clearly costs involved—69 percent acknowledged that participating in the research could cause unpleasant side effects. More than one-third (34 percent) had concerns that the vaccine might cause further health problems for them. So why go through this? The answer is altruism. All of the participants expressed that they were taking part in these trials because they wanted to help the global HIV community (Balfour, Corace, Tasca, Tremblay, Routy, & Angel, 2010).

We will begin by considering the basic origins of prosocial behaviour and altruism. Why do people help others? Few questions have intrigued observers of the human condition as much as this one. Is the willingness to help a basic impulse with genetic roots? Is it something that must be taught and nurtured in childhood? Is there a pure motive for helping, such that people are willing to aid their fellow human beings even when they have nothing to gain? Or are people willing to help only when there is something in it for them? Let's see how psychologists have addressed these centuries-old questions.

Evolutionary Psychology: Instincts and Genes

According to Charles Darwin's (1859) theory of evolution, natural selection favours genes that promote the survival of the individual (see Chapter 9). Any gene that furthers our survival and increases the probability that we will produce offspring is likely to be passed on from generation to generation. Genes that lower our chances of survival, such as those that cause life-threatening diseases, reduce the chances that we will produce offspring and thus are less likely to be passed on. Several psychologists have pursued these ideas, spawning the field of evolutionary psychology, which is the attempt to explain social behaviour in terms of genetic factors that evolved over time according to the principles of natural selection (Buss, 2005; Ketelaar & Ellis, 2000; Pinker, 2002; Simpson & Beches, 2010).

Altruism based on kin selection is the enemy of civilization. If human beings are to a large extent guided to favor their own relatives and tribe, only a limited amount of global harmony is possible.

—E. O. Wilson, *On Human Nature*, 1978

Darwin realized early on that a potential problem exists with evolutionary theory. How can it explain altruism? If people's overriding goal is to ensure their own survival, why would they ever help others at a cost to themselves? It would seem that over the centuries, altruistic behaviour would disappear because people who acted that way would, by putting themselves at risk, produce fewer offspring than would people who acted selfishly. Genes promoting selfish behaviour would be more likely to be passed on—or would they?

Kin Selection One way that evolutionary psychologists attempt to resolve this dilemma is with the notion of **kin selection**, the idea that behaviours that help a genetic relative are favoured by natural selection (Hamilton, 1964; Meyer, 1999). People can increase the chances that their genes will be passed along not only by having their own children but also by ensuring that their genetic relatives have children. Because a person's blood relatives share some of his or her genes, the more that person ensures his or her survival, the greater the chance that that person's genes will flourish in future generations. Thus, natural selection should favour altruistic acts directed toward genetic relatives. Consistent with this view, a recent analysis of wills probated in British Columbia found that genetic relatedness was a strong predictor of estate allocations. In other words, the closer the genetic link, the greater the designated inheritance (Webster, Bryan, Crawford, McCarthy, & Cohen, 2008).

Kin Selection

The idea that behaviour that helps a genetic relative is favoured by natural selection

People also report that they would be more likely to help genetic relatives than nonrelatives in life-and-death situations, such as a house fire, but not when the situation was non–life threatening. Interestingly, both men and women, as well as American and Japanese participants, follow this rule of kin selection in life-threatening situations (Burnstein, Crandall, & Kitayama, 1994; Graziano, Habashi, Sheese, & Tobin, 2007). Of course, in this research, people only report what they would do; this doesn't prove

According to evolutionary psychology, prosocial behaviour occurs in part because of kin selection.

that in a real fire they would indeed be more likely to save their sibling than their friend. Some anecdotal evidence from real emergencies, however, is consistent with these results. Sime (1983) interviewed survivors of a fire at a vacation complex and found that when people became aware that there was a fire, they were much more likely to search for family members before exiting the building than they were to search for friends.

Evolutionary psychologists do not mean to imply that people consciously weigh the biological importance of their behaviour before deciding whether to help. It is not as if people crassly compute the likelihood that their genes will be passed on before deciding whether to help someone push his or her car out of a ditch. According to evolutionary theory, however, the genes of people who follow this "biological importance" rule are more likely to survive than the genes of people who do not. Thus, they argue that over the millennia, kin selection became ingrained in human behaviour.

In an interesting twist on this issue, Korchmaros and Kenny (2006) asked participants to list the names of immediate and extended family members and to report how close they felt to each of them. Next, they were presented with a variety of possible helping situations and were asked to report which family member they would be most likely to help. Contrary to the idea of kin selection, the degree of genetic relatedness did not predict willingness to help. Instead, the critical variable was the degree of closeness: Participants were most likely to help the family members to whom they had the closest emotional ties, rather than those to whom they were most closely related. The researchers suggest that evolution may actually have created the tendency to help those who are close to us, rather than the tendency to help those who are related to us. Clearly, additional research will be required to further disentangle this issue.

Norm of Reciprocity

The expectation that helping others will increase the likelihood that they will help us in the future

The Reciprocity Norm To explain altruism, evolutionary psychologists also point to the **norm of reciprocity**, which is the expectation that helping others will increase the likelihood that they will help us in the future. The idea is that as human beings were evolving, a group of completely selfish individuals, each living in his or her own cave, would have found it more difficult to survive than a group composed of members who had learned to cooperate with one another. Of course, if people cooperated too readily, they might have been exploited by an adversary who never helped in return. Those who were most likely to survive, the argument goes, were people who developed an understanding with their neighbours about reciprocity: "I will help you now, with the agreement that when I need help, you will return the favour." Because of its survival value, such a norm of reciprocity may have become genetically based (Cosmides & Tooby, 1992; De Waal, 1996; Shackelford & Buss, 1996; Trivers, 1971).

According to a fascinating set of studies recently conducted at Queen's University, reciprocity can already be detected in infancy (Dunfield & Kuhlmeier, 2010). In this research, 21-month-old infants were seated across a table from two female confederates who offered—but did not give—the infant an attractive toy. In the "unwilling" condition, the confederate pulled the toy away before the infant could take it. In the "unable" condition, the toy "accidentally" rolled off the table before the confederate could hand it over. In the next phase of the study, the confederates produced an attractive new toy, but it dropped. The situation was staged so that both of the confederates reached for the toy but couldn't recover it, leaving it for the infant to retrieve.

One-third of the infants who picked up the toy kept it for themselves. Those who were willing to part with it were significantly more likely to give the toy to the confederate who had intended, but was unable to, give them a toy earlier, than to the confederate who had been unwilling. In another study, the researchers compared infants' reactions to confederates who were willing, but unable, to give them the toy with a condition in which the confederate actually handed over the toy. When an attractive toy was dropped, the infants were as likely to give the toy to the confederate with helpful intentions as to the confederate who had actually been helpful (i.e., had given them the toy earlier). Thus, even infants reciprocate good deeds. What is even more amazing is that they can pick up on whether someone *intends* to help them and reciprocate accordingly (Dunfield & Kuhlmeier, 2010).

According to William Brown and Chris Moore (2000) at Dalhousie University, from an evolutionary perspective it would also be adaptive to be able to detect pure altruists from those who are cheaters (free riders who have no plans of reciprocating helpful acts in the future). In a series of studies using hypothetical scenarios, they demonstrated that people are remarkably adept at discerning true acts of altruism. In Chapter 9, we also discussed a recent study in which groups of participants had to decide whether to donate their money so the entire group could benefit or keep their money and benefit from the donations of others. People did not react favourably to freeloaders and developed complex strategies to try to get them to change their ways (Kiyonari & Barclay, 2008).

The accompanying Try It! exercise describes how the reciprocity norm can work to increase helping in everyday life.

Learning Social Norms Nobel laureate Herbert Simon (1990) offered one more link between evolution and altruism. He argued that it is highly adaptive for individuals to learn social norms from other members of a society. Over the centuries, a culture learns such things as which foods are poisonous and how members of the culture should cooperate with one another; the person who learns these rules is more likely to survive than the person who does not. Consequently, through natural selection, the ability to learn social norms has become part of our genetic makeup. One norm that people learn is the value of helping others; this is considered to be a valuable norm in virtually all societies. In short, people are genetically programmed to learn social norms, and one of these norms is altruism (Hoffman, 1981; Kameda, Takezawa, & Hastie, 2003). In the same vein, Dacher Keltner (2008) recently has argued that it is to our evolutionary advantage to engage in prosocial behaviours toward others. Those who cooperate are more likely to survive.

TRY IT! Does the Reciprocity Norm Increase Helping?

Have you ever gotten a fundraising appeal from a charity that included a little gift, such as address labels with your name on them? If so, did the gift make you more inclined to donate money to the charity? If so, you were subject to the reciprocity norm—because the charity did something for you, you felt more obligated to do something for the charity. The same norm applies when stores offer free samples of a product they are selling. It can feel rude not to reciprocate by buying the product, even though the people are strangers trying to sell us something rather than friends doing us a favour. What about in everyday life? Can you think of times that the reciprocity norm influenced how likely you were to help a friend? Have you found that doing a favour for a friend makes it more likely that your friend will do a favour for you? Give this a try and see if it works.

In sum, evolutionary psychologists believe that people help others because of three factors that have become ingrained in our genes: kin selection, the norm of reciprocity, and the ability to learn and follow social norms. As we saw in Chapter 9, evolutionary psychology is a challenging and creative approach, but it does have its critics (Batson, 1998; Buller, 2005; Caporael & Brewer, 2000; Gould, 1997; Wood & Eagly, 2002). How, for example, can evolutionary theory explain why complete strangers help each other, even when there is no reason for them to assume that they share the same genes or that their favour will ever be returned? It seems absurd to say that 14-year-old Justice Peck somehow calculated how genetically similar the occupants of the burning house were to him before deciding to save their lives. Tina Moores, who lost her life while trying to save a drowning child would not have expected that, down the road, the child would return the favour. Clearly, other factors must be considered to explain why people help under such conditions. We turn to these factors next.

Social Exchange: The Costs and Rewards of Helping

Although some social psychologists disagree with evolutionary approaches to prosocial behaviour, they do agree that altruistic behaviour can be based on self-interest. In fact, social exchange theory (see Chapter 9) argues that much of what we do stems from the desire to maximize our rewards and minimize our costs (Homans, 1961; Lawler & Thye, 1999; Thibaut & Kelley, 1959). What might be the rewards of helping? There are actually a number of them. First, as we saw with the norm of reciprocity, helping someone is an investment in the future, the social exchange being that someday someone will help you when you need it. Helping can also relieve the distress of the bystander. Considerable evidence indicates that people are aroused and disturbed when they see another person suffer, and that they help at least in part to relieve their own distress (Dovidio, 1984; Dovidio, Piliavin, Gaertner, Schroeder, & Clark, 1991; Piferi, Jobe, & Jones, 2006). Finally, by helping others, we can also gain such rewards as social approval from others and increased feelings of self-worth.

Let him who neglects to raise the fallen, fear lest, when he falls, no one will stretch out his hand to lift him up.

—Saadi, The Orchard, *1257*

I once saw a man out of courtesy help a lame dog over a stile, and [the dog] for requital bit his fingers.

—William Chillingworth *(1602–1644)*

The other side of the coin, of course, is that helping can be costly. Helping decreases when the costs are high, as when it would put us in physical danger, result in pain or embarrassment, or take too much time (Dovidio et al., 1991; Piliavin, Piliavin, & Rodin, 1975). Not surprisingly, under such conditions, people are less likely to help. Thus, the basic assumption of social exchange theory is that people help only when the benefits outweigh the costs. True altruism, in which people help even when doing so is costly, does not exist, according to this theory.

If you are like many of our students, you may be experiencing discomfort over this view of helping behaviour, finding it to be a rather cynical portrayal of human nature. Is true altruism, motivated only by the desire to help someone else, really such a mythical act? Must we trace all prosocial behaviour to the self-interest of the helper? Well, a social exchange theorist might reply that there are many ways in which people can obtain gratification and we should be thankful that one way is by helping others. After all, wealthy people could decide to get pleasure only from lavish vacations, expensive cars, and gourmet meals at fancy restaurants. We should applaud their decision to give money to the disadvantaged, even if, ultimately, it is just another way for them to feel good about themselves. Prosocial acts are doubly rewarding in that they help both the giver and the recipient of the aid. Thus, it is to everyone's advantage to promote and praise such acts.

Still, many people are dissatisfied with the argument that all helping stems from self-interest. How can it explain why people go so far as to risk their lives for others, as Justice Peck did when he entered a burning house or Murray Aklwenzie did when he intervened when a woman was being harassed on the street? According to some social psychologists, people do have hearts of gold and sometimes help only for the sake of helping—as we shall see now.

Calvin and Hobbes by Bill Watterson

Empathy and Altruism: The Pure Motive for Helping

C. Daniel Batson (1991) acknowledges that people sometimes help others for selfish reasons; however, he argues that people's motives are sometimes purely altruistic, in that their only goal is to help the other person, even if doing so involves some cost. Pure altruism is likely to come into play, he maintains, when we feel empathy for the person in need of help. **Empathy** is defined as the ability to put ourselves in the shoes of another person, experiencing events and emotions the way that person experiences them. Suppose, for example, that you are at the grocery store and see a man holding a baby and a bag full of diapers, toys, and rattles. As the man reaches for a box of Cheerios, he loses his grip on the bag and its contents spill on the floor. Will you stop to help him pick up his things? According to Batson, it depends first on whether you feel empathy for him; if you do, you will help, regardless of what you have to gain. Your goal will be to relieve the man's distress, not to gain something for yourself. This is the crux of Batson's **empathy-altruism hypothesis.**

Empathy
The ability to experience events and emotions (e.g., joy, sadness) the way another person experiences them

Empathy-Altruism Hypothesis
The idea that when we feel empathy for a person, we will attempt to help him or her purely for altruistic reasons, regardless of what we have to gain

What if you do not feel empathy? If, for whatever reason, you do not share the other person's distress, then Batson says social exchange comes into play. What's in it for you? If there is something to be gained, such as obtaining approval from the man in the mall or from onlookers, you will help the man pick up his things. If you will not profit from helping, you will go on your way without stopping. (Batson's empathy-altruism hypothesis is summarized in Figure 10.1.) Batson would, however, be the first to acknowledge that it can be very difficult to isolate the exact causes of complex social behaviours.

Consider a famous story about Abraham Lincoln. One day, while riding in a coach, Lincoln and a fellow passenger were debating the very question we are considering: Is helping ever truly altruistic? Lincoln argued that helping always stems from self-interest, whereas the other passenger took the view that true altruism exists. Suddenly, the men were interrupted by the screeching whine of a sow trying to save her piglets from drowning in a creek beside the coach track. Lincoln promptly called out, "Driver, can't you stop for just a moment?" He jumped out of the coach, ran to the creek, and lifted the piglets to the safety of the bank. When he returned, his companion said, "Now, Abe, where does selfishness come in on this little episode?" "Why, bless your soul, Ed," Lincoln replied. "That was the very essence of selfishness. I should have had no peace of mind all day had I gone on and left that suffering old sow worrying over those pigs. I did it to get peace of mind, don't you see?" (Sharp, 1928). As this example shows, an act that seems truly altruistic is sometimes motivated by self-interest. How, then, can we tell which is which?

Batson and his colleagues have devised a series of clever experiments to unravel people's motives (Batson & Powell, 2003; Batson, Ahmad, & Stocks, 2004; Batson, Ahmad, Powell, & Stocks, 2008; see Batson, 2010, for a review). Imagine you were one of the participants (Introductory Psychology students) in a study by Miho Toi and Daniel Batson (1982). You are asked to evaluate some tapes of new programs for

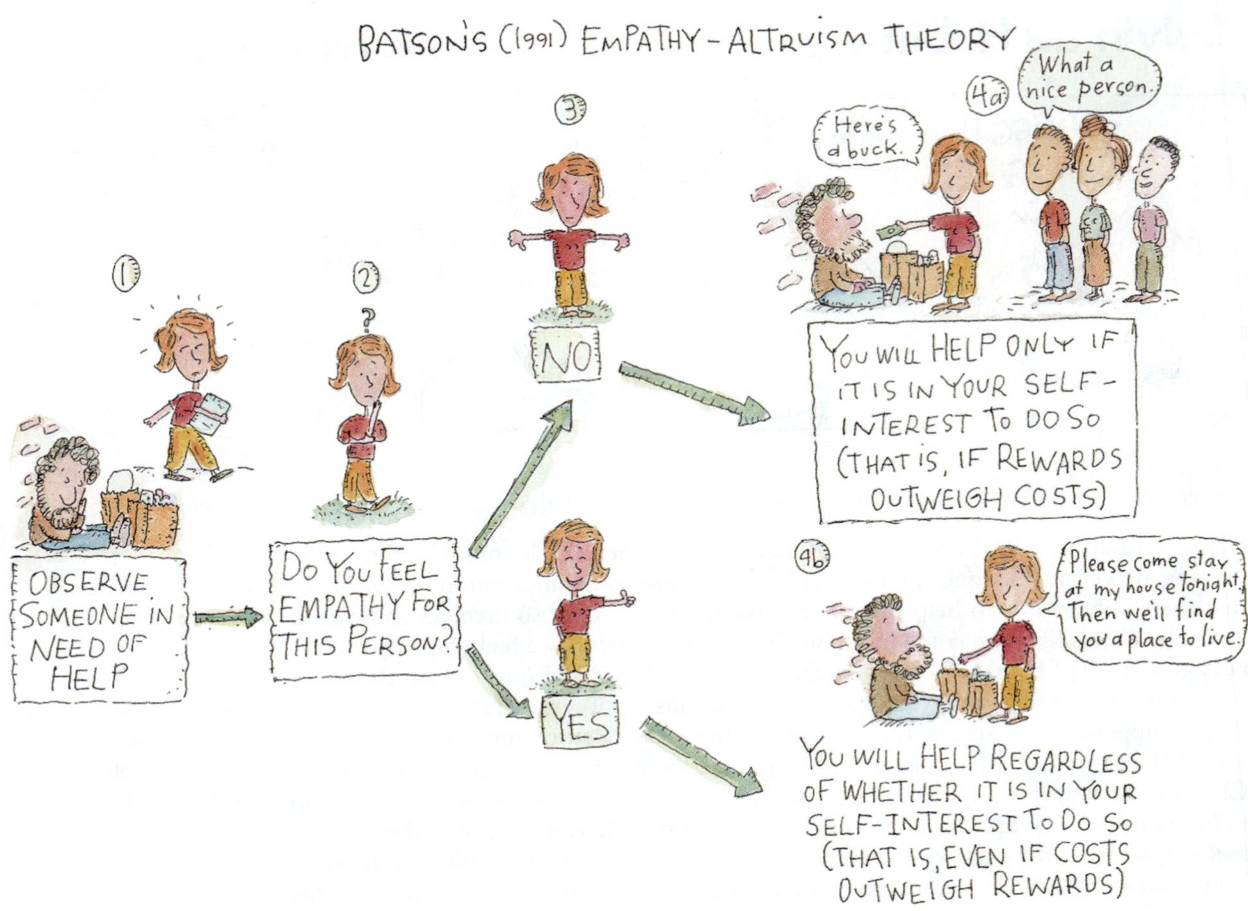

FIGURE 10.1
Batson's (1991) empathy-altruism theory.

your university's radio station. The tape you hear is an interview with a student named Carol Marcy. She describes a bad automobile accident and explains that because she is still in a wheelchair, it has been very difficult to keep up with her course work. Carol mentions that she will have to drop her introductory psychology course unless she can find a student from whom she can borrow lecture notes. After you listen to the tape, the experimenter hands you an envelope marked "To the student listening to the Carol Marcy pilot tape" and says that it came from the professor supervising the research. The envelope contains a note from the professor, asking if the student who listened to this tape would be willing to meet with Carol and share his or her introductory psychology lecture notes.

As you have probably guessed, the point of the study was to look at the conditions under which people agreed to help Carol. Toi and Batson (1982) pitted two motives against each other: self-interest and empathy. First, they varied how much empathy people felt toward Carol: In the high-empathy condition, people were told to try to imagine how Carol felt about what had happened to her and how it had changed her life; in the low-empathy condition, they were told to try to be objective and to not be concerned with how Carol felt. As expected, participants in the high-empathy condition reported feeling more empathy with Carol than did those in the low-empathy condition.

The researchers varied how costly it would be *not* to help Carol. In the high-cost condition, participants learned that Carol would start coming back to class the following week and happened to be in the same Introductory Psychology section as they were. Obviously, it would be unpleasant to refuse to help Carol and then run into her every week in class. In the low-cost condition, people learned that Carol would be

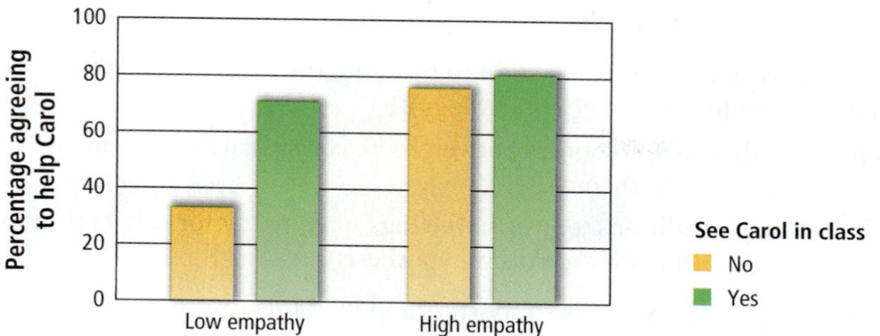

FIGURE 10.2

Altruism versus self-interest.

Under what conditions did people agree to help Carol with the work she missed in her Introductory Psychology class? When empathy was high, people helped regardless of the costs and rewards (i.e., regardless of whether they would encounter her in class). When empathy was low, people were more concerned with the rewards and costs for them—they helped only if they would encounter Carol in class and thus feel guilty about not helping.

(Adapted from Toi & Batson, 1982)

studying at home and would not be coming to class; thus, they would never have to face her in her wheelchair and feel guilty about not helping her out.

When deciding whether to help Carol, did people take into account the costs involved? According to the empathy-altruism hypothesis, if empathy was high, people should have been motivated by genuine altruistic concern and should have helped regardless of the costs (see Figure 10.1). As you can see on the right side of Figure 10.2, this prediction was confirmed: in the high-empathy condition, about as many people agreed to help when they thought they would see Carol in class as when they thought they would not see her in class. This suggests that people had Carol's interests in mind, not their own. In the low-empathy condition, however, many more people agreed to help when they thought they would see Carol in class than when they thought they would not see her in class (see the left side of Figure 10.2). This suggests that when empathy was low, social exchange came into play, in that people based their decision to help on the costs and benefits to themselves. They helped when it was in their interests to do so (i.e., when they would see Carol in her wheelchair and feel guilty for not helping) but not otherwise (i.e., when they thought they would never see her again).

These sorts of findings are not limited to laboratory experiments. For example, Piferi and colleagues (2006) examined helping in the wake of the September 11, 2001, terrorist attacks in the United States. In this study, the researchers assessed a number of variables, including empathy, help given immediately after September 11, help given one year later, reasons for helping, and so on. The first finding of note was that participants who were high in empathy reported providing more help (e.g., donating money, giving blood) both immediately after 9/11 and one year later, compared with those who were low in empathy. Also consistent with Batson's empathy-altruism hypothesis, those whose primary motivation was to alleviate their distress were more likely to provide help immediately after the attacks but not one year later (when, presumably, their distress had lessened). In contrast, those who were motivated by altruistic motives were more likely to engage in sustained help provision—giving help both immediately after the attack and a year later (Piferi, Jobe, & Jones, 2006).

The important role of empathy also has been demonstrated in studies conducted with children. For example, a study conducted with children in British Columbia found that those who were able to put themselves in another person's shoes were more likely to behave in prosocial ways toward him or her (e.g., helping an experimenter who dropped a box of paper clips, letting a friend have a turn at an enjoyable game). In fact, empathy was related to helping among children as young as five years old (Roberts & Strayer, 1996). Thus, as Batson's altruism-empathy hypothesis suggests, sometimes people do behave in truly altruistic ways.

This touching story of early hominid prosocial behaviour is intriguing to think about in terms of different theories of prosocial behaviour. Evolutionary psychologists might argue that the caregivers helped the dwarf because he was a relative and that people are programmed to help those who share their genes (i.e., kin selection). Social exchange theory would maintain that the dwarf's caregivers received sufficient rewards from their actions to outweigh the costs of caring for him. The empathy-altruism hypothesis would hold that the caregivers helped out of strong feelings of empathy and compassion for him—an interpretation supported by the article's final paragraph.

Study: Cavemen helped disabled

United Press International

NEW YORK—The skeleton of a dwarf who died about 12,000 years ago indicates that cave people cared for physically disabled members of their communities, a researcher said yesterday.

The skeleton of the 3-foot-high youth was initially discovered in 1963 in a cave in southern Italy but was lost to anthropologists until American researcher David W. Frayer reexamined the remains and reported his findings in the British journal Nature.

Frayer, a professor of anthropology at the University of Kansas at Lawrence, said in a telephone interview that the youth "couldn't have taken part in normal hunting of food or gathering activities so he was obviously cared for by others."

Archaeologists have found the remains of other handicapped individuals who lived during the same time period, but their disabilities occurred when they were adults, Frayer said.

"This is the first time we've found someone who was disabled since birth . . . .", Frayer said. He said there was no indication that the dwarf, who was about 17 at the time of his death, had suffered from malnutrition or neglect.

He was one of six individuals buried in the floor of a cave and was found in a dual grave in the arms of a woman, about 40 years old.

To sum up, we've identified three basic motives underlying prosocial behaviour:

1. Helping is an instinctive reaction to promote the welfare of those genetically similar to us (evolutionary psychology).
2. The rewards of helping often outweigh the costs, so helping is in our self-interest (social exchange theory).
3. Under some conditions, powerful feelings of empathy for others prompt selfless giving (the empathy-altruism hypothesis).

Each of these approaches has its supporters and its critics.

Connect to MyPsychLab
Are you a hero? To take a survey about if you could be a hero, go to MyPsychLab

Personal Determinants of Prosocial Behaviour: Why Do Some People Help More than Others?

If basic human motives were all there was to it, how could we explain the fact that some people are much more helpful than others? Clearly, we need to consider the personal determinants of prosocial behaviour that distinguish the helpful person from the selfish one.

Individual Differences: The Altruistic Personality

When you read the examples at the beginning of this chapter, did you think about the different personalities of the people involved? It is natural to assume that people such as Tina Moores, who lost her life while saving a drowning child, and Neil Bauman (introduced in Chapter 1), who left behind his young family to travel to Haiti to build shelters for earthquake victims, are cut from a different cloth—selfless, caring people who would never dream of ignoring someone's pleas for help. Psychologists have been quite interested in the nature of the **altruistic personality**—those aspects of a person's makeup that cause him or her to help others in a wide variety of situations (Eisenberg, Spinrad, Sadovsky, 2006; Mikulincer & Shaver, 2005, 2010; Penner, 2002).

Altruistic Personality
Aspects of a person's makeup that cause him or her to help others in a wide variety of situations

Although some people are obviously more helpful than others, personality alone does not determine behaviour. Studies of both children and adults, for example, find that people with high scores on personality tests of altruism are not that much more likely to help than those with lower scores (Batson, 1998; Magoo & Khanna, 1991; Piliavin & Charng, 1990). Why not? We need to consider several other critical factors as well, such as the situational pressures that are affecting people, their gender, the culture in which they grew up, and even their current mood. Indeed, the view that currently prevails in this area of research is that people's personalities interact with the situation to determine whether or not they will engage in prosocial behaviours (Graziano, Habashi, Sheese, & Tobin, 2007; Knafo & Israel, 2010; Penner & Orom, 2010).

Clearly, some people have more of an altruistic personality than others, causing them to engage in more prosocial behaviour. Personality, however, is not the whole story; the nature of the social situation also determines whether people help.

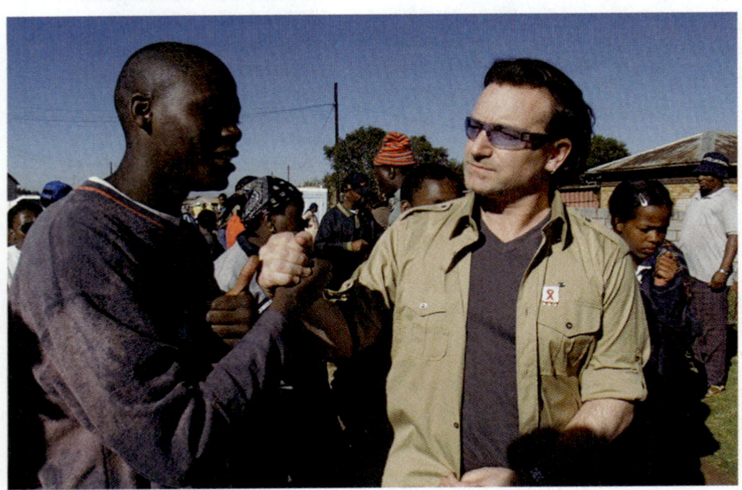

Gender Differences in Prosocial Behaviour

Consider two scenarios: (1) passing by a house, hearing the cries of young children, and smelling smoke, and then entering the house to rescue the children; and (2) helping an elderly disabled neighbour with household chores. Are women or men most likely to help in each situation? As you've probably guessed, the answer is men in the first situation and women in the second situation (Eagly, 1987; Eagly & Crowley, 1986; Eagly & Koenig, 2006). In virtually all cultures, norms prescribe different traits and behaviours for males and females, learned as children grow up. In Western cultures, the male sex role includes being chivalrous and heroic; females are expected to be nurturant and caring and to value close, long-term relationships.

On reflecting at dinner that he had done nothing to help anybody all day, he uttered these memorable and praiseworthy words: 'Friends, I have lost a day.'

—Suetonius, *Lives of the Twelve Caesars,second century* CE

Consistent with these gender roles, the recipients of the Medal of Bravery bestowed by Canada's governor general for "acts of bravery in hazardous circumstances" tend to be men. For example, in 2010, bravery medals were awarded to 46 males but only 6 females. Now consider the Governor General's Caring Canadian Award. This award honours Canadians who "have given extraordinary help or care to individuals, families, or groups, or supported community service or humanitarian causes." In 2007, 59 women received this award, compared to 35 men (Governor General of Canada, n.d.). (More recent statistics are not available because according to the governor general's website, the Caring Canadian Awards program is currently under review.)

Both men and women belie their nature when they are not kind.

—Gamaliel Bailey (1807–1859)

Researchers at the University of British Columbia recently interviewed recipients of the governor general's bravery and caring awards and also administered standard personality tests to them. The winners of these awards were more likely than a comparison group of adults to have been helpers in early life, to be securely attached, and to show a pattern of nurturant compassion coupled with decisive action-taking. Recipients of caring awards were higher in nurturance, more optimistic, and generally tended to be more focused on close relationships than recipients of bravery awards (Walker & Frimer, 2007). Women typically possess these qualities to a greater degree than do men.

Indeed, there is considerable evidence that helping that involves nurturance and commitment is more likely to be performed by women than by men (Fehr, 2010; George, Carroll, Kersnick, & Calderon, 1998; Otten, Penner, & Waugh, 1988; Smith, Wheeler, & Diener, 1975). For example, in national survey data gathered in the United States, women reported having spent an average of 95.7 hours providing emotional support to kin in the last month, compared to an average of 54.2 hours reported by men. Women also provided more practical help to kin than did men (Marks & Song, 2009).

Whereas men are more likely to perform chivalrous and heroic acts, women are more likely to be helpful in long-term relationships that involve greater commitment.

Socioeconomic Status Differences in Prosocial Behaviour

Does being poor make you more helpful? The answer is yes. In a series of studies conducted in Canada and the United States, Piff and colleagues found that people who are of lower socioeconomic status (SES) gave more of the money they earned during an experiment to their partner in the experiment, were more likely to help their partner in an experiment complete his or her tasks, and, in another study, when asked what percentage of one's income should be donated to charity, gave a higher number than did participants with a higher SES (Piff, Kraus, Côté, Cheng, & Keltner, 2010). To find out whether greater helpfulness could be induced in people with high SES, the researchers primed compassion by having participants watch a film clip on child poverty (participants in a control condition watched a conversation between two people). Priming compassion had the effect of making people with high SES just as generous as people with low SES typically are. Piff and colleagues (2010) conclude that people who have a lower SES are more concerned with the needs of others than those who have a higher SES, and this concern leads them to act in prosocial ways (Piff et al., 2010).

Cultural Differences in Prosocial Behaviour

In previous chapters, we noted that people who grow up in Western cultures tend to be individualist and have an independent view of the self, whereas people who grow up

In-Group

The group with which an individual identifies, and of which he or she feels a member

Out-Group

A group with which the individual does not identify

in Eastern cultures tend to be collectivist and have an interdependent view of the self. Does this cultural difference affect people's willingness to help others? Because people with an interdependent view of the self are more likely to define themselves in terms of their social relationships and have more of a sense of "connectedness" to others, we might predict that they'd be more likely to help a person in need.

However, it turns out that people in all cultures are more likely to help someone they define as a member of their **in-group**—the group with which an individual identifies. We are more likely to feel empathy for in-group members and this, in turn, leads to increased helping (Stürmer, Snyder, & Omoto, 2005). In contrast, people are less likely to help someone they perceive to be a member of an **out-group**—a group with which the individual does not identify (Brewer & Brown, 1998; see Chapter 12). Cultural factors come into play in determining how strongly people draw the line between in-groups and out-groups. In many interdependent cultures, the needs of in-group members are considered more important than those of out-group members. Consequently, members of these cultures are more likely to help in-group members than are members of individualist cultures (Leung & Bond, 1984; Miller, Bersoff, & Harwood, 1990; Moghaddam, Taylor, & Wright, 1993). However, because the line between "us" and "them" is more firmly drawn in interdependent cultures, people in these cultures are *less* likely to help members of out-groups than are people in individualist cultures (L'Armand & Pepitone, 1975; Leung & Bond, 1984; Triandis, 1994). According to McCrae and colleagues, this is why people in a collectivist culture, namely China, score lower on scales that assess the altruistic personality type than people in an individualist culture, namely Canada (McCrae, Yik, Trapnell, Bond, & Paulhus, 1998). Similarly, when Osamu Iwata (1992) compared the altruistic intentions of students in Canada and Japan by type of relationship, Canadian students expressed greater altruism toward "a person one happens to see occasionally but with whom he or she has no relation." However, Canadians and Japanese students did not differ when altruism was directed toward a person with whom one has "personal and close relations." Thus, to be helped by other people, it is important that they view you as a member of their in-group—as "one of them"—and this is especially true in interdependent cultures (Ting & Piliavin, 2000).

Before leaving this topic, we should point out that cultural norms about taking credit for helping others may also contribute to the perception that people from Asian cultures are less altruistic overall than people from Western cultures. According to Lee and colleagues, in Asian cultures, children are taught to be modest and self-effacing—and this includes not seeking recognition for helpful acts. These researchers presented scenarios about helping to children (aged 7 to 11) in Canada and China. In one scenario, a girl named Kelly knew that her friend Anne had lost the money she needed for a class trip. Kelly secretly put some of her own money in Anne's pocket so that Anne could go on the trip. Later, a teacher asked Kelly if she knew who had given the money to Anne. Canadian children believed that Kelly should acknowledge this helpful act (thereby garnering the praise of the teacher); Chinese children believed that Kelly should not admit that she had done so because begging for praise would violate social norms of modesty (Lee, Cameron, Xu, Fu, & Board, 1997). These researchers subsequently replicated this study with adults (university students, elementary school teachers, and parents) in Canada and China, and found the same results (Fu, Lee, Cameron, & Xu, 2001).

The Effects of Mood on Prosocial Behaviour

Imagine you are at your local shopping mall. As you walk from one store to another, a fellow in front of you suddenly drops a manila folder, and papers flutter in all directions. He looks around in dismay, and then bends down and starts to pick up the papers. Would you stop to help him? What do you think the average shopper would do? By now, you know that thinking about how many altruistic people there are in the world won't predict the answer. Other factors, including the mood people happen to be in at the time, can strongly affect behaviour—in this case, whether they will help.

Effects of Positive Moods: Feel Good, Do Good In a classic study, Alice Isen and Paul Levin (1972) explored the effect of good moods on prosocial behaviour in shopping malls in two US cities. They boosted the mood of shoppers in a simple way: by leaving a dime in the coin-return slot of a pay telephone at the mall and waiting for someone to find it. As the lucky shoppers left the phone with their newly found dime, a confederate played the role of the man with the manila folder. He deliberately dropped the folder about a metre in front of the shopper, to see whether the shopper would stop to help him pick up his papers. It turned out that finding the dime had a dramatic effect on helping. Only 4 percent of the people who did not find a dime helped the man pick up his papers. In comparison, 84 percent of the people who found a dime helped.

Researchers have found this "feel good, do good" effect in diverse situations. For example, people are more likely to help others after doing well on a test, receiving a gift, when they are thinking happy thoughts, or listening to pleasant music (North, Tarrant, & Hargreaves, 2004). And when people are in a good mood for any of these reasons, they are more helpful in many ways, including contributing money to charity, helping someone find a lost contact lens, tutoring another student, donating blood, and helping co-workers on the job (Carlson, Charlin, & Miller, 1988; Isen, 1999; Salovey, Mayer, & Rosenhan, 1991). See the accompanying Try It! exercise for a way of doing your own test of the "feel good, do good" hypothesis.

What is it about being in a good mood that makes people more altruistic? Being in a good mood can increase helping for three reasons. First, a good mood makes us look on the bright side of life. If you saw the man drop his manila folder full of papers, you could view this incident in at least two ways. "What a klutz," you might think. "Let him clean up his own mess." Or you might have more sympathy for him, thinking, "Oh, that's too bad. The poor guy, he probably feels really frustrated." When we are in a good mood, we tend to see the good side of other people, giving them the benefit of the doubt. A victim who might normally seem clumsy or annoying will, when we are feeling cheerful, seem like a decent, needy person who is worthy of our help (Carlson, Charlin, & Miller, 1988; Forgas & Bower, 1987).

Second, helping other people is an excellent way of prolonging our good mood. If we see someone in need of help, being a good Samaritan spawns even more good feelings, and we can walk away feeling terrific. In comparison, not helping when we know we should is a surefire downer, deflating our good mood (Clark & Isen, 1982; Isen, 1987; Lyubomirsky, Sheldon, & Schkade, 2005).

Finally, good moods increase self-awareness. As we noted in Chapter 5, at any given time, people vary in how much attention they pay to their feelings and values versus the world around them. Sometimes, we are particularly attuned to our internal worlds and, sometimes, we are not. Good moods increase the amount of attention we pay to

TRY IT! Do Good, Feel Good?

Suppose you found a $20 bill on the ground and could spend it on yourself (e.g., buy yourself a nice lunch) or on someone else (e.g., treat a friend to lunch). Which would you rather do? If your goal is to improve your mood, the answer might surprise you—spend it on your friend! Research by Dunn, Aknin, and Norton (2008) found that people who spent money on others were happier than people who spent money on themselves. Try this yourself the next time you have a little money to spend. Rather than buying yourself a treat, try treating a friend or donating the money to charity. You might be surprised by how good you feel!

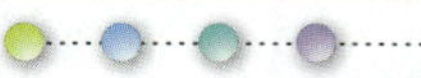

ourselves, and this factor in turn makes us more likely to behave according to our values and ideals (Berkowitz, 1987; Carlson, Charlin, & Miller, 1988; Salovey & Rodin, 1985). A recent, fascinating study suggests that people are, indeed, more helpful when they are self-aware (Shariff & Norenzayan, 2007). In this study, students at the University of British Columbia were primed with God concepts (participants were given scrambled sentences that made references to God which they had to "unscramble") or with morality concepts. Those in a control condition did not receive any prime. Participants who were primed with God donated the most money to their partner in the experiment (regardless of whether the participant actually believed in God). Those who were primed with morality were nearly as generous as those who were primed with God. Participants in the control condition were least generous. The researchers suggest that the primes served to increase self-awareness which, in turn, made people more likely to behave in line with their altruistic values.

> *If you want to be happy, practise compassion.*
>
> —14th Dalai Lama *(1935–)*

Negative-State Relief: Feel Bad, Do Good What about when we are in a bad mood? Suppose that when you saw the fellow in the mall drop his folder, you were feeling down in the dumps. Would this influence the likelihood that you would help the man? One kind of bad mood clearly leads to an increase in helping—feeling guilty (Baumeister, Stillwell, & Heatherton, 1994; Estrada-Hollenbeck & Heatherton, 1998). People often act on the idea that good deeds cancel out bad deeds. When they have done something that makes them feel guilty, helping another person balances things out, thereby reducing their guilty feelings. For example, in one study, it was found that churchgoers were more likely to donate money to charities before attending confession than afterward, presumably because confessing to a priest reduced their guilt (Harris, Benson, & Hall, 1975). Thus, if you just realized you had forgotten your best friend's birthday, you would be more likely to help the fellow in the mall to repair your guilty feelings.

But suppose you just had a fight with a friend or just found out you did poorly on a test, and you are feeling sad. Given that feeling happy leads to greater helping, it might seem that feeling sad would decrease helping. Surprisingly, however, sadness can also lead to an increase in helping, at least under certain conditions (Carlson & Miller, 1987; Salovey, Mayer, & Rosenhan, 1991). When people are sad, they are motivated to engage in activities that make them feel better (Wegener & Petty, 1994). The idea that people help in order to alleviate their own sadness and distress is called the **negative-state relief hypothesis** (Cialdini, Darby, & Vincent, 1973; Cialdini & Fultz, 1990; Cialdini et al., 1987). It is an example of the social exchange theory approach to helping discussed earlier. People help someone else with the goal of helping themselves: to relieve their own sadness and distress. In this way, if you are feeling down, you are more likely to donate money to a charity. The warm glow of helping the charity lifts us out of the doldrums (Cialdini, Darby, & Vincent, 1973).

Negative-State Relief Hypothesis
The idea that people help in order to alleviate their own sadness and distress

Emotional Numbness: Feel Nothing, Do Nothing The emotional numbness that people feel when they are excluded by a group of people they care about can interfere with prosocial behaviour. In a series of studies, Twenge and colleagues (2007) demonstrated that when people are excluded from social groups, they are less likely to engage in prosocial acts. For example, in one experiment, participants interacted in same-sex groups. Later, they were asked to name the two group members with whom they would most like to work. Participants in the acceptance condition were told that "everyone chose you," whereas those in the exclusion condition were told that they had been rejected by the group ("no one chose you"). Next, participants were told that the experiment was over and that they could leave or, if they wished, stay and help out with some other experiments. The results were dramatic—90 percent of the participants who were accepted by the group agreed to help, whereas only 20 percent of those who were rejected by the group offered to do so (Twenge et al., 2007). Other studies have found that participants who were excluded from a group were less likely to donate money to a charity or help someone clean up after a mishap (e.g., knocking over a cup of pencils). The reason was *not* that social rejection put people in a bad mood; in fact, people who were rejected seemed to experience a temporary inability to feel anything too deeply. By shutting down emotionally, people avoided the pain of being rejected by others. But it also made them less able to feel empathy toward someone who needed their help (DeWall & Baumeister, 2006; Twenge, Baumeister, DeWall, Ciarocco, & Bartels, 2007).

Situational Determinants of Prosocial Behaviour: When Will People Help?

Personality, gender, culture, and moods each contribute a piece to the puzzle of why people help others, but they are not the complete picture. To understand more fully why people help, we need to consider the social situation in which they find themselves.

Environment: Rural versus Urban

Suppose you are walking down the street one day when you see a man suddenly fall down and cry out in pain. He rolls up his pant leg, revealing a bandaged shin that is bleeding heavily. What would you do? When this event was staged in a small town, about half of the people who walked by stopped and offered to help. In large cities, only 15 percent of passersby stopped to help (Amato, 1983). Other studies have found that people in small towns are more likely to help when asked to help a lost child, give directions, or return a lost letter. The finding that help is more likely to be offered in small towns than in large cities has been reported in several countries, including Canada, the United States, Israel, Australia, Turkey, Great Britain, and Sudan (Hedge & Yousif, 1992; Steblay, 1987).

Why are people more likely to help in small towns? One possibility is that people who grow up in a small town are more likely to internalize altruistic values. If this were the case, people who grew up in small towns would be more likely to help, even if they were visiting a big city. Alternatively, the immediate surroundings, and not people's internalized values, might be the key. Stanley Milgram (1970) proposed an urban-overload hypothesis, which holds that people living in cities are constantly being bombarded with stimulation, and therefore they keep to themselves to avoid being overloaded by it. According to this **urban-overload hypothesis**, if you put urban dwellers in a calmer, less stimulating environment, they would be as likely as anyone else to reach out to others.

Do not wait for extraordinary circumstances to do good action; try to use ordinary situations.

—Jean Paul Richter *(1763–1825)*

Urban-Overload Hypothesis

The theory that because people living in cities are constantly being bombarded with stimulation, they keep to themselves to avoid being overloaded by it

People are less helpful in big cities than in small towns, not because of a difference in values but because the stress of urban life causes them to keep to themselves.

Interestingly, the evidence supports the urban-overload hypothesis more than it does the idea that living in cities makes people less altruistic by nature. A review of dozens of studies found that when an opportunity for helping arises, it matters more whether the incident occurs in a rural or urban area than which kind of person happens to be there (Steblay, 1987). Further, in field studies conducted in 36 cities in the United States, it was found that population density (the number of people per square kilometre) was more related to helping than was population size (Levine, Martinez, Brase, & Sorenson, 1994). The greater the density of people, the less likely people were to help. This makes sense, according to the urban-overload hypothesis: There should be more stimulation in an area packed with a lot of people than in an area in which people are more spread out. The hustle and bustle in cities can be so overwhelming that even caring, altruistic people turn inward, responding less to those around them.

CONNECTIONS

Does Belonging to a Community Make You More Helpful?

In many parts of the world, it is common for people to move far away from where they were raised (Hochstadt, 1999). As it turns out, people who have lived in one place for a long time are more likely to engage in prosocial acts that help the community. Living in one place for a long time leads to greater attachment to the community and more interdependence with one's neighbours, thereby increasing the likelihood that help and support will be reciprocated (Baumeister, 1986; Oishi, Rothman, Snyder, Su, Zehm, Hertel, Gonzalez, & Sherman, 2007; Twenge, Baumeister, DeWall, Ciarocco, & Bartles, 2007). For example, Oishi and colleagues (2007) found that people who had lived in the Minneapolis–St. Paul area for a long time were more likely to purchase "critical habitat" licence plates compared with people who had recently moved to the area. (These licence plates cost an extra $30 per year and provide funds for the state to purchase and manage natural habitats.)

Perhaps it is not surprising that people who have lived in one place for a while feel more of a stake in their community. However, Oishi and colleagues (2007) found that helpfulness can increase quite quickly even in a one-time laboratory setting. Imagine you are in a study in which you are playing a trivia contest against four other students. The winner will receive a $10 gift certificate. The experimenter says that people in the group can help one another if they want, but that doing so might lower a person's chances of winning the prize. As the game progresses, one of your fellow group members keeps sighing and commenting that he doesn't know the answers to the questions. Would you offer him help or let him struggle on his own?

The answer, it turns out, depends on how long you have been in the group with the struggling student. The actual study by Oishi and colleagues had four tasks in all (the trivia contest was the last one). Half of the participants remained together and worked on all the tasks throughout the study, whereas the other half switched to a new group after each task. Thus, in the former condition, people had more of an opportunity to get to know one another and form a sense of community, whereas the experience of the latter group was more analogous to moving from one community to another. As the researchers predicted, people in the stable community condition were more likely to help the struggling student in their group than those in the more "transient" community condition. The bottom line? Prosocial behaviour is much more likely when people feel part of a group or a community.

Research on residential mobility found that people who had lived for a long time in the Minneapolis–St. Paul area in the United States were more likely to purchase "critical habitat" license plates, such as the one pictured here, than were people who had recently moved to the area.

Bystander Intervention: The Latané and Darley Model

Explore on mypsychlab
Bystander Intervention

Remember Kitty Genovese? We have just seen one reason why her neighbours may have turned a deaf ear to her cries for help. Her murder took place in New York City, one of the most densely populated areas in the world. Perhaps her neighbours were so overloaded with urban stimulation that they dismissed Genovese's cries as one small addition to the surrounding din. Although it is true that people help less in urban environments, this is not the only explanation for Genovese's neighbours' failure to help. Her desperate cries surely must have risen above the everyday noise of garbage trucks and car horns.

Bibb Latané and John Darley (1970) are two social psychologists who taught at universities in New York at the time of the Genovese murder. As we discussed in Chapter 2, they, too, were unconvinced that the only reason her neighbours failed to help were the stresses and stimulation of urban life. They focused on the fact that many people heard her cries. Paradoxically, they thought, it might be that the greater the number of bystanders who observe an emergency, the less likely it is that any one of them will help. As Bibb Latané (1987) put it, "We came up with the insight that perhaps what made the Genovese case so fascinating was itself what made it happen—namely, that not just one or two, but 38 people had watched and done nothing" (p. 78).

In a series of now-classic experiments, Latané and Darley (1970) found that in terms of receiving help, there is no safety in numbers. Think back to the seizure experiment we discussed in Chapter 2. In this study, a participant was taken to a cubicle, supposedly to take part in a group discussion of university life with students in other cubicles via an intercom system. One of the other students suddenly had a seizure, crying out for help, choking, and finally, falling silent. There was actually only one real participant in the study; the others, including the one who had the seizure, were prerecorded voices. The point of the study was to see whether the real participant tried to help the seizure victim, by trying to find him or by summoning the experimenter, or whether—like Kitty Genovese's neighbours—he or she simply sat there and did nothing. As Darley and Latané (1968) anticipated, the answer depended on how many people the participant thought witnessed the emergency. When people believed they were the only one listening to the student have the seizure, most of them (85 percent) helped within a minute. By 2.5 minutes, 100 percent of the people who thought they were the only bystander had offered assistance (see Figure 10.3). In comparison, when the research participants believed there was one other student listening, fewer people helped—only 62 percent in the first minute. As you can see in Figure 10.3, helping occurred more slowly when there were two bystanders, and never reached 100 percent, even after six minutes, at which point the experiment was terminated. Finally, when the participants believed there were four other students listening in addition to themselves, the percentage of people who helped dropped even more dramatically. Only 31 percent helped in the first minute, and after six minutes only 62 percent had offered help. Dozens of other studies, conducted both in the laboratory and in the field, have found the same thing. The greater the number of bystanders who witness an emergency, the less likely any one of them is to help the victim—a phenomenon called the **bystander effect**.

Bystander Effect
The finding that the greater the number of bystanders who witness an emergency, the less likely it is that any one of them will help

Why is it that people are less likely to help when other bystanders are present? Latané and Darley (1970) developed a step-by-step description of how people decide whether to intervene in an emergency (see Figure 10.4). Part of this description, as we will see, is an explanation of how the number of bystanders can make a difference. But let's begin with the first step: whether people notice that someone needs help.

Noticing an Event Obviously, if people don't notice that an emergency has occurred, they will not intervene and offer to help. But what determines whether people notice an emergency? John Darley and Daniel Batson (1973) demonstrated that something as seemingly trivial as how much of a hurry people are in can make more of a difference than what kind of person they are. These researchers conducted

Simulate on mypsychlab
Helping a Stranger

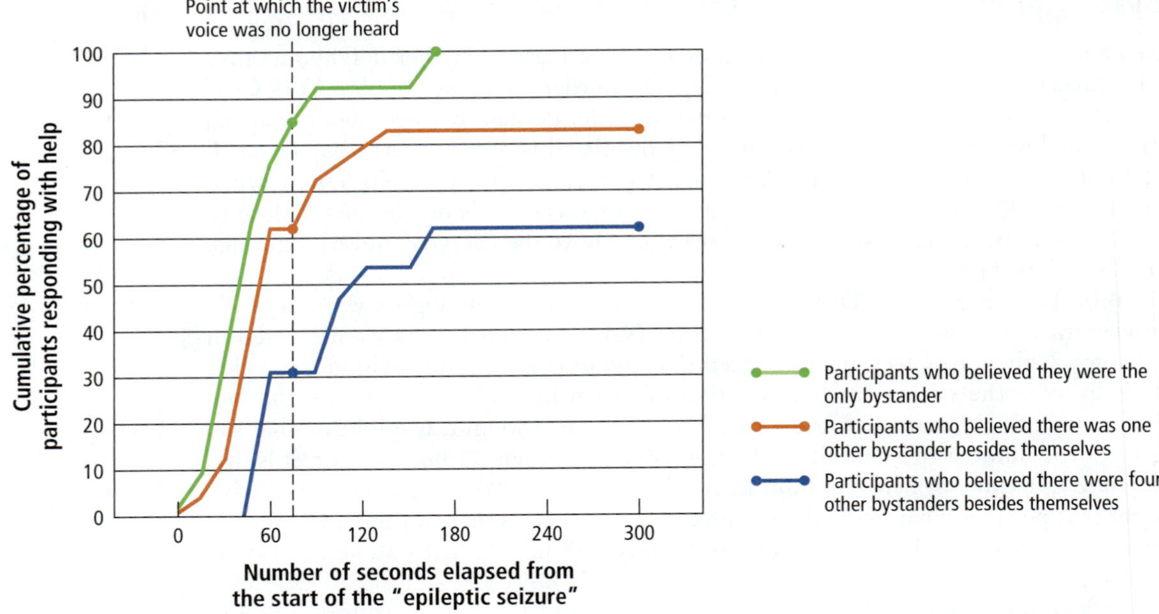

FIGURE 10.3

Bystander intervention: The presence of bystanders reduces helping.

When people believed that they were the only person hearing a student having a seizure—when they were the lone bystander—most of them helped him immediately, and all did so within 2.5 minutes. When they believed that someone else was listening as well—that there were two bystanders—they were less likely to help and did so more slowly. And when they believed that four others were listening—that there were five bystanders—they were even less likely to help.

(Adapted from Darley & Latané, 1968)

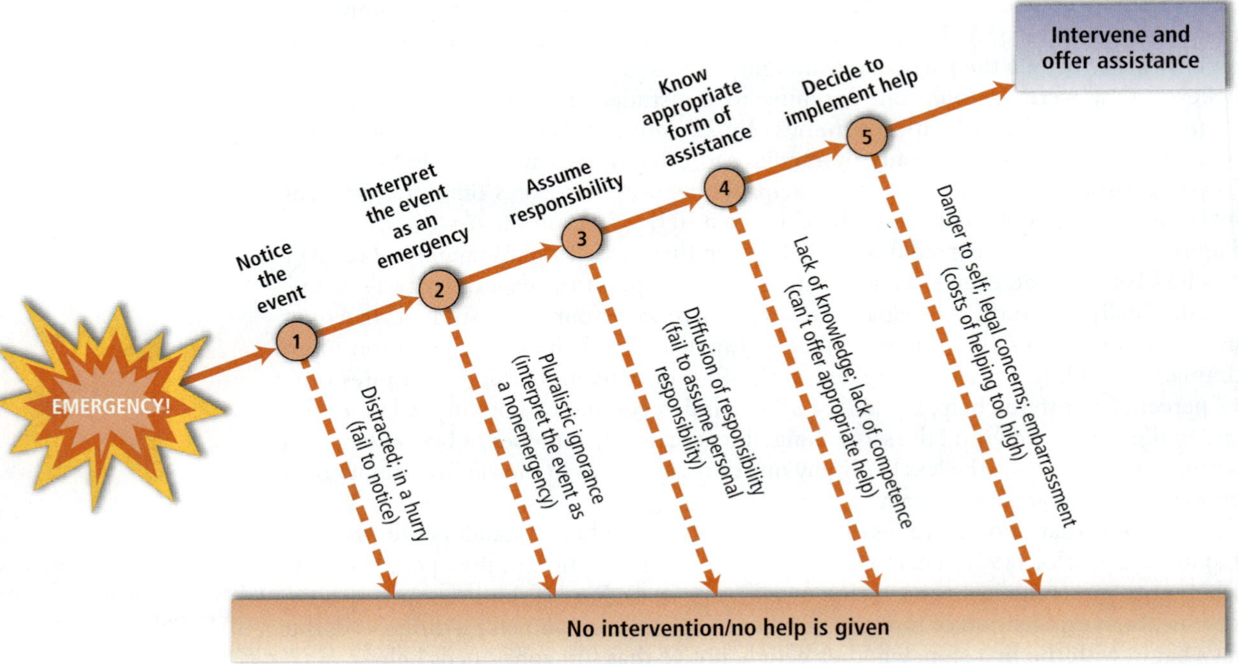

FIGURE 10.4

Bystander intervention decision tree: Five steps to helping in an emergency.

According to Latané and Darley (1970), people go through five decision-making steps before they help someone in an emergency. If bystanders fail to take any one of the five steps, they will not help. Each step, as well as the possible reasons why people decide not to intervene, is outlined.

(Adapted from Latané & Darley, 1970)

a study that mirrored the parable of the good Samaritan, wherein many passersby failed to stop to help a man lying unconscious on the side of the road. The research participants were people we might think would be extremely altruistic—seminary students preparing to devote their lives to the ministry. The students were asked to walk to another building, where the researchers would record them making a brief speech. Some were told that they were late and should hurry to keep their appointment. Others were told that there was no rush, because the assistant in the other building was a few minutes behind schedule. As they walked to the other building, each of the students passed a man (an accomplice of the experimenters) who was slumped in a doorway. The man coughed and groaned as each student walked by. Did the seminary students stop to help him? If they were not in a hurry, most of them (63 percent) did. However, only 10 percent of the people hurrying to keep their appointment stopped to help. Many of the students who were in a hurry did not even notice the man.

It is perhaps unsurprising that when people are in a rush, they pay less attention to what's going on around them, making them less likely to help someone in need. What is surprising is that such a seemingly trivial matter as how much of a hurry we are in can overpower the kind of people we are. Darley and Batson (1973) tested the seminary students on a variety of personality measures that assessed how religious they were. They also varied the topic of the speech. Specifically, some students were asked to speak on the parable of the good Samaritan—surely, seminary students speaking on this topic would be especially likely to stop and help a man slumped in a doorway, given the similarity of this incident to the parable. However, if the students were in a hurry, they were unlikely to help, even if they were very religious individuals preparing to give a speech about the good Samaritan. We should note that Darley and Batson did find one variable that made a difference: whether the students saw religion as a quest (an open-minded search for truth) versus a set of traditions. Those who viewed religion as a quest were no more likely to stop, but those who did stop were more responsive to the man's needs than those who viewed religion as a set of traditions.

Interpreting the Event as an Emergency Even if people do notice someone slumped in a doorway, they might not stop and help. The next determinant of helping is whether the bystander interprets the event as an emergency—that is, as a situation in which help is needed (see Figure 10.4). Is the person in the doorway drunk, or seriously ill? If we see white smoke coming out of a vent, is it something innocuous, such as mist from an air conditioner, or a sign that the building is on fire? Did that scream we just heard come from someone having a good time at a party, or is someone being attacked? If people assume that nothing is wrong when an emergency is taking place, obviously they will not help.

Interestingly, when other bystanders are present, people are more likely to assume that an emergency is something innocuous. To understand why, think back to our discussion of informational social influence in Chapter 7. This type of social influence occurs when we use other people to help us define reality. When we are uncertain about what's going on, such as whether or not the smoke we see is a sign of a fire, one of the first things we do is look around to see how other people are responding. If other people look up, shrug, and go about their business, we are likely to assume that there is nothing to worry about. If other people look panic-stricken and yell, "Fire!," we immediately assume that the building is, indeed, on fire. As we saw in Chapter 7, it's often a good strategy to use other people as a source of information when we are uncertain about what's going on. The danger in doing so, however, is that sometimes no one is sure what is happening. Since an emergency is frequently a sudden and confusing event, bystanders tend to freeze, watching and listening with blank expressions as they try to figure out what's taking place. When they glance at each other, they see an apparent lack of concern on the part of other bystanders. This results in a state of **pluralistic ignorance**: Bystanders assume that nothing is wrong in an emergency because no one else looks concerned.

Pluralistic Ignorance
The phenomenon whereby bystanders assume that nothing is wrong in an emergency because no one else looks concerned

Consider another classic experiment by Latané and Darley (1970). Imagine that you are participating in a study of people's attitudes toward the problems of urban life, and you arrive at the appointed time. A sign instructs you to fill out a questionnaire while you are waiting for the study to begin. You take a copy of the questionnaire, sit down, and work on it for a few minutes, when something odd happens. White smoke starts coming into the room through a small vent in the wall. Before long, the room is so filled with smoke you can barely see the questionnaire. What will you do? In fact, there was no real danger—the experimenters were pumping smoke into the room to see how people would respond to this potential emergency. Not surprisingly, when people were by themselves, most of them took action. Within two minutes, 50 percent of the participants left the room and found the experimenter down the hall, reporting that there was a potential fire in the building; by six minutes, 75 percent of the participants left the room to alert the experimenter.

But what would happen if people were not alone? Given that 75 percent of the participants who were by themselves reported the smoke, it would seem that the larger the group, the greater the likelihood that someone would report the smoke. In fact, this can be figured mathematically: If there is a 75 percent chance that any one person will report the smoke, there is a 98 percent chance that at least one person in a three-person group will do so. To find out whether more bystanders would increase the chances of helping, Latané and Darley (1970) included a condition in which everything was identical except that three people instead of one sat in the room as the smoke began to seep in. Surprisingly, in only 12 percent of the three-person groups did someone report the smoke within two minutes, and in only 38 percent of the groups did someone report the smoke within six minutes. In the remaining groups, the participants sat there filling out questionnaires even when they had to wave away the smoke with their hands to see what they were writing. What went wrong?

Because it was not clear that the smoke constituted an emergency, the participants used one another as a source of information. If the people next to you glance at the smoke and then go on filling out their questionnaires, you will feel reassured that nothing is wrong—otherwise, why would they be acting so unconcerned? The problem is that they are probably looking at you out of the corner of their eyes and, seeing that you appear to be not overly concerned, they, too, are reassured that everything is okay. Group members gain false reassurance from one another whenever each person assumes that the others know more about what's going on than he or she does. And when the event is ambiguous—as when smoke is coming from a vent—people

Emergency situations can be confusing. Does this man need help? Have the bystanders failed to notice him? Or has the behaviour of the others led each of them to interpret the situation as a nonemergency—an example of pluralistic ignorance?

Kitty Genovese (inset) and the alley in which she was murdered. Ironically, she would probably be alive today had fewer people heard her desperate cries for help.

will convince one another that nothing is wrong (Clark & Word, 1972; Solomon, Solomon, & Stone, 1978).

Assuming Responsibility Sometimes, it is obvious that an emergency is occurring, as when Kitty Genovese cried out, "Oh my God, he stabbed me! Please help me! Please help me!" (Rosenthal, 1964). Genovese's neighbours must have believed that something terrible was happening and that she desperately needed help. That they did nothing indicates that even if we interpret an event as an emergency, we have to decide that it is *our* responsibility—not someone else's—to do something about it. Here, again, the number of bystanders is a crucial variable. Think back to the Darley and Latané (1968) seizure experiment, in which participants believed they were the only one listening to the student while he had a seizure. The responsibility rested totally on their shoulders. If they didn't help, no one would, and the student might die. As a result, in this condition most people helped almost immediately, and all helped within a few minutes.

But what happens when there are many witnesses? A **diffusion of responsibility** occurs, whereby each bystander's sense of responsibility to help decreases as the number of witnesses to an emergency or crisis increases. Because other people are present, no single bystander feels strong personal responsibility to take action. Recall from our earlier discussion that helping often entails costs; we can place ourselves in danger, and we can look foolish by overreacting or doing the wrong thing. Why should we risk these costs when many other people who can help are present? The problem is that everyone is likely to feel this way, making all of the bystanders less likely to help. This is particularly true if people cannot tell whether someone else has already intervened. When participants in the seizure experiment believed that other students were also hearing the crisis, they couldn't tell whether another student had already helped because the intercom system transmitted only the voice of the student having the seizure. Each student probably assumed that he or she did not have to help, because surely someone else had already done so. Similarly, Kitty Genovese's neighbours had no way of knowing whether someone else had called the police. Most likely, they assumed that someone else had already made the call. Tragically, everyone assumed it was somebody else's responsibility to take action, thereby leaving Genovese to fight her assailant alone. The sad irony of Genovese's murder is that she might have received help and survived the attack had *fewer* people heard her cries for help.

Diffusion of Responsibility

Each bystander's sense of responsibility to help decreases as the number of witnesses to an emergency or crisis increases

Knowing How to Help Even if people have made it this far in the helping sequence—noticing an event has occurred, interpreting it as an emergency, and taking responsibility—an additional condition must still be met. The person must decide what form of help is appropriate (Step 4 in Figure 10.4). Suppose, for example, that on a hot summer day you see a woman collapse in the street and you determine she is gravely ill. No one else seems to be helping, so you decide that it is up to you. But what should you do? Has the woman had a heart attack? Or is she suffering from heat stroke? Should you call an ambulance, administer CPR, or try to get her out of the sun? If people don't know what form of assistance to give, obviously, they will be unable to help.

Deciding to Implement Help Finally, even if you know exactly what kind of help is appropriate, there are still reasons why you might decide not to intervene. For one thing, you might not be qualified to deliver the right kind of help. Even if the woman on the street is complaining of chest pains, suggesting a heart attack, if you don't know how to administer CPR, you'll be unable to help her. Or you might be afraid of making a fool of yourself. It can be embarrassing to intervene, only to discover that a situation actually wasn't an emergency. Even some forms of helping can be embarrassing. For example, Edwards (1975) conducted a study in South Africa in which a female confederate "accidentally" dropped either her purse or a box of tampons while walking down a street. Nearly everyone (95 percent) who saw the woman drop her purse returned it. In comparison, 59 percent of bystanders returned the tampons. One potential helper was about to return the tampons but quickly dropped the box when he realized what it contained! This study was replicated in Canada by James McDonald and Stuart McKelvie (1992) at Bishop's University. In their study, a male confederate dropped either a mitten or a box of condoms while walking through a shopping mall. Nearly half (47 percent) of the people who saw him drop the mitten retrieved it. In contrast, only 17 percent of bystanders returned the condoms. One man "helped" by kicking the condoms along the floor of the mall until they caught up with the confederate! Thus, costs of helping such as embarrassment can be barriers to providing help.

Another cost of helping is fear of doing the wrong thing and making matters worse, or even of placing yourself in danger by trying to help. We began this chapter with the story of Murray Aklwenzie, a good Samaritan who intervened when a panhandler was harassing a woman. The panhandler then turned on Aklwenzie and viciously attacked him. Aklwenzie had to relearn to walk and talk after the attack. Sadly, the injuries he sustained have left him permanently brain damaged. He is under constant care in a nursing home and does not even recognize his daughter or his grandchildren (McIntyre, 2006). In short, this single act of helping destroyed Aklwenzie's life.

In sum, five steps have to be taken before people will intervene in an emergency. They have to notice the event, interpret it as an emergency, decide it is their responsibility to help, know how to help, and decide to act. If people fail to take any one of these steps, they will not intervene. Given how difficult it can be to take all five steps, it is not surprising that incidents such as Kitty Genovese's murder can occur.

The Nature of the Relationship: Communal versus Exchange Relationships

A great deal of research on prosocial behaviour has looked at helping between strangers, such as Latané and Darley's research on bystander intervention. Although this research is very important, most helping in everyday life occurs between people who know each other well, such as family members and close friends. In Chapter 9, we distinguished between communal and exchange relationships. *Communal relationships* are those in which people's primary concern is the welfare of the other person (e.g., a child), whereas *exchange relationships* are those governed by concerns about equity—that what you put into the relationship equals what you get out of it. How does helping occur in communal relationships? It turns out that when the person in need of help is someone close to us, we are less concerned about the benefits that we may reap from helping and more concerned with simply responding to his or her needs (Clark & Monin, 2006; LeMay, Clark, & Feeney, 2007).

In communal relationships, such as those between parents and their children, people are concerned less with who gets what and more with how much help the other person needs.

How Can Helping Be Increased?

Most religions stress some version of Christianity's Golden Rule, urging us to do unto others as we would have others do unto us. There are many saintly people in the world who succeed in following this rule, devoting their lives to the welfare of others. We would all be better off, however, if prosocial behaviour were more common than it is. How can we get people, when faced with an emergency, to act more like Murray Aklwenzie and less like Kitty Genovese's neighbours?

Before addressing this question, we should point out that people do not always want to be helped. Imagine that you are sitting at a computer terminal in the library and are struggling to access a particular website. You can't figure out why the address you're trying isn't working, and you become increasingly frustrated as the computer responds with incomprehensible messages. A confident-looking guy strides into the room and peers over your shoulder for a few minutes. "You sure have a lot to learn," he says. "Move over and let me show you how this works." How would you react? You might feel some gratitude; but you would probably also feel some resentment. His offer of help comes with a message: "You are too stupid to figure this out for yourself." Receiving help can make us feel inadequate and dependent. As a result, we do not always react positively when someone offers us aid. When we do not want to appear incompetent, we may suffer in silence—even if doing so lowers our chances of successfully completing a task (Brown, Nesse, & Vinokur, 2003; Nadler & Fisher, 1986; Schneider, Major, Luhtanen, & Crocker, 1996).

When death, the great reconciler, has come, it is never our tenderness that we repent of, but our severity.

—George Eliot (Marian Evans), *Adam Bede, 1859*

Nonetheless, the world would be a better place if more people helped their fellow human beings. How can we increase everyday acts of kindness, such as looking out for an elderly neighbour or volunteering to read to kids at the local school? One answer is to cultivate helping behaviour early on. There also are ways of increasing the likelihood that bystanders will intervene.

Instilling Helpfulness with Rewards and Models

Developmental psychologists have discovered that prosocial behaviour occurs early in life. Even children as young as 18 months frequently help others, such as assisting a parent with household tasks or trying to make a crying infant feel better (Volling, Kolak, & Kennedy, 2009). One powerful way to encourage prosocial behaviour is for parents and others to reward such acts with praise, smiles, and hugs. Several studies suggest that these kinds of rewards increase prosocial behaviour in children (Fischer, 1963; Grusec, 1991). Rewards should not, however, be emphasized too much. As you may recall from our discussion of the overjustification effect in Chapter 5, rewarding people too strongly for performing a behaviour can lower their intrinsic interest in it because they come to believe they are doing it only to get the reward. The trick is to encourage children to act prosocially but not to be too heavy-handed with rewards. One way of accomplishing this is to tell children, after they have helped, that they did so because they are kind and helpful people. Such comments encourage children to perceive themselves as altruistic people, so they will help in future situations even when no rewards are forthcoming (Grusec, Kuczynski, Rushton, & Simutis, 1979).

Another way for parents to increase prosocial behaviour in their children is to behave prosocially themselves. Children generally model behaviours they observe in others, including prosocial behaviours (Batson, 1998; Dodge, 1984; Mussen & Eisenberg-Berg, 1977). Children who observe their parents helping others (e.g., volunteering to help the homeless) learn that helping others is a valued act. Interviews with people who have gone to great lengths to help others—such as Christians who helped Jews escape from Nazi Germany during World War II—indicate that their parents were also dedicated helpers (London, 1970; Rosenhan, 1970).

Closer to home, a recent Statistics Canada report found that people whose parents had done volunteer work are more likely to engage in prosocial behaviours such as charitable giving (Statistics Canada, 2009). Similarly, S. Mark Pancer and Michael Pratt (1999) found that Canadian youths who spend time volunteering are likely to have parents who have instilled values of kindness and helping, and who model those behaviours. The response of one 17-year-old girl who participated in this research is illustrative. This girl's sister had been in an accident and, therefore, was temporarily unable to continue her after-school position working with a high-needs handicapped child. Here's her response:

> And so my mom and my sister convinced me to work [her] hours for her . . .. And this child, you really have to care for her to work with her. She's a really sad case . . .. You have to not lose patience with her . . .. My mom's a really caring person and she has a really strong bond with this little girl. She and my sister *should* be able to rely on me to help out on this.

The lesson for parents and other adults is clear: If you want children to be altruistic, act in altruistic ways yourself.

Increasing the Likelihood that Bystanders Will Intervene

There is evidence that simply being aware of the barriers to helping can increase people's chances of overcoming those barriers. Several years ago at Cornell University,

An increasing number of schools and businesses are requiring people to perform community service (in fact, high schools in Ontario require students to have served 40 hours of "community involvement" to graduate). These programs can actually lower interest in volunteering if people feel they are doing so because of an external requirement. Encouraging people to volunteer while preserving the sense that they freely choose to do so is likely to increase people's intentions to volunteer again in the future.

some students intervened to prevent another student from committing suicide. As is often the case with emergencies, the situation was a very confusing one, and at first the bystanders were not sure what was happening or what they should do. The student who led the intervention said she was reminded of a lecture she had heard on bystander intervention in her Introductory Psychology class a few days earlier and had realized that if she didn't act, no one might (Savitsky, 1998). A similar incident took place at Vassar College, where some students looked outside their dormitory and saw a student being attacked by a mugger. Like Kitty Genovese's neighbours, most of them did nothing, probably because they assumed that someone else had already called the police. One of the students, however, immediately called the campus police because she was struck by how similar the situation was to the studies on bystander intervention she had read about in her Social Psychology course—even though she had taken the course more than a year earlier (Coats, 1998).

These are not controlled experiments, of course, and, therefore, we cannot be certain that the people who intervened were really spurred on by what they had learned in their psychology classes. Perhaps they were especially helpful people who would have helped anyway. Fortunately, this issue has been addressed experimentally. Beaman and colleagues (1978) randomly assigned students to listen to a lecture on Latané and Darley's (1970) bystander intervention research or a lecture on an unrelated topic. Two weeks later, all of the students participated in what they thought was a completely unrelated sociology study, during which they encountered a student lying on the floor. Was he in need of help? Had he fallen and injured himself, or was he simply a student who had fallen asleep after pulling an all-nighter? As we have seen, when in an ambiguous situation such as this, people look to see how other people are reacting. Because an accomplice of the experimenter—posing as another participant—purposefully acted unconcerned, the natural thing for participants to do was assume that nothing was wrong. This is exactly what most participants did if they had not heard the lecture about bystander intervention research; in this condition, only 25 percent of them stopped to help the student. However, if participants had heard the lecture about bystander intervention, 43 percent stopped to help the student (Beaman, Barnes, Klentz, & McQuirk, 1978). Thus, knowing how we can unwittingly be influenced

The Lost Letter Technique

An interesting way to study prosocial behaviour is to leave some stamped letters lying on the ground and see whether people pick them up and mail them. This procedure, called the *lost letter technique*, was invented by Stanley Milgram (1969). He found that people were more likely to mail letters addressed to organizations that they supported; for example, 72 percent of letters addressed to "Medical Research Associates" were mailed, whereas only 25 percent of letters addressed to "Friends of the Nazi Party" were mailed. (All were addressed to the same post office box so that Milgram could count how many were returned.)

Try the lost letter technique yourself. Put your address on the letters so that you can count how many are returned but vary where you put the letters or to whom they are addressed. For example, drop some letters in a small town and some in an urban area to see whether people in small towns are more likely to mail them. Be sure to mark the envelopes in some way that will let you know where they were dropped. Studies have found that people living in small towns were more likely to mail the letters (Bridges & Coady, 1996; Hansson & Slade, 1977). Or, you might vary the ethnicity of the name of the person on the address to see if people are more likely to help members of some ethnic groups than others. Be creative!

A final note: It is best to use a fairly large number of letters (e.g., a minimum of 15 to 20 in each condition) to get reliable results. Obviously, you should not leave more than one letter in the same location. You might want to team up with some classmates on this project, so that you can split the cost of the stamps.

by others can by itself help us overcome this type of social influence. We can only hope that knowing about other barriers to prosocial behaviour will also make them easier to overcome.

If you want to learn more about the conditions under which people help others, try an experiment of your own design in the Try It! exercise.

HOW WOULD YOU USE THIS?

We hope it never happens, but suppose you are injured in an accident in a public place and need help. Based on what you have learned in this chapter, how could you make sure that someone comes to your aid as soon as possible? As we saw in the section on the bystander effect, the trick is to persuade people to notice that you need help, to interpret it as an emergency, and to assume that they (and not someone else) are responsible for helping. One way to avoid a diffusion of responsibility is to point to one person and ask for his or her help. That is, instead of shouting, "Will someone please help me?," single out one person—"Hey, you in the blue shirt and sunglasses—could you please call 911?" That makes one person feel responsible and also communicates to him or her how to help. Based on what you have read in this chapter, you should also know more about what to do if you witness an emergency—don't assume that someone else will help.

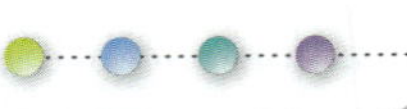

Summary

- **Why Do People Help?** This chapter examined the causes of prosocial behavior, acts performed with the goal of benefiting another person. What are the basic origins of prosocial behavior?
  - **Evolutionary Psychology: Instincts and Genes** Evolutionary theory explains prosocial behaviour in four ways. The first is kin selection, the idea that behaviours that help a genetic relative are favoured by natural selection. The second is the norm of reciprocity, which is the expectation that helping others will increase the likelihood that they will help us in the future. The third is that it is adaptive for people to learn social norms of all kinds, and one of these norms is the value of helping others.
  - **Social Exchange: The Costs and Rewards of Helping** Social exchange theory argues that prosocial behaviour is not necessarily rooted in our genes. Instead, people help others in order to maximize social rewards and minimize social costs.
  - **Empathy and Altruism: The Pure Motive for Helping** People can be motivated by altruism, the desire to help another person even if it involves a cost to the helper. According to the empathy-altruism hypothesis, when people feel empathy toward another person (they experience events and emotions the other person experiences), they will help that person purely for altruistic reasons.
- **Personal Determinants of Prosocial Behaviour: Why Do Some People Help More than Others?** Social psychologists have conducted research to try to understand why some people are more helpful than others.
  - **Individual Differences: The Altruistic Personality** Although some people have personality qualities that make them more likely to help than others, personality factors have not been shown to be strong predictors of who will help across a variety of social situations. Situational factors need to be taken into account as well.
  - **Gender Differences in Prosocial Behaviour** In many cultures, the male sex role includes helping in chivalrous and heroic ways, whereas the female sex role includes helping in close, long-term relationships.
  - **Socioeconomic Status Differences in Prosocial Behaviour** Recent research shows that people who are of low socioeconomic status are more helpful and generous than those who have a high socioeconomic status. Poor people are generous because they are more likely to feel compassion toward those in need.

- **Cultural Differences in Prosocial Behaviour** People in all cultures are more likely to help someone they define as a member of their in-group, the group with which an individual identifies. People everywhere are less likely to help someone they perceive to be a member of an out-group, a group with which they do not identify. Cultural factors come into play in determining how strongly people draw the line between in-groups and out-groups.
- **The Effects of Mood on Prosocial Behaviour** People are more likely to help if they are in especially good moods, but also if they are in especially bad moods. Feeling emotionally numb (e.g., because of social exclusion) interferes with helping.

Situational Determinants of Prosocial Behaviour: When Will People Help? To understand why people help others, we also need to consider the nature of the social situation.

- **Environment: Rural versus Urban** People are less likely to help in dense, urban settings because of the urban-overload hypothesis—the idea that people living in cities are constantly bombarded with stimulation and that they keep to themselves to avoid being overwhelmed by it.

  People who have lived for a long time in one place are more likely to engage in prosocial behaviours than people who have recently moved to an area.
- **Bystander Intervention: The Latané and Darley Model** To help in an emergency, people must meet five conditions: They must notice the event, interpret it as an emergency, assume responsibility, know the appropriate form of assistance, and implement their decision to help. As the number of bystanders who witness an emergency increases, the more difficult it is to meet two of these conditions: interpreting the event as an emergency and assuming responsibility. This produces the bystander effect: The larger the number of bystanders, the less likely any one of them is to help.
- **The Nature of the Relationship: Communal versus Exchange Relationships** People in *exchange relationships*—those governed by concerns about equity—are concerned primarily with the benefits they will receive by helping others. People in *communal relationships*—those in which the primary concern is the welfare of the other person—are less concerned with the benefits they will receive and more with simply satisfying the needs of the other person.

How Can Helping Be Increased? Prosocial behaviour can be increased in a number of ways.

- **Instilling Helpfulness with Rewards and Models** One way to instill helpfulness is for parents to reward their children for helping. Rewards must be used carefully, however, or they will undermine the child's intrinsic interest in helping, causing an overjustification effect. Children also are more likely to be helpful when they observe adults engaging in helpful behaviours.
- **Increasing the Likelihood that Bystanders Will Intervene** Research shows that teaching people about the barriers to bystander intervention increases the likelihood that they will help in emergencies.

11 Aggression

Why We Hurt Other People

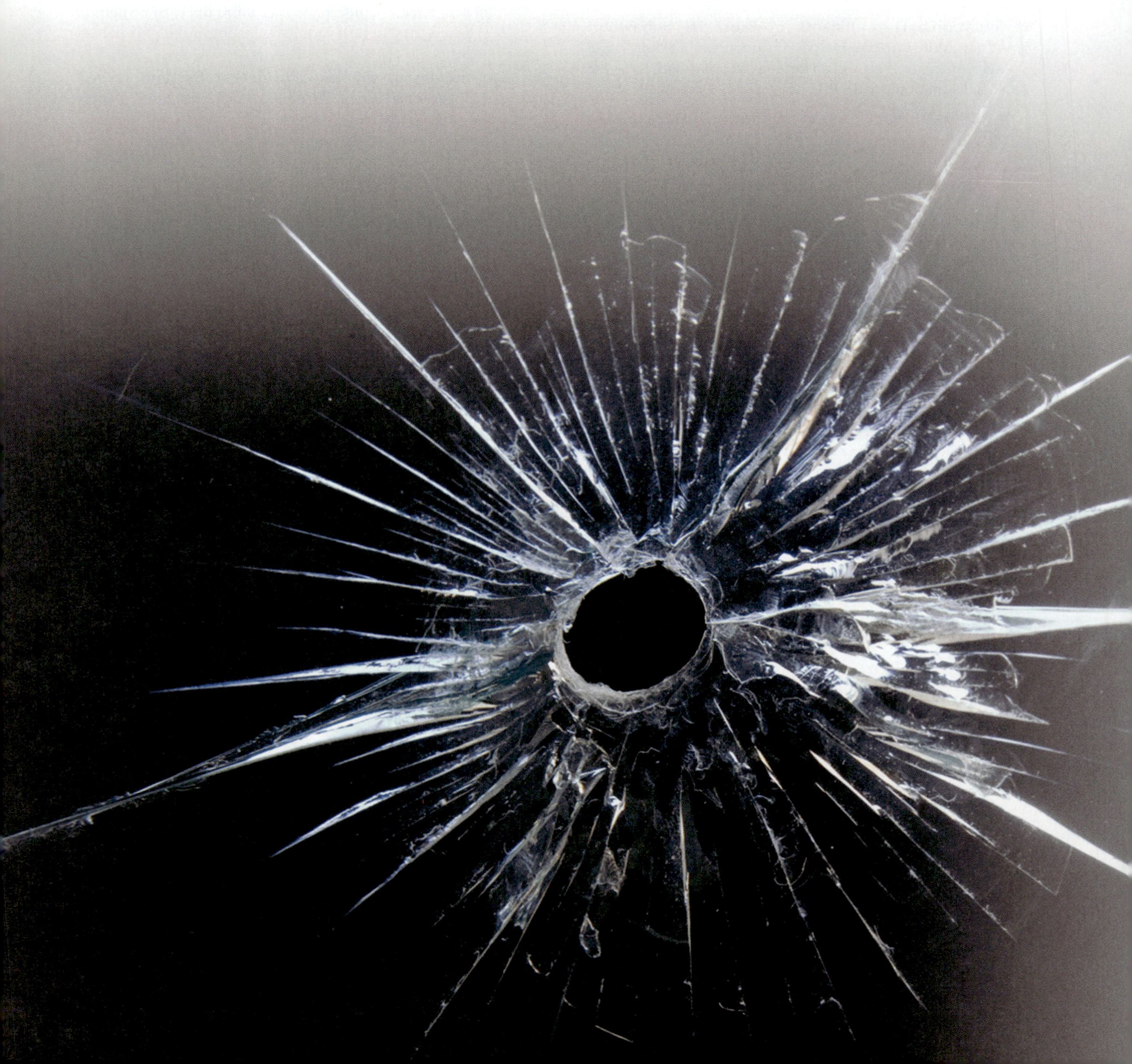

OCTOBER 28, 2006. MICHAEL LEVY, THEN 18 YEARS OLD, was dancing with his girlfriend at a birthday party held at a hall in Surrey, British Columbia, when he was swarmed by a group of teens who viciously assaulted him. He had done nothing to provoke them. After punching him, smashing a bottle on his head, and spraying him with mace, one of the teens, Enrique Quintana, attacked him with an axe, severing his spine and leaving him paralyzed. In February 2008, Quintana was given a 10-year jail term. He appealed, and in March 2009 his sentence was reduced by 8 months. In July 2010, Quintana applied for parole. His request was denied on the basis that his behaviour in jail suggested that there was a significant risk that he would reoffend. Tuan Minh Nguyen, a teen who also participated in the attack, was sentenced to house arrest under a 20-month conditional sentence in December 2007. There was outrage when television stations broadcast footage of him laughing with his friends in an elevator following his sentencing. In April 2008, the Crown appealed, asking for jail time. According to Crown prosecutor Joyce DeWitt-Van Oosten, "[The attackers] robbed a young man not only of his physical well-being but his dream . . . anything less [than a jail sentence] must be appealed" (Lazaruk, 2008). In June 2008, the B.C. Court of Appeal overturned the conditional sentence and ordered Tuan Minh Nguyen to serve 8 months in a youth detention centre. The court called the swarming of Michael Levy "a violent and cowardly attack on a defenceless person" (Canadian Press, 2008). Why would a group of teens brutally attack a young man who had done nothing to provoke them?

In an article titled "Kids Who Kill," the *Winnipeg Free Press* documents a series of homicides in 2007 in which teens were charged with murder: Thirty-eight-year-old Thomas Roy Phillips was sitting in his vehicle when he was shot to death by teens. Twenty-two-year-old Ernestine Pascal was found in an abandoned building, the victim of blunt-force trauma inflicted by an 18-year-old woman and two teenage girls. She later died in a Winnipeg hospital. Twenty-one-year-old Kyle Boss, a father of two young children, was beaten to death on a Winnipeg street. Two boys, 14 and 16 years of age, were charged with second-degree murder (Owen, 2007).

OUTLINE

Michael Levy, a former weightlifter, is wheelchair bound as the result of a brutal attack by a group of teens.

Why is the rate of teen homicide rising at a time when the crime rate, in general, is declining? A newspaper writer asks, "Does violence in video games and the glorification of the gangster lifestyle in rap music have any influence on kids who kill?" (Owen, 2007, p. B4). Does social psychology have an answer to this disturbing question? Stay tuned.

In this chapter, we begin with the fundamental question "What is aggression?" and then move on to another fundamental question, "What causes it?" Are human beings instinctively aggressive? Can situational factors cause "normal people" to commit violence? Can aggression be prevented or reduced? These are social psychological questions of the utmost importance. Needless to say, we don't have all the answers. By the time you reach the end of this chapter, however, we hope you will have gained some insight into the issues. But first, we explain what we mean by the term.

What Is Aggression?

Man's inhumanity to man Makes countless thousands mourn!

—Robert Burns, *"Man Was Made to Mourn,"* 1784

For social psychologists, aggression is intentional behaviour aimed at causing either physical or psychological pain. It should not be confused with assertiveness—even though people often loosely refer to others as "aggressive" when they stand up for their rights, write letters to the editor complaining about real or imagined injustices, work extra hard, display a great deal of ambition, or are "go-getters." Similarly, in a sexist society, a woman who simply speaks her mind or makes the first move in a relationship might be called "aggressive" by some. Our definition is much more specific: **Aggression** is an intentional action aimed at doing harm or causing pain; as such, aggression might be physical or verbal. Whether or not a harmful action succeeds in its goal, it is still aggression. If someone throws a beer bottle at your head, and because you duck the bottle misses, the throwing was still an aggressive act. By the same token, if a drunk driver unintentionally runs you down while you're attempting to cross the street, that is not an act of aggression, even though the damage would be far greater than that caused by a flying beer bottle. The important thing is the intention.

Aggression
Intentional behaviour aimed at causing either physical or psychological pain

It is also useful to distinguish between hostile and instrumental aggression (Berkowitz, 1993). **Hostile aggression** is an act of aggression stemming from feelings of anger and aimed at inflicting pain or injury. With **instrumental aggression**, there is an intention to hurt the other person, but the hurting takes place as a means to some goal other than causing pain. For example, in a professional football game, a defensive lineman will usually do whatever it takes to thwart his opponent (the blocker) and tackle the ball carrier. This typically includes intentionally inflicting pain on his opponent if doing so is useful in helping him get the blocker out of the way so he can get to the ball carrier. This is instrumental aggression. On the other hand, if he believes his opponent has been playing dirty, he might become angry and go out of his way to hurt the other player, even if doing so does not increase his opportunity to tackle the ball carrier. This is hostile aggression.

Hostile Aggression
An act of aggression stemming from feelings of anger and aimed at inflicting pain or injury

Instrumental Aggression
Aggression as a means to some goal other than causing pain

Is Aggression Inborn or Learned?

For centuries, scientists, philosophers, and other serious thinkers have been arguing about the human capacity for aggressiveness. Some are convinced that aggression is an inborn, instinctive phenomenon. Others are just as certain that aggressive behaviour must be learned (Baron & Richardson, 1994; Berkowitz, 1993; Green, 1998). The political philosopher Thomas Hobbes, in his classic work *Leviathan* (1651), took the view that we human beings, in our natural state, are brutes and that only by enforcing the law and order of society could we curb our natural instinct toward aggression. A century later, Jean-Jacques Rousseau argued just the opposite. Humans, he wrote in 1762, are "noble savages"—naturally gentle creatures born into a restrictive society that forces them to become hostile and aggressive.

Hobbes' more pessimistic view was elaborated on in the twentieth century by Sigmund Freud (1930), who theorized that human beings are born with an instinct toward life, which he called **Eros**, and an equally powerful death instinct, **Thanatos**, which leads to aggressive actions. Freud believed that aggressive energy must come out somehow, lest it continue to build up and produce illness. The analogy is one of water pressure building up in a container: unless energy is released, it will produce some sort of explosion. According to Freud, society performs an essential function in regulating this instinct and in helping people to *sublimate* it—that is, to turn the destructive energy into acceptable or useful behaviour.

Eros
The instinct toward life, posited by Freud

Thanatos
According to Freud, an instinctual drive toward death, leading to aggressive actions

Is Aggression Instinctual? Situational? Optional?

The Evolutionary Argument In recent years evolutionary psychologists (Buss, 2004; Buss & Duntley, 2006) have entered into the discussion by arguing that aggression is genetically programmed into men because it enables them to perpetuate their genes. Males are theorized to aggress for two reasons: First, males behave aggressively to establish dominance over other males. The idea here is that the female will choose the male who is most likely to provide the best genes and the greatest protection and resources for offspring. Second, males aggress "jealously" to ensure that their mate(s) are not copulating with others. This ensures their paternity. (Note that, as discussed in the last chapter, some evolutionary theorists recently have argued that compassionate, prosocial behaviour also is genetically programmed, not just aggression; Keltner, 2009).

Is this kind of aggression "only natural"?

The evolutionary perspective receives tangential support from crime statistics, which show that males are most likely to engage in violence during their peak reproductive years—their teens and twenties (Canada, 2005e). Among young males, violence is typically initiated by issues related to "respect." For the males involved, the stakes seem high: They believe that they are fighting for their status in the group. Jealousy is another major reason why males aggress against each other and their mates (Wilson, Daly, & Weghorst, 1982; Schützwohl, 2004; Wells, Graham, & Tremblay, 2009).

In most contemporary societies, social dominance and hence access to females is still largely (but certainly not entirely) based on status. But nowadays, status has taken on a different meaning. In most societies, the ability to physically intimidate other males in the group is no longer the primary attribute that attracts females. Rather, power is now based on attributes related to success such as high-status careers, wealth, and celebrity. These speculations from evolutionary social psychologists are interesting and provocative, but ultimately . . . well, speculative. (Conduct your own research following the steps in the accompanying Try It! exercise.)

Aggression among Animals As we have just discussed, the research supporting the evolutionary

TRY IT! Fighting and Its Attractiveness

Interview several of your male friends and ask them to reflect on their childhood and adolescent experiences with physical fighting or simply being challenged to fight. Ask them what they think was at stake in the fight. How difficult was it to back down? Ask them to elaborate on their answers.

Now, interview several of your female friends. Ask them the same questions you asked the men. Are their responses wildly different from those of the men? Why or why not? Now, ask the women to think about men they know in terms of possible relationships. Determine to what extent they consider physical aggressiveness to be attractive. Ask them to elaborate on their response. Do your findings support the evolutionary argument?

perspective is provocative but inconclusive because it is impossible to conduct a definitive experiment. Scientists have turned to experiments with non-human species to gain additional insight into the extent to which aggression may be hard-wired. Consider, for example, a common belief about cats and rats. Most people assume that cats will instinctively stalk and kill rats. Almost half a century ago, biologist Zing Yang Kuo (1961) attempted to demonstrate that this was a myth. He raised a kitten in the same cage with a rat. What did he find? Not only did the cat refrain from attacking the rat, but the two became close companions. Moreover, when given the opportunity, the cat refused either to chase or to kill other rats; thus, the benign behaviour was not confined to his buddy but was generalized to rats the cat had never encountered before.

Although this demonstration is charming, it fails to prove that aggressive behaviour is not instinctive; it merely demonstrates that the aggressive instinct can be inhibited by early experience. What if an organism grows up without any experience with other organisms? Will it or won't it show aggressive tendencies? It turns out that rats raised in isolation (i.e., without any experience in fighting other rats) will attack a fellow rat when one is introduced into the cage. Moreover, the isolated rat uses the same pattern of threat and attack that experienced rats use (Eibl-Eibesfeldt, 1963). Thus, although aggressive behaviour can be modified by experience (as shown by Kuo's experiment), aggression apparently does not need to be learned.

We can gain still greater insight by observing the behaviour of those animals with which we have the most genetic similarity. Our closest relatives in the animal kingdom are two primates: the chimpanzees and the bonobos. Both species have 98 percent of their DNA in common with human beings. The chimpanzee is known for the aggressive behaviour of its male members (Watts, Muller, Amsler, Mbabazi, & Mitani, 2006; Watts & Mitani, 2001). In fact, chimps kill each other at about the same rate that humans in hunter-gatherer societies kill each other (Wrangham, Wilson, & Muller, 2006). Based on this research, we might conclude that humans, especially males, are genetically programmed for aggressive behaviour.

The bonobo, our equally close genetic relative, has been known for its nonaggressive behaviour, often referred to as the "make love, not war" ape (de Waal, 1995). For example, when the bonobos arrive at a feeding ground, they first engage in sexual play and then proceed to eat peacefully. In contrast, when chimps arrive at a feeding ground, they compete aggressively for the food. Also, unlike the chimps, bonobos form into female-dominated societies (Parish & de Waal, 2000). This image of the peaceful, love-making, "hippie" apes has widespread appeal. However, more recent research in which bonobos have been observed in their natural habitat (rather than in zoos) is casting doubt on this image. Apparently, all bonobos actually do hunt and kill other apes (Parker, 2007; Kahn, 2008), although perhaps not at the rate exhibited by chimps.

When people say that aggression is "natural," they often point to our primate relatives, such as chimpanzees (top) and bonobos (bottom).

The near universality of aggression strongly suggests that aggressiveness has evolved and has been maintained because it has survival value (Lore & Schultz, 1993; Buss, 2004). At the same time, researchers underscore the point that nearly all organisms also seem to have evolved strong inhibitory mechanisms that enable them to suppress aggression when it is in their best interests to do so. Aggression is an optional strategy. Whether it is expressed is determined by the animal's previous social experiences as well as by the specific social context in which the animal finds itself.

Aggression and Culture

Social psychologists agree that aggression is an optional strategy. Moreover, where humans are concerned, because of the complexity and importance of our social interactions, the social situation takes on even greater importance than it does among the lower organisms (Bandura, 1973; Berkowitz, 1968, 1993; Lysak, Rule, & Dobbs, 1989). Indeed, there is a lot of support for the view that for humankind, innate patterns of behaviour are infinitely modifiable and flexible. Cross-cultural studies have found that human cultures vary widely in their degree of aggressiveness. European history, when condensed, consists of one major war after another; in contrast, certain so-called primitive peoples, such as the Lepcha of Sikkim, the Baka of central Africa, and the Arapesh of New Guinea, live in apparent peace and harmony, with acts of aggression being extremely rare (Baron & Richardson, 1994).

Changes in Aggression over Time Within a given culture, changing social conditions frequently lead to striking changes in aggressive behaviour. For example, for hundreds of years, the Iroquois of North America lived peacefully as a hunting nation, without engaging in aggression against other tribes. But in the seventeenth century, barter with the newly arrived Europeans brought the Iroquois into direct competition with the neighbouring Huron over furs, which dramatically increased in value because they could then be traded for manufactured goods. A series of skirmishes with the Huron ensued, and within a short time, the Iroquois developed into ferocious warriors. It would be difficult to argue that they were spectacular warriors because of uncontrollable aggressive instincts; rather, their aggressiveness almost certainly came about because a social change produced increases in competition (Hunt, 1940).

Aggression and a Culture of Honour In more recent research, Vandello and Cohen (2003) have explored the idea that violence may be seen as more acceptable in *honour cultures*—that is, cultures that define male honour in terms of power, toughness, and the ability to protect one's property (e.g., Mediterranean; Middle Eastern and Arabic; Latin and South American cultures with Iberian roots; southern American states). Specifically, they found that participants from male honour cultures (e.g., Brazil, southern American states) were more likely than participants from non-honour cultures (e.g., northern American states) to believe that the infidelity of a female partner was damaging to the male partner's reputation and that his reputation could be restored through the use of violence against her. There was also the belief that the female partner should remain loyal, even if her male partner was violent.

Other research has shown that within the United States, homicide rates for white southern males are substantially higher than those for white northern males, especially in rural areas (Nisbett, 1993). Because of a "culture of honour" in the Deep South, southerners are more inclined to endorse violence for protection and in response to insults—a pattern that persists to this day. For example, in a recent analysis of pitcher aggression in baseball, it was found that pitchers often deliberately hit batters to restore justice, such as payback for having hit a home run earlier in the game or retaliation for a teammate having been hit. Interestingly, white pitchers who were born in the American South are 40 percent more likely to hit a batter than are non-southerners (Timmerman, 2007).

Closer to home, Graham and Wells and colleagues (1998) suggest that a code of male honour exists among security staff at bars (i.e., bouncers) and among bar patrons.

In a series of studies conducted in various bars in London, Ontario, they found that bouncers were most likely to engage in excessive aggression against bar patrons when they perceived that their authority or masculinity was being threatened (Wells, Graham, & West, 1998). Observations of bar patrons revealed a "macho" subculture in which males bullied one another or made threatening comments in response to little or no provocation. In one incident, for example, a group of males gathered around two men embroiled in a confrontation. Then two of the onlookers started fighting with each other, while the others placed bets on who would win (Graham & Wells, 2001a, 2001b; Graham, West, & Wells, 2000). To gain further insight into this culture of honour, these researchers conducted in-depth interviews with young men (ages 18 to 25) living in London, Ontario (Wells, Graham, & Tremblay, 2009). The picture of barroom aggression that emerged was summed up as "every male in there is your competition."

Taking these findings into account, we would conclude that although there may be an evolved tendency for humans to be aggressive, these tendencies are modifiable by the social context. As we have seen, there are clear examples of situational and social events that can produce aggressive behaviour.

Connect to MyPsychLab
How does your brain work? To participate in an experiment on hemispheric specialization, go to MyPsychLab

Neural and Chemical Influences on Aggression

Amygdala
An area in the core of the brain that is associated with aggressive behaviour

Aggressive behaviour in human beings, as well as in lower animals, is associated with an area in the core of the brain called the **amygdala**. When the amygdala is stimulated, docile organisms become violent; similarly, when neural activity in that area is blocked, violent organisms become docile (Moyer, 1976). But there is flexibility here also: The impact of neural mechanisms can be modified by social factors, even in subhumans. For example, if a male monkey is in the presence of other, less dominant monkeys, he will indeed attack the other monkeys when the amygdala is stimulated. But if the amygdala is stimulated while the monkey is in the presence of more dominant monkeys, he will not attack but instead will run away.

Serotonin
A chemical in the brain that may inhibit aggressive impulses

Certain chemicals have been shown to influence aggression as well. For example, **serotonin**, a chemical substance that occurs naturally in the midbrain, seems to have an inhibiting effect on impulsive aggression. In animals, when the flow of serotonin is disrupted, increases in aggressive behaviour frequently follow. Among humans, researchers have found that violent criminals have particularly low levels of naturally produced serotonin (Davidson, Putnam, & Larson, 2000). Moreover, in laboratory experiments on normal people, when the natural production of serotonin is interrupted, aggressive behaviour increases (Bjork, Dougherty, Moeller, Cherek, & Swann, 1999).

Testosterone
A male sex hormone associated with aggression

Too little serotonin can lead to increases in aggression but so can too much **testosterone**, a male sex hormone. Laboratory animals injected with testosterone become more aggressive (Moyer, 1983). There is a parallel finding in humans; naturally occurring testosterone levels are significantly higher among prisoners convicted of violent crimes than among those convicted of nonviolent crimes. Also, once incarcerated, prisoners with higher testosterone levels violate more prison rules, especially those involving overt confrontation (Dabbs, Carr, Frady, & Riad, 1995; Dabbs et al., 1988). Similarly, juvenile delinquents have higher testosterone levels than do college students (Banks & Dabbs, 1996).

Turning to research conducted with noncriminal populations, comparisons of fraternities at a U.S. college have found that those generally considered most rambunctious, less socially responsible, and "cruder" have the highest average testosterone levels (Dabbs, 2000; Dabbs, Hargrove, & Heusel, 1996). Research conducted with lower-class 12- and 13-year-old boys in Quebec found that testosterone was not strongly related to physical aggression but was associated with social dominance (Tremblay, Schaal, Boulerice, Arseneault, Soussignan, Paquette, & Laurent, 1998). A recent study conducted at Brock University found that testosterone levels can fluctuate depending on situational factors. In this study, men's testosterone levels were assessed before they played a computer game with a fictitious opponent and again during the game (Carré, Gilchrist, Morrissey, & McCormick, 2010). The game was set up so that the participant was either provoked (the opponent stole points from them) or not (no points stolen). The rewards of aggression also were manipulated, such that aggression was either rewarded (you get to keep the points that you steal from your opponent) or costly (you don't get to keep stolen points, and, while you're stealing, you can't earn points for yourself). Participants who were provoked and for whom aggression was costly showed an increase in testosterone (from before the game to during the game). After the game, all participants were given the choice of playing a competitive game against the same opponent or helping the experimenter validate a computer program. Those men who showed the largest increase in testosterone and who were most aggressive during the earlier computer game were most likely to choose the competitive game.

What are we to conclude? When researchers at Queen's University conducted a meta analysis of 45 studies, they found that overall a weak positive correlation exists between testosterone and aggression; the average correlation was 0.14 (Brook, Starzyk, & Quinsey, 2001). (Recall from Chapter 2 that correlations range from 0—no relation—to 1.00—a perfect correlation.) This result is not surprising given the recent findings that testosterone fluctuates depending on situational factors. Thus, while testosterone may be a factor in some cases of aggression, it, too, is modifiable by the situation the person is in.

Gender and Aggression

If testosterone levels affect aggressiveness—at least to some degree—does that mean that men are more aggressive than women? Apparently so. In a classic survey of research on children, Eleanor Maccoby and Carol Jacklin (1974) found that boys appear to be more aggressive than girls. In one study, for example, the investigators closely observed children at play in a variety of different cultures, including the United States, Switzerland, and Ethiopia. There was far more nonplayful pushing, shoving, and hitting among boys than among girls (Deaux & LaFrance, 1998).

But the research on gender differences is a bit more complicated than it might seem on the surface. For example, although research shows that young boys tend to be more overtly aggressive than young girls (in the sense that they lash out directly at the target person), girls tend to express their aggressive feelings more covertly—by gossiping, engaging in backbiting, and spreading false rumours about the target person (Coie, Cillessen, Dodge, Hubbard, Schwartz, Lemerise, & Bateman, 1999; Dodge & Schwartz, 1997; Pepler et al., 2004, 2005). Moreover, a meta analysis of 64 separate experiments found that while it is true that men are far more aggressive than women under ordinary circumstances, the gender difference becomes much smaller when men and women are actually provoked (Bettencourt & Miller, 1996). In fact, a study conducted at McGill University found that women were just as aggressive as men when subjected to strong provocation from a confederate (Hoaken & Pihl, 2000).

In other words, in everyday life situations, under ordinary circumstances, men behave far more aggressively than women. It seems as though men are more likely than women to interpret ambiguous situations as provocative and are therefore more likely to react aggressively in what we would consider everyday situations. A good example is road rage: Many men seem to regard being cut off in traffic as a personal insult and respond aggressively. Women are more likely to take such occurrences in stride. However, when women are subjected to frustration or insult, they will react almost as aggressively as men.

Men's greater inclination to respond to "everyday" provocations with aggression might help explain why the great majority of persons arrested for aggressive offences are men. When women are arrested, it is usually for property crimes (e.g., forgery, fraud, larceny) rather than for violent crimes (e.g., murder, aggravated assault). How can we explain these differences? Are males naturally predisposed to be more physically aggressive than females, or have they learned to behave that way? In short, does biology or social learning have the greater influence? We cannot be sure. In Canada, serious violent crime by female youths has more than doubled over the past two decades (from 1986 to 2005; Statistics Canada, 2008). The rate of serious violent crime among female adults has nearly doubled over this period. These statistics might indicate the influence of social learning (e.g., the loosening of restrictions on girls and women to behave in "feminine" ways). However, the rate of violent crime committed by men is still four times that of the female rate, which might suggest a biological difference (Statistics Canada, 2008).

It is important to keep in mind that even if gender differences in aggression are at least partly attributable to biological factors, it does not excuse violent behaviour, nor does it mean that such behaviour cannot be altered by a social intervention—as we shall see later in this chapter.

Does the Target Make a Difference? When examining the issue of gender differences, we must also consider another situational factor: the target of aggression. Men's aggression is generally directed at other men, is more likely to take place in bars or other public places, and is more likely to involve alcohol consumption (Graham & Wells, 2001a, 2001b; Statistics Canada, 2008; Tremblay, Graham, & Wells, 2008). Women's aggression is much more likely to be directed at a romantic partner (Statistics Canada, 2008). For example, Straus (2004) examined rates of physical violence against dating partners among university students in 16 different countries, including Canada. There were a few exceptions, but overall women were more likely to report engaging in physical violence than were men (see left side of Table 11.1). A meta analysis of well over 100 studies confirms that women are more likely than men to be physically aggressive toward their partners (Archer, 2000; for examples of Canadian studies that have found this gender difference, see also DeKeseredy & Kelly, 1993; Kwong, Bartholomew, & Dutton, 1999; Scott & Straus, 2007; Sharpe & Taylor, 1999). Recent studies conducted with students in junior and senior high schools in various parts of Canada have found this gender difference as well. Thus, females appear to be more physically aggressive toward their dating partners than are males, right at the onset of dating (Connolly, Nocentini, Menesini, Peplar, Craig, & Williams, 2010; Ellis, Crooks, & Wolfe, 2009; Josephson & Proulx, 2008; Sears & Bryers, 2010).

However, there are some important qualifiers. First, men are much more likely to engage in more severe forms of violence than are women. For example, Statistics Canada (2009) data show that women are about three times more likely than men to report having experienced severe violence at the hands of their current or former spouse (e.g., beaten, choked). Men are much more likely to report having experienced the mildest forms of violence surveyed (e.g., threatened to hit, threw something). Second, women are much more likely to suffer serious physical injury at the hands of their male partner than the other way around. In the Straus (2004) study reported earlier, even though female university students generally were more likely to physically assault their dating partner than were men, the gender difference reversed when the analysis focused

TABLE 11.1 Percentage of Canadian University Students Who Physically Assaulted a Dating Partner in the Last 12 Months

	Overall Assault Perpetration (%)			Severe Injury Perpetration (%)		
City	Total	Male	Female	Total	Male	Female
London, ON	36.3	25.9	44.2	8.9	10.3	7.8
Montreal, QC	22.8	20.6	23.4	0.7	1.6	0.4
Winnipeg, MB	29.0	38.5	27.7	0.9	0.0	1.0
Hamilton, ON	23.0	13.5	24.5	3.0	5.4	2.6

Source: Based on Straus, 2004.

on perpetration of severe injuries—a greater percentage of male than female students had inflicted severe injury on their partner (see right-hand side of Table 11.1). Recent Statistics Canada data also show that women are more than twice as likely as men to report being physically injured as a result of spousal violence (42 percent of women versus 18 percent of men). In fact, women are at far greater risk of being murdered by their partners. Over the past 30 years, the rate of spousal homicides against women has consistently been about three or four times higher than that for men (Statistics Canada, 2009). As one health official remarked, "Women worry when they go out; perhaps they should worry when they stay in" (as quoted in Goode, 2000, p. F1).

Finally, there is evidence that male violence does more emotional and psychological damage than female violence. For example, research conducted with junior high and high school students in New Brunswick (Sears & Byers, 2010) and Ontario (Ellis et al., 2009) has found that female victims of dating violence report poorer emotional adjustment and greater upset than do male victims. Studies of spousal violence similarly find that women are much more likely to report negative emotional effects (e.g., feeling upset, confused, depressed) as a result of partner violence than are men (Statistics Canada, 2009).

What is the risk of experiencing partner violence for women and men in Canada? See the accompanying Try It! exercise to find out.

Does Culture Make a Difference? Sex differences in aggressive behaviour tend to hold up across cultures. In one study, teenagers from 11 countries, mostly in Europe and Asia, were asked to read stories involving conflict among people and then write how the stories would end (Archer & McDaniel, 1995). In every one of the 11 countries, young men showed a greater tendency toward violent solutions to conflict than did young women. However, culture also played a major role; for example, women from Australia and New Zealand produced more violent responses than did men from Sweden and Korea. Overall, teenagers in New Zealand reported the most violent responses to these stories; Koreans generated the least violent responses. Young people from the United States ranked fourth and those from Canada ranked seventh.

TRY IT! The Incidence of Violence in Intimate Relationships

Violence in intimate relationships is usually assessed using the Conflict Tactics Scale (Straus, Hamby, McCoy, & Sugarman, 1996), or variations of it, in which people report whether their partner has used any of the following types of violence:

- threatened to hit
- threw something
- pushed, grabbed, or shoved
- slapped
- kicked, bit, or hit
- hit with something
- beat
- choked
- used, or threatened to use, a gun or knife
- sexually assaulted

To see how knowledgeable you are about the incidence of spousal violence (including common-law relationships) in Canada, answer the following questions:

1. Which of the above kinds of violence do you think is most common in marriages?
2. Which of the above kinds of violence is more likely to be experienced by women?
3. Which of the above kinds of violence is more likely to be experienced by men?

Go to www.MyPsychLab.com for answers.

Alcohol and Aggression

As most socially active college and university students know, alcohol is a social lubricant that lowers people's inhibitions against committing behaviours frowned on by society, including acts of aggression. The link between the consumption of alcoholic beverages and aggressive behaviour has been well established. For example, researchers at the Centre for Addiction and Mental Health in London, Ontario, analyzed data from the Canadian Campus Survey, in which more than 4000 students from 40 different Canadian universities were asked about alcohol and aggression. The bottom line was clear—the greater the reported consumption of alcohol, the greater the reported aggression (Mihic, Wells, Graham, Tremblay, & Demers, 2009; Wells, Mihic, Tremblay, Graham, & Demers, 2008). This research also has shown that people who tend to be physically aggressive to begin with are more likely to report getting into fights when drinking, as are people who say that they drink in order to get drunk or high (rather than for social reasons). A recent study found that heavier men are more likely to be aggressive when they have been drinking than are lighter men (weight did not affect the link between alcohol and aggression in women; DeWall, Bushman, Giancola, & Webster, 2010). Big guys have a better chance of winning fights and therefore are less likely to inhibit aggression than are smaller men.

The setting also plays a role. For example, a survey of students at six different Canadian universities found that more severe violence was reported when alcohol was consumed at a bar or a party rather than at home. Further, fights are more likely to break out in "jock" bars or student bars than in "classy establishments" (Tremblay, Graham, & Wells, 2008; Tremblay, Mihic, Graham, & Jelley, 2007; Wells, Graham, & Tremblay, 2009). Thus, the strength of the relation between alcohol and aggression varies, depending on the person and the situation. But the link between alcohol and aggression cannot be denied.

You may be thinking, so far you've just presented survey data—what people say they do. Is there any "hard" evidence that people are more aggressive when they drink? To answer this question, Graham and Wells (2001a, 2001b; Graham, West, & Wells, 2000), recorded incidents of aggression (physical and nonphysical) in various bars in London, Ontario. The role of alcohol was clear: The more people drank, the more likely they were to engage in aggression, especially severe forms of physical aggression (e.g., punching, kicking, brawling). Intoxication has been implicated as a factor in cases of air rage (Bronskill, 2007). And crime statistics reveal that more than half of individuals who have committed violent crimes were drinking heavily at the time of the crime (Murdoch, Pihl, & Ross, 1990; Pihl & Peterson, 1995).

Family violence also is often associated with alcohol use. Consider, for example, the following statistics: If a spouse drinks heavily, the rate of marital violence is six times higher than if a spouse drinks moderately or not at all (Canada, 2005a). Marital violence is between four and six times more likely if the husband is an alcoholic than if the husband is not an alcoholic (O'Farrell & Murphy, 1995). Not only is violence more likely to occur when alcohol is involved, but it also tends to be more severe (Dutton, 1995; Johnson, 2001; Wekerle & Wall, 2002; Wells, Graham, & West, 2000). Sadly, it appears that the stage for alcohol-related aggression is set early on. York University psychologist Debra Pepler and her colleagues (2002) conducted a large-scale study of alcohol use and aggression in a sample of nearly 1000 youths in early adolescence. The researchers discovered that by grade 8, close to 35 percent of the boys and 25 percent of the girls reported alcohol use. When the researchers examined the relation between bullying and alcohol use, the results were shocking: "Both boys and girls who bullied others were almost five times more likely to report alcohol use than boys and girls who did not report bullying (Pepler, Craig, Connolly, & Henderson, 2002, p. 159). Similarly, dating aggression was up to five times more likely among adolescents who used alcohol compared with those who did not (see also Howard & Wang, 2003). This research suggests that interventions aimed at reducing relationship violence and alcohol abuse must be introduced well before high school, given how early these detrimental patterns are established.

You may have noticed that the data we have been presenting are correlational, and as you well know by now, one cannot draw causal conclusions from correlational data. Is there any evidence that alcohol increases aggression in a direct manner? In other words, can we be sure that alcohol is a direct cause of aggression? Controlled laboratory experiments demonstrate that when individuals ingest enough alcohol to make them legally drunk, they tend to respond more violently to provocation than do those who have ingested little or no alcohol (Bushman, 1993; Lipsey et al., 1997; Taylor & Leonard, 1983). For example, research conducted at McGill University has found that intoxicated men who are provoked administer stronger shocks to a fictitious opponent than participants who are not intoxicated (Hoaken & Pihl, 2000; Pihl & Hoaken, 2002; Pihl, Young, Harden, Plotnick, Chamberlain, & Ervin, 1995).

The implications of these effects for close relationships were explored by MacDonald, Zanna, and Holmes (2000). In their study, male students at the University of Waterloo who were dating or married were asked to describe a conflict in their relationship. Participants in the alcohol condition then drank enough vodka to bring their blood alcohol level to Ontario's legal limit of 0.08. Participants in a placebo condition ingested a drink that smelled of alcohol but contained only a minuscule amount. Those in the control group did not receive drinks of any kind. The participants were then asked to evaluate the conflict they had previously described. The results were disturbing: Intoxicated participants reported more negative emotions when thinking about the conflict and had more negative perceptions of their partner's feelings than did participants in the other two conditions—who did not differ from one another. The researchers concluded that "alcohol can play a causal role in exacerbating relationship conflict" (MacDonald, Zanna, & Holmes, 2000, p. 190). In short, it appears that whenever people are intoxicated, the stage is set for aggression.

Pain, Discomfort, and Aggression

If an animal experiences pain and cannot flee the scene, it will almost invariably attack; this is true of rats, mice, hamsters, foxes, monkeys, crayfish, snakes, raccoons, alligators, and a host of other creatures (Azrin, 1967; Hutchinson, 1983). In these circumstances, animals will attack members of their own species, members of different species, or anything else in sight, including stuffed dolls and tennis balls. Do you think this is true of human beings as well? When Russell and Fehr (1994) asked students at the University of British Columbia to describe an experience of anger, physical pain was among the causes mentioned. Most of us probably can relate to the student who wrote that he experienced intense anger when he bashed his kneecap on the edge of a swimming pool. Most of us probably also know the feeling of wanting to lash out at the nearest available target in such situations. Indeed, in a series of experiments, Leonard Berkowitz (1983, 1988) showed that students who underwent the pain of having their hand immersed in very cold water showed a sharp increase in their likelihood to aggress against other students.

By the same token, many theorists have postulated that other forms of bodily discomfort—such as heat, humidity, air pollution, and offensive odours—might act to lower the threshold for aggressive behaviour (Stoff & Cairns, 1997). Research conducted in the United States has found that the hotter it is on a given day, the greater the likelihood that riots and violent crimes will occur (Anderson & Anderson, 1984; Anderson, Bushman, & Groom, 1997; Bushman, Wang, & Anderson, 2005a, 2005b; Harries & Stadler, 1988). In the desert city of Phoenix, Arizona, drivers without air-conditioned cars are more likely to honk their horns in traffic jams than are drivers with air-conditioned cars (Kenrick & MacFarlane, 1986). And believe it or not, in major league baseball games, significantly more batters are hit by pitches when the temperature is above 32°C than when it is below that temperature (Reifman, Larrick, & Fein, 1988).

Watch on mypsychlab
Heat Aggression

As you know by now, one has to be cautious about interpreting events that take place in natural settings. For example, the scientist in you might be tempted to ask whether increases in aggression are due to the temperature itself or merely due to the fact that more people are apt to be outside—getting in one another's way!—on hot days than on cool or rainy days. Fortunately, we can test this by conducting laboratory experiments. In one such experiment, students at the University of Alberta read ambiguous stories that could end with aggression or nonaggression. Here's an example of one of the stories:

> Todd was on his way home from work one evening when he had to brake quickly for a yellow light. The person in the car behind him . . . crashed into the back of Todd's car, causing a lot of damage to both vehicles. Fortunately, there were no injuries. Todd got out of his car and surveyed the damage. He then walked over to the other car.

The researchers found that participants who read these stories in an uncomfortably hot room (32°C) were more likely to complete the stories with aggressive responses than were participants who performed the task at room temperature (21°C; Rule, Taylor, & Dobbs, 1987). This study shows that people are more likely to have aggression on their minds when they are uncomfortably hot. But do they actually behave more aggressively? To find out, Griffitt and Veitch (1971) had students take a test in either a room with normal temperature or a room in which the temperature was allowed to soar to 32°C. The students in the hot room not only reported feeling more aggressive, but also expressed more hostility to a stranger.

Recently, researchers have found that simply being exposed to heat-related words is enough to increase aggressive thoughts. DeWall and Bushman (2009) exposed participants to either heat-related words (e.g., *burning*, *hot*), cold-related words (e.g., *shivers*, *frozen*) or neutral words. Later, participants received word fragments that could be completed with aggression words or nonaggression words. For example, "ki—" can be completed as either *kill* (an aggressive word) or *kiss* (a nonaggressive word). Participants who had been exposed to heat-related terms came up with more aggressive word completions than those in the other conditions. A follow-up study showed that exposure to heat-related words also was associated with attributing more hostility to another person compared to exposure to cold-related or neutral words. See the accompanying Try It! exercise to conduct your own observational research on heat and aggression.

Situational Causes of Aggression

We've seen the effects of body chemistry, alcohol, and unpleasant physical experiences such as pain and heat on aggression. Certain social situations also are conducive to aggression—so conducive that even the most docile, laid-back person among us might resort to aggressive behaviour. What might some of these situations be?

Heat, Humidity, and Aggression

The next time you find yourself caught in a traffic jam, try doing a simple, natural replication of the Kenrick and MacFarlane (1986) experiment. Consider the following hypothesis: The greater the heat and humidity, the greater the aggression.

- Take notes on how much aggression you observe (in the form of horn honking).
- Note the heat and humidity that day.
- The next two or three times you get caught in a traffic jam, do the same thing.

Can you discern a relationship between heat and humidity, and horn honking?

Frustration as a Cause of Aggression

Imagine that your friend Alain is driving you to the airport so you can fly home for the holidays. Alain has picked you up a bit later than you feel comfortable with; but, when you mention it, he accuses you of being overly anxious and assures you that he knows the route well and that you will arrive with time to spare. Halfway to the airport, you grind to a halt in bumper-to-bumper traffic. Once again, Alain assures you that there is plenty of time—but this time he sounds less confident. After a few minutes, your palms are sweating. You open the car door and survey the road ahead: There is nothing but gridlock as far as you can see. You get back in the car, slam the door, and glare at Alain. He smiles lamely and says, "How was I supposed to know there would be so much traffic?" Should he be prepared to duck?

As this all-too-familiar story suggests, frustration is a major cause of aggression. Frustration occurs when a person is thwarted on the way to an expected goal or gratification. All of us experience some degree of frustration from time to time; indeed, it's unlikely we can get through a week without experiencing it. According to **frustration-aggression theory**, people's perception that they are being prevented from obtaining a goal will increase the probability of an aggressive response (Dollard, Doob, Miller, Mowrer, & Sears, 1939). This does not mean that frustration *always* leads to aggression—but it frequently does, especially when the frustration is a decidedly unpleasant experience. In a classic experiment by Barker, Dembo, and Lewin (1941), young children were shown a roomful of attractive toys that were kept out of reach by a wire screen. After a painfully long wait, the children were finally allowed to play with the toys. In a control condition, other children were allowed to play with the toys, without first being frustrated by a wait. These children played joyfully with the toys. However, when children in the frustrated group were finally given access to the toys, they were extremely destructive. Many smashed the toys, threw them against the wall, and stepped on them.

Frustration-Aggression Theory

The theory that frustration—the perception that you are being prevented from obtaining a goal—will increase the probability of an aggressive response

Several factors can increase frustration and accordingly will increase the probability that some form of aggression will occur. One such factor involves your closeness to the goal or the object of your desire. The closer the goal, the greater the expectation of pleasure that is thwarted; and the greater the expectation, the more likely the aggression. This was demonstrated in a field experiment by Mary Harris (1974), who

Road rage is often caused by frustration.

instructed confederates to cut in line in front of people who were waiting in a variety of places—for movie tickets, outside crowded restaurants, or at the checkout counter of a supermarket. On some occasions, the confederates cut in front of the second person in line; at other times, they cut in front of the twelfth person in line. The results were clear: The people standing behind the intruder were much more aggressive when the confederate cut in to the second place in line.

Aggression also increases when the frustration is unexpected. James Kulik and Roger Brown (1979) hired students to telephone strangers and ask for donations to a charity. The students were hired on a commission basis—that is, they received a small fraction of each dollar pledged. Some of the students were led to expect a high rate of contributions; others were led to expect far less success. The experiment was rigged so none of the potential donors agreed to make a contribution. The experimenters found that the callers with high expectations directed more verbal aggression toward the non-donors, speaking more harshly and slamming down the phone with more force than the callers with low expectations.

As we've already said, frustration does not always produce aggression. Rather, it seems to produce anger or annoyance and a readiness to aggress if other things about the situation are conducive to aggressive behaviour (Berkowitz, 1978, 1988, 1989, 1993; Gustafson, 1989). What are those things? For one, the size and strength of the person responsible for your frustration—as well as that person's ability to retaliate—will influence whether you react with aggression. It is undoubtedly easier to slam the phone down on a reluctant donor who is miles away and has no idea who you are, than to take out your anger against your frustrater if he turns out to be a defensive lineman for the Edmonton Eskimos and is staring you in the face. Similarly, if the frustration is understandable, legitimate, and unintentional, the tendency to aggress will be reduced. In an experiment by Burnstein and Worchel (1962), for example, when a confederate "unwittingly" sabotaged the problem solving of his groupmates because his hearing aid stopped working, the resulting frustration did not lead to a measurable degree of aggression.

Relative Deprivation We should also point out that frustration is not the same as deprivation. For example, children who simply don't have toys do not aggress more than children who do have toys. In the toy experiment discussed earlier, frustration and aggression occurred because the children had every reason to expect to play with the toys, and their reasonable expectation was thwarted; this thwarting was what caused the children to behave destructively.

The Reverend Jesse Jackson (1981), with great insight, pointed out that the race riots that occurred in the United States in 1967 and 1968 took place in the middle of rising expectations and increased, though inadequate, social spending. In short, Jackson was suggesting that thwarted expectations were largely responsible for the frustration and aggression. A similar phenomenon occurred when the Berlin Wall came down and East Germans began to expect higher employment rates and wages. When these changes did not immediately materialize, high levels of anger and frustration ensued.

Relative Deprivation

The perception that you have less than you deserve, less than what you have been led to expect, or less than what people similar to you have

What causes aggression, then, is not deprivation but **relative deprivation**—the perception that you (or your group) have less than you deserve, less than what you have been led to expect, or less than what people similar to you have. For example, researchers from universities in Canada and France tested whether South Africans who felt relative deprivation (e.g., in terms of their economic status relative to other South Africans) would report more negative attitudes toward immigrants to their country than those who felt less deprived. And that was exactly what they found (Dambrun, Taylor, McDonald, Crush, & Méot, 2006). Closer to home, Tougas and her colleagues found that some Canadian policewomen experienced relative deprivation—they believed that they were excluded from opportunities and activities that were available to their male colleagues (Tougas, Rinfret, Beaton, De la Sablonnière, 2005). More recently, Grant (2008) examined feelings of relative deprivation among skilled immigrants from Asia and Africa who were experiencing credentialing problems (i.e., problems getting their credentials and work experience from their country of origin recognized in Canada). Most of the participants were professionally trained, yet two-thirds of them had an income of less than $20 000 per year. The perception that their credentials are not recognized in Canada was associated with feelings of anger, frustration, and resentment, as well as intentions to protest or challenge their situation.

Feelings of relative deprivation have also been created in the laboratory (Wright, 1997; Wright, Taylor, & Moghaddam, 1990). For example, in one experiment, students at McGill University were told that everyone would begin as a member of a low-status group, but that there would be an opportunity to become a member of a high-status group depending on how participants performed on a decision-making task. The many benefits of being in the high-status group were described—among them, the chance to win $100. After completing the decision-making task, some participants were told that the high-status group had decided to accept only those who had scored at least 8.5, and that their mark was only 6.0. Other participants were told that they had just missed the cut-off with their mark of 8.2. All participants were then given various options for responding to the high-status group's decision not to accept them. Those who nearly made it into the high-status group were most likely to write a letter of protest demanding that the high-status group reverse its decision, even though they were told that the decision was final and that the high-status group disapproved of protest action. They also perceived greater injustice in the situation than did those who were far from being accepted. Participants in the latter group were more likely to passively resign themselves to remaining in the low-status group for the rest of the experiment (Wright, Taylor, & Moghaddam, 1990).

Direct Provocation and Reciprocation

Suppose that you are having lunch in the cafeteria, quietly minding your own business. While you're eating, you notice two guys whispering to each other and occasionally glancing in your direction. One of the guys picks up his lunch tray and walks toward you. He dumps his tray in the garbage next to you, dropping leftovers all over you. How would you respond?

This was one of the scenarios presented to male high school students in Nova Scotia in a study by Van Oostrum and Horvath (1997). The researchers found that the participants' response to situations such as this one depended on whether they perceived the other student's behaviour as intentional. Those who attributed hostile intentions (e.g., believed that the student spilled the tray "to be mean") reported that they would respond with aggression—more so than students who interpreted the event as an accident or who believed that the other student's motives were ambiguous. Interestingly, the participants who reported the greatest use of aggression in their everyday lives were also the most likely to attribute hostile intent in the scenarios.

In more recent research, more than 1000 students from six different Canadian universities were presented with a number of provocation scenarios (e.g., you are waiting in line to get into a bar/club and a group of people cut in line ahead of you; you catch your boyfriend/girlfriend flirting with his or her ex). It was found that provocation was associated with the motivation to aggress; moreover, the desire to be aggressive was stronger when participants imagined being intoxicated, rather than sober, in the provocation situation (Tremblay, Mihic, Graham, & Jelley, 2007).

One cause of aggression, then, stems from the urge to reciprocate after being provoked by aggressive behaviour from another person. Although the Christian plea to "turn the other cheek" is wonderful advice, it does not appear to be the typical reaction of most human beings. This has been illustrated in countless experiments in and out of the laboratory. Typical of this line of research is an experiment by Robert Baron (1988) in which participants prepared an advertisement for a new product. Their ad was then evaluated and criticized by an accomplice of the experimenter. In one condition, the criticism, while strong, was done in a gentle and considerate manner ("I think there's a lot of room for improvement"); in the other condition, the criticism was given in an insulting manner ("I don't think you could be original if you tried"). When provided with an opportunity to retaliate, subjects who were treated harshly were far more likely to do so than were those in the "gentle" condition.

Similarly, as discussed earlier in the study on testosterone, male participants at Brock University who were provoked by an opponent during a computer game (i.e., the opponents stole points from them) were more aggressive (i.e., stole points from their opponent at the cost of earning points for themselves) than those who were not provoked and later were more likely to choose to play a competitive game against their opponent rather than help the experimenter validate a new computer program (Carré et al., 2010).

Nothing is more costly, nothing is more sterile, than revenge.

—Winston Churchill *(1874–1965)*

It is important to point out that when provoked, people do not always reciprocate. First, we ask ourselves whether or not the provocation was intentional. When convinced it was unintentional, most of us will not reciprocate (Kremer & Stephens, 1983). But to curtail an aggressive response, these mitigating circumstances must be known at the time of the provocation, as demonstrated in a study conducted at the University of Alberta. In this experiment, students were insulted by the experimenter's assistant. Half of the students were first told that the assistant was upset because he had just received an unfair grade on a chemistry exam; the other students received this information only after the insult was delivered. All participants later had an opportunity to retaliate by choosing the level of unpleasant noise with which to zap the assistant. Those students who knew about the mitigating circumstances before being insulted delivered less intense bursts of noise than did those who learned about the circumstances after they had been insulted (Johnson & Rule, 1986). Why the difference? At the time of the insult, the informed students simply did not take it personally and therefore had no strong need to retaliate. This interpretation is bolstered by evidence of their physiological arousal. At the time of the insult, the heartbeat of the insulted students did not increase as rapidly if they knew beforehand about the assistant's unhappy state of mind.

Social Exclusion

The following theme is becoming all-too-common: A high school or a university student shows up at school one day with a gun and goes on a killing rampage. Analyses of these tragedies paint a picture of the killers as socially isolated individuals who experienced rejection by their peers. They then deal with the pain of rejection by mounting a lethal attack on those whose acceptance they craved most. Is there validity to these kinds of analyses? Does social exclusion actually lead to aggressive behaviour? An extensive program of research suggests that it does (Baumeister, DeWall, Ciarocco, & Twenge, 2005; Twenge, Baumeister, Tice, & Stucke, 2001).

Imagine you were a participant in one of these studies. You arrive at a laboratory along with four or five other students. First, you spend 15 minutes chatting as part of a getting-acquainted exercise. Then, you are informed that the actual experiment involves working in groups on a task. You and the other students are asked to name the two people with whom you would most like to work. You eagerly write down the names of the two people you enjoyed most during the getting-acquainted discussion. The experimenter then collects the names and tells you she will be back shortly to announce the group assignments. To your horror, when she returns she says, "I hate to tell you this, but no one chose you as someone they wanted to work with." How would you react?

If you are like the actual participants in this study, you would react with aggression. The rest of the experiment was set up so participants were given an opportunity to deliver loud bursts of white noise to a confederate who insulted them. Those participants who had been rejected earlier were much more aggressive toward the confederate (i.e., gave longer and louder bursts of noise) than those who were told they had been accepted by the group. It is remarkable that the experience of being excluded from a group of strangers in a laboratory can provoke considerable levels of aggression. It is perhaps little wonder that those who experience the sting of rejection from classmates on a daily basis end up reacting with extreme aggression.

Before leaving this topic, we should note that even though the research we have been discussing was conducted with university students, the effects of social exclusion have been documented among elementary school children as well. For example, studies conducted with Dutch and Canadian children, ages 8 to 13, have found that children who are rejected by their peers behave more aggressively than those who do not experience rejection. This effect has been found in both correlational studies (Orbio de Castro, Brendgen, Van Boxtel, Vitaro, & Schaepers, 2007) and in carefully controlled experiments (Reijntjes, Thomaes, Bushman, Boelen, Orbio de Castro, & Telch, 2010).

We end with a silver lining: There is some evidence that social exclusion can motivate us to form new social bonds. In a series of studies, it was found that when participants (university students) were socially excluded, they were more interested in forming new friendships with other students or becoming socially reconnected in other ways (Maner, DeWall, Baumeister, & Schaller, 2007).

Aggressive Objects as Aggressive Cues

Is it conceivable that the mere presence of an object associated with aggressive responses (e.g., a gun) might increase the probability of aggression? This sort of object is called an **aggressive stimulus**. In a classic experiment by Leonard Berkowitz and Anthony LePage (1967), university students were made angry. Some of them were made angry in a room in which a gun was left lying around (ostensibly from a previous experiment), and others were made angry in a room in which a neutral object (a badminton racket) was substituted for the gun. Participants were then given the opportunity to administer electric shocks to a fellow student. Those individuals who had been made angry in the presence of the gun administered more intense electric shocks than did those made angry in the presence of the badminton racket (see Figure 11.1).

Aggressive Stimulus

An object associated with aggressive responses (e.g., a gun) whose mere presence can increase the probability of aggression

These basic findings have been borne out a great many times (Frodi, 1975; Turner & Leyens, 1992; Turner & Simons, 1974; Turner, Simons, Berkowitz, & Frodi, 1977). The findings are provocative and point to a conclusion opposite to a familiar slogan often used by opponents of gun control: "Guns don't kill; people do." Guns do kill. Leonard Berkowitz (1981) put it this way, "An angry person can pull the trigger of his gun if he wants to commit violence; but the trigger can also pull the finger or otherwise elicit aggressive reactions from him, if he is ready to aggress and does not have strong inhibitions against such behaviour" (p. 12).

Connect to MyPsychLab

To access the Critical Thinking question on guns and aggression, go to MyPsychLab

Consider Seattle, Washington, and Vancouver, British Columbia. They are virtually twin cities; they have similar climates, populations, economies, general crime rates, and rates of physical assault. They differ, however, in two respects: (1) Vancouver severely restricts handgun ownership, whereas Seattle does not, and (2) the murder rate in Seattle is more than twice as high as that in Vancouver (Sloan et al., 1988). Can the difference in murder rates be attributed to the difference in restrictions on guns? We cannot be sure. But the laboratory experiments discussed above strongly suggest that the ubiquitous presence of that aggressive stimulus in the United States might be a factor. This speculation receives additional support from Dane Archer and Rosemary Gartner (1984), who found that the homicide rate in countries all over the world is highly correlated with the availability of handguns. Britain, for example, where handguns are banned, has one-quarter the population of the United States but just one-sixteenth as many homicides. In Canada, gun control has become a hot-button issue as the Conservative government under Prime Minister Stephen Harper seeks to dismantle the gun registry. However, statistics show that the rates of death and injury have fallen dramatically since the introduction of stricter gun laws in 1991 (Bill C-17) and in 1995 (Bill C-68). For example, data gathered in 2007 show that suicides committed by firearm have dropped by 52 percent since the introduction of stricter

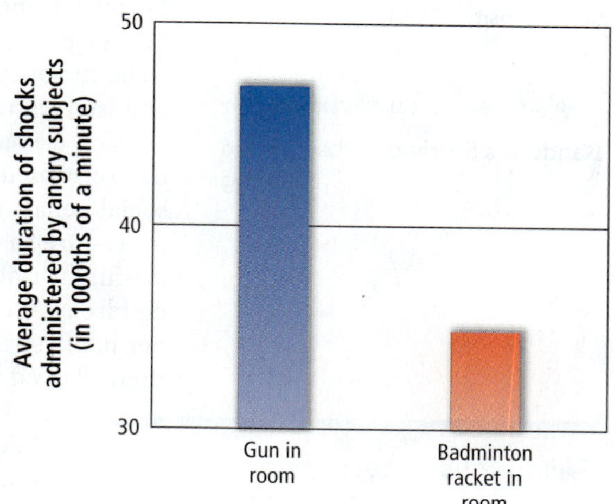

FIGURE 11.1

The trigger can pull the finger.

Aggressive cues, such as weapons, tend to increase levels of aggression.

(Adapted from Berkowitz & LePage, 1967)

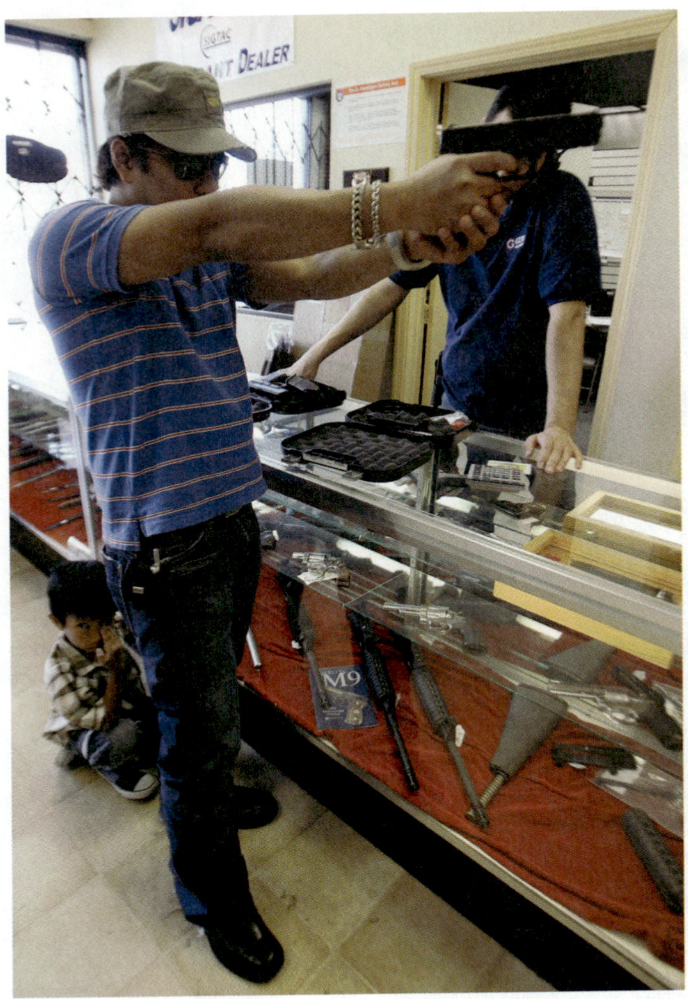

Guns to the left of me, guns to the right of me . . . Does the ready availability of guns in the United States contribute to the frequency and intensity of violence?

gun laws in 1991 (Coalition for Gun Control, n.d.). According to Statistics Canada's (2009) report on family violence, the rate of spousal homicides involving firearms fell by 74 percent from 1980 to 2009. These statistics are consistent with the argument that if guns aren't readily available, people are less likely to use them.

It is important to note that the aggressive stimulus effect occurs only when we actually link an object with aggression. For example, Bartholow and colleagues (2004) found that hunting guns were associated with aggression for non-hunters but not for hunters, whereas assault guns were associated with aggression for both groups (Bartholow, Anderson, Carnagey, & Benjamin, 2004). We should also point out that aggression can be cued by any aggressive stimulus—not just guns. For example, Josephson (1987) demonstrated that even neutral objects can come to be associated with aggression. In her study, some of the participants (young boys) were shown a violent television segment in which snipers communicated via walkie-talkies. Later, they played a game of floor hockey while observers recorded instances of aggression by speaking into either a walkie-talkie or a tape recorder. Participants showed greater aggression when the observers used walkie-talkies than when they used tape recorders. Thus, the walkie-talkie had become a violence-related cue—simply from having been associated with violence in the television show the participants had seen earlier.

Imitation and Aggression

Children frequently learn to solve conflicts aggressively by imitating adults and their peers, especially when they see that the aggression is rewarded. For example, in many high-contact sports (e.g., football and hockey), the more aggressive players achieve the greatest fame and the highest salaries, and the more aggressive teams win more games. In these sports, it usually doesn't pay to be a gentle soul. Famed baseball manager Leo Durocher once said, "Nice guys finish last!" The data bear him out. For instance, the hockey players most frequently sent to the penalty box for overly aggressive play tend to be the ones who score the most goals (McCarthy & Kelly, 1978). What lessons are children learning from observing aggression among athletes and other adults?

Explore on **mypsychlab**
Bandura's Study on Observation Learning

In a classic series of experiments, Albert Bandura and his associates (1961, 1963) demonstrated the power of social learning. Social learning theory holds that we learn social behaviour (e.g., aggression) by observing others and imitating them. The basic procedure in the Bandura experiments was to have an adult knock around a plastic, air-filled "Bobo" doll (the kind that bounces back after it's been knocked down) while children observed. The adult would smack the doll around with the palm of his or her hand, strike it with a mallet, kick it, and yell aggressive things at it. The kids were then allowed to play with the doll. In these experiments, the children imitated the aggressive models and treated the doll in an abusive manner. Moreover, these children used identical actions and identical aggressive words to those of the adult. In addition, many went beyond mere imitation—they also engaged in novel forms of aggressive behaviour. In contrast, children in a control condition, who did not see the aggressive adult in action, almost never unleashed any aggression against the hapless doll.

Children have never been very good at listening to their elders, but they have never failed to imitate them.

—James Baldwin, Nobody Knows My Name, *1961*

Given findings such as these, it probably comes as no surprise that numerous studies have found that a large percentage of physically abusive people were themselves abused by their parents when they were kids (Dutton &

Hart, 1992a, 1992b; Silver, Dublin, & Lourie, 1969; Straus & Gelles, 1980). When children experience aggressive treatment at the hands of their parents, they learn that violence is the way to respond to conflict or anger.

People may also imitate acts of violence performed by their peers. In April 1999, the shooting rampage of two students at Columbine High School in Littleton, Colorado, made news headlines around the world. Eric Harris and Dylan Klebold shot and killed 13 people at their high school before fatally shooting themselves. Later that month, a 14-year-old boy (who cannot be named because he was a minor) attending W. R. Myers High School in Taber, Alberta, opened fire, killing one student and wounding another. It was believed that the Taber tragedy was an imitation of the Columbine massacre. According to Kevin Cameron, the social worker who led the crisis unit team sent to Taber, critical periods, such as the anniversary of the shootings, are associated with increased threats for at least three to five years afterward (Cameron, 2000). Indeed, on the one-year anniversary of the Columbine shootings, four students and one staff member at Cairine Wilson Secondary School in Orleans, Ontario, were wounded when they were attacked by a knife-wielding student. A decade later, the Columbine massacre continued to have an impact around the world. On April 16, 2007, 32 students and staff died in the Virginia Tech massacre, which was widely believed to be an anniversary shooting. And on September 24, 2008, Matti Saari, a student at a trade school in Finland opened fire on his fellow students and teachers. He killed 10 people before turning his gun on himself. This was the second school shooting in Finland in less than a year. In both cases, the gunmen had been fascinated by the Columbine shootings (Turula, 2008).

Shootings on college and university campuses are becoming all too familiar. On September 13, 2006, Kimveer Gill went on a shooting rampage at Dawson College near Montreal. One person was killed; 19 others were injured. Kimveer then shot and killed himself.

The Effects of Violence in the Media

Simulate on **mypsychlab**
Media Violence

If just watching people behave aggressively causes children to mistreat dolls, how does watching violence on television or in movies affect them—affect all of us? And what about violent video games in which children participate in the destruction of cities or the lopping off of heads and limbs of characters?

Most children in North America are immersed in television violence. It has been estimated that by the time the average American child finishes elementary school, he or she will have seen 8000 murders and more than 100 000 other acts of violence (Eron, 2001). Analyses of the content of television shows have revealed that 58 percent of all television programs contain violence; of those programs, 78 percent show no remorse, criticism, or penalty for the violence (Seppa, 1997). Indeed, some 40 percent of violent incidents seen on television are initiated by characters portrayed as heroes or other attractive role models for children (Cantor, 1994; Kunkel et al., 2001).

> *Television has brought murder back into the home—where it belongs.*
>
> —Alfred Hitchcock, *1965*

Exactly what do children learn from watching violence on television? In an impressive longitudinal program of research, Eron and Huesmann and their colleagues (Eron, 1982, 1987; Eron, Huesmann, Lefkowitz, & Walder, 1996) assessed television viewing habits of nearly 900 eight-year-old children. The children were asked to report which shows they watched on television and how frequently they watched them. (The shows were independently rated by judges as to how violent they were.) Then, the general aggressiveness of the children was rated by their teachers and classmates. The researchers found a significant correlation between the amount of violent television shows watched and the children's aggressiveness. More striking was the finding that the impact of watching violent television shows accumulated over time—10 years later, when the original research participants were 18 years old, the correlation between television violence and aggression was stronger than it had been at age eight!

Death has been tidied up, cleansed of harmful ingredients, and repackaged in prime-time segments that pander to baser appetites but leave no unpleasant aftertaste. The Caesars of network television permit no mess on the living room floor.

—Donald Goddard, 1977

These sorts of findings have been obtained for adolescents and adults as well, as shown in a large-scale longitudinal study in which the behaviour of more than 700 families was monitored over a period of 17 years (Johnson, Cohen, Smailes, Kasen, & Brook, 2002). The findings were striking: There was a significant association between the amount of time spent watching television during adolescence and early adulthood and the likelihood of subsequent violent acts against others. This association was significant regardless of parental education, family income, and neighbourhood violence. Moreover, unlike most laboratory experiments on aggression, which understandably must use rather pallid measures of aggression (e.g., administering fake electric shocks or loud noises to the victim), this study—because it took place in the real world over a long period of time—was able to examine severe aggressive behaviour such as assault and armed robbery (Johnson et al., 2002).

Although these data are powerful, they do not definitively prove that watching a lot of violence on television causes children and adolescents to become violent adults. After all, it is at least conceivable that the aggressive kids were born with a tendency to enjoy violence and that this enjoyment manifested itself in both their aggressive behaviour and their liking for watching violence on television. Once again, we see the value of the controlled experiment in sorting out what causes what. To demonstrate conclusively that watching violence on television actually causes violent behaviour, the relationship must be shown experimentally.

Because this issue is of great importance to society, it has been well researched. Although not all of the research is consistent, the overwhelming thrust of the experimental evidence is that watching violence does indeed increase the frequency of aggressive behaviour in children (see reviews of the literature by Cantor et al., 2001; Geen, 1998; Huesmann & Miller, 1994; Wood, Wong, & Chachere, 1991). For example, in an early experiment on this issue, Robert Liebert and Robert Baron (1972) exposed a group of children to an extremely violent television episode of a police drama. In a control condition, a similar group of children was exposed to an exciting but nonviolent television sporting event for the same length of time. Each child was then allowed to play in another room with a group of other children. Those who had watched the violent police drama showed far more aggression against their playmates than did those who had watched the sporting event.

Earlier we referred to an experiment by Josephson (1987), who found that watching violence on television has the greatest impact on youngsters who are somewhat prone to violence to begin with. In this experiment, nearly 400 boys from various Winnipeg schools were exposed to either a film depicting a great deal of police violence or an exciting, nonviolent film about bike racing. The boys then played a game of floor hockey. Exposure to the violent film had the effect of increasing the number of aggressive acts committed during the game—primarily by those boys who had previously been rated as highly aggressive by their teachers. These boys hit others with their sticks, threw elbows, and yelled aggressive things at their opponents to a much greater extent than nonaggressive boys, who had also watched the violent film, or the boys rated as aggressive (by their teachers), who had watched the nonviolent film. Thus, it may be that watching media violence in effect serves to give aggressive children "permission" to express their aggression. Josephson's results suggest that children who do not have aggressive tendencies to begin with do not necessarily act aggressively—at least, not on the basis of seeing only one violent film.

This last phrase is an important one, because research has shown that even children who are not prone to aggression will become more aggressive if exposed to a steady diet of violent films over a long period (Leyens, Camino, Parke, & Berkowitz, 1975; Parke et al., 1977).

It is important to point out that the kinds of effects we have been discussing extend to violence portrayed in the media more generally—not just in television programming. For example, there is evidence that listening to songs with violent lyrics increases aggressive thoughts and feelings of hostility for both males and females (Anderson, Carnagey, & Eubanks, 2003). The Columbine High School killings raised the disturbing question of whether violent entertainment, such as violent video games, can contribute to aggression. Apparently Harris and Klebold enjoyed playing a bloody, extremely violent video game licensed by the U.S. military to train soldiers how to kill. For a class project, Harris and Klebold produced a videotape that was an eerie rendition of the killings they subsequently carried out. Their videotape, modelled after the video game, featured the two of them wearing trench coats, carrying guns, and killing school athletes.

Many people are unconcerned about the impact of watching violent entertainment; however, research shows that viewing violent content can have lasting ill effects.

Does playing violent video games actually produce aggressive behaviour? The answer is yes. Specifically, there is evidence that violent video game playing is positively correlated with aggressive behaviour and delinquency in children (Anderson & Dill, 2000). Laboratory experiments conducted with university students confirm that exposure to violent video games increases aggressive thoughts and behaviours (Anderson & Dill, 2000; Bartholow & Anderson, 2002; Bushman & Anderson, 2002). (If this isn't enough to persuade you to curb time spent playing video games, note that Anderson and Dill [2000] also found that the more time the participants spent playing video games—violent or not—the lower their grades became!)

Recently Anderson and colleagues (2010) conducted a meta analysis of 130 studies on the effects of playing violent video games. This is the most comprehensive meta analysis of the effects of violent video games that has been conducted to date. Their conclusion? "The evidence strongly suggests that exposure to violent video games is a causal risk factor for increased aggressive behavior, aggressive cognition, and aggressive affect and for decreased empathy and prosocial behaviour" (Anderson, Shibuya, Ihori, Swing, Bushman, Sakamoto, Rothstein, & Saleem, 2010, p. 151). D. Gentile and J. R. Gentile (2008) have suggested that video games are extremely effective at teaching aggression because they accomplish three elements of "best" instructional practises: teaching the same content across several contexts, distributing the practise over time, and inducing emotional and physiological responses.

Watch on **mypsychlab**

Violence and Video Games: Douglas Gentile

Listen on **mypsychlab**

Psychology in the News: Social Psychology

Media violence may serve to give kids already prone to aggression permission to be aggressive. It also may make generally nonaggressive children behave aggressively.

Research suggests that playing violent video games makes children and adults more prone to aggression.

Watch on mypsychlab Television Violence

The Numbing Effect of Media Violence Repeated exposure to difficult or unpleasant events tends to have a numbing effect on our sensitivity to those events. In one experiment, Victor Cline and his colleagues (1973) measured the physiological responses of several young men while they were watching a rather brutal and bloody boxing match. Those who watched a lot of television in their daily lives seemed relatively indifferent to the mayhem in the ring—that is, they showed little physiological evidence of excitement or anxiety. They treated the violence in a lackadaisical manner. On the contrary, those who typically watched relatively little television underwent major physiological arousal—the violence really bothered them (Cline, Croft, & Courrier, 1973).

Studies also have found that viewing violence on television can subsequently numb people's reactions when they are faced with real-life aggression. In one study, participants watched either a violent police drama or an exciting but nonviolent volleyball game (Thomas, Horton, Lippincott, & Drabman, 1977). After a short break, they observed a verbally and physically aggressive interaction between two preschoolers. Those who had watched the police show responded less emotionally—as measured by changes in galvanic skin response—than did those who had watched the volleyball game. It seems that viewing the initial violence served to desensitize them to further acts of violence; they were not upset by an incident that should have upset them. While such a reaction may psychologically protect us from upset, it may also have the unintended effect of increasing our indifference to victims of violence and perhaps rendering us more accepting of violence as a necessary aspect of modern life. In a follow-up experiment, Margaret Thomas (1982) took this reasoning a step further. She demonstrated that students exposed to a great deal of violence on television not only showed physiological evidence of greater acceptance of violence, but also, when subsequently given the opportunity to administer electric shocks to a fellow student, delivered more powerful electric shocks than did those in the control condition.

In a related fashion, recently researchers have shown that people who play violent video games are more likely to be oblivious to the needs of others. Bushman and Anderson (2009) ran an experiment in which participants had the opportunity to help an injured person. Those who previously had been playing violent video games took much longer to respond than those who were playing a nonviolent game. In a follow-up study, these researchers found that people who had just watched a violent movie took longer to help a confederate who dropped her crutches outside of the theatre than people who had watched a nonviolent show. Bushman and Anderson (2009) concluded that violent media make people numb to the pain and suffering of others.

Violent Pornography and Violence against Women

If viewing aggression in films and on television contributes to aggressiveness, doesn't it follow that exposure to pornographic material could increase the incidence of sexual aggression, such as rape? Many people think so. Lavoie, Robitaille, and Hébert (2000), for example, conducted discussion groups with youths who frequented a teen drop-in centre in Quebec City. Both males and females perceived pornography as a cause of sexual violence in relationships. Moreover, participants reported that it was not uncommon for them or their partners to imitate acts of sexual violence observed in pornographic movies or magazines. Similarly, Sommers and Check (1987) found that women living in shelters or attending counselling groups for battered women in the Toronto area reported much greater consumption of pornographic material by their partner than did a comparison group of women who were not battered. The battered women experienced higher levels of verbal aggression, physical aggression, and sexual aggression from their partners than did the control group. In addition, 39 percent of the battered women—versus 3 percent of the control group—answered yes to the question "Has your partner ever upset you by trying to get you to do what he'd seen in pornographic pictures, movies, or books?"

Careful scientific research suggests an important distinction between simple pornography and violent pornography. By "violent pornography" we mean exactly what you might think: pornographic material that includes an element of violence against women. The findings from carefully conducted research over the past 30 years confirm that exposure to violent pornography is associated with greater acceptance of sexual violence toward women and is almost certainly a factor associated with actual aggressive behaviour toward women (Dean & Malamuth, 1997; Donnerstein & Berkowitz, 1981; Donnerstein & Linz, 1994; Malamuth & Brière, 1986; Malamuth, Linz, Heavey, Barnes, & Acker, 1995). For example, Neil Malamuth and James Check (1981) asked students at the University of Manitoba to watch a movie shown at a campus theatre, supposedly as part of a study on the evaluation of movies. The participants saw either a movie that contained sexual violence against women or a nonviolent movie that portrayed a positive, caring relationship. Several days later, the students were asked to complete a sexual attitudes survey in their psychology class. The researchers found that male students who had viewed the movie containing sexual violence were more accepting of violence against women than were those who had seen the nonviolent movie.

But do laboratory studies show that men who view violent pornography actually behave aggressively toward women? Sadly, the answer is yes. In one experiment (Donnerstein & Berkowitz, 1981), male participants were angered by a female accomplice. They were then shown one of three films—an aggressive erotic film involving rape, a purely erotic film without violence, or a film depicting non-erotic violence against women. After viewing one of these films, the men took part in a supposedly unrelated experiment that involved teaching the female accomplice by means of administering electric shocks to her whenever she gave incorrect answers. They were allowed to choose whatever level of shock they wished to use. (As with other experiments using this procedure, no shocks were actually received.) Only men who had previously seen the violent pornographic film subsequently administered intense shocks to the female accomplice.

There is also evidence showing that those who view violent pornographic films will administer more intense shocks to a female confederate than to a male confederate (Donnerstein, 1980). Unfortunately, these are not isolated findings. Researchers at the Canadian National Foundation for Family Research and Education conducted a meta analysis of 46 Canadian and U.S. studies on the effects of pornography and concluded that exposure to pornographic material (which, in their analysis, included violent pornography) has far-reaching negative consequences, such as an increased risk of developing sexually deviant tendencies, committing sexual offences, accepting the rape myth, and experiencing difficulties in one's intimate relationships (Paolucci-Oddone, Genius, & Violato, 2000).

How to Reduce Aggression

"Stop hitting your brother!" "Turn off the TV and go to your room!" Trying to curb the aggressive behaviour of their children, most parents use some form of punishment. Some deny privileges; others use force, believing in the old saying, "Spare the rod and spoil the child." How well does punishment work?

Watch on mypsychlab
Bandura's Bobo Doll Experiment

Does Punishing Aggression Reduce Aggressive Behaviour?

Punishment is a complex event, especially as it relates to aggression. On the one hand, you might guess that punishing any behaviour, including aggression, would reduce its frequency. On the other hand, severe punishment itself usually takes the form of an aggressive act. The punishers are actually modelling aggressive behaviour for the person whose aggressive behaviour they are trying to stamp out, and their punishment might induce that person to imitate the action. This seems to be true—for children. As we mentioned earlier in this chapter, children who grow up with punitive, aggressive parents tend to be prone toward violence when they grow up (Vissing, Straus, Gelles, & Harrop, 1991).

All punishment is mischief; all punishment itself is evil.

—Jeremy Bentham, *Principles of Morals and Legislation, 1789*

Moreover, as we saw in Chapter 6, several experiments with preschoolers have demonstrated that the threat of relatively severe punishment for committing a transgression does not make the transgression less appealing to the child. However, the threat of mild punishment—of a degree just powerful enough to get the child to cease the undesired activity temporarily—can induce the child to try to justify his or her restraint and can make the behaviour less appealing (Aronson & Carlsmith, 1963; Freedman, 1965).

What about adults? The criminal justice system of most cultures administers harsh punishments as a means of retribution and to deter violent crimes. Does the threat of harsh punishments for violent crimes make such crimes less likely? Do people who are about to commit such crimes say to themselves, "I'd better think twice about this, because if I get caught, I'll be severely punished"? Here, the scientific evidence is mixed. Laboratory experiments indicate that punishment can act as a deterrent but only if two ideal conditions are met: (1) The punishment must be both prompt and certain; and (2) it must be unavoidable (Bower & Hilgard, 1981). Needless to say, in the real world these conditions are almost never met. The probability that a person who has committed a violent crime will be apprehended, charged, tried, and convicted is not high. Moreover, promptness is rarely possible—punishment is typically delayed by months or even years. Consequently, in the complex world of the criminal justice system, severe punishment is unlikely to have the kind of deterrent effect it does in the laboratory.

Indeed, there is evidence that severe punishment does not seem to deter violent crimes. For example, the United States—where many states invoke the death penalty for murder—has a much higher rate of homicide than many other industrial countries, including Canada (Archer & Gartner, 1984). Moreover, the American states that have abolished the death penalty have not experienced the increase in capital crimes that some experts predicted (Archer & Gartner, 1984; Nathanson, 1987; Peterson & Bailey, 1988). A study by the National Academy of Sciences (see Berkowitz, 1993) demonstrated that consistency and certainty of punishment were far more effective deterrents of violent behaviour than was severe punishment.

Closer to home, in 1990, Manitoba instituted a family violence court to deal specifically with cases of family violence; in 1997, Ontario established similar courts. Other territories and provinces (Yukon, Saskatchewan, Alberta, New Brunswick, and Newfoundland) have followed. These specialized courts are part of an overall response to family violence that includes a zero-tolerance policy for arrest, early intervention in domestic abuse situations, the use of Crown attorneys with expertise in family violence issues (e.g., sensitivity to victims' reluctance to testify, ensuring that the legal process does not revictimize victims of violence), and treatment programs for offenders and victims of family violence. The message being sent from these courts is that family violence is a serious crime with immediate, serious consequences.

The establishment of family violence courts has had several effects. The first has been a dramatic increase in the number of arrests and convictions. For example, in the first two years that the Court was operating in Winnipeg, there was a 150 percent increase in spousal abuse charges (Chin, 2011). Importantly, the high rate of convictions has been coupled with an emphasis on rehabilitation; for example, most offenders are required to participate in treatment groups. It is encouraging that an analysis of a domestic violence court in Calgary, Alberta, found that the rates of recidivism among the accused are now lower than they were prior to the implementation of the court (Tutty, McNichol, & Christensen, 2008).

Catharsis and Aggression

It is generally believed that one way to reduce feelings of aggression is to do something aggressive. "Get it out of your system" has been common advice for a great many years. So, if you are feeling angry, the belief goes, don't try to ignore it, but instead yell, scream, curse, throw a plate at the wall. Express the anger and it won't build up into something uncontrollable. This common belief is based on an oversimplification of the psychoanalytic notion of **catharsis** (Dollard, Doob, Miller, Mowrer, & Sears, 1939; Freud, 1933). As we noted earlier, Freud had a "hydraulic" idea of aggressive impulses: He believed that unless people were allowed to express their aggression in relatively harmless ways, the aggressive energy would be dammed up, pressure would build, and the energy would seek an outlet, either exploding into acts of extreme violence or manifesting itself as symptoms of mental illness.

Catharsis

The notion that "blowing off steam"—by performing an aggressive act, watching others engage in aggressive behaviour, or engaging in a fantasy of aggression—relieves built-up aggressive energies and hence reduces the likelihood of further aggressive behaviour

Freud was a brilliant and complex thinker who invariably stopped short of giving simplistic advice. Unfortunately, his theory of catharsis has been boiled down to the dictum that people should "vent" their anger. The idea is that blowing off steam will not only make angry people feel better, but also serve to make them less likely to engage in subsequent acts of destructive violence. Does this square with the data?

Consider a study by Bushman, Baumeister, and Stack (1999). They asked university students to read an article, supposedly published in *Science*, titled, "Research Shows that Hitting Inanimate Objects Is an Effective Way to Vent Anger." In the article, a Harvard psychologist claimed that people who vent their anger by hitting a punching bag subsequently behave less aggressively toward others. Other participants read the same article, except that the word *Effective* in the title was changed to *Ineffective*, and the article stated that venting one's anger did *not* reduce aggression. Later, all the participants were insulted by a confederate. Some participants were given a chance to vent their anger by hitting a punching bag; other participants were not. Then, everyone was given an opportunity to deliver bursts of noise either to the person who insulted them or to a different person. It turned out that the most aggressive participants (i.e., those who delivered the longest and loudest blasts of noise) were those who had read the pro-catharsis message and had hit the punching bag. Moreover, they were equally aggressive, regardless of whether the target was the person who had angered them or an innocent person. Thus, it appears that venting anger actually increases anger rather than reduces it.

In more recent research, Bushman and Whitaker (2010) had participants read the same articles. Some participants were then insulted; others were not. Later, all participants rated how much they wanted to play a number of video games, which varied in terms of violence. Participants who read the pro-catharsis article and who were angered wanted to play the violent video games more than participants in the other conditions. In a follow-up study, catharsis beliefs were measured rather than manipulated. It was found that people who believe in catharsis were more likely to choose violent video games when angered than people who did not believe in catharsis. As one participant remarked, "How could I squelch the urge to set my manager on fire if I couldn't get people on fire in video games?" (Bushman & Whitaker, 2010, p. 791).

Something of vengeance I had tasted for the first time; an aromatic wine it seemed, on swallowing, warm and racy; its after-flavour, metallic and corroding, gave me a sensation as if I had been poisoned.

—Charlotte Brontë, *Jane Eyre, 1847*

Studies have also examined whether participating in aggressive sports has a cathartic effect. For example, Patterson (1974) measured the hostility of high school football players, rating them both one week before and one week after the football season. If it were true that the intense competitiveness and aggressive behaviour that are part of playing football serve to reduce the tension caused by pent-up aggression, the players would be expected to exhibit a decline in hostility over the course of the season. Instead, the results showed a significant *increase* in feelings of hostility. This is not to say that people do not get pleasure from these games—they do. Engaging in these games, however, does not decrease participants' aggressive feelings; if anything, it increases them.

Some people believe in another variation of the catharsis hypothesis: that watching competitive and aggressive games is a safe way to get rid of our aggressive impulses. Gordon Russell (1983), a sports psychologist at the University of Lethbridge, tested this proposition by measuring the hostility of spectators at an especially violent hockey game. As the game progressed, the spectators became increasingly belligerent; toward the end of the final period, their level of hostility skyrocketed and did not return to the pre-game level until several hours after the game was over. Similar results have been found among spectators at football games and wrestling matches (Arms, Russell, & Sandilands, 1979; Branscombe & Wann, 1992; Goldstein & Arms, 1971). As with participating in an aggressive sport, watching one serves to increase, rather than reduce, aggressive behaviour.

Blaming the Victim of Our Aggression When somebody angers us, venting our hostility against that person may relieve tension and make us feel better, at least temporarily, assuming that the person we vent on doesn't decide to vent back on us. But "feeling better" should not be confused with a reduction in hostility. Aggressing the first time can reduce your inhibitions against committing other such actions; in a sense, the aggression is legitimized, making it easier to carry out such assaults. Further, and more importantly, the main thrust of the research on this issue indicates that committing an overt act of aggression against a person changes one's feelings about that person—in a negative direction—thereby increasing the probability of future aggression against that person.

Does sound familiar? It should. As we saw in Chapter 6, when one person does harm to another person, it sets in motion cognitive processes aimed at justifying the act of cruelty. Specifically, when you hurt another person, you experience cognitive dissonance. The cognition "I have hurt Charlie" is dissonant with the cognition "I am a decent, reasonable person." A good way for you to reduce dissonance is somehow to convince yourself that hurting Charlie was not an indecent, unreasonable, bad thing to do. You can accomplish this by convincing yourself that Charlie is a terrible human being who deserved to be hurt. This will reduce dissonance, all right—but it also sets

Fans watching aggressive sports do not become less aggressive—contrary to the idea of catharsis.

the stage for further aggression; once a person has succeeded in derogating someone, he or she finds it easier to do further harm to the victim in the future.

If our reasoning is correct, it might help explain why it is that when two nations are at war, a relatively small percentage of the members of the victorious nation feel much sympathy for the innocent victims of their nation's actions. Near the end of World War II, when U.S. planes dropped atom bombs on Hiroshima and Nagasaki, more than 100 000 Japanese civilians—including many children—were killed, and countless thousands suffered severe injuries. Shortly thereafter, a poll of the American people indicated that less than 5 percent felt that those weapons should not have been used, whereas 23 percent felt that many more of them should have been used before giving Japan the opportunity to surrender. Why would so many U.S. citizens favour the wanton death and destruction of innocent victims? Our guess is that in the course of the war, a sizeable proportion of Americans adopted increasingly derogatory attitudes toward the Japanese, which made it easier to accept that the U.S. military was causing them a great deal of misery. The more misery the Americans inflicted on them, the more the Americans derogated them—leading to an endless spiral of aggression and its justification, even to the point of favouring a delay in ending the war so that more destruction might be inflicted.

In war, the state is sanctioning murder. Even when the war is over, this moral corruption is bound to linger for many years.

—Desiderius Erasmus, *1514*

Closer to home, what percentage of Canadians do you suppose have paused to feel sadness about the civilian lives lost as a result of Canada's involvement in Afghanistan? Considerable media attention has been placed on the tragic deaths of Canadian soldiers in Afghanistan: 157 Canadian members of the Canadian Forces have died between the first deployment in February 2002 and September 2011 (the time of writing). It is certainly appropriate to recognize and mourn these losses. What is not highlighted in the media, however, is the thousands of Afghani civilians who have lost their lives. It is difficult to get an exact count; but, according to NATOs International Security Assistance Force, 2537 civilians were killed in 2009 and 2010 alone. The United Nations sets this figure at 5191 deaths over this two-year period (Bohannon, 2011). Research shows that there is little sympathy for the innocent victims in such situations (see Aronson, Wilson, & Akert, 2007). Afghan President Hamid Karzai would agree. Although he received an apology from NATO for an air strike that killed nine children in March 2011, President Karzai felt it was "not enough." Sadly, a few days later the president's cousin was fatally shot in his home, allegedly by coalition soldiers. NATO is currently conducting an investigation into the killing (Abma, 2011).

When a nation is at war, the impact of that situation extends even beyond feelings of hostility toward the enemy. Specifically, being at war makes the population—even the noncombatants—more prone to commit aggressive actions against one another. Dane Archer and Rosemary Gartner (1976, 1984) compared the crime rates for 110 countries starting with the year 1900. They found that compared with similar nations that remained at peace, countries that fought wars exhibited substantial postwar increases in their homicide rates. This should not be surprising; it is consistent with everything we have been saying about the social causes of

During World War II, Americans depicted the Japanese enemy as being vampires and other creatures. Dehumanizing images, such as that shown in this poster (top), helped justify the use of the atom bomb on Hiroshima (bottom) and Nagasaki, causing the deaths of hundreds of thousands of civilians.

aggression. The fact that a nation is at war (1) weakens the population's inhibitions against aggression; (2) leads to imitation of aggression; (3) makes aggressive responses more available; and (4) numbs our senses to the horror of cruelty and destruction, making us less sympathetic toward the victims. In addition, being at war serves to legitimize the use of violent solutions to address difficult problems to the general population. This phenomenon is likely to be more powerful now than ever before because, thanks to satellite transmission, we and our children can watch the war unfold in our living room as it happens, 24 hours a day.

What Are We Supposed to Do with Our Anger?

If violence leads to self-justification, which in turn breeds more violence, then what are we to do when we are feeling angry with someone? Stifling anger and sulking around the house, hoping that someone will read our mind, doesn't seem to be a good solution. Neither is brooding and ruminating by ourselves, which just prolongs and intensifies anger (Rusting & Nolen-Hoeksema, 1998). But if keeping our feelings bottled up and expressing them are both harmful, what are we supposed to do? This dilemma isn't as difficult as it might seem. First, it is possible to control our anger by actively enabling it to dissipate. "Actively enabling" means using such simple techniques as counting to 10 before shooting your mouth off (Tavris, 1989). Taking deep breaths or engaging in a distracting activity (working on a crossword puzzle, listening to soothing music, taking a bike ride, or even doing a good deed) are good ways of actively enabling the anger to fade away. But there is more to anger than simply controlling it, as we shall see.

To jaw-jaw is better than to war-war.

—Winston Churchill, *1954*

I was angry with my friend: I told my wrath, my wrath did end.

—William Blake, *"A Poison Tree," 1789–1794*

Communication and Problem Solving It is impossible to go through life—or sometimes to get through the day—without feeling frustrated, annoyed, or angry. Feeling anger is part of being human, but anger itself is not the problem. The problem is the *expression* of anger in violent or cruel ways. Yet, we are not born knowing how to express anger or annoyance constructively and nonviolently. Indeed, it seems almost natural to lash out when we are angry. However, it is possible to express anger in a nonviolent and nondemeaning way. You can do this (after counting to 10!) by making a clear, calm, and simple statement indicating that you are feeling angry and describing, nonjudgmentally, precisely what the other person did to bring about those feelings. Such a statement in itself will probably relieve tension and make you feel better. At the same time, because you haven't actually harmed the target of your anger, such a response does not set in motion the cognitive processes that would lead you to justify your behaviour by ridiculing or derogating him or her. The person with whom you are angry also is more likely to react in a constructive manner. For example, in a study conducted at the University of Winnipeg, it was found that if participants were angry with their partner, they expected that their partner would react more positively if they, themselves, expressed their anger in positive, constructive ways (e.g., talking it over, expressing hurt feelings). On the contrary, participants expected that if they expressed anger in negative ways (e.g., with direct or indirect aggression), their partner would be likely to respond in negative ways (Fehr, Baldwin, Collins, Patterson, & Benditt, 1999).

When feelings of anger are expressed in a clear, open, nonpunitive manner, the result can be greater mutual understanding and a strengthening of the relationship. It almost seems too simple; yet, we have found such behaviour to be a reasonable option that will have more beneficial effects than, on the one hand, shouting, name calling, and throwing dishes or, on the other hand, suffering in silence as you grin and bear it (Aronson, 2008).

What about people who lack the social skills that are required to communicate anger or criticism in constructive ways? There is some evidence that formal training in communication and problem solving can be an effective means of reducing aggression (Studer, 1996). For example, in a classic experiment by Joel Davitz (1952), children were allowed to play in groups of four. Some of these groups were taught constructive ways to relate to one another, and they were rewarded for such behaviour; others were rewarded for aggressive or competitive behaviour. Next, the children were deliberately frustrated. They were told that they would be shown entertaining movies and be allowed to have fun. The experimenter began to show a movie and to hand out candy bars but, then, he abruptly terminated the movie at the point of highest interest and took the candy bars away. Now, the children were allowed to play freely, as the researchers watched for constructive or aggressive behaviours. The results? Children who had been trained for constructive behaviour displayed far more constructive activity and far less aggressive behaviour than did those who had been rewarded for aggression. Many elementary and secondary schools now train students to employ such nonaggressive strategies for resolving conflict (Eargle, Guerra, & Tolan, 1994; Educators for Social Responsibility, 2001).

Defusing Anger through Apology Earlier, we noted that when people had been frustrated by someone and then learned that the person simply couldn't do any better, frustration was less likely to bubble over into anger or aggression. This suggests that an effective way to reduce aggression in another person is to take some action aimed at diminishing the anger and annoyance that caused it.

Suppose you are scheduled to be at your friend's house at 7:30 P.M. to drive her to a concert scheduled to start at 8:00. She has been looking forward to the concert for months. You rush out of your house with just barely enough time to get there, but after driving for a few minutes you discover that you have a flat tire. By the time you change the tire and get to her house, you are already 20 minutes late for the concert. Imagine her response if you (a) casually walk in, grin at her, and say, "Oh well, it probably wouldn't have been such a good concert anyway. Lighten up; it's not a big deal," or (b) run in clearly upset, show her your dirty hands, explain what happened, apologize sincerely and profusely, and vow to find a way to make it up to her.

We would predict that your friend would be prone toward aggression in the first instance but not in the second, and a host of experiments supports our prediction (Baron, 1988, 1990; Ohbuchi & Sato, 1994; Weiner et al., 1987). Typically, any apology sincerely given and in which the perpetrator takes full responsibility is effective at reducing aggression.

With this in mind, one of the authors of this book (Elliot Aronson) has speculated about the great advantages that might be gained by equipping automobiles with "apology" signals. Picture the scene: You are at a stop sign and then proceed, but too late you realize that the right of way wasn't really yours. What happens? In most urban centres, the offended driver will honk his or her horn angrily at you, or open the window and give you that nearly universal one-fingered gesture of anger and contempt. Because nobody likes to be the recipient of such abuse, you might be tempted to honk back, thereby escalating the anger and aggression. Such escalation might be avoided, though, if in addition to the horn (which throughout the world is most often used as an instrument of aggression), every car were equipped with an apology signal—perhaps at the push of a button, a little flag would pop up, announcing, "Oops! Sorry!" In the foregoing scenario, had you pushed such a button as soon as you became aware of your transgression, doing so might well have defused the cycle of anger and retaliation that is all too frequently a part of the driving experience. One of our Eastern European readers wrote to tell us that in Poland and Hungary, people apologize by using their emergency flashing lights. If and when techniques such as these become widely used, road rage may become a thing of the past.

The Modelling of Nonaggressive Behaviour We've seen that children will be more aggressive—toward dolls as well as other children—if they witness others behaving aggressively in similar situations. What if we reverse things and expose children to nonaggressive models—to people who, when provoked, express themselves in a restrained, rational, pleasant manner? This has been tested in several experiments and found to work (Baron, 1972; Donnerstein & Donnerstein, 1976; Vidyasagar &

Mahatma Gandhi was effective in bringing about the independence of India from Britain, using and modelling nonviolent resistance. Being nonviolent in the face of violence is difficult but effective.

Mishra, 1993). In these experiments, children first witnessed the behaviour of youngsters who behaved nonaggressively when provoked. When the children were subsequently placed in a situation in which they themselves were provoked, they showed a much lower frequency of aggressive responses than did children who were not exposed to the nonaggressive models.

Building Empathy Let's look at horn honking again. Picture the following scene: A long line of cars is stopped at a traffic light at a busy intersection; the light turns green; the lead car hesitates for 10 seconds. What happens? Almost inevitably, there will be an eruption of honking horns. In a controlled experiment, Robert Baron (1976) found that when the lead car failed to move after the light turned green, almost 90 percent of the drivers of the second car honked their horn in a relentless, aggressive manner. As part of the same experiment, a pedestrian crossed the street between the first and second cars while the light was still red and was out of the intersection by the time the light turned green. As you might imagine, this did not have an effect on the behaviour of the drivers of the next car in line—almost 90 percent honked their horn when the light turned green. In another condition the pedestrian was on crutches but managed to hobble across the street before the light turned green. Interestingly, in this condition the percentage of drivers who honked their horn dropped to 57 percent. Why? Apparently, seeing a person on crutches evoked feelings of empathy, which as you will recall from Chapter 10, is the ability to put oneself in the shoes of another person and experience some of the same feelings that person is experiencing. In this instance, once evoked, the feeling of empathy infused the consciousness of the potential horn honkers and decreased their urge to be aggressive.

> *Man must evolve for all human conflict a method which rejects revenge, aggression, and retaliation.*
>
> —Martin Luther King, Jr., *Nobel Peace Prize acceptance speech, 1964*

In a similar vein, Takaku (2006) performed a clever experiment in which he tested the hypothesis that road rage could be decreased if drivers were made aware of the fact that they are capable of the same "reckless" mistakes as the person they were enraged at. The researcher set up a driving simulation in which the participants first made the mistake of cutting someone off prior to being cut off by another driver. Participants who had made a mistake earlier were more forgiving of the driver who cut them off. Thus, becoming aware of our own fallibility creates greater empathy for other drivers, thereby reducing the possibility of road rage.

CONNECTIONS 

Teaching Empathy in School

"What would the world look like to you if you were as small as a cat?" "What birthday presents would make each member of your family happiest?" These questions form the basis of exercises designed by Norma Feshbach, who has pioneered the teaching of empathy in elementary schools. Thinking hard about the answers to such questions expands children's ability to put themselves in another's situation. This empathy-building program also involves having children listen to stories and then retell them from the point of view of each character. The children are then videotaped, playing the role of the different characters. Later, they view the tapes and analyze how people feel and look when they express different feelings.

Not only do children learn empathy, but this program also has several other positive effects. At the end of the program, children show higher self-esteem, greater generosity, more positive attitudes, and less aggressiveness compared with children who have not participated in it (Feshbach, 1989, 1997; Feshbach & Cohen, 1988).

At first glance, such a program may seem unrelated to academics. Yet, role playing and close analysis of stories is just what students do when putting on a play or analyzing a piece of literature. In reminiscing about his childhood, the Nobel Prize–winning physicist

Children who are taught to put themselves in others' shoes often have higher self-esteem, are more generous, and are less aggressive than children who lack empathy skills.

Richard Feynman reported that his father challenged his intellect by asking him to pretend he was a tiny creature who dwelled in their living room carpet. To deal with that challenge, Feynman needed, in effect, to crawl into the skin and persona of that creature and get a feel for what his life would be like in those circumstances. Such questions also encourage the kind of cognitive flexibility taught in corporate creativity programs. Thus, it should not surprise us that Norma Feshbach (1989, 1997) reports that students who have learned to develop greater empathic ability also tend to have higher academic achievement.

The important role of empathy is underscored in a series of studies conducted by Wohl and McGrath (2007) at Carleton University. This research focused on various kinds of interpersonal transgressions (e.g., your friend offers to drop off a job application for you but fails to do so, and as a result, you lose out on a great job). Participants in the close condition were made to focus on how recently the event occurred. Participants in the distant condition were induced to put the event "behind them" (by emphasizing that the event took place in the past). Those in the distant condition—who put the event behind them—reported more empathy for the aggressor than those in the close condition. And, importantly, the greater the empathy experienced, the lower the desire to seek revenge for the transgression.

Clearly, empathy is an important human phenomenon. As Feshbach (1989, 1997) observed, most people find it difficult to inflict pain on another human being unless they can find some way to dehumanize their victim. As we mentioned in Chapter 6, when Canadian soldiers were on a peacekeeping mission to Somalia, they referred to Somali people as "gimmes," "smufties," or "nignogs." We see this as a dehumanizing rationalization for acts of cruelty, such as the torture and killing of Shidane Arone; it's easier to commit violent acts against a "gimme" or a "nignog" than against a fellow human being. This kind of rationalization not only makes it possible for us to aggress against another person, but also guarantees we will *continue* to aggress against him or her. Once we succeed in convincing ourselves that our enemy is not really a human being at all but just a "nignog," it lowers our inhibitions for committing all kinds of atrocities.

Understanding the process of dehumanization is the first step toward reversing it. Specifically, if it is true that most individuals must dehumanize their victims in order to commit an extreme act of aggression, then by building empathy among people, aggressive acts should become more difficult to commit. The research data lend strong support to this contention. In one study, students who had been trained to empathize—that is, to take the perspective of the other person—behaved less aggressively toward that person than students who had not received the training (Richardson, Hammock, Smith, & Gardner, 1994). In research along the same lines, Japanese students were told to shock another student as part of a learning experiment (Ohbuchi & Baba, 1988; Ohbuchi, Ohno, & Mukai, 1993). In one condition, the "victims" first disclosed something personal about themselves; in the other condition, they were not given this opportunity. Participants administered less severe shocks to the victim who had revealed personal information. Thus, there is reason to be hopeful that people's tendencies toward aggression can be reduced.

HOW WOULD YOU USE THIS?

Imagine that you have a younger brother who is in high school. In a conversation with your parents, you learn that he seems to be having a problem with anger management. He has been getting into fistfights with some of his classmates and has even beaten up smaller boys. Your father has recommended that he try out for the high school football team as a way of "burning off" some of his excess aggressive energy. Your mother is not sure that this is a good idea. They say to you, "You're taking a course in psychology, what would you recommend?"

What questions would you ask them about your brother's hobbies and activities? Based on what you learn, what would you recommend?

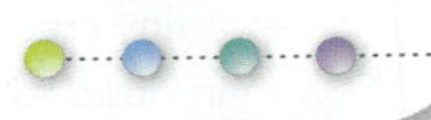

Summary

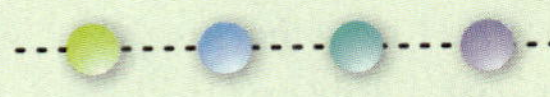

- **What Is Aggression?** Aggression is intentional behaviour aimed at doing harm or causing pain to another person. Hostile aggression is defined as having as one's goal the harming of another; instrumental aggression uses inflicting harm as a means to some other end.
  - **Is Aggression Inborn or Learned?** Over the centuries philosophers and psychologists have argued about whether or not humans are aggressive by nature. Some argued that it is in human nature to be aggressive, whereas others argued that humans are fundamentally malleable and thus the qualities of a society determine how aggressive its members are.
  - **Is Aggression Instinctual? Situational? Optional?** Evolutionary psychologists argue that aggression is inherited because of its survival value—that is, it increased the individual's chances of reproducing. Observations of other species suggest that animals are naturally aggressive; however, there is substantial variation in the degree of aggressiveness. Social psychologists argue that although aggressive behaviour may be hard-wired into humans, it is influenced by situational and cultural factors and is infinitely modifiable.
  - **Aggression and Culture** The levels of aggression of individuals living in different cultures vary greatly. It is also the case that within a given society, the degree of aggressiveness can change across time because of changes in the situation faced by the culture. The key point here is that multiple factors shape whether or not a culture tends to nurture aggressive behaviour.
- **Neural and Chemical Influences on Aggression** The area in the brain called the amygdala is thought to control aggression. Evidence suggests that the chemical serotonin serves to inhibit aggressive behaviour and that testosterone is positively correlated with aggressive behaviour.
  - **Gender and Aggression** Men are much more likely than women to behave aggressively in provocative situations. Men are also more likely to interpret a given situation as provocative; however, gender differences are reduced when women are actually provoked. Crime statistics show that males commit violent crimes at much higher rates than females. Women report more aggression toward their dating or marital partner than do men. However, men's aggression tends to be more severe, inflicts more physical injury, and does more emotional damage than women's aggression.
  - **Alcohol and Aggression** Alcohol can increase aggressive behaviour because it serves as a disinhibitor—it reduces one's social inhibitions. People report behaving more aggressively when intoxicated, and laboratory studies confirm this.
  - **Pain, Discomfort, and Aggression** When people experience pain they are far more likely to act aggressively. Discomfort, such as heat and humidity, increases the likelihood of hostile and violent behaviour.

- **Situational Causes of Aggression** Many social situations lead to aggression.
  - **Frustration as a Cause of Aggression** Frustration-aggression theory states that frustration can increase the probability of an aggressive response. Frustration is more likely to produce aggression if one is thwarted on the way to a goal in a manner that is either illegitimate or unexpected. Relative deprivation—the feeling that you have less than what you deserve or less than people similar to you have—can lead to aggressive behaviour.
  - **Direct Provocation and Reciprocation** Individuals frequently aggress when provoked. They also tend to reciprocate the aggressive behaviour of others. Aggression is reduced if there are mitigating circumstances.
  - **Social Exclusion** Correlational and laboratory studies show that when people experience social exclusion they are likely to respond with aggression.
  - **Aggressive Objects as Aggressive Cues** Research suggests that the mere presence of a violent object in a situation increases the degree of aggressive behaviour. In a classic study, participants angered in the presence of a gun administered more intense electric shock to their "victim" than those angered in the presence of a nonaggressive object such as a badminton racket.
  - **Imitation and Aggression** Social learning theory holds that we learn social behaviour (e.g., aggression) by observing others and imitating them. People, especially children, learn to behave aggressively by observing aggressive behaviour in adults and peers.
  - **The Effects of Violence in the Media** Most children are exposed to a great deal of violence through watching television and movies and playing violent video games. Long-term studies show that the more violence on television observed by children, the greater the amount of violence they exhibit as teenagers and young adults. Exposure to violent media has also been shown to increase violent behaviour in adults.
  - **Violent Pornography and Violence against Women** Exposure to violent pornography increases acceptance of violence toward women.
- **How to Reduce Aggression**
  - **Does Punishing Aggression Reduce Aggressive Behaviour?** If the punishment is itself aggressive, it actually models aggressive behaviour to children and may engender greater aggression. For punishment to serve as a deterrent to crime it must be both prompt and certain. These ideal conditions are rarely met in real life.
  - **Catharsis and Aggression** The theory of catharsis would predict that venting one's anger or watching others behave aggressively would serve to make one less likely to engage in subsequent acts of aggression. Research shows the contrary: Acting aggressively or observing aggressive events (such as a violent hockey game) actually increases the likelihood of future aggressive behaviour. At a national level, violent acts against another nation lead to increasingly negative attitudes toward that nation and greater willingness to inflict further violence because it triggers the tendency to justify that action. When a nation is at war, even one that is far away, its people are more likely to commit aggressive acts against one another.
  - **What Are We Supposed to Do with Our Anger?** Aggression can be reduced in a number of constructive ways. These include making clear and constructive statements about the reasons for anger and training people in communication skills. Anger and aggression also can be diffused through apologizing, modelling nonaggressive behaviour, and building people's empathy toward others. Building empathy is particularly useful as a means of thwarting the human tendency to dehumanize one's victim.

12 Prejudice

Causes and Cures

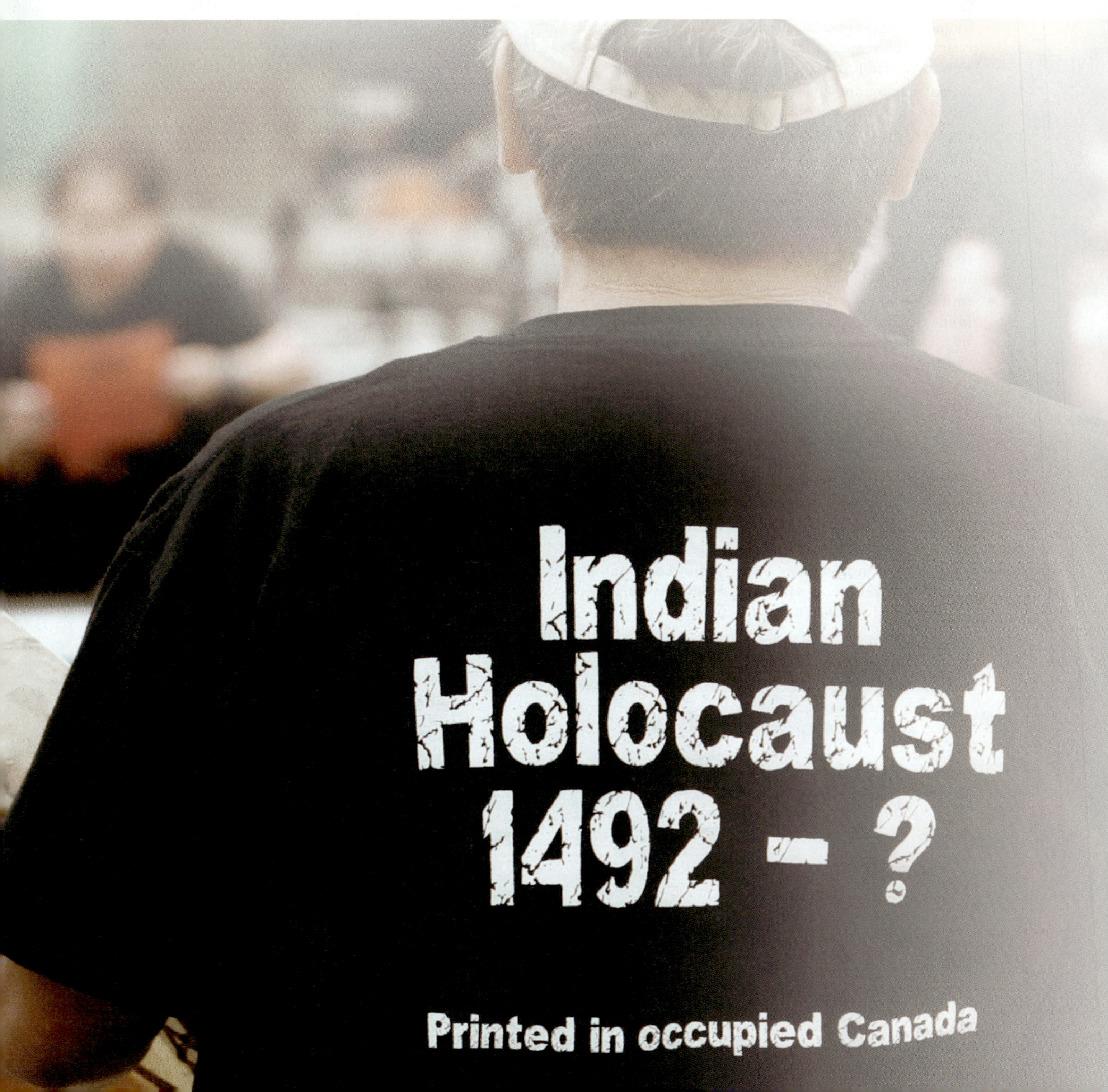

MEET MARY YOUNG, DIRECTOR OF THE ABORIGINAL Student Services Centre at the University of Winnipeg. Mary grew up as a member of Bloodvein First Nation, an Anishinabe (Ojibway) community in northern Manitoba. When she was growing up, Mary understood that she was a Treaty Indian according to the federal Indian Act, but being Indian was not part of her identity. She thought of herself as Anishinabe and she was comfortable with that identity. At the age of 14, she moved to Winnipeg with the dream of being the first person from Bloodvein to graduate from high school. With that move came the startling discovery that the other students thought of her as Indian. Moreover, *Indian* was not a neutral term—it was laden with negative connotations. Mary was forced to adopt a new identity, and she learned quickly that this new identity meant she was less acceptable, less deserving, and less worthy than the white students attending her high school.

In reflecting on these experiences, Mary comments, "When I left home at the age of fourteen . . . my goal was to finish high school. I never expected that I would have difficulty with my identity, my cultural background, nor did I think I was going to allow myself to feel ashamed of my family, including my own shame of being an 'Indian.'" To express her feelings about this life-shattering experience, Mary wrote the following poem:

AFRAID

I heard
"The Only Good Indian
Is a Dead Indian"
I never heard that on
The reserve
I was fine before I
Came to the city
What is wrong with me
Now?

I have no answer
All I know is that
I am afraid of making
A mistake
I am afraid if I succeed
It will not make any
Difference.

There was a time
Laughing at myself
Came easily
Now all I feel is
Shame
I am afraid to open
My mouth
I know that I am not dead
Does this mean
I am no good?
I must be no good
Because I feel ugly
I hate being Indian
Why was I born on the
Reserve anyway?

There is nothing I can do
To change that
I can't change who I am
I'm afraid I am
Not prepared to die
Just yet
So I have to try
Harder
"To Be a Good Indian"

OUTLINE

Mary Young felt the impact of racism in her life when she moved from her First Nations community to Winnipeg to attend high school.

Of all the social behaviours we discuss in this book, prejudice is perhaps the most widespread and certainly among the most dangerous. Prejudice touches nearly everyone's life. We are all victims or potential victims of stereotyping and discrimination, for no other reason than our membership in an identifiable group—whether it be related to ethnicity, religion, gender, national origin, sexual preference, obesity, skin colour, language, age, or disability. However, clearly some people are more victimized than others. People who are members of visible minorities report experiencing the greatest prejudice and discrimination, and if they are of a minority status in more than one way, they are especially likely to be discriminated against. Researchers at Wilfrid Laurier University (Foster, 2005) and at York University (Patterson, Cameron, & Lalonde, 1996) have found, for example, that women of colour feel that both gender and racial stereotypes are applied to them. Similarly, black-skinned immigrants to Canada experience more prejudice and discrimination than do white-skinned immigrants, and this experience is compounded for a black person who is Muslim or is female (Dion, 2001; Dion & Dion, 2001). Granted, many manifestations of prejudice are less frequent and less flagrant than they used to be. For example, a recent Environics poll showed that 75 percent of Canadians believe that Muslims make a positive contribution to Canada. In fact, in a recent comparison of 23 Western nations, Canadians showed the least prejudice toward Muslims (Borooah & Mangan, 2007). However, as the story of Mary Young illustrates, prejudice continues to exact a heavy toll on its targets. In this chapter, we will examine prejudice as a social psychological phenomenon. We will focus on two fundamental questions: What causes prejudice? And how can prejudice be reduced?

Prejudice: The Ubiquitous Social Phenomenon

The story of Mary Young illustrates that members of minority groups are often targets of prejudice at the hands of the dominant majority. Needless to say, this aspect of prejudice is extremely powerful and poignant. However, the truth is that prejudice is a two-way street; it flows from a minority group to the majority group, as well as from the majority to a minority. Any group can be a target of stereotyping and prejudice. However, stereotypes are most likely to be held for social groups (e.g., racial and ethnic groups) rather than other groups such as jury members or the cast of a play, as shown by research conducted at the University of Victoria (Spencer-Rodgers, Hamilton, & Sherman, 2007). Let us take one of the most superordinate social groups to which you belong—your nationality. Canadians are typically stereotyped as the nice, dull, boring "country cousins" of their more adventurous, exciting counterparts to the south. American television host Tucker Carlson put it this way: "Canada is a sweet country. It is like your retarded cousin . . .. You know he's nice but you don't take him seriously" (Gorham, 2005, p. A3). (Interestingly, research shows that Canadians and Americans actually have very similar personalities; Terracciano et al., 2005.) Even worse, some nations view Canada as hypocritical for calling other countries to task on unfair treatment of minority groups while allowing Aboriginal peoples in Canada to live in poverty.

Your nationality is only one aspect of your identity that can cause you to be labelled and discriminated against. Racial and ethnic identity is a major focal point for prejudiced attitudes. Canada views itself as a country that embraces multiculturalism—a country that appreciates the diversity that different racial and ethnic groups contribute to its social fabric. However, all you have to do is ask a sample of Canadians about their attitudes toward Aboriginals, Pakistanis, East Asians, and Sikhs and you quickly become aware that diversity is not always celebrated or even tolerated (Esses & Gardner, 1996; Pruegger & Rogers, 1993). In fact, people who belong to such groups are common targets of prejudice. (The accompanying Try It! exercise raises some interesting issues about the merits of multiculturalism.) Even particular subgroups of white

TRY IT! Multiculturalism: Is It Working?

In the United States, members of different nationalities or ethnic groups are expected to assimilate with the majority. In contrast, in Canada, cultural groups are encouraged to maintain their values and customs while participating in Canadian society. The American image is a "melting pot"; the Canadian image is a "cultural mosaic." Canada formally passed the Multiculturalism Act in 1987. Slogans such as "celebrating differences" reflect our country's multicultural orientation. Is this a good idea? Queen's University researcher John Berry and colleagues have found that immigrant youth in this country fare best when they retain a sense of their own cultural identity as well as develop an identity as Canadians (Berry, Phinney, Sam, & Vedder, 2006; Sabatier & Berry, 2008). Thus, multiculturalism appears to be beneficial for people who come to this country. But does multiculturalism foster positive relationships between majority and minority group members? Research conducted in the Netherlands, a country that also promotes multiculturalism, suggests that such policies can be beneficial. In a series of studies, it was found that members of the majority group (Dutch people) and a minority group (Turkish people living in the Netherlands) who favoured multiculturalism evaluated the minority group (Turks) more positively than those who advocated assimilation (Verkuyten, 2005). (Proponents of multiculturalism actually held the same stereotypes of these groups as did proponents of assimilation.)

Based on this research, we might conclude that promoting multiculturalism is an effective way to reduce prejudice. But before plunging headlong into a multiculturalism promotion campaign, it might be wise to consider the results of a recent program of research conducted at the University of Manitoba (Vorauer & Sasaki, 2010; Vorauer, Gagnon, & Sasaki, 2009). In this research, students who were high and low in prejudice were exposed to information on the merits of multiculturalism (e.g., "Each ethnic group within Canada can contribute in its own unique way"). Other students did not receive pro-multiculturalism information. Later, all participants sent and received written messages from an Aboriginal Canadian student whom they expected to meet (none of the participants was Aboriginal). Low-prejudice students who had contemplated the benefits of multiculturalism communicated more warmth (e.g., liking, personal self-disclosure) in these messages than did low-prejudice students who did not receive this message.

However, promoting multiculturalism seemed to backfire for the high-prejudice participants—they actually communicated less warmth to the Aboriginal student compared to high-prejudice participants who did not receive this message. Interestingly, Vorauer and Sasaki (2010) found that participants exposed to the merits of multiculturalism actually felt that there were greater differences between themselves and Canadians who are of a different colour than did participants in the control condition.

However, as you may recall from Chapter 9, similarity is one of the best predictors of attraction and liking. Indeed, a study of English Canadians, French Canadians, Jews, and people from India, Algeria, and Greece living in Montreal found that the more similar the respondents perceived a group to be to their own group, the greater their willingness to associate with members of that group (Osbeck, Moghaddam, & Perreault, 1997). This result suggests that it might be more effective to promote similarities between groups than to highlight differences. What are we to make of this? If we want to reduce prejudice, should we promote multiculturalism or not?

The answer is "It depends." More specifically, it depends on how prejudiced people are. Vorauer and Sasaki (2010) suggest that low-prejudice people may find the prospect of interacting with others who are different to be stimulating and exciting (which is why pro-multiculturalism arguments are effective), whereas high-prejudice people may find differences threatening.

This research prompts some intriguing questions (which you may want to discuss with a friend):

1. What are the implications of the research findings for Canada's policy of multiculturalism?
2. Is it actually possible to "celebrate differences"?
3. Are there ways in which basic similarities between groups could be highlighted, while allowing for an appreciation of differences? Might you go about this differently, depending on whether you are dealing with someone who is prejudiced?

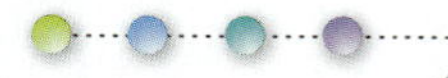

Canadians are subjected to prejudice, as witnessed by the long-standing popularity of Newfie jokes, the tensions between anglophones and francophones in Quebec, and "centre of the universe" comments about Torontonians.

Other aspects of your identity also leave you vulnerable to prejudice: your gender, your sexual orientation, your religion, your weight, and even your age. For example, research conducted at several Canadian universities shows that prejudice toward gays and lesbians continues (Clow & Olson, 2010; Morrison, Morrison, & Franklin, 2009). In fact, Canadians are more prejudiced toward homosexuals than toward Muslims (Borooah & Mangan, 2007). Prejudice and discrimination against those who are overweight or obese is on the rise in many countries (Crandall D'Anello, Sakalli, Lazarus, & Wieczorkowska, 2001), including Canada (Brochu & Esses, 2009; Brochu & Morrison, 2007; Clarke & Lawson, 2009). Regarding age, researchers at Bishop's University found that people recommended harsher punishments for murder if the perpetrator was a 40-year-old man rather than a 20- or 60-year-old man (Bergeron & McKelvie, 2004; see Pozzulo, Dempsey, Maeder, & Allen, 2010, for similar findings).

Even the labels used to refer to people can invoke prejudice (Donakowski & Esses, 1996). In a series of studies on the "Ms. stereotype," University of Toronto researchers found that women who preferred the title *Ms.* were rated more negatively (i.e., perceived as less likeable) than women who preferred a traditional form of address (i.e., *Miss* or *Mrs.*; Dion, 1987, 1999; Dion & Schuller, 1991). More than 20 years later, research conducted at the University of Winnipeg showed that women who use *Ms.* are still rated as more competitive, more independent, and less warm and nurturing than those who use the title *Miss* or *Mrs.* (Malcolmson & Sinclair, 2007).

If a child of colour believes that white dolls are more desirable than black dolls, what stereotypes has she internalized?

Finally, your profession or your hobbies can also lead to you being stereotyped. We are all familiar with the "dumb jock" and "computer nerd" stereotypes. Some people have negative attitudes about blue-collar workers; others stereotype people in high-status occupations, such as lawyers, as witnessed by the popularity of lawyer jokes (Olson, Maio, & Hobden, 1999). The point is that none of us emerges completely unscathed from the effects of prejudice; it is a problem of and for all humankind.

In addition to being widespread, prejudice is dangerous. Simple dislike of a group can be relentless and can lead to extreme hatred, to thinking of its members as less than human, and to behaviour such as torture, murder, and genocide. But even when murder or genocide is not the culmination of prejudiced beliefs, the targets of prejudice will suffer in less dramatic ways. In a classic experiment conducted in the late 1940s, social psychologists Kenneth Clark and Mamie Clark (1947) demonstrated that African-American children—some of them only three years old—were already convinced that it was not particularly desirable to be black. In this experiment, the children were offered a choice between playing with a white doll or a black doll. The great majority of them rejected the black doll, feeling that the white doll was prettier and generally superior.

You may be thinking, "But that was more than 70 years ago, and it took place in the United States. Surely these findings are no longer relevant, and surely they wouldn't apply to Canada!" As it turns out, all you have to do is substitute "Aboriginal Canadian" for "African-American." Corenblum and Annis (1993; Corenblum, Annis, & Young, 1996) presented white and Native children attending schools in Brandon,

Manitoba, with drawings of white and Native boys and girls. When asked which child they would like to play with, Native children were slightly more likely to choose a white child than a Native child. (White children overwhelmingly chose a white child.) Native children also attributed more positive qualities (e.g., friendliness) to a white child than to a Native child. Conversely, they attributed more negative qualities to a Native child (e.g., is bad, gets into fights) than to a white child.

A little black girl yearns for the blue eyes of a little white girl, and the horror at the heart of her yearning is exceeded only by the evil of fulfillment.

—Toni Morrison, *The Bluest Eye*, *1970*

We should note that significant changes have taken place. For example, African-American children have gradually become more content with black dolls than they were in 1947 (Gopaul-McNicol, 1987; Porter, 1971; Porter & Washington, 1979, 1989). As we have already mentioned, there is evidence that people are less prejudiced toward some stigmatized groups than they used to be. Recent research conducted with Canadian university students shows that interventions targeted at reducing prejudice toward homosexuals tend to be effective (Hodson, Choma, & Costello, 2009; Rye & Meaney, 2009). Thus, attitudes are changing, and can be changed, although, as shall be seen, this is no easy feat.

Measurement of Prejudice

Watch on **mypsychlab**
Prejudice

As the norm swings toward tolerance for out-groups, many people have become more careful to outwardly act unprejudiced even if they inwardly maintain their prejudiced views. This phenomenon is known as *modern prejudice* (Dovidio & Gaertner, 1996; Gaertner & Dovidio, 1986; McConahay, 1986). In other words, people have learned to hide their prejudice to avoid being labelled *racist* or *sexist*, but when the situation is "safe," their prejudice will be revealed. For example, Evans, Garcia, Garcia, and Baron (2003) found that participants rated various ethnic groups much more positively when an experimenter was in the room than they did when alone in the room or completing the same scale over the Internet. In fact, when an experimenter was present, participants rated various out-groups even more positively than their own group—presumably to show just how unprejudiced they were. In another study, Allen Hart and Marian Morry (1997) showed white students a videotape of a black person and a white person making speeches. When the performance was poor, participants attributed more negative characteristics to the black speaker than to the white speaker. When the speakers performed well, however, participants bent over backward to show that they were not prejudiced and rated the black speaker even more positively than the white speaker.

We all decry prejudice, yet all are prejudiced.

—Herbert Spencer, *biologist and philosopher, 1873*

Given the properties of modern prejudice, social psychologists conducting research on prejudice face a rather formidable challenge. The kinds of attitudes they are most interested in studying are the kinds of attitudes people may be least willing to admit. Thus, it has been necessary to develop subtle or unobtrusive measures. As mentioned in Chapter 6, researchers are now beginning to measure attitudes by using the Implicit Association Test (IAT). The IAT is particularly well-suited to assess the kinds of attitudes that people may not be willing to report on a questionnaire—namely, prejudiced attitudes—but that can be detected by using more subtle measures. In the IAT, the task for participants is to respond to words or pictures presented on a computer screen, allowing the researcher to see whether, for example, a participant responds more quickly to unpleasant words when a black face has been shown on the computer than when a white face is shown. (To try out the Implicit Association Test, see https://implicit.harvard.edu/implicit.)

Recently, researchers at the University of Western Ontario have developed methodology along the same lines that involves presenting images (e.g., black faces and white faces) on a computer screen for a very brief duration. The task for participants is to rate the pleasantness of a neutral stimulus (e.g., a Chinese character) that appears on the next screen. People who are prejudiced rate the neutral stimulus as less pleasant when it is preceded by a black face than a white face (Gawronski, Peters, Brochu, & Strack, 2008).

Clow and Olson (2010), also at the University of Western Ontario, have developed another promising avenue for assessing prejudice in a subtle manner. In this research, participants were told that they were in a study of memory associations. Homosexual (e.g., *gay*) and heterosexual (e.g., *straight*) words were displayed on a computer screen. Participants could either pull the word toward them with the mouse (making the words larger) or push them away (making them shrink and disappear). Those who were high in prejudice toward homosexuals were more likely to push away the homosexual words than were those who were low prejudice, and they did so more quickly (Clow & Olson, 2010). What is common to these kinds of techniques is that people are required to respond extremely quickly; because there isn't time to control their responses, people's "true" attitudes come through.

There has also been an effort to construct questionnaires in a way that assesses prejudice more unobtrusively. For example, the Modern Racism Scale is a subtle, indirect measure of racial prejudice (McConahay, 1986). It turns out that people who are reluctant to express blatant prejudice nevertheless are quite willing to agree with statements such as "Minorities are getting too demanding in their push for special rights." Research conducted in Canada, the United States, and Britain has shown that those who score high on modern prejudice scales are more likely to be prejudiced against black people than those who score low (Kawakami, Dion, & Dovidio, 1998; Lepore & Brown, 1997; Tougas, Desruisseaux, Desrochers, St-Pierre, Perrino, & De la Sablonnière, 2004; Wittenbrink, Judd, & Park, 1997).

At the University of Ottawa, Francine Tougas and her colleagues have developed the Neosexism Scale to assess sexist attitudes in a more subtle manner (Tougas, Brown, Beaton, & Joly, 1995). Parallel to the issue of racism, these researchers reasoned that people who are opposed to equality for women may be reluctant to say so directly but might find it acceptable to express disagreement with social policies aimed at increasing the status of women. Accordingly, the Neosexism Scale asks respondents to indicate how much they agree with statements such as "Women will make more progress by being patient and not pushing too hard for change." Women and men who score high in this scale tend to show a pro-male bias when evaluating women's and men's competence (e.g., believing that male managers are more competent in general than female managers). The researchers also found that male managers who score high on this scale are less willing to support women in the workplace than managers who score low. In addition, secretaries who score high are more opposed to affirmative action programs for women than those who score low (Beaton, Tougas, & Joly, 1996; Tougas, Brown, Beaton, & St-Pierre, 1999). A study conducted with students at the University of Windsor found that neosexism was also associated with negative attitudes toward the feminist movement and toward gays and lesbians (Campbell, Schellenberg, & Senn, 1997).

Finally, because it has become less socially acceptable to openly express prejudice toward gays and lesbians, researchers at the University of Saskatchewan have recently developed a more subtle measure called the Modern Homonegativity Scale (Morrison, Morrison, & Franklin, 2009). Students at Canadian and American universities are reluctant to agree with statements such as "Male homosexuality is a perversion," which appear on traditional scales that measure prejudice toward gay men and lesbians in a direct way. However, those who are prejudiced toward these groups are willing to agree with statements such as "If gay men want to be treated like everyone else, they then need to stop making such a fuss about their sexuality/culture." It may interest you to know that the researchers found that American university students expressed more negative attitudes toward gays and lesbians than did Canadian students.

We will encounter both subtle and not-so-subtle ways of assessing prejudice in this chapter (see also Olson, 2009, for a review of measures of prejudice). As will be seen, in areas in which people are willing to admit prejudice, social psychologists continue to use direct measures (e.g., attitude questionnaires). However, indirect measures such as those discussed above are becoming increasingly common.

Prejudice, Stereotyping, and Discrimination Defined

Connect to MyPsychLab
To access the Critical Thinking question on institutional racism, go to MyPsychLab

Prejudice is an attitude. As we discussed in Chapter 6, attitudes are made up of three components: an affective or emotional component, representing the type of emotion linked with the attitude (e.g., anger, warmth); a cognitive component, involving the beliefs or thoughts (cognition) that make up the attitude; and a behavioural component, relating to one's actions. People don't simply hold attitudes; they usually act on them as well.

Prejudice: The Affective Component

Simulate on **mypsychlab**
Prejudice and Discrimination

Prejudice refers to a general attitude and its affective (emotional) component. Technically, prejudice can involve either positive or negative affect (Crandall & Schaller, 2005; Wright & Taylor, 2003). For example, you could be prejudiced against or in favour of Torontonians. In one case, your emotional reaction is negative: When a person is introduced to you as "Michael from Toronto," you will expect him to act in particular ways that you associate with "those snobbish Torontonians." Conversely, if your emotional reaction is positive, you will be delighted to meet another one of those "sophisticated, cosmopolitan Torontonians." While prejudice can involve either positive or negative affect, social psychologists—and people in general—use the word *prejudice* primarily when referring to negative attitudes about others. Consistent with general usage, we will define **prejudice** as a hostile or negative attitude toward people in a distinguishable group, based *solely* on their membership in that group. For example, when we say that an individual is prejudiced against Aboriginal peoples, we mean that he or she feels hostility or disliking toward Aboriginal peoples as a whole.

Prejudice
A hostile or negative attitude toward people in a distinguishable group, based *solely* on their membership in that group

Stereotypes: The Cognitive Component

Stereotype
A generalization about a group of people in which identical characteristics are assigned to virtually all members of the group, regardless of actual variation among the members

Close your eyes for a moment and imagine the appearance and characteristics of the following people: a high school cheerleader, a Sikh taxi driver, a Jewish doctor, a black musician. Our guess is that this task was not difficult. We all walk around with images of various "types" of people in our heads. The distinguished journalist Walter Lippmann (1922), who was the first to introduce the term *stereotype*, described the distinction between the world out there and stereotypes, "the little pictures we carry around inside our heads." Within a given culture, these pictures tend to be remarkably similar. For example, we would be surprised if your image of the cheerleader was anything but a person who is bouncy, full of pep, pretty, nonintellectual, and (of course!) female. We would also be surprised if the Jewish doctor or the Sikh taxi driver in your head were female—or if the black musician was playing classical music.

It goes without saying that there are male cheerleaders, female doctors and taxi drivers, and black classical musicians. Deep down, we know that taxi drivers come in every size, shape, race, and gender. But we tend to categorize according to what we regard as normative within a culture. Stereotyping, however, goes a step beyond simple categorization. A **stereotype** is a generalization about a group of people in which identical characteristics are assigned to virtually all members of the group, regardless of actual variation among the members. Once formed, stereotypes are resistant to change on the basis of new information.

It is important to point out that stereotyping does not necessarily lead to negative or harmful behaviours. Often stereotyping is merely a way to simplify how we look at the world—and we all do it to some extent. Gordon Allport (1954), for example, described stereotyping as "the law of least effort." According to Allport, the world is just too complicated for us to have a highly differentiated attitude about everything. Instead, we maximize our cognitive time and energy by developing elegant, accurate attitudes about some topics, while

Is this roughly the stereotypical image that came to mind when you were asked to imagine a Sikh taxi driver?

Stereotype Content: Where Does It Come From?

Have you ever wondered where stereotypes come from? Who decides whether positive or negative characteristics apply to a given group? And who decides which particular positive or negative characteristics apply? These questions have been addressed in a program of research conducted at the University of British Columbia by Mark Schaller and colleagues (Schaller & Conway, 1999, 2001, 2005; Schaller, Conway, & Tanchuk, 2002; Schaller & O'Brien, 1992). According to these researchers, the traits or characteristics of a group that other people are most likely to talk about are the traits that become part of the stereotype of that group. Moreover, the more these traits are talked about, the more likely it is that they will remain part of the group's stereotype over time. In short, the traits that have the highest communicability, or "gossip" value, will become part of the stereotype of a particular group. You may wish to test this hypothesis yourself or with a group of friends.

First, list the traits or characteristics you would be most likely to mention if you were talking about the following groups:

- White Canadians (more specifically, white Canadians living in Vancouver)
- Chinese
- East Indians
- First Nations peoples

Now, check whether any of the traits you (or your friends) mentioned are part of the following stereotypes of these groups, as identified by a multicultural group of students at the University of British Columbia (Schaller, Conway, & Tanchuk, 2002):

- White Canadians: athletic, individualistic, pleasure-loving, straightforward, sportsmanlike
- Chinese: ambitious, loyal to family ties, intelligent, efficient, conservative
- East Indians: very religious, tradition-loving, aggressive, loyal to family ties, physically dirty
- First Nations peoples: poor, physically dirty, lazy, tradition-loving, superstitious

Schaller and colleagues' research suggests that you and your friends would be most likely to list the traits that are part of the stereotype of that group. These researchers also found that positive traits are more likely to become part of the stereotype of the largest groups in a society (in Vancouver, white Canadians, followed by Chinese people), whereas negative traits are more likely to become part of the stereotype of smaller groups (First Nations people). To make matters even worse, negative traits are more likely than positive traits to persist over time. In other words, once a negative trait becomes part of a stereotype of a group, it is very difficult to shed. Schaller and colleagues conclude, "In a sense, traits are like viruses: Those that are more highly communicable are more likely to infect the stereotypic beliefs of a population and are less likely to be gotten rid of" (Schaller, Conway, & Tanchuk, 2002).

relying on simple, sketchy beliefs for others. (This should remind you of the discussion of schemas in Chapter 3.) Given our limited information-processing capacity, it is reasonable, on the one hand, for us to take shortcuts and adopt certain heuristics in our attempt to understand other people (Fiske, 1989b; Fiske & Depret, 1996; Taylor, 1981; Taylor & Falcone, 1982). On the other hand, if a stereotype blinds us to individual differences within a class of people, it is maladaptive and unfair, and can lead to discrimination. For one insight into where stereotypes come from, see the accompanying Try It! exercise.

cathy® by Cathy Guisewite

Consider, for a moment, the stereotype associated with your gender. Research conducted in Canada and in Belgium shows that even young children associate dolls and doll houses with girls, and trucks, cars, and tools with boys (Banse, Gawronski, Rebetez, Gutt, & Morton, 2010). In one study, children aged 5 to 11 years old played a computer game in which they pretended to be Santa giving toys such as dolls and trucks to other girls and boys. It turned out that when children were told that Sarah wanted a doll and Marc wanted a truck, they were much faster at "delivering" the toys than when they were told that Pierre wanted a doll and Isabelle wanted a truck (i.e., information that contradicted gender stereotypes). This study demonstrates how knowledge of stereotypes allows us to make quick, efficient judgments, thereby saving cognitive energy. It also shows how early on stereotypes are established. What are the implications? Considerable research has shown that children face ostracism and ridicule from their peers for behaving in counter-stereotypic ways. Boys, in particular, face negative social consequences for engaging in behaviours that are considered feminine.

Needless to say, the implications of gender stereotyping are evident in adulthood as well. In a recent study, students at several Ontario universities were given a list of job descriptions and asked a number of questions about each job, such as whether the typical jobholder would be male or female and what the salary should be for that job (Alksnis, Desmarais, & Curtis, 2008). There was a high degree of agreement on the gender associated with the various jobs. For example, 100 percent of the male participants indicated that a crystal/china clerk would be female, and 94 percent of them perceived an automotive magazine editor to be male; 100 percent of the female participants perceived a home economics teacher to be female. Research conducted at the University of Waterloo found that advertisements for jobs in male-dominated areas (e.g., plumber, electrician) contain more stereotypically masculine words (e.g., *competitive*, *dominate*) than advertisements for jobs in female-dominated areas (e.g., nurse, administrative assistant; see Figure 12.1). However, the presence of stereotypically feminine words (e.g., *support*, *understand*) did not differ for male- and female-dominated occupations. Similar to Alksnis and colleagues' results, participants perceived that there were more men in occupations which were advertised using masculine wording (Gaucher, Friesen, & Kay, 2011).

So, you may be thinking, what difference does word choice in job advertising make? It turns out that it matters a lot. One big difference has to do with salary. In Alksnis and colleagues' study (2008), participants assigned higher salaries to jobs that they considered to be "male" jobs than those they considered to be "female" jobs (average salary of $39,651 for male jobs versus $36,527 for female jobs). There is another very sobering consequence: Gaucher and colleagues (2011) found that when jobs were advertised using masculine wording, women were reluctant to apply—not because they felt they did not have the requisite skills for the job but because they felt that they would not belong in that work environment. The researchers conclude that wording of job ads in terms of gender stereotypes has the subversive effect of maintaining gender inequality in our society.

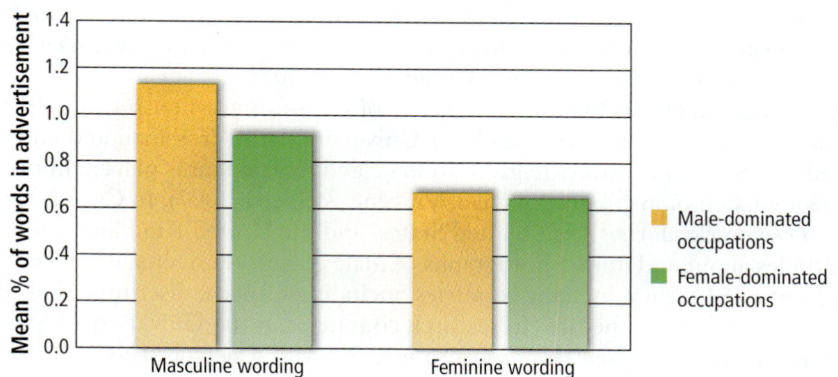

FIGURE 12.1

Mean percentage of gendered wording as a function of occupation area.

Job advertisements for male-dominated occupations contain more stereotypically masculine words than job advertisements for female-dominated occupations. However, the presence of stereotypically feminine words did not differ for male- and female-dominated occupations.

Gaucher, D., Friesen, J., and Kay, A. C. (2011, March 7). Evidence that Gendered Wording in Job Advertisements Exists and Sustains Gender Inequality. *Journal of Personality and Social Psychology*. Advance online publication. Copyright© 2011 by the American Psychological Association. Reprinted with Permission.

Discrimination: The Behavioural Component

Discrimination

Unjustified negative or harmful action toward a member of a group simply because of his or her membership in that group

This brings us to the final component of prejudice—the action component. Stereotypic beliefs often result in unfair treatment. We call this **discrimination**—unjustified negative or harmful action toward a member of a group simply because of his or her membership in that group. If you are a grade 4 math teacher and you have the stereotypic belief that girls are hopeless at math, you might spend less time in the classroom coaching a girl than you would a boy. If you are a police officer and you have the stereotypic belief that black people are more violent than white people, this might affect your behaviour toward a specific black man you are trying to arrest.

> *Prejudices are the props of civilization.*
>
> —André Gide, *1939*

Discrimination can affect every area of a person's life. Consider the very basic issue of where you live. There is considerable evidence that people who are members of disadvantaged groups have much more difficulty finding housing because of discrimination. Stewart Page (1999) examined discriminatory behaviour by landlords in various cities in Ontario and in Detroit, Michigan. In one study, a caller inquiring about accommodation that had been advertised in a local paper identified himself or herself as gay/lesbian ("I guess it's only fair to tell you that I'm a gay person [or lesbian]"), or did not mention his or her sexual orientation. Landlords were most likely to claim that the accommodation was unavailable when they believed the caller was gay or lesbian. In a subsequent study, Page (1999) found that landlords were five times more likely to say that the accommodation was unavailable when the caller mentioned that she or he had AIDS. More recently, Barata and Stewart (2010) had a female confederate call 181 landlords to ask if rental apartments advertised in Toronto were still available. If she mentioned that she was currently staying at a women's shelter, the landlord was nearly 10 times more likely to say that the accommodation was not available compared to a control condition in which the caller did not mention her current living situation.

It will not surprise you that there is also evidence of housing discrimination based on race or ethnicity. A recent report on homelessness in Winnipeg concluded that "racism, especially against Aboriginal people, is common when looking for housing" (Winnipeg Street Health Report, 2010, p. 13). The 170 Aboriginal respondents relayed experiences of being told over the telephone that an apartment was available, but when they showed up to see it, the landlord would say it was not available after all. One participant was told an apartment was not available when she went to see it, but when a white friend inquired about the same place, it was shown to her. Among those who managed to find housing, Aboriginal tenants were more likely than white tenants to experience discrimination in the form of unfair evictions and demands for sexual favours from landlords.

Discrimination also rears its ugly head in school settings. For example, Riley and Ungerleider (2008) presented Canadian teacher candidates with the academic records of elementary school students and asked them to recommend the placement each student should have the following year in high school (ranging from a remedial program to an advanced program). The same academic record received a lower placement recommendation when it contained information that the student was of Aboriginal (versus non-Aboriginal) ancestry. These effects are not limited to racial or ethnic bias. A study of high school teacher candidates in Ontario found that those who were homophobic expressed less commitment to, and less willingness to help, students who were non-heterosexual (Dowling, Rodger, & Cummings, 2007).

Discrimination affects many other aspects of life—not just housing, employment, and academic opportunities. At Lakehead University, Jane Crossman and colleagues analyzed the newspaper coverage given to male and female tennis players in the 2004 Wimbledon Championships (Crossman, Vincent, & Speed, 2007). In Canada (specifically in *The Globe and Mail*), the United States, and the United Kingdom, there were more articles about and more photographs of male players than female players.

As mentioned earlier, in many countries, including Canada, discrimination against overweight people is on the rise. In research conducted at the University of Saskatchewan, participants expressed less desire to interact with a person who was described as overweight than with someone who was described as average weight (Brochu & Morrison, 2007). In follow-up research conducted at the University of Western Ontario, it was found that people who were high in anti-fat prejudice were more likely to support a policy denying medically necessary surgeries to overweight people (Brochu & Esses, 2009).

Finally, recent research suggests that in Canadian courts, black defendants still receive harsher sentences than white defendants, despite the establishment of procedures that are intended to screen jury members for racial bias (Schuller, Kazoleas, & Kawakami, 2009). And although Aboriginals make up only 2 percent of the Canadian population, they represent 18 percent of inmates in jails. In the Prairie provinces, Aboriginals constitute 6 percent of the general population and a shocking 41 percent of the prison population (Jackiw, Arbuthnott, Pfeifer, Marcon, & Meissner, 2008).

In summary, discrimination is sometimes blatant and sometimes subtle; but it is undeniable that discrimination pervades virtually all aspects of life.

What Causes Prejudice?

As you might expect, there is no single answer to the question of what causes prejudice. However, social psychologists have made huge strides in understanding the kinds of factors that lead to prejudice. Some of these centre on the person—the way we process information, what we believe, and how we are feeling (e.g., our mood). Social psychologists have also examined the kinds of societal factors that are likely to lead to prejudice (e.g., social norms, conflict over resources). We begin with the former.

The Way We Think: Social Cognition

Our first explanation for what causes prejudice is that it is the inevitable by-product of the way we process and organize information; in other words, it is the dark side of human social cognition (see Chapter 3). Our tendency to categorize and group information together, to form schemas and to use these to interpret new or unusual information, to rely on potentially inaccurate heuristics (shortcuts in mental reasoning), and to depend on what are often faulty memory processes can lead us to form negative stereotypes and to apply them in a discriminatory way. Let's examine this dark side of social cognition more closely.

Social Categorization: Us versus Them The first step in prejudice is the creation of groups—putting some people into one group based on certain characteristics and others into another group based on their different characteristics. This kind of categorization is the underlying theme of human social cognition (Brewer & Brown, 1998; Rosch & Lloyd, 1978; Taylor, 1981). For example, we make sense of the physical world by grouping animals and plants into taxonomies based on their physical characteristics; similarly, we make sense of our social world by grouping people according to characteristics such as their gender, nationality, and ethnicity. When we encounter a person with certain characteristics (e.g., old, male), we rely on our perceptions of what people with similar characteristics have been like in the past to help us determine how to react to this person. Thus, social categorization is both useful and necessary; however, this simple cognitive process has profound implications because the process of classifying people into groups is rarely a neutral one.

Wearing our school colours is a way of demonstrating that we are a member of the in-group.

In-Group Bias
The tendency to evaluate in-group members more positively than out-group members

In-Group Bias It probably comes as no surprise that we evaluate in-group members more positively than out-group members. This is known as **in-group bias**. When researchers at Queen's University assessed the attitudes of more than 3000 Canadians toward 14 different ethnic groups, the results were clear—people assigned the most favourable ratings to their own ethnic group (Kalin & Berry, 1996). Similarly, a recent study found that French Canadians rated their group more positively than they rated North Africans (Yabar & Hess, 2007). In contrast, out-group members are often seen as possessing negative traits and are often disliked. Lalonde, Moghaddam, and Taylor (1987) found evidence of this among fans at home games of the McGill University hockey team. The fans rated the opposing teams higher in negative characteristics, such as arrogance and aggressiveness, than they did their own team. In fact, as the season progressed, the ratings of the two teams increasingly diverged. Recent research has shown that even the same behaviour (e.g., a smile) is perceived more negatively when it comes from an out-group than an in-group member, as shown in research conducted with students at the University of Western Ontario (Gawronski, Bodenhausen, & Banse, 2005); people of European, African, or Asian descent living in Quebec (Beaupré & Hess, 2003); and American and Canadian university students (Inzlicht, Kaiser, & Major, 2008).

This tendency to favour the in-group while denigrating the out-group is so pervasive that people show this bias even under the most minimal conditions. Such effects have been demonstrated by British social psychologist Henri Tajfel and colleagues, who have created entities that they refer to as minimal groups (Tajfel, 1982a, 1982b; Tajfel & Billig, 1974; Tajfel & Turner, 1979). In these experiments, complete strangers are formed into groups by using the most trivial criteria imaginable. For example, in one experiment, participants watched a coin toss that randomly assigned them to either group X or group W. In another experiment, participants were first asked to express their opinions about artists they had never heard of and were then randomly assigned to a group that appreciated either the "Klee style" or the "Kandinsky style," ostensibly by their picture preferences. The striking thing about the Tajfel research is that despite the fact that the participants were strangers prior to the experiment and didn't interact with one another during it, they behaved as if those who shared the same meaningless label were their dear friends or close kin. They liked the members of their own group better; they rated the members of their in-group as more likely than out-group members to have pleasant personalities and to have done better work. Most striking, the participants allocated more money and other rewards to those who shared their label, and did so in a rather hostile, cutthroat manner—that is, when given a clear choice, they preferred to give themselves only $2 if it meant giving an out-group person $1, rather than give themselves $3 if that meant the out-group member would receive $4. These findings have been replicated in Canada (Amiot & Bourhis, 2003).

From these results, you can see that it doesn't take much to produce feelings of "us" and "them." In fact, researchers at the University of Alberta found that an in-group can be created simply by photographing people together (Burgess, Enzle, & Morry, 2000). Specifically, Burgess and colleagues (2000) found that pairs of strangers who were photographed together were more likely to use terms such as *we* and *us* and to report greater liking than pairs of strangers who sat next to each other but were not photographed together. (Note that taking a picture of each person separately did not produce this "we" feeling.)

Before leaving this topic, it is important to point out that the tendency to discriminate against the out-group is even stronger when people have chosen their group rather than being randomly assigned to it. Perreault and Bourhis (1999) demonstrated this by letting some research participants (French-speaking Acadians in New Brunswick) choose whether they wanted to be in Group K or Group W, whereas other participants were randomly assigned to Group K. These effects are likely to be even stronger in the real world than in the laboratory studies that we've been discussing.

Why Do We Show In-Group Bias? Why do we show this tendency to favour the in-group and discriminate against the out-group, even when group membership is based on something as trivial as the toss of a coin or having a photo taken together? The answer to this question has two parts. The first part is that belonging to a group gives us a social identity. The second part is that having a social identity contributes to feelings of self-esteem.

Social Identity Benefits If it is true that belonging to a group provides us with a social identity, we would expect that individuals who strongly identify with a group would be more likely to favour their group than individuals who only weakly identify with their group. Evidence of this was found in research conducted at the University of Waterloo (Sahdra & Ross, 2007). Canadian students were induced to feel either high or low identification with Canada. They were then asked to recall specific negative acts that Canadians have committed toward other groups (e.g., violence, hatred) as well as specific positive acts (e.g., kindness, bravery). Participants in the high-identification group were more likely to recall good deeds done by Canadians and less likely to recall bad deeds than those in the low-identification group. On a related note, Grant (2008) found that immigrants to Canada who adopted a Canadian identity were less likely to feel that Canada discriminated against immigrants compared to their counterparts who did not identify as strongly with Canada. These findings are interesting, given that the participants in this research were professionals who were frustrated and angry because of difficulties with getting their credentials recognized in this country.

Recent research suggests that threats to identity also cause people to "circle their wagons" and become even more protective of the in-group, as shown in a study conducted with French Canadians living in Quebec. Participants in a threat condition were given information indicating that, in the future, French Canadian culture might merge with anglophone culture. (Participants in a control condition read an article about Quebec geography.) Those who had a strong French Canadian identity reacted to this threat by expressing greater support for Quebec sovereignty than those who did not identify as strongly with being French Canadian (and participants in the threat condition expressed greater support than participants in the control condition; Wohl, Giguère, Branscombe, & McVicar, 2011). In follow-up research, students at Carleton University in the threat condition were given information that Canada was at risk of losing its sovereignty because of American interest in forming a shared security agency. Parallel to the findings of the first study, those who had a strong Canadian identity were more likely to endorse actions to protect the sovereignty of our nation than those who identified more weakly with being Canadian (Wohl et al., 2011). Other research conducted at York University has shown that when people's identities as Canadians are threatened, they take steps to restore it (Giguère & Lalonde, 2009).

There is also evidence that the more strongly one identifies with one's own group, the more likely one is to discriminate against an out-group. In a study by Gagnon and Bourhis (1996), French Canadian university students were told that they were in Group K or Group W (based on a coin toss) and would be deciding how to allocate five percentage points to other participants' psychology grades. As predicted, those who identified most strongly with their group discriminated most against the other group when awarding grade points. Moreover, the more these participants discriminated, the more they liked being a member of their group. Similar results have been obtained in a real-world study conducted with prospective Canadian military officers (Guimond, 2000).

Findings such as these suggest that if a person's sense of social identity is threatened, he or she might be especially likely to discriminate against an out-group. This prediction was tested in a series of studies by Peter Grant (1992, 1993). Students at the University of Saskatchewan who cared about either a "women's issue" (e.g., women should be encouraged to apply for high-status jobs) or a "men's issue" (e.g., men's roles have become confusing and unclear) discussed these topics in same-sex groups. They were told that later they would also exchange ideas with an opposite-sex group. Before doing so, those in the high-threat condition were informed that the opposite-sex group couldn't care less about their issue and didn't see a need for change. Participants in the low-threat condition were told that the other group thought the issue was important and had come up with some strategies for change. As expected, participants whose identities were threatened (i.e., those who were told the other group didn't care about their issue) rated the other group more negatively than did those whose identities were not threatened. Once again, these laboratory findings have been confirmed in real-world research. For example, Corenblum and Stephan (2001) found that the more Native people identified with their own group, the more likely they were to perceive white people as threatening their values and beliefs. These feelings of threat, in turn, predicted prejudice toward white people.

Self-Esteem Benefits Clearly, there is evidence that dividing the world into "us" and "them" gives us a sense of social identity. Why is this important? According to Tajfel (1982a, 1982b; Turner, Hogg, Oakes, Reicher, & Wetherell, 1987), it gives people a self-esteem boost if they believe that their group is superior and that other groups are inferior. Evidence of this was found in a study conducted by Louise Lemyre and Phillip Smith (1985). Participants were University of British Columbia students who were simply told that they were in the "red" group or the "blue" group. Some participants were then given an opportunity to discriminate against the out-group (by giving them fewer points), whereas others were not. Those who discriminated against the out-group showed higher self-esteem than did those who were not given the chance to discriminate. The researchers also included a condition in which participants were not assigned to any group but were allowed to discriminate against one of the groups. Interestingly, these participants did not show an increase in self-esteem. This result suggests that discriminating against others improves our self-esteem, but only when our social identity is involved.

As you might expect, when our self-esteem is threatened, we are especially likely to denigrate the out-group as a means of restoring feelings of self-worth. In a classic study, Meindl and Lerner (1984) threatened the self-esteem of some of their participants (English-speaking Canadians) by making them feel responsible for an accident in the laboratory. Participants in a control condition were not made to feel responsible for the accident. Feelings of group identification were manipulated by asking participants to rate various issues related to Quebec, either from the perspective of "a member of the English-speaking majority in Canada" or simply "as an individual." Participants who experienced a threat to their self-esteem rated French Canadians more negatively than those whose self-esteem had not been threatened, especially if their identity as an English-speaking Canadian had been made salient. Similar effects have been obtained in more recent research conducted at the University of Waterloo focusing on discrimination toward Native people (Jordan, Spencer, & Zanna, 2005). Thus, if we are feeling defensive and threatened, we are more likely to engage in discrimination than if our self-esteem is in good shape.

Watch on **mypsychlab**
We versus They: Robert Cialdini

Implications of Social Categorization for Reducing Prejudice We have seen that people gain social identity benefits from dividing the world into "us" and "them." Further, people can boost their self-esteem by discriminating against "them." Is there a way to minimize such effects? Recent research provides some encouraging answers. One approach is to change people's perceptions of "us" and "them"—either by promoting a common identity or by emphasizing the superordinate groups to which both in-group and out-group members belong. Another approach is to provide people with an alternative route to self-esteem, so they won't have to step on others.

There is evidence that prejudice is diminished when groups share a common identity. In a series of studies with francophone and anglophone students at the University of Ottawa, Richard Clément and colleagues have found that competence in the other group's language promoted feelings of identity with that group (Clément, Baker, & MacIntyre, 2003; Clément, Noels, & Deneault, 2001; Noels & Clément, 1996; Rubenfeld, Clément, Vinograd, Lussier, Amireault, Auger, & Lebrun, 2007). The researchers suggest that at a very basic level, speaking the same language can help blur the distinction between "us" and "them."

More recently, researchers have attempted to reduce prejudice by making salient the superordinate group to which members of both groups belong (Dovidio, ten Vagert, Stewart, Gaertner, Johnson, & Esses, 2004; Esses, Wagner, & Wolf, 2006; Levin, Prosser, Evans, & Reicher, 2005; Van Bavel & Cunningham, 2007). For example, Wohl and Branscombe (2005) asked members of the Jewish Students' Association at two Canadian universities questions such as "Should Germans be forgiven for the Holocaust?" and "How guilty should contemporary Germans feel?" In the social identity condition, the Holocaust was described as "an event in which Germans behaved aggressively toward Jews." In the human identity condition, the Holocaust was described as "an event in which humans behaved aggressively toward other humans." As predicted, participants in the human identity condition were more willing to forgive and assigned less guilt to Germans today than those in the social identity condition. These effects were replicated with Native Canadian students attending the University of Alberta, who were asked to think about the treatment of Native peoples in Canadian history (Wohl & Branscombe, 2005). We find these results encouraging. They suggest that prejudice and discrimination can be reduced when people's focus shifts from membership in their specific in-group to a broader group that includes members of the out-group.

Another avenue for minimizing discrimination against out-groups is to provide people with alternative routes to self-esteem. Based on self-affirmation theory (see Chapter 6), Fein and Spencer (1997) predicted that if people were affirmed in some way, they would be less likely to need to boost their self-esteem by derogating out-group members. To test this, participants in the self-affirmation condition were asked to write why certain values were important to them. Participants in the control condition did not engage in this self-affirmation exercise. Next, all participants saw a video of a woman who was portrayed as Jewish, a group that was negatively stereotyped by the participants. Those who had not been affirmed rated the woman more negatively than those in the self-affirmation condition. Other research has also shown that if we can find some other domain in which to give our self-esteem a boost, we are less likely to derogate others to feel good about ourselves (Correll, Spencer, & Zanna, 2004; Fein, Hoshino-Browne, Davies, & Spencer, 2003; Sherman & Kim, 2005; Shira & Martin, 2005). Recent research conducted at York University has shown that people who are especially likely to derogate out-groups may need a "double dose" of affirmation (i.e., engage in more than one kind of self-affirmation exercise) in order to reduce discrimination (McGregor, Haji, & Kang, 2008). The bottom line is that if you want to reduce prejudice against stigmatized groups, remind in-group members of our common identity as human beings. It also wouldn't hurt to give them a self-esteem boost by telling them how great they are—this should reduce their need to put other people down.

What We Believe: Stereotypes

If we have a negative stereotype of a group, we will show prejudice toward members of that group. Right? While that is often the case, it's actually not that simple. It turns out that the relationship between stereotyping and prejudice is highly complex. One of the complexities is that our stereotypes are not activated in every situation. As you will see, whether our stereotypes are turned on or off has important implications for prejudice. It is also the case that our attitudes toward members of another group are determined not only by our stereotype of that group, but also by our perception of that group's stereotype of "us."

The Activation of Stereotypes Imagine this scenario. You are a member of a group engaged in judging another person's performance, and someone in your group makes an ugly, stereotypical comment about that individual. Will the comment affect your judgment of the performance? "No," you are probably thinking, "I'd disregard it completely." But would you be able to do so? Is it possible that the comment would trigger in your mind all the other negative stereotypes and beliefs about people in that

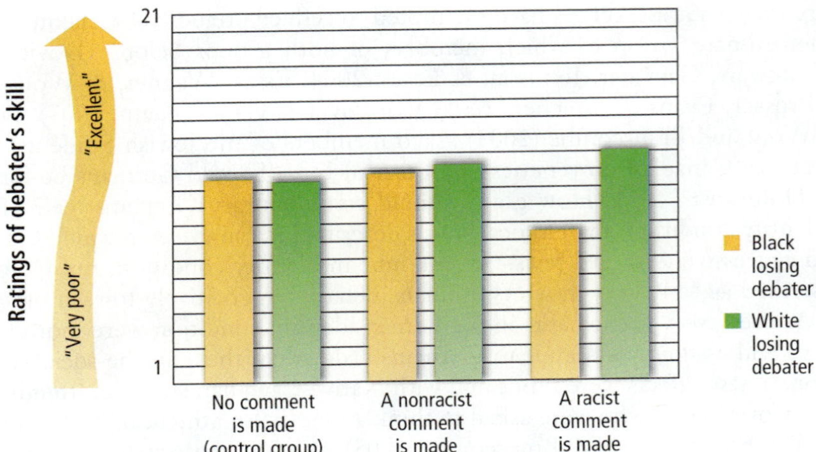

FIGURE 12.2

Activation of stereotypical belief.

When a derogatory comment was made about the black debater, it activated the latent stereotype held by the observers, causing them to lower their rating of his performance.

(Adapted from Greenberg & Pyszczynski, 1985)

group and affect your judgment about that particular individual—even if you neither believe the stereotype nor consider yourself prejudiced against that group?

In a classic study, Greenberg and Pyszczynski (1985) had participants watch a debate between a black person and a white person. When a confederate made a racist comment about the black debater, participants rated the black debater's performance lower than the white debater's performance. When no racist remark was made, the black and white debaters were rated as equally skilled. In other words, the derogatory comment activated other negative stereotypical beliefs about black people, so that the participants who heard it rated the same performance as less skilled than did those who had not heard the racist remark (see Figure 12.2).

CONNECTIONS

Can Social Categorization Affect Your Reaction to Terrorism?

For many people, September 11, 2001, marks the day that the threat of terrorism became a reality in their lives. The terrorist attacks that followed—such as the train bombings in Spain in 2004 and in India in 2005; the tourist bombings in Bali, Saudi Arabia, Egypt, and Jordan; and the subway bombings in England in 2005 have served to reinforce people's feelings of fear and vulnerability. Former Canadian prime minister Paul Martin warned, "This is a dangerous world and Canadians must not be complacent" (Martin, as quoted in Robson, 2005, p. A3). Martin was implying that Canadians are not immune from the threat of terrorism. Indeed, in March 2011, two students who had attended the University of Manitoba were arrested because they were suspected of plotting terrorism. A month later, in April 2011, a Toronto man was arrested at Pearson Airport because of suspicions that he was part of a terrorist organization in Somalia. How afraid did the terrorist attacks on September 11 make you feel? Research suggests that your level of fear may depend on whether or not you include Americans in your in-group. Let's take a look at the details.

One week after the attacks on the World Trade Center in New York, European researchers conducted a series of studies in which they manipulated participants' sense of identity (Dumont, Yzerbyt, Wigboldus, & Gordijn, 2003). In one condition, participants were asked to focus on their identity as Europeans versus Americans. This condition was intended to make Americans the out-group. In the other condition, participants were asked to focus on their identity as Westerners versus Arabs. This condition was intended to make Americans part of the in-group. The researchers found that when Europeans included Americans in their in-group (i.e., their "Westerners" identity was made salient), greater fear was reported in response to the terrorist attacks than when Americans were portrayed as the out-group. Including Americans in the in-group also had some interesting behavioural implications: Participants were more willing to offer support and help to the victims, and were more likely to seek out information concerning how to prevent future attacks (e.g., lobbying NATO to intervene). Thus, reactions to terrorism were quite different, depending on whether participants were induced to regard Americans as part of the in-group or the out-group.

Henderson-King and Nisbett (1996) subsequently showed that all it took was one negative action by one African-American (actually a confederate of the experimenters) to activate the negative stereotypes of African-Americans and to discourage the participants from wanting to interact with different African-Americans. These findings suggest that in most of us stereotypes lurk just beneath the surface. It doesn't take much to activate a stereotype. And, once activated, the stereotype can have dire consequences for how a particular member of that out-group is perceived and treated.

Automatic and Controlled Processing of Stereotypes How does this activation process work? Patricia Devine differentiates between the automatic processing of information and the controlled processing of information (Devine, 1989a, 2003; Zuwerink, Montieth, Devine, & Cook, 1996). As discussed in Chapter 3, an automatic process is one over which we have no control. For example, even if you score very low on a prejudice scale, you are certainly familiar with certain stereotypes that exist in our culture, such as "Aboriginals are lazy," "Jews are money hungry," or "Homosexual men are effeminate." These stereotypes are automatically triggered under certain conditions—

Simulate on mypsychlab
Unconscious Stereotyping

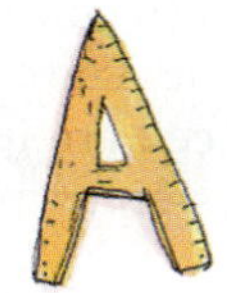

FIGURE 12.3
A two-step model of the cognitive processing of stereotypes.

According to Devine's theory, we exhibit both automatic and controlled processing of information. So, even though your automatic response to this man might reflect prejudice, you could override the stereotypes behind that response by more controlled processing.

they just pop into one's mind. For people who are not deeply prejudiced, however, controlled processes can suppress or override these stereotypes. For example, such a person can say to himself or herself, "Hey, that stereotype isn't fair and it isn't right—Jews are no more money hungry than non-Jews. Ignore the stereotype about this person's ethnicity." What Devine's theory suggests, therefore, is a two-step model of cognitive processing: The automatic processing brings up information—in this case, stereotypes—but the controlled (or conscious) processing can refute or ignore it (see Figure 12.3).

While the activation of stereotypes is a frequent occurrence, research suggests that there are some conditions under which we do not automatically do this. What are those conditions? Stay tuned.

The Motivation to Control Prejudice One factor that influences whether stereotypes are automatically activated is the motivation to control prejudice—in other words, whether we want to be non-prejudiced. In a series of studies, Maddux and colleagues (2004) showed participants (white students) photographs of black or white faces presented on a computer screen. The researchers varied the background of each photograph to be either neutral (e.g., a church) or consistent with the negative stereotype of black people (e.g., a jail). When the background cued the stereotype (e.g., the jail), participants who were high in motivation to control prejudice were less likely to show automatic negative responses to black faces than were those who were low in motivation to control prejudice. Motivation to control prejudice did not affect responses when the context was neutral (e.g., the church). The researchers conclude that those of us who want to be non-prejudiced are less likely to activate negative stereotypes automatically when we encounter stereotype-relevant cues.

Research conducted at the University of Ottawa confirms that those who are motivated to control prejudice are less likely to show prejudice (Legault, Green-Demers, & Eadie, 2009; Legault, Green-Demers, Grant, & Chung, 2007). For example, in a recent study, these researchers found that people who are high in motivation to control prejudice inhibit the application of stereotypes. Specifically, these people were less likely to read hostility into ambiguous behaviours performed by a black man than were people who are lower in motivation to control prejudice (Legault et al., 2009).

The Need to Feel Good about Ourselves Another factor that determines whether we automatically activate stereotypes is whether we will get a self-esteem boost by doing so. Consider Michael, a university student who receives a negative evaluation on a term paper he wrote for a course taught by a black professor. Michael's stereotype of black people is that they are not very competent. How might Michael repair the damage to his self-esteem caused by receiving a low grade? Based on our discussion so far, you can probably answer this question. Michael can activate his stereotype of black people as incompetent. This allows him to dismiss the criticism of his work as stemming from an incompetent source, with the result that Michael will not feel as bad about his negative evaluation.

Now, consider Chris, a classmate of Michael. Chris also subscribes to a stereotype of black people as incompetent. Unlike Michael, however, Chris received a very positive evaluation of his term paper. On the one hand, Chris is eager to accept the professor's praise and enjoy the boost in self-esteem that it produces. On the other hand, it is difficult to feel good about praise that comes from a person who has been stereotyped as incompetent. How can Chris resolve this dilemma? According to a groundbreaking program of research by Lisa Sinclair at the University of Winnipeg and Ziva Kunda at the University of Waterloo, Chris might inhibit (i.e., push out of his mind) his stereotype of black people. This would allow him to revel in the praise he received.

In a series of studies, Sinclair and Kunda (1999) demonstrated that we not only selectively activate stereotypes, but also inhibit stereotypes in the service of self-enhancement. In one of their studies, male students—none of whom was black—were asked to participate in research on managers' evaluations of employees' interpersonal skills. The participants first answered questions that supposedly assessed their interpersonal skills and then received an evaluation (via videotape) from either a white manager or a black manager (both confederates). Half of the participants received a positive evaluation (e.g., "I was very impressed with this person; I think he has really good interpersonal skills"), whereas the others received a negative evaluation (e.g., "I was not very impressed with this person").

Sinclair and Kunda predicted that participants who received negative feedback from the black manager would activate their (negative) stereotype of black people. In contrast, participants who were praised by the black manager were expected to inhibit the black stereotype. How could the researchers tell whether participants activated or inhibited their stereotype of black people? In the next phase of the experiment, the students participated in a supposedly unrelated study on word completions. The word fragments could be completed to form either racial or nonracial words. For example, _ _*ACK* could be completed as *BLACK* or as any number of nonracial words (e.g., *SNACK*); *CR*_ _ _ could be completed as *CRIME* or as a nonracial word (e.g., *CREEK*). The researchers reasoned that participants who activated their stereotype of black people would be most likely to use racial word completions, whereas those who inhibited their stereotype of black people would show the fewest racial word completions.

The results are shown in Figure 12.4. In interpreting these findings, you may wish to think of the participants who were evaluated by a white manager as the control group. These participants give us a sense of how many racial word completions came to mind for participants who were not motivated to either activate or inhibit their stereotype of black people. As you can see, participants who received negative feedback from a black manager generated more racial words than did those who received negative feedback from a white manager. This is evidence of stereotype activation. In contrast, those who were praised by the black manager pushed the stereotype of black people out of their minds—they came up with even fewer racial word completions than did participants who were praised by a white manager. This is evidence of stereotype inhibition. Finally, as you might expect, participants who were criticized by the black manager rated his skill at evaluating them lower than did participants who were praised by a black manager. (White managers who gave negative feedback also were rated as less skilled than white managers who gave positive feedback, but this difference was not nearly so pronounced as it was for black managers.)

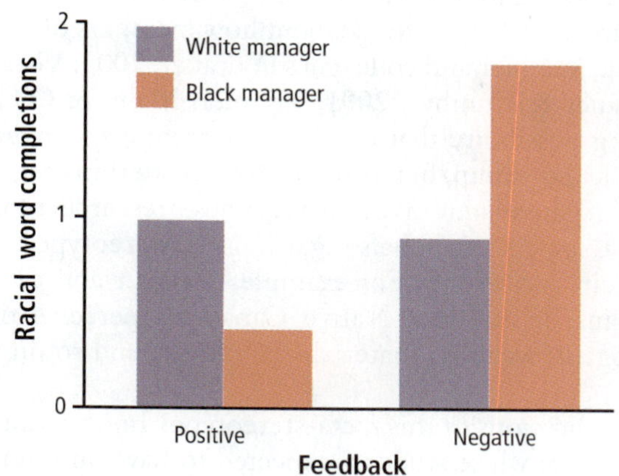

FIGURE 12.4

Number of racial completions as a function of feedback favourability and manager race.

(Sinclair & Kunda, 1999)

In subsequent research on stereotypes of women, Sinclair and Kunda (1999) found that students at the University of Waterloo rated their female professors as less competent than their male professors when they received a low grade in the course—but not when they received a high grade. As the researchers put it, "She's fine if she praised me but incompetent if she criticized me." In contrast, the ratings of male professors did not depend as much on the grades that students received from them.

Finally, in conceptually related research, Livingston and Sinclair (2008) examined reactions to Aboriginal and white speakers who delivered a threatening message to University of Winnipeg students—namely, that the university was considering implementing an exit exam that students would have to pass to graduate. The speakers, who were portrayed as university administrators, presented arguments in favour of exit exams. The Aboriginal speaker was rated more negatively (e.g., less competent, less professional), less persuasive, and as presenting lower-quality arguments than the white speaker, even though both speakers delivered the identical message. Students who were non-prejudiced were just as likely to show these effects as those who were high in prejudice toward Aboriginals. The researchers conclude, "Regardless of degree of prejudice, people may derogate stigmatized individuals and their messages when it suits their purposes" (Livingston & Sinclair, 2008, p. 220).

Before leaving this topic, we should point out that in everyday life, stereotype activation and inhibition can be quite a complex process. Most people belong to multiple groups, which means that a number of stereotypes can apply to the same person (Dunn & Spellman, 2003). Sinclair and Kunda (1999) suggest that we "pick and choose" which stereotypes to activate or inhibit—once again, depending on what will produce the greatest self-enhancement. For example, in one study, they focused on two stereotypes that have opposing implications for competence—the negative stereotype of black people and the positive stereotype of doctors. As in their earlier study, participants received either a positive or a negative evaluation, but this time it came from either a white doctor or a black doctor. The researchers predicted that when the black doctor delivered praise, the doctor stereotype would be activated (to bolster their desired positive impression of him) and the black stereotype would be inhibited (to prevent it from interfering with a positive impression of him). When he delivered criticism, just the opposite was expected: participants would bring the black stereotype to mind and push the doctor stereotype out of their minds. And that is exactly what happened.

In short, this research suggests that if we can salvage our self-esteem by activating negative stereotypes about a group, we will do so. However, if a negative stereotype will interfere with a self-esteem boost (e.g., when we are praised by a member of a stereotyped group), we simply push that stereotype out of our minds.

Meta-Stereotypes Research on stereotyping usually focuses on our perceptions of other groups. We are less likely to think about how members of other groups perceive *us*. However, Jacquie Vorauer and colleagues (Vorauer, 2003; Vorauer, Hunter, Main, & Roy, 2000; Vorauer & Kumhyr, 2001; Vorauer, Main, & O'Connell, 1998) have raised the intriguing possibility that our level of prejudice depends not only on our stereotype of a particular group, but also on whether we think members of that group have a positive or negative stereotype of us. These researchers use the term **meta-stereotype** to refer to a person's beliefs regarding the stereotype that out-group members hold about their own group. For example, Vorauer and colleagues have found that white Canadians believe that Native Canadians perceive them as prejudiced, unfair, selfish, arrogant, wealthy, materialistic, phony, and so on (Vorauer, Main, & O'Connell, 1998).

Meta-Stereotype

A person's beliefs regarding the stereotype that out-group members hold about their own group

What are the implications of this meta-stereotype? In one study, Vorauer and colleagues found that when white students expected to have an interaction with an Aboriginal person, those who thought that they personally would be perceived in terms of the meta-stereotype (i.e., the stereotype that they believe Aboriginal people have of white people) anticipated that the interaction would be unpleasant. These participants also expressed the greatest amount of prejudice (Vorauer, Main, & O'Connell, 1998).

Perhaps most striking, the participants' beliefs about whether an Aboriginal person would stereotype them predicted their attitudes and reactions more strongly than did their own stereotypes of Aboriginals. In other words, the way in which participants expected to be perceived by an out-group member was the most important determinant of their reactions—even more so than their own evaluation of that group.

These findings offer a different perspective on the value of getting people to take an empathic stance when interacting with others. In prejudice reduction literature, it is often recommended that people try to take the perspective of out-group members and to empathize with them. This may be good advice in general, but it may not work so well when people are actually engaged in an interaction with an out-group member. Here's why: If you are asked to take the perspective of an out-group member with whom you are having an interaction, you are likely to also start thinking about how that person perceives you and your group (i.e., meta-stereotypes). Concerns that you will be perceived in terms of a negative meta-stereotype then become the dominant focus. The ironic result is that people can actually end up being more prejudiced toward an out-group member if they are asked to take that person's perspective than if they are not asked to do so (Vorauer & Sasaki, 2009; Vorauer, Martens, & Sasaki, 2009).

We have seen that people report greater prejudice when they expect to be perceived in terms of the stereotype they believe others hold of their group. But does this actually happen? Do other people perceive us in terms of meta-stereotypes? To find out, Vorauer and Kumhyr (2001) had pairs of Aboriginal and white Canadian students at the University of Manitoba engage in a getting-acquainted conversation. Afterward, each person rated their conversation partner and how they believed their conversation partner perceived them. The results were striking—white Canadians who were high in prejudice felt that they were stereotyped by their Aboriginal partner when, in reality, they were not. Low-prejudice white participants did not feel as though they were stereotyped by their Aboriginal conversation partner, and they were right. Interestingly, neither high- nor low-prejudice participants stereotyped their Aboriginal partner, and indeed the Aboriginal participants did not feel as though they had been the targets of prejudice. This story does not have a happy ending, however. It turned out that Aboriginal participants who were paired with a high-prejudice white participant reported feeling self-critical, ashamed, and angry with themselves. In other words, the Aboriginal participants attributed the negativity they experienced during the interaction to themselves rather than to prejudice.

Finally, recent research shows that meta-stereotypes influence people's behaviour during interactions. Specifically, Goff and colleagues (2008) found that white participants who were reminded of the negative stereotype of whites as racist sat farther away from a black person than a white person during an interaction. The distance was even greater when they were told that the topic of discussion would be racial profiling (as opposed to a neutral topic). The researchers suggest that the distancing was due to anxiety about confirming the meta-stereotype (Goff, Steele, & Davies, 2008).

> *A fanatic is one who can't change his mind and won't change the subject.*
>
> —Winston Churchill, *1944*

Can Prejudice Be Reduced by Revising Stereotypical Beliefs? It may seem obvious that if we want to reduce prejudice, we should simply change people's stereotypes. This makes a lot of sense, except for one problem: Stereotypes are very resistant to change. After all, proof that they are accurate is always out there—when our beliefs guide us to see it. Moreover, we "hang on to" our stereotypes even in the face of contradictory evidence (Barbéra, 2003; Ickes, Patterson, Rajecki, & Tanford, 1982). This was demonstrated in a study by Taylor and Gardner (1969), who had anglophone students listen to a tape recording in which a French Canadian speaker described himself in ways that were either consistent or inconsistent with English Canadians' stereotype of French Canadians as religious, emotional, talkative, sensitive, and proud. Even if the speaker completely contradicted the stereotype, he was still perceived in stereotypical terms (although less so than when he confirmed the stereotype).

Sometimes the person we encounter may be so contrary to our stereotype that it is impossible to interpret the person's behaviour in stereotype-consistent terms. What do

Can the image of an articulate African-American president on the world stage change entrenched stereotypes? A recent study found that exposure to President Obama reduced implicit prejudice toward blacks among non-black Americans (Columb & Plant, 2011).

we do then? According to Ziva Kunda and Kathryn Oleson (1995, 1997), we may simply create a new subtype for this deviant member, particularly if we are able to come up with some justification for doing so. For example, in one study, the researchers presented University of Waterloo students with a description of a monogamous gay man—thereby contradicting the stereotype of gays as promiscuous. Some participants were given additional, neutral information—namely, that the man was an accountant. The researchers found that this irrelevant information was used as grounds for creating a new subtype, thereby leaving the original stereotype intact. In effect, these participants were saying, "Gay men, in general, are promiscuous. The one exception is gay men who are accountants."

This tendency to create a new subcategory of exceptions to the rule can place the targets of stereotyping in a no-win situation. Consider, for example, the remarks of Sajjad, a participant in a study on discrimination experienced by Muslim students in Canadian schools (Zine, 2001). Sajjad moved to Canada from Guyana when he was seven years old. By junior high school he was all too aware that stereotypes are virtually impossible to overcome. In his words, "I'd given up a long time ago trying to impress other people, or trying to prove to other people that I'm a good black person, or I'm a good Indian person . . .. Even if I were to be a good person . . . they have a certain image of coloured people, so it's like, 'Well, all coloured people are bad, but he's a good one . . . he's an exception'" (Sajjad, as quoted in Zine, 2001, p. 411).

By now you may be feeling unconvinced that stereotypes actually can be changed. The good news is that when people are bombarded with many examples that are inconsistent with the stereotype, they do gradually modify their beliefs (Webber & Crocker, 1983). Thus, if you encounter someone who holds a stereotype that we find particularly annoying—namely, that professors are lazy—providing that person with information about many professors who contradict the stereotype (not just your Social Psychology professor) should lead that person to change his or her views.

Connect to MyPsychLab
Could your emotions influence your beliefs? To take a survey on how you deal with your emotions, go to MyPsychLab

The Way We Feel: Affect and Mood

So far, we have focused on the cognitive aspect of prejudice: the stereotypes we hold of different groups. As we have seen, under certain conditions stereotyping is indeed linked to prejudice. However, as Esses, Haddock, and Zanna (1993) point out, "There is more to prejudice than merely the attribution of stereotypes to groups." In their view, other factors must be considered, including emotion, symbolic beliefs, and behaviour. More specifically, Esses and colleagues suggest that the emotions elicited by a particular group are the most important determinant of our level of prejudice—even more important than our stereotype of that group (see also Brochu & Esses, 2009; Cottrell & Neuberg, 2005; Cuddy, Fiske, & Glick, 2007; Fiske, Cuddy, Glick, & Xu, 2002). Prejudice is also a product of our symbolic beliefs—the perception that a particular group promotes or hinders values that we cherish. Finally, prejudice is also a product of our behaviour and our experiences with members of the group (Haddock, Zanna, & Esses, 1994; Maio, Esses, & Bell, 1994). Let's take a look at some of the evidence.

In one of their studies, Haddock, Zanna, and Esses (1993, 1994) assessed University of Waterloo students' attitudes toward four ethnic groups (English Canadians, French Canadians, Native Canadians, and Pakistanis) and toward gays and lesbians. To find out what best predicted attitudes, the researchers asked the participants to describe the emotions they experienced when thinking about members of each group, their stereotypic beliefs (i.e., "characteristics you would use to describe the group"), and their symbolic beliefs (i.e., "the values that you believe members of the group promote or hinder"). Behaviour was assessed by asking participants to describe the frequency of contact and quality of their most recent experiences with members of these groups.

It turns out that all of these variables were related to attitudes. However, overall, the strongest effects were found for emotion. There was some variability, though, depending on the group that was being rated. Specifically, emotion was the best predictor of attitudes for the groups toward which participants were least prejudiced (English Canadians and Native Canadians). For these groups, knowing how someone feels about members of the group would allow you to predict his or her level of prejudice with the greatest accuracy. Symbolic beliefs best predicted attitudes for the groups toward which participants were most prejudiced (Pakistanis and gays/lesbians). (Researchers at the University of Manitoba also have found that symbolic beliefs predict attitudes toward gays and lesbians; Mohipp & Morry, 2004.) For these groups, prejudice would be predicted most accurately by asking whether the group threatens people's important beliefs or values. Stereotypes did not strongly predict attitudes toward any of these groups when emotions, symbolic beliefs, and behaviour were taken into account.

Research by Corenblum and Stephan (2001) suggests that emotion is also a strong predictor of the prejudice that minority groups feel toward majority groups. In their study, white Canadians and Native Canadians were asked about their stereotypes, symbolic beliefs (i.e., agreement with statements such as "Natives and white Canadians have many incompatible values"), and emotions (specifically, anxiety about interacting with out-group members). All of these variables predicted the level of prejudice that white Canadians felt toward Native Canadians, but the strongest predictor was emotion. The same held true when researchers predicted the level of prejudice that Native Canadians felt toward white Canadians. Thus, the more negative emotion people expect to feel while interacting with members of another group, the greater their prejudice toward that group—regardless of whether their group is in a majority or minority position.

It is important to point out that the research we have been discussing is correlational and, therefore, does not actually prove that negative emotions *cause* people to be prejudiced toward certain groups. It may be the other way around: Prejudice may produce nasty feelings in people. How might we untangle this? One way would be to change people's emotions and see whether or not that affects their attitudes. Esses and colleagues did just that (Bell & Esses, 1997; Esses & Zanna, 1995). In a series of experiments conducted with students at Ontario universities, the researchers induced a positive, negative, or neutral mood (e.g., by having participants describe events in their lives that made them feel extremely happy, unhappy, or neutral). The findings were clear: Participants in a bad mood described various ethnic groups in more negative terms than did those who were in a good mood or a neutral mood.

We want to be clear on the point that these researchers are making. They are not saying that stereotyping never produces prejudice. Indeed, earlier in this chapter we presented evidence to the contrary. However, this research does suggest that an even stronger determinant of prejudice is how we feel about a group.

Reducing Prejudice by Changing People's Emotions These findings suggest that if we want to reduce prejudice, it might be best to design interventions that will speak to people's hearts rather than to their heads. Esses and Dovidio (2002; Dovidio, ten Vergert, Stewart, Gaertner, Johnson, Esses, & Pearson, 2004) took on this challenge. They showed white participants a videotape of a black man experiencing discrimination

Research has suggested that mood affects prejudice; people in a good mood feel more favourably toward other racial or ethnic groups.

in several situations. Some participants were instructed to pay attention to their feelings; others were told to pay attention to their thoughts. Those who focused on their feelings subsequently expressed more willingness to engage in future contact with black people than did those who focused on their thoughts. Why? The researchers discovered that focusing on feelings about the discriminatory situations did not affect people's symbolic beliefs or their stereotypes of blacks. However, it did affect their emotions: They now felt more positive toward blacks and therefore were more willing to interact with blacks in the future.

The Way We Assign Meaning: Attributional Biases

The human tendency to make attributions for people's behaviour can also serve to perpetuate stereotyping and prejudice. As we discussed in Chapter 4, it is in our nature to make dispositional (internal) attributions—that is, to leap to the conclusion that a person's behaviour is due to his or her personality and not the situation or the person's life circumstances. This is the familiar correspondence bias. Although attributing people's behaviour to their dispositions is often accurate, human behaviour is also shaped by situational factors. Thus, relying too heavily on dispositional attributions can lead us to make attributional mistakes. Many problems and complications arise when we overzealously act out the correspondence bias for a whole group of people. Thomas Pettigrew (1979) has called this the **ultimate attribution error** because we apply this bias to entire groups of people.

> *The cause is hidden, but the result is known.*
>
> —Ovid, *first century* CE

Ultimate Attribution Error

Our tendency to make dispositional attributions about an entire group of people

To use gender stereotypes as an example, Janet Swim and Lawrence Sanna (1996) carefully studied some 58 separate experiments completed over the previous 20 years. They found that if a man was successful on a task, observers attributed his success to ability; if a woman was successful at that same task, observers attributed her success to hard work (see also Deaux & Emsweiler, 1974; Feldman-Summers & Kiesler, 1974).

As you might expect, such effects are not limited to gender stereotypes. Corenblum, Annis, and Young (1996) showed white and Native children attending elementary schools in Brandon, Manitoba, videos in which a white child and a Native child performed a task. When a white child performed well, both Native and white participants made dispositional attributions for the child's performance (e.g., being smart); when a white child performed poorly, both Native and white participants made external attributions (e.g., bad luck). Exactly the opposite pattern was observed when making attributions for the performance of a Native child—good performance was attributed to external factors (e.g., luck, an easy task) by both Native and white children; poor performance was attributed to internal factors (e.g., not being smart).

These findings suggest that when people conform to our stereotype, we tend to blind ourselves to clues about why they might have behaved as they did. Instead, we assume that their behaviour is due to something about their character or disposition, and not their situation. In other words, we explain the behaviour of out-group members in a way that perpetuates our stereotypes of them, thereby fostering prejudice.

Prejudice and Economic Competition: Realistic Conflict Theory

One of the most obvious sources of conflict and prejudice is competition—for scarce resources, for political power, and for social status. Indeed, it can be said that whatever problems result from the simple in-group versus out-group phenomenon, they will be magnified by real economic, political, or status competition. **Realistic conflict theory** holds that limited resources lead to conflict among groups and result in increased prejudice and discrimination (Cottrell & Neuberg, 2005; Jackson, 1993; Sherif, 1966; White, 1977). More specifically, conflict and prejudice are most likely to result when we perceive that our group may miss out on a limited resource and when we perceive that another group (an out-group) is competing with us for that resource (Esses, Dovidio, Danso, Jackson, & Semenya, 2005). Thus, prejudiced attitudes tend to increase when times are tense and conflict exists between groups over mutually exclusive goals.

Realistic Conflict Theory
The theory that limited resources lead to conflict among groups and result in increased prejudice and discrimination

Economic and Political Competition Whenever people compete for any scarce resource, the stage is set for prejudice. In his classic study of prejudice in a small U.S. industrial town, John Dollard (1938) was among the first to document the relation between discrimination and economic competition. While initially there was no discernible prejudice against new German immigrants to the town, as jobs grew scarce, prejudice flourished. Similarly, in the nineteenth century, when Chinese immigrants in the United States joined the gold rush in California, in direct competition with white miners of Anglo-Saxon origin, they were described as "depraved and vicious . . . gross gluttons, . . . bloodthirsty and inhuman" (Jacobs & Landau, 1971). However, only a few years later, when they were willing to accept back-breaking work as labourers on the Transcontinental Railroad—work that few white Americans were willing to do—they were regarded as sober, industrious, and law abiding. With the end of the Civil War came an influx of former soldiers into an already tight job market. This change was immediately followed by a dramatic increase in negative attitudes toward the Chinese. The stereotype changed to one characterizing them as criminal, conniving, crafty, and stupid (Jacobs & Landau, 1971).

Closer to home, prejudice toward First Nations peoples has increased in Caledonia, Ontario, as a result of a dispute over a land claim. Six Nations Aboriginals claim that a housing development in the town sits on land that was stolen from them more than 200 years ago. Aboriginal protesters began to occupy the land in 2006, resulting in violent confrontations between town residents and the protesters. Three years later, tensions escalated when a cigarette-selling shack was set up on the property of a local resident. Frustrations over a perceived lack of intervention by the Ontario Provincial Police prompted some residents to form an unarmed citizens' militia in June 2009. David Boyter, a Caledonia resident, comments, "When we moved into Caledonia nobody ever thought of who was native or who was white. Now there's a terrific rift, and the rift will be there for generations to come" ("Caledonia Land Conflict," 2007).

These real-world examples suggest that when times are tough and resources are scarce, in-group members feel more threatened by members of the out-group, with

Conflict over valuable land has fuelled racial tension between non-Native residents of Caledonia, Ontario, and Native protestors who claim that the land belongs to them.

the result that incidents of prejudice, discrimination, and violence toward out-group members increase. How might this hypothesis be tested scientifically?

We might look for increases in prejudice toward minority group members during times of economic hardship. Douglas Palmer (1996) did just that by tracking attitudes toward immigration along with unemployment rates in Canada. Between 1975 and 1995, the unemployment rate increased and so did negative attitudes about immigration. Between 1996 and 1998, the unemployment rate dropped and—you guessed it—so did opposition to immigration (Palmer, 2000). In conceptually similar research, Tougas and colleagues (2003) found that francophones living in Quebec who believed that the percentage of immigrants was increasing tended to agree with statements such as "In comparison with immigrants, the Québécois are disadvantaged in terms of job opportunities." These feelings of threat, in turn, predicted negative attitudes toward immigrants (Tougas, de la Sablonnière, Legace, & Kocum, 2003). More recently, there has been a documented increase in prejudice toward immigrants to Canada, which has been attributed to the economic recession in our country (see Sinclair, Fehr, Wan, & Regehr, 2011).

The astute reader will have noticed that, once again, the research we have been describing is correlational; experimental research designs allow us to make cause-and-effect statements with far more confidence than we can on the basis of correlational research (see Chapter 2). What evidence is there that competition actually *causes* prejudice?

In what has become a classic experiment, Muzafer Sherif and colleagues (1961) tested realistic conflict theory by using the natural environment of a Boy Scout camp. The participants in the camp were normal, well-adjusted, 12-year-old boys who were randomly assigned to one of two groups, the Eagles or the Rattlers. Each group stayed in its own cabin, and the cabins were located quite a distance apart. The boys were placed in situations designed to increase the cohesiveness of their own group by arranging enjoyable activities, such as hiking and swimming, and by having them work on various building projects, preparing group meals, and so on. After feelings of cohesiveness developed within each group, the researchers set up a series of competitive activities in which the two groups were pitted against each other—for example, in games such as football, baseball, and tug-of-war. Prizes were awarded to the winning team. These competitive games aroused feelings of conflict and tension between the two groups. In addition, the investigators created other situations to further intensify the conflict. For example, a camp party was arranged, but each group was told it started at a different time, thereby ensuring that the Eagles would arrive well before the Rattlers.

Half of the food at the party was fresh, appealing, and appetizing; the other half was squashed, ugly, and unappetizing. As you'd expect, the early-arriving Eagles ate well, and the late-coming Rattlers were not happy with what they found. They began to call the exploitive group some rather uncomplimentary names. Because the Eagles believed that they deserved what they got (first come, first served), they resented the name calling and responded in kind. Name calling escalated into food throwing, and within a short time the boys were throwing punches and a full-scale riot ensued. In short, competition led to high levels of dislike and hostility (Sherif, Harvey, White, Hood, & Sherif, 1961). (In a moment, we will discuss how Sherif and colleagues went about trying to reduce the hostility that they had created.)

Closer to home, Esses, Jackson, and Armstrong (1998; Esses, Dovidio, Jackson, & Armstrong, 2001) conducted a series of experiments to see whether perceived competition for resources causes unfavourable attitudes toward immigrants. Participants in these experiments read one of two editorials on immigration to Canada. In the competition condition, the editorial focused on the scarcity of jobs in Canada and the high rate of participation of skilled immigrants in the job market; in the no-competition condition, the job market was not mentioned. Next, participants were told that because of a natural disaster in the country of Sandir (a fictitious country), a new group of immigrants, the Sandirians, would be arriving in Canada. The researchers described the Sandirians in positive terms: ambitious, hard-working, smart, family-oriented, spiritual, and religious. Participants in the competition condition later construed the traits of the Sandirians more negatively than did those in the no-competition condition (e.g., "Since they are family-oriented, they are probably not too accepting of others outside the family."). These participants also expressed more negative attitudes toward the idea of Sandirian immigration to Canada and toward immigrants in general than did participants in the no-competition condition.

Reducing Prejudice by Fostering Common Goals Let's return to Sherif and colleagues' summer camp experiment. How did they reduce hostility between the groups of boys? Their first step was to eliminate competitive games and promote a great deal of nonconflictual social contact. Once hostility had been aroused, however, simply eliminating the competition did not eliminate the hostility. Indeed, hostility continued to escalate, even when the two groups were engaged in such benign activities as watching movies together. But these researchers eventually did succeed. How? By having the boys experience **mutual interdependence**—a situation in which two or more groups need each other and must depend on each other to accomplish a superordinate goal (a goal that is important to both groups). For example, the investigators set up an emergency situation by damaging the water supply system. The only way the system could be repaired was for all of the Rattlers and the Eagles to cooperate immediately. On another occasion, the camp truck broke down while the boys were on a camping trip. To get the truck going again, it was necessary to pull it up a steep hill. This could be accomplished only if all of the boys pulled together, regardless of whether they were Eagles or Rattlers. Eventually, these sorts of situations brought about a diminution of hostile feelings and negative stereotyping among the campers. In fact, after these cooperative situations were introduced, the number of boys who said their closest friend was in the other group increased dramatically (see Figure 12.5).

Mutual Interdependence
A situation in which two or more groups need each other and must depend on each other to accomplish a goal that is important to both groups

"I wish we could have met under different circumstances . . . "

OLIPHANT © UNIVERSAL UCLICK. Reprinted with permission. All rights reserved.

The Way We Conform: Normative Rules

We've seen that prejudice is created and maintained by many forces in the social world. Some operate within the individual, such as the way we process information and assign meaning to events; some operate on whole groups of people, such as the effects of competition, conflict, and frustration. Our final explanation for what

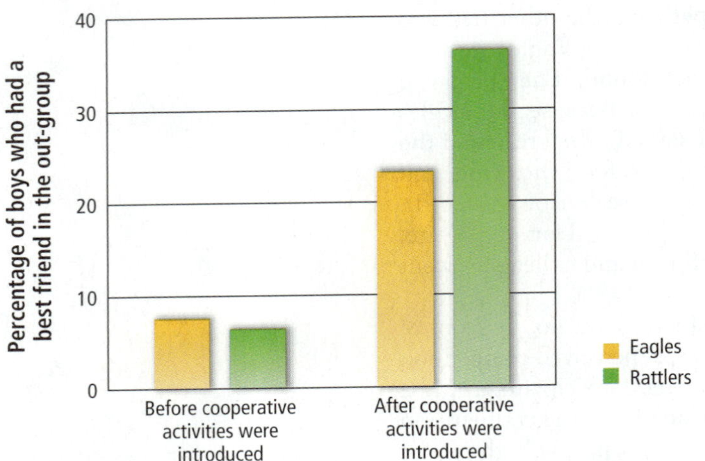

FIGURE 12.5
Intergroup relations.

Intergroup tensions were eased only after members engaged in cooperative activities.

(Adapted from Sherif et al., 1961)

causes prejudice also occurs at the group level: conformity to normative standards or rules in the society. As Thomas Pettigrew (1958, 1985, 1991) has noted, many people hold prejudiced attitudes and engage in discriminatory behaviour in order to conform to, or fit in with, the prevailing majority view of their culture. It's as if people say, "Hey, everybody else thinks X's are inferior; if I treat X's with respect, people might not like me. I think I'll just go along with everybody else." Pettigrew argues convincingly that although economic competition, frustration, and social cognition processes do account for some prejudice, a powerful determinant of prejudice is slavish conformity to social norms.

Research underscores the important role that social norms play in perpetuating prejudice. For example, in a series of studies, Stangor and colleagues (2001) assessed European-American students' stereotypes of African-Americans. They were also asked to estimate the beliefs that other students at their university held about African-Americans. Later, participants received (false) feedback that their estimate of the other students' beliefs was actually incorrect. Some participants were told that the other students actually held more positive beliefs about African-Americans than what they had estimated. Other participants were told that the students at their university actually had more negative beliefs about African-Americans than they had estimated. What was the effect of learning these social norms? Those who discovered that other students were actually more positive in their views of African-Americans expressed more positive attitudes toward African-Americans than before they learned about this social norm. Sadly, the opposite was true as well: Those who learned that the other students felt negatively toward African-Americans subsequently became more negative as well (Stangor, Sechrist, & Jost, 2001).

In another program of research, Christian Crandall and colleagues (2002) asked participants to rate a large number of social groups in terms of how acceptable it is to have negative feelings toward each group. Other participants rated how positively or negatively they personally felt toward each of these groups. The correlation between the two sets of ratings was astonishingly high: 0.96. (Recall that a perfect correlation is 1.00.) In other words, "to ask people about the norms regarding prejudice is, in practical terms, the same as asking people how they personally feel" (Crandall, Eshleman, & O'Brien, 2002, p. 374). The researchers note that although we may start out being hesitant to accept the norms of any given group, over time, as we begin to identify with the group, we internalize its norms and make them our own. Other research has shown that we are particularly likely to rely on social norms (i.e., what other people think) when developing attitudes toward groups with which we have little familiarity (Sechrist, Stangor, & Killen, 2005).

Watch on **mypsychlab**

Sexism and Adolescent Girls: Campbell Leaper

Injunctification

A motivated tendency to see the status quo (the ways things are) as the most desirable state of affairs (the way things should be)

Injunctification A recent program of research conducted at the University of Waterloo by Aaron Kay, Danielle Gaucher, and colleagues (2009) suggests that people take social norms ("the way things are") one step further and draw the inference that the way things are is how "things are supposed to be," a process referred to as **injunctification** (Kay & Zanna, 2009; Kay, Gaucher, Peach, Laurin, Friesen, Zanna, & Spencer, 2009). This effect is most likely to occur when people are motivated to justify the current system. For example, in one of Kay and colleagues' (2009) studies, students at the University of Waterloo were reminded of the important impact that either their country (Canada) or their university has on their lives. Next, the students were given information that the "system" distributed its funds unequally (for participants in the Canada condition, the unequal treatment was directed at provinces; for participants in the university condition, the unequal treatment was directed at academic departments). Participants who had just been reminded how dependent they were on their country were most likely to regard the Canadian government's distribution of funding to the provinces as being more fair and reasonable (i.e., the way it should be) than their university's distribution of funding to departments. Participants who had just been reminded of how dependent they were on their university for their life's outcomes did just the opposite: They defended the university's unequal allocation of funds but not the government's unequal funding decisions.

What are the consequences of justifying the system? Research by Lau and colleagues (2008) shows that when people are highly motivated to justify their systems (i.e., under system threat), they are more likely to endorse stereotypical or "traditional" gender roles. Specifically, men whose faith in the federal government system was threatened were more attracted to a woman who was described using terms and phrases that reinforce gender inequality (e.g., *vulnerable*, *making a man feel "complete"*) than a woman who was described in nonstereotypical terms (e.g., *career-oriented*, *athletic*; Lau, Kay, & Spencer, 2008). Kay and colleagues have also shown that when people are motivated to believe that the status quo reflects how things should be, they react negatively to someone who does not conform to prevailing social norms. More specifically, these researchers found that under conditions of system threat (which were created by having participants read an article about the social and economic downturn of Canada), female participants who were given information that Canada had very few women in CEO positions later rated a female business student as less likable and competent than did participants who were told that Canada has many women in CEO positions (Kay et al., 2009).

Finally, in a recent series of studies along the same lines, Julia Becker at Philipps University in Germany and Stephen Wright at Simon Fraser University (2011) found that when women were exposed to benevolent sexism (portrayals of women as wonderful but childlike and needy), they were less likely to take action to improve the rights of women (e.g., less likely to sign petitions advocating women's rights) compared to women who were exposed to hostile sexism (portrayals of women as nasty and less competent than men). Why the failure to act? Exposure to benevolent sexism caused women to justify the system (i.e., to agree with statements such as "In general, relations between women and men are fair") and to see less need for change than women exposed to hostile sexism. The researchers conclude that even though benevolent sexism may be seen as more positive than hostile sexism, in some ways it is even more insidious because gender equality is perpetuated when people justify the system and fail to take action.

Watch on **mypsychlab**
Sexism in Education

Individual Differences in Prejudice

As we have mentioned repeatedly throughout this chapter, no one is immune from prejudice. The simple act of classifying people into groups tends to bring with it value judgments about which groups are better than others. However, as you probably have observed, some people do seem to hold more prejudiced attitudes than others. Indeed, research confirms that certain kinds of people are especially likely to hold negative attitudes toward members of out-groups. More specifically, those who are high in right-wing authoritarianism, religious fundamentalism, and social dominance orientation are more likely to be more prejudiced than those who are low in these dimensions.

Right-Wing Authoritarianism

Bob Altemeyer (1981, 1988, 1996) has identified an individual difference variable—right-wing authoritarianism—that is strongly associated with prejudice. *Right-wing authoritarianism* is defined in terms of three clusters of attitudes:

- authoritarian submission—a high degree of submission to authority figures in society;
- authoritarian aggression—aggression directed toward groups that are seen as legitimate targets by authority figures; and
- conventionalism—a high degree of conformity to the rules and conventions that are established by authority figures.

Right-wing authoritarians agree with statements such as "Once our government leaders give us the 'go ahead,' it will be the duty of every patriotic citizen to help stomp out the rot that is poisoning our country from within" (Altemeyer, 1998).

In extensive research conducted at the University of Manitoba, Altemeyer (1981, 1996, 1998) has found strong positive correlations between right-wing authoritarianism and racial prejudice. Similarly, at the University of Waterloo, Haddock, Zanna, and Esses (1993) found that participants who are high in right-wing authoritarianism express more negative attitudes than those who are low on this trait toward French Canadians, First Nations peoples, and Pakistanis. Not surprisingly, right-wing authoritarianism also is correlated with prejudice toward immigrants to Canada (Hodson, Hogg, & MacInnis, 2009). Right-wing authoritarians also hold traditional, nonegalitarian attitudes toward women (e.g., believing that women should be subservient to men; Altemeyer, 1996, 1998; Perrott, Miller, & Delaney, 1997) and have negative attitudes toward feminists (Haddock & Zanna, 1994). Finally, those right-wing authoritarians show especially high levels of prejudice toward gays and lesbians (Altemeyer, 1996, 1998; Altemeyer & Hunsberger, 1992; Haddock, Zanna, & Esses, 1993; Hunsberger, 1996; Whitley, 1999).

Reducing Prejudice among Right-Wing Authoritarians Can the attitudes of right-wing authoritarians be changed? This is a tall order, indeed. Given that right-wing authoritarians are especially prejudiced toward gays and lesbians, Altemeyer (1988, 2001) has focused on ways of changing attitudes toward this group. One strategy that has proven effective is to create awareness that attitudes generally have become more positive toward the gay and lesbian community (Altemeyer, 2001). When right-wing authoritarians are shown that their attitudes are more negative than other people's, they tend to change them because conforming to social norms is important to them (see also Nicol, 2009).

Another strategy for reducing prejudice is to encourage interaction with members of out-groups. (The benefits of contact are discussed more fully at the end of this chapter.) Altemeyer decided to find out if right-wing authoritarians would change their attitudes if they personally knew a gay or lesbian person. He did so by telling one of his psychology classes that he was gay and was actively involved in the gay rights movement. (Altemeyer actually is not gay, although a newspaper article describing this demonstration reported that he was, which apparently came as quite a surprise to his in-laws!) What effect did this revelation have on the right-wing authoritarians in his class? They subsequently became more positive in their attitudes toward gays as a group (see Altemeyer, 2001). Thus, there is reason to be optimistic that prejudice can be reduced, even among right-wing authoritarians.

Religious Fundamentalism

Research conducted at Wilfrid Laurier University by Bruce Hunsberger (1995, 1996) and at the University of Manitoba (Altemeyer & Hunsberger, 1992, 1993) suggests that religious fundamentalism is another individual difference variable that is related to prejudice. *Religious fundamentalism* is defined as a belief in the absolute and literal truth of one's religious beliefs. People who are high in fundamentalism also believe that their religion is the "right" one and that forces of evil are constantly threatening to undermine its truth. (Note that the term *fundamentalism* does not refer to a specific religion but, rather, to any religious beliefs that are seen as portraying the ultimate truth.)

Studies conducted with university students and community samples have shown that religious fundamentalism is correlated with racial prejudice as well as with negative attitudes toward single mothers and gays and lesbians (the behaviour of these latter groups is seen as immoral; Altemeyer & Hunsberger, 1992, 1993; Jackson & Esses, 1997). For example, Hunsberger (1996) assessed religious fundamentalism and attitudes toward gays and lesbians among Muslims, Jews, and Hindus living in Toronto. Within each group, the greater the fundamentalism, the greater the hostility toward the gay and lesbian community.

It may have crossed your mind that there are similarities between religious fundamentalism and right-wing authoritarianism. Indeed, Altemeyer and Hunsberger (1993) have reached the conclusion that fundamentalism is a religious manifestation of right-wing authoritarianism.

Finally, we want to emphasize that these researchers are not saying that religion *per se* is associated with prejudice but, rather, that there is a relation between prejudice and the way in which certain people hold their religious beliefs. Those who regard their beliefs as the absolute truth that must be zealously followed are likely to be prejudiced. This is not true for those who have a flexible, open, and questioning orientation to religion (known as religious quest). In fact, religious quest tends to be negatively correlated with prejudice (Altemeyer & Hunsberger, 1992, 1993).

Social Dominance Orientation

Another individual difference variable that is related to prejudice is *social dominance orientation* (Pratto, Sidanius, Stallworth, & Malle, 1994; Sidanius, Levin, & Pratto, 1996). Individuals who are high in social dominance orientation believe that groups of people are inherently unequal and that it is acceptable for some groups in society to benefit more than others. They prefer to be in the advantaged group, even if it means treating other groups badly. For example, people high in social dominance orientation agree with statements such as "To get ahead in life, it is sometimes necessary to step on others." For example, a study conducted with officer cadets at the Royal Military College of Canada found that leaders high in social dominance orientation do not consider it important to relate to subordinates but rather see subordinates as tools for getting work done (Nicol, 2009).

Research conducted in many countries, including Canada, has shown that social dominance orientation is associated with racial prejudice, sexism, and negative attitudes toward gays and lesbians (Altemeyer, 1998; Pratto et al., 1994, 2000; Sidanius, Levin, & Pratto, 1996; Whitley, 1999). Not surprisingly, those who are high on this trait also are opposed to interracial dating and transracial adoptions, as shown in a study conducted by York University researchers (Lalonde, Giguère, Fontaine, & Smith, 2007). Brock University researcher Gordon Hodson and colleagues (2010) have recently shown that university students who are high in social dominance orientation prefer jokes directed at low-status out-groups (Mexicans) to jokes directed at a high-status out-group (Americans) or a high-status in-group (Canadians; Hodson, Rush, & MacInnis, 2010; Hodson, MacInnis, & Rush, 2010). The researchers argue that this humour preference serves to perpetuate prejudice toward these lower-status out-groups. People who are high in social dominance orientation also hold negative attitudes toward immigrants. They oppose offering assistance to immigrant groups because they believe that any gains made by immigrants occur at their expense (Esses, Jackson, & Armstrong, 1998; Esses, Dovidio, Jackson, & Armstrong, 2001). In research along the same lines, Hodson and colleagues have found that social dominance orientation is associated with perceiving immigrants to Canada as a threat, a lack of empathy for immigrants, and, most disturbingly, dehumanization of immigrants (Costello & Hodson, 2010; Hodson et al., 2009). Similarly, refugees are seen as immoral and as trying to unjustly sneak into Canada (Esses, Veenvliet, Hodson, & Mihic, 2008). It probably comes as no surprise that organizational leaders who are high in social dominance orientation are more likely to make unethical decisions (e.g., exploiting the labour pool of poor countries) than those who are low in this trait, as shown in a series of experiments conducted at Guelph University and the University of Waterloo (Son Hing, Bobocel, Zanna, & McBride, 2007).

Finally, it may interest you to know that a study conducted with French Canadian university students found that law students score higher on social dominance orientation (and prejudice) than do psychology students. Moreover, upper-year law students score higher on social dominance orientation than first-year law students, whereas the opposite is true for psychology students (Guimond, Dambrun, Michinov, & Durarte, 2003).

Reducing Prejudice among People High in Social Dominance Orientation How do you reduce prejudice among people who think it's fine for them to be on top?

Esses and colleagues (2001) have tried several approaches, including trying to persuade those who are high in social dominance orientation that they do not necessarily lose out when others get ahead. This didn't work. In fact, it made things worse. The researchers also attempted to create feelings of a sense of shared identity between people high in social dominance orientation and immigrant groups. This approach had some success in Canada (Esses et al., 2001) but backfired when it was tried in Germany (Esses, Wagner, & Wolf, 2006). Thus, reducing prejudice among those high in social dominance orientation will continue to be a challenge, given that people with this trait do not see a need for prejudice to be reduced (Hodson & Esses, 2005).

Effects of Stereotyping, Prejudice, and Discrimination

Stereotyping, prejudice, and discrimination can have insidious effects, such as poverty, war, torture, and genocide. Even when prejudice doesn't cost an individual's life, he or she can still pay a very high price in terms of the psychological consequences of prejudice and discrimination. For example, a recent study documented that among First Nations adults in Canada, feeling discriminated against was correlated with symptoms of depression (Bombay, Matheson, & Anisman, 2010). Prejudice and discrimination also have behavioural consequences. When a member of a majority group mistreats a member of a disadvantaged group, the disadvantaged person is unlikely to perform well, thereby confirming the majority group member's negative stereotype and, in turn, perpetuating the discrimination. You probably recognize our old friend the *self-fulfilling prophecy* once again rearing its head. Moreover, fears that one will confirm the negative stereotype of one's group also can impede performance, as we shall see shortly. Perhaps most tragic of all, even when the poor performance of disadvantaged groups is clearly the result of discrimination, they may nevertheless blame themselves rather than place the blame where it deserves to be placed—on the shoulders of those who are engaging in the discriminatory behaviour.

Self-Fulfilling Prophecies

All other things being equal, if you believe that Amy is stupid and treat her accordingly, chances are that she will not say a lot of clever things in your presence. This is the well-known self-fulfilling prophecy, discussed in Chapter 3. How does this come about? If you believe that Amy is stupid, you probably will not ask her interesting questions and you will not listen intently while she is talking; indeed, you might even look out the window or yawn. You behave this way because of a simple expectation: Why waste energy paying attention to Amy if she is unlikely to say anything smart or interesting? This is bound to have an important impact on Amy's behaviour, for if you aren't paying attention when she is talking to you, she will feel uneasy and will probably clam up, and not come out with the poetry and wisdom within her. This in turn serves to confirm your initial belief about her. The circle is closed; the self-fulfilling prophecy is complete.

The relevance of this phenomenon to stereotyping and discrimination was demonstrated in an elegant experiment by Carl Word, Mark Zanna, and Joel Cooper (1974). They asked white university students to interview several job applicants; some of the applicants were white and others were African-Americans. Unwittingly, the students displayed discomfort and lack of interest when interviewing African-American applicants; for example, they sat farther away, they tended to stammer when talking, and they terminated the interview far sooner than when they were interviewing white applicants. Can you guess how this behaviour might have affected the African-American applicants? To find out, the researchers, in a second experiment, systematically varied the behaviour of the interviewers (actually confederates) so it coincided with the way the real interviewers had treated the African-American or white interviewees in the first experiment. But in the second experiment, all of the interviewees were white. The researchers videotaped the proceedings and had the applicants rated by independent judges. They found that those applicants who were interviewed the way African-Americans had been interviewed in the first experiment were judged to be far more nervous and far less effective than those who were interviewed the way white applicants had been interviewed in the first experiment. In sum, these experiments clearly demonstrated that when African-Americans are interviewed by whites, they are unintentionally placed at a disadvantage and are not likely to perform as well as their white counterparts (see Figure 12.6).

In a recent program of research conducted at the University of Waterloo, Christine Logel and colleagues have examined how men in mathematics and engineering fields who hold sexist attitudes behave in ways that cause their female colleagues to underperform (Logel, Walton, Spencer, Iserman, von Hippel, & Bell, 2009). In their first study, male engineering students completed a subtle measure of sexism and then had an interaction with a female confederate posing as another engineering student. The men who were sexist displayed more dominance and more sexual interest in the female confederate than men who were less sexist. To find out how these behaviours affect the performance of women in the field of engineering, the researchers conducted a second study in which they trained male confederates to behave exactly like the sexist male engineering students in the first study (e.g., showing dominance and sexual interest) or to behave in a nonsexist way. The results showed that female engineering students actually reported greater attraction to the male confederates who behaved in a sexist way than the confederates who acted in a nonsexist way. However, women in the sexist condition subsequently scored much lower on an engineering test than women in the nonsexist condition. Logel and colleagues (2009) suggest that the confederate's sexist behaviour activated the stereotype that women are not very good at math and engineering and that anxiety about confirming this negative stereotype interfered with the women's performance. But wait, you may be thinking. Maybe these women performed poorly because they were distracted by their feelings of attraction to the sexist male confederate, rather than because of fears about confirming a negative stereotype about their gender. To find out, the researchers replicated the study (this time with women from math, sciences, and engineering), but this time some women were given a math test whereas other women were given an English test (English is a domain in which women are not negatively stereotyped). When a male confederate behaved in a sexist way, women performed worse on the math test compared to women who interacted with a nonsexist confederate. However, the confederate's sexism did not affect performance on the English test. This finding supports the conclusion that when women in male-dominated fields encounter sexist behaviour, it

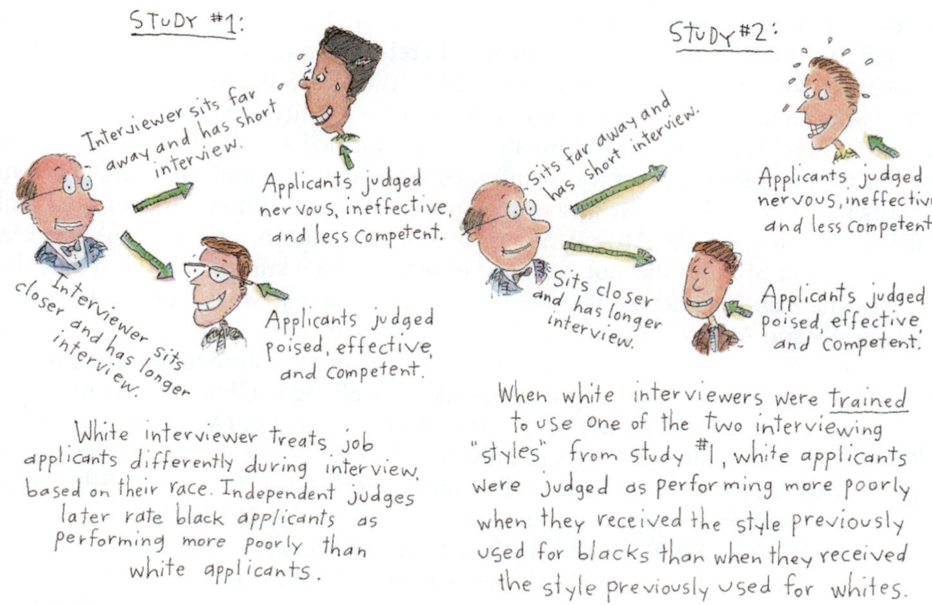

FIGURE 12.6

An experiment demonstrating self-fulfilling prophecies.

makes them feel anxious about confirming the negative stereotype that women do not perform well in these domains, and voila, the prophecy is fulfilled.

These are not isolated findings. In a series of studies conducted by University of Toronto researcher Glenn Adams and colleagues (2006), it was found that the mere suggestion of sexism (a female confederate casually mentioning that the male experimenter seemed sexist) caused women to perform more poorly on a logic test compared with women who did not hear the sexism remark (Adams, Garcia, Purdie-Vaughns, & Steele, 2006).

On a societal level, the insidiousness of the self-fulfilling prophecy goes even farther. Suppose there is a general belief that a particular group is irredeemably stupid, uneducable, and fit only for menial jobs. Why waste educational resources on them? Hence, they are given inadequate schooling. What do you find 30 years later? An entire group that, with few exceptions, is fit only for menial jobs. "See? I was right all the time," says the bigot. "How fortunate that we didn't waste our precious educational resources on such people!" The self-fulfilling prophecy strikes again.

Stereotype Threat

It is well established that academic test performance varies among different cultural groups. For example, in the United States, it has been found that although there is considerable overlap, Asian-Americans perform slightly better than European-Americans, who in turn perform better than African-Americans. Why does this occur? There may be any number of explanations: economic, cultural, historical, or political. Social psychologists have discovered another factor having to do with the anxiety that is produced by negative stereotypes—specifically, the fear that one's behaviour will conform to the stereotype of one's group (J. Aronson, Jannone, McGlone, & Johnson-Campbell, 2009; J. Aronson, Quinn, & Spencer, 1998; Steele, 1997; Steele & J. Aronson, 1995a, 1995b; Steele, Spencer, & J. Aronson, 2002). This phenomenon is referred to as **stereotype threat.** When African-American students, for example, find themselves in highly evaluative educational situations, most tend to experience apprehension about confirming the existing negative cultural stereotype of intellectual inferiority. In effect, an African-American student is saying, "If I perform poorly on this test, it will reflect poorly on me and on my race." This extra burden of apprehension in turn interferes with the student's ability to perform well in these situations. Thus, the self-fulfilling prophecy strikes again—in this case, triggered by fears that one will confirm the stereotype of one's group.

Stereotype Threat

The apprehension experienced by members of a minority group that they might behave in a manner that confirms an existing cultural stereotype

In one of their experiments, Claude Steele and Joshua Aronson (1995a) administered a difficult verbal test, the GRE, individually to African-American and white students at Stanford University. Half of the students of each race were led to believe that the investigator was interested in measuring their intellectual ability; the other half were led to believe that the investigator was merely trying to develop the test itself—and because the test was not yet valid or reliable, they were assured that their performance would mean nothing in terms of their actual ability. The results confirmed the researchers' speculations: White students performed equally well regardless of whether they believed the test was being used as a diagnostic tool. African-American students who believed the test was nondiagnostic of their abilities performed as well as white students. But the African-American students who thought that the test was measuring their abilities did not perform as well as white students or as well as the African-American students in the other group. In subsequent experiments in the same series, Steele and Aronson also found that if race is made more salient, the decrement in performance among African-American students is even more pronounced.

I will look at any additional evidence to confirm the opinion to which I have already come.

—Lord Hugh Molson, *British politician (1950s–1960s)*

Stereotype threat applies to gender as well. As you know, a common stereotype is that men are better at math than women. (According to recent research conducted at Laval University, the fewer the number of women in math and science programs, the more likely it is that women will buy into this stereotype; Delisle, Guay, Senécal, & Larose, 2009). Spencer, Steele, and Quinn (1999) showed that when women were led to believe that a particular test was designed to show gender differences in math abilities, they did not perform as well as men. When women in another condition were told that the same test had nothing to do with male–female differences, they performed just as well as men. These effects have been replicated by many other researchers in the United States (e.g., Brown & Pinel, 2003); in Germany (Keller & Dauenheimer, 2003); and in Canada, with university students in Newfoundland (Walsh, Hickey, & Duffy, 1999), and with French Canadian women from a number of different academic programs (Beaton, Tougas, Rinfret, Huard, & Delisle, 2007).

Recent research conducted with Canadian and American female university students shows that trying to keep negative stereotypes about women and math out of mind (i.e., thought suppression), and trying to suppress anxiety about confirming negative stereotypes, taxes valuable cognitive resources to the point where test performance is impaired (Johns, Inzlicht, & Schmader, 2008; Logel, Iserman, Davies, Quinn, & Spencer, 2009).

Sadly, stereotype threat has widespread effects (Davies, Spencer, & Claude, 2005; Davies, Spencer, & Steele, 2005; von Hippel, von Hippel, Conway, Preacher, Schooler, & Radvansky, 2005). In a series of studies, Jennifer Steele, at York University, and Nalini Ambady (2006) showed that simply reminding women of their gender (e.g., by subliminally presenting female stereotype words) resulted in the women having more negative attitudes toward math compared to women in the other conditions who were exposed to either male stereotype words or neutral words. And it isn't just attitudes that are affected. Davies and colleagues (2002) found that stereotype threat can lead women—even women who are good at math—to avoid taking math tests and to shy away from math-related careers (Davies, Spencer, Quinn, & Gerhardstein, 2002).

Here's an interesting twist: What if you happen to be an Asian woman and you also are aware of the stereotype that Asians are good at math? Might you perform differently depending on which stereotype about you is activated? Shih, Pittinsky, and Ambady (1999) raised the intriguing possibility that performance might differ depending on which of an individual's identities is activated: her identity as an Asian or as a woman. The researchers conducted a fascinating study in which they administered the Canadian Math Competition Test to a group of female Asian-American university students. Some of the women were reminded of their ethnicity before they took the test; others were reminded of their gender (a control group was not reminded of any identity before taking the test). Remarkably, the participants who had been reminded that they were Asian had the highest performance on the test, whereas those who had been reminded that they were women had the lowest performance (the control group scored in between these two groups).

These findings suggest that although stereotype threat usually has negative effects, being reminded of a positive stereotype associated with one's identity (e.g., Asians are good at math) can lead to improved performance. But even reminders of positive stereotypes can be a mixed blessing. For example, there is evidence that people sometimes choke under the pressure of having to live up to the high expectations that others have of their group (Cheryan & Bodenhausen, 2000; Shih, Ambady, Richeson, Fujita, & Gray, 2002).

Stereotype threat occurs when people feel they are being evaluated against an existing negative cultural stereotype.

Before leaving this topic, we should note that the effects we have been discussing are not limited to women. In a series of studies, Joshua Aronson and colleagues (1999) demonstrated that white men do not perform as well on math exams when competing with Asian men (Aronson, Lustina, Good, Keough, Steele, & Brown, 1999). These effects also are not limited to academic performance. For example, Stone and colleagues (1999) found that when a game of miniature golf was framed as a measure of "sport strategic intelligence," black athletes performed worse than whites. When the game was framed as "natural athletic ability," the pattern reversed, such that the black athletes outperformed the white athletes (Stone, Lynch, Sjomeling, & Darley, 1999). More recently, University of Toronto researchers found that elderly women paired with a young female confederate did worse (recalled less information) when told they were taking a memory test than when they were told it was a reading comprehension test (Kang & Chasteen, 2009).

Can the effects of stereotype threat be overcome? Research conducted over the last decade points to a number of ways that the effects of stereotype threat can be reduced. One particularly promising avenue is to change people's mindset when taking a test. For example, the effects of stereotype threat are diminished if students are given a reminder that they are good students just before taking a test (Good, Aronson, & Harder, 2008; McGlone & Aronson, 2006) or if they are made aware that it is normal for members of stereotyped groups to experience test anxiety (Aronson & Williams, 2009; Johns, Schmader, & Martens, 2005). Stereotype threat also is reduced if people are reminded that abilities are improvable rather than fixed (Aronson, Fried, & Good, 2002; Good, Aronson, & Inzlicht, 2003). Stereotype threat is reduced in women if they are told that gender differences in math performance are the result of differences in experience, rather than genetics, as shown in research conducted at the University of British Columbia (Dar-Nimrod & Heine, 2006) or if they are told that there are no gender differences in the performance domain, as demonstrated in several studies conducted at the University of Waterloo (Davies et al., 2005; Logel et al., 2009). In fact, under these conditions, women perform as well as men. Recent research conducted with female Canadian and American university students has found that cognitive reappraisal (e.g., being told to approach a math test in an objective, neutral manner) also improves performance on a math test (relative to a stereotype threat condition in which women were told that the test was diagnostic of their true strengths and weaknesses in the math domain; Johns et al., 2008).

Finally, another effective strategy is to have people engage in self-affirmation before they begin an evaluative task. For example, research conducted at the University of Alberta (Schimel, Arndt, Banko, & Cook, 2004) and by a team of researchers at several American universities and the University of Waterloo (Sherman, Cohen, Nussbaum, Bunyan, & Garcia, 2009) found that female students who were given a self-affirmation exercise before taking a math test performed better than those in a control condition. Interestingly, Sherman and colleagues (2009) found that self-affirmation worked even when the intervention was implicit (i.e., occurred outside of conscious awareness).

Interventions for Reducing Prejudice and Discrimination

It is never too late to give up our prejudices.

—Henry David Thoreau, *Walden, 1854*

Sometimes subtle, sometimes brutally overt, prejudice is indeed ubiquitous. Does this mean that prejudice is an essential aspect of human social interaction and will therefore always be with us? We social psychologists do not take such a pessimistic view. People can change. But how? We have offered several clues throughout this chapter. We have shown that getting people to focus on positive aspects of themselves (self-affirmation) reduces the need to denigrate others to get a boost in self-esteem. We have also seen that blurring the distinction between "us" and "them" can improve attitudes toward out-groups. We have discussed how promoting common goals—mutual interdependence—fosters cooperation and liking between groups. We will now focus on a few more general strategies for eliminating, or at least reducing, this noxious aspect of human social behaviour.

Learning Not to Hate

While social psychologists disagree on whether or not humans are naturally prejudiced, most would agree that the *specifics* of prejudice must be learned. How easy is it to learn prejudice? Sinclair and colleagues (2004) found that children in grades 4 and 5 shared their parents' racial attitudes, especially if they identified with their parents (Sinclair, Dunn, & Lowery, 2004). What about when children become adults? Do they still adopt their parents' prejudices? Researchers at the University of Waterloo took a close look at the folk wisdom that "the apple never falls far from the tree" by examining attitude and value similarity between parents and their adult children (Rohan & Zanna, 1996). They found that similarity was significantly stronger between children and parents when parents held egalitarian attitudes and values than when parents held prejudice-related attitudes and values. Why might this be? Our guess is that this discrepancy occurs because the culture as a whole is more egalitarian than the bigoted parents. Thus, when children of bigoted parents leave home (e.g., to go off to university), they are more likely to be exposed to competing views.

Teachers also play a crucial role in educating children to treat others in a nondiscriminatory manner, as was illustrated by the life-altering lesson in prejudice that Jane Elliott (1977), a teacher in Riceville, Iowa, taught her grade 3 class. Elliott was concerned that her young students were leading too sheltered a life. The children all lived in rural Iowa, they were all white, and they were all Christian. Elliott felt it was important to give them some direct experience about what stereotyping and discrimination felt like, from both sides. To achieve this end, Elliott divided her class by eye colour. She told her students that blue-eyed people were superior to brown-eyed people—smarter, nicer, more trustworthy, and so on. The brown-eyed youngsters were required to wear special collars around their necks so they would be instantly recognizable as a member of the inferior group. She gave special privileges to the blue-eyed youngsters; for example, they got to play longer at recess, could have second helpings at the cafeteria, and received extra praise in the classroom. How did the children respond?

In a matter of hours, Elliott succeeded in creating a microcosm of a prejudiced society in her classroom. Just a few hours before the experiment began, the children had been a cooperative, cohesive group; once the seeds of divisiveness were planted, there was trouble. The "superior" blue-eyed kids made fun of the brown-eyed kids, refused to play with them, tattled on them to the teacher, thought up new restrictions and punishments for them, and even started a fistfight in the schoolyard. The "inferior" brown-eyed kids became self-conscious, depressed, and demoralized. They performed poorly on classroom tests that day.

The world is full of pots jeering at kettles.

—François de la Rochefoucauld, *Maxims, 1665*

The next day, Elliott switched the stereotypes about eye colour. She said she'd made a dreadful mistake—that brown-eyed people were really the superior ones. She told the brown-eyed kids to put their collars on the blue-eyed kids. They gleefully did so. The tables had turned—and the brown-eyed kids exacted their revenge.

On the morning of the third day, Elliott explained to her students that they had been learning about prejudice and discrimination, and how it feels to be a person of colour. The children discussed the two-day experience and clearly understood its message. In a follow-up, Elliott met with these students at a class reunion when they were in their mid-twenties. Their memories of the exercise were startlingly clear; they reported that the experience had a powerful and lasting impact on their lives. They felt that they were less prejudiced and more aware of discrimination against others because of this childhood experience.

Jane Elliott's eye colour exercise has been used widely in classrooms in many countries, including Canada, and in other settings (e.g., with prison staff) with the hope that experiencing discrimination first-hand will make people less likely to behave in discriminatory ways.

Although adults obviously play an important role in socializing children not to be prejudiced, an intriguing study by Aboud and Doyle (1996) suggests that children also may be effective at teaching one another. Participants in this research were white students in grades 3 and 4 attending various schools in Quebec. First, their attitudes toward whites, blacks, and Chinese-Canadians were assessed. Then, the researchers paired a high-prejudice child with a low-prejudice child and asked them to discuss their perceptions of different racial groups. Low-prejudice children were more likely than high-prejudice children to point out negative characteristics of whites and similarities across racial groups. For example, if a prejudiced child mentioned that a black classmate or a Chinese classmate had been mean, a low-prejudice child would point out white classmates who had been mean as well. Importantly, these discussions had the effect of reducing prejudice among the high-prejudice children. Happily, the opposite did not occur—high-prejudice children did not create prejudice among low-prejudice children. These findings are encouraging and suggest that peers also may play an important role in teaching one another not to hate.

The Contact Hypothesis

As you have perhaps experienced in your own life, repeated contact with members of an out-group can have a positive effect on stereotypes and prejudice. People often feel anxious, however, about interacting with out-group members (Mendes, Gray, Mendoza-Denton, Major, & Epel, 2007). One worry is that out-groups might be hostile and unfriendly toward us (Plant & Devine, 2003). Another worry is that we might say or do something that makes us look prejudiced—even if we're not. According to Vorauer and Turpie (2004), people may choke under the pressure of trying to appear unprejudiced to the point where they actually show less warmth and responsiveness than they otherwise would. These researchers had white students at the University of Manitoba engage in an interaction (via videotape) with an Aboriginal person. Ironically, it was the participants who were least prejudiced who were most likely to show these "choking" effects.

There is yet another complicating factor: Jacquie Vorauer and colleagues have found that when interacting with out-group members, we believe that it is obvious that we are showing interest and friendliness—when it actually may not be all that obvious to our interaction partner. This perception sets up a vicious cycle—the other person doesn't seem to be reciprocating our friendly overtures, and, therefore, we aren't very keen on pursuing a friendship with him or her. These effects have been demonstrated in interactions between white Canadian and Native Canadian (Vorauer, 2005) and between white Canadian and Chinese students at the University of Manitoba (Vorauer & Sakamoto, 2006). Low-prejudice people are most likely to overestimate the friendliness they've shown, leading to the counterintuitive result that their interactions with out-group members can actually be more negative than those of high-prejudice people.

CONNECTIONS

Can Playing Video Games Make You Less Prejudiced?

Is there a way to overcome people's reluctance to interact with members of out-groups? An intriguing study conducted at York University offers some promise. Kawakami and colleagues (2007) had non-black participants play a video game in which they were trained to either approach photos of white faces and avoid photos of black faces by using a joystick or do the opposite (i.e., approach blacks and avoid whites). Participants in a control group simply moved the joystick to the left or the right. Those who were in the "approach blacks" condition later showed lower levels of prejudice toward blacks compared with those in the "avoid blacks" group and the control group. In a subsequent study, the researchers found that participants who approached photographs of black faces in the video game sat closer to a black confederate during an interaction after the game compared with participants in the other groups. Thus, approaching blacks in a video game actually translated into more positive behaviours in a real-life contact situation (Kawakami, Phills, Steele, & Dovidio, 2007).

Thus, although it may seem obvious that the first step toward reducing prejudice would be to bring members of different groups into contact with one another, it isn't as easy as it may seem. In his strikingly prescient masterwork *The Nature of Prejudice*, Gordon Allport stated the contact hypothesis in this way:

> Prejudice may be reduced by equal status contact between majority and minority groups in the pursuit of common goals. The effect is greatly enhanced if this contact is sanctioned by

> institutional supports (i.e., by law, custom or local atmosphere), and provided it is of a sort that leads to the perception of common interests and common humanity between members of the two groups. (Allport, 1954)

In other words, Allport is not talking about mere contact; he is clear that contact must be between people who are of equal status and in pursuit of common goals. Let's now turn to a discussion of these conditions.

Two of the key factors in the success of contact are *mutual interdependence* and a *common goal* (Amir, 1969, 1976). We have already seen the importance of these factors when discussing Sherif and colleagues' (1961) classic study of cooperation between hostile groups of Boy Scouts at a summer camp.

The third condition is *equal status.* At the boys' camp (Sherif et al., 1961), the group members were very much the same in terms of status and power. When status is unequal, however, interactions can easily follow stereotypical patterns: The bosses will act like stereotypical bosses, the employees will act like stereotypical subordinates—and no one will learn new, disconfirming information about the other group (Pettigrew, 1969; Wilder, 1984). The whole point of contact is to allow people to learn that their stereotypes are inaccurate; contact and interaction should lead to disconfirmation of negative stereotyped beliefs.

Fourth, contact must occur in a *friendly, informal setting*, where in-group members can interact with out-group members on a one-to-one basis (Brewer & Miller, 1984; Cook, 1984; Wilder, 1986). Simply placing two groups in contact in a room where they can remain segregated will do little to promote their understanding or knowledge of one another.

Fifth, through friendly, informal interactions *with multiple members* of the out-group, an individual will learn that his or her beliefs about the out-group are wrong. It is crucial for the individual to believe that the out-group members he or she comes to know are typical of their group; otherwise, the stereotype can be maintained by labelling one out-group member as the exception (Wilder, 1984).

Sixth and last, contact is most likely to lead to reduced prejudice when *social norms that promote and support equality* among groups are operating in the situation (Amir, 1969; Wilder, 1984). We know the power of social norms; here, they can be harnessed to motivate people to reach out to members of the out-group. If the boss in a work setting, or the professor in a classroom, creates and reinforces a norm of acceptance and tolerance, group members will modify their own behaviour to fit the norm.

To sum up, suspicious or even hostile groups will reduce their stereotyping, prejudice, and discriminatory behaviour when these six conditions of contact are met: mutual interdependence; a common goal; equal status; informal, interpersonal contact; multiple contacts; and social norms of equality. It might seem a tall order to structure contact situations in a way in which all of these conditions are met. Fortunately, according to a recent meta analysis of 515 studies on the contact hypothesis, although these conditions facilitate the reduction of prejudice, it is not essential that all of them be met for contact to have beneficial effects (Pettigrew & Tropp, 2006; Pettigrew & Tropp, 2011).

We must recognize that beneath the superficial classification of sex and race the same potentialities exist, recurring generation after generation only to perish because society has no place for them.

—Margaret Mead, Male and Female, *1943*

Cooperation and Interdependence: The Jigsaw Classroom

Let's paint a scenario. Imagine a grade 6 student of Mexican origin, whom we will call Carlos. Carlos has been attending schools in an underprivileged neighbourhood for his entire life. Because the schools in his neighbourhood were not well equipped or well staffed, his first five years of education were somewhat deficient. Suddenly, without much warning or preparation, he is bused to a school in a predominantly white, middle-class neighbourhood. Carlos must now compete against white, middle-class students who have had better preparation than he has had and who have been reared to hold white, middle-class values, which include working hard in pursuit of good grades, raising one's hand enthusiastically whenever the teacher asks a question, and so on. In effect, Carlos has been thrust into a highly competitive situation for which he is unprepared and in which payoffs are made for abilities he has not yet developed. The white kids might quickly conclude that Carlos is stupid, unmotivated, and sullen—just as they had suspected (Wilder & Shapiro, 1989). Moreover, Carlos might conclude that the white kids are arrogant showoffs. This is an example of the self-fulfilling prophecy we discussed earlier.

Is it possible to get white students and minority students to have equal status, be mutually dependent, and pursue common goals? One of the authors of this textbook (Elliot Aronson) got to find out. In 1971, the school system of Austin, Texas, was desegregated. Within a few weeks, the schools were in turmoil. African-American, white, and Mexican-American children were in open conflict; fistfights broke out between the various racial groups in the corridors and the schoolyards. The school superintendent invited Elliot Aronson, who was then a professor at the University of Texas, to enter the system with the mandate to do anything within reason to create a more harmonious environment. After spending a few days observing the dynamics of several classrooms, Aronson and his graduate students were strongly reminded of the situation that existed in Sherif and colleagues' (1961) camp experiment. With the findings of that study in mind, they developed a technique that created an interdependent classroom atmosphere, designed to encourage the students of various racial and ethnic groups to pursue common goals. They called it the **jigsaw classroom**, because it resembled the assembling of a jigsaw puzzle (Aronson, 1992; Aronson & Bridgeman, 1979; Aronson & Gonzalez, 1988; Aronson & Patnoe, 1997; Aronson, Stephan, Sikes, Blaney, & Snapp, 1978).

Jigsaw Classroom

A classroom setting designed to reduce prejudice between children by placing them in small, desegregated groups and making each child dependent on the other children in the group to learn the course material and do well in the class

How the Jigsaw Classroom Works Students are placed in diverse six-person learning groups. The day's lesson is divided into six paragraphs, so that each student has one segment of the written material. For example, if the students are to learn about the life of Mother Teresa, her biography is arranged in six parts; each student has possession of a unique and vital part of the information, which, like the pieces of a jigsaw puzzle, must be put together before anyone can learn the whole picture. The individual must learn his or her own section and teach it to the other members of the group who do not have any other access to that material. So, if Debbie wants to do well on the ensuing exam about the life of Mother Teresa, she must pay close attention to Carlos (who is reciting on Mother Teresa's childhood), to Natalie (who is reciting on Mother Teresa's humanitarian actions), and so on. Through the jigsaw process, the children begin to pay more attention to each other and to show respect for each other. As you might expect, a child like Carlos would respond to this treatment by simultaneously becoming more relaxed and more engaged; this would inevitably produce an improvement in his ability to communicate. And the other students would begin to realize that Carlos is a lot smarter than they thought he was. They begin to like him. Carlos begins to enjoy school more; his academic performance begins to improve and so does his self-esteem. The vicious circle has been broken.

Listen on mypsychlab
Prejudice

The formal data that Aronson and his colleagues gathered from the jigsaw experiments were clear and striking. Compared with students in traditional classrooms, students in jigsaw groups showed a decrease in prejudice and stereotyping, as well as an increase in their liking for their group mates, both within and across ethnic boundaries. In addition, children in the jigsaw classrooms performed better on objective exams, liked school more, and showed a significantly greater increase in self-esteem than did children in traditional classrooms. Moreover, children in schools where the jigsaw technique was practised developed a greater ability to empathize with others and showed substantial evidence of true integration—that is, in the schoolyard there was far more intermingling among the various races and ethnic groups than in the yards of schools using more traditional classroom techniques (Aronson & Bridgeman, 1979).

Two are better than one because they have a good reward for their toil. For if they fail, one will lift up his fellow, but woe to him who is alone when he falls and has not another to lift him up. Again, if two lie together, they are warm; but how can one be warm alone?

—Ecclesiastes 4:9–12

When the classroom is structured so that students of various ethnic groups work together cooperatively, prejudice decreases.

The jigsaw approach was first tested in 1971; since then, several similar cooperative techniques have been developed (Cook, 1985; Johnson & Johnson, 1987, 1989; Meier, 1995; Sharan, 1980; Slavin, 1980, 1996). The striking results originally obtained by Aronson and colleagues have been successfully replicated in thousands of classrooms (Jürgen-Lohmann, Borsch, & Giesen, 2001). What began as a simple experiment in one school setting is slowly becoming an important force in the field of public education. Unfortunately, the operative word is *slowly*. The educational system, like all bureaucracies, tends to resist change, and the consequences can be tragic (Aronson, 2000, 2004).

The Extended Contact Hypothesis

We have seen that contact between groups can be highly effective in reducing prejudice. However, the practicalities of bringing members of different racial, ethnic, and other social groups together can be formidable. Fortunately, research on the **extended contact hypothesis** conducted by Stephen Wright at Simon Fraser University and Art Aron at Stony Brook University in New York and their colleagues suggests that prejudice can be reduced simply by informing people that a member of their own group has a close relationship with an out-group member (e.g., Aron, Wright, Eberhardt, & Slatcher, 2009; Brody, Wright, Aron, McLaughlin-Volpe, 2009; Wright, Brody, & Aron, 2005; Wright, Aron, McLaughlin, & Ropp, 1997). Take a moment to think about a racial or ethnic group to which you do not belong. Then ask yourself how many people in your racial or ethnic group are friends with members of that group. Wright and colleagues have found that the greater the number of people in our group who have friendships with out-group members, the less prejudiced we are toward that group. These effects hold for both majority and minority groups.

Extended Contact Hypothesis

The mere knowledge that a member of one's own group has a close relationship with a member of another group can reduce one's prejudice toward that group

These findings imply that prejudice between groups could be reduced by creating cross-group friendships and making members of each group aware of these friendships. Is that possible? Wright and colleagues (1997) decided to find out. In a fascinating study, they recreated Sherif and colleagues' (1961) summer camp study in which conflict was created between two groups of boys, except they did so in their laboratory. Here's how it worked. At the beginning of the four-day study, university students were assigned to either the blue group or the green group. Over the next few days, the groups engaged in activities that were designed to create conflict and hostility between them. Then, one member of each group was selected to participate in a supposedly unrelated experiment, which was actually a friendship-building exercise. Later, these participants were asked to describe the experience to their group. Remarkably, the discovery that one of the group members was now friends with the "enemy" caused the remaining group members to adopt more positive attitudes toward the out-group as a whole. They also became more generous to the out-group when allocating monetary rewards (Wright et al., 1997).

Other research by Wright, Aron, and colleagues confirms that the more friends you have in a particular out-group, the more positive your attitudes are toward their group as a whole. Moreover, the closer you are to these friends, the more you like the entire group (Brody et al., 2009; McLaughlin-Volpe, Aron, Wright, & Reis, 2000; Wright & van der Zande, 1999). These results are highly encouraging. The take-home message is that if you make the effort to become friends with a member of an out-group, it can have rather far-reaching effects. You are likely to feel more positively about the out-group as a whole. Moreover, as members of the groups to which you belong learn about this friendship, they will become less prejudiced toward that group as well. Thus, you alone truly can make a difference.

Summary

- **Prejudice: The Ubiquitous Social Phenomenon** Prejudice is a widespread phenomenon, present in all walks of life. People can be the targets of prejudice for any number of reasons, including their race or ethnicity, gender, age, sexual preference, religion, and even their weight.
  - **Measurement of Prejudice** Nowadays, people have learned to hide their prejudice in situations in which it would lead them to be labelled as *racist* or *sexist*, a phenomenon known as modern prejudice. Because of this, social psychologists have had to develop subtle measures to assess prejudice. These include assessing prejudice at an implicit (unconscious) level as well as using more indirect, subtle wording on prejudice scales.
- **Prejudice, Stereotyping, and Discrimination Defined**
  - **Prejudice: The Affective Component** Social psychologists define prejudice as a hostile or negative attitude toward a distinguishable group of people based solely on their group membership.
  - **Stereotypes: The Cognitive Component** While prejudice is defined in terms of a negative attitudinal and emotional response, stereotypes denote both the positive and negative traits that people assign to members solely by virtue of their membership in a particular social group.
  - **Discrimination: The Behavioural Component** Discrimination denotes actual behaviour. It is defined as an unjustified negative or harmful action toward members of a group solely because of their membership in that group.
- **What Causes Prejudice?** As a broad-based and powerful attitude, prejudice has many causes. We discussed five aspects of social life that bring about prejudice: the way we think, the way we feel, the way we assign meaning or make attributions, the way we allocate resources, and the way we conform to social norms.
  - **The Way We Think: Social Cognition** Prejudice is enabled by the human tendency to organize people into in-groups and out-groups. In-group bias means that we will treat members of our own group more positively than members of the out-group. Another consequence of categorization is the perception of out-group homogeneity—namely, that members of out-groups are more similar to one another than members of in-groups.
  - **What We Believe: Stereotypes** Stereotypes are widely known; even if you do not believe them, they can affect how you process information about an out-group member. Stereotypes can be selectively activated or inhibited, depending on motivational factors, most notably, self-enhancement. The stereotypes that we believe out-group members have of us are known as meta-stereotypes. We expect more negative interactions with, and show more prejudice toward, members of groups who we believe hold negative stereotypes of us.
  - **The Way We Feel: Affect and Mood** Our emotions or moods also determine how prejudiced we are. When we are in a good mood we tend to evaluate out-group members more positively than when we are in a bad mood.
  - **The Way We Assign Meaning: Attributional Biases** The correspondence bias applies to prejudice—we tend to overestimate the role of dispositional forces when making sense out of others' behaviour. Stereotypes can be described as the ultimate attribution error—making negative dispositional attributions about an entire out-group. When out-group members act non-stereotypically, we tend to make situational attributions about them, thereby maintaining our stereotypes.

- **Prejudice and Economic Competition: Realistic Conflict Theory** Realistic conflict theory states that prejudice is the inevitable by-product of real conflict between groups for limited resources, such as economics, power, or status. Competition for resources leads to derogation of and discrimination against the competing out-group.
- **The Way We Conform: Normative Rules** Normative conformity, or the desire to be accepted and "fit in," leads many people to go along with stereotyped beliefs and not challenge them. People are especially likely to embrace the status quo when they are feeling threatened.

Individual Differences in Prejudice Several individual difference variables are associated with prejudice. Those who are high in right-wing authoritarianism, religious fundamentalism, and social dominance are more likely to be prejudiced against out-groups than are those who are low in these traits.

- **Right-Wing Authoritarianism** People who are high in right-wing authoritarianism, a trait that is defined in terms of authoritarian submission, authoritarian aggression, and conventionalism, are prejudiced toward racial groups, women, and especially homosexuals.
- **Religious Fundamentalism** Religious fundamentalists believe that their religious beliefs are the only correct beliefs. These people are especially prejudiced toward people whose behaviour they believe is immoral (e.g., gays, single mothers).
- **Social Dominance Orientation** People high in social dominance orientation believe that groups of people are unequal and that it is acceptable to step on other people in order to be "on top." They show prejudice toward many groups but are especially prejudiced toward groups that they perceive as competing for resources (e.g., immigrants). For example, they believe any gains made by other groups come at their expense.

Effects of Stereotyping, Prejudice, and Discrimination Prejudice, stereotyping, and discrimination can have devastating effects on their targets.

- **Self-Fulfilling Prophecies** Research on self-fulfilling prophecies suggests that we may unknowingly create stereotypical behaviour in out-group members through our treatment of them.
- **Stereotype Threat** Members of an out-group also may experience stereotype threat—a fear that they will behave in a manner that confirms an existing stereotype about their group. This fear interferes with their ability to perform well.

Interventions for Reducing Prejudice and Discrimination

- **Learning Not to Hate** One approach for reducing prejudice is to nip it in the bud by teaching children not to be prejudiced.
- **The Contact Hypothesis** Another effective approach is to reduce prejudice through contact—bringing in-group and out-group members together. Contact situations should ideally include the following six conditions: mutual interdependence; a common goal; equal status; informal, interpersonal contact; multiple contacts; and social norms of equality.
- **Cooperation and Interdependence: The Jigsaw Classroom** The jigsaw classroom, a learning atmosphere in which children must depend on each other and work together to reach a common goal has been very successful at reducing prejudice among children of different ethnicities.
- **The Extended Contact Hypothesis** Research on the extended contact hypothesis has shown that the mere knowledge that a member of an in-group is friends with an out-group member can reduce prejudice toward that group.

SOCIAL PSYCHOLOGY IN ACTION

1 Social Psychology and the Environment

OUTLINE

THE NEWS IS FULL OF STORIES ABOUT COUNTRIES WREAKING havoc on the environment. The destruction of the rainforests in Brazil, industrial pollution in China—the list goes on and on. Which region do you think is considered "one of the world's top environmental hot zones" by the United Nations? It may surprise you to learn that the answer is Alberta's tar sands. This region of northern Alberta has become a hotbed of energy production, mining bitumen, an oil product, from the tar sands that span a vast area along the Athabasca River. In fact, the tar sands project is considered to be the largest energy project in the world. One of the resources that is being expended in order to produce bitumen is natural gas, which accounts for 60 percent of the operating costs of the tar sands projects. Andrew Nikiforuk, author of *Tar Sands: Dirty Oil and the Future of a Continent*, reports that "using natural gas to melt a resource as dirty as bitumen, is, as one executive said, like 'burning a Picasso for heat'" (2008, p. 15). Wasted natural gas is not the only cost. The production of each barrel of bitumen requires three barrels of fresh water from the Athabasca River. Ninety percent of that water ends up in what is known as the tailing ponds—one of the world's largest collections of toxic waste. The death of ducks on the tailing ponds, located along the Athabaska River, is one of the consequences, but the effects are more widespread. According to a report released by the University of Toronto's Munk Centre in October 2008, the environmental impact of Alberta's tar sands will not be limited to Western Canada but will extend all the way to the Great Lakes, threatening water and air quality around the world's largest body of fresh water (Mittelstaedt, 2008). Toxins from the tailing ponds are seeping into groundwater that serves nearby communities. Over the last 10 years, rare cancers have been documented among residents of Fort Chipewyan, a community downstream from the tailing ponds. Dr. John O'Connor, a family physician in the area, was concerned that these cancers were the result of toxins in the environment, and in December 2006, he issued a health warning. Government officials from Health Canada responded by filing a complaint with the Alberta College of Physicians and Surgeons, accusing the doctor of raising "undue alarm." O'Connor was then called before the registrar of the College of Physicians and Surgeons to defend himself against these charges. He never anticipated that speaking out about his concerns would result in a career-threatening struggle that could cost him his medical licence.

A series of government studies has concluded that there is no need to be alarmed about the health effects of the tar sands project. However, quite a different conclusion was drawn by an Alberta ecologist and statistician, Kevin Timoney, who released an independent report in November 2007. According to Timoney, "The findings of my study indicate that there is cause for concern in that there are contaminants in the food supply that are associated with . . . types of cancer observed in the community. Certainly, these contaminants come from tar sands" (Timoney, as quoted in De Souza, 2007). More recently, the government has taken steps to improve the tar sands' bad reputation. Federal Minister of the Environment Peter Kent unveiled a new monitoring plan on July 21, 2011, that is intended to protect air and water quality and biodiversity in the area. Environmentalists argue that more monitoring isn't the issue; instead, the government has to actually impose legally binding regulations on the oil-producing companies (Galloway, 2011).

Imagine living in an area described as Canada's worst toxic waste site and hearing that people who live where you do show particularly high rates of cancer. How would this affect you? Sadly, the residents of Fort Chipewyan are not the only Canadians in this type of circumstance. Residents of Nova Scotia living near the Sydney tar ponds have faced such a situation for years. For nearly a century, emissions and waste products from Sydney's Sysco steel plant have been dumped there. There are high levels of carcinogenic materials in this hazardous toxic site. To find out how people are affected by living in such an environment, researchers at the University College of Cape Breton interviewed junior high school students attending a school near the tar ponds (O'Leary & Covell, 2002). These adolescents reported worrying about environmental issues and about their own health and that of their families—more so than students attending a school 40 kilometres away. Worse still, the adolescents who worried most about health showed the highest level of depression. (Overall, depression levels were higher than the national average among both groups of adolescents. The researchers suggest that even the students who lived 40 kilometres away may have felt affected by this environmental hazard.) People who live on contaminated land report high rates of deaths from cancer and high levels of illness among children in the community. On July 6, 2011, after a lengthy legal battle, residents of Sydney finally got the green light from a Supreme Court judge to proceed with a class-action lawsuit against the federal and provincial governments (CBC News, 2011).

Clearly, even among 12- to 14-year-olds, living in a toxic environment creates stress. A study conducted with two communities in Ontario found that even nonhazardous landfill sites create stress and reduce well-being among residents (Wakefield & Elliott, 2000). These researchers found that decision-making processes (e.g., whether or not the government allowed public input, divisions in the community over the effects of the site) often created as much stress as the final outcome.

In short, it is clear that Canada's physical environment is being harmed in multiple ways, and it is taking a toll on the planet's inhabitants. However, as long as people continue to consume massive amounts of energy, projects such as Alberta's tar sands will go on. Changes in attitudes and behaviour are urgently needed to avoid environmental

Alberta's tar sands region has been designated as one of the world's top environmental "hot zones."

catastrophe. But it isn't easy. University of Victoria researcher Robert Gifford (2008, 2011) recently identified some of the psychological barriers (what he referred to as "the dragons of inaction") that impede pro-environmental behaviours pertaining to climate change. The list is depressingly long, ranging from denial, to system justification, to concerns about freeloaders ("Why should I put effort into making things better when other people do nothing?"). Fortunately, social psychologists have studied a number of techniques involving social influence and social interaction that encourage people to behave in more environmentally sustainable ways (Geller, 2002; Gifford, 2008; Oskamp, 1995; Sundstrom, Bell, Busby, & Asmus, 1996; Vining & Ebreo, 2002). We turn to these now.

Applied Research in Social Psychology

Connect to MyPsychLab
Time to review! To take a survey on what you know about psychology, go to MyPsychLab

Since its inception, the field of social psychology has been interested in applying what it knows to solve practical problems. Kurt Lewin (1946), generally recognized as the founder of empirical social psychology, made three key points:

- Social psychological questions are best tested with the experimental method.
- These studies can be used to understand basic psychological processes and to develop theories about social influence.
- Social psychological theories and methods can be used to address pressing social problems.

If you've read the first 12 chapters of this book, you know a lot about these points—especially the first two. In Chapter 2, you read about the importance of using the experimental method to test causal hypotheses, and in subsequent chapters, you read about numerous social psychological experiments and how they have increased our understanding of important theoretical questions, such as how people think about themselves and the social world, respond to social influence, change their attitudes, and help and hurt their fellow humans.

Much of this research dealt directly with important applied issues, such as bullying, racism, bystander intervention, and decision making. To many of us in the field, the beauty of social psychology is that by its very nature it addresses both basic and applied questions about human behaviour. Research on stereotyping and prejudice, for example, investigates basic theoretical questions about the ways in which people form impressions of each other, as well as applied questions about how stereotyping and prejudice might be reduced.

As we discussed in Chapter 2, though, a distinction can still be made between *basic research*, which is concerned primarily with theoretical issues, and *applied research*, which is concerned primarily with addressing specific real-world problems. Although much of the research we have discussed so far has touched on practical problems, it falls squarely in the category of basic research. As Kurt Lewin (1951) said, "There is nothing so practical as a good theory," by which he meant that to solve difficult social problems, we must first understand the underlying psychological dynamics of human nature and social influence. Increasingly, though, social psychologists are conducting studies designed specifically to address practical problems. In fact, social psychologists are better equipped than many other disciplines to study applied problems.

Why would we dare make such a bold claim? For two reasons: First, the field of social psychology is a rich source of theories about human behaviour that people can draw on to devise solutions to social problems. Second, but of equal importance, social psychologists know how to perform rigorous experimental tests of these solutions to see if they work (Wilson, 2005). Only by conducting experiments (as opposed to observational or correlational studies; see Chapter 2) can we hope to discover which solutions to applied questions, such as getting people to reduce energy consumption, will work best.

Most people seem to understand this lesson in other domains, such as research on medical treatments. Suppose that a chemist found a new compound that seems to be an effective pain killer—the initial studies with rats look very promising, but studies on humans have not yet been conducted. Should we allow a drug company to go ahead and market the drug to people? Not so fast, most of us would think. Who knows how safe the drug is for humans? It might turn out to have dangerous side effects, as has happened all too often. There should be extensive clinical trials in humans, in which people are randomly assigned to receive the new drug or a placebo, to see whether it really does reduce pain, and whether it has any serious side effects. Indeed, federal law requires extensive testing and approval before drugs become available to the public.

We have laxer standards when it comes to testing psychological and social "treatments." If someone wants to try a new energy conservation technique, a new educational initiative, or a program to reduce prejudice, they can usually do so without a lot of rigorous testing of the intervention. A company might try a new program to reduce energy usage or institute a mandatory diversity training program, for example, before such techniques have been tested experimentally.

Well, you might think, what's the harm? Trying a new energy conservation program hardly puts people at risk, and we certainly don't want to inhibit innovation by subjecting people to cumbersome testing guidelines. And can't we find out whether these interventions work by interviewing people afterward or seeing whether their behaviour changes (e.g., do they use less energy after the conservation program)? Unfortunately, the solution is not so simple. It is difficult to test the effectiveness of an intervention in the absence of a randomly assigned control group, and failing to conduct such tests can have serious consequences.

Take, for example, the case of trying to persuade people to use less energy by giving them information on how much energy the average member of their community uses. Given everything we know about conforming to social norms, such social comparison information should be helpful, it, shouldn't it? When social psychologists tried this approach, they found that people did, indeed, change their energy usage to conform to the norms of their community (Shultz, Nolan, Cialdini, Goldstein, & Griskevicius, 2007). However, this turned out to be a mixed blessing. People who were using a lot of energy, did, in fact, reduce energy consumption. But this approach has a boomerang effect for those people who were already using low amounts of energy. Once they learned what their neighbours were doing (using electricity like crazy), they actually increased their consumption! But social psychology came to the rescue in coming up with a solution. The researchers hypothesized that low energy users might keep up the good work if they were given positive feedback about their low energy consumption. So, they introduced a very simple manipulation—they drew a "smiley" face next to the energy consumption information if the consumer had used less than the average amount of energy and a sad face if they had used more than the average. Consumers who got the "smiley face" reward maintained the same low rate of energy use that they had before the experiment began. The smiley face reminded them that they were doing the right thing and, as a result, they kept on doing it. (The "sad face" treatment was effective in getting high usage consumers to use less, as was information about the average use in the neighbourhood.)

This study has had a major impact on energy conservation strategies in the United States. The use of smiley faces and sad faces, combined with social norm information about average energy use, is now being used by utility companies in 10 major metropolitan areas, including Chicago, Sacramento, and Seattle (Kaufman, 2009).

Using Social Psychology to Achieve a Sustainable Future

Connect to MyPsychLab
To access the Critical Thinking question on recycling, go to MyPsychLab

Social psychologists have adopted a variety of approaches to try to get people to behave in more environmentally responsible ways. What these approaches have in common is that they are inspired by social psychological theories and they use the experimental method to evaluate whether the approach is effective.

Resolving Social Dilemmas

Be honest: When you think about the topic of energy conservation, how do you feel? If you are like us, you know that you should conserve energy and reduce CO_2 emissions, but the prospect of changing habits doesn't seem very appealing. It involves personal sacrifice, such as using our cars less, turning down the thermostat in winter and the air conditioner in summer, and buying fewer consumer goods. "Why should I be the one to do these things," you might think, "when I see plenty of other people driving SUVs, heating and cooling their houses with abandon, and buying stuff they don't really need?" As we mentioned earlier, there is ample evidence that people do think along these lines (Gifford, 2011).

Good question. What we have here is a classic social dilemma. As we discussed in Chapter 8, a social dilemma is a conflict in which the most beneficial action for an individual will, if chosen by most people, have a harmful effect on everyone. It is in everyone's self-interest to use as much energy as he or she wants; after all, one person's contribution to global warming is minuscule. But if we all adopt that attitude, we will all suffer the consequences.

Of particular relevance to energy conservation is a type of social dilemma called the *commons dilemma*, a situation in which everyone takes from a common pool of goods that will replenish itself if used in moderation but will disappear if overused. Examples include the use of limited resources such as water and energy. Individuals benefit by using as much as they need, but if everyone does so, shortages result (Brucks & Van Lange, 2008; Dawes, 1980; Kortenkamp & Moore, 2001; Levine & Moreland, 1998; Pruitt, 1998; Sibley & Liu, 2003; Weber, Kopelman, & Messick, 2004). Or, to give another example, Canada's National Parks face the dilemma of development for tourism, when doing so can potentially destroy the very beauty that tourists are coming to see (Jackson, 1987).

The earth we abuse and the living things we kill, in the end, take their revenge; for in exploiting their presences we are diminishing our future.

—Marya Mannes, *1958*

How can we resolve social dilemmas and persuade people to act for the greater good of everyone, rather than purely out of self-interest? Social psychologists have devised some fascinating laboratory games to try to answer this question. Imagine you arrive for a study and discover that there are six other participants you have never met. The experimenter gives you and the other participants $6 and says that each of you can keep the money. There is, however, another option. Each person can donate his or her money to the rest of the group, to be divided equally among the six other members. If anyone does so, the experimenter will double the contribution. For example, if you donate your money, it will be doubled to $12 and divided evenly among the six other participants. If other group members donate their money to the pot, it will be doubled and you will get a share.

Think about the dilemma you face. If everyone (including you) cooperates by donating his or her money to the group, once it is doubled and divided up, your share will be $12—double what you started with. Donating your money is risky, however; if you are the only one who does so, you will end up with nothing, while having increased everyone else's winnings (see Table SPA1.1). Clearly, the most selfish—and safest—course of action is to keep your money, hoping that everyone else donates theirs. That way, you would make up to $18—your $6 plus your share of the money everyone else threw into the pot. Of course, if everyone thinks this way, you'll make only $6, because no one will donate any money to the group.

If you are like most of the participants in the actual study, you will keep your six bucks (Orbell, van de Kragt, & Dawes, 1988). After all, as you can see in Table SPA1.1, you will always earn more money by keeping what you have than by giving it away (i.e., the winnings in the top row of Table SPA1.1 are always higher than the winnings in the bottom row). The problem with this strategy is that because most people adopt it, everyone suffers. That is, the total pool of money to be divided remains low, because few people donate to the group, which would allow the experimenter to double the money. As with many social dilemmas, most people look out for themselves, and as a result, everyone loses.

How can people be persuaded to trust their fellow group members, cooperating in such a way that everyone benefits? It is notoriously difficult to resolve social dilemmas, as indicated by the effort required to get people to conserve water when there are droughts, recycle their waste goods, clean up a common area in a dormitory or apartment, or reduce the use of pesticides and thereby lower the production level and visual appeal of produce. In another condition of the experiment discussed, the researchers discovered an intriguing result: Simply allowing the group to talk together for 10 minutes dramatically increased the number of members who donated money to the group—from 38 percent to 79 percent (Orbell et al., 1988).

Communication works in two ways. First, when people make a public commitment to help, it is more difficult to back out. If people can take the selfish route privately, undiscovered by their peers, they will often do so. However, if their actions are public, the kinds of normative pressures we discussed in Chapter 7 come into play, making people's behaviour more consistent with group norms. There is another way in which

TABLE SPA1.1 Amount of Money You Stand to Win in the Orbell, van de Kragt, and Dawes (1988) Experiment

You can either keep your $6 or donate it to the six other group members. If you donate it, the money will be doubled, so that each group member will receive $2. Most people who play this game want to keep their money to maximize their own gains. The more people who keep their money, however, the more everyone loses.

Other People's Decisions:	6 Keep, 0 Give	5 Keep, 1 Gives	4 Keep, 2 Give	3 Keep, 3 Give	2 Keep, 4 Give	1 Keeps, 5 Give	0 Keep, 6 Give
Your Decision							
Keep your $6	$6	$8	$10	$12	$14	$16	$18
Give your $6	$0	$2	$4	$6	$8	$10	$12

Source: Adapted from Orbell, van de Kragt, & Dawes, 1988.

communication works: When people communicate, they are more likely to establish a sense of group identity or solidarity, which makes them more likely to act for the good of the group (Weber, Kopelman, & Messick, 2004). Another way to increase cooperation is for one person to set an example by cooperating consistently and without exception. When people observe someone else acting in such a selfless manner, they contribute more to the group as a result (Weber & Murnighan, 2008).

These findings are encouraging, but may be limited to small groups that are able to communicate face to face. What happens when an entire community is caught in a social dilemma? When large groups are involved, alternative approaches are needed.

How can we encourage people to act in selfless ways that help the environment? One way is to set an example by acting that way ourselves. When people observe someone else acting in a selfless manner, they are likely to follow suit and cooperate as well.

Conveying and Changing Social Norms

One approach is to remind people of social norms: the rules a group has for the acceptable behaviours, values, and beliefs of its members (see Chapter 7). For example, Scott (1999) found that residents of the Greater Toronto Area recycled a higher number of products when they felt social pressure to do so. As one respondent remarked, "[People] feel they have to because their neighbours put out a blue box." People follow two kinds of social norms: **injunctive norms**, which are people's perceptions of the behaviour that is approved or disapproved of by others, and **descriptive norms**, which are people's perceptions of how others actually behave in a given situation (Cialdini, 2003).

Injunctive Norms

People's perceptions of the behaviour that is approved or disapproved of by others

Descriptive Norms

People's perceptions of how other people actually behave in a given situation, regardless of whether the behaviour is approved or disapproved of by others

Robert Cialdini and colleagues have illustrated the power of social norms in persuading people to stop engaging in behaviours that harm the environment, such as littering, stealing wood from national park forests, and laundering towels after a single use (Cialdini, Kallgren, & Reno, 1991; Cialdini, Reno, & Kallgren, 1990; Griskevicius, Cialdini, & Goldstein, 2008; Kallgren, Reno, & Cialdini, 2000). Compared with other environmental problems, littering may not seem all that serious a matter. Many people think that it isn't a big deal to toss their paper cup on the side of the road instead of putting it in a garbage can (or even better, a recycling bin!). Unfortunately, those paper cups add up. For example, in the state of California, each year $41 million is spent cleaning up litter ("Litter Bugs," 2005). The stuff we discard is polluting North American water systems, endangering wildlife, and costing millions of dollars.

How can people be persuaded not to litter? Reno, Cialdini, and Kallgren (1993) conducted a field experiment to investigate the power of injunctive norms. As people left a local library and approached their cars in the parking lot, a confederate walked by them, picked up a fast-food bag that had been discarded on the ground, and put the bag in the trash. In a control condition, no bag was on the ground, and the confederate simply walked by the library patrons. When the patrons got to their car, they found a pamphlet on their windshield. The question was how many of these people would litter by throwing the pamphlet on the ground. Reno and colleagues hypothesized that seeing the confederate pick up the fast-food bag would be a vivid reminder of the injunctive norm—littering is bad, and other people disapprove of it—and hence would reduce the participant's own inclination to litter. They were right. In this condition, only 7 percent of the people tossed the pamphlet on the ground, compared with 37 percent in the control condition.

We live in an environment whose principal product is garbage.

—Russell Baker, *1968*

Although descriptive norms (i.e., communicating what other people actually are doing) also can be effective in promoting pro-environmental behaviours (Cialdini, Reno, & Kallgren, 1991), in situations such as getting people to clean up litter, injunctive norms actually work better (Kallgren et al., 2000). This should not surprise you because injunctive norms tap into normative conformity (see Chapter 7)—we conform (e.g., refrain from littering) because someone's behaviour has reminded us that our society disapproves of littering. If you would like to try to replicate this effect in an experiment of your own, see the accompanying Try It! exercise.

TRY IT! Reducing Littering by Using Injunctive Norms

See if you can get people to pick up litter by invoking injunctive norms, using the techniques discovered by Reno, Cialdini, and Kallgren (1993). This exercise is easier to complete with a friend who can unobtrusively observe if people littler. Here's how it works:

Find an environment in which people are likely to litter. In the psychology building at one of our universities, for example, the place where people pick up the student newspaper would be appropriate. The paper often comes with an advertising insert, and when people pick up the paper, they often discard the insert on the floor.

Next, plant a conspicuous piece of litter in this environment. Reno and colleagues (1993) used a fast-food bag stuffed with litter. Place it in a location where people are sure to see it, such as near a doorway.

In one condition, wait until an individual enters the environment and is in full view of the piece of trash you have planted. Then, pick up the trash, throw it away, and go on your way. It is critical that the person realizes it wasn't your bag but that you decided to pick it up and throw it away anyway. In a second condition, walk by the trash, glance at it, and continue on your way without picking it up.

The observer should watch to see whether people litter; for example, whether they throw the paper's advertising insert on the floor or put it in a garbage can or recycling bin.

Reno, Cialdini, and Kallgren (1993) found that when people saw someone pick up another person's litter, they were much less likely to litter themselves. Did you replicate this effect? Why or why not?

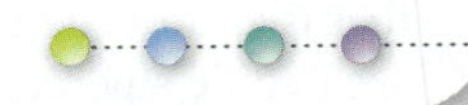

What happens when there are no norms for acting in environmentally responsible ways, or are even norms for behaving in the opposite manner? In this situation, the first step is to change the norm. This isn't always easy, of course, but sometimes people underestimate what they can do to change injunctive norms, particularly if they are high-status members of a group. Suppose, for example, that among your group of friends, many people drive gas-guzzling SUVs. Perhaps that is the vehicle of choice—maybe it's even a sign of status and prestige. No one likes to "break the rules," and though you might have been thinking about trading in your Jeep Grand Cherokee for a car with a hybrid engine such as the Toyota Prius, you worry about what your friends will say.

But would it really be so bad? People often overestimate the strength of an injunctive norm—for example, how much our friends would really care if we traded in our SUV. Several studies have shown that university students tend to overestimate other injunctive norms, such as what their friends think about drinking alcohol. As we discussed in Chapter 7, many college and university students believe that their peers are more in favour of drinking than they actually are. The same might be true about cars. Other people in your social group might be thinking about getting more fuel-efficient cars but are reluctant to say so.

Even if your friends would look disparagingly at your purchase of a Toyota Prius, someone has to be the first to change an injunctive norm. As we saw in Chapter 7, it is easier to buck the tide if we can get just one other person to go along with us, so you might first try to convince a friend who is looking to buy a car to consider a hybrid. If this doesn't work, just go for it. You might be surprised by how much you alone can change a norm, especially if you keep reminding people how much you are saving on gas and that SUVs are not nearly as safe as people think they are (Gladwell, 2005).

Besides being unsightly, litter can cost millions of dollars to clean up. Social psychologists have found that emphasizing various kinds of social norms against littering is an effective way to prevent it.

Making It Easy to Keep Track of Energy Consumption

A problem with some environmental social dilemmas is that it is not easy for people to keep track of how much of a resource they are using, such as water or electricity. During a drought, for example, people may be asked to conserve water, but it is not easy for them to monitor how many litres a day they are using. One pair of researchers reasoned that making it easy for people to keep track of their water use would make it easier for them to act on their concern for the greater good (Van Vugt & Samuelson, 1999). They compared two communities in the Hampshire region of England during a severe drought in the summer of 1995. The houses in one community had been equipped with water meters that allowed residents to monitor how much water they were consuming. The houses in the other community did not have meters. As expected, when people felt that the water shortage was severe, those in the metered houses consumed less water than those in the unmetered houses. Further, there was evidence that they did so not purely out of self-interest (i.e., using less water would save money) but out of concern for the collective good. Similar results have been found in studies that make it easier for people to track how much electricity they are using (Abrahamse, Steg, Vlek, & Rothengatter, 2005).

What if we got people to keep track of the energy they were saving, rather than the energy they were consuming? For example, what if we asked drivers to keep track of the miles they *avoided* driving, by walking, riding a bike, taking public transportation, or getting a ride with a friend? Making people more mindful of opportunities to avoid driving might make people more willing to leave their car at home. To find out, Graham, Koo, and Wilson (2011) asked college students to keep track of the number of miles they avoided driving and to record that figure on a website every other day for two weeks. As predicted, students who kept track of the miles they saved drove their cars less than did students in a control group who did not keep track of the miles they saved. This finding is consistent with research showing that simply keeping track of one's behaviour is the first step to changing it.

Graham and colleagues (2011) also examined whether giving the students different kinds of feedback about the miles they saved would influence their driving habits. After students entered how many miles they had avoided driving, some received feedback about how much money they had saved on gas and maintenance costs. Others received feedback about savings in air pollution (e.g., how many carbon dioxide and hydrocarbon emissions weren't emitted). Some got both kinds of feedback. It turned out that this latter group—that learned both how much money they had saved and how much pollution wasn't emitted—was especially likely to avoid driving their cars. Keeping track of one's behaviour that avoids environmental damage and receiving concrete feedback about the savings turned out to be an effective way to get college students to drive their cars less. (If you would like to try this on your own, you can download a spreadsheet with instructions at http://people.virginia.edu/~tdw/Driving.file.htm).

Introducing a Little Competitiveness

Other researchers have demonstrated that a little competitiveness helps people conserve energy (Staats, Harland, & Wilke, 2004). For example, in a study by Siero and colleagues (1996), employees at one unit of a factory in the Netherlands were urged to engage in energy-saving behaviour. Announcements were placed in the company magazine asking people to perform behaviours such as closing windows during cold weather and turning off lights when leaving a room. In addition, the employees received weekly feedback on their behaviour; graphs were posted that showed how much they had improved their energy-saving behaviour. This intervention resulted in modest improvement. By the end of the program, the number of times people left the lights on, for example, decreased by 27 percent (Siero, Bakker, Dekker, & van den Burg, 1996).

Another unit of the factory took part in an identical program, with one difference. In addition to receiving weekly feedback on their own energy-saving actions, they received feedback about how the other unit was doing. The researchers hypothesized that this social comparison information would motivate people to do better than their colleagues in the other unit. As seen in Figure SPA1.1, they were right: By the end of the program,

FIGURE SPA1.1

Effects of comparative feedback on energy-saving behaviour.

Two units of a factory were urged to conserve energy and then received feedback about how their unit was doing. Only one of the units, however, received comparative feedback about how they were doing relative to the other unit. As seen in the graph, workers in this second unit showed a greater improvement in their behaviour, especially by turning off the lights more often.

(Adapted from Siero et al., 1996)

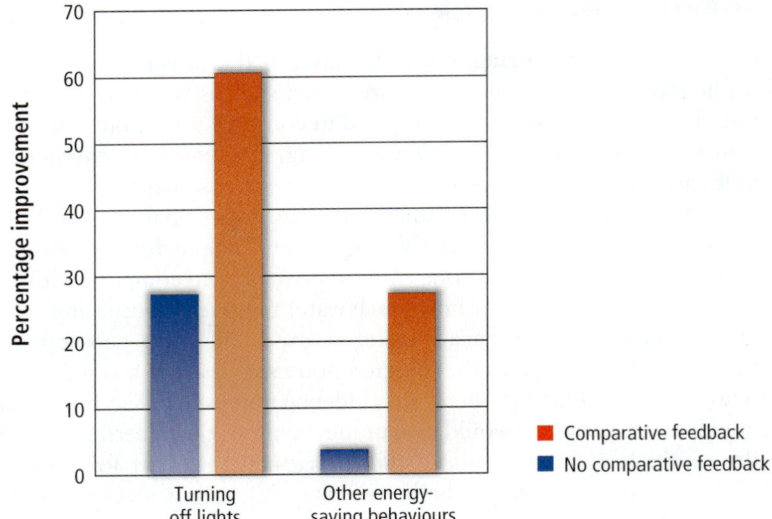

the number of times people left the lights on had decreased by 61 percent. Clearly, engaging people's competitive spirit can have a significant impact on their behaviour.

Using Intrinsic Motivation and Implementation Plans

In Chapter 5, we introduced the concepts of intrinsic motivation—doing something because you enjoy it or find it interesting—versus extrinsic motivation—doing something because of external rewards or pressures. A large body of evidence shows that people who are high in intrinsic motivation are much more likely to engage in a variety of pro-environmental behaviours and to sustain these behaviours over time. An extensive program of research conducted by Luc Pelletier and colleagues at the University of Ottawa shows that being internally motivated to preserve the environment (versus feeling external pressure to do so) is associated with pro-environmental behaviours such as sustained curbside recycling, as well as more effortful forms of recycling (e.g., recycling away from home), environmental activism, conserving water, and buying biodegradable products (see Pelletier & Sharp, 2008, for a review). Moreover, people who are high in intrinsic motivation engage in a greater number of different pro-environmental behaviours—not just one. Similarly, a recent study conducted with high school students in Montreal found that intrinsic motivation was associated with engaging in environmental behaviours such as recycling (Renaud-Dubé, Taylor, Lekes, Koestner, & Guay, 2010).

So, then, the important question becomes "How can we increase people's intrinsic motivation to engage in environmentally sustainable behaviours?" Pelletier and Sharp (2008) point out that the first step is to make people aware that a problem exists. Here fear appeals can be useful (e.g., clear information on the impact of driving your car), as long as they are not so threatening that people tune out the message (see our discussion of this issue in Chapter 6). The next step is to shift the focus to solutions that can be implemented now to avoid the feared negative outcomes. At this step, Pelletier and Sharp advocate taking a more positive approach and emphasizing what can be gained by engaging in specific pro-environmental behaviours.

Implementation Plan

People's specific plans about where, when, and how they will fulfill a goal

Finally, and importantly, people need to develop an **implementation plan**—people's specific plans about where, when, and how they will fulfill a goal (Koestner, Lekes, Powers, & Chicone, 2002; Koestner, 2008; Koestner et al., 2006). In one study, for example, the researchers measured the extent to which office workers recycled plastic cups, which had to be taken to a central location (i.e., the workers did not have boxes in their offices in which they could deposit used cups). Workers in the implementation intention condition were first asked to visualize and write down exactly when, where, and how they would recycle their cups, whereas workers in a control condition were not. People in the former condition recycled nearly four times as many cups as those in the latter, suggesting that the best-laid plans often go awry *unless* we first visualize how we are going to make those plans come true (Holland, Aarts, & Langendam, 2006).

Inducing Hypocrisy

In many areas of the world, water is becoming an increasingly scarce resource. One cause is population growth in areas that have limited water supplies. Another is droughts, which are becoming more frequent as the temperature of Earth rises. Thirty years ago, 10 to 15 percent of Earth was drought-stricken; today, that figure is closer to 30 percent ("Drought's Growing Reach," 2005).

Several years ago, when California was experiencing severe water shortages, the administrators at one campus of the University of California realized that an enormous amount of water was being wasted by students using the university athletic facilities. The administrators posted signs in the shower rooms of the gymnasiums, exhorting students to conserve water by taking briefer, more efficient showers. The signs appealed to the students' conscience by urging them to take brief showers and to turn off the water while soaping up. The administrators were confident that the signs would be effective because the vast majority of students at this campus were ecology-minded and believed in preserving natural resources. However, systematic observation revealed that fewer than 15 percent of the students complied with the conservation message on the posted signs.

The administrators were puzzled—perhaps the majority of the students hadn't paid attention to the signs? After all, a sign on a wall is easy to ignore. So, administrators made each sign more obtrusive, putting it on a tripod at the entrance to the showers so the students needed to walk around the sign to get into the shower room. While this increased compliance slightly (19 percent turned off the shower while soaping up), it apparently made a great many students angry. The sign was continually being knocked over and kicked around, and a large percentage of students took inordinately *long* showers, apparently as a reaction against being told what to do. The sign was doing more harm than good, which puzzled the administrators even more. It was time to call in the social psychologists.

Elliot Aronson and his students (Dickerson, Thibodeau, Aronson, & Miller, 1992) decided to apply the hypocrisy technique used successfully in an earlier study to increase condom purchases (see Chapter 6). The procedure involved intercepting female students who were on their way from the swimming pool to the women's shower room, introducing the experimental manipulations, and then having a research assistant casually follow them into the shower room, where the assistant unobtrusively timed their showers. Research participants in one condition were asked to respond to a brief questionnaire about their water use, a task designed to make them mindful of how they sometimes wasted water while showering. In another condition, research participants made a public commitment, exhorting others to take steps to conserve water. Specifically, these participants were asked to sign their names to a public poster that read "Take Shorter Showers. Turn Shower Off While Soaping Up. If I Can Do It, So Can YOU!" In the crucial condition—the "hypocrisy" condition—the participants did both; that is, they were made mindful of their own wasteful behaviour and indicated publicly (on the poster) that they were practising water conservation. In short, they were made aware that they were preaching behaviour that they themselves were not practising. Just as in the condom study (Chapter 6), participants who were made to feel like hypocrites changed their behaviour so they could feel good about themselves. In this case, they took very brief showers. Indeed, the procedure was so effective that the average time students in this condition spent showering was reduced to 3.5 minutes. The hypocrisy procedure has also been found to increase other environmentally sound practices, such as recycling (Fried & Aronson, 1995).

Removing Small Barriers to Achieve Big Changes

Sometimes the best way to change people's behaviour is simply to make it easy for them to do so. To reduce the amount of garbage that ends up in landfills, many cities are encouraging people to recycle materials such as glass, paper, and aluminum. However, as you know, it can be inconvenient to do so; in some areas, you have to load your car with boxes of cans and bottles and drop them off at a recycling centre, which might be

In a study by Dickerson, Thibodeau, Aronson, and Miller (1992), university students who were made aware that they were advocating conservation behaviour that they themselves were not practising changed their behaviour by taking shorter showers.

several kilometres from your house. Other cities have curbside recycling, whereby a truck picks up recycling materials that you put out on the curb on a designated day. Even then, though, you have to remember to separate your cans, bottles, and newspapers, and find a place to store them until pick-up day. We therefore have another social dilemma—a behaviour (recycling) that, while good for us all, is effortful and unpleasant for individuals. As you might imagine, several social psychologists have turned their attention to ways of getting people to recycle more.

There have been two general approaches to this problem. First, some psychologists have focused on ways of changing people's attitudes and values in a pro-environmental direction, with the assumption that behaviour will follow. This assumption is consistent with social psychological research on attitudes, which has found that under certain conditions people's attitudes are good predictors of their behaviour (see Chapter 6). Indeed, several studies have found that people's attitudes toward recycling are good predictors of their recycling behaviour (Ewing, 2001; Knussen, Yule, & MacKenzie, 2004; Oskamp, Burkhardt, Schultz, Hurin, & Zelezny, 1998; Valle, Rebelo, & Reis, 2005). For example, a recent nationwide survey of more than 1000 Canadians found that people who have environmentally friendly attitudes are more likely to engage in behaviours to lower greenhouse gas emissions in their homes (e.g., turning off lights, recycling, keeping temperatures moderate) than those who hold less environmentally friendly attitudes (Ngo, West, & Calkins, 2009). Findings such as these suggest that a mass media campaign that targets people's attitudes is a good way to go.

Sometimes, though, we might fail to act consistently with our attitudes, despite our best intentions. Perhaps the recycling centre is too far away, or we just can't find the time to sort our trash, even though we know we should. For example, research conducted with residents of Cornwall, Ontario, found that a major reason why people failed to engage in pro-environmental actions was "I just can't seem to make the effort to change my habits" (Pelletier, Dion, Tuson, & Green-Demers, 1999). Similarly, commuters in Victoria who thought it would be difficult to take the bus or cycle to work were more likely to report using their cars (Abrhamse et al., 2009). Kurt Lewin (1947), one of the founders of social psychology, made the observation that big social changes can sometimes occur by removing small barriers from people's environments. When it comes to behaviours such as recycling, it might be better to simply make it hassle-free, such as by instituting curbside recycling, than to try to change people's attitudes toward the environment. Indeed, the results of studies on recycling conducted with residents of Edmonton (Wall, 1995) and four communities in the Greater Toronto Area (Scott, 1999), as well as a 1991 Statistics Canada survey on the environment (Berger, 1997), all converge on the same conclusion: "People will take pro-environmental actions if they have access to a convenient way of doing so" (Berger, 1997). Increasing the number of recycling bins in a community, instituting curbside recycling, and allowing residents to mix materials instead of having to sort them have all been found to increase people's recycling behaviour (Domina & Koch, 2002; Ludwig, Gray, & Rowell, 1998; Schultz, Oskamp, & Mainieri, 1995). Similarly, a recent study found that providing office workers with a recycling box that they could keep next to their desks dramatically increased the amount of paper they recycled (Holland et al., 2006). The simple convenience of putting paper in a box next to their desk—as opposed to taking it to a central location—was enough to alter people's behaviour.

The moral? There are two ways to get people to act in more environmentally sound ways. One method is to try to change people's attitudes in a pro-environmental direction; this will motivate them to act in environmentally friendly ways, even if barriers, such as finding a box for bottles and cans and then taking them to a recycling centre, make it difficult to do so. It is often easier, however, simply to remove the barriers,

Social psychologists have identified several ways of increasing the likelihood that people will recycle materials such as bottles, cans, and newspapers. One way is to make it as convenient as possible—for example, by offering curbside pickup, as shown in this photo of a recycling service.

such as by instituting curbside recycling and giving people containers. When it is easy to comply, many people will, even if they do not have strong pro-environmental attitudes. Now that you have read about several ways of changing people's behaviour in ways that help the environment, you are in a position to try them out yourself. See the accompanying Try It! exercise.

TRY IT! Changing Environmentally Damaging Behaviour

Use the techniques discussed in this chapter to change people's behaviour in ways that help the environment. Here's how to proceed:

1. Choose the behaviour you want to change. You might try to increase the amount that you and your roommates recycle, reduce the amount of energy wasted in your dorm, or increase water conservation.
2. Choose the technique you will use to change the behaviour. You might, for example, use the comparative feedback technique used by Frans Siero and colleagues (1996) to increase energy conservation. Encourage two areas of your dormitory to reduce energy use or to recycle, and give each feedback about how they are doing relative to the other area. (To do this, you will have to have an easy, objective way of measuring people's behaviour, such as the number of times lights are left on at night or the number of cans that are recycled.) Or you might try the hypocrisy technique used by Elliot Aronson and colleagues (Aronson et al., 1991; Dickerson et al., 1992) to increase water conservation, whereby you ask people to sign a public poster that encourages recycling and have them fill out a questionnaire that makes them mindful of times they have failed to recycle. Be creative and feel free to use more than one technique.
3. Measure the success of your intervention. Find an easy way to measure people's behaviour, such as the amount they recycle. Assess their behaviour before and after your intervention. If possible, include a control group of people who do not receive your intervention (randomly assigned, of course). In the absence of such a control group, it will be difficult to gauge the success of your intervention; for example, if people's behaviour changes over time, you won't be able to tell if it is because of your intervention or some other factor (e.g., an article on recycling that happened to appear in the newspaper). By comparing the changes in behaviour in your target group to the control group, you will have a better estimate of the success of your intervention.

Summary

- **Applied Research in Social Psychology** By its very nature, social psychology addresses both basic and applied questions about human behaviour. Social psychologists have conducted a good deal of applied research on important social and psychological issues, such as how people can adopt a more sustainable lifestyle. Social psychologists are in a unique position to find solutions to applied problems. First, the field of social psychology is a rich source of theories about human behaviour that people can draw upon to devise solutions to problems. Second, social psychologists know how to perform rigorous experimental tests of these solutions to see if they work.
- **Using Social Psychology to Achieve a Sustainable Future** The human population is expanding at an exponential rate with severe environmental consequences. Famine and malnutrition are spreading, natural resources are being depleted, and global warming is an alarming, immediate problem. Social psychologists have devised a number of different approaches to encourage people to adopt a more sustainable lifestyle.
    - **Resolving Social Dilemmas** Energy conservation is a type of social dilemma called a *commons dilemma*, a situation in which everyone takes from a common pool of goods that will replenish itself if used in moderation but will disappear if overused. It is in any individual's interest to consume as much as possible; but, if everyone acts that way, everyone loses—there are no resources left. Social psychologists have studied the conditions under which people are most likely to act for the common good, such as encouraging people to communicate with one another.
    - **Conveying and Changing Social Norms** Another approach is to remind people of both injunctive and descriptive norms against environmentally damaging acts, such as littering. For example, communicating descriptive norms—that other people act in environmentally friendly ways—has been shown to reduce the extent to which passersby litter and increase the extent to which hotel room guests reuse their towels.
    - **Making It Easy to Keep Track of Energy Consumption** One simple technique is to make it easier for people to know how much energy they are using—for example, by providing them with water meters that are easy to read or by providing them with information about the number of kilometres they avoid driving if they walk or take the bus.
    - **Introducing a Little Competitiveness** Units in a company that were competing with each other to conserve energy were more successful than units that were encouraged to save but did not compete.
    - **Using Intrinsic Motivation and Implementation Plans** People who are internally motivated to preserve the environment engage in more sustainable behaviours. Internal motivation can be encouraged by making people aware of issues, encouraging them to come up with solutions in a positive way, and making an implementation plan—a specific plans about where, when, and how they will fulfill a goal, such as the goal to recycle.
    - **Inducing Hypocrisy** It works to arouse dissonance in people by making them feel that they are not practicing what they are preaching—for example, that even though they believe in water conservation, they are taking long showers.
    - **Removing Small Barriers to Achieve Big Changes** Removing barriers that make pro-environmental behaviours difficult, such as instituting curbside recycling and providing people with recycling bins, has been shown to be effective.

SOCIAL PSYCHOLOGY IN ACTION

2 Social Psychology and Health

OUTLINE

MEET ELVIRA TOEWS, A DYNAMIC, VIVACIOUS, 76-YEAR-OLD woman. At social gatherings, Elvira's infectious, joyous laugh can be heard above the sounds of the crowd. Indeed, Elvira's trademark qualities are enthusiasm, humour, and *joie de vivre*. You might think that someone with such a sparkling personality and hearty laugh has had an easy life. Not at all. Elvira has experienced some of life's most traumatic and difficult stressors. Her husband suffered from manic depression all of his adult life. Their 42-year marriage ended tragically when he committed suicide. Two years after this devastating loss, in 2000, Elvira was faced with other major stressors, including heart surgery. Although the surgery was helpful, her ability to engage in physical activity, such as walking, remains limited. In more recent years, Elvira has had to cope with painful arthritis in her back, which further restricts how much she can get around.

On June 5, 2010, Elvira was dealt another crushing blow when her daughter, Marj, who had endured a long battle with mental illness, followed her father's footsteps and committed suicide. A few months after Marj's death, Elvira decided to move to Toronto, where her other daughter lives.

This elderly woman, originally from a small town in Manitoba, is embracing Canada's largest city with her characteristic zest and enthusiasm. She has mastered using the subway system, riding streetcars, and driving in this urban metropolis. Elvira also explores on foot. If a pedestrian traffic sign indicates that there are only 2 seconds left to cross a four-lane street before the opposite light turns green, Elvira forges ahead. "If I'm going to be killed," she says, "it might as well happen while I'm doing something I enjoy."

Many people would crumble under the pain and stress that Elvira has experienced. But she is determined to make the most of life. One of her most valued resources is the knowledge that she and her husband loved each other and that he wanted her to be happy. She also draws strength from the close relationship she had with her daughter Marj and the close relationship she enjoys with her other daughter. Elvira has also cultivated many long-term friendships and has forged fulfilling new friendships in her new home. In addition to these assets, Elvira possesses a large measure of resilience and extraordinary determination. When it became apparent that her physical mobility was not likely to improve, Elvira decided that she would rely on her cognitive abilities to keep her active and give her life meaning. Given her love of words, she pursued competitive Scrabble playing and has achieved an advanced ranking. Although travel is difficult and challenging, Elvira manages to make her way to Scrabble competitions in various cities across North America. She can even be found giving her opponents a run for their money on Scrabble cruises!

People who know Elvira are struck by the fact that her feisty spirit, her pleasant smile, and the sparkle in her eyes have not diminished, despite the life-shattering events she has undergone. How does Elvira manage to live such a rewarding life? Is it her positive outlook or is she simply blessed with good genes? As you will see, it may be more than a coincidence that Elvira is so upbeat and in control of her life, despite the unspeakably painful events she has had to endure and the chronic health problems she copes with on a daily basis.

In this module, we're concerned with the application of social psychology to physical and mental health, which is a flourishing area of research (Bailis & Segall, 2004; Cohen & Herbert, 1996; Salovey, Rothman, & Rodin, 1998; Taylor, 1995). We will focus on topics related to the interface of social psychology and health: how people cope with stress in their lives, the relationship between their coping styles and their physical and mental health, and how we can get people to behave in more healthful ways.

Connect to MyPsychLab
Do you manage your stress well? To take a survey about how you take care of your mental health, go to MyPsychLab

Stress and Human Health

There is more to health than germs and disease; we also need to consider the amount of stress in our lives and how we deal with that stress (Inglehart, 1991). A great deal of anecdotal evidence indicates that stress can affect the body in dramatic ways. Consider the following examples, reported by the psychologist W. B. Cannon (1942):

- A New Zealand woman eats a piece of fruit and then learns that it came from a forbidden supply reserved for the chief. She is horrified and her health deteriorates. The next day she dies—even though it was a perfectly fine piece of fruit.
- A man in Africa has breakfast with a friend, eats heartily, and goes on his way. A year later, he learns that his friend made the breakfast from a wild hen, a food strictly forbidden in the man's culture. The man immediately begins to tremble and is dead within 24 hours.
- An Australian man's health deteriorates after a witch doctor casts a spell on him. He recovers only when the witch doctor removes the spell.

These examples probably sound pretty bizarre. But if we fast-forward to the beginning of the twenty-first century, we find many similar cases of sudden death following a psychological trauma. When people undergo a major upheaval in their lives, such as losing a spouse, declaring bankruptcy, or being forced to resettle in a new culture, their chance of dying increases (Morse, Martin, & Moshonov, 1991). Or consider the plight of an older person who is institutionalized in a long-term health-care facility. In many such institutions in Canada, the residents have little responsibility for, or control over, their own lives: They cannot choose what to eat, what to wear, or even when to go to the bathroom. Residents in such institutions often become passive and withdrawn, and fade into death as if they have simply given up. Quite a contrast from the zest shown by Elvira Toews as she proceeds through her seventies!

Stress also takes a toll on its victims in other ways. According to research conducted at McGill University, Holocaust survivors—particularly those who were adolescents or young adults at the end of World War II—continue to experience negative psychological effects, such as paranoia and depression, more than 40 years after they were persecuted (Sigal & Weinfeld, 2001). Similarly, the cruelty and abuse some First Nations children suffered in residential schools during the twentieth century continue to have traumatic effects on the survivors (Hanson & Hampton, 2000). Finally, as you know all too well, university life is fraught with stress. A large-scale study of university students across Canada found that psychological distress (e.g., anxiety, depression) was significantly higher among students than in Canada's general population (Adlaf, Gliksman, Demers, & Newton-Taylor, 2001). The good news was that distress declined with each successive year in university. So rest assured—things will get better as you go along!

As these examples suggest, our physical and psychological health is closely tied to the amount of stress in our lives. As we will see, we need to consider not only the amount of stress in our lives, but also how we deal with that stress.

Effects of Negative Life Events

Among the pioneers in research on stress was Hans Selye (1956, 1976), who defined *stress* as the body's physiological response to threatening events. Selye focused on how the human body adapts to threats from the environment, regardless of the source of a threat, be it a psychological or physiological trauma. Later researchers have examined what it is about a life event that makes it threatening. Holmes and Rahe (1967), for example, suggested that stress is the degree to which people have to change and readjust their lives in response to an external event. The more change required, the more stress occurs. Thus, if a spouse or partner dies, just about every aspect of a person's life is disrupted, leading to a great deal of stress. This definition of stress applies to happy events in one's life as well, if the event causes a person to change his or her daily routine. Graduating from university is a happy occasion, but it can be stressful because of the major changes it sets in motion in one's life. Similarly, many people look forward to retirement, failing to anticipate the extent of life change that occurs as a result of this transition. A study of Bell Canada retirees, for example, found that for many people, retirement caused considerable instability and stress (Marshall, Clarke, & Ballantyne, 2001).

To assess such life changes, Holmes and Rahe (1967) developed a measure called the Social Readjustment Rating Scale. Here's how the scale works: Respondents get a list of life events such as "divorce" and "trouble with boss," each of which has been assigned a certain number of points, depending on how stressful it is (e.g., "divorce" gets 73 points, whereas "trouble with boss" gets 23). People check all events that have occurred in their lives over the past year. The points assigned to each event are added up to get an overall "life change" score. Several studies have found that the higher people's score, the worse their physical and mental health (Seta, Seta, & Wang, 1990; Tesser & Beach, 1998).

The original scale is a bit dated and did not include events that many college or university students find stressful, such as taking final exams. The accompanying Try It! exercise contains a version that has been developed specifically for students. Take it and figure out your score. How did you do? When the researchers who developed the scale gave it to a sample of undergraduates, the average score was 1247 (Renner & Mackin, 1998).

It seems pretty obvious that people who are experiencing a lot of change and upheaval in their lives are more likely to feel anxious and get sick. But a closer look reveals that these findings aren't all that straightforward. One problem, as you may have recognized, is that most studies in this area use correlational designs rather than experimental designs. Just because life changes are correlated with health problems, this does not mean that the life changes *caused* the health problems. (See our discussion in Chapter 2 of correlation and causality.) Some researchers have argued persuasively that it is not life changes that cause health problems; rather, people with certain personality traits, such as the tendency to experience negative moods, or who are low in optimism or hardiness are more likely to experience life difficulties and to have health problems (Schroeder & Costa, 1984; Watson & Pennebaker, 1989).

The College Life Stress Inventory

Simulate on mypsychlab
How Stressed Are You?

Copy the stress rating number into the last column for any event that has occurred in your life in the past year; then add your scores.

Event	Stress Rating	Your Score
Being raped	100	______
Finding out that you are HIV-positive	100	______
Being accused of rape	98	______
Death of a close friend	97	______
Death of a close family member	96	______
Contracting a sexually transmitted disease (other than AIDS)	94	______
Concerns about being pregnant	91	______
Finals week	90	______
Concerns about your partner being pregnant	90	______
Oversleeping for an exam	89	______
Flunking a class	89	______
Having a boyfriend or girlfriend cheat on you	85	______
Ending a steady dating relationship	85	______
Serious illness in a close friend or family member	85	______
Financial difficulties	84	______
Writing a major term paper	83	______
Being caught cheating on a test	83	______
Driving drunk	82	______
Sense of overload in school or work	82	______
Two exams in one day	80	______
Cheating on your boyfriend or girlfriend	77	______
Getting married	76	______
Negative consequences of drinking or drug use	75	______
Depression or crisis in your best friend	73	______
Difficulties with parents	73	______
Talking in front of a class	72	______
Lack of sleep	69	______
Change in housing situation (hassles, moves)	69	______
Competing or performing in public	69	______
Getting in a physical fight	66	______
Difficulties with a roommate	66	______
Job changes (applying, new job, work hassles)	65	______
Declaring a major or concerns about future plans	65	______
A class you hate	62	______
Drinking or use of drugs	61	______
Confrontations with professors	60	______
Starting a new semester	58	______
Going on a first date	57	______
Registration	55	______
Maintaining a steady dating relationship	55	______
Commuting to campus or work, or both	54	______
Peer pressures	53	______

Being away from home for the first time	53	______
Getting sick	52	______
Concerns about your appearance	52	______
Getting straight As	51	______
A difficult class that you love	48	______
Making new friends; getting along with friends	47	______
Fraternity or sorority rush	47	______
Falling asleep in class	40	______
Attending an athletic event (e.g., football game)	20	______
Sum of Your Scores	______	______

Another problem with inventories such as Holmes and Rahe's original scale is that it focuses on stressors experienced by the middle class and under-represents stressors experienced by the poor and members of minority communities. Variables such as poverty and racism are potent causes of stress (Clark, Anderson, Clark, & Williams, 1999; Gibbons, Gerrard, & Cleveland, 2004; Giscombé & Lobel, 2005). To understand the relationship between stress and health, we need a better understanding of such community-level and cultural-level variables as poverty and racism.

Perceived Stress and Health

There is another problem: Simply adding up the number of negative life events that people experience—such as divorcing or losing one's job—violates a basic principle of social psychology, namely that subjective situations have more of an impact on people than objective situations (Dohrenwend, 2006; Griffin & Ross, 1991). Of course, some situations are objectively bad for our health, regardless of how we interpret them (Jackson & Inglehart, 1995; Taylor, Repetti, & Seeman, 1997). Still, there are events that seem to have negative effects only on the people who construe them in negative ways. For some students, writing a term paper is a major hassle; for others, it's a minor inconvenience (or even an enjoyable experience). Some people view a major life change such as getting divorced as a liberating escape from an abusive relationship, whereas others view it as a devastating personal failure. As recognized by Richard Lazarus (1966, 2000) in his pioneering work on stress, it is subjective, not objective, stress that causes problems. An event is stressful for people only if they interpret it as stressful; thus, we can define **stress** as the negative feelings and beliefs that occur whenever people feel unable to cope with demands from their environment (Lazarus & Folkman, 1984).

Stress
The negative feelings and beliefs that occur whenever people feel unable to cope with demands from their environment

Consider the number of losses Elvira Toews has experienced. If she filled out the Holmes and Rahe (1967) Social Readjustment Rating Scale—even just for the year 2010—she would score a very high number of life change units. According to the theory, she should be experiencing a great deal of stress, enough to put her at considerable risk for a health crisis. The fact that she comes through major life stressors with such grace and strength suggests that there are limits to trying to predict people's reactions from a count of the number of stressful events in their lives. We need to take into account how different people *interpret* disruptions and challenges in their lives.

Studies using this subjective definition of stress confirm that it is the life experiences that we perceive as negative that are bad for our health. For example, a recent study conducted with gay and bisexual men living in Ontario found that the greater the number of stressful events experienced, the greater the risk of HIV infection (Burchell, Calzavara, Myers, Remis, Raboud, Corey, & Swantee, 2010). More specifically, when these men were stressed, they were more likely to engage in risky sexual behaviours, which, in turn, increased the risk of HIV infection. A recent program of research

Some of these events are happy; yet, they cause stress. Which of these situations might cause you to experience stress?

conducted with University of Waterloo students found that people who have high levels of interpersonal stress are more likely to report health problems (e.g., missing class due to illness). Those who have low self-esteem are especially likely to experience interpersonal stress, and their health pays the price (Stinson, Logel, Zanna, Holmes, Cameron, Wood, & Spencer, 2008). Lefrançois and colleagues (2000) administered a French version of the Holmes and Rahe (1967) Social Readjustment Rating Scale (modified to focus on the life changes associated with aging) to elderly people in Quebec. It was the life changes regarded as negative that were associated with the greatest psychological distress (Lefrançois, Leclerc, Hamel, & Gaulin, 2000).

Stress caused by negative interpretations of events can even affect our immune systems, making us more susceptible to disease. Consider the common cold. When people are exposed to the virus that causes a cold, 20 to 60 percent of them become sick. Is it possible that stress is a determinant of who will become ill? To find out, Cohen, Tyrrell, and Smith (1991, 1993) asked volunteers to spend a week at a research institute in southern England. As a measure of stress, the participants listed recent events that had had a negative impact on their lives. (Consistent with our definition of stress, the participants listed only events that they perceived to be negative.) The researchers then gave participants nasal drops that contained either the virus that causes the common cold or saline (salt water). The participants were subsequently quarantined for several days so that they had no contact with other people.

The results? The people who were experiencing a great deal of stress in their lives were more likely to catch a cold from the virus (see Figure SPA2.1). Among people who reported the least amount of stress, about 27 percent came down with a cold. This rate increased steadily in relation to the amount of stress people reported, topping out at a rate of nearly 50 percent in the group that was experiencing the most stress. This effect of stress was found even when several other factors that influence catching a cold

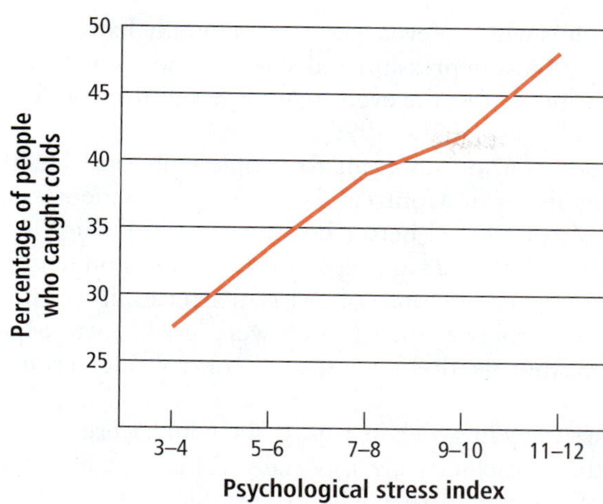

FIGURE SPA2.1

Stress and the likelihood of catching a cold.

People were first exposed to the virus that causes the common cold, and then isolated. The greater the amount of stress they were experiencing, the greater the likelihood that they caught a cold from this virus.

(Adapted from Cohen, Tyrell, & Smith, 1991)

were taken into account, such as the time of year and the participant's age, weight, and sex. This study, along with others like it, shows that the more stress people experience, the lower their immunity to diseases (Doyle, Gentile, & Cohen, 2006; O'Leary, 1990; Stone, Bovbjerg, Neale, Napoli, Valdimarsdottir, Cox, Hayden, & Gwaltney, 1992).

The results from Cohen and colleagues' correlational study have been confirmed in research using experimental designs. For example, there are studies in which people's immune responses are measured before and after undergoing mildly stressful tasks in the laboratory, such as solving mental arithmetic problems continuously for six minutes or giving speeches on short notice. It turns out that even relatively mild stressors such as these can lead to a suppression of the immune system (Cacioppo, 1998; Cacioppo et al., 1998).

The finding that stress has negative effects on people's health raises an important question: What exactly is it that makes people perceive a situation as stressful? One important determinant, as we will now see, is the amount of control that they believe they have over the event.

Feeling in Charge: The Importance of Perceived Control

How much control do you have over your own life? Are you able to decide what to do with each day? When and what to eat? When to study? When to go out with friends? Research in social psychology suggests that the feeling that we don't have control is detrimental to our psychological and physical health. Shelley Taylor and her colleagues (1984), for example, interviewed women with breast cancer and found that many of them believed that they could control whether their cancer returned. Here is how one man described his wife: "She got books, she got pamphlets, she studied, she talked to cancer patients. She found out everything that was happening to her and she fought it. She went to war with it. She calls it 'taking in her covered wagons and surrounding it'" (as quoted in Taylor, 1989; Taylor, Lichtman, & Wood, 1984). The researchers found that women who believed that their cancer was controllable were better adjusted psychologically (see also Folkman & Moskowitz, 2000).

Subsequent studies have found that a high sense of **perceived control**, defined as the belief that we can influence our environment in ways that determine whether we experience positive or negative outcomes, is associated with good mental and physical health (Burger, 1992; Lachman, 2006; Skinner, 1995; Thompson, 1999). For example, research conducted at the University of Manitoba found that first-year students who felt that they had control over their academic performance reported less anxiety, stress, boredom, and depression. Importantly, these students also achieved better grades than those who perceived less control (Perry, 2003; Perry, Hladkyj, Pekrun, & Pelletier, 2001; Ruthig, Haynes, Stupnisky, & Perry, 2009).

Perceived Control

The belief that we can influence our environment in ways that determine whether we experience positive or negative outcomes

The benefits of perceived control have been demonstrated in a variety of other domains. A study conducted with clients at sexual assault centres in southern Ontario found that rape victims who believed that they generally had control over outcomes in their lives experienced less depression and showed fewer symptoms of post-traumatic stress six months or more after the event than rape victims who felt that they had little control (Regehr, Cadell, & Jansen, 1999).

Perceived control is also important to people's physical health. A recent survey of nearly 900 adults living in Montreal found that respondents who reported higher perceived control also reported better health (Moore, Daniel, Bockenholt, Gauvin, Richard, & Stewart, 2010). In a study specifically focused on patients who had undergone a coronary angioplasty because of diseased arteries, it was found that those who had a high sense of control over their futures were less likely to experience subsequent heart problems than those with a low sense of control (Helgeson, 2003; Helgeson & Fritz, 1999).

A Canada-wide survey in which nearly 10 000 adults were surveyed over the course of 8 years found that the elderly are especially vulnerable to feelings of loss of control. Specifically, it was found that when older people experienced multiple stressors, they felt a much greater loss of control than younger people going through the same thing (Cairney & Krause, 2008). Similarly, results from the Aging in Manitoba project found that the "old-old" (ages 85 and older) experienced a larger decrease in feelings of perceived control after a fall than did the "young-old" (younger than 85 years; Ruthig, Chipperfield, Newall, Perry, & Hall, 2007). The researchers suggest that with age, people have fewer resources (e.g., support from friends) to help cope with stress. This is unfortunate because elderly people who do perceive control in their lives reap many benefits. For example, longitudinal research conducted by the Canadian Aging Research Network with elderly residents of Manitoba found that those who perceived that they had control over housework and outdoor work were more likely to see themselves as having good health—more so than elderly people who perceived less control. Importantly, those who perceived control actually were in better health (Chipperfield, Perry, & Menec, 1999), engaged in more physical activity (Ruthig et al., 2007), saw themselves as more active than their peers (Bailis, Chipperfield, Perry, Newall, & Haynes, 2008), believed that they were at less risk for hip fractures (Ruthig, Chipperfield, Bailis, & Perry, 2008), and actually tended to live longer (Menec & Chipperfield, 1997).

Of course, studies such as these are using correlational rather than experimental designs. Researchers measure the amount of control people are experiencing and correlate this with their psychological and physical adjustment. Such studies cannot prove that feelings of control *cause* good physical or emotional health; for example, it is possible that good physical or emotional health causes one to feel more in control. Indeed, Menec, Chipperfield, and Perry (1999) found that elderly people who believed that they were in good health were also more likely to perceive control over their lives and engage in control-enhancing strategies. It is also possible that some third variable contributes to both good health and feelings of control (Johnson & Krueger, 2005). To address the question of whether feelings of control have beneficial causal effects, we need to conduct experimental studies in which people are randomly assigned to conditions of "high" versus "low" perceived control. Fortunately, a number of such experimental studies have been conducted (Heckhausen & Schulz, 1995; Ratelle, Baldwin, & Vallerand, 2005; Rodin, 1986).

One of the most famous series of studies on the importance of perceived control was conducted by David Glass and Jerome Singer (1972). In a typical experiment, participants were given several problems to solve, such as complex addition problems or a proofreading task. While they worked on these problems, they heard loud bursts of noise coming from various sources: a mimeograph machine, a typewriter, or two people speaking in Spanish. The noise was played at 108 decibels—about what you would hear if you were operating a riveting machine or standing near the runway when a large commercial jet took off.

In one condition, the bursts of noise occurred at unpredictable lengths and at unpredictable intervals over the course of the 25-minute session. In a second condition, people heard the same sequence of noises but were given a sense of control over them.

The experimenter told participants that they could stop the noise at any point by pressing a button. "Whether or not you press the button is up to you," explained the experimenter. "We'd prefer that you do not, but that's entirely up to you" (Glass & Singer, 1972). A key fact to remember is that *no one* actually pressed the button. People in this condition heard the same amount of noise as people in the uncontrollable noise condition; the only difference was that they believed they could stop the noise whenever they wanted to. Finally, a third condition was included wherein people worked on the problem in peace and quiet. After the 25-minute session was over, people in all conditions worked on new problems without any noise present.

Interestingly, the noise had little effect on people during the initial 25-minute session. As long as a task was not too complex, people could bear down and ignore unpleasant noises, doing just as well on the problems as people who worked on them in quiet surroundings. A different picture emerged, however, when people worked on problems in the next session, in which everyone could work in peace and quiet. Those who had endured the uncontrollable noises made significantly more errors during this session than did people who had not heard noises during the first session. In contrast, the people who heard the noises but believed they could control them did almost as well on the subsequent problems as those who heard no noise at all. When people knew they could turn off the noise at any point, the noise was much easier to tolerate and did not impair later performance—even though these people had never actually turned it off.

Subsequent research conducted at the University of Manitoba underscores the importance of perceived control. Cramer, Nickels, and Gural (1997) found that participants who were told that there was nothing they could do to escape bursts of loud noise (78 decibels) resembling sirens of emergency vehicles felt more helpless than did those who were told they had some control. Interestingly, among those who were told that they had some control, helplessness was reduced to the same extent, regardless of whether they were told that they had 25 percent, 50 percent, or 75 percent control. As the researchers put it, "A little control may go far to shield a person from feelings of helplessness, and additional control provides little extra protection" (Cramer et al., 1997, p. 623).

Increasing Perceived Control in Nursing Homes Some of the most dramatic effects of perceived control have been found in studies of older people in nursing homes. Many people who live in nursing homes and hospitals feel that they have lost control of their lives (Raps, Peterson, Jonas, & Seligman, 1982). People are often placed in long-term care facilities against their wishes, and once there, have little say in what they do, whom they see, or what they eat. For example, an observational study of residents at a nursing home in Alberta found that patients tended to sit passively and rely on nursing staff to initiate contact (Intrieri & Morse, 1997).

Ellen Langer and Judith Rodin (1976) believed that it would be beneficial for residents of a nursing home if their feelings of control were increased. They asked the director of a nursing home in Connecticut to convey to the residents that contrary to what they might think, they had a lot of responsibility for their own lives. Here is an excerpt of his speech:

> Take a minute to think of the decisions you can and should be making. For example, you have the responsibility of caring for yourselves, of deciding whether or not you want to make this a home you can be proud of and happy in. You should be deciding how you want your rooms to be arranged—whether you want it to be as it is or whether you want the staff to help you rearrange the furniture. You should be deciding how you want to spend your time . . .. If you are unsatisfied with anything here, you have the influence to change it . . .. These are just a few of the things you could and should be deciding and thinking about now and from time to time every day. (Langer & Rodin, 1976)

The director went on to say that a movie would be shown on two nights the following week and that the residents should decide on which night they wanted to attend. Finally, he gave each resident a gift of a houseplant, emphasizing that it was up to the resident to take care of it.

Giving senior citizens a sense of control over their lives has been found to have positive benefits, both physically and psychologically.

The director also gave a speech to residents assigned to a comparison group. This speech was different in one crucial way—all references to making decisions and residents being responsible for themselves were deleted. The director emphasized that he wanted the residents to be happy, but he did not say anything about the control they had over their lives. He said that a movie would be shown on two nights the next week and that the residents would be assigned to see it on one night or the other. He gave plants to these residents as well, but said that the nurses would take care of the plants.

The director's speech might not seem like a major change in the lives of the residents. The people in the induced control group heard one speech about the responsibility they had for their lives and were given one plant to water. That doesn't seem like very strong stuff, does it? But to an institutionalized person who feels helpless and constrained, even a small boost in control can have a dramatic effect. Indeed, residents in the induced control group became happier and more active than did residents in the comparison group (Langer & Rodin, 1976). Most dramatic of all, the induced control intervention affected the residents' health and mortality. One and a half years after the director's speech, 30 percent of residents in the comparison condition had died, compared with only 15 percent of residents in the induced control group (Rodin & Langer, 1977; see left side of Figure SPA2.2).

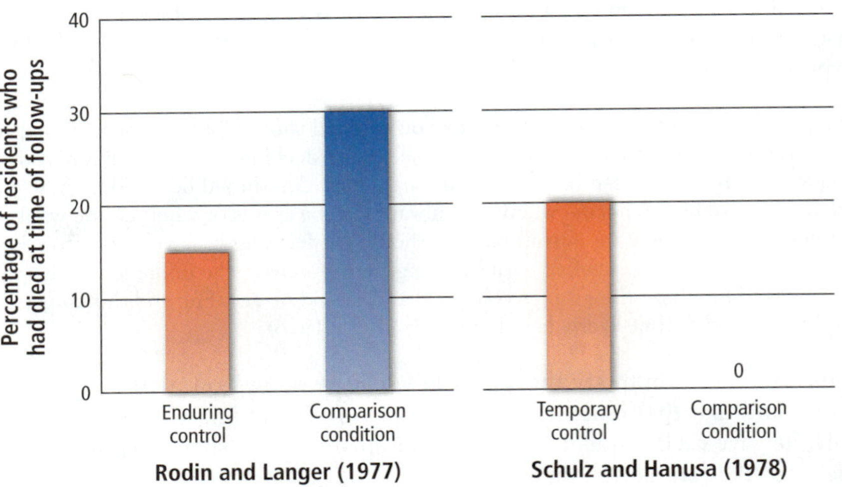

FIGURE SPA2.2

Perceived control and mortality.

In two studies, elderly residents in nursing homes were made to feel more in control of their lives. In one (Rodin & Langer, 1977), the intervention endured over time so that people continued to feel in control. As seen in the left side of the figure, this intervention had positive effects on mortality rates. Those who received it were more likely to be alive 18 months later than those who did not. In the other study (Schulz & Hanusa, 1978), the intervention was temporary. Being given control and then having it taken away had negative effects on mortality rates, as seen in the right side of the figure.

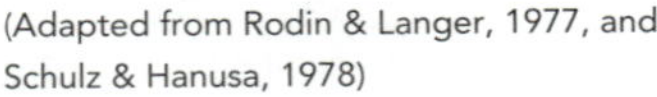
(Adapted from Rodin & Langer, 1977, and Schulz & Hanusa, 1978)

Richard Schulz (1976) increased feelings of control in residents of nursing homes in a different way. Schulz started a program in a North Carolina nursing home in which undergraduates visited the residents once a week for two months. In the induced control condition, the residents decided when the visits would occur and how long they would last. In a randomly assigned comparison condition, it was the students, not the residents, who decided when the visits would occur and how long they would last. While residents received visits in both conditions, in only one could they control the visits' frequency and duration. This may seem like a minor difference but, again, giving the residents some semblance of control over their lives had dramatic effects. After two months, those in the induced control condition were happier, healthier, and more active, and they were taking fewer medications than those in the comparison group. Schulz returned to the nursing home several months later to assess the long-term effects of his intervention, including its effect on mortality rates. Based on the results of the Langer and Rodin (1976) study, we might expect that those residents who could control the students' visits would be healthier and more likely to still be alive than residents who could not. However, there is a crucial difference between the two studies; the residents in the Langer and Rodin study were given an enduring sense of control, whereas the residents in the Schulz study experienced control and then lost it when the students' visits ceased. Langer and Rodin's participants could continue to choose which days to participate in different activities, to take care of their plant, and to feel they could make a difference in what happened to them—even after the study ended. By contrast, when Schulz's study was over and the students stopped visiting, the residents who could control the visits suddenly had that control removed.

Unfortunately, Schulz's intervention had an unintended effect. Once the program ended, the people in the induced control group did worse (Schulz & Hanusa, 1978). Compared with people in the comparison group, they were more likely to have experienced deteriorating health and zest for life, and they were more likely to have died (see the right side of Figure SPA2.2). This study has sobering implications for the many programs in which volunteers visit residents of nursing homes, prisons, and mental hospitals. These programs might be beneficial in the short run but do more harm than good after they end.

Disease, Control, and Well-Being We end this discussion with some words of caution. First, the link between perceived control and stress is stronger in Western cultures than in Asian cultures. Sastry and Ross (1998) found that Asians reported that perceived control was less important to them than did Westerners and that there was less of a relationship between perceived control and psychological distress among Asians. The researchers argue that in Western cultures, in which individualism and personal achievement are prized, people are more likely to feel stressed when they cannot control their destinies. A sense of control is less of an issue in Asian cultures because Asians tend to place greater value on collectivism and putting the social group ahead of individual goals.

Second, even in Western societies, there is a danger in exaggerating the relationship between perceived control and physical health. The social critic Susan Sontag (1978, 1988) perceptively observed that when a society is plagued by a deadly but poorly understood disease, such as tuberculosis in the nineteenth century and AIDS today, the illness is often blamed on some kind of human frailty, such as lack of faith, moral weakness, or a broken heart. As a result, people sometimes blame themselves for their illnesses, even to the point where they do not seek effective treatment. Even though it is beneficial for people to feel that they are in control of their illnesses, the downside of this strategy is that if they do not get better, they may blame themselves for failing to recover. Tragically, diseases such as cancer can be fatal no matter how much control a person feels. One of the doctors who treated the world-famous cyclist Lance Armstrong when he battled cancer put it this way, "I've seen wonderful, positive people not make it in the end . . . and some of the most miserable, ornery people survive to resume their ornery lives" (Armstrong, 2000, p. 127). It only adds to the tragedy if people with serious diseases feel a sense of moral failure, blaming themselves for an unavoidable disease.

For people living with serious illness, maintaining some form of control when their health is failing has important benefits. Researchers have found that even when people who are seriously ill with cancer or AIDS feel no control over the disease, many of them believe that they can still control the *consequences* of the disease (e.g., their emotional reactions and some of the physical symptoms, such as how tired they feel; Thompson, Nanni, & Levine, 1994). And the more people feel they can control the consequences of their illness, the better adjusted they are, even if they know they cannot control the eventual course of the disease. In short, it is important to feel in control of something—even if it is not the disease itself (Heckhausen & Schulz, 1995; Morling & Evered, 2006; Thompson, 2002).

Knowing You Can Do It: Self-Efficacy

Self-Efficacy
The belief in one's ability to carry out specific actions that produce desired outcomes

Believing we have control over our lives is one thing; believing that we can actually execute the specific behaviours that will get us what we want is another. Sam might have a general sense that he is in control of his life, but will this mean that he will find it easy to stop smoking? According to Albert Bandura, a highly influential social psychologist (who was born in Alberta and studied at the University of British Columbia), we have to examine his **self-efficacy**, which is the belief in one's ability to carry out specific actions that produce desired outcomes (Bandura, 1997; Bandura & Locke, 2003; Benight & Bandura, 2004). If Sam believes that he can perform the behaviours that will enable him to quit smoking—throwing away his cigarettes, avoiding situations in which he is most tempted to smoke, distracting himself when he craves a cigarette—then chances are he will succeed. If he has low self-efficacy in this domain, believing that he can't perform the behaviour necessary to quit, then he is likely to fail.

Again, it is not a general sense of control that predicts engaging in healthier behaviour, but the confidence that one can perform the specific behaviour in question. A person might have high self-efficacy in one domain, such as high confidence that he or she can lose weight, but low self-efficacy in another domain, such as low confidence that he or she can quit smoking.

People's level of self-efficacy has been found to predict a number of other important health behaviours, such as the likelihood that they will quit smoking, lose weight, lower their cholesterol, and exercise regularly (Bandura, 1997; Hyde, Hankins, Deale, & Marteau, 2008; Salovey, Rothman, Detweiler, & Steward, 2000; Sullivan, O'Connor, & Burris, 2006). For example, a study of more than 1000 high school students in Toronto found that those who were high in self-efficacy in the area of exercise were more likely to engage in vigorous physical exercise than those who had low self-efficacy in this area (Allison, Dwyer, & Makin, 1999). Similarly, recent research conducted with kinesiology students at the University of Saskatchewan found a positive relation between self-efficacy and engaging in levels of physical activity recommended by Health Canada (Nickel & Spink, 2010a). Finally, a review of the more than 350 interventions designed to promote safer sex confirms that they work because they increase people's self-efficacy about condom use (Albarracín, Durantini, & Earl, 2006; Albarracín, Gillette, Earl, Glasman, Durantini, & Ho, 2005; Noguchi, Albarracín, Durantini, & Glasman, 2007)

Self-efficacy increases the likelihood that people will engage in the desired behaviour in two ways. First, it influences people's persistence and effort at a task. People with low self-efficacy tend to give up easily, whereas people high in self-efficacy set higher goals, try harder, and persist more in the face of failure—thereby increasing the likelihood that they will succeed (Cervone & Peake, 1986; Litt, 1988; Steel, 2007). Second, self-efficacy influences the way our bodies react while we are working toward our goals. For example, people with high self-efficacy experience less anxiety while working on a difficult task, and their immune system functions more optimally (Bandura, Cioffi, Taylor, & Brouillard, 1988; Wiedenfield, O'Leary, Bandura, Brown, Levine, & Raska, 1990). In short, self-efficacy operates as a kind of self-fulfilling prophecy. The more you believe that you can accomplish something, such as quitting smoking, the greater the likelihood that you will.

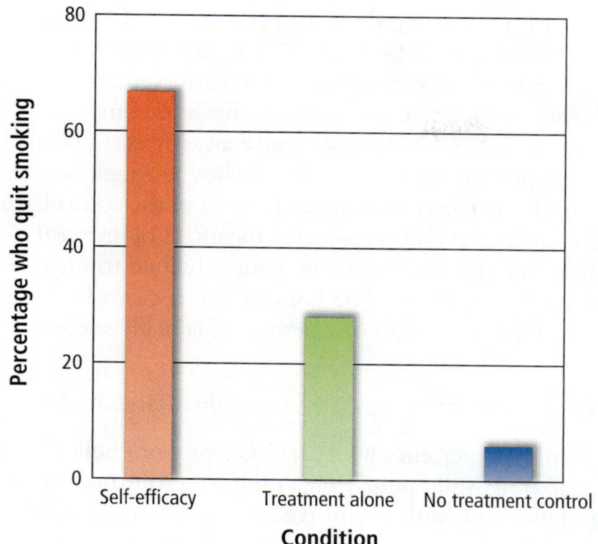

FIGURE SPA2.3

The role of self-efficacy in smoking cessation.

Adult smokers were randomly assigned to one of three conditions. In the self-efficacy condition, people were told that they were selected for the study because they had great potential to quit. They then underwent a 14-week smoking cessation program. People in the treatment-alone condition participated in the same program but were told that they had been randomly selected for it. People in the no-treatment control condition did not take part in the program. At the end of the 14-week period, substantially more people in the self-efficacy condition had quit smoking. Believing that we have the ability to carry out beneficial behaviour—having high self-efficacy—is an important determinant of whether we succeed.

(Adapted from Blittner, Goldberg, & Merbaum, 1978)

How can self-efficacy be increased? In one study, for example, participants signed up for a program to help them quit smoking (Blittner, Goldberg, & Merbaum, 1978). In the self-efficacy condition, participants were told that they had been chosen for the 14-week program because they "showed that they had strong willpower and great potential to control and conquer their desires and behaviour" (Blittner et al., 1978, p. 555). Participants in the treatment-alone condition underwent the same program, with one important difference: they were told that they had been chosen randomly for the treatment program. Finally, participants in the no-treatment control condition were told that they would be contacted for the study at a later time.

As seen in Figure SPA2.3, the self-efficacy instructions were quite effective. By the end of the treatment period, 67 percent of people in the self-efficacy condition had quit smoking, compared with only 28 percent in the treatment-alone group and 6 percent in the no-treatment control group (Blittner et al., 1978). It is important to keep in mind that the people in the self-efficacy condition did not have stronger willpower than anyone else; they were randomly assigned to receive this feedback. The *belief* that they were likely to succeed, however, contributed to greater success.

Researchers at York University and Wilfrid Laurier University have recently shown that another way to increase self-efficacy is to visualize or picture success (Vasquez & Buehler, 2007). In a series of studies, university students were asked about an important academic task such as a test or an essay that they would be writing in the next few weeks. Participants who were asked to imagine that they were an observer, seeing themselves carrying out the task successfully, subsequently reported higher achievement motivation than participants who did not engage in this kind of visualization.

Finally, research by Koestner and colleagues (2006) suggests yet another way in which self-efficacy can be increased. These researchers had students at McGill University come to the laboratory early in January and report one of their New Year's resolutions. (Most resolutions pertained to academic or social goals.) Participants in the self-efficacy condition were asked to think about past instances of mastering a similar goal, to think of someone who could provide support to them while pursuing their goal, and to think of a person similar to themselves who had mastered a similar goal. Other participants were asked to write out an implementation plan—the specific steps they were going to take to achieve their goals. (We discussed implementation plans in the Social Psychology and the Environment module.) Participants in a third condition received the self-efficacy intervention and were asked to write out their implementation plan. Five months later, the participants were contacted again to assess whether their New Year's resolutions had been achieved. The greatest success was found among those who had received the self-efficacy intervention and who had spelled out their plan for achieving their goal (Koestner, Horberg, Gaudreau, Powers, Di Dio, Jochum, & Salter, 2006). In research along the same lines, female postgraduate students at the University of Alberta underwent an intervention that involved attending sessions in which they spelled out specific plans for attending fitness training sessions. (Participants in the control group did not receive any intervention.) Those who formulated implementation plans were more likely to follow through and attend fitness training sessions over an 11-week period than participants in the control group. Importantly, the implementation plan intervention also had the effect of increasing self-efficacy (specifically, confidence that you could arrange your schedule to include regular exercise; Murray, Rodgers, & Fraser, 2009). The bottom line is clear: Believing that we can do something is a powerful determinant of whether we actually succeed.

Simulate on **mypsychlab**
Learned Helplessness

Explaining Negative Events: Learned Helplessness

What happens when we experience a setback? Despite our belief in ourselves, perhaps we failed to quit smoking or did poorly on a midterm. Another important determinant of our physical and mental health is how we explain to ourselves why a negative event occurred. Consider two university students who both get poor grades on their first calculus test. Student A says to herself, "I'll bet the professor deliberately made the test difficult, to motivate us to do better. I'll just have to study harder. If I really buckle down for the next test, I'll do better." Student B says to himself, "Wow, I guess I can't really cut it. I was worried that I wasn't smart enough to make it in university and, boy, was I ever right." Which student do you think will do better on the next test? Clearly the first one, because she has explained her poor performance in a way that is more flattering to herself and makes her feel more in control. In contrast, the second student is expressing **learned helplessness**—pessimism that results from attributing a negative event to stable, internal, and global factors (Abramson, Seligman, & Teasdale, 1978; Overmier, 2002; Peterson & Park, 2007; Wise & Rosqrist, 2006).

Learned Helplessness
Pessimism that results from attributing a negative event to stable, internal, and global factors

Stable Attribution
The belief that the cause of an event is a result of factors that will not change over time, as opposed to unstable factors that will change over time

Internal Attribution
The inference that a person is behaving in a certain way because of something about him or her, such as his or her attitude, character, or personality

Global Attribution
The belief that the cause of an event is a result of factors that apply in a large number of situations, as opposed to the belief that the cause is specific and applies in only a limited number of situations

If we think that a negative event has a stable cause, we've made a **stable attribution:** We believe that the event was caused by things that will not change over time (e.g., our intelligence) as opposed to factors that can change over time (e.g., the amount of effort we put into a task). Explaining this negative event as stemming from an internal cause—that is, making an **internal attribution**—means we believe that something about us caused the event (e.g., our own ability or effort) as opposed to factors that are external to us (e.g., the difficulty of a test). Finally, explaining an event as the result of a global or widespread cause—that is, making a **global attribution**—is the belief that the event is caused by factors that apply in a large number of situations (e.g., our general intelligence, which will influence our performance in many areas) rather than factors that are specific and apply in only a limited number of situations (e.g., how good we are at math, which will affect our performance in math courses but not in other courses). According to learned helplessness theory, making stable, internal, and global attributions for negative events leads to hopelessness, depression, reduced effort, and difficulty in learning (see Figure SPA2.4).

Student B, for example, believes that the cause of his poor grade is stable (being unintelligent will last forever), internal (something about him is to blame), and global (being unintelligent will affect him in many situations other than calculus classes). This kind of explanation will lead to learned helplessness, thereby producing depression, reduced effort, and the inability to learn new things. Student A, in contrast, believes that the cause of her poor grade is unstable (the professor will make the tests easier, and she can study harder next time), external (the professor intentionally made the test hard), and specific (the things that caused her poor calculus grade are unlikely to affect anything else, such as her grade in English). People who explain bad events in this more optimistic way are less likely to be depressed and in better health, and do better in school and in their careers, as indicated by research conducted in Canada and the United States (Dweck, 1999; Hyde, Mezulis, & Abramson, 2008; Nickel & Spink, 2010b; Perry, 2003; Perry, Stupinsky, Daniels, & Haynes, 2008; Peterson & Seligman, 1984; Sweeney, Anderson, & Bailey, 1986).

FIGURE SPA2.4

The theory of learned helplessness.

Explaining a negative event in a pessimistic manner leads to learned helplessness (i.e., depression, lowered effort, poor learning).

Other research has shown that the way in which people explain negative relationship issues also has important implications. For example, a recent study conducted with more than 1000 elderly people living in Manitoba found that those who believed that relationships are formed through external factors (e.g., luck) reported greater loneliness and less social participation than those who believed that the formation of relationships depends on internal, controllable factors (e.g., effort; Newall, Chipperfield, Clifton, Perry, Swift, & Ruthig, 2009). Research by Rempel, Ross, and Holmes (2001) suggests that the kinds of attributions that couples make for negative events in their relationship have important consequences. In their study, married couples living in the Waterloo area were asked to discuss a problem in their relationship. The researchers found that couples who were high in trust tended to make positive global attributions for their partner's behaviour. Even when discussing a conflict, these couples were optimistic; they focused on the enduring, positive aspects of their partner and the relationship. In contrast, low-trust couples showed a pattern of negative, pessimistic attributions; in other words, for these couples, learned helplessness had set in.

Returning to the example of Student A and Student B, note that we do not know the real reason our hypothetical students did poorly on their calculus test. Instead, learned helplessness theory states that it is more important to consider people's perceptions of these causes. The real causes, of course, are not irrelevant. Students who truly lack ability in calculus are likely to do poorly on future calculus tests. Often in life, however, what actually causes our behaviour is not so clear-cut or fixed. In such situations, people's attributions about the causes of their problems can be very important.

Consider, for example, cyclist Lance Armstrong's comeback after he had recovered from cancer. In his first races, he did fairly well, finishing fourteenth in a five-day race through Spain and nineteenth in an eight-day race from Nice to Paris. He was used to winning, however, and initially explained his failure to do so in this way: "Well, I've just been through too much. I've been through three surgeries, three months of chemo, and a year of hell, and that's the reason I'm not riding well. My body is just never going to be the same" (Armstrong, 2000, p. 188). Note that he attributed his poor performance to a cause that was internal (his lowered physical abilities), stable (a condition that would not change), and global (a condition that would influence many aspects of his life, not just one race). Had he persisted in explaining his performance in this way, surely he would not have gone on to win the Tour de France. Instead, he had the insight to recognize that every cyclist has ups and downs and that no one wins every race. "What I really should have been saying," Armstrong realized, "was, 'Hey, it's just a bad day'"—an attribution to a cause that was external (the particular circumstances, not something about him), unstable (something likely to change), and specific (something limited to that one situation).

Can learned helplessness be overcome? To find out, Tim Wilson and Patricia Linville (1982, 1985) conducted a study with first-year university students. They assumed that many first-year students experience academic difficulties because of a damaging pattern of attributions. Because of the difficulty of adjusting to a new academic and social environment, the first year of university has its rough spots for nearly everyone. The problem is that many first-year students do not realize how common such adjustment problems are and assume that their problems come from personal predicaments that are unlikely to change—just the kind of attribution that leads to learned helplessness. Wilson and Linville tried to combat this pessimism by convincing first-year students that the causes of poor performance are often temporary. In the treatment condition, the students watched videotaped interviews of four senior students, each of whom mentioned that his or her grades had been poor or mediocre during the first year of study but had improved significantly since then. The students were also given statistics indicating that academic performance is often poor in the first year of university but improves thereafter. The researchers hypothesized that this simple message would help prevent learned helplessness, increasing the students' motivation to try harder and removing needless worries about their abilities. Judging by the students' subsequent performance, this is just what happened. Compared with students in a control group who participated in the study but did not watch the videotaped interviews or see the statistics, students in the treatment condition improved their grades more in the following year and were less likely to drop out.

Similar results have been found in studies that have administered attributional retraining programs to first-year students in Belgium (Van Overwalle & De Metsenaere, 1990; Wilson, Damiani, & Shelton, 2002) and at the University of Manitoba (Haynes, Daniels, Stupinsky, Perry, & Hladkyj, 2008; Menec, Perry, Struthers, Schonwetter, Hechter, & Eichholz, 1994). In fact, in a recent study in this series, the researchers found that students at the University of Manitoba who received attributional retraining were 73 percent less likely to fail their Introductory Psychology course compared to students who did not receive this training (Haynes, Clifton, Daniels, Perry, Chipperfield, & Ruthig, 2011). Thus, teaching students to attribute academic outcomes to controllable rather than uncontrollable factors can have rather dramatic effects on their performance.

Finally, we note that a recent study conducted by researchers at the University of Sport Sciences in France and at St. Thomas University in Fredericton found that attribution interventions such as those used in the academic domain also can enhance persistence and performance when people are learning a new sport (Le Foll, Rascle, & Higgins, 2008).

In summary, our feelings of control and self-efficacy, and the kinds of attributions we make for negative events, are important determinants of our psychological and physical health. The power of our minds over our bodies is, of course, limited. But research shows that people's psychological reactions to life events can have a big influence on their mental and physical well-being.

Watch on mypsychlab
Learned Optimism

Students who realize that poor academic performance in the first year of university is common and that they are likely to improve will probably do better than students who believe that poor performance is a result of personal shortcomings that are unlikely to change.

Coping with Stress

No one always feels in control, of course, and sometimes it is difficult to avoid being pessimistic after something bad happens. The death of a loved one, an acrimonious divorce, and the loss of a job are extremely stressful events. Considerable research indicates that people exhibit various reactions, or **coping styles**, in the face of potentially stressful events (e.g., Aspinwall & Taylor, 1997; Lazarus & Folkman, 1984; Lehman, Davies, DeLongis, & Wortman, 1993; Salovey, Rothman, Detweiler, & Steward, 2000; Somerfield & McCrae, 2000). What are these styles, and how successful are they? We examine a few coping styles here, beginning with research on differences in the way that men and women cope with stress.

Coping Styles
The ways in which people react to stressful events

Gender Differences in Coping with Stress

If you have ever been to a dog park, you know that dogs respond in one of two ways when they are attacked: Sometimes they respond in kind and a dogfight ensues. Other times, the dog that is attacked will take off as fast as he or she can, tail between its legs. Walter Cannon (1932) termed this the **fight-or-flight response**, defined as responding to stress by either attacking the source of the stress or fleeing from it. The fight-or-flight response has been viewed as the way in which all mammals respond to stress. When under threat, mammals are energized by the release of hormones such as norepinephrine and epinephrine, and like the dogs in the park, they either attack or retreat as quickly as they can.

Explore on **mypsychlab**
Coping Strategies and Their Effects

Fight-or-Flight Response
Responding to stress by either attacking the source of the stress or fleeing from it

That, at least, has been the accepted story for many years. Shelley Taylor and her colleagues (2000) pointed out a little-known fact about research on the fight-or-flight syndrome: Most of it has been done on males, particularly male rats. Taylor and her colleagues argue that the fight-or-flight response does not work well for females because they typically play a greater role in caring for children. Fighting is not a good option for a pregnant female or one tending offspring. Consequently, Taylor and her colleagues argue, a different way of responding to stress has evolved in females, the **tend-and-befriend response**. Instead of fighting or fleeing, women respond to stress with nurturant activities designed to protect themselves and their offspring (tending) and by creating social networks that provide protection from threats (befriending). Tending has a number of benefits for both the mother and the child. For example, a quiet child is less likely to be noticed by predators, and nurturing behaviour leads to

Tend-and-Befriend Response
Responding to stress with nurturant activities designed to protect oneself and one's offspring (tending) and by creating social networks that provide protection from threats (befriending)

lower stress and improved immune functioning. Befriending involves the creation of close ties with other members of the species, which also confers a number of advantages. A close-knit group can exchange resources, watch out for predators, and share child care (Taylor, 2006; Taylor, Klein, Lewis, Gruenewald, Gurung, & Updegraff, 2000). As we saw in Chapter 5, women are more likely than men to develop intimate friendships, cooperate with others, and focus their attention on social relationships (Fehr, 1996). Women are especially likely to seek out others when stressed, especially other women, as shown by research conducted in the United States (Matud, 2004; Tamres, Janicki, & Helgeson, 2002) and in the Canadian Maritimes (Day & Livingstone, 2003).

We hasten to point out that although gender differences in coping do exist, the magnitude of these differences is not very large (Tamres et al., 2002). Further, seeking social support can benefit both women and men, as we'll see next.

Social Support: Getting Help from Others

Simulate on mypsychlab
Closer Look Simulation: Stress

One of the striking things about cyclist Lance Armstrong's recovery from cancer was the amount of support he received from his family and friends. His mother, to whom he was very close, took an active role in his treatment and recovery. She stayed by his side as much as possible and organized his schedule, prescription medicines, and diet. A close circle of friends stayed with him as well, many travelling great distances to visit him in the hospital and support him during his treatments. For example, 24 hours after his brain surgery, a group of friends took him to dinner at a restaurant across the street from the hospital. Armstrong also developed close friendships with many of the doctors and nurses who treated him.

Social Support

The perception that others are responsive and receptive to one's needs

Social support, defined as the perception that others are responsive and receptive to one's needs, is very helpful when dealing with stress (Helgeson & Cohen, 1996; Ryff & Singer, 2001; Sarason, Sarason, & Pierce, 1990; Stroebe & Stroebe, 1996; Uchino, Uno, & Holt-Lunstad, 1999; Taylor, 2007). Responsiveness is the key ingredient in social support, as demonstrated in a program of research by Nancy Collins and colleagues (Collins & Feeney, 2000, 2004). In a recent study, they had participants come to the lab with their romantic partner. The participants were told that they would be cliff-walking in a virtual world. The researchers created avatars resembling the participant who were required to navigate an obstacle course that was rather terrifying in places. For example, there were steep canyons and rocks would tumble down around the participant while the wind howled through the canyon. For some participants, an avatar of their partner was created and inserted into the virtual world. The researchers made it look as though the participant's romantic partner was controlling what his or her avatar did. In reality, the researchers manipulated the behaviour of the partner avatars. In the attentive support condition, the partner avatar oriented toward the participant, waved at him or her, and clapped when he or she navigated a particularly harrowing segment of the cliff walk. In the inattentive support condition, the partner's avatar did not orient toward the partner and often stared off into the distance while the participant struggled with a challenging stretch of the cliff walk. Participants in a control condition navigated the course on their own, without an avatar of their partner present.

In research by Collins and colleagues, participants create an avatar to represent their partner, such as the one pictured here, and then navigate a difficult trail in virtual reality in the presence of their "avatar partner".

The results? Participants in the attentive support condition found the task much less stressful than those who did the cliff walk alone. Moreover, having an inattentive partner present was slightly—but not significantly—better than going it alone. Those who received attentive support also reported feeling safer and more secure in the virtual world than participants in the inattentive support condition. Finally, on a later task, it was found that people whose partners had been inattentive in the cliff walking task later kept greater physical distance from their partner than those with an attentive partner or no partner present. The researchers conclude that "mere presence is not enough"; social support requires that those around us are responsive to our needs (Kane, McCall, Collins, & Blascovich, 2011).

As we shall see, responsive social support has been shown to have a number of beneficial physical and psychological effects across a variety of stressors—both acute and chronic. Let's start with the acute stressor of life-threatening illness. In one study, David Spiegel and his colleagues (1989) randomly assigned women with advanced breast cancer to a social support condition or a control condition. Women in the social support condition met weekly with doctors and other patients to discuss their problems and fears, whereas people in the control group did not have access to this support system. Social support not only improved women's moods and reduced their fears, but also lengthened their lives by an average of 18 months. Other studies have shown that interventions designed to increase social support and decrease stress in cancer patients improve immune system functioning (Antoni & Lutgendorf, 2007; Andersen, Farrar, Golden-Kreutz, Glaser, Emery, & Crespin, 2004; McGregor, Antoni, Boyers, Alferi, Cruess, Kilbourn, Blomberg, & Carver, 2004).

Researchers at McMaster University, the University of Saskatchewan and at Acadia University recently examined the effects of social support in a sample of people who had suffered heart attacks (mostly men). Participants who reported receiving high levels of social support reported greater self-efficacy when it came to maintaining a long-term rehabilitation exercise program and reported better health, overall, compared to those who reported less support (Woodgate, Brawley, & Shields, 2007).

Social support also makes a huge difference when people are coping with challenges in relationships or dealing with the loss of relationships. Research conducted with parents of children with a disability (recruited from the Society for Manitobans with Disabilities) found that feeling a lack of support from one's spouse while trying to cope with the many stresses of having a disabled child was associated with psychological distress (Marin, Holtzman, DeLongis, & Robinson, 2007). In another study, the effects of social support were evaluated among a group of Canadian women who had been widowed in the previous two years (Stewart, Craig, MacPherson, & Alexander, 2001). The women met weekly in small groups led by a peer—a woman who also was widowed—and a mental health professional. At the end of the 20-week program, the participants showed a number of improvements, including increased positive affect and increased hope and confidence.

Social support also plays an important role in the workplace, particularly for those in high-stress occupations. In a study of more than 800 Canadian and American firefighters, it was found that those who received social support at work and from

Women are somewhat more likely than men to develop intimate friendships, cooperate with others, and focus their attention on social relationships, particularly when under stress. Shelley Taylor and colleagues (2000) have referred to this as a tend-and-befriend strategy in which people respond to stress with nurturant activities designed to protect themselves and their offspring (tending) and by creating social networks that provide protection from threats (befriending).

their families were less likely to suffer from post-traumatic stress disorder (Corneil, Beaton, Murphy, Johnson, & Pike, 1999). Similarly, a study of physicians, nurses, and technicians employed at cancer clinics in southern Ontario found that stress was less likely to impair job performance for those health-care professionals who perceived that social support was available in their workplace (Stewart & Barling, 1996). Similar results were found in a study of more than 2000 Ontario nurses. Specifically, those who reported having a friend to confide in experienced fewer stress-related health problems, although this relation was more likely to hold for women than for men (Walters, Lenton, French, Eyles, Mayr, & Newbold, 1996). Some of you may classify the life of a university or college student as a "high-stress occupation." Here again, the research shows that having social support is associated with lower levels of stress and depression, as shown by a recent study conducted at the University of Manitoba. Moreover, the researchers found that lower levels of stress and depression, in turn, were positively correlated with students' grades (Ruthig et al., 2009).

We should point out that even people who are not dealing with huge life crises suffer if they don't have social support. For example, a study of elderly women and men living in Quebec found that those who had adequate social support experienced less psychological distress (e.g., depression, anxiety) than those who were lacking in social support (Lefrançois et al., 2000). Social support also can affect how long you live—even if you aren't experiencing a health crisis. In a study using a large sample of American men and women in the years 1967 to 1969, it was found that men with a low level of social support were 2 to 3 times more likely to die over the next 12 years than were men with a high level of social support; women with a low level of social support were 1.5 to 2 times more likely to die (House, Robbins, & Metzner, 1982), Interestingly, it is not just receiving social support that is beneficial: A study of people aged 65 and over found that those who *gave* support to others, such as helping family members with child care or doing errands for a neighbour, lived longer than people who did not (Brown, Nesse, & Vinokur, 2003).

It may seem obvious that social support is beneficial, but exactly when and how does it help? When times are tough—you've just broken up with your girlfriend or boyfriend, or your parents have gone off the deep end again—social support helps in two ways. First, it can help you interpret an event as less stressful than you would otherwise interpret it. Suppose you've just found out that you have midterms in your psychology and calculus classes on the same day. If you have several friends in these classes who can commiserate with you and help you study, you are likely to find the tests less of a big deal than if you had to cope with them on your own. Second, even if we do interpret an event as stressful, social support can help us cope. Suppose you've just done poorly on a midterm and feel bad about it. It's best to have close friends to help you deal with this and figure out how to do better on the next test (Stroebe & Stroebe, 1996). To get an idea of the amount of social support you feel is available in your life, complete the accompanying Try It! questionnaire.

Finally, social support operates differently in different cultures. Who do you think is more likely to seek support from others when things get tough: members of Western cultures that emphasize individualism and independence or members of Eastern cultures that emphasize collectivism and interdependence? It might seem as though people in collectivist cultures would be more likely to seek help from one another, but Shelley Taylor and colleagues have found just the opposite: When under stress, members of East Asian cultures are *less* likely to seek social support than members of Western cultures (Kim, Sherman, & Taylor, 2008; Taylor, Kim, & Sherman, 2004; Taylor, Welch, Kim, & Sherman, 2007). The reason? Members of collectivistic cultures are concerned that seeking support will disrupt the harmony of the group and open them up to criticism from others.

Does this mean that members of collectivistic cultures receive less support and benefit less when they receive it? Not at all—the main difference is in *how* people in difference cultures seek and obtain support. Members of collectivistic cultures are less likely to directly ask for help in a way that shows that they are having problems. But they do benefit from interacting with supportive others (Kim et al., 2008). In fact, there is some evidence that people who live in cultures that stress interdependence and

TRY IT! Social Support

This scale is made up of a list of statements, each of which may or may not be true about you. For each statement, choose T (for probably true) if the statement is true about you, or F (for probably false) if the statement is not true about you.

You may find that many of the statements are neither clearly true nor clearly false. If so, try to decide quickly whether probably true or probably false is more descriptive of you. Although some questions will be difficult to answer, it is important that you pick one alternative or the other. Remember to circle only one of the alternatives for each statement.

Read each item quickly but carefully before responding. Remember that this is not a test and there are no right or wrong answers.

1. There is at least one person I know whose advice I really trust.	T	F
2. There is really no one I can trust to give me good financial advice.	T	F
3. There is really no one who can give me objective feedback about how I'm handling my problems.	T	F
4. When I need suggestions for how to deal with a personal problem, I know there is someone I can turn to.	T	F
5. There is someone whom I feel comfortable going to for advice about sexual problems.	T	F
6. There is someone I can turn to for advice about handling hassles over household responsibilities.	T	F
7. I feel that there is no one with whom I can share my most private worries and fears.	T	F
8. If a family crisis arose, few of my friends would be able to give me good advice about how to handle it.	T	F
9. There are very few people I trust to help solve my problems.	T	F
10. There is someone I could turn to for advice about changing my job or finding a new one.	T	F

Scoring: You get one point each time you answered true (T) to questions 1, 4, 5, 6, and 10 and one point for each time you answered false (F) to questions 2, 3, 7, 8, and 9.

This scale was developed to measure what the researchers call appraisal social support, or "the perceived availability of someone to talk to about one's problems" (Cohen, Mermelstein, Kamarach, & Hoberman, 1985, pp. 75–76). One of their findings was that when people were not under stress, those low in social support had no more physical symptoms than those high in social support. However, when people were under stress, those low in social support had more physical symptoms than those high in social support. We need social support the most when times are tough. Another finding was that women scored reliably higher on the social support scale than men did. If you scored lower than you would like, you might want to consider reaching out to others more when you are under stress.

(Adapted from Cohen et al., 1985)

collectivism suffer less from stress-related diseases (Bond, 1991; Brislin, 1993; Cross & Vick, 2001). The bottom line is clear regardless of the culture that we live in: When we believe that we have someone to lean on, we can deal better with life's stresses.

Personality and Coping Styles

Some people, of course, are more likely to seek help from others or, more generally, to react in adaptive ways when under stress. Others seem to react badly when the going gets tough. As seen earlier in our discussion of learned helplessness, part of this comes from the way people explain the causes of a particular setback; explaining the setback in an optimistic way leads to better coping than explaining events in a pessimistic way. Other researchers have looked at this from the vantage point of individual differences, the aspects of people's personalities that make them different from other people.

Optimism Some people are by nature optimistic, generally expecting the best out of life, whereas others always see life's dark underside. As you might have guessed, there is evidence that optimistic people react better to stress and are generally healthier than pessimists (Carver & Scheier, 2003; Fischer & Chalmers, 2008; Nes & Segerstrom, 2006; Smith, 2006). For example, University of Manitoba researchers found that elderly people who were high in optimism reported that they were more physically active than other people their age (Bailis et al., 2008) and, in another study, reported better health in general than their less optimistic counterparts (Ruthig et al., 2007). These researchers also have found that first-year university students with high optimism are less stressed, less depressed, and more likely to feel in control of their lives than those who are less optimistic (Ruthig et al., 2009). All of these studies have used the Life Orientation Test to assess optimism. To get an idea of how optimistic you tend to be, you can complete this test for yourself (see the accompanying Try It! exercise).

The Life Orientation Test

Indicate the extent of your agreement or disagreement with each of the following 10 statements, using the scale below. Be as accurate and honest as you can on each item, and try not to let your answer to one question influence your answer to other questions. There are no right or wrong answers.

0	1	2	3	4
strongly disagree	disagree	neutral	agree	strongly agree

1. In uncertain times, I usually expect the best. ______
2. It's easy for me to relax. ______
3. If something can go wrong for me, it will. ______
4. I'm always optimistic about my future. ______
5. I enjoy my friends a lot. ______
6. It's important for me to keep busy. ______
7. I hardly ever expect things to go my way. ______
8. I don't get upset too easily. ______
9. I rarely count on good things happening to me. ______
10. Overall, I expect more good things to happen to me than bad. ______

Scoring: First, reverse your answers to questions 3, 7, and 9. That is, for these questions, change 0 to 4, 1 to 3, 3 to 1, and 4 to 0. Then, total these reversed scores and the scores you gave to questions 1, 4, and 10. (Ignore questions 2, 5, 6, and 8, because they were filler items.)

This measure of dispositional optimism was created by Scheier, Carver, and Bridges (1994). According to these researchers, the higher your score, the more optimistic your approach to life. The average score for university students in their study was 14.3, with no significant differences between women and men. Several studies have found that optimistic people cope better with stress and are healthier than their pessimistic counterparts.

The good news is that most people have been found to have an optimistic outlook on life. In fact, there is evidence that most people are *unrealistically* optimistic about their lives (Armor & Taylor, 1998; Taylor & Brown, 1988, 1994). We tend to expect that good events are more likely to happen to us than to our peers and that negative events are less likely to happen to us than our peers.

Between the optimist and the pessimist the difference is droll; The optimist sees the doughnut, The pessimist the hole.

—McLandburgh Wilson, *1915*

This kind of unrealistic optimism would be a problem if it caused people to make serious mistakes about their prospects in life. Obviously, it would not be a good idea to convince ourselves that we will never get lung disease and therefore we're free to smoke as much as we want. Fortunately, most people have a healthy balance of optimism and reality monitoring. We manage to put a positive spin on many aspects of our lives, which leads to increased feelings of control and self-efficacy. At the same time, most people are able to keep their optimistic biases in check when they are faced with a real threat and need to take steps to deal with that threat (Armor & Taylor, 1998). Consider cyclist Lance Armstrong's battle with cancer. In one sense, he was quite realistic, finding out all he could about the disease and the latest treatments and seeking the advice of many experts. He even learned to read X-rays as well as the doctors. Despite the severity of his disease, however, and the very real possibility that it might kill him, he was able to maintain a sense of optimism: "What is stronger, fear or hope? . . . Initially, I was very fearful and without much hope, but, as I sat there and absorbed the full extent of my illness, I refused to let the fear completely blot out my optimism" (Armstrong, 2000, p. 99).

Hardiness
A personality trait defined as a combination of self-esteem and a sense of control

Resilience
The ability to recover from negative experiences and adapt to the demands of life

Connect to MyPsychLab
To access the Critical Thinking question on trauma, go to MyPsychLab

Hardiness Other personality traits are also related to stress and coping. Kenneth Dion examined the personality variable of hardiness in relation to a particular kind of stress: the stress of being a victim of prejudice and discrimination (Dion, 2002, 2003). **Hardiness** is a combination of self-esteem and a sense of control that helps people interpret and deal with stressful events in a positive, effective manner. In one study, Dion and his colleagues assessed hardiness, stress symptoms, and perceptions of discrimination among members of Toronto's Chinese community (Dion, Dion, & Pak, 1992). They found that discrimination was correlated with psychological stress—but only for those who were low in hardiness. People with hardy personalities reported just as much discrimination but much less stress.

People are surprisingly resilient in the face of stressful events. Studies of reactions to the 9/11 terrorist attacks, for example, have found that relatively few people showed long-term signs of depression or other mental health problems.

Recently, hardiness has been studied among Canadian Forces officer candidates undergoing basic training. Hardiness was associated with fewer health symptoms, finding the training less stressful, greater satisfaction with training and with general life satisfaction (Skomorovsky & Sudom, 2011).

Why might this be? Foster and Dion (2001) wondered whether people make different attributions for negative events, depending on their level of hardiness. To find out, they conducted a study on gender discrimination and found that hardy women tended to attribute discrimination to specific, unstable factors rather than to global, stable factors. In other words, the hardy participants, unlike their less hardy counterparts, treated the discrimination they experienced as an isolated event, and not as an ongoing issue that pervaded all aspects of their lives.

Resilience Recently, researchers have turned their attention to yet another personality trait: resilience. **Resilience** is defined as the ability to recover from negative experiences and adapt to the demands of life. People who are high in resilience showed higher life satisfaction, greater optimism, more positive emotions, and less depression than those who are low in resilience (Fredrickson, Tugade, Waugh, & Larkin, 2003). Other research has shown

Watch on **mypsychlab**
Grieving a Loss part 1: Bob, 81 Years Old

that people are able to "bounce back" fairly quickly from traumatic events, such as the September 11, 2001, terrorist attacks (Bonanno, 2004, 2005; Bonanno & Mancini, 2008; McNally & Breslau, 2008; Seery, Silver, Holman, Ence, & Chu, 2008; Updegraff, Silver, & Holman, 2008). In fact, resilience may be the norm rather than the exception. Studies of bereaved spouses, for example, typically find that fewer than half show signs of significant, long-term distress. The remainder show no signs of depression and are able to experience positive emotions (Bonanno, Boerner, & Wortman, 2008; Bonanno, Moskowitz, Papa, & Folkman, 2005).

Watch on mypsychlab Grieving a Loss part 2: Bob, 81 Years Old

Investigations such as these fall largely in the domain of personality psychology in that they focus on traits that set people apart. What is it about one person that makes him or her more resistant to health problems than another person? The social psychologist takes a different tack, asking instead, "Can we identify ways of coping with stress that everyone can adopt to make it easier to deal with the challenges of life?"

Opening Up: Making Sense of Traumatic Events

When something traumatic happens to you, is it best to try to bury it as deeply as you can and never talk about it, or to spend time thinking about the event and discussing it with others? Although folk wisdom has long held that it is best to open up, only recently has this assumption been put to the test. James Pennebaker and colleagues (Niederhoffer & Pennebaker, 2002; Pennebaker 1990, 1997, 2004; Sloan & Marx, 2004) have conducted a number of interesting experiments on the value of opening up about traumatic events. Pennebaker and Beale (1986), for example, asked university students to write for 15 minutes on each of four consecutive nights about a traumatic event that they experienced. The traumas they chose to write about were highly personal and in many cases quite tragic, including such events as rape and the death of a sibling. Students in a control condition wrote for the same amount of time about a trivial event.

Writing about these events certainly was upsetting in the short term: Students who wrote about traumatic events reported more negative moods and showed greater increases in blood pressure. But there were dramatic long-term benefits: These same students were less likely to visit the student health centre during the next six months, and they reported having fewer illnesses. Similarly, in other research, first-year university students who wrote about the problems of entering university (Pennebaker, Colder, & Sharp, 1990) and survivors of the Holocaust who disclosed the most about their World War II experiences improved their health over the next several months (Pennebaker, Barger, & Tiebout, 1989; Pennebaker, Colder, & Sharp, 1990).

What is it about opening up that leads to better health? Pennebaker (1997) argues that people who write or talk about negative events construct a more meaningful narrative or story that explains the events. He has analyzed hundreds of pages of writing from his participants and finds that the people who improve the most are those who

Research by Pennebaker (1990) shows that there are long-term health benefits to writing or talking about one's personal traumas.

began with rather incoherent, disorganized descriptions of their problem and ended with coherent, organized stories that explained the event and gave it meaning. Once people are able to gain insight into an experience and feel they understand it, they are better able to put it behind them (Hemenover, 2003; Kelly, Klusas, von Weiss, & Kenny, 2001). Further, people might be less inclined to suppress thoughts about a traumatic event if they have written about it. As we discussed in Chapter 3, trying to suppress thoughts can lead to a preoccupation with those very thoughts, because the act of not trying to think about them can actually make us think about them more (Wegner, 1994). Thus, writing about or confiding in others about a traumatic event can help us gain a better understanding of the event and move forward with life. Subsequent research has shown that this kind of understanding is especially likely to occur when people take a step back and analyze a negative life event as an observer would, rather than immersing themselves in the event and trying to relive it (Ayduk & Kross, 2008; Kross & Ayduk, 2008). If you would like to try this writing exercise, you can find instructions at http://homepage.psy.utexas.edu/homepage/faculty/pennebaker/home2000/writingandhealth.html.

Using Social Psychological Interventions to Promote Healthier Behaviour

In addition to helping people reduce stress, social psychologists can offer some insight into how to get people to change their health habits more directly: to stop smoking, to lose weight, to eat a more healthful diet, and to stop abusing alcohol or other drugs. In fact, this is an area in which social psychology can be especially helpful.

North Americans are doing a pretty good job of improving some of their health habits; for instance, the percentage of the Canadian population aged 15 and over who are smokers has been declining slowly and steadily. Currently, this figure is down to 18 percent (Health Canada, 2010). People today are also more likely to avoid high-cholesterol and fatty foods than they were a few years ago, and more women are getting Pap smears to detect cervical cancer. In addition, a recent survey found an increase in seat belt usage, an increase in mammography exams for women aged 40 and over, and an increase in flu shots for people over the age of 65 (Nelson, Bland, Powell-Griner, Klein, Wells, Hogelin, & Marks, 2002).

There is definitely room for improvement, however. The number of obese Canadian adults and children has increased substantially over the last 25 years. According to the Obesity in Canada report released in 2011, obesity rates doubled between 1981 and 2007–2009. Canada's obesity rate is currently 24 percent. When obesity rates are combined with rates of being overweight, this figure rises to 62 percent. The largest increase in obesity has occurred for adults between the ages of 25 and 34; in this age group, obesity has nearly tripled over the last 25 years. There is also widespread concern about the increase in obesity among children. According to a House of Commons Health Committee Report, in 1978, 15 percent of Canadian children were overweight or obese. By 2004, this number had risen to 26 percent (O'Neill, 2007). Rob Merrifield, who chaired the House of Commons report, made the shocking statement that "For the first time in recorded history, our younger generations are expected to live shorter lives than their parents due to obesity" (Merrifield, as quoted in O'Neill, 2007).

In addition, binge drinking on university campuses is occurring at an alarmingly high rate (Wechsler, Lee, Kuo, Siebring, Nelson, & Lee, 2002). A study conducted at York University found that students who drink alcohol tend to do so two to three times per week, and on each occasion generally consume five or six standard drinks (e.g., five or six bottles of beer). For male students, this results in an average of 16 drinks per week; for female students, the weekly average is 13 drinks. According to the researchers, this level of alcohol consumption qualifies as "heavy social drinking" (Wall, Hinson, & McKee, 1998). Binge drinkers are more likely to have a number of health problems, including high blood pressure, heart disease, meningitis, difficulties performing sexually, and sexually transmitted diseases. They are also more likely to be in car accidents, die by drowning, and experience domestic violence (Naimi, Brewer, Mokdad, Serdula, Denny, & Marks, 2003; "Quick stats," 2008).

Finally, as we discussed in Chapter 6, people who are at risk for getting AIDS are not taking as many precautions as they should. For example, a study conducted in Ontario found that only 29 percent of young adults who had engaged in casual sex over the past year had always used a condom (Herold & Mewhinney, 1993). A more recent Canada-wide health survey reported similar findings—namely, that 30 percent of young people reported not having used a condom the last time they had sex. This percentage was even higher (nearly 44 percent) among adults aged 20 to 24 (Canada, 2005d).

We realize that we have just maligned what many people consider to be the chief pleasures of life: sex, eating, drinking, and smoking. Health problems resulting from these behaviours are prevalent precisely because they are so pleasurable—and, in some cases (e.g., smoking), addictive. It is thus a challenge to find ways to change people's attitudes and behaviours in ways that lead to better health habits. How might we do so?

Let's rewind and think back to Chapter 6, in which we discussed social psychological research on attitude change. In that chapter, we focused on a number of ways in which people's attitudes can be changed. For example, we discussed the use of fear-arousing communications to persuade people to change their attitudes and behaviours. As we mentioned in that chapter, the Canadian government is placing even more graphic photographs of people suffering from lung cancer and other smoking-related diseases on cigarette packages, with the intent of frightening people into quitting, or not starting, smoking. Many public service advertisements take this approach, trying to scare people into applying sunscreen, using condoms, and wearing seat belts or helmets. These approaches can be effective as long as the level of fear is not so threatening that people tune out the message. It is also important to provide people with specific recommendations for how they can avoid the feared event.

We also discussed the use of cognitive dissonance to promote attitude change. One program of research relevant to health issues is Aronson and colleagues' use of hypocrisy to induce cognitive dissonance (Aronson et al., 1991; Stone et al., 1994). As you may recall from Chapter 6, in this research, participants in the hypocrisy condition were reminded of their own failures to use condoms and were asked to make a videotape advocating the use of condoms that would be shown to high school students. The researchers hypothesized that these students would reduce the resultant dissonance by subsequently purchasing more condoms than participants in the other conditions (for whom dissonance was not created). And that is exactly what was found.

In Chapter 6, we also presented research showing that interventions based on the theory of planned behaviour are also effective in getting people to use condoms. As we discussed in that chapter, people are more likely to use condoms when they believe other people approve of condom use (subjective norms), when they believe that condom use is an issue that they can control, and when they have strong intentions to use condoms. These variables are also important in promoting other healthy behaviours.

Message Framing: Stressing Gains versus Losses

Attitude change also depends on the way in which persuasive messages are framed. Suppose, for example, that you were devising a public service ad to lower fatalities from skin cancer. Your goal is to get people to examine their skin regularly for cancer and to use sunscreen when they are exposed to the sun. You could frame your message in terms of what people have to lose by not performing these behaviours; for example, you might emphasize that most skin cancers are fatal if not detected at an early stage. Or you could frame your message in a more positive way by emphasizing what people have to gain; for example, you could say that skin cancers are curable if detected early and that people can decrease their chances of getting skin cancer by using sunscreen.

It might seem that these different messages would have the same effect; after all, they convey the same information—that it is a good idea to examine your skin regularly and use sunscreen. It turns out, though, that framing messages in terms of losses versus gains can make a big difference (Jones, Sinclair, & Courneya, 2003; Rothman &

Salovey, 1997; Yi & Baumgartner, 2008, 2009). When trying to get people to engage in behaviour that will *prevent* disease, it is best to use a "gain frame," emphasizing what they have to gain by engaging in this behaviour (e.g., using sunscreen; Linville, Fischer, & Fischhoff, 1993; Rothman, Martino, Bedell, Detweiler, & Salovey, 1999). When trying to get people to *detect* the presence of a disease, it is best to use a "loss frame," emphasizing what they have to lose by avoiding this behaviour (e.g., the costs of not examining one's skin for cancer; Meyerowitz & Chaiken, 1987; Rothman, 2000). To give an example, Rothman and colleagues presented women with information trying to get them to avoid skin cancer (Rothman, Salovey, Antone, Keough, & Martin, 1993). Some participants received a message that focused on the positive benefits of being concerned about skin cancer (e.g., "If they are detected early, most of these cancers are curable"). Other participants received a message framed in terms of the negative consequences of not being concerned about skin cancer (e.g., "Unless they are detected and treated early, most of these cancers are not curable"). It turned out that the gain-framed message worked best with prevention behaviour (i.e., requesting a sample of sunscreen). The loss-framed message worked best on detection behaviour (i.e., the women's intention to perform exams of their skin.

Watch on **mypsychlab**
Effects of Sun Tanning on Skin

Why does the way in which a message is framed make a difference? It may change the way we think about our health (Rothman & Salovey, 1997). A loss frame focuses our attention on the possibility that we might have a problem that can be dealt with by performing detection behaviours (e.g., examining our skin for cancer). A gain frame focuses our attention on the fact that we are in a good state of health and that to stay that way, we should perform preventive behaviours (e.g., using sunscreen when exposed to the sun and condoms when having sex).

So, before designing your public health ad, decide which kind of behaviour you are going to target—a prevention or detection behaviour—and design your ad accordingly.

Now that you have read about several of the factors that influence health behaviour, see if you can improve your habits by taking the advice in the accompanying Try It! exercise.

Changing Your Health Habits

Pick a health habit of yours and try to improve it, using the principles we have discussed in this chapter. For example, you might try to lose a few kilograms, exercise more, or cut down on your smoking. This is not easy, of course—if it were, we would all be svelte, physically fit nonsmokers! We suggest that you start small with a limited goal; try to lose 2 kilograms, for example, or increase your exercise by one or two hours a week. Here are some specific suggestions as to how to change your behaviour:

- Increase your feelings of control over your behaviour, particularly your self-efficacy in this domain. One way to do this is to start small. If you are trying to lose weight, for example, begin slowly with some easy-to-control behaviour. You might start by eliminating one food or beverage from your diet that you do not like all that much but that is pretty fattening. Suppose, for example, that you drink a 200-calorie fruit juice five times a week. Replacing the juice with water will save 52 000 calories a year, which is equivalent to 6 kilograms! The idea is to gain mastery over your behaviour slowly, improving your feelings of self-efficacy. When you've mastered one behaviour, try another. You can do it!
- If you experience a setback, such as eating two pieces of cake at a birthday party, avoid a damaging pattern of attributions. Do not assume that the setback was a result of internal, stable, global causes—this will cause learned helplessness. Remember that almost everyone fails the first time they try to diet or quit smoking. It often takes people several attempts; therefore, a setback or two is not because of something unchangeable about you. Keep trying.
- It can be stressful to change a well-ingrained habit, and it is at times of stress that social support is most important. Talk with your friends and family about your attempts to change your behaviour. Seek their advice and support. Even better, convince several friends to try these techniques with you. Make it a group project, in which you and your friends support one another's efforts to alter your behaviour.

Summary

- **Stress and Human Health** The relationship between stress and human health has received a great deal of attention from social psychologists.
  - **Effects of Negative Life Events** Stressful events can have debilitating effects on people's psychological and physical health. Some studies calculate the number of stressful events people are experiencing and use that to predict their health.
  - **Perceived Stress and Health** Stress is best defined as the negative feelings and beliefs that arise when people feel unable to cope with demands from their environment. The more stress people experience, the more likely they are to get sick (e.g., catch a cold).
  - **Feeling in Charge: The Importance of Perceived Control** People perceive negative events as stressful if they feel they cannot control them. The less control people believe they have, the more likely it is that the event will cause them physical and psychological problems. For example, the loss of control experienced by many older people in nursing homes can have negative effects on their health.
  - **Knowing You Can Do It: Self-Efficacy** It is also important for people to have high self-efficacy in a particular domain, which is the belief in their ability to carry out specific actions that produce desired outcomes.
  - **Explaining Negative Events: Learned Helplessness** The way in which people explain the causes of negative events is also critical to how stressful those events will be. When bad things happen, learned helplessness results if people make stable, internal, and global attributions for those events.
- **Coping with Stress** Coping styles refer to the ways in which people react to stressful events.
  - **Gender Differences in Coping with Stress** Men are more likely to react to stress with a fight-or-flight reaction, in which they respond to stress by either attacking the source of the stress or fleeing from it. Women are more likely to react to stress with a tend-and-befriend reaction, in which they respond to stress with nurturant activities designed to protect themselves and their offspring (tending) and by creating social networks that provide protection from threats (befriending).
  - **Social Support: Getting Help from Others** Social support—the perception that other people are responsive to one's needs—is beneficial for men and women. Social support is especially helpful in times of stress. People from collectivistic cultures prefer to receive support without disclosing that they are having problems.
  - **Personality and Coping Styles** Research on personality traits, such as optimism, hardiness, and resilience focuses on how different types of people deal with stress and how these different styles are related to their physical health. Optimistic, hardy, and resilient people tend to react better to stress and to be healthier than people who are low on these traits.
  - **Opening Up: Making Sense of Traumatic Events** Several studies show that opening up, by writing or talking about one's problems, has long-term health benefits.
- **Using Social Psychological Interventions to Promote Healthier Behaviour** It is also important to find ways to help people change their health habits more directly. One strategy is to present people with persuasive communications urging them to adopt better health habits. For example, fear messages can persuade people to change their attitudes and behaviour. Techniques that arouse cognitive dissonance, such as making people feel hypocritical about their failures to use condoms, are effective as well because people will change their health habits to reduce the unpleasantness of dissonance.
  - **Message Framing: Stressing Gains versus Losses** It is also important to tailor persuasive messages to the kinds of behaviour you want people to adopt. To get people to perform detection behaviour, such as examining their skin for cancer, it is best to use messages framed in terms of losses (the negative consequences of failing to act). To get people to perform preventive behaviour, such as using sunscreen, it is best to use messages framed in terms of gains (the positive consequences of performing the behaviour).

SOCIAL PSYCHOLOGY IN ACTION

3 Social Psychology and the Law

TWO DAYS BEFORE CHRISTMAS IN 1981, 16-YEAR-OLD BARBARA Stoppel was found strangled in the Winnipeg doughnut shop where she worked. Several people reported that they had seen a tall, lanky man wearing a cowboy hat near the doughnut shop around the time she was killed. Police artists composed a sketch of the suspect based on the descriptions offered by these eyewitnesses. The police sketch looked a lot like Thomas Sophonow, a tall, lanky hotel doorman from Vancouver who was in Winnipeg at the time. Moreover, several witnesses testified that they had seen him leaving the doughnut shop around the time that Stoppel was strangled.

On the basis of this evidence, Sophonow was charged with murder. His trial in 1982 resulted in a hung jury (i.e., jury members were unable to reach a verdict). Sophonow was tried a second time in 1983; that jury found him guilty of second-degree murder after only four hours of deliberation. Sophonow appealed the conviction and was tried a third time in 1985. This time, after five days of deliberation (a record in Canada), a "problematic" juror was removed, after which the remaining jurors rendered their verdict: guilty of second-degree murder. Sophonow again appealed. At this point, he had spent four years in prison for a murder he claimed he did not commit. In December 1985, after conducting an extensive examination of this case, the Manitoba Court of Appeal argued that Sophonow should not face a fourth trial and set him free—but did not declare him innocent. Many people, including Winnipeg's chief of police, continued to believe that Sophonow was Stoppel's killer.

In 1998, Winnipeg police reopened the case because Sophonow lobbied for DNA testing of gloves that had been found at the scene of the crime. (DNA testing was not available at the time of Sophonow's trials.) It is unclear whether the DNA tests resulted in any useful evidence because many people, including Sophonow and a Crown attorney, had tried on the gloves in court. However, police did finally reach the conclusion that Sophonow was not Stoppel's killer and announced that they had a new suspect. On June 8, 2000, after more than 18 years of agony, a sobbing Sophonow accepted apologies from the Winnipeg police and the Crown for sending him to prison for a crime he had not committed.

Life did not return to normal for Sophonow, however. The following year, he had to relive the trauma of his arrest, wrongful conviction, and imprisonment during an inquiry into what went wrong. The judge presiding over the inquiry awarded Sophonow $2.6 million in compensation. However, collecting the compensation turned out to be an uphill battle. More than a year after the inquiry, the city of

OUTLINE

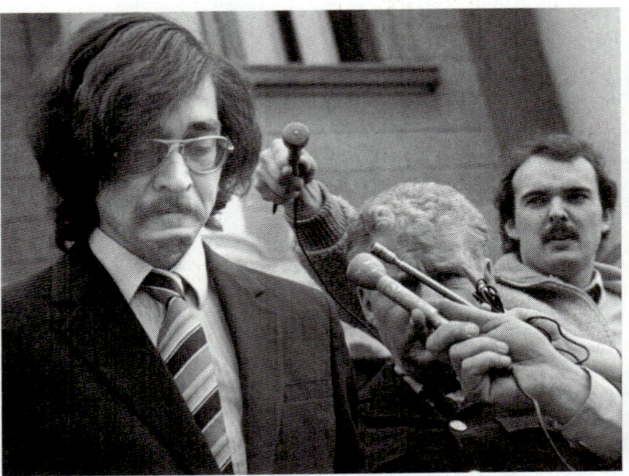

Thomas Sophonow (left) endured three trials and spent four years in jail for a murder he did not commit. His wrongful conviction was due in part to his resemblance to the police sketch circulated at the time. Terry Samuel Arnold (right), who became the prime suspect in the Barbara Stoppel case, bore a striking resemblance to Sophonow. Although we will probably never know whether he was Stoppel's killer, Arnold had a long history of violent crime. He committed suicide on March 29, 2005, before his case went to trial.

Winnipeg and the province of Manitoba were still embroiled in a controversy over whose responsibility it was to pay up. A cheque was eventually issued to Sophonow on February 22, 2003. He decided to accept the settlement so that he could begin to get on with his life.

The case of Thomas Sophonow raises a number of important questions. If he was innocent, why did eyewitnesses say that he was the person leaving the scene of the crime? And why did two juries believe them? How common are such miscarriages of justice? In this module, we will discuss the answers to these and other questions, focusing on the role that social psychological processes play in the legal system.

The Canadian Justice System

Let's begin with a brief review of the Canadian justice system, which consists of criminal and civil law. In civil cases, one party (the plaintiff) brings a complaint against another (the defendant) for violating the former's rights in some way. In this module, we are mostly interested in criminal law. When someone commits a crime and the police arrest a suspect, the Crown attorney's office usually decides whether there is enough evidence to press formal charges. (Sometimes at a preliminary hearing, a judge decides whether there will be a trial.) If there is adequate evidence to press charges, lawyers for the defence and the prosecution gather additional evidence and negotiate with each other. As a result of these negotiations, the defendant may plead guilty to a lesser charge. About a quarter of cases go to trial, during which a jury or a judge decides the defendant's fate.

All of these steps in the legal process are intensely social psychological. In criminal cases, first impressions of the accused and of witnesses have a powerful effect on police investigators and jurors. Attributions about what caused the criminal behaviour are made by police, lawyers, jurors, and the judge; prejudiced beliefs and stereotypical ways of thinking affect those attributions. Attitude change and persuasion techniques abound in the courtroom, as lawyers for each side argue their case and as jurors later debate with one another; and the processes of social cognition affect the jurors' decision making when deciding guilt or innocence. Social psychologists have studied the legal system a great deal in recent years, both because it offers an excellent applied setting in which to examine basic psychological processes and because of its immense importance in daily life. If you, through no fault of your own, are accused of a crime—as Thomas Sophonow was—what do you need to know to convince the system of your innocence?

As we progress through this module, we will from time to time refer to the Sophonow case, which vividly illustrates many of the points we want to make. We will begin our discussion with the most troubling aspect of the Sophonow case: eyewitness testimony. How accurate are people at identifying someone who has committed a crime?

Eyewitness Testimony

Connect to MyPsychLab
To access the Critical Thinking question on wrongful convictions, go to MyPsychLab

In countries such as Canada, the legal system assigns a great deal of significance to eyewitness testimony. If you are fingered by an eyewitness as the culprit, you are quite likely to be convicted, even if considerable circumstantial evidence indicates you are innocent. Thomas Sophonow was convicted largely because of the testimony of eyewitnesses who claimed that they had seen him near the doughnut shop at about the time of the murder. There were, however, reasons to be suspicious of this testimony. Some witnesses admitted that they had come forward because of the rewards being offered for information on the case. One witness told a dramatic tale of having chased Sophonow after the murder, finally catching him on a bridge, where a fight ensued. This story was never corroborated. Numerous witnesses claimed that, with each trial, their initially sketchy memories had become sharper and more accurate. There also should have been skepticism about the clarity with which witnesses could have seen Sophonow, given that the murder occurred between 8:15 and 8:45 P.M. on a winter evening. Moreover, witnesses offered conflicting reports of the direction in which he had headed. Despite the lack of physical evidence linking Sophonow to the scene of the crime, the eyewitness testimony that he had been in the vicinity of the doughnut shop was enough to convict him—twice.

It turns out that the most common cause of an innocent person's being convicted of a crime is an erroneous eyewitness (Brandon & Davies, 1973; Sporer, Koehnken, & Malpass, 1996; Wells, Memon, & Penrod, 2006). Systematic experiments have confirmed that jurors rely heavily on eyewitness testimony when they are deciding whether someone is guilty. Unfortunately, jurors also tend to overestimate the accuracy of eyewitnesses (Ellsworth & Mauro, 1998; Loftus, 1979; Potter & Brewer, 1999; Wells & Olson, 2003; Wells & Hasel, 2008), as confirmed in a recent study conducted at the University of Victoria (Boyce, Lindsay, & Brimacombe, 2008). Rod Lindsay and colleagues (1981) conducted a clever experiment that illustrates both of these points. The researchers staged the theft of a calculator in front of unsuspecting University of Alberta students, and then tested how accurately the students could pick out the "thief" from a set of six photographs. In one condition, it was difficult to identify the thief because he had worn a knit cap pulled over his ears and was in the room for only 12 seconds. In the second condition, the thief had worn the knit cap higher on his head, revealing some of his hair, so it was easier to identify him. In the third condition, the thief had worn no hat and had stayed in the room for 20 seconds, making it easiest to identify him. The first set of results reflected what we'd expect: The more visual information available about the thief, the higher the percentage of students who correctly identified him in the photo lineup (see Figure SPA3.1).

In the next stage of the experiment, a researcher playing the role of lawyer questioned the students about their eyewitness identifications, just as a real lawyer would cross-examine witnesses in a trial. These question-and-answer sessions were videotaped. A new group of participants, playing the role of jurors, watched the videotapes of these cross-examinations and rated the extent to which they believed the witnesses had correctly identified the thief. As shown in Figure SPA3.1, the jurors overestimated the accuracy of the witnesses, especially in the condition in which the thief was difficult to identify (Lindsay, Wells, & Rumpel, 1981).

Researchers have documented many cases of wrongful arrest, and in a remarkably high proportion of these cases, the wrong person was convicted because an eyewitness mistakenly identified him or her as the criminal (Penrod & Cutler, 1999; Sporer, Koehnken, & Malpass, 1996; Wells, Wright, & Bradfield, 1999; Yarmey, 2001a; for a review of this literature in the context of Canadian law, see Read, Connolly, & Turtle, 2001). Gary Wells and colleagues (1998), for example, examined 40 cases in which DNA evidence—obtained after the conviction of a suspect—indicated that the suspect was innocent. In 36 of these cases, an eyewitness had falsely identified the suspect as

FIGURE SPA3.1

The accuracy of eyewitness identification.

The accuracy of eyewitness identification depends on the viewing conditions at the time the crime was committed. As in this study, however, most jurors believe that witnesses can correctly identify the criminal even when viewing conditions are poor.

(Adapted from Lindsay, Wells, & Rumpel, 1981)

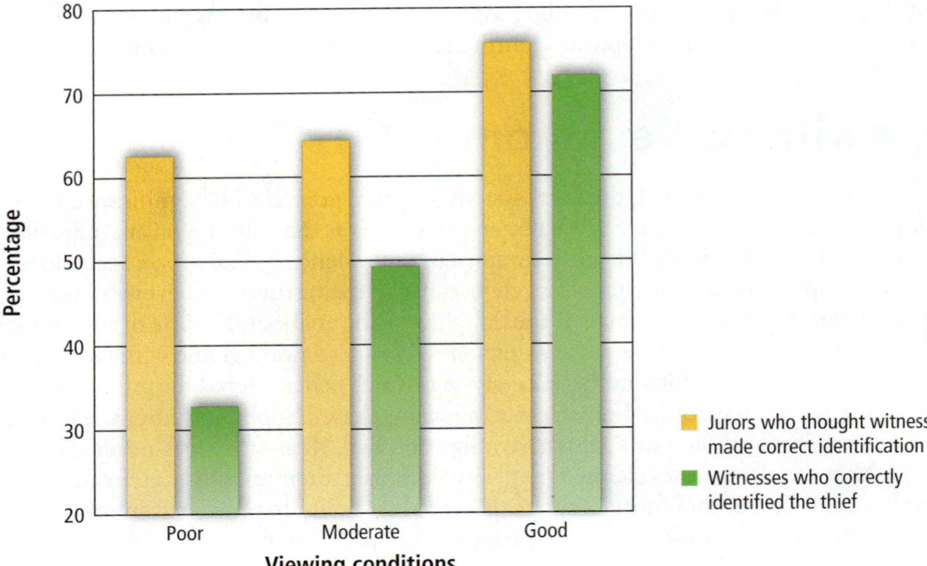

the criminal; five of these falsely accused people were on death row when they were exonerated. According to University of Guelph psychologist A. Daniel Yarmey, "Mistaken eyewitness identification is responsible for more wrongful convictions than all other causes combined" (Yarmey, 2001a, p. 92).

Connect to MyPsychLab

How's your memory? To participate in an experiment on digit span, go to MyPsychLab

Why Are Eyewitnesses Often Wrong?

The problem is that our minds are not like video cameras, which can record an event, store it over time, and play it back later with perfect accuracy. Think back to our discussion of social perception in Chapter 4, the study of how we form impressions of, and make inferences about, other people. We saw that a number of distortions can occur. Because eyewitness identification is a form of social perception, it is subject to similar problems, particularly those involving memory. To be an accurate witness, a person must successfully complete three stages of memory processing: acquisition, storage, and retrieval of the events witnessed. **Acquisition** refers to the process by which people notice and pay attention to information in the environment. Because people cannot perceive everything that is happening around them, they acquire only a subset of the information available in the environment. **Storage** refers to the process by which people store in memory information they have acquired from the environment. **Retrieval** refers to the process by which people recall information stored in their memory (see Figure SPA3.2). Eyewitnesses can be inaccurate because of problems at any of these three stages.

Acquisition

The process by which people notice and pay attention to information in the environment; people cannot perceive everything that is happening around them, so they acquire only a subset of the information available in the environment

Storage

The process by which people store in memory information they have acquired from the environment

Retrieval

The process by which people recall information stored in their memory

Acquisition A number of factors limit the amount of information about a crime that people take in, such as how much time they have to watch an event and the nature of the viewing conditions. As obvious as this may sound, people sometimes forget how these factors limit eyewitness reports of crimes (Read, Connolly, & Turtle, 2001; Yarmey, Jacob, & Porter, 2002). Crimes usually occur under the very conditions that make acquisition difficult: quickly, unexpectedly, and under poor viewing conditions, such as at night. As we have already mentioned, Barbara Stoppel's murder took place after dark on a winter evening. Presumably, it would have been quite difficult for eyewitnesses to get a good look at the murderer making his getaway.

Consider a more recent case that took place in the United States: In October 1997, four young men in Fairbanks, Alaska, went on a rampage, attacking passersby at random. By the end of the night, they had killed a teenage boy and severely wounded an older man, Franklin Dayton. Eventually, four suspects were arrested and convicted of the crimes, largely on the basis of eyewitness testimony of Fairbanks resident Arlo Olson. Olson testified that he had seen the defendants attack Dayton from "a couple of blocks away"—a distance that was later determined to be 137 metres, one and a half lengths of a football field.

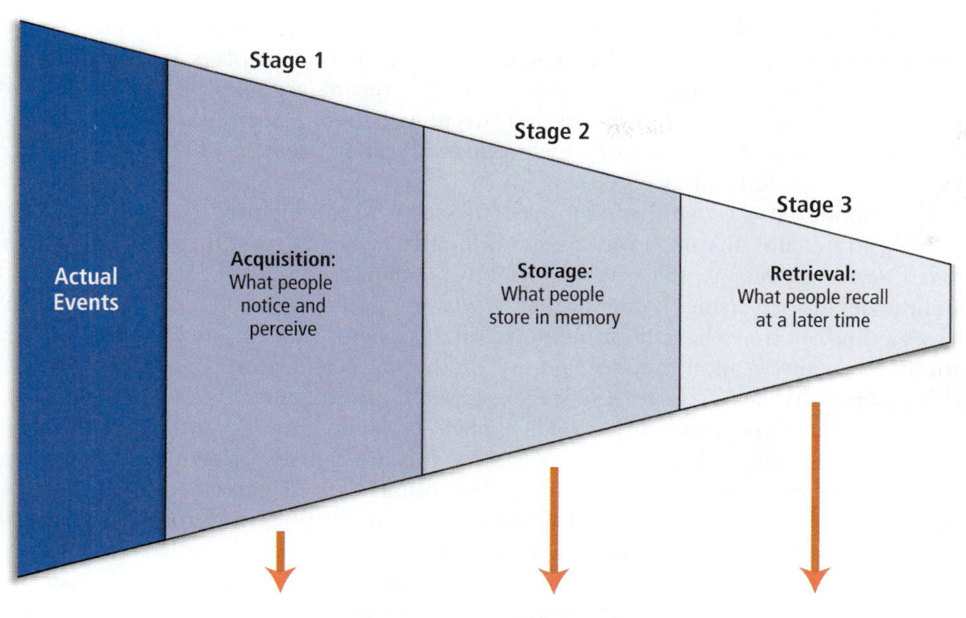

FIGURE SPA3.2

Acquisition, storage, and retrieval.

To be an accurate eyewitness, people must complete these three stages of memory processing. There are sources of error at each of the three stages.

How much should we trust Olson's testimony? To answer this question, Geoffrey Loftus and Erin Harley (2005) calculated the amount of detail that is lost in the perception of a face as distance increases. As an illustration, look at the photographs of Julia Roberts below. The one on the left shows how Roberts's face would appear if she were standing 1.6 metres away from you. No problem recognizing her here; perhaps you would ask Roberts for her autograph. The middle picture is how her face would appear if Roberts were standing 13 metres away from you. In this case, you might think, "Hmm, that woman looks kind of like Julia Roberts; maybe I'll get a closer look." The picture on the right is how Roberts would appear if she were standing 52 metres away. Here, it would probably never dawn on you that a famous celebrity was in the vicinity.

When Loftus and Harley (2005) showed photographs like these to research participants, they found that accuracy in identifying the celebrities began to drop when the simulated distance exceeded 7.5 metres. At 10 metres only 75 percent of the participants

How easy is it to recognize Julia Roberts from these photos? These images are how she would appear from a distance of 1.6 metres, 13 metres, and 52 metres.

recognized the face, and at 23 metres, only 25 percent of the participants did so. It thus seems unlikely that Arlo Olson could have identified the suspects in the Fairbanks murder case from a distance of 137 metres. A more recent large-scale study conducted by researchers at Queen's University and two universities in Australia confirms that as distance increases, the accuracy of eyewitness identification decreases (Lindsay, Semmler, Weber, Brewer, & Lindsay, 2008).

We should also remember that eyewitnesses who are victims of a crime will be terribly afraid, and this alone can make it difficult to take in everything that is happening. The more stress people are under, the worse their memory for people involved in and the details of a crime (Deffenbacher, Bornstein, & Penrod, 2004). Another reason why victims of crimes have poor memory for a suspect is that they tend to focus their attention on any weapon they see and less on the suspect's features (Hope & Wright, 2007; Loftus, Miller, & Burns, 1978; Pickel, 2007). If someone points a gun at you and demands your money, your attention is likely to be on the gun rather than on whether the robber has blue or brown eyes. (Note that this is also true for people who witness crimes. Tollestrup, Turtle, and Yuille [1994] found that 73 percent of eyewitnesses correctly identified a police suspect when no weapon was present during a crime; this figure dropped to 31 percent when a weapon was present.)

When an actual perceptual fact is in conflict with expectation, expectation may prove a stronger determinant of perception and memory than the situation itself.

—Gordon Allport and Leo Postman, The Psychology of Rumor, *1947*

Finally, the information people notice and pay attention to is also influenced by what they expect to see. Consider our friend Alan, a social psychologist who is an expert on social perception. One Sunday, Alan was worried because his neighbour, a frail woman in her eighties, did not appear for church. After knocking on her door repeatedly and receiving no response, Alan jimmied open a window and searched her house. Soon his worst fears were realized: The woman was lying dead on the floor of her bedroom. Shaken, Alan returned to his house and telephoned the police. After spending a great deal of time in the woman's house, a detective came over and asked Alan some pointed questions, such as whether he had noticed any suspicious activity in the past day or two. Alan was confused by this line of questioning and finally burst out, "Why are you asking me these questions? Isn't it obvious that she died of old age? Shouldn't we be notifying her family?" Now it was the detective's turn to look puzzled. "Aren't you the one who discovered the body?" he asked. Alan said he was. "Well," said the detective, "didn't you notice that her bedroom had been ransacked, that there was broken glass everywhere, and that there was a belt tied around her neck?"

It turned out that Alan's neighbour had been strangled by a man who had come to spray her house for insects. There had been a fierce struggle, and the fact that the woman was murdered could not have been more obvious. But Alan saw none of the signs. He was worried that his elderly neighbour had passed away. When he discovered that she had in fact died, he was quite upset, and the furthest thing from his mind was that she had been murdered. As a result, he saw what he expected to see and failed to see the unexpected. When the police later showed him photographs of the crime scene, he felt as though he had never been there. He recognized almost nothing.

Research confirms that people are poor at noticing the unexpected. In one study, participants watched a videotape of two teams passing a basketball back and forth and counted the number of times one team passed the ball to the other. Thirty-five seconds into the film, something weird happened: A woman in a gorilla suit walked into the middle of the basketball game, turned toward the camera, thumped her chest, and then walked away. Meanwhile, the basketball players continued with their passing game. Although it seems like everyone would notice such a bizarre interruption, only half did. The other half simply didn't see the gorilla at all (Simons & Chabris, 1999). Given that crimes are almost always highly unexpected events, it is no surprise that people often fail to notice key details in the crime scene (Rensink, 2002; Simons & Ambinder, 2005).

Own-Race Bias

The finding that people are better at recognizing faces within their own race than those of other races

Even if we notice a person or an event, we might not remember it well if we are unfamiliar with it. Unfamiliar events or people are also more difficult to remember than familiar events or people. For example, people are better at recognizing faces within their own race, a phenomenon known as **own-race bias.** White people are better at recognizing white faces than black or Asian faces, black people are better at recognizing black than white faces, and Asians are better at recognizing Asian than white faces (Brigham, Bennett, Meissner, & Mitchell, 2007; Johnson & Fredrickson, 2005; Levin, 2000). Similarly, University of Regina researchers found that white Canadians are better at recognizing white faces than faces of First Nations people, and First Nations people are better at recognizing faces of First Nations people than faces of white people (Jackiw, Arbuthnott, Pfeifer, Marcon, & Meissner, 2008). Own-race bias occurs because people have more contact with members of their own race, allowing them to better learn how to distinguish one individual from another (Meissner & Brigham, 2001b). Another recent study looked at how well three different groups could recognize white and Asian faces: white residents of France, Koreans who grew up in Korea, and Koreans who had been adopted by white French families when they were children. As expected, the first two groups showed own-race bias: The whites had better recall for white faces, and the Koreans had better recall for Asian faces. What about the Koreans who grew up in white families? They had better memory for white faces, which is consistent with the idea that we are best at remembering faces that are of the race with which we have the most contact (Sangrigoli, Pallier, Argenti, Ventureyra, & Schonen, 2005).

Suppose you were watching a video of two groups of people passing a basketball back and forth and counting the number of passes one team threw to the other. Would you notice that a person dressed in a gorilla suit entered the scene, faced the camera, and thumped her chest? Only 50 percent of the participants noticed the gorilla in a study by Simons & Chabris (1999). People often fail to notice changes in their environments that are unexpected, especially if they are concentrating on something else (e.g., counting the passes). (From Simons & Chabris, 1999)

These effects are evident at an early age. For example, Corenblum and Meissner (2006) showed Euro-Canadian children (in grades 2 to 8) and university students in Brandon, Manitoba, photos of African-American faces, Native-Canadian faces, and Euro-Canadian faces. Later, they were given a large set of photographs and asked to identify which ones they had seen earlier (some of the photographs had, in fact, been presented earlier; others were new). Participants were most accurate at identifying own-race faces (i.e., Euro-Canadian faces), followed by Native-Canadian faces, and then African-American faces. The researchers point out that accuracy rates reflected the amount of contact these students had with each of these racial groups. Overall, younger children (in grades 2 to 6) were not as accurate as those in grades 7 and 8 or the students in university. However, even the youngest children still showed own-race bias.

Another reason for the own-race bias is that when people examine same-race faces, they pay close attention to individuating features that distinguish that face from others, such as the height of the cheekbones or the contour of the forehead. When people see the face of a person of another race, they tend to classify the face in terms of race and stop at that. Daniel Levin (2000), a researcher who has investigated this hypothesis, observes, "When a White person looks at another White person's nose, they're likely to think to themselves, 'That's John's nose.' When they look at a Black person's nose, they're likely to think, 'That's a Black nose'" (as quoted in Carpenter, 2000, p. 44). In a series of studies, Levin demonstrated that when people are required to move beyond their initial snap judgments and pay attention to individuating information, they are actually quite capable of discriminating between cross-race faces.

Storage Many people think that memory is like a collection of photographs. We record a picture of an event, such as the face of a robber, and place it in our memory "album." In reality, few of us have a photographic memory. Further, memories, like real photographs, fade with age. However, it is tempting to believe that the picture, once stored, cannot be altered or retouched, and that details cannot be added to or subtracted from the image. If the robber we saw was clean-shaven, surely we will not pencil in a moustache at some later time. Or will we?

Patricia Tollestrup, John Turtle, and John Yuille (1994) examined records of robbery and fraud cases handled by the RCMP in Vancouver in which a suspect was caught and confessed to the crime. The researchers compared the descriptions of the criminals given by eyewitnesses and victims with the criminals' actual physical characteristics (e.g., were witnesses correct that a criminal had blond hair and a moustache?). Eyewitnesses weren't too bad at remembering some details. For example, 100 percent of bystanders correctly remembered whether the criminal had facial hair (although crime victims correctly remembered this only 60 percent of the time). However, only 48 percent of the bystanders and 38 percent of the victims correctly remembered the suspect's hair colour. Most important, neither bystanders nor victims did a very good job of picking the criminal out of a lineup; they correctly identified the criminal only 48 percent of the time.

As this study illustrates, unfortunately, our memories are far from indelible. People can become confused about where they heard or saw something; memories in one "album" get confused with memories in another. As a result, people can have quite inaccurate recall about what they saw.

Reconstructive Memory

The process by which memories of an event become distorted by information encountered after the event has occurred

In the case of Thomas Sophonow, the police—who were under extreme pressure to make an arrest—arranged for a key witness to meet Sophonow "accidentally" at the remand centre where he was being held. Is it possible that actually seeing Sophonow altered the witness's memory of the appearance of the "tall, lanky man with a cowboy hat" he allegedly had seen the night of the murder? The answer to this question is yes. This answer is based on years of research on **reconstructive memory**, the distortion of memories of an event by information encountered after the event has occurred (Davis & Loftus, 2007; Lindsay & Read, 2006; Loftus, 1979, 2005; McDonald & Hirt, 1997). According to this research, information that we obtain after witnessing an event can change our memory of the event. In a classic study, Elizabeth Loftus and colleagues showed students 30 slides depicting different stages of an automobile accident (Loftus, Miller, & Burns, 1978). The content of one slide varied; some students saw a car stopped at a stop sign, whereas others saw the same car stopped at a yield sign (see the photos on the next page). After the slide show, the students were asked several questions about the car accident they had "witnessed." The key question varied how the traffic sign was described. In one version, the question was "Did another car pass the red Datsun while it was stopped at the stop sign?" In another version, the question was "Did another car pass the red Datsun while it was stopped at the yield sign?" Thus, for half of the participants, the question described the traffic sign as they had in fact seen it. But for the other half, the wording of the question subtly introduced new information—for example, if they had seen a stop sign, the question described it as a yield sign. Would this small change—akin to what might occur when witnesses are being questioned by police investigators or attorneys—influence people's memories of the actual event?

All of the participants were shown the two pictures reproduced on the next page and were asked which one they had originally seen. Most people (75 percent) who were asked about the sign they had actually seen chose the correct picture; that is, if they had seen a stop sign and were asked about a stop sign, most of them correctly identified the stop sign photograph. (Note that 25 percent of people made a crucial mistake on what would seem to be an easy question.) However, of those who had received the misleading question, only 41 percent chose the correct photograph (Loftus et al., 1978). In subsequent experiments, Loftus (1979) found that misleading questions can change people's minds about how fast a car was going, whether broken glass was at the scene of an accident, whether a traffic light was green or red, or whether a robber had a moustache.

> *Give us a dozen healthy memories, well-formed, and . . . we'll guarantee to take any one at random and train it to become any type of memory we might select—hammer, screwdriver, wrench, stop sign, yield sign, Indian chief—regardless of its origin or the brain that holds it.*
>
> —Elizabeth Loftus and Hunter Hoffman *(1989)*

In research along the same lines, Jennifer Tomes and Albert Katz (1997) showed students at the University of Western Ontario crime episodes from various films. For example, one episode from *Talons of the Eagle* showed a woman at an airport, putting her luggage in a red convertible car. A man in a truck drove up and stole her luggage and coat. The woman screamed at him, and he drove away. Later, when questioned about the incident, some participants received incorrect information. For example, one question made reference to the assailant's blue truck, when in fact the truck was rust-coloured; another question mentioned that the woman dropped her purse—even though she had not carried one. When participants were again questioned about the crimes, those who had been exposed to misinformation were more likely to

Research participants saw one of these pictures and then tried to remember whether they had seen a stop sign or a yield sign. Many of those who heard leading questions about the street sign made mistaken reports about which sign they had seen.

(From Loftus, Miller, & Burns, 1978)

have incorporated it into their memory of the event compared with a control group that had not been exposed to misinformation.

Researchers at Dalhousie University have found that people are especially likely to incorporate misinformation into their memories when the event they have witnessed produces negative emotion—which is likely to be the case whenever people witness crimes (Porter, Spencer, & Birt, 2003). University of British Columbia researchers recently found that adults with intellectual disabilities may be especially vulnerable to being swayed by leading questions (Ternes & Yuille, 2008).

Misleading questions cause a problem with **source monitoring**, the process by which people try to identify the source of their memories (Johnson, Hashtroudi, & Lindsay, 1993; Lyle & Johnson, 2006; Johnson, Verfaellie, & Dunlosky, 2008; Mitchell & Johnson, 2000; Qin, Ogle, & Goodman, 2008).

Source Monitoring
The process by which people try to identify the source of their memories

In research conducted at Bishop's University, for example, when participants received information about a crime via a radio broadcast and in written form, there was a tendency to confuse the source of these statements. Most frequently, this took the form of thinking they'd heard something on the radio that they had actually read about (Eberman & McKelvie, 2002). Similarly, in the Tomes and Katz (1997) study we discussed earlier, people who saw a rust-coloured truck but received the misleading question about a blue truck now had two pieces of information in memory: the rust-coloured truck and the blue truck. This is all well and good, as long as they could remember where these memories came from: the rust-coloured truck from the crime they saw earlier and the blue truck from the question they were asked later. The problem is that people often become mixed up about where they heard or saw something—in this case, mistakenly believing that the truck in the crime scene was blue. In short, when information is stored in memory, it is not always well tagged as to where it came from.

The implications for legal testimony are sobering. Eyewitnesses who are asked misleading questions often report seeing things that were not really there. In addition, eyewitnesses might be confused as to why a suspect looks familiar. Thomas Sophonow might have looked familiar to eyewitnesses because he happened to resemble the police sketch or because they had seen him in the earlier trials or, as in the case of one witness, because he had seen Sophonow at the remand centre.

Retrieval Suppose the police have arrested a suspect and want to see if you, the eyewitness, can identify the person. Typically, the police arrange a lineup of suspects at the police station, where you will be asked whether one of several people is the perpetrator. Sometimes you will be asked to look through a one-way mirror at an actual lineup of the suspect and some foils (people known not to have committed the crime). Other times you will be asked to examine videotapes of a lineup or photographs of the suspect and the foils. In each case, if a witness identifies a suspect as the culprit, the suspect is likely to be charged and convicted of the crime. After all, the argument goes, if an eyewitness saw the suspect commit the crime and then picked the suspect out of a lineup later, that's pretty good evidence the suspect is the guilty party.

Research shows that if a witness selects a suspect from a lineup, jurors, police investigators, and judges are likely to assume that the witness is right (e.g., a study by

Boyce et al., 2008, at the University of Victoria; studies by Pozzulo & Dempsey, 2009a; 2009b; Pozzulo, Lemieux, Wilson, Crescini, & Girardi, 2009, at Carleton University).

Do lineups actually result in correct identifications? Research conducted with people living in southern Ontario suggests that lineups have a higher success rate than the alternative of showing eyewitnesses only one person (Yarmey, Yarmey, & Yarmey, 1996). More specifically, Yarmey and colleagues found that if only one person was shown and that person was innocent, a mistaken identification was four times more likely than when the same person appeared in a six-person lineup. Errors were especially likely if the innocent person wore clothing similar to that worn by the person who committed the crime. Thus, the use of lineups appears to be better than the alternative of presenting only one person and asking eyewitnesses whether that person committed the crime.

This is not to say, however, that lineups are without problems. Just as there are problems with acquisition and storage of information, so too can there be problems with how people retrieve information from their memory (Charman & Wells, 2007; Malpass, Tredoux, & McQuiston-Surrett, 2007; Wells, 2008; Wells & Hasel, 2008; Wells & Olson, 2003). A number of things other than the image of a person that is stored in memory can influence whether eyewitnesses will pick someone out of a lineup. Witnesses often choose the person in a lineup who most resembles the criminal, even if the resemblance is not strong.

Suppose, for example, that a 19-year-old woman commits a robbery and the police mistakenly arrest you, a 19-year-old woman, for the crime. They put you in a lineup and ask witnesses to pick out the criminal. Which do you think would be more fair: if the other people in the lineup were a 20-year-old man, a 3-year-old child, and an 80-year-old woman; or if the other people were all 19-year-old women? In the former case, the witnesses might pick you only because you are the one who most resembles the actual criminal (Buckhout, 1974). In the latter case, it is much less likely that the witnesses will mistake you for the criminal, because everyone in the lineup is the same age and sex as the culprit (Wells, 1993; Wells & Luus, 1990).

In the Thomas Sophonow case, apparently witnesses were asked by police to identify the man with the cowboy hat they had seen outside the doughnut shop from a photographic lineup. Nine of the photographs had been taken indoors and none of the people wore hats. The tenth photo—the photo of Thomas Sophonow—was larger than the others, was taken outdoors, and showed him wearing a cowboy hat. Police later admitted that the photo gallery was biased and presented a less biased lineup to the witnesses. According to Elizabeth Loftus, who testified at the inquiry into Sophonow's wrongful conviction, it is highly unlikely that the new, fairer lineup would have reversed the damage done by the first one. In her words, "That's like trying to squeeze toothpaste back in the tube" (Loftus, as quoted in Janzen, 2001).

To avoid this "best guess" problem, wherein witnesses pick the person who looks most like the suspect, as well as other problems with lineup identifications, social psychologists recommend that police follow these steps:

- **Ensure that everyone in the lineup resembles the witness's description of the suspect.** Doing so will minimize the possibility that the witness will simply choose the person who looks most like the culprit (Wells et al., 1998).
- **Tell the witnesses that the person suspected of the crime may or may not be in the lineup.** If witnesses believe that the culprit is present, they are much more likely to choose the person who looks most like the culprit, rather than saying that they aren't sure or that the culprit is not present. In short, false identifications are more likely to occur when people believe that the culprit is in the lineup (Clark, 2005; Malpass & Devine, 1981; Wells et al., 1998, 2000).
- **Do not always include the suspect in an initial lineup.** If a witness picks out someone as the culprit from a lineup that includes only foils (i.e., a blank lineup), you will know the witness is not reliable (Pozzulo & Demsey, 2009b). In a study conducted at the University of Alberta, for example, 61 percent of the research participants who made an identification from a blank lineup failed to identify the correct person later when he was actually present in a photo lineup.

In contrast, of participants who correctly indicated that the suspect was not in the blank lineup, only 31 percent later made a mistaken identification when shown a lineup containing the suspect (Wells, 1984).

- **Make sure that the person conducting the lineup does not know which person in the lineup is the suspect.** This precaution avoids the possibility that the person will unintentionally communicate to the witness who the suspect is (Perlini & Silvaggio, 2007; Wells et al., 1998). Researchers at the University of Ontario Institute of Technology and at several American universities have recently developed a computer-based program in which photographs are displayed by a "virtual" officer that can respond to simple voice commands (Cutler, Daugherty, Babu, Hodges, & Van Wallendael, 2009). The early results from using this program were encouraging. Thus, in the future, it may be possible to bypass human investigators and, instead, have computers administer photo lineups
- **Present pictures of people sequentially instead of simultaneously.** Doing so makes it more difficult for witnesses to compare all of the pictures, choosing the one that most resembles the criminal, even when the criminal is not actually in the lineup (Meissner, Tredoux, & Parker, 2005; Sporer, 1994; Steblay, Dysart, Fulero, & Lindsay, 2001). For example, in a study conducted at Queen's University, 35 percent of research participants exposed to a simultaneous lineup mistakenly identified an innocent person as the perpetrator, whereas only 18 percent of those exposed to a sequential lineup made a mistaken identification (Lindsay & Wells, 1985). Findings along the same lines were obtained in recent research conducted at Laurentian University (Perlini & Silvaggio, 2007).
- **Present witnesses with photographs of people and sound recordings of their voices.** Witnesses who both see and hear members of a lineup are much more likely to identify the person they saw commit a crime than are people who only see pictures or only hear voice recordings (Melara, DeWitt-Rickards, & O'Brien, 1989). In fact, Yarmey and colleagues (2001) found that people are really quite inaccurate when identifying voices—much less accurate than they think they are. For example, if a voice was unfamiliar to the participants, the false identification rate was 45 percent (Yarmey, Yarmey, Yarmey, & Parliament, 2001).
- **Don't use composite face programs.** Sometimes witnesses are asked to reconstruct the face of a suspect, using computer programs that are designed for this purpose. Typically, the faces that witnesses generate with these programs do not look much like the actual suspect. Even worse, research shows that people who generate faces with these programs actually have a worse memory for the suspect than people who did not (Wells, Charman, & Olson, 2005; Wells & Hasel, 2008).
- **Try to minimize the time between the crime and the identification of suspects.** Studies based on staged crimes (Yarmey, Yarmey, & Yarmey, 1996) and actual crimes reported in RCMP records (Tollestrup, Turtle, & Yuille, 1994) have found that the longer the time that elapses between when witnesses see a suspect and when they are asked to identify the person from a lineup, the greater the likelihood of error (Read, Connolly, & Turtle, 2001).

Judging Whether Eyewitnesses Are Mistaken

Suppose you are a police detective or a member of a jury who is listening to a witness describe a suspect. How can you tell whether the witness's memory is accurate or whether he or she is making one of the many mistakes in memory we have just documented? It might seem that the answer to this question is pretty straightforward: Pay careful attention to how confident the witness is. Suppose the witness stands up in the courtroom, points her finger at the defendant, and says, "That's the man I saw commit the crime. There's absolutely no doubt in my mind—I'd recognize him anywhere." Sounds pretty convincing, doesn't it? Compare this testimony with a witness who says, "Well, gee, I'm really not sure, because it all happened so quickly. If I had to guess, I'd say it was the defendant, but I could be wrong." Which witness would you be more likely to believe? The eyewitness who was more confident, of course. And you would not be alone. There is evidence that confident witnesses are more likely to be believed by police investigators, judges, and jurors (Read, Connolly, & Turtle, 2001).

In the Thomas Sophonow case, Sophonow testified that on the evening of Barbara Stoppel's murder, he had stopped at a store to buy some food. While he was there, he decided to purchase stockings filled with treats to distribute to children who would have to spend Christmas in a hospital. At the second trial, the court heard testimony from a ward clerk at a Winnipeg hospital, who testified that a man fitting Sophonow's description had arrived at her desk between 8:10 and 8:30 P.M. on December 23 with Christmas stockings for sick children. The clerk had told him that her hospital didn't have a children's ward, but she gave him directions to three hospitals that did. Employees of those hospitals verified that a tall, slim man had arrived with Christmas stockings; however, none of them was certain that the man had been Sophonow, nor was any clerk certain of the exact date that the stockings had been delivered. In contrast, the eyewitnesses who identified Sophonow as the man near the doughnut shop became more confident of their descriptions with each trial. Who did the jurors believe? The witnesses who presented their testimony with greater confidence, apparently.

Does Certainty Mean Accuracy? The only problem—and it is a big one—is that numerous studies have shown that a witness's confidence is not strongly related to his or her accuracy (Brewer & Weber, 2008; Brewer & Wells, 2006; Olsson, 2000; Read, Connolly, & Turtle, 2001; Wells, Olson, & Charman, 2002; Yarmey, Jacob, & Porter, 2002). It is dangerous to assume that because a witness is very confident, he or she must therefore be correct. For example, in the calculator theft experiment we discussed earlier, witnesses who saw the crime under poor viewing conditions (the "thief" wore the cap over his ears) had as much confidence in their identifications as did witnesses who saw the crime under moderate or good viewing conditions, even though the former were considerably less accurate (Lindsay et al., 1981; see Figure SPA3.1 on page 466).

No subjective feeling of certainty can be an objective criterion for the desired truth.

—Hugo Münsterberg, *On the Witness Stand*, 1908

Similar results were obtained at the University of Alberta when Wells, Lindsay, and Ferguson (1978) conducted another version of the calculator theft study described earlier (Lindsay et al., 1981). Participants in this study were asked to identify the calculator "thief" from a photo lineup as well as to indicate how certain they were that they had identified the correct person. The correlation between participants' confidence that they had made a correct identification and the accuracy of their identifications was only 0.29 (recall that a perfect correlation is 1.00). Participants also were asked questions about the event, as if under cross-examination in a trial. Other research participants, serving as jurors, observed the cross-examinations. It turned out that jurors were more likely to believe confident, rather than unconfident, witnesses—a disturbing finding, given the weak relation between accuracy and confidence. Unfortunately, judges do the same thing (Wise & Safer, 2004).

Signs of Accurate Testimony How, then, can we tell whether a witness's testimony is correct? It is by no means easy, but research by David Dunning and Lisa Beth Stern (1994; Stern & Dunning, 1994) suggests some answers. They showed participants a film in which a man stole some money from a woman's wallet, asked participants to pick the man out of a photo lineup, and then asked participants to describe how they had made up their minds. Accurate witnesses tended to say that they didn't really know how they recognized the man, that his face just "popped out" at them. Inaccurate witnesses tended to say that they used a process of elimination whereby they deliberately compared one face with another. Ironically, taking more time and thinking more carefully about the pictures was associated with making more mistakes. We should, therefore, be more willing to believe a witness who says, "I knew it was the defendant as soon as I saw him in the lineup" than one who says, "I compared everyone in the lineup, thought about it, and decided it was the defendant." Subsequent research has shown that people are most accurate when they make their judgment quickly—in 10 seconds or less (Dunning & Perretta, 2002; Weber, Brewer, & Wells, 2004).

The Problem with Verbalization It would seem that another way to improve accuracy of eyewitness identification would be to tell people to write down a description of the suspect as soon as they can, to help them remember what they saw. Studies by Jonathan Schooler and Tonya Engstler-Schooler (1990), however, show that trying to put an image of a face into words can make people's memory worse. They showed students a film of a bank robbery. Participants in the verbalization condition were asked to write a detailed description of the robber's face. Those in the no-verbalization condition spent the same amount of time completing an unrelated task. All students then tried to identify the robber from a photo lineup of eight faces. The results? Only 38 percent of the people in the verbalization condition correctly identified the robber, compared with 64 percent of the people in the no-verbalization condition.

Schooler and Engstler-Schooler (1990; see also Chin & Schooler, 2008) suggest that trying to put a face into words is difficult and impairs memory for that face. Using the word *squinty* to describe a robber's eyes, for example, might be a general description of what his eyes looked like but probably does not capture the subtle contours of his eyes, eyelids, eyelashes, eyebrows, and upper cheeks. When you see the photo lineup, if you look for eyes that are squinty, doing so interferes with your attention to the finer details of the faces. If you ever witness a crime, then, you should not try to put into words what the criminal looked like. And if you hear someone say she or he wrote down a description of the criminal and then deliberated long and hard before deciding whether the person was present at a lineup, you might doubt the accuracy of the witness's identification.

To sum up, several factors make eyewitness testimony inaccurate, leading to all too many false identifications. Based on their meta analysis, Sarah Desmarais at the University of South Florida and J. Don Read at Simon Fraser University concluded that the average "person on the street" who would be a candidate for jury duty knows about some, but certainly not all, of the pitfalls of eyewitness testimony and identifications. Moreover, even if people are aware of issues discussed earlier, that doesn't mean they won't be persuaded by a confident witness in an actual trial (Desmarais & Read, 2011; see also Read & Desmarais, 2009). It doesn't help that television crime dramas fail to portray the limitations of eyewitness evidence (Desmarais, Price, & Read, 2008). The results of years of scientific research suggest a clear bottom line: The criminal law system in Canada should rely less on eyewitness testimony than it currently does. This might mean that some guilty people go free, but it would avoid many false convictions. To see how accurate you and your friends are at eyewitness testimony, and to illustrate some of the pitfalls we have discussed, tackle the accompanying Try It! exercise.

Judging Whether Eyewitnesses Are Lying

There is yet another reason eyewitness testimony can be inaccurate: Even if witnesses have very accurate memories for what they saw, they might deliberately lie when on the witness stand. In the Thomas Sophonow case, some witnesses admitted that they testified because they wanted a reward. It also turned out that the man who told the wild tale of chasing and catching Sophonow on a bridge was lying. To make matters worse, the Crown relied on jailhouse informants who claimed that Sophonow had confessed to them that he was Barbara Stoppel's killer. Deals had been struck with these informants in exchange for their testimony. Why couldn't two different sets of jurors see through these stories?

Sadly, the Sophonow case is not unique in this regard. In other cases of wrongful conviction, such as those of David Milgaard and Donald Marshall, police and jury members believed the false stories of the acquaintances who testified against them. Sometimes, the truth is never established.

How can we tell whether witnesses are lying or telling the truth? Several studies have tested people's ability to detect deception (Bond & Atoum, 2000; Bond & DePaulo, 2008; Ekman, 2002; Gordon & Miller, 2000). In a typical study, participants watch a video or listen to an audiotape of people who are lying half of the time and telling the truth half of the time. The participants' task is to distinguish the lies from the truths. In a review of more than 250 such studies, Bond and DePaulo (2006) found that whereas people are better than chance at telling lies from truths, their level of accuracy is not

TRY IT! The Accuracy of Eyewitness Testimony

Try this demonstration with a group of friends who you know will be gathered in one place, such as a dorm room or an apartment. The idea is to stage an incident in which someone comes into the room suddenly, acts in a strange manner, and then leaves. Your friends will then be asked to recall as much as they can about this person, to see if they are good eyewitnesses. Here are some specific instructions about how you might do this:

1. Take one friend, whom we will call the actor, into your confidence before you do this exercise. Ideally, the actor should be a stranger to the people who will be the eyewitnesses. The actor should suddenly rush into the room where you and your other friends are gathered and act in a strange (but nonthreatening) manner. For example, the actor could hand someone a flower and say, "The flower man cometh!" Or, he or she could go up to each person and say something unexpected, such as "Meet me in Moscow at New Year's." Ask the actor to hold something in his or her hand during this episode, such as a pencil, a shoelace, or a banana. Keep track of how long the episode takes. Remember: The actor should not act in a violent or threatening way, or make the eyewitnesses uncomfortable. The goal is to act in unexpected and surprising ways, not to frighten people.
2. After a few minutes, the actor should leave the room. Inform your friends that you staged this event as a demonstration of eyewitness testimony and that if they are willing, they should try to remember, in as much detail as possible, what occurred. Ask them to write down answers to these questions:
   a. What did the actor look like? Write down a detailed description.
   b. What did the actor say? Write down his or her words as best as you can remember.
   c. How much time passed between the moment the actor entered the room and the point at which he or she left?
   d. Did the actor touch anyone? If so, whom did he or she touch?
   e. What was the actor holding in his or her hand?
3. After everyone has answered these questions, ask your friends to read their answers out loud. How much did they agree? How accurate were people's answers? Discuss with your friends why they were correct or incorrect in their descriptions.

Note: This demonstration will work best if you have access to a video camera and can record the actor's actions. That way, you can play the video to assess the accuracy of the eyewitnesses' descriptions. If you cannot record it, you can ask the actor to repeat his or her actions.

impressive: On average, people were correct only 54 percent of the time (where 50 percent would be guessing at chance levels). According to a review by Michel Sabourin at the Université de Montreal, accuracy rates are even lower when people try to detect deception in members of other ethnic groups (Sabourin, 2007). To make matter worse, as with eyewitness testimony, confidence that you have correctly identified the lies and truths is not strongly correlated with accuracy, as demonstrated by researchers at Dalhousie University (Porter, Woodworth, & Birt, 2000; see also Porter, ten Brinke, & Gustaw, 2010).

> *A man's most valuable trait is a judicious sense of what not to believe.*
>
> —Euripides (*c. 480–406* BCE)

Interestingly, people with a lot of experience dealing with liars (e.g., U.S. customs officers, detectives, judges) are no more accurate at detecting deception than are university students (e.g., DePaulo & Pfeiffer, 1986). Porter and colleagues (2000) obtained similar findings when comparing Canadian federal parole officers with Dalhousie University students—both groups performed at, or below, chance levels. These researchers found that if people—in this case, parole officers and university students—are given extensive training, their accuracy at detecting deception can improve—but their performance remains far from perfect (Porter et al., 2000).

Polygraph
A machine that measures people's physiological responses (e.g., heart rate); polygraph operators attempt to tell if someone is lying by observing how that person responds physiologically while answering questions

Are Polygraph Machines Accurate at Detecting Lies? If people are poor lie detectors, perhaps machines can do better. You've probably heard of a **polygraph** or "lie detector"—a machine that measures people's physiological responses, such as their heart rate and breathing rate. Polygraph operators attempt to tell if someone is lying by observing how that person responds physiologically while answering questions. The assumption is that when people lie they become anxious, and this anxiety can be detected by increases in heart rate, breathing rate, and so on.

How well do these tests work? Several years ago, a board of distinguished scientists conducted an extensive review of the literature and concluded that the polygraph reveals whether someone is lying or telling the truth at levels better than chance (National Research Council, 2003). The accuracy rate, averaging over dozens of studies, was 0.86—that is, people were correctly labelled as lying or telling the truth 86 percent of the time. Although this might seem like an impressive rate of accuracy, it still allows for a substantial number of errors, including false positives, where people who are telling the truth are incorrectly labelled as liars, as has been found in a research study conducted with inmates in a B.C. prison (Patrick & Iacono, 1989; see Iacono, 2008, for a review). Think of it this way: If you were wrongly accused of a serious crime, would you be willing to take a test that had a 14 percent chance of landing you in prison? Because of these high error rates, the Canadian justice system does not allow the results of polygraph evidence to be used in court. The National Research Council summarized it like this: "Almost a century of research in scientific psychology and physiology provides little basis for the expectation that a polygraph test could have extremely high accuracy" (2003, p. 212).

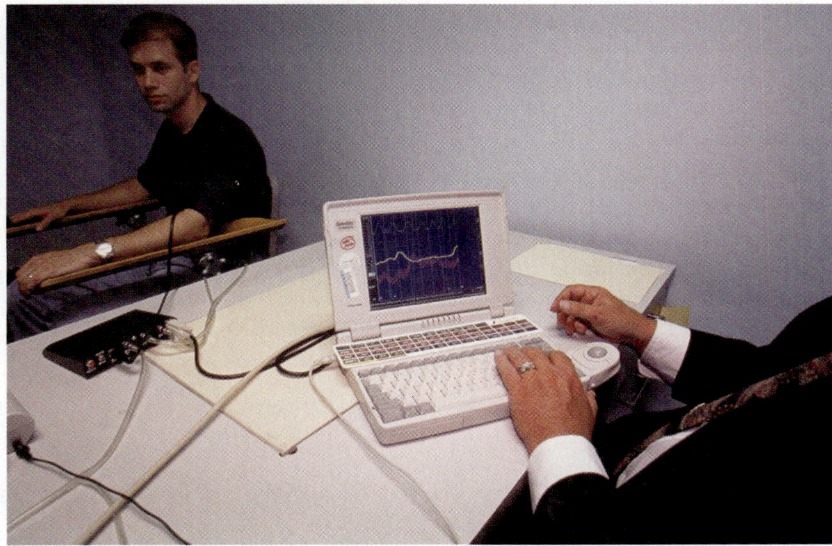

Although polygraphs can detect whether someone is lying at levels better than chance, they are by no means infallible. Because of the rate of error, the Canadian justice system does not allow the results of polygraph tests to be used in court.

Researchers continue to try to develop better lie detectors, using measures such as patterns of brain waves, involuntary eye movements, and blood flow in the face by using high-definition thermal imaging technology (Knight, 2004; Pavlidis, Eberhardt, & Levine, 2002). So far, however, none of these measures has proved to be any better than the polygraph (National Research Council, 2003; Sip, Roepstorff, McGregor, & Frith, 2008). A concern with all physiological measures of deception is whether guilty people can learn to beat the tests. There is some evidence that people can deliberately act in ways that reduce the validity of the results of polygraph tests, such as biting their tongue and doing mental arithmetic. The search continues, but there is still no perfect lie detection machine that can always differentiate lies from the truth (Iacono, 2000; Kleiner, 2002).

If falsehood, like truth, had only one face, we would be in better shape. For we would take as certain the opposite of what the liar said. But the reverse of truth has a hundred thousand shapes.

—Montaigne, *Essays, 1575*

To see how well you and your friends can tell whether someone is lying, complete the accompanying Try It! exercise.

TRY IT! Lie Detection

The purpose of this exercise, which should be done with a group of friends, is to see how well people can tell if someone is lying. Ask for a volunteer to be the speaker and the others to be the audience. The speaker's job will be to lie about how much he or she likes five acquaintances from high school, and to tell the truth about how much he or she likes five other acquaintances from high school. The audience's job is to try to guess when the speaker is telling the truth and when he or she is lying. Here are some specific instructions:

Instructions for the speaker: Make a list of 10 people you knew in high school and think about how much you liked each person. Randomly choose 5 people and put a T next to their names. These are the people about whom you will be truthful. Put an L next to the other names. These are the people about whom you will lie. Take a few minutes to think about what you will say. When you are ready, describe your feelings toward each person (truthfully or not) to the audience. Give a few sentences about each person.

Instructions for the audience: The speaker will be describing his or her feelings about 10 acquaintances from high school. He or she will be telling the truth about half of the people and lying about the other half. Listen carefully and try to guess when the speaker is telling the truth and when he or she is lying. You may use any cues you want to make your decision. Write down the numbers 1 to 10, and put "Truth" or "Lie" next to the number of each person the speaker describes.

Variation: Here is an interesting variation you can try. Have half of the audience sit with their backs to the speaker so they can hear but not see him or her. The other half of the audience should sit facing the speaker. Which group was better at detecting when the speaker was lying? Bella DePaulo, Dan Lassiter, and Julie Stone (1983) found that people who were instructed to pay special attention to a speaker's tone of voice did better at lie detection than did people instructed to pay attention to how the speaker looked. When people can see a speaker, they tend to focus on facial cues that they think are good indications of lying but which, in fact, are not. Therefore, the group of people who cannot see the speaker might rely more on tone of voice and may, as a result, be more accurate.

Go to www.MyPsychLab.com for scoring instructions.

Can Eyewitness Testimony Be Improved?

We have seen a number of ways in which eyewitness testimony can go wrong. Given the importance of such testimony in criminal trials, are there ways to improve it? Two general approaches have been tried but, unfortunately, neither has proven to be very successful.

The first involves hypnosis. You may have seen movies in which a witness to a terrible crime has no memory of what occurred—until he or she is put under hypnosis. Then, while in a trance-like state, the person is able to describe the murderer in great detail. Unfortunately, this is one area in which the movies do not reflect real life. University of Toronto psychologist Marilyn Smith (1983) conducted a review of the literature and concluded that there is no hard evidence that people's memories improve when they are hypnotized. A subsequent review confirms this conclusion (Read, Connolly, & Turtle, 2001). In fact, there is some evidence that when people are under hypnosis they are more susceptible to suggestion, coming to believe they saw things that they did not (Patry, Stinson, & Smith, 2009). Even worse, people tend to become more confident in their memories after they have been hypnotized, even if they are no more accurate (Lynn, Lock, Loftus, Krackow, & Lilienfeld, 2003; Mazzoni & Lynn, 2007; Scoboria, Mazzoni, Kirsch, & Milling, 2002). This is dangerous because, as we saw earlier, juries often interpret a witness's confidence as a gauge of his or her accuracy, even though confidence is not strongly related to accuracy. Given these concerns, in 2007, the Supreme Court of Canada ruled that witness testimony that has been obtained under hypnosis is not admissible in court (Patry et al., 2009).

Cognitive Interview

A technique in which a trained interviewer tries to improve eyewitnesses' memories by focusing their attention on the details and context of the event

The second way people have tried to increase eyewitness accuracy is with the use of the **cognitive interview** (Geiselman & Fischer, 1989). With this technique, a trained interviewer tries to improve an eyewitness's memory by focusing the individual's attention on the details and context of the event. This is done chiefly by asking the person to recall the event several times from different starting points (e.g., from the beginning of the event and from the middle of the event) and by asking the person to create a mental image of the scene. Research on this technique has been mixed. Its designers claim that it improves witnesses' recall (Fisher & Schreiber, 2007). In a recent study, researchers at Wilfrid Laurier University and at Martine Powell-Deakin University in Australia found that children had better memories for activities that they had engaged in over a two-week period when they were asked to mentally "return to the scene" and picture the activities they had performed, what the surroundings were, and so on (Drohan-Jennings, Roberts, & Powell, 2010). Others claim that the cognitive interview may, in fact, increase errors and confabulations of memory, especially when used with children (Finger & Pezdek, 1999; Fisher, Brennan, & McCauley, 2001; Whitehouse, Orne, Dinges, Bates, Nadon, & Orne, 2005). Rather than having people mentally go back to a crime scene, researchers at Simon Fraser University recently conducted a study in which participants saw a staged theft and then returned to the room in which the theft happened one week later and answered questions about the crime. Other participants answered the same questions but in a different room. Reinstating the context (i.e., returning to the same room) had some positive effects (e.g., better memory for what had happened) but also some negative effects (e.g., being more willing to identify someone from a lineup, regardless of accuracy; Wong & Read, 2011).

So far, then, researchers have not found a tried-and-true way to improve eyewitnesses' memories. However, what can be done is to take steps to avoid the pitfalls we have discussed. According to a leading expert in this area, Gary Wells, the most effective approach for reducing the rate of false convictions in the legal system is to improve how police conduct eyewitness interviews and identification procedures. Wells has assisted in developing a National Institute of Justice guide for law enforcement on eyewitness evidence, which outlines procedures for obtaining more accurate information from eyewitnesses. Recommendations include avoiding leading or suggestive questions when interviewing witnesses, telling witnesses that the suspect may or may not be in a lineup, and so on. The hope is that these procedures will prevent witness bias from occurring in the first place (Cynkar, 2007).

The Recovered Memory Debate Another form of eyewitness memory has received a great deal of attention: the case in which a person recalls having been the victim of a crime, typically sexual abuse, after many years of being consciously unaware of that fact. Not surprisingly, the accuracy of such **recovered memories** has been hotly debated (McNally, 2003; Pezdek & Banks, 1996; Schooler & Eich, 2000). This debate received extensive media attention in Canada in 1992, when John Popowich, a Saskatoon police officer, was charged with sexually assaulting children at a daycare centre. The children claimed that he and other adults had forced them to drink blood, perform sexual acts, and watch people having their eyes plucked out. These charges came at a time when *recovered memories* were receiving a lot of attention in the media and the courts; as a result, the children's testimony was believed. After a 10-year fight that took a tremendous toll on his personal and professional life, Popowich managed to establish his innocence. In the summer of 2002, Saskatchewan's justice minister issued an apology to Popowich for his wrongful conviction and agreed to pay $1.3 million in compensation (Millin, 2002).

Recovered Memories
Recollections of an event, such as sexual abuse, that have been forgotten or repressed

The question of the accuracy of recovered memories is highly controversial. On one side are writers such as Ellen Bass and Laura Davis (1994), who claim that it is not uncommon for women who were sexually abused to repress these traumas so that they have absolutely no memory of them. The abuse and its subsequent repression, according to this view, are responsible for many psychological problems, such as depression and eating disorders. Later in life, often with the help of a psychotherapist, these events can be "recovered" and brought back into memory. On the other side of the controversy are academic psychologists who argue that the accuracy of recovered memories cannot be accepted on faith (e.g., Loftus, 2003; Loftus, Garry, & Hayne, 2008; Schacter, 1996; Schooler, 1999). These psychologists acknowledge that sexual abuse and other childhood traumas are a terrible problem and more common than we would like to think. They further agree that claims of sexual abuse should be taken very seriously and fully investigated, and that when sufficient evidence of guilt exists, the person responsible for the abuse should be prosecuted.

But here's the problem: What is "sufficient evidence"? Is it enough that someone remembers, years later, that he or she has been abused, in the absence of any other evidence of abuse? According to many researchers, the answer is no, because of **false memory syndrome**: People can recall a past traumatic experience that is objectively false but that they believe is true (Kihlstrom, 1996). There is evidence that people can acquire vivid memories of events that never occurred, especially if another person—such as a psychotherapist—suggests that the events occurred (Johnson & Raye, 1981; Kealy, Kuiper, & Klein, 2006; Loftus et al., 2008; Schooler & Eich, 2000).

False Memory Syndrome
Remembering a past traumatic experience that is objectively false but nevertheless accepted as true

Simulate on **mypsychlab**
Creating False Memories

In addition to numerous laboratory demonstrations of false memories, evidence from everyday life also indicates that memories of abuse or other traumas can be false. Often, these memories are contradicted by objective evidence (e.g., no evidence of satanic murders can be found); sometimes, people who suddenly acquire such memories decide later that the events never occurred; and, sometimes, the memories are so bizarre (e.g., that people were abducted by aliens) as to strain credulity. Unfortunately, some psychotherapists do not sufficiently consider that by suggesting past abuse, they may be planting false memories rather than helping clients remember real events.

This is not to say, however, that all recovered memories are inaccurate. While scientific evidence for repression and recovery—the idea that something can be forgotten for years and then recalled with great accuracy—is sparse, there may be instances in which people do suddenly remember traumatic events that really did occur (Schooler, 1999). Thus, any claim of abuse should be taken with the utmost seriousness. Unfortunately, however, it is very difficult to distinguish the accurate memories from the false ones in the absence of any corroborating evidence. In a recent large-scale study conducted in several countries, including Canada, participants were presented with a description of a 25-year-old woman who claimed that through therapy, she began to remember that her father had sexually abused her when she was a child. The father denied the allegations. The researchers also presented some participants with testimony from an expert, arguing that such memories tend to be false. Other participants received testimony in which an expert argued that such memories tend to be accurate. Overall, participants were more likely to believe the daughter's allegation than the father's denial. However, people also were swayed by whatever expert testimony they were exposed to. One implication of these findings is that when such cases go to court, it is important to bring in experts from both sides of this debate (Nachson, Read, Seelau, Goodyear-Smith, Lobb, Davies . . . & Brimacombe, 2007). (Incidentally, it may interest you to know that of all of the countries included in this study, participants from Canada and the United States had the most knowledge of the recovered memory debate.)

Watch on **mypsychlab**
Memory: Elizabeth Loftus

Recently, researchers at Dalhousie University and at Grant MacEwan College have taken a first step in trying to untangle truthful versus fabricated reports of traumatic experiences (Porter, Peace, & Emmett, 2007). In this research, participants were asked to describe an actual traumatic experience and to also make up a traumatic experience. Participants then answered a number of questions, such as how stressful each experience was, how intense its impact, what their emotional reaction was, and so on. It turned out that descriptions of fabricated traumatic events contained fewer specific details about time and place than did descriptions of actual traumas and were rated as less believable by coders (who didn't know which accounts were real and which were fabricated). When asked about their reactions to these events, participants reported stronger emotional reactions to the fabricated traumas than to the actual traumas—even though when describing these events, fabricated accounts actually were less emotional than accounts of actual traumas. This tendency to "go over the top" when reporting on reactions to fabricated traumas was also reflected in participants' reports of how much they thought about the event, their level of traumatic stress, and their experience of post-traumatic stress disorder symptoms—all of these reactions were reported more strongly when describing a fake, rather than a real, traumatic event. Thus, when attempting to determine whether an accusation is true or false, investigators might do well to rely on the signs of fabrication identified in this work.

We note that in more recent research along the same lines conducted at the University of British Columbia, ten Brinke and colleagues (in press) had participants describe a transgression of theirs for which they truly were sorry; in the fabricated condition, participants were asked them to pretend that they were truly sorry. Similar to the traumatic events study described above, people who were fabricating remorse were more likely to show more extreme emotional displays (in the words of the researchers, "crocodile tears"). They also exhibited more speech hesitations and made more references to other people than those who were expressing genuine remorse (ten Brinke, MacDonald, Porter, & O'Connor, in press). These findings are important given that whether a person seems genuinely remorseful for having committed a crime influences sentencing and parole decisions.

Other Kinds of Evidence

Police investigators, judges, and juries can rely on a number of other kinds of evidence when reaching decisions about the guilt or innocence of people accused of crimes. They can turn to experts for information (e.g., about an accused person's mental state). They also can rely on physical evidence such as fingerprints or DNA tests conducted on hair samples or blood. Legal professionals and juries also can base their verdicts on statistical evidence—the probability that the accused committed the crime. As we shall see, juries find some of these kinds of evidence more persuasive than others.

Expert Testimony

A number of thorny issues surround the use of expert testimony in court (Pfeifer, 1997). Research conducted at York University suggests that jurors may not always understand judges' instructions about the kinds of evidence that are permissible from an expert witness and the kinds of evidence that should be disregarded (Schuller & Paglia, 1999; see Schuller & Yarmey, 2001, for a review). It is important that jurors know how to properly evaluate expert testimony, because research has shown that jurors are influenced by such information.

In one study, for example, students at York University and visitors to the Ontario Science Centre were presented with a transcript of a homicide case based on an actual case in which an abused woman shot and killed her husband (Schuller & Hastings, 1996). Participants in the expert testimony condition read that a psychologist had testified that the woman's behaviour should be understood in terms of battered wife syndrome. The psychologist explained that battered wife syndrome resembles post-traumatic stress disorder in terms of its emotional and psychological consequences. Participants in the control condition were not exposed to any expert testimony. Did expert testimony have an effect on the mock jurors' verdicts? The answer is yes. Participants who received expert testimony were more likely to conclude that the woman acted out of self-defence than were participants who did not hear expert testimony. Importantly, those who received expert testimony also rendered a more lenient verdict.

In a more recent study, researchers at York University presented participants with mock court documents in which a woman alleged that a man had given her a "date rape" drug and sexually assaulted her. The man claimed that they had mutually consenting sex. Some participants were shown a report indicating that medical tests did not find any traces of drugs in the woman's blood or urine. In this condition, only 9 percent of the participants decided that the man was guilty. Other participants received the same information but also read the report of an expert forensic scientist who argued that the tests that were used could not conclusively prove that the woman hadn't been given a drug. This expert testimony was influential as evidenced by the fact that 30 percent of the participants in this condition rendered a guilty verdict (Jenkins & Schuller, 2007).

In Canada, the courts have shown a tendency to move away from expert testimony or at least impose more stringent criteria for using it (Glancy & Bradford, 2007; Peters, 2001; Yarmey, 2001b; but see Saunders, 2001, for a different opinion). Why is this the case? According to Martin Peters, a Toronto criminal lawyer, some judges believe that much of what experts—in particular, psychological experts—have to offer is common sense. In other words, jury members are assumed to already know whatever a psychologist might have to offer. Other judges are concerned that jury members will rely too heavily on what the experts say, rather than critically evaluate information themselves (Peters, 2001). Not surprisingly, psychologists argue that they do have something to offer the legal system. As A. Daniel Yarmey (2001b) points out, research on the accuracy of eyewitness testimony and on identification of suspects from lineups has revealed important information that is not part of common sense knowledge. Given that wrongful convictions are generally a result of mistaken eyewitness identification, experts can provide the kind of information that would enable jurors to properly evaluate such evidence. Fortunately, some judges agree. According to the Honourable

Mr. Justice Jamie W. S. Saunders of the Nova Scotia Court of Appeal, expert testimony does have a place in Canadian courts, provided that certain guidelines are followed (e.g., experts must be independent and objective).

It is not only jurors who would benefit from being informed about research on errors and biases in eyewitness testimony. In a survey administered by Wise and Safer (2004), U.S. judges were correct on only 55 percent of the questions asked about eyewitness testimony and its unreliability. Psychologists with expertise in eyewitness testimony are now being used to educate judges in the U.S. legal system on the various inaccuracies in eyewitness testimony. The intent is for judges to pass on this information when instructing jury members on how to evaluate eyewitness testimony. Gary Wells, one of the experts who has given lectures to groups of judges, points out that this approach holds considerable promise (Cynkar, 2007). One advantage is that judges can disseminate information on the pitfalls of eyewitness testimony each time they preside over a case, rather than having an expert brought in for each trial to instruct jury members (who would use this information on a one-time basis).

We end this section on a cautionary note. University of British Columbia researcher John Yuille and colleagues (2010) point out that the majority of studies on eyewitness testimony are conducted in the laboratory with staged crimes. They point out that although there are some similarities between witnessing a "crime" in the laboratory and witnessing a crime that researchers have staged in the real world (i.e., a field study), there are also differences. Yuille and colleagues recommend that experts differentiate between the results of studies conducted in the real world and field studies (i.e., crimes that are staged in the real world, so that the research more closely resembles actual crimes). By doing so, experts can ensure that the findings they present are relevant and applicable to real-world crime situations. Yuille and colleagues also encourage additional research comparing how laboratory eyewitnesses differ from actual eyewitnesses (Yuille, Ternes, & Cooper, 2010).

Physical Evidence

When crimes occur, forensic experts scrutinize the scene for footprints, fingerprints, and samples of hair or fibres. In addition, in recent years, DNA testing has become much more accurate, and courts increasingly rely on this kind of evidence. When Larry Fisher was tried for the murder of Gail Miller—the murder for which David Milgaard had been wrongfully convicted—DNA testing proved that he had raped Miller. The jury then used this information to infer that he had killed her as well. The same kind of evidence that was used to convict Larry Fisher was also used to exonerate Guy Paul Morin. Morin was wrongfully convicted of sexually assaulting and killing his neighbour's nine-year-old daughter in 1986. In 1995, he was exonerated on the basis of DNA evidence. To give a final example, in 1990, James Driskoll was charged with the first-degree murder of Perry Dean Harder. DNA evidence played an important role in securing his release after he had spent 13 years in prison. In September 2008, the city of Winnipeg and the province of Manitoba agreed to a $4 million settlement as compensation for his wrongful conviction.

Although DNA testing is more conclusive than many other kinds of evidence, based on their program of research, Puzzolo and colleagues at Carleton University caution that jurors may be quick to convict based on DNA evidence, without fully understanding its limitations (Pozzulo et al., 2009).

And what about other kinds of physical evidence? Research conducted by Elizabeth Loftus (1974, 1983) suggests that other kinds of physical evidence tend not to be very persuasive. In one study, for example, Loftus (1974) presented research participants with a description of a robbery of a grocery store and the murder of its owner. Participants in the physical evidence condition read that the defendant had been found with large sums of cash and that traces of the cleaning solution used on the store's floor had been found on his shoes. Those in the eyewitness testimony condition read that a store clerk had identified the defendant as the killer. Participants in a third condition received both physical and eyewitness evidence, but the eyewitness testimony was

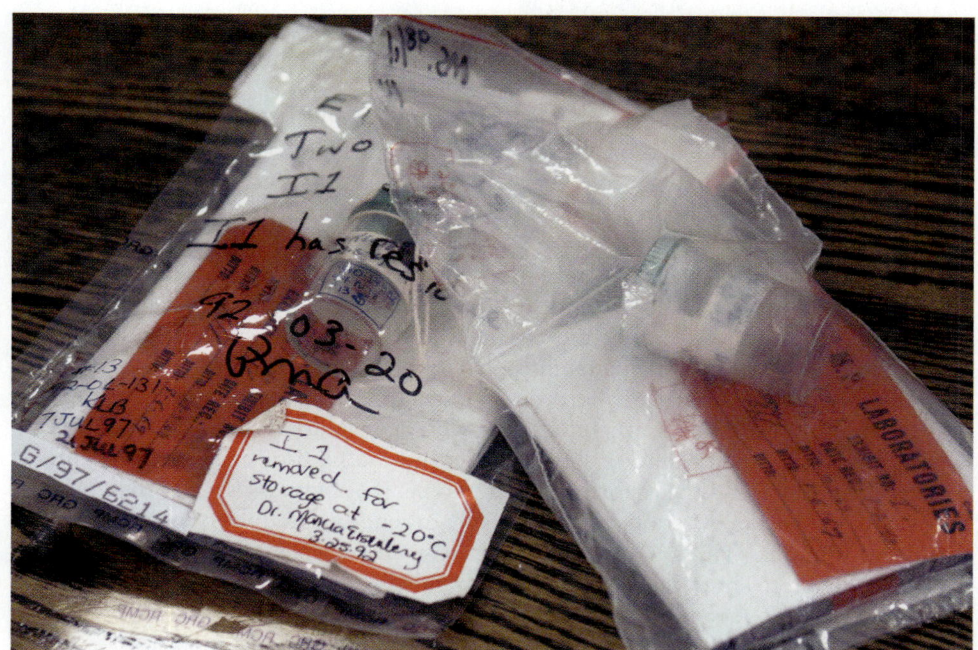

A vial of melted snow containing semen samples found at the scene where Gail Miller was murdered in 1969 was the source of DNA evidence used to exonerate David Milgaard and to convict Larry Fisher. In 2005–2006, the government held a public inquiry into Milgaard's wrongful conviction and imprisonment.

discredited; specifically, participants were told that the eyewitness had poor vision. It turned out that physical evidence alone was not very convincing to these mock jurors—only 18 percent of them rendered a guilty verdict. In sharp contrast, 72 percent of participants who received eyewitness testimony believed that the defendant was guilty. Perhaps most disturbing, 68 percent of participants who received eyewitness testimony that was later discredited nevertheless considered the defendant to be guilty.

In the Thomas Sophonow case, physical evidence was presented at the third trial that made it unlikely that he could have been at the doughnut shop at the time of Barbara Stoppel's murder. Sophonow testified that he had telephoned his mother in Vancouver before delivering the Christmas stockings to the hospitals. Telephone records confirmed that he had placed the call at 7:56 P.M. from a location that would have made it difficult to reach the doughnut shop by the time the murder took place (between 8:15 and 8:45 P.M.). Consistent with Loftus's research, jurors obviously did not find this evidence very convincing, choosing instead to believe the reports of people who claimed to have seen Sophonow at the scene of the crime.

Statistical Evidence

Consider a hypothetical case that legal scholars have frequently debated. A bus hits and kills a dog. Although it is not known to which company the bus belongs, 80 percent of the buses on the route where the dog was killed are owned by the Blue Bus company. The key question is whether the Blue Bus company should be held liable for this accident based on this statistical information alone. According to civil law—which applies to cases such as this—the Blue Bus company should be held responsible if it is "more likely than not" that a Blue Bus killed the dog.

Gary Wells (1992) presented this case to students at the University of Alberta. He found that participants who were told that 80 percent of the buses on the route were owned by the Blue Bus company were extremely reluctant to assign guilt to the Blue Bus company on this basis; only 8 percent of them held the Blue Bus company liable. In another condition, participants were told that a weigh station attendant had seen a Blue Bus on that road earlier that day but that his reports tended to be only 80 percent accurate; remarkably, in this case, 67 percent of participants assigned responsibility for the accident to the Blue Bus company. Even though the probabilities were the same in each condition (80 percent), participants were much more swayed by eyewitness testimony than by statistical evidence (i.e., 67 percent versus 8 percent convictions).

Interestingly, when Wells presented the Blue Bus case to experienced judges, he found that they were no more likely than university students to assign guilt based on statistical evidence alone.

Might there be conditions under which people would be willing to place more weight on statistical evidence? Edward Wright and colleagues (1996) designed a study to answer this question. They presented the Blue Bus case to students at St. Francis Xavier University, varying the amount of time participants had before presenting their verdict, to determine whether having a lot of time to think about this kind of evidence might cause people to rely on it more. Some participants were also given the opportunity to discuss the evidence with others, to see if group discussion might increase reliance on statistical evidence. However, neither extended decision-making time nor group discussion made participants more likely to assign guilt to the Blue Bus company (Wright, MacEachern, Stoffer, & MacDonald, 1996).

Based on these findings, it appears that when considering different kinds of evidence, juries and judges tend to be persuaded by the kind of evidence that is most likely to be unreliable—the reports of other people. If eyewitnesses claim that they saw the person (or bus) in question, juries are likely to render a guilty verdict based on that testimony. Physical evidence and especially statistical evidence apparently are not very persuasive at all. In short, it seems that what is most likely to convince us of something is hearing another person say that it is so.

Juries: Group Processes in Action

Juries are of particular interest to social psychologists because the way they reach verdicts is directly relevant to social psychological research on group processes and social interaction. The right to be tried by a jury of one's peers has a long tradition in Canadian law. Trial by jury was an established institution in England at the beginning of the seventeenth century, and this tradition was adopted by Canada in 1867. Despite this tradition, the jury system has often come under attack. We have already discussed several cases in which juries in Canada have reached the wrong decision and convicted innocent people.

'Tis with our judgments as our watches, None go just alike, yet each believes his own.

—Alexander Pope, *Essay on Criticism*, 1711

The jury system also has been criticized on grounds that jurors may lack the ability to understand complex evidence and reach a dispassionate verdict (Arkes & Mellers, 2002; Devine, Clayton, Dunford, Seying, & Pryce, 2001). According to research conducted at Simon Fraser University, jury members' comprehension of the instructions given to them by judges is remarkably low. In one of the studies in this research program, participants acting as mock jurors understood just over 60 percent of what they had been told (Rose & Ogloff, 2001). A former dean of the Harvard Law School put it this way: "Why should anyone think that 12 persons brought in from the street, selected in various ways for their lack of general ability, should have any special capacity for deciding controversies between persons?" (as quoted in Kalven & Zeisel, 1966).

The jury system has its staunch supporters, of course, and few people argue that it should be abolished altogether. The point is that it is not a perfect system and that based on research in social psychology, there are ways we might expect it to go wrong (Levett, Danielsen, Kovera, & Cutler, 2005; Winter & Greene, 2007). Problems can arise at all phases of a jury trial, including the way in which jurors process information during the trial and the way in which they deliberate in the jury room after all of the evidence has been presented.

How Jurors Process Information during the Trial

How do individual jurors think about the evidence they hear during a trial? As we saw in Chapter 3, people often construct theories and schemas to interpret the world around them, and the same is true of jurors. Some psychologists suggest that jurors decide on one story that best explains all of the evidence; they then try to fit this story to the possible verdicts they are allowed to render. If one of those verdicts fits well with their preferred story, they are likely to vote to convict on that charge (Hastie, 2008; Hastie & Pennington, 2000). This possibility has important implications for how lawyers present their cases. Lawyers typically present the evidence in one of two ways: In the first, called *story order*, they present the evidence in the sequence in which events occurred, corresponding as closely as possible to the story they want the jurors to believe. In the second, called *witness order*, they present witnesses in the sequence they think will have the greatest impact, even if this means that events are described out of order. A lawyer might save his or her best witness for last, for example, so that the trial ends on a dramatic and memorable note, even if this witness describes events that occurred early in the alleged crime.

If you were a lawyer, in which order would you present the evidence? You probably can guess which order researchers in this area would hypothesize to be most successful. If jurors are ultimately swayed by the story or schema they think best explains the sequence of events, the best strategy should be to present the evidence in story order and not in witness order. To test this hypothesis, Pennington and Hastie (1988) asked mock jurors to listen to a simulated murder trial. The researchers varied the order in which the defence attorney and the prosecuting attorney presented their cases. In one condition, both used the story order, whereas in another condition, both used the witness order. In other conditions, one attorney used the story order, whereas the other used the witness order.

The results provided clear and dramatic support for the story order strategy. As seen in Table SPA3.1, when the prosecutor used the story order and the defence used the witness order, the jurors were most likely to believe the prosecutor—78 percent voted to convict the defendant. When the prosecutor used the witness order and the defence used the story order, the tables were turned—only 31 percent voted to convict. One reason the conviction rate in felony trials is so high (approximately 80 percent in the United States) is that in real trials, prosecutors usually present evidence in story order, whereas defence attorneys usually use witness order. To those of our readers who are budding lawyers, remember this when you are preparing for your first trial!

Confessions: Are They Always What They Seem?

Imagine that you are a member of a jury at a murder trial. The prosecution presents what seems to be some pretty damning evidence: a video of the defendant confessing to the crime. "OK, I admit it," you hear the defendant say. "I was the one who pulled the trigger." More than likely you would vote to convict. Why would the defendant admit to the crime if he or she was innocent? Many cases never even go to trial because the defendant pleads guilty after confessing to the crime.

TABLE SPA3.1 How Lawyers Should Present Their Cases

Lawyers can present their cases in a variety of ways. This study found that story order, in which lawyers present the evidence in the order that corresponds most closely to the story they want the jurors to believe, works best.

Percentage of People Voting to Convict the Defendant

	Defence Evidence	
Prosecution Evidence	**Story Order(%)**	**Witness Order (%)**
Story order	59	78
Witness order	31	63

Source: Adapted from Pennington & Hastie, 1988.

Confessions, however, are not always what they seem. Consider the case of a woman who was raped and brutally beaten while jogging in New York City's Central Park in 1989. The woman was in a coma for several days and when she awoke she had no memory of the attack. Soon, however, the police arrested five African-American and Hispanic teenagers who had been in the park that night. The boys confessed to the crime and provided lurid details of what happened. Four of the confessions were videotaped and played at the trial, and largely on this basis, all of the teenagers were convicted and given long prison sentences.

The only problem is that it is now clear that the boys were innocent. Thirteen years later Matias Reyes, in prison for three rapes and a murder, confessed to the crime, claiming he had acted alone. His DNA matched semen recovered from the victim (none of the teenagers' DNA matched), and he gave details of the crime scene that were known only to the police. In 2002, a judge vacated the convictions of all five boys.

If the boys were innocent, why did they confess to the crime? Research by Saul Kassin (2007, 2008) and others has shown that the interrogation process can go wrong in ways that elicit false confessions, even to the point where innocent suspects come to believe that they actually did commit the crime. One problem is that police investigators are often convinced that the suspect is guilty, and this belief biases how they conduct the interrogation. They ask leading questions, isolate suspects and put them under considerable stress, claim that an eyewitness has identified the suspect, and sometimes make false promises. The suspects in the Central Park jogger case, for example, were questioned for up to 30 hours, and the police detectives implied that the suspects could go home if they signed a confession (Kassin, 2007, 2008). This is all well and good if a suspect really is guilty, and if the techniques succeed in making him or her confess. As we saw earlier, however, people—even trained investigators—are not very good at detecting whether someone is lying, which means that innocent people are sometimes subjected to these techniques. It is also the case that after many hours of prolonged interrogation innocent people can become so psychologically fatigued that they don't know what to think, and may even come to believe that they are guilty, as has been found in research conducted in the United States (Kassin & Kiechel, 1996). According to recent research conducted at Simon Fraser University, this is especially likely to happen with people who are highly suggestible (Klaver, Lee, & Rose, 2008). In fact, in a large number of cases in which DNA evidence exonerated defendants who had been falsely convicted of a crime, the defendant had confessed ("False Confessions," 2006).

In a recent study titled "Peering inside a Canadian interrogation room," Memorial University researchers analyzed videotapes of 44 police interrogations in Atlantic Canada. The researchers found that some of the recommended guidelines were strictly followed (e.g., in every case, interrogators complied with the guideline not to have suspects in handcuffs or shackles during the interrogation). Overall, it was found that the greater the use of influence tactics (e.g., confronting the suspect with existing evidence of guilt) and the greater the use of coercive tactics (e.g., threatening the suspect with psychological pain), the higher the rate of confessions. (Note that coercive tactics were not frequently used.) So, people do confess when they are pressured to do so, but, unfortunately, it is not known whether these were "true" confessions or whether innocent people ended up confessing to crimes they did not commit (King & Snook, 2009).

Researchers at St. Mary's University also have expressed concerns that the "Mr. Big" technique used in Canada to elicit confessions may be susceptible to false confessions (Smith, Stinson, & Patry, 2009). This technique tends to be used in serious criminal cases and involves undercover officers enticing the suspect to commit small crimes in exchange for money, the promise of gang membership, and so on. At some point, the suspect is told that he will be meeting the head of the gang or organization (i.e., "Mr. Big") and reasons will be given for why the suspect needs to "come clean" before he can be accepted into the gang. Sometimes the suspect will be told that police have evidence that he is guilty of the crime that is under investigation. This technique has produced a high rate of confessions (75 percent). However, given the intense pressure that is put on suspects, there is evidence that at least some suspects cave in and confess to serious crimes that they did not commit. As Smith and colleagues point out, such mistakes are easily made, but they are not at all easy to identify and undo.

In a recent study, 211 inmates at a Quebec penitentiary were asked what influenced their decision to confess or not to confess to police. It turned out that the interrogation techniques that were used did play a role, but by far the most important factor was police evidence. Offenders who believed that the police had strong evidence against them were more likely to confess than those who believed that the evidence was weak (Deslauriers-Varin, Beauregard, & Wong, 2011).

People sometimes confess to crimes they did not commit when they are subjected to long, stressful interrogations.

One remedy to the confessions issue is to require that interrogations be videotaped so that a jury can view the recording and judge for themselves whether the defendant was coerced into admitting things he or she didn't do. In Canada, interrogations are now generally recorded (Smith, Stinson, & Paltry, 2009). Although this is a step forward, it raises other potential problems. Almost all videos of interrogations focus on the suspect rather than on the interrogator asking the questions. Well, of course they do, you might think—the whole point is to judge how the suspect is responding to the questioning, so it is no surprise that the camera focuses on him or her. The dedicated student of social psychology, however, will recognize this as a problem. As we discussed in Chapter 4, people's judgments about the causes of another person's behaviour are influenced by what is visually salient to them. When we focus our attention on one person in a group, we tend to think that he or she is having a disproportionately large influence on the conversation. Dan Lassiter and colleagues (2004; Ware, Lassister, Patterson, & Ransom, 2008) showed people a video of the same confession from different camera angles and asked them to judge how voluntary or coerced the confession was. People thought that the confession was most voluntary (i.e., the least coerced) when the camera focused on the suspect; here, people had the sense that the suspect was in charge of what was happening. When the camera showed both the suspect and the interrogator, people thought the confession was less voluntary. When the camera focused only on the interrogator, people thought the confession was the least voluntary (the most coerced). Remember, everyone heard the same confession; all that differed was their visual perspective. In part because of this research, at least one American state (Wisconsin) now requires that both the suspect and the questioner be shown in video interviews. It also has been argued that by videotaping only the interrogation session, juries and judges fail to see the interactions between the suspect and police investigators that took place before the videotaped session and, therefore, important contextual information may be missing (e.g., interactions that took place in the police car; Smith et al., 2009).

Deliberations in the Jury Room

As any lawyer can tell you, a crucial part of the jury process occurs out of sight, when jurors deliberate before deciding on the verdict. Even if most jurors are inclined to vote to convict, there might be a persuasive minority that changes their fellow jurors' minds. Sometimes, this can be a minority of one, as in the classic movie *12 Angry Men*. When this film begins, a jury has just finished listening to the evidence in a murder case and all of the jurors except one vote to convict the defendant. Over the next 90 minutes, however, the lone holdout, played by Henry Fonda, convinces his peers that there is reason to doubt that the young Hispanic defendant is guilty. At first, the other jurors pressure Fonda to change his mind by using techniques of normative and informational conformity (as discussed in Chapter 7); but, in the end, reason triumphs and the other jurors come to see that Fonda is right.

As entertaining as this movie is, research indicates that it does not reflect the reality of most jury deliberations (Devine, Clayton, Dunford, Seying, & Pryce, 2001; Ellsworth & Mauro, 1998). In a study of more than 200 juries in actual criminal trials, the researchers found that in 97 percent of cases, the jury's final decision was the same as the one favoured by a majority of the jurors on the initial vote (Kalven & Zeisel, 1966). Just as we saw in Chapter 7 on conformity, majority opinion usually carries the day, bringing dissenting jurors into line. And what happens if a dissenting juror does not succumb to pressure to go along with the majority opinion? In Chapter 7, we found that dissenters may eventually be ejected from the group. This may have been the case in the third Sophonow trial, in which jurors were unable to reach a unanimous verdict after five long days of deliberation—apparently because one juror refused to go along with the rest of the group. In a startling move, the judge dismissed this juror because she supposedly had claimed to possess "psychic powers and special gifts." The juror who was removed maintains that she said no such thing. Once the "problematic" juror was removed, the remaining 11 members swiftly rendered their guilty verdict.

A court is no better than each . . . of you sitting before me on this jury. A court is only as sound as its jury, and a jury is only as sound as the [people] who make it up.

—Harper Lee, To Kill a Mockingbird, *1960*

If jury deliberation is stacked toward the initial majority opinion, why not just abandon the deliberation process, letting the jury's initial vote determine a defendant's guilt or innocence? This would not be a good idea for two reasons: First, forcing juries to reach a unanimous verdict makes them consider the evidence more carefully, rather than simply assuming that their initial impressions of the case were correct (Hastie, Penrod, & Pennington, 1983). Second, even if minorities seldom succeed in persuading the majority to change their minds about guilt or innocence, minorities often do change people's minds about *how* guilty a person is. In criminal trials, juries usually have some discretion about the type of guilty verdict they can reach. In a murder trial, for example, they can often decide whether to convict the defendant of first-degree murder, second-degree murder, or manslaughter. Pennington and Hastie (1990) found that people on a jury who have a minority point of view often convince the majority to change their minds about the specific verdict to render. Thus, although a minority of jurors is unlikely to convince a majority to change its verdict from first-degree murder to not guilty, they may well persuade the majority to change the verdict to second-degree murder.

Why Do People Obey the Law?

Ultimately, the success of the legal system depends on keeping people out of it. We should, of course, find ways to improve the accuracy of eyewitness testimony and help juries make better decisions. Even more important, though, is finding ways to prevent people from committing crimes in the first place. We therefore close with a discussion of how to get people to obey the law.

Do Severe Penalties Deter Crime?

Crime rates, overall, have been dropping. For example, the overall violent crime rate declined by 4 percent between 1997 and 2006 (Statistics Canada, 2008). Analysts have attributed the decrease in crime to the aging of the population (most violent crimes are committed by adolescents and young adults), Canada's economy, and new approaches to preventing and solving crimes. Similar reasons have been given for the decline in violent crime that has been observed in the United States; however, in 1997, the U.S. attorney general at the time believed that stiffer penalties for crimes were at least partly responsible ("Juveniles Committing Fewer Violent Crimes," 1997). Similarly, in Canada, "getting tough on crime" continues to be a major objective of Stephen Harper's Conservative government. It seems to make perfect sense that the harsher the penalty for a crime, the less likely people would be to commit it. As we have seen many times in this book, however, common sense is not always correct, and in the case of crime and prison sentences, the story is not as straightforward as it might seem.

Deterrence Theory

The theory that people refrain from criminal activity because of the threat of legal punishment, as long as the punishment is perceived as relatively severe, certain, and swift

Let's begin with a theory that stiff penalties do prevent crimes. According to **deterrence theory**, people refrain from criminal activity because of the threat of legal punishment, as long as the punishment is perceived as relatively severe, certain, and swift (Carlsmith, Darley, & Robinson, 2002; Pratt, Cullen, Blevins, Daigle, & Madensen, 2006; Williams & Hawkins, 1986). Undoubtedly, this theory is correct under some circumstances. As we mentioned in Chapter 11, several Canadian provinces have set up special family violence courts to ensure that penalties for domestic violence are relatively severe, certain, and swift. There are promising signs that these courts are effective in reducing family violence. Note that because these courts combine certain, swift punishment with rehabilitation, it is difficult to determine whether reductions in violence are attributable to punishment or to rehabilitation, or to both.

Consider another example. Imagine you are heading to downtown Edmonton for an important interview one day and become ensnarled in a traffic jam. At last the traffic clears; but, unless you hurry, you will be late. "Maybe I'll speed up just a little," you think, as the speedometer creeps up to 125 kilometres per hour. Your decision to exceed the speed limit was probably based on a consideration of the fact that you are unlikely to get caught, and if you are, the penalty won't be too severe. However, suppose you knew that the Yellowhead Trail is always patrolled by the Edmonton Police Service and that the penalty for speeding is a five-year prison sentence. Chances are you would not dare to press too hard on the accelerator.

In this example, we have made a couple of important assumptions. First, we assumed that you know the penalties for speeding. Second, we assumed that you have control over your behaviour and that whether you speed is a rational decision that you make after reflecting on the consequences. For many crimes, however, these assumptions do not hold. Surveys have found that many people are ignorant of the penalties for different crimes; if they do not know what the penalties are, the penalties cannot act as a deterrent. (To see how well you know the penalties for various federal crimes, complete the accompanying Try It! quiz.) Further, other types of crimes are not based on a rational decision-making process. Many murders, for example, are impulsive crimes of passion committed by people in highly emotional states, not by people who carefully weigh the pros and cons. In general, severe penalties will work as a deterrent only when people know what the penalties are, believe that they are relatively certain to be caught, and weigh the consequences before deciding whether to commit a crime (Freeman & Watson, 2006; Williams, 2005).

American legislators suffer from a monumental illusion in their belief that long prison sentences will reduce the crime rate.

—Jack Gibbs, *1985*

TRY IT! Are You Aware of the Penalties for Crimes?

Deterrence theory holds that legal penalties will prevent crimes if they are perceived to be relatively severe, certain, and swift. If people are unaware that a crime has a severe penalty, however, those penalties cannot act as a deterrent. Are you aware of the penalties specified in the Criminal Code of Canada for the crimes listed below? Take the following quiz to find out.

What Are the Penalties for These Crimes?

1. First-degree murder (deliberate, planned murder). Note that first-degree murder charges also apply if someone dies as a result of another crime being committed (e.g., a bank teller or store clerk is killed during a robbery).
2. Second-degree murder (deliberate, but unplanned, murder)
3. Manslaughter (causing the death of another person accidentally or through carelessness)
4. Communication for prostitution
5. Break and enter
6. Drug trafficking
7. Impaired driving (or having a blood-alcohol content of more than 0.08)
8. False pretence (e.g., forging a cheque)
9. Assisting suicide
10. Sexual assault

Go to www.MyPsychLab.com for the answers.

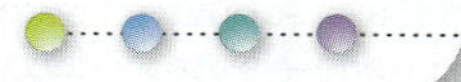

To illustrate these points, let's consider two different kinds of crimes: drunk driving and murder. The decision about whether to drink and drive is one that most of us can control; when we go to a party or a bar and know that we will be driving home afterward, we can decide how much we will drink. Given that this decision is a fairly rational one—at least, under most circumstances—we would expect that certain, severe penalties would act as a deterrent. Researchers in the United States have found some support for this conclusion by comparing states with different drunk-driving laws. (Such research cannot be conducted in Canada because drunk driving falls under the federal Criminal Code, and, therefore, penalties are the same from province to province.) These U.S. studies have found that increasing the severity of penalties for drunk driving is not related, by itself, to a lower rate of alcohol-related motor vehicle fatalities. Consistent with deterrence theory, however, increasing the certainty of being caught for drunk driving—by checking the blood alcohol level of all motorists stopped at sobriety checkpoints—is associated with a lower rate of alcohol-related accidents (Tippetts, Voas, & Fell, 2005; Voas, Holder, & Gruenewald, 1999; Wagenaar & Maldonado-Molina, 2007). These results suggest that severity of the penalty itself does not act as a deterrent but that an increase in the certainty of being caught does.

Now, consider a very different crime and a very different penalty: murder and capital punishment. Canadians who favour capital punishment tend to believe that it has a deterrent effect (Haddock & Zanna, 1998; Vidmar, 1974), even though capital punishment has been abolished in Canada. A majority of U.S. citizens support the death penalty for murder, in part because they believe that it acts as a deterrent. Of course, there is no more severe penalty than death, and if the death penalty prevents even a few murders, it might be worth it—or so the argument goes. To see if this argument is valid, several studies have compared the murder rates in states that have the death penalty with those that do not; the murder rates in states before and after they adopted the death penalty; and the murder rates in other countries before and after they adopted the death penalty. The results are clear: There is no evidence that the death penalty prevents murders (Archer & Gartner, 1984; Bedau, 1997; Donohue & Wolfers, 2006; Ellsworth & Mauro, 1998).

Opponents of the death penalty point out, as we mentioned earlier, that most murders are crimes of passion that are not preceded by a rational consideration of the consequences. Because people are not considering the consequences of their actions, the death penalty does not act as a deterrent. A further argument for not using the death penalty is that an astonishing number of innocent people have been sentenced to death.

Increasing the certainty that people will be caught when drunk driving—by checking the blood alcohol level of every motorist stopped at a sobriety checkpoint such as this one—is associated with a lower rate of alcohol-related accidents.

Proponents of the death penalty say that severity of the crime is not enough; as argued by deterrence theory, severe penalties must be applied with certainty and speed. The last of these conditions is almost never met. In the United States, the time between a conviction for murder and the execution of the convicted murderer is often many years because of the slowness of the judicial system and the many avenues of appeal open to prisoners on death row. Were the process sped up, this argument goes, the death penalty *could* act as a deterrent.

There is reason to doubt that the death penalty would act as a deterrent even if it were applied swiftly. We refer to a few studies that have found that executions are followed not by a decrease but by an *increase* in murders (Archer & Gartner, 1984; Bailey & Peterson, 1997; Sakamoto, Sekiguchi, & Shinkyu, 2003). This finding might seem bizarre. Why would the execution of a convicted murderer *increase* the likelihood that someone else would commit a murder? If you recall our discussion on aggression in Chapter 11, the finding makes sense. As we saw, observing someone else commit a violent act weakens people's inhibitions against aggression, leads to imitation of aggression, and numbs their sense of horror over violence. Could it be that observing the government put someone to death lowers other people's inhibitions, making them more likely to commit murders? While the data are not conclusive, this argument makes social psychological sense—and some evidence supports it (Bailey & Peterson, 1997).

Procedural Justice: People's Sense of Fairness

We have just seen that one reason people obey the law is their fear of being caught and punished. An even more important reason, however, is their moral values about what constitutes good behaviour. People will obey a law if they think that it is just, even if they are unlikely to be caught breaking it. For example, many people are honest on their tax returns because they think that cheating is wrong, not because they fear being caught for cheating. Thus, if you were a lawmaker, you could try to prevent crime in one of two ways: You could increase the penalties for breaking the law and the probability that people will be caught, or you could try to convince people that the law is just and fair. As we have seen, the former approach is difficult and sometimes ineffective. If we wanted to prevent people from driving through red lights, we could increase the penalties for doing so and station a police officer at every intersection; it would be far simpler, however, to convince people that it is wrong to run red lights, so that they comply with the law even when no police officers are around.

What determines whether people think a law is just? One important factor is their perception of the fairness of legal proceedings. **Procedural justice** is defined as people's judgments about the fairness of the procedures used to determine outcomes, such as whether they are innocent or guilty of a crime (Blader & Tyler, 2003; Kelley & Thibaut, 1978; Napier & Tyler, 2008; Skarlicki, Ellard, & Kelln, 1998; Skitka, 2002; Wenzel, 2000). People who feel that they have been treated fairly are more likely to comply with the law than are people who feel that they have been treated unfairly (Tyler, 1990). Consider, for example, what happens when the police are called because of a domestic assault. What determines whether the person accused of assault will repeat this crime in the future? It turns out that one factor is whether suspects feel that they were treated fairly by the police ("Misconceptions about why people obey laws," 1997).

Procedural Justice

People's judgments about the fairness of the procedures used to determine outcomes, such as whether they are innocent or guilty of a crime

In summary, social psychological research indicates that the Canadian legal system can go wrong in a number of ways. Juries rely heavily on eyewitness testimony, when in fact such testimony is often incorrect. Determining when witnesses are telling the truth is difficult, even with the use of polygraphs. And because juries are groups of people who try to reach consensus by discussing, arguing, and bargaining, the kinds of conformity pressures and group processes we discussed in Chapter 7 can lead to faulty decisions. By illuminating these problems in their research, however, social psychologists can help initiate change in the legal system—change that will lead to greater fairness and equity and to a greater sense of procedural justice. Most important of all, heeding psychological research on these questions might reduce the number of cases in which people such as Thomas Sophonow languish in prison for crimes they did not commit.

Summary

- **The Canadian Justice System** The Canadian justice system deals with civil cases and criminal cases. When someone commits a crime and there is adequate evidence to press charges, lawyers for the defence and the prosecution gather additional evidence and negotiate with each other. If a case goes to trial, a jury or a judge decides the defendant's fate. All of these steps in the legal process are intensely social psychological (e.g., attributions about what caused the criminal behaviour are made by police, lawyers, jurors, and the judge; prejudiced beliefs and stereotypical ways of thinking affect those attributions).

- **Eyewitness Testimony** Eyewitness testimony is often of questionable accuracy because of the limitations of memory.
  - **Why Are Eyewitnesses Often Wrong?** A number of factors bias the acquisition, storage, and retrieval of what people observe, sometimes leading to the false identification of criminals. For example, research on own-race bias shows that people find it more difficult to recognize members of other races than members of their own race. Research on reconstructive memory indicates that errors in source monitoring can occur when people become confused about where they saw or heard something. Recognizing the problems people have retrieving information from memory, social psychologists have issued guidelines for how police lineups should be conducted.
  - **Judging Whether Eyewitnesses Are Mistaken** There is no surefire way of telling whether a witness is making an accurate or inaccurate identification, although there is some evidence that people who identify a suspect from an array of pictures quickly are more likely to be correct.
  - **Judging Whether Witnesses Are Lying** Humans are not very good at telling whether another person is lying. The polygraph can detect lying at above-chance levels but is not perfect and often yields inaccurate results.
  - **Can Eyewitness Testimony Be Improved?** Not only does hypnosis fail to improve people's memory, it also makes people more susceptible to suggestion and increases their confidence in their memories. A new interview technique called the cognitive interview offers some promise in improving accuracy, but research on its effectiveness has produced mixed findings.

- **Other Kinds of Evidence** Other kinds of evidence are admitted in court as well, including expert testimony, physical evidence, and statistical evidence (information on the probability that the accused committed the crime).
  - **Expert Testimony** The use of experts in courtroom proceedings is controversial. Psychologists have been used to alert judges and jurors to the pitfalls of eyewitness testimony, although studies done in the laboratory may not generalize to "real world" crime situations.
  - **Physical Evidence** Although it might seem as though physical evidence such as DNA testing would be conclusive, there still are pitfalls. Jurors tend not to find other kinds of physical evidence very convincing.
  - **Statistical Evidence** Jurors also are not very convinced by statistical evidence (e.g., being told that there is an 80 percent chance that a company was liable for an accident).

- **Juries: Group Processes in Action** Juries are of particular interest to social psychologists because the way they reach verdicts is directly relevant to social psychological research on group processes and social interaction. Jurors are susceptible to the same kinds of biases and social pressures we documented in earlier chapters.
  - **How Jurors Process Information During the Trial** During a trial, jurors attempt to make sense out of the testimony and often decide on one story that explains all of the evidence. Juries are thus most swayed by lawyers who present the evidence in a way that tells a consistent story.
  - **Confessions: Are They Always What They Seem?** The interrogation techniques used by police can sometimes produce false confessions. The video recording of interrogations is a safeguard against this, although focusing the camera solely on the suspect increases the likelihood that viewers will think he or she voluntarily confessed.
  - **Deliberations in the Jury Room** During deliberations, jurors with minority views are often pressured into conforming to the view of the majority; thus, verdicts usually correspond to the initial feelings of the majority of jurors.

- **Why Do People Obey the Law?** It is important to examine people's perception of the legal system because these perceptions have a lot to do with how likely people are to obey the law.
  - **Do Severe Penalties Deter Crime?** Deterrence theory holds that people refrain from criminal activity if they view penalties as relatively severe, certain, and swift. Deterrence theory may be correct about crimes that are the result of rational thought but is unlikely to apply to crimes of passion that are not rational, such as many murders. There is no evidence, for example, that the death penalty deters murders, and there is even some evidence that it increases the murder rate.
  - **Procedural Justice: People's Sense of Fairness** People are more likely to obey the law if their sense of procedural justice is high; that is, if they believe that the procedures used to determine their guilt or innocence are fair.

Glossary

Accessibility The extent to which schemas and concepts are at the forefront of people's minds and are therefore likely to be used when making judgments about the social world

Acquisition The process by which people notice and pay attention to information in the environment; people cannot perceive everything that is happening around them, so they acquire only a subset of the information available in the environment

Actor/Observer Difference The tendency to see other people's behaviour as dispositionally caused, while focusing more on the role of situational factors when explaining one's own behaviour

Affect Blend A facial expression in which one part of the face registers one emotion while another part of the face registers a different emotion

Affectively Based Attitude An attitude based primarily on people's emotions and feelings about the attitude object

Aggression Intentional behaviour aimed at causing either physical or psychological pain

Aggressive Stimulus An object associated with aggressive responses (e.g., a gun) whose mere presence can increase the probability of aggression

Altruism The desire to help others, even if it involves a cost to the helper

Altruistic Personality Aspects of a person's makeup that cause him or her to help others in a wide variety of situations

Amygdala An area in the core of the brain that is associated with aggressive behaviour

Analytic Thinking Style A type of thinking in which people focus on the properties of objects without considering their surrounding context; this type of thinking is common in Western cultures

Anxious/Ambivalent Attachment Style An attachment style characterized by a concern that others will not reciprocate one's desire for intimacy, resulting in higher-than-average levels of anxiety

Applied Research Studies designed specifically to solve a particular social problem; building a theory of behaviour is usually secondary to solving the specific problem

Archival Analysis A form of the observational method whereby the researcher examines the accumulated documents, or archives, of a culture (e.g., diaries, novels, magazines, and newspapers)

Attachment Styles The expectations people develop about relationships with others based on the relationship they had with their primary caregiver when they were infants

Attachment Theory The theory that our behaviour in adult relationships is based on our experiences as infants with our parents or caregivers

Attitude An evaluation of a person, object, or idea

Attitude Inoculation The process of making people immune to attempts to change their attitudes by exposing them to small doses of the arguments against their position

Attribution Theory A description of the way in which people explain the causes of their own and other people's behaviour

Automatic Thinking Thinking that is nonconscious, unintentional, involuntary, and effortless

Availability Heuristic A mental shortcut whereby people base a judgment on the ease with which they can bring something to mind

Avoidant Attachment Style An attachment style characterized by a suppression of attachment needs, because attempts to be intimate have been rebuffed; people with this style find it difficult to develop intimate relationships

Base Rate Information Information about the frequency of members of different categories in the population

Basic Research Studies that are designed to find the best answer as to why people behave the way they do and that are conducted purely for reasons of intellectual curiosity

Behaviourally Based Attitude An attitude based primarily on observations of how one behaves toward an attitude object

Belief in a Just World A form of defensive attribution wherein people assume that bad things happen to bad people and that good things happen to good people

Bystander Effect The finding that the greater the number of bystanders who witness an emergency, the less likely it is that any one of them will help

Catharsis The notion that "blowing off steam"—by performing an aggressive act, watching others engage in aggressive behaviour, or engaging in a fantasy of aggression—relieves built-up aggressive energies and hence reduces the likelihood of further aggressive behaviour

Causal Theories Theories about the causes of one's own feelings and behaviours; typically, we learn such theories from our culture (e.g., "absence makes the heart grow fonder")

Cognitive Dissonance A feeling of discomfort caused by the realization that one's behaviour is inconsistent with one's attitudes or that one holds two conflicting attitudes

Cognitive Interview A technique in which a trained interviewer tries to improve eyewitnesses' memories by focusing their attention on the details and context of the event

Cognitively Based Attitude An attitude based primarily on a person's beliefs about the properties of an attitude object

Communal Relationships Relationships in which people's primary concern is being responsive to the other person's needs

Companionate Love The feelings of intimacy and affection we feel toward someone with whom our lives are deeply intertwined

Comparison Level People's expectations about the levels of rewards and costs that they deserve in a relationship

Comparison Level for Alternatives People's expectations about the level of rewards and punishments they would receive in an alternative relationship

Complementarity Attraction to people who are opposite to us

Compliance A change in behaviour in response to a direct request from another person

Conformity A change in behaviour as a result of the real or imagined influence of other people

Consensus Information Information about the extent to which other people behave the same way as the actor does toward the same stimulus

Consistency Information Information about the extent to which the behaviour between one actor and one stimulus is the same across time and circumstances

Construal The way in which people perceive, comprehend, and interpret the social world

Contagion The rapid transmission of emotions or behaviour through a crowd

Contingency Theory of Leadership The theory that leadership effectiveness depends both on how task-oriented or relationship-oriented the leader is, and on the amount of control and influence the leader has over the group

Controlled Thinking Thinking that is conscious, intentional, voluntary, and effortful

Coping Styles The ways in which people react to stressful events

Correlation Coefficient A statistic that assesses how well you can predict one variable based on another (e.g., how well you can predict people's weight from their height)

Correlational Method The technique whereby researchers systematically measure two or more variables and assess the relation between them (i.e., how much one can be predicted from the other)

Correspondence Bias The tendency to infer that people's behaviour corresponds to or matches their disposition (personality)

Counter-Attitudinal Advocacy The process that occurs when a person states an opinion or attitude that runs counter to his or her private belief or attitude

Counterfactual Thinking Mentally changing some aspect of the past as a way of imagining what might have been

Covariation Model A theory stating that to form an attribution about what caused a person's behaviour, we systematically note the pattern between the presence (or absence) of possible causal factors and whether or not the behaviour occurs

Cover Story A description of the purpose of a study given to participants that is different from its true purpose; cover stories are used to maintain psychological realism

Cross-Cultural Research Research conducted with members of different cultures to see whether the psychological processes of interest are present across cultures or whether they are specific to a single culture

Debriefing Explaining to the participants, at the end of the experiment, the true purpose of the study and exactly what transpired

Deception The procedure whereby participants are misled about the true purpose of a study or the events that will actually transpire

Decode To interpret the meaning of the nonverbal behaviour other people express, such as deciding that a pat on the back was an expression of condescension and not kindness

Defensive Attributions Explanations for behaviour that avoid feelings of vulnerability and mortality

Deindividuation The loosening of normal constraints on behaviour when people are in a group, leading to an increase in impulsive and deviant acts

Dependent Variable The variable a researcher measures to see if it is influenced by the independent variable; the researcher hypothesizes that the dependent variable will be influenced by the level of the independent variable

Descriptive Norms People's perceptions of how other people actually behave in a given situation, regardless of whether the behaviour is approved or disapproved of by others

Deterrence Theory The theory that people refrain from criminal activity because of the threat of legal punishment, as long as the punishment is perceived as relatively severe, certain, and swift

Diffusion of Responsibility Each bystander's sense of responsibility to help decreases as the number of witnesses to an emergency or crisis increases

Discrimination Unjustified negative or harmful action toward a member of a group simply because of his or her membership in that group

Dismissive Avoidant Style A type of avoidant attachment in which the person is self-sufficient and claims not to need close relationships

Display Rules Culturally determined rules about which emotional expression are appropriate to show

Distinctiveness Information Information about the extent to which one particular actor behaves in the same way to different stimuli

Door-in-the-Face Technique A technique to get people to comply with a request, whereby people are presented first with a large request, which they are expected to refuse, and then with a smaller, more reasonable request, to which it is hoped they will acquiesce

Downward Social Comparison The process whereby we compare ourselves with people who are worse than we are on a particular trait or ability

Elaboration Likelihood Model The theory that there are two ways in which persuasive communications can cause attitude change: the *central route* occurs when people are motivated and have the ability to pay attention to the arguments in the communication, and the *peripheral route* occurs when people do not pay attention to the arguments but are instead swayed by surface characteristics (e.g., who gave the speech)

Emblems Nonverbal gestures that have well-understood definitions within a given culture; they usually have direct verbal translations, such as the "okay" sign

Empathy The ability to experience events and emotions (e.g., joy, sadness) the way another person experiences them

Empathy-Altruism Hypothesis The idea that when we feel empathy for a person, we will attempt to help him or her purely for altruistic reasons, regardless of what we have to gain

Encode To express or emit nonverbal behaviour, such as smiling or patting someone on the back

Equity Theory The theory that people are happiest with relationships in which the rewards and costs that a person experiences, and the contributions that he or she makes to the relationship are roughly equal to the rewards, costs, and contributions of the other person

Eros The instinct toward life, posited by Freud

Ethnography The method by which researchers attempt to understand a group or culture by observing it from the inside without imposing any preconceived notions they might have

Evolutionary Approach An approach derived from evolutionary biology that states that men and women are attracted to different characteristics in each other—men are attracted by women's appearance; women are attracted by men's resources—because this maximizes their reproductive success

Evolutionary Psychology The attempt to explain social behaviour in terms of genetic factors that evolved over time according to the principles of natural selection

Exchange Relationships Relationships governed by the need for equity (i.e., for a comparable ratio of rewards and costs)

Experimental Method The method in which the researcher randomly assigns participants to different conditions and ensures that these conditions are identical except for the independent variable (the one thought to have a causal effect on people's responses)

Explicit Attitudes Attitudes that we consciously endorse and can easily report

Extended Contact Hypothesis The mere knowledge that a member of one's own group has a close relationship with a member of another group can reduce one's prejudice toward that group

External Attribution The inference that a person is behaving a certain way because of something about the situation he or she is in; the assumption is that most people would respond the same way in that situation

External Justification A person's reason or explanation for dissonant behaviour that resides outside the individual (e.g., to receive a large reward or avoid a severe punishment)

External Validity The extent to which the results of a study can be generalized to other situations and to other people

Extrinsic Motivation The desire to engage in an activity because of external rewards or pressures, not because we enjoy the task or find it interesting

False Memory Syndrome Remembering a past traumatic experience that is objectively false but nevertheless accepted as true

Fear-Arousing Communication A persuasive message that attempts to change people's attitudes by arousing their fears

Fearful Avoidant Style A type of avoidant attachment in which close relationships are avoided because of mistrust and fears of being hurt

Field Experiments Experiments conducted in natural settings, rather than in the laboratory

Fight-or-Flight Response Responding to stress by either attacking the source of the stress or fleeing from it

Foot-in-the-Door Technique A technique to get people to comply with a request, whereby people are presented first with a small request, to which they are expected to acquiesce, followed by a larger request, to which it is hoped they will also acquiesce

Frustration-Aggression Theory The theory that frustration—the perception that you are being prevented from obtaining a goal—will increase the probability of an aggressive response

Fundamental Attribution Error The tendency to overestimate the extent to which people's behaviour stems from internal, dispositional factors and to underestimate the role of situational factors

Gestalt Psychology A school of psychology stressing the importance of studying the subjective way in which an object appears in people's minds, rather than the objective physical attributes of the object

Global Attribution The belief that the cause of an event is a result of factors that apply in a large number of situations, as opposed to the belief that the cause is specific and applies in only a limited number of situations

Great Person Theory The theory that certain key personality traits make a person a good leader, regardless of the situation the leader faces

Group A collection of three or more people who interact with one another and are interdependent, in the sense that their needs and goals cause them to rely on one another

Group Cohesiveness Qualities of a group that bind members together and promote liking among them

Group Polarization The tendency for groups to make decisions that are more extreme than the initial inclinations of their members

Groupthink A kind of thinking in which maintaining group cohesiveness and solidarity is more important than considering the facts in a realistic manner

Hardiness A personality trait defined as a combination of self-esteem and a sense of control

Heuristic-Systematic Model of Persuasion The theory that there are two ways in which persuasive communications can cause attitude change: people either process the merits of the arguments (known as *systematic processing*) or are swayed by factors that are peripheral to the message itself, such as "Experts are always right" (known as *heuristic processing*)

Hindsight Bias The tendency for people to exaggerate how much they could have predicted the outcome after knowing that it occurred

Holistic Thinking Style A type of thinking in which people focus on the overall context, particularly the ways in which objects relate to one another; this type of thinking is common in East Asian cultures (e.g., China, Japan, Korea)

Hostile Aggression An act of aggression stemming from feelings of anger and aimed at inflicting pain or injury

Hypothesis A testable statement or idea about the relationship between two or more variables

Idiosyncrasy Credits The credits a person earns, over time, by conforming to a group's norms; if enough idiosyncrasy credits are earned, the person can, on occasion, behave in a deviant manner without retribution from the group

Implementation Plan People's specific plans about where, when, and how they will fulfill a goal

Implicit Attitudes Attitudes that are involuntary, uncontrollable, and at times unconscious

Implicit Personality Theory A type of schema people use to group various kinds of personality traits together; for example, many people believe that if someone is kind, he or she is generous as well

Independent Variable The variable a researcher changes or varies to see if it has an effect on some other variable

Independent View of the Self Defining oneself in terms of one's own internal thoughts, feelings, and actions, and not in terms of the thoughts, feelings, and actions of other people

Individual Differences The aspects of people's personalities that make them different from other people

Informational Social Influence Conforming because we believe that others' interpretation of an ambiguous situation is more correct than ours and will help us choose an appropriate course of action

Informed Consent Agreement to participate in an experiment, granted in full awareness of the nature of the experiment which has been explained in advance

In-Group The group with which an individual identifies, and of which he or she feels a member

In-Group Bias The tendency to evaluate in-group members more positively than out-group members

Injunctification A motivated tendency to see the status quo (the ways things are) as the most desirable state of affairs (the way things should be)

Injunctive Norms People's perceptions of the behaviour that is approved or disapproved of by others

Instrumental Aggression Aggression as a means to some goal other than causing pain

Insufficient Punishment The dissonance aroused when individuals lack sufficient external justification for having resisted a desired activity or object, usually resulting in individuals devaluing the forbidden activity or object

Integrative Solution A solution to a conflict whereby the parties make trade-offs on issues according to their different interests; each side concedes the most on issues that are unimportant to it but important to the other side

Interdependent View of the Self Defining oneself in terms of one's relationships to other people; recognizing that one's behaviour is often determined by the thoughts, feelings, and actions of others

Interjudge Reliability The level of agreement between two or more people who independently observe and code a set of data; by showing that two or more judges independently come up with the same observations, researchers ensure that the observations are not the subjective impressions of one individual

Internal Attribution The inference that a person is behaving in a certain way because of something about him or her, such as his or her attitude, character, or personality

Internal Justification The reduction of dissonance by changing something about oneself (e.g., one's attitude or behaviour)

Internal Validity Ensuring that nothing other than the independent variable can affect the dependent variable; this is accomplished by controlling all extraneous variables and by randomly assigning people to different experimental conditions

Intrinsic Motivation The desire to engage in an activity because we enjoy it or find it interesting, not because of external rewards or pressures

Introspection The process whereby people look inward and examine their own thoughts, feelings, and motives

Investment Model The theory that people's commitment to a relationship depends on their satisfaction with the relationship in terms of rewards, costs, and comparison level; their comparison level for alternatives; and how much they have invested in the relationship that would be lost by leaving it

Jigsaw Classroom A classroom setting designed to reduce prejudice between children by placing them in small, desegregated groups and making each child dependent on the other children in the group to learn the course material and do well in the class

Judgmental Heuristics Mental shortcuts people use to make judgments quickly and efficiently

Justification of Effort The tendency for individuals to increase their liking for something they have worked hard to attain

Kin Selection The idea that behaviour that helps a genetic relative is favoured by natural selection

Learned Helplessness Pessimism that results from attributing a negative event to stable, internal, and global factors

Looking-Glass Self The idea that we see ourselves through the eyes of other people and incorporate their views into our self-concept

Lowballing An unscrupulous strategy whereby a salesperson induces a customer to agree to purchase a product at a very low cost, and then subsequently raises the price; frequently, the customer will still make the purchase at the inflated price

Mass Psychogenic Illness The occurrence of similar physical symptoms in a group of people for which there is no known physical or medical cause

Mere Exposure Effect The finding that the more exposure we have to a stimulus, the more apt we are to like it

Meta Analysis A statistical technique that averages the results of two or more studies to see if the effect of an independent variable is reliable

Meta-Stereotype A person's beliefs regarding the stereotype that out-group members hold about their own group

Minority Influence The case in which a minority of group members influences the behaviour or beliefs of the majority

Misattribution of Arousal The process whereby people make mistaken inferences about what is causing them to feel the way they do

Mundane Realism The extent to which an experiment is similar to real-life situations

Mutual Interdependence A situation in which two or more groups need each other and must depend on each other to accomplish a goal that is important to both groups

Natural Selection The process by which heritable traits that promote survival in a particular environment are passed along to future generations, because organisms with that trait are more likely to reproduce

Negative-State Relief Hypothesis The idea that people help in order to alleviate their own sadness and distress

Negotiation A form of communication between opposing sides in a conflict, in which offers and counter-offers are made and a solution occurs only when both parties agree

Nonverbal Communication The way in which people communicate, intentionally or unintentionally, without words; nonverbal cues include facial expressions, tone of voice, gestures, body position and movement, the use of touch, and eye gaze

Norm of Reciprocity The expectation that helping others will increase the likelihood that they will help us in the future

Normative Social Influence The influence of other people that leads us to conform in order to be liked and accepted by them; this type of conformity results in public compliance with the group's beliefs and behaviours but not necessarily in private acceptance

Obedience Conformity in response to the commands of an authority figure

Observational Method The technique whereby a researcher observes people and systematically records measurements of their behaviour

Operational Definition The precise specification of how variables are measured or manipulated

Out-Group A group with which the individual does not identify

Overconfidence Barrier The barrier that results when people have too much confidence in the accuracy of their judgments; people's judgments are usually not as correct as they think they are

Overjustification Effect The case whereby people view their behaviour as caused by compelling extrinsic reasons, making them underestimate the extent to which their behaviour was caused by intrinsic reasons

Own-Race Bias The finding that people are better at recognizing faces within their own race than those of other races

Passionate Love The feelings of intense longing, accompanied by physiological arousal, we feel for another person; when our love is reciprocated, we feel great fulfillment and ecstasy; but, when it is not, we feel sadness and despair

Perceived Control The belief that we can influence our environment in ways that determine whether we experience positive or negative outcomes

Perceptual Salience Information that is the focus of people's attention; people tend to overestimate the causal role of perceptually salient information

Performance-Contingent Rewards Rewards that are based on how well we perform a task

Persuasive Communication Communication (e.g., a speech or television advertisement) advocating a particular side of an issue

Pluralistic Ignorance The phenomenon whereby bystanders assume that nothing is wrong in an emergency because no one else looks concerned

Polygraph A machine that measures people's physiological responses (e.g., heart rate); polygraph operators attempt to tell if someone is lying by observing how that person responds physiologically while answering questions

Positive Illusions Idealization of our romantic relationships and partners in order to maintain the relationship

Post-Decision Dissonance Dissonance that is inevitably aroused after a person makes a decision; such dissonance is typically reduced by enhancing the attractiveness of the chosen alternative and devaluing the rejected alternatives

Prejudice A hostile or negative attitude toward people in a distinguishable group, based *solely* on their membership in that group

Priming The process by which recent experiences increase the accessibility of a schema, trait, or concept

Private Acceptance Conforming to other people's behaviour out of a genuine belief that what they are doing or saying is right

Probability Level (*p*-Value) A number, calculated with statistical techniques, that tells researchers how likely it is that the results of their experiment occurred by chance and not because of the independent variable(s); the convention in science, including social psychology, is to consider results significant if the probability level is less than 5 in 100 that the results might be attributable to chance factors and not the independent variables studied

Procedural Justice People's judgments about the fairness of the procedures used to determine outcomes, such as whether they are innocent or guilty of a crime

Process Loss Any aspect of group interaction that inhibits good problem solving

Propinquity Effect The finding that the more we see and interact with people, the more likely they are to become our friends

Prosocial Behaviour Any act performed with the goal of benefiting another person

Psychological Realism The extent to which the psychological processes triggered in an experiment are similar to psychological processes that occur in everyday life; psychological realism can be high in an experiment, even when mundane realism is low

Public Compliance Conforming to other people's behaviour publicly, without necessarily believing in what they are doing or saying

Random Assignment to Condition The process whereby all participants have an equal chance of taking part in any condition of an experiment; through random assignment, researchers can be relatively certain that differences in the participants' personalities or backgrounds are distributed evenly across conditions

Random Selection A way of ensuring that a sample of people is representative of a population, by giving everyone in the population an equal chance of being selected for the sample

Rationalization Trap The potential for dissonance reduction to produce a succession of self-justifications that ultimately result in a chain of stupid or immoral actions

Realistic Conflict Theory The theory that limited resources lead to conflict among groups and result in increased prejudice and discrimination

Reciprocal Liking When you like someone and that person also likes you

Reciprocity Norm A social norm by which the receipt of something positive from another person requires you to reciprocate, or behave similarly, in response

Reconstructive Memory The process by which memories of an event become distorted by information encountered after the event has occurred

Recovered Memories Recollections of an event, such as sexual abuse, that have been forgotten or repressed

Relationship-Oriented Leader A leader who is concerned primarily with the feelings of and relationships among the workers

Relative Deprivation The perception that you have less than you deserve, less than what you have been led to expect, or less than what people similar to you have

Replication Repeating a study, generally with different subject populations, in different settings, or by using different methods

Representativeness Heuristic A mental shortcut whereby people classify something according to how similar it is to a typical case

Retrieval The process by which people recall information stored in their memory

Reward/Cost Ratio The notion that there is a balance between the rewards that come from a relationship and the personal cost of maintaining the relationship; if the ratio is not favourable, the result is dissatisfaction with the relationship

Schemas Mental structures people use to organize their knowledge about the social world around themes or subjects and that influence the information people notice, think about, and remember

Secure Attachment Style An attachment style characterized by trust, a lack of concern with being abandoned, and the view that one is worthy and well liked

Self-Affirmation Theory A theory suggesting that people will reduce the impact of a dissonance-arousing threat to their self-concept by focusing on and affirming their competence on some dimension unrelated to the threat

Self-Awareness The act of thinking about ourselves

Self-Awareness Theory The idea that when people focus their attention on themselves, they evaluate and compare their behaviour with their internal standards and values

Self-Concept The contents of the self; that is, our knowledge about who we are

Self-Discrepancy Theory The theory that we become distressed when our sense of who we truly are—our actual self—is discrepant from our personal standards or desired self-conceptions

Self-Efficacy The belief in one's ability to carry out specific actions that produce desired outcomes

Self-Enhancement An unrealistically positive view of oneself

Self-Esteem People's evaluations of their own self-worth—that is, the extent to which they view themselves as good, competent, and decent

Self-Fulfilling Prophecy The case whereby people have an expectation about what another person is like, which influences how they act toward that person, which, in turn, causes that person to behave consistently with their original expectations

Self-Perception Theory The theory that when our attitudes and feelings are uncertain or ambiguous, we infer these states by observing our behaviour and the situation in which it occurs

Self-Reference Effect The tendency for people to remember information better if they relate it to themselves

Self-Schemas An organized body of knowledge about the self (e.g., attitudes, preferences, traits) that influences what people notice, think about, and remember about themselves

Self-Serving Attributions Explanations for one's successes that credit internal, dispositional factors and explanations for one's failures that blame external, situational factors

Self-Verification Theory A theory suggesting that people have a need to seek confirmation of their self-concept, whether the self-concept is positive or negative; in some circumstances, this tendency can conflict with the desire to uphold a favourable view of oneself

Serotonin A chemical in the brain that may inhibit aggressive impulses

Similarity Attraction to people who are like us

Social Cognition How people think about themselves and the social world; more specifically, how people select, interpret, remember, and use social information

Social Comparison Theory The idea that we learn about our own abilities and attitudes by comparing ourselves with other people

Social Dilemma A conflict in which the most beneficial action for an individual, if chosen by most people, will have harmful effects on everyone

Social Exchange Theory The theory that how people feel about a relationship depends on their perceptions of the rewards and costs of the relationship, the kind of relationship they deserve, and the probability that they could have a better relationship with someone else

Social Facilitation The tendency for people to do better on simple tasks, but worse on complex tasks, when they are in the presence of others and their individual performance can be evaluated

Social Impact Theory The theory that conforming to social influence depends on the strength of the group, its immediacy, and the number of other people in the group

Social Learning Theory The theory that we learn social behaviour (e.g., aggression) by observing others and imitating them

Social Loafing The tendency for people to do worse on simple tasks, but better on complex tasks, when they are in the presence of others and their individual performance cannot be evaluated

Social Norms The implicit or explicit rules a group has for the acceptable behaviours, values, and beliefs of its members

Social Perception The study of how we form impressions of and make inferences about other people

Social Psychology The scientific study of the way in which people's thoughts, feelings, and behaviours are influenced by the real or imagined presence of other people

Social Roles Shared expectations by group members about how particular people in the group are supposed to behave

Social Support The perception that others are responsive and receptive to one's needs

Source Monitoring The process by which people try to identify the source of their memories

Stable Attribution The belief that the cause of an event is a result of factors that will not change over time, as opposed to unstable factors that will change over time

Stereotype A generalization about a group of people in which identical characteristics are assigned to virtually all members of the group, regardless of actual variation among the members

Stereotype Threat The apprehension experienced by members of a minority group that they might behave in a manner that confirms an existing cultural stereotype

Storage The process by which people store in memory information they have acquired from the environment

Stress The negative feelings and beliefs that occur whenever people feel unable to cope with demands from their environment

Subliminal Messages Words or pictures that are not consciously perceived but that supposedly influence people's judgments, attitudes, and behaviours

Surveys Research in which a representative sample of people are asked questions about their attitudes or behaviour

Task-Contingent Rewards Rewards that are given for performing a task, regardless of how well the task is done

Task-Oriented Leader A leader who is concerned more with getting the job done than with the feelings of and relationships among the workers

Tend-and-Befriend Response Responding to stress with nurturant activities designed to protect oneself and one's offspring (tending) and by creating social networks that provide protection from threats (befriending)

Testosterone A male sex hormone associated with aggression

Thanatos According to Freud, an instinctual drive toward death, leading to aggressive actions

Theory An organized set of principles that can be used to explain observed phenomena

Theory of Planned Behaviour A theory that the best predictors of a person's planned, deliberate behaviours are the person's attitudes toward specific behaviours, subjective norms, and perceived behavioural control

Thought Suppression The attempt to avoid thinking about something a person would prefer to forget

Tit-for-Tat Strategy A means of encouraging cooperation by at first acting cooperatively but then always responding the way your opponent did (i.e., cooperatively or competitively)on the previous trial

Transactional Leaders Leaders who set clear, short-term goals and reward people who meet them

Transactive Memory The combined memory of two people that is more efficient than the memory of either individual

Transformational Leaders Leaders who inspire followers to focus on common, long-term goals

Two-Step Process of Attribution Analyzing another person's behaviour first by making an automatic internal attribution and only then thinking about possible situational reasons for the behaviour, after which one may adjust the original internal attribution

Ultimate Attribution Error Our tendency to make dispositional attributions about an entire group of people

Upward Social Comparison The process whereby we compare ourselves with people who are better than we are on a particular trait or ability

Urban-Overload Hypothesis The theory that because people living in cities are constantly being bombarded with stimulation, they keep to themselves to avoid being overloaded by it

Yale Attitude Change Approach The study of the conditions under which people are most likely to change their attitudes in response to persuasive messages; researchers in this tradition focus on "who said what to whom"—that is, on the source of the communication, the nature of the communication, and the nature of the audience

References

Abada, T., Hou, F., & Ram, B. (2008). The effects of harassment and victimization on self-rated health and mental health among Canadian adolescents. *Social Science & Medicine*, 67(4), 557–567.

Abela, J. R. Z., Webb, C. A., Wagner, C., Ho, M-H. R, & Adams, P. (2006). The role of self-criticism, dependency, and hassles in the course of depressive illness: A multiwave longitudinal study. *Personality and Social Psychology Bulletin*, *32*, 328–338.

Abelson, R. P., Kinder, D. R., Peters, M. D., & Fiske, S. T. (1982). Affective and semantic components in political person perception. *Journal of Personality and Social Psychology*, *42*, 619–630.

Aboud, F. E., & Doyle, A.B. (1996). Does talk of race foster prejudice or tolerance in children? *Canadian Journal of Behavioural Science*, *28*, 161–170.

Abrahamse, W., Steg, L., Gifford, R., & Vlek, C. (2009). Factors influencing car use for commuting and the intention to reduce it: A question of self-interest or morality? *Transportation Research Part F: Traffic Psychology and Behaviour*, *12*(4), 317–324.

Abrahamse, W., Steg, L., & Vlek, C. (2005). A review of intervention studies aimed at household energy conservation. *Journal of Environmental Psychology*, *25*, 273–291.

Abrahamse, W., Steg, L., Vlek, C., & Rothengatter, T. (2005). A review of intervention studies aimed at household energy conservation. *Journal of Environmental Psychology*, *25*, 273–291.

Abrams, D., Marques, J. M., Bown, N., & Henson, M. (2000). Pro-norm and anti-norm deviance within and between groups. *Journal of Personality and Social Psychology*, *78*, 906–912.

Abrams, D., Wetherell, M., Cochrane, S., Hogg, M. A., & Turner, J. C. (1990). Knowing what to think by knowing who you are: Self-categorization and the nature of norm formation, conformity, and group polarization. *British Journal of Social Psychology*, *29*, 97–119.

Abramson, L. Y., Seligman, M. E. P., & Teasdale, J. D. (1978). Learned helplessness in humans: Critique and reformulation. *Journal of Abnormal Psychology*, *87*, 49–74.

Adams, G., Anderson, S. L., & Adonu, J. K. (2004). The cultural grounding of closeness and intimacy. In D. J. Mashek & A. Aron (Eds.), *Handbook of Closeness and Intimacy* (pp. 321–342). Mahwah, NJ: Lawrence Erlbaum Associates.

Adams, G., Garcia, D. M., Purdie-Vaughns, V., & Steele, C. M. (2006). The detrimental effects of a suggestion of sexism in an instruction situation. *Journal of Experimental Social Psychology*, *42*, 602–615.

Adlaf, E. M., Demers, A., & Gliksman, L. (Eds). (2005). Canadian Campus Survey 2004. CAMH. Toronto, ON: Centre for Addiction and Mental Health.

Adlaf, E. M., Gliksman, L., Demers, A., & Newton-Taylor, B. (2001). The prevalence of elevated psychological distress among Canadian undergraduates: Findings from the 1998 Canadian Campus Survey. *Journal of American College Health*, *50*, 67–72.

Adlag, R. J., & Fuller, S. R. (1993). Beyond fiasco: A reappraisal of the groupthink phenomenon and a new model of group decision processes. *Psychological Bulletin*, *113*, 533–552.

Agrell, S. (2008, April 19). The perils of legislating a healthy aesthetic. *Globe and Mail*. Retrieved form www.theglobeandmail.com/servlet/story/RTGAM.20080419.wthinNEW0419_2/BNStory/specialScienceandHealth/home

Ahlfinger, N. R., & Esser, J. K. (2001). Testing the groupthink model: Effects of promotional leadership and conformity predisposition. *Social Behavior and Personality*, *29*, 31–41.

Aiello, J. R., & Douthitt, E. A. (2001). Social facilitation from Triplett to electronic performance monitoring. *Group Dynamics: Theory, Research, and Practice*, *5*, 163–80.

Ainsworth, M. D. S., Blehar, M. C., Waters, E., & Wall, S. (1978). *Patterns of attachment: A psychological study of the strange situation*. Hillsdale, NJ: Erlbaum.

Ajzen, I. (1985). From intentions to actions: A theory of planned behavior. In J. Kuhl & J. Beckmann (Eds.), *Action-control: From cognition to behavior* (pp. 11–39). Heidelberg, Germany: Springer.

Ajzen, I. (2001). Nature and operation of attitudes. *Annual Review of Psychology*, *52*, 27–58.

Ajzen, I., & Fishbein, M. (1980). *Understanding attitudes and predicting social behavior*. Englewood Cliffs, NJ: Prentice Hall.

Ajzen, I., & Fishbein, M. (2005). The influence of attitudes on behavior. In D. Albarracín, B. T. Johnson, & M. P. Zanna (Eds.), *The handbook of attitudes* (pp. 173–221). Mahwah, NJ: Erlbaum.

Ajzen, I., & Sexton, J. (1999). Depth of processing, belief congruence, and attitude-behavior correspondence. In S. Chaiken & Y. Trope (Eds.), *Dual-process theories in social psychology* (pp. 117–138). New York: Guilford Press.

Akert, R. M. (1998). *Terminating romantic relationships: The role of personal responsibility and gender*. Unpublished manuscript, Wellesley College.

Albarracín, D., Durantini, M. R., & Earl, A. N. (2006). Empirical and theoretical conclusions of an analysis of outcomes of HIV-prevention interventions. *Current Directions in Psychological Science*, *15*, 73–78.

Albarracín, D., Gillette, J. C., Earl, A. N., Glasman, L. R., Durantini, M. R., & Ho, M. (2005). A test of major assumptions about behavior change: A comprehensive look at the effects of passive and active HIV-prevention interventions since the beginning of the epidemic. *Psychological Bulletin*, *131*, 856–897.

Albright, L., & Forziati, C. (1995). Cross-situational consistency and perceptual accuracy in leadership. *Personality and Social Psychology Bulletin*, *21*, 1269–1276.

Alksnis, C., Desmarais, S., & Curtis, J. (2008). Workforce segregation and the gender wage gap: Is 'women's' work valued as highly as 'men's'? *Journal of Applied Social Psychology*, *38*(6), 1416–1441.

Allen, V. L., & Levine, J. M. (1969). Consensus and conformity. *Journal of Personality and Social Psychology*, *5*, 389–399.

Allison, K. R., Dwyer, J. M., & Makin, S. (1999). Self-efficacy and participation in vigorous physical activity by high school students. *Health Education and Behavior*, *26*, 12–24.

Allison, P. D. (1992). The cultural evolution of beneficient norms. *Social Forces*, *71*, 279–301.

Allport, G. (1954). *The nature of prejudice*. Reading, MA: Addison-Wesley.

Allport, G. W. (1985). The historical background of social psychology. In G. Lindzey & E. Aronson (Eds.), *The handbook of social psychology* (Vol. 1, pp. 1–46). Reading, MA: Addison-Wesley.

Altemeyer, B. (1981). *Right-wing authoritarianism*. Winnipeg, MB: The University of Manitoba Press.

Altemeyer, B. (1988). *Enemies of freedom: Understanding right-wing authoritarianism*. San Francisco, CA: Jossey-Bass Publishers.

Altemeyer, B. (1996). *The authoritarian specter*. Cambridge, MA: Harvard University Press.

Altemeyer, B. (1998). The other "authoritarian personality." In M. P. Zanna (Ed.), *Advances in experimental social psychology* (Vol. 30). San Diego, CA: Academic Press Limited.

Altemeyer, B. (2001). Changes in attitudes toward homosexuals. *Journal of Homosexuality, 42*, 63–75.

Altemeyer, B., & Hunsberger, B. (1992). Authoritarianism, religious fundamentalism, quest, and prejudice. *The International Journal for the Psychology of Religion, 2*, 113–133.

Altemeyer, B., & Hunsberger, B. (1993). Reply to Gorsuch. *International Journal for the Psychology of Religion, 3*, 33–37.

Amato, P. R. (1983). Helping behavior in urban and rural environments: Field studies based on a taxonomic organization of helping episodes. *Journal of Personality and Social Psychology, 45*, 571–586.

Ambady, N., Bernieri, F. J., & Richeson, J. A. (2000). Toward a histology of social behavior: Judgmental accuracy from thin slices of the behavioral stream. In M. P. Zanna (Ed.), *Advances in experimental social psychology* (Vol. 32, pp. 201–271). San Diego, CA: Academic Press.

Ambady, N., & Rosenthal, R. (1992). Thin slices of expressive behavior as predictors of interpersonal consequences: A meta-analysis. *Psychological Bulletin, 111*, 256–274.

Ambady, N., & Rosenthal, R. (1993). Half a minute: Predicting teacher evaluations from thin slices of nonverbal behavior and physical attractiveness. *Journal of Personality and Social Psychology, 64*, 431–441.

American Psychological Association. (2003). *Ethical principles of psychologists and code of conduct.* Retrieved from *www.apa.org/ethics*

Amiot, C. E., & Bourhis, R. Y. (2003). Discrimination and the positive-negative asymmetry effects: Ideological and normative process. *Personality and Social Psychology Bulletin, 29*:5, 597–608.

Amiot, C. E., Vallerand, R. J., & Blanchard, C. M. (2006). Passion and psychological adjustment: A test of the person-environment fit hypothesis. *Personality and Social Psychology Bulletin, 32*, 220–229.

Amir, I. (1969). Contact hypothesis in ethnic relations. *Psychological Bulletin, 71*, 319–342.

Amir, Y. (1976). The role of intergroup contact in change of prejudice and ethnic relations. In P. Katz (Ed.), *Towards the elimination of racism*. New York: Pergamon Press.

Andersen, B., Farrar, W.B., Golden-Kreutz, D.M., Glaser, R., Emery, C. F., & Crespin, T.R. (2004). Psychological, behavioral, and immune changes after a psychological intervention: A clinical trial. *Journal of Clinical Oncology, 22*, 3570–3580.

Andersen, S. M. (1984). Self-knowledge and social inference: II. The diagnosticity of cognitive/affective and behavioral data. *Journal of Personality and Social Psychology, 46*, 294–307.

Andersen, S. M., & Bem, S. L. (1981). Sex typing and androgyny in dyadic interaction: Individual differences in responsiveness to physical attractiveness. *Journal of Personality and Social Psychology, 41*, 74–86.

Andersen, S. M., & Klatzky, R. L. (1987). Traits and social stereotypes: Levels of categorization in person perception. *Journal of Personality and Social Psychology, 53*, 235–246.

Andersen, S. M., & Ross, L. D. (1984). Self-knowledge and social inference: I. The impact of cognitive/affective and behavioral data. *Journal of Personality and Social Psychology, 46*, 280–293.

Anderson, C. A. (1995). Implicit personality theories and empirical data: Biased assimilation, belief perseverance and change, and covariation detection sensitivity. *Social Cognition, 13*, 25–48.

Anderson, C. A. (1999). Attributional style, depression, and loneliness: A cross-cultural comparison of American and Chinese students. *Personality and Social Psychology Bulletin, 25*, 482–499.

Anderson, C. A., & Anderson, D. C. (1984). Ambient temperature and violent crime: Tests of the linear and curvilinear hypotheses. *Journal of Personality and Social Psychology, 46*, 91–97.

Anderson, C. A., Bushman, B. J., & Groom, R. W. (1997). Hot years and serious and deadly assault: Empirical tests of the heat hypothesis. *Journal of Personality and Social Psychology, 73*, 1213–1223.

Anderson, C. A., Carnagey, N. L., & Eubanks, J. (2003). Exposure to violent media: The effects of songs with violent lyrics of aggressive thoughts and feelings. *Journal of Personality and Social Psychology, 84*, 960–971.

Anderson, C. A., & Dill, K. E. (2000). Video games and aggressive thoughts, feelings, and behavior in the laboratory and in life. *Journal of Personality and Social Psychology, 78*, 772–790.

Anderson, C. A., Lepper, M. R., & Ross, L. (1980). The perseverance of social theories: The role of explanation in the persistence of discredited information. *Journal of Personality and Social Psychology, 39*, 1037–1049.

Anderson, C. A., & Lindsay, J. J. (1998). The development, perseverance, and change of naive theories. *Social Cognition, 16*, 8–30.

Anderson, J. L., Crawford, C. B., Nadeau, J., & Lindberg, T. (1992). Was the Duchess of Windsor right? A cross-cultural review of the socioecology of ideals of female body shape. *Ethology and Sociobiology, 13*, 197–227.

Anderson, J. E., Kay, A. C., & Fitzsimons, G. M. (2010). In search of the silver lining: The justice motive fosters perceptions of benefits in the later lives of tragedy victims. *Psychological Science, 21*(11), 1599–1604.

Anthony, D. B., Holmes, J. G., & Wood, J. V. (2007). Social acceptance and self-esteem: Tuning the sociometer to interpersonal value. *Journal of Personality and Social Psychology, 92*, 1024–1039.

Antoni, M. H., & Lutgendorf, S. (2007). Psychosocial factors and disease progression in cancer. *Current Directions in Psychological Science, 16*, 42–46.

Aquino, K., Reed, A., II, Thau, S., & Freeman, D. (2007). A grotesque and dark beauty: How moral identity and mechanisms of moral disengagement influence cognitive and emotional reactions to war. *Journal of Experimental Social Psychology, 43*, 385–392.

Arbour-Nicitopoulos, K. P., Kwan, M. W., Lowe, D., Taman, S., & Faulkner, G. J. (2010). Social norms of alcohol, smoking, and marijuana use within a Canadian university setting. *Journal of American College Health, 59*(3), 191–196.

Archer, D. (1997). Unspoken diversity: Cultural differences in gestures. *Qualitative Sociology, 20*, 79–105.

Archer, D., & Akert, R. M. (1980). The encoding of meaning: A test of three theories of social interaction. *Sociological Inquiry, 50*(3–4), 393–419.

Archer, D., & Akert, R. M. (1984). Problems of context and criterion in nonverbal communication: A new look at the accuracy issue. In M. Cook (Ed.), *Issues in person perception* (pp. 114–144). London and New York: Methuen.

Archer, D., & Gartner, R. (1976). Violent acts and violent times: A comparative approach to postwar homicide rates. *American Sociological Review, 41*, 937–963.

Archer, D., & Gartner, R. (1984). *Violence and crime in cross-national perspective*. New Haven, CT: Yale University Press.

Archer, D., & McDaniel, P. (1995). Violence and gender: Differences and similarities across societies. In R. B. Ruback & N. A. Weiner (Eds.), *Interpersonal violent behaviors: social and cultural aspects* (pp. 63–88). New York: Springer Publishing.

Archer, J. (2000). Sex differences in aggression between heterosexual partners: A meta-analytic review. *Psychological Bulletin, 126*, 651–680.

Arendt, H. (1965). *Eichmann in Jerusalem: A report on the banality of evil.* New York: Viking.

Arkes, H. R., & Mellers, B. A. (2002). Do juries meet our expectations? *Law and Human Behavior, 26*, 625–639.

Armor, D. A., & Taylor, S. E. (1998). Situated optimism: Specific outcome expectancies and self-regulation. In M. P. Zanna (Ed.), *Advances in experimental social psychology* (Vol. 30, pp. 309–379). San Diego, CA: Academic Press.

Arms, R. L., Russell, G. W., & Sandilands, M. L. (1979). Effects on the hostility of spectators of viewing aggressive sports. *Social Psychology Quarterly, 42*, 275–279.

Armstrong, L. (2000). *It's not about the bike: My journey back to life.* New York: Putnam.

Arnett, J. (1995). The young and the reckless: Adolescent reckless behavior. Current Directions in *Psychological Science, 4*(June), 67–71.

Arnocky, S., Stroink, M., & De Cicco, T. (2007). Self-construal predicts environmental concern, cooperation, and conservation. *Journal of Environmental Psychology, 27*(4), 255–264.

Arnold, K. A., Turner, N., Barling, J., Kelloway, E., & McKee, M. C. (2007). Transformational leadership and psychological well-being: The mediating role of meaningful work. *Journal of Occupational Health Psychology, 12*(3), 193–203.

Aron, A., & Aron, E. N. (1986a). Falling in love: Prospective studies of self-concept change. *Journal of Personality and Social Psychology, 69*, 1102–1112.

Aron, A., & Aron, E. N. (1986b). *Love and the expansion of the self.* New York: Hemisphere.

Aron, A., & Aron, E. N. (1996). Self and self-expansion in relationships. In G. J. O. Fletcher & J. Fitness (Eds.), *Knowledge structures in close relationships: A social psychological approach* (pp. 325–344). Mahwah, NJ: Erlbaum.

Aron, A., Fisher, H. E., Strong, G., Acevedo, B., Riela, S., & Tsapelas, I. (2008). Falling in love. In S. Sprecher, A. Wenzel, & J. Harvey (Eds.), *Handbook of relationship initiation* (pp. 315–336). New York: Taylor & Francis.

Aron, A., Mashek, D., & Aron, E. N. (2004). Closeness, intimacy, and including the other in the self. In D. Mashek & A. Aron (Eds.), *Handbook of closeness and intimacy* (pp. 27–41). Mahwah, NJ: Lawrence Erlbaum.

Aron, A., & Westbay, L. (1996). Dimensions of the prototype of love. *Journal of Personality and Social Psychology, 70*, 535–551.

Aronson, E. (1968). Dissonance theory: Progress and problems. In R. P. Abelson, E. Aronson, W. J. McGuire, T. M. Newcomb, M. J. Rosenberg, and P. H. Tannenbaum (Eds.), *Theories of cognitive consistency: A sourcebook* (pp. 5–27). Chicago, IL: Rand McNally.

Aronson, E. (1969). The theory of cognitive dissonance: A current perspective. In L. Berkowitz (Ed.), *Advances in experimental social psychology* (Vol. 4, pp. 1–34). New York: Academic Press.

Aronson, E. (1990). Applying social psychology to prejudice reduction and energy conservation. *Personality and Social Psychology Bulletin, 16*, 118–132.

Aronson, E. (1992). Stateways can change folkways. In R. Baird & S. Rosenbaum (Eds.), *Bigotry, prejudice and hatred: Definitions, causes and solutions.* Buffalo, NY: Prometheus Books.

Aronson, E. (1997a). The giving away of psychology—and condoms. *APS Observer, 10*, 17–35.

Aronson, E. (1997b). The theory of cognitive dissonance: The evolution and vicissitudes of an idea. In C. McGarty & S. Alexander Haslam (Eds.), *The message of social psychology: Perspectives on mind in society* (pp. 20–35). Oxford, UK: Blackwell.

Aronson, E. (1998). Dissonance, hypocrisy, and the self-concept. In E. Harmon-Jones & J. S. Mills (Eds.), *Cognitive dissonance theory: Revival with revisions and controversies.* Washington, DC: American Psychological Association.

Aronson, E. (2000). *Nobody left to hate: Teaching compassion after Columbine.* New York: Worth/Freeman.

Aronson, E. (2002). Drifting my own way: Following my nose and my heart. In R. Sternberg (Ed.), *Psychologists defying the crowd: Stories of those who battled the establishment and won* (pp. 3–31). Washington, DC: American Psychological Association.

Aronson, E., & Bridgeman, D. (1979). Jigsaw groups and the desegregated classroom: In pursuit of common goals. *Personality and Social Psychology Bulletin, 5*, 438–446.

Aronson, E., & Carlsmith, J. M. (1963). Effect of severity of threat in the devaluation of forbidden behavior. *Journal of Abnormal and Social Psychology, 66*, 584–588.

Aronson, E., & Carlsmith, J. M. (1968). Experimentation in social psychology. In G. Lindzey & E. Aronson (Eds.), *The handbook of social psychology* (Vol. 2, pp. 1–79). Reading, MA: Addison-Wesley.

Aronson, E., Chase, T., Helmreich, R., & Ruhnke, R. (1974). A two-factor theory of dissonance reduction: The effect of feeling stupid or feeling awful on opinion change. *International Journal for Research and Communication, 3*, 59–74.

Aronson, E., Ellsworth, P. C., Carlsmith, J. M., & Gonzalez, M. H. (1990). *Methods of research in social psychology* (2nd ed.). New York: McGraw-Hill.

Aronson, E., Fried, C., & Stone, J. (1991). Overcoming denial and increasing the intention to use condoms through the induction of hypocrisy. *American Journal of Public Health, 81*, 1636–1638.

Aronson, E., & Gonzales, M. (1990). The social psychology of energy conservation. In J. Edwards (Ed.), *Social influence processes and prevention.* New York: Plenum.

Aronson, E., & Gonzalez, A. (1988). Desegregation, jigsaw, and the Mexican-American experience. In P. A. Katz & D. Taylor (Eds.), *Towards the elimination of racism: Profiles in controversy* (pp. 310–30). New York: Plenum.

Aronson, E., & Mettee, D. (1968). Dishonest behavior as a function of differential levels of induced self-esteem. *Journal of Personality and Social Psychology, 9*, 121–127.

Aronson, E., & Mills, J. (1959). The effect of severity of initiation on liking for a group. *Journal of Abnormal and Social Psychology, 59*, 177–181.

Aronson, E., & Patnoe, S. (1997). *Cooperation in the classroom: The jigsaw method.* New York: Longman.

Aronson, E., Stephan, C., Sikes, J., Blaney, N., & Snapp, M. (1978). *The jigsaw classroom.* Beverly Hills, CA: Sage.

Aronson, E., Wilson, T. D., & Akert, R. M. (2007). *Social psychology.* Upper Saddle River, NJ: Pearson/Prentice Hall.

Aronson, E., Wilson, T. D., & Brewer, M. (1998). Experimental methods. In D. Gilbert, S. Fiske, & G. Lindzey (Eds.), *The handbook of social psychology* (4th ed., Vol. 1, pp. 99–142). New York: Random House.

Aronson, E., & Yates, S. (1985). Social psychological aspects of energy conservation. In D. Hafemeister, H. Kelly, & B. Levi (Eds.), *Energy sources: Conservation and renewables* (pp. 81–91). New York: American Institute of Physics Press.

Aronson, J., Jannone, S., McGlone, M., & Johnson-Campbell, T. (2009). The Obama effect: An experimental test. *Journal of Experimental Social Psychology, 45*(4), 957–960.

Aronson, J., & Williams, J. (2004). *Stereotype threat: Forewarned is forearmed.* New York: New York University.

Aronson, J. M., Cohen, J., & Nail, P. (1998). Self-affirmation theory: An update and appraisal. In E. Harmon-Jones & J. S. Mills (Eds.), *Cognitive dissonance theory: Revival with revisions and controversies.* Washington, DC: American Psychological Association.

Aronson, J. M., Lustina, M. J., Good, C., Keough, K., Steele, C. M., & Brown, J. (1999). When white men can't do math: Necessary and sufficient factors in stereotype threat. *Journal of Experimental Social Psychology, 35*, 29–46.

Aronson, J. M., Quinn, D., & Spencer, S. (1998). Stereotype threat and the academic underperformance of women and minorities. In J. K. Swim & C. Stangor (Eds.), *Stigma: The target's perspective* (pp. 83–103). San Diego, CA: Academic Press.

Arthur, B. (2008, August 12). Humidity wears down Dancevic. *National Post*, p. B3.

Arthur, K. (2006, April 11). A new fugue for handicappers: Interactive and unpredictable, 'American Idol.' *New York Times*, p. B3.

Asch, S. E. (1946). Forming impressions of personality. *Journal of Abnormal and Social Psychology, 41*, 258–290.

Asch, S. E. (1951). Effects of group pressure upon the modification and distortion of judgment. In H. Guetzkow (Ed.), *Groups, leadership, and men*. Pittsburgh, PA: Carnegie Press.

Asch, S. E. (1955). Opinions and social pressure. *Scientific American, 193*, 31–35.

Asch, S. E. (1956). Studies of independence and conformity: A minority of one against a unanimous majority. *Psychological Monographs, 70*, 9 (Whole No. 416).

Asch, S. E. (1957). An experimental investigation of group influence. In *Symposium on preventive and social psychiatry* (pp. 15–17). Walter Reed Army Institute of Research. Washington, DC: U.S. Government Printing Office.

Ashmore, R. D., Solomon, M. R., & Longo, L. C. (1996). Thinking about fashion models' looks: A multidimensional approach to the structure of perceived physical attractiveness. *Personality and Social Psychology Bulletin, 22*, 1083–1104.

Aspenlieder, L., Buchanan, C. M., McDougall, P., & Sippola, L. K. (2009). Gender nonconformity and peer victimization in pre- and early adolescence. *European Journal of Developmental Science, 3*(1), 3–16.

Aspinwall, L. G., & Taylor, S. E. (1993). Effects of social comparison direction, threat, and self-esteem on affect, evaluation, and expected success. *Journal of Personality and Social Psychology, 64*, 708–722.

Aspinwall, L. G., & Taylor, S. E. (1997). A stitch in time: Self-regulation and proactive coping. *Psychological Bulletin, 121*, 417–436.

Associated Press. (2000, April 3). Parents led kids to death: Childhood seen as sinful by cult.

Associated Press (2002, November 1). Halloween is debated by French. *Boston Globe*, p. A20.

Atlas, R. S., & Pepler, D. J. (1998). Observations of bullying in the classroom. *Journal of Educational Research, 92*, 86–99.

Aune, K. S., & Aune, R. K. (1996). Cultural differences in the self-reported experience and expression of emotions in relationships. *Journal of Cross-Cultural Psychology, 27*, 67–81.

Aviezer, H., Hassin, R. R., Ryan, J., Grady, C., Susskind, J., Anderson, A., . . . Bentin, S. (2008). Angry, disgusted, or afraid? Studies on the malleability of emotion perception. *Psychological Science, 19*, 724–732.

Axelrod, R. (1984). *The evolution of cooperation*. New York: Basic Books.

Ayduk, Ö., & Kross, E. (2008). Enhancing the pace of recovery: Self-distanced analysis of negative experiences reduces blood pressure reactivity. *Psychological Science, 19*, 229–231.

Ayman, R., Korabik, K., & Morris, S. (2009). Is transformational leadership always perceived as effective? Male subordinates' devaluation of female transformational leaders. *Journal of Applied Social Psychology, 39*(4), 852–879.

Azrin, N. H. (1967, May). Pain and aggression. *Psychology Today*, 27–33.

Babad, E. (1993). Pygmalion—25 years after interpersonal expectations in the classroom. In P. D. Blank (Ed.), *Interpersonal expectations: Theory, research, and applications* (pp. 125–153). New York: Cambridge University Press.

Back, M. D., Schmukle, S. C., & Egloff, B. (2008). Becoming friends by chance. *Psychological Science, 19*(5), 439–440.

Bader, B., Horman, J., & Lapointe, C. (2010). Fostering community and civic engagement in low-income multicultural schools through transformative leadership. *Exceptionality Education International, 20*(2), 25–37.

Badr, L. K., & Abdallah, B. (2001). Physical attractiveness of premature infants affects outcome at discharge from the NICU. *Infant Behavior and Development, 24*, 129–133.

Bailey, D. S., & Taylor, S. P. (1991). Effects of alcohol and aggressive disposition on human physical aggression. *Journal of Research in Personality, 25*, 334–342.

Bailey, W. C., & Peterson, R. D. (1997). Murder, capital punishment, and deterrence: A review of the literature. In H. A. Bedau (Ed.), *The death penalty in America: Current controversies* (pp. 135–161). New York: Oxford University Press.

Bailis, D. S., Chipperfield, J. G., Perry, R. P., Newall, N. E., & Haynes, T. L. (2008). Exploring the commonalities between adaptive resources and self-enhancement in older adults' comparative judgments of physical activity. *Journal of Aging and Health, 20*(8), 899–919.

Bailis, D. S., & Segall, A. (2004). Self-determination and social comparison in a health-promotion setting. *Basic and Applied Social Psychology, 26*, 25–33.

Balcetis, E., & Dunning, D. A. (2008). A mile in moccasins: How situational experience diminishes dispositionism in social inference. *Personality and Social Psychology Bulletin, 34*(1), 102–114.

Baldwin, M. W. (1992). Relational schemas and the processing of social information. *Psychological Bulletin, 112*, 461–484.

Baldwin, M. W., Carrell, S. E., & Lopez, D. F. (1990). Priming relationship schemas: My advisor and the pope are watching me from the back of my mind. *Journal of Experimental Social Psychology, 26*, 435–454.

Baldwin, M. W., & Fehr, B. (1995). On the instability of attachment style ratings. *Personal Relationships, 2*, 247–261.

Baldwin, M. W., Fehr, B., Keedian, E., Seidel, M., & Thomson, D. W. (1993). An exploration of the relational schemata underlying attachment styles: Self-report and lexical decision approaches. *Personality and Social Psychology Bulletin, 19*, 746–754.

Baldwin, M. W., Granzberg, A., Pippus, L., & Pritchard, E. T. (2003). Cued activation of relational schemas: Self-evaluation and gender effects. *Canadian Journal of Behavioural Science, 35*, 153–163.

Baldwin, M. W., & Holmes, J. O. (1987). Salient private audiences and awareness of the self. *Journal of Personality and Social Psychology, 52*, 1087–1098.

Baldwin, M. W., Keelan, J. P. R., Fehr, B., Enns, V., & Koh-Rangarajoo, E. (1996). Social-cognitive conceptualizations of attachment working models: Availability and accessibility effects. *Journal of Personality and Social Psychology, 71*, 94–109.

Baldwin, M. W., & Meunier, J. (1999). The cued activation of attachment relational schemas. *Social Cognition, 17*, 209–227.

Baldwin, M. W., & Sinclair, L. (1996). Self-esteem and "if . . . then" contingencies of interpersonal acceptance. *Journal of Personality and Social Psychology, 71*, 1130–1141.

Balfour, L., Corace, K., Tasca, G. A., Tremblay, C., Routy, J., & Angel, J. B. (2010). Altruism motivates participation in a therapeutic HIV vaccine trial (CTN 173). *AIDS Care, 22*(11), 1403–1409.

Ballard, E. J., & Suedfeld, P. (1988). Performance ratings of Canadian prime ministers: Individual and situational factors. *Political Psychology, 9*, 291–302.

Bandura, A. (1973). *Aggression: A social learning analysis*. Englewood Cliffs, NJ: Prentice Hall.

Bandura, A. (1997). *Self-efficacy: The exercise of control*. New York: Freeman.

Bandura, A., Cioffi, D., Taylor, C. B., & Brouillard, M. E. (1988). Perceived self-efficacy in coping with cognitive stressors and opioid activation. *Journal of Personality and Social Psychology, 55*, 479–488.

Bandura, A., & Locke, E. A. (2003). Negative self-efficacy and goal effects revisited. *Journal of Applied Psychology, 88*, 87–99.

Bandura, A., Ross, D., & Ross, S. (1961). Transmission of aggression through imitation of aggressive models. *Journal of Abnormal and Social Psychology, 63*, 575–582.

Bandura, A., Ross, D., & Ross, S. (1963). Imitation of film-mediated aggressive models. *Journal of Abnormal and Social Psychology, 66*, 3–11.

Bane, C. H., Cornish, M., Erspamer, N., & Kampman, L. (2010). Self-disclosure through weblogs and perceptions of online and 'real-life' friendships among female bloggers. *Cyberpsychology, Behavior, and Social Networking, 13*(2), 131–139.

Banks, T., & Dabbs, J. M., Jr. (1996). Salivary testosterone and cortisol in delinquent and violent urban subculture. *Journal of Social Psychology, 136*, 49–56.

Banse, R., Gawronski, B., Rebetez, C., Gutt, H., & Morton, J. (2010). The development of spontaneous gender stereotyping in childhood: Relations to stereotype knowledge and stereotype flexibility. *Developmental Science, 13*(2), 298–306.

Barata, P. C., & Stewart, D. E. (2010). Searching for housing as a battered woman: Does discrimination affect reported availability of a rental unit? *Psychology of Women Quarterly, 34*(1), 43–55.

Barbéra, E. (2003). Gender schemas: Configuration and activation process. *Canadian Journal of Behavioural Science, 35*, 176–184.

Bargh, J. A. (1994). The four horseman of automaticity: Awareness, intention, efficiency, and control in social cognition. In R. S. Wyer, Jr. & T. K. Srull (Eds.), *Handbook of Social Cognition* (Vol. 1, pp. 1–40). Hillsdale, NJ: Erlbaum.

Bargh, J. A. (1996). Automaticity in social psychology. In E. T. Higgins & A. W. Kruglanski (Eds.), *Social psychology: Handbook of basic principles* (pp. 169–183). New York: Guilford.

Bargh, J. A. (Ed). (2007). *Social psychology and the unconscious: The automaticity of higher mental processes*. Philadelphia, PA: Psychology Press.

Bargh, J. A., & Chartrand, T. L. (1999). The unbearable automaticity of being. *American Psychologist, 54*, 462–479.

Bargh, J. A., & Ferguson, M. J. (2000). Beyond behaviorism: On the automaticity of higher mental processes. *Psychological Bulletin, 126*, 925–945.

Bargh, J. A., Gollwitzer, P. M., Lee-Chai, A., Barndollar, K., & Trötschel, R. (2001). The automated will: Nonconscious activation and pursuit of behavioral goals. *Journal of Personality and Social Psychology, 81*, 1014–1027.

Bargh, J. A., & McKenna, K. Y. A. (2004). The internet and social life. *Annual Review of Psychology, 55*, 573–590.

Bargh, J. A., & McKenna, K. Y. A., & Fitzsimons, G. M. (2002). Can you see the real me? Activation and expression of the "true self" on the Internet. *Journal of Social Issues, 58*, 33–48.

Bargh, J. A., & Morsella, E. (2008). The unconscious mind. *Perspectives on Psychological Science, 3*, 73–79.

Bargh, J. A., & Pietromonaco, P. (1982). Automatic information processing and social perception: The influence of trait information presented outside of conscious awareness on impression formation. *Journal of Personality and Social Psychology, 43*, 437–49.

Barker, R., Dembo, T., & Lewin, K. (1941). Frustration and aggression: An experiment with young children. *University of Iowa Studies in Child Welfare, 18*, 1–314.

Barley, S. R., & Bechky, B. A. (1994). In the backrooms of science: The work of technicians in science labs. *Work and Occupations, 21*, 85–126.

Baron, R. A. (1972). Reducing the influence of an aggressive model: The restraining effects of peer censure. *Journal of Experimental Social Psychology, 8*, 266–275.

Baron, R. A. (1976). The reduction of human aggression: A field study on the influence of incompatible responses. *Journal of Applied Social Psychology, 6*, 95–104.

Baron, R. A. (1988). Negative effects of destructive criticism: Impact on conflict, self-efficacy, and task performance. *Journal of Applied Psychology, 73*, 199–207.

Baron, R. A. (1990). Countering the effects of destructive criticism: The relative efficacy of four interventions. *Journal of Applied Psychology, 75*, 235–245.

Baron, R. A. (1997). The sweet smell of . . . helping: Effects of pleasant ambient fragrance on prosocial behavior in shopping malls. *Personality and Social Psychology Bulletin, 23*, 498–503.

Baron, R. A., & Richardson, D. R. (1994). *Human aggression*. (2nd ed). New York: Plenum.

Baron, R. S. (1986). Distraction/conflict theory: Progress and problems. In L. Berkowitz (Ed.), *Advances in experimental social psychology* (Vol. 19, pp. 1–40). Orlando, FL: Academic Press.

Baron, R. S. (2005). So right it's wrong: Groupthink and the ubiquitous nature of polarized group decision making. In M. P. Zanna (Ed.), *Advances in experimental social psychology* (Vol. 37, pp. 219–253). San Diego, CA: Academic Press.

Baron, R. S., Vandello, J. A., & Brunsman, B. (1996). The forgotten variable in conformity research: Impact of task importance on social influence. *Journal of Personality and Social Psychology, 71*, 915–927.

Barrett, L. F., Lane, R. D., Sechrest, L., & Schwartz, G. E. (2000). Sex differences in emotional awareness. *Personality and Social Psychology Bulletin, 26*, 1027–1035.

Barriga, C. A., Shapiro, M. A., & Jhaveri, R. (2009). Media context, female body size and perceived realism. *Sex Roles, 60*, 128–141.

Bartels, A., & Zeki, S. (2000, November 27). The neural basis of romantic love. *Neuroreport, 11*, 3829–3834.

Bartels, A., & Zeki, S. (2004). The neural correlates of maternal and romantic love. *Neuroimage, 21*, 1155–1166.

Bartholomew, K. (1990). Avoidance of intimacy: An attachment perspective. *Journal of Social and Personal Relationships, 7*, 147–178.

Bartholomew, K., & Horowitz, L. M. (1991). Attachment styles among young adults: A test of a four-category model. *Journal of Personality and Social Psychology, 61*, 226–244.

Bartholomew, R., & Wessely, S. (2007). Canada's "toxic bus": The new challenge for law enforcement in the post-9/11 world/Mass psychogenic illness. *Canadian Journal of Criminology and Criminal Justice, 49*, 657–671.

Bartholomew, R. E., & Wessely, S. (2002). Protean nature of mass sociogenic illness: From possessed nuns to chemical and biological terrorism. *British Journal of Psychiatry, 180*, 300–306.

Bartholow, B. D., & Anderson, C. A. (2002). Effects of violent video games on aggressive behavior: Potential sex differences. *Journal of Experimental Social Psychology, 38*, 283–290.

Bartholow, B. D., Anderson, C. A., Carnagey, N. L., & Benjamin, A. J., Jr. (2004). Interactive effects of life experience and situational cues on aggression: The weapons priming effect in hunters and nonhunters. *Journal of Experimental Social Psychology, 41*, 48–60.

Bartlett, D. C. (1932). *Remembering*. Cambridge: Cambridge University Press.

Bartz, J. A., & Lydon, J. E. (2006). Navigating the interdependence dilemma: Attachment goals and the use of communal norms with potential close others. *Journal of Personality and Social Psychology, 91*, 77–96.

Bass, B. M. (1990). *Bass and Stogdill's handbook of leadership: Theory, research, and managerial applications* (3rd ed.). New York: Free Press.

Bass, B. M. (1997). Does the transactional-transformational leadership paradigm transcend organizational and national boundaries? *American Psychologist, 52*, 130–139.

Bass, E., & Davis, L. (1994). *The courage to heal: A guide for women survivors of child sexual abuse* (3rd ed.). New York: HarperCollins.

Bassili, J. N. (2003). The minority slowness effect: Subtle inhibitions in the expression of views not shared by others. *Journal of Personality and Social Psychology, 84*, 261–276.

Bassili, J. N. (2008). Media richness and social norms in the choice to attend lectures or to watch them online. *Journal of Educational Multimedia and Hypermedia, 17*(4), 453-475.

Bassili, J. N., & Brown, R. D. (2005). Implicit and explicit attitudes: Research, challenges, and theory. In D. Albarracín, B. T. Johnson,

& M. P. Zanna (Eds.), *The handbook of attitudes* (pp. 543–574). Mahwah, NJ: Erlbaum.

Batson, C., Ahmad, N., Powell, A., & Stocks, E. (2008). Prosocial motivation. In J. Y. Shah & W. L. Gardner (Eds.), *Handbook of motivation science* (pp. 135–149). New York: Guilford Press.

Batson, C. D. (1991). *The altruism question: Toward a social-psychological answer*. Hillsdale, NJ: Erlbaum.

Batson, C. D. (1998). Altruism and prosocial behavior. In D. Gilbert, S. Fiske, & G. Lindzey (Eds.), *The handbook of social psychology*. (4th ed., Vol. 2, pp. 282–316). New York: McGraw-Hill.

Batson, C. D., & Ahmad, N. (2001). Empathy-induced altruism in a prisoner's dilemma II: What if the target of empathy has defected? *European Journal of Social Psychology, 31*, 25–36.

Batson, C. D., Ahmad, N., & Stocks, E. L. (2004). Benefits and liabilities of empathy-induced altruism. In A. G. Miller (Ed.), *The social psychology of good and evil* (pp. 359–385). New York: Guilford.

Batson, C. D., & Powell, A. A. (2003). Altruism and prosocial behavior. In T. Millon & M. J. Lerner (Eds.), *Handbook of psychology: Personality and social psychology* (Vol. 5, pp. 463–484). New York: Wiley.

Bauer, I., & Wrosch, C. (2011). Making up for lost opportunities: The protective role of downward social comparisons for coping with regrets across adulthood. *Personality and Social Psychology Bulletin, 37*(2), 215–228.

Baumeister, R. F. (1986). *Identity: Cultural change and the struggle for self.* New York: Oxford University Press.

Baumeister, R. (Ed). (1993). *Self-esteem: The puzzle of low self-regard*. New York: Plenum.

Baumeister, R., Vohs, K., & Tice, D. (2007). The strength model of self-control. *Current Directions in Psychological Science, 16*, 351–355.

Baumeister, R. F. (1991). *Escaping the self: Alcoholism, spirituality, masochism, and other flights from the burden of selfhood*. New York: Basic Books.

Baumeister, R. F. (1998). The self. In D. T. Gilbert, S. T. Fiske, & G. Lindzey (Eds.), *The handbook of social psychology* (4th ed., Vol. 1, pp. 680–740). New York: McGraw-Hill.

Baumeister, R. F., & Bratslavsky, E. (1999). Passion, intimacy, and time: Passionate love as a function of change in intimacy. *Personality and Social Psychology Review, 3*, 49–67.

Baumeister, R. F., DeWall, C. N., Ciarocco, N. J., & Twenge, J. M. (2005). Social exclusion impairs self-regulation. *Journal of Personality and Social Psychology, 88*(4), 589–604.

Baumeister, R. F., & Hetherington, T. F. (1996). Self-regulation failure: An overview. *Psychological Inquiry, 7*, 1–15.

Baumeister, R. F., & Leary, M. R. (1995). The need to belong: Desire for interpersonal attachment as a fundamental human motivation. *Psychological Bulletin, 117*, 497–529.

Baumeister, R. F., Muraven, M., & Tice, D. M. (2000). Ego depletion: A resource model of volition, self-regulation, and controlled processing. *Social Cognition, 18*, 130–150.

Baumeister, R. F., & Vohs, K. D. (2003). Self-regulation and the executive function of the self. In M. R. Leary & J. P. Tangney (Eds.), *Handbook of self and identity* (pp. 197–217). New York: Guilford Press.

Baumeister, R. F., & Sommer, K. L. (1997). What do men want? Gender differences and two spheres of belongingness: Comment on Cross and Madson (1997). *Psychological Bulletin, 122*, 38–44.

Baumeister, R. F., Stillwell, A. M., & Heatherton, T. F. (1994). Guilt: An interpersonal approach. *Psychological Bulletin, 115*, 243–267.

Baxter, L. A. (1982). Strategies for ending relationships: Two studies. *Western Journal of Speech Communication, 47*, 85–98.

Baxter, L. A. (1985). Accomplishing relationship disengagement. In S. Duck & D. Perlman (Eds.), *Understanding personal relationships* (pp. 243–265). London, UK: Sage.

Baym, N. K., & Ledbetter, A. (2009). Tunes that bind? Predicting friendship strength in a music-based social network. *Information, Communication & Society, 12*(3), 408–427.

Beaman, A. L., Barnes, P. J., Klentz, B., & McQuirk, B. (1978). Increasing helping rates through informational dissemination: Teaching pays. *Personality and Social Psychology Bulletin, 4*, 406–411.

Beaman, A. L., Klentz, B., Diener, E., & Svanum, S. (1979). Objective self-awareness and transgression in children: A field study. *Journal of Personality and Social Psychology, 37*, 1835–1846.

Bearman, S. K., Stice, E., & Chase, A. (2003). Evaluation of an intervention targeting both depressive symptoms and bulimic pathology: A randomized prevention trial. *Behavior Therapy, 34*, 277–293.

Beaton, A., Tougas, F., Rinfret, N., Huard, N., & Delisle, M. (2007). Strength in numbers? Women and mathematics. *European Journal of Psychology of Education, 22*(3), 291–306.

Beaton, A. M., Tougas, F., & Joly, S.(1996). Neosexism among male managers: Is it really a matter of numbers? *Journal of Applied Social Psychology, 26*, 2189–2203.

Beaupré, M. G., & Hess, U. (2003). In my mind we all smile: A case of in-group favoritism. *Journal of Experimental Social Psychology, 39*, 371–377.

Beaupré, M. G., & Hess, U. (2006). An ingroup advantage for confidence in emotion recognition judgments: The moderating effect of familiarity with the expressions of outgroup members. *Personality and Social Psychology Bulletin, 32*, 16–26.

Becker, D. V., Kenrick, D. T., Neuberg, S. L., Blackwell, K. C., & Smith, D. M. (2007). The confounded nature of angry men and happy women. *Journal of Personality and Social Psychology, 92*(2), 179–190.

Becker, J. C., & Wright, S. C. (2011). Yet another dark side of chivalry: Benevolent sexism undermines and hostile sexism motivates collective action for social change. *Journal of Personality and Social Psychology, 101*(1), 62–77.

Becker, M. H., & Josephs, J. G. (1988). AIDS and behavioral change to reduce risk: A review. *American Journal of Public Health, 78*, 394–410.

Bedau, H. A. (Ed). (1997). *The death penalty in America: Current controversies*. New York: Oxford University Press.

Behrmann, M., Winocur, G., & Moscovitch, M. (1992). Dissociation between mental imagery and object recognition in a brain- damaged patient. *Nature, 359*, 636–637.

Bell, D. W., & Esses, V. (1997). Ambivalence and response amplification toward Native peoples. *Journal of American Social Psychology, 27*, 1063–1084.

Bell, D. W., & Esses, V. M. (2002). Ambivalence and response amplification: A motivational perspective. *Personality and Social Psychology Bulletin, 28*, 1143–1152.

Bell, S. T., Kuriloff, P. J., & Lottes, I. (1994). Understanding attributions of blame in stranger rape and date rape situations: An examination of gender, race, identification, and students' social perceptions of rape victims. *Journal of Applied Social Psychology, 24*, 1719–1734.

Bem, D. J. (1972). Self-perception theory. In L. Berkowitz (Ed.), *Advances in experimental social psychology* (Vol. 6, pp. 1–62). New York: Academic Press.

Benham, G., Woody, E. Z., Wilson, K. S., & Nash, M. R. (2006). Expect the unexpected: Ability, attitude, and responsiveness to hypnosis. *Journal of Personality and Social Psychology, 91*, 342–350.

Benight, C. C., & Bandura, A. (2004). Social cognitive theory of posttraumatic recovery: The role of perceived self-efficacy. *Behaviour Research and Therapy, 42*, 1129–1148.

Ben-Shakhar, G., & Elaad, E. (2003). The validity of psychophysiological detection of information with the guilty knowledge test: A meta-analytic review. *Journal of Applied Psychology, 88*, 131–151.

Berger, I. E. (1997). The demographics of recycling and the structure of environmental behavior. *Environment and Behavior, 29*, 515–531.

Bergeron, C. E., & McKelvie, S. J. (2004). Effects of defendant age on severity of punishment for different crimes. *Journal of Social Psychology, 144*, 75–90.

Bergstrom, R. L., & Neighbors, C. (2006). Body image disturbance and the social norms approach: An integrative review of literature. *Journal of Social and Clinical Psychology, 25*, 995–1020.

Beran, T., Hughes, G., & Lupart, J. (2008). A model of achievement and bullying: Analyses of the Canadian National Longitudinal Survey of Children and Youth data. *Educational Research, 50*(1), 25–39.

Berkow, J. H. (1989). *Darwin, sex, and status: Biological approaches to mind and culture*. Toronto, ON: University of Toronto Press.

Berkowitz, A. D. (2004). An overview of the social norms approach. In L. Lederman & L. Stewart (Eds.), *Changing the culture of college drinking* (pp. 193-214). Cresskill, NJ: Hampton Press.

Berkowitz, L. (1968, September). Impulse, aggression, and the gun. *Psychology Today*, 18–22.

Berkowitz, L. (1978). Whatever happened to the frustration-aggression hypothesis? *American Behavioral Scientist, 21*, 691–708.

Berkowitz, L. (1981, June). How guns control us. *Psychology Today*, 11–12.

Berkowitz, L. (1983). Aversively simulated aggression. *American Psychologist, 38*, 1135–1144.

Berkowitz, L. (1987). Mood, self-awareness, and willingness to help. *Journal of Personality and Social Psychology, 52*, 721–729.

Berkowitz, L. (1988). Frustrations, appraisals, and aversively stimulated aggression. *Aggressive Behavior, 14*, 3–11.

Berkowitz, L. (1989). Frustration-aggression hypothesis: Examination and reformulation. *Psychological Bulletin, 106*, 59–73.

Berkowitz, L. (1993). *Aggression: Its causes, consequences, and control*. New York: McGraw-Hill.

Berkowitz, L., & LePage, A. (1967). Weapons as aggression-eliciting stimuli. *Journal of Personality and Social Psychology, 7*, 202–207.

Berkowitz, L., & Troccoli, B., (1990). Feelings, direction of attention, and expressed evaluations of others. *Cognition and Emotion, 4*, 305–325.

Bernard, M. M., Maio, G. R., & Olson, J. M. (2003). The vulnerability of values to attack: Inoculation of values and value-relevant attitudes. *Personality and Social Psychology Bulletin, 29*, 63–75.

Berns, G. S., Chappelow, J., Zink, C. F., Pagnoni, G., Martin-Skurski, M. E., & Richards, J. (2005). Neurobiological correlates of social conformity and independence during mental rotation. *Biological Psychiatry, 58*, 245–253.

Bernstein, D. M., Erdfelder, E., Meltzoff, A. N., Peria, W., & Loftus, G. R. (2001). Hindsight bias from 3 to 95 years of age. *Journal of Experimental Psychology: Learning, Memory, and Cognition, 37*, 378–391.

Berry, D. S. (1995). Beyond beauty and after affect: An event perception approach to perceiving faces. In R. A. Eder (Ed.), *Craniofacial anomalies: Psychological perspectives* (pp. 48–75). New York: Springer-Verlag.

Berry, J. W. (1967). Independence and conformity in subsistence-level societies. Journal of *Personality and Social Psychology, 7*, 415–418.

Berscheid, E. (1985). Interpersonal attraction. In G. Lindzey & E. Aronson (Eds.), *The handbook of social psychology* (pp. 413–484). New York: McGraw-Hill.

Berscheid, E., & Peplau, L. A. (1983). The emerging science of relationships. In H. H. Kelley, E. Berscheid, A. Christensen, J. H. Harvey, T. L. Huston, G. Levinger, E. D. R. Peterson (Eds.), *Close relationships* (pp. 1–19). New York: Freeman.

Berscheid, E., & Reis, H. T. (1998). Attraction and close relationships. In D. Gilbert, S. Fiske, & G. Lindzey (Eds.), *The handbook of social psychology* (4th ed., Vol. 2, pp. 193–281). New York: McGraw-Hill.

Berscheid, E., & Walster (Hatfield), E. (1974). A little bit about love. In T. L. Huston (Ed.), *Foundations of interpersonal attraction* (pp. 355–381). New York: Academic Press.

Berscheid, E., & Walster (Hatfield), E. (1978). *Interpersonal attraction*. Reading, MA: Addison-Wesley.

Bessenoff, G. R. (2006). Can the media affect us? Social comparison, self-discrepancy, and the thin ideal. *Psychology of Women Quarterly, 30*, 239–251.

Bettencourt, B. A., & Miller, N. (1996). Gender differences in aggression as a function of provocation: A meta-analysis. *Psychological Bulletin, 119*, 422–447.

Bettencourt, B. A., & Sheldon, K. (2001). Social roles as mechanism for psychological need satisfaction within social groups. *Journal of Personality and Social Psychology, 81*, 1131–1143.

Bickman, L. (1974). The social power of a uniform. *Journal of Applied Social Psychology, 4*, 47–61.

Biehl, M., Matsumoto, D., Ekman, P., Hearn, V., Heider, K., . . . Ton, V. (1997). Matsumoto and Ekman's Japanese and Caucasian facial expressions of emotion (JACFEE): Reliability and cross-national differences. *Journal of Nonverbal Behavior, 21*, 3–21.

Biernat, M., Crandall, C. S., Young, L. V., Kobrynowicz, D., & Halpin, S. M. (1998). All that you can be: Stereotyping of self and others in a military context. *Journal of Personality and Social Psychology, 75*, 301–317.

Biesanz, J. C., West, S. G., & Millevoi, A. (2007). What do you learn about someone over time? The relationship between length of acquaintance and consensus and self-other agreement in judgments of personality. *Journal of Personality and Social Psychology, 92*, 119–135.

Bils, J., & Singer, S. (1996, August 16). Gorilla saves tot in Brookfield ape pit. *Chicago Tribune*, p. 1.

Bird, B. (2001, January 28). Love as fleeting as a bus ride. *Winnipeg Free Press*, p. B5.

Bjork, J. M., Dougherty, D. M., Moeller, F. G., Cherek, D. R., & Swann, A. C. (1999). The effects of tryptophan depletion and loading on laboratory aggression in men: Time course and a food-restricted control. *Psychopharmacology, 142*, 24–30.

Blader, S. L., & Tyler, T. R. (2003). A four-component model of procedural justice: Defining the meaning of a "fair" process. *Personality and Social Psychology Bulletin, 6*, 747–758.

Blair, I. V. (2002). The malleability of automatic stereotypes and prejudice. *Personality and Social Psychology Review, 6*, 242–261.

Blais, J. J., Craig, W. M., Pepler, D., & Connolly, J. (2008). Adolescents online: The importance of Internet activity choices to salient relationships. *Journal of Youth and Adolescence, 37*(5), 522–536.

Blais, M. R., Sabourin, S., Boucher, C., & Vallerand, R. (1990). Toward a motivational model of couple happiness. *Journal of Personality and Social Psychology, 59*, 1021–1031.

Blanchette, I., Richards, A., Melnyk, L., & Lavda, A. (2007). Reasoning about emotional contents following shocking terrorist attacks: A tale of three cities. *Journal of Experimental Psychology: Applied, 13*(1), 47–56.

Blanchfield, M. (2000, June 21). I will never be able to trust my leaders again. *Ottawa Citizen*. Retrieved from www.ottawacitizen.com/national/ 000227/3666380.html.

Blanchfield, M. (2005, November 4). Study ignores Gulf War syndrome symptoms. *Winnipeg Free Press*, p. A17.

Blank, P. D. (Ed). (1993). *Interpersonal expectations: Theory, research, and applications*. New York: Cambridge University Press.

Blanton, H., Pelham, B. W., De Hart, T., & Carvallo, M. (2001). Overconfidence as dissonance reduction. *Journal of Experimental Social Psychology, 37*, 373–385.

Blascovich, J., Mendes, W. B., Hunter, S. B., & Salomon, K. (1999). Social "facilitation" as challenge and threat. *Journal of Personality and Social Psychology, 77*, 68–77.

Blaskovich, J., Ginsburg, G. P., & Veach, T. L. (1975). A pluralistic explanation of choice shifts on the risk dimension. *Journal of Personality and Social Psychology, 31*, 422–429.

Blass, T. (2000). *Obedience to authority: Current perspectives on the Milgram paradigm*. Mahwah, NJ: Erlbaum.

Blass, T. (1999). The Milgram paradigm after 31 years: Some things we now know about obedience to authority. *Journal of Applied Social Psychology, 29*(5), 955–978.

Blass, T. (2004). *The man who shocked the world: The life and legacy of Stanley Milgram*. New York: Basic Books.

Blau, P. M. (1964). *Exchange and power in social life*. New York: Wiley.

Bless, H., Strack, F., & Walther, E. (2001). Memory as a target of social influence? Memory distortions as a function of social influence and metacognitive knowledge. In J. P. Forgas & W. D. Kipling (Eds.), *Social influence: Direct and indirect processes* (pp. 167–183). Philadelphia: Psychology Press.

Blittner, M., Goldberg, J., & Merbaum, M. (1978). Cognitive self-control factors in the reduction of smoking behavior. *Behavior Therapy, 9*, 553–561.

Boadle, A. (1994, November 8). Pictures of Somali beaten to death shock Canadians [Reuters]. Retrieved from http://burn.ucsd.edu/archives/riot-l/1994.Nov/0012.html

Bochner, S. (1994). Cross-cultural differences in the self-concept: A test of Hofstede's individualism/collectivism distinction. *Journal of Cross-Cultural Psychology, 25*, 273–283.

Bogaert, A. F., Fawcett, C. C., & Jamieson, L. K. (2009). Attractiveness, body size, masculine sex roles and 2D:4D ratios in men. *Personality and Individual Differences, 47*(4), 273–278.

Bombay, A., Matheson, K., & Anisman, H. (2010). Decomposing identity: Differential relationships between several aspects of ethnic identity and the negative effects of perceived discrimination among First Nations adults in Canada. *Cultural Diversity and Ethnic Minority Psychology, 16*(4), 507–516.

Bonanno, G. (2005). Resilience in the face of potential trauma. *Current Directions in Psychological Science, 14*, 135–138.

Bonanno, G., Boerner, K., & Wortman, C. (2008). Trajectories of grieving. In M. S. Stroebe, R. O. Hansson, H. Schut, W. Stroebe, & E. Van den Blink (Eds.), *Handbook of bereavement research and practice: Advances in theory and intervention* (pp. 287–307). Washington, DC: American Psychological Association.

Bonanno, G. A. (2004). Loss, trauma, and human resilience: Have we underestimated the human capacity to thrive after extremely aversive events? *American Psychologist, 59*, 20–28.

Bonanno, G. A., Moskowitz, J.T., Papa, A., & Folkman, S. (2005). Resilience to loss in bereaved spouses, bereaved parents, and bereaved gay men. *Journal of Personality and Social Psychology, 88*, 827–843.

Bonanno, G. A., Rennicke, C., & Dekel, S. (2005). Self-enhancement among high-exposure survivors of the September 11th terrorist attack: Resilience or social maladjustment? *Journal of Personality and Social Psychology, 88*, 984–998.

Bond, C. F., Atoum, A. O., & VanLeeuwen, M. D. (1996). Social impairment of complex learning in the wake of public embarrassment. *Basic and Applied Social Psychology, 18*, 31–44.

Bond, C. F., & Titus, L. J. (1983). Social facilitation: A meta-analysis of 241 studies. *Psychological Bulletin, 94*, 264–292.

Bond, C. F., Jr. & Atoum, A. O. (2000). International deception. *Personality and Social Psychology Bulletin, 26*, 385–395.

Bond, C. F., Jr., & DePaulo, B. M. (2006). Accuracy of deception judgments. *Personality and Social Psychology Review, 10*, 214–234.

Bond, M. H. (Ed). (1988). *The cross-cultural challenge to social psychology*. Newbury Park, CA: Sage.

Bond, M. H. (1991). Chinese values and health: A culture-level examination. *Psychology and Health, 5*, 137–152.

Bond, M. H. (1996). Chinese values. In M. H. Bond (Ed.), *The handbook of Chinese psychology* (pp. 208–226). Hong Kong: Oxford University Press.

Bond, R., & Smith, P. B. (1996). Culture and conformity: A meta-analysis of studies using Asch's (1952b, 1956) Line Judgment task. *Psychological Bulletin, 119*, 111–137.

Bonta, B. D. (1997). Cooperation and competition in peaceful societies. *Psychological Bulletin, 121*, 299–320.

Boon, S. D., & Pasveer, K. A. (1999). Charting the topography of risky relationship experiences. *Personal Relationships, 6*, 317–336.

Boothroyd, L. G., Jones, B. C., Burt, D. M., DeBruine, L. M., & Perrett, D. I. (2008). Facial correlates of sociosexuality. *Evolution and Human Behavior, 29*, 211–219.

Bornstein, R. F. (1989). Exposure and affect: Overview and meta-analysis of research, 1968–1987. *Psychological Bulletin, 106*, 265–289.

Bornstein, R. F., & D'Agostino, P. R. (1992). Stimulus recognition and the mere exposure effect. *Journal of Personality and Social Psychology, 63*, 545–552.

Bornstein, R. F., & Pittman, T. S. (Eds). (1992). *Perception without awareness: Cognitive, clinical, and social perspectives*. New York: Guilford.

Borsari, B., & Carey, K. B. (2005). Descriptive and injunctive norms in college drinking: A meta-analytic integration. *Journal of Studies on Alcohol, 64*, 331–341.

Bourgeois, M. J., & Bowen, A. (2001). Self-organization of alcohol-related attitudes and beliefs in a campus housing complex: An initial investigation. *Health Psychology, 20*, 434–437.

Bourgeois, P., & Hess, U. (2008). The impact of social context on mimicry. *Biological Psychology, 77*, 434–352.

Bowker, A. (2006). The relationship between sports participation and self-esteem during early adolescence. *Canadian Journal of Behavioural Science, 38*, 214–229.

Bower, G. H., & Hilgard, E. R. (1981). *Theories of learning* (15th ed). Englewood Cliffs, NJ: Prentice Hall.

Bowlby, J. (1969). *Attachment and loss: Vol. 1. Attachment*. New York: Basic Books.

Bowlby, J. (1973). *Attachment and loss: Vol. 2. Separation: Anxiety and anger*. New York: Basic Books.

Bowlby, J. (1980). *Attachment and loss: Vol. 3. Loss*. New York: Basic Books.

Boyce, M. A., Lindsay, S. D., & Brimacombe, C. E. (2008). Investigating investigators: Examining the impact of eyewitness identification evidence on student-investigators. *Law and Human Behavior, 32*(5), 439–453.

Bradbury, T. N., & Fincham, F. D. (1991). A contextual model for advancing the study of marital relationships. In G. J. O. Fletcher & F. D. Fincham (Eds.), *Cognition in close relationships* (pp. 127–147). Hillsdale, NJ: Erlbaum.

Bradfield, A., & Wells, G. L. (2005). Not the same old hindsight bias: Outcome information distorts a broad range of retrospective judgments. *Memory & Cognition, 33*, 120–130.

Bradley, J. P., Nicol, A. A. M., Charbonneau, D., & Meyer, J. P. (2002). Personality correlates of leadership development in Canadian Forces officer candidates. *Canadian Journal of Behavioural Science, 34*, 92–103.

Bradshaw, R. H., Bubier, N. E., & Sullivan, M. (1994). The effects of age and gender on perceived facial attractiveness: A reply to McLellan and McKelvie. *Canadian Journal of Behavioural Science, 26*, 199–204.

Branscombe, N. R., Owen, S., Garstka, T. A., & Coleman, J. (1996). Rape and accident counterfactuals: Who might have done otherwise and would it have changed the outcome? *Journal of Applied Social Psychology, 26*, 1042–1067.

Branscombe, N. R., & Wann, D. L. (1992). Role of identification with a group, arousal, categorization processes, and self-esteem in sports spectator aggression. *Human Relations, 45*, 1013–1033.

Branswell, B. (1998, June 1). Pain and pride. *Maclean's, 111*(22), 21.

Branzei, O., Vertinsky, I., & Camp, R. (2007). Culture-contingent signs of trust in emergent relationships. *Organizational Behavior and Human Decision Processes, 104*(1), 61–82.

Brassard, A., Shaver, P. R., & Lussier, Y. (2007). Attachment, sexual experience, and sexual pressure in romantic relationships: A dyadic approach. *Personal Relationships, 14*(3), 475–493.

Breckler, S. J., & Wiggins, E. C. (1989). On defining attitude and attitude theory: Once more with feeling. In A. R. Pratkanis, S. J. Breckler, & A. G. Greenwald (Eds.), *Attitude structure and function* (pp. 407–427). Hillsdale, NJ: Erlbaum.

Brehm, J. W. (1956). Postdecision changes in the desirability of alternatives. *Journal of Abnormal and Social Psychology, 52*, 384–389.

Brewer, M. B., & Brown, R. J. (1998). Intergroup relations. In D. Gilbert, S. Fiske, & G. Lindzey (Eds.), *The handbook of social psychology* (4th ed., Vol. 2, pp. 554–594). New York: McGraw-Hill.

Brewer, M. B., & Gardner, W. L. (1996). Who is this "we"? Levels of collective identity and self representations. *Journal of Personality and Social Psychology, 71*, 83–93.

Brewer, M. B., & Miller, N. (1984). Beyond the contact hypothesis: Theoretical perspectives on desegregation. In N. Miller & M. B. Brewer (Eds.), *Groups in contact: The psychology of desegregation* (pp. 281–302). New York: Academic Press.

Brewer, N., & Weber, N. (2008). Eyewitness confidence and latency: Indices of memory processes not just markers of accuracy. *Applied Cognitive Psychology, 22*, 827–840.

Brewer, N., & Wells, G. L. (2006). The confidence-accuracy relationship in eyewitness identification: Effects of lineup instructions, foil similarity, and target-absent base rates. *Journal of Experimental Psychology: Applied, 12*, 11–30.

Bridges, F. S., & Coady, N. P. (1996). Affiliation, urban size, urgency, and cost of responses to lost letters. *Psychological Reports, 79*, 775–780.

Brigham, J., Bennett, L., Meissner, C., & Mitchell, T. (2007). The influence of race on eyewitness memory. In R. C. L. Lindsay, D. F. Ross, D. J. Read, & M. P. Toglia (Eds.), *The handbook of eyewitness psychology: Vol. II. Memory for people* (pp. 257–281). Mahwah, NJ: Lawrence Erlbaum.

Brigham, J. C. (1980). Limiting conditions of the "physical attractiveness stereotype": Attributions about divorce. *Journal of Research in Personality, 14*, 365–375.

Brislin, R. (1993). *Understanding culture's influence on behavior*. Fort Worth, TX: Harcourt Brace.

Brochu, P. M., & Esses, V. M. (2009). Weight prejudice and medical policy: Support for an ambiguously discriminatory policy is influenced by prejudice-colored glasses. *Analyses of Social Issues and Public Policy, 9*(1), 117–133.

Brochu, P. M., & Morrison, M. A. (2007). Implicit and explicit prejudice toward overweight and average-weight men and women: Testing their correspondence and relation to behavioral intentions. *Journal of Social Psychology, 147*(6), 681–706.

Brody, S., Wright, S. C., Aron, A., & McLaughlin-Volpe, T. (2009). Compassionate love for individuals in other social groups. In B. Fehr, S. Sprecher, & L. Underwood, L. (Eds.). *The science of compassionate love: Theory, research, and applications* (pp. 283–308). Malden, MA: Blackwell Publishers.

Bronskill, J. (2007, May 19). Feds have plan to help airlines combat "air rage." *Winnipeg Free Press*, p. A9.

Brook, A. S., Starzyk, K. B., & Quinsey, V. L. (2001). The relationship between testosterone and aggression: A meta-analysis. *Aggression and Violent Behavior, 6*, 579–599.

Brophy, J. E. (1983). Research on the self-fulfilling prophecy and teacher expectations. *Journal of Educational Psychology, 75*, 631–661.

Brown, D. J., Ferris, D., Heller, D., & Keeping, L. M. (2007). Antecedents and consequences of the frequency of upward and downward social comparisons at work. *Organizational Behavior and Human Decision Processes, 102*(1), 59–75.

Brown, J. D. (1990). Evaluating one's abilities: Shortcuts and stumbling blocks on the road to self-knowledge. *Journal of Experimental Social Psychology, 26*, 149–167.

Brown, R. (1965). *Social psychology*. New York: Free Press.

Brown, R. (1986). *Social psychology: The second edition*. New York: Free Press.

Brown, R. P., & Pinel, E. C. (2003). Stigma on my mind: Individual differences in the experience of stereotype threat. *Journal of Experimental Social Psychology, 39*, 626–33.

Brown, S. L., Nesse, R. M., & Vinokur, A D. (2003). Providing social support may be more beneficial than receiving it: Results from a prospective study of mortality. *Psychological Science, 14*, 320–327.

Brown, T. C., & Latham, G. P. (2006). The effect of training in verbal self-guidance on performance effectiveness in an MBA program. *Canadian Journal of Behavioural Science, 38*, 1–11.

Brown, W. M., & Moore, C. (2000). Is prospective altruist-detection an evolved solution to the adaptive problem of subtle cheating in cooperative ventures? Supportive evidence using the Wason selection task. *Evolution and Human Behavior, 21*, 25–37.

Broyles, S. (2006). Misplaced paranoia over subliminal advertising: What's the big uproar this time? *Journal of Consumer Marketing, 23*, 312–313.

Brucks, W., & Van Lange, P. (2008). No control, no drive: How noise may undermine conservation behavior in a commons dilemma. European *Journal of Social Psychology, 38*, 810–822.

Brunet, P. M., & Schmidt, L. A. (2010). Sex differences in the expression and use of computer-mediated affective language: Does context matter? *Social Science Computer Review, 28*(2), 194–205.

Bryden, J. (2008, May 9). Dion weak, but at least he's likable. *Winnipeg Free Press*, p. A13.

Buchtel, E. E., & Norenzayan, A. (2008). Which should you use, intuition or logic? Cultural differences in injunctive norms about reasoning. *Asian Journal of Social Psychology, 11*(4), 264–273.

Buckle, L., Gallup, G. G., & Rodd, Z. A. (1996). Marriage as a reproductive contract: Patterns of marriage, divorce and remarriage. *Ethology and Sociobiology, 17*, 363–377.

Budworth, M., & Mann, S. L. (2010). Becoming a leader: The challenge of modesty for women. *Journal of Management Development, 29*(2), 177–186.

Buehler, R., & Griffin, D. (1994). Change-of-meaning effects in conformity and dissent: Observing construal processes over time. *Journal of Personality and Social Psychology, 67*, 984–996.

Buehler, R., Griffin, D. W., & Ross, M. (2002). Inside the planning fallacy: The causes and consequences of optimistic time preferences. In T. Gilovich, D. W. Griffin, & D. Kahneman (Eds.), *Heuristics and biases: The psychology of intuitive judgment* (pp. 250–270). New York: Cambridge University Press.

Buller, D. J. (2005). *Adapting minds: Evolutionary psychology and the persistent quest for human nature*. Cambridge, MA: MIT Press.

Buote, V. M., Wood, E., & Pratt, M. (2009). Exploring similarities and differences between online and offline friendships: The role of attachment style. *Computers in Human Behavior, 25*(2), 560–567.

Burchell, A. N., Calzavara, L. M., Myers, T., Remis, R. S., Raboud, J., Corey, P., & Swantee, C. (2010). Stress and increased HIV infection risk among gay and bisexual men. *AIDS, 24*(11), 1757–1764.

Burger, J. M. (1981). Motivational biases in the attribution of responsibility for an accident: A meta-analysis of the defensive-attribution hypothesis. *Psychological Bulletin, 90*, 496–512.

Burger, J. M. (1986). Increasing compliance by improving the deal: The that's-not-all technique. *Journal of Personality and Social Psychology, 51*, 277–283.

Burger, J. M. (1992). Desire for control: Personality, social, and clinical perspectives. New York: Plenum.

Burger, J. M. (1999). The foot-in-the-door compliance procedure: A multiple-process analysis and review. *Personality and Social Psychology Review, 3,* 303–325.

Burger, J. M. (2009). Replicating Milgram: Would people still obey today? *American Psychologist, 64* (1), 1-11.

Burgess, M., Enzle, M. E., & Morry, M. (2000). The social psychological power of photography: Can the image-freezing machine make something out of nothing? *European Journal of Social Psychology, 30,* 595–612.

Burke, R.J., & Greenglass, E. R. (1990). Type A Behavior and non-work activities. *Personality and Individual Differences, 11,* 945–952.

Burkley, E. (2008). The role of self-control in resistance to persuasion. *Personality and Social Psychology Bulletin, 34,* 419-431.

Burleson, B. R. (1994). Friendship and similarities in social-cognitive and communicative abilities: Social skill bases of interpersonal attraction in childhood. *Personal Relationships, 1,* 371–389.

Burleson, B. R., & Samter, W. (1996). Similarity in the communication skills of young adults: Foundations of attraction, friendship, and relationship satisfaction. *Communication Reports, 9,* 127–139.

Burnstein, E., Crandall, C., & Kitayama, S. (1994). Some neo- Darwinian decision rules for altruism: Weighing cues for inclusive fitness as a function of the biological importance of the decision. *Journal of Personality and Social Psychology, 67,* 773–789.

Burnstein, E., & Sentis, K. (1981). Attitude polarization in groups. In R. E. Petty, T. M. Ostrom, & T. C. Brock (Eds.), *Cognitive responses in persuasion* (pp. 197–216). Hillsdale, NJ: Erlbaum.

Burnstein, E., & Vinokur, A. (1977). Persuasive argumentation and social comparison as determinants of attitude polarization. *Journal of Experimental Social Psychology, 13,* 315–332.

Burnstein, E., & Worchel, P. (1962). Arbitrariness of frustration and its consequences for aggression in a social situation. *Journal of Personality, 30,* 528–540.

Burt, M. R. (1980). Cultural myths and supports for rape. *Journal of Personality and Social Psychology, 38,* 217–230.

Burton, K. D., Lydon, J. E., D'Alessandro, D. U., & Koestner, R. (2006). The differential effects of intrinsic and identified motivation on well-being and performance: Prospective, experimental, and implicit approaches to self-determination theory. *Journal of Personality and Social Psychology, 91,* 750–762.

Bushman, B. J. (1993). Human aggression while under the influence of alcohol and other drugs: An integrative research review. *Current Directions in Psychological Science, 2,* 148–152.

Bushman, B. J., & Anderson, C. A. (2009). Comfortably numb: Desensitizing effects of violent media on helping others. *Psychological Science, 21*(3), 273–277.

Bushman, B. J., Baumeister, R. F., & Stack, A. D. (1999). Catharsis, aggression, and persuasive influence: Self-fulfilling or self-defeating prophecies? *Journal of Personality and Social Psychology, 76,* 367–376.

Bushman, B. J., & Cooper, H. M. (1990). Alcohol and human aggression: An integrative research review. *Psychological Bulletin, 107,* 341–354.

Bushman, B. J., Wang, M. C., & Anderson, C. A. (2005a). Is the curve relating temperature to aggression linear or curvilinear? Assaults and temperature in Minneapolis re-examined. *Journal of Personality and Social Psychology, 89,* 62–66.

Bushman, B. J., Wang, M. C., & Anderson, C. A. (2005b). Is the curve relating temperature to aggression linear or curvilinear? A response to Bell (2005) and to Cohn and Rotton (2005). *Journal of Personality and Social Psychology, 89,* 74–77.

Buss, D. M. (1985). Human mate selection. *American Scientist, 73,* 47–51.

Buss, D. M. (1988a). The evolution of human intrasexual competition. *Journal of Personality and Social Psychology, 54,* 616–628.

Buss, D. M. (1988b). Love acts: The evolutionary biology of love. In R. J. Sternberg & M. L. Barnes (Eds.), *The psychology of love* (pp. 110–118). New Haven, CT: Yale University Press.

Buss, D. M. (1989). Sex differences in human mate preferences: Evolutionary hypotheses tested in 37 cultures. *Behavioral and Brain Sciences, 12,* 1–49.

Buss, D. M. (1994). *The evolution of desire.* New York: Basic Books.

Buss, D. M. (1996a). The evolutionary psychology of human social strategies. In E. T. Higgins & A. W. Kruglanski (Eds.), *Social psychology: Handbook of basic principles* (pp. 3–38). New York: Guilford.

Buss, D. M. (1996b). Sexual conflict: Evolutionary insights into feminism and the "battle of the sexes." In D. Buss & N. Malamuth (Eds.), *Sex, power, conflict: Evolutionary and feminist perspectives* (pp. 296–318). New York: Oxford University Press.

Buss, D. M. (1999). *Evolutionary psychology: The new science of the mind.* Needham Heights, MA: Allyn & Bacon.

Buss, D. M. (2004). *Evolutionary psychology: The new science of the mind* (2nd ed.). Boston: Allyn & Bacon.

Buss, D. M. (Ed). (2005). *The handbook of evolutionary psychology.* Hoboken, NJ: Wiley.

Buss, D. M., Abbott, M., Angleitner, A., Biaggio, A., Blanco-Villasenor, A., Bruchon-Schweitzer, M., . . . Yang, K. (1990). International preferences in selecting mates: A study of 37 cultures. *Journal of Cross-Cultural Psychology, 21,* 5–47.

Buss, D. M., & Barnes, M. (1986). Preferences in human mate selection. *Journal of Personality and Social Psychology, 50,* 559–570.

Buss, D. M., & Duntley, J. D. (2006). The evolution of aggression. In M. Schaller, J. A. Simpson, & D. T. Kenrick (Eds.), *Evolution and social psychology* (pp. 263–285). Madison, CT: Psychosocial Press.

Buss, D. M., & Kenrick, D. T. (1998). Evolutionary social psychology. In D. Gilbert, S. Fiske, & G. Lindzey (Eds.), *The handbook of social psychology* (4th ed., Vol. 2, pp. 982–1026). New York: Random House.

Buss, D. M., & Schmitt, D. P. (1993). Sexual strategies theory: An evolutionary perspective on human mating. *Psychological Bulletin, 100,* 204–232.

Buston, P. M., & Emlem, S. T. (2003). Cognitive processes underlying human mate choice: The relationship between self-perception and mate preference in Western society. *Proceedings of the National Academy of Sciences, 100,* 8805–8810.

Butler, D., & Geis, F. L. (1990). Nonverbal affect responses to male and female leaders: Implications for leadership evaluations. *Journal of Personality and Social Psychology, 58,* 48–59.

Butler, E. A., Egloff, B., Wilhelm, F. H., Smith, N. C., Erickson, E. A., & Gross, J. J. (2003). The social consequences of expressive suppression. *Emotion, 3,* 48–67.

Button, C. M., & Collier, D. R. (1991, June). *A comparison of people's concepts of love and romantic love.* Paper presented at the Canadian Psychological Association Conference, Calgary, Alberta.

Buunk, B. P., Oldersma, F. L., & de Dreu, C. K. W. (2001). Enhancing satisfaction through downward comparison: The role of relational discontent and individual differences in social comparison orientation. *Journal of Experimental Social Psychology, 37,* 452–467.

Buunk, B. P., & Prins, K. S. (1998). Loneliness, exchange orientation, and reciprocity in friendships. *Personal Relationships, 5,* 1–14.

Byrne, D. (1997). An overview (and underview) of research and theory within the attraction paradigm. *Journal of Social and Personal Relationships, 14,* 417–431.

Byrne, D., & Clore, G. L. (1970). A reinforcement model of evaluative processes. *Personality: An International Journal, 1,* 103–128.

Byrne, D., Clore, G. L., & Smeaton, G. (1986). The attraction hypothesis: Do similar attitudes affect anything? *Journal of Personality and Social Psychology, 51,* 1167–1170.

Byrne, D., & Nelson, D. (1965). Attraction as a linear function of positive reinforcement. *Journal of Personality and Social Psychology, 1,* 659–663.

Cacioppo, J. T. (1998). Somatic responses to psychological stress: The reactivity hypothesis. *Advances in Psychological Science, 2,* 87–112.

Cacioppo, J. T., Berntson, G. G., Malarkey, W. B., Kiecolt-Glaser, J. K., Sheridan, J. F., Poehlmann, K. M., . . . Glaser, R. (1998). Autonomic, neuroendocrine, and immune responses to psychological stress: The reactivity hypothesis. *Annals of the New York Academy of Sciences, 840*, 664–673.

Cadsby, C., Hamaguchi, Y., Kawagoe, T., Maynes, E., & Song, F. (2007). Cross-national gender differences in behavior in a threshold public goods game: Japan versus Canada. *Journal of Economic Psychology, 28*(2), 242–260.

Cafri, G., & Thompson, J. K. (2004). Measuring male body image: A review of the current methodology. *Psychology of Men and Masculinity, 5*, 18–29.

Cafri, G., Thompson, J. K., Ricciardelli, L., McCabe, M., Smolak, L., & Yesalis, C. (2005). Pursuit of the muscular ideal: Physical and psychological consequences and putative risk factors. *Clinical Psychology Review, 25*, 215–239.

Cairney, J., & Krause, N. (2008). Negative life events and age-related decline in mastery: Are older more vulnerable to the control-eroding effect of stress? The *Journals of Gerontology: Series B: Psychological Sciences and Social Sciences, 63B*(3), S162–S170.

Caledonia land conflict convoy comes to Queen's Park. (2007, May 2). Retrieved from www.citynews.ca/news/news_10544

Calder, B. J., & Staw, B. M. (1975). Self-perception of intrinsic and extrinsic motivation. *Journal of Personality and Social Psychology, 31*, 599–605.

Callan, M. J., Ellard, J. H., & Nicol, J. E. (2006). The belief in a just world and immanent justice reasoning in adults. *Personality and Social Psychology Bulletin, 32*, 1646–1658.

Callan, M. J., Kay, A. C., Olson, J. M., Brar, N., & Whitefield, N. (2010). The effects of priming legal concepts on perceived trust and competitiveness, self-interested attitudes, and competitive behavior. *Journal of Experimental Social Psychology, 46*(2), 325–335.

Callan, M. J., Sutton, R. M., & Dovale, C. (2010). When deserving translates into causing: The effect of cognitive load on immanent justice reasoning. *Journal of Experimental Social Psychology, 46*(6), 1097–1100.

Cameron, J. E. (1999). Social identity and the pursuit of possible selves: Implications for the psychological well-being of university students. *Group Dynamics: Theory, Research and Practice, 3*, 179–189.

Cameron, J. J., Ross, M., & Holmes, J. G. (2002). Loving the one you hurt: Positive effects of recounting a transgression against an intimate partner. *Journal of Experimental Social Psychology, 38*, 307–314.

Cameron, K. (2000). Student threats in the aftermath of the Taber and Littleton school shootings: How seriously do we take them? *Psynopsis, Fall*, 13.

CAMH (2003). The 2003 Ontario student drug use drug report: Executive summary. The Centre for Addiction and Mental Health. Retrieved from www. camh.net/pdf/osdus2003-execsummary.pdr

Campbell, B., Schellenberg, E. G., & Senn, C. Y. (1997). Evaluating measures of contemporary sexism. *Psychology of Women Quarterly, 21*, 89–102.

Campbell, D. T., & Stanley, J. C. (1967). Experimental and quasi- experimental designs for research. Chicago, IL: Rand McNally.

Campbell, J., & Stasser, G. (2006). The influence of time and task demonstrability on decision-making in computer-mediated and face-to-face groups. *Small Group Research, 37*, 271–294.

Campbell, J. D. (1986). Similarity and uniqueness: The effects of attribute type, relevance, and individual differences in self-esteem and depression. *Journal of Personality and Social Psychology, 50*, 281–294.

Campbell, J. D. (1990). Self-esteem and clarity of the self-concept. *Journal of Personality and Social Psychology, 59*, 538–549.

Campbell, J. D., Assanand, S., & DiPaula, A. (2000). Structural features of the self-concept and adjustment. In A. Tesser, R. B. Felson, & J. M. Suls (Eds.), *Psychological perspectives on self and identity* (pp. 67–87). Washington, DC: American Psychological Association.

Campbell, J. D., & Fairey, P. J. (1989). Informational and normative routes to conformity: The effect of faction size as a function of norm extremity and attention to the stimulus. *Journal of Personality and Social Psychology, 57*, 457–468.

Campbell, J. D., & Fehr, B. (1990). Self-esteem and perceptions of conveyed impressions: Is negative affectivity associated with greater realism? *Journal of Personality and Social Psychology, 58*, 122–133.

Campbell, J. D., Trapnell, P. D., Heine, S. J., Katz, I. M., Lavallee, L. F., & Lehman, D. R. (1996). Self-concept clarity: Measurement, personality correlates, and cultural boundaries: Correction. *Journal of Personality and Social Psychology, 70*, 141–156.

Campbell, L., Lackenbauer, S. D., & Muise, A. (2006). When is being known or adored by romantic partners most beneficial? Self- perceptions, relationship length, and responses to partner's verifying and enhancing appraisals. *Personality and Social Psychology Bulletin, 32*, 1283–1294.

Campbell, L., Simpson, J. A., Boldry, J., & Kashy, D. A. (2005). Perceptions of conflict and support in romantic relationships: The role of attachment anxiety. *Journal of Personality and Social Psychology, 88*, 510–531.

Canada (1997). Report of the Somalia Commission of Inquiry. Ottawa, ON: Department of National Defence. Retrieved from www.dnd.ca/somalia/somaliae.htm/Canada

Canada (2001). Shaping the nation's workforce: Immigrants, demand for skills, and an aging population. *2001 Census*. Statistics Canada .Retrieved from www12.statcan.ca/english/census01/products/analytic/companion/paid/canada.cfm#3

Canada (2002, May 4). Divorces, 2001, 2002. Statistics Canada. *The Daily*. Retrieved from www.statcan.ca/Daily/English/040504/d04050a.htm

Canada (2005a, July 14). Family violence in Canada: A statistical profile. Statistics Canada. *The Daily*. Retrieved from www.statcan.ca/Daily/English/050714/d050714a.htm

Canada (2005b, August 11). Canadian tobacco use monitoring survey, February–December 2004. Statistics Canada. *The Daily*. Retrieved from www.statcan.ca/Daily/English/050811/d050811c.htm

Canada (2005c, July 6). Canadian community health survey, 2004: Obesity among children and adults. Statistics Canada. *The Daily*. Retrieved from www.statcan.ca/Daily/English/050706/d050706a.htm

Canada (2005d, May 3). Canadian community health survey, 2003: Early sexual intercourse, condom use, and sexually transmitted diseases, 1998/99 to 2000/01 and 2003. Statistics Canada. *The Daily*. Retrieved from www.statcan.ca/Daily/English/050503/d050503a.htm

Canada. (2005e, July 21). Crime statistics. *The Daily*. Retrieved from www.statcan.ca/ Daily/English/050721/d050721a.htm.

Canada. (2005f). Women in Canada: A guide to understanding the changing roles of women and men in Canada. Retrieved from www.statcan.gc.ca/ ads-annonces/89-503-x/index-eng.htm

Canada (2007). Deaths, by selected grouped causes and sex, Canada, provinces and territories. Statistics Canada, Table 102-0552. Retrieved from http://cansim2.statcan.ca/cgi-win/ cnsmcgi.exe?Lang=E&RootDir=CII/&ResultTemplate=CII/CII___&Array_Pick=1&ArrayId=1020552

Canada (2008). Family violence in Canada: A statistical profile. Statistics Canada, Catalogue No. 85-224-X. Retrieved from www.statcan.gc.ca/ pub/85-224-x/85-224-x2008000-eng.pdf.

Canadian Psychological Association (2000). "Canadian Code of Ethics for Psychologists." Retrieved from www.cpa.ca/cpasite/userfiles/Documents/Canadian Code of Ethics for Psycho.pdf

Canary, D. J., & Stafford, L. (2001). Equity in the preservation of personal relationships. In J. Harvey & A. Wenzel (Eds.), *Close romantic relationships: Maintenance and enhancement* (pp. 133–151). Mahwah, NJ: Erlbaum.

Cannon, W. B. (1932). *The wisdom of the body*. New York: Norton.

Cannon, W. B. (1942). "Voodoo" death. *American Anthropologist, 44*, 169–181.

Cantor, J. (1994). Confronting children's fright responses to mass media. In D. Zillmann, J. Bryant, & Aletha C. Huston (Eds.), *Media, children, and the family: Social scientific, psychodynamic, and clinical perspectives* (pp. 139–150). Hillsdale, NJ: Erlbaum.

Cantor, J., Bushman, B. J., Huesmann, L. R., Groebel, J., Malamuth, N. M., Impett, . . . Smith, S. (2001). Some hazards of television viewing: Fears, aggression, and sexual attitudes. In D. G. Singer & J. L. Singer (Eds.), *Handbook of children and the media* (pp. 207–307). Thousand Oaks, CA: Sage.

Cantril, H. (1940). *The invasion from Mars: A study in the psychology of panic*. New York: Harper & Row.

Caporael, L. R., & Brewer, M. B. (2000). Metatheories, evolution, and psychology: Once more with feeling. *Psychological Inquiry, 11*, 23–26.

Carli, L. L. (1999). Cognitive reconstruction, hindsight, and reactions to victims and perpetrators. *Personality and Social Psychology Bulletin, 25*, 966–979.

Carli, L. L., & Eagly, A. H. (1999). Gender effects on social influence and emergent leadership. In G. N. Powell (Ed.), *Handbook of gender and work* (pp. 203–222). Thousand Oaks, CA: Sage.

Carlsmith, K. M., Darley, J. M., & Robinson, P. H. (2002). Why do we punish? Deterrence and just deserts as motives for punishment. *Journal of Personality and Social Psychology, 83*, 284–299.

Carlson, M., Charlin, V., & Miller, N. (1988). Positive mood and helping behavior: A test of six hypotheses. *Journal of Personality and Social Psychology, 55*, 211–229.

Carlson, M., & Miller, N. (1987). Explanation of the relationship between negative mood and helping. *Psychological Bulletin, 102*, 91–108.

Carlston, D. E., & Skowronski, J. J. (1994). Savings in the relearning of trait information as evidence of spontaneous inference generation. *Journal of Personality and Social Psychology, 66*, 840–856.

Carnevale, P. J. (1986). Strategic choice in mediation. *Negotiation Journal, 2*, 41–56.

Carpenter, J. (2008, February 9). Agony of Japan's Diana. *Express*, p. 38.

Carpenter, S. (2000, December). Why do "they all look alike"? *Monitor on Psychology*, 44–45.

Carré, J., Gilchrist, J., Morrissey, M., & McCormick, C. (2010). Motivational and situational factors and the relationship between testosterone dynamics and human aggression during competition. *Biological Psychology, 84*(2), 346-353.

Carroll, J. M., & Russell, J. A. (1996). Do facial expressions signal specific emotions? Judging emotion from the face in context. *Journal of Personality and Social Psychology, 70*, 205–218.

Cartwright, D. (1979). Contemporary social psychology in historical perspective. *Social Psychology Quarterly, 42*, 82–93.

Cartwright, D., & Zander, A. (Eds). (1968). *Group dynamics: Research and theory* (3rd ed). New York: Harper & Row.

Carvalho, S. W., Samu, S., & Sivaramakrishnan, S. (2011). The effect of country-related brand associations and product attributes on attitude toward unfamiliar foreign brands: A schema congruity perspective. *Journal of International Consumer Marketing, 23*(2), 135–150.

Carvallo, M., & Pelham, B. W. (2006). When fiends become friends: The need to belong and perceptions of personal and group discrimination. *Journal of Personality and Social Psychology, 90*, 94–108.

Carver, C. S. (2003). Self-awareness. In M. R. Leary & J. P. Tangney (Eds.), *Handbook of self and identity* (pp. 179–196). New York: Guilford Press.

Carver, C. S., & Scheier, M. F. (1981). *Attention and self-regulation: A control-theory approach to human behavior*. New York: Springer-Verlag.

Carver, C. S., & Scheier, M. F. (1998). *On the self-regulation of behavior*. New York: Cambridge University Press.

Cassidy, W., Jackson, M., & Brown, K. (2009). Sticks and stones can break my bones, but how can pixels hurt me? Students' experiences with cyber-bullying. *School Psychology International, 30*(4), 383–402.

Catalyst. (2008). *Catalyst Expanding Opportunities for Women and Business*. Retrieved from http://www.catalyst.org/publication/132/us-women-in-business

Cate, R. M., & Lloyd, S. A. (1992). *Courtship*. Newbury Park, CA: Sage.

CAUT survey shows PSE gender inequity widespread. (2006, April). *CAUT Bulletin*, p. A9.

CBC News (2011, July 6). Sydney residents closer to day in court: Tar ponds lawsuit can go ahead. *Globe and Mail*. Retrieved from www.cbc.ca/news/politics/story/2011/07/06/ns-tarponds-class-action-decision.html

Cervone, D., & Peake, P. (1986). Anchoring, efficacy, and action: The influence of judgmental heuristics on self-efficacy judgments and behavior. *Journal of Personality and Social Psychology, 50*, 492–501.

Cesario, J., Plaks, J. E., Hagiwara, N., Navarrete, C., & Higgins, E. (2010). The ecology of automaticity: How situational contingencies shape action semantics and social behavior. *Psychological Science, 21*(9), 1311–1317.

Chaiken, S. (1980). Heuristic versus systematic information processing and the use of source versus message cues in persuasion. *Journal of Personality and Social Psychology, 39*, 752–766.

Chaiken, S. (1987). The heuristic model of persuasion. In M. P. Zanna, J. M. Olson, & C. P. Herman (Eds.), *Social influence: The Ontario Symposium* (Vol. 5, pp. 3–39). Hillsdale, NJ: Erlbaum.

Chaiken, S., & Baldwin, M. W. (1981). Affective–cognitive consistency and the effect of salient behavioral information on the self perception of attitudes. *Journal of Personality and Social Psychology, 41*, 1–12.

Chaiken, S., Liberman, A., & Eagly, A. H. (1989). Heuristic and systematic information processing within and beyond the persuasion context. In J. S. Uleman & J. A. Bargh (Eds.), *Unintended thought* (pp. 212–252). New York: Guilford Press.

Chaiken, S., Wood, W., & Eagly, A. H. (1996). Principles of persuasion. In E. T. Higgins & A. W. Kruglanski (Eds.), *Social psychology: Handbook of basic principles* (pp. 702–742). New York: Guilford.

Chan, J. (2009). Where is the imbalance? *Journal of School Violence, 8*(2), 177–190.

Chang, C., & Chen, J. (1995). Effects of different motivation strategies on reducing social loafing. *Chinese Journal of Psychology, 37*, 71–81.

Charman, S., & Wells, G. (2007). Applied lineup theory. *The handbook of eyewitness psychology, Vol II: Memory for people* (pp. 219–254). Mahwah, NJ: Lawrence Erlbaum.

Chassin, L., Presson, C. G., & Sherman, S. J. (1990). Social psychological contributions to the understanding and prevention of adolescent cigarette smoking. *Personality and Social Psychology Bulletin, 16*, 133–151.

Cheadle, B. (2005, January 17). Volunteers recall grim work for Martin. *Winnipeg Free Press*. Retrieved from www.winnipegfreepress.com

Chebat, J., El Hedhli, K., Gélinas-Chebat, C., & Boivin, R. (2007). Voice and persuasion in a banking telemarketing context. *Perceptual and Motor Skills, 104*(2), 419–437.

Chemers, M. M. (2000). Leadership research and theory: A functional integration. *Group Dynamics: Theory, Research, and Practice, 4*, 27–43.

Chemers, M. M., Watson, C. B., & May, S. T. (2000). Dispositional affect and leadership effectiveness: A comparison of self-esteem, optimism, and efficacy. *Personality and Social Psychology Bulletin, 26*, 267–277.

Chen, M., & Bargh, J. A. (1997). Nonconscious behavioral confirmation processes: The self-fulfilling consequences of automatic stereotype activation. *Journal of Experimental Social Psychology, 33*, 541–560.

Chen, S., & Andersen, S. M. (1999). Relationships from the past in the present: Significant-other representations and transference in interpersonal life. In M. P. Zanna (Ed.), *Advances in experimental social psychology* (Vol. 31, pp. 123–190). San Diego, CA: Academic Press.

Chen, S., Bond, M., Chan, B., Tang, D., & Buchtel, E. E. (2009). Behavioral manifestations of modesty. *Journal of Cross-Cultural Psychology, 40*(4), 603–626.

Chen, S., & Chaiken, S. (1999). The heuristic-systematic model in its broader context. In S. Chaiken & Y. Trope (Eds.), *Dual-process theories in social psychology* (pp. 73–96). New York: Guilford Press.

Cheryan, S., & Bodenhausen, G. V. (2000). When positive stereotypes threaten intellectual performance: The psychological hazards of "model minority" status. *Psychological Science, 11*(5), 399–402.

Cheung, S. F., Chan, D. K., & Wong, Z. S. (1999). Reexamining the theory of planned behavior in understanding wastepaper recycling. *Environment and Behavior, 31*, 587–612.

Chia, A., & Costigan, C. L. (2006). Understanding the multidimensionality of acculturation among Chinese Canadians. *Canadian Journal of Behavioural Science, 38*, 311–324.

Chin, J., & Schooler, J. (2008). Why do words hurt? Content, process, and criterion shift accounts of verbal overshadowing. *European Journal of Cognitive Psychology, 20*, 396–413.

Chipperfield, J. G., Perry, R. P., & Menec, V. H. (1999). Primary and secondary control-enhancing strategies: Implications for health in later life. *Journal of Aging and Health, 11*, 517–539.

Chiu, C., Morris, M. W., Hong, Y., & Menon, T. (2000). Motivated cultural cognition: The impact of implicit cultural theories on dispositional attribution varies as a function of need for closure. *Journal of Personality and Social Psychology, 78*, 247–259.

Choi, I., Dalal, R., Kim-Prieto, C., & Park, H. (2003). Culture and judgment of causal relevance. *Journal of Personality and Social Psychology, 84*, 46–59.

Choi, I., & Nisbett, R. E. (1998). Situational salience and cultural differences in the correspondence bias and in the actor-observer bias. *Personality and Social Psychology Bulletin, 24*, 949–960.

Christensen, L. (1988). Deception in psychological research: When is its use justified? *Personality and Social Psychology Bulletin, 14*, 664–675.

Christianson, S. (1992). Emotional stress and eyewitness memory: A critical review. *Psychological Bulletin, 112*, 284–309.

Church, A. H. (1993). Estimating the effects of incentives on mail survey response rates: A meta-analysis. *Public Opinion Quarterly, 57*, 62–79.

Cialdini, R. B. (1993). *Influence: Science and practice* (3rd ed). New York: HarperCollins.

Cialdini, R. B. (2000). *Influence: Science and practice* (4th ed). Boston: Allyn & Bacon.

Cialdini, R. B. (2003). *Crafting normative messages to protect the environment. Current Directions in Psychological Science, 12*, 105–109.

Cialdini, R. B., Cacioppo, J., Basset, R., & Miller, J. (1978). Low-ball procedure for producing compliance: Commitment then cost. *Journal of Personality and Social Psychology, 36*, 463–476.

Cialdini, R. B., Darby, B. L., & Vincent, J. E. (1973). Transgression and altruism: A case for hedonism. *Journal of Experimental Social Psychology, 9*, 502–516.

Cialdini, R. B., & Fultz, J. (1990). Interpreting the negative mood-helping literature via "mega"-analysis: A contrary view. *Psychological Bulletin, 107*, 210–214.

Cialdini, R. B., & Goldstein, N. J. (2004). Social influence: Compliance and conformity. *Annual Review of Psychology, 55*, 591–621.

Cialdini, R. B., Green, B. L., & Rusch, A. J. (1992). When tactical pronouncements of change become real change: The case of reciprocal persuasion. *Journal of Personality and Social Psychology, 63*, 30–40.

Cialdini, R. B., Kallgren, C. A., & Reno, R. R. (1991). A focus theory of normative conduct: A theoretical refinement and reevaluation of the role of norms in human behavior. In M. P. Zanna (Ed.), *Advances in experimental social psychology* (Vol. 24, pp. 201–234). San Diego, CA: Academic Press.

Cialdini, R. B., Reno, R. R., & Kallgren, C. A. (1990). A focus theory of normative conduct: Recycling the concept of norms to reduce littering in public places. *Journal of Personality and Social Psychology, 58*, 1015–1026.

Cialdini, R. B., Schaller, M., Houlihan, D., Arps, K., Fultz, J., & Beaman, A. L. (1987). Empathy-based helping: Is it selflessly or selfishly motivated? *Journal of Personality and Social Psychology, 52*, 749–758.

Cialdini, R. B., & Trost, M. R. (1998). Social influence: Social norms, conformity, and compliance. In D. Gilbert, S. Fiske, & G. Lindzey (Eds.), *The handbook of social psychology* (4th ed., Vol. 2, pp. 151–192). New York: McGraw-Hill.

Cialdini, R. B., Trost, M. R., & Newsom, J. T. (1995). Preference for consistency: The development of a valid measure and the discovery of surprising behavioral implications. *Journal of Personality and Social Psychology, 69*, 318–328.

Cialdini, R. B., Vincent, J. E., Lewis, S. K., Catalan, J., Wheeler, D., & Darby, B. L. (1975). Reciprocal concessions procedure for inducing compliance: The door-in-the-face technique. *Journal of Personality and Social Psychology, 31*, 206–215.

Clark, A. P. (2008). Attracting interest: Dynamic displays of proceptivity increase the attractiveness of men and women. *Evolutionary Psychology, 6*(4), 563–574.

Clark, D. A., & Purdon, C. (2009). Mental control of unwanted intrusive thoughts: A phenomenological study of nonclinical individuals. *International Journal of Cognitive Therapy, 2*(3), 267–281.

Clark, K., & Clark, M. (1947). Racial identification and preference in Negro children. In T. M. Newcomb & E. L. Hartley (Eds.), *Readings in social psychology* (pp. 169–178). New York: Holt.

Clark, M. S. (1984). Record keeping in two types of relationships. *Journal of Personality and Social Psychology, 47*, 549–577.

Clark, M. S., & Chrisman, K. (1994). Resource allocation in intimate relationships: Trying to make sense of a confusing literature. In M. J. Lerner & G. Mikula (Eds.), *Entitlement and the affectional bond: Justice in close relationships* (pp. 65–88). New York: Plenum.

Clark, M. S., & Grote, N. K. (1998). Why aren't indices of relationship costs always negatively related to indices of relationship quality? *Personality and Social Psychology Review, 2*, 2–17.

Clark, M. S., & Isen, A. M. (1982). Toward understanding the relationship between feeling states and social behavior. In A. H. Hastorf & A. M. Isen (Eds.), *Cognitive social psychology* (pp. 73–108). New York: Elsevier.

Clark, M. S., & Mills, J. (1979). Interpersonal attraction in exchange and communal relationships. *Journal of Personality and Social Psychology, 37*, 12–24.

Clark, M. S., & Mills, J. (1993). The difference between communal and exchange relationships: What it is and is not. *Personality and Social Psychology Bulletin, 19*, 684–691.

Clark, M. S., Mills, J., & Corcoran, D. M. (1989). Keeping track of needs and inputs of friends and strangers. *Personality and Social Psychology Bulletin, 15*, 533–542.

Clark, M. S., & Monin, J. K. (2006). Giving and receiving communal responsiveness as love. In R. J. Sternberg & K. Weis (Eds.), *The new psychology of love* (pp. 200–221). New Haven, CT: Yale University Press.

Clark, M. S., & Waddell, B. (1985). Perception of exploitation in communal and exchange relationships. *Journal of Social and Personal Relationships, 2*, 403–413.

Clark, R., Anderson, N. B., Clark, V. R., & Williams, D. R. (1999). Racism as a stressor for African Americans. *American Psychologist, 54*, 805–816.

Clark, R. D., III & Word, L. E. (1972). Why don't bystanders help? Because of ambiguity? *Journal of Personality and Social Psychology, 24*, 392–400.

Clarke, A. K., & Lawson, K. L. (2009). Women's judgments of a sexual assault scenario: The role of prejudicial attitudes and victim weight. *Violence and Victims, 24*(2), 248–264.

Clarke, L., & Griffin, M. (2007). The body natural and the body unnatural: Beauty work and aging. *Journal of Aging Studies, 21*(3), 187–201.

Clarke, V. A., Lovegrove, H., Williams, A., & Macpherson, M. (2000). Unrealistic optimism and the Health Belief Model. *Journal of Behavioral Medicine, 23*, 367–376.

Clément, R. Baker, S. C., & MacIntyre, P. D. (2003). Willingness to communicate in a second language: The effects of context, norms, and vitality. *Journal of Language and Social Psychology, 22*, 190–209.

Clément, R., Noels, K. A., & Deneault, B. (2001). Interethnic contact, identity, and psychological adjustment: The mediating and moderating roles of communication. *Sex Roles, 57*, 559–577.

Cline, V. B., Croft, R. G., & Courrier, S. (1973). Desensitization of children to television violence. *Journal of Personality and Social Psychology, 27*, 360–365.

Clow, K. A., & Esses, V. M. (2007). Expectancy effects in social stereotyping: Automatic and controlled processing in the neely paradigm. *Canadian Journal of Behavioural Science, 39*, 161–173.

Clow, K. A., & Olson, J. M. (2010). Conceptual-motor compatibility and homonegativity: Approaching and avoiding words associated with homosexuality. *Canadian Journal of Behavioural Science, 42*(4), 222–233.

Coates, L. (1997). Causal attributions in sexual assault trial judgments. *Journal of Language and Social Psychology, 16*, 278–296.

Coats, E. (1998). Bystander intervention (E-mail response to G. Mumford, Tobacco update 3/20/98). Retrieved from www.stolaf.edu/cgi-bin/mailarchivesearch.pl?directory=/home/www/people/huff/SPSP&listname=archive98&location=683178

Coalition for Gun Control (n.d.). Gun control works: Gun death and injury decline. Retrieved from www.guncontrol.ca/English/Home/Works/GunDeathandInjuryDecline.pdf

Cohen, D., Hoshino-Browne, E., & Leung, A. (2007). Culture and the structure of personal experience: Insider and outsider phenomenologies of the self and social world. In M. P. Zanna (Ed.), *Advances in experimental social psychology* (Vol. 39, pp. 1–67). San Diego, CA: Elsevier Academic Press.

Cohen, S., & Herbert, T. B. (1996). Health psychology: Psychological factors and physical disease from the perspective of human psychoneuroimmunology. *Annual Review of Psychology, 47*, 113–142.

Cohen, S., Mermelstein, R., Kamarack, T., & Hoberman, H. (1985). Measuring the functional components of social support. In I. G. Sarason & B. R. Sarason (Eds.), *Social support: Theory, research, and applications* (pp. 73–94). The Hague, Netherlands: Martines Nijhoff.

Cohen, S., Tyrrell, D. A. J., & Smith, A. P. (1991). Psychological stress in humans and susceptibility to the common cold. *New England Journal of Medicine, 325*, 606–612.

Cohen, S., Tyrrell, D. A. J., & Smith, A. P. (1993). Negative life events, perceived stress, negative affect, and susceptibility to the common cold. *Journal of Personality and Social Psychology, 64*, 131–140.

Cohen, S., & Wills, T. A. (1985). Stress, social support, and buffering. *Psychological Bulletin, 98*, 310–357.

Cohen, T. R., & Insko, C. A. (2008). War and peace: Possible approaches to reducing intergroup conflict. *Perspectives on Psychological Science, 3*, 87–93.

Cohn, L. D., & Adler, N. E. (1992). Female and male perceptions of ideal body shapes. *Psychology of Women Quarterly, 16*, 69–79.

Coie, J. D., Cillessen, A. H. N., Dodge, K. A., Hubbard, J. A., Schwartz, D., Lemerise, E. D., & Bateman, H. (1999). It takes two to fight: A test of relational factors and a method for assessing aggressive dyads. *Developmental Psychology, 35*, 1179–1188.

Colligan, M. J., Pennebaker, J. W., & Murphy, L. R. (Eds). (1982). *Mass psychogenic illness: A social psychological analysis.* Hillsdale, NJ: Erlbaum.

Collins, R. L. (1996). For better or worse: The impact of upward social comparison on self-evaluations. *Psychological Bulletin, 119*, 51–69.

Coltrane, S., Archer, D., & Aronson, E. (1986). The social-psychological foundations of successful energy conservation programs. *Energy Policy, 14*, 133–148.

Combating childhood obesity. (2007, Fall/Winter). *True Azure*, pp. 14–16.

Condon, J. W., & Crano, W. D. (1988). Inferred evaluation and the relation between attitude similarity and interpersonal attraction. *Journal of Personality and Social Psychology, 54*, 789–797.

Connolly, J., Friedlander, L., Pepler, D., Craig, W., & Laporte, L. (2010). The ecology of adolescent dating aggression: Attitudes, relationships, media use, and socio-demographic risk factors. *Journal of Aggression, Maltreatment & Trauma, 19*(5), 469–491.

Connolly, J., Nocentini, A., Menesini, E., Pepler, D., Craig, W., & Williams, T. (2010). Adolescent dating aggression in Canada and Italy: A cross-national comparison. *International Journal of Behavioral Development, 34*(2), 98–105.

Correll, J., Park, B., Judd, C. M., & Wittenbrink, B. (2002). The police officer's dilemma: Using ethnicity to disambiguate potentially threatening individuals. *Journal of Personality and Social Psychology, 83*, 1314–1329.

Conway, L. G., III & Schaller, M. (2005). When authorities' commands backfire: Attributions about consensus and effects on deviant decision making. *Journal of Personality and Social Psychology, 89*, 311–326.

Conway, M., & Dubé, L. (2002). Humor in persuasion on threatening topics: Effectiveness is a function of audience sex role orientation. *Personality and Social Psychology Bulletin, 28*, 863–873.

Cook, S. W. (1984). Cooperative interaction in multiethnic contexts. In N. Miller & M. Brewer (Eds.), *Groups in contact: The psychology of desegregation.* New York: Academic Press.

Cook, S. W. (1985). Experimenting on social issues: The case of school desegration. *American Psychologist, 40*, 452–460.

Cooley, C. H. (1902). *Human nature and social order.* New York: Scribner's.

Cooper, W. H., Gallupe, R. B., Pollard, S., & Cadsby, J. (1998). Some liberating effects of anonymous electronic brainstorming. *Small Group Research, 29*, 147–178.

Corcoran, K. M., & Woody, S. R. (2009). Effects of suppression and appraisals on thought frequency and distress. *Behaviour Research and Therapy, 47*(12), 1024-1031.

Corenblum, B. (2003). What children remember about ingroup and outgroup peers: Effects of stereotypes on children's processing of information about group members. *Journal of Experimental Child Psychology, 86*, 32–66.

Corenblum, B., & Annis, R. (1993). Development of racial identity in minority and majority children: An affect discrepancy model. *Canadian Journal of Behavioural Science, 25*, 499–521.

Corenblum, B., Annis, R., & Young, S. (1996). Effects of own group success or failure on judgments of task performance by children of different ethnicities. *European Journal of Social Psychology, 26*, 777–798.

Corenblum, B., & Meissner, C. A. (2006). Recognition of faces of ingroup and outgroup children and adults. *Journal of Experimental Child Psychology, 93*, 187–206.

Corenblum, B., & Stephan, W. G. (2001). White fears and Native apprehensions: An integrated threat theory approach to intergroup attitudes. *Canadian Journal of Behavioural Science, 33*, 251–268.

Corneil, W., Beaton, R., Murphy, S., Johnson, C., & Pike, K. (1999). Exposure to traumatic incidents and prevalence of post-traumatic stress symptomatology in urban firefighters in two countries. *Journal of Occupational Health Psychology, 4*, 131–141.

Correll, J., Park, B., Judd, C. M., & Wittenbrink, B. (2002). The police officer's dilemma: Using ethnicity to disambiguate potentially threatening individuals. *Journal of Personality and Social Psychology, 83*, 1314–1329.

Correll, J., Spencer, S. J., & Zanna, M. P. (2004). An affirmed sense and an open mind: Self-affirmation and sensitivity to argument strength. *Journal of Experimental Social Psychology, 40*, 350–356.

Cosmides, L., & Tooby, J. (1992). Cognitive adaptations for social exchange. In J. H. Barkow, L. Cosmides, & J. Tooby (Eds.), *The adapted mind: Evolutionary psychology and the generation of culture* (pp. 163–228). New York: Oxford University Press.

Costello, K., & Hodson, G. (2010). Exploring the roots of dehumanization: The role of animal--human similarity in promoting immigrant humanization. *Group Processes & Intergroup Relations, 13*(1), 3–22.

Cottrell, C. A., & Neuberg, S. L. (2005). Different emotional reactions to different groups: A sociofunctional threat-biased approach to "prejudice." *Journal of Personality and Social Psychology, 88*, 770–789.

Cottrell, N. B. (1968). Performance in the presence of other human beings: Mere presence, audience, and affiliation effects. In E. C. Simmel, R. A. Hoppe, & G. A. Milton (Eds.), *Social facilitation and imitative behavior* (pp. 91–110). Boston, MA: Allyn & Bacon.

Cottrell, N. B., Wack, K. L., Sekerak, G. J., & Rittle, R. (1968). Social facilitation in dominant responses by the presence of an audience and the mere presence of others. *Journal of Personality and Social Psychology, 9*, 245–250.

Courage, M. L., Edison, S. C., & Howe, M. L. (2004). Variability in the early development of visual self-recognition. *Infant Behavior and Development, 27*, 509–532.

Courneya, K. S., & Friedenreich, C. M. (1997). Determinants of exercise during colorectal cancer treatment: An application of the theory of planned behavior. *Oncology Nursing Forum, 24*, 1715–1723.

Courneya, K. S., & Friedenreich, C. M. (1999). Utility of the theory of planned behavior for understanding exercise during breast cancer treatment. *Psycho-Oncology, 8*, 112–122.

Craig, W. M., & Pepler, D. J. (1997). Observations of bullying and victimization in the school yard. *Canadian Journal of School Psychology, 13*, 41–60.

Cramer, K. M., Nickels, J. B., & Gural, D. M. (1997). Uncertainty of outcomes, prediction of failure, and lack of control as factors explaining perceived helplessness. *Journal of Social Behavior and Personality, 12*, 611–630.

Crandall, C. S., D'Anello, S., Sakalli, N., Lazarus, E., Wieczorkowska, G., & Feather, N. T. (2001). An attribution-value model of prejudice: Anti-fat attitudes in six nations. *Personality and Social Psychology Bulletin, 27*, 30–37.

Crandall, C. S., Eshelman, A., & O'Brien, L. (2002). Social norms and the expression and suppression of prejudice: The struggle for internalization. *Journal of Personality and Social Psychology, 82*, 359–378.

Crandall, C. S., & Schaller, M. (Eds). (2005). *Social psychology of prejudice: Historical and contemporary issues*. Lawrence, KS: Lewinian Press.

Crano, W., & Prislin, R. (2006). Attitudes and persuasion. *Annual Review of Psychology, 57*, 345–374.

Crawford, C., & Krebs, D. L. (1998). *Handbook of evolutionary psychology*. Mahwah, NJ: Erlbaum.

Crawford, T. (2004, June 25). Dangerous chemical discovered as probable cause of toxic bus mystery. *The Canadian Press*.

Crites, S. L., Jr., Fabrigar, L. R., & Petty, R. E. (1994). Measuring the affective and cognitive properties of attitudes: Conceptual and methodological issues. *Personality and Social Psychology Bulletin, 20*, 619–634.

Crocker, J., & Major, B. (1989). Social stigma and self-esteem: The self-protective properties of stigma. *Psychological Review, 96*, 608–630.

Cross, S. E., Bacon, P. L., & Morris, M. L. (2000). The relational-interdependent self-construal and relationships. *Journal of Personality and Social Psychology, 78*, 791–808.

Cross, S. E., & Madson, L. (1997). Elaboration of models of the self: Reply to Baumeister and Sommer (1997) and Martin and Rubble (1997). *Psychological Bulletin, 122*, 51–55.

Cross, S. E., & Vick, N. V. (2001). The interdependent self-construal and social support: The case of persistence in engineering. *Personality and Social Psychology Bulletin, 27*, 820–832.

Crossman, J., Vincent, J., & Speed, H. (2007). 'The times they are a-changing': Gender comparisons in three national newspapers of the 2004 Wimbledon Championships. *International Review for the Sociology of Sport, 42*(1), 27–41.

Crowley, A. E., & Hoyer, W. D. (1994). An integrative framework for understanding two-sided persuasion. *Journal of Consumer Research, 20*, 561–574.

Croyle, R. T., & Jemmott, J. B., III (1990). Psychological reactions to risk factor testing. In J. A. Skelton & R. T. Croyle (Eds.), *The mental representation of health and illness* (pp. 121–157). New York: Springer-Verlag.

Crutchfield, R. A. (1955). Conformity and character. *American Psychologist, 10*, 191–198.

Csikszentmihalyi, M., & Figurski, T. J. (1982). Self-awareness and aversive experience in everyday life. *Journal of Personality, 50*, 15–28.

Cuddy, A. J. C., Fiske, S. T., & Glick, P. (2007). The BIAS map: Behaviors from intergroup affect and stereotypes. *Journal of Personality and Social Psychology, 92*, 631–648.

Cullen, M. C., & Bradley, M. T. (2004). Positions of truthfully answered controls on control question test with the polygraph. *Canadian Journal of Behavioural Science, 36*, 167–176.

Cunningham, M. R. (1986). Measuring the physical in physical attractiveness: Quasi-experiments on the sociobiology of female facial beauty. *Journal of Personality and Social Psychology, 50*, 925–935.

Cunningham, M. R., Barbee, A. R., & Pike, C. L. (1990). What do women want? Facial metric assessment of multiple motives in the perception of male facial physical attractiveness. *Journal of Personality and Social Psychology, 59*, 61–72.

Cunningham, M. R., Roberts, A. R., Barbee, A. P., Druen, P. B., & Wu, C. (1995). "Their ideas of beauty are, on the whole, the same as ours": Consistency and variability in the cross-cultural perception of female physical attractiveness. *Journal of Personality and Social Psychology, 68*, 261–279.

Curtis, R. C., & Miller, K. (1986). Believing another likes or dislikes you: Behaviors making the beliefs come true. *Journal of Personality and Social Psychology, 51*, 284–290.

Cusumano, D. L., & Thompson, J. K. (1997). Body image and body shape ideals in magazines: Exposure, awareness, and internalization. *Sex Roles, 37*, 701–721.

Cutler, B. L., Daugherty, B., Babu, S., Hodges, L., & Van Wallendael, L. (2009). Creating blind photoarrays using virtual human technology: A feasibility test. *Police Quarterly, 12*(3), 289–300.

Cutler, B. L., & Kovera, M. (2011). Expert psychological testimony. *Current Directions in Psychological Science, 20*(1), 53–57.

Cynkar, A. (June, 2007). Order in the court. *Monitor on Psychology*, pp. 48–49.

Dabbs, J. M., Jr., (2000). *Heroes, rogues, and lovers*. New York: McGraw-Hill.

Dabbs, J. M., Jr., Carr, T. S., Frady, R. L., & Riad, J. K. (1995). Testosterone, crime, and misbehavior among 692 male prison inmates. *Personality and Individual Differences, 18*, 627–633.

Dabbs, J. M., Jr., Hargrove, M. F., & Heusel, C. (1996). Testosterone differences among college fraternities: Well-behaved vs. rambunctious. *Personality and Individual Differences, 20*, 157–161.

Dabbs, J. M., Jr., Ruback, R. B., Frady, R. L., Hopper, C. H., & Sgoutas, D. S. (1988). Saliva testosterone and criminal violence among women. *Personality and Individual Differences, 7*, 269–275.

Dahl, D. W., Gorn, G. J., & Weinberg, C. B. (1998). Condom carrying behavior among college students. *Canadian Journal of Public Health, 89*, 368–370.

Dambrun, M., Taylor, D. M., McDonald, D. A., Crush, J., & Méot, A. (2006). The relative deprivation-gratification continuum and the attitudes of South Africans toward immigrants: A test of the V-curve hypothesis. *Journal of Personality and Social Psychology, 91*, 1032–1044.

D'Angelo, A. M. (2000, February 14). No charges in bridge fall. *North Shore News*. Retrieved from www.nsnews.com/issues00/w021400/02110001.html

Daniel, M., & Nelson, K. (2004, August 20). In search of rush teens risk lives surfing on cars. *Boston Globe*, pp. B1, B4.

Darke, P. R., & Chaiken, S. (2005). The pursuit of self-interest: Self- interest bias in attitude judgment and persuasion. *Journal of Personality and Social Psychology, 89*, 864–883.

Darley, J. M. (1995). Constructive and destructive obedience: A taxonomy of principal-agent relationships. *Journal of Social Issues, 51*, 125–154.

Darley, J. M., & Akert, R. M. (1993). *Biographical interpretation: The influence of later events in life on the meaning of and memory for earlier events*. Unpublished manuscript, Princeton University.

Darley, J. M., & Batson, C. D. (1973). From Jerusalem to Jericho: A study of situational and dispositional variables in helping behavior. *Journal of Personality and Social Psychology, 27*, 100–108.

Darley, J. M., & Latané, B. (1968). Bystander intervention in emergencies: Diffusion of responsibility. *Journal of Personality and Social Psychology, 8*, 377–383.

Dar-Nimrod, I., & Heine, S. J. (2006). Exposure to scientific theories affects women's math performance. *Science, 314*, 435.

Darwin, C. (1872). *The expression of emotions in man and animals*. London, UK: John Murray.

Darwin, C. R. (1859). *The origin of species*. London, UK: John Murray.

Das, E., Bushman, B. J., Bezemer, M. D., Kerkhof, P., & Vermeulen, I. E. (2009). How terrorism news reports increase prejudice against outgroups: A Terror Management account. *Journal of Experimental Social Psychology, 45*, 453–459.

Das, E. H. J., de Wit, J. B. F., & Stroebe, W. (2003). Fear appeals motivate acceptance of action recommendations: Evidence for a positive bias in the processing of persuasive messages. *Personality and Social Psychology Bulletin, 29*, 650–664.

Davidson, A. R., & Jaccard, J. J. (1979). Variables that moderate the attitude behavior relation: Results of a longitudinal survey. *Journal of Personality and Social Psychology, 37*, 1364–1376.

Davidson, R., Putnam, K., & Larson, C. (2000). Dysfunction in the neural circuitry of emotion regulation: A possible prelude to violence. *Science, 289*, 591–594.

Davies, M. F. (1997). Belief persistence after evidential discrediting: The impact of generated versus provided explanations on the likelihood of discredited outcomes. *Journal of Experimental Social Psychology, 33*, 561–578.

Davies, P. G., Spencer, S. J., & Claude, M. (2005). Clearing the air: Identity safety moderates the effects of stereotype threat on women's leadership aspirations. *Journal of Personality and Social Psychology, 88*, 276–287.

Davies, P. G., Spencer, S. J., Quinn, D. M., & Gerhardsteine, R. (2002). Consuming images: How television commercials that elicit stereotype threat can restrain women academically and professionally. *Personality and Social Psychology Bulletin, 28*, 1615–1628.

Davies, P. G., Spencer, S. J., & Steele, C. M. (2005). Clearing the air: Identity safety moderates the effects of stereotype threat on women's leadership aspirations. *Journal of Personality and Social Psychology, 88*, 276–287.

Davies, R. (1991). *Murther and walking spirits*. Toronto, ON: McClelland and Stewart.

Davis, C., Lehman, D., Cohen Silver, R., Wortman, C., & Ellard, J. (1996). Self-blame following a traumatic event: The role of perceived avoidability. *Personality and Social Psychology Bulletin, 22*, 557–567.

Davis, C. G., & Lehman, D. R. (1995). Counterfactual thinking and coping with traumatic life events. In N. J. Roese & J. M. Olson (Eds.), *What might have been: The social psychology of counterfactual thinking* (pp. 353–374). Mahwah, NJ: Erlbaum.

Davis, C. G., Lehman, D. R., Wortman, C. B., Silver, R. C., & Thompson, S. C. (1995). The undoing of traumatic life events. *Personality and Social Psychology Bulletin, 21*, 109–124.

Davis, D., & Loftus, E. F. (2007). Internal and external sources of misinformation in adult witness memory. In M. P. Toglia, J. D. Read, D. F. Ross, & R. C. L. Lindsay (Eds.) *The handbook of eyewitness psychology: Vol. I. Memory for events* (pp. 195–237). Mahwah, NJ: Lawrence Erlbaum.

Davis, D. D., & Harless, D. W. (1996). Group versus individual performance in a price-searching experiment. *Organizational Behavior and Human Decision Processes, 66*, 215–227.

Davis, K. E., & Jones, E. E. (1960). Changes in interpersonal perception as a means of reducing cognitive dissonance. *Journal of Abnormal and Social Psychology, 61*, 402–410.

Davison, K. P., Pennebaker, J. W., & Dickerson, S. S. (2000). Who talks? The social psychology of illness support groups. *American Psychologist, 55*, 205–217.

Davitz, J. (1952). The effects of previous training on post-frustration behavior. *Journal of Abnormal and Social Psychology, 47*, 309–315.

Dawes, R. M. (1980). Social dilemmas. *Annual Review of Psychology, 31*, 169–193.

Day, A. L., & Livingstone, H. A. (2003). Gender differences in perceptions of stressors and utilization of social support among university students. *Canadian Journal of Behavioural Science, 35*, 73–83.

Dean, K. E., & Malamuth N. M. (1997). Characteristics of men who aggress sexually and of men who imagine aggressing: Risk and moderating variables. *Journal of Personality and Social Psychology, 72*, 499–455.

Deaux, K., & Emsweiler, T. (1974). Explanations of successful performance of sex-linked tasks: What is skill for male is luck for the female. *Journal of Personality and Social Psychology, 29*, 80–85.

Deaux, K., & La France, M. (1998). Gender. In D. T. Gilbert, S. T. Fiske, & G. Lindzey (Eds.), *The handbook of social psychology* (4th ed., Vol. 1, pp. 788–828). New York: McGraw-Hill.

Deaux, K., & Major, B. (1987). Putting gender into context: An interactive model of gender-related behavior. *Psychological Review, 94*, 369–389.

DeBono, K. G., & Snyder, M. (1995). Acting on one's attitudes: The role of a history of choosing situations. *Personality and Social Psychology Bulletin, 21*, 629–636.

Deci, E. L., Koestner, R., & Ryan, R. M. (1999a). A meta-analytic review of experiments examining the effects of extrinsic rewards. *Psychological Bulletin, 125*, 627–668.

Deci, E. L., Koestner, R., & Ryan, R. M. (1999b). The undermining effect is a reality after all—extrinsic rewards, task interest, and self-determination: Reply to Eisenberger, Pierce, and Cameron (1999) and Lepper, Henderlong, and Gingras (1999). *Psychological Bulletin, 125*, 692–700.

Deci, E. L., & Ryan, R. M. (1985). *Intrinsic motivation and self- determination in human behavio*r. New York: Plenum.

Deci, E. L., & Ryan, R. M. (Eds). (2002). *Handbook of self-determination research*. Rochester, NY: University of Rochester Press.

De Dreu, C., Nijstad, B., & van Knippenberg, D. (2008). Motivated information processing in group judgment and decision making. *Personality and Social Psychology Review, 12*, 22–49.

De Dreu, C. K. W., & De Vries, N. K. (Eds). (2001). *Group consensus and minority influence: Implications for innovation*. Oxford, UK: Blackwell Publishers.

De Dreu, C. K. W., Weingart, L. R., & Kwon, S. (2000). Influence of social motives on integrative negotiation: A meta-analytic review and test of two theories. *Journal of Personality and Social Psychology, 78*, 889–905.

Deffenbacher, K. A., Bornstein, B. H., & Penrod, S. D. (2004). A meta-analytic review of the effects of high stress on eyewitness memory. *Law and Human Behavior, 28*, 687–706.

De Hoog, N., Stroebe, W., & de Wit, J. B. (2005). The impact of fear appeals on processing and acceptance of action recommendations. *Personality and Social Psychology Bulletin, 31*, 24–33.

DeJong, W., & Winsten, J. A. (1989). *Recommendations for future mass media campaigns to prevent preteen and adolescent substance abuse.* Unpublished manuscript, Center for Health Communication, Harvard School of Public Health.

DeKeseredy, W. S., & Kelly, K. (1993). Woman abuse in university and college dating relationships: The contribution of the ideology of familial patriarchy. *Journal of Human Justice, 4*, 25–52.

Delisle, M., Guay, F., Senécal, C., & Larose, S. (2009). Predicting stereotype endorsement and academic motivation in women in science programs: A longitudinal model. *Learning and Individual Differences, 19*(4), 468–475.

De Marco, P. (1994, September 28). "Dear diary." *New York Times*, p. C2.

Dempsey, J. L., & Pozzulo, J. D. (2008). Identification accuracy of eyewitnesses for a multiple perpetrator crime: Examining the simultaneous and elimination lineup procedures. *American Journal of Forensic Psychology, 26*(4), 67–81.

De Neys, W., & Glumicic, T. (2008). Conflict monitoring in dual process theories of thinking. *Cognition, 106*(3), 1248–1299.

Dennett, D. C. (1991). *Consciousness explained.* Boston: Little, Brown.

Depape, A. R., Hakim-Larson, J., Voelker, S., Page, S., & Jackson, D. L. (2006). Self-talk and emotional intelligence in university students. *Canadian Journal of Behavioural Science, 38*, 250–260.

De Paulo, B. M., Epstein, J. A., & Wyer, M. M. (1993). Sex differences in lying: How women and men deal with the dilemma of deceit. In M. Lewis & C. Saarni (Eds.), *Lying and deception in everyday life* (pp. 126–147). New York: Guilford Press.

De Paulo, B. M., & Friedman, H. S. (1998). Nonverbal communication. In D. Gilbert, S. Fiske, & G. Lindzey (Eds.), *The handbook of social psychology* (4th ed., Vol. 2, pp. 3–40). New York: McGraw Hill.

De Paulo, B. M., Kenny, D. A., Hoover, C. W., Webb, W., & Oliver, P. (1987). Accuracy of person perception: Do people know what kinds of impressions they convey? *Journal of Personality and Social Psychology, 52*, 303–315.

DePaulo, B. M., Lassiter, G. D., & Stone, J. I. (1983). Attentional determinants of success at detecting deception and truth. *Personality and Social Psychology Bulletin, 8*, 273–279.

DePaulo, B. M., & Pfeiffer, R. L. (1986). On-the-job experience and skill at detecting deception. *Journal of Applied Social Psychology, 16*, 249–267.

Desjarlais, M., & Willoughby, T. (2010). A longitudinal study of the relation between adolescent boys and girls' computer use with friends and friendship quality: Support for the social compensation or the rich-getricher hypothesis? *Computers in Human Behavior, 26*(5), 896–905.

Deslauriers-Varin, N., Beauregard, E., & Wong, J. 2011). Changing their mind about confessing to police: The role of contextual factors in crime confession. *Police Quarterly, 14*, 5–24.

Desmarais, S. L., Price, H. L., & Read, J. (2008). Objection, your honor! Television is not the relevant authority: Crime drama portrayals of eyewitness issues. *Psychology, Crime & Law, 14*(3), 225–243.

Desmond, E. W. (1987, November 30). Out in the open. *Time*, pp. 80–90.

De Souza, M. (2007, November 12). Doctor alleges oilsands coverup. CanWest News Service. Calgary Herald. Retrieved from www.canada.com/calgaryherald/news/story.html?id=8c9ccc7f-9ea7-4564-a8b3-d7f2dfc099e9

Desportes, J. P., & Lemaine, J. M. (1998). The sizes of human groups: An analysis of their distributions. In D. Canter, J. C. Jesuino, L. Soczka, & G. M. Stephenson (Eds.), *Environmental social psychology* (pp. 57–65). Dordrecht, Netherlands: Kluwer.

Deutsch, M. (1973). *The resolution of conflict: Constructive and destructive processes.* New Haven, CT: Yale University Press.

Deutsch, M. (1990). Cooperation, conflict, and justice. In S. A. Wheelan, E. A. Pepitone, & V. Abt (Eds.), *Advances in field theory* (pp. 149–164). Newbury Park, CA: Sage.

Deutsch, M., & Gerard, H. G. (1955). A study of normative and informational social influence upon individual judgment. *Journal of Abnormal and Social Psychology, 51*, 629–636.

Deutsch, M., & Krauss, R. M. (1960). The effect of threat upon interpersonal bargaining. *Journal of Abnormal and Social Psychology, 61*, 181–189.

Deutsch, M., & Krauss, R. M. (1962). Studies of interpersonal bargaining. *Journal of Conflict Resolution, 6*, 52–76.

Devine, D. J., Clayton, L. D., Dunford, B. B., Seying, R., & Pryce, J. (2001). Jury decision making: 45 years of empirical research on deliberating groups. *Psychology, Public Policy, and Law, 7*, 622–727.

Devine, P. G. (1989a). Automatic and controlled processes in prejudice: The roles of stereotypes and personal beliefs. In A. R. Pratkanis, S. J. Breckler, & A. G. Greenwald (Eds.), *Attitude structure and function* (pp. 181–212). Hillsdale, NJ: Erlbaum.

Devine, P. G. (1989b). Stereotypes and prejudice: Their automatic and controlled components. *Journal of Personality and Social Psychology, 56*, 5–18.

Devine, P. G. (2003). A modern perspective on the classic American dilemma. *Psychological Inquiry, 14*(3), 244–250.

Devine, P. G., & Monteith, M. J. (1999). Automaticity and control in stereotyping. In S. Chaiken & Y. Trope (Eds.), *Dual-process theories in social psychology* (pp. 339–360). New York: Guilford Press.

de Waal, F. B. M. (1995, March). Bonobo sex and society: The behavior of a close relative challenges assumptions about male supremacy in human evolution. *Scientific American*, 82–88.

de Waal, F. (1996). *Good natured: The origins of right and wrong in humans and other animals.* Cambridge, MA: Harvard University Press.

DeWall, C. N., & Baumeister, R. F. (2006). Alone but feeling no pain Effects of social exclusion on physical pain tolerance and pain threshold, affective forecasting, and interpersonal empathy. *Journal of Personality and Social Psychology, 91*, 1–15.

Dickerson, C., Thibodeau, R., Aronson, E., & Miller, D. (1992). Using cognitive dissonance to encourage water conservation. *Journal of Applied Social Psychology, 22*, 841–854.

Diener, E. (1980). Deindividuation: The absence of self-awareness and self-regulation in group members. In P. B. Paulus (Ed.), *Psychology of group influence* (pp. 209–242). Hillsdale, NJ: Erlbaum.

Diener, E., & Wallbom, M. (1976). Effects of self-awareness on antinormative behavior. *Journal of Research in Personality, 10*, 107–111.

Dijksterhuis, A. (2004). Think different: The merits of unconscious thought in preference development and decision making. *Journal of Personality and Social Psychology, 87*, 586–598.

Dijksterhuis, A., & Aarts, H. (2002). *The power of the subliminal: On subliminal persuasion and other potential applications.* Unpublished manuscript.

Dijksterhuis, A., Aarts, H., & Smith, P. K. (2005). The power of the subliminal: On subliminal persuasion and other potential applications. In R. R. Hassin, J. S. Uleman, & J. A. Bargh (Eds.), *The new unconscious* (pp. 77–106). New York: Oxford University Press.

Dijksterhuis, A., & Nordgren, L. F. (2005). *A theory of unconscious thought* (Vol. I, pp. 95–109). University of Amsterdam.

Dijksterhuis, A., & Nordgren, L. F. (2006). A theory of unconscious thought. *Perspectives on Psychological Science, 1*(2), 95–109.

Dijksterhuis, A., Preston, J., Wegner, D. M., & Aarts, H. (2008). Effects of subliminal priming of self and god on self-attribution of authorship for events. *Journal of Experimental Social Psychology, 44*, 2–9.

Dijksterhuis, A., & van Knippenberg, A. (1996). The knife that cuts both ways: Facilitated and inhibited access to traits as a result of stereotype activation. *Journal of Experimental Social Psychology, 32*, 271–288.

Dillard, J. P. (1991). The current status of research on sequential- request compliance techniques. *Personality and Social Psychology Bulletin, 17*, 283–288.

Dillard, J. P., Plotnick, C. A., Godbold, L. C., Freimuth, V. S., & Edgar, T. (1996). The multiple affective outcomes of AIDS PSAs: Fear appeals do more than scare people. *Communication Research, 23*, 44–72.

Dion, Karen K. (2002). Cultural perspectives on facial attractiveness. In G. Rhodes (Ed.), *Facial attractiveness: Evolutionary, cognitive, and social perspectives* (pp. 239–259). Westport, CT: Ablex Publishing.

Dion, K. K., Berscheid, E., & Walster (Hatfield), E. (1972). What is beautiful is good. *Journal of Personality and Social Psychology, 24*, 285–290.

Dion, K. K., & Dion, K. L. (1996). Cultural perspectives on romantic love. *Personal Relationships, 3*, 5–17.

Dion, K. K., & Dion, K. L. (2001). Gender and cultural adaptation in immigrant families. *Journal of Social Issues, 57*, 511–521.

Dion, Kenneth L. (1985). Social distance norms in Canada: Effects of stimulus characteristics and dogmatism. *International Journal of Psychology, 20*, 743–749.

Dion, K. L. (1987). What's in a title? The Ms. stereotype and images of women's titles of address. *Psychology of Women Quarterly, 11*(1), 21–36.

Dion, K. L. (1999). Ms. as a title of address. In H. Tierney (Ed.), *Women's studies encyclopedia: Revised and expanded edition* (Vol. 2, G–P, pp. 954–957). Westport, CT: Greenwood Press.

Dion, K. L. (2000). Canada. In A. E. Kazdin (Ed.), *Encyclopedia of psychology* (Vol. 2, pp. 5–12). Washington, DC/New York: American Psychological Association & Oxford University Press.

Dion, K. L. (2001). Immigrants' perceptions of discrimination in Toronto, ON: The Housing New Canadians project. *Journal of Social Issues, 57*, 523–539.

Dion, K. L. (2002). The social psychology of perceived prejudice and discrimination. *Canadian Psychology, 43*, 1–10.

Dion, K. L. (2003). Prejudice, racism, and discrimination. In T. Millon & M. J. Lerner (Eds.), *Handbook of psychology: Personality and social psychology* (Vol. 5, pp. 507–536). Hoboken, NJ: John Wiley & Sons.

Dion, K. L., & Dion, K. K. (1973). Correlates of romantic love. *Journal of Consulting and Clinical Psychology, 41*, 51–56.

Dion, K. L., & Dion, K. K. (1987). Belief in a just world and physical attractiveness stereotyping. *Journal of Personality and Social Psychology, 52*, 775–780.

Dion, K. L., & Dion, K. K. (1993). Gender and ethnocultural comparisons in styles of love. *Psychology of Women Quarterly, 17*, 463–473.

Dion, K. L., Dion, K. K., & Pak, A. W. (1992). Personality-based hardiness as a buffer for discrimination-related stress in members of Toronto's Chinese community. *Canadian Journal of Behavioural Science, 24*, 517–536.

Dion, K. L., & Kawakami, K. (1996). Ethnicity and perceived discrimination in Toronto, ON: Another look at the personal/group discrimination discrepancy. *Canadian Journal of Behavioural Science, 28*, 203–213.

Dion, K. L., Pak, A., & Dion, K. K. (1990). Stereotyping physical attractiveness. *Journal of Cross Cultural Psychology, 21*, 158–179.

Dion, K. L., & Schuller, R. A. (1991). The Ms. stereotype: Its generality and its relation to managerial and marital status stereotypes. *Canadian Journal of Behavioural Science, 23*, 25–40.

Dittman, M. (2004, October). What makes good people do bad things? *Monitor on Psychology*, 68–69.

Dix, T. (1993). Attributing dispositions to children: An interactional analysis of attribution in socialization. *Personality and Social Psychology Bulletin, 19*, 633–643.

Djikic, M., Chan, I., & Peterson, J. B. (2007). Reducing memory distortions in egoistic self-enhancers: Effects of indirect social facilitation. *Personality and Individual Differences, 42*(4), 723–731.

Dodge, K. A., & Schwartz, D. (1997). Social information processing mechanisms in aggressive behavior. In D. M. Stoff & J. Breiling (Eds.), *Handbook of antisocial behavior* (pp. 171–180). New York: Wiley.

Dodge, M. K. (1984). Learning to care: Developing prosocial behavior among one- and two-year-olds in group settings. *Journal of Research and Development in Education, 17*, 26–30.

Dohrenwend, B. (2006). Inventorying stressful life events as risk factors for psychopathology: Toward resolution of the problem of intracategory variability. *Psychological Bulletin, 132*, 477–495.

Doi, T. (1988). An experimental investigation of the validity of the characteristic space theory and the measurement of social motivation. *Japanese Journal of Experimental Social Psychology, 27*, 139–148.

Dolin, D. J., & Booth-Butterfield, S. (1995). Foot-in-the-door and cancer prevention. *Health Communication, 7*, 55–66.

Dollard, J. (1938). Hostility and fear in social life. *Social Forces, 17*, 15–26.

Dollard, J., Doob, L., Miller, N., Mowrer, O. H., & Sears, R. R. (1939). *Frustration and aggression*. New Haven, CT: Yale University Press.

Domina, T., & Koch, K. (2002). Convenience and frequency of recycling: Implications for including textiles in curbside recycling programs. *Environment and Behavior, 34*, 216–238.

Donakowski, D. W., & Esses, V. M. (1996). "Native Canadians," "First Nations," and "Aboriginals": The effect of labels on attitudes toward Native peoples. *Canadian Journal of Behavioural Science, 28*, 86–91.

Donnellan, M. B., Burt, S. A., Levendosky, A. A., & Klump, K. L. (2008). Genes, personality, and attachment in adults: A multivariate behavioral genetic analysis. *Personality and Social Psychology Bulletin, 34*, 3–16.

Donnerstein, E. (1980). Aggressive erotica and violence against women. *Journal of Personality and Social Psychology, 39*, 269–272.

Donnerstein, E., & Berkowitz, L. (1981). Victim reactions in aggressive erotic films as a factor in violence against women. *Journal of Personality and Social Psychology, 41*, 710–724.

Donnerstein, E., & Donnerstein, M. (1976). Research in the control of interracial aggression. In R. G. Green & E. C. O'Neal (Eds.), *Perspectives on aggression* (pp. 133–168). New York: Academic Press.

Donnerstein, E., & Linz, D. (1994). Sexual violence in the mass media. In M. Costanzo, S. Oskamp et al. (Eds.), *Violence and the law: Claremont symposium on applied social psychology* (Vol. 7, pp. 9–36). Thousand Oaks, CA: Sage.

Don't stand by . . . stand up! (2006, October). *Our Schools*, p. 4.

Donohue, J., & Wolfers, J. J. (2006). Uses and abuses of empirical evidence in the death penalty debate. *Stanford Law Review, 58*, 791–845.

Double deception. (2000, April 1). *Winnipeg Free Press.* [Letter to editor.]

Dovidio, J. F. (1984). Helping behavior and altruism: An empirical and conceptual overview. In L. Berkowitz (Ed.), *Advances in experimental social psychology* (Vol. 17, pp. 361–427). New York: Academic Press.

Dovidio, J. F., & Gaertner, S. L. (1996). Affirmative action, unintentional racial biases, and intergroup relations. *Journal of Social Issues, 52*, 51–75.

Dovidio, J. F., Kawakami, K., & Gaertner, S. L. (2002). Implicit and explicit prejudice and interracial interaction. *Journal of Personality and Social Psychology, 82*, 62–68.

Dovidio, J. F., Piliavin, J. A., Gaertner, S. L., Schroeder, D. A., & Clark, III R. D. (1991). The arousal cost-reward model and the process of intervention. In M. S. Clark (Ed.), *Review of personality and social psychology* (Vol. 12, pp. 86–118). Newbury Park, CA: Sage.

Dovidio, J. F., ten Vergert, M., Stewart, T. L., Gaertner, S. L., Johnson, J. D., Esses, V. M., & Pearson, A. R. (2004). Perspective and prejudice: Antecedents and mediating mechanisms. *Personality and Social Psychology Bulletin, 30*(12), 1537–1549.

Dowling, K. B., Rodger, S., & Cummings, A. L. (2007). Exploring attitudes of future educators about sexual minority youth. *Alberta Journal of Educational Research, 53*(4), 401–413.

Doyle, W. J., Gentile, D. A., & Cohen, S. (2006). Emotional style, nasal cytokines, and illness expression after experimental rhinovirus exposure. *Brain, Behavior and Immunity, 20*, 175–181.

Drohan-Jennings, D. M., Roberts, K. P., & Powell, M. B. (2010). Mental context reinstatement increases resistance to false suggestions after children have experienced a repeated event. *Psychiatry, Psychology and Law, 17*(4), 594–606.

Dryer, D. C., & Horowitz, L. M. (1997). When do opposites attract? Interpersonal complementarity versus similarity. *Journal of Personality and Social Psychology, 72*, 592–603.

Duck, J., Hogg, M., & Terry, D. (1995). Me, us and them: Political identification and the third-person effect in the 1993 Australian federal election. *European Journal of Social Psychology, 25*, 195–215.

Dugas, D. (2005, January 14). Canadians opened wallets in record numbers: polls. *Winnipeg Free Press*, p. A14.

Dumont, M., Yzerbyt, V., Wigboldus, D., & Gordijn, E. (2003). Social categorization and fear reactions to the September 11th terrorist Attacks. *Personality and Social Psychology Bulletin, 29*, 1509–1520.

Duncan, L. A., & Schaller, M. (2009). Prejudicial attitudes toward older adults may be exaggerated when people feel vulnerable to infectious disease: Evidence and implications. *Analyses of Social Issues and Public Policy, 9*(1), 97–115.

Dunfield, K. A., & Kuhlmeier, V. A. (2010). Intention-mediated selective helping in infancy. *Psychological Science, 21*(4), 523–527.

Dunn, E. W., Aknin, L. B., & Norton, M. I. (2008). Spending money on others promotes happiness. *Science, 319*, 1687–1688.

Dunn, E. W., Biesanz, J. C., Human, L. J., & Finn, S. (2007). Misunderstanding the affective consequences of everyday social interactions: The hidden benefits of putting one's best face forward. *Journal of Personality and Social Psychology, 92*, 990–1005.

Dunn, E. W., Brackett, M. A., Ashton-James, C., Schneiderman, E., & Salovey, P. (2007). On emotionally intelligent time travel: Individual differences in affective forecasting ability. *Personality and Social Psychology Bulletin, 33*, 85–93.

Dunn, E. W., & Spellman, B. A. (2003). Forgetting by remembering: Stereotype inhibition through rehearsal of alternative aspects of identity. *Journal of Experimental Social Psychology, 39*, 420–433.

Dunning, D., & Perretta, S. (2002). Automaticity and eyewitness accuracy: A 10- to 12-second rule for distinguishing accurate from inaccurate positive identifications. *Journal of Applied Psychology, 87*, 951–962.

Dunning, D., & Stern, L. B. (1994). Distinguishing accurate from inaccurate eyewitness identifications via inquiries about decision processes. *Journal of Personality and Social Psychology, 67*, 818–835.

Dupéré, V., Lacourse, É., Willms, J., Vitaro, F., & Tremblay, R. (2007). Affiliation to youth gangs during adolescence: The interaction between childhood psychopathic tendencies and neighborhood disadvantage. *Journal of Abnormal Child Psychology, 35*(6), 1035–1045.

Durik, A., & Harackiewicz, J. (2007). Different strokes for different folks: How individual interest moderates the effects of situational factors on task interest. *Journal of Educational Psychology, 99*, 597–610.

Dussault, M., Payette, D., & Leroux, M. (2008). Principals' transformational leadership and teachers' collective efficacy. *Psychological Reports, 102*(2), 401–410.

Dutton, D. G. (1995). *The domestic assault of women: Psychological and criminal justice perspectives*. Vancouver, BC: UBC Press.

Dutton, D. G., & Aron, A. P. (1974). Some evidence for heightened sexual attraction under conditions of high anxiety. *Journal of Personality and Social Psychology, 30*, 510–517.

Dutton, D. G., & Hart, S. D. (1992a). Evidence for long-term, specific effects of childhood abuse and neglect on criminal behavior in men. *International Journal of Offender Therapy and Comparative Criminology, 36*, 129–137.

Dutton, D. G., & Hart, S. D. (1992b). Risk markers for family violence in a federally incarcerated population. *International Journal of Law and Psychiatry, 15*, 101–112.

Duval, S., & Wicklund, R. A. (1972). *A theory of objective self-awareness*. New York: Academic Press.

Duval, T. S., & Silvia, P. J. (2002). Self-awareness, probability of improvement, and the self-serving bias. *Journal of Personality and Social Psychology, 82*, 49–61.

Dweck, C. S. (1999). *Self-theories: Their role in motivation, personality, and development*. Bristol, PA: Taylor & Francis.

Eagly, A., & Chaiken, S. (2007). The advantages of an inclusive definition of attitude. *Social Cognition, 25*, 582–602.

Eagly, A. H. (1987). *Sex differences in social behavior: A social-role interpretation*. Hillsdale, NJ: Erlbaum.

Eagly, A. H., Ashmore, R. D., Makhijani, M. G., & Longo, L. C. (1991). What is beautiful is good, but . . . : A meta-analytic review of research on the physical attractiveness stereotype. *Psychological Bulletin, 110*, 109–128.

Eagly, A. H., & Carli, L. L. (1981). Sex of researchers and sex-typed communications as determinants of sex differences in influenceability: A meta-analysis of social influence studies. *Psychological Bulletin, 90*, 1–20.

Eagly, A. H., & Carli, L. L. (2003). The female leadership advantage: An evaluation of the evidence. *Leadership Quarterly, 14*, 807–834.

Eagly, A. H., & Chaiken, S. (1975). An attribution analysis of communicator characteristics on opinion change: The case of communicator attractiveness. *Journal of Personality and Social Psychology, 32*, 136–244.

Eagly, A. H., & Chaiken, S. (1998). Attitude structure and function. In D. T. Gilbert, S. T. Fiske, & G. Lindzey (Eds.), *The handbook of social psychology* (4th ed., Vol. 1, pp. 269–322). New York: McGraw-Hill.

Eagly, A. H., & Crowley, M. (1986). Gender and helping behavior: A meta-analytic review of the social psychological literature. *Psychological Bulletin, 100*, 283–308.

Eagly, A. H., & Diekman, A. B. (2003). The malleability of sex differences in response to changing social roles. In L. G. Aspinwall, & U. M. Staudinger (Eds.), *A psychology of human strengths: Fundamental questions and future directions for a positive psychology* (pp. 103–115). Washington, D.C.: American Psychological Association.

Eagly, A. H., Diekman, A. B., Johannesen-Schmidt, M. C., & Koenig, A. M. (2004). Gender gaps in sociopolitical attitudes: A social psychological analysis. *Journal of Personality and Social Psychology, 87*, 796–798.

Eagly, A. H., Johannesen-Schmidt, M. C., & van Engen, M. L. (2003). Transformational, transactional, and laissez-faire leadership styles: A meta-analysis comparing women and men. *Psychological Bulletin, 129*, 569–591.

Eagly, A. H., & Karau, S. J. (2002). Role congruity theory of prejudice toward female leaders. *Psychological Review, 109*, 573–598.

Eagly, A. H., Karau, S. J., & Makhijani, M. G. (1995). Gender and the effectiveness of leaders: A meta-analysis. *Psychological Bulletin, 117*, 125–145.

Eagly, A. H., & Koenig, A. M. (2006). Social role theory of sex differences and similarities: Implication for prosocial behavior. In K. Dindia & D. J. Canary (Eds.), *Sex differences and similarities in communication* (2nd ed., pp. 161–177). Mahwah, NJ: Erlbaum.

Eagly, A. H., Makhijani, M. G., & Klonsky, B. G. (1992). Gender and the evaluation of leaders: A meta-analysis. *Psychological Bulletin, 111*, 3–22.

Eagly, A. H., & Steffen, V. J. (2000). Gender stereotypes stem from the distribution of women and men into social roles. In C. Stangor (Ed.), *Stereotypes and prejudice: Essential readings* (pp. 142–160). Philadelphia: Psychology Press.

Eargle, A., Guerra, N., & Tolan, P. (1994). Preventing aggression in inner-city children: Small group training to change cognitions, social skills, and behavior. *Journal of Child and Adolescent Group Therapy, 4*, 229–242.

Eberhardt, J. L., Goff, P. A., Purdie, V. J., & Davies, P. G. (2004). Seeing Black: Race, crime, and visual processing. *Journal of Personality and Social Psychology, 87*(6), 876–893.

Eberman, C., & McKelvie, S. J. (2002). Vividness of visual memory and source memory for audio and text. *Applied Cognitive Psychology, 16*, 87–95.

Edmonds, S. (2000, May 5). Judge agrees anthrax vaccine unsafe. The Canadian Press. Retrieved from www.canoe.ca/Health0005/05_ anthrax. html

Educators for Social Responsibility (2001). *About the Resolving Conflict Creatively Program.* Retrieved from www.esrnational. org/about-rccp.html

Edwards, D. J. A. (1975). Returning a dropped object: Effect of response cost and number of potential helpers. *Journal of Social Psychology, 97*, 169–171.

Edwards, K. (1990). The interplay of affect and cognition in attitude formation and change. *Journal of Personality and Social Psychology, 59*, 202–216.

Edwards, K., & von Hippel, W. (1995). Hearts and minds: The priority of affective versus cognitive factors in person perception. *Personality and Social Psychology Bulletin, 21*, 996–1011.

Ehrlinger, J., Gilovich, T., & Ross, L. (2005). Peering into the bias blind spot: People's assessments of bias in themselves and others. *Personality and Social Psychology Bulletin, 31*, 680–692.

Eibach, R. P., & Mock, S. E. (2011). Idealizing parenthood to rationalize parental investments. *Psychological Science, 22*(2), 203–208.

Eibl-Eibesfeldt, I. (1963). Aggressive behavior and ritualized fighting in animals. In J. H. Masserman (Ed.), *Science and psychoanalysis: Vol. 6. Violence and war*. New York: Grune & Stratton.

Eisenberg, N., Spinrad, T. L., & Sadovsky, A. (2006). Empathy-related responding in children. In M. Killen & J. G. Smetana (Eds.), *Handbook of moral development* (pp. 517–549). Mahwah, NJ: Erlbaum.

Eiser, J. R., & Ford, N. (1995). Sexual relationships on holidays: A case of situational disinhibition. *Journal of Social and Personal Relationships, 12*, 323–339.

Ekman, P. (1965). Communication through nonverbal behavior: A source of information about an interpersonal relationship. In S. S. Tomkins & C. E. (Eds.), *Affect, cognition, and personality* (pp. 390–442). New York: Springer-Verlag.

Ekman, P. (1993). Facial expression and emotion. *American Psychologist, 48*, 384–392.

Ekman, P. (1994). Strong evidence for universals in facial expressions: A reply to Russell's mistaken critique. *Psychological Bulletin, 115*, 268–287.

Ekman, P. (2002). *Telling lies: Clues to deceit in the marketplace, politics, and marriage.* New York: Norton.

Ekman, P., & Davidson, R. J. (Eds). (1994). *The nature of emotion: Fundamental questions.* New York: Oxford University Press.

Ekman, P., & Friesen, W. V. (1969). The repertoire of nonverbal behavior: Categories, origins, usage, and coding. *Semiotica, 1*, 49–98.

Ekman, P., & Friesen, W. V. (1971). Constants across cultures in the face and emotion. *Journal of Personality and Social Psychology, 17*, 124–129.

Ekman, P., & Friesen, W. V. (1975). *Unmasking the face*. Englewood Cliffs, NJ: Prentice Hall.

Ekman, P., & Friesen, W. V. (1986). A new pan-cultural facial expression of emotion. *Motivation and Emotion, 10*, 159–168.

Ekman, P., Friesen, W. V., O'Sullivan, M., Chan, A., Diacoyanni-Tarlatzis, I., . . . Tzavras, A. (1987). Universals and cultural differences in the judgments of facial expressions of emotions. *Journal of Personality and Social Psychology, 53*, 712–717.

Ekman, P., & O'Sullivan, M. (1988). The role of context in interpreting facial expression: Comment on Russell & Fehr (1987). *Journal of Experimental Psychology: General, 117*, 86–88.

Ekman, P., O'Sullivan, M., & Matsumoto, D. (1991). Confusions about content in the judgment of facial expression: A reply to "Contempt and the relativity thesis." *Motivation and Emotion, 15*, 169–176.

Ekos Research Associates and Canadian Policy Research Networks. (1999, April). *Analysis of Volunteering: Results from the 1997 National Survey of Giving, volunteering and Participating*. Ottawa, ON: Applied Research Branch: Strategic Policy, Human Resources Canada.

Elfenbein, H., Beaupré, M., Lévesque, M., & Hess, U. (2007). Toward a dialect theory: Cultural differences in the expression and recognition of posed facial expressions. *Emotion*, 7(1), 131-146.

Elfenbein, H. A., & Ambady, N. (2002). On the universality and cultural specificity of emotion recognition: A meta-analysis. *Psychological Bulletin, 128*, 203–235.

Elliott, J. (1977). The power and pathology of prejudice. In P. Zimbardo & F. Ruch (Eds.), *Psychology and life* (9th ed., diamond printing). Glenview, IL: Scott Foresman.

Ellis, A. P. J., Porter, C. O. L. H., & Wolverton, S. A. (2008). Learning to work together: An examination of transactive memory system development in teams. In V. I. Sessa & M. London (Eds.), *Work group learning: Understanding, improving and assessing how groups learn in organizations* (pp. 91–115). New York: Erlbaum.

Ellis, W., Crooks, C., & Wolfe, D. (2009). Relational aggression in peer and dating relationships: Links to psychological and behavioral adjustment. *Social Development, 18*(2), 253–269.

Ellsworth, P. C., & Mauro, R. (1998). Psychology and law. In D. Gilbert, S. Fiske, & G. Lindzey (Eds.), *The handbook of social psychology* (4th ed., Vol. 2, pp. 684–732). New York: McGraw Hill.

Emery, N. J, & Clayton, N. S. (2005). Animal cognition. In. J. J. Bolhuis (Ed.), *Behavior of animals: Mechanisms, function, and evolution* (pp. 170–196). Malden, MA: Blackwell.

Endo, Y., Heine, S. J., & Lehman, D. R. (2000). Culture and positive illusions in close relationships: How my relationships are better than yours. *Personality and Social Psychology Bulletin, 26*, 1571–1586.

Eraker, S. A., & Politser, P. (1988). How decisions are reached: Physicians and the patient. In J. Dowie & A. S. Elstein (Eds.), *Professional judgment: A reader in clinical decision making* (pp. 379–394). Cambridge, UK: Cambridge University Press.

Erdelyi, M. H. (1994). Hypnotic hypermnesia: The empty set of hypermnesia. *International Journal of Clinical and Experimental Hypnosis, 42*, 379–390.

Eron, L. D. (1982). Parent–child interaction, television violence, and aggression of children. *American Psychologist, 37*, 197–211.

Eron, L. D. (1987). The development of aggressive behavior from the perspective of a developing behaviorism. *American Psychologist, 42*, 425–442.

Eron, L. D. (2001) Seeing is believing: How viewing violence alters attitudes and aggressive behavior. In A. C. Bohart & D. J. Stipek (Eds.), *Constructive and destructive behavior: Implications for family, school, and society* (pp. 49–60). Washington, DC: American Psychological Association.

Eron, L. D., Huesmann, L. R., Lefkowitz, M. M., & Walder, L. O. (1996). Does television violence cause aggression? In D. F. Greenberg (Ed.), *Criminal careers. The international library of criminology, criminal justice, and penology* (Vol. 2, pp. 311–321). Aldershot, UK: Dartmouth Publishing Company Limited.

Esses, V., Jackson, L., & Armstrong, T. (1998). Intergroup competition and attitudes toward immigrants and immigration: An instrumental model of group conflict. *Journal of Social Issues, 54*, 699–724.

Esses, V. M., & Dovidio, J. F. (2002). The role of emotions in determining willingness to engage in intergroup contact. *Personality and Social Psychology Bulletin, 28*, 1202–1214.

Esses, V. M., Dovidio, J. F., Danso, H. A., Jackson, L. M., & Semenya, A. (2005). Historical and modern perspectives on group competition. In C. S. Crandall & M. Schaller (Eds.). *Social psychology of prejudice: Historical and contemporary issues* (pp. 94–112). Lawrence, KS: Lewinian Press.

Esses, V. M., Dovidio, J. F., Jackson, L., & Armstrong, T. L. (2001). The immigration dilemma: The role of perceived group competition, ethnic prejudice, and national identity. *Journal of Social Issues, 57*, 389–412.

Esses, V. M., & Gardner, R. C. (1996). Multiculturalism in Canada: Context and current status. *Canadian Journal of Behavioural Science, 28*, 145–152.

Esses, V. M., Haddock, G., & Zanna, M. P. (1993). Values, stereotypes, and emotions as determinants of intergroup attitudes. In D. M. Mackie & D. L. Hamilton (Eds.), *Affect, cognition, and stereotyping: Interactive processes in group perception*. San Diego, CA: Academic Press, Inc.

Esses, V. M., Veenvliet, S., Hodson, G., & Mihic, L. (2008). Justice, morality, and the dehumanization of refugees. *Social Justice Research, 21*, 4–25.

Esses, V. M., Wagner, U., & Wolf, C. (2006). Perceptions of national identity and attitudes toward immigrants and immigration in Canada and Germany. *International Journal of Intercultural Relations, 30*, 653–669.

Esses, V. M., & Zanna, M. P. (1995). Mood and the expression of ethnic stereotypes. *Journal of Personality and Social Psychology, 69*, 1052–1068.

Estabrooks, P., & Carron, A. V. (1999). The influence of the group with elderly exercisers. *Small Group Research, 30*, 438–452.

Estrada-Hollenbeck, M., & Heatherton, T. F. (1998). Avoiding and alleviating guilt through prosocial behavior. In J. Bybee (Ed.), *Guilt and children* (pp. 215–231). San Diego, CA: Academic Press.

Evans, D. C., Garcia, D. J., Garcia, D. M., & Baron, R. S. (2003). In the privacy of their own homes: Using the Internet to assess racial bias. *Personality and Social Psychology Bulletin, 29*(2), 273–284.

Evans, W. N., Neville, D., & Graham, J. D. (1991). General deterrence of drunk driving: Evaluation of American policies. *Risk Analysis, 11*, 279–289.

Ewing, G. (2001). Altruistic, egoistic, and normative effects on curbside recycling. *Environment and Behavior, 33*, 733–764.

Fabrigar, L. R., & Petty, R. E. (1999). The role of affective and cognitive bases of attitudes in susceptibility to affectively and cognitively based persuasion. *Personality and Social Psychology Bulletin, 25*, 363–381.

Fabrigar, L. R., Petty, R. E., Smith, S. M., & Crites, S. L. J. (2006). Understanding knowledge effects on attitude-behavior consistency: The role of relevance, complexity, and amount of knowledge. *Journal of Personality and Social Psychology, 90*, 556–577.

Faiola, A. (2004, August 31). Japanese women live, and like it, on their own. *Washington Post*, p. A01.

Falck, R., & Craig, R. (1988). Classroom-oriented, primary prevention programming for drug abuse. *Journal of Psychoactive Drugs, 20*, 403–408.

Falk, C. F., Heine, S. J., Yuki, M., & Takemura, K. (2009). Why do Westerners self-enhance more than East Asians? *European Journal of Personality, 23*(3), 183–203.

False Confessions (2006). Innocence Project. Retrieved from www .innocenceproject. org/understand/False-Confessions.php

Farber, E. W., & Burge-Callaway, K. (1998). Differences in anger, hostility, and interpersonal aggression in Type A and Type B adolescents. *Journal of Clinical Psychology, 54*, 945–952.

Fazio, R. H. (1990). Multiple processes by which attitudes guide behavior: The MODE model as an integrative framework. In M. P. Zanna (Ed.), *Advances in experimental social psychology* (Vol. 23, pp. 75–109). San Diego: Academic Press.

Fazio, R. H. (2000). Accessible attitudes as tools for object appraisal: Their costs and benefits. In G. Maio & J. Olson (Eds.), *Why we evaluate: Functions of attitudes* (pp. 1–36). Mahwah, NJ: Erlbaum.

Fazio, R. H. (2007). Attitudes as object-evaluation associations of varying strength. *Social Cognition, 25*, 603–637.

Fazio, R. H., & Olson, M. A. (2003). Implicit measures in social cognition research: Their meaning and uses. *Annual Review of Psychology,54*, 297–327.

Feeney, J. R., Polivy, J., Pliner, P., & Sullivan, M. D. (2011). Comparing live and remote models in eating conformity research. *Eating Behaviors, 12*(1), 75–77.

Fehr, B. (1988). Prototype analysis of the concepts of love and commitment. *Journal of Personality and Social Psychology, 55*, 557–579.

Fehr, B. (1993). How do I love thee? Let me consult my prototype. In S. Duck (Ed.), *Individuals in relationships* (pp. 87–120). Newbury Park, CA: Sage.

Fehr, B. (1994). Prototype-based assessment of laypeople's views of love. *Personal Relationships, 1*, 309–331.

Fehr, B. (1996). *Friendship processes*. Thousand Oaks, CA: Sage Publications.

Fehr, B. (2001). The status of theory and research on love and commitment. In G. Fletcher and M. Clark (Eds.), *The Blackwell handbook of social psychology: Interpersonal processes* (pp. 331–356). Oxford, UK: Blackwell Publishers.

Fehr, B. (2006). A prototype approach to studying love. In R. J. Sternberg & K. Weis (Eds.). *The new psychology of love* (pp. 225–246). New Haven, CT: Yale University Press.

Fehr, B. (2008). Friendship formation. In S. Sprecher, A. Wenzel, & J. Harvey (Eds.). *Handbook of relationship initiation* (pp. 29–54). New York: Taylor & Francis.

Fehr, B. (in press). The social psychology of love. In J. A. Simpson and L. Campbell (Eds.), *Handbook of Close Relationships*. New York: Oxford University Press.

Fehr, B., & Baldwin, M. (1996). Prototype and script analyses of laypeople's knowledge of anger. In G. J. O. Fletcher, and J. Fitness (Eds.), *Knowledge structures in close relationships: A social psychological approach* (pp. 219–245). Mahwah, NJ: Erlbaum.

Fehr, B., Baldwin, M., Collins, L., Patterson, S., & Benditt, R. (1999). Anger in close relationships: An interpersonal script analysis. *Personality and Social Psychology Bulletin, 25*, 299–312.

Fehr, B., & Broughton, R. (2001). Gender and personality differences in conceptions of love: An interpersonal theory analysis. *Personal Relationships, 8*, 115–136.

Fehr, B., & Russell, J. A. (1991). The concept of love viewed from a prototype perspective. *Journal of Personality and Social Psychology, 60*, 425–438.

Fein, S., Hoshino-Browne, E., Davies, P. G., & Spencer, S. J. (2003). Self-image maintenance goals and sociocultural norms in motivated social perception. In S. Spencer & S. Fein (Eds). *Motivated social perception: The Ontario symposium* (Vol. 99, pp. 21–44). Mahwah, NJ: Erlbaum.

Fein, S., & Spencer, S. J. (1997). Prejudice as self-image maintenance: Affirming the self through derogating others. *Journal of Personality and Social Psychology, 73*, 31–44.

Fein, S., von Hippel, W., & Spencer, S. J. (2000). To stereotype or not to stereotype: Motivation and stereotype activation, application, and inhibition. *Psychological Inquiry, 10*, 49–54.

Feingold, A. (1990). Gender differences in effects of physical attractiveness on romantic attraction: A comparison across five research paradigms. *Journal of Personality and Social Psychology, 59*, 981–993.

Feingold, A. (1992a). Gender differences in mate selection preferences: A test of the parental investment model. *Psychological Bulletin, 112*, 125–139.

Feingold, A. (1992b). Good-looking people are not what we think. *Psychological Bulletin, 111*, 304–341.

Feld, S. L. (1982). Social structural determinants of similarity among associates. *American Sociological Review, 47*, 797–801.

Feldman-Summers, S., & Kiesler, S. B. (1974). Those who are number two try harder: The effect of sex on attributions of causality. *Journal of Personality and Social Psychology, 38*, 846–855.

Felmlee, D. H. (1995). Fatal attractions: Affection and dissatisfaction in intimate relationships. *Journal of Social and Personal Relationships, 12*, 295–311.

Feshbach, N. D. (1989). Empathy training and prosocial behavior. In J. Groebel & R. A. Hinde (Eds.), *Aggression and war: Their biological and social bases* (pp. 101–111). New York: Cambridge University Press.

Feshbach, N. D. (1997). Empathy: The formative years—implications for clinical practice. In A. C. Bohart & L. S. Greenberg (Eds.), *Empathy reconsidered: New directions in psychotherapy* (pp. 33–59). Washington, DC: American Psychological Association.

Feshbach, N. D., & Cohen, S. (1988). Training affect comprehension in young children: An experimental evaluation. *Journal of Applied Developmental Psychology, 9*, 201–210.

Fessel, F., Epstude, K., & Roese, N. J. (2009). Hindsight bias refined: It's about time. *Organizational Behavior and Human Decision Processes, 110*, 56–64.

Festinger, L. (1954). A theory of social comparison processes. *Human Relations, 7*, 117–140.

Festinger, L. (1957). *A theory of cognitive dissonance*. Stanford, CA: Stanford University Press.

Festinger, L., & Carlsmith, J. M. (1959). Cognitive consequences of forced compliance. *Journal of Abnormal and Social Psychology, 58*, 203–211.

Festinger, L., & Maccoby, N. (1964). On resistance to persuasive communications. *Journal of Abnormal and Social Psychology, 68*, 359–366.

Festinger, L., Riecken, H. W., & Schachter, S. (1956). *When prophecy fails*. Minneapolis, MN: University of Minnesota Press.

Festinger, L., Schachter, S., & Back, K. (1950). *Social pressures in informal groups: A study of human factors in housing*. New York: Harper & Bros.

Festinger, L., & Thibaut, J. (1951). Interpersonal communication in small groups. *Journal of Abnormal and Social Psychology, 46*, 92–99.

Fiedler, F. (1967). *A theory of leadership effectiveness*. New York: McGraw-Hill.

Fiedler, F. (1978). The contingency model and the dynamics of the leadership process. In L. Berkowitz (Ed.), *Advances in experimental social psychology* (Vol. 11, pp. 59–112). Orlando, FL: Academic Press.

Fiedler, K., Walther, E., & Nickel, S. (1999). Covariation-based attribution: On the ability to assess multiple covariations of an effect. *Personality and Social Psychology Bulletin, 25*, 607–622.

Fincham, F. D., & Bradbury, T. N. (1993). Marital satisfaction, depression, and attributions: A longitudinal analysis. *Journal of Personality and Social Psychology, 64*, 442–452.

Fincham, F. D., Bradbury, T. N., Arias, I., Byrne, C. A., & Karney, B. R. (1997). Marital violence, marital distress, and attributions. *Journal of Family Psychology, 11*, 367–372.

Fine, G. A., & Elsbach, K. D. (2000). Ethnography and experiment in social psychological theory building: Tactics for integrating qualitative field data with quantitative lab data. *Journal of Experimental Social Psychology, 36*, 51–76.

Finger, K., & Pezdek, K. (1999). The effect of cognitive interview on face identification accuracy: Release from verbal overshadowing. *Journal of Applied Social Psychology, 84*, 340–348.

Fink, B., & Penton-Voak, I. (2002). Evolutionary psychology of facial attractiveness. *Current Directions in Psychological Science, 11*, 154–158.

Finney, P. D. (1987). When consent information refers to risk and deception: Implications for social research. *Journal of Social Behavior and Personality, 2*, 37–48.

Fischer, R., & Chalmers, A. (2008). Is optimism universal? A meta-analytical investigation of optimism levels across 22 nations. *Personality and Individual Differences, 45*, 378–382.

Fischer, W. F. (1963). Sharing in preschool children as a function of amount and type of reinforcement. *Genetic Psychology Monographs, 68*, 215–245.

Fischhoff, B., Gonzalez, R., Lerner, J. S., & Small, D. A. (2005). Evolving judgments of terror risks: Foresight, hindsight, and emotion. *Journal of Experimental Psychology: Applied, 11*, 124–139.

Fishbein, M., & Ajzen, I. (1975). *Belief, attitude, intention, and behavior: An introduction to theory and research*. Reading, MA: Addison-Wesley.

Fishbein, M., Chan, D., O'Reilly, K., Schnell, D., Wood, R., Beeker, C., & Cohn, C. (1993). Factors influencing gay men's attitudes, subjective norms, and intentions with respect to performing sexual behaviors. *Journal of Applied Social Psychology, 23*, 417–438.

Fisher, H. E. (2004). *Why we love: The nature and chemistry of romantic love*. New York: Henry Holt.

Fisher, R. P., Brennan, K. H., & McCauley, M. R. (2001). The cognitive interview method to enhance eyewitness recall. In M. L. Eisen (Ed.), *Memory and suggestibility in the forensic interview* (pp. 265–286). Mahwah, NJ: Erlbaum.

Fisher, R. P., & Schreiber, N. (2007). Interview protocols to improve eyewitness memory. In M. P. Toglia, J. D. Read, D. F. Ross, & R. C. L. Lindsay (Eds.), *The handbook of eyewitness psychology: Vol. I. Memory for events* (pp. 53–80). Mahwah, NJ: Lawrence Erlbaum.

Fiske, A. P., Kitayama, S., Markus, H. R., & Nisbett, R. E. (1998). The cultural matrix of social psychology. In D. Gilbert, S. Fiske, & G. Lindzey (Eds.), *The handbook of social psychology* (4th ed., Vol. 2, pp. 915–981). New York: McGraw Hill.

Fiske, S. T. (1989a). Examining the role of intent: Toward understanding its role in stereotyping and prejudice. In J. S. Uleman & J. A. Bargh (Eds.), *Unintended thought* (pp. 253–283). New York: Guilford.

Fiske, S. T. (1989b). *Interdependence and stereotyping: From the laboratory to the Supreme Court (and back)*. Invited address, American Psychological Association, New Orleans.

Fiske, S. T., Cuddy, A. J. C., Glick, P., & Xu, J. (2002). A model of (often mixed) stereotype content: Competence and warmth respectively follow from perceived status competition. *Journal of Personality and Social Psychology, 82*, 878–902.

Fiske, S. T., & Depret, E. (1996). Control, interdependence, and power: Understanding social cognition in its social context. In W. Stroebe & M. Hewstone (Eds.), *European Review of Social Psychology, 7*, 31–61. New York: Wiley.

Fiske, S. T., & Taylor, S. E. (1991). *Social cognition* (2nd ed). New York: McGraw-Hill.

Flanagan, C. A., Bowes, J. M., Jonsson, B., Csapo, B., & Sheblanova, E. (1998). Ties that bind: Correlates of adolescents' civic commitments in seven countries. *Journal of Social Issues, 54*, 457–475.

Fletcher, G. J. O., & Ward, C. (1988). Attribution theory and processes: A cross-cultural perspective. In M. H. Bond (Ed.), *The cross-cultural challenge to social psychology*. Newbury Park, CA: Sage.

Flowers, M. L. (1977). A lab test of some implications of Janis' groupthink hypothesis. *Journal of Personality and Social Psychology, 35*, 888–897.

Folkman, S., & Moskowitz, J. T. (2000). The context matters. *Personality and Social Psychology Bulletin, 26*, 150–151.

Fong, G. T., Krantz, D. H., & Nisbett, R. E. (1986). The effects of statistical training on thinking about everyday problems. *Cognitive Psychology, 18*, 253–292.

Foot, R. (2007, May 30). Believers plan new journey to centre of the Earth. *Winnipeg Free Press*, p. A2.

Forer, B. R. (1949). The fallacy of personal validation: A classroom demonstration of gullibility. *Journal of Abnormal and Social Psychology, 44*, 118–123.

Forgas, J. P., & Bower, G. H. (1987). Mood effects on person-perception judgments. *Journal of Personality and Social Psychology, 53*, 53–60.

Forster, J., Liberman, N., & Higgins, E. T. (2005). Accessibility from active and fulfilled goals. *Journal of Experimental Social Psychology, 41*, 220–239.

Foster, G. (2005). Making friends: A nonexperimental analysis of social pair formation. *Human Relations, 58*, 1443–1465.

Foster, M. (2005, June). *Double jeopardy in coping with discrimination: Differences between white and visible minority women.* Paper presented at the Canadian Psychological Association Conference, Montreal, Quebec.

Foster, M., & Dion, K. L. (2001, June). Hardiness and responses to perceived discrimination: Buffer or denial? In K. L. Dion (Chair), *Social psychology of prejudice: Cognitive perspectives.* Symposium conducted at the American Psychological Association Convention, Toronto, Ontario.

Foster, M., & Matheson, K. (1999). Perceiving and responding to the personal/group discrimination discrepancy. *Personality and Social Psychology Bulletin, 25*, 1319–1329.

Foster, M. D., & Tsarfati, E. M. (2005). The effects of meritocracy beliefs on women's well-being after first-time gender discrimination. *Personality and Social Psychology Bulletin, 31*, 1730–1738.

Fouts, G., & Burggraf, K. (1999). Television situation comedies: Female body images and verbal reinforcements. *Sex Roles, 40*, 473–479.

Fouts, G., & Burggraf, K. (2000). Television situation comedies: Female weight, male negative comments, and audience reactions. *Sex Roles, 42*,925–932.

Fox, C. (2006). The availability heuristic in the classroom: How soliciting more criticism can boost your course ratings. *Judgment and Decision Making, 1*, 86–90.

Fox, J. (1980). Making decisions under the influence of memory. *Psychological Review, 87*, 190–211.

Frager, R. (1970). Conformity and anticonformity in Japan. *Journal of Personality and Social Psychology, 15*, 203–210.

Fraidin, S. N. (2004). When is one head better than two? Interdependent information in group decision making. *Organizational Behavior and Human Decision Processes, 93*, 102–113.

Fraley, R. C. (2002). Attachment stability from infancy to adulthood: Meta-analysis and dynamic modeling of developmental mechanisms. *Personality and Social Psychology Review, 6*, 123–151.

Fraley, R. C., & Shaver, P. R. (2000). Adult romantic attachment: Theoretical developments, emerging controversies, and unanswered questions. *Review of General Psychology, 4*, 132–154.

Frank, M. G., & Gilovich, T. (1988). The dark side of self and social perceptions: Black uniforms and aggression in professional sports. *Journal of Personality and Social Psychology, 54*, 74–85.

Frankel, Glenn. (2005, 24 July). London Police Had Expressed "Deep Regret" for Bystander Shooting. Retrieved from www.washingtonpost.com

Fredrickson, B. L., Roberts, T., Noll, S. M., Quinn, D. M., & Twenge, J. M. (1998). That swimsuit becomes you: Sex differences in self-objectification, restrained eating, and math performance. *Journal of Personality and Social Psychology, 75*, 269–284.

Fredrickson, B. L., Tugade, M., Waugh, C., & Larkin, G. (2003). What good are positive emotions in crises? A prospective study of resilience and emotions following the terrorist attacks on the United States on September 11th, 2001. *Journal of Personality and Social Psychology, 84*, 365–376.

Freedman, D., Pisani, R., Purves, R., & Adhikari, A. (1991). *Statistics* (2nd ed). New York: Norton.

Freedman, J. L. (1965). Long-term behavioral effects of cognitive dissonance. *Journal of Experimental and Social Psychology, 1*, 145–155.

Freedman, J. L., & Fraser, S. C. (1966). Compliance without pressure: The foot-in-the-door technique. *Journal of Personality and Social Psychology, 4*, 195–202.

French, M. (2002). Physical appearance and earnings: Further evidence. *Applied Economics, 34*, 569–572.

Freud, S. (1930). *Civilization and its discontents.* Joan Rivière (Trans). London, UK: Hogarth Press.

Freud, S. (1933). *New introductory lectures on psycho-analysis.* New York: Norton.

Fried, C., & Aronson, E. (1995). Hypocrisy, misattribution, and dissonance reduction: A demonstration of dissonance in the absence of aversive consequences. *Personality and Social Psychology Bulletin, 21*, 925–933.

Frodi, A. (1975). The effect of exposure to weapons on aggressive behavior from a cross-cultural perspective. *International Journal of Psychology, 10*, 283–292.

Fu, G., Lee, K., Cameron, C. A., & Xu, F. (2001). Chinese and Canadian adults' categorization and evaluation of lie- and truth-telling about prosocial and antisocial behaviors. *Journal of Cross-Cultural Psychology, 32*, 720–727.

Funder, D. C., & Colvin, C. R. (1988). Friends and strangers: Acquaintanceship, agreement, and the accuracy of personality judgment. *Journal of Personality and Social Psychology, 55*, 149–158.

Gabriel, S., & Gardner, W. L. (1999). Are there "his" and "hers" types of interdependence? The implications of gender differences in collective versus relational interdependence for affect, behavior, and cognition. *Journal of Personality and Social Psychology*, 77, 642–655.

Gabriel, S., & Gardner, W. L. (2004). Are there "his" and "hers" types of interdependence? The implications of gender differences in collective versus relational interdependence for affect, behavior, and cognition. In H. T. Reis & C. E. Rusbult (Eds.), *Close relationships: Key readings* (pp. 405–420). Philadelphia, PA: Taylor & Francis.

Gackle, P. (2008, August 9). McLean funeral picketers fear backlash. *Winnipeg Free Press*, p. A5.

Gaertner, S. L., & Dovidio, J. F. (1986). The aversive form of racism. In J. F. Dovidio & S. L. Gaertner (Eds.), *Prejudice, discrimination, and racism: Theory and research* (pp. 61–89). New York: Academic Press.

Gagné, F., Khan, A., Lydon, J., & To, M. (2008). When flattery gets you nowhere: Discounting positive feedback as a relationship maintenance strategy. *Canadian Journal of Behavioural Science/Revue canadienne des sciences du comportement, 40*(2), 59–68.

Gagné, F., Lydon, J. E., & Bartz, J. (2003). Effects of mindset on the predictive validify of relationship constructs. *Journal Personality and Social Psychology, 35*, 292–304.

Gagné, F. M., & Lydon, J. E. (2001). Mind-set and close relationships: When bias leads to (in)accurate predictions. *Journal of Personality and Social Psychology, 81*, 85–96.

Gagné, F. M., & Lydon, J. E. (2003). Identification and the commitment shift: Accounting for gender differences in relationship illusions. *Personality and Social Psychology Bulletin, 29*(7), 907–919.

Gagné, J., & Earls, C. M. (2010). L'impact de l'information saillante et du niveau de gravité du crime sur la décision du jury (The impact of salient information and the level of the crime on the decision of the jury). *Canadian Journal of Behavioural Science, 42*(4), 247–253.

Gagnon, A., & Bourhis, R. Y. (1996). Discrimination in the minimal group paradigm: Social identity or self-interest? *Personality and Social Psychology Bulletin, 22*, 1289–1301.

Galef, B. G., & Whiskin, E. E. (2008). 'Conformity' in Norway rats? *Animal Behaviour, 75*(6), 2035–2039.

Galinsky, A. D., Mussweiler, T., & Medvec, V. H. (2002). Disconnecting outcomes and evaluations: The role of negotiator focus. *Journal of Personality and Social Psychology, 83*, 1131–1140.

Gallese, V., Fadiga, L., Fogassi, L., & Rizzolatti, G. (1996). Action recognition in the premotor cortex. *Brain, 119(2)*, 593–609.

Galloway, G. (2011, July 21). Oil-sands monitoring regime aims to protect air and water quality. *Globe and Mail.* Retrieved from www.theglobeandmail.com/news/politics/ottawa-notebook/oil-sands-monitoring-regimeaims-to-protect-air-and-water-quality/article2104903/?from=sec368

Gallup, G. G. (1977). Self-recognition in primates: A comparative approach to the bidirectional properties of consciousness. *American Psychologist, 32*, 329–338.

Gallup, G. G. Jr., Anderson, J. R., & Shillito, D. J. (2002). The mirror test. In M. Bekoff & C. Allen (Eds.), *Cognitive animal: Empirical and theoretical perspectives on animal cognition* (pp. 325–333). Cambridge, MA: MIT Press.

Gallup, G. G., & Suarez, S. D. (1986). Self-awareness and the emergence of mind in humans and other primates. In J. Suls & A. G. Greenwald (Eds.), *Psychological perspectives on the self* (Vol. 3, pp. 3–26). Hillsdale, NJ: Erlbaum.

Gangestad, S. W. (1993). Sexual selection and physical attractiveness: Implications for mating dynamics. *Human Nature, 4*, 205–235.

Gao, G. (1993, May). *An investigation of love and intimacy in romantic relationships in China and the United States.* Paper presented at the annual conference of the International Communication Association, Washington, DC.

Gao, G. (1996). Self and other: A Chinese perspective on interpersonal relationships. In W. B. Gudykunst, S. Ting-Toomey, & T. Nishida (Eds.), *Communication in personal relationships across cultures* (pp. 81–101). Thousand Oaks, CA: Sage.

Gao, G., & Gudykunst, W. B. (1995). Attributional confidence, perceived similarity, and network involvement in Chinese and European American romantic relationships. *Communication Quarterly, 43*, 431–445.

Gardner, R. C., MacIntyre, P. D., & Lalonde, R. N. (1995). The effects of multiple social categories on stereotyping. *Canadian Journal of Behavioural Science, 27*, 466–483.

Gardner, W. L., Pickett, C. L., & Brewer, M. B. (2000). Social exclusion and selective memory: How the need to belong influences memory for social events. *Personality and Social Psychology Bulletin, 26*, 486–496.

Garfinkle, H. (1967). *Studies in ethnomethodology*. Englewood Cliffs, NJ: Prentice Hall.

Gaucher, D., Friesen, J., & Kay, A. C. (2011, March 7). Evidence that gendered wording in job advertisements exists and sustains gender inequality. *Journal of Personality and Social Psychology*. Advance online publication. doi:10.1037/a0022530.

Gaucher, D., Hafer, C. L., Kay, A. C., & Davidenko, N. (2010). Compensatory rationalizations and the resolution of everyday undeserved outcomes. *Personality and Social Psychology Bulletin, 36*(1), 109–118.

Gauthier, I., Behrmann, M., & Tarr, M. J. (1999). Can face recognition really be disassociated from object recognition? *Journal of Cognitive Neuroscience, 11*, 249–370.

Gawronski, B. (2003a). Implicational schemata and the correspondence bias: On the diagnostic value of situationally constrained behavior. *Journal of Personality and Social Psychology, 84*, 1154–1171.

Gawronski, B. (2003b). On difficult questions and evident answers: Dispositional inference from role-constrained behavior. *Personality and Social Psychology Bulletin, 29*, 1459–1475.

Gawronski, B., & Bodenhausen, G. V. (2005). Accessibility effects on implicit social cognition: The role of knowledge activation and retrieval experiences. *Journal of Personality and Social Psychology, 89*, 672–685.

Gawronski, B., & Bodenhausen, G. V. (2006). Associative and propositional processes in evaluation: An integrative review of implicit and explicit attitude change. *Psychological Bulletin, 132*, 692–731.

Gawronski, B., Bodenhausen, G. V., & Becker, A. P. (2007). I like it, because I like myself: Associative self-anchoring and post-decisional change of implicit evaluations. *Journal of Experimental Social Psychology, 43*(2), 221–232.

Gawronski, B., Bodenhausen, G. V., & Banse, R. (2005). We are, therefore they aren't: Ingroup construal as a standard of comparison for outgroup judgments. *Journal of Experimental Social Psychology, 41*, 515–526.

Gawronski, B., Bodenhausen, G. V., & Becker, A. P. (2007). I like it, because I like myself: Associative self-anchoring and post-decisional change of implicit evaluations. *Journal of Experimental Social Psychology, 43*, 221–232.

Gawronski, B., & LeBel, E. P. (2008). Understanding patterns of attitude change: When implicit measures show change, but explicit measures do not. *Journal of Experimental Social Psychology, 44*(5), 1355–1361.

Gawronski, B., Peters, K. R., Brochu, P. M., & Strack, F. (2008). Understanding the relations between different forms of racial prejudice: A cognitive consistency perspective. *Personality and Social Psychology Bulletin, 34*(5), 648–665.

Geddes, J. (2008, March 10). The Chuck Cadman affair—from someone who was there. Macleans.ca. Retrieved from www.macleans.ca/article.jsp?content=20080310_093557_2860

Geen, R. (1998). Aggression and anti-social behavior. In D. Gilbert, S. Fiske, & G. Lindzey (Eds.), *The handbook of social psychology* (4th ed., Vol. 2, pp. 317–356). New York: McGraw Hill.

Geen, R. G. (1989). Alternative conceptions of social facilitation. In P. B. Paulus (Ed.), *Psychology of group influence* (2nd ed., pp. 15–51). Hillsdale, NJ: Erlbaum.

Geiselman, R. E., & Fischer, R. P. (1989). The cognitive interview technique for victims and witnesses of crime. In D. C. Raskin (Ed.), *Psychological methods in criminal investigation and evidence* (pp. 191–215). New York: Springer.

Geldart, S. (2008). Tall and good-looking? The relationship between raters' height and perceptions of attractiveness. *Journal of Individual Differences, 29*(3), 148–156.

Geller, E. S. (2002). The challenge of increasing proenvironmental behavior. In R. B. Bechtel & A. Churchman (Eds.), *Handbook of environmental psychology* (pp. 525–540). New York: Wiley.

Gentile, D. A., & Gentile, J. R. (2008). Violent video games as exemplary teachers: A conceptual analysis. *Journal of Youth and Adolescence, 37*(2), 127–141.

George, D. M., Carroll, P., Kersnick, R., & Calderon, K. (1998). Gender-related patterns of helping among friends. *Psychology of Women Quarterly, 22*, 685–704.

George, J. M. (1990). Personality, affect, and behavior in groups. *Journal of Applied Psychology, 75*, 107–116.

Gerard, H. B. (1953). The effect of different dimensions of disagreement on the communication process in small groups. *Human Relations, 6*, 249–271.

Gerard, H. B., & Mathewson, G. C. (1966). The effects of severity of initiation on liking for a group: A replication. *Journal of Experimental Social Psychology, 2*, 278–287.

Gerard, H. B., Wilhelmy, R. A., & Conolley, E. S. (1968). Conformity and group size. *Journal of Personality and Social Psychology, 8*, 79–82.

Gerbner, G., Gross, L., Morgan, M., Signorielli, N., & Shanahan, J. (2002). Growing up with television: Cultivation processes. In J. Bryant & D. Zillmann (Eds.), *Media effects: Advances in theory and research* (pp. 43–67). Mahwah, NJ: Erlbaum.

Gerdes, E. P. (1979). College students' reactions to social psychological experiments involving deception. *Journal of Social Psychology, 107*, 99–110.

Gergen, K. J., Gergen, M. M., & Barton, W. H. (1973, July). Deviance in the dark. *Psychology Today*, 129–130.

Gibbons, F. X. (1978). Sexual standards and reactions to pornography: Enhancing behavioral consistency through self-focused attention. *Journal of Personality and Social Psychology, 36*, 976–987.

Gibbons, F. X., Gerrard, M., & Cleveland, M. J. (2004). Perceived discrimination and substance use in African American parents and their children: A panel study. *Journal of Personality and Social Psychology, 86*, 517–529.

Gibbs, J. P. (1985). Deterrence theory and research. *Nebraska Symposium on Motivation, 33*, 87–130.

Giesler, R., Josephs, R., & Swann, W. (1996). Self-verification in clinical depression: The desire for negative evaluation. *Journal of Abnormal Psychology, 105*, 358–368.

Gifford, R. (1991). Mapping nonverbal behavior on the interpersonal circle. *Journal of Personality and Social Psychology, 61*, 279–288.

Gifford, R. (1994). A lens-mapping framework for understanding the encoding and decoding of interpersonal dispositions in nonverbal behavior. *Journal of Personality and Social Psychology, 66*, 398–412.

Gifford, R. (2008). Psychology's essential role in alleviating the impacts of climate change. *Canadian Psychology, 49*, 273–280.

Gifford, R. (2011). The dragons of inaction: Psychological barriers that limit climate change mitigation and adaptation. *American Psychologist, 66*(4), 290–302.

Gifford-Smith, M. E., & Brownell, C. A. (2003). Childhood peer relationships: Social acceptance, friendships, and peer networks. *Journal of School Psychology, 41*, 235–284.

Gigerenzer, G. (2000). *Adaptive thinking: Rationality in the real world.* Oxford, UK: Oxford University Press.

Gigerenzer, G. (2008). Why heuristics work. *Perspectives on Psychological Science, 3*, 20–29.

Giguère, B., Lalonde, R., & Lou, E. (2010). Living at the crossroads of cultural worlds: The experience of normative conflicts by second generation immigrant youth. *Social and Personality Psychology Compass, 4*(1), 14–29.

Giguère, B., & Lalonde, R. N. (2009). The effects of social identification on individual effort under conditions of identity threat and regulatory depletion. *Group Processes & Intergroup Relations, 12*(2), 195–208.

Gilbert, D. T. (1989). Thinking lightly about others: Automatic components of the social inference process. In J. S. Uleman & J. A. Bargh (Eds.), *Unintended thought* (pp. 189–211). New York: Guilford Press.

Gilbert, D. T. (1991). How mental systems believe. *American Psychologist, 46*, 107–119.

Gilbert, D. T. (1993). The assent of man: Mental representation and the control of belief. In D. M. Wegner & J. W. Pennebaker, (Eds.), *The handbook of mental control* (pp. 57–87). Englewood Cliffs, NJ: Prentice Hall.

Gilbert, D. T. (1998a). Ordinary personology. In D. T. Gilbert, S. T. Fiske, & G. Lindzey (Eds.), *The handbook of social psychology* (4th ed., Vol. 2, pp. 89–150). New York: McGraw-Hill.

Gilbert, D. T. (1998b). Speeding with Ned: A personal view of the correspondence bias. In J. M. Darley & J. Cooper (Eds.), *Attribution and social interaction* (pp. 5–36). Washington, DC: American Psychological Association.

Gilbert, D. T. (2006). *Stumbling on happiness*. New York: Knopf.

Gilbert, D. T., & Ebert, J. E. J. (2002). Decisions and revisions: The affective forecasting of changeable outcomes. *Journal of Personality and Social Psychology, 82*, 503–514.

Gilbert, D. T., & Hixon, J. G. (1991). The trouble of thinking: Activation and applications of stereotypical beliefs. *Journal of Personality and Social Psychology, 60*, 509–517.

Gilbert, D. T., & Malone, P. S. (1995). The correspondence bias. *Psychological Bulletin, 117*, 21–38.

Gilbert, D. T., & Osborne, R. E. (1989). Thinking backward: Some curable and incurable consequences of cognitive busyness. *Journal of Personality and Social Psychology, 57*, 940–949.

Gilbert, D. T., Pelham, B. W., & Krull, D. S. (1988). On cognitive busyness: When person perceivers meet persons perceived. *Journal of Personality and Social Psychology, 54*, 733–740.

Gill, R., & Matheson, K. (2006). Responses to discrimination: The role of emotion and expectations for emotional regulation. *Personality and Social Psychology Bulletin, 32*, 149–161.

Gilovich, T. (1991). *How we know what isn't so: The fallibility of human reasoning in everyday life*. New York: Free Press.

Gilovich, T., & Griffin, D. W. (2002). Introduction: Heuristics and biases, now and then. In T. Gilovich, D. W. Griffin, & D. Kahneman (Eds.), *Heuristics and biases: The psychology of intuitive judgment* (pp. 1–18). New York: Cambridge University Press.

Gilovich, T., & Medvec, V. H. (1995). The experience of regret: What, when, and why. *Psychological Review, 102*, 379–395.

Gilovich, T., Medvec, V. H., & Chen, S. (1995). Commission, omission, and dissonance reduction: Coping with regret in the "Monty Hall" problem. *Personality and Social Psychology Bulletin, 21*, 182–190.

Gilovich, T., & Savitsky, K. (2002). Like goes with like: The role of representativeness in erroneous and pseudoscientific beliefs. In T. Gilovich, D. W. Griffin, & D. Kahneman (Eds.), *Heuristics and biases: The psychology of intuitive judgment* (pp. 617–624). New York: Cambridge University Press.

Gimlin, D. (1994). The anorexic as overconformist: Toward a reinterpretation of eating disorders. In K. A. Callaghan (Ed.), *Ideals of feminine beauty: Philosophical, social, and cultural dimensions* (pp. 99–111). Westport, CN: Greenwood.

Gire, J. T. (1997). The varying effect of individualism-collectivism on preference for methods of conflict resolution. *Canadian Journal of Behavioural Science, 29*, 38–43.

Girl born to Japan's princess. (2001, December 1). *New York Times*, p. 8.

Giscombé, C., & Lobel, M. (2005). Explaining disproportionately high rates of adverse birth outcomes among African Americans: The impact of stress, racism, and related factors in pregnancy. *Psychological Bulletin, 131*, 662–683.

Gladwell, M. (2004). Big and bad. *New Yorker, 79*, 28–33.

Glass, D. C. (1964). Changes in liking as a means of reducing cognitive discrepancies between self-esteem and aggression. *Journal of Personality, 32*, 531–549.

Glass, D. C., & Singer, J. E. (1972). *Urban stress: Experiments on noise and social stressors*. New York: Academic Press.

Glenn, S. A., & Byers, E. (2009). The roles of situational factors, attributions, and guilt in the well-being of women who have experienced sexual coercion. *Canadian Journal of Human Sexuality, 18*(4), 201–219.

Godin, G., Maticka-Tyndale, E., Adrien, A., Manson-Singer, S., Willams, D., & Cappon, P. (1996). Cross-cultural testing of three social cognitive theories: An application to condom use. *Journal of Applied Social Psychology, 26*, 1556–1586.

Goerzen, M. (February 19, 2011). No casino for Brandon: Decter Hirst. Retrieved from http://findarticles.com/p/news-articles/brandon-sun-the/mi_8087/is_20110219/casino-brand

Goethals, G. R., & Darley, J. M. (1977). Social comparison theory: An attributional approach. In J. M. Suls & R. L. Miller (Eds.), *Social comparison processes: Theoretical and empirical perspectives* (pp. 259–278). Washington, DC: Hemisphere/Halsted.

Goff, P. A., Steele, C. M., & Davies, P. G. (2008). The space between us: Stereotype threat and distance in interracial contexts. *Journal of Personality and Social Psychology, 94*, 91–107.

Goffin, R. D., Jelley, R., Powell, D. M., & Johnston, N. G. (2009). Taking advantage of social comparisons in performance appraisal: The relative percentile method. *Human Resource Management, 48*(2), 251–268.

Gold, J. A., Ryckman, R. M., & Mosley, N. R. (1984). Romantic mood induction and attraction to a dissimilar other: Is love blind? *Personality and Social Psychology Bulletin, 10*, 358–368.

Goldberg, C. (2008, March 3). Cultural insights: Brain scans support surprising differences in perception between Westerners and Asians. *The Boston Globe*, pp. C1, C3.

Goldstein, J. H., & Arms, R. L. (1971). Effect of observing athletic contests on hostility. *Sociometry, 34*, 83–90.

Goldstein, N., Cialdini, R. B., & Griskevicius, V. (2008). A room with a viewpoint: Using social norms to motivate environmental conservation in hotels. *Journal of Consumer Research, 35*, 475–482.

Goldstein, N. J., Cialdini, R. B., & Griskevisius, V. (2008). A room with a viewpoint: Using social norms to motivate environmental conservation in hotels. *Journal of Consumer Research, 35*, 472–482.

Goleman, D. (1982, January). Make-or-break resolutions. *Psychology Today*, 19.

Golmier, I., Chebat, J., & Gélinas-Chebat, C. (2007). Can cigarette warnings counterbalance effects of smoking scenes in movies?. *Psychological Reports, 100*(1), 3–18.

Gonzales, A. L., & Hancock, J. T. (2011). Mirror, mirror on my Facebook wall: Effects of exposure to Facebook on self-esteem. *Cyberpsychology, Behavior, and Social Networking, 14*(1-2), 79–83.

Gonzales, M. H., Aronson, E., & Costanzo, M. (1988). Using social cognition and persuasion to promote energy conservation: A quasi-experiment. *Journal of Applied Social Psychology, 18*, 1049–1066.

Good, C. Aronson, J., & Harder, J. (2008). Problems in the pipeline: Stereotype threat and women's achievement in high-level math courses. *Journal of Applied Developmental Psychology, 29*(1), 17–28.

Goode, E. (2000, February 15). When women find love is fatal. *New York Times*, pp. F1*ff.*

Gopaul-McNicol, S.-A. A. (1987). A cross-cultural study of the effects of modeling, reinforcement, and color meaning word association on doll color preference of Black preschool children and White preschool children in New York and Trinidad. *Dissertation Abstracts International, 48*, 340–341.

Gorassini, D. R., & Olson, J. M. (1995). Does self-perception change explain the foot-in-the-door effect? *Journal of Personality and Social Psychology, 69*, 91–105.

Gordon, A. K., & Miller, A. G. (2000). Perspective differences in the construal of lies: Is deception in the eye of the beholder? *Personality and Social Psychology Bulletin, 26*, 46–55.

Gorham, B. (2005, December 20). We're slow and "stalking" America, says TV pundit. *Winnipeg Free Press*, p. A3.

Gould, S. J. (1997, June 26). Evolution: The pleasures of pluralism. *The New York Review*, pp. 47–52.

Governor General of Canada (n.d.). *It's an honour: Governor General's awards.* Retrieved from http://www.gg.ca/document.aspx?id=187

Grabe, S., Ward, L. M., & Hyde, J. S. (2008). The role of media in body image concerns among women: A meta-analysis of experimental and correlational studies. *Psychological Bulletin, 134*(3), 460–476.

Graham, J., Koo, M., & Wilson, T. D. (2011). Conserving energy by inducing people to drive less. *Journal of Applied Social Psychology. 41*(1), 106–118.

Graham, K., & Wells, S. (2001a). The two worlds of aggression for men and men. *Sex Roles, 45*, 595–622.

Graham, K., & Wells, S. (2001b). Aggression among young adults in the social context of the bar. *Addiction Research & Theory, 9*, 193–219.

Graham, K., West, P., & Wells, S. (2000). Evaluating theories of alcohol- related aggression using observations of young adults in bars. *Addiction, 95*, 847–863.

Granberg, D., & Brown, T. (1989). On affect and cognition in politics. *Social Psychology Quarterly, 52*, 171–182.

Grant, M. J., Button, C. M., Hannah, T. E., & Ross, A. S. (2003). The role of ideological consistency in attitude inferences. *Current Research in Social Psychology, 9*(3), 32–49.

Grant, P. R. (1992). Ethnocentrism between groups of unequal power in response to perceived threat to social identity and valued resources. *Canadian Journal of Behavioural Science, 24*, 348–370.

Grant, P. R. (1993). Reactions to intergroup similarity: Examination of the similarity-differentiation and the similarity-attraction hypothesis. *Canadian Journal of Behavioural Science, 25*, 28–44.

Grant, P. R. (2008). The protest intentions of skilled immigrants with credentialing problems: A test of a model integrating relative deprivation theory with social identity theory. *British Journal of Social Psychology, 47*(4), 687–705.

Graziano, W. G., Habashi, M. M., Sheese, B. E., & Tobin, R. M. (2007). Agreeableness, empathy, and helping: A person × situation perspective. *Journal of Personality and Social Psychology, 93*, 583–599.

Graziano, W. G., Jensen-Campbell, L. A., & Finch, J. F. (1997). The self as a mediator between personality and adjustment. *Journal of Personality and Social Psychology, 73*, 392–404.

Graziano, W. G., Jensen-Campbell, L. A., Shebilske, L. J., & Lundgren, S. R. (1993). Social influence, sex differences, and judgments of beauty: Putting the interpersonal back in interpersonal attraction. *Journal of Personality and Social Psychology, 65*, 522–531.

Greenberg, J., & Musham, C. (1981). Avoiding and seeking self- focused attention. *Journal of Research in Personality, 15*, 191–200.

Greenberg, J., & Pyszczynski, T. (1985). The effect of an overheard slur on evaluations of the target: How to spread a social disease. *Journal of Experimental Social Psychology, 21*, 61–72.

Greenberg, J., Pyszczynski, T., & Solomon, S. (1986). The causes and consequences of the need for self-esteem: A terror management theory. In R. F. Baumeister (Ed.), *Public self and private self* (pp. 189–212). New York: Springer-Verlag.

Greenberg, J., Solomon, S., & Pyszczynski, T. (1997). Terror management theory of self-esteem and cultural worldviews: Empirical assessments and conceptual refinements. In M. P. Zanna (Eds.), *Advances in experimental social psychology* (Vol. 29, pp. 61–139). San Diego, CA: Academic Press.

Green-Demers, I., Pelletier, L. G., Stewart, D. G., & Gushue, N. R. (1998). Coping with the less interesting aspects of training. Toward a model of interest and motivation enhancement in individual sports. *Basic and Applied Social Psychology, 20*, 251–261.

Greenglass, E. R. (1991). Type A behavior, career aspirations, and role conflict in professional women. In M. J. Strube (Ed.), *Type A Behavior*. Newbury Park, CA: Sage.

Greenwald, A. G., & Banaji, M. R. (1989). The self as a memory system: Powerful, but ordinary. *Journal of Personality and Social Psychology, 57*, 41–54.

Greenwald, A. G., & Banaji, M. R. (1995). Implicit social cognition: Attitudes, self-esteem, and stereotypes. *Psychological Review, 102*, 4–27.

Greenwald, A. G., McGhee, D. E., & Schwartz, J. L. K. (1998). Measuring individual differences in implicit cognition: The Implicit Association Test. *Journal of Personality and Social Psychology, 74*, 1464–1480.

Greenwald, A. G., & Nosek, B. A. (2001). Health of the Implicit Association Test at age 3. *Zeitschrift für Experimentelle Psychologie, 48*, 85–93.

Greenwald, A. G., Spangenberg, E. R., Pratkanis, A. R., & Eskenazi, J. (1991). Double-blind tests of subliminal self-help audiotapes. *Psychological Science, 2*, 119–122.

Griffin, D., & Buehler, R. (1993). Role of construal processes in conformity and dissent. *Journal of Personality and Social Psychology, 65*, 657–669.

Griffin, D., & Buehler, R. (1999). Frequency, probability, and prediction: Easy solutions to cognitive illusions. *Cognitive Psychology, 38,* 48–78.

Griffin, D., & Kahneman, D. (2003). Judgmental heuristics: Human strengths or human weaknesses? In L. G. Aspinwall, & U. M. Staudinger (Eds.), *A psychology of human strengths: Fundamental questions and future directions for a positive psychology* (pp. 165–178). Washington, DC: American Psychological Association.

Griffin, D. W., & Ross, L. (1991). Subjective construal, social inference, and human misunderstanding. In L. Berkowitz (Ed.), *Advances in experimental social psychology* (Vol. 24, pp. 319–359). San Diego, CA: Academic Press.

Griffin, E., & Sparks, G. G. (1990). Friends forever: A longitudinal exploration of intimacy in same-sex pairs and platonic pairs. *Journal of Social and Personal Relationships,* 7, 29–46.

Griffitt, W., & Veitch, R. (1971). Hot and crowded: Influences of population density and temperature on interpersonal affective behavior. *Journal of Personality and Social Psychology, 17,* 92–98.

Griskevicius, V., Cialdini, R. B., & Goldstein, N. J. (2008). Applying (and resisting) peer influence. *MIT Sloan Management Review, 49,* 83–88.

Groopman, J. (2007, January 29). What's the trouble? *New Yorker,* pp. 36–41.

Gross, J. J. (1998). Antecedent- and response-focused emotion regulation: Divergent consequences for experience, expression, and physiology. *Journal of Personality and Social Psychology, 74,* 224–237.

Gross, J. J., & Levenson, R. W. (1993). Emotional suppression: Physiology, self-report, and expressive behavior. *Journal of Personality and Social Psychology, 64,* 970–986.

Gross, J. J., & Levenson, R. W. (1997). Hiding feelings: The acute effects of suppressing negative and positive emotion. *Journal of Abnormal Psychology, 106,* 95–103.

Grossbard, H, R, Lee, C. M., Neighbors, C., & Larimer, M. E. (2009). Body image concerns and contingent self-esteem in male and female college students. *Sex Roles, 60,* 198–297.

Grouzet, F. M. E., Kasser, T., Ahuvia, A., Dols, J. M. F., Kim, Y., Lau, S. . . . Kennon, M. (2005). The structure of goal contents across 15 cultures. *Journal of Personality and Social Psychology, 89,* 800–816.

Grusec, J. E. (1991). The socialization of altruism. In M. S. Clark (Ed.), Review of personality and social psychology (Vol. 12, pp. 9–33). Newbury Park, CA: Sage.

Grusec, J. E., Kuczynski, L., Rushton, J. P., & Simutis, Z. M. (1979). Modeling, direct instruction, and attributions: Effects on altruism. *Developmental Psychology, 14,* 51–57.

Guay, F., Mageau, G. A., & Vallerand, R. J. (2003). On the hierarchical structure of self-determined motivation: A test of top-down, bottom-up, reciprocal, and horizontal effects. *Personality and Social Psychology Bulletin, 29*(8), 992–1004.

Gudykunst, W. B., Ting-Toomey, S., & Nishida, T. (1996). *Communication in personal relationships across cultures.* Thousand Oaks, CA: Sage Publications.

Guerin, B. (1993). Social facilitation. Cambridge, UK: Cambridge University Press.

Guilbault, R. L., Bryant, F. B., Brockway, J. H., & Posavac, E. J. (2004). A meta-analysis of research on hindsight bias. *Basic and Applied Social Psychology, 26,* 103–117.

Guimond, S. (1999). Attitude change during college: Normative or informational social influence? *Social Psychology of Education, 2,* 237–261.

Guimond, S. (2000). Group socialization and prejudice: The social transmission of intergroup attitudes and beliefs. *European Journal of Social Psychology, 30,* 335–354.

Guimond, S., Chatard, A., Martinot, D., Crisp, R. J., & Redersdorff, S. (2006). Social comparison, self-stereotyping, and gender differences in self-construals. *Journal of Personality and Social Psychology, 90,* 221–242.

Guimond, S., Dambrun, M., Michinov, N., & Durarte, S. (2003). Does social dominance generate prejudice? Integrating individual and contextual determinants of intergroup cognitions. *Journal of Personality and Social Psychology, 84*(4), 697–721.

Guimond, S., & Dubé, L. (1989). La representation des causes de l'inferiorité economique des québequois francophones. *Canadian Journal of Behavioural Science, 21,* 28–39.

Guimond, S., & Palmer, D. L. (1996). The political socialization of commerce and social science students: Epistemic authority and attitude change. *Journal of Applied Social Psychology, 26,* 1985–2013.

Guisinger, S., & Blatt, S. J. (1994). Individuality and relatedness: Evolution of a fundamental dialect. *American Psychologist, 49,* 104–111.

Gulli, C. (2005, September 17). Why I gave a stranger a kidney. *National Post,* p. A1.

Gustafson, R. (1989). Frustration and successful vs. unsuccessful aggression: A test of Berkowitz' completion hypothesis. *Aggressive Behavior, 15,* 5–12.

Guthrie, M. (2005, January 11). "Housewives" drives home ad. *New York Daily News.* Retrieved from www.nydailynews.com/entertainment/ent_radio/story/269947p-231207c.html

Haddock, G., Maio, G. R., Arnold, K., & Huskinson, T. (2008). Should persuasion be affective or cognitive? The moderating effects of need for affect and need for cognition. *Personality and Social Psychology Bulletin, 34,* 769–778.

Haddock, G., & Zanna, M. P. (1994). Preferring "housewives" to "feminists": Categorization and the favorability of attitudes toward women. *Psychology of Women Quarterly, 18,* 25–52.

Haddock, G., & Zanna, M. P. (1998). Assessing the impact of affective and cognitive information in predicting attitudes toward capital punishment. *Law and Human Behavior, 22,* 325–339.

Haddock, G., Zanna, M. P., & Esses, V. M. (1993). Assessing the structure of prejudicial attitudes: The case of attitudes toward homosexuals. *Journal of Personality and Social Psychology, 65,* 1105–1118.

Haddock, G., Zanna, M. P., & Esses, V. M. (1994). The (limited) role of trait-laden stereotypes in predicting attitudes toward Native peoples. *British Journal of Social Psychology, 33,* 83–106.

Hadjistavropoulos, T., & Genest, M. (1994). The understanding of the role of physical attractiveness in dating preferences: Ignorance or taboo? *Canadian Journal of Behavioural Science, 26,* 298–318.

Hafer, C. L. (2000a). Do innocent victims threaten the belief in a just world? Evidence from a modified Stroop task. *Journal of Personality and Social Psychology, 79,* 165–173.

Hafer, C. L. (2000b). Investment in long-term goals and commitment to just means drive the need to believe in a just world. *Personality and Social Psychology Bulletin, 26,* 1059–1073.

Hafer, C. L. (2002). Why we reject innocent victims. In M. Ross & D. T. Miller (Eds). *The justice motive in everyday life* (pp. 109–126). New York: Cambridge University Press.

Hafer, C. L., & Bègue, L. (2005). Experimental research on just-world theory: Problems, developments, and future challenges. *Psychological Bulletin, 131,* 128–167.

Hafer, C. L., Reynolds, K. L., & Obertynski, M. A. (1996). Message comprehensibility and persuasion: Effects of complex language in counter attitudinal appeals to laypeople. *Social Cognition, 14,* 317–337.

Hakkarainen, K. K., & Olson, D. R. (2009). The uses of evidence in accident analysis by professionally versus scientifically trained investigators. *European Review of Applied Psychology/Revue Européenne de Psychologie Appliquée, 59*(4), 253–264.

Haidt, J., & Keltner, D. (1999). Culture and facial expression: Open-ended methods find more faces and a gradient of recognition. *Cognition and Emotion, 13,* 225–266.

Halberstadt, J. B., & Rhodes, G. (2000). The attractiveness of nonface averages: Implications for an evolutionary explanation of the attractiveness of average faces. *Psychological Science, 11*, 285–289.

Hall, E. T. (1969). *The hidden dimension*. Garden City, NY: Doubleday.

Hall, J. A. (1979). *A cross-national study of gender differences in nonverbal sensitivity*. Unpublished manuscript, Northeastern University.

Hall, J. A. (1984). *Nonverbal sex differences: Communication accuracy and expressive style*. Baltimore, MD: Johns Hopkins University Press.

Hall, V. (2008, August 12). Out of ammo. *National Post*, p. B1.

Hamamura, T., Heine, S. J., & Paulhus, D. L. (2007). Cultural differences in response styles: The role of dialectical thinking. *Personality and Individual Differences, 44*, 932–942.

Hamamura, T., Heine, S. J., & Takemoto, T. R. S. (2007). Why the better-than-average effects is a worse-than-average measure of self-enhancement: An investigation of conflicting findings from studies of East Asian self-evaluations. *Motivation and Emotion, 31*(4), pp. 247–259.

Hamilton, V. L., Sanders, J., & McKearney, S. J. (1995). Orientations toward authority in an authoritarian state: Moscow in 1990. *Personality and Social Psychology Bulletin, 21*, 356–365.

Hamilton, W. D. (1964). The genetical evolution of social behavior. *Journal of Theoretical Biology*, 7, 1–52.

Hammond, D., Fong, G. T., Borland, R., Cummings, M., McNeill, A., & Driezen, P. (2007). Text and graphic warnings on cigarette packages: Findings from the International Tobacco Control Country study. *American Journal of Preventive Medicine, 32*, 202–209.

Han, S., & Shavitt, S. (1994). Persuasion and culture: Advertising appeals in individualistic and collectivistic societies. *Journal of Experimental Social Psychology, 30*, 326–350.

Haney, C., Banks, C., & Zimbardo, P. (1973). Interpersonal dynamics in a simulated prison. *International Journal of Criminology and Penology, 1*, 69–97.

Hankin, B. L., Fraley, R. C., & Abela, J. R. Z. (2005). Daily depression and cognitions about stress: Evidence for a traitlike depressogenic cognitive style and the prediction of depressive symptoms in a prospective daily diary study. *Journal of Personality and Social Psychology, 88*, 673–685.

Hansen, C. H., & Hansen, R. D. (1988). Finding the face in the crowd: An anger superiority effect. *Journal of Personality and Social Psychology, 17*, 917–924.

Hansen, E. M., Kimble, C. E., & Biers, D. W. (2001). Actors and observers: Divergent attributions of constrained unfriendly behavior. *Social Behavior and Personality, 29*, 87–104.

Hanson, I., & Hampton, M. R. (2000). Being Indian: Strengths sustaining First Nations Peoples in Saskatchewan residential schools. *Canadian Journal of Community Mental Health, 19*, 127–142.

Hansson, R. O., & Slade, K. M. (1977). Altruism toward a deviant in a city and small town. *Journal of Applied Social Psychology*, 7, 272–279.

Harackiewicz, J. M. (1979). The effects of reward contingency and performance feedback on intrinsic motivation. *Journal of Personality and Social Psychology, 37*, 1352–1363.

Harackiewicz, J. M. (1989). Performance evaluation and intrinsic motivation processes: The effects of achievement orientation and rewards. In D. M. Buss & N. Cantor (Eds.), *Personality psychology: Recent trends and emerging directions* (pp. 128–137). New York: Springer-Verlag.

Harackiewicz, J. M., Durik, A. M., & Barron, K. E. (Eds). (2005). *Multiple goals, optimal motivation, and the development of interest*. New York: Cambridge University Press.

Harackiewicz, J. M., & Elliot, A. J. (1993). Achievement goals and intrinsic motivation. *Journal of Personality and Social Psychology, 65*, 904–915.

Harackiewicz, J. M., & Elliot, A. J. (1998). The joint effects of target and purpose goals on intrinsic motivation: A mediational analysis. *Personality and Social Psychology Bulletin, 24*(7), 675–689.

Harackiewicz, J. M., Manderlink, G., & Sansone, C. (1984). Rewarding pinball wizardry: Effects of evaluation and cue value on intrinsic interest. *Journal of Personality and Social Psychology, 47*, 287–300.

Harasymchuk, C. (2008, February). *Relational boredom and its correlates: Validation of a scale using individual and couple level analyses*. Paper presented at the Society for Personality and Social Psychology conference, Albuquerque, New Mexico.

Harasymchuk, C., & Fehr, B. (2008, July). Relational boredom: Correlates and unique contribution to satisfaction. In C. Harasymchuk and G. Strong (Chairs), *Routine, rituals, and boredom in relationships*. Symposium conducted at the International Association for Relationship Research, Providence, Rhode Island.

Hare, B., & Tomasello, M. (2005). Human-like social skills in dogs? *Trends in Cognitive Sciences, 9*(9), 439–444.

Hareli, S., Shomrat, N., & Hess, U. (2009). Emotional versus neutral expressions and perceptions of social dominance and submissiveness. *Emotion, 9*(3), 378–384.

Haritos-Fatouros, M. (1988). The official torturer: A learning model for obedience to the authority of violence. *Journal of Applied Social Psychology, 18*, 1107–1120.

Harmon-Jones, E., & Mills, J. S. (1998). *Cognitive dissonance theory: Revival with revisions and controversies*. Washington, DC: American Psychological Association.

Harries, K. D., & Stadler, S. J. (1988). Heat and violence: New findings from Dallas field data, 1980–1981. *Journal of Applied Social Psychology, 18*, 129–138.

Harrigan, J. A., & O'Connell, D. M. (1996). How do you feel when feeling anxious? Facial displays of anxiety. *Personality and Individual Differences, 21*, 205–212.

Harris, C. R., & Pashler, H. (2004). Attention and the processing of emotional words and names: Not so special after all. *Psychological Science, 15*, 171–178.

Harris, M. (1974). Mediators between frustration and aggression in a field experiment. *Journal of Experimental and Social Psychology, 10*, 561–571.

Harris, M. (1986). Helping the person with an altered self-image. *Geriatric Nursing*, 7, 90–92.

Harris, M. (2008). How do I love thee? Let me do the chores. *Winnipeg Free Press*, p. A16.

Harris, M. B., Benson, S. M., & Hall, C. (1975). The effects of confession on altruism. *Journal of Social Psychology, 96*, 187–192.

Harris, P. (1996). Sufficient grounds for optimism? The relationship between perceived controllability and optimistic bias. *Journal of Social and Clinical Psychology, 15*, 9–52.

Harrison, J. A., & Wells, R. B. (1991). Bystander effects on male helping behavior: Social comparison and diffusion of responsibility. *Representative Research in Social Psychology, 19*, 53–63.

Harrison, L. A., & Abrishami, G. (2004). Dating violence attributions: Do they differ for in-group and out-group members who have a history of dating violence? *Sex Roles, 51*, 543–550.

Hart, A. J., & Morry, M. M. (1997). Trait inferences based on racial and behavioral cues. *Basic & Applied Social Psychology, 19*, 33–48.

Hart, D., & Damon, W. (1986). Developmental trends in self-understanding. *Social Cognition, 4*, 388–407.

Hartshorne, H., & May, M. A. (1929). *Studies in the nature of character: Studies in service and self-control* (Vol. 2). New York: Macmillan.

Hartstone, M., & Augoustinos, M. (1995). The minimal group paradigm: Categorization into two versus three groups. *European Journal of Social Psychology, 25*, 179–193.

Hartup, W. W., & Laursen, B. (1999). Relationships as developmental contexts: Retrospective themes and contemporary issues. In W. A. Collins & B. Laursen (Eds.), *Relationships as developmental contexts: Minnesota Symposia on Child Psychology* (Vol. 30, pp. 13–35). Mahwah, NJ: Erlbaum.

Hartup, W. W., & Stevens, N. (1997). Friendships and adaptation in the life course. *Psychological Bulletin, 121*, 355–370.

Hassin, R. R., Uleman, J. S., & Bargh, J. A. (Eds). (2005). *The new unconscious*. New York: Oxford University Press.

Hastie, R. (2008). What's the story? Explanations and narratives in civil jury decisions. In B, H. Bornstein, R. L. Wiener, R. Schopp, & S. L. Willborn (Eds.), *Civil juries and civil justice: Psychological and legal perspectives* (pp. 23–34). New York: Springer.

Hastie, R., & Pennington, N. (2000). Explanation-based decision making. In T. Connolly & H. R. Arkes (Eds.), *Judgment and decision making: An interdisciplinary reader* (2nd ed., pp. 212–228). New York: Cambridge University Press.

Hastie, R., Penrod, S. D., & Pennington, N. (1983). *Inside the jury*. Cambridge, MA: Harvard University Press.

Hatfield, E., Greenberger, E., Traupmann, J., & Lambert, P. (1982). Equity and sexual satisfaction in recently married couples. *Journal of Sex Research, 18*, 18–32.

Hatfield, E., & Rapson, R. L. (1993). *Love, sex, and intimacy: Their psychology, biology, and history*. New York: HarperCollins.

Hatfield, E., & Rapson, R. L. (1996). *Love and sex: Cross-cultural perspectives*. Needham Heights, MA: Allyn & Bacon.

Hatfield, E., & Rapson, R. L. (2002). Passionate love and sexual desire: Cultural and historical perspectives. In A. L. Vangelisti, H. T. Reis, & M. A. Fitzpatrick (Eds.), *Stability and change in relationships* (pp. 306–324). New York: Cambridge University Press.

Hatfield, E., & Sprecher, S. (1986a). *Mirror, mirror: The importance of looks in everyday life*. Albany, NY: State University of New York Press.

Hatfield, E., & Sprecher, S. (1986b). Measuring passionate love in intimate relationships. *Journal of Adolescence, 9*, 383–410.

Hatfield, E., & Sprecher, S. (1995). Men's and women's preferences in marital partners in the United States, Russia, and Japan. *Journal of Cross-Cultural Psychology, 26*, 728–750.

Hatfield, E., & Walster, G. W. (1978). *A new look at love*. Reading, MA: Addison-Wesley.

Haugtvedt, C. P., & Wegener, D. T. (1994). Message order effects in persuasion: An attitude strength perspective. *Journal of Consumer Research, 21*, 205–218.

Hawa, R., Munro, B. E., & Doherty-Poirier, M. (1998). Information, motivation and behaviour as predictors of AIDS risk reduction among Canadian first-year university students. *Canadian Journal of Human Sexuality, 7*, 9–18.

Haynes, G. A., Sorrentino, R. M., Olson, J. M., Szeto, A. H., Wirkki, J., & O'Connor, M. C. (2007). The effects of temporal framing on counterfactual thinking and self-appraisal: An individual differences perspective. *Social Cognition, 25*(3), 339–366.

Haynes, T. L., Daniels, L. M., Stupnisky, R. H., Perry, R. P., & Hladkyj, S. (2008). The effect of attributional retraining on mastery and performance motivation among first-year college students. *Basic and Applied Social Psychology, 30*(3), 198–207.

Haynes Stewart, T. L., Clifton, R. A., Daniels, L. M., Perry, R. P., Chipperfield, J. G., & Ruthig, J. C. (2011). Attributional retraining: Reducing the likelihood of failure. *Social Psychology of Education, 14*(1), 75–92.

Hazan, C., & Shaver, P. (1987). Romantic love conceptualized as an attachment process. *Journal of Personality and Social Psychology, 52*, 511–524.

Hébert, Y., Bernard, J., deMan, A. F., & Farrar, D. (1989). Factors related to the use of condoms among French-Canadian university students. *Journal of Social Psychology, 129*, 707–709.

Hebl, M., Foster, J., Bigazzi, J., Mannix, L., & Dovidio, J. (2002). Formal and interpersonal discrimination: A field study of bias toward homosexual applicants. *Personality and Social Psychology Bulletin, 28*, 815–825.

Heckhausen, J., & Schulz, R. (1995). A life-span theory of control. *Psychological Review, 102*, 284–304.

Hedden, T., Ketay, S., Aron, A., Markus, H. R., & Gabrieli, J. D. E. (2008). Cultural influences on neural substrates of attentional control. *Psychological Science, 19*(1), 12–17.

Hedge, A., & Yousif, Y. H. (1992). Effects of urban size, urgency, and cost on helpfulness. *Journal of Cross-Cultural Psychology, 23*, 107–115.

Heider, F. (1958). *The psychology of interpersonal relations*. New York: Wiley.

Heine, S. J. (2001). Self as cultural product: An examination of East Asian and North American selves. *Journal of Personality, 69*, 881–906.

Heine, S. J. (2003). Making sense of East Asian self-enhancement. *Journal of Cross-Cultural Psychology, 34*, 596–602.

Heine, S. J. (2005). Where is the evidence for pancultural self-enhancement? A reply to Sedikides, Gaertner, and Toguchi (2003). *Journal of Personality and Social Psychology, 89*, 531–538.

Heine, S. J. (2008). *Cultural psychology*. New York: Norton.

Heine, S. J., & Buchtel, E. E. (2009). Personality: The universal and the culturally specific. *Annual Review of Psychology, 60*, 369–394.

Heine, S. J., Buchtel, E. E., & Norenzayan, A. (2008). What do cross-national comparisons of personality tell us? *Psychological Science, 19*, 309–313.

Heine, S. J., Foster, J. B., & Spina, R. (2009). Do birds of a feather universally flock together? Cultural variation in the similarity-attraction effect. *Asian Journal of Social Psychology, 12*(4), 247–258.

Heine, S. J., & Hamamura, T. (2007). In search of East Asian self-enhancement. *Personality and Social Psychology Review, 11*, 1–24.

Heine, S. J., Kitayama, S., & Lehman, D. R. (2001). Cultural differences in self-evaluation: Japanese readily accept negative self- relevant information. *Journal of Cross-Cultural Psychology, 32*, 434–443.

Heine, S. J., & Lehman, D. R. (1995). Cultural variation in unrealistic optimism: Does the West feel more vulnerable than the East? *Journal of Personality and Social Psychology, 68*, 595–607.

Heine, S. J., & Lehman, D. R. (1997a). Culture, dissonance, and self-affirmation. *Personality and Social Psychology Bulletin, 23*, 389–400.

Heine, S. J., & Lehman, D. R. (1997b). The cultural construction of self-enhancement: An examination of group serving biases. *Journal of Personality and Social Psychology, 72*, 1268–1283.

Heine, S. J., & Lehman, D. R. (1999). Culture, self-discrepancies, and self-satisfaction. *Personality and Social Psychology Bulletin, 25*, 915–925.

Heine, S. J., Lehman, D. R., Markus, H. R., & Kitayama, S. (1999). Is there a universal need for positive self-regard? *Psychological Review, 106*, 766–794.

Heine, S. J., Lehman, D. R., Peng, K., & Greenholtz, J. (2002). What's wrong with cross-cultural comparisons of subjective Likert scales? The reference-group effect. *Journal of Personality and Social Psychology, 82*, 903–918.

Heine, S. J., Proulx, T., & Vohs, K. D. (2006). The meaning maintenance model: On the coherence of social motivations. *Personality and Social Psychology Review, 10*, 88–110.

Heine, S. J., & Raineri, A. (in press). Self-improving motivations and collectivism: The case of Chileans. *Journal of Cross-Cultural Psychology*.

Heine, S. J., & Renshaw, K. (2002). Interjudge agreement, self- enhancement, and liking: Cross-cultural perspectives. *Personality and Social Psychology Bulletin, 28*, 578–587.

Heine, S. J., Takata, T., & Lehman, D. R. (2000). Beyond self- presentation: Evidence for self-criticism among Japanese. *Personality and Social Psychology Bulletin, 26*, 71–78.

Heine, S. J., Takemoto, T., Moskalenko, S., Lasaleta, J., & Henrich, J. (2008). Mirrors in the head: Cultural variation in objective self-awareness. *Personality and Social Psychology Bulletin, 34*, 879–887.

Hejmadi, A., Davidson, R. J., & Rozin, P. (2000). Exploring Hindu Indian emotion expressions: Evidence for accurate recognition by Americans and Indians. *Psychological Science, 11*, 183–187.

Helgeson, V. S. (1994). The effects of self-beliefs and relationship beliefs on adjustment to a relationship stressor. *Personal Relationships, 1*, 241–258.

Helgeson, V. S. (2003). Cognitive adaptation, psychological adjustment, and disease progression among angioplasty patents: 4 years later. *Health Psychology, 22*, 30–38.

Helgeson, V. S., & Cohen, S. (1996). Social support and adjustment to cancer: Reconciling descriptive, correlational, and intervention research. *Health Psychology, 15*, 135–148.

Helgeson, V. S., & Fritz, H. L. (1999). Cognitive adaptation as a predictor of new coronary events after percutaneous transluminal coronary angioplasty. *Psychosomatic Medicine, 61*, 488–495.

Hemenover, S. H. (2003). The good, the bad, and the healthy: Impacts of emotional disclosure of trauma on resilient self- concept and psychological distress. *Personality and Social Psychology Bulletin, 29*(10), 1236–1244.

Henderson-King, E., & Nisbett, R. E. (1996). Anti-black prejudice as a function of exposure to the negative behavior of a single black person. *Journal of Personality and Social Psychology, 71*, 654–664.

Hendrick, S. S., & Hendrick, C. (1986). A theory and method of love. *Journal of Personality and Social Psychology, 50*, 392–402.

Hendrick, S. S., & Hendrick, C. (1995). Gender differences and similarities in sex and love. *Personal Relationships, 4*, 281–297.

Hendrick, S. S, Hendrick, C., & Adler, N. L. (1988). Romantic relationships: Love, satisfaction, and staying together. *Journal of Personality and Social Psychology, 54*, 980–988.

Henley, N. M. (1977). *Body politics: Power, sex, and nonverbal communication*. Englewood Cliffs, NJ: Prentice Hall.

Henningsen, D., Henningsen, M., Eden, J., & Cruz, M. (2006). Examining the symptoms of groupthink and retrospective sensemaking. *Small Group Research, 37*, 36–64.

Henry, R. A. (1995). Using relative confidence judgments to evaluate group effectiveness. *Basic and Applied Social Psychology, 16*, 333–350.

Herold, E. S., & Mewhinney, D. (1993). Gender differences in casual sex and AIDS prevention: A survey of dating bars. *Journal of Sex Research, 30*, 36–42.

Hersh, S. M. (1970). *My Lai 4: A report on the massacre and its aftermath*. New York: Vintage Books.

Hersh, S. M. (2004, April 30). Annals of National Security: Torture at Abu Ghraib, *The New Yorker*. Retrieved from www.newyorker.com/fact/content/ ?040510fa_fact

Hershcovis, M., & Barling, J. (2010). Comparing victim attributions and outcomes for workplace aggression and sexual harassment. *Journal of Applied Psychology, 95*(5), 874–888.

Heschl, A., & Burkart, J. (2006). A new mark test for mirror self-recognition in non-human primates. *Primates, 47*, 187–198.

Hess, U., & Blairy, S. (2001). Facial mimicry and emotional contagion to dynamic emotional facial expressions and their influence on decoding accuracy. *International Journal of Psychophysiology, 40*, 129–141.

Hess, U., & Bourgeois, P. (2010). You smile-I smile: Emotion expression in social interaction. *Biological Psychology, 84*(3), 514–520.

Hess, U., Philippot, P., & Blairy, S. (1998). Facial reactions to emotional facial expressions: Affect or cognition? *Cognition and Emotion, 12*, 509–531.

Heuer, L., Penrod, S., Hafer, C. L., & Cohn, I. (2002). The role of resource and relational concerns for procedural justice. *Personality and Social Psychology Bulletin, 28*(11), 1468–1482.

Heunemann, R. L., Shapiro, L. R., Hampton, M. C., & Mitchell, B. W. (1966). A longitudinal study of gross body composition and body conformation and their association with food and activity in the teenage population. *American Journal of Clinical Nutrition, 18*, 325–338.

Hewstone, M., & Jaspars, J. (1987). Covariation and causal attribution: A logical model of the intuitive analysis of variance. *Journal of Personality and Social Psychology, 53*, 663–672.

Hicks, B. (2010, February 27). Bernard runs out of magic. Retrieved from http://www.cbc.ca/olympics/curling/story/2010/02/27/spo-bernard-nmkr.html

Higgins, E. T. (1987). Self-discrepancy: A theory relating self and affect. *Psychological Review, 94*, 319–340.

Higgins, E. T. (1989). Self-discrepancy theory: What patterns of self-beliefs cause people to suffer? In L. Berkowitz (Ed.), *Advances in experimental social psychology* (Vol. 22, pp. 93–136). New York: Academic Press.

Higgins, E. T. (1996). Knowledge application: Accessibility, applicability, and salience. In E. T. Higgins and A. R. Kruglanski (Eds.), *Social psychology: Handbook of basic principles* (pp. 133–168). New York: Guilford.

Higgins, E. T. (1997). Beyond pleasure and pain. *American Psychologist, 52*, 1280–1300.

Higgins, E. T. (1998). Promotion and prevention: Regulatory focus as a motivational principle. In M. P. Zanna (Ed.), *Advances in experimental social psychology* (Vol. 30, pp. 1–46). San Diego, CA: Academic Press.

Higgins, E. T. (1999). Self-discrepancy: A theory relating self and affect. In R. F. Baumeister (Ed.), *The self in social psychology* (pp. 150–181). Philadelphia: Psychology Press.

Higgins, E. T. (2005). Value from regulatory fit. *Current Directions in Psychological Science, 14*, 209–213.

Higgins, E. T., & Bargh, J. A. (1987). Social cognition and social perception. *Annual Review of Psychology, 38*, 369–425.

Higgins, E. T., Bond, R. N., Klein, R., & Strauman, T. (1986). Self- discrepancies and emotional vulnerability: How magnitude, accessibility, and type of discrepancy influence affect. *Journal of Personality and Social Psychology, 51*, 5–15.

Higgins, E. T., & Brendl, C. M. (1995). Accessibility and applicability: Some "activation rules" influencing judgment. *Journal of Experimental Social Psychology, 31*, 218–243.

Higgins, E. T., Klein, R., & Strauman, T. (1987). Self-discrepancies: Distinguishing among self-states, self-state conflicts, and emotional vulnerabilities. In K. M. Yardley & T. M. Honess (Eds.), *Self and identity: Psychosocial perspectives* (pp. 173–186). New York: Wiley.

Higgins, E. T., Rholes, W. S., & Jones, C. R. (1977). Category accessibility and impression formation. *Journal of Experimental Social Psychology, 13*, 141–154.

Hill, A. J., Boudreau, F., Amyot, E., Dery, D., & Godin, G. (1997). Predicting the stages of smoking acquisition according to the theory of planned behavior. *Journal of Adolescent Health, 21*, 107–115.

Hill, A. J., Oliver, S., & Rogers, P. J. (1992). Eating in the adult world: The rise of dieting in childhood and adolescence. *British Journal of Clinical Psychology, 31*, 95–105.

Hill, E., & Pfeifer, J. E. (1992). Nullification instructions and juror guilt ratings: An examination of modern racism. *Contemporary Social Psychology, 16*, 6–10.

Hilton, A., Potvin, L., & Sachdev, I. (1989). Ethnic relations in rental housing: A social psychological approach. *Canadian Journal of Behavioural Science, 21*, 121–131.

Hilton, J. L., Fein, S., & Miller, D. T. (1993). Suspicion and dispositional inference. *Journal of Personality and Social Psychology, 19*, 501–512.

Hinduja, S., & Patchin, J. (2007). Offline consequences of online victimization: School violence and delinquency. *Journal of School Violence, 6*(3), 89–112.

Hirt, E. R., Kardes, F. R., & Markman, K. D. (2004). Activating a mental simulation mind-set through generation of alternatives:

Implications for debiasing in related and unrelated domains. *Journal of Experimental Social Psychology, 40*(3), 374–383.

Hoaken, P. N. S., & Pihl, R. O. (2000). The effects of alcohol intoxication on aggressive responses in men and women. *Alcohol and Alcoholism, 35*, 471–477.

Hobbes, T. (1986 [1651]). *Leviathan*. Harmondsworth, UK: Penguin Press.

Hobden, K. L., & Olson, J. M. (1994). From jest to antipathy: Disparagement humor as a source of dissonance-motivated attitude change. *Basic and Applied Social Psychology, 15*, 239–249.

Hochstadt, S. (1999). *Mobility and modernity: Migration in Germany, 1820–1989*. Ann Arbor, MI: University of Michigan Press.

Hodges, B. H., & Geyer, A. L. (2006). A nonconformist account of the Asch experiments: Values, pragmatics, and moral dilemmas. *Personality and Social Psychology Review, 10*, 2–19.

Hodson, G., Choma, B. L., & Costello, K. (2009). Experiencing alien-nation: Effects of a simulation intervention on attitudes toward homosexuals. *Journal of Experimental Social Psychology, 45*(4), 974–978.

Hodson, G., & Esses, V. M. (2002). Distancing oneself from negative attributes and the personal/group discrimination discrepancy. *Journal of Experimental Social Psychology, 38*, 500–507.

Hodson, G., & Esses, V. M. (2005). Lay perceptions of ethnic prejudice: Causes, solutions, and individual differences. *European Journal of Social Psychology, 35*, 329–344.

Hodson, G., Hogg, S. M., & MacInnis, C. C. (2009). The role of 'dark personalities' (narcissism, Machiavellianism, psychopathy), Big Five personality factors, and ideology in explaining prejudice. *Journal of Research in Personality, 43*(4), 686–690.

Hodson, G., MacInnis, C. C., & Rush, J. (2010). Prejudice-relevant correlates of humor temperaments and humor styles. *Personality and Individual Differences, 49*(5), 546–549.

Hodson, G., & Olson, J. M. (2005). Testing the generality of the name letter effect: Name initials and everyday attitudes. *Personality and Social Psychology Bulletin, 31*, 1099–1111.

Hodson, G., Rush, J., & MacInnis, C. C. (2010). A joke is just a joke (except when it isn't): Cavalier humor beliefs facilitate the expression of group dominance motives. *Journal of Personality and Social Psychology, 99*(4), 660–682.

Hodson, G., & Sorrentino, R. M. (1997). Groupthink and uncertainty orientation: Personality differences in reactivity to the group situation. *Group Dynamics, 1*, 144–155.

Hodson, R. (2004). A meta-analysis of workplace ethnographies: Race, gender, and employee attitudes and behavior. *Journal of Contemporary Ethnography, 33*, 4–38.

Hoffman, A. J., Gillespie, J. J., Moore, D. A., Wade-Benzoni, K. A., Thompson, L. L., & Bazerman, M. H. (1999). A mixed-motive perspective on the economics versus environmental debate. *American Behavioral Scientist, 42*, 1254–1276.

Hoffman, B., Monge, P., Chou, C., & Valente, T. (2007). Perceived peer influence and peer selection on adolescent smoking. *Addictive Behaviors, 32*, 1546–1554.

Hoffman, C., Lau, I., & Johnson, D. R. (1986). The linguistic relativity of person cognition: An English-Chinese comparison. *Journal of Personality and Social Psychology, 51*, 1097–1105.

Hoffman, H. G., Granhag, P. A., See, S. T. K., & Loftus, E. F. (2001). Social influences on reality-monitoring decisions. *Memory and Cognition, 29*, 394–404.

Hoffman, M. L. (1981). Is altruism a part of human nature? *Journal of Personality and Social Psychology, 40*, 121–137.

Hofmann, W., Gawronski, B., Gschwendner, T., Le, H., & Schmitt, M. (2005). A meta-analysis on the correlation between the Implicit Association Test and explicit self-report measures. *Personality and Social Psychology Bulletin, 31*, 1369–1385.

Hofstede, G. (1984). *Culture's consequences: International differences in work-related values*. Newbury Park, CA: Sage.

Hofstede, G. (1986). Cultural differences in teaching and learning. *International Journal of Intercultural Relations, 10*, 301–320.

Hogg, M. A. (1992). *The social psychology of group cohesiveness: From attraction to social identity*. London, UK: Harvester-Wheatsheaf.

Hogg, M. A. (1993). Group cohesiveness: A critical review and some new directions. In W. Stroebe & M. Hewstone (Eds.), *European review of social psychology* (Vol. 4, pp. 85–111). Chichester, UK: Wiley.

Hogg, M. A. (2001). A social identity theory of leadership. *Personality and Social Psychology Review, 5*, 184–200.

Hogg, M. A., & Hains, S. C. (1998). Friendship and group identification: A new look at the role of cohesiveness in groupthink. *European Journal of Social Psychology, 28*, 323–341.

Holland, R. W., Aarts, H., & Langendam, D. (2006). Breaking and creating habits on the working floor: A field-experiment on the power of implementation intentions. *Journal of Experimental Social Psychology, 42*, 776–783.

Hollander, E. P. (1958). Conformity, status, and idiosyncrasy credit. *Psychological Review, 65*, 117–127.

Hollander, E. P. (1960). Competence and conformity in the acceptance of influence. *Journal of Abnormal and Social Psychology, 61*, 361–365.

Hollander, E. P. (1985). Leadership and power. In G. Lindzey & E. Aronson (Eds.), *Handbook of social psychology* (3rd ed., Vol. 2, pp. 485–537). New York: McGraw-Hill.

Hollingshead, A. B. (2001). Cognitive interdependence and convergent expectations in transactive memory. *Journal of Personality and Social Psychology, 81*, 1080–1089.

Holmberg, D., & MacKenzie, S. (2002). So far so good: Scripts for romantic relationship development as predictors of relational well-being. *Journal of Social and Personal Relationships, 19*, 777–796.

Holmes, J. G., Miller, D. T., & Lerner, M. J. (2002). Committing altruism under the cloak of self-interest: The exchange fiction. *Journal of Experimental Social Psychology, 38*, 144–151.

Holmes, T. H., & Rahe, R. H. (1967). The social readjustment rating scale. *Journal of Psychosomatic Research, 11*, 213–218.

Holtz, R. (1997). Length of group membership, assumed similarity, and opinion certainty: The dividend for veteran members. *Journal of Applied Social Psychology, 27*, 539–555.

Holtz, R. (2004). Group cohesion, attitude projection, and opinion certainty: Beyond interaction. *Group Dynamics: Theory, Research, and Practice, 8*, 112–125.

Homans, G. C. (1961). *Social behavior: Its elementary forms*. New York: Harcourt Brace & World.

Hong, J. J., & Woody, S. R. (2007). Cultural mediators of self-reported social anxiety. *Behaviour Research and Therapy, 45*(8), 1779–1789.

Honts, C. R. (1994). Psychophysiological detection of deception. *Current Directions in Psychological Science, 3*, 77–82.

Hope, L., & Wright, D. (2007). Beyond unusual? Examining the role of attention in the weapon focus effect. *Applied Cognitive Psychology, 21*, 951–961.

Horne, S. G., & Biss, W. J. (2009). Equality discrepancy between women in same-sex relationships: The mediating role of attachment in relationship satisfaction. *Sex Roles, 60*(9-10), 721–730.

Hornsey, M. J., & Jetten, J. (2004). The individual within the group: Balancing the need to belong with the need to be different. *Personality and Social Psychology Review, 8*, 248–264.

Hornsey, M. J., & Jetten, J. (2005). Loyalty without conformity: Tailoring self-perception as a means of balancing belonging and differentiation. *Self and Identity, 4*, 81–95.

Hornsey, M. J., Jetten, J., McAuliffe, B. J., & Hogg, M. A. (2006). The impact of individualist and collectivist group norms on evaluations of dissenting group members. *Journal of Experimental Social Psychology, 42*, 57–68.

Hoshino-Browne, E., Zanna, A. S., Spencer, S. J., Zanna, M. P., Kitayama, S., & Lackenbauer, S. (2005). On the cultural guises of cognitive dissonance: The case of easterners and westerners. *Journal of Personality and Social Psychology, 89*, 294–310.

Hosking, W., Borland, R., Yong, H., Fong, G., Zanna, M., Laux, F., . . . Omar, M. (2009). The effects of smoking norms and attitudes on quitting intentions in Malaysia, Thailand and four Western nations: A crosscultural comparison. *Psychology & Health, 24*(1), 95–107.

House, J. S., Robbins, C., & Metzner, H. L. (1982). The association of social relationships and activities with mortality: Prospective evidence from the Tecumseh Community Health Study. *American Journal of Epidemiology, 116*, 123–140.

House, R. J. (1971). A path-goal theory of leadership effectiveness. *Administrative Science Quarterly, 16*, 321–338.

Hovland, C. I., Janis, I. L., & Kelley, H. H. (1953). *Communication and persuasion: Psychological studies of opinion change*. New Haven, CT: Yale University Press.

Hovland, C. I., & Sears, R. R. (1940). Minor studies in aggression: 6. Correlation of lynchings with economic indices. *Journal of Psychology, 9*, 301–310.

Hovland, C. I., & Weiss, W. (1951). The influence of source credibility on communication effectiveness. *Public Opinion Quarterly, 15*, 635–650.

Howard, D. E., & Wang, M. Q. (2003). Risk profiles of adolescent girls who were victims of dating violence. *Adolescence, 38*, 1–14.

Hsu, S. S. (1995, April 8). Fredericksburg searches its soul after clerk is beaten as 6 watch. *Washington Post*, pp. A1, A13.

Hudson, S., Hudson, D., & Peloza, J. (2008). Meet the parents: A parents' perspective on product placement in children's films. *Journal of Business Ethics, 80*(2), 289–304.

Huesmann, L. R., & Miller, L. S. (1994). Long-term effects of repeated exposure to media violence in childhood. In L. R. Huesmann (Ed.), *Aggressive behavior: Current perspectives* (pp. 153–186). New York: Plenum.

Huffman, K. T., Grossnickle, W. F., Cope, J. G., & Huffman, K. P. (1995). Litter reduction: A review and integration of the literature. *Environment and Behavior, 27*, 153–183.

Huguet, P., Galvaing, M. P., Monteil, J. M., & Dumas, F. (1999). Social presence effects in the Stroop task: Further evidence for an attentional view of social facilitation. *Journal of Personality and Social Psychology*, 77, 1011–1025.

Hui, C. H., & Triandis, H. C. (1986). Individualism-collectivism: A study of cross-cultural researchers. *Journal of Cross-Cultural Psychology, 17*, 225–248.

Hull, J. G. (1981). A self-awareness model of the causes and effects of alcohol consumption. *Journal of Personality and Social Psychology, 90*, 586–600.

Hull, J. G., & Young, R. D. (1983). Self-consciousness, self-esteem, and success-failure as determinants of alcohol consumption in male social drinkers. *Journal of Personality and Social Psychology, 44*, 1097–1109.

Hull, J. G., Young, R. D., & Jouriles, E. (1986). Applications of the self-awareness model of alcohol consumption: Predicting patterns of use and abuse. *Journal of Personality and Social Psychology, 51*, 790–796.

Human, L. J., & Biesanz, J. C. (2011). Through the looking glass clearly: Accuracy and assumed similarity in well-adjusted individuals' first impressions. *Journal of Personality and Social Psychology, 100*(2), 349–364.

Hunsberger, B. (1995). Religion and prejudice: The role of religious fundamentalism, quest, and right-wing authoritarianism. *Journal of Social Issues, 51*, 113–129.

Hunsberger, B. (1996). Religious fundamentalism, right-wing authoritarianism and hostility toward homosexuals in non-Christian religious groups. *International Journal for the Psychology of Religion, 6*, 39–49.

Hunt, G. T. (1940). *The wars of the Iroquois*. Madison, WI: University of Wisconsin Press.

Hurley, D., & Allen, B. P. (1974). The effect of the number of people present in a nonemergency situation. *Journal of Social Psychology, 92*, 27–29.

Hurley, E., & Allen, B. (2007). Asking the how questions: Quantifying group processes behaviors. *Journal of General Psychology, 134*, 5–21.

Hutchinson, R. R. (1983). The pain-aggression relationship and its expression in naturalistic settings. *Aggressive Behavior, 9*, 229–242.

Hyde, J., Hankins, M., Deale, A., & Marteau, T. (2008). Interventions to increase self-efficacy in the context of addiction behaviours: A systematic literature review. *Journal of Health Psychology, 13*, 607–623.

Hynie, M., & Lydon, J. E. (1995). Women's perceptions of female contraceptive behavior: Experimental evidence of the sexual double standard. *Psychology of Women Quarterly, 19*, 563–581.

Hynie, M., & Lydon, J. E. (1996). Sexual attitudes and contraceptive behavior revisited: Can there be too much of a good thing? *Journal of Sex Research, 33*, 127–134.

Hynie, M., Lydon, J. E., Cote, S., & Wiener, S. (1998). Relational sexual scripts and women's condom use: The importance of internalized norms. *Journal of Sex Research, 35*, 370–380.

Hynie, M., MacDonald, T. K., & Marques, S. (2006). Self-conscious emotions and self-regulation in the promotion of condom use. *Personality and Social Psychology Bulletin, 32*, 1072–1084.

Iacono, W. G. (2000). The detection of deception. In J. T. Cacioppo & L. G. Tassinary (Eds.), *Handbook of psychophysiology* (2nd ed., pp. 772–793). New York: Cambridge University Press.

Iacono, W. G.. (2008). Polygraph testing. In E. Borgida and S. T. Fiske (Eds.), Beyond common sense: Psychological science in the courtroom (pp. 219–235). Malden, MA: Blackwell Publishing.

Iacono, W. G., & Patrick, C. J. (1999). Polygraph ("lie detector") testing: The state of the art. In A. K. Hess & I. B. Weiner (Eds.), *The handbook of forensic psychology* (2nd ed., pp. 440–473). New York: Wiley.

Ibrahim, J., & Glantz, S. (2007). The rise and fall of tobacco control media campaigns, 1967-2006. *American Journal of Public Health, 97*, 1383–1396.

Ickes, W., Patterson, M. L., Rajecki, D. W., & Tanford, S. (1982). Behavioral and cognitive consequences of reciprocal versus compensatory responses to preinteraction expectancies. *Social Cognition, 1*, 160–190.

Igou, E. R., & Bless, H. (2003). Inferring the importance of arguments: Order effects and conversational rules. *Journal of Experimental Social Psychology, 39*, 91–99.

Inglehart, M. R. (1991). *Reactions to critical life events: A social psychological analysis*. New York: Praeger.

Insko, C. A., & Schopler, J. (1998). Differential trust of groups and individuals. In C. Sedikides & J. Schopler (Eds.), *Intergroup cognition and intergroup behavior* (pp. 75–107). Mahwah, NJ: Erlbaum.

Intrieri, R. C., & Morse, J. M. (1997). A sequential analysis of verbal and nonverbal interaction of two long-term care residents. *Journal of Applied Gerontology, 16*, 477–494.

Inzlicht, M., Aronson, J., Good, C., & McKay, L. (2006). A particular resiliency to threatening environments. *Journal of Experimental Social Psychology, 42*(3), 323–336.

Inzlicht, M., & Gutsell, J. N. (2007). Running on empty: Neural signals for self-control failure. *Psychological Science, 18*(11), 933–937.

Inzlicht, M., Kaiser, C. R., & Major, B. (2008). The face of chauvinism: How prejudice expectations shape perceptions of facial affect. *Journal of Experimental Social Psychology, 44*(3), 758–766.

Inzlicht, M., & Kang, S. (2010). Stereotype threat spillover: How coping with threats to social identity affects aggression, eating, decision making, and attention. *Journal of Personality and Social Psychology, 99*(3), 467–481.

Ip, K., & Jarry, J. L. (2008). Investment in body image for self-definition results in greater vulnerability to the thin media than does investment in appearance management. *Body Image, 5*(1), 59–69.

Isen, A. M. (1987). Positive affect, cognitive processes, and social behavior. In L. Berkowitz (Ed.), *Advances in experimental social psychology* (Vol. 20, pp. 203–253). San Diego, CA: Academic Press.

Isen, A. M. (1999). Positive affect. In T. Dalgleish & M. J. Power (Eds.), *Handbook of cognition and emotion* (pp. 521–539). Chichester, UK: Wiley.

Isen, A. M., & Levin, P. A. (1972). Effect of feeling good on helping: Cookies and kindness. *Journal of Personality and Social Psychology, 21*, 384–388.

Isenberg, D. J. (1986). Group polarization: A critical review and meta-analysis. *Journal of Personality and Social Psychology, 50*, 1141–1151.

Ito, K., Masuda, T., & Hioki, K. (2011, January 17). Affective information in context and judgment of facial expression: Cultural similarities and variations in context effects between North Americans and East *Asians. Journal of Cross-Cultural Psychology.* Advanced online publication. doi:10.1177/0022022110395139.

Ivey, G. W., & Kline, T. B. (2010). Transformational and active transactional leadership in the Canadian military. *Leadership & Organization Development Journal, 31*(3), 246–262.

Iwata, O. (1992). A comparative study of person perception and friendly altruistic behavior intentions between Canadian and Japanese undergraduates. In S. Iwawaki, Y. Kashima, & K. Leving (Eds.), *Innovations in cross cultural psychology*. Amsterdam, Netherlands: Swets & Zeitlinger.

Iyer, A., & Ryan, M. K. (2009). Why do men and women challenge gender discrimination in the workplace? The role of group status and in-group identification in predicting pathways to collective action. *Journal of Social Issues, 65*(4), 791–814.

Izard, C. E. (1994). Innate and universal facial expressions: Evidence from developmental and cross-cultural research. *Psychological Bulletin, 115*, 288–299.

Jackiw, L. B., Arbuthnott, K. D., Pfeifer, J. E., Marcon, J. L., & Meissner, C. A. (2008). Examining the cross-race effect in lineup identification using Caucasian and First Nations samples. *Canadian Journal of Behavioural Science, 40*(1), 52–57.

Jackson, E. L. (1985). Environmental attitudes and preferences for energy resource options. *Journal of Environmental Education, 17*, 23–30.

Jackson, E. L. (1987). Outdoor recreation participation and views on resource development and preservation. *Leisure Sciences, 9*, 235–250.

Jackson, J. (1981, July 19). Syndicated newspaper column.

Jackson, J. M., & Williams, K. D. (1985). Social loafing on difficult tasks: Working collectively can improve performance. *Journal of Personality and Social Psychology, 49*, 937–942.

Jackson, J. S., Brown, T. N., Williams, D. R., Torres, M., Sellers, S. L., & Brown, K. (1996). Racism and the physical and mental health status of African Americans: A thirteen-year national panel study. *Ethnicity and Disease, 6*, 132–147.

Jackson, J. S., & Inglehart, M. R. (1995). Reverberation theory: Stress and racism in hierarchically structured communities. In S. E. Hobfoll & M. W. de Vries (Eds.), *Extreme stress and communities: Impact and intervention* (pp. 353–373). Dordrecht, Netherlands: Kluwer Academic Publishers.

Jackson, J. W. (1993). Realistic group conflict theory: A review and evaluation of the theoretical and empirical literature. *Psychological Record, 43*, 395–413.

Jackson, L. A. (1992). *Physical appearance and gender: Socio-biological and sociocultural perspectives*. Albany, NY: State University of New York Press.

Jackson, L. A., Hunter, J. E., & Hodge, C. N. (1995). Physical attractiveness and intellectual competence: A meta-analytic review. *Social Psychology Quarterly, 58*, 108–122.

Jackson, L. M., & Esses, V. M. (1997). Of scripture and ascription: The relation between religious fundamentalism and intergroup helping. *Personality and Social Psychology Bulletin, 23*, 893–906.

Jacobs, P., & Landau, S. (1971). *To serve the devil* (Vol. 2, p. 71). New York: Vintage Books.

Jain, S. P., & Posavac, S. S. (2001). Prepurchase attribute verifiability, source credibility, and persuasion. *Journal of Consumer Psychology, 11*(3), 169–180.

James, J. M., & Bolstein, R. (1992). Large monetary incentives and their effect on mail survey response rates. *Public Opinion Quarterly, 56*, 442–453.

James, K. (2008). Terrorism and hazardous material trucking: Promoting perceived collective efficacy for terrorism prevention. *Journal of Occupational Health Psychology, 13*(1), 24–31.

James, W. (1890). *The principles of psychology*. New York: Holt.

Jamieson, D. W., Lydon, J. E., & Zanna, M. P. (1987). Attitude and activity preference similarity: Differential bases of interpersonal attraction for low and high self-monitors. *Journal of Personality and Social Psychology, 53*, 1052–1060.

Janes, L. M., & Olson, J. M. (2000). Jeer pressure: The behavioral effects of observing ridicule of others. *Personality and Social Psychology Bulletin, 26*, 474–485.

Janicik, G. A., & Larrick, R. P. (2005). Social network schemas and the learning of incomplete networks. *Journal of Personality and Social Psychology, 88*, 348–364.

Janis, I. L. (1972). *Victims of groupthink*. Boston, MA: Houghton Mifflin.

Janis, I. L. (1982). *Groupthink* (2nd ed). Boston, MA: Houghton Mifflin.

Janis, I. L., & Feshbach, S. (1953). Effects of fear-arousing communications. *Journal of Abnormal and Social Psychology, 49*, 78–92.

Jankowiak, W. (1995). Introduction. In W. Jankowiak (Ed.), *Romantic passion: A universal experience?* (pp. 1–19). New York: Columbia University Press.

Jankowiak, W. R., & Fischer, E. F. (1992). A cross-cultural perspective on romantic love. *Ethnology, 31*, 149–155.

Janzen, L. (2001, May 13). Police photos, lineups faulted in Sophonow case. *Winnipeg Free Press*, p. A3.

Jarry, J. L., & Kossert, A. L. (2007). Self-esteem threat combined with exposure to thin media images leads to body image compensatory self-enhancement. *Body Image, 4*(1), 39–50.

Jecker, J., & Landy, D. (1969). Liking a person as a function of doing him a favor. *Human Relations, 22*, 371–378.

Jenkins, G., & Schuller, R. A. (2007). The impact of negative forensic evidence on mock jurors' perceptions of a trial of drug-facilitated sexual assault. *Law and Human Behavior, 31*(4), 369–380.

Jepson, C., & Chaiken, S. (1990). Chronic issue-specific fear inhibits systematic processing of persuasive communications. *Journal of Social Behavior and Personality, 5*, 61–84.

Jewell, L. M., & Morrison, M. A. (2010). "But there's a million jokes about everybody . . .": Prevalence of, and reasons for, directing negative behaviors toward gay men on a Canadian university campus. *Journal of Interpersonal Violence, 25*(11), 2094–2112.

Job, R. F. S. (1988). Effective and ineffective use of fear in health promotion campaigns. *American Journal of Public Health, 78*, 163–167.

Johns, M., Inzlicht, M., & Schmader, T. (2008). Stereotype threat and executive resource depletion: Examining the influence of emotion regulation. *Journal of Experimental Psychology: General, 137*(4), 691–705.

Johns, M., Schmader, T., & Martens, A. (2005). Knowing is half the battle: Teaching stereotype threat as a means of improving women's math performance. *Psychological Science, 16*, 175–179.

Johnson, D. W., & Johnson, R. T. (1987). *Learning together and alone: Cooperative, competitive, and individualistic learning* (2nd ed.). Englewood Cliffs, NJ: Prentice Hall.

Johnson, D. W., & Johnson, R. T. (1989). *A meta-analysis of cooperative, competitive, and individualistic goal structures*. Hillsdale, NJ: Erlbaum.

Johnson, H. (2001). Contrasting views of the role of alcohol in cases of wife assault. *Journal of Interpersonal Violence, 16*, 54–72.

Johnson, J. G., Cohen, P., Smailes, E. M., Kasen, S., & Brook, J. (2002). Television viewing and aggressive behavior during adolescence and adulthood. *Science, 295*, 2468–2471.

Johnson, K. J., & Fredrickson, B. L. (2005). We all look the same to me: Positive emotions eliminate the own-race bias in face recognition. *Psychological Science, 16*, 875–881.

Johnson, M., Verfaellie, M., & Dunlosky, J. (2008). Introduction to the special section on integrative approaches to source memory. *Journal of Experimental Psychology: Learning, Memory, and Cognition, 34*, 727–729.

Johnson, M. K., Hashtroudi, S., & Lindsay, D. S. (1993). Source monitoring. *Psychological Bulletin, 114*, 3–28.

Johnson, M. K., & Raye, C. L. (1981). Reality monitoring. *Psychological Review, 88*, 67–85.

Johnson, M. K., Raye, C. L., Wang, A. Y., & Taylor, T. H. (1979). Fact and fantasy: The roles of accuracy and variability in confusing imaginations with perceptual experiences. *Journal of Experimental Psychology: Human Learning and Memory, 5*, 229–240.

Johnson, R. D., & Downing, R. L. (1979). Deindividuation and valence of cues: Effects of prosocial and antisocial behavior. *Journal of Personality and Social Psychology, 37*, 1532–1538.

Johnson, T. E., & Rule, B. G. (1986). Mitigating circumstance information, censure, and aggression. *Journal of Personality and Social Psychology, 50*, 537–542.

Joiner, T. E., Jr. & Wagner, K. D. (1995). Attributional style and depression in children and adolescents: A meta-analytic review. *Clinical Psychology Review, 15*, 777–798.

Johnson, W., & Krueger, R. F. (2005). Higher perceived life control decreases genetic variance in physical health: Evidence from a national twin study. *Journal of Personality and Social Psychology, 88*, 165–173.

Johnston, V. S., Hagel, R., Franklin, M., Fink, B., & Grammer, K. (2001). Male facial attractiveness: Evidence for hormone-mediated adaptive design. *Evolution and Human Behavior, 22*, 251–267.

Jonas, E., Schimel, J., Greenberg, J., & Pyszczynski, T. (2002). The scrooge effect: Evidence that mortality salience increases prosocial attitudes and behavior. *Personality and Social Psychology Bulletin, 28*(10), 1342–1353.

Jones, D., & Hill, K. (1993). Criteria of facial attractiveness in five populations. *Human Nature, 4*, 271–296.

Jones, E. E. (1979). The rocky road from acts to dispositions. *American Scientist, 34*, 107–117.

Jones, E. E. (1990). *Interpersonal perception*. New York: Freeman.

Jones, E. E., & Davis, K. E. (1965). From acts to dispositions: The attribution process in social psychology. In L. Berkowitz (Ed.), *Advances in experimental social psychology* (Vol. 2, pp. 219–266). New York: Academic Press.

Jones, E. E., & Harris, V. A. (1967). The attribution of attitudes. *Journal of Experimental Social Psychology, 3*, 1–24.

Jones, E. E., & Nisbett, R. E. (1972). The actor and the observer: Divergent perceptions of the causes of behavior. In E. E. Jones, D. E. Kanouse, H. H. Kelley, R. E. Nisbett, S. Valins, & B. Weiner (Eds.), *Attribution: Perceiving the causes of behavior* (pp. 79–94). Morristown, NJ: General Learning Press.

Jones, L. W., Sinclair, R. W., & Courneya, K. S. (2003). The effects of source credibility and message framing on exercise intentions, behavior and attitudes: An integration of the elaboration likelihood model and prospect theory. *Journal of Applied Social Psychology, 33*, 179–196.

Jordan, C. H., Spencer, S. J., & Zanna, M. P. (2005). Types of high self-esteem and prejudice: How implicit self-esteem relates to ethnic discrimination among high explicit self-esteem individuals. *Personality and Social Psychology Bulletin, 31*, 693–702.

Jordan, C. H., Whitfield, M., & Zeigler-Hill, V. (2007). Intuition and the correspondence between implicit and explicit self-esteem. *Journal of Personality and Social Psychology, 93*, 1067–1079.

Joseph, J., & Kuo, B. H. (2009). Black Canadians' coping responses to racial discrimination. *Journal of Black Psychology, 35*(1), 78-101.

Josephson, W. (1987). Television violence and children's aggression: Testing the priming, social script, and disinhibition prediction. *Journal of Personality and Social Psychology, 53*, 882–890.

Josephson, W., & Proulx, J. (2008). Violence in young adolescents' relationships: A path model. *Journal of Interpersonal Violence, 23*(2), 189–208.

Judd, C. M., & Park, B. (1988). Out-group homogeneity: Judgments of variability at the individual and group levels. *Journal of Personality and Social Psychology, 54*, 778–788.

Judge rules ACLU discrimination suit against Continental Airlines can go forward (2002). Retrieved from www.aclu.org/RacialEquality/RacialEquality.cfm?ID=10994&c=133.

Jürgen-Lohmann, J., Borsch, F., & Giesen, H. (2001). Kooperatives Lernen an der Hochschule: Evaluation des Gruppenpuzzles in Seminaren der Pädagogischen Psychologie. *Zeitschrift für Pädagogische Psychologie, 15*, 74–84

Jussim, L. (1986). Self-fulfilling prophecies: A theoretical and integrative review. *Psychological Review, 93*, 429–445.

Jussim, L., & Harber, K. (2005). Teacher expectations and self-fulfilling prophecies: Knowns and unknowns, resolved and unresolved controversies. *Personality and Social Psychology Review, 9*, 131–155.

Juveniles committing fewer violent crimes (1997, Oct. 3). *Charlottesville Daily Progress*, pp. A1, A9.

Kahn, M. (1966). The physiology of catharsis. *Journal of Personality and Social Psychology, 3*, 278–298.

Kahn, M. (2008, October 15). "Hippie" apes not all peace and love. *Globe and Mail*. Retrieved from www.theglobeandmail.com/servlet/story/RTGAM.20081015.wbonobo1015/BNStory/Science/home

Kahneman, D., & Frederick, S. (2002). Representativeness revisited: Attribute substitution in intuitive judgment. In T. Gilovich, D. W. Griffin, & D. Kahneman (Eds). *Heuristics and biases: The psychology of intuitive judgment* (pp. 49–81). New York: Cambridge University Press.

Kahneman, D., & Miller, D. T. (1986). Norm theory: Comparing reality to its alternatives. *Psychological Review, 93*, 136–153.

Kahneman, D., & Tversky, A. (1973). On the psychology of prediction. *Psychological Review, 80*, 237–251.

Kahneman, D., & Tversky, A. (1982). The simulation heuristic. In D. Kahneman, P. Slovic, & A. Tversky (Eds.), *Judgment under uncertainty: Heuristics and biases* (pp. 201–208). New York: Cambridge University Press.

Kalin, R., & Berry, J. W. (1996). Interethnic attitudes in Canada: Ethnocentrism, consensual hierarchy and reciprocity. *Canadian Journal of Behavioural Sciences, 28*, 253–261.

Kallgren, C. A., Reno, R. R., & Cialdini, R. B. (2000). A focus theory of normative conduct: When norms do and do not affect behavior. *Personality and Social Psychology Bulletin, 26*, 1002–1012.

Kalven, H., Jr. & Zeisel, H. (1966). *The American jury*. Boston, MA: Little, Brown.

Kameda, T., Takezawa, M., & Hastie, R. (2003). The logic of social sharing: An evolutionary game analysis of adaptive norm development. *Personality and Social Psychology Review, 7*, 2–19.

Kammrath, L. K., & Dweck, C. (2006). Voicing conflict: Preferred conflict strategies among incremental and entity theorists. *Personality and Social Psychology Bulletin, 32*, 1497–1508.

Kang, S. K., & Chasteen, A. L. (2009). The moderating role of age-group identification and perceived threat on stereotype threat among older adults. *The International Journal of Aging & Human Development, 69*(3), 201–220.

Kappas, A. (1997). The fascination with faces: Are they windows to our soul? *Journal of Nonverbal Behavior, 21*, 157–162.

Karau, S. J., & Williams, K. D. (1993). Social loafing: A meta-analytic review and theoretical integration. *Journal of Personality and Social Psychology, 65*, 681–706.

Karau, S. J., & Williams, K. D. (2001). Understanding individual motivation in groups: The collective effort model. In M. E. Turner (Ed.), *Groups at work—theory and research: Applied social research* (pp. 113–141). Mahwah, NJ: Erlbaum.

Karney, B. R., & Bradbury, T. N. (2000). Attributions in marriage: State or trait? A growth curve analysis. *Journal of Personality and Social Psychology, 78*, 295–309.

Kashima, Y., Siegel, M., Tanaka, K., & Kashima, E. S. (1992). Do people believe behaviors are consistent with attitudes? Towards a cultural psychology of attribution process. *British Journal of Social Psychology, 31*, 111–124.

Kassarjian, H., & Cohen, J. (1965). Cognitive dissonance and consumer behavior. *California Management Review, 8*, 55–64.

Kassin, S. (2007). Internalized false confessions. In M. P. Toglia, J. D. Read, D. F. Ross, & R. C. L. Lindsay (Eds.) *The handbook of eyewitness psychology, Vol I: Memory for events* (pp. 175–192). Mahwah, NJ: Lawrence Erlbaum.

Kassin, S. (2008). Expert testimony on the psychology of confessions: A pyramidal framework of the relevant science. In E. Borgida and S. T. Fiske (Eds.), *Beyond common sense: Psychological science in the courtroom* (pp. 195–218). Malden, MA: Blackwell Publishing.

Kassin, S. M. (2005). On the psychology of confessions: Does innocence put innocents at risk? *American Psychologist, 60*, 215–228.

Kassin, S. M., & Kiechel, K. L. (1996). The social psychology of false confessions: Compliance, internalization, and confabulation. *Psychological Science*, 7(3), pp. 125–128.

Katz, D. (1960). The functional approach to the study of attitudes. *Public Opinion Quarterly, 24*, 163–204.

Katz, J., & Joiner, T. E. (2002). Being known, intimate, and valued: Global self-verification and dyadic adjustment in couples and roommates. *Journal of Personality, 70*, 33–58.

Kawakami, K., Dion, K. L., & Dovidio, J. F. (1998). Racial prejudice and stereotype activation. *Personality and Social Psychology Bulletin, 24*, 407–416.

Kawakami, K., Phills, C. E., Steele, J. R., & Dovidio, J. F. (2007). (Close) distance makes the heart grow fonder: Improving implicit racial attitudes and interracial interactions through approach behaviors. *Journal of Personality and Social Psychology, 92*, 957–971.

Kay, A. C., Gaucher, D., Peach, J. M., Laurin, K., Friesen, J., Zanna, M. P., & Spencer, S. J. (2009). Inequality, discrimination, and the power of the status quo: Direct evidence for a motivation to see the way things are as the way they should be. *Journal of Personality and Social Psychology, 97*(3), 421–434.

Kay, A. C., Moscovitch, D. A., & Laurin, K. (2010). Randomness, attributions of arousal, and belief in God. *Psychological Science, 21*(2), 216–218.

Kealy, K. L. K., Kuiper, N. A., & Klein, D. N. (2006). Characteristics associated with real and made-up events: The effects of event valence, event elaboration, and individual differences. *Canadian Journal of Behavioural Science, 38*, 158–175.

Kebbell, M. R., & Wagstaff, G. F. (1998). Hypnotic interviewing: The best way to interview eyewitnesses? *Behavioral Sciences and the Law, 16*, 115–129.

Keelan, J. P. R., Dion, K. L., & Dion, K. K. (1994). Attachment style and heterosexual relationships among young adults: A short-term panel study. *Journal of Social and Personal Relationships, 11*, 201–214.

Keenan, J. P., Gallup, G. G.., & Falk, D. (2003). *The face in the mirror: The search for the origins of consciousness.* New York: HarperCollins.

Keller, J., & Dauenheimer, D. (2003). Stereotype threat in the classroom: Dejection mediates the disrupting threat effect on women's math performance. *Personality and Social Psychology Bulletin, 29*, 371–381.

Kelley, H. H. (1950). The warm-cold variable in first impressions of persons. *Journal of Personality, 18*, 431–439.

Kelley, H. H. (1955). The two functions of reference groups. In G. E. Swanson, T. M. Newcomb, & E. L. Hartley (Eds.), *Readings in social psychology* (2nd ed., pp. 410–414). New York: Holt.

Kelley, H. H. (1967). Attribution theory in social psychology. In D. Levine (Ed.), *Nebraska Symposium on Motivation* (Vol. 15, pp. 192–238). Lincoln, NE: University of Nebraska Press.

Kelley, H. H. (1972). Attribution in social interaction. In E. E. Jones, D. E. Kanouse, H. H. Kelley, R. E. Nisbett, S. Valins, & B. Weiner (Eds.), *Attribution: Perceiving the causes of behavior* (pp. 1–26). Morristown, NJ: General Learning Press.

Kelley, H. H. (1973). The process of causal attribution. *American Psychologist, 28*, 107–128.

Kelley, H. H. (1983). Love and commitment. In H. H. Kelley, E. Berscheid, A. Christensen, J. H. Harvey, T. L. Huston, G. Levinger, . . . D. R. Peterson (Eds.), *Close relationships* (pp. 265–314). New York: Freeman.

Kelley, H. H., & Thibaut, J. (1978). *Interpersonal relations: A theory of interdependence.* New York: Wiley.

Kelly, A. E., Klusas, J. A., von Weiss, R. T., & Kenny, C. (2001). What is it about revealing secrets that is beneficial? *Personality and Social Psychology Bulletin, 27*, 651–665.

Kelly, J. R., & Karau, S. J. (1999). Group decision making: The effects of initial preferences and time pressure. *Personality and Social Psychology Bulletin, 25*, 1342–1354.

Kelman, H. C. (1997). Group processes in the resolution of inter national conflicts: Experiences from the Israeli–Palestinian case. *American Psychologist, 52*, 212–220.

Keltner, D. (1995). The signs of appeasement: Evidence for the distinct displays of embarrassment, amusement, and shame. *Journal of Personality and Social Psychology, 68*, 441–454.

Keltner, D., & Shiota, M. N. (2003). New displays and new emotions: A commentary on Rozin and Cohen. *Emotion, 3*, 86–91.

Kerr, N. L., & Tindale, R. S. (2004). Groups performance and decision making. *Annual Review of Psychology, 55*, 623–655.

Kenny, D. A. (1994). Using the social relations model to understand relationships. In R. Erber & R. Gilmour (Eds.), *Theoretical Frameworks for Personal Relationships* (pp. 111–127). Hillsdale, NJ: Erlbaum.

Kenrick, D. T., & Keefe, R. C. (1992). Age preferences in mates reflect sex differences in human reproductive strategies. *Behavioral and Brain Sciences, 15*, 75–133.

Kenrick, D. T., & MacFarlane, S. W. (1986). Ambient temperature and horn honking: A field study of the heat/aggression relationship. *Environment and Behavior, 18*, 179–191.

Kent, M. V. (1994). The presence of others. In A. P. Hare, H. H. Blumberg, M. F. Davies, & M. V. Kent (Eds.), *Small group research: A handbook* (pp. 81–105). Norwood, NJ: Ablex.

Kerr, N. L., & Kaufman-Gilliland, C. M. (1994). Communication, commitment, and cooperation in social dilemmas. *Journal of Personality and Social Psychology, 66*, 513–529.

Kerr, N. L., & Tindale, R. S. (2004). Groups performance and decision making. *Annual Review of Psychology, 55*, 623–655.

Ketelaar, T., & Ellis, B. J. (2000). Are evolutionary explanations unfalsifiable? Evolutionary psychology and the Lakatosian philosophy of science. *Psychological Inquiry, 11*, 1–21.

Key, W. B. (1973). *Subliminal seduction*. Englewood Cliffs, NJ: Signet.

Key, W. B. (1989). *Age of manipulation: The con in confidence and the sin in sincere.* New York: Holt.

Kiesler, C. A., & Kiesler, S. B. (1969). *Conformity*. Reading, MA: Addison-Wesley.

Kihlstrom, J. F. (1987). The cognitive unconscious. *Science, 237*, 1445–1452.

Kihlstrom, J. F. (1996). The trauma-memory argument and recovered memory therapy. In K. Pezdek & W. P. Banks (Eds.), *The recovered memory/false memory debate* (pp. 297–311). San Diego, CA: Academic Press.

Kihlstrom, J. F., Beer, J. S., & Klein, S. B. (2003). Self and identity as memory. In M. R. Leary & J. P. Tangney (Eds.), *Handbook of self and identity* (pp. 68–90). New York: Guilford Press.

Killen, J. D. (1985). Prevention of adolescent tobacco smoking: The social pressure resistance training approach. *Journal of Child Psychology and Psychiatry, 26*, 7–15.

Kim, H. S., Sherman, D. K., & Taylor, S. E. (2008). Culture and social support. *American Psychologist, 63*, 518–526.

Kim, M. P., & Rosenberg, S. (1980). Comparison of two structural models of implicit personality theory. *Journal of Personality and Social Psychology, 38*, 375–389.

Kim, U., & Berry, J. W. (1993). *Indigenous psychologies: Research and experience in cultural context*. Newbury Park, CA: Sage.

Kim, U., Triandis, H. C., Kagitcibasi, C., Choi, S. C., & Yoon, G. (Eds). (1994). *Individualism and collectivism: Theory, method and applications*. Thousand Oaks, CA: Sage.

King, L., & Snook, B. (2009). Peering inside a Canadian interrogation room: An examination of the Reid model of interrogation, influence tactics, and coercive strategies. *Criminal Justice and Behavior, 36*(7), 674–694.

Kirkpatrick, L. A., & Hazan, C. (1994). Attachment styles and close relationships: A four-year prospective study. *Personal Relationships, 1*, 123–142.

Kitayama, S., & Cohen, D. (Eds.). (2007). *Handbook of cultural psychology*. New York: Guilford.

Kitayama, S., & Markus, H. R. (1994). Culture and the self: How cultures influence the way we view ourselves. In D. Matsumoto (Ed.), *People: Psychology from a cultural perspective* (pp. 17–37). Pacific Grove, CA: Brooks/Cole.

Kitayama, S., & Masuda, T. (1997). *Cultural psychology of social inference: The correspondence bias in Japan*. Unpublished manuscript, Kyoto University.

Kitayama, S., & Uchida, Y. (2003). Explicit self-criticism and implicit self-regard: Evaluating self and friend in two cultures. *Journal of Experimental Social Psychology, 39*, 476–482.

Kitayama, S., & Uchida, Y. (2005). Interdependent agency: An alternative system for action. In R. M. Sorrentino & D. Cohen (Eds.), *Cultural and social behavior: The Ontario Symposium* (Vol. 10, pp. 137–164). Mahwah, NJ: Erlbaum.

Kiyonari, T., & Barclay, P. (2008). Cooperation in social dilemmas: Free riding may be thwarted by second-order reward rather than by punishment. *Journal of Personality and Social Psychology, 95*(4), 826–842.

Klaver, J. R., Lee, Z., & Rose, V. (2008). Effects of personality, interrogation techniques and plausibility in an experimental false confession paradigm. *Legal and Criminological Psychology, 13*(1), 71–88.

Klein, W. M. (1996). Maintaining self-serving social comparisons: Attenuating the perceived significance of risk-increasing behaviors. *Journal of Social and Clinical Psychology, 15*, 120–142.

Kleiner, M. (Ed). (2002). *Handbook of polygraph testing*. San Diego, CA: Academic Press.

Klenke, K. (1996). *Women and leadership: A contextual perspective*. New York: Springer.

Kliewer, W., Lepore, S. J., & Evans, G. W. (1990). The costs of Type B behavior: Females at risk in achievement situations. *Journal of Applied Social Psychology, 20*, 1369–1382.

Kliman, A. M., & Rhodes, R. (2008). Do government brochures affect physical activity cognition? A pilot study of Canada's physical activity guide to healthy active living. *Psychology, Health & Medicine, 13*(4), 415–422.

Knapp, M., & Hall, J. A. (2006). *Nonverbal communication in human interaction*. Belmont, CA: Thomson Wadsworth.

Knäuper, B., Kornik, R., Atkinson, K., Guberman, C., & Aydin, C. (2005). Motivation influences the underestimation of cumulative risk. *Personality and Social Psychology Bulletin, 31*, 1511–1523.

Knee, C. R., Lonsbary, C., Canevello, A., & Patrick, H. (2005). Self-determination and conflict in romantic relationships. *Journal of Personality and Social Psychology, 89*, 997–1009.

Knowles, E., & Linn, J. (Eds.) (2004). *Resistance and persuasion*. Mahwah, NJ ; Erlbaum.

Knowles, E. D., Morris, M. W., Chiu, C., & Hong, Y. (2001). Culture and the process of person perception: Evidence for automaticity among East Asians in correcting for situational influences on behavior. *Personality and Social Psychology Bulletin*, 27, 1344–1356.

Knox, R. E., & Inkster, J. A. (1968). Postdecision dissonance at post time. *Journal of Personality and Social Psychology, 8*, 319–323.

Knussen, C., Yule, F., & MacKenzie, J. (2004). An analysis of intentions to recycle household waste: The roles of past behaviour, perceived habit, and perceived lack of facilities. *Journal of Environmental Psychology, 24*, 237–246.

Koch, E. J., & Metcalfe, K. P. (2011). The bittersweet taste of success: Daily and recalled experiences of being an upward social comparison target. *Basic and Applied Social Psychology, 33*(1), 47–58.

Koehler, D. J., & Poon, C. S. K. (2006). Self-predictions overweight strength of current intentions. *Journal of Experimental Social Psychology, 42*, 517–524.

Koestner, R., Horberg, E. J., Gaudreau, P., Powers, T., Di Dio, P., Bryan, C., . . . Salter, N. (2006). Bolstering implementation plans for the long haul: The benefits of simultaneously boosting self-concordance or self-efficacy. *Personality and Social Psychology Bulletin, 32*, 1547–1558.

Koestner, R., & Losier, G. F. (2002). Distinguishing three ways of being internally motivated: A closer look at introjection, identification, and intrinsic motivation. In E. L. Deci & R. M. Ryan (Eds.), *Handbook of self-determination research* (pp. 101–121). Rochester, NY: University of Rochester Press.

Kogan, N., & Wallach, M. A. (1964). *Risk-taking: A study in cognition and personality*. New York: Holt.

Kojetin, B. A. (1993). *Adult attachment styles with romantic partners, friends, and parents*. Unpublished doctoral dissertation, University of Minnesota, Minneapolis.

Kollack, P., Blumstein, P. & Schwartz, P., (1994). The judgment of equity in intimate relationships. *Social Psychology Quarterly, 57*, 340–351.

Konishi, C., & Hymel, S. (2009). Bullying and stress in early adolescence: The role of coping and social support. *The Journal of Early Adolescence, 29*(3), 333–356.

Koopman, C., Hermanson, K., Diamond, S., Angell, K., & Spiegel, D. (1998). Social support, life stress, pain and emotional adjustment to advanced breast cancer. *Psycho-Oncology*, 7, 101–111.

Korchmaros, J. D., & Kenny, D. A. (2006). An evolutionary and close-relationship model of helping. *Journal of Social and Personal Relationships, 23*, 21–43.

Koriat, A., Goldsmith, M., & Pansky, A. (2000). Toward a psychology of memory accuracy. *Annual Review of Psychology, 51*, 481–537.

Kortenkamp, K. V., & Moore, C. F. (2001). Ecocentrism and antropocentrism: Moral reasoning about ecological commons dilemmas. *Journal of Environmental Psychology, 21*, 261–272.

Krajick, K. (1990, July 30). Sound too good to be true? Behind the boom in subliminal tapes. *Newsweek, 116*, 60–61.

Krakow, A., & Blass, T. (1995). When nurses obey or defy inappropriate physician orders: Attributional differences. *Journal of Social Behavior and Personality, 10*, 585–594.

Krantz, D. S, & McCeney, M. K. (2002). Effects of psychological and social factors on organic disease: A critical assessment of research on coronary heart disease. *Annual Review of Psychology, 53*, 341–369.

Krauss, R. M., & Deutsch, M. (1966). Communication in interpersonal bargaining. *Journal of Personality and Social Psychology, 4*, 572–577.

Kremer, J. F., & Stephens, L. (1983). Attributions and arousal as mediators of mitigation's effects on retaliation. *Journal of Personality and Social Psychology, 45*, 335–343.

Kressel, K., & Pruitt, D. G. (1989). A research perspective on the mediation of social conflict. In K. Kressel & D. G. Pruitt (Eds.), *Mediation research: The process and effectiveness of third party intervention* (pp. 394–435). San Francisco, CA: Jossey-Bass.

Kristiansen, C. M., & Giulietti, R. (1990). Perceptions of wife abuse: Effects of gender, attitudes toward women, and just-world beliefs among college students. *Psychology of Women Quarterly, 14*, 177–189.

Krosnick, J. A., & Alwin, D. F. (1989). Aging and susceptibility to attitude change. *Journal of Personality and Social Psychology, 57*, 416–425.

Kross, E., & Ayduk, O. (2008). Facilitating adaptive emotional analysis: Distinguishing distanced-analysis of depressive experiences from immersed-analysis and distraction. *Personality and Social Psychology Bulletin, 34*, 924–938.

Krueger, J., Ham, J. J., & Linford, K. (1996). Perceptions of behavioral consistency: Are people aware of the actor-observer effect? *Psychological Science, 7*, 259–264.

Kruger, K., Epley, N., Packer, J., & Ng, Z. (2005). Egocentricism over e-mail: Can we communicate as well as we think? *Journal of Personality and Social Psychology, 89*(6), 925–936.

Kruglanski, A. W., & Mayseless, O. (1990). Classic and current social comparison research: Expanding the perspective. *Psychological Bulletin, 108*, 195–208.

Kruglanski, A. W., & Webster, D. M. (1991). Group members' reactions to opinion deviates and conformists at varying degrees of proximity to decision deadline and of environmental noise. *Journal of Personality and Social Psychology, 61*, 212–225.

Krull, D. S. (1993). Does the grist change the mill? The effect of the perceiver's inferential goal on the process of social inference. *Personality and Social Psychology Bulletin, 19*, 340–348.

Krull, D. S., Loy, M. H., Lin, J., Wang, C., Chen, S., & Zhao, X. (1999). The fundamental correspondence bias in individualist and collectivist cultures. *Personality and Social Psychology Bulletin, 25*, 1208–1219.

Kubitschek, W. N., & Hallinan, M. T. (1998). Tracking and students' friendships. *Social Psychology Quarterly, 61*, 1–15.

Kuhl, J. (1983). Emotion, cognition, and motivation: I. Towards a systems-oriented theory of the development of emotions. English abstract of German article Emotion, kognition und motivation: I. auf dem wege zu einer systemtheoretischen betrachtung der emotionsgenese. *Sprache & Kognition, 2*, 1–27.

Kulik, J., & Brown, R. (1979). Frustration, attribution of blame, and aggression. *Journal of Experimental Social Psychology, 15*, 183–194.

Kunda, Z. (1990). The case for motivated reasoning. *Psychological Bulletin, 108*, 480–498.

Kunda, Z. (1999). *Social cognition: Making sense of people*. Cambridge, MA,: MIT Press.

Kunda, Z., Davies, P. G., Adams, B. D., & Spencer, S. J. (2002). The dynamic time course of stereotype activation: Activation, dissipation, and resurrection. *Journal of Personality and Social Psychology, 82*, 283–299.

Kunda, Z., Fong, G. T., Sanitioso, R., & Reber, E. (1993). Directional questions about self-conceptions. *Journal of Experimental Social Psychology, 29*, 63–86.

Kunda, Z., & Oleson, K. C. (1995). Maintaining stereotypes in the face of disconfirmation: Constructing grounds for subtyping deviance. *Journal of Personality and Social Psychology, 68*, 565–579.

Kunda, Z., & Oleson, K. C. (1997). When exceptions prove the rule: How extremity of deviance determines the impact of deviant examples on stereotypes. *Journal of Personality and Social Psychology, 72*, 965–979.

Kunda, Z., Sinclair, L., & Griffin, D. (1997). Equal ratings but separate meanings: Stereotypes and the construal of traits. *Journal of Personality and Social Psychology, 72*, 720–734.

Kunkel, D., Wilcox, B., Hill-Scott, K., Greenberg, B. S., Rampoldi-Hnilo, L., Montgomery, K. C., . . . Trotta, L. (2001). Part III: Policy issues and advocacy. In D. G. Singer, & J. L. Singer (Eds.), *Handbook of children and the media* (pp. 587–719). Thousand Oaks, CA: Sage Publications.

Kunz, P. R., & Woolcott, M. (1976). Season's greetings: From my status to yours. *Social Science Research, 5*, 269–278.

Kuo, Z. Y. (1961). Genesis of the cat's response to the rat. In *Instinct* (p. 24). Princeton, NJ: Van Nostrand.

Kwong, M. J., Bartholomew, K., & Dutton, D. G. (1999). Gender differences in patterns of relationship violence in Alberta. *Canadian Journal of Behavioural Science, 31*, 150–160.

Lachman, M. (2006). Perceived Control Over Aging-Related Declines: Adaptive Beliefs and Behaviors. *Current Directions in Psychological Science, 15*, 282–286.

La France, M., Hecht, M. A., & Paluck, E. L. (2003). The contingent smile: A meta-analysis of sex differences in smiling. *Psychological Bulletin, 129*, 305–334.

La Gaipa, J. J. (1982). Rules and rituals in disengaging from relationships. In S. Duck (Ed.), *Personal relationships: Vol. 4. Dissolving personal relationships.* (pp. 189–210). London, UK: Academic Press.

Lalancette, M. F., & Standing, L. (1990). Asch fails again. *Social Behavior and Personality, 18*, 7–12.

Lalonde, R. N., & Giguère, B. (2008). When might the two cultural worlds of second generation biculturals collide? *Canadian Diversity, Spring*, 58–62.

Lalonde, R. N., Jones, J. M., & Stroink, M. L. (2008). Racial identity, racial attitudes, and race socialization among Black Canadian parents. *Canadian Journal of Behavioural Science, 40*(3), 129–139.

Lalonde, R. N., Moghaddam, F. M., & Taylor, D. M. (1987). The process of group differentiation in a dynamic intergroup setting. *Journal of Social Psychology, 127*, 273–287.

Lam, K. C. H., Buehler, R., McFarland, C., Ross, M., & Cheung, I. (2005). Cultural differences in affective forecasting: The role of focalism. *Personality and Social Psychology Bulletin, 31*, 1296–1309.

Lamb, C. S., Jackson, L. A., Cassiday, P. B., & Priest, D. J. (1993). Body figure preferences of men and women: A comparison of two generations. *Sex Roles, 28*, 345–358.

Lambert, A. J., & Raichle, K. (2000). The role of political ideology in mediating judgments of blame in rape victims and their assailants: A test of the just world, personal responsibility, and legitimization hypotheses. *Personality and Social Psychology Bulletin, 26*, 853–863.

Lampert, R., Baron, S. J., McPherson, C. A., & Lee, F. A. (2002). Heart rate variability during the week of September 11, 2001. *Journal of the American Medical Association, 288*, 575.

Langer, E. J. (1975) The illusion of control. *Journal of Personality and Social Psychology, 32*, 311–328.

Langer, E. J., & Rodin, J. (1976). The effects of choice and enhanced personal responsibility for the aged: A field experiment. *Journal of Personality and Social Psychology, 34*, 191–198.

Langlois, J. H., Kalakanis, L., Rubenstein, A. J., Larson, A., Hallam, M., & Smoot, M. (2000). Maxims or myths of beauty? A meta-analytic and theoretical review. *Psychological Bulletin, 126*, 390–423.

Langlois, J. H., & Roggman, L. A. (1990). Attractive faces are only average. *Psychological Science, 1*, 115–121.

Langlois, J. H., Roggman, L. A., & Musselman, L. (1994). What is average and what is not average about attractive faces? *Psychological Science, 5*, 214–220.

LaPiere, R. T. (1934). Attitudes vs. actions. *Social Forces, 13*, 230–237.

L'Armand, K., & Pepitone, A. (1975). Helping to reward another person: A cross-cultural analysis. *Journal of Personality and Social Psychology, 31*, 189–198.

Larson, J. R., Jr., Christensen, C., Franz, T. M., & Abbott, A. S. (1998). Diagnosing groups: The pooling, management, and impact of shared and unshared case information in team-based medical decision making. *Journal of Personality and Social Psychology, 75*, 93–108.

Larson, J. R., Jr., Foster-Fishman, P. G., & Franz, T. M. (1998). Leadership style and the discussion of shared and unshared information in decision-making groups. *Personality and Social Psychology Bulletin, 24*, 482–495.

Laschinger, H., Finegan, J., & Wilk, P. (2011). Situational and dispositional influences on nurses' workplace well-being: The role of empowering unit leadership. *Nursing Research, 60*(2), 124-131.

Lassiter, G. D. (2002). Illusory causation in the courtroom. *Current Directions in Psychological Science, 11*, 204–208.

Lassiter, G. D. (2004). *Interrogations, confessions, and entrapment*. New York: Kluwer Academic/Plenum.

Lassiter, G. D., Diamond, S. S., Schmidt, H. C., & Elek, J. K. (2007). Evaluating videotaped confessions: Expertise provides no defense against the camera-perspective effect. *Psychological Science, 18*(3), 224–226.

Lassiter, G. D., Ratcliff, J. J., Ware, L. J., & Irvin, C. R. (2006). Vidoetaped confessions: Panacea or Pandora's box? *Law & Policy, 28*, 192–210.

Latané, B. (1981). The psychology of social impact. *American Psychologist, 36*, 343–356.

Latané, B. (1987). From student to colleague: Retracing a decade. In N. E. Grunberg, R. E. Nisbett, J. Rodin, & J. E. Singer (Eds.), *A distinctive approach to psychological research: The influence of Stanley Schachter* (pp. 66–86). Hillsdale, NJ: Erlbaum.

Latané, B., & Bourgeois, M. J. (2001). Successfully simulating dynamic social impact: Three levels of prediction. In J. P. Forgas & K. D. Williams (Eds.), *Social influence: Direct and indirect processes* (pp. 61–76). Philadelphia, PA: Psychology Press.

Latané, B., & Dabbs, J. M. (1975). Sex, group size, and helping in three cities. *Sociometry, 38*, 108–194.

Latané, B., & Darley, J. M. (1968). Group inhibition of bystander intervention. *Journal of Personality and Social Psychology, 10*, 215–221.

Latané, B., & Darley, J. M. (1970). *The unresponsive bystander: Why doesn't he help?* Englewood Cliffs, NJ: Prentice Hall.

Latané, B., & L'Herrou, T. (1996). Spatial clustering in the conformity game: Dynamic social impact in electronic games. *Journal of Personality and Social Psychology, 70*, 1218–1230.

Latané, B., & Nida, S. (1981). Ten years of research on group size and helping. *Psychological Bulletin, 89*, 308–324.

Latané, B., Williams, K., & Harkins, S. (1979). Many hands make light work: The causes and consequences of social loafing. *Journal of Personality and Social Psychology, 37*, 822–832.

Lau, G. P., Kay, A. C., & Spencer, S. J. (2008). Loving those who justify inequality: The effects of system threat on attraction to women who embody benevolent sexist ideals. *Psychological Science, 19*(1), 20–21.

Lau, R. R., & Russell, D. (1980). Attributions in the sports pages: A field test of some current hypotheses about attribution research. *Journal of Personality and Social Psychology, 39*, 29–38.

Laughlin, P. R. (1980). Social combination processes of cooperative problem-solving groups as verbal intellective tasks. In M. Fishbein (Ed.), *Progress in social psychology* (Vol. 1, pp. 127–155). Hillsdale, NJ: Erlbaum.

Laughlin, P. R., Hatch, E. C., Silver, J. S., & Boh, L. (2006). Groups perform better than the best individuals on letters-to-numbers problems: Effects of group size. *Journal of Personality and Social Psychology, 90*, 644–651.

Laursen, B., & Hartup, W. W. (2002). The origins of reciprocity and social exchange in friendships. In L. Brett & W. G. Graziano (Eds.), *Social exchange in development: New directions for child and adolescent development* (pp. 27–40). San Francisco, CA: Jossey-Bass/Pfeiffer.

Laver, R. (1994, October 17). Apocolypse now. *Maclean's*, 14.

Lavergne, K. J., Sharp, E. C., Pelletier, L. G., & Holtby, A. (2010). The role of perceived government style in the facilitation of self-determined and non self-determined motivation for pro-environmental behavior. *Journal of Environmental Psychology, 30*(2), 169–177.

Lavine, H., Sweeney, D., & Wagner, S. H. (1999). Depicting women as sex objects in television advertising: Effects on body dissatisfaction. *Personality and Social Psychology Bulletin, 25*, 1049–1058.

Lavoie, F., Robitaille, L., & Hébert, M. (2000). Teen dating relationships and aggression. *Violence Against Women, 6*, 6–36.

Law, D., Shapka, J., & Olson, B. (2010). To control or not to control? Parenting behaviours and adolescent online aggression. *Computers in Human Behavior, 26*(6), 1651–1656.

Lawler, E. J., & Thye, S. R. (1999). Bringing emotions into social exchange theory. *Annual Review of Sociology, 25*, 217–244.

Lawson, K. L. (2003). Perceptions of deservedness of social aid as a function of prenatal diagnostic testing. *Journal of Applied Social Psychology, 33*(1), 76–90.

Lazaruk, S. (2008, April 13). Crown appeals sentence. *The Province*. Retrieved from www.canada.com/theprovince/news/story.html?id=cd87b3e8-3b2e-4ddd-9981-ec9a4e3ca27b

Lazarus, R. S. (1966). *Psychological stress and the coping process*. New York: McGraw-Hill.

Lazarus, R. S. (2000). Toward better research on stress and coping. *American Psychologist, 55*, 665–673.

Lazarus, R. S., & Folkman, S. (1984). *Stress, appraisal, and coping*. New York: Springer-Verlag.

Lea, M., & Spears, R. (1995). Love at first byte: Building personal relationships over computer networks. In J. T. Wood & S. W. Duck (Eds.), *Understudied relationships: Off the beaten track* (pp. 197–233). Thousand Oaks, CA: Sage.

Lea, M., Spears, R., & de Groot, D. (2001). Knowing me, knowing you: Anonymity effects on social identity processes within groups. *Personality and Social Psychology Bulletin, 27*, 526–537.

Leadbeater, B., Banister, E., Ellis, W., & Yeung, R. (2008). Victimization and relational aggression in adolescent romantic relationships: The influence of parental and peer behaviors, and individual adjustment. *Journal of Youth and Adolescence, 37*(3), 359–372.

Leary, M. R. (2004). The self we know and the self we show: Self-esteem, self-presentation, and the maintenance of interpersonal relationships. In M. B. Brewer & M. Hewstone (Eds.), *Emotion and motivation* (pp. 204–224). Malden, MA: Blackwell.

Leary, M. R., & Tangney, J. P. (2003). The self as an organizing construct in the behavioral and social sciences. In M. R. Leary & J. P. Tangney (Eds.), *Handbook of self and identity* (pp. 3–14). New York: Guilford Press.

Leathers, D. G. (1997). *Successful nonverbal communication: Principles and applications*. Boston, MA: Allyn & Bacon.

Lederman, L. C., Stewart, L. P., Goodheart, F. W., & Laitman, L. (2003). A case against "binge" as a term of choice: Convincing college students to personalize messages about dangerous drinking. *Journal of Health Communication, 8*, 79–91.

Lee, E. (2004). Effects of visual representation on social influence in computer-mediated communication: Experimental tests of the social identity model of deindividuation effects. *Human Communication Research, 30*, 234–259.

Lee, F., Hallahan, M., & Herzog, T. (1996). Explaining real-life events: How culture and domain shape attributions. *Personality and Social Psychology Bulletin, 22*, 732–741.

Lee, J., & Lemyre, L. (2009). A social-cognitive perspective of terrorism risk perception and individual response in Canada. *Risk Analysis, 29*(9), 1265–1280.

Lee, J., Lemyre, L., & Krewski, D. (2010). A multi-method, multi-hazard approach to explore the uniqueness of terrorism risk perceptions and worry. *Journal of Applied Social Psychology, 40*(1), 241–272.

Lee, J., Gibson, S., Markon, M., & Lemyre, L. (2009). A preventive coping perspective of individual response to terrorism in Canada. *Current Psychology: A Journal for Diverse Perspectives on Diverse Psychological Issues, 28*(2), 69–84.

Lee, K., Ashton, M. C., Pozzebon, J. A., Visser, B. A., Bourdage, J. S., & Ogunfowora, B. (2009). Similarity and assumed similarity in personality reports of well-acquainted persons. *Journal of Personality and Social Psychology, 96*(2), 460–472.

Lee, K., Cameron, C. A., Xu, F., Fu, G., & Board, J. (1997). Chinese and Canadian children's evaluations of lying and truth telling: Similarities and differences in the context of pro- and antisocial behaviors. *Child Development, 68*, 924–934.

Lee, Y., & Seligman, M. E. P. (1997). Are Americans more optimistic than the Chinese? *Personality and Social Psychology Bulletin, 23*, 32–40.

Lee-Flynn, S. C., Pomaki, G., DeLongis, A., Biesanz, J. C., & Puterman, E. (2011). Daily cognitive appraisals, daily affect, and long-term depressive symptoms: The role of self-esteem and self-concept clarity in the stress process. *Personality and Social Psychology Bulletin, 37*(2), 255–268.

Le Foll, D., Rascle, O., & Higgins, N. C. (2008). Attributional feedback-induced changes in functional and dysfunctional attributions, expectations of success, hopefulness, and short-term persistence in a novel sport. *Psychology of Sport and Exercise, 9*(2), 77–101.

Lefrançois, R., Leclerc, G., Hamel, S., & Gaulin, P. (2000). Stressful life events and psychological distress of the very old: Does social support have a moderating effect? *Archives of Gerontology and Geriatrics, 31*, 243–255.

Legault, L., Green-Demers, I., & Eadie, A. L. (2009). When internalization leads to automatization: The role of self-determination in automatic stereotype suppression and implicit prejudice regulation. *Motivation and Emotion, 33*(1), 10–24.

Legault, L., Green-Demers, I., Grant, P., & Chung, J. (2007). On the self-regulation of implicit and explicit prejudice: A self- determination theory perspective. *Personality and Social Psychology Bulletin, 33*, 732–749.

Lehman, D. R., Davies, C. G., DeLongis, A., & Wortman, C. B. (1993). Positive and negative life changes following bereavement and their relkations to adjustment. *Journal of Social and Clinical Psychology, 12*, 90–112.

Leippe, M., & Eisenstadt, D. (1998). A self-accountability model of dissonance reduction: Multiple modes on a continuum of elaboration. In E. Harmon-Jones & J. S. Mills (Eds.), *Cognitive dissonance theory: Revival with revisions and controversies*. Washington, DC: American Psychological Association.

Leippe, M. R., & Eisenstadt, D. (1994). Generalization of dissonance reduction: Decreasing prejudice through induced compliance. *Journal of Personality and Social Psychology, 67*, 395–413.

Leishman, K. (1988, February). Heterosexuals and AIDS. *Atlantic Monthly*.

Lemay, E. P., & Clark, M. S. (2008). How the head liberates the heart: Projection of communal responsiveness guides relationship promotion. *Journal of Personality and Social Psychology, 94*(4), 647–671.

Lemay, E. P., Clark, M. S., & Feeney, B. C. (2007). Projection of responsiveness to needs and the construction of satisfying communal relationships. *Journal of Personality and Social Psychology, 92*, 834–853.

Lemyre, L., & Smith, P. M. (1985). Intergroup discrimination and self-esteem in the minimal group paradigm. *Journal of Personality and Social Psychology, 49*, 660–670.

Lenton, A. P., & Bryan, A. (2005). An affair to remember: The role of sexual scripts in perceptions of sexual intent. *Personal Relationships, 12*, 483–498.

Leone, T., Herman, C., & Pliner, P. (2008). Perceptions of undereaters: A matter of perspective?. *Personality and Social Psychology Bulletin, 34*(12), 1737–1746.

Leone, T., Pliner, P., & Herman, C. (2007). Influence of clear versus ambiguous normative information on food intake. *Appetite, 49*(1), 58–65.

Lepore, L., & Brown, R. (1997). Category and stereotype activation: Is prejudice inevitable? *Journal of Personality and Social Psychology, 72*, 275–287.

Lepper, M. (1995). Theory by numbers? Some concerns about meta-analysis as a theoretical tool. *Applied Cognitive Psychology, 9*, 411–422.

Lepper, M. (1996). Intrinsic motivation and extrinsic rewards: A commentary on Cameron and Pierce's meta-analysis. *Review of Educational Research, 66*, 5–32.

Lepper, M. R., Corpus, J. H., & Iyengar, S. S. (2005). Intrinsic and extrinsic motivational orientations in the classroom: Age differences and academic correlates. *Journal of Educational Psychology, 97*, 184–196.

Lepper, M. R., Greene, D., & Nisbett, R. E. (1973). Undermining children's intrinsic interest with extrinsic reward: A test of the overjustification hypothesis. *Journal of Personality and Social Psychology, 28*, 129–137.

Lepper, M. R., Henderlong, J., & Gingras, I. (1999). Understanding the effects of extrinsic rewards on intrinsic motivation—uses and abuses of meta-analysis: Comment on Deci, Koestner, and Ryan (1999). *Psychological Bulletin, 125*, 669–676.

Lepper, M. R., Keavney, M., & Drake, M. (1996). Intrinsic motivation and extrinsic rewards: A commentary on Cameron and Pierce's meta analysis. *Review of Educational Research, 66*, 5–32.

Lerner, M. J. (1980). *The belief in a just world: A fundamental decision*. New York: Plenum.

Lerner, M. J., & Miller, D. T. (1978). Just world research and the attribution process: Looking back and ahead. *Psychological Bulletin, 85*, 1030–1051.

Lerner, M. J., & Simmons, C. H. (1966). Observer's reaction to the "innocent victim": Compassion or rejection? *Journal of Personality and Social Psychology, 4*, 203–210.

Leu, J., Mesquita, B., Ellsworth, P. C., ZhiYong, Z., Huijuan, Y., Buchtel, E., . . . Masuda, T. (2010). Situational differences in dialectical emotions: Boundary conditions in a cultural comparison of North Americans and East Asians. *Cognition and Emotion, 24*(3), 419–435.

Leung, K. (1996). Beliefs in Chinese culture. In M. H. Bond (Ed.), *The handbook of Chinese psychology* (pp. 247–262). Hong Kong: Oxford University Press.

Leung, K., & Bond, M. H. (1984). The impact of cultural collectivism on reward allocation. *Journal of Personality and Social Psychology, 47*, 793–804.

Leventhal, H., Watts, J. C., & Pagano, F. (1967). Effects of fear and instructions on how to cope with danger. *Journal of Personality and Social Psychology, 6*, 313–321.

Levett, L. M., Danielsen, E. M., Kovera, M. B., & Cutler, B. L. (2005). The psychology of jury and juror decision making. In N. Brewer, K. D. Williams (Eds.), *Psychology and law: An empirical perspective* & (pp. 365–406). New York, Guilford Press.

Levin, D. T. (2000). Race as a visual feature: Using visual search and perceptual discrimination tasks to understand face categories and the cross-race recognition deficit. *Journal of Experimental Psychology: General, 129*, 559–574.

Levin, M., Prosser, A., Evans, D., & Reicher, S. (2005). Identity and emergency intervention: How social group membership and inclusiveness of group boundaries shape helping behavior. *Journal of Personality and Social Psychology Bulletin, 31*(4), 443–453.

Levine, J. M. (1989). Reaction to opinion deviance in small groups. In P. B. Paulus (Ed.), *Psychology of group influence* (2nd ed., pp. 187–231). Hillsdale, NJ: Erlbaum.

Levine, J. M. (1999). Solomon Asch's legacy for group research. *Personality and Social Psychology Review, 3*, 358–364.

Levine, J. M., Higgins, E. T., & Choi, H.-S. (2000). Development of strategic norms in groups. *Organizational Behavior and Human Decision Processes, 82*, 88–101.

Levine, J. M., & Moreland, R. L. (1998). Small groups. In D. Gilbert, S. Fiske, & G. Lindzey (Eds.), *The handbook of social psychology* (4th ed., Vol. 2, pp. 415–469). New York: McGraw Hill.

Levine, J. M., & Moreland, R. L. (2006). Small groups: An overview. In J. M. Levine & R. L. Moreland (Eds.), *Small groups* (pp. 1–10). New York: Psychology Press.

Levine, J. M., Moreland, R. L., & Choi, S. (2001). Group socialization and newcomer innovation. In M. Hogg & S. Tindale (Eds.), *Blackwell Handbook of Social Psychology: Group Processes* (pp. 86–106). Oxford, UK: Blackwell Publishers.

Levine, J. M., & Thompson, L. (1996). Conflict in groups. In E. T. Higgins & A. W. Kruglanski (Eds.), *Social psychology: Handbook of basic principles* (pp. 745–776). New York: Guilford.

Levine, M. P., & Smolak, L. (1996). Media as a context for the development of disordered eating. In L. Smolak, M. P. Levine, & R. Striegel-Moore (Eds.), *Developmental psychopathology of eating disorders: Implications for research, prevention, and treatment* (pp. 235–257). Mahwah, NJ: Erlbaum.

Levine, R., Sato, S., Hashimoto, T., & Verma, J. (1995). Love and marriage in eleven cultures. *Journal of Cross Cultural Psychology, 26*, 554–571.

Levine, R. V., Martinez, T. S., Brase, G., & Sorenson, K. (1994). Helping in 36 U.S. cities. *Journal of Personality and Social Psychology, 67*, 69–82.

Levitan, L. C., & Visser, P. S. (2008). The impact of the social context on resistance to persuasion: Effortful versus effortless responses to counter-attitudinal information. *Journal of Experimental Social Psychology, 44*, 640–649.

Levy, J. S., & Morgan, T. C. (1984). The frequency and seriousness of war: An inverse relationship? *Journal of Conflict Resolution, 28*, 731–749.

Lewin, K. (1943). Defining the "field at a given time." *Psychological Review, 50*, 292–310.

Lewin, K. (1946). Action research and minority problems. *Journal of Social Issues, 2*, 34–46.

Lewin, K. (1947). Frontiers in group dynamics. *Human Relations, 1*, 5–41.

Lewin, K. (1948). *Resolving social conflicts: Selected papers in group dynamics*. New York: Harper.

Lewin, K. (1951). Problems of research in social psychology. In D. Cartwright (Ed.), *Field theory in social science* (pp. 155–169). New York: Harper & Row.

Lewis, I., Watson, B., & Tay, R. (2007). Examining the effectiveness of physical threats in road safety advertising: The role of the third-person effect, gender, and age. *Transportation Research Part F: Traffic Psychology and Behaviour, 10*(1), 48–60.

Lewis, K., Belliveau, M., Herndon, B., & Keller, J. (2007). Group cognition, membership change, and performance: Investigating the benefits and detriments of collective knowledge. *Organizational Behavior and Human Decision Processes, 103*, 159–178.

Lewis, M., & Ramsay, D. (2004). Development of self-recognition, personal pronoun use, and pretend play during the 2nd year. *Child Development, 75*, 1821–1831.

Lewis, M. A., Lee, C. M., Patrick, M. E., & Fossos, N. (2007). Gender-specific normative misperceptions of risky sexual behavior and alcohol-related risky sexual behavior. *Sex Roles, 57*, 81–90.

Lewis, R.S., Goto, S. G., & Kong, L. L. (2008). Culture and context: East Asian American and European American differences in P3 event-related potentials and self construal. *Personality and Social Psychology Bulletin, 34*(5), 623–634.

Leyens, J. P., Camino, L., Parke, R. D., & Berkowitz, L. (1975). Effects of movie violence on aggression in a field setting as a function of group dominance and cohesion. *Journal of Personality and Social Psychology, 32*, 346–360.

L'Heureux-Dubé, C. (2001). Beyond the myths: Equality, impartiality, and justice. *Journal of Social Distress and the Homeless, 10*, 87–104.

Li, J., & Chignell, M. (2010). Birds of a feather: How personality influences blog writing and reading. *International Journal of Human-Computer Studies, 68*(9), 589–602.

Li, Q. (2007). New bottle but old wine: A research of cyberbullying in schools. *Computers in Human Behavior, 23*(4), 1777–1791.

Li, Q. (2008). A cross-cultural comparison of adolescents' experience related to cyberbullying. *Educational Research, 50*(3), 223–234.

Li, Q. (2010). Cyberbullying in high schools: A study of students' behaviors and beliefs about this new phenomenon. *Journal of Aggression, Maltreatment & Trauma, 19*(4), 372–392.

Liang, D. W., Moreland, R., & Argote, L. (1995). Group versus individual training and group performance: The mediating role of transactive memory. *Personality and Social Psychology Bulletin, 21*, 384–393.

Liberman, A., & Chaiken, S. (1992). Defensive processing of personally relevant health messages. *Personality and Social Psychology Bulletin, 18*, 669–679.

Liberman, V., Samuels, S. M., & Ross, L. D. (2004). The name of the game: Predictive power of reputations versus situational labels in determining Prisoner's Dilemma Game moves. *Personality and Social Psychology Bulletin, 30*, 1175–1185.

Lieberman, M. D., Jarcho, J. M., & Obayashi, J. (2005). Attributional inference across cultures: Similar automatic attributions and different controlled corrections. *Personality and Social Psychology Bulletin, 31*(7), 889–901.

Liebert, R. M., & Baron, R. A. (1972). Some immediate effects of televised violence on children's behavior. *Developmental Psychology, 6*, 469–475.

Lim, T.-S., & Choi, S.-H. (1996). Interpersonal relationships in Korea. In W. B. Gudykunst, S. Ting-Toomey, & T. Nishida (Eds.), *Communication in personal relationships across cultures* (pp. 122–136). Thousand Oaks, CA: Sage.

Linardatos, L., & Lydon, J. E. (2011a). A little reminder is all it takes: The effects of priming and relational self-construal on responses to partner transgressions. *Self and Identity, 10*(1), 85–100.

Linardatos, L., & Lydon, J. E. (2011b). Relationship-specific identification and spontaneous relationship maintenance processes. *Journal of Personality and Social Psychology, 101*(4), 737–753. Advance online publication.

Linden-Andersen, S., Markiewicz, D., & Doyle, A. (2009). Perceived similarity among adolescent friends: The role of reciprocity, friendship quality, and gender. *The Journal of Early Adolescence, 29*(5), 617–637.

Lindsay, D. S., & Read, J. D. (2006). Adults' memories of long-past events. In L. Nilsson & N. Ohta (Eds.), *Memory and society: Psychological perspectives* (pp. 51–72). New York: Psychology Press.

Lindsay, R. C. L., & Wells, G. L. (1985). Improving eyewitness identifications from lineups: Simultaneous versus sequential lineup presentation. *Journal of Applied Psychology, 70*, 556–564.

Lindsay, R. C. L., Wells, G. L., & Rumpel, C. M. (1981). Can people detect eyewitness-identification accuracy within and across situations? *Journal of Applied Psychology, 66*, 79–89.

Lindsay, R. L., Semmler, C., Weber, N., Brewer, N., & Lindsay, M. R. (2008). How variations in distance affect eyewitness reports and identification accuracy. *Law and Human Behavior, 32*(6), 526–535.

Linville, P. W., Fischer, G. W., & Fischhoff, B. (1993). AIDS risk perceptions and decision biases. In J. B. Pryor & G. D. Reeder (Eds.), The social psychology of HIV infection (pp. 5–38). Hillsdale, NJ: Erlbaum.

Linville, P. W., Fischer, G. W., & Salovey, P. (1989). Perceived distributions of characteristics of in-group and out-group members: Empirical evidence and a computer simulation. *Journal of Personality and Social Psychology, 57*, 165–188.

Linz, D. G., Donnerstein, E., & Penrod, S. (1984). The effects of multiple exposures to filmed violence against women. *Journal of Communication, 34*, 130–147.

Linz, D. G., Donnerstein, E., & Penrod, S. D. (1988). Effects of long-term exposure to violent and sexually degrading depictions of women. *Journal of Personality and Social Psychology, 55*, 758–768.

Lippmann, W. (1922). *Public opinion*. New York: Free Press.

Lipsey, M. W., Wilson, D. B., Cohen, M. A., & Derzon, J. H. (1997). Is there a causal relationship between alcohol use and violence? A synthesis of evidence. In M. Galanter (Ed.), *Recent developments in alcoholism: Vol. 13. Alcohol and violence: Epidemiology, neurobiology, psychology, and family issues* (pp. 245–282). New York: Plenum.

Litt, M. D. (1988). Self-efficacy and perceived control: Cognitive mediators of pain tolerance. *Journal of Personality and Social Psychology, 54*, 149–160.

Little, A. C., Burriss, R. P., Jones, B. C., DeBruine, L. M., & Caldwell, C. A. (2008). Social influence in human face preference: Men and women are influenced more for long-term than short-term attractiveness decisions. *Evolution and Human Behavior, 29*, 140–146.

Little, A. C., & Perrett, D. I. (2002). Putting beauty back in the eye of the beholder. *Psychologist, 15*, 28–32.

Livingston, S. D., & Sinclair, L. (2008). Taking the watchdog off its leash: Personal prejudices and situational motivations jointly predict derogation of a stigmatized source. *Personality and Social Psychology Bulletin, 34*, 210–223.

Lloyd, S. A., & Cate, R. M. (1985). The developmental course of conflict in dissolution of premarital relationships. *Journal of Social and Personal Relationships, 2*, 179–194.

Lobchuk, M. M., McClement, S. E., McPherson, C., & Cheang, M. (2008). Does blaming the patient with lung cancer affect the helping behavior of primary caregivers? *Oncology Nursing Forum, 35*(4), 681–689.

Lockwood, P. (2002). Could it happen to you? Predicting the impact of downward social comparison on the self. *Journal of Personality and Social Psychology, 82*, 343–358.

Lockwood, P., & Kunda, Z. (1997). Superstars and me: Predicting the impact of role models on the self. *Journal of Personality and Social Psychology, 73*, 91–103.

Lockwood, P., & Kunda, Z. (1999). Increasing salience of one's best selves can undermine inspiration by outstanding role models. *Journal of Personality and Social Psychology, 76*, 214–228.

Lockwood, P. & Kunda, Z. (2000). Outstanding role models: Do they inspire or demoralize us? In A. Tesser, R. B. Felson, & J. M. Suls (Eds.), *Psychological perspectives on self and identity* (pp. 147–170). Washington, DC: American Psychological Association.

Lockwood, P., Marshall, T. C., & Sadler, P. (2005). Promoting success or preventing failure: Cultural differences in motivation by positive and negative role models. *Personality and Social Psychology Bulletin, 31*(3), 379–392.

Lockwood, P., Sadler, P., Fyman, K., & Tuck, S. (2004). To do or not to do: Using positive and negative role models to harness motivation. *Social Cognition, 22*(4), 422–450.

Lodish, L. M., Abraham, M., Kalmenson, S., Lievelsberger, J., Lubetkin, B., Richardson, B., & Stevens, M. E. (1995). How TV advertising works: A meta-analysis of 389 real-world split-cable TV advertising experiments. *Journal of Marketing Research, 32*, 125–139.

Loftus, E. F. (1974). Reconstructing memory. The incredible eyewitness. *Psychology Today, 8*, 116–119.

Loftus, E. F. (1979). *Eyewitness testimony*. Cambridge, MA: Harvard University Press.

Loftus, E. F. (1983). Silence is not golden. *American Psychologist, 38*, 564–572.

Loftus, E. F. (1993). The reality of repressed memories. *American Psychologist, 48*, 518–537.

Loftus, E. F. (2003). The dangers of memory. In R. J. Sternberg (Ed.). *Psychologists defying the crowd: Stories of those who battled the establishment and won* (pp. 105–117). Washington, DC: American Psychological Association.

Loftus, E. F. (2005). Planting misinformation in the human mind: A 30-year investigation of the malleability of memory. *Learning and Memory, 12*, 361–366.

Loftus, E. F., Garry, M., & Hayne, H. (2008). Repressed and recovered memory. In E. Borgida and S. T. Fiske (Eds.), Beyond common sense: Psychological science in the courtroom (pp. 177–194). Malden, MA: Blackwell Publishing.

Loftus, E. F., & Hoffman, H. G. (1989). Misinformation and memory: The creation of new memories. *Journal of Experimental Psychology: General, 118*, 100–104.

Loftus, E. F., Miller, D. G., & Burns, H. J. (1978). Semantic integration of verbal information into a visual memory. *Journal of Experimental Psychology: Human Learning and Memory, 4*, 19–31.

Loftus, G. R., & Harley, E. M. (2005). Why is it easier to identify someone close than far away? *Psychonomic Bulletin and Review, 12*, 43–65.

Logel, C., Iserman, E. C., Davies, P. G., Quinn, D. M., & Spencer, S. J. (2009). The perils of double consciousness: The role of thought suppression in stereotype threat. *Journal of Experimental Social Psychology, 45*(2), 299–312.

Logel, C., Walton, G. M., Spencer, S. J., Iserman, E. C., von Hippel, W., & Bell, A. E. (2009). Interacting with sexist men triggers social identity threat among female engineers. *Journal of Personality and Social Psychology, 96*(6), 1089–1103.

London, P. (1970). The rescuers: Motivational hypotheses about Christians who saved Jews from the Nazis. In J. R. Macaulay & L. Berkowitz (Eds.), *Altruism and helping behavior* (pp. 241–250). New York: Academic Press.

Lonner, W., & Berry, J. (Eds). (1986). *Field methods in cross-cultural research*. Beverly Hills, CA: Sage.

Lord, C. G., Lepper, M. R., & Preston, E. (1984). Considering the opposite: A corrective strategy for social judgment. *Journal of Personality and Social Psychology, 47*, 1231–1243.

Lord, C. G., Scott, K. O., Pugh, M. A., & Desforges, D. M. (1997). Leakage beliefs and the correspondence bias. *Personality and Social Psychology Bulletin, 23*, 824–836.

Lore, R. K., & Schultz, L. A. (1993). Control of human aggression. *American Psychologist, 48*, 16–25.

Lorenzo, G. L., Biesanz, J. C., & Human, L. J. (2010). What is beautiful is good and more accurately understood: Physical attractiveness and accuracy in first impressions of personality. *Psychological Science, 21*(12), 1777–1782.

Losier, G. F., & Koestner, R. (1999). Intrinsic versus identified regulation in distinct political campaigns: The consequences of following politics for pleasure versus personal meaningfulness. *Personality and Social Psychology Bulletin, 25*, 287–298.

Lott, A. J., & Lott, B. E. (1974). The role of reward in the formation of positive interpersonal attitudes. In T. Huston (Ed.), *Foundations of interpersonal attraction*. New York: Academic Press.

Luby, V., & Aron, A. (1990, July). *A prototype structuring of love, like, and being in love.* Paper presented at the Fifth International Conference on Personal Relationships, Oxford, UK.

Ludwig, T. D., Gray, T. W., & Rowell, A. (1998). Increasing recycling in academic buildings: A systematic replication. *Journal of Applied Behavior Analysis, 31*, 683–686.

Lumsdaine, A. A., & Janis, I. L. (1953). Resistance to "counterpropaganda"; produced by one-sided and two-sided "propaganda" presentations. *Public Opinion Quarterly, 17*, 311–318.

Lundy, D. E., Tan, J., & Cunningham, M. R. (1998). Heterosexual romantic preferences: The importance of humor and physical attractiveness for different types of relationships. *Personal Relationships, 5*, 311–325.

Lupaschuk, D., & Yewchuk, C. (1998). Student perceptions of gender roles: Implications for counsellors. *International Journal for the Advancement of Counseling, 20*, 301–318.

Lussier, Y., Sabourin, S., & Turgeon, C. (1997). Coping strategies as moderators of the relationship between attachment and marital adjustment. *Journal of Social and Personal Relationships, 14*, 777–791.

Lydon, J. E. (1999). Commitment and adversity: A reciprocal relation. In A. Jeffrey & J. Warren (Eds.), *Handbook of interpersonal commitment and relationship stability*. New York: Plenum Publishers.

Lydon, J. E., Fitzsimons, G. M., & Naidoo, L. (2003). Devaluation versus enhancement of attractive alternatives: A critical test using the calibration paradigm. *Personality and Social Psychology Bulletin, 29*, 349–359.

Lydon, J. E., Meana, M., Sepinwall, D., Richards, N., & Mayman, S. (1999). The commitment calibration hypothesis: When do people devalue attractive partners? *Personality and Social Psychology Bulletin, 25*, 152–161.

Lydon, J. E., Menzies-Tolman, D., Burton, K., & Bell, C. (2008). If-then contingencies and the differential effects of availability of an attractive alternative on relationship maintenance for men and women. *Journal of Personality and Social Psychology, 95*, 50–65.

Lydon, J. E., & Zanna, M. P. (1990). Commitment in the face of adversity: A value-affirmation approach. *Journal of Personality and Social Psychology, 58*, 1040–1047.

Lykken, D. T. (1998). *A tremor in the blood: Uses and abuses of the lie detector*. New York: Plenum.

Lyle, K. B., & Johnson, M. K. (2006). Importing perceived features into false memories. *Memory, 14*, 197–213.

Lynn, S. J., Lock, T., Loftus, E., Krackow, E., & Lilienfeld, S. O. (2003). The remembrance of things past: Problematic memory recovery techniques in psychotherapy. In S. O. Lilienfeld & S. J. Lynn (Eds.), *Science and pseudoscience in clinical psychology* (pp. 205–239). New York: Guilford Press.

Lysak, H., Rule, B. G., & Dobbs, A. R. (1989). Conceptions of aggression: Prototype or defining features? *Personality and Social Psychology Bulletin, 15*, 233–243.

Lyubomirsky, S., Caldwell, N. D., & Nolen-Hoeksema, S. (1993). Effects of ruminative and distracting responses to depressed mood on retrieval of autobiographical memories. *Journal of Personality and Social Psychology, 75*, 166–177.

Lyubomirsky, S., Sheldon, K. M., & Schkade, D. (2005). Pursuing happiness: The architecture of sustainable change. *Review of General Psychology, 9*, 111–131.

Madon, S., Guyll, M., Buller, A. A., Scherr, K., Willard, J., & Spoth, R. (2008). The mediation of mothers' self-fulfilling effects on their children's alcohol use: Self-verification, informational conformity, and modeling processes. *Journal of Personality and Social Psychology, 95*(2), 369–384.

Madon, S., Guyll, M., Spoth, R., & Willard, J. (2004). The synergistic accumulative effect of parents' beliefs on childrens' drinking behavior. *Psychological Science, 15*, 837–845.

Maddux, W. W., Barden, J., Brewer, M. B., & Petty, R. E. (2004). Saying no to negativity: The effects of context and motivation to control prejudice on automatic evaluative responses. *Journal of Experimental Social Psychology, 41*, 19–35.

Magaro, P. A., & Ashbrook, R. M. (1985). The personality of societal groups. *Journal of Personality and Social Psychology, 48*, 1479–1489.

Magoo, G., & Khanna, R. (1991). Altruism and willingness to donate blood. *Journal of Personality and Clinical Studies, 7*, 21–24.

Maier, N. R. F., & Solem, A. R. (1952). The contribution of a discussion leader to the quality of group thinking: The effective use of minority opinions. *Human Relations, 5*, 277–288.

Maio, G. R., Bell, D. W., & Esses, V. M. (1996). Ambivalence in persuasion: The processing of messages about immigrant groups. *Journal of Experimental Social Psychology, 32*, 513–536.

Maio, G. R., Esses, V. M., & Bell, D. W. (1994). The formation of attitudes toward new immigrant groups. *Journal of Applied Social Psychology, 24*, 1762–1776.

Maio, G. R., & Olson, J. M. (1995). Relations between values, attitudes, and behavioral intentions: The moderating role of attitude function. *Journal of Experimental Social Psychology, 31*, 266–285.

Maio, G. R., Olson, J. M., & Bush, J. E. (1997). Telling jokes that disparage groups: Effects on the joke teller's stereotypes. *Journal of Applied Social Psychology, 27*, 1986–2000.

Major, B., & Gramzow, R. H. (1999). Abortion as stigma: Cognitive and emotional implications of concealment. *Journal of Personality and Social Psychology, 77*, 735–745.

Major, B., Quinton, W. J., & McCoy, S. K. (2002). Antecedents and consequences of attributions to discrimination: Theoretical and empirical advances. In M. P. Zanna (Ed.), *Advances in Experimental Social Psychology* (Vol. 34, pp. 251–330). San Diego, CA: Academic Press.

Major, B., Kaiser, C. R., & McCoy, S. K. (2003). It's not my fault: When and why attributions to prejudice protect self-esteem. *Personality and Social Psychology Bulletin, 29*(6), 772–781.

Major, B., Spencer, S., Schmader, T., Wolfe, C., & Crocker, J. (1998). Coping with negative stereotypes about intellectual performance: The role of psychological disengagement. *Personality and Social Psychology Bulletin, 24*, 34–50.

Malamuth, N. (1983). Human sexuality. In D. Perlman & P. C. Cozby (Eds.), *Social psychology*. New York: Holt, Rinehart & Winston.

Malamuth, N. M. (1981). Rape fantasies as a function of exposure to violent sexual stimuli. *Archives of Sexual Behavior, 10*, 33–47.

Malamuth, N. M., & Brière, J. (1986). Sexual violence in the media: Indirect effects on aggression against women. *Journal of Social Issues, 42*, 75–92.

Malamuth, N. M., & Check, J. U. (1981). The effects of mass media exposure on acceptance of violence against women: A field experiment. *Journal of Sex Research, 15*, 436–446.

Malamuth, N. M., Linz, D., Heavey, C. L., Barnes, G., & Acker, M. (1995). Using the confluence model of sexual aggression to predict men's conflict with women: A 10-year follow-up study. *Journal of Personality and Social Psychology, 69*, 353–369.

Malcolmson, K. A., Reynolds, M. G., & Smilek, D. (2007). Collaboration during visual search. *Psychonomic Bulletin & Review, 14*(4), 704–709.

Malcolmson, K. A., & Sinclair, L. (2007). The Ms. stereotype revisited: Implicit and explicit facets. *Psychology of Women Quarterly, 31*, 305–310.

Malle, B. F., & Knobe, J. (1997). Which behaviors do people explain? A basic actor-observer asymmetry. *Journal of Personality and Social Psychology, 72*, 288–304.

Malloy, T. E. (2001). Difference to inference: Teaching logical and statistical reasoning through on-line interactivity. *Behavior Research Methods, Instruments, and Computers, 33*, 270–273.

Malpass, R. S., & Devine, P. G. (1981). Eyewitness identification: Lineup instructions and the absence of the offender. *Journal of Applied Psychology, 66*(4), 482–489.

Malpass, R. S., Tredoux, C. G., & McQuiston-Surrett, D. (2007). Lineup construction and lineup fairness. *The handbook of eyewitness psychology: Vol. II. Memory for people* (pp. 155-178). Mahwah, NJ: Lawrence Erlbaum.

Mandal, M. K., Bryden, M. P., & Bulman-Fleming, M. B. (1996). Similarities and variations in facial expressions of emotions: Cross-cultural evidence. *International Journal of Psychology, 31*, 49–58.

Mandel, D. R., & Dhami, M. K. (2005). "What I did" versus "what I might have done": Effect of factual versus counterfactual thinking on blame, guilt, and shame in prisoners. *Journal of Experimental Social Psychology, 41*, 627–635.

Mandel, D. R., & Lehman, D. R. (1996). Counterfactual thinking and ascriptions of cause and preventability. *Journal of Personality and Social Psychology, 71*, 450–463.

Mandler, G. (1975). *Mind and emotion*. New York: Wiley.

Maner, J. K., DeWall, C. N., Baumeister, R. F., & Schaller, M. (2007). Does social exclusion motivate interpersonal reconnection? Resolving the "porcupine problem." *Journal of Personality and Social Psychology, 92*, 42–55.

Manstead, A. S. R. (1997). Situations, belongingness, attitudes, and culture: Four lessons learned from social psychology. In G. McGarty & H. S. Haslam (Eds.), *The message of social psychology: Perspectives on mind and society* (pp. 238–251). Oxford: Blackwell.

Mantler, J., Schellenberg, E. G., & Page, J. S. (2003). Attributions for serious illness: Are controllability, responsibility, and blame different constructs. *Canadian Journal of Behavioural Science, 35*(2), 142–152.

Maracek, J., & Mettee, D. R. (1972). Avoidance of continued success as a function of self-esteem, level of esteem certainty, and responsibility for success. *Journal of Personality and Social Psychology, 22*, 90–107.

Marigold, D. C., Holmes, J. G., & Ross, M. (2007). More than words: Reframing compliments from romantic partners fosters security in low self-esteem individuals. *Journal of Personality and Social Psychology, 92*, 232–248.

Marin, T. J., Holtzman, S., DeLongis, A., & Robinson, L. (2007). Coping and the response of others. *Journal of Social and Personal Relationships, 24*, 951–969.

Marion, R. (1995, August). The girl who mewed. *Discover*, 38–40.

Markman, K. D., Gavanski, I., Sherman, S. J., & McMullen, M. N. (1995). The impact of perceived control on the imagination of better and worse possible worlds. *Personality and Social Psychology Bulletin, 21*, 588–595.

Markus, H. (1977). Self-schemata and processing information about the self. *Journal of Personality and Social Psychology, 35*, 63–78.

Markus, H., & Kitayama, S. (1991). Culture and the self: Implications for cognition, emotion, and motivation. *Psychological Review, 98*, 224–253.

Markus, H. R., & Kitayama, S. (2001). The cultural construction of selfand emotion: Implications for social behavior. In W. G. Parrott (Ed.), *Emotions in social psychology: Essential readings* (pp. 119–137). Philadelphia: Psychology Press.

Markus, H. R., Kitayama, S., & Heiman, R. J. (1996). Culture and "basic" psychological principles. In E. T. Higgins & A. W. Kruglanski (Eds.), *Social psychology: Handbook of basic principles* (pp. 857–913). New York: Guilford.

Markus, H. R., & Zajonc, R. B. (1985). The cognitive perspective in social psychology. In G. Lindzey & E. Aronson (Eds.), *Handbook of social psychology* (3rd ed., Vol. 1, pp. 137–230). New York: McGraw-Hill.

Marshall, V. W., Clarke, P. J., & Ballantyne, P. J. (2001). Instability in the retirement transition. *Research on Aging, 23*, 379–409.

Martin, A. J., Berenson, K. R., Griffing, S., Sage, R. E., Madry, L., Bingham, L. E., & Primm, B. J. (2000). The process of leaving an abusive relationship: The role of risk assessments and decision certainty. *Journal of Family Violence, 15*, 109–122.

Martin, L. L., & Tesser, A. (1996). Some ruminative thoughts. In R. S. Wyer, Jr. (Ed.), *Advances in social cognition* (Vol. 9, pp. 1–47). Hillsdale, NJ: Erlbaum.

Martin, R., Hewstone, M., & Martin, P. Y. (2003). Resistance to persuasive messages as a function of majority and minority source status. *Journal of Experimental Social Psychology, 39*(6), 585–593.

Martin, R., & Randal, J. (2009). How Sunday, price, and social norms influence donation behaviour. *The Journal of Socio-Economics, 38*(5), 722–727.

Marx, D. M., & Roman, J. S. (2002). Female role models: Protecting women's math test performance. *Personality and Social Psychology Bulletin, 28*, 1183–1193.

Masters, K. S., Lacaille, R. A., & Shearer, D. S. (2003). The acute affective response of type A behaviour pattern individuals to competitive and noncompetitive exercise. *Canadian Journal of Behavioural Science, 35*, 25–34.

Masuda, T., Ellsworth, P. C., Mesquita, B., Leu, J., Tanida, S., & Van de Veerdonk, E. (2008). Placing the face in context: Cultural differences in the perception of facial emotion. *Journal of Personality and Social Psychology, 94*, 365–381.

Masuda, T., & Kitayama, S. (1996). *Correspondence bias in Japan*. Unpublished manuscript, Kyoto University.

Masuda, T., & Kitayama, S. (2003). Perceiver-induced constraint and attitude attribution in Japan and the US: A case for the cultural dependence of the correspondence bias. *Journal of Experimental Social Psychology, 40*, 409–416.

Masuda, T., & Nisbett, R. E. (2006). Culture and change blindness. *Cognitive Science: A Multidisciplinary Journal, 30*, 381–399.

Maticka-Tyndale, E. (1992). Social construction of HIV transmission and prevention among heterosexual young adults. *Social Problems, 39*, 238–252.

Maticka-Tyndale, E., Herold, E. S., & Mewhinney, D. (1998). Casual sex on spring break: Intentions and behaviors of Canadian students. *Journal of Sex Research, 35*, 254–264.

Maticka-Tyndale, E., Herold, E. S., & Mewhinney, D. (2001). Casual sex on spring break: Intentions and behaviors of Canadian students. In R. F. Baumeister (Ed.), *Social psychology and human sexuality: Key readings in social psychology* (pp. 173–186). Philadelphia, PA: Psychology Press.

Matsumoto, D., & Ekman, P. (2004). The relationship among expressions, labels, and descriptions of contempt. *Journal of Personality and Social Psychology, 87*(4), 529–540.

Matsumoto, D., Yoo, S., Fontaine, J., Anguas-Wong, A., Arriola, M., Ataca, B., . . . Grossi, E. (2008). Mapping expressive differences around the world: The relationship between emotional display rules and individualism versus collectivism. *Journal of Cross-Cultural Psychology, 39*(1), 55–74.

Matthews, K. A. (1988). Coronary heart disease and Type A behaviors: Update on and alternative to the Booth-Kewley and Friedman (1987) quantitative review. *Psychological Bulletin, 104*, 373–380.

Matud, M. P. (2004). Gender differences in stress and coping styles. *Personality and Individual Differences, 37*, 1401–1415.

Maupin, H. E., & Fisher, R. J. (1989). The effects of superior female performance and sex-role orientation on gender conformity. *Canadian Journal of Behavioural Science, 21*, 55–69.

Mazzoni, G., & Lynn, S. J. (2007). Using hypnosis in eyewitness memory: Past and current issues. In M. P. Toglia, J. D. Read, D. F. Ross, & R. C. L. Lindsay (Eds.) *The handbook of eyewitness psychology: Vol. I. Memory for events* (pp. 321–338). Mahwah, NJ: Lawrence Erlbaum.

Mazar, N., & Zhong, C. (2010). Do green products make us better people? *Psychological Science, 21*(4), 494–498.

McAlister, A., Perry, C., Killen, J., Slinkard, L. A., & Maccoby, N. (1980). Pilot study of smoking, alcohol, and drug abuse prevention. *American Journal of Public Health, 70*, 719–721.

McAllister, H. A. (1996). Self-serving bias in the classroom: Who shows it? Who knows it? *Journal of Educational Psychology, 88*, 123–131.

McArthur, L. (1972). The how and what of why: Some determinants and consequences of causal attribution. *Journal of Personality and Social Psychology*, *22*, 171–193.

McArthur, L. Z., & Baron, R. M. (1983). Toward an ecological theory of social perception. *Psychological Review*, *90*, 215–238.

McArthur, L. Z., & Berry, D. S. (1987). Cross cultural agreement in perceptions of babyfaced adults. *Journal of Cross-Cultural Psychology*, *18*, 165–192.

McCabe, M. P., & Ricciardelli, L. A. (2003a). Sociocultural influences on body image and body changes among adolescent boys and girls. *Journal of Social Psychology*, *143*, 5–26.

McCabe, M. P., & Ricciardelli, L. A. (2003b). A longitudinal study of body change strategies among adolescent males. *Journal of Youth and Adolescence*, *32*, 105–113.

McCann, S. J. (1992). Alternative formulas to predict the greatness of U.S. presidents: Personological, situational, and zeitgeist factors. *Journal of Personality and Social Psychology*, *62*, 469–479.

McCann, S. J. H. (2001). The precocity-longevity hypothesis: Earlier peaks in career achievement predict shorter lives. *Personality and Social Psychology Bulletin*, *27*, 1429–1439.

McCann, S. J. H. (2003). Younger achievement age predicts shorter life for governors: Testing the precocity-longevity with artifact controls. *Personality and Social Psychology Bulletin*, *29*, 164–169.

McCarthy, J. F., & Kelly, B. R. (1978). Aggressive behavior and its effect on performance over time in ice hockey athletes: An archival study. *International Journal of Sport Psychology*, *9*, 90–96.

McCauley, C. (1989). The nature of social influence in groupthink: Compliance and internalization. *Journal of Personality and Social Psychology*, *57*, 250–260.

McCloskey, M., & Zaragoza, M. (1985). Misleading postevent information and memory for events: Arguments and evidence against memory impairment hypotheses. *Journal of Experimental Psychology: General*, *114*, 1–16.

Maccoby, E. E., & Jacklin, C. N. (1974). *The psychology of sex differences*. Stanford, CA: Stanford University Press.

McClure, M., Lydon, J. E., Baccus, J. R., & Baldwin, M. W. (2010). A signal detection analysis of chronic attachment anxiety at speed dating: Being unpopular is only the first part of the problem. *Personality and Social Psychology Bulletin*, *36*(8), 1024–1036.

McConahay, J. B. (1986). Modern racism, ambivalence, and the Modern Racism Scale. In J. F. Dovidio & S. L. Gaertner (Eds.), *Prejudice, discrimination, and racism: Theory and research* (pp. 91–125). New York: Academic Press.

McCormack, G. R., Spence, J. C., Berry, T., & Doyle-Baker, P. K. (2009). Does perceived behavioral control mediate the association between perceptions of neighborhood walkability and moderate- and vigorousintensity leisure-time physical activity? *Journal of Physical Activity & Health*, *6*(5), 657-666.

McCoy, S. K., & Major, B. (2003). Group identification moderates emotional responses to perceived prejudice. *Personality and Social Psychology Bulletin*, *29*(8), 1005–1017.

McCrae, R. R., Yik, M. S. M., Trapnell, P. D., Bond, M. H., & Paulhus, D. L. (1998). Interpreting personality profiles across cultures: Bilingual, acculturation, and peer rating studies of Chinese undergraduates. *Journal of Personality and Social Psychology*, *74*, 1041–1055.

MacDonald, G., Nail, P. R., & Harper, J. R. (2011). Do people use reverse psychology? An exploration of strategic self-anticonformity. *Social Influence*, *6*(1), 1–14.

MacDonald, G., Zanna, M. P., & Holmes, J. G. (2000). An experimental test of the role of alcohol in relationship conflict. *Journal of Experimental Social Psychology*, *36*, 182–193.

McDonald, H. E., & Hirt, E. R. (1997). When expectancy meets desire: Motivational effects in reconstructive memory. *Journal of Personality and Social Psychology*, *72*, 5–23.

McDonald, J., & McKelvie, S. J. (1992). Playing safe: Helping rates for a dropped mitten and a box of condoms. *Psychological Reports*, *71*, 113–114.

MacDonald, T. K., Fong, G. T., Zanna, M. P., & Martineau A. M. (2000). Alcohol myopia and condom use: Can alcohol intoxication be associated with more prudent behaviour? *Journal of Personality and Social Psychology*, *78*, 605–619.

MacDonald, T. K., & Martineau, A. M. (2002). Self-esteem, mood, and intentions to use condoms: When does low self-esteem lead to risky health behaviors? *Journal of Experimental Social Psychology*, *38*, 299–306.

MacDonald, T. K., & Ross, M. (1999). Assessing the accuracy of predictions about dating relationships. How and why do lovers' predictions differ from those made by observers? *Personality and Social Psychology Bulletin*, *25*, 1417–1429.

MacDonald, T. K., & Zanna, M. P. (1998). Cross-dimension ambivalence toward social groups: Can ambivalence affect intentions to hire feminists? *Personality and Social Psychology Bulletin*, *24*, 427–441.

MacDonald, T. K., Zanna, M., & Fong, G. (1996). Why common sense goes out the window: Effects of alcohol on intentions to use condoms. *Personality and Social Psychology Bulletin*, *22*, 763–775.

McElwain, A. K., Korabik, K., & Rosin, H. M. (2005). An examination of gender differences in work-family conflict. *Canadian Journal of Behavioural Science*, *37*, 283–298.

McFarland, C., Beuhler, R., von Rüti, R., Nguyen, L., & Alvaro, C. (2007). The impact of negative moods on self-enhancing cognitions: The role of reflective versus ruminative mood orientations. *Journal of Personality and Social Psychology*, *93*, 728–750.

McFarland, C., Cheam, A., & Buehler, R. (2007). The perseverance effect in the debriefing paradigm: Replication and extension. *Journal of Experimental Social Psychology*, *43*(2), 233–240.

McFarland, C., & Miller, D. (1990). Judgments of self-other similarity. *Personality and Social Psychology Bulletin*, *16*, 475–484.

McFarlane, J., Martin, C. L., & Williams, T. M. (1988). Mood fluctuations: Women versus men and menstrual versus other cycles. *Psychology of Women Quarterly*, *12*, 201–233.

McFarland, C., & Miller, D. T. (1994). The framing of relative performance feedback: Seeing the glass as half empty or half full. *Journal of Personality and Social Psychology*, *66*, 1061–1073.

McFarlane, J., Martin, C. L., & Williams, T. M. (1988). Mood fluctuations: Women versus men and menstrual versus other cycles. *Psychology of Women Quarterly*, *12*, 201–233.

McGlone, M., & Aronson, J. (2006). Stereotype threat, identity salience, and spatial reasoning. *Journal of Applied Developmental Psychology*, *27*(5), 486–493.

McGraw, A. P., Mellers, B. A., & Tetlock, P. E. (2005). Expectations and emotions of Olympic athletes. *Journal of Experimental Social Psychology*, *41*, 438–446.

McGregor, B., Antoni, M., Boyers, A., Alferi, S., Cruess, D., Kilbourn, K., . . . Carver, C. S. (2004). Cognitive behavioral stress management increases benefit finding and immune function among women with early stage breast cancer. *Journal of Psychosomatic Research*, *54*, 1–8.

McGregor, C., Darke, S., Ali, R., & Christie, P. (1998). Experience of non-fatal overdose among heroin users in Adelaide, Australia: Circumstances and risk perceptions. *Addiction*, *93*, 701–711.

McGregor, I., Gailliot, M. T., Vasquez, N. A., & Nash, K. A. (2007). Ideological and personal zeal reactions to threat among people with high self-esteem: Motivated promotion focus. *Personality and Social Psychology Bulletin*, *33*, 1587–1599.

McGregor, I., Haji, R., & Kang, S. (2008). Can ingroup affirmation relieve outgroup derogation? *Journal of Experimental Social Psychology*, *44*(5), 1395–1401.

McGregor, I., Nail, P. R., Marigold, D. C., & Kang, S. (2005). Defensive pride and consensus: Strength in imaginary numbers. *Journal of Personality and Social Psychology, 89*, 978–996.

McGuire, W. J. (1964). Inducing resistance to persuasion. In L. Berkowitz (Ed.), *Advances in experimental social psychology* (Vol. 1, pp. 192–229). New York: Academic Press.

McGuire, W. J. (1968). Personality and susceptibility to social influence. In E. F. Borgatta & W. W. Lambert (Eds.), *Handbook of personality theory and research* (pp. 1130–1187). Chicago, IL: Rand McNally.

McHugo, G. J., & Smith, C. A. (1996). The power of faces: A review of John T. Lanzetta's research on facial expression and emotion. *Motivation and Emotion, 21*, 85–120.

McIntrye, M. (2006, June 3). Could no one have helped samaritan? *Winnipeg Free Press*, p. A3.

McIntyre, R. B, Paulson, R. M., & Lord, C. G. (2003). Alleviating women's mathematics stereotype threat through salience of group achievements. *Journal of Experimental Social Psychology, 39*(1), 83–90.

McKay, R., Arnold, D., Fratzl, J., & Thomas, R. (2008). Workplace bullying in academia: A Canadian study. *Employee Responsibilities and Rights Journal, 20*(2), 77–100.

McKelvie, S. J. (1995). Biases in the estimated frequency of names. *Perceptual and Motor Skills, 81*, 1331–1338.

McKelvie, S. J. (1997). The availability heuristic: Effects of fame and gender on the estimated frequency of male and female names. *Journal of Social Psychology, 137*, 63–78.

McKelvie, S. J., & McLellan, B. (1993). "Effects of age and gender on perceived facial attractiveness." Reply. *Canadian Journal of Behavioural Science, 26*, 205–209.

McKelvie, S. J., & McLellan, B. (1994). Effects of age and gender on perceived facial attractiveness: Reply. *Canadian Journal of Behavioural Science, 26*, 205–209.

McKenna, K. Y. A. (2008). MySpace or your place: Relationship initiation and development in the wired and wireless world. In S. Sprecher, A. Wenzel, & J. Harvey (Eds.), *Handbook of relationship initiation* (pp. 235–247). New York: Taylor & Francis.

McKenna, K. Y. A., & Bargh, J. A. (2000). Plan 9 from cyberspace: The implications of the Internet for personality and social psychology. *Personality and Social Psychology Review, 4*, 57–75.

McKenna, K. Y. A., Green, A. S., & Gleason, M. J. (2002). Relationship formation on the Internet: What's the big attraction? *Journal of Social Issues, 58*, 9–31.

McKenzie-Mohr, D., Nemiroff, L. S., Beers, L., & Desmarais, S. (1995). Determinants of responsible environmental behavior. *Journal of Social Issues, 51*, 139–156.

Mackie, D. M. (1987). Systematic and nonsystematic processing of majority and minority persuasive communications. *Journal of Personality and Social Psychology, 53*, 41–52.

McLaughlin-Volpe, T., Aron, A., Wright, S. C., & Reis, H. T. (2000). *Intergroup social interactions and intergroup prejudice: Quantity versus quality*. Unpublished manuscript. As cited in Brody et al. (2009).

McNally, R., & Breslau, N. (2008). Does virtual trauma cause posttraumatic stress disorder? *American Psychologist, 63*, 282–283.

McNally, R. J. (2003). *Remembering trauma.* Cambridge, MA: Harvard University Press.

McNally, R. J., Bryant, R. A., & Ehlers, A. (2003). Does early psychological intervention promote recovery from posttraumatic stress? *Psychological Science in the Public Interest, 4*, 45–79.

McPherson, M., Smith-Lovin, L., & Cook, J. M. (2001). Birds of a feather: Homophily in social networks. *Annual Review of Sociology, 27*, 415–444.

Marshall, T. C. (2010). Love at the cultural crossroads: Intimacy and commitment in Chinese Canadian relationships. *Personal Relationships, 17*(3), 391–411.

Mead, G. H. (1934). *Mind, self, and society*. Chicago, IL: University of Chicago Press.

Medvec, V. H., Madey, S. F., & Gilovich, T. (1995). When less is more: Counterfactual thinking and satisfaction among Olympic medalists. *Journal of Personality and Social Psychology, 69*, 603–610.

Medvec, V. H., Madey, S. F., & Gilovich, T. (2002). When less is more: Counterfactual thinking and satisfaction among Olympic medalists. In T. Gilovich, D. Griffin, & D. Kahneman (Eds.), *Heuristics and biases: The psychology of intuitive judgment* (pp. 625–635). Cambridge, UK: Cambridge University Press.

Meeus, W. H. J., & Raaijmakers, Q. A. W. (1995). Obedience in modern society: The Utrecht Studies. *Journal of Social Issues, 51*, 155–175.

Mehta, N., Chen, X., & Narasimhan, O. (2008). Informing, transforming, and persuading: Disentangling the multiple effects of advertising on brand choice decisions. *Marketing Science, 27*(3), 334–355.

Meier, D. (1995). *The power of their ideas*. New York: Beacon.

Meindl, J. R., & Lerner, M. J. (1984). Exacerbation of extreme response to an out-group. *Journal of Personality and Social Psychology, 47*, 71–83.

Meissner, C. A., & Brigham, J. C. (2001) A meta-analysis of the verbal overshadowing effect in face identification. *Applied Cognitive Psychology, 15*, 603–616.

Meissner, C. A., Tredoux, C. G., & Parker, J. F. (2005). Eyewitness decisions in simultaneous and sequential lineups: A dual-process signal detection theory analysis. *Memory and Cognition, 33*, 783–792.

Melara, R. D., DeWitt-Rickards, T. S., & O'Brien, T. P. (1989). Enhancing lineup identification accuracy: Two codes are better than one. *Journal of Applied Psychology, 74*, 706–713.

Melisurgo, L. (2010, May 26). Lee DeWyze is named "American Idol" winner. Retrieved from http://www.nj.com/entertainment/tv/index.ssf/2010/05/lee_dewyze_is_named_american_i.html

Mendes, W. B., Gray, H. M., Mendoza-Denton, R., Major, B., & Epel, E. S. (2007). Why egalitarianism might be good for your health: Physiological thriving during stressful intergroup encounters. *Psychological Science, 18*(11), 991–998.

Menec, V. H., & Chipperfield, J. G. (1997). The interactive effect of perceived control and functional status on health and mortality among young-old and old-old adults. *Journal of Gerontology: Psychological Sciences, 52B*, 118–126.

Menec, V. H., Chipperfield, J. G., & Perry, R. P. (1999). Self-perceptions of health: A prospective analysis of mortality, control, and health. *Journal of Gerontology: Psychological Sciences, 54B*, 85–93.

Menec, V. H., & Perry, R. P. (1998). Reactions to stigmas among Canadian students: Testing attribution-affect-help judgment model. *Journal of Social Psychology, 138*, 443–453.

Menec, V. H., Perry, R. P., Struthers, C. W., Schonwetter, D. J., Hechter, F. J., & Eichholz, B. L. (1994). Assisting at-risk college students with attributional retraining and effective teaching. *Journal of Applied Social Psychology, 24*, 675–701.

Menzies-Toman, D. A., & Lydon, J. E. (2005). Commitment-motivated benign appraisals of partner transgressions: Do they facilitate accommodation? *Journal of Social and Personal Relationships, 22*, 111–128.

Merikle, P. M. (1988). Subliminal auditory messages: An evaluation. *Psychology and Marketing, 5*, 355–372.

Merton, R. K. (1948). The self-fulfilling prophecy. *Antioch Review, 8*, 193–210.

Messick, D., & Liebrand, W. B. G. (1995). Individual heuristics and the dynamics of cooperation in large groups. *Psychological Review, 102*, 131–145.

Meston, C. M., & Frohlich, P. F. (2003). Love at first fright: Partner salience moderates roller-coaster-induced excitation transfer. *Archives of Sexual Behavior, 32*(6), 537–544.

Metcalfe, J. (1998). Cognitive optimism: Self-deception or memory-based processing heuristics? *Personality and Social Psychology Review*, *2*, 100–110.

Metcalfe, J., & Finn, B. (2011). People's hypercorrection of high-confidence errors: Did they know it all along? *Journal of Experimental Psychology: Learning, Memory, and Cognition*, *37*, 437–448.

Mewhinney, D. M., Herold, E. S., & Maticka-Tyndale, E. (1995). Sexual scripts and risk taking of Canadian university students on spring break in Daytona Beach, Florida. *Canadian Journal of Human Sexuality*, *4*, 273–288.

Meyer, P. (1999). The sociobiology of human cooperation: The interplay of ultimate and proximate causes. In J. M. G. van der Dennen & D. Smillie (Eds.), *The Darwinian heritage and sociobiology: Human evolution, behavior, and intelligence* (pp. 49–65). Westport, CT: Praeger.

Meyerowitz, B. E., & Chaiken, S. (1987). The effect of message framing on breast self-examination attitudes, intentions, and behavior. *Journal of Personality and Social Psychology*, *52*, 500–510.

Mezulis, A. H., Abramson, L. Y., Hyde, J. S., & Hankin, B. L. (2004). Is there a universal positivity bias in attributions? A meta-analytic review of individual, developmental, and cultural differences in the self-serving attributional bias. *Psychological Bulletin*, *130*(5), 711–747.

Michalos, A. C., & Zumbo, B. D. (2001). Ethnicity, modern prejudice, and the quality of life. *Social Indicators Research*, *53*, 189–222.

Michaels, J. W., Blommel, J. M., Brocato, R. M., Linkous, R. A., & Rowe, J. S. (1982). Social facilitation and inhibition in a natural setting. *Replications in Social Psychology*, *2*, 21–24.

Middleton, W., Harris, P., & Surman, M. (1996). Give 'em enough rope: Perception of health and safety risks in bungee jumpers. *Journal of Social and Clinical Psychology*, *15*, 68–79.

Migration and geographic mobility in metropolitan and nonmetropolitan America, 1995–2000 (2003). United States Census Bureau. www.census.gov/prod/2003pubs/censr-9.pdf. Accessed April 2006.

Mihic, L., Wells, S., Graham, K., Tremblay, P., & Demers, A. (2009). Situational and respondent-level motives for drinking and alcohol-related aggression: A multilevel analysis of drinking events in a sample of Canadian university students. *Addictive Behaviors*, *34*(3), 264–269.

Mikulincer, M., & Shaver, P. R. (2005). Attachment theory and emotions in close relationships: Exploring the attachment-anxiety dynamics of emotional reactions to relational events. *Personal Relationships*, *12*, 149–168.

Mikulincer, M., & Shaver, P. R. (2007). *Attachment in adulthood: Structure, dynamics, and change*. New York: Guilford Press.

Mikulincer, M., & Shaver, P. R. (2010). *Prosocial motives, emotions, and behavior: The better angels of our nature*. Washington, DC: APA Press.

Milgram, S. (1963). Behavioral study of obedience. *Journal of Abnormal and Social Psychology*, *67*, 371–378.

Milgram, S. (1969, March). The lost letter technique. *Psychology Today*, 30–33, 67–68.

Milgram, S. (1970). The experience of living in cities. *Science*, *167*, 1461–1468.

Milgram, S. (1974). *Obedience to authority: An experimental view*. New York: Harper & Row.

Milgram, S. (1976). Obedience to criminal orders: The compulsion to do evil. In T. Blass (Ed.), *Contemporary social psychology: Representative readings* (pp. 175–184). Itasca, IL: F. E. Peacock.

Milgram, S., & Sabini, J. (1978). On maintaining urban norms: A field experiment in the subway. In A. Baum, J. E. Singer, & S. Valins (Eds.), *Advances in environmental psychology* (Vol. 1, pp. 9–40). Hillsdale, NJ: Erlbaum.

Mill, D., Gray, T., & Mandel, D. R. (1994). Influence of research methods and statistics courses on everyday reasoning, critical abilities, and belief in unsubstantiated phenomena. *Canadian Journal of Behavioural Science*, *26*, 246–258.

Miller, A. F. (1995). Constructions of the obedience experiments: A focus upon domains of relevance. *Journal of Social Issues*, *51*, 33–53.

Miller, A. G. (1986). *The obedience experiments: A case study of controversy in social science*. New York: Praeger.

Miller, A. G., Ashton, W., & Mishal, M. (1990). Beliefs concerning the features of constrained behavior: A basis for the fundamental attribution error. *Journal of Personality and Social Psychology*, *59*, 635–650.

Miller, C. E., & Anderson, P. D. (1979). Group decision rules and the rejection of deviates. *Social Psychology Quarterly*, *42*, 354–363.

Miller, C. T. (1982). The role of performance-related similarity in social comparison of abilities: A test of the related attributes hypothesis. *Journal of Experimental Social Psychology*, *18*, 513–523.

Miller, D. T., & McFarland, C. (1986). Counterfactual thinking and victim compensation: A test of norm theory. *Personality and Social Psychology Bulletin*, *12*, 513–519.

Miller, D. T., & McFarland, C. (1987). Pluralistic ignorance: When similarity is interpreted as dissimilarity. *Journal of Personality and Social Psychology*, *53*, 298–305.

Miller, D. T., & Ratner, R. K. (1996). The power of the myth of self-interest. In L. Montada & M. Lerner (Eds.), *Current societal concerns about justice* (pp. 25–48). New York: Plenum.

Miller, D. T., & Ross, M. (1975). Self-serving biases in the attribution of causality: Fact or fiction? *Psychological Bulletin*, *82*, 213–225.

Miller, D. T., & Taylor, B. R. (2002). Counterfactual thought, regret, and superstition: How to avoid kicking yourself. In T. Gilovich, D. Griffin, & D. Kahneman (Eds.), *Heuristics and biases: The psychology of intuitive judgment* (pp. 367–378). Cambridge, UK: Cambridge University Press.

Miller, D. T., Turnbull, W., & McFarland, C. (1990). Counterfactual thinking and social perception: Thinking about what might have been. In M. P. Zanna (Ed.), *Advances in experimental social psychology* (Vol. 23, pp. 305–331). San Diego, CA: Academic Press.

Miller, J. G. (1984). Culture and the development of everyday social explanation. *Journal of Personality and Social Psychology*, *46*, 961–978.

Miller, J. G., Bersoff, D. M., & Harwood, R. L. (1990). Perceptions of social responsibilities in India and the United States: Moral imperatives or personal decisions? *Journal of Personality and Social Psychology*, *58*, 33–47.

Miller, N., & Campbell, D. T. (1959). Recency and primacy in persuasion as a function of the timing of speeches and measurements. *Journal of Abnormal and Social Psychology*, *59*, 1–9.

Miller, P. J. E., Niehuis, S., & Huston, T. L. (2006). Positive illusions in marital relationships: A 13-year longitudinal study. *Personality and Social Psychology Bulletin*, *32*, 1579–1594.

Millin, L. (2002, August 7). Just forget recovered memory. *Winnipeg Free Press*, p. A12.

Mills, J. (1958). Changes in moral attitudes following temptation. *Journal of Personality*, *26*, 517–531.

Mills, J., & Clark, M. S. (1982). Communal and exchange relationships. In L. Wheeler (Ed.), *Review of personality and social psychology* (Vol. 2, pp. 121–144). Beverly Hills, CA: Sage.

Mills, J., & Clark, M. S. (1994). Communal and exchange relationships: Controversies and research. In R. Erber & R. Gilmour (Eds.), *Theoretical frameworks for personal relationships* (pp. 29–42). Hillsdale, NJ: Erlbaum.

Mills, J., & Clark, M. S. (2001). Viewing close romantic relationships as communal relationships: Implications for maintenance and enhancement. In J. Harvey & A. Wenzel (Eds.), *Close romantic relationships: Maintenance and enhancement* (pp. 13–25). Mahwah, NJ: Erlbaum.

Mills, J. S., Polivy, J., Herman, C. P., & Tiggemann, M. (2002). Effects of exposure to thin media images: Evidence of self-enhancement among restrained eaters. *Personality and Social Psychology Bulletin*, *28*, 1687–1699.

Misconceptions about why people obey laws and accept judicial decisions (1997, September). *American Psychological Society Observer*, *5*, 12–13, 46.

Mitchell, K. J., & Johnson, M. K. (2000). Source monitoring: Attributing mental experiences. In E. Tulving & F. I. Craik (Eds.), *Oxford handbook of memory* (pp. 179–195). New York: Oxford University Press.

Mitchell, K. J., Johnson, M. K., & Mather, M. (2003). Source monitoring and suggestibility to misinformation: Adult age-related differences. *Applied Cognitive Psychology, 17,* 107–119.

Mittelstaedt, M. (2008, October 8). Oil sands will pollute Great Lakes, report warns. *Globe and Mail.* Retrieved from www.theglobeandmail.com/servlet/ story/RTGAM.20081008.wlakes08/BNStory/National/home

Miyamoto, Y., Nisbett, R. E., & Masuda, T. (2006). Culture and the physical environment: Holistic versus analytic perceptual affordances. *Psychological Science, 17,* 113–119.

Mobius, M. M., & Rosenblat, T. S. (2006).Why beauty matters. *American Economic Review, 96*(1), 222–235.

Modigliani, A., & Rochat, F. (1995). The role of interaction sequences and the timing of resistance in shaping obedience and defiance to authority. *Journal of Social Issues, 51,* 107–123.

Moghaddam, F. M., Taylor, D. M., & Wright, S. C. (1993). *Social psychology in cross-cultural perspective.* New York: Freeman.

Mohamed, A. A., & Wiebe, F. A. (1996). Toward a process theory of groupthink. *Small Group Research, 27,* 416–430.

Mohipp, C., & Morry, M. M. (2004). The relationship of symbolic beliefs and prior contact to heterosexuals' attitudes toward gay men and lesbian women. *Canadian Journal of Behavioural Science, 36,* 36–44.

Mok, D., Wellman, B., & Basu, R. (2007). Did distance matter before the Internet? Interpersonal contact and support in the 1970s. *Social Networks, 29*(3), 430–461.

Montaya, R. M., Horton, R. S., & Kirchner, J. (2008). Is actual similarity necessary for attraction? A meta-analysis of actual and perceived similarity. *Journal of Social and Personal Relationships, 25*(6), 889–922.

Montemayor, R., & Eisen, M. (1977). The development of self- conceptions from childhood to adolescence. *Developmental Psychology, 13,* 314–319.

Moore, C., Mealiea, J., Garon, N., & Povinelli, D. J. (2007). The development of body self-awareness. *Infancy, 11*(2), 157–174.

Moore, R. L. (1998). Love and limerance with Chinese characteristics: Student romance in the PRC. In V. C. de Munck (Ed.), *Romantic love and sexual behavior* (pp. 251–283). Westport, CT: Praeger.

Moore, S., Daniel, M., Bockenholt, U., Gauvin, L., Richard, L., & Stewart, S. (2010). Associations among socioeconomic status, perceived neighborhood control, perceived individual control, and self-reported health. *Journal of Community Psychology, 38*(6), 729–741.

Moore, T. E. (1995). Subliminal self-help tapes: An empirical test of perceptual consequences. *Canadian Journal of Behavioural Science, 27,* 9–20.

Moran, S., & Ritov, I. (2007). Experience in integrative negotiations: What needs to be learned? *Journal of Experimental Social Psychology, 43,* 77–90.

Moray, N. (1959). Attention in dichotic listening: Affective cues and the influence of instructions. *Quarterly Journal of Experimental Psychology, 11,* 56–60.

Moreland, R. L. (1987). The formation of small groups. In C. Hendrick (Ed.), *Review of personality and social psychology* (Vol. 8, pp. 80–110). Newbury Park, CA: Sage.

Moreland, R. L. (1999). Transactive memory: Learning who knows what in work groups and organizations. In L. L. Thompson & J. M. Levine (Eds.), *Shared cognition in organizations: The management of knowledge* (pp. 3–31). Mahwah, NJ: Erlbaum.

Moreland, R. L., Argote, L., & Krishnan, R. (1996). Socially shared cognition at work: Transactive memory and group performance. In J. L. Nye & A. M. Brower (Eds.), *What's social about social cognition?* (pp. 57–84). Thousand Oaks, CA: Sage.

Moreland, R. L., & Beach, R. (1992). Exposure effects in the classroom: The development of affinity among students. *Journal of Experimental Social Psychology, 28,* 255–276.

Moreland, R. L., & Zajonc, R. B. (1982). Exposure effects in person perception: Familiarity, similarity, and attraction. *Journal of Experimental Social Psychology, 18,* 395–415.

Morling, B., & Evered, S. (2006). Secondary control reviewed and defined. *Psychological Bulletin, 132,* 269–296.

Moroschan, G., Hurd, P., & Nicoladis, E. (2009). Sex differences in the use of indirect aggression in adult Canadians?. *Evolutionary Psychology,* 7(2), 146–159.

Morris, M. W., & Peng, K. (1994). Culture and cause: American and Chinese attributions for social and physical events. *Journal of Personality and Social Psychology, 67,* 949–971.

Morris, W. N., & Miller, R. S. (1975). The effects of consensus- breaking and consensus-preempting partners on reduction of conformity. *Journal of Experimental Social Psychology, 11,* 215–223.

Morrison, M. A., Morrison, T. G., & Franklin, R. (2009). Modern and old-fashioned homonegativity among samples of Canadian and American university students. *Journal of Cross-Cultural Psychology, 40*(4), 523–542.

Morrison, T. G., & Bearden, A. G. (2007). The construction and validation of the Homopositivity Scale: An instrument measuring endorsement of positive stereotypes about gay men. *Journal of Homosexuality, 52*(3-4), 63–89.

Morrongiello, B. A., & Mark, L. (2008). 'Practice what you preach': Induced hypocrisy as an intervention strategy to reduce children's intentions to risk take on playgrounds. *Journal of Pediatric Psychology, 33*(10), 1117–1128.

Morry, M. M. (2005a). Relationship satisfaction as a predictor of similarity ratings: A test of the attraction-similarity hypothesis. *Journal of Social and Personal Relationships, 22,* 561–584.

Morry, M. M. (2005b). Allocentrism and friendship satisfaction: The mediating roles of disclosure and closeness. *Canadian Journal of Behavioural Science, 37*(3), 211–222.

Morry, M. M. (2007). The attraction-similarity hypothesis among cross-sex friends: Relationship satisfaction, perceived similarities, and self-serving perceptions. *Journal of Social and Personal Relationships, 24,* 117–138.

Morry, M. M., & Harasymchuk, C. (2005). Perceptions of locus of control and satisfaction in friendships: The impact of problem-solving strategies. *Journal of Social and Personal Relationships, 22,* 183–206.

Morry, M. M., Reich, T., & Kito, M. (2010). How do I see you relative to myself? Relationship quality as a predictor of self- and partner-enhancement within cross-sex friendships, dating relationships, and marriages. *The Journal of Social Psychology, 150*(4), 369–392.

Morry, M. M., & Staska, S. L. (2001). Magazine exposure: Internalization, self-objectification, eating attitudes, and body satisfaction in male and female university students. *Canadian Journal of Behavioural Science, 33,* 269–279.

Morry, M. M., & Winkler, E. (2001). Student acceptance and expectation of sexual assault. *Canadian Journal of Behavioural Science, 33,* 188–192.

Morse, D. R., Martin, J., & Moshonov, J. (1991). Psychosomatically induced death: Relative to stress, hypnosis, mind control, and voodoo: Review and possible mechanisms. *Stress Medicine,* 7, 213–232.

Moscovitch, M., Winocur, G., & Behrmann, M. (1997). What is special about face recognition? Nineteen experiments on a person with visual object agnosia and dyslexia but normal face recognition. *Journal of Cognitive Neuroscience, 9,* 555–604.

Moscovici, S. (1985). Social influence and conformity. In G. Lindzey & E. Aronson (Eds.), *Handbook of social psychology* (Vol. 2, pp. 347–412). New York: McGraw-Hill.

Moscovici, S. (1994). Three concepts: Minority, conflict, and behavioral style. In S. Moscovici, A. Mucchi-Faina, & A. Maass (Eds.), *Minority Influence* (pp. 233–251). Chicago, IL: Nelson-Hall.

Moscovici, S., & Nemeth, C. (1974). Minority influence. In C. Nemeth (Ed.), *Social psychology: Classic and contemporary integrations* (pp. 217–249). Chicago, IL: Rand McNally.

Moscovitch, M., Winocur, G., & Behrmann, M. (1997). What is special about face recognition? Nineteen experiments on a person with visual object agnosia and dyslexia but normal face recognition. *Journal of Cognitive Neuroscience, 9*, 555–604.

Moskalenko, S., & Heine, S. (2003). Watching your troubles away: Television viewing as a stimulus for subjective self-awareness. *Personality and Social Psychology Bulletin, 29*, 76–85.

Moyer, K. E. (1983). The physiology of motivation: Aggression as a model. In C. J. Scheier & A. M. Rogers (Eds.), *G. Stanley Hall Lecture Series* (Vol. 3). Washington, DC: American Psychological Association.

Mukai, T. (1996). Mothers, peers, and perceived pressure to diet among Japanese adolescent girls. *Journal of Research in Adolescence, 6*, 309–324.

Mukai, T., Kambara, A., & Sasaki, Y. (1998). Body dissatisfaction, need for social approval, and eating disturbances among Japanese and American college women. *Sex Roles, 39*, 751–771.

Mullen, B. (1986). Atrocity as a function of lynch mob composition: A self-attention perspective. *Personality and Social Psychology Bulletin, 12*, 187–197.

Mullen, B., Rozell, D., & Johnson, C. (2001). Ethnophaulisms for ethnic immigrant groups: The contributions of group size and familiarity. *European Journal of Social Psychology, 31*, 231–246.

Mullen, J. E., & Kelloway, E. (2009). Safety leadership: A longitudinal study of the effects of transformational leadership on safety outcomes. *Journal of Occupational and Organizational Psychology, 82*(2), 253–272.

Muller, D., Atzeni, T., & Fabrizio, B. (2004). Coaction and upward social comparison reduce the illusory conjunction effect: Support for distraction-conflict theory. *Journal of Experimental Social Psychology, 40*, 659–665.

Muller, D., & Butera, F. (2007). The focusing effect of self-evaluation threat in coaction and social comparison. *Journal of Personality and Social Psychology, 93*, 194–211.

Mummery, W. K., & Wankel, L. M. (1999). Training adherence in adolescent competitive swimmers: An application of the theory of planned behavior. *Journal of Sport and Exercise Psychology, 21*,313–328.

Muraven, M., Rosman, H., & Gagné, M. (2007). Lack of autonomy and self-control: Performance contingent rewards lead to greater depletion. *Motivation and Emotion, 31*(4), 322–330.

Muraven, M., Tice, D. M., & Baumeister, R. F. (1998). Self-control as limited resource: Regulatory depletion patterns. *Journal of Personality and Social Psychology, 74*, 774–789.

Murdoch, D., Pihl, R. O., & Ross, D. (1990). Alcohol and crimes of violence: Present issues. *International Journal of Addictions, 25*, 1065–1081.

Murnaghan, D., Blanchard, C., Rodgers, W., La Rosa, J., Macquarrie, C., MaClellan, D., & Gray, B. (2009). The influence of student-level normative, control and behavioral beliefs on staying smoke-free: An application of Ajzen's theory of planned behavior. *Addiction Research & Theory, 17*(5), 469-480.

Murnaghan, D. A., Blanchard, C. M., Rodgers, W. M., LaRosa, J. N., MacQuarrie, C. R., MacLellan, D. L., & Gray, B. J. (2010). Predictors of physical activity, healthy eating and being smoke-free in teens: A theory of planned behaviour approach. *Psychology & Health, 25*(8), 925–941.

Murray, D. R., Trudeau, R., & Schaller, M. (2011). On the origins of cultural differences in conformity: Four tests of the pathogen prevalence hypothesis. *Personality and Social Psychology Bulletin, 37*(3), 318–329.

Murray, S. L., Bellavia, G., Feeney, B., Holmes, J. G., & Rose, P. (2001). The contingencies of interpersonal acceptance: When romantic relationships function as a self-affirmational resource. *Motivation and Emotion, 25*, 163–189.

Murray, S. L., Griffin, D. W., Rose, P., & Bellavia, G. M. (2003). Calibrating the sociometer: The relational contingencies of self-esteem. *Journal of Personality and Social Psychology, 85*(1), 63–84.

Murray, S. L., Haddock, G., and Zanna, M. P. (1996). On creating value-expressive attitudes: An experimental approach. In Seligman, Olson, & Zanna (Eds.), *The psychology of values: The Ontario symposium* (Vol. 8). Mahwah, NJ: Erlbaum.

Murray, S. L., & Holmes, J. G. (1993). Seeing virtues in faults: Negativity and the transformation of interpersonal narratives in close relationships. *Journal of Personality and Social Psychology, 65*, 707–722.

Murray, S. L., Holmes, J. G., Aloni, M., Pinkus, R. T., Derrick, J. L., & Leder, S. (2009). Commitment insurance: Compensating for the autonomy costs of interdependence in close relationships. *Journal of Personality and Social Psychology, 97*(2), 256–278.

Murray, S. L., Holmes, J. G., & Pinkus, R. T. (2010). A smart unconscious? Procedural origins of automatic partner attitudes in marriage. *Journal of Experimental Social Psychology, 46*(4), 650-656.

Murray, S. L., & Holmes, J. G. (1997). A leap of faith? Positive illusions in romantic relationships. *Personality and Social Psychology Bulletin, 23*, 586–604.

Murray, S. L., & Holmes, J. G. (1999). The (mental) ties that bind: Cognitive structures that predict relationship resilience. *Journal of Personality and Social Psychology, 77*, 1228–1244.

Murray, S. L., Holmes, J. G., Bellavia, G., Griffin, D. W., & Dolderman, D. (2002). Kindred spirits? The benefits of egocentrism in close relationships. *Journal of Personality and Social Psychology, 82*, 563–581.

Murray, S. L., Holmes, J. G., Dolderman, D., & Griffin, D. W. (2000). What the motivated mind sees: Comparing friends' perspectives to married partners' views of each other. *Journal of Experimental Social Psychology, 36*, 600–620.

Murray, S. L., Holmes, J. G., & Griffin, D. W. (1996a). The benefits of positive illusions: Idealization and the construction of satisfaction in close relationships. *Journal of Personality and Social Psychology, 70*, 79–98.

Murray, S. L., Holmes, J. G., & Griffin, D. W. (1996b). The self-fulfilling nature of positive illusions in romantic relationships: Love is not blind, but prescient. *Journal of Personality and Social Psychology, 71*, 1155–1180.

Murray, S. L., Holmes, J. G., MacDonald, G., & Ellsworth, P. C. (1998). Through the looking glass darkly? When self-doubts turn into relationship insecurities. *Journal of Personality and Social Psychology, 75*, 1459–1480.

Murray, S. L., Rose, P., Holmes, J. G., Derrick, J., Podchaski, E. J., Bellavia, G., & Griffin, D. W. (2005). Putting the partner within reach: A dyadic perspective on felt security in close relationships. *Journal of Personality and Social Psychology, 88*, 327–347.

Murray, T. C., Rodgers, W. M., & Fraser, S. N. (2009). Examining implementation intentions in an exercise intervention: The effects on adherence and self-efficacy in a naturalistic setting. *Journal of Applied Social Psychology, 39*(10), 2303–2320.

Murru, E. C., & Martin Ginis, K. A. (2010). Imagining the possibilities: The effects of a possible selves intervention on self-regulatory efficacy and exercise behavior. *Journal of Sport & Exercise Psychology, 32*(4), 537–554.

Mussen, P., & Eisenberg-Berg, N. (1977). *Roots of caring, sharing, and helping: The development of prosocial behavior in children*. San Francisco, CA: Freeman.

Mussweiler, T., Strack, F., & Pfeiffer, T. (2000). Overcoming the inevitable anchoring effect: Considering the opposite compensates for selective accessibility. *Personality and Social Psychology Bulletin, 26*, 1142–1150.

NBC.com (2011). Love in the Wild [Promotional material]. Retrieved from www.nbc.com/love-in-the-wild/

Nachson, I., Read, J., Seelau, S. M., Goodyear-Smith, F., Lobb, B., Davies, G., . . . Brimacombe, E. (2007). Effects of prior knowledge and expert statement on belief in recovered memories: An international perspective. *International Journal of Law and Psychiatry, 30*(3), 224–236.

Nadler, A., & Fisher, J. D. (1986). The role of threat to self-esteem and perceived control in recipient reactions to help: Theory development and empirical validation. In L. Berkowitz (Ed.), *Advances in experimental social psychology* (Vol. 19, pp. 81–123). New York: Academic Press.

Nail, P. R., McDonald, G., & Levy, D. A. (2000). Proposal of a four-dimensional model of social response. *Psychological Bulletin, 126*, 454–470.

Naimi, T., Brewer, B., Mokdad, A., Serdula, M., Denny, C., & Marks, J. (2003). Binge drinking among U.S. adults. *Journal of the American Medical Association, 289*, 70–75.

Napier, J., & Tyler, T. (2008). Does moral conviction really override concerns about procedural justice? A reexamination of the value protection model. *Social Justice Research, 21*, 509–528.

Nasco, S. A., & Marsh, K. L. (1999). Gaining control through counterfactual thinking. *Personality and Social Psychology Bulletin, 25*, 556–568.

Nathanson, S. (1987). *An eye for an eye? The morality of punishing by death*. Totowa, NJ: Roman & Littlefield.

Neal, A. (2000, July 7). The handbag. *The other story*. [Radio broadcast.] Canadian Broadcasting Corporation. www.ottawa.cbc.ca/ theotherstory/handbag.html. Broadcast November 14, 2000.

Neisser, U. (1976). *Cognition and reality: Principles and implications of cognitive psychology*. San Francisco, CA: Freeman.

Nelson, D. E., Bland, S., Powell-Griner, E., Klein, R., Wells, H. E., Hogelin, G., & Marks, J. S. (2002). State trends in health risk factors and receipt of clinical preventive services among US adults during the 1990s. *Journal of the American Medical Association, 287*, 2659–2667.

Nemeroff, C. J., Stein, R. I., Diehl, N. S., & Smilack, K. M. (1995). From the Cleavers to the Clintons: Role choices and body orientation as reflected in magazine article content. *International Journal of Eating Disorders, 16*, 167–176.

Nemeth, C. J., & Chiles, C. (1988). Modeling courage: The role of dissent in fostering independence. *European Journal of Social Psychology, 18*, 275–280.

Nes, L., & Segerstrom, S. (2006). Dispositional Optimism and Coping: A Meta-Analytic Review. *Personality and Social Psychology Review, 10*, 235–251.

Newby-Clark, I. R., McGregor, I., & Zanna, M. P. (2002). Thinking and caring about cognitive inconsistency: When and for whom does attitudinal ambivalence feel uncomfortable? *Journal of Personality and Social Psychology, 82*, 157–166.

Newcomb, T. M. (1961). *The acquaintance process*. New York: Holt, Rinehart & Winston.

Newall, N. E., Chipperfield, J. G., Clifton, R. A., Perry, R. P., Swift, A. U., & Ruthig, J. C. (2009). Causal beliefs, social participation, and loneliness among older adults: A longitudinal study. *Journal of Social and Personal Relationships, 26*(2-3), 273–290.

Newman, L. S. (1991). Why are traits inferred spontaneously? A developmental approach. *Social Cognition, 9*, 221–253.

Newman, L. S. (1996). Trait impressions as heuristics for predicting future behavior. *Personality and Social Psychology Bulletin, 22*, 395–411.

Newman, P. C. (2005). *The secret Mulroney tapes: Confessions of a prime minister*. Toronto, ON: Random House.

Ngo, A., West, G. E., & Calkins, P. H. (2009). Determinants of environmentally responsible behaviours for greenhouse gas reduction. *International Journal of Consumer Studies, 33*(2), 151–161.

Nguyen, M., Beland, F., Otis, J., & Potvin, L. (1996). Diet and exercise profiles of 30- to 60-year-old male smokers: Implications for community heart health programs. *Journal of Adolescent Health, 21*, 107–115.

Nickel, D., & Spink, K. S. (2010a). Attributions and self-regulatory efficacy for health-related physical activity. *Journal of Health Psychology, 15*(1), 53–63.

Nickel, D., & Spink, K. S. (2010b). Attributions for health-related physical activity. *Journal of Applied Social Psychology, 40*(11), 2927–2945.

Nicol, A. M. (2009). Social dominance orientation, right-wing authoritarianism, and their relation with leadership styles. *Personality and Individual Differences, 47*(6), 657–661.

Niederhoffer, K. G., & Pennebaker, J. W. (2002). Sharing one's story: On the benefits of writing or talking about emotional experience. In C. R. Snyder & S. J. Lopez (Eds.), *Handbook of positive psychology* (pp. 573–583). London, UK: Oxford University Press.

Nikiforuk, A. (2008). *Tar sands: Dirty oil and the future of the continent*. Vancouver, BC: Greystone Books.

NIMH Multisite HIV Prevention Trial Group (1998, June 19). The NIMH Multisite HIV Prevention Trial: Reducing sexual HIV risk behavior. *Science, 280*, 1889–1894.

NIMH Multisite HIV Prevention Trial Group (2001). Social-cognitive theory mediators of behavior change in the National Institute of Mental Health Multisite HIV Prevention Trial. *Health Psychology, 20*, 369–376.

Nisbett, R. E. (1993). Violence and U.S. regional culture. *American Psychologist, 48*, 441–449.

Nisbett, R. E. (2003). *The geography of thought: How Asians and Westerners think differently . . . and why*. New York: Free Press.

Nisbett, R. E., Fong, G. T., Lehman, D. R., & Cheng, P. W. (1987). Teaching reasoning. *Science, 238*, 625–631.

Nisbett, R. E., Krantz, D. H., Jepson, C., & Kunda, Z. (1983). The use of statistical heuristics in everyday inductive reasoning. *Psychological Review, 90*, 339–363.

Nisbett, R. E., & Ross, L. (1980). *Human inference: Strategies and shortcomings of human judgment*. Englewood Cliffs, NJ: Prentice Hall.

Nisbett, R. E., & Wilson, T. D. (1977a). Telling more than we can know: Verbal reports on mental processes. *Psychological Review, 84*, 231–259.

Nisbett, R. E., & Wilson, T. D. (1977b). The halo effect: Evidence for unconscious alteration of judgments. *Journal of Personality and Social Psychology, 35*, 250–256.

Noels, K. A., & Clément, R. (1996). Communicating across cultures: Social determinants and acculturative consequences. *Canadian Journal of Behavioural Science, 28*, 214–228.

Noels, K. A., Clément, R., Pelletier, L. G. (1999). Perceptions of teachers' communicative style and students' intrinsic and extrinsic motivation. *Modern Language Journal, 83*, 23–34.

Noguchi, K., Albarracín, D., Durantini, M., & Glasman, L. (2007). Who participates in which health promotion programs? A meta-analysis of motivations underlying enrollment and retention in HIV-prevention interventions. *Psychological Bulletin, 133*, 955–975.

Nolan, J. M., Schultz, P. W., Cialdini, R. B., Goldstein, N. J., & Griskevicius, V. (2008). Normative social influence is underdetected. *Personality and Social Psychology Bulletin, 34*(7), 913–923.

Norenzayan, A., Choi, I., & Nisbett, R. E. (1999). Eastern and Western perceptions of causality for social behavior: Lay theories about personalities and situations. In D. A. Prentice & D. T. Miller (Eds.), *Cultural divides: Understanding and overcoming group conflict* (pp. 239–272). New York: Russell Sage Foundation.

Norenzayan, A., Choi, I., & Peng, K. (2007). Perception and cognition. In S. Kitayama & D. Cohen (Eds.), *Handbook of cultural psychology* (pp. 569–594). New York: Guilford.

Norenzayan, A., & Hansen, I. G. (2006). Belief in supernatural agents in the face of death. *Personality and Social Psychology Bulletin, 32*, 174–187.

Norenzayan, A., & Heine, S. J. (2005). Psychological universals: What are they and how can we know? *Psychological Bulletin, 131*, 763–784.

Norenzayan, A., & Lee, A. (2010). It was meant to happen: Explaining cultural variations in fate attributions. *Journal of Personality and Social Psychology, 98*(5), 702–720.

Norenzayan, A., & Nisbett, R. E. (2000). Culture and causal cognition. *Current Direction in Psychological Science, 9*, 132–135.

Norman, R. G., Sorrentino, R. M., Windell, D., Ye, Y., Szeto, A. H., & Manchanda, R. (2010). Predicting behavioural intentions to those with mental illness: The role of attitude specificity and norms. *International Journal of Social Psychiatry, 56*(3), 239–254.

North, A. C., Tarrant, M., & Hargreaves, D. J. (2004). The effects of music on helping behavior: A field study. *Environment and Behavior, 36*, 266–275.

Nosek, B. A., Banaji, M. R., & Greenwald, A. G. (2002). Math = male, me = female, therefore math fi me. *Journal of Personality and Social Psychology, 83*, 44–59.

Nosen, E., & Woody, S. R. (2009). Applying lessons learned from obsessions: Metacognitive processes in smoking cessation. *Cognitive Therapy and Research, 33*(2), 241–254.

Nosko, A., Wood, E., & Molema, S. (2010). All about me: Disclosure in online social networking profiles: The case of FACEBOOK. *Computers in Human Behavior, 26*(3), 406–418.

Nowak, A., Szamrej, J., & Latané, B. (1990). From private attitude to public opinion: A dynamic theory of social impact. *Psychological Review, 97*, 362–376.

Nowatzki, J., & Morry, M. M. (2009). Women's intentions regarding, and acceptance of, self-sexualizing behaviour. *Psychology of Women Quarterly, 33*, 95–107 .

Nussbaum, A. D., & Steele, C. M. (2007). Situational disengagement and persistence in the face of adversity. *Journal of Experimental Social Psychology, 43*, 831–844.

Ochsner, K. (2007). Social cognitive neuroscience: Historical development, core principles, and future promise. In A. W. Kruglanski & E. T. Higgins (Eds.), *Social psychology: Handbook of basic principles* (2nd ed., pp. 39–66). New York: Guilford.

O'Connor, K. M., & Carnevale, P. J. (1997). A nasty but effective negotiation strategy: Misrepresentation of a common-value issue. *Personality and Social Psychology Bulletin, 23*, 504–515.

O'Farrell, T. J., & Murphy, C. M. (1995). Marital violence before and after alcoholism treatment. *Journal of Consulting and Clinical Psychology, 63*, 256–262.

O'Hara, J. (2000, March 6). The hell of hazing. *Maclean's*, 50–52.

Ohbuchi, K., & Baba, R. (1988). Selection of influence strategies in interpersonal conflicts: Effects of sex, interpersonal relations, and goals. *Tohoku Psychologica Folia, 47*, 63–73.

Ohbuchi, K., Ohno, T., & Mukai, H. (1993). Empathy and aggression: Effects of self-disclosure and fearful appeal. *Journal of Social Psychology, 133*, 243–253.

Ohbuchi, K., & Sato, K. (1994). Children's reactions to mitigating accounts: Apologies, excuses, and intentionality of harm. *Journal of Social Psychology, 134*, 5–17.

Ohtsubo, Y., Masuchi, A., & Nakanishi, D. (2002). Majority influence process in group judgment: Test of the social judgment scheme model in a group polarization context. *Group Processes and Intergroup Relations, 5*, 249–261.

Oishi, S., Rothman, A. J., Snyder, M., Su, J., Zehm, K., Hertel, A. W., . . . Sherman, G. D. (2007). The socioecological model of procommunity action: The benefits of residential stability. *Journal of Personality and Social Psychology, 93*, 831–844.

Oishi, S., Schimmack, U., & Colcombe, S. J. (2003). The contextual and systematic nature of life satisfaction judgments. *Journal of Experimental Social Psychology, 39*, 232–247.

Oishi, S., Wyer, R. S., & Colcombe, S. J. (2000). Cultural variation in the use of current life satisfaction to predict the future. *Journal of Personality and Social Psychology, 78*, 434–445.

O'Leary, J., & Covell, K. (2002). The tar ponds kids: Toxic environments and adolescent well-being. *Canadian Journal of Behavioural Science, 34*, 34–43.

Olson, J. M., Goffin, R. D., & Haynes, G. A. (2007). Relative versus absolute measures of explicit attitudes: Implications for predicting diverse attitude-relevant criteria. *Journal of Personality and Social Psychology, 93*, 907–926.

Olson, J. M., Maio, G. R., & Hobden, K. L. (1999). The (null) effects of exposure to disparagement humor on stereotypes and attitudes. *Humor: International Journal of Humor Research, 12*, 195–219.

Olson, M. A., & Fazio, R. H. (2008). Implicit and explicit measures of attitudes: The perspective of the MODE model. In R. E. Petty, R. H. Fazio, P. Briñol, R. E. Petty, R. H. Fazio, & P. Briñol (Eds.), *Attitudes: Insights from the new implicit measures* (pp. 19–63). New York: Psychology Press.

Olson, J. M., & Zanna, M. P. (1993). Attitudes and attitude change. *Annual Review of Psychology, 44*, 117–154.

Olsson, N. (2000). A comparison of correlation, calibration, and diagnosticity as measures of the confidence-accuracy relationship. *Journal of Applied Psychology, 85*, 504–511.

Olweus, D. (1996). Bullying at school: Knowledge base and an effective intervention program. In C. Ferris & T. Grisso (Eds.), *Understanding aggressive behavior in children* (New York Academy of Sciences, Annals of the New York Academy of Sciences. Vol. 794, pp. 265–276). New York: Academy of Sciences.

Olweus, D. (1997). Tackling peer victimization with a school-based intervention program. In D. Fry & K. Bjorkqvist (Eds.), *Cultural variation in conflict resolution: Alternatives to violence* (pp. 215–231). Mahwah, NJ: Erlbaum.

Olweus, D. (2004). The Olewus Bullying Prevention Programme: Design implementation issues and a new national initiative in Norway. In P. K. Smith, D. Pepler, & K. Rigby (Eds.), *Bullying in schools: How successful can interventions be?* (pp. 13–36). Cambridge, UK: Cambridge University Press.

O'Neill, J. (2007, March 28). Obesity expected to shorten kids' lives. *Winnipeg Free Press*, p. A12.

O'Neill, P. (2000). Cognition in social context. In J. Rappaport & E. Seidman (Eds), *Handbook of community psychology* (pp. 115–132). New York: Springer Publishing.

Onishi, N. (2004, August 7). A princess's distress pierces Japan's veil of secrecy. *New York Times*. Retrieved from http://query.nytimes.com/gst/fullpage.html?res=9B01EEDD103CF934A3575BC0A9629C 8B63& sec=health&spon=&pagewanted=all

Oppenheimer, D. M. (2004). Spontaneous discounting of availability in frequency judgment tasks. *Psychological Science, 15*, 100–105.

Opposition MPs grill PM again about Cadman affair (2008, March 5). *CBC News*/cbc.ca. Retrieved from www.cbc.ca/canada/story/2008/03/ 05/harper-cadman.html

Orbell, J. M., van de Kragt, A. J. C., & Dawes, R. M. (1988). Explaining discussion-induced comparison. *Journal of Personality and Social Psychology, 54*, 811–819.

Orobio de Castro, B., Brendgen, M., Van Boxtel, H., Vitaro, F., & Schaepers, L. (2007). 'Accept me, or else': Disputed overestimation of social competence predicts increases in proactive aggression. *Journal of Abnormal Child Psychology, 35*(2), 165–178.

Osbeck, L. M., Moghaddam, F. M., & Perrault. (1997). Similarity and attraction among majority and minority groups in a multicultural context. *International Journal of Intercultural Relations, 21*, 113–123.

Oskamp, S. (1995). Applying social psychology to avoid ecological disaster. *Journal of Social Issues, 51*, 217–238.

Oskamp, S. (2000). A sustainable future for humanity? How can psychology help? *American Psychologist, 55*, 496–508.

Oskamp, S., Burkhardt, R. I., Schultz, P. W., Hurin, S., & Zelezny, L. (1998). Predicting three dimensions of residential curbside recycling: An observational study. *Journal of Environmental Education, 29*, 37–42.

Osofsky, M. J., Bandura, A., & Zimbardo, P. G. (2005). The role of moral disengagement in the execution process. *Law and Human Behavior, 29*, 371–393.

Ostrom, T., & Sedikides, C. (1992). Out-group homogeneity effects in natural and minimal groups. *Psychological Bulletin, 112*, 536–552.

Otten, C. A., Penner, L. A., & Waugh, G. (1988). That's what friends are for: The determinants of psychological helping. *Journal of Social and Clinical Psychology, 7*, 34–41.

Outten, H., Giguère, B., Schmitt, M. T., & Lalonde, R. N. (2010). Racial identity, racial context, and ingroup status: Implications for attributions to discrimination among Black Canadians. *Journal of Black Psychology, 36*(2), 172–196.

Ovcharchyn, C. A., Johnson, H. H., & Petzel, T. P. (1981). Type A behavior, academic aspirations, and academic success. *Journal of Personality, 49*, 248–256.

Overmier, J. B. (2002). On learned helplessness. *Integrative Physiological and Behavioral Science, 37*, 4–8.

Owen, B. (2007, October, 14). Kids who kill. *Winnipeg Free Press*, pp. B1, B4.

Owen, K. I., Wright, S. C., & Brody, S. M. (2001). *Bicultural friends: When group membership salience matters.* Paper presented at the Western Psychological Association Conference, Maui, Hawaii.

Oyserman, D., Kemmelmeier, M., Fryberg, S., Brosh, H., & Hart-Johnson, T. (2003). Racial-ethnic self-schemas. *Social Psychology Quarterly, 66*, 333–347.

Oyserman, D., & Lee, S. (2008). Does culture influence what and how we think? Effects of priming individualism and collectivism. *Psychological Bulletin, 134*, 311–342.

Packer, D. J. (2008). Identifying systematic disobedience in Milgram's obedience experiments. *Psychological Science, 3*, 301–304.

Packer, D. J., & Chasteen, A. L. (2010). Loyal deviance: Testing the normative conflict model of dissent in social groups. *Personality and Social Psychology Bulletin, 36*(1), 5–18.

Page, S. (1998). Accepting the gay person: Rental accommodation in the community. *Journal of Homosexuality, 36*, 31–39.

Page, S. (1999). Accommodating persons with AIDS: Acceptance and rejection in rental situations. *Journal of Applied Social Psychology, 29*, 261–270.

Page-Gould, E., Mendoza-Denton, R., & Tropp, L. R. (2008). With a little help from my cross-group friend: Reducing anxiety in intergroup contexts through cross-group friendship. *Journal of Personality and Social Psychology, 95*(5), 1080–1094.

Page-Gould, E., Mendoza-Denton, R., Alegre, J., & Siy, J. (2010). Understanding the impact of cross-group friendship on interactions with novel outgroup members. *Journal of Personality and Social Psychology, 98*(5), 775–793.

Paik, J., MacDougall, B. L., Fabrigar, L. R., Peach, J. M., & Jellous, K. (2009). Altering category-level beliefs: The impact of level of representation at belief formation and belief disconfirmation. *Personality and Social Psychology Bulletin, 35*(8), 1112–1125.

Palmer, D. L. (1996). Determinants of Canadian attitudes toward immigration: More than just racism? *Canadian Journal of Behavioural Science, 28*, 180–192.

Palmer, D. L. (2000). *Canadian attitudes in the wake of the boats from China*. Submitted to Citizenship and Immigration Canada.

Pancer, S. M., & Pratt, M. W. (1999). Social and family determinants of community service involvement in Canadian youth. In M. Yates & J. Youniss (Eds.), *Roots of civic identity: International perspectives on community service and activism in youth*. Cambridge, UK: Cambridge University Press.

Panetta, A. (2005, December 14). The Harper effect: The more we see him, the more we dislike him, poll suggests. *Winnipeg Free Press*, pp. A1, A11.

Panetta, A. (2008, January 10). Canada's first female PM springs to defence of Hillary Clinton. Canadian Press. Retrieved from http://cnews.canoe.ca/ CNEWS/Canada/2008/01/10/4766419-cp.html

Paolucci-Oddone, E., Genius, M., & Violato, C. (2000). A meta-analysis of the published research on the effects of pornography. In C. Violato (Ed.), *The changing family and child development* (pp. 48–59). Burlington, VT: Ashgate Publishing.

Parish, A. R., & De Waal, F. B. M. (2000). The other "closest living relative": How bonobos (pan paniscus) challenge traditional assumptions about females, dominance, intra- and intersexual interactions, and hominid evolution. In D. LeCroy & P. Moller (Eds.), *Evolutionary perspectives on human reproductive behavior* (pp. 97–113). New York: New York Academy of Sciences.

Parke, R. D., Berkowitz, L., Leyens, J. P., West, S. G., & Sebastian, R. J. (1977). Some effects of violent and nonviolent movies on the behavior of juvenile delinquents. In L. Berkowitz (Ed.), *Advances in experimental social psychology* (Vol. 10, pp. 135–172). New York: Academic Press.

Parker, I. (2007, July 30). Swingers: Bonobos are celebrated as peace-loving, matriarchal, and sexually liberated. Are they? *New Yorker*. Retrieved from www.newyorker.com/reporting/2007/07/30/070730fa_fact_parker?printable=true

Parks, C. D., & Rumble, A. C. (2001). Elements of reciprocity and social value orientation. *Personality and Social Psychology Bulletin, 27*, 1301–1309.

Patch, M. E., Hoang, V. R., & Stahelski, A. J. (1997). The use of metacommunication in compliance: Door-in-the-face and single- request strategies. *Journal of Social Psychology, 137*, 88–94.

Patrick, C. J., & Iacono, W. G. (1989). Psychopathy, threat, and polygraph test accuracy. *Journal of Applied Psychology, 74*, 347–355.

Patry, M. W., Stinson, V., & Smith, S. M. (2009). Supreme Court of Canada addresses admissibility of posthypnosis witness evidence: R. v.Trochym (2007). *Canadian Psychology, 50*(2), 98–105.

Patterson, A. (1974, September). *Hostility catharsis: A naturalistic quasi-experiment.* Paper presented at the meeting of the American Psychological Association, New Orleans.

Patterson, L. A., Cameron, J. E., & Lalonde, R. N. (1996). The intersection of race and gender: Examining the politics of identity in women's studies. *Canadian Journal of Behavioural Science, 28*, 229–239.

Patton, E., & Johns, G. (2007). Women's absenteeism in the popular press: Evidence for a gender-specific absence culture. *Human Relations, 60*, 1579–1612.

Paulhus, D. L. (1998). Interpersonal and intrapsychic adaptiveness of trait self-enhancement: A mixed blessing? *Journal of Personality and Social Psychology, 74*, 1197–1208.

Paulhus, D. L., & Bruce, M. N. (1992). The effect of acquaintanceship on the validity of personality impressions: A longitudinal study. *Journal of Personality and Social Psychology, 63*, 816–824.

Paulhus, D. L., & Morgan, K. L. (1997). Perceptions of intelligence in leadership groups: The dynamic effects of shyness and acquaintance. *Journal of Personality and Social Psychology, 72*, 581–591.

Paulhus, D. L., & Reynolds, S. (1995). Enhancing target variance in personality impressions: Highlighting the person in person perception. *Journal of Personality and Social Psychology, 69*, 1233–1242.

Pavlidis, I., Eberhardt, N. L., & Levine, J. A. (2002). Seeing through the face of deception: Thermal imaging offers a promising hands-off approach to mass security screening. *Nature, 415*, 35.

Payne, B. (2006). Weapon bias: Split-second decisions and unintended stereotyping. *Current Directions in Psychological Science, 15*, 287-291.

Payne, B. K. (2001). Prejudice and Perception: The role of automatic and controlled processes in misperceiving a weapon. *Journal of Personality and Social Psychology, 81*, 1–12.

Payne, B. K., Shimizu, Y., & Jacoby, L. L. (2005). Mental control and visual illusions: Toward explaining race-biased weapon misidentifications. *Journal of Experimental Social Psychology, 41*, 36–47.

Peebles, F. (2008, April 10). Teen saves family from fire. *Prince George Citizen*. Retrieved from www.princegeorgecitizen.com/20080410126500/local/news/teen-saves-family-from-fire.html

Pelletier, L. G. (2002). A motivational analysis of self-determination for pro-environmental behaviors. In E. L. Deci & R. M. Ryan (Eds.), *Handbook of self-determination research* (pp. 205–232). Rochester, NY: University of Rochester Press.

Pelletier, L. G., Dion, S., Tuson, K., & Green-Demers, I. (1999). Why do people fail to adopt environmental protective behaviors? Toward a taxonomy of environmental amotivation. *Journal of Applied Social Psychology, 29*, 2481–2504.

Pelletier, L. G., Fortier, M. S., Vallerand, R. J., & Brière, N. M. (1996). *Perceived autonomy support, motivation, and persistence in physical activity: A longitudinal investigation*. Unpublished manuscript, University of Ottawa.

Pelletier, L. G., & Sharp, E. (2008). Persuasive communication and proenvironmental behaviours: How message tailoring and message framing can improve the integration of behaviours through self-determined motivation. *Canadian Psychology, 49*(3), 210–217.

Pennebaker, J. W. (1990). *Opening up: The healing powers of confiding in others*. New York: William Morrow.

Pennebaker, J. W. (1997). Writing about emotional experiences as a therapeutic process. *Psychological Science, 8*, 162–166.

Pennebaker, J. W. (2004). Theories, therapies, and taxpayers: On the complexities of the expressive writing paradigm. *Clinical Psychology: Science and Practice, 11*, 138–142.

Pennebaker, J. W., Barger, S. D., & Tiebout, J. (1989). Disclosure of traumas and health among Holocaust survivors. *Psychosomatic Medicine, 51*, 577–589.

Pennebaker, J. W., & Beale, S. K. (1986). Confronting a traumatic event: Toward an understanding of inhibition and disease. *Journal of Abnormal Psychology, 95*, 274–281.

Pennebaker, J. W., Colder, M., & Sharp, L. K. (1990). Accelerating the coping process. *Journal of Personality and Social Psychology, 58*, 528–537.

Penner, L. A. (2002). Dispositional and organizational influences on sustained volunteerism: An interactionist perspective. *Journal of Social Issues, 58*, 447–467.

Penner, L. A., Dovidio, J. F., Piliavin, J. A., & Schroeder, D. A. (2005). Prosocial behavior: Multilevel perspectives. *Annual Review of Psychology, 56*, 365–392.

Pennington, N., & Hastie, R. (1988). Explanation-based decision making: Effects of memory structure on judgment. *Journal of Experimental Psychology: Learning, Memory, and Cognition, 14*, 521–533.

Pennington, N., & Hastie, R. (1990). Practical implications of psychological research on juror and jury decision making. *Personality and Social Psychology Bulletin, 16*, 90–105.

Pennington, N., & Hastie, R. (1992). Explaining the evidence: Tests of the story model for juror decision making. *Journal of Personality and Social Psychology, 62*, 189–206.

Pennington, N., & Hastie, R. (1993). Reasoning in explanation-based decision making. *Cognition, 49*, 123–163.

Penton-Voak, I. S., & Chang, H. Y. (2008). Attractiveness judgements of individuals vary across emotional expression and movement conditions. *Journal of Evolutionary Psychology, 6*(2), 89–100.

Peplau, L. A., & Perlman, D. (1982). Perspectives on loneliness. In L. A. Peplau & D. Perlman (Eds.), *Loneliness: A sourcebook of current theory, research, and therapy* (pp. 1–18). New York: Wiley.

Pepler, D., Craig, W. M., O'Connell, P., Atlas, R., & Charach, A. (2004). Making a difference in bullying: Evaluation of a systemic school-based programme in Canada. In P. K. Smith, D. Pepler & K. Rigby (Eds.), *Bullying in schools: How successful can interventions be?* (pp. 125–140). Cambridge, UK: Cambridge University Press.

Pepler, D., Jiang, D., & Craig, W. (2006, July). *Who benefits from bullying prevention programs? A generalized mixed model analysis.* Paper presented at the Biennial Meeting of the International Society for the Study of Behavioural Development, Melbourne, Australia.

Pepler, D., Smith, P. K., & Rigby, K. (2004). Looking back and looking forward: Implications for making interventions work effectively. In P. K. Smith, D. Pepler, & K. Rigby (Eds.), *Bullying in schools: How successful can interventions be?* (pp. 307–324). Cambridge, UK: Cambridge University Press.

Pepler, D. J., & Craig, W. M. (1995). A peek behind the fence: Naturalistic observations of aggressive children with remote audiovisual recording. *Developmental Psychology, 31*, 548–553.

Pepler, D. J., Craig, W. M., Connolly, J., & Henderson, K. (2002). Bullying, sexual harassment, dating violence, and substance abuse among adolescents. In C. Wekerle & A. Wall (Eds.), *The violence and addiction equation* (pp. 153–168). New York: Taylor & Francis.

Pepler, D. J., Craig, W. M., Ziegler, S., & Charach, A. (1994). An evaluation of anti-bullying intervention in Toronto schools. *Canadian Journal of Community Mental Health, 13*, 95–110.

Perkins, H. W. (2007). Misperceptions of peer drinking norms in Canada: Another look at the "reign of error" and its consequences among college students. *Addictive Behaviors, 32*, 2645–2656.

Perkins, H. W., Haines, M. P., & Rice, R. (2005). Misperceiving college drinking norms and related problems: A nationwide study of exposure to prevention information, perceived norms and student alcohol misuse. *Journal of Studies on Alcohol, 66*, 470–478.

Perlini, A. H., Bertolissi, S., & Lind, D. L. (1999). The effect of women's age and physical appearance on evaluations of attractiveness and social desirability. *Journal of Social Psychology, 139*, 343–351.

Perlini, A. H., & Silvaggio, A. D. (2007). Eyewitness misidentification: Single vs double-blind comparison of photospread administration. *Psychological Reports, 100*(1), 247–256.

Perlini, A. H., & Ward, C. (2000). HIV prevention intentions: The effects of role-play and behavioural commitment on knowledge and attitudes. *Canadian Journal of Behavioural Science, 32*, 133–143.

Perreault, S., & Bourhis, R. Y. (1999). Ethnocentrism, social identification, and discrimination. *Personality and Social Psychology Bulletin, 25*, 92–103.

Perrett, D. I., May, K. A., & Yoshikawa, S. (1994). Facial shape and judgments of female attractivenesss. *Nature, 368*, 239–242.

Perrott, S., & Webber, N. (1996). Attitudes toward male and female victims of sexual assault: Implications for services to the male victim. *Journal of Psychology and Human Sexuality, 8*, 19–38.

Perrott, S. B., Miller, Y. M., & Delaney, M. E. (1997). Attitudes toward the mandatory arrest response to domestic battering: Gender and institutional differences from a traditional and a women's university. *Legal and Criminological Psychology, 2*, 35–49.

Perry, R. P. (2003). Perceived (academic) control and causal thinking in achievement settings. *Canadian Psychology, 44*(4), 312–331.

Perry, R. P., Hladkyj, S., Pekrun, R. H., & Pelletier, S. T. (2001). Academic control and action control in the achievement of college students: A longitudinal field study. *Journal of Educational Psychology, 93*, 776–789.

Perry, R. P., Stupnisky, R. H., Daniels, L. M., & Haynes, T. L. (2008). Attributional (explanatory) thinking about failure in new achievement settings. *European Journal of Psychology of Education, 23*(4), 459–475.

Peters, L. H., Hartke, D. D., & Pohlmann, J. T. (1985). Fiedler's contingency theory of leadership: An application of the meta-analysis procedures of Schmidt and Hunter. *Psychological Bulletin, 97*, 274–285.

Peters, M. (2001). Forensic psychological testimony: Is the courtroom door now locked and barred? *Canadian Psychology, 42*, 101–108.

Petersen, L., & Dietz, J. (2008). Employment discrimination: Authority figures' demographic preferences and followers' affective organizational commitment. *Journal of Applied Psychology, 93*(6), 1287–1300.

Peterson, C., & Park, N. (2007). Explanatory style and emotion regulation. In J. J. Gross (Ed.), *Handbook of emotion regulation* (pp. 159–179). New York: Guilford Press.

Peterson, C., & Seligman, M. E. P. (1984). Causal explanations as a risk factor for depression: Theory and evidence. *Psychological Review, 91*, 347–374.

Peterson, R. D., & Bailey, W. C. (1988). Murder and capital punishment in the evolving context of the post–Furman era. *Social Forces, 66*, 774–807.

Petrie, K. J., Booth, R. J., & Pennebaker, J. W. (1998). The immunological effects of thought suppression. *Journal of Personality and Social Psychology, 75*, 1264–1272.

Petrie, T. A., Austin, L. J., Crowley, B. J., Helmcamp, A., Johnson, C. E., Lester, R., . . . Walbrick, K. (1996). Sociocultural expectations for attractiveness for males. *Sex Roles, 35*, 581–602.

Pettigrew, T., & Tropp, L. (2006). A meta-analytic test of intergroup contact theory. *Journal of Personality and Social Psychology, 90*, 751–783.

Pettigrew, T. F. (1958). Personality and sociocultural factors and intergroup attitudes: A cross-national comparison. *Journal of Conflict Resolution, 2*, 29–42.

Pettigrew, T. F. (1969). Racially separate or together? *Journal of Social Issues, 25*, 43–69.

Pettigrew, T. F. (1979). The ultimate attribution error: Extending Allport's cognitive analysis of prejudice. *Personality and Social Psychology Bulletin, 5*, 461–476.

Pettigrew, T. F. (1985). New black-white patterns: How best to conceptualize them? *Annual Review of Sociology, 11*, 329–346.

Pettigrew, T. F. (1991). Normative theory in intergroup relations: Explaining both harmony and conflict. Special Issue: Conflict and harmony in pluralistic societies. *Psychology and Developing Societies, 3*, 3–16.

Pettijohn, T. F., II & Jungeberg, B. J. (2004). Playboy playmate curves: Changes in facial and body feature preferences across social and economic conditions. *Personality and Social Psychology Bulletin, 30*(9), 1186–1197.

Petty, R. E., Cacioppo, J. T., Strathman, A. J., & Priester, J. R. (2005). To think or not to think: Exploring two routes to persuasion. In T. C. Brock & M. C. Green (Eds.), *Persuasion: Psychological insights and perspectives* (pp. 81–116). Thousand Oaks, CA: Sage Publications, Inc.

Petty, R. E. (1995). Attitude change. In A. Tesser (Ed.), *Advanced social psychology* (pp. 195–255). New York: McGraw-Hill.

Petty, R. E., & Cacioppo, J. T. (1986). *Communication and persuasion: Central and peripheral routes to attitude change*. New York: Springer-Verlag.

Petty, R. E., Haugtvedt, C. P., & Smith, S. M. (1995). Elaboration as a determinant of attitude strength. In R. E. Petty & J. A. Krosnick (Eds.), *Attitude strength: Antecedents and consequences* (pp. 93–130). Mahwah, NJ: Erlbaum.

Petty, R. E., & Wegener, D. T. (1999). The elaboration likelihood model: Current status and controversies. In S. Chaiken & Y. Trope (Eds.), *Dual-process theories in social psychology* (pp. 41–72). New York: Guilford Press.

Petty, R. E., Wegener, D. T., & Fabrigar, L. R. (1997). Attitudes and attitude change. *Annual Review of Psychology, 48*, 609–647.

Pezdek, K., & Banks, W. P. (Eds). (1996). *The recovered memory/false memory debate*. San Diego, CA: Academic Press.

Pfeifer, J. E. (1997). Social psychology in the courtroom. In S. W. Sadava & D. R. McCreary (Eds.), *Applied social psychology*. Upper Saddle River, New Jersey: Prentice-Hall.

Pfeifer, J. E., & Ogloff, J. R. P. (1991). Ambiguity and guilt determinations: A modern racism perspective. *Journal of Applied Social Psychology, 21*, 1713–1725.

Pfeifer, J. E., & Ogloff, J. R. P. (2003). Mock juror ratings of guilt in Canada: Modern racism and ethnic heritage. *Social Behavior and Personality, 31*(3), 301–312.

Philippe, F. L., Vallerand, R. J., Houlfort, N., Lavigne, G. L., & Donahue, E. G. (2010). Passion for an activity and quality of interpersonal relationships: The mediating role of emotions. *Journal of Personality and Social Psychology, 98*(6), 917–932.

Phillips, A. G., & Silvia, P. J. (2005). Self-awareness and the emotional consequences of self-discrepancies. *Personality and Social Psychology Bulletin, 31*, 703–713.

Pickel, K. (2007). Remembering and identifying menacing perpetrators: Exposure to violence and the weapon focus effect. In R. C. L. Lindsay, D. F. Ross, J. D. Read, & M. P. Toglia (Eds.), *The handbook of eyewitness psychology, Vol II: Memory for people* (pp. 339–360). Mahwah, NJ: Lawrence Erlbaum.

Pickel, K. L. (1998). Unusualness and threat as possible causes of "weapons focus." *Memory, 6*, 277–295.

Pickett, C. L., Silver, M. D., & Brewer, M. B. (2002). The impact of assimilation and differentiation needs on perceived group importance and judgments of ingroup size. *Personality and Social Psychology Bulletin, 28*, 546–558.

Pierce, R. S., Frone, M. R., Russell, M., & Cooper, M. L. (1996). Financial stress, social support, and alcohol involvement: A longitudinal test of the buffering hypothesis in a general population survey. *Health Psychology, 15*, 38–47.

Pierce, T., & Lydon, J. E. (2001). Global and specific relational models in the experience of social interactions. *Journal of Personality and Social Psychology, 80*, 613–631.

Piferi, R. L., Jobe, R. L., & Jones, W. H. (2006). Giving to others during national tragedy: The effects of altruistic and egoistic motivations on long-term giving. *Journal of Social and Personal Relationships, 23*, 171–184.

Piff, P. K., Kraus, M. W., Côté, S., Cheng, B., & Keltner, D. (2010). Having less, giving more: The influence of social class on prosocial behavior. *Journal of Personality and Social Psychology, 99*(5), 771–784.

Pihl, R. O., & Hoaken, P. N. S. (2002). Biological bases of addiction and aggression in close relationships. In C. Wekerle, & A. Wall (Eds.), *The violence and addiction equation* (pp. 25–43). New York: Taylor & Francis.

Pihl, R. O., & Peterson, J. (1995). Drugs and aggression: Correlations, crime and human manipulative studies and some proposed mechanisms. *Journal of Psychiatric Neuroscience, 20*, 141–149.

Pihl, R. O., Young, S. N., Harden, P., Plotnick, S., Chamberlain, B., & Ervin, F. R. (1995). Acute effect of altered tryptophan levels and alcohol on aggression in normal human males. *Psychopharmacology, 119*, 353–360.

Pika, S., Nicoladis, E., & Marentette, P. (2009). How to order a beer: Cultural differences in the use of conventional gestures for numbers. *Journal of Cross-Cultural Psychology, 40*(1), 70–80.

Piliavin, I. M., Piliavin, J. A., & Rodin, J. (1975). Costs, diffusion, and the stigmatized victim. *Journal of Personality and Social Psychology, 32*, 429–438.

Piliavin, J. A., & Charng, H. (1990). Altruism: A review of recent theory and research. *Annual Review of Sociology, 16*, 27–65.

Piliavin, J. A., Dovidio, J. F., Gaertner, S., & Clark, R. D., II (1981). *Emergency intervention*. New York: Academic Press.

Piliavin, J. A., & Piliavin, I. M. (1972). The effect of blood on reactions to a victim. *Journal of Personality and Social Psychology, 23*, 253–261.

Pincus, W. (2006, February 10). Ex-CIA official faults use of data on Iraq. *Washington Post*, p. A1.

Pinker, S. (2002). *The blank slate: The modern denial of human nature*. New York: Viking.

Pinkus, R. T., Lockwood, P., Schimmack, U., & Fournier, M. A. (2008). For better and worse: Everyday social comparisons between romantic partners. *Journal of Personality and Social Psychology, 95*, 1180–1201.

Pitman, R., & Scharfe, E. (2010). Testing the function of attachment hierarchies during emerging adulthood. *Personal Relationships, 17*(2), 201–216.

Plaks, J. E., & Stecher, K. (2007). Unexpected improvement, decline, and stasis: A prediction confidence perspective on achievement success and failure. *Journal of Personality and Social Psychology, 93*, 667–684.

Plant, E. A., & Devine, P. G. (2003). The antecedents and implication of interracial anxiety. *Personality and Social Psychology Bulletin, 29*(6), 790–801.

Plante, I., Théorêt, M., & Favreau, O. (2009). Student gender stereotypes: Contrasting the perceived maleness and femaleness of mathematics and language. *Educational Psychology, 29*(4), 385–405.

Pliner, P., Rizvi, S., & Remick, A. K. (2009). Competition affects food choice in women. *International Journal of Eating Disorders, 42*(6), 557–564.

Pliner, P., & Zec, D. (2007). Meal schemas during a preload decrease subsequent eating. *Appetite, 48*(3), 278–288.

Pope, H. G., Jr., Olivardia, R., Gruber, A. J., & Borowiecki, J. (1999). Evolving ideals of male body image as seen through action toys. *International Journal of Eating Disorders, 26*, 65–72.

Pope, H. G., Jr., Phillips, K. A., & Olivardia, R. (2000). *The Adonis complex: The secret crisis of male body obsession*. New York: Freeman.

Porter, J. R. (1971). *Black child, white child: The development of racial attitudes*. Cambridge, MA: Harvard University Press.

Porter, J. R., & Washington, R. E. (1979). Black identity and self-esteem, 1968–1978. *Annual Review of Sociology*. Stanford, CA: Annual Reviews.

Porter, J. R., & Washington, R. E. (1989). Developments in research on black identity and self-esteem, 1979–1988. *Revue Internationale de Psychologie Sociale, 2*, 339–353.

Porter, S., Peace, K. A., & Emmett, K. A. (2007). You protest too much, methinks: Investigating the features of truthful and fabricated reports of traumatic experiences. *Canadian Journal of Behavioural Science, 39*, 79–91.

Porter, S., Spencer, L., & Birt, A. R. (2003). Blinded by emotion? Effect of the emotionality of a scene on susceptibility to false memories. *Canadian Journal of Behavioural Science, 35*, 165–175.

Porter, S., Woodworth, M., & Birt, A. (2000). Truth, lies, and videotape: An investigation of the ability of federal parole officers to detect deception. *Law and Human Behavior, 24*, 643–658.

Posada, S., & Colell, M. (2007). Another gorilla (Gorilla gorilla gorilla) recognizes himself in a mirror. *American Journal of Primatology, 69*(5), 576–583.

Post, S. G., Underwood, L.G., Schloss, J. P., & Hurlbut, W. B. (Eds). (2002). *Altruism & altruistic love: Science, philosophy, and religion in dialogue*. New York: Oxford University Press.

Postmes, T., & Spears, R. (1998). Deindividuation and antinormative behavior: A meta-analysis. *Psychological Bulletin, 123*, 238–259.

Postmes, T., Spears, R., & Cihangir, S. (2001). Quality of decision making and group norms. *Journal of Personality and Social Psychology, 80*, 918–930.

Potter, R., & Brewer, N. (1999). Perceptions of witness behavior-accuracy relationships held by police, lawyers, and mock-jurors. *Psychiatry, Psychology, and Law, 6*, 97–103.

Pozzulo, J. D., Crescini, C., & Lemieux, J. T. (2008). Are accurate witnesses more likely to make absolute judgments? *International Journal of Law and Psychiatry, 31*(6), 495–501.

Pozzulo, J. D., Crescini, C., & Panton, T. (2008). Does methodology matter in eyewitness identification research? The effect of live versus video exposure on eyewitness identification accuracy. *International Journal of Law and Psychiatry, 31*(5), 430–437.

Pozzulo, J. D., Dempsey, J., Maeder, E., & Allen, L. (2010). The effects of victim gender, defendant gender, and defendant age on juror decision making. *Criminal Justice and Behavior, 37*(1), 47–63.

Pozzulo, J. D., & Dempsey, J. L. (2009a). The effect of eyewitness testimonial consistency and type of identification decision on juror decision making. *American Journal of Forensic Psychology, 27*, 49–69.

Pozzulo, J. D., & Dempsey, J. L. (2009b). Witness factors and their influence on jurors' perceptions and verdicts. *Criminal Justice and Behavior, 36*, 923–934.

Pozzulo, J. D., Lemieux, J. T., Wilson, A., Crescini, C., & Girardi, A. (2009). The influence of identification decision and DNA evidence on juror decision making. *Journal of Applied Social Psychology, 39*(9), 2069–2088.

Pratkanis, A. R. (1992). The cargo-cult science of subliminal persuasion. *Skeptical Inquirer, 16*, 260–272.

Pratkanis, A. R., & Aronson, E. (1991). Subliminal sorcery: Who is seducing whom? *USA Today, 120*, 64–66.

Pratt, T. C., Cullen, F. T., Blevins, K. R., Daigle, L. E., & Madensen, T. D. (Eds.) (2006). *The empirical status of deterrence theory*. New Brunswick, NJ: Transaction.

Pratto, F., Sidanius, J., Stallworth, L. M., & Malle, B. F. (1994). Social dominance orientation: A personality variable predicting social and political attitudes. *Journal of Personality and Social Psychology, 67*, 741–763.

Pratto, F., Sidanius, J., Stallworth, L. M., & Malle, B. F. (2000). Social dominance orientation: A personality variable predicting social and political attitudes. In C. Stangor, & C. Stangor (Eds.), *Stereotypes and prejudice: Essential readings* (pp. 259–288). New York: Psychology Press.

Prentice-Dunn, S., & Rogers, R. W. (1989). Deindividuation and the self-regulation of behavior. In P. B. Paulus (Ed.), *Psychology of group influence* (2nd ed., pp. 87–109). Hillsdale, NJ: Erlbaum.

Proctor, J. (2007, June 21). Talk of the devil. The Current. [Radio broadcast.] Canadian Broadcasting Corporation.

Pronin, E., Berger, J., & Molouki, S. (2007). Alone in a crowd of sheep: Asymmetric perceptions of conformity and their roots in an introspection illusion. *Journal of Personality and Social Psychology, 92*(4), 585–595.

Pronin, E., Lin, D. Y., & Ross, L. (2002). The bias blind spot: Perceptions of bias in self versus others. *Personality and Social Psychology Bulletin, 28*, 369–381.

Pronin, E., Gilovich, T., & Ross, L. (2004). Objectivity in the eye of the beholder: Divergent perceptions of bias in self versus others. *Psychological Review, 111*, 781–799.

Pruegger, V. J., & Rogers, T. B. (1993). Development of a scale to measure cross-cultural sensitivity in the Canadian context. *Canadian Journal of Behavioural Science, 25*, 615–621.

Pruitt, D. G. (1998). Social conflict. In D. Gilbert, S. Fiske, & G. Lindzey (Eds.), *The handbook of social psychology* (4th ed., Vol. 2, pp. 470–503). New York: McGraw Hill.

Pruitt, D. G., & Kimmel, M. J. (1977). Twenty years of experimental gaming: Critique, synthesis, and suggestions for the future. *Annual Review of Psychology, 28*, 363–392.

Qin, J., Ogle, C., & Goodman, G. (2008). Adults' memories of childhood: True and false reports. *Journal of Experimental Psychology: Applied, 14*, 373–391.

Quan-Haase, A. (2007). University students' local and distant social ties: Using and integrating modes of communication on campus. *Information, Communication & Society, 10*(5), 671–693.

Quattrone, G. A. (1982). Behavioral consequences of attributional bias. *Social Cognition, 1*, 358–378.

Quattrone, G. A. (1986). On the perception of a group's variability. In S. Worchel & W. G. Austin (Eds.), *Psychology of intergroup relations* (2nd ed). Chicago, IL: Nelson-Hall.

Quattrone, G. A., & Jones, E. E. (1980). The perception of variability within ingroups and outgroups: Implications for the law of small numbers. *Journal of Personality and Social Psychology, 38*, 141–152.

Quick stats binge drinking (2008). Department of Health and Human Services, Center for Disease Control and Prevention. Retrieved from http://www.cdc.gov/alcohol/quickstats/binge_drinking.htm

Quinn, K. A., Macrae, C. N., & Bodenhausen, G. V. (2003). Stereotyping and impression formation: How categorical thinking shapes person perception. In M. A. Hogg & J. Cooper (Eds.), *Sage handbook of social psychology* (pp. 87–109). Thousand Oaks, CA: Sage.

Quinn, K. A., Roese, N. J., Penington, G. L., & Olson, J. M. (1999). The personal/group discrimination discrepancy: The role of informational complexity. *Personality and Social Psychology Bulletin, 25*, 1430–1440.

R. v. *Ewanchuk* (1998). Alberta Court of Appeal, 52. Retrieved from www.albertacourts.ab.ca/webpage/jdb/current_judgments-ca.htm

Rajecki, D. W., Kidd, R. F., & Ivins, B. (1976). Social facilitation in chickens: A different level of analysis. *Journal of Experimental Social Psychology, 12*, 233–246.

Ramsey, S. J. (1981). The kinesics of femininity in Japanese women. *Language Sciences, 3*, 104–123.

Rapoport, A., & Chammah, A. M. (1965). *Prisoner's Dilemma: A study in conflict and cooperation*. Ann Arbor, MI: University of Michigan Press.

Raps, C. S., Peterson, C., Jonas, M., & Seligman, M. E. P. (1982). Patient behavior in hospitals: Helplessness, reactance, or both? *Journal of Personality and Social Psychology, 42*, 1036–1041.

Raskin, D. C., Honts, C. R., & Kircher, J. C. (1997). The scientific status of research on polygraph techniques: The case for polygraph tests. In D. L. Faigman, D. H. Kaye, M. J. Saks, & J. Sanders (Eds.), *Modern scientific evidence: The law and science of expert testimony* (pp. 565–582). St. Paul, MN: West.

Ratelle, C. F., Baldwin, M. W., & Vallerand, R. J. (2005). On the cued activation of situational motivation. *Journal of Experimental Social Psychology, 41*, 482–487.

Read, J. D., Connolly, D., & Turtle, J. W. (2001). Memory in legal contexts: Remembering events, circumstances, and people. In R. A. Schuller & J. R. P. Ogloff (Eds), *Introduction to psychology and law: Canadian perspectives* (pp. 95–125). Toronto, ON: University of Toronto Press.

Redersdorff, S., & Guimond, S. (2006). Comparing oneself over time: the temporal dimension of social comparison. In S. Guimond (Ed.), *Social comparison and social psychology* (pp. 76–96). New York: Cambridge University Press.

Reeves, R. A., Baker, G. A., Boyd, J. G., & Cialdini, R. B. (1991). The door-in-the-face technique: Reciprocal concessions vs. self- presentational explanations. *Journal of Social Behavior and Personality, 6*, 545–558.

Regan, P. C. (1998). Of lust and love: Beliefs about the role of sexual desire in romantic relationships. *Personal Relationships, 5*, 139–157.

Regan, P. C., & Berscheid, E. (1995). Gender differences in beliefs about the causes of male and female sexual desire. *Personal Relationships, 2*, 345–358.

Regan, P. C., & Berscheid, E. (1997). Gender differences in characteristics desired in a potential sexual and marriage partner. *Journal of Psychology and Human Sexuality, 9*, 25–37.

Regan, P. C., & Berscheid, E. (1999). *Lust: What we know about human sexual desire*. Thousand Oaks, CA: Sage.

Regan, P. C., Snyder, M., & Kassin, S. M. (1995). Unrealistic optimism: Self-enhancement or person positivity? *Personality and Social Psychology Bulletin, 21*, 1073–1082.

Regehr, C., Cadell, S., & Jansen, K. (1999). Perceptions of control and long-term recovery from rape. *American Journal of Orthopsychiatry, 69*, 110–115.

Regoeczi, W. (2008). Crowding in context: An examination of the differential responses of men and women to high-density living environments. *Journal of Health and Social Behavior, 49*(3), 254–268.

Rehm, J., Steinleitner, M., & Lilli, W. (1987). Wearing uniforms and aggression: A field experiment. *European Journal of Social Psychology, 17*, 357–360.

Reifman, A. S., Larrick, R., & Fein, S. (1988). *The heat-aggression relationship in major-league baseball*. Paper presented at the meeting of the American Psychological Association, San Francisco.

Reis, H. T., Clark, M. S., & Holmes, J. G. (2004). Perceived partner responsiveness as an organizing construct in the study of intimacy and closeness. In D. J. Mashek & A. Aron (Eds.), *Handbook of closeness and intimacy* (pp. 201–225). New York: Oxford University Press.

Reis, H. T., & Judd, C.M. (Eds). (2000). *Handbook of research methods in social and personality psychology*. New York, NY: Cambridge University Press.

Reis, H. T., Maniaci, M. R., Caprariello, P. A., Eastwick, P. W., & Finkel, E. J. (2011, March 7). Familiarity does indeed promote attraction in live interaction. *Journal of Personality and Social Psychology, 101*(3), 557–570. Advance online publication.

Reis, H. T., Nezlek, J., & Wheeler, L. (1980). Physical attractiveness in social interaction. *Journal of Personality and Social Psychology, 38*, 604–617.

Reis, H. T., Wheeler, L., Speigel, N., Kernis, M. H., Nezlek, J., & Perri, M. (1982). Physical attractiveness in social interaction 2: Why does appearance affect social experience? *Journal of Personality and Social Psychology, 43*, 979–996.

Reiss, D., & Marino, L. (2001). Mirror self-recognition in the bottlenose dophin: A case of cognitive convergence. *Proceedings of the National Academy of Sciences, 98*, 5937–5942.

Reiter, S. M., & Samuel, W. (1980). Littering as a function of prior litter and the presence or absence of prohibitive signs. *Journal of Applied Social Psychology, 10*, 45–55.

Rempel, J. K., & Burris, C. T. (2006). Push-you-pull-you: The boundaried self in close relationships. *Personality and Social Psychology Bulletin, 32*, 256–269.

Rempel, J. K., Ross, M., & Holmes, J. G. (2001). Trust and communicated attributions in close relationships. *Journal of Personality and Social Psychology, 81*, 57–64.

Renaud, J. M., & McConnell, A. R. (2002). Organization of the self-concept and the suppression of self-relevant thoughts. *Journal of Experimental Social Psychology, 38*, 79–86.

Renaud-Dubé, A., Taylor, G., Lekes, N., Koestner, R., & Guay, F. (2010). Adolescents' motivation toward the environment: Age-related trends and correlates. *Canadian Journal of Behavioural Science, 42*(3), 194–199.

Renner, M. J., & Mackin, R. S. (1998). A life stress instrument for classroom use. *Teaching of Psychology, 25*, 46–48.

Reno, R. R., Cialdini, R. B., & Kallgren, C. A. (1993). The transsituational influence of social norms. *Journal of Personality and Social Psychology, 64*, 104–112.

Rensink, R. A. (2002). Change detection. *Annual Review of Psychology, 53*, 245–277.

Rentfrow, P. J., & Gosling, S. D. (2006). Message in a ballad: The role of music preferences in interpersonal perception. *Psychological Science, 17*, 236–242.

Reynolds, L. (2000, March 22). Some folks call Tillie "a miracle worker." *Winnipeg Free Press*, p. D3.

Rhodes, G., Yoshikawa, S., Clark, A., Lee, K., McKay, R., & Akamatsu, S. (2001). Attractiveness of facial averageness and symmetry in non-Western cultures: In search of biologically based standards of beauty. *Perception, 30*, 611–625.

Rhodes, N., & Wood, W. (1992). Self-esteem and intelligence affect influenceability: The mediating role of message reception. *Psychological Bulletin, 111*, 156–171.

Rhodes, R. E., & Blanchard, C. M. (2008). Do sedentary motives adversely affect physical activity? Adding cross-behavioural cognitions to the theory of planned behaviour. *Psychology & Health, 23*(7), 789–805.

Rholes, W. S., Newman, L. S., & Ruble, D. N. (1990). Understanding self and other: Developmental and motivational aspects of perceiving persons in terms of invariant dispositions. In E. T. Higgins & R. M. Sorrentino (Eds.), *Handbook of motivation and cognition: Foundations of social behavior* (Vol. 2). New York: Guilford.

Ricciardelli, L. A., & McCabe, M. P. (2003). A longitudinal analysis of the role of psychosocial factors in predicting body change strat egies among adolescent boys. *Sex Roles, 48*, 349–360.

Richards, J. M., & Gross, J. J. (1999). Composure at any cost? The cognitive consequences of emotion suppression. *Personality and Social Psychology Bulletin, 25*, 1033–1044.

Richardson, D., Hammock, G., Smith, S., & Gardner, W. (1994). Empathy as a cognitive inhibitor of interpersonal aggression. *Aggressive Behavior, 20*, 275–289.

Richardson, H. R. L., Beazley, R. P., Delaney, M. E., & Langille, D. E. (1997). Factors influencing condom use among students attending high school in Nova Scotia. *Canadian Journal of Human Sexuality*, 6, 185–196.

Rigby, K., & Johnson, B. (2006–2007). Playground heroes. *Greater Good, 3*(2), 14–17.

Rigby, K., Smith, P. K., & Pepler, D. (2004). Working to prevent school bullying: Key issues. In P. K. Smith, D. Pepler, & K. Rigby (Eds.), *Bullying in schools: How successful can interventions be?* (pp. 1–12). Cambridge, UK: Cambridge University Press.

Riggs, J. M., & Gumbrecht, L. B. (2005). Correspondence bias and American sentiment in the wake of September 11, 2001. *Journal of Applied Social Psychology, 35*, 15–28.

Riley, S. (2011, March 8). The orgy of pointless polling analysis. *Winnipeg Free Press*, p. A10.

Riley, T., & Ungerleider, C. (2008). Preservice teachers' discriminatory judgments. *Alberta Journal of Educational Research, 54*(4), 378–387.

Ringelmann, M. (1913). Recherches sur les moteurs animés: Travail de l'homme. *Annales de l'Institut National Argonomique, 12*, 2e srie, 1–40.

Riordan, C. A. (1978). Equal-status interracial contact: A review and revision of a concept. *International Journal of Intercultural Relations, 2*, 161–185.

Risen, J. L., & Gilovich, T. (2007). Target and observer differences in the acceptance of questionable apologies. *Journal of Personality and Social Psychology, 92*(3), 418–433.

Roberts, M. (2008, July 22). Polygamist leader charged with sexual assault. Associated Press. *Globe and Mail.*

Roberts, M. (2008, August 5). Texas child welfare officials want 8 children from sect back in state care. Associated Press. *Globe and Mail.*

Roberts, W., & Strayer, J. (1996). Empathy, emotional expressiveness, and prosocial behavior. *Child Development, 67*, 449–470.

Robins, R. W., & Beer, J. S. (2001). Positive illusions about the self: Short-term benefits and long-term costs. *Journal of Personality and Social Psychology, 80*, 340–352.

Robins, R. W., Spranca, M. D., & Mendelsohn, G. A. (1996). The actor-observer effect revisited: Effects of individual differences and repeated social interactions on actor and observer attributions. *Journal of Personality and Social Psychology, 71*, 375–389.

Robinson, A. (2010, January 22). Heading to Haiti to help. Retrieved from http://telgraphjournal.canadaeast.com/rss/article/929057

Robson, M. (2005, July 30). We must fight terror: PM. *Winnipeg Free Press*, p. A3.

Rodin, J. (1986). Aging and health: Effects of the sense of control. *Science, 233*, 1271–1276.

Rodin, J., & Langer, E. J. (1977). Long-term effects of a control- relevant intervention with the institutional aged. *Journal of Personality and Social Psychology, 35*, 897–902.

Rodrigo, M. F., & Ato, M. (2002). Testing the group polarization hypothesis by using logit models. *European Journal of Social Psychology, 32*, 3–18.

Roesch, S. C., & Amirkhan, J. H. (1997). Boundary conditions for self-serving attributions: Another look at the sports pages. *Journal of Applied Social Psychology, 27*, 245–261.

Roese, N. J. (1994). The functional basis of counterfactual thinking. *Journal of Personality and Social Psychology, 66*, 805–818.

Roese, N. J. (1997). Counterfactual thinking. *Psychological Bulletin, 121*, 133–148.

Roese, N. J., & Olson, J. M. (1993). Self-esteem and counterfactual thinking. *Journal of Personality and Social Psychology, 65*, 199–206.

Roese, N. J., & Olson, J. M. (1995). Outcome controllability and counterfactual thinking. *Personality and Social Psychology Bulletin, 21*, 620–628.

Roese, N. J., & Olson, J. M. (1996). Counterfactuals, causal attributions, and the hindsight bias: A conceptual integration. *Journal of Experimental Social Psychology, 32*, 197–227.

Roese, N. J., & Olson, J. M. (1997). Counterfactual thinking: The intersection of affect and function. In M. Zanna (Ed.), *Advances in experimental social psychology* (Vol. 29). San Diego, CA: Academic Press.

Rogers, P. (1998). The cognitive psychology of lottery gambling: A theoretical review. *Journal of Gambling Studies, 14*, 111–134.

Rogers, R. (1983). Cognitive and physiological processes in fear appeals and attitude change: A revised theory of protection motivation. In J. T. Cacioppo & R. E. Petty (Eds.), *Social psychophysiology: A sourcebook* (pp. 153–176). New York: Guilford Press.

Rohan, M., & Zanna, M. (1996). Value transmission in families. In C. Seligman, J. Olson, & M. Zanna (Eds.), *The psychology of values: The Ontario symposium on personality and social psychology* (Vol. 8, pp. 253–276). Mahwah, NJ: Erlbaum.

Rokach, A., & Wanklyn, S. (2009). Motivation to volunteer: Helping empower sick children. *Psychology and Education: An Interdisciplinary Journal, 46*(1), 7–25.

Rollason, K. (2008, June 21). Teen's last words haunt family. *Winnipeg Free Press*, p. A5.

Rollason, K. (2011, February, 18). Bullying posted on Facebook. Retrieved from http://www.winnipegfreepress.com/local/bullying-posted-on-facebook-116459638.html

Rosch, E., & Lloyd, B. (Eds). (1978). *Cognition and categorization.* Hillsdale, NJ: Erlbaum.

Rose, V. G., & Ogloff, J. R. P. (2001). Evaluating the comprehensibility of jury instructions: A method and an example. *Law and Human Behavior, 25*, 409–431.

Rosenbaum, M. E. (1986). The repulsion hypothesis: On the non development of relationships. *Journal of Personality and Social Psychology, 51*, 1156–1166.

Rosenberg, L. A. (1961). Group size, prior experience, and conformity. *Journal of Abnormal and Social Psychology, 63*, 436–437.

Rosenberg, M. J., Davidson, A. J., Chen, J., Judson, F. N., & Douglas, J. M. (1992). Barrier contraceptives and sexually transmitted diseases in women: A comparison of female-dependent methods and condoms. *American Journal of Public Health, 82*, 669–674.

Rosenblatt, P. C. (1974). Cross-cultural perspectives on attraction. In T. L. Huston (Ed.), *Foundations of interpersonal attraction* (pp. 79–99). New York: Academic Press.

Rosenhan, D. L. (1970). The natural socialization of altruistic autonomy. In J. R. Macaulay & L. Berkowitz (Eds.), *Altruism and helping behavior* (pp. 251–268). New York: Academic Press.

Rosenman, R. H. (1993). Relationship of the Type A behavior pattern with coronary heart disease. In L. Goldberger & S. Breznitz (Eds.), *Handbook of stress: Theoretical and clinical aspects* (2nd ed., pp. 449–476). New York: Free Press.

Rosenthal, A. M. (1964). *Thirty-eight witnesses*. New York: McGraw-Hill.

Rosenthal, R. (1994). Interpersonal expectancy effects: A 30-year perspective. *Current Directions in Psychological Science, 3*, 176–179.

Rosenthal, R. (1995). Critiquing Pygmalion: A 25-year perspective. *Current Directions in Psychological Science, 4*, 171–172.

Rosenthal, R., & De Paulo, B. M. (1979). Sex differences in accommodation in nonverbal communication. In R. Rosenthal (Ed.), *Skill in nonverbal communication: Individual differences* (pp. 68–103). Cambridge, MA: Oelgeschlager, Gunn & Hain.

Rosenthal, R., & Jacobson, L. (1968). *Pygmalion in the classroom: Teacher expectation and student intellectual development.* New York: Holt, Rinehart & Winston.

Ross, L. (1977). The intuitive psychologist and his shortcomings: Distortions in the attribution process. In L. Berkowitz (Ed.), *Advances in experimental social psychology* (Vol. 10, pp. 173–220). Orlando, FL: Academic Press.

Ross, L. (1998). Comment on Gilbert. In J. M. Darley & J. Cooper (Eds.), *Attribution and social interaction* (pp. 53–66). Washington, DC: American Psychological Association.

Ross, L., Amabile, T. M., & Steinmetz, J. L. (1977). Social roles, social control, and biases in social perception. *Journal of Personality and Social Psychology, 35*, 485–494.

Ross, L., Lepper, M. R., & Hubbard, M. (1975). Perseverance in self perception and social perception: Biased attributional processes in the debriefing paradigm. *Journal of Personality and Social Psychology, 32*, 880–892.

Ross, L., & Nisbett, R. E. (1991). *The person and the situation: Perspectives of social psychology*. New York: McGraw-Hill.

Ross, L., & Samuels, S. M. (1993). *The predictive power of personal reputation versus labels and construal in the Prisoner's Dilemma game.* Unpublished manuscript, Stanford University.

Ross, L., & Ward, A. (1995). Psychological barriers to dispute resolution. In M. P. Zanna (Ed.), *Advances in experimental social psychology* (Vol. 27, pp. 255–304). San Diego, CA: Academic Press.

Ross, L., & Ward, A. (1996). Naive realism: Implications for social conflict and misunderstanding. In T. Brown, E. Reed, & E. Turiel (Eds.), *Values and knowledge* (pp. 103–135). Hillsdale, NJ: Erlbaum.

Ross, L. R., & Spinner, B. (2001). General and specific attachment representations in adulthood: Is there a relationship? *Journal of Social and Personal Relationships, 18*, 747–766.

Ross, M., Heine, S. J., Wilson, A. E., & Sugimori, S. (2005). Cross- cultural discrepancies in self-appraisals. *Personality and Social Psychology Bulletin, 31*, 1175–1188.

Ross, M., McFarland, C., Conway, M., & Zanna, M. P. (1983). Reciprocal relation between attitudes and behavior recall: Committing people to newly formed attitudes. *Journal of Personality and Social Psychology, 45*, 257–267.

Ross, M., & Olson, J. M. (1981). An expectancy-attribution model of the effects of placebos. *Psychological Review, 88*, 408–437.

Ross, M., & Sicoly, F. (1979). Egocentric biases in availability and attribution. *Journal of Personality and Social Psychology, 45*, 257–267.

Ross, M., & Wilson, A. E. (2002). It feels like yesterday: Self-esteem, valence of personal past experiences, and judgments of subjective distance. *Journal of Personality and Social Psychology, 82*, 792–803.

Ross, M., Xun, W. Q. E., & Wilson, A. E. (2002). Language and the bicultural self. *Personality and Social Psychology Bulletin, 28*, 1040–1050.

Ross, W., & La Croix, J. (1996). Multiple meanings of trust in negotiation theory and research: A literature review and integrative model. *International Journal of Conflict Management, 7*, 314–360.

Roszell, P., Kennedy, D., & Grabb, E. (1989). Physical attractiveness and income attainment among Canadians. *Journal of Psychology, 123*, 547–559.

Rotenberg, K. J. (1998). Stigmatizations of transitions in loneliness. *Journal of Social and Personal Relationships, 15*, 565–576.

Rothman, A. J. (2000). Toward a theory-based analysis of behavioral maintenance. *Health Psychology, 19*, 64–69.

Rothman, A. J., & Hardin, C. D. (1997). Differential use of the availability heuristic in social judgment. *Personality and Social Psychology Bulletin, 23*, 123–138.

Rothman, A. J., Martino, S. C., Bedell, B. T., Detweiler, J. B., & Salovey, P. (1999). The systematic influence of gain- and loss-framed messages on interest in and use of different types of health behavior. *Personality and Social Psychology Bulletin, 25*, 1355–1369.

Rothman, A. J., & Salovey, P. (1997). Shaping perceptions to motivate healthy behavior: The role of message framing. *Psychological Bulletin, 121*, 3–19.

Rothman, A. J., Salovey, P., Antone, C., Keough, K., & Martin, C. D. (1993). The influence of message framing on intentions to perform health behaviors. *Journal of Experimental Social Psychology, 29*, 408–432.

Rubenfeld, S., Clément, R., Vinograd, J., Lussier, D., Amireault, V., Auger, R., & Lebrun, M. (2007). Becoming a cultural intermediary: A further social corollary of second-language learning. *Journal of Language and Social Psychology, 26*(2), 182–203.

Rubenfeld, S., Sinclair, L., & Clément, R. (2007). Second language learning and acculturation: The role of motivation and goal congruence. *Canadian Journal of Applied Linguistics, 10*, 309–324.

Rubin, Z. (1970). Measurement of romantic love. *Journal of Personality and Social Psychology, 16*, 265–273.

Rubin, Z. (1973). *Liking and loving: An invitation to social psychology*. New York: Holt, Rinehart & Winston.

Rubin, Z., Peplau, L. A., & Hill, C. T. (1981). Loving and leaving: Sex differences in romantic attachments. *Sex Roles, 7*, 821–835.

Rudman, L. A. (2004). Sources of implicit attitudes. *Current Directions in Psychological Science, 13*, 79–82.

Rudman, L. A., & Borgida, E. (1995). The afterglow of construct accessibility: The behavioral consequences of priming men to view women as sexual objects. *Journal of Experimental Social Psy chology, 31*, 493–517.

Rudman, L. A., Phelan, J. E., & Heppen, J. (2007). Developmental sources of implicit attitudes. *Personality and Social Psychology Bulletin, 33*(12), 1700–1713.

Ruggiero, K. M., & Taylor, D. M. (1995). Coping with discrimination: How disadvantaged group members perceive the discrimination that confronts them. *Journal of Personality and Social Psychology, 68*, 826–838.

Ruggiero, K. M., & Taylor, D. M. (1997). Why minority group members perceive or do not perceive the discrimination that confronts them: The role of self-esteem and perceived control. *Journal of Personality and Social Psychology, 72*, 373–389.

Rule, B. G., Taylor, B. R., & Dobbs, A. R. (1987). Priming affects of heat on aggressive thoughts. *Social Cognition, 5*, 131–143.

Rusbult, C. E. (1980). Commitment and satisfaction in romantic associations: A test of the investment model. *Journal of Experimental Social Psychology, 16*, 172–186.

Rusbult, C. E. (1983). A longitudinal test of the investment model: The development (and deterioration) of satisfaction and commitment in heterosexual involvements. *Journal of Personality and Social Psychology, 45*, 101–117.

Rusbult, C. E. (1991). *Commitment processes in close relationships: The investment model.* Paper presented at the meeting of the American Psychological Association, San Francisco.

Rusbult, C. E., & Buunk, A. P. (1993). Commitment processes in close relationships: An interdependence analysis. *Journal of Social and Personal Relationships, 10*, 175–204.

Rusbult, C. E., & Martz, J. M. (1995). Remaining in an abusive relationship: An investment model analysis of nonvoluntary dependence. *Personality and Social Psychology Bulletin, 21*, 558–571.

Rusbult, C. E., Martz, J. M., & Agnew, C. R. (1998). The investment model scale: Measuring commitment level, satisfaction level, quality of alternatives, and investment size. *Personal Relationships, 5*, 357–391.

Rusbult, C. E., Olsen, N., Davis, N. L., & Hannon, P. (2001). Committment and relationship maintenance mechanisms. In J. H. Harvey & A. Wenzel (Eds.), *Close romantic relationships: Maintenance and enhancement* (pp. 87–113). Mahwah, NJ: Lawrence Erlbaum Associates.

Rusbult, C. E., & Van Lange, P. A. M. (2003). Interdependence, interaction and relationships. *Annual Review of Psychology, 54*, 351–375.

Russell, F. (2008, March 12). Reckless, mean-spirited partisan without limit. *Winnipeg Free Press*, p. A13.

Russell, G. W. (1983). Psychological issues in sports aggression. In J. H. Goldstein (Ed.), *Sports violence* (pp. 157–181). New York: Springer-Verlag.

Russell, G. W., & Arms, R. L. (1998). Toward a social psychological profile of would-be rioters. *Aggressive Behavior, 24*, 219–226.

Russell, J. A. (1994). Is there universal recognition of emotion from facial expressions? A review of the cross-cultural studies. *Psychological Bulletin, 115*, 102–141.

Russell, J. A., & Fehr, B. (1987). Relativity in the perception of emotion in facial expressions. *Journal of Experimental Psychology: General, 116*, 223–237.

Russell, J. A., & Fehr, B. (1988). The role of context in interpreting facial expression: Reply to Ekman and O'Sullivan. *Journal of Experimental Psychology: General, 117*, 89–90.

Russell, J. A., & Fehr, B. (1994). Fuzzy concepts in a fuzzy hierarchy: Varieties of anger. *Journal of Personality and Social Psychology, 67*, 186–205.

Russell, J. A., Suzuki, N., & Ishida, N. (1993). Canadian, Greek, and Japanese freely produced emotion labels for facial expressions. *Motivation and Emotion, 17*, 337–351.

Rusting, C. L., & Nolen-Hoeksema, S. (1998). Regulating responses of anger: Effects of rumination and distraction on angry mood. *Journal of Personality and Social Psychology, 74*, 790–803.

Rutherford, M D., Chattha, H., & & Krysko, K. M. (2008) . The use of aftereffects in the study of relationships among emotion categories. *Journal of Experimental Psychology: Human Perception and Performance, 34* (1), 27–40.

Ruthig, J. C., Chipperfield, J. G., Bailis, D. S., & Perry, R. P. (2008). Perceived control and risk characteristics as predictors of older adults' health risk estimates. *Journal of Social Psychology, 148*(6), 667–688.

Ruthig, J. C., Chipperfield, J. G., Newall, N. E., Perry, R. P., & Hall, N. C. (2007). Detrimental effects of falling on health and well-being in later life: The mediating roles of perceived control and optimism. *Journal of Health Psychology, 12*(2), 231–248.

Ruthig, J. C., Haynes, T. L., Stupnisky, R. H., & Perry, R. P. (2009). Perceived academic control: Mediating the effects of optimism and social support on college students' psychological health. *Social Psychology of Education, 12*(2), 233–249.

Rutter, D. R., Quine, L., & Albery, I. P. (1998). Perceptions of risk in motorcyclists: Unrealistic optimism, relative realism, and predictions of behaviour. *British Journal of Psychology, 89*, 681–696.

Ryan, B., Jr. (1991). *It works! How investment spending in advertising pays off.* New York: American Association of Advertising Agencies.

Ryan, M. K., Haslam, S. A., Hersby, M. D., Kulich, C., & Atkins, C. (2008). Opting out or pushed off the edge? The glass cliff and the precariousness of women's leadership positions.Opting out or pushed off the edge? The glass cliff and the precariousness of women's leadership positions. *Social and Personality Psychology Compass, 2.* Retrieved from http://www.blackwell-compass.com/subject/socialpsychology/

Ryan, R. M., & Deci, E. L. (1996). When paradigms clash: Comments on Cameron and Pierce's claim that rewards do not undermine intrinsic motivation. *Review of Educational Research, 66*, 33–38.

Ryan, R. M., & Deci, E. L. (2000). Intrinsic and extrinsic rewards: Classic definitions and new directions. *Current Educational Psychology, 25*, 54–67.

Rydell, R. J., & Gawronski, B. (2009). I like you, I like you not: Understanding the formation of context-dependent automatic attitudes. *Cognition and Emotion, 23*(6), 1118–1152.

Rye, B. J., & Meaney, G. J. (2009). Impact of a homonegativity awareness workshop on attitudes toward homosexuality. *Journal of Homosexuality, 56*(1), 31–55.

Ryff, C. D., & B. H. Singer (Eds). (2001). *Emotion, social relationships, and health.* New York: Oxford University Press.

Sabatier, C., & Berry, J. W. (2008). The role of family acculturation, parental style, and perceived discrimination in the adaptation of second-generation immigrant youth in France and Canada. *European Journal of Developmental Psychology, 5*(2), 159–185.

Sabbane, L., Bellavance, F., & Chebat, J. (2009). Recency versus repetition priming effects of cigarette warnings on nonsmoking teenagers: The moderating effects of cigarette-brand familiarity. *Journal of Applied Social Psychology, 39*(3), 656–682.

Sabourin, M. (2007). The assessment of credibility: An analysis of truth and deception in a multiethnic environment. *Canadian Psychology, 48*(1), 24–31.

Sacks, O. (1987). *The man who mistook his wife for a hat and other clinical tales.* New York: Harper & Row.

Saewyc, E. M., Poon, C. S., Homma, Y., & Skay, C. L. (2008). Stigma management? The links between enacted stigma and teen pregnancy trends among gay, lesbian, and bisexual students in British Columbia. *Canadian Journal of Human Sexuality, 17*(3), 123–139.

Safdar, S., Friedlmeier, W., Matsumoto, D., Yoo, S.H., Kwantes, C.T., Kakai, H., & Shigemasu, E. (2009). Variations of emotional display rules within and across cultures. A comparison between Canada, USA, and Japan. *Canadian Journal of Behavioural Science, 41*(1), 1–10.

Saffrey, C., & Ehrenberg, M. (2007). When thinking hurts: Attachment, rumination, and postrelationship adjustment. *Personal Relationships, 14*(3), 351–368.

Sagarin, B. J., Cialdini, R. B., Rice, W. E., & Serna, S. B. (2002). Dispelling the illusion of invulnerability: The motivations and mechanisms of resistance to persuasion. *Journal of Personality and Social Psychology, 83*, 526–541.

Sahdra, B., & Ross, M. (2007). Group identification and historical memory. *Personality and Social Psychology Bulletin, 33*, 384–395.

Sakellaropoulo, M., & Baldwin, M. W. (2007). The hidden sides of self-esteem: Two dimensions of implicit self-esteem and their relation to narcissistic reactions. *Journal of Experimental Social Psychology, 43*, 995–1001.

Salganik, M. J., Dodds, P. S., & Watts, D. J. (2006). Experimental study of inequality and unpredictability in an artificial cultural market. *Science, 311*, 854–856.

Salovey, P., Mayer, J. D., & Rosenhan, D. L. (1991). Mood and helping: Mood as a motivator of helping and helping as a regulator of mood. In M. S. Clark (Ed.), *Prosocial behavior: Review of personality and social psychology* (Vol. 12, pp. 215–237). Newbury Park, CA: Sage.

Salovey, P., & Rodin, J. (1985). Cognitions about the self: Connecting feeling states and social behavior. In P. Shaver (Ed.), *Self, situations, and social behavior: Review of personality and social psychology* (Vol. 6, pp. 143–166). Beverly Hills, CA: Sage.

Salovey, P., Rothman, A. J., Detweiler, J. B., & Steward, W. T. (2000). Emotional states and physical health. *American Psychologist, 55*, 110–121.

Salovey, P., Rothman, A. J., & Rodin, J. (1998). Social psychology and health behavior. In D. Gilbert, S. Fiske, & G. Lindzey (Eds.), *The handbook of social psychology* (4th ed., Vol. 2, pp. 633–683). New York: McGraw-Hill.

Sande, G., Goethals, G., Ferrari, L., & Worth, L. (1989). Value guided attributions: Maintaining the moral self-image and the diabolical enemy-image. *Journal of Social Issues, 45*, 91–118.

Sande, G. H., Goethals, G. R., & Radloff, C. E. (1988). Perceiving one's own traits and others': The multifaceted self. *Journal of Personality and Social Psychology, 54*, 13–20.

Sande, G. N., Ellard, J. H., & Ross, M. (1986). Effect of arbitrarily assigned status labels on self-perceptions and social perceptions: The mere position effect. *Journal of Psychology and Social Psychology, 50*, 684–689.

Sanders, C. (2006, July 20). Canadian fathers stepping up. *Winnipeg Free Press*, p. A5.

Sanger, D. E. (1993, May 30). The career and the kimono. *New York Times Magazine*, 18–19.

Sangrigoli, S., Pallier, C., Argenti, A. M., Ventureyra, V. A. G., & de Schonen, S. (2005). Reversibility of the other-race effect in face recognition during childhood. *Psychological Science, 16*, 440–444.

Sanitioso, R., Kunda, Z., & Fong, G. T. (1990). Motivated recruitment of autobiographical memories. *Journal of Personality and Social Psychology, 59*, 229–241.

Sanna, L. J. (1992). Self-efficacy theory: Implications for social facilitation and social loafing. *Journal of Personality and Social Psychology, 62*, 774–786.

Sanna, L. J., Carter, S. E., & Small, E. M. (2006). The road not taken: Counterfactual thinking over time. In L. J. Sanna & E. C. Chang (Eds.), *Judgments over time: The interplay of thoughts, feelings, and behaviors* (pp. 163–181). New York: Oxford University Press.

Sanna, L. J., & Schwarz, N. (2004). Integrating temporal biases: The interplay of focal thoughts and accessibility experiences. *Psychological Science, 15*, 474–481.

Sansone, C., & Harackiewicz, J. M. (1996). "I don't feel like it": The function of interest in self-regulation. In L. L. Martin & A. Tesser (Eds.), *Striving and feeling: Interactions among goals, affect, and self-regulation* (pp. 203–228). Mahwah, NJ: Erlbaum.

Sarason, I. G., Sarason, B. R., & Pierce, G. R. (Eds). (1990). *Social support: An interactional view*. New York: Wiley.

Sargent, J. D., Dalton, M. A., Beach, M. L., Mott, L. A., Tickle, J. J., Ahrens, M. B., & Heatherton, T. F. (2002). Viewing tobacco use in movies: Does it shape attitudes that mediate adolescent smoking? *American Journal of Preventive Medicine, 22*, 137–145.

Sastry, J., & Ross, C. E. (1998). Asian ethnicity and the sense of personal control. *Social Psychology Quarterly, 61*, 101–120.

Sato, T., & Cameron, J. E. (1999). The relationship between collective self-esteem and self construal in Japan and Canada. *Journal of Social Psychology, 139*, 426–435.

Satzewich, V., & Shaffir, W. (2009). Racism versus professionalism: Claims and counter-claims about racial profiling. *Canadian Journal of Criminology and Criminal Justice, 51*(2), 199–226.

Saunders, J. W. S. (2001). Experts in court: A view from the bench. *Canadian Psychology, 42*, 109–118.

Savitsky, K. (1998). Embarrassment study [e-mails]. Society for Personal and Social Psychology e-mail list archive. Retrieved from www.stolaf.edu/cgi-bin/mailarchivesearch.pl?directory=/ home/www/people/huff/SPSP&listname=archive98

Saxe, L. (1994). Detection of deception: Polygraph and integrity tests. *Current Directions in Psychological Science, 3*, 69–73.

Schachter, S. (1951). Deviation, rejection, and communication. *Journal of Abnormal and Social Psychology, 46*, 190–207.

Schachter, S., Silverstein, B., & Perlick, D. (1977). Studies of the interaction of psychological and pharmacological determinants of smoking: V. psychological and pharmacological explanations of smoking under stress. *Journal of Experimental Psychology: General, 106*(1), 31–40.

Schacter, D. L. (1996). *Searching for memory: The brain, the mind, and the past*. New York: Basic Books.

Schafer, M., & Crichlow, S. (1996). Antecedents of groupthink: A quantitative study. *Journal of Conflict Resolution, 40*, 415–435.

Schaller, M., Asp, C. H., Rosell, M. C., & Heim, S. J. (1996). Training in statistical reasoning inhibits formation of erroneous group stereotypes. *Personality and Social Psychology Bulletin, 22*, 829–844.

Schaller, M., & Conway, L. G., III (1999). Influence of impression-management goals on the emerging contents of group stereotypes: Support for social-evolutionary process. *Personality and Social Psychology Bulletin, 25*, 819–833.

Schaller, M., & Conway, L. G., III (2001). From cognition to culture: The origins of stereotypes that really matter. In G. B. Moskowitz (Ed.), *Cognitive social psychology: The Princeton symposium on the legacy and future of social cognition* (pp. 163–176). Mahwah, NJ: Erlbaum.

Schaller, M., & Conway, L. G., III (2005). The substance of prejudice: Biological- and social- evolutionary perspectives on cognition, culture, and the contents of stereotypical beliefs. In C. S. Crandall & M. Schaller (Eds.), *Social psychology of prejudice: Historical and contemporary issues* (pp. 145–160). Lawrence, KS: Lewinian Press.

Schaller, M., Conway, L. G., III & Tanchuk, T. L. (2002). Selective pressures on the once and future contents of ethnic stereotypes: Effects of the communicability of traits. *Journal of Personality and Social Psychology, 82*, 861–877.

Schaller, M., O'Brien, M. (1992). "Intuitive analysis of covariance" and group stereotype formation. *Personality and Social Psychology Bulletin, 18*, 776–785.

Schaller, M., Park, J. H., & Mueller, A. (2003). Fear of the dark: Interactive effects of beliefs about danger and ambient darkness on ethnic stereotypes. *Personality and Social Psychology Bulletin, 29*(5), 637–649.

Schaller, M., Simpson, J., & Kenrick, D. (Eds.) (2006). *Evolution and social psychology*. Madison, CT: Psychosocial Press.

Scheier, M. F., Carver, C. S., & Bridges, M. W. (1994). Distinguishing optimism from neuroticism (and trait anxiety, self-mastery, and self-esteem): A revision of the Life Orientation Test. *Journal of Personality and Social Psychology, 67*, 1063–1078.

Schemo, D. J. (2003, July 24). Study of campus faults some antidrinking drives. *New York Times*, p. A17.

Schimel, J., Arndt, J., Banko, K. M., & Cook, A. (2004). Not all self-affirmations were created equal: The cognitive and social benefit of affirming the intrinsic (vs. extrinsic) self. *Social Cognition, 22*(1), 75–99.

Schimel, J., Hayes, J., Williams, T., & Jahrig, J. (2007). Is death really the worm at the core? Converging evidence that worldview threat increases death-thought accessibility. *Journal of Personality and Social Psychology, 92*, 789–803.

Schimmack, U., & Oishi, S. (2005). The influence of chronically and temporarily accessible information on life satisfaction judgements. *Journal of Personality and Social Psychology, 89*, 395–406.

Schlenger, W. E., Caddell, J. M., Ebert, L., Jordan, B. K., Rourke, K. M., Wilson, D., . . . Kulka, R. A. (2002). Psychological reactions to terrorist attacks: Findings from the National Study of Americans' Reactions to September 11. *Journal of the American Medical Association, 288*, 581–588.

Schmeichel, B. J., & Baumeister, R. F. (2004). Self-regulatory strength. In R. F. Baumeister, & K. D. Vohs (Eds.), *Handbook of self-regulation: Research, theory, and applications* (pp. 84–98). New York: Guilford.

Schmitt, B. H., Gilovich, T., Goore, N., & Joseph, L. (1986). Mere presence and social facilitation: One more time. *Journal of Experimental Social Psychology, 22*, 228–241.

Schmitt, D. P., Youn, G., Bond, B., Brooks, S., Frye, H., Johnson, S., . . . Stoka, C. (2009). When will I feel love? The effects of culture, personality, and gender on the psychological tendency to love. *Journal of Research in Personality, 43(5)*, 830–846.

Schneider, D. J. (1973). Implicit personality theory: A review. *Psychological Bulletin, 79*, 294–309.

Schneider, M. E., Major, B., Luhtanen, R., & Crocker, J. (1996). Social stigma and the potential costs of assumptive help. *Personality and Social Psychology Bulletin, 22*, 201–209.

Schoeneman, T. J., & Rubanowitz, D. E. (1985). Attributions in the advice columns: Actors and observers, causes and reasons. *Personality and Social Psychology Bulletin, 11*, 315–325.

Scholten, L., van Knippenberg, D., Nijstad, B. A., & De Dreu, C. K. W. (2007). Motivated information processing and group decision-making: Effects of process accountability on information processing and decision quality. *Journal of Experimental Social Psychology, 43*, 539–552.

Schooler, J. W. (1999). Seeking the core: The issues and evidence surrounding recovered accounts of sexual trauma. In L. M. Williams & V. L. Banyard (Eds.), *Trauma and memory* (pp. 203–216). Thousand Oaks, CA: Sage.

Schooler, J. W., & Eich, E. (2000). Memory for emotional events. In E. Tulving & F. I. M. Craik (Eds.), *The Oxford handbook of memory* (pp. 379–392). Oxford, UK: Oxford University Press.

Schooler, J. W., & Engstler-Schooler, T. Y. (1990). Verbal overshadowing of visual memories: Some things are better left unsaid. *Cognitive Psychology, 22*, 36–71.

Schooler, J. W., Fiore, S. M., & Brandimonte, M. A. (1997). At a loss from words: Verbal overshadowing of perceptual memories. *Psychology of Learning and Motivation, 37*, 291–340.

Scott-Ladd, B., & Chan, C. A. (2008). Using action research to teach students to manage team learning and improve teamwork satisfaction. *Active Learning in Higher Education, 9*(3), 231–248.

Schriesheim, C. A., Tepper, B. J., & Tetrault, L. A. (1994). Least preferred co-worker score, situational control, and leadership effectiveness: A meta-analysis of contingency model performance predictions. *Journal of Applied Psychology, 79*, 561–573.

Schroeder, D. H., & Costa, P. T., Jr. (1984). Influence of life event stress on physical illness: Substantive effects or methodological flaws? *Journal of Personality and Social Psychology, 46*, 853–863.

Schuller, R. A., & Hastings, P. A. (1996). Trials of battered women who kill: The impact of alternative forms of expert evidence. *Law and Human Behavior, 20*, 167–187.

Schuller, R. A., Kazoleas, V., & Kawakami, K. (2009). The impact of prejudice screening procedures on racial bias in the courtroom. *Law and Human Behavior, 33*(4), 320–328.

Schuller, R. A., & Paglia, A. (1999). An empirical study: Juror sensitivity to variations in hearsay conveyed via expert evidence. *Law and Psychology Review, 23*, 131–152.

Schuller, R. A., & Yarmey, M. (2001). The jury: Deciding guilt and innocence. In R. A. Schuller, & J. R. P. Ogloff (Eds), *Introduction to psychology and law: Canadian perspectives* (pp. 157–187). Toronto, ON: University of Toronto Press.

Schulte-Hostedde, A. I., Eys, M. A., & Johnson, K. (2008). Female mate choice is influenced by male sport participation. *Evolutionary Psychology, 6*(1), 113–124.

Schultz, P. W., Oskamp, S., & Mainieri, T. (1995). Who recycles and when? A review of personal and situational factors. *Journal of Environmental Psychology, 15*, 105–121.

Schulz, R. (1976). Effects of control and predictability on the physical and psychological well-being of the institutionalized aged. *Journal of Personality and Social Psychology, 33*, 563–573.

Schulz, R., & Hanusa, B. H. (1978). Long-term effects of control and predictability-enhancing interventions: Findings and ethical issues. *Journal of Personality and Social Psychology, 36*, 1202–1212.

Schuman, H., & Kalton, G. (1985). Survey methods. In G. Lindzey & E. Aronson (Eds.), *Handbook of social psychology* (3rd ed., Vol. 1, pp. 635–697). New York: McGraw-Hill.

Schützwohl, A. (2004). Which infidelity type makes you more jealous? Decision strategies in a forced-choice between sexual and emotional infidelity. *Evolutionary Psychology, 2*, 121–128.

Schwartz, S. H. (1992). Universals in the content and structure of values: Theoretical advances and empirical tests in 20 countries. In M. P. Zanna (Ed.), *Advances in experimental social psychology* (Vol. 25, pp. 1–65). San Diego, CA: Academic Press.

Schwartz, S. H., & Gottlieb, A. (1976). Bystander reactions to a violent theft: Crime in Jerusalem. *Journal of Personality and Social Psychology, 34*, 1188–1199.

Schwarz, N. (1999). Self-reports: How the questions shape the answers. *American Psychologist, 54*, 93–105.

Schwarz, N., Bless, H., Strack, F., Klumpp, G., Rittenauer-Schatka, H., & Simmons, A. (1991). Ease of retrieval as information: Another look at the availability heuristic. *Journal of Personality and Social Psychology, 61*, 195–202.

Schwarz, N., Groves, R. M., & Schuman, H. (1998). Survey methods. In D. Gilbert, S. Fiske, & G. Lindzey (Eds.), *The handbook of social psychology* (4th ed., Vol. 1, pp. 143–179). New York: Random House.

Schwarz, N., Hippler, H. J., Deutsch, B., & Strack, F. (1985). Response scales: Effects of category range on reported behavior and comparative judgments. *Public Opinion Quarterly, 49*, 388–395.

Schwarz, N., & Sudman, S. (Eds). (1996). *Answering questions*. San Fransisco, CA: Jossey-Bass Publishers.

Schwarz, N., & Vaughn, L. A. (2002). The availability heuristic revisited: Ease of recall and content of recall as distinct sources of information. In T. Gilovich, D. W. Griffin, & D. Kahneman (Eds.), *Heuristics and biases: The psychology of intuitive judgment* (pp. 103–119). New York: Cambridge University Press.

Sciangula, A. M., & Morry, M. M. (2009). Self-esteem and perceived regard: How I see myself affects my relationship satisfaction. *Journal of Social Psychology, 149*, 143–158.

Scoboria, A., Mazzoni, G., Kirsch, I., & Milling, L. S. (2002). Immediate and persisting effects of misleading questions and hypnosis on memory reports. *Journal of Experimental Psychology: Applied, 8*, 26–32.

Scott, D. (1999). Equal opportunity, unequal results: Determinants of household recycling intensity. *Environment and Behavior, 31*, 267–290.

Scott, K., & Straus, M. (2007). Denial, minimization, partner blaming, and intimate aggression in dating partners. *Journal of Interpersonal Violence, 22*(7), 851-871.

Scott, S. (2002, October). The man who reads faces. *Elm Street*, 78–91.

Sears, D. O. (1981). Life stage effects on attitude change, especially among the elderly. In S. B. Kiesler, J. N. Morgan, & V. K. Oppenheimer (Eds.), *Aging: Social change* (pp. 183–204). New York: Academic Press.

Sears, H., & Byers, E. (2010). Adolescent girls' and boys' experiences of psychologically, physically, and sexually aggressive behaviors in their dating relationships: Co-occurrence and emotional reaction. *Journal of Aggression, Maltreatment & Trauma, 19*(5), 517–539.

Sechrist, G. B., Stangor, C., & Killen, M. (2005). Prejudice as social norms. In C. S. Crandall & M. Schaller (Eds.), *Social psychology of prejudice: Historical and contemporary issues* (pp. 163–183). Lawrence, KS: Lewinian Press.

Sechrist, G. B., Swim, J. K., & Stangor, C. (2004). When do the stigmatized make attributions to discrimination occurring to the self and others? The roles of self-presentation and need for control. *Journal of Personality and Social Psychology, 87*(1), 111–122.

Secord, P. F., & Backman, C. W. (1964). *Social psychology*. New York: McGraw-Hill.

Sedikides, C., & Anderson, C. A. (1994). Causal perceptions of intertrait relations: The glue that holds person types together. *Personality and Social Psychology Bulletin, 21*, 294–302.

Seery, M., Silver, R., Holman, E., Ence, W., & Chu, T. (2008). Expressing thoughts and feelings following a collective trauma: Immediate responses to 9/11 predict negative outcomes in a national sample. *Journal of Consulting and Clinical Psychology, 76*, 657–667.

Segal, M. W (1974). Alphabet and attraction: An unobtrusive measure of the effect of propinquity in a field setting. *Journal of Personality and Social Psychology, 30*, 654–657.

Segerstrom, S. C. (2005). Optimism and immunity: Do positive thoughts always lead to positive effects? *Brain, Behavior, and Immunity, 19*(3), 195–200.

Séguin, C., Pelletier, L. G., & Hunsley, J. (1999). Predicting environmental behaviors: The influence of self-determined motivation and information about perceived environmental health risks. *Journal of Applied Social Psychology, 29*, 1582–1604.

Seijts, G. H., & Latham, G. P. (2000). The effects of goal setting and group size on performance in a social dilemna. *Canadian Journal of Behavioural Science, 32*, 104–116.

Seligman, M. E. P. (1975). *Helplessness: On depression, development, and death*. San Francisco, CA: W. H. Freeman.

Seligman, M. E. P., & Schulman, P. (1986). Explanatory style as a predictor of productivity and quitting among life insurance agents. *Journal of Personality and Social Psychology, 50*, 832–838.

Selye, H. (1956). *The stress of life*. New York: McGraw-Hill.

Selye, H. (1976). *Stress in health and disease*. Woburn, MA: Butterworth.

Semin, G. R., Higgins, E. T., de Montes, L. G., Estourget, Y., & Valencia, J. F. (2005). Linguistic signatures of regulatory focus: How abstraction fits promotion more than prevention. *Journal of Personality and Social Psychology, 89*, 36–45.

Seppa, N. (1997). Children's TV remains steeped in violence. *APA Monitor, 28*, p. 36.

Sergios, P. A., & Cody, J. (1985). Physical attractiveness and social assertiveness skills in male homosexual dating behavior and partner selection. *Journal of Social Psychology, 125*, 505–514.

Seta, J. J., Seta, C. E., & Wang, M. A. (1990). Feelings of negativity and stress: An averaging-summation analysis of impressions of negative life experiences. *Personality and Social Psychology Bulletin, 17*, 376–384.

Shackelford, T. K., & Buss, D. M. (1996). Betrayal in mateships, friendships, and coalitions. *Personality and Social Psychology Bulletin, 22*, 1151–1164.

Shadel, W. G., Cervone, D., Niaura, R., & Abrams, D. B. (2004). Developing an integrative social-cognitive strategy for personality assessment at the level of the individual: An illustration with regular cigarette smokers. *Journal of Research in Personality, 38*, 394–419.

Shang, J., Basil, D. Z., & Wymer, W. (2010). Using social marketing to enhance hotel reuse programs. *Journal of Business Research, 63*(2), 166–172.

Sharan, S. (1980). Cooperative learning in small groups. *Review of Educational Research, 50*, 241–271.

Shariff, A. F., & Norenzayan, A. (2007). God is watching you: Priming God concepts increases prosocial behavior in an anonymous economic game. *Psychological Science, 18*(9), 803–809.

Sharpe, D., Adair, J. G., & Roese, N. J. (1992). Twenty years of deception research: A decline in subjects' trust? *Personality and Social Psychology Bulletin, 18*, 585–590.

Sharpe, D., & Taylor, J. K. (1999). An examination of variables from a social-developmental model to explain physical and psychological dating violence. *Canadian Journal of Behavioural Science, 31*, 165–175.

Sharp, F. C. (1928). *Ethics*. New York: Century.

Shavitt, S. (1989). Operationalizing functional theories of attitude. In A. R. Pratkanis, S. J. Breckler, & A. G. Greenwald (Eds.), *Attitude structure and function* (pp. 311–337). Hillsdale, NJ: Erlbaum.

Shavitt, S. (1990). The role of attitude objects in attitude function. *Journal of Experimental Social Psychology, 26*, 124–148.

Shaw, J. I., & Skolnick, P. (1999). Weapon focus and gender differences in eyewitness accuracy: Arousal versus salience. *Journal of Applied Social Psychology, 29*, 2328–2341.

Sheldon, K. M. (1999). Learning the lessons of tit-for-tat: Even competitors can get the massage. *Journal of Personality and Social Psychology, 77*, 1245–1253.

Sheppard, J., & Young, M. (2007). The routes of moral development and the impact of exposure to the Milgram obedience study. *Journal of Business Ethics, 75*(4), 315–333.

Shepperd, J. A., & Taylor, K. M. (1999). Social loafing and expectancy-value theory. *Personality and Social Psychology Bulletin, 25*, 1147–1158.

Sherif, M. (1936). *The psychology of social norms*. New York: Harper.

Sherif, M. (1966). *In common predicament: Social psychology of intergroup conflict and cooperation*. Boston, MA: Houghton Mifflin.

Sherif, M., Harvey, O. J., White, J., Hood, W., & Sherif, C. (1961). *Intergroup conflict and cooperation: The robber's cave experiment*. Norman: University of Oklahoma, Institute of Intergroup Relations.

Sherman, D. K., Cohen, G. L., Nelson, L. D., Nussbaum, A., Bunyan, D. P., & Garcia, J. (2009). Affirmed yet unaware: Exploring the role of awareness in the process of self-affirmation. *Journal of Personality and Social Psychology, 97*(5), 745–764.

Sherman, D. K., & Kim, H. S. (2002). Affective perseverance: The resistance of affect to cognitive invalidation. *Personality and Social Psychology Bulletin, 28*, 224–237.

Sherman, D. K., & Kim, H. S. (2005). Is there an "I" in "Team"? The role of the self in group-serving judgments. *Journal of Personality and Social Psychology, 88*, 108–120.

Sherman, J. W., & Klein, S. B. (1994). Development and representation of personality impressions. *Journal of Personality and Social Psychology, 67*, 972–983.

Sherrod, D. R. (1974). Crowding, perceived control, and behavioral aftereffects. *Journal of Applied Social Psychology, 4*, 171–186.

Shestowsky, D., Wegener, D. T., & Fabrigar, L. R. (1998). Need for cognition and interpersonal influence: Individual differences in impact on dyadic decisions. *Journal of Personality and Social Psychology, 74*, 1317–1328.

Shih, M., Ambady, N., Richeson, J. A., Fujita, K., & Gray, H. M. (2002). Stereotype performance boosts: The impact of self-relevance and that manner of stereotype activation. *Journal of Personality and Social Psychology, 83*, 638–647.

Shih, M., Pittinsky, T. L., & Ambady, N. (1999). Stereotype susceptibility: Identity salience and shifts in quantitative performance. *Psychological Science, 10*, 80–83.

Shira, I., & Martin, L. L. (2005). Stereotyping, self-affirmation, and the cerebral hemispheres. *Personality and Social Psychology Bulletin, 31*, 846–856.

Shotland, R. L., & Straw, M. K. (1976). Bystander response to an assault: When a man attacks a woman. *Journal of Personality and Social Psychology, 34*, 990–999.

Showers, C., & Zeigler-Hill, V. (2003). Organization of self-knowledge: Features, functions, and flexibility. In M. R. Leary & J. P. Tangney (Eds.), *Handbook of self and identity* (pp. 47–67). New York: Guilford Press.

Shultz, T. R., Léveillé, E., & Lepper, M. R. (1999). Free choice and cognitive dissonance revisited: Choosing "lesser evils" versus "greater goods." *Personality and Social Psychology Bulletin, 25*, 40–48.

Sibley, C. G., & Liu, J. H. (2003). Differentiating active and passive littering: A two-stage process model of littering behavior in public spaces. *Environment and Behavior, 35*, 415–433.

Sidanius, J., Levin, S., & Pratto, F. (1996). Consensual social dominance orientation and its correlates within the hierarchical structure of American society. *International Journal of Intercultural Relations, 20*, 385–408.

Siero, F. W., Bakker, A. B., Dekker, G. B., & van den Burg, M. T. C. (1996). Changing organizational energy consumption behavior through comparative feedback. *Journal of Environmental Psychology, 16*, 235–246.

Sigal, J. J., & Weinfeld, M. (2001). Do children cope better than adults with potentially traumatic stress? A 40-year follow-up of Holocaust survivors. *Psychiatry, 64*, 69–80.

Silver, L. B., Dublin, C. C., & Lourie, R. S. (1969). Does violence breed violence? Contributions from a study of the child abuse syndrome. *American Journal of Psychiatry, 126*, 404–407.

Silver, R., Holman, E., A., McIntosh, D. N., Poulin, M., & Gil-Rivas, V. (2002). Nationwide longitudinal study of psychological responses to September 11. *Journal of the American Medical Association, 2882*, 1235–1244.

Silverstein, B., Perdue, L., Peterson, B., & Kelly, E. (1986). The role of the mass media in promoting a thin standard of bodily attractiveness for women. *Sex Roles, 14*, 519–532.

Silvia, P. J., & Abele, A. E. (2002). Can positive affect induce self- focused attention? Methodological and measurement issues. *Cognition and Emotion, 16*, 845–853.

Sime, J. D. (1983). Affiliative behavior during escape to building exits. *Journal of Environmental Psychology, 3*, 21–41.

Simmie, S. (1999, November 20). Pumping up the "level of cruelty." *Toronto Star*, p. A3.

Simmons, R. E., & Scheepers, L. (1996). Winning by a neck: Sexual selection in the evolution of giraffe. *The American Naturalist, 148*, 771–786.

Simms, D. C., & Byers, E. (2009). Interpersonal perceptions of desired frequency of sexual behaviours. *Canadian Journal of Human Sexuality, 18*(1-2), 15–25.

Simon, D., Craig, K. D., Gosselin, F., Belin, P., & Rainville, P. (2008). Recognition and discrimination of prototypical dynamic expressions of pain and emotions. *Pain, 135*(1-2), 55–64.

Simon, H. A. (1990). A mechanism for social selection and successful altruism. *Science, 250*, 1665–1668.

Simons, D. J., & Ambinder, M. S. (2005). Change blindness: Theory and consequences. *Current Directions in Psychological Science, 14*, 44–48.

Simons, D. J., & Chabris, C. F. (1999). Gorillas in our midst: Sustained inattentional blindness for dynamic events. *Perception, 1999, 28*, 1059–1074.

Simonton, D. K. (1985). Intelligence and personal influence in groups: Four nonlinear models. *Psychological Review, 92*, 532–547.

Simonton, D. K. (1987). *Why presidents succeed: A political psychology of leadership*. New Haven, CT: Yale University Press.

Simonton, D. K. (1999). Significant samples: The psychological study of eminent individuals. *Psychological Methods, 4*, 425–451.

Simonton, D. K. (2001). Predicting presidential performance in the United States: Equation replication on recent survey results. *Journal of Social Psychology, 141*, 293–307.

Simpson, G. E., & Yinger, J. M. (1958). *Racial and cultural minorities: An analysis of prejudice and discrimination*. New York: Harper.

Simpson, J. A., & Kenrick, D. T. (Eds). (1997). *Evolutionary social psychology*. Mahwah, NJ: Erlbaum.

Simpson, J. A., Rholes, W. S., Campbell, L., & Wilson, C. L. (2003). Changes in attachment orientations across the transition to parenthood. *Journal of Experimental Social Psychology, 39*, 317–331.

Sinclair, L., & Kunda, Z. (1999). Reactions to a black professional: Motivated inhibition and activation of conflicting stereotypes. *Journal of Personality and Social Psychology, 77*, 885–904.

Sinclair, L., & Kunda, Z. (2000). Motivated stereotyping of women: She's fine if she praised me but incompetent if she criticized me. *Personality and Social Psychology Bulletin, 26*, 1329–1342.

Sinclair, R. C., Lovsin, T. K., & Moore, S. E. (2007). Mood state, issue involvement, and argument strength on responses to persuasive appeals. *Psychological Reports, 101*(3), 739–753.

Sinclair, R. C., Moore, S. E., Mark, M. M., Soldat, A. S., & Lavis, C. A. (2010). Incidental moods, source likeability, and persuasion: Liking motivates message elaboration in happy people. *Cognition and Emotion, 24*(6), 940–961.

Sinclair, S., Dunn, E., & Lowery, B. S. (2004). The relationship between parental racial attitudes and children's implicit prejudice. *Journal of Experimental Social Psychology, 41*, 283–289.

Singer, T., & Frith, C. D. (2006). The emergence of the "social" in cognitive neuroscience: The study of interacting brains. In P. A. M. van Lange (Ed.), *Bridging social psychology: Benefits of transdisciplinary approaches* (pp. 97–102). Mahwah, NJ: Erlbaum.

Sip, K., Roepstorff, A., McGregor, W., & Frith, C. (2008). Detecting deception: The scope and limits. *Trends in Cognitive Sciences, 12*, 48–53.

Sirois, F. (1982). Perspectives on epidemic hysteria. In M. J. Colligan, J. W. Pennebaker, & L. R. Murphy (Eds.), *Mass psychogenic illness: A social psychological analysis* (pp. 217–236). Hillsdale, NJ: Erlbaum.

Sirois, F. M., Monforton, J., & Simpson, M. (2010). "If only I had done better": Perfectionism and the functionality of counterfactual thinking. *Personality and Social Psychology Bulletin, 36*(12), 1675–1692.

Sistrunk, F., & McDavid, J. W. (1971). Sex variable in conforming behavior. *Journal of Personality and Social Psychology, 17*, 200–207.

Skarlicki, D. P., Ellard, J. H., & Kelln, B. R. C. (1998). Third-party perceptions of a layoff: Procedural, derogation, and retributive aspects of justice. *Journal of Applied Psychology, 83*, 119–127.

Skerritt, J. (2007, July 10). Manitoba teens are out-puffing their peers. *Winnipeg Free Press*, p. A3.

Skinner, B. F. (1938). *The behavior of organisms*. New York: Appleton-Century-Crofts.

Skinner, E. A. (1995). *Perceived control, motivation, and coping*. Thousand Oaks, CA: Sage.

Skinner, E. A. (1996). A guide to constructs of control. *Journal of Personality and Social Psychology, 71*, 549–570.

Skitka, L. J. (2002). Do the means always justify the ends, or do the ends sometimes justify the means? A value protection model of justice reasoning. *Personality and Social Psychology Bulletin, 28*, 588–597.

Skomorovsky, A., & Sudom, K. A. (2011). Role of hardiness in the psychological well-being of Canadian forces officer candidates. *Military Medicine, 176*(1), 7–12.

Slavin, R. E. (1980). *Cooperative learning and desegregation.* Paper presented at the meeting of the American Psychological Association.

Slavin, R. E. (1996). Cooperative learning in middle and secondary schools. *Clearing House, 69, Young adolescents at risk* (special ed.), 200–205.

Sloan, D. M., & Marx, B. P. (2004). Taking pen to hand: Evaluating theories underlying the written disclosure paradigm. *Clinical Psychology: Science and Practice, 11*, 121–137.

Sloan, J. H., Kellerman, A. L., Reay, D. T., Ferris, J. A., Koepsell, T., Rivara, F. P., . . . LoGerfo, J. (1988). Handgun regulations, crime, assaults, and homicide: A tale of two cities. *New England Journal of Medicine, 319*, 1256–1261.

Slovic, P., & Lichtenstein, S. (1971). Comparison of Bayesian and regression approaches to the study of information processing in judgment. *Organizational Behavior and Human Performance, 6*, 649–744.

Slusher, M. P., & Anderson, C. A. (1989). Belief perseverance and self-defeating behavior. In R. Curtis (Ed.), *Self-defeating behaviors: Experimental research, clinical impressions, and practical implications* (pp. 11–40). New York: Plenum.

Smith, A. E., Jussim, L., & Eccles, J. (1999). Do self-fulfilling prophecies accumulate, dissipate, or remain stable over time? *Journal of Personality and Social Psychology, 77*, 548–565.

Smith, M. B., Bruner, J., & White, R. W. (1956). *Opinions and personality*. New York: Wiley.

Smith, M. C. (1983). Hypnotic memory enhancement of witnesses: Does it work? *Psychological Bulletin, 94*, 387–407.

Smith, P. B., & Bond, M. H. (1999). *Social psychology across cultures* (2nd ed.). Needham Heights, MA: Allyn & Bacon.

Smith, P. K., Pepler, D., & Rigby, K. (Eds.). (2004). *Bullying in schools: How successful can interventions be?* Cambridge, UK: Cambridge University Press.

Smith, R. E., Wheeler, G., & Diener, E. (1975). Faith without works: Jesus people, resistance to temptation, and altruism. *Journal of Applied Psychology, 5*, 320–330.

Smith, S. M., Fabrigar, L. R., Powell, D. M., & Estrada, M. (2007). The role of information-processing capacity and goals in attitude- congruent selective exposure effects. *Personality and Social Psychology Bulletin, 33*, 948–960.

Smith, S. M., Stinson, V., & Patry, M. W. (2009). Using the "Mr. Big" technique to elicit confessions: Successful innovation or dangerous development in the Canadian legal system? *Psychology, Public Policy, and Law, 15*(3), 168–193.

Smith, S. S., & Richardson, D. (1983). Amelioration of deception and harm in psychological research: The important role of debriefing. *Journal of Personality and Social Psychology, 44*, 1075–1082.

Smith, T. (2006). Personality as Risk and Resilience in Physical Health. *Current Directions in Psychological Science, 15*, 227–231.

Smith, T. W. (2003). Hostility and health: Current status of a psychosomatic hypothesis. In P. Salovey & A. J. Rothman (Eds.), *Social psychology of health* (pp. 325–341). New York: Psychology Press.

Smith, V. L., & Ellsworth, P. C. (1987). The social psychology of eyewitness accuracy: Misleading questions and communicator expertise. *Journal of Applied Psychology, 72*, 294–300.

Smith, V. L., Kassin, S. M., & Ellsworth, P. C. (1989). Eyewitness accuracy and confidence: Within- versus between-subjects correlations. *Journal of Applied Psychology, 74*, 356–359.

Snook, B., Grant, M. J., & Button, C. M. (2009). A judgement analysis of social perceptions of attitudes and ability. *Thinking & Reasoning, 15*(4), 319–336.

Snyder, C. R., Irving, L. M., & Anderson, J. R. (1991). Hope and health. In C. R. Snyder & D. R. Forsyth (Eds.), *Handbook of clinical and social psychology* (pp. 285–305). New York: Pergamon.

Snyder, M. (1984). When belief creates reality. In L. Berkowitz (Ed.), *Advances in experimental social psychology* (Vol. 18, pp. 247–305). Orlando, FL: Academic Press.

Snyder, M., & DeBono, K. G. (1989). Understanding the functions of attitudes: Lessons for personality and social behavior. In A. R. Pratkanis, S. J. Breckler, & A. G. Greenwald (Eds.), *Attitude structure and function* (pp. 339–359). Hillsdale, NJ: Erlbaum.

Snyder, M., Tanke, E. D., & Berscheid, E. (1977). Social perception and interpersonal behavior: On the self-fulfilling nature of social stereotypes. *Journal of Personality and Social Psychology, 35*, 656–666.

Soames, R. F. (1988). Effective and ineffective use of fear in health promotion campaigns. *American Journal of Public Health, 78*, 163–167.

Solomon, L. Z., Solomon, H., & Stone, R. (1978). Helping as a function of number of bystanders and ambiguity of emergency. *Personality and Social Psychology Bulletin, 4*, 318–321.

Solomon, S., Greenberg, J., & Pyszczynski, T. (1991). Terror management theory of self-esteem. In C. R. Snyder, D. R. Forsyth (Eds.), *Handbook of social and clinical psychology: The health perspective* (pp. 21–40). Elmsford, NY: Pergamon Press.

Sommers, E. K., & Check, J. V. (1987). An empirical investigation of the role of pornography in the verbal and physical abuse of women. *Violence and Victims, 2*, 189–209.

Song, F. (2009). Intergroup trust and reciprocity in strategic interactions: Effects of group decision-making mechanisms. *Organizational Behavior and Human Decision Processes, 108*(1), 164–173.

Son Hing, L. S., Bobocel, D. R., Zanna, M. P., & McBride, M. V. (2007). Authoritarian dynamics and unethical decision making: High social dominance orientation leaders and high right-wing authoritarianism followers. *Journal of Personality and Social Psychology, 92*, 67–81.

Sontag, S. (1978). *Illness as metaphor*. New York: Farrar, Straus & Giroux.

Sontag, S. (1988). *AIDS and its metaphors*. New York: Farrar, Straus & Giroux.

Sorensen, J., Wrinkle, R. Brewer, V., & Marquart, J. (1999). Capital punishment and deterrence: Examining the effect of executions on murder in Texas. *Crime and Delinquency, 45*, 481–493.

Sorkin, A. R. (2003, June 5). Despite shuffle, Stewart still in charge. *New York Times*, p. C1, C5.

Sorkin, R. D., Hays, C. J., & West, R. (2001). Signal-detection analysis of group decision making. *Psychological Review, 108*, 183–203.

Sorokowski, P., Szmajke, A., Sorokowska, A., Cunen, M., Fabrykant, M., Zarafshani, K., . . . Fang, T. (2011). Attractiveness of leg length: Report from 27 nations. *Journal of Cross-Cultural Psychology, 42*(1), 131–139.

Sorrels, J. P., & Kelley, J. (1984). Conformity by omission. *Personality and Social Psychology Bulletin, 10*, 302–305.

Spencer, S., Steele, C. M., & Quinn, D. (1997). *Under suspicion of inability: Stereotype threat and women's math performance*. Unpublished manuscript, Stanford University.

Spencer, S. J., Josephs, R. A., & Steele, C. M. (1993). Low self-esteem: The uphill battle for self-integrity. In R. F. Baumeister (Ed.), *Self-esteem and the puzzle of low self-regard* (pp. 21–36). New York: Wiley.

Spencer, S. J., Steele, C. M., & Quinn, D. M. (1999). Stereotype threat and women's math performance. *Journal of Experimental Social Psychology, 35*, 4–28.

Spencer-Rodgers, J., & Collins, N. L. (2006). Risk and resilience: Dual effects of perceptions of group disadvantage among Latinos. *Journal of Experimental Social Psychology, 42*, 729–737.

Spencer-Rodgers, J., Hamilton, D. L., & Sherman, S. J. (2007). The central role of entitativity in stereotypes of social categories and task groups. *Journal of Personality and Social Psychology, 92*, 369–388.

Spencer-Rodgers, J., Williams, M. J., Hamilton, D. L., Peng, K., & Wang, L. (2007). Culture and group perception: Dispositional and stereotypic inferences about novel and national groups. *Journal of Personality and Social Psychology, 93*, 525–543.

Spiegel, D., Bloom, J. R., Kraemer, H. C., & Gottheil, E. (1989). Psychological support for cancer patients. *Lancet, 2*, 1447.

Spiegel, H., & Spiegel, D. (1987 [1978]). *Trance and treatment: Clinical uses of hypnosis*. Washington, DC: American Psychiatric Press.

Spina, R. R., Ji, L., Guo, T., Zhang, Z., Li, Y., & Fabrigar, L. (2010). Cultural differences in the representativeness heuristic: Expecting a correspondence in magnitude between cause and effect. *Personality and Social Psychology Bulletin, 36*(5), 583–597.

Spitzberg, B. H., & Rhea, J. (1999). Obsessive relational intrusion and sexual coercion victimization. *Journal of Interpersonal Violence, 14*, 3–20.

Spitzer, B. L., Henderson, K. A., & Zivian, M. T. (1999). Gender differences in population versus media body sizes: A comparison over four decades. *Sex Roles, 40*, 545–565.

Sporer, S. L. (1994). Decision times and eyewitness identification accuracy in simultaneous and sequential lineups. In D. F. Ross, J. D. Read, & M. P. Toglia (Eds.), *Adult eyewitness testimony: Current trends and developments* (pp. 300–327). New York: Cambridge University Press.

Sporer, S. L., Koehnken, G., & Malpass, R. S. (1996). Introduction: 200 years of mistaken identification. In S. L. Sporer, R. S. Malpass, & G. Koehnken (Eds.), *Psychological issues in eyewitness identification* (pp. 1–6). Mahwah, NJ: Erlbaum.

Sprecher, S. (1994). Two sides to the breakup of dating relationships. *Personal Relationships, 1*, 199–222.

Sprecher, S. (1998). The effect of exchange orientation on close relationships. *Social Psychology Quarterly, 61*, 230–231.

Sprecher, S., Aron, A., Hatfield, E., Cortese, A., Potapova, E., & Levitskaya, A. (1994). Love: American style, Russian style, and Japanese style. *Personal Relationships, 1*, 349–369.

Sprecher, S., & Fehr, B. (1998). The dissolution of close relationships. In J. H. Harvey (Ed.), Perspectives on loss: A sourcebook (pp. 99–112). Philadelphia, PA: Taylor & Francis.

Sprecher, S., Felmlee, D., Metts, S., Fehr, B., & Vanni, D. (1998). Factors associated with distress following the breakup of a close relationship. *Journal of Social and Personal Relationships, 15*, 791–809.

Sprecher, S., & Metts, S. (1989). Development of the "Romantic Beliefs Scale" and examination of the effects of gender and gender-role orientation. *Journal of Social and Personal Relationships, 6*, 387–411.

Sprecher, S., & Schwartz, P. (1994). Equity and balance in the exchange of contributions in close relationships. In M. J. Lerner & G. Mikula (Eds.), *Entitlement and the affectional bond: Justice in close relationships* (pp. 11–42). New York: Plenum.

Sprecher, S., Schwartz, P., Harvey, J., & Hatfield, E. (2008). TheBusinessofLove.com: Relationship initiation at Internet matchmaking services. In S. Sprecher, A. Wenzel, & J. Harvey (Eds.), *Handbook of relationship initiation* (pp. 249–265). New York: Taylor & Francis.

Sprecher, S., Wenzel, A., & Harvey, J. (Eds). (2008). *Handbook of relationship initiation*. New York: Taylor & Francis.

Sprink, K. S., & Carron, A. V. (1994). Group cohesion effects in exercise classes. *Small Group Research, 25*, 26–42.

Sritharan, R., Heilpern, K., Wilbur, C. J., & Gawronski, B. (2010). I think I like you: Spontaneous and deliberate evaluations of potential romantic partners in an online dating context. *European Journal of Social Psychology, 40*(6), 1062–1077.

Staats, H., Harland, P., & Wilke, H. A. M. (2004). Effecting durable change: A team approach to improve environmental behavior in the household. *Environment and Behavior, 36*, 341–367.

Standing Committee on Communication and Culture (1993). Television violence: Fraying our social fabric. Retrieved from www.media-awareness.ca/english/resources/research_documents/reports/violence/upload/Television-Violence-Fraying-Our-Social-Fabric-Report-pdf.pdf

Stangor, C., Sechrist, G. B., & Jost, J. T. (2001). Changing racial beliefs by providing consensus information. *Personality and Social Psychology Bulletin, 27*, 484–494.

Stanley, D., Phelps, E., & Banaji, M. (2008). The neural basis of implicit attitudes. *Current Directions in Psychological Science, 17*, 164–170.

Stapel, D. A., & Koomen, W. (2000). How far do we go beyond the information given? The impact of knowledge activation on interpretation and inference. *Journal of Personality and Social Psychology, 78*, 19–37.

Stapel, D., & Koomen, W. (2006). The flexible unconscious: Investigating the judgmental impact of varieties of unaware perception. *Journal of Experimental Social Psychology, 42*(1), 112–119.

Starzyk, K. B., Fabrigar, L. R., Soryal, A. S., & Fanning, J. J. (2009). A painful reminder: The role of level and salience of attitude importance in cognitive dissonance. *Personality and Social Psychology Bulletin, 35*(1), 126–137.

Starzyk, K. B., Holden, R. R., Fabrigar, L. R., & MacDonald, T. K. (2006). The personal acquaintance measure: A tool for appraising one's acquaintance with any person. *Journal of Personality and Social Psychology, 90*, 833–847.

Stasser, G. (2000). Information distribution, participation, and group decision: Explorations with the DISCUSS and SPEAK models. In D. R. Ilgen & C. L. Hulin (Eds.), *Computational modeling of behavior in organizations: The third scientific discipline* (pp. 135–161). Washington, DC: American Psychological Association.

Stasser, G., & Birchmeier, Z. (2003). Group creativity and collective choice. In P. B. Paulus, & B. A. Nijstad (Eds.), *Group creativity: Innovation through collaboration* (pp. 85–109). New York: Oxford University Press.

Stasser, G., Stewart, D. D., & Wittenbaum, G. M. (1995). Expert roles and information exchange during discussion: The importance of knowing who knows what. *Journal of Experimental and Social Psychology, 31*, 244–265.

Stasser, G., & Titus, W. (1985). Pooling of unshared information in group decision making: Biased information sampling during discussion. *Journal of Personality and Social Psychology, 48*, 1467–1478.

Staub, E. (1974). Helping a distressed person: Social, personality, and stimulus determinants. In L. Berkowitz (Ed.), *Advances in experimental social psychology* (Vol. 7, pp. 293–341). New York: Academic Press.

Staub, E. (1989). *The roots of evil: The origins of genocide and other group violence*. Cambridge, UK: Cambridge University Press.

Steblay, N. M. (1987). Helping behavior in rural and urban environments: A meta-analysis. *Psychological Bulletin, 102*, 346–356.

Steblay, N. M., Dysart, J., Fulero, S. M., & Lindsay, R. C. L. (2001). Eyewitness accuracy rates in sequential and simultaneous lineup presentations: A meta-analytic comparison. *Law and Human Behavior, 25*, 459–473.

Steel, P. (2007). The nature of procrastination: A meta-analytic and theoretical review of quintessential self-regulatory failure. *Psychological Bulletin, 133*(1), 65–94.

Steele, C. M. (1988). The psychology of self-affirmation: Sustaining the integrity of the self. In L. Berkowitz (Ed.), *Advances in experimental social psychology* (Vol. 21, pp. 261–302). New York: Academic Press.

Steele, C. M. (1997). A threat in the air: How stereotypes shape intellectual identity and performance. *American Psychologist, 52*, 613–629.

Steele, C. M., & Aronson, J. M. (1995a). Stereotype threat and the intellectual test performance of African-Americans. *Journal of Personality and Social Psychology, 69*, 797–811.

Steele, C. M, & Aronson, J. (1995b). Stereotype vulnerability and intellectual performance. In E. Aronson (Ed.), *Readings about the social animal* (7th ed). New York: Freeman.

Steele, C. M., Spencer, S. J., & Aronson, J. M. (2002). Contending with group image: The psychology of stereotype and social identity threat. In M. P. Zanna (Ed.), *Advances in experimental social psychology* (Vol. 34, pp. 379–440). San Diego, CA: Academic Press.

Steele, C. M., Spencer, S. J., & Josephs, R. (1992). *Seeking self-relevant information: The effects of self-esteem and stability of the information.* Unpublished manuscript, University of Michigan.

Steele, C. M., Spencer, S. J., & Lynch, M. (1993). Self-image resilience and dissonance: The role of affirmational resources. *Journal of Personality and Social Psychology, 64*, 885–896.

Steele, J. R., & Ambady, N. (2006). "Math is hard!" The effect of gender priming on women's attitudes. *Journal of Experimental Social Psychology, 42*, 428–436.

Steiner, I. D. (1972). *Group process and productivity*. New York: Academic Press.

Stelzl, M., & Seligman, C. (2009). Multiplicity across cultures: Multiple national identities and multiple value systems. *Organization Studies, 30*(9), 959–973.

Stern, L. B., & Dunning, D. (1994). Distinguishing accurate from inaccurate eyewitness identifications: A reality monitoring approach. In D. F. Ross, J. D. Read, & M. P. Toglia (Eds.), *Adult eyewitness testimony: Current trends and developments* (pp. 273–299). New York: Cambridge University Press.

Sternberg, R. J., & Beall, A. E. (1991). How can we know what love is? An epistemological analysis. In G. J. O. Fletcher & F. D. Fincham (Eds.), *Cognition in close relationships* (pp. 257–278). Hillsdale, NJ: Erlbaum.

Sternberg, R. J., & Vroom, V. (2002). The person versus the situation in leadership. *Leadership Quarterly, 13*, 301–323.

Stewart, D. D., & Stasser, G. (1995). Expert role assignment and information sampling during collective recall and decision making. *Journal of Personality and Social Psychology, 69*, 619–628.

Stewart, M., Craig, D., MacPherson, K., & Alexander, S. (2001). Promoting positive affect and diminishing loneliness of widowed seniors through a support intervention. *Public Health Nursing, 18*, 54–63.

Stewart, T. L., Latu, I. M., Kawakami, K., & Myers, A. C. (2010). Consider the situation: Reducing automatic stereotyping through situational attribution training. *Journal of Experimental Social Psychology, 46*(1), 221–225.

Stewart, W., & Barling, J. (1996). Daily work stress, mood, and interpersonal job performance: A mediational model. *Work and Stress, 10*, 336–351.

Stice, E., & Shaw, H. E. (2002). Role of body dissatisfaction in the onset and maintenance of eating pathology: A synthesis of research findings. *Journal of Psychosomatic Research, 53*, 961–962.

Stickney, L. T., & Konrad, A. M. (2007). Gender-role attitudes and earnings: A multinational study of married women and men. *Sex Roles, 57*(11-12), 801–811.

Stinson, D., Logel, C., Holmes, J. G., Wood, J. V., Forest, A. L., Gaucher, D., . . . Kath, J. (2010). The regulatory function of self-esteem: Testing the epistemic and acceptance signaling systems. *Journal of Personality and Social Psychology, 99*(6), 993–1013.

Stinson, D., Logel, C., Zanna, M. P., Holmes, J. G., Cameron, J. J., Wood, J. V., & Spencer, S. J. (2008). The cost of lower self-esteem: Testing a self- and social-bonds model of health. *Journal of Personality and Social Psychology, 94*(3), 412–428.

Stobbe, M. (2010, November 10). Hyper-texting teens more likely to have sex, do drugs. *Winnipeg Free Press*, p. D1.

Stoff, D. M., & Cairns, R. B. (Eds). (1997). *Aggression and violence: Genetic, neurobiological, and biosocial perspectives.* Mahwah, NJ: Erlbaum.

Stogdill, R. M. (1974). *Handbook of leadership*. New York: Free Press.

Stone, A. A., Bovbjerg, D. H., Neale, J. M., Napoli, A., Valdimarsdottir, H., Cox, . . . Gwaltney, J. M. (1992). Development of common cold symptoms following experimental rhinovirus infection is related to prior stressful life events. *Behavioral Medicine, 18*(3), 115–120.

Stone, J., Aronson, E., Crain, A. L., Winslow, M. P., & Fried, C. (1994). Inducing hypocrisy as a means of encouraging young adults to use condoms. *Personality and Social Psychology Bulletin, 20*, 116–128.

Stormo, K. J., Lang, A. R., & Stritzke, W. G. K. (1997). Attributions about acquaintance rape: The role of alcohol and individual differences. *Journal of Applied Social Psychology, 27*, 279–305.

Storms, M. D. (1973). Videotape and the attribution process: Reversing actors' and observers' points of view. *Journal of Personality and Social Psychology, 27*, 165–175.

Storms, M. D., & Nisbett, R. E. (1970). Insomnia and the attribution process. *Journal of Personality and Social Psychology, 16*, 319–328.

Strahan, E. J., Lafrance, A., Wilson, A. E., Ethier, N., Spencer, S. J., & Zanna, M. P. (2008). Victoria's dirty secret: How sociocultural norms influence adolescent girls and women. *Personality and Social Psychology Bulletin, 34*(2), 288–301.

Strahan, E. J., Spencer, S. J., & Zanna, M. P. (2002). Subliminal priming and persuasion: Striking while the iron is hot. *Journal of Experimental Social Psychology, 38*, 556–568.

Straus, M. A. (2004). Prevalence of violence against dating partners by male and female university students worldwide. *Violence Against Women, 10*, 790–811.

Strauss, M. A., & Gelles, R. J. (1980). *Behind closed doors: Violence in the American family*. New York: Anchor/Doubleday.

Stroebe, W., & Stroebe, M. (1996). The social psychology of social support. In E. T. Higgins & A. W. Kruglanski (Eds.), *Social psychology: Handbook of basic principles* (pp. 597–621). New York: Guilford.

Struthers, C., Eaton, J., Mendoza, R., Santelli, A. G., & Shirvani, N. (2010). Interrelationship among injured parties' attributions of responsibility, appraisal of appropriateness to forgive the transgressor, forgiveness, and repentance. *Journal of Applied Social Psychology, 40*(4), 970–1002.

Struthers, C., Eaton, J., Santelli, A. G., Uchiyama, M., & Shirvani, N. (2008). The effects of attributions of intent and apology on forgiveness: When saying sorry may not help the story. *Journal of Experimental Social Psychology, 44*(4), 983–992.

Struthers, C. W., Dupuis, R., & Eaton, J. (2005). Promoting forgiveness among co-workers following a workplace transgression: The effects of social motivation training. *Canadian Journal of Behavioural Science, 37*, 299–308.

Studer, J. (1996). Understanding and preventing aggressive responses in youth. *Elementary School Guidance and Counseling, 30*, 194–203.

Stuhlmacher, A. F., & Citera, M. (2005). Hostile behavior and profit in virtual negotiation: A meta-analysis. *Journal of Business and Psychology, 20*, 69–93.

Stürmer, S., Snyder, M., & Omoto, A. (2005). Prosocial emotions and helping: The moderating role of group membership. *Journal of Personality and Social Psychology, 88*(3), 532–546.

Stuster, J. W., & Blowers, M. A. (1995). *Experimental evaluation of sobriety checkpoint programs.* Report No. DTNH22-91-C-07204. Washington, DC: National Highway Safety Administration.

Sudman, S., Bradburn, N., & Schwarz, N. (1996). *Thinking about answers: The application of cognitive processes to survey methodology*. San Fransisco, CA: Jossey-Bass Publishers.

Suedfeld, P. (2003). Specific and general attributional patterns of holocaust survivors. *Canadian Journal of Behavioural Science, 35*(2), 133–141.

Suedfeld, P., Conway, L. G., III & Eichorn, D. (2001). Studying Canadian leaders at a distance. In O. Feldman & L. O. Valenty (Eds.), *Profiling political leaders: Cross-cultural studies of personality and behavior* (pp. 3–19). Westport, CT: Praeger Publishers/ Greenwood Publishing Group.

Sullivan, B., O'Connor, K., & Burris, E. (2006). Negotiator confidence: The impact of self-efficacy on tactics and outcomes. *Journal of Experimental Social Psychology, 42*, 567–581.

Suls, J., & Fletcher, B. (1983). Social comparison in the social and physical sciences: An archival study. *Journal of Personality and Social Psychology, 44*, 575–580.

Suls, J. M., Martin, R., & Wheeler, L. (2000). Three kinds of opinion comparison: The triadic model. *Personality and Social Psychology Review, 4*, 219–237.

Suls, J. M., & Miller, R. L. (Eds). (1977). *Social comparison processes: Theoretical and empirical perspectives*. Washington, DC: Hemisphere/ Halstead.

Summers, G., & Feldman, N. S. (1984). Blaming the victim versus blaming the perpetrator: An attributional analysis of spouse abuse. *Journal of Social and Clinical Psychology, 2*, 339–347.

Sundstrom, E., Bell, P. A., Busby, P. L., & Asmus, C. (1996). Environmental psychology. *Annual Review of Psychology, 47*, 485–512.

Surian, L., Caldi, S., & Sperber, D. (2007). Attribution of beliefs by 13-month-old infants. *Psychological Science, 18*(7), 580–586.

Susskind, J.M., Lee, D.H., Cusi, A., Feiman, R., Grabski, W., & Anderson, A. K. (2008). Expressing fear enhances sensory acquisition. *Nature Neuroscience, 11*(7), 843–850.

Swann, W. B., Jr. (1990). To be adored or to be known? The interplay of self-enhancement and self-verification. In R. M. Sorrentino & E. T. Higgins (Eds.), *Motivation and cognition* (pp. 404–448). New York: Guilford Press.

Swann, W. B., Jr. (1996). *Self-traps: The elusive quest for higher self-esteem*. New York: W. H. Freeman.

Swann, W. B., Jr. Bosson, J. K., & Pelham, B. W. (2002). Different partners, different selves: Strategic self-verification of circumscribed identities. *Personality and Social Psychology Bulletin, 28*, 1215–1228.

Swann, W. B., Jr. & Ely, Jr., R. J. (1984). A battle of wills: Self- verification versus behavioral confirmation. *Journal of Personality and Social Psychology, 46*, 1287–1302.

Swann, W. B., Jr. & Hill, C. A. (1982). When our identities are mistaken: Reaffirming self-conceptions through social interaction. *Journal of Personality and Social Psychology, 43*, 59–66.

Swann, W. B., Jr. & Pelham, B. W. (1988). *The social construction of identity: Self-verification through friend and intimate selection*. Unpublished manuscript, University of Texas-Austin.

Swann, W. B., Jr. & Schroeder, D. B. (1995). The search for beauty and truth: A framework for understanding reactions to evaluations. *Personality and Social Psychology Bulletin, 21*, 1307–1318.

Swann, W. B., Jr. Stein-Seroussi, A., & McNulty, S. E. (1992). Outcasts in a white-lie society: The enigmatic worlds of people with negative self-concepts. *Journal of Personality and Social Psychology, 62*, 618–624.

Swap, W. C. (1977). Interpersonal attraction and repeated exposure to rewarders and punishers. *Personality and Social Psychology Bulletin, 3*, 248–251.

Sweeney, P. D., Anderson, K., & Bailey, S. (1986). Attributional style in depression: A meta-analytic review. *Journal of Personality and Social Psychology, 50*, 974–991.

Swim, J., & Sanna, L. (1996). He's skilled, she's lucky: A meta-analysis of observers' attributions for women's and men's successes and failures. *Personality and Social Psychology Bulletin, 22*, 507–519.

Sykes, R. E. (1983). Initial interaction between strangers and acquaintances: A multivariate analysis of factors affecting choice of communication partners. *Human Communication Research, 10*, 27–63.

Symons, C. S., & Johnson, B. T. (1997). The self-reference effect in memory: A meta-analysis. *Psychological Bulletin, 121*, 371–394.

Symons, D. (1979). *The evolution of human sexuality*. New York: Oxford University Press.

Tafarodi, R. W., Kang, S., & Milne, A. B. (2002). When different becomes similar: Compensatory conformity in bicultural visible minorities. *Personality and Social Psychology Bulletin, 28*, 1131–1142.

Tajfel, H. (1982a). *Social identity and intergroup relations*. Cambridge, UK: Cambridge University Press.

Tajfel, H. (1982b). Social psychology of intergroup relations. *Annual Review of Psychology, 33*, 1–39.

Tajfel, H., & Billig, M. (1974). Familiarity and categorization in intergroup behavior. *Journal of Experimental Social Psychology, 10*, 159–170.

Tajfel, H., & Turner, J. C. (1979). An integrative theory of social contact. In W. Austin & S. Worchel (Eds.), *The social psychology of intergroup relations* (pp. 33–47). Monterey, CA: Brooks/Cole.

Takaku, S. (2006). Reducing road rage: An application of the dissonance-attribution model of interpersonal forgiveness. *Journal of Applied Social Psychology, 36*, 2362–2378.

Tamres, L. K., Janicki, D., & Helgeson, V. S. (2002). Sex differences in coping behavior: A meta-analytic review. *Personality and Social Psychology Review, 6*, 2–30.

Tanford, S., & Penrod, S. (1984). Social influence model: A formal integration of research on majority and minority influence processes. *Psychological Bulletin, 95*, 189–225.

Tang, K. (2000). Cultural stereotypes and the justice system: The Canadian case of *R.* v. *Ewanchuk*. *International Journal of Offender Therapy and Comparative Criminology, 44*, 681–691.

Tang, S., & Hall, V. C. (1995). The overjustification effect: A meta-analysis. *Applied Cognitive Psychology, 9*, 365–404.

Tavris, C. (1984). On the wisdom of counting to ten: Personal and social dangers of anger expression. *Review of Personality and Social Psychology, 5*, 170–191.

Tavris, C. (1989). *Anger: The misunderstood emotion* (Rev. Ed.). New York: Touchstone Books/Simon & Schuster.

Tavris, C., & Aronson, E. (2007). *Mistakes were made (but not by me)*. New York: Harcourt.

Taylor, D. M., & Gardner, R. C. (1969). Ethnic stereotypes: There effects on the perception of communicators of varying credibility. *Canadian Journal of Psychology, 23*, 161–173.

Taylor, D. M., Ruggiero, K. M., & Louis, W. R. (1996). Personal/group discrimination discrepancy: Towards a two-factor explanation. *Canadian Journal of Behavioural Science, 28*, 193–202.

Taylor, D. M., Wright, S. C., Moghaddam, F. M, & Lalonde, R. M. (1990). The personal/group discrimination discrepancy: Perceiving my group, but not myself, to be a target fro discrimination. *Personality and Social Psychology Bulletin, 16*, 254–262.

Taylor, S. (2006). Tend and Befriend: Biobehavioral Bases of Affiliation Under Stress. *Current Directions in Psychological Science, 15*, 273–277.

Taylor, S. E. (1981). A categorization approach to stereotyping. In D. L. Hamilton (Ed.), *Cognitive processes in stereotyping and intergroup relations* (pp. 418–429). Hillsdale, NJ: Erlbaum.

Taylor, S. E. (1989). *Positive illusions: Creative self-deception and the healthy mind*. New York: Basic Books.

Taylor, S. E. (1995). *Health psychology* (3rd ed.). New York: McGraw-Hill.

Taylor, S.E. (2007). Social support. In H.S. Friedman & R.C. Silver (Eds.), *Foundations of health psychology* (pp. 145-171). New York: Oxford University Press.

Taylor, S. E., & Brown, J. (1988). Illusion and well-being: A social psychological perspective on mental health. *Psychological Bulletin, 103*, 193–210.

Taylor, S. E., & Brown, J. D. (1994). Positive illusions and well-being revisited: Separating fact from fiction. *Psychological Bulletin, 116*, 21–27.

Taylor, S. E., & Falcone, H. (1982). Cognitive bases of stereotyping: The relationship between categorization and prejudice. *Personality and Social Psychology Bulletin, 8*, 426–432.

Taylor, S. E., & Fiske, S. T. (1975). Point of view and perceptions of causality. *Journal of Personality and Social Psychology, 32*, 439–445.

Taylor, S. E., Klein, L. C., Lewis, B. P., Gruenewald, T. L., Gurung, R. A. R., & Updegraff, J. A. (2000). Biobehavioral responses to stress in females: Tend-and-befriend, not fight-or-flight. *Psychological Review, 107*, 411–429.

Taylor, S. E., Lichtman, R. R., & Wood, J. V. (1984). Attributions, beliefs about control, and adjustment to breast cancer. *Journal of Personality and Social Psychology, 46*, 489–502.

Taylor, S. E., Repetti, R. L., & Seeman, T. (1997). Health psychology: What is an unhealthy environment and how does it get under the skin? *Annual Review of Psychology, 48*, 411–447.

Taylor, S. E., Welch, W., Kim, H. S., & Sherman, D. K. (2007). Cultural differences in the impact of social support on psychological and biological stress responses. *Psychological Science, 18*, 831–837.

Taylor, S. P., & Leonard, K. E. (1983). Alcohol and human physical aggression. In R. Geen & E. Donnerstein (Eds.), *Aggression: Theoretical and empirical reviews*. New York: Academic Press.

Teger, A. L., & Pruitt, D. G. (1967). Components of group risk taking. *Journal of Experimental Social Psychology, 3*, 189–205.

ten Brinke, L., McDonald, S., Porter, S., & O'Connor, B. (in press). Crocodile tears: Facial, verbal and body language behaviour associated with genuine and fabricated remorse. *Law and Human Behaviour*.

Teng, L., Laroche, M., & Zhu, H. (2007). The effects of multiple-ads and multiple-brands on consumer attitude and purchase behavior. *Journal of Consumer Marketing, 24*(1), 27–35.

Ternes, M., & Yuille, J. C. (2008). Eyewitness memory and eyewitness identification performance in adults with intellectual disabilities. *Journal of Applied Research in Intellectual Disabilities, 21*(6), 519–531.

Terracciano, A., Abdel-Khalek, A. M., Ádám, N., Adamovová, L., Ahn, C.-k., Ahn, H.-n., . . . McCrae, R. R. (2005). National character does not reflect mean personality trait levels in 49 cultures. *Science, 310*, 96–100.

Tesser, A., & Beach, S. R. H. (1998). Life events, relationship quality, and depression: An investigation of judgment discontinuity in vivo. *Journal of Personality and Social Psychology, 74*, 36–52.

Tesser, A., Campbell, J., & Mickler, S. (1983). The role of social pressure, attention to the stimulus, and self-doubt in conformity. *European Journal of Social Psychology, 13*, 217–233.

Tetlock, P. E., Peterson, R. S., McGuire, C., Chang, S., & Field, P. (1992). Assessing political group dynamics: A test of the groupthink model. *Journal of Personality and Social Psychology, 63*, 403–425.

Thibault, P., Bourgeois, P., & Hess, U. (2006). The effect of group-identification on emotion recognition: The case of cats and basketball players. *Journal of Experimental Social Psychology, 42*, 676–683.

Thibaut, J. W., & Kelley, H. H. (1959). *The social psychology of groups*. New York: Wiley.

Thibodeau, R., & Aronson, E. (1992). Taking a closer look: Reasserting the role of the self-concept in dissonance theory. *Personality and Social Psychology Bulletin, 18*, 591–602.

Thomas, C. R., & Gadbois, S. A. (2007). Academic self-handicapping: The role of self-clarity and students' learning strategies. *British Journal of Educational Psychology*, 77(1), 101–119.

Thomas, M. (1982). Physiological arousal, exposure to a relatively lengthy aggressive film, and aggressive behavior. *Journal of Research in Personality, 16*, 72–81.

Thomas, M. H., Horton, R., Lippincott, E., & Drabman, R. (1977). Desensitization to portrayals of real-life aggression as a function of exposure to television violence. *Journal of Personality and Social Psychology, 35*, 450–458.

Thomas, S. L., Skitka, L. J., Christen, S., & Jurgena, M. (2002). Social facilitation and impression formation. *Basic and Applied Social Psychology, 242*, 67–70.

Thomas, W. I. (1928). *The child in America*. New York: Alfred A. Knopf.

Thompson, J. K., & Heinberg, L. J. (1999). The media's influence on body image disturbance and eating disorders: We've reviled them, now can we rehabilitate them? *Journal of Social Issues, 55*, 339–353.

Thompson, L. (1997). *The mind and heart of the negotiator*. Englewood Cliffs, NJ: Prentice-Hall.

Thompson, L. L. (2005). *The heart and mind of the negotiator* (3rd ed.). Upper Saddle River, NJ: Prentice-Hall.

Thompson, S. C. (1999). Illusions of control: How we overestimate our personal influence. *Current Directions in Psychological Science, 8*, 187–190.

Thompson, S. C. (2002). The role of personal control in adaptive functioning. In C. R. Snyder & S. J. Lopez (Eds.), *Handbook of positive psychology* (pp. 202–213). London, UK: Oxford University Press.

Thompson, S. C., Nanni, C., & Levine, A. (1994). Primary versus secondary and central versus consequence-related control in HIV-positive men. *Journal of Personality and Social Psychology, 67*, 540–547.

Tiggemann, M., & Polivy, J. (2010). Upward and downward: Social comparison processing of thin idealized media images. *Psychology of Women Quarterly, 34*(3), 356–364.

Tihanyi, E. (1999). Who I am because of who she was. In G. Valle (Ed). *Our grandmothers, ourselves: Reflections of Canadian women* (pp. 102–108). Vancouver, BC: Raincoast Books.

Timmerman, T. A. (2007). "It was a thought pitch": Personal, situational, and target influences on hit-by-pitch events across time. *Journal of Applied Psychology, 92*, 876–884.

Ting, J., & Piliavin, J. A. (2000). Altruism in comparative international perspective. In J. Phillips, B. Chapman, & D. Stevens (Eds.), *Between state and market: Essays on charities law and policy in Canada* (pp. 51–105). Montreal, QC, and Kingston, ON: McGill-Queen's University Press.

Ting-Toomey, S., & Chang, L. (1996). Cross cultural interpersonal communication: Theoretical trends and research directions. In W. B. Gudykunst, S. Ting-Toomey, & T. Nishada (Eds.), *Communication in personal relationships across cultures*. Thousand Oaks, CA: Sage.

Toch, H. (1980). *Violent men* (rev. ed). Cambridge, MA: Schenkman.

Toi, M., & Batson, C. D. (1982). More evidence that empathy is a source of altruistic motivation. *Journal of Personality and Social Psychology, 43*, 281–292.

Tollestrup, P., Turtle, J., & Yuille, J. (1994). Actual victims and witnesses to robbery and fraud: An archival analysis. In D. F. Ross, J. D. Read, & M. P. Toglia (Eds.), *Adult eyewitness testimony: Current trends and developments* (pp. 144–160). New York: Cambridge University Press.

Tomes, J. L., & Katz, A. N. (1997). Habitual susceptibility to misinformation and individual differences in eyewitness memory. *Applied Cognitive Psychology, 11*, 233–251.

Tormala, Z. L., & Petty, R. E. (2002). What doesn't kill me makes me stronger: The effect of resisting persuasion on attitude certainty. *Journal of Personality and Social Psychology, 83:6*, 1298–1313.

Toronto (2000). *Research group on drug use*. Toronto, ON: Department of Public Health.

Tougas, F., Brown, R., Beaton, A. M., & Joly, S. (1995). Neosexism: *Plus ça change, plus c'est pareil. Personality and Social Psychology Bulletin, 21*, 842–849.

Tougas, F., Brown, R., Beaton, A., & St-Pierre, L. (1999). Neosexism among women: The role of personally experienced social mobility attempts. *Personality and Social Psychology Bulletin, 25*, 1487–1497.

Tougas, F., de la Sablonnière, R., Lagacé, M., & Kocum, L. (2003). Intrusiveness of minorities: Growing pains for the majority group? *Journal of Applied Social Psychology, 33*(2), 283–298.

Tougas, F., Desruisseaux, J.-C., Desrochers, A., St-Pierre, L., Perrino, A., & de la Sablonnière, R. (2004). Two forms of racism and their related outcomes: The bad and the ugly. *Canadian Journal of Behavioural Science, 36*(3), 177–189.

Tougas, F., Rinfret, N., Beaton, A. M., & de la Sablonnière, R. (2005). Policewomen acting in self-defense: Can psychological disengagement protect self-esteem from the negative outcomes of relative deprivation? *Journal of Personality and Social Psychology, 88*(5), 790–800.

Trach, J., Hymel, S., Waterhouse, T., & Neale, K. (2010). Bystander responses to school bullying: A cross-sectional investigation of grade and sex differences. *Canadian Journal of School Psychology, 25*(1), 114–130.

Tracy, J. L., & Matsumoto, D. (2008). The spontaneous expression of pride and shame: Evidence for biologically innate nonverbal displays. *Proceedings of the National Academy of Sciences, 105*(33), 11655-11660.

Tracy, J. L., & Robins, R. W. (2006). Appraisal antecedents of shame and guilt: Support for a theoretical model. *Personality and Social Psychology Bulletin, 32*, 1339–1351.

Tracy, J. L., & Robins, R. W. (2007). The psychological structure of pride: A tale of two facets. *Journal of Personality and Social Psychology, 92*, 506–525.

Tracy, J. L., & Robins, R. W. (2008). The nonverbal expression of pride: Evidence for cross-cultural recognition. *Journal of Personality and Social Psychology, 94*(3), 516–530.

Trampe, D., Stapel, D. A., & Siero, F. W. (2007). On models and vases: Body dissatisfaction and proneness to social comparison effects. *Journal of Personality and Social Psychology, 92*, 106–118.

Trappey, C. (1996). A meta-analysis of consumer choice and subliminal advertising. *Psychology and Marketing, 13*, 517–530.

Traupmann, J., Petersen, R., Utne, M., & Hatfield, E. (1981). Measuring equity in intimate relations. *Applied Psychology Measurement, 5*, 467–480.

Travis, C. B., Phillippi, R. H., & Tonn, B. E. (1989). Judgment heuristics and medical decisions. *Patient Education and Counseling, 13*, 211–220.

Travis, C. B., & Yeager, C. P. (1991). Sexual selection, parental investment, and sexism. *Journal of Social Issues, 47*, 117–129.

Tremblay, P., Graham, K., & Wells, S. (2008). Severity of physical aggression reported by university students: A test of the interaction between trait aggression and alcohol consumption. *Personality and Individual Differences, 45*(1), 3–9.

Tremblay, P., Mihic, L., Graham, K., & Jelley, J. (2007). Role of motivation to respond to provocation, the social environment, and trait aggression in alcohol-related aggression. *Aggressive Behavior, 33*(5), 389–411.

Tremblay, R. E., Schaal, B., Boulerice, B., Arseneault, L., Soussignan, R. G., Paquette, D., & Laurent, D. (1998). Testosterone, physical aggression, dominance, and physical development in early adolescence. *International Journal of Behavioral Development, 22*, 753–777.

Triandis, H. C. (1989). The self and social behavior in differing cultural contexts. *Psychological Review, 96*, 506–520.

Triandis, H. C. (1990). Cross-cultural studies of individualism and collectivism. In J. J. Berman (Ed.), *Nebraska Symposium on Motivation, 1989* (pp. 41–133). Lincoln, NE: University of Nebraska Press.

Triandis, H. C. (1994). *Culture and social behavior*. New York: McGraw-Hill.

Triandis, H. C. (1995). *Individualism and collectivism*. Boulder, CO: Westview Press.

Triplett, N. (1898). The dynamogenic factors in pace making and competition. *American Journal of Psychology, 9*, 507–533.

Trivers, R. L. (1971). The evolution of reciprocal altruism. *Quarterly Review of Biology, 46*, 35–57.

Trope, Y., & Gaunt, R. (2000). Processing alternative explanations of behavior: Correction of integration? *Journal of Personality and Social Psychology, 79*(3), 344–354.

Trope, Y., & Gaunt, R. (2003). Attribution and person perception. In M. A. Hogg & J. Cooper (Eds.), *The sage handbook of social psychology* (pp.190–210). Thousand Oaks, CA: Sage.

Tropp, L. R., & Wright, S. C. (2001). Ingroup identification as the inclusion of ingroup in the self. *Personality and Social Psychology Bulletin, 27*, 585–600.

Trottier, K., Polivy, J., & Herman, C. (2007). Effects of exposure to thin and overweight peers: Evidence of social comparison in restrained and unrestrained eaters. *Journal of Social and Clinical Psychology, 26*(2), 155–172.

Tsai, M. (2006). Sociable resources and close relationships: Intimate relatives and friends in Taiwan. *Journal of Social and Personal Relationships, 23*, 151–169.

Tseëlon, E. (1995). *The presentation of woman in everyday life*. Thousand Oaks, CA: Sage.

Tucker, P., Pfefferbaum, B., Doughty, D. B., Jones, D. E., Jordan, F. B., & Nixon, S. J. (2002). Body handlers after terrorism in Oklahoma City: Predictors of posttraumatic stress and other symptoms. *American Journal of Orthopsychiatry, 72*, 469–475.

Tucker, S., Turner, N., Barling, J., & McEvoy, M. (2010). Transformational leadership and childrens' aggression in team settings: A short-term longitudinal study. *The Leadership Quarterly, 21*(3), 389–399.

Turner, C., & Leyens, J. (1992). The weapons effect revisited: The effects of firearms on aggressive behavior. In P. Suedfeld & P. Tetlock (Eds.), *Psychology and social policy* (pp. 201–221). New York: Hemispheres.

Turner, C., & Simons, L. (1974). Effects of subject sophistication and evaluation apprehension on aggressive responses to weapons. *Journal of Personality and Social Psychology, 30*, 341–348.

Turner, C., Simons, L., Berkowitz, L., & Frodi, A. (1977). The stimulating and inhibiting effects of weapons on aggressive behavior. *Aggressive Behavior, 3*, 355–378.

Turner, J. C., Hogg, M. A., Oakes, P. J., Reicher, S. D., & Wetherell, M. S. (1987). *Rediscovering the social group: A self-categorization theory*. Oxford, UK: Blackwell Publishers.

Turner, M., Pratkanis, A., Probasco, P., & Leve, C. (2006). Threat, cohesion, and group effectiveness: Testing a social identity maintenance perspective on groupthink. In J. M. Levine & R. L. Moreland (Eds.), *Small groups* (pp. 241–264). New York: Psychology Press.

Turner, M., Pratkanis, A., & Struckman, C. (2007). Groupthink as social identity maintenance. *The science of social influence: Advances and future progress* (pp. 223–246). New York: Psychology Press.

Turner, M. E., & Horvitz, T. (2001). The dilemma of threat: Group effectiveness and ineffectiveness under adversity. In M. E. Turner (Ed.), *Groups at work: Theory and research* (pp. 445–470). Mahwah, NJ: Erlbaum.

Turner, N., Chmiel, N., Hershcovis, M., & Walls, M. (2010). Life on the line: Job demands, perceived co-worker support for safety, and hazardous work events. *Journal of Occupational Health Psychology, 15*(4), 482–493.

Turula, M. (2007, August 11). Eight shot dead at Finnish school. *Winnipeg Free Press*. Retrieved from www.winnipegfreepress.com/historic/ 32558084.html

Turula, M. (2008, November 8). 8 shot dead at Finnish school. *Winnipeg Free Press*, p. A3.

Tversky, A., & Kahneman, D. (1973). Availability: A heuristic for judging frequency and probability. *Cognitive Psychology, 5*, 207–232.

Tversky, A., & Kahneman, D. (1974). Judgment under uncertainty: Heuristics and biases. *Science, 185*, 1124–1131.

Twenge, J. M., Baumeister, R. F., DeWall, C., Ciarocco, N. J., & Bartels, J. M. (2007). Social exclusion decreases prosocial behaviour. *Journal of Personality and Social Psychology, 92*, 56–66.

Twenge, J. M., Baumeister, R. F., Tice, D. M., & Stucke, T. S. (2001). If you can't join them, beat them: Effects of social exclusion on aggressive behavior. *Journal of Personality and Social Psychology, 81*, 1058–1069.

Tyler, T. R. (1990). *Why people obey the law*. New Haven, CT: Yale University Press.

Uchino, B. N., Uno, D., & Holt-Lunstad, J. (1999). Social support, physiological processes, and health. *Current Directions in Psychological Science, 8*, 145–148.

Uehara, E. S. (1995). Reciprocity reconsidered: Gouldner's "moral norm of reciprocity" and social support. *Journal of Social and Personal Relationships, 12*, 483–502.

Updegraff, J., Silver, R., & Holman, E. (2008). Searching for and finding meaning in collective trauma: Results from a national longitudinal study of the 9/11 terrorist attacks. *Journal of Personality and Social Psychology, 95*, 709–722.

Usborne, E., & Taylor, D. M. (2010). The role of cultural identity clarity for self-concept clarity, self-esteem, and subjective well-being. *Personality and Social Psychology Bulletin, 36*(7), 883–897.

Uskul, A. K., Lalonde, R. N., & Cheng, L. (2007). Views on interracial dating among Chinese and European Canadians: The roles of culture, gender, and mainstream cultural identity. *Journal of Social and Personal Relationships, 24*, 891–911.

Uzzell, D. (2000). Ethnographic and action research. In G. M. Breakwell, S. Hammond, & C. Fife-Schaw (Eds.), *Research methods in psychology* (2nd ed., pp. 326–337). Thousand Oaks, CA: Sage.

Vaananen, A., Buunk, B. P., Kivimaki, M., Pentti, J., & Vahteva, J. (2005). When is it better to give than to receive? Long-term health effects of perceived reciprocity in support exchange. *Journal of Personality and Social Psychology, 89*, 176–193.

Vaillancourt, T., Brittain, H., Bennett, L., Arnocky, S., McDougall, P., Hymel, S., . . . Cunningham, L. (2010). Places to avoid: Population-based study of student reports of unsafe and high bullying areas at school. *Canadian Journal of School Psychology, 25*(1), 40–54.

Vaillancourt, T., McDougall, P., Hymel, S., Krygsman, A., Miller, J., Stiver, K., & Davis, C. (2008). Bullying: Are researchers and children/youth talking about the same thing? *International Journal of Behavioral Development, 32*(6), 486–495.

Valins, S. (1966). Cognitive effects of false heart-rate feedback. *Journal of Personality and Social Psychology, 4*, 400–408.

Valle, P. O. D., Rebelo, E., & Reis, E. (2005). Combining behavioral theories to predict recycling involvement. *Environment and Behavior, 37*, 364–396.

Van Vugt, M. (2006). Evolutionary origins of leadership and followership. *Personality and Social Psychology Review, 10*(4), 354–371.

Van Vugt, M., & De Cremer, D. C. (1999). Leadership in social dilemmas: The effects of group identification on collective actions to provide public goods. *Journal of Personality and Social Psychology, 76*, 587–599.

Vallerand, R. J. (1997). Toward a hierarchical model of intrinsic and extrinsic motivation. *Advances in Experimental Social Psychology, 29*, 271–360.

Vallerand, R. J., Fortier, M. S., & Guay, F. (1997). Self-determination and persistence in real-life setting: Toward a motivational model of high school dropout. *Journal of Personality and Social Psychology, 72*, 1161–1176.

Vallerand, R. J., & Ratelle, C. F. (2002). Intrinsic and extrinsic motivation: A hierarchical model. In E. L. Deci & R. M. Ryan (Eds.), *Handbook of self-determination research* (pp. 37–63). Rochester, NY: University of Rochester Press.

Vallone, R. P., Griffin, D. W., Lin, S., & Ross, L. (1990). The overconfident prediction of future actions and outcomes by self and others. *Journal of Personality and Social Psychology, 58*, 582–592.

Van Bavel, J. J., & Cunningham, W. A. (2007, June). *Shifting intergroup evaluations using arbitrary coalitions*. Paper presented at the Canadian Psychological Association Conference, Ottawa, Ontario.

Van Boven, L., White, K., Kamanda, A., & Gilovich, T. (2003). Intuitions about situational correction in self and others. *Journal of Personality and Social Psychology, 85*(2), 249–258.

Vandello, J. A., & Cohen, D. (2003) Male honor and female fidelity: Implicit cultural scripts that perpetuate domestic violence. *Journal of Personality and Social Psychology, 84*, 997–1010.

van de Vijver, F., & Leung, K. (1997). *Methods and data analyses for cross-cultural research*. Thousand Oaks, CA: Sage.

Van Lange, P. A. M., Ouwerkerk, J. W., & Tazelaar, M. J. A. (2002). How to overcome the detrimental effects of noise in social interaction: The benefits of generosity. *Journal of Personality and Social Psychology, 82*, 768–780.

Vanneman, R. D., & Pettigrew, T. (1972). Race and relative deprivation in the urban United States. *Race, 13*, 461–486.

VanOostrum, N., & Horvath, P. (1997). The effects of hostile attribution on adolescents' aggressive responses to social situations. *Canadian Journal of School Psychology, 13*, 729–738.

Van Overwalle, F., & De Metsenaere, M. (1990). The effects of attribution-based intervention and study strategy training on academic achievement in college freshmen. *British Journal of Educational Psychology, 60*, 299–311.

Van Vugt, M. (2001). Community identification moderating the impact of financial incentives in a natural social dilemma: Water conservation. *Personality and Social Psychology Bulletin, 27*, 1440–1449.

Van Vugt, M., & Samuelson, C. (1999). The impact of personal metering in the management of a natural resource crisis: A social dilemma analysis. *Personality and Social Psychology Bulletin, 25*, 731–745.

Van Winkle, C. M., & MacKay, K. J. (2008). Self-serving bias in visitors' perceptions of the impacts of tourism. *Journal of Leisure Research, 40*(1), 69–89.

Van Yperen, N. W., & Buunk, B. P. (1994). Social comparison and social exchange in marital relationships. In M. J. Lerner & G. Mikula (Eds.), *Entitlement and the affectional bond: Justice in close relationships* (pp. 89–116). New York: Plenum.

Vasquez, N. A., & Buehler, R. (2007). Seeing future success: Does imagery perspective influence achievement motivation? *Personality and Social Psychology Bulletin, 33*, 1392–1405.

Verkuyten, M. (2005). Ethnic group identification and group evaluation among minority and majority groups: Testing the multiculturalism hypothesis. *Journal of Personality and Social Psychology, 88*, 121–138.

Vidmar, N. (1974). Retributive and ulitarian motives and other correlates of Canadian attitudes toward the death penalty. *Canadian Psychologist, 15*, 337–356.

Vidyasgar, P., & Mishra, H. (1993). Effect of modelling on aggression. *Indian Journal of Clinical Psychology, 20*, 50–52.

Vining, J., & Ebreo, A. (2002). Emerging theoretical and methodological perspectives on conservation behavior. In R. B. Bechtel & A. Churchman (Eds.), *Handbook of environmental psychology* (pp. 541–558). New York: Wiley.

Vissing, Y., Straus, M., Gelles, R., & Harrop, J. (1991).Verbal aggression by parents and psychosocial problems of children. *Child Abuse and Neglect, 15*, 223–238.

Voas, R. B., Holder, H. D., & Gruenewald, P. J. (1999). The effect of drinking and driving interventions on alcohol-related traffic crashes within a comprehensive community trial. *Addiction, 92*, S221–S236.

Voelpel, S. C., Eckhoff, R. A., & Forster, J. (2008). David against Goliath? Group size and bystander effects in virtual knowledge sharing. *Human Relations, 61*, 271–295.

Vohs, K. D., Baumeister, R. F., & Ciarocco, N. J. (2005). Self-regulation and self-presentation: Regulatory resource depletion impairs impression management and effortful self-presentation depletes regulatory resources. *Journal of Personality and Social Psychology, 88*, 632–657.

Volling, B. L., Kolak, A. M., & Kennedy, D. E. (2009). Empathy and compassionate love in early childhood: Development and family influence. In B. Fehr, S. Sprecher, & L. Underwood (Eds.), *The science of compassionate love: Theory, research, and applications* (pp. 161–200). Malden, MA: Blackwell Publishers.

von Hippel, W., Hawkins, C., & Schooler, J. W. (2001). Stereotype distinctiveness: How counterstereotypic behavior shapes the self-concept. *Journal of Personality and Social Psychology, 81*, 193–205.

von Hippel, W., von Hippel, C., Conway, L., Preacher, K. J., Schooler, J. W., & Radvansky, G. A. (2005). Coping with stereotype threat: Denial as an impression management strategy. *Journal of Personality and Social Psychology, 89*, 22–35.

Voracek, M., Fisher, M. L., Rupp, B., Lucas, D., & Fessler, D. T. (2007). Sex differences in relative foot length and perceived attractiveness of female feet: Relationships among anthropometry, physique, and preference ratings. *Perceptual and Motor Skills, 104*(3, Pt2), 1123–1138.

Vorauer, J. D. (2001). The other side of the story: Transparency estimation in social interaction. In G. B. Moskowitz (Ed.), *Cognitive social psychology: The Princeton symposium on the legacy and future of social cognition* (pp. 261–276). Mahwah, NJ: Erlbaum.

Vorauer, J. D. (2003). Dominant group members in intergroup interaction: Safety or vulnerability in numbers? *Personality and Social Psychology Bulletin, 29*, 498–511.

Vorauer, J. D. (2005). Miscommunications surrounding efforts to reach out across group boundaries. *Personality and Social Psychology Bulletin, 31*, 1653–1664.

Vorauer, J. (2008). Unprejudiced and self-focused: When intergroup contact is experienced as being about the ingroup rather than the outgroup. *Journal of Experimental Social Psychology, 44*, 912–919.

Vorauer, J. D., & Cameron, J. J. (2002). So close, and yet so far: Does collectivism foster transparency overestimation? *Journal of Personality and Social Psychology, 83*, 1344–1352.

Vorauer, J. D., Cameron, J. J., Holmes, J. G., & Pearce, D.G. (2003). Invisible overtures: Fears of rejection and the signal amplification bias. *Journal of Personality and Social Psychology, 84*(4), 793–812.

Vorauer, J. D., & Claude, S. D. (1998). Perceived versus actual transparency of goals in negotiation. *Personality and Social Psychology Bulletin, 24*, 371–385.

Vorauer, J. D., Hunter, A. J., Main, K., & Roy, S. (2000). Meta- stereotype activation: Evidence from indirect measures for specific evaluative concerns experienced by members of dominant groups in intergroup interaction. *Journal of Personality and Social Psychology, 78*, 690–707.

Vorauer, J. D., & Kumhyr, S. M. (2001). Is this about you or me? Self-versus other-directed judgments and feelings in response to intergroup interaction. *Personality and Social Psychology Bulletin, 27*, 706–719.

Vorauer, J. D., Main, K., & O'Connell, G. B. (1998). How do individuals expect to be viewed by members of lower status groups? Content and implications of meta stereotypes. *Journal of Personality and Social Psychology, 75*, 917–937.

Vorauer, J. D., Martens, V., & Sasaki, S. J. (2009). When trying to understand detracts from trying to behave: Effects of perspective taking in intergroup interaction. *Journal of Personality and Social Psychology, 96*(4), 811–827.

Vorauer, J. D., & Miller, D. T. (1997). Failure to recognize the effect of implicit social influence on the presentation of self. *Journal of Personality and Social Psychology, 73*, 281–295.

Voraurer, J. D., & Ross, M. (1999). Self-awareness and feeling transparent: Failing to suppress one's self. *Journal of Experimental Social Psychology, 35*, 415–440.

Vorauer, J. D., & Sasaki, S. J. (2009). Helpful only in the abstract? Ironic effects of empathy in intergroup interaction. *Psychological Science, 20*(2), 191–197.

Vorauer, J. D., & Sasaki, S. J. (2010). In need of liberation or constraint? How intergroup attitudes moderate the behavioral implications of intergroup ideologies. *Journal of Experimental Social Psychology, 46*(1), 133–138.

Vorauer, J. D., & Sakamoto, Y. (2006). I thought we could be friends, but . . . : Systematic miscommunication and defensive distancing as obstacles to cross-group friendship formation. *Psychological Science, 17*, 326–331.

Vorauer, J. D., & Turpie, C. A. (2004). Disruptive effects of vigilance on dominant group members' treatment of outgroup members: Choking versus shining under pressure. *Journal of Personality and Social Psychology, 87*(3), 384–399.

Wagenaar, A., & Maldonado-Molina, M. (2007). Effects of drivers' license suspension policies on alcohol-related crash involvement: Long-term follow-up in forty-six states. *Alcoholism: Clinical and Experimental Research, 31*, 1399–1406.

Wakefield, S., & Elliott, S. J. (2000). Environmental risk perception and well-being: Effects of the landfill siting process in two southern Ontario communities. *Social Science & Medicine, 50*, 1139–1154.

Wakefield, M., Flay, B., & Nichter, M. (2003). Role of the media in influencing trajectories of youth smoking. *Addiction, 98*(Suppl1), Special issue: Contexts and adolescent tobacco use trajectories, 79–103.

Walker, L. J., & Frimer, J. A. (2007). Moral personality of brave and caring exemplars. *Journal of Personality and Social Psychology, 93*, 845–860.

Wall, A., Hinson, R. E., & McKee, S. A. (1998). Alcohol outcome expectancies, attitude toward drinking and the theory of planned behavior. *Journal of Studies on Alcohol, 59*, 409–419.

Wall, G. (1995). Barriers to individual environmental action: The influence of attitudes and social experiences. *Canadian Review of Sociology and Anthropology, 32*, 465–489.

Wallach, M. A., Kogan, N., & Bem, D. J. (1962). Group influences on individual risk taking. *Journal of Abnormal and Social Psychology, 65*, 75–86.

Walsh, M., Hickey, C., & Duffy, J. (1999). Influence of item content and stereotype situation on gender differences in mathematical problem solving. *Sex Roles, 41*, 219–240.

Walster, E. (1966). Assignment of responsibility for an accident. *Journal of Personality and Social Psychology, 3*, 73–79.

Walster, E., Aronson, V., Abrahams, D., & Rottman, L. (1966). Importance of physical attractiveness in dating behavior. *Journal of Personality and Social Psychology, 5*, 508–516.

Walster, E., & Festinger, L. (1962). The effectiveness of "overheard" persuasive communication. *Journal of Abnormal and Social Psychology, 65*, 395–402.

Walster (Hatfield), E., Aronson, V., Abrahams, D., & Rottman, L. (1966). Importance of physical attractiveness in dating behavior. *Journal of Personality and Social Psychology, 5*, 508–516.

Walster (Hatfield), E., Walster, G. W., & Berscheid, E. (1978). *Equity: Theory and research*. Needham Heights, MA: Allyn & Bacon.

Walters, V., Lenton, R., French, S., Eyles, J., Mayr, J., & Newbold, B. (1996). Paid work, unpaid work and social support: A study of the health of male and female nurses. *Social Science Medical, 43*, 1627–1636.

Walther, E., Bless, H., Strack, F., Rackstraw, P., Wagner, D., & Werth, L. (2002). Conformity effects in memory as a function of group size, dissenters and uncertainty. *Applied Cognitive Psychology, 16*, 793–810.

Wang, H., Masuda, T., & Ishii, K. (2008, February). *Comparing patterns of attention between Canadians and East Asian international students.* Paper presented at the Society for Social Psychology and Personality Conference, Albuquerque, New Mexico.

Wang, H., Masuda, T., Ito, K., & Rashid, M. (under review). How much information? East Asian and North American cultural products and information search performance. Manuscript submitted for publication, University of Alberta.

Wang, T., Brownstein, R., & Katzev, R. (1989). Promoting charitable behavior with compliance techniques. *Applied Psychology: An International Review, 38*, 165–184.

Want, S. C., Vickers, K., & Amos, J. (2009). The influence of television programs on appearance satisfaction: Making and mitigating social comparisons to "Friends." *Sex Roles, 60*(9-10), 642–655.

Ware, L., Lassiter, G., Patterson, S., & Ransom, M. (2008). Camera perspective bias in videotaped confessions: Evidence that visual attention is a mediator. *Journal of Experimental Psychology: Applied, 14*, 192–200.

Wasswa, H. (2002, March 16). Uganda cult deaths remain a mystery. Associated Press. Retrieved from www.rickross.com/reference/tencommand ments/tencommandments117.html

Watkins, D., Adair, J., Akande, A., Gerong, A., McInerney, D., Sunar, . . . Wondimu, H. (1998). Individualism-collectivism, gender and the self-concept: A nine-culture investigation. *Psychologia: An International Journal of Psychology in the Orient, 41*, 259–271.

Watkins, D., Akande, A., Fleming, J., Ismail, M., Lefner, K., Regmi, M., . . . Wondimu, H. (1998). Cultural dimensions, gender, and the nature of self-concept: A fourteen-country study. *International Journal of Psychology, 33*, 17–31.

Watson, D., & Pennebaker, J. W. (1989). Health complaints, stress, and distress: Exploring the central role of negative affectivity. *Psychological Review, 96*, 234–254.

Watson, J. (1924). *Behaviorism*. Chicago, IL: University of Chicago Press.

Watson, R. I. (1973). Investigation into deindividuation using a cross-cultural survey technique. *Journal of Personality and Social Psychology, 25*, 342–345.

Watson, W. E., Johnson, L., Kumar, K., & Critelli, J. (1998). Process gain and process loss: Comparing interpersonal processes and performance of culturally diverse and non-diverse teams across time. *International Journal of Intercultural Relations, 22*, 409–430.

Watts, D. P., Muller, M., Amsler, S. J., Mbabazi, G., and Mitani, J. C. (2006, February). Lethal intergroup aggression by chimpanzees in Kibale National Park, Uganda. *American Journal of Primatology, 68*(2), 161–180.

Wayment, H. A. (2006). Attachment style, empathy, and helping following a collective loss: Evidence from the September 11 terrorist attacks. *Attachment and Human Development, 8*, 1–9.

Webber, R., & Crocker, J. (1983). Cognitive processes in the revision of stereotypic beliefs. *Journal of Personality and Social Psychology, 45*, 961–977.

Weber, J. M., Kopelman, S., & Messick, D. M. (2004). A conceptual review of decision making in social dilemmas: Applying a logic of appropriateness. *Personality and Social Psychology Review, 8*, 281–307.

Weber, E. U., Bockenholt, U., Hilton, D. J., & Wallace, B. (1993). Determinants of diagnostic hypothesis generation: Effects of information, base rates, and experience. *Journal of Experimental Psychology: Learning, Memory, and Cognition, 19*, 1151–1164.

Weber, J., & Murnighan, J. (2008). Suckers or saviors? Consistent contributors in social dilemmas. *Journal of Personality and Social Psychology, 95*(6), 1340–1353.

Webster, D. M. (1993). Motivated augmentation and reduction of the overattributional bias. *Journal of Personality and Social Psychology, 65*, 261–271.

Webster, G. D., Bryan, A., Crawford, C. B., McCarthy, L., & Cohen, B. H. (2008). Lineage, sex, and wealth as moderators of kin investment: Evidence from inheritances. *Human Nature, 19*(2), 189–210.

Wechsler, H., Lee, J. E., Kuo, M., Siebring, M., Nelson, T. F., & Lee, H. (2002). Trends in college binge drinking during a period of increased prevention efforts: Findings from 4 Harvard School of Public Health college alcohol study surveys, 1993–2001. *Journal of American College Health, 50*, 203–217.

Wechsler, H., Nelson, T., Lee, J. E., Seiber, M., Lewis, C., & Keeling, R. (2003). Perception and reality: A national evaluation of social norms marketing interventions to reduce college students' heavy alcohol use. *Quarterly Journal of Studies on Alcohol, 49*, 85–92.

Weeden, J., & Sabini, J. (2005). Physical attractiveness and health in Western societies: A review. *Psychological Bulletin, 131*, 635–653.

Wegener, D. T., & Petty, R. E. (1994). Mood management across affective states: The hedonic contingency hypothesis. *Journal of Personality and Social Psychology, 66*, 1034–1048.

Wegener, D. T., & Petty, R. E. (1995). Flexible correction processes in social judgment: The role of naive theories in corrections for perceived bias. *Journal of Personality and Social Psychology, 68*, 36–51.

Wegner, D. M. (1992). You can't always think what you want: Problems in the suppression of unwanted thoughts. In M. P. Zanna (Ed.), *Advances in experimental social psychology* (pp. 193–225). San Diego, CA: Academic Press.

Wegner, D. M. (1994). Ironic processes of mental control. *Psychological Review, 101*, 34–52.

Wegner, D. M. (1995). A computer network model of human transactive memory. *Social Cognition, 13*, 319–339.

Wegner, D. M. (2002). *The illusion of conscious will.* Cambridge, MA: MIT Press.

Wegner, D. M. (2004). Precis of "The illusion of conscious will." *Behavioral & Brain Sciences, 27*, 649–659.

Wegner, D. M., & Bargh, J. A. (1998). Control and automaticity in social life. In D. Gilbert, S. Fiske, & G. Lindzey (Eds.), *The handbook of social psychology* (4th ed., Vol. 1, pp. 446–498). New York: McGraw Hill.

Wegner, D. M., Erber, R., & Raymond, P. (1991). Transactive memory in close relationships. *Journal of Personality and Social Psychology, 61*, 923–929.

Wegner, D. M., Wenzlaff, R. M., & Kozak, M. (2004). Dream rebound: The return of suppressed thoughts in dreams. *Psychological Science, 15*, 232–236.

Wehrle, T., Kaiser, S., Schmidt, S., & Scherer, K. R. (2000). Studying the dynamics of emotional expression using synthesized facial muscle movements. *Journal of Personality and Social Psychology, 78*, 105–119.

Wei, M., Fischer, E., & Main, K. J. (2008). An examination of the effects of activating persuasion knowledge on consumer response to brands engaging in covert marketing. *Journal of Public Policy & Marketing, 27*(1), 34–44.

Weiner, B., Amirkhan, J., Folkes, V. S., & Verette, J. A. (1987). An attributional analysis of excuse giving: Studies of a naive theory of emotion. *Journal of Personality and Social Psychology, 52*, 316–324.

Weingardt, K. R., Toland, H. K., & Loftus, E. F. (1994). Reports of suggested memories: Do people truly believe them? In D. F. Ross, J. D. Read, & M. P. Toglia (Eds.), *Adult eyewitness testimony: Current trends and developments* (pp. 3–26). New York: Cambridge University Press.

Weinstein, N. D. (1980). Unrealistic optimism about future life events. *Journal of Personality and Social Psychology, 39*, 806–820.

Weinstein, N. D., & Klein, W. M. (1996). Unrealistic optimism: Present and future. *Journal of Social and Clinical Psychology, 15*, 1–8.

Weir, W. (1984, October 15). Another look at subliminal "facts." *Advertising Age*, p. 46.

Wekerle, C., & Wall, A. (2002). Introduction: The overlap between relationship violence and substance abuse. In C. Wekerle, & A. Wall (Eds.), *The violence and addiction equation* (pp. 1–21). New York: Taylor & Francis.

Wells, G. (2008). Theory, logic and data: Paths to a more coherent eyewitness science. *Applied Cognitive Psychology, 22*, 853–859.

Wells, G., & Hasel, L. (2008). Eyewitness identification: Issues in common knowledge and generalization. In E. Borgida & S. T. Fiske (Eds.), *Beyond common sense: Psychological science in the courtroom* (pp. 159–176). Malden, MA: Blackwell Publishing.

Wells, G., Memon, A., & Penrod, S. (2006). Eyewitness Evidence: Improving its Probative Value. *Psychological Science in the Public Interest, 7*, 45–75.

Wells, G. L. (1984). The psychology of lineup identifications. *Journal of Applied Social Psychology, 14*, 89–103.

Wells, G. L. (1992). Naked statistical evidence of liability: Is subjective probability enough? *Journal of Personality and Social Psychology, 62*, 739–752.

Wells, G. L. (1993). What do we know about eyewitness identification? *American Psychologist, 48*, 553–571.

Wells, G. L., Charman, S. D., & Olson, E. A. (2005). Building face composites can harm lineup identification performance. *Journal of Experimental Psychology: Applied, 11*, 147–156.

Wells, G. L., Lindsay, R. C. L., & Ferguson, T. (1978). Accuracy, confidence, and juror perceptions in eyewitness identification. *Journal of Applied Psychology, 64*, 440–448.

Wells, G. L., & Luus, C. A. E. (1990). Police lineups as experiments: Social methodology as a framework for properly conducted lineups. *Personality and Social Psychology Bulletin, 16*, 106–117.

Wells, G. L., Malpass, R. S., Lindsay, R. C. L., Fisher, R. P., Turtle, J. W., & Fulero, S. M. (2000). From the lab to the police station. *American Psychologist, 55*, 581–598.

Wells, G. L., & Olson, E. A. (2003). Eyewitness testimony. *Annual Review of Psychology, 54*, 277–295.

Wells, G. L., Olson, E. A., & Charman, S. D. (2002). The confidence of eyewitnesses in their identifications from lineups. *Current Directions in Psychological Science, 11*, 151–154.

Wells, G. L., Small, M., Penrod, S. D., Malpassq, R. S., Fulero, S. M., & Brimacombe, C. A. E. (1998). Eyewitness identification pro cedures: Recommendations for lineups and photospreads. *Law and Human Behavior, 22*, 603–645.

Wells, G. L., Wright, E. F., & Bradfield, A. L. (1999) Witnesses to crime: Social and cognitive factors governing the validity of people's reports. In R. Roesch, S. D. Hart, & J. R. P. Ogloff (Eds.), *Psychology and law: The state of the discipline* (pp. 53–88). New York: Kluwer.

Wells, S., Graham, K., & Tremblay, P. (2009). "Every male in there is your competition": Young men's perceptions regarding the role of the drinking setting in male-to-male barroom aggression. *Substance Use & Misuse, 44*(9-10), 1434–1462.

Wells, S., Graham, K., & West, P. (1998). "The good, the bad, and the ugly": Responses by security staff to aggressive incidents in public drinking settings. *Journal of Drug Issues, 28*, 817–836.

Wells, S., Graham, K., & West, P. (2000). Alcohol-related aggression in the general population. *Journal of Studies on Alcohol, 61*, 626–632.

Wells, S., Mihic, L., Tremblay, P., Graham, K., & Demers, A. (2008). Where, with whom, and how much alcohol is consumed on drinking events involving aggression? Event-level associations in a Canadian National Survey of University Students. *Alcoholism: Clinical and Experimental Research, 32*(3), 522–533.

Wells, W. D. (Ed). (1997). *Measuring advertising effectiveness*. Mahwah, NJ: Erlbaum.

Wenzlaff, R. M., & Bates, D. E. (2000). The relative efficacy of concentration and suppression strategies of mental control. *Personality and Social Psychology Bulletin, 26*, 1200–1212.

Werhun, C. D., & Penner, A. J. (2010). The effects of stereotyping and implicit theory on benevolent prejudice toward Aboriginal Canadians. *Journal of Applied Social Psychology, 40*(4), 899–916.

Werner, C., & Parmelee, P. (1979). Similarity of activity preferences among friends: Those who play together stay together. *Social Psychology Quarterly, 42*, 62–66.

Werth, L., & Foerster, J. (2002). Implicit person theories influence memory judgments: The circumstances under which metacognitive knowledge is used. *European Journal of Social Psychology, 32*, 353–362.

Weyant, J. M. (1996). Application of compliance techniques to direct-mail requests for charitable donations. *Psychology and Marketing, 13*, 157–170.

Whatley, M. A., Webster, J. M., Smith, R. H., & Rhodes, A. (1999). The effect of a favor on public and private compliance: How internalized is the norm of reciprocity? *Basic and Applied Social Psychology, 21*, 251–259.

Wheeler, L., & Kim, Y. (1997). What is beautiful is culturally good: The physical attractiveness stereotype has different content in collectivistic cultures. *Personality and Social Psychology Bulletin, 23*, 795–800.

Wheeler, L., Koestner, R., & Driver, R. (1982). Related attributes in the choice of comparison others: It's there, but it isn't all there is. *Journal of Experimental Social Psychology, 18*, 489–500.

White, H. (1997). Longitudinal perspective on alcohol and aggression during adolescence. In M. Galanter (Ed.), *Recent developments in alcoholism: Vol. 13. Alcohol and violence: Epidemiology, neurobiology, psychology, and family issues* (pp. 81–103). New York: Plenum.

White, K., & Argo, J. J. (2009). Social identity threat and consumer preferences. *Journal of Consumer Psychology, 19*(3), 313–325.

White, K., & Willness, C. (2009). Consumer reactions to the decreased usage message: The role of elaborative processing. *Journal of Consumer Psychology, 19*(1), 73–87.

White, K., & Lehman, D. R. (2005a). Culture and social comparison seeking: The role of self-motives. *Personality and Social Psychology Bulletin, 31*, 232–242.

White, K., & Lehman, D. R. (2005b). Looking on the bright side: Downward counterfactual thinking in response to negative life events. *Personality and Social Psychology Bulletin, 31*, 1413–1424.

White, K., Lehman, D. R., & Cohen, D. (2006). Culture, self-construal, and affective reactions to successful and unsuccessful others. *Journal of Experimental Social Psychology, 42*, 582–592.

White, L. K. (1990). Determinants of divorce: A review of research in the eighties. *Journal of Marriage and the Family, 52*, 904–912.

White, P. A. (2002). Causal attribution from covariation information: The evidential evaluation model. *European Journal of Social Psychology, 32*, 667–684.

White, R. K. (1977). Misperception in the Arab–Israeli conflict. *Journal of Social Issues, 33*, 190–221.

Whitehouse, W. G., Orne, E. C., Dinges, D. F., Bates, B. L., Nadon, R., & Orne, M. T. (2005). The cognitive interview: Does it successfully avoid the dangers of forensic hypnosis? *American Journal of Psychology, 118*(2), 213–234.

Whitley, B. E., Jr. (1999). Right-wing authoritarianism, social dominance orientation, and prejudice. *Journal of Personality and Social Psychology*, 77, 126–134.

Whorf, B. L. (1956). *Language, thought, and reality*. New York: Wiley.

Wicker, A. W. (1969). Attitudes versus actions: The relationship between verbal and overt behavioral responses to attitude objects. *Journal of Social Issues, 25*, 41–78.

Wicker, B., Keysers, C., Plailly, J., Royet, J. P., Gallese, V., & Rizzolatti, G. (2003). Both us disgusted in my insula: The common neural basis of seeing and feeling disgust. *Neuron, 40*(3), 655–664.

Wickham, L. H. V., & Swift, H. (2006). Articulatory suppression attenuates the verbal overshadowing effect: A role for verbal encoding in face identification. *Applied Cognitive Psychology, 20*(2), 157–169.

Wiedenfeld, S. A., O'Leary, A., Bandura, A., Brown, S., Levine, S., & Raska, K. (1990). Impact of perceived self-efficacy in coping with stressors on components of the immune system. *Journal of Personality and Social Psychology, 59*, 1082–1094.

Wiekens, C. J., & Stapel, D. A. (2008). The mirror and I: When private opinions are in conflict with public norms. *Journal of Experimental Social Psychology, 44*, 1160–1166.

Wilder, D. A. (1984). Intergroup contact: The typical member and the exception to the rule. *Journal of Experimental Psychology, 20*, 177–194.

Wilder, D. A. (1986). Social categorization: Implications for creation and reduction of intergroup bias. In L. Berkowitz (Ed.), *Advances in experimental social psychology* (Vol. 19, pp. 291–355). New York: Academic Press.

Wilder, D. A., & Shapiro, P. N. (1989). Role of competition-induced anxiety in limiting the beneficial impact of positive behavior by an out-group member. *Journal of Personality and Social Psychology, 56*, 60–69.

Wiles, M. A., & Danielova, A. (2009). The worth of product placement in successful films: An event study analysis. *Journal of Marketing, 73*(4), 44–63.

Williams, K. R., & Hawkins, R. (1986). Perceptual research on general deterrence: A critical review. *Law and Society Review, 20*, 545–572.

Williams, L., Fisher, M., & Cox, A. (2008). The impact of sexual history and desired relationship duration on evaluations of attractiveness and recall. *Journal of Evolutionary Psychology, 6*(1), 1–23.

Williams, R. B. (2002). Hostility, neuroendocrine changes, and health outcomes. In H. G. Koenig & H. J. Cohen (Eds.), *The link between religion and health: Psychoneuroimmunology and the faith factor* (pp. 160–173). London, UK: Oxford University Press.

Williams, R. H., & Ross, M. H. (1980, March–April). Drilling for oil and gas in our houses. *Technology Review*, pp. 24–36.

Williams, S. S., Kimble, D. L., Covell, N. H., Weiss, L. H., Newton, K. J., Fisher, J. D., & Fisher, W. A. (1992). College students use implicit personality theory instead of safer sex. *Journal of Applied Social Psychology, 22*, 921–933.

Williams, T. P., & Sogon, S. (1984). Group composition and conforming behavior in Japanese students. *Japanese Psychological Research, 26*, 231–234.

Williamson, G. M., & Clark, M. S. (1989). Providing help and desired relationship type as determinants of changes in moods and self-evaluations. *Journal of Personality and Social Psychology, 56*, 722–734.

Williamson, G. M., & Clark, M. S. (1992). Impact of desired relationship type on affective reactions to choosing and being required to help. *Personality and Social Psychology Bulletin, 18*, 10–18.

Wilson, A. E., & Ross, M. (2000). The frequency of temporal-self and social comparisons in people's personal appraisals. *Journal of Personality and Social Psychology, 78*, 928–942.

Wilson, A. E., & Ross, M. (2001). From chump to champ: People's appraisals of their earlier and current selves. *Journal of Personality and Social Psychology, 80*, 572–584.

Wilson, K. S., & Spink, K. S. (2009). Social influence and physical activity in older females: Does activity preference matter? *Psychology of Sport and Exercise, 10*(4), 481–488.

Wilson, M., Daly, M., & Weghorst, S. J. (1982). Male sexual jealousy. *Ethology and Sociobiology, 3*, 11–27.

Wilson, T. D. (1985). Strangers to ourselves: The origins and accuracy of beliefs about one's own mental states. In J. H. Harvey & G. Weary (Eds.), *Attribution in contemporary psychology* (pp. 9–36). New York: Academic Press.

Wilson, T. D. (1994). The proper protocol: Validity and completeness of verbal reports. *Psychological Science, 5*, 249–252.

Wilson, T. D. (2002). *Strangers to ourselves: Self-insight and the adaptive unconscious*. Cambridge, MA: Harvard University Press.

Wilson, T. D. (2005). The message is the method: Celebrating and exporting the experimental approach. *Psychological Inquiry, 16*, 185–193.

Wilson, T. D., Aronson, E., & Carlsmith, K. (in press). Data (Laboratory Experimentation). In S. T. Fiske, D. T. Gilbert, & G. Lindzey (Eds.), *Handbook of social psychology* (5th ed.). New York: Wiley.

Wilson, T. D., & Brekke, N. C. (1994). Mental contamination and mental correction: Unwanted influences on judgments and evaluations. *Psychological Bulletin, 116*, 117–142.

Wilson, T. D., Centerbar, D. B., & Brekke, N. (2002). Mental contamination and the debiasing problem. In T. Gilovich, D. W. Griffin, & D. Kahneman (Eds.), *Heuristics and biases: The psychology of intuitive judgment* (pp. 185–200). New York: Cambridge University Press.

Wilson, T. D., Damiani, M., & Shelton, N. (2002). Improving the academic performance of college students with brief attributional interventions. In J. Aronson (Eds.), *Improving academic achievement: Impact of psychological factors on education* (pp. 88–108). San Diego, CA: Academic Press.

Wilson, T. D., & Dunn, E. W. (2004). Self-knowledge: Its limits, value and potential for improvement. *Annual Review of Psychology, 55*, 493–518.

Wilson, T. D., Gilbert, D. T., & Wheatley, T. (1998). Protecting our minds: The role of lay beliefs. In V. Yzerbyt, G. Lories, & B. Dardenne (Eds.), *Metacognition: Cognitive and social dimensions* (pp. 171–201). Thousand Oaks, CA: Sage.

Wilson, T. D., Houston, C. E., & Meyers, J. M. (1998). Choose your poison: Effects of lay beliefs about mental processes on attitude change. *Social Cognition, 16*(1), 114–132.

Wilson, T. D., Laser, P. S., & Stone, J. I. (1982). Judging the predictors of one's own mood: Accuracy and the use of shared theories. *Journal of Experimental Social Psychology, 18*, 537–556.

Wilson, T. D., Lindsey, S., & Schooler, T. Y. (2000). A model of dual attitudes. *Psychological Review, 107*, 101–126.

Wilson, T. D., & Linville, P. W. (1982). Improving the academic performance of college freshmen: Attribution therapy revisited. *Journal of Personality and Social Psychology, 42*, 367–376.

Wilson, T. D., & Linville, P. W. (1985). Improving the performance of college freshmen using attributional techniques. *Journal of Personality and Social Psychology, 49*, 287–293.

Wilson, T. D., Lisle, D., Schooler, J., Hodges, S. D., Klaaren, K. J., & LaFleur, S. J. (1993). Introspecting about reasons can reduce post-choice satisfaction. *Personality and Social Psychology Bulletin, 19*, 331–339.

Wilson, T. D., & Stone, J. I. (1985). Limitations of self-knowledge: More on telling more than we can know. In P. Shaver (Ed.), *Review of personality and social psychology* (Vol. 6, pp. 167–183). Beverly Hills, CA: Sage.

Winerman, L. (2005). The mind's mirror. *Monitor on Psychology, 36*(9), 48–50.

Winslow, R. W., Franzini, L. R., & Hwang, J. (1992). Perceived peer norms, casual sex, and AIDS risk prevention. *Journal of Applied Social Psychology, 22*, 1809–1827.

Winter, R., & Greene, E. (2007). Juror decision-making. In F. T. Durso, R. S. Nickerson, S. T. Dumais, S. Lewandowsky, & T. J. Perfect (Eds.), *Handbook of applied cognition* (2nd ed., pp. 739–761). Hoboken, NJ: John Wiley & Sons.

Wintre, M. G., & Bowers, C. D. (2007). Predictors of persistence to graduation: Extending a model and data on the transition to university model. *Canadian Journal of Behavioural Science, 39*, 220–234.

Wise, D., & Rosqvist, J. (2006). Explanatory style and well-being. In J. C. Thomas, D. L. Segal, & M. Hersen (Eds.), *Comprehensive handbook of personality and psychopathology: Vol. 1, Personality and everyday functioning* (pp. 285–305). Hoboken, NJ: Wiley.

Wise, R. A., & Safer, M. A. (2004). What US judges know and believe about eyewitness testimony. *Journal of Applied Cognitive Psychology, 18*, 427–443.

Wisman, A., & Goldenberg, J. L. (2005). From the grave to the cradle: Evidence that mortality salience engenders a desire for offspring. *Journal of Personality and Social Psychology, 89*, 46–61.

Wittenbrink, B., Judd, C. M., & Park, B. (1997). Evidence for racial prejudice at the implicit level and its relationship with questionnaire measures. *Journal of Personality and Social Psychology, 72*, 262–274.

Wohl, M. J. A., & Branscombe, N. R. (2005). Forgiveness and collective guilt assignment to historical perpetrator groups depend on level of social category inclusiveness. *Journal of Personality and Social Psychology, 88*(2), 288–303.

Wohl, M. J. A., & McGrath, A. L. (2007). The perception of time heals all wounds: Temporal distance affects willingness to forgive following an interpersonal transgression. *Personality and Social Psychology Bulletin, 33*, 1023–1035.

Wojtowicz, A. E., & von Ranson, K. M. (2006). Psychometric evaluation of two scales examining muscularity concerns in men and women. *Psychology of Men and Masculinity, 7*, 56–66.

Wolfgang, A., & Wolofsky, Z. (1991). The ability of new Canadians to decode gestures generated by Canadians of Anglo-Celtic backgrounds. *International Journal of Intercultural Relations, 15*, 47–64.

Wong, C. K., & Read, J. (2011). Positive and negative effects of physical context reinstatement on eyewitness recall and identification. *Applied Cognitive Psychology, 25*(1), 2–11.

Wong, R. Y., & Hong, Y. (2005). Dynamic influences of culture on cooperation in a Prisoner's Dilemma game. *Psychological Science, 16*, 429–434.

Wood, J. V. (1996). What is social comparison and how should we study it? *Personality and Social Psychology Bulletin, 22*, 520–537.

Wood, J. V., Heimpel, S. A., Newby-Clark, I. R., & Ross, M. (2005). Snatching defeat from the jaws of victory: Self-esteem differences in the experience and anticipation of success. *Journal of Personality and Social Psychology, 89*, 764–780.

Wood, J. V., Michela, J. L., & Giordano, C. (2000). Downward comparison in everyday life: Reconciling self-enhancement models with the mood-cognition priming model. *Journal of Personality and Social Psychology, 79*, 563–579.

Wood, J. V., Taylor, S. E., & Lichtman, R. R. (1985). Social comparison in adjustment to breast cancer. *Journal of Personality and Social Psychology, 49*, 1169–1183.

Wood, W. (1987). Meta-analytic review of sex differences in group performance. *Psychological Bulletin, 102*, 53–71.

Wood, W., & Eagly, A. H. (2002). A cross-cultural analysis of the behavior of women and men: Implications for the origins of sex differences. *Psychological Bulletin, 128*, 699–727.

Wood, W., Lundgren, S., Ouellette, J. A., Busceme, S., & Blackstone, J. (1994). Minority influence: A meta-analytic review of social influence processes. *Psychological Bulletin, 115*, 323–345.

Wood, W., Pool, G. J., Leck, K., & Purvis, D. (1996). Self-definition, defensive processing, and influence: The normative impact of majority and minority groups. *Journal of Personality and Social Psychology, 71*, 1181–1193.

Wood, W., & Quinn, J. M. (2003). Forewarned and forearmed? Two meta-analytic syntheses of forewarnings of influence appeals. *Psychological Bulletin, 129*, 119–138.

Wood, W., Wong, F. Y., & Chachere, G. (1991). Effects of media violence on viewers' aggression in unconstrained social interaction. *Psychological Bulletin, 109*, 371–383.

Woodgate, J., Brawley, L. R., & Shields, C. A. (2007). Social support in cardiac rehabilitation exercise maintenance: Associations with self-efficacy and health-related quality of life. *Journal of Applied Social Psychology, 37*(5), 1041–1059.

Word, C. O., Zanna, M. P., & Cooper, J. (1974). The nonverbal mediation of self-fulfilling prophecies in interracial interaction. *Journal of Experimental Social Psychology, 10*, 109–120.

Wrangham, R. W., Wilson, M. L., & Muller, M. N. (2006, January). Comparative rates of violence in chimpanzees and humans. *Primates, 47*(1), 14–26.

Wright, E. F., Luus, C. A. E., & Christie, S. D. (1990). Does group discussion facilitate the use of consensus information in making causal attributions? *Journal of Personality and Social Psychology, 59*, 261–269.

Wright, E. F., MacEachern, L., Stoffer, E., & MacDonald, N. (1996). Factors affecting the use of naked statistical evidence of liability. *Journal of Social Psychology, 136*, 677–688.

Wright, E. F., Rule, B., Ferguson, T., McGuire, G., & Wells, G. (1992). Misattribution of dissonance and behaviour-consistent attitude change. *Canadian Journal of Behavioural Science, 24*, 456–464.

Wright, R. (1994). *The moral animal: Why we are the way we are: The new science of evolutionary psychology*. New York: Random House.

Wright, S. C. (1997). Ambiguity, social influence, and collective action: Generating collective protest in response to tokenism. *Personality and Social Psychology Bulletin, 23*, 1277–1290.

Wright, S. C., Aron, A., McLaughlin, T., & Ropp, S. A. (1997). The extended contact effect: Knowledge of cross-group friendships and prejudice. *Journal of Personality and Social Psychology, 73*, 73–90.

Wright, S. C., Brody, S. M., & Aron, A. (2005). Intergroup contact: Still our best hope for improving intergroup relations. In C. S. Crandall & M. Schaller (Eds.), *Social psychology of prejudice: Historical and contemporary issues* (pp. 115–142). Lawrence, KS: Lewinian Press.

Wright, S. C., & Taylor, D. M. (2003). The social psychology of cultural diversity: Social stereotyping, prejudice, and discrimination. In M. A. Hogg & J. Cooper (Eds.), *Sage Handbook of Social Psychology* (pp. 432–457). London, UK: Sage.

Wright, S. C., Taylor, D., & Moghaddam, F. (1990). Responding to membership in a disadvantaged group: From acceptance to collective protest. *Journal of Social and Personality Psychology, 58*, 994–1003.

Wright, S. C., & van der Zande, C. C. (1999, October). *Bicultural friends: When cross-group friendships cause improved intergroup attitudes.* Paper presented at the Society for Experimental Social Psychology Conference, St. Louis, MO.

Wrosch, C., Miller, G. E., Scheier, M. F., & de Pontet, S. B. (2007). Giving up on unattainable goals: Benefits for health? *Personality and Social Psychology Bulletin, 33*, 251–265.

Wyer, R. S., & Srull, T. K. (1989). *Memory and cognition in its social context.* Hillsdale, NJ: Erlbaum.

Yabar, Y., & Hess, U. (2007). Display of empathy and perception of out-group members. *New Zealand Journal of Psychology, 36*(1), 42–49.

Yarmey, A. D. (2001a). Expert testimony: Does eyewitness memory research have probative value for the courts? *Canadian Psychology, 42*, 92–100.

Yarmey, A. D. (2001b). Police investigations. In R. A. Schuller & J. R. P. Ogloff (Eds), *Introduction to psychology and law: Canadian perspectives* (pp. 59–94). Toronto, ON: University of Toronto Press.

Yarmey, A, D. Jacob, J., & Porter, A. (2002). Person recall in field settings. *Journal of Applied Social Psychology, 32*(11), 2354–2367.

Yarmey, A. D., Yarmey, A. L., Yarmey, M. J., & Parliament, L. (2001). Commonsense beliefs and the identification of familiar voices. *Applied Cognitive Psychology, 15*, 283–299.

Yarmey, A. D., Yarmey, M. J., & Yarmey, A. L. (1996). Accuracy of eyewitness identifications in showups and lineups. *Law and Human Behavior, 20*, 459–477.

Yi, S., & Baumgartner, H. (2008). Motivational compatability and the role of anticipated feelings in positively valenced persuasive message framing. *Psychology & Marketing, 25*(11), 1007–1026.

Yi, S., & Baumgartner, H. (2009). Regulatory focus and message framing: A test of three accounts. *Motivation and Emotion, 33*(4), 435–443.

Yik, M. S., Bond, M. H., & Paulhus, D. L. (1998). Do Chinese self-enhance or self-efface? It's a matter of domain. *Personality and Social Psychology Bulletin, 24*, 399–406.

Yik, M. S. M., Meng, Z., & Russell, J. A. (1998). Adults' freely produced emotion labels for babies' spontaneous facial expressions. *Cognition and Emotion, 12*, 723–730.

Yik, M. S. M., & Russell, J. A. (1999). Interpretation of faces: A cross-cultural study of a prediction from Fridlund's theory. *Cognition and Emotion, 13*, 93–104.

York, A. (2001, April 26). The product placement monster that E.T. spawned. *Salon*. Retrieved from http://archive.salon.com/tech/feature/2001/ 04/26/product_placement/print.html

Yuille, J. C., Ternes, M., & Cooper, B. S. (2010). Expert testimony on laboratory witnesses. *Journal of Forensic Psychology Practice, 10*(3), 238–251.

Yuki, M., Maddux, W. W., & Masuda, T. (2007). Are the windows to the soul the same in the East and West? Cultural differences in using the eyes and mouth as cues to recognize emotions in Japan and the United States. *Journal of Experimental Social Psychology, 43*(2), 303–311.

Zillmann, D. (1978). Attribution and misattribution of excitatory reactions. In J. H. Harvey, W. J. Ickes, & R. F. Kidd (Eds.), *New directions in attribution research* (Vol. 2, pp. 335–370). Hillsdale, NJ: Erlbaum.

Yum, Y., & Schenck-Hamlin, W. (2005). Reactions to 9/11 as a function of terror management and perspective taking. *Journal of Social Psychology, 145*, 265–286.

Zajonc, R. B. (1965). Social facilitation. *Science, 149*, 269–274.

Zajonc, R. B. (1968). Attitudinal effects of mere exposure. *Journal of Personality and Social Psychology, 9*, Monograph Suppl. 2, Pt. 2.

Zajonc, R. B. (1980). Compresence. In P. B. Paulus (Ed.), *Psychology of group influence* (pp. 35–60). Hillsdale, NJ: Erlbaum.

Zajonc, R. B., Heingartner, A., & Herman, E. M. (1969). Social enhancement and impairment of performance in the cockroach. *Journal of Personality and Social Psychology, 13*, 83–92.

Zajonc, R. B., & Sales, S. M. (1966). Social facilitation of dominant and subordinate responses. *Journal of Experimental Social Psychology, 2*, 160–168.

Zanna, M., & Cooper, J. (1974). Dissonance and the pill: An attribution approach to studying the arousal properties of dissonance. *Journal of Personality and Social Psychology, 29*, 703–709.

Zanna, M., Goethals, G. R., & Hill, J. (1975). Evaluating a sex-related ability: Social comparison with similar others and standard setters. *Journal of Experimental Social Psychology, 11*, 86–93.

Zanna, M., & Rempel, J. K. (1988). Attitudes: A new look at an old concept. In D. Bar-Tal & A. W. Kruglanski (Eds.), *The social psychology of attitudes* (pp. 315–334). New York: Cambridge University Press.

Zanna, M. P., & Fazio, R. H. (1982). The attitude-behavior relation: Moving toward a third generation of research. In M. P. Zanna, E. T. Higgins, & C. P. Herman (Eds.), *Consistency in social behavior: The Ontario Symposium* (Vol. 2, pp. 283–301). Hillsdale, NJ: Erlbaum.

Zanna, M. P., & Sande, G. N. (1987). The effects of collective actions on the attitudes of individual group members: A dissonance analysis. In M. P. Zanna, J. M. Olson, & C. P. Herman's (Eds.), *Consistency in social behavior: The Ontario Symposium* : Vol. 5. Social influence. Hillsdale, NJ: Erlbaum.

Zanot, E. J., Pincus, J. D., & Lamp, E. J. (1983). Public perceptions of subliminal advertising. *Journal of Advertising, 12*, 39–45.

Zebrowitz, L. A. (1997). *Reading faces: Window to the soul?* Boulder, CO: Westview Press.

Zebrowitz, L. A., & Montepare, J. M. (1992). Impressions of babyfaced individuals across the life-span. *Developmental Psychology, 28*, 1143–1152.

Zebrowitz-McArthur, L. (1988). Person perception in cross-cultural perspective. In M. H. Bond (Ed.), *The cross-cultural challenge to social psychology* (pp. 245–265). Newbury Park, CA: Sage.

Zhang, S., & Kline, S. L. (2009). Can I make my own decision? A cross-cultural study of perceived social network influence in mate selection. *Journal of Cross-Cultural Psychology, 40*(1), 3–23.

Zillman, D., & Bryant, J. (1984). Effects of massive exposure to pornography. In N. M. Malamuth & E. Donnerstein (Eds.), *Pornography and sexual aggression* (pp. 115–138). Orlando, FL: Academic Press.

Zimbardo, P. (2007). *The Lucifer effect: Understanding how good people turn evil*. New York: Random House.

Zimbardo, P. G. (1970). The human choice: Individuation, reason, and order versus deindividuation, impulse, and chaos. In W. J. Arnold & D. Levine (Eds.), *Nebraska Symposium on Motivation: 1969* (Vol. 17, pp. 237–307). Lincoln, NE: University of Nebraska Press.

Zimbardo, P. G., & Andersen, S. (1993). Understanding mind control: Exotic and mundane mental manipulations. In M. D. Langone (Ed.), *Recovery from cults* (pp. 104–125). New York: Norton.

Zine, J. (2001). Muslim youth in Canadian schools: Education and the politics of religious identity. *Anthropology & Education Quarterly, 32*, 399–423.

Zuber, J. A., Crott, H. W., & Werner, J. (1992). Choice shift and group polarization: An analysis of the status of arguments and social decision schemes. *Journal of Personality and Social Psychology, 62*, 50–61.

Zuwerink, J., Monteith, M., Devine, P., & Cook, D. (1996). Prejudice toward Blacks: With and without compunction? *Basic and Applied Social Psychology, 18*, 131–150.

Credits

Chapter 1 Pages 2–3: © Davor Lovincic/iStockPhoto; Page 4: Courtesy of the University of Vermont; Page 8: AP Photo/Laura Rauch; Page 10: Paul Chesley/National Geographic Image Collection; Page 14: Getty Images; Page 15: Archives of the History of American Psychology, University of Akron; Page 15: Archives of the History of American Psychology, University of Akron; page 16: Photograph courtesy of Trudy Festinger. Reprinted by permission; Page 17: Photo by: Will Hart/NBC/NBCU Photo Bank, (C) NBC [2010] all rights reserved; Page 22: AP Photo/The Canadian Press, Health Canada

Chapter 2 Pages 26–27: AP Photo/Michael Schmelling; Page 30: Henry Groskinsky/Getty Images/Time Life Pictures; Page 33: © Andia/Alamy; Page 34 (left): The Advertising Archives; Page 34 (right): Richard B. Levine/Newscom; Page 34: Fashion B/Shutterstock; Page 37: Courtesy of the Library of Congress; Page 38: Joe Bryska/Winnipeg Free Press; Page 44: © Laurent/Aubourg/MaxxImages; Page 48 (left): © Marion Bull/Alamy; Page 48 (right): © Jake Lyell / Alamy; Page 49: © Arif ÖSÜN/iStockPhoto

Chapter 3 Pages 54–55: Sean Nel/Shutterstock; Page 56 (top): Photograph by KC Armstrong; Page 56 (bottom): Konstantin Sutyagin/Shutterstock; Page 58: Joshua Correll/Courtesy Charles Judd, University of Colorado; Page 61 (left): Mark Lyons/AP Wide World Photos; Page 61 (right): Mark Lyons/AP Wide World Photos; Page 63: wrangler/Shutterstock; Page 67: GG Pro Photo/Shutterstock; Page 70: Creatas Images/ Thinkstock; Page 76: © Stacy Walsh Rosenstock/Alamy; Page 78 (left): AP Photo/Gerry Broome; Page 78 (right): The Canadian Press/Nathan Denette; Page 83: Courtesy of Drs. Masuda & Nisbett

Chapter 4 Pages 88–89: Getty Images; Page 92 (top left): Jupiterimages/ Thinkstock; Page 92 (top center): © Jodi Matthews/iStockPhoto; Page 92 (top right): © drbimages/iStockPhoto; Page 92 (bottom left): Ryan McVay/Thinkstock; Page 92 (bottom center): Jupiterimages/ Thinkstock; Page 92 (bottom right): iStockphoto/Thinkstock; Page 93: Paul Ekman, Ph.D./ Paul Ekman Group, LLC; Page 96 (right): Paul Ekman, Ph.D./ Paul Ekman Group, LLC; Page 96 (left): Paul Ekman, Ph.D./ Paul Ekman Group, LLC; Page 97 (top left): © Karen Kasmauski/Corbis; Page 97 (bottom left): © travelib pakistan/Alamy; Page 97 (center): Andresr/Shutterstock; Page 97 (top right): © Vadim Balantsev/iStockPhoto; Page 97 (bottom right): © Ragnar Schmuck/ fstop/Corbis; Page 101(left): Chris Scwarz/Ponopresse; Page 101 (right): Amos Morgan/PhotoDisc/Thinkstock; Page 103: Toronto Star / GetStock.com; Page 113: © Pixel 8/Alamy; Page 115: ZUMA Press/ Newscom

Chapter 5 Pages 122–123: Adri Berger/Getty Images; Page 123: Photographer: Antal Tihanyi. Used with permission from Eva Tihanyi; Page 124: Constance Bannister Corp/Getty Images; Page 127: AP Wide World Photos; Page 138 (left); Mark Baldwin; Page 138 (center): Mark Baldwin; Page 138 (right): Shutterstock; Page 145: Peter Close/ Shutterstock

Chapter 6 Pages 152–153: Gaslight Advertising Archives, Inc. N.Y.; Page 154: Michael Ponomareff/Ponopresse; Page 155: Kevin Dietsch/ UPI/Landov; Page 158: © Moodboard/Corbis; Page 165: Courtesy McNeil Consumer Healthcare; Page 167: Shaun Best/Reuters /Landov; Page 169: © Bill Aron/PhotoEdit; Page 170: California Department of Public Health; Page 171: American Association of Advertising Agencies; Page 174: Walden Media/The Kobal Collection; Page 176: Digital Vision/Thinkstock; Page 178: © G P Bowater/Alamy; Page 179: Yellow Dog Productions/The Image Bank/Getty Images; Page 180: Image IHC88-12-2, Canadian Forces, National Defence. Reproduced with the permission of the Minister of Public Works and Government Services, 2011; Page 181: Shutterstock; Page 184 (top): imDream/Shutterstock; Page 184 (bottom): Jack.Q/Shutterstock; Page 185:Shidane Arone, Corporal Clayton Matchee, National Defence, 1993. Reproduced with the permission of the Minister of Public Works and Government Services, 2011

Chapter 7 Pages 192–193: Stockbyte/Thinkstock; Page 194: Peter Blashill/The Province; Page 198: Associated Press; Page 202: © Lonely Planet Images/Alamy; Page 203: Photo William Vandivert and Scientific American. From “Opinions and Social Pressure” by Solomon E. Asch, November 1955. Reproduced with permission. Copyright © 1955 Scientific American, Inc. All rights reserved; Page 208: Bill Becker/CP Photo; Page 210: © Alaska Stock/Alamy; Page 213: Keith Morison, Morision Communications; Page 214: © Anne Clark/iStockPhoto; Page 216: The Kobal Collection; Page 217: CSA Plastock/Getty Images; Page 223: World History Archive/Newscom; Page 224 (top): John Florea/Time & Life Pictures/Getty Images; Page 224 (bottom left): From the film Obedience © 1968 by Stanley Milgram; © renewed 1993 by Alexandra Milgram, distributed by Penn State Media Sales; Page 224 (bottom right): From the film Obedience © 1968 by Stanley Milgram; © renewed 1993 by Alexandra Milgram, distributed by Penn State Media Sales.

Chapter 8 Page 234–235: © Tommy (Louth)/Alamy; Page 236 (left): Louise Richard LT (N) ret'd RN, Gulf War Veteran Freelance Advocate for Disabled Veterans & Families, Ottawa, Ontario, Canada; Page 236 (right): The Canadian Press/Maclean's/Mike Pinder; Page 237: Jupiterimages/Thinkstock; Page 238: Quiet Rage: The Stanford Prison Experiment, reprinted by permission of Dr. Philip Zimbardo.; Page 239: AP Photo; Page 243: © Andrew Fox/Alamy; Page 247: CP PHOTO/ Toronto Star-Rick Madonik; Page 253:© PhotoSpin, Inc./Alamy; Page 256 (top): © Supreme Court of Canada. Photo by Andrew Balfour; Page 256 (bottom): Photo Jean-Marc Carisse. www.carisse.org; Page 260: AP Photo/Evan Vucci; Page 261: © Design Pics Inc./Alamy; Page 266: Fred Cattroll;

Chapter 9 Pages 270–271: © Spencer Grant/MaXxImages; Page 273: Goodshoot/Thinkstock; Page 277: © webphotographeer/iStockPhoto; Page 280 (top left): DVS/ABACAUSA.COM/Newscom; Page 280 (top right): Getty Images; Page 280 (bottom left): Photo by Willi Schneider/ Rex Features; Page 280 (bottom right): Allstar Picture Library/GetStock. com; Page 284: Hemera/Thinkstock; Page 287: © AF archive/Alamy; Page 289: © Blend Images/Alamy; Page 294: four photos: Reprinted from Evolution and Human Behavior, 29(3), Lynda G. Boothroyd,Benedict C. Jones,D. Michael Burt,Lisa M. DeBruine,David I. Perrett, Facial correlates of sociosexuality, pp. 211–218, Copyright (May 2008), with permission from Elsevier; Page 295: © Carey Hope/iStockPhoto; Page 300 (left): wavebreakmedia ltd/Shutterstock; Page 300 (right): Dmitriy Shironosov/ Shutterstock; Page 306: John Penezic/Shutterstock

Chapter 10 Pages 310–311: © Lynsey Addario/VII Network/Corbis; Page 312: Prince George Citizen/Brent Braaten; Page 314: Steve Mason/Photodisc/Thinkstock; Page 319: Study: Cavemen helped disabled © United Press International, Inc. All Rights Reserved.; Page 320: AP Photo/Themba Hadebe; Page 321: Alexander Raths/Shutterstock; Page 325 (left): © Hemis/Alamy; Page 325 (right): © Brownstock/ Alamy; Page 326: Copyright © NM DNR Reprinted with Permission; Page 330: © Stock Connection Distribution/Alamy; Page 331 (inset): © The New York Times Photo Archives; Page 331: © The New York Times Photo Archives; Page 333: auremar/Shutterstock; Page 334: © Gunter Marx/SW/Alamy

Chapter 11 Pages 338–339: iStockphoto/Thinkstock; Page 340: Jason Payne/The Province; Page 341: © Cultura RM/Alamy; Page 342 (top): Karl Ammann/Nature Picture Library; Page 342 (bottom): Karl Ammann/Nature Picture Library; Page 351: Ryan McVay/Photodisc/ Thinkstock; Page 356: AFP/Getty Images; Page 357: Reuters/ vampirefreaks.com/Landov; Page 359: New Regency Pictures/The Kobal Collection; Page 360: © David Young-Wolff / PhotoEdit; Page 364: Getty Images; Page 365: U.S. Army Photograph; Page 365: DPA/ Landov; Page 368: CP Photo; Page 369: © PhotoEdit

Chapter 12 Pages 372–373: Andy Clark/REUTERS; Page 374: © Mary Young; Page 376: Jupiterimages/Thinkstock; Page 379: Christoph

Wilhelm/Taxi/Getty Images; Page 383: The Canadian Press Images/Maclean's Magazine/Andrew Tolson; Page 390: Blend Images/Hill Street Studios/Getty Images; Page 394: The Canadian Press/Adrian Wyld; Page 396: iofoto/Shutterstock; Page 398: CP PHOTO/Nathan Denette; Page 407: Creatas/Thinkstock; Page 413: iStockphoto/Thinkstock

Spa 1 Pages 416–417: © Chico Batata/epa/Corbis; Page 419: CP PHOTO/Larry MacDougal; Page 423: © Jani Bryson/iStockPhoto; Page 424: Pearson Education/PH College; Page 428: Pedrick/The Image Works; Page 429: Toronto Star/GetStock.com

Spa 2 Pages 432–433: Photograph courtesy of Elvira Toews; Page 438 (top left): Maria Teijeiro/Photodisc/Thinkstock; Page 438 (top right): Ryan McVay/Getty Images; Page 438 (bottom left): Jade Brookbank/The Image Bank/Getty Images; Page 438 (bottom right): Comstock Images/Thinkstock; Page 442: Jupiterimages/Thinkstock; Page 449: lightpoet/Shutterstock; Page 450: Reprinted from Journal of Experimental Psychology, Available online 12 July 2011, Heidi S. Kane, Cade McCall, Nancy L. Collins and Jim Blascovich, Mere presence is not enough: Responsive support in a virtual world, Copyright (2011), with permission from Elsevier; Page 451: © digitalskillet/iStockPhoto; Page 455: AFP/Getty Images; Page 456: iStockphoto/Thinkstock

Spa 3 Pages 462–463: Dick Hemingway; Page 464 (left): CP PHOTO/Winnipeg Free Press-Ken Gigliotti; Page 464 (right): Winnipeg Free Press; Page 467: Arnaldo Magnani/Getty Images; Page 469: From: Simons, D.J. & Chabris, C.F., "Gorillas in Our Midst: Sustained inattentional blindness for dynamic events". Perception 1999, 28, p. 1070. Figure provided by Daniel Simons; Page 471: Loftus EF. Miller DG, Burns HJ, (1978). Semantic integration of verbal information into a visual memory. "Journal of Experimental Psychology"; Human Learning and Memory, 4, 19–31; Page 477: John Boykin Stock Connection Worldwide/Newscom; Page 483: CP PHOTO/Jacques Boissinot; Page 487: A/T MEDIA SERVICES/Pearson Education/PH College; Page 490: Toronto Star/GetStock.com

Name Index

A

B

C

H

L

M

N

O

S

W

Z

Subject Index

Note: Page numbers followed by "f" refer to figures; those followed by "t" refer to tables.

A

D

E

N

O

P

R

S

T

U

W

Z